Handbook of
Sociological
Theory

Handbooks of Sociology and Social Research

Series Editor:
Howard B. Kaplan, *Texas A&M University, College Station, Texas*

Handbook of Sociological Theory

Edited by

Jonathan H. Turner

University of California
Riverside, California

 Springer

Library of Congress Cataloging-in-Publication Data

Handbook of sociological theory/edited by Jonathan H. Turner.
   p. cm. — (Handbooks of sociology and social research)
  Includes bibliographical references and index.
  ISBN 0-406-46554-X
  I. Sociology—Philosophy. I. Turner, Jonathan H. II. Series.

HM585 .H36 2001
301'.01—dc21
                                          2001023467

ISBN-10: 0-387-32458-5 soft cover
ISBN-13: 978-0387-32458-6

ISBN: 0-406-46554-X hardcover

Printed on acid-free paper.

First softcover printing, 2006

Printed in the United States of America.

9 8 7 6 5 4 3 2 1

springer.com

Contributors

Jeffrey Alexander, Department of Sociology, Yale University, New Haven, Connecticut 06520

Kenneth D. Bailey, Department of Sociology, University of California, Los Angeles, California 90095

Jens Beckert, Department of Sociology, Free University of Berlin, 14195 Berlin, Germany

Judith R. Blau, Department of Sociology, University of North Carolina, Chapel Hill, North Carolina 27599

Peter M. Blau, Department of Sociology, University of North Carolina, Chapel Hill, North Carolina 27599

David E. Boyns, Department of Sociology, University of California, Riverside, California 92521

Michael Burawoy, Department of Sociology, University of California, Berkeley, California 94720

Craig Calhoun, Social Research Council, and Department of Sociology, New York University, New York, New York 10003

Kathleen M. Carley, Department of Social and Decision Sciences, Carnegie Mellon University, Pittsburgh, Pennsylvania 15213

Janet Saltzman Chafetz, Department of Sociology, University of Houston, Houston, Texas 77204

Christopher Chase-Dunn, Department of Sociology, University of California-Riverside, Riverside, California 92521

Randall Collins, Department of Sociology, University of Pennsylvania, Philadelphia, Pennsylvania 19104

Karen S. Cook, Department of Sociology, Stanford University, Stanford, California 94305

Stephan Fuchs, Department of Sociology, University of Virginia, Charlottesville, Virginia 22903

Douglas Goodman, Department of Sociology, Wellesley College, Wellesley, Massachusetts 02481

Guillermina Jasso, Department of Sociology, New York University, New York, New York 10003

Hans Joas, Department of Sociology, Free University of Berlin, 14195 Berlin, Germany

Michèle Lamont, Department of Sociology, Princeton University, Princeton, New Jersey 08540

Siegwart Lindenberg, Department of Sociology/ICS, University of Groningen, Groningen, The Netherlands

Joseph Lopreato, Austin, Texas 78701

John D. McCarthy, Department of Sociology, Pennsylvania State University, University Park, Pennsylvania 16802

Jim Murphy, Department of Sociology, University of Maryland, College Park, Maryland 20742

Eric R. W. Rice, Department of Sociology, Stanford University, Stanford, California 94305

Cecilia L. Ridgeway, Department of Sociology, Stanford University, Stanford, California 94305

George Ritzer, Department of Sociology, University of Maryland, College Park, Maryland 20742

Jörg Rössell, Department of Science of Culture, Universitat Leipzig, Leipzig, Germany

Stephen K. Sanderson, Department of Sociology, Indiana University of Pennsylvania, Indiana, Pennsylvania 15705

Thomas J. Scheff, Department of Sociology, University of California, Santa Barbara, California 93106

Emanuel A. Schegloff, Department of Sociology, University of California, Los Angeles, California 90095

Alan Sica, Department of Sociology, Pennsylvania State University, University Park, Pennsylvania 16802

Philip Smith, Department of Sociology and Anthropology, Queensland University, Brisbane, Australia

Sheldon Stryker, Department of Sociology, Indiana University, Bloomington, Indiana 47405

Charley Tilly, Department of Sociology, Columbia University, New York, New York 10027

Jonathan H. Turner, Department of Sociology, University of California, Riverside, California 92521

Ralph H. Turner, Department of Sociology, University of California, Los Angeles, California 90095

Erik Olin Wright, Department of Sociology, University of Wisconsin-Madison, Madison, Wisconsin 53706

Mayer N. Zald, Department of Sociology, University of Michigan, Ann Arbor, Michigan 48109

Shanyang Zhao, Department of Sociology, Temple University, Philadelphia, Pennsylvania 19122

Preface

One of the most obvious trends in sociology over the last 30 years is differentiation of substantive specialties. What is true in the discipline as a whole is particularly evident in sociological theory. Where once there were just a few theoretical perspectives, e.g., functionalism, symbolic interactionism, conflict theory, exchange theory, now there are many. In one sense this differentiation is exciting and signals the emergence of new ideas, while in another light the splintering of theory indicates that there is no consensus over how sociology should proceed to explain the social world.

I assembled the authors in this "handbook" (more like an "armbook") with an eye to capturing the diversity of theoretical activity in sociology. Even my original list of authors did not cover all of theory and as the months went by I lost four or five authors who, for various reasons, could not complete their chapters. The result is that the volume is not quite as broad as I had hoped, but it still covers most theoretical approaches in sociology today.

This is a handbook, implying that it is to be used as a basic reference, but it is a special kind of handbook: it is about the forefront of theory. I asked authors to tell the reader about what they are doing, right now, rather than what others have done in the past. Those looking for textbook summaries or "annual review" type chapters will be disappointed; those seeking to gain insight into theory as it is unfolding today will be pleased. Thus, the goal of this volume is to allow prominent theorists working in a variety of traditions to review their work. This is a handbook, but it is one devoted to theorists telling us about their latest work. I did not seek textbooklike reviews of fields, but rather forefront work in a field. Of course, in presenting their ideas, the authors of the chapters in this volume place their arguments in an intellectual context, but only to explain what they are doing at the forefront.

As will be evident, the authors took my charge in different directions. All asked me how much summary of the field and how much of their own work they should present. My answer was to do what they wanted but with an emphasis on their own work. What are they doing? In what tradition is this work? What are the problems and issues? How are they to be resolved? The result is a volume that provides overviews of traditions but more importantly that shows where theoretical sociology is going.

I hope that the reader finders these chapters as engaging as I do.

JONATHAN H. TURNER

Contents

VII. THEORIZING FROM ASSUMPTIONS OF RATIONALITY

CHAPTER 1

Sociological Theory Today

Jonathan H. Turner

If we placed ourselves back in 1950, what would we see in theoretical circles? Functional theorizing was about to become the dominant perspective; Marxist-oriented conflict theory in America was still in the closet imposed by McCarthyism, although alive and well in Europe in many guises but most prominently in the tradition of the Frankfurt School (Turner, 1998, pp. 545–557; Held, 1980; Schroyer, 1973); and symbolic interactionism was carrying forth the legacy of George Herbert Mead. At the general level, this is all there was, although many more specific theories of meso processes could be observed, theories such as urban ecology, differential association, and anomie theory in criminology, phenomenology, theories from the Gestalt tradition (e.g., cognitive dissonance, congruity, and balance theories) in social psychology, and perhaps a half dozen other narrow theories.[1] A little over a decade later, functionalism was being challenged by European conflict theorists who prodded a new generation of Marxist theorists in America to take up the challenge, structuralism was emerging in Europe and about to infect America, and exchange theory was just making its entrance. Still, there were few general approaches, but things were about to change. The 1960s and 1970s saw a proliferation of theoretical perspectives that continues to this day.

Today, sociology is experiencing what can only be described as hyperdifferentiation of theories; and if Randall Collins' (1998) "law of small numbers" has any merit, there are now too many approaches competing for an attention space that in the intellectual arena can manage at best seven approaches. From this perspective, we should see a weeding out of theories to a smaller number, but in fact, this is not likely to occur because each of the many theoretical perspectives has a resource base of adherents, a place in academia, and a series of outlets for scholarly publications (Turner & Turner, 1990). As a result, theories in sociology do not compete head on with each other as much as they coexist. One of the effects of hyper-differentiation is that many new resource niches are created, allowing scholars and their students to operate without having to justify their importance vis-à-vis other theories, and this

---

[1]Textbooks in theory tended to list many more theoretical perspectives, but the distinctions made by authors in the 1950s, for the most part, were labels that they imposed. Actual theorizing was confined to a few general approaches, plus a larger number of more specific theories on specific substantive topics.

Jonathan H. Turner • Department of Sociology, University of California, Riverside, California 92521.

Handbook of Sociological Theory, edited by Jonathan H. Turner. Kluwer Academic / Plenum Publishers, New York, 2002.

is especially so as sociological theory has abandoned the requirement that it be tested against empirical facts.

True, the most prominent theoretical orientations do indeed compete, and here we see the law of small numbers operating since there are probably no more than seven major approaches dominating the spotlight.[2] But backstage, there is lots of activity among less prominent theoretical programs that often pay scant attention to the actors on the center stage. The result is for many diverse theoretical approaches to persist. No one theoretical perspective in sociology has any chance of becoming hegemonic, even to the extent of functionalism in the 1950s or conflict theory in the 1960s. Indeed, the diversity of approaches has led to a smug cynicism about the prospects of theory being anything more than texts produced people who call themselves sociologists and who, for many, should not have a privileged voice. Thus, sociological theory will never be fully scientific (see Chapter 2, this volume, on what makes sciences "scientific").

The chapters in this volume represent a mix of theoretical orientations and strategies, but as is evident, these theories are very diverse, and the selection in this volume does not include some important approaches; to name a few, structuration, network, and ecological theories. But the pages to follow do give a sense for the range of activities pursued by sociological theorists. In this chapter, I do not intend to summarize specific chapters; rather, I want to offer my own impressions of what has occurred to theoretical sociology over the last five decades, freely venting my own views and prejudices as I try to review at least the major axes along which theories have differentiated.

DIVERSE STANCES ON EPISTEMOLOGY

Is Sociological Theory to Be Scientific?

From sociology's inception, the prospects for theories resembling those in the natural sciences have been debated. August Comte (1830–1842), of course, argued for a theoretically driven positivism in which the laws of human organization were to be very much like those in the physics of his time. Comte found ready allies in Herbert Spencer and Émile Durkheim and perhaps Georg Simmel, but Karl Marx and Max Weber had doubts about the scientific prospects of sociology—doubts that persist to this day. Marx saw theory as part of a critique of existing social conditions and as a way to mobilize opposition to these conditions. Weber did not hold this view, but he believed that much of social reality involves the chance confluence of events, thereby making general laws of human organization difficult; instead of theoretical laws, objective descriptions of phenomena with analytical ideal types could be undertaken, but these analytical descriptions would not constitute a subject matter amenable to universal laws (see Chapter 23, this volume, on Weberian theory today). Thus, by the turn into the 20th century, three positions could be discerned: (1) those who saw sociology as a natural science that would discover the laws of human organization; (2) those who emphasized theory as critique and as a call for action; and (3) those who saw sociological "explanation" as revolving around interpreting empirical events in terms of analytical schemes consisting of categories describing classes of empirical phenomena.

These positions still exist today, but like all else in sociology, they have many variants. A minority of theorists are positivists in this sense: they see their goal as developing general

[2]At center stage, there are from four to seven major perspectives, conforming to Collins' law of small numbers. But, in the wings are many more theoretical orientations that persist because they have a resource base.

scientific principles and models of generic social processes (see Chapters 3 and 4). Many are critical theorists of many stripes: Marxists who continue to use theory as both an analysis and critique of the existing system of oppression (see Chapter 22, for an example); descendants of the Frankfurt School who carry the emancipatory spirit of Marx and the pessimism of Weber, and who as a result see the role of the theorist as constructing analytical schemes exposing patterns of domination (e.g., Habermas 1962, 1970, 1984; see Chapter 5, this volume); world systems theorists who take Marxian analysis global and conduct both analysis and critique of capitalism on the world stage (e.g., Wallerstein, 1974; Chapter 27, this volume); and post-modernists who carry on a double critique of science as a failed epistemology and of capital-ism as a system whose technologies and markets destroy local cultures, compress time and space, commodify virtually everything, and fracture the individual (e.g., Lyotard, 1984; Chapters 6 and 8, this volume). Probably the largest group of theorists, many of whom have doubts about science, construct analytical schemes of categories for "interpreting" current events; and although their respective styles of scheme-building vary, they all see theory as an interpretative enterprise using a conceptual system of categories denoting important phenom-ena (e.g., Giddens, 1984; Bourdieu, 1984).

Over the whole of the last decade of the 20th century, increasing cynicism about the prospects of scientific theory was evident. Looking back 50 years ago, especially in America, there was real optimism that sociology would sit at the table of science, but today a much smaller proportion of sociological theorists hold such a position. Many of those who see themselves as social theorists do not consider the goal of sociological theory to be the articulation of general laws of human organization. These theorists may differ radically on what they propose as an alternative, but they are all critical of the epistemology of science.

My views on the epistemiological wars in theory circles are well known. I will simply repeat what I have said before: If sociological theory is not scientific, then what is it? My an-swer is that it becomes various mixes of journalism, ideological preaching, critique of perceived wrongs, and vague philosophizing. Such alternatives to the epistemology science do not, I believe, take sociology in a very healthy direction. They assure that we will be a watered-down humanities and that we will be irrelevant to policymakers and even our fellow academics.

Is Sociological Theory to Be Micro or Macro?

Outside of the epistemological arena, the most debated issue in sociological theory is the linkages among micro-level and macro-level phenomena. How are theories of action, behav-ior, and interpersonal processes, on the one side, to be reconciled with theories of population-level and societal-level forces, on the other? All sciences reveal a micro–macro divide, and even the most advanced sciences have not reconciled the two levels theoretically. In sociology, however, the issue appears to have persisted and pestered theorists for several decades (e.g., Alexander et al., 1987; Huber, 1991; Emirbayer & Mische, 1999; Ritzer & Gindoff, 1994), and we can ask why this should be so, especially in a discipline where much theory does not aspire to be scientific.

One reason for the persistence of the issue is that it is conflated with other questions that pull theorists back into epistemological issues. In Europe but also in America, micro–macro issues are often conflated with agency–structure questions (e.g., Archer, 1982, 1988; Giddens, 1984; Smart, 2001). If one gives primacy to action, then structure and culture are at best constraints on such action; but more fundamentally, action is not determinative and predict-able, which in turn makes the scientific pretensions of sociology just that—pretensions. If, on the other hand, action is constrained by culture and structure, it is more predictable, and hence amenable to study in scientific terms. I have simplified the antagonists here, but the important point is that agency–structure questions take us right back to epistemological doubts about sociology as a scientific enterprise. And most approaches that try to reconcile the two (e.g., Giddens, 1976) are decidedly antiscience, seeing agency as only loosely constrained by structure and as indeterminate in the production and reproduction of structure. All of these approaches are incredibly vague and metaphorical about the relations between agency and structure, and this vagueness merely labels the issue but with an antiscience bias.

Another reason the micro–macro, or agency–structure, debate continues is because of what I call "micro-chauvinism," whereby a good many theorists argue for the primacy of the micro (e.g., Berger & Luckman, 1967; Coleman, 1990; Collins, 1981a,b). Micro-chauvinists vary in whether or not they are willing to acknowledge the reality of the macro as more than a reification of the analyst, but they all argue that reality is to be explained by reference to the micro-social processes. Modern-day symbolic interactionists were the first to make this extreme assertion (e.g., Blumer, 1969); others such as ethnomethodologists, at least in the early years (e.g., Garfinkel, 1967), also made this assertion, as did the extreme behaviorists (e.g., Homans, 1961). But over the last three decades, a growing number of theorists in other traditions has made the argument that the macro, if it exists, is to be explained by the micro. Rational choice theory is one prominent example of this emphasis (e.g., Hechter, 1987; Coleman, 1990; Chapter 29, this volume); interaction ritual theory is another (e.g., Collins, 1975; Chapter 24, this volume). When reality is reducible to theories of micro-processes, a good part of social reality is in essence not considered the proper subject matter of theory. Naturally, to defend their turf, those working at the meso- and macro-levels spin out counter-arguments, thus proliferating theories in sociology, which if they do not criticize each other, will ignore the pronouncements of micro-chauvinists.

There are also more macro-chauvinists (e.g., Blau, 1994, 1977a,b; Mayhew, 1981a,b; see also Chapter 17, this volume), but this chauvinism is generally more tempered, simply arguing that there are emergent realities that need to be explained in their own terms (Turner, 2000, 2002). While these emergent realities do indeed constrain action and interaction at the micro-level, they do not determine in any precise manner micro processes.

There has been a number of strategies to reconcile the micro-macro divide that are less chauvinistic (Turner, 1983, 2002; see also Chapter 18, this volume). Perhaps the most popular is implied by Max Weber's (1921/1968) analysis of building conceptual staircases from "action" to "social relationships" to "associations" to "legitimated orders." Talcott Parsons (1951) followed a similar strategy in his analysis of "modes of orientation and motivation" leading to actions that form relationships in "social systems" composed of "status-roles" and typified by the "pattern variables." The general argument of these approaches is that as one adds more actors and relationships, additional concepts are introduced to account for the emergent properties of each new level of reality, but the problem with most such approaches is that they become much like Weber's sociology, a series of analytical categories that describe but do not explain the dynamics of each level of reality.

Another approach comes from Simmel (1895) and his advocacy for a formal sociology. Here, emphasis is on the forms of the relationships rather than the properties of the actors in the relationship, with the theories thereby explaining the dynamics of relationships among both individuals and collective actors. Network theory and more significantly exchange network theory (e.g., Emerson, 1962; Molm & Cook, 1995) take this approach; while considerable insight has come from these theories (see Chapter 31, this volume), it is probably true that the nature of the actor sometimes does make a difference in the dynamics of their relationships. Isomorphism does exist no doubt across levels of reality, but this fact cannot explain away the emergent and unique properties of each level.

Yet another strategy for dealing with the micro–macro gap is what might be termed deductive reductionism in which axioms or higher-order propositions about behavior or other micro-processes stand at the top of a deductive system of propositions, with the laws of social structure and culture derived from, and hence explained by, these axioms (e.g., Homans, 1961; Emerson, 1972; Blau, 1994; see also Chapter 3, this volume). Such an approach acknowledges the reality of the meso and macro and the laws of sociology that explain their operation, but it emphasizes that these laws are deducible from the laws of micro-processes. In this way, the gap in explanations at different levels of reality is closed by the deductive structure of the theory.

The recent rise in cultural theory in some respects is an effort to deal with the micro–macro problem, although it obviously is much more (Lamont & Wuthnow, 1990; see also Chapters 7, 9, and 10, this volume). When attention shifts from social structures to systems of symbols, it is much easier to see how culture becomes part of the individual, and conversely, how thoughts and acts of individuals generate, change, or reproduce culture. For ultimately culture is either inside of people's heads or deposited in warehouses, such as libraries, and it is used by people in action and interaction. Thus a more macro force—culture—is more readily connected to a micro force—thoughts, actions, and interactions of people who have internalized culture—than is the case when structure as networks of relationships must be reconciled with individuals' actions. This is why, I suspect, that structuralism became so popular; it allowed sociologists to see structure as cultural symbols, and as such, it is far easier to connect macro- and micro-levels of analysis. Anthony Giddens' (1984) structuration theory is a good example, because structure as "rules and resources" that are used by actors in micro-settings allows for an easier reconciliation of micro and macro. Similarly, Pierre Bourdieu's (1984) notion of "habitus" is a name for the nexus between culture and the individual, again connecting micro and macro. Of course, culture is not all that there is to the macro-realm; and these approaches do not solve the problem of how to conceive of structure as anything more than rules and other cultural processes. The cultural turn in sociology, then, only gives the illusion of resolving the micro–macro problem.

Some who have advocated this cultural turn (e.g., Alexander, 1982–1984) argue for a multidimensional approach to theorizing about micro- and macro-processes. Action and order are each considered important dimensions of the social world and each is conceptualized, but in fact, such conceptualizations simply label the problem rather than resolve it. Action has certain properties, and order or structure–culture has its own distinctive properties; but the question remains: How is a *theoretical* integration to occur beyond simply stating that action is constrained by order and that order is reproduced and changed by action? Other multidimensional approaches, such as Ritzer's (1985, 1988a,b, 1990) "integrated paradigm," categorize reality along two intersecting dimensions: microscopic–macroscopic and objective–subjective. And then, various approaches are placed in the four quadrants created by these two continua—that is, micro-subjective, macro-subjective, micro-objective, macro-objective—but all this does is once again categorize approaches. It does not reconcile them theoretically or produce integrated explanations.

One of the most famous approaches for reconciling micro–macro theorizing was Robert Merton's (1968) advocacy for "theories of the middle range." In this approach, sociology would abandon the grand analytical schemes like Talcott Parsons' "action theory" in favor of theories about specific substantive topics, awaiting a later Einstein to come along and integrate these middle-range theories with the equivalent of general relativity theory. The end result of this advocacy was to produce "theories of" each substantive area in sociology, which of course only proliferated the number of specialized theories in the discipline. Since these theories were so specialized, and indeed, since they often elevated empirical generalizations to the status of laws, there was little hope that they would be integrated in ways that would resolve any theoretical problem, much less the micro–macro linkage question.

The most obvious solution to the micro–macro problem has not, in my view, been pursued with any commitment (Turner, 2002). This solution involves recognizing that social reality does indeed unfold along micro, meso, and macro dimensions; that each of these levels reveals its own emergent properties; that these properties are driven by forces distinctive to each level; that theory is to be about the dynamics of the forces operating at each level; and that theoretical integration will always be about how the properties of one level load the values for the unique forces operating at other levels. This kind of synthesis does not produce a "unified theory" but rather a series of theoretical models and principles on forces of one level of reality, as these are influenced by structures at other levels of reality (as David Boyns and I explore in Chapter 18; see also Turner, 2000, 2002).

Thus, sociological theory has not resolved its micro-macro divide any more than other sciences, although sociological theorists seem rather more obsessed with the problem. Added to this are the disagreements over epistemology, and we can see why sociological theory has moved in so many diverse directions. There is no accepted epistemology among theorists, and efforts to resolve the micro–macro gap have tended to produce "solutions" that further differentiate theory. The end result is a hyperdifferentiated discipline, at both the theoretical and substantive levels.

DIVERSE THEORY TRADITIONS
IN SOCIOLOGY

Functional Theory

Functionalism was sociology's first theoretical orientation, and for a brief time in the 1950s and early 1960s, it dominated sociological theorizing (see Turner & Maryanski, 1979, for a history). Today, functionalism is virtually dead, except for a few dedicated theorists who continue to work in the tradition (e.g., Münch, 1982). Functional theory always asks the question of how a particular phenomenon operates to meet the survival needs or requisites of a larger social system, as the latter seeks to adapt to its environment. The notion of "needs" or "requisites" always poses a problem in such theorizing because it often appears that the need for something brings this something about; or alternatively, the reasoning becomes circular: system parts exist to allow the system to meet its needs for survival in an environment; and we know that a part of this system is meeting these needs because the system is surviving.

Early functionalism, however, avoided these problems by examining differentiation as a kind of master social process. Herbert Spencer (1874–1896) emphasized the axes along which social systems differentiate, whereas Émile Durkheim (1893) examined the new bases for integration of social systems undergoing differentiation. From their respective analyses, it is rather easy to extract testable propositions. Thus, it is not functionalism per se that creates problems, but rather it was the particular mode of analysis conducted by Talcott Parsons. Parsons' functionalism emphasized requisites (the famous, A,G,I,L) and built an elaborate category system around these requisites (Parsons, Bales, & Shils, 1953; Parsons & Smelser, 1956). Such an approach saw explanation as placing an empirical case into an analytical category. This approach had no real theoretical legs because to categorize a phenomenon in a rather elaborate conceptual scheme does not explain it. This problem of believing that classification is explanation was far more fatal to functionalism than its supposed ideological conservatism (e.g., Dahrendorf, 1958; Lockwood, 1956).

Neofunctionalism (e.g., Alexander, 1985; Alexander & Colomy, 1985) abandoned the notion of requisites—the defining feature of all functional analysis—and emphasized the master process of differentiation and relatedly cultural processes. As a result, neofunctional-ism is not functional theory (Turner & Maryanski, 1988). Even with the abandonment of the notion of needs or requisites, neofunctional sociology never really was accepted as theory, although it can be credited with bringing back into focus the central problematic of early functional sociology: the process of differentiation with a special emphasis on cultural bases of integration in differentiated social systems (see Chapter 7). Neofunctionalism, then, helped bring culture back to prominence within sociological theory but did not make functionalism any more acceptable.

The demise of functionalism left the door open for many new approaches to gain prominence or to regain prominence lost under the brief hegemony of Parsonian functional-ism. The most obvious benefactor was the approach most responsible for the demise of functionalism: conflict theory.

Conflict Theory

With the exception of a few persistent souls (e.g., Mills, 1956), conflict theory remained closeted during the McCarthy era in America (1950s); but as Europeans began to criticize functionalism (e.g., Dahrendorf, 1958; Lockwood, 1956) and as the repression of the Cold War era lessened, conflict theory emerged in America and during the cultural changes of the 1960s and 1970s became the most dominant theoretical orientation. Even those who were not conflict theorists began to label themselves in this manner, if only to get attention or appear in vogue. Indeed, for a time all theories were "required" by the new (in)sensibilities to talk about power and conflict—as if this is all that there is in the social universe.

As a critique of functionalism, conflict theorists were rather unfair; and out of the ex-tremes of this critique, sociologists discovered the obvious: social systems reveal both integra-tive and conflict processes. Only in an environment where the conflict theorists had gone overboard would such an obvious statement be taken seriously, as somehow profound. What conflict theory did do, however, is shift the focus of theoretical sociology to the conditions under which varying types of conflict emerge in social systems; once this shift in emphasis had occurred, many diverse conflict approaches developed.

One was the Marxian and Weberian emphasis on how inequality and stratification generate conflicts between social classes (e.g., Dahrendorf, 1959). Another was an effort to update Marx to deal with the fact that a revolution never occurred in capitalism, and moreover that classes do not polarize in capitalist system but on the contrary they proliferate (Wright, 1985, 1997; see also Chapter 22). Social movements theorizing got an enormous boost, moving from a subfield within collective behavior to the study of mobilizations (see Chapter 25, as well as Chapter 26). Exchange theories often saw themselves in conflict terms (e.g., Collins, 1975; Blau, 1964), although few proposed the obvious point that much conflict theory is a subcase of exchange theory (or what transpires when the exchange of resources is unequal in a social system). World systems theory (Wallerstein, 1974; Frank, 1979) also emerged in the heady days of the conflict revival, and this approach has evolved from its purely Marxian roots into a variety of approaches examining globalization issues (e.g., Chase-Dunn, 1989; Chase-Dunn & Hall, 1997; Sanderson, 1988, 1995); and indeed, theorizing about globalization is the new hot area in sociology (see Chapter 27). Perhaps the most interesting offshoot of conflict theory was the rise of comparative–historical sociology, which disproportionately perhaps, has focused on revolutions but which nonetheless became the entry point for a new historical sociology that represents one of the brighter branches of sociology today (see Chapter 26).

Today, sociologists do not go around thumping their chests, proclaiming themselves to be conflict theorists as they once did in the 1960s. This is due, perhaps, to the widespread acceptance of all varieties of conflict theory in sociology; somehow we are more secure in studying conflict, which itself is a rather remarkable admission. Today, conflict theory is often specialized, focusing on specific forms of inequality and conflict, such as ethnic antagonism or gender tensions (see Chapter 28, for an illustration in the area of gender).

Many early conflict theories implied a critique (of functionalism, of capitalism, of imperialism, of colonialism, and of lots of things). European sociology had a much longer legacy on this score than American social theory, and this critical focus has evolved into a distinctive perspective in both Europe and America (see Chapter 6).

Critical Theorizing

Sociological theory always has had a critical edge. The discipline emerged in response to the transformations associated with modernity; and theorists often posited pathological conditions, such as alienation, exploitation, anomie, marginality, iron cages, and other ills associated with the rise of capitalism. In America, despite the high-sounding rhetoric about being scientific, sociology began with a "social problems" emphasis, seeing the goals of sociology as revolving around amelioration (Turner & Turner, 1990). Some such as Auguste Comte (1830–1842) and perhaps Émile Durkheim saw scientific theory as the vehicle for social reconstruction, but most critical theory has been antiscience, often portraying science as part of the problem.

In the 20th century, critical theory first became codified within the Frankfurt School, which had the emancipatory zeal of Marx but the realistic and pessimistic assessment of Weber as to the power of rational–legal authority to dominate individuals. Like most critical theorists, the Frankfurt School wanted to expose patterns of domination and control even if they had no real program to deal with these oppressive patterns. The goal of much critical theory thus became one of criticizing, usually within the secure confines of academia, leaving the question of how to manage the problems exposed by such criticism to others, or perhaps to another time in the future when conditions were more favorable to emancipation.

Contemporary critical theory has not really moved from this stance in the 21st century. Scholars like Jurgen Habermas (1962, 1970, 1979, 1984), the direct descendant of the Frankfurt School, continue to agonize over the loss of "the public sphere" (assuming that it actually had existed) and the invasion of the "life world" by a rationalized–bureaucratized economy and by a politico-administrative apparatus. Such critiques tend to be more philosophical than sociological, but they have inspired many to make similar claims about the power of the forces unleashed by capitalism to invade local cultures and personal self.

Postmodernism is perhaps the most prominent form of critical theory today, but it really builds on themes that were evident with the early founders of sociology (Allan & Turner, 2001; see also Chapter 8). For postmodernists, the development of communication and transportation technologies, the expansions of capitalism to a global scale, and the capacity of high-volume and far-reaching markets to commodify just about anything, including symbols and lifestyles, are destroying local cultures, symbols of groups, and the integrity of the individual. Because all can be commodified and marketed on a global scale, cultural symbols are lifted from their local context and marketed, thus reducing the power of symbols to regulate the activities of local groups. Similarly, because people can now buy in markets the trappings of a new self, persons have become incapable of having a unified sense of who they are, particularly as the power of local cultures has declined with commodification of symbols. Among these postmodern theorists, the retread Marxists (e.g., Jameson, 1984; Lash & Urry, 1994; Harvey, 1989) appear to have the analysis of the transformations ushered in by globalization correct, but the more culturally oriented wing of postmodernism (e.g., Braudrillard, 1994; Lyotard, 1984) appears to go off the deep end in asserting without any hard data how these trends are changing the social world and person in fundamental ways.

The great problem with critical theory is not so much the critical dimension to this work but the theory part. Theory in the hands of most critical theorists becomes a license to say just about anything one wants about the social world, apparently without the requirement to check these pronouncements against data. Evil forces are posited and bad consequences are seen to ensue from these forces. While there is almost always an element of insight in these diagnoses, they almost always are too extreme to have much credibility. For we can ask: Have local cultures been destroyed? Have people lost a sense of their own self? Are people less embedded in groups than 100 years ago? Has commodification trivialized the symbols of groups? And so on. Scant amounts of systematic data have been brought to bear on these and related empirical questions; and until such data are forthcoming, we can take with a grain of salt many of the pronouncements of critical theory (see Chapters 6 and 8, for another assessment of postmodern theory). Critical theory has, like conflict theory in general, become more specialized, roughly paralleling social movements such as the civil rights and feminist movements. Feminist theory is clearly the most prominent of these more specialized critical theories (Chafetz, 1988, 1990; see also Chapter 28, for an assessment).

Evolutionary Theory

Sociological theory always has had an evolutionary bent. Every one of the founders of sociology saw societies as changing toward increased complexity, and each emphasized particular aspects of this transformation. Some were explicitly evolutionary, others less so, but all saw society as moving in a particular direction. While stage models of evolution came under relentless attack in the early decades of the 20th century, these models reappeared in the last decades of the century, in a variety of forms. One direction was a revival of the stage model, with theorists viewing societies as moving through identifiable stages (e.g., Parsons, 1966; Lenski, 1966). Another was world systems analysis that tended to see capitalism as evolving to a global level, with scholars differing on whether the contradictions of capitalism would indeed now lead to the destruction of this economic form (see Chapter 27, this volume). Others have blended stage models with world systems theories (e.g., Sanderson, 1988, 1995). Evolutionary stage models also can be found in critical theories (e.g., Habermas, 1979), and almost all postmodern theorists carry an evolutionary argument. Thus, evolutionary thinking is back in vogue within sociological theory.

But evolutionary theory involves much more than portrayals of societal movements from simple to complex forms. Early on, more purely biological arguments about evolutionary processes can be found in stage model theories (see also Chapter 21, this volume). For example, both Herbert Spencer (1874–1896) and Émile Durkheim (1893) offered ecological analyses more in tune with Darwinian theory, seeing competition among actors over resources as one of the driving forces behind specialization of activities (the sociological equivalent of the speciation of life forms). Such ecological theories have continued in both grand forms (e.g., Hawley, 1986; Turner, 1995) or more specialized incarnations within urban ecology (Berry & Kasarda, 1977; Hawley, 1950; Frisbie & Kasarda, 1988; Bidwell & Kasarda, 1985; Kasarda, 1972) and organizational ecology (Hannan & Freeman, 1977, 1989).

Another form of evolutionary theorizing has been more controversial because it often appears to be reductionist (see Chapter 20). Variously labeled "sociobiology" and "evolutionary psychology," this theory posits that key patterns of social organization are ultimately explained by reference to genic fitness (e.g., Barash, 1977; van den Berghe, 1981). Genes seek to survive and maximize their fitness or ability to stay in the gene pool and so; the behaviors of individuals and by extension their patterns of sociocultural organization will reflect drives for fitness by genes. Most of the formal modeling in evolutionary psychology was borrowed from economics, with notions of maximizing utilities and even of equilibrium processes transferred to biological arguments about what genes do. When organisms cannot think, as is the case with insects, perhaps the models of sociobiology have some utility—to make a bad pun. But once animals are able to create complex social structures mediated by culture, the effects of genic fitness are diminished. There can be no doubt that humans created social structures to survive and reproduce themselves, but once created these structures and their cultures have emergent properties that drive behavior and patterns of social organization above and beyond the pressures exerted by genes to remain in the gene pool. Indeed, most explanations from sociobiology become "just so" stories about how a particular structure can be explained by genic pressures to maximize fitness. The problems with such stories is that they are easily constructed, and they almost always are post hoc and ad hoc. They can never be tested because they are fabricated after the fact, typically making vague references to what must have happened in the evolutionary past.

There is a final form of evolutionary theorizing that has received the least amount of attention. Humans evolved like any other animal, and so it is reasonable to ask how natural selection shaped the nature of this animal. By looking at humans' closest relatives, the Great Apes of Africa (chimpanzees and gorillas), it is possible to get some clues about human nature because the hominid ancestors of humans split from this line about 5 to 8 million years ago (see Maryanski & Turner, 1992; Turner, 2001). Since humans share over 98% of their genes with these primate relatives, it is possible to use comparative anatomy and evolutionary theory to get hints of what human nature is really like at the biological level. Most sociologists are very hostile to this kind of theorizing because it strikes at their core commitments to a "socially constructed" view of the world and because it hints at reductionism. Humans are, most sociologists would argue, the product of purely sociocultural forces, and hence, human behavior and social structures can only be understood in these terms. This kind of extremism will only hurt sociology because humans are obviously an animal with an evolutionary history, and this history does influence human behavior, interaction, and organization. And advances in biology will increasingly expose sociology to ridicule as we stick to the view that genes have nothing to do with human behavior. We need to be reductionists to draw insights from evolutionary biology, but most theorists in sociology remain hostile to any form of biological theorizing.

Utilitarian Theory

Adam Smith was a great sociologist, although we often allow economics claim him as its founder. But Smith's *The Theory of Moral Sentiments* (1759) was highly sociological and in many ways set the agenda for sociological theorizing in the 19th century, especially the concern for how highly differentiated social systems were to become integrated. But except for hints of utilitarian arguments in George Herbert Mead's (1934) pragmatism and in Georg Simmel's (1907) analysis of money, utilitarian theories were not prominent at the beginnings of sociology. Of course, Karl Marx saw his great work on *Capital* (1867) as an effort to extend and correct Smith's *On the Wealth of Nations* (1776), and so in this sense Marx was a utilitarian. But the analysis of behavior in terms of individuals' efforts to realize utilities and avoid costs is for the most part a concern of later 20th-century theorizing. Moreover, this emphasis was often blended with behaviorism, another late 19th- and early 20th-century theory emphasizing that organisms, including humans, learn and retain in their repertoires those behaviors than provide reinforcement (Pavlov, 1928; Thorndike, 1932; Watson, 1913; Skinner, 1938).

The revival of this mode of theorizing occurred in the late 1950s and early 1960s, with both behaviorist (e.g., Homans, 1961) and utilitarian (e.g., Coleman, 1966) variants that persist to this day (see Chapter 31, this volume). But perhaps the most important advances in these theories came with the development of exchange theory in a guise first proposed by Georg Simmel (1907). Peter Blau's (1964) approach sought to analyze the power dimension of all exchange relations at both the micro- and macro levels of social organization; and in seeking power as the central dynamic of exchange and in trying to posit isomorphism in the process influencing both individual and collective actors, Blau brought Simmel's ideas to the modern era. In a very different mode, but still inspired by Simmel, Richard Emerson (1962) blended a theory of power-dependence relations with network theory, seeing the properties of network structures organizing individual and collective actors as a reflection of efforts to balance power relations. While the Blau tradition has receded, and unfortunately so, the network approach has flowered within two basic traditions; one self-consciously following Emerson (see Chapter 31) and in another, often termed "elementary theory," that pursues the same questions but with a somewhat different vocabulary (e.g., Willer & Anderson, 1981).

In the last two decades of the 20th century, rational choice theory asserted itself as a prominent variant of utilitarian theory (see Chapter 29, this volume). Consciously borrowing from key assumptions from economics, this approach has sought to see sociocultural arrangements as the result of efforts by individuals to maximize their utilities (rewards less costs and investments). Indeed, much like the explanatory logic of sociobiology, an ad hoc and post hoc story is told about how a structure reflects the rational decisions of individuals (this similarity to sociobiology should not be surprising, of course, because sociobiology and rational choice theory have borrowed key ideas from economics). But unlike sociobiology, rational choice theories have proliferated, and they have been used to explain many diverse phenomena and even to make predictions as opposed to post hoc interpretations. The real question is how far such explanations can go in explaining social phenomena, which to my view reveal emergent forces above and beyond the utilitarian calculations of individuals (see Chapter 30 for a form of theorizing where extreme rationality is played down but where predictions can be made from key assumptions about how humans make assessments and comparisons).

Interactionist Theorizing

The legacy of George Herbert Mead (1934, 1938) has endured throughout the decades since his death, but it has been supplemented and extended in many directions. There is, of course, the symbolic interactionist tradition (e.g., Blumer, 1969; Stryker, 1980; Burke, 1991) that carries forth Mead's emphasis on the importance of self (see Chapter 11), but even this tradition has been blended with other perspectives, such as role theory (see Chapter 12), exchange theory (McCall & Simmons, 1966), action theory (see Chapter 14), and sociology of emotions (see Chapter 13). But there also is the Durkheimian (1912) tradition of interactionism emphasizing rituals and emotional arousal, as can be seen in Erving Goffman's (1959, 1967) dramaturgical approach or Randall Collins' (1975) interaction ritual theory (see Chapter 24). While symbolic interactionists often claim dramaturgy to be within their tradition, its roots are entirely different (Durkheim's analysis of religion as opposed to G. H. Mead and American pragmatism); moreover, individuals are not considered to have stable and enduring self-conceptions as they are in all symbolic interactionist approaches.

In addition to the split between dramaturgy and symbolic interaction are more phenomenologically oriented approaches, ultimately coming to sociology from Edmund Husserl through Alfred Schutz (1932). Here emphasis is not on self, but on the practices used by individuals to create a sense of intersubjectivity or the illusion that they share a common world. Ethnomethodology has been the most robust of the phenomenological approaches, although this perspective has evolved into a rather routine analysis of conversations. Indeed, after the rather loud and shrill proclamations of early ethnomethodologists (e.g., Garfinkel, 1967; Handel, 1979) that the metaphysics of symbolic interactionists and in fact all of sociology were wrong, ethnomethodology has become a rather tame and routine enterprise, although creative theoretical work can still be found (see Chapter 15, this volume, for an example).

Probably the most interesting forefront within interactionist theorizing is the study of emotions. It is rather remarkable that George Herbert Mead never developed an analysis of emotions, and perhaps this fact explains why the study of human emotions did not really begin until the late 1970s (e.g., Heise, 1979; Hochschild, 1979; Kemper, 1979; Shott, 1979), but since this time, the leading edge of microsociology clearly has been the study of emotions. Some stay within the symbolic interactionist tradition as it has been extended, but most approaches bring in other theoretical perspectives in analyzing emotions, thereby providing a hook for integrating the concerns of symbolic interactionists with psychoanalysis (Turner, 1999), dramaturgy (Hochschild, 1979), gestalt-oriented theories (Heise, 1979; Smith-Lovin, 1990), evolutionary biology (Turner, 2001), power-status theory (Kemper & Collins, 1990), expectations states theory (Ridgeway, 1994), exchange theory (McCall & Simmons, 1966), network analysis (Markovsky & Lawler, 1994), conflict theory (Collins, 1984), and other approaches. Thus, the newfound concern with emotions has allowed interactionist theory to become less parochial and one dimensional (with the heavy emphasis on self and identity), and as a result, real integration of microsociology is currently underway (see Chapter 13, this volume for one approach that links psychoanalytical theory with symbolic interactionism).

At the microlevel, one of the most systematic approaches to the study of interaction is expectation-states theory, which ultimately extends assumptions from gestalt psychological to the analysis of the status structure of groups (Berger & Conner, 1969). While initially a rather narrow approach, studying the expectations associated with status in experimental groups, the approach has proliferated into many areas and to new topics (see Berger & Zelditch, 1985, 1998; Berger, Wagner, & Zelditch, 1989; Berger, Fisek, Norman, & Zelditch, 1977; Berger, Conner, & Fisek, 1974; Webster & Foschi, 1988, for reviews and anthologies); as this theoretical growth has occurred, the theory has become much more robust and general, analyzing the effects of expectations and the cultural beliefs that guide these expectations in diverse situations (see Chapter 16).

Structural and Structuralist Theory

Sociologists, of course, have always been concerned with social structure, and on the rise of "structuralism" as a broad intellectual movement has influenced some approaches in sociology that can be labeled structural or structuralist. Structuralism comes from Émile Durkheim's (1893) sociology, as it was turned on its head by Claude Lévi-Strauss (1953), and while structuralism enjoyed a brief moment in the sun (perhaps less than the normal 15 minutes of fame), the imagery of structuralism still remains in much theory (Lemert, 1990). The view that there is an underlying structural form to surface empirical events is intriguing (regardless of whether or not this is seen to reside in the neurology of the brain); and it has inspired diverse perspectives, such as Anthony Giddens' (1984) structural theory, Pierre Bourdieu's (1984) analysis of habitus, and Robert Wuthnow's (1987) study of cultural meanings. None of these approaches goes so far as Lévi-Strauss (1953) or Noam Chomsky (1980) in seeing the biology of the brain as the critical source of the generative rules of structure, but the vocabulary and metaphors of structuralism are employed in these and a number of sociological perspectives.

Another kind of structuralism, also rooted in Durkheim, is network analysis, which has both European and American roots through psychology and social psychology but all converging in modern-day views of structure as consisting of matrices of ties among nodes (Mitchell, 1974). Here, concern is with the dynamics of various properties or forms of ties, such as strength, centrality, density, transitivity, equivalence, brokerage, and bridges. Much network analysis is atheoretical, with an overemphasis on the methodologies for analyzing networks rather than the explanatory principles explaining their dynamics. Yet, more theoretical works can be found (e.g., Burt, 1980, 1982, 1992) particularly so when network analysis is combined with exchange theory (see Molm & Cook, 1995, for a review).

Yet another form of structuralism focuses on how structural constraints influence rates of interaction. Here structures are seen as parameters that influence opportunities for interaction, with these opportunities determining general rates of contact among individuals. The most prominent theory along these lines is that produced by Peter Blau (see Chapter 17), but other approaches often reveal the same underlying imagery. For example, much network theory argues that the place in a network will influence opportunities for ties, and hence, rates of contact among actors. Similarly, ecological theories often carry this view of distribution of characteristics in social space as influencing rates of interaction (e.g., McPherson & Ranger-Moore, 1991).

A final form of structural analysis—general systems theory—seeks to portray phenomena in terms of systems of relationships. These relationships often are considered to hold across different domains of the universe—physical, biological, mechanical, and social. As a result, the goal is to develop a common set of concepts and principles than can account for the systemic properties of widely diverse phenomena. While the general systems movement once enjoyed great popularity in the late 1950s and 1960s, relatively few dedicated scholars now work in this tradition, despite its promise of unifying science (see Chapter 19, this volume).

CONCLUSION

Let me end where I began: Sociological theory is now so diverse that it is difficult to see any unity ever emerging. Sociologists do not agree on what is real, what our core problems are, what our epistemology is, and what our theories should look like. As is evident in the chapters in this volume, some very interesting if not brilliant work is being done by sociological theorists, but it would be difficult to see much unity among the theoretical positions argued in each chapter. Some perspectives overlap and/or draw upon similar traditions, but most go their own way, defining problems and performing analysis without great regard for the whole of activity that constitutes theory today.

I could have added another 10 or 15 perspectives to the volume; indeed, I have lost five or six chapters along the way that were to be part of this volume. Thus, the chapters in this volume only begin to reflect the differentiated intellectual state of sociological theory today. For me, this diversity spells trouble for the discipline. True, this diversity also signals a certain vitality, but in the end, sciences must reveal consensus on problems and epistemology. Sociological theory does not have, nor will it ever have, such consensus; and there is danger here. If sociologists cannot speak with one voice, or at least many voices in a contrapuntal chorus, we will be overshadowed by those disciplines—such as economics—that can. We will not be considered useful in the halls of power, nor will our knowledge be respected by those inside or outside academia. Sociological knowledge has accumulated over the last half century (no doubt about this), but this knowledge has not been consolidated; as a result, it is difficult to see sociology as a cumulative science. Of course, many consider science a failed epistemology, and hence, there is no problem with the lack of cumulation that was a chimera anyway in the eyes of these critics. But if we are simply a discipline housed in the tower of babel (and babble), sociology will remain a weak discipline, operating at the fringes of academic and public life. Only with some degree of theoretical unity—on epistemology and problems—will sociology become an important discipline.

REFERENCES

Alexander, J. C. (1982–1984). *Theoretical logic in sociology*, 4 volumes. Berkeley: University of California Press.
Alexander, J. C. (Ed.). (1985). *Neofunctionalism*. Beverly Hills, CA: Sage.
Alexander, J. C., & Colomy, P. (1985). Toward neofunctionalism. *Sociological Theory, 3*, 11–23.
Alexander, J. C., Giesen, B., Münch, R., & Smelser, N. (Eds.). (1987). *The micro–macro link*. Berkeley: University of California Press.
Allan, K., & Turner, J. H. (2001). A formalization of postmodern theory. *Sociological Perspectives, 43*, 364–385.
Archer, M. S. (1982). Morphogenesis versus structuration: On combining structure and action. *British Journal of Sociology, 33*, 455–483.
Archer, M. S. (1988). *Culture and agency: The place of culture in social theory*. Cambridge: Cambridge University Press.
Barash, D. P. (1977). *Sociobiology and behavior*. New York: Elsevier.
Barnes, B. (2001). The micro/macro problem and the problem of structure and agency. In G. Ritzer & B. Smart (Eds.), *Handbook of sociological theory* (pp. 339–354). London: Sage.
Berger, J., & Conner, T. L. (1969). Performance expectations and behavior in small groups. *Acta Sociologica, 12*, 186–198.
Berger, J., & Zelditch, Jr., M. (1985). *Status, rewards, and influence*. San Francisco: Jossey-Bass.
Berger, J., & Zelditch, Jr., M. (1998). *Status, power and legitimacy: Strategies and theories*. New Brunswick, NJ: Transaction Books.
Berger, J., Conner, T. L., & Fisek, M. H. (Eds.). (1974). *Expectation states theory: A theoretical research program*. Cambridge, MA: Winthrop.
Berger, J., Fisek, M. H., Norman, R. Z., & Zelditch, Jr., M. (1977). *Status characteristics and social interaction: An expectation states approach*. New York: Elsevier.
Berger, J., Wagner, D. G., & Zelditch, M. (1989). The growth, social processes, and meta theory. In J. H. Turner (Ed.), *Theory building*. Newbury Park, CA: Sage.
Berger, P., & Luckman, T. (1967). *The social construction of reality*. Garden City, NY: Anchor.
Berry, B. J. L., & Kasarda, J. D. (1977). *Contemporary urban ecology*. New York: Macmillan.
Bidwell, C. E., & Kasarda, J. D. (1985). *The organization and its ecosystem: A theory of structuring in organizations*. Greenwich, CT: JAI Press.
Blau, P. M. (1964). *Exchange and power in social life*. New York: Wiley.
Blau, P. M. (1977a). *Inequality and heterogeneity: A primitive theory of social structure*. New York: Free Press.
Blau, P. M. (1977b). A macrosociological theory of social structure. *American Sociological Review, 83*, 245–254.
Blau, P. M. (1994). *Structural context of opportunities*. Chicago: University of Chicago Press.
Blumer, H. (1969). *Symbolic interactionism: Perspective and method*. Englewood Cliffs, NJ: Prentice-Hall.

Bourdieu, P. (1984). *Distinction: A social critique of the judgement of taste*. Cambridge, MA: Harvard University Press.

Braudrillard, J. (1994). *Simulacra and simulation*. Ann Arbor: University of Michigan Press.

Burke, P. J. (1991). Identity processes and social stress. *American Sociological Review, 56*, 836–849.

Burt, R. S. (1980). Models of network structure. *Annual Review of Sociology, 6*, 79–141.

Burt, R. S. (1982). *Toward a structural theory of action*. New York: Academic Press.

Burt, R. S. (1992). *Structural holes: The social structure of competitiveness*. Cambridge, MA: Harvard University Press.

Chafetz, J. S. (1988). *Feminist sociology: An overview of contemporary theories*. Itasca, IL: Peacock.

Chafetz, J. S. (1990). *Gender equity: An integrated theory of stability and change*. Newbury Park, CA: Sage.

Chase-Dunn, C. K. (1989). *Global formation: Structures of the world economy*. Cambridge, MA: Blackwell.

Chase-Dunn, C. K., & Hall, T. D. (1997). *Rise and demise: Comparing world systems*. Boulder, CO: Westview.

Chomsky, N. (1980). *Rules and representations*. New York: Columbia University Press.

Coleman, J. S. (1966). The possibility of a social welfare function. *American Sociological Review, 56*, 1105–1122.

Coleman, J. S. (1990). *Foundations of social theory*. Cambridge, MA: Belknap.

Collins, R. (1975). *Conflict sociology: Toward an explanatory science*. New York: Academic Press.

Collins, R. (1981a). Micro-translation as a theory-building strategy. In K. Knorr-Cetina & A. Cicourel (Eds.), *Advances in social theory and methodology* (pp. 76–84). New York: Methuen.

Collins, R. (1981b). On the micro-foundations of macro-sociology. *American Journal of Sociology, 86*, 984–1014.

Collins, R. (1984). The role of emotion in social structure. In K. R. Scherer & P. Ekman (Eds.), *Approaches to emotion* (pp. 385–396). Hillsdale, NJ: Erlbaum.

Collins, R. (1998). *The sociology of philosophies: A global theory of intellectual change*. Cambridge, MA: The Belknap Press.

Comte, A. (1830–1842). *Cours de philosophie positive, les préliminares généraux et ca philosophie mathématique*. Paris: Bachelier.

Dahrendorf, R. (1958). Out of utopia: Toward a reorientation of sociological analyses. *American Journal of Sociology, 74*, 115–127.

Dahrendorf, R. (1959). *Class and class conflict in industrial society*. Stanford, CA: Stanford University Press.

Durkheim, É. (1893). *The division of labor in society*. New York: Free Press.

Durkheim, É. (1912). *The elementary forms of the religious life*. New York: Free Press.

Emerson, R. M. (1962). Power–dependence relations. *American Sociological Review, 17*, 31–41.

Emerson, R. A. (1972). Exchange theory, part I: A psychological basis for social exchange and part II: Exchange relations and network structures. In J. Berger, M. Zelditch, Jr., & B. Anderson (Eds.), *Sociological theories in progress*. New York: Houghton-Mifflin.

Emirbayer, M., & Mische, A. (1999). What is agency? *American Journal of Sociology, 106*, 187–211.

Frank, A. G. (1979). *Dependent accumulation and underdevelopment*. New York: Monthly Review Press.

Frisbie, P. W., & Kasarda, J. D. (1988). Spatial processes. In N. J. Smelser (Ed.), *Handbook of sociology* (pp. 629–666). Newbury Park, CA: Sage.

Garfinkel, H. (1967). *Ethnomethodology*. Englewood Cliffs, NJ: Prentice-Hall.

Giddens, A. (1976). *New rules of sociological method*. London: Hutchinson Ross.

Giddens, A. (1984). *The constitution of society: Outline of the theory of structuration*. Berkeley, CA: University of California Press.

Goffman, E. (1959). *The presentation of self in everyday life*. Garden City, NY: Anchor Books.

Goffman, E. (1967). *Interaction ritual: Essays on face-to-face behavior*. Garden City, NY: Anchor Books.

Habermas, J. (1962). *Struckturwandel de offentlichkeit*. Neuwied: Luchterhand.

Habermas, J. (1970). *Knowledge and human interest*. London: Heinemann.

Habermas, J. (1979). *Communication and the evolution of society*. London: Heinemann.

Habermas, J. (1984). *The theory of communicative action*. Volume I. Boston: Beacon Press.

Handel, W. (1979). Normative expectations and the emergence of meaning as solutions to problems: Convergence of structural and interactionist views. *American Journal of Sociology, 84*, 855–881.

Hannan, M. T., & Freeman, J. (1977). The population ecology of organizations. *American Journal of Sociology, 82*, 929–964.

Hannan, M. T., & Freeman, J. (1989). *Organizational ecology*. Cambridge, MA: Harvard University Press.

Harvey, D. (1989). *The conditions of postmodernity: An inquiry into the origins of cultural change*. Oxford, England: Blackwell.

Hawley, A. H. (1950). *Human ecology*. New York: Ronald Press.

Hawley, A. H. (1986). *Human ecology: A theoretical essay*. Chicago, IL: University of Chicago Press.

Hecter, M. (1987). *Principles of group solidarity*. Berkeley and Los Angeles: University of California Press.

16   JONATHAN H. TURNER

Heise, D. (1979). *Understanding events: Affect and the construction of social action*. New York: Cambridge University Press.
Held, D. (1980). *Introduction to critical theory*. Berkeley: University of California Press.
Hochschild, A. R. (1979). Emotion work, feeling rules, and social structure. *American Journal of Sociology, 85*, 551–575.
Homans, G. C. (1961). *Social behavior: Its elementary forms*. New York: Harcourt & Brace.
Huber, J. (1991). *Macro–micro linkages in sociology*. Newbury Park, CA: Sage.
Jameson, F. (1984). *The postmodern condition*. Minneapolis: University of Minnesota Press.
Kasarda, J. D. (1972). The theory of ecological expansion: An empirical test. *Social Forces, 51*, 165–175.
Kemper, T. D. (1979). *A social interactional theory of emotions*. New York: Wiley.
Kemper, T., & Collins, R. (1990). Dimensions of microinteraction. *American Journal of Sociology, 96*, 32–68.
Lamont, M., & Wuthnow, R. (1990). Betwixt and between: Recent cultural sociology in Europe and the United States. In G. Ritzer (Ed.), *Frontiers of social theory* (pp. 287–315). New York: Columbia University Press.
Lash, S., & Urry, J. (1994). *Economies of signs and space*. Newbury Park, CA: Sage.
Lemert, C. C. (1990). The uses of French structuralisms in sociology. In G. Ritzer (Ed.), *Frontiers of social theory* (pp. 230–254). New York: Columbia University Press.
Lenski, G. (1966). *Power and privilege: A theory of stratification*. New York: McGraw-Hill.
Lévi-Strauss, C. (1953). Social structure. In A. Kroeber (Ed.), *Anthropology today* (pp. 524–553). Chicago: University of Chicago Press.
Lockwood, D. (1956). Some remarks on "The Social System." *British Journal of Sociology, 7*, 134–146.
Lyotard, J.-F. (1984). *The post modern condition*. Minneapolis: University of Minnesota Press.
Markovsky, B., & Lawler, E. J. (1994). A new theory of group solidarity. *Advances in Group Processes, 11*, 113–138.
Marx, K. (1867). *Capital: A critical analysis of capitalist production*, Volume 1. New York: International Publishers in 1967.
Maryanski, A. R., & Turner, J. H. (1992). *The social cage: Human nature and the evolution of society*. Stanford, CA: Stanford University Press.
Mayhew, B. H. (1981a). Structuralism vs. individualism. part I. *Social Forces, 59*, 335–375.
Mayhew, B. H. (1981b). Structuralism vs. individualism. part II. *Social Forces, 59*, 627–648.
McCall, G. J., & Simmons, J. L. (1966). *Identities and interactions*. New York: Free Press.
McPherson, M. J., & Ranger-Moore, J. (1991). Evolution on a dancing landscape: Organizations and networks in dynamic Blau-space. *Social Forces, 70*, 19–42.
Mead, G. H. (1934). *Mind, self, and society*. Chicago: University of Chicago Press.
Mead, G. H. (1938). *The philosophy of the act*. Chicago: University of Chicago Press.
Merton, R. K. (1968). *Social theory and social structure*, enlarged ed. New York: Free Press.
Mills, C. W. (1956). *The power elite*. New York: Oxford University Press.
Mitchell, C. (1974). Social networks. *Annual Review of Anthropology, 3*, 279–299.
Molm, L. D., & Cook, K. S. (1995). Social exchange and exchange networks. In K. S. Cook, G. A. Fine, & J. S. House (Eds.), *Sociological perspectives on social psychology* (pp. 48–74). Boston, MA: Allyn & Bacon.
Münch, R. (1982). *Theory of action: Reconstructing the contributions of Talcott Parsons, Émile Durkheim, and Max Weber*, 2 volumes. Frankfurt: Suhrkamp.
Parsons, T. (1951). *The social system*. New York: Free Press.
Parsons, T. (1966). *Societies: Evolutionary and comparative perspectives*. Englewood Cliffs, NJ: Prentice-Hall.
Parsons, T., & Smelser, N. J. (1956). *Economy and society*. New York: Free Press.
Parsons, T., Bales, R. F., & Shils, E. A. (1953). *Working papers in the theory of action*. Glencoe, IL: Free Press.
Pavlov, I. P. (1928). *Lectures on conditioned reflexes*, 3rd ed. New York: International Publishers.
Ridgeway, C. L. (1994). Affect. In M. Foschi & E. Lawler (Eds.), *Group processes: Sociological analyses* (pp. 205–220). Chicago: Nelson-Hall.
Ritzer, G. (1985). The rise of micro-sociological theory. *Sociological Theory, 3*, 88–98.
Ritzer, G. (1988a). The micro-macro link: Problems and prospects. *Contemporary Sociology, 17*, 703–706.
Ritzer, G. (1988b). *Sociological theory*, 2nd ed. New York: Alfred Knopf.
Ritzer, G. (1990). Micro-macro linkage in sociological theory. In *Frontiers of social theory: The new synthesis* (pp. 64–79). New York: Columbia University Press.
Ritzer, G., & Gindoff, P. (1994). Agency-structure, micro-macro, individualism–holism–relationalism: A meta-theoretical explanation of theoretical convergence between the United States and Europe. In *Agency and structure: Reorienting social theory* (pp. 107–118). London: Gordon & Breach.
Sanderson, S. K. (1988). *Macrosociology: An introduction to human societies*. New York: Harper & Row.
Sanderson, S. K. (1995). *Social transformations: A general history of historical development*. Cambridge, MA: Blackwell.

Schroyer, T. (1973). *The critique of domination: The origins and development of critical theory.* New York: Braziller.

Schutz, A. (1932). *The phenomenology of the social world.* Evanston, IL: Northwestern University Press (edition published in 1967).

Shott, S. (1979). Emotion and social life: A symbolic interactionist analysis. *American Journal of Sociology, 84,* 1317–1334.

Simmel, G. (1895). The problem of sociology. *Annals of the American Academy of Political and Social Science, 6,* 412–423.

Simmel, G. (1907). *The philosophy of money,* trans. T. Bottomore & D. Frisby. Boston: Routledge (edition 1990).

Skinner, B. F. (1938). *The behavior of organisms: An experimental analysis.* New York: Appleton-Century-Crofts.

Smith, A. (1759). *The theory of moral sentiments.* Indianapolis, IN: Liberty Press.

Smith, A. (1776). *An inquiry into the nature and causes of the wealth of nations.* Indianapolis, IN: Liberty Press.

Smith-Lovin, L. (1990). Emotion as confirmation and disconfirmation of identity: An affect control model. In T. D. Kemper (Ed.), *Research agendas in the sociology of emotions.* New York: Gordon & Breach.

Spencer H. (1874–1896). *The principles of sociology,* three volumes. New York: Appleton-Century.

Stryker, S. (1980). *Symbolic interactionism.* Menlo Park, CA: Benjamin-Cummings.

Thorndike, E. L. (1932). *The fundamentals of learning.* New York: Teachers College Press.

Turner, J. H. (1983). Theoretical strategies for linking micro and macro processes. *Western Sociological Review, 14,* 4–15.

Turner, J. H. (1995). *Macrodynamics: Toward a theory on the organization of human populations.* New Brunswick, NJ: Rutgers University Press for Rose Monograph Series of the American Sociological Association.

Turner, J. H. (1998). *The structure of sociological theory,* 6th ed. Belmont, CA: Wadsworth.

Turner, J. H. (1999). Toward a general sociological theory of emotions. *Journal for the Theory of Social Behavior, 29,* 109–162.

Turner, J. H. (2000). A theory of embedded encounters. *Advances in Group Processes, 17,* 285–322.

Turner, J. H. (2001). *On the origins of human emotions: A sociological inquiry into the evolution of human affect.* Stanford, CA: Stanford University Press.

Turner, J. H. (2002). *Face-to-face: A sociological theory of interpersonal behavior.* Stanford, CA: Stanford University Press.

Turner, J. H., & Maryanski, A. R. (1979). *Functionalism.* Menlo Park, NJ: Benjamin-Cummings.

Turner, J. H., & Maryanski, A. R. (1988). Is neofunctionalism really functional? *Sociological Theory, 6,* 110–121.

Turner, S. P., & Turner, J. H. (1990). *The impossible science: An institutional history of American sociology.* Newbury Park, CA: Sage.

van den Berghe, P. (1981). *The ethnic phenomenon.* New York: Elsevier.

Wallerstein, I. (1974). *The modern world-system.* New York: Academic Press.

Watson, J. B. (1913). Psychology as the behaviorist views it. *Psychological Review, 20,* 158–177.

Weber, M. (1921/1968). *Economy and society,* 3 volumes. Totowa, NJ: Bedminster Press.

Webster, Jr., M., & Foschi, M. (1988). *Status generalization: New theory and research.* Stanford, CA: Stanford University Press.

Willer, D., & Anderson, B. (Eds.). (1981). *Networks, exchange and coercion.* New York: Elsevier.

Wright, E. O. (1985). *Classes.* London: Verso Press.

Wright, E. O. (1997). *Class counts.* Cambridge: Cambridge University Press.

Wuthnow, R. (1987). *Meaning and moral order: Explorations in cultural analysis.* Berkeley: University of California Press.

PART I

THEORETICAL METHODOLOGIES AND STRATEGIES

CHAPTER 2

What Makes Sciences "Scientific"?

STEPHAN FUCHS

The first serious difficulty raised in the titular question of this chapter is that there does not seem to be a unified "science," in the singular. At least, "unity" ought to be operationalized as a variable, not fixed, in advance and a priori, as a constant property of the "nature" of science. Empirical research on the sciences suggests a manifest cultural, structural, and organizational disunity (Galison, 1997). There also are considerable differences between the frontiers of a science and its more routine or normal areas. Sciences change over time as well, and some of them, such as the locations where rapid discoveries are being made, change very quickly, with little respect or eye toward philosophical definitions, criteria, or rules of method.

The evidence supports the suspicion that the unity of science is a myth and exaggeration. Significantly, the mythical properties of logic and rationality also are a core theme in neo-institutionalist theories of organizations (Meyer & Rowan, 1977). They find widespread loose coupling between formal and informal systems. Similar loose coupling exists between logic and practice of a science. There are many sciences now, and new sciences or specialties emerge all the time. Worse for unity, within a science there are specialties, clusters, and research fronts that behave in ways not necessarily consonant with unity. The sciences look more like a patchwork quilt than a logically unified pyramid.

To say the sciences are historical, social, and cultural is true, but only the beginning of a problem, not its solution. Logic is a poor predictor for what an actual science does, in the here and now of its occurring and happening. What a science does is the result of its own previous operations, not its philosophy. Most active scientists are too busy to pay much attention to philosophical puzzles and enigmata. They might become more involved in philosophy once their active careers are over, or when an outside observer, such as postmodernism, appears to be saying there are no truth and objectivity in science. Major upheavals in a culture, including revolutions, also tend to generate so much uncertainty and novelty that it is hard to separate "science" from "metaphysics." A major metaphysical controversy during the Scientific Revolution opposed natural philosophers to scholastics and humanists on the question of whether *any* "contrived" experiments, that is, "the experiment as such," could ever be true to the essence of nature.

The sciences do have philosophical dimensions, but once they become "normal," they no

STEPHAN FUCHS • Department of Sociology, University of Virginia, Charlottesville, Virginia 22903.

Handbook of Sociological Theory, edited by Jonathan H. Turner. Kluwer Academic / Plenum Publishers, New York, 2002.

longer reflect on them. To be sure, normalization and establishment need not happen and are rather unlikely, since most organizational upstarts fail due to a widespread "liability of newness" (Hannan & Freeman, 1989). However, if a science does take off toward maturity and institutionalization, it begins to forget the origins and transcendental foundations of science itself. As a science becomes more normal and mature, with a well-established and -defined niche in the world, it gradually sediments its core operations and building blocks. These become routines, hardwired into the blueprints and black boxes of a particular culture (Berger & Luckman, 1967).

Whether experiments "as such" are "true to nature" is not a problem a mature science could understand let alone turn into a viable research puzzle. Who would fund such research and how could research prove that research as such captures the essence of nature? Once doing research becomes the prevalent intellectual mode of relating to the world, metaphysics becomes obsolete and eventually disappears into academic and professional philosophy. The "truth" is now the outcome of scientific research, not metaphysics. After a while, systematic philosophy turns into naturalism, that is, global advocacy and endorsement of science.

A mature science solves the problems it has posed for itself. It does so on the basis of its previous problems and solutions. It can change these, of course, but mature and professionalized sciences do not wonder about the metaphysical or ontological foundations. They might remain skeptical, but not about themselves. The truths of a science also change, together with advances and discoveries, but as its maturity increases, so does a science's inability or unwillingness to engage in metaphysics. It no longer has a protocol for handling metaphysical mysteries, or it operationalizes these into empirically decidable propositions.

With Medawar (1963/1990), a science becomes more scientific when it has mastered the "art of the soluble." A metaphysics, in contrast, does not "solve" anything but wonders whether "solving" some problem or puzzle might not be just one way among others to practice the intellectual craft. Unlike science, a religion becomes weaker and more secular when the great mysteries disappear.

FROM PHILOSOPHICAL TO LOCAL UNITY

Call the epistemological sort of unity "strong." More in tune with recent evidence from science studies is the much weaker assumption that unity is local and temporary, the result of actual mergers or hybrids between various sciences (Shapin, 1995). This unity lasts as long as it does and extends as far as it does until further notice, that is, until the configurations of sciences and specialties change yet again. Unity is not global or transcendental, and it can be lost and found. Unity also is a matter of degree. Rarely is a unity "complete." This weaker empirical or contingent, as opposed to conceptual, unity is not the realization of philosophical analysis or reduction. Rather, it follows from the observable movements, alignments, and coalitions among the sets of networks within which science actually occurs or happens.

There is, then, no agreeable and robust philosophical criterion or set of criteria that made a science "scientific" (Laudan, 1996). Even within philosophy, the suspicion grows that the very search for such criteria might be in vain (Rorty, 1991). It turns out that such criteria change over time; they are not the same for different sciences, and what follows from them for the way an actual science assembles and reassembles itself is uncertain. No doubt there are rules of method, but they rarely lead to concise and clear proscriptions for rationality.

Troubles with rationality surface not just in science, though it is here that rationality has traditionally been placed with privilege. Rationality is not a good empirical metaphor for action generally (Collins, 1993), and this includes the decisions scientists might make in advancing a certain project, program, or line of research.

The unity of science is an exaggeration, observed within a segment of analytical epistemology. This particular observer is placed at a large distance from where science actually gets done. Philosophy observes science from far away and from within its own networks and traditions. The farther away an observer is from a referent, the more unity that observer tends to attribute to what is being observed (Collins, 1988; Fleck, 1935/1979). Observers at a far distance depend on their observing strongly on the more or less official front stage self-presentations of that which they observe. Such presentations summarize and condense select features and data into rational versions or formats, maybe for the benefit of instruction or popularization. Move closer to an actual science, into the laboratory, and that unity dissolves into multiple clusters and networks. What happens in these networks is, at best, loosely coupled to epistemological rules and regulations, much as the informal systems in organizations separate, to a variable degree, from the official manuals, charts, and handbooks.

The closer an observer gets to the local assembly of a science, the less "consensus" is being measured. A widespread criterion for making a science scientific has been that the "harder" and more "mature" a science becomes, the more consensus it displays. This is not false, but needs modification. More consensus is being claimed than exists or can be cashed in when needed, and science is no exception (Gilbert & Mulkay, 1984). You think other reasonable people do, will, or would agree with the reasonable opinions you hold yourself. Probe deeper into consensus, however, and it tends to become brittle, fall apart, or become vague and empty, as in "universal values." Actual consensus—that is, not the quasi-transcendental fictions of Habermas and not the ideological appeals to "the people"—shrinks and expands over time and according to how concretely it specifies what is to be said and done. An empirical consensus cannot extend both its range or width and depth simultaneously. At the frontiers of a culture, where breakthroughs occur, conflict and controversy undermine consensus.

What the sciences do not have, however, is dissensus on whether it is a good thing to do science or whether it might be better to do something else instead, maybe criticism, moralizing, or the latest fad in social and cultural theory—writing about yourself. Nonsciences keep arguing and dissenting on what they are, really, and what they should do. Sciences also do not have multiple fragmentation along political or ideological cleavages, including sex and race.

A science becomes more scientific as it externalizes its outcomes to "reality," instead of attributing them to "standpoints" or "perspectives." This is the difference between science and ideology (more on this later). The more scientific a science, the more it will generate its own foci of attention and reputational structures, and the less attention it will pay to what it observes as nonscience, prescience, or pseudo-science. In turn, those non-, pre-, and pseudo-sciences either imitate or challenge and debunk science.

Some constructivists conclude from the empirical record of science studies that method, progress, cumulation, and rational reconstructions are "fictions," but this is premature and triggers misleading connotations and "science wars" (Fuchs, 1996). Confronted with critical debunkings of their core possessions, the scientists feel provoked and outraged, since their sacred symbols are being desecrated. This reaction is not particularly surprising, since any profession will respond to attacks on its front stage myths with emotionally charged vehemence. Constructivists also would rightly be upset if the integrity of their motives were being challenged. As far as they are still doing science or doing work commensurate with science, constructivists will insist that their contributions to scholarship are based on methodical and objective research, not perspectival or political biases.

To call something a "fiction" suggests unreality, maybe deception. But method and rationality are very real and they are not deceptions. Instead, they surface in certain places, at certain times, to do certain kinds of cultural work. In some areas of a science, where more routine puzzles are being solved, "method" is indeed more of an empirical presence. Method appears prominently in low-level science instruction, as well as in grant proposals or written reports of findings. Likewise, rationality appears regularly when a science is asked or invited to tell its history, which then appears as cumulative progress or, in more dramatic cases, as victory over superstition and the forces of unreason. No science "follows" rational rules of method, especially not when it is making breakthroughs, but no science can do without method and rationality on certain occasions and in certain areas of its work.

BOUNDARIES AND DEMARCATIONS

"What makes a science scientific" as opposed to different ways of knowing? This is the problem of demarcation (Ward, 1996). In philosophy, demarcation is essentialist; that is, demarcation of science from nonscience by means of separating the "nature" of scientific knowing from other ways or other cultures. Various candidates for demarcation have been suggested and dropped. These include distinctions between facts and values, subjective and objective, internal and external, and logical versus contingent. By its very nature science is objective, rational, empirical, disinterested, cumulative, and truthful. Nonscientific ways of knowing, such as religion, metaphysics, or art, are valuable forms of culture but they do not correspond to anything real, outside of themselves. Outside of science there are superstition, faith, tastes, money, or power.

Not one of these "demarcation criteria" has proven operational or successful for separating science from the rest of culture in all possible worlds. Start with the distinction of science–metaphysics. A science does have some metaphysical or paradigmatic structures in the cores of its networks, where the black boxes and routine equipment are being housed (Latour, 1987). These are metaphysical, in the sense that they are not themselves the themes, topics, and puzzles of research, at least not within the science whose "presuppositions" are in question. "Materialism" belongs to the "metaphysics" of any modern science, but no modern science could turn the truth of materialism itself into a soluble experimental puzzle. A science also could not establish by means of an experiment that experiments as such are "true to Nature."

To say science is "objective," as opposed to art, for example, is misleading as well, since there is very little objective consensus on objectivity (Fuchs, 1997). At its frontiers, where a science produces rapid breakthroughs and innovations, there is less "objectivity" than in its settled and established parts. Virtuoso performance in science and art appear phenomenally similar, colored by ecstacy, charisma, and genius (Schneider, 1993; Heinich, 1996). A science is not without "faith"; it has faith in itself and the overall soundness of its accomplishments. It trusts that more progress will be made in the very near future, as soon as the new equipment can be funded and delivered. During major upheavals and ruptures, "prophets" might appear in the history of science as well. In fact, this happens under much the same structural conditions as in the history of a religion (Spengler, 1923/1993). A science that were utterly "disinterested" would be a very poor science indeed, since an active science is very keenly interested in itself and in its continuation and expansion.

We find, then, actual sciences and cultures in unruly disregard for proper philosophical conduct and procedure. Some allegedly "subjective" arts look surprisingly objective; think of socialist realism, with its centralized rules and regulations for politically correct art. A revolutionary science has much in common, at least in its beginning and emergence, with avant-gardes in music (Mullins, 1973). To say science is based on "observation" raises a host of difficulties as well, even within the analytical movement (Lakatos, 1970). Aristotle did a good bit of observing; there are theoretical entities and unobservables in any science; how observation relates to theory also is controversial.

AFTER PHILOSOPHY

Sociologically, demarcation criteria are not logical or analytical but empirical and temporal. They are the various empirical and therefore revisable boundary markers a culture employs to distinguish itself from that which it is not, not anymore, or not yet. All cultures perform some boundary work, and the robustness of boundaries varies together with the strength and confidence of a culture. Establishing a boundary also varies with the environment against which a specialty, network, or culture distinguishes itself. Distinctions lead to "identity" (White, 1992). This identity is not essential, constant, or written in stone. Rather, an identity is the current summary or definition of a previously accomplished identity.

A specialty with high-velocity changes its boundaries and demarcations very rapidly, without pause for philosophical reflection and solidification. When the environment of related specialties changes rapidly as well, turbulence breaks out. Weak boundaries surround specialties-in-formation; stronger boundaries signal a consolidated culture with a known and celebrated history of recognized achievements and successes. However, weak and strong are matters of degree, not principle, and the weaker might become stronger over time, or the other way around. As boundaries grow very strong and as a culture or specialty consolidates into the smooth and confident continuity of a normal tradition, its demarcations from rivals or other cultures tend to grow firmer as well, approaching analytical, definitional, and possibly tautological status (Quine, 1964). Tautologies can be found in the redundant and fortified cores of cultures and their institutions (Fuchs, 2000).

Demarcation criteria are variable distinctions an observer draws to distinguish its—not his or hers—identity from the identity of other observers. Distinctions drawn by observers run both ways; there are self-observations and observations by other observers (Baecker, 1999). When the latter happen to be rivals or competitors over a certain niche or territory, the conflicts over demarcations may heat up into intellectual property struggles. Occasionally, a specialty invades another one and conquers it without indigenous rest. Now, a local unity and new identity emerge, distinguishing itself in new ways from past identities and from the related specialties in the larger networks among specialties.

A "reduction" of one specialty or even discipline to another one occurs not as a result of some philosopher claiming to have demonstrated that one entity is really another entity, the latter being more fundamental, basic, or original than the reduced entities (Spear, 1999). Sociologically, reduction is an improbable and contingent event in the competitive relations between specialties and cultures. Reduction is an event that either happens or not. If it happens, it happens locally, not globally; that is, interdisciplinarity tends to involve a fairly small number of specialties. In some cases, "interdisciplinarity" may just be a ritualistic and fashionable buzzword the administrators, funders, and planners of science like to use, but rarely does interdisciplinarity involve more than, say, three or four disciplines, and even then, it tends to become its own discipline, complete with special institutes specializing in interdisciplinarity.

SOCIOLOGICAL PHILOSOPHY

The evidence from science studies does not resonate well with analytical philosophical criteria for what makes a theory and science truly or essentially scientific. But there might be sociological ways for distinguishing science from other cultures, ways of knowing, and nonsciences. Sociological demarcation refers to variable cultural boundaries, not essential or logical criteria. To make the step from philosophy to sociology, we need to switch to a second-order mode of observation (Luhmann, 1992). In this observational mode, the observer sociology observes how actual sciences, not philosophy of science, distinguish themselves from that which they are not, not yet, or not anymore. Sociology theorizes such distinctions as the variable cultural markers and boundaries that professions employ to lay claim to intellectual property and turf.

Avoid, again, the mistake to conclude there are no truth, objectivity, or rationality in science. Far from it. But as a second-order observer, sociology cannot simply confirm or repeat, en bloc, scientific claims to truth and objectivity. Neither, of course, can it deny them (Bloor, 1976). What is left, then, is to explore when and how truth and objectivity and progress are made to "happen" and how this is accomplished. This observational Gestalt–switch marks the transition from philosophy to sociology of science. Sociology cannot really say: That which makes a science scientific are its truth and rationality. For it has no independent way to decide anything about a science's claims to truth *other than* its own claims to truth.

Science is indeed "objective," but in a sociological, not philosophical, sense. Sociologically, objectivity is an internal accomplishment of cultures committed to objectivity. It does not fall out of the sky, but must be accomplished or not. Objectivity is contingent; it either is made to happen or not. Therefore, it has a history and semantic career (Daston, 1992). Sociologically, objectivity is not adequate representation, lack of bias, or simply the opposite of "subjective." To say objectivity is "intersubjective" comes a bit closer, but conversations and traffic signs are intersubjective as well.

Think of objectivity as a semantic currency running through certain intellectual networks. By means of this currency, the network explains to itself or an audience how it behaves, and why. In this mode of formal or official self-observation, the outcomes and results of a network are, by and large and in the long run, "objective," because they reflect actual states in the world. If they are "subjective," someone has made a mistake, and that mistake ought to be corrected, since objective is better than subjective. The subjective is "merely" so, indicating that something is lacking and amiss. The same applies to "perspectives." If a fact is objective only within a perspective, then it is not really objective, so that the idea is to overcome perspectives, not celebrate them, as happens in networks that are fragmenting into ideological politics.

Objectivity deserves trust. At first, this was trust in the honor of gentlemen (Shapin, 1994). Since these have long since departed, trust in honor has transformed into trust in reputation and procedure. This trust trusts that the scientific mistakes are generally honest, not deceptive. Deceptions are misconduct, to be investigated and sanctioned harshly, usually by ostracism from the tribe, since a sacred object has been violated (Fuchs & Westervelt, 1996).

Objectivity is the "code" that structures how the communications in the network should be handled and rewarded (Luhmann, 1992). According to the code, the contributions are generally based on solid evidence, sound research, and plausible explanations, not on sexual bias or racial prejudice. The outcomes offered are the results of research, not intuition, charismatic vision, or prophetic revelation. Or, how the insights communicated were gathered is irrelevant; what counts is whether they survived the usual tests. No reputation goes to those offering the merely subjective or perspectival. This does not mean that the culture the network sustains were in close contact with the way the world really is; only that "objective" is the way in which recursively networked communications that cherish and institutionalize objectivity are coupled within a network. When this happens, when networks with objectivity emerge, we may get "science": "For the scientific truth is but that which *aspires* to be true only to those who want the scientific truth" (Weber, 1904/1982, p. 184).

SOCIOLOGICAL DEMARCATION

What makes a science scientific? What makes a religion religious? Search now for sociological, not philosophical, distinctions. Max Scheler (1924) leads the way. He compares the modern sciences, metaphysics, and religion as social structures and historical cultures. The modern *sciences* are organized as reputational and professional networks. Doing science is the career path for credentialed and specialist workers trained by teachers and drills or exercises. The sciences do "research," that is, they solve the puzzles they pose to themselves with their own means and devices. Research is done on soluble problems for which exists a protocol of decidability. Research is administered in projects and programs; it is organized into small and competitive specialties. The organizational nucleus of science is the laboratory or, more correctly, a network among laboratories. Laboratories are sites of controlled experiments. To do those, much equipment is needed.

A *metaphysics* surrounds a virtuoso "master." The metaphysician still belongs to generations of metaphysicians and often gathers admirers, but metaphysics is not organized as a professional work organization. When this happens nevertheless, when metaphysics becomes part of a specialist academic curriculum, metaphysics comes to an end. It dies with the likes of Nietzsche, Heidegger, Adorno, and Sartre. As Max Weber (1919/1982), who had his own metaphysical moments, predicted, there are no longer any genuine metaphysical virtuosos and masters. The remaining prophets have become "false," that is, prophethood becomes visible as being constructed and accomplished.

The closest we currently have to metaphysics is "theory," but theory is also located in institutions of specialties, so that one can specialize in it and become a "theorist." Another successor to the metaphysician is the "scholar," particularly of the humanist variety; but scholars are experts also, which means they are not experts, but amateurs, outside their particular area of expertise. The "popular intellectual" belongs in this set of heirs to metaphysics as well, although the last thing on a genuine metaphysician's mind is to become popular and commercial. The irony about popular intellectuals is that they deride those very forces that created a niche for them in the first place. There is still something metaphysical about a Habermas or Luhmann, but both praise "postmetaphysical" thinking.

As opposed to the professional philosopher, who hurries from conference to conference, the metaphysician is not comfortably at home in the contemporary university and its networks. Metaphysicians prefer solitude; Heidegger had his cabin in the Black Forest around Todtnauberg and Nietzsche fled to the mountains of Sils Maria. This does not mean the metaphysician wants to be left alone or that he or she does not like other people, only that they dislike being part of a *Betrieb*. Metaphysics is often snobbish about academic politics and elitist about popular culture or common sense. Plato preferred ideas to experiences.

Metaphysics must be "lived," not taught. In this, it behaves much like a cult. Admission to the cult resembles an initiation rite more than admission by examination or credential. The new recruits are being transformed, not educated. They participate in a Truth unavailable to nonmembers. Membership does have its privileges. Metaphysics, at least in its self-understanding, is not a set of propositions or assertions that could be "tested" in some way against "the evidence." Neither does it advertise itself as one "worldview" among others. Metaphysics has no "method," or declares method to be secondary and subordinate to "substance." The substance of metaphysics are the perennial and foundational mysteries: the essence of Being, the nature of reality, or how to live the good life.

What makes a science scientific, in contrast, is its relationalism and antiessentialism (Cassirer, 1969). In a science, things are what they are because the relations and forces working on them have made them what they are. Change these relations and forces and a different thing emerges. A number, for example, is a position in a set of operations and relations among numbers. The number is defined by those relations, not by any "intrinsic meaning." In antiessentialism, a thing is nothing but a temporary balance of forces impinging on it. A thing has no intrinsic properties. There is no "thing-in-itself." All that which exists exists empirically; that is, until further notice, or until new evidence suggests something different might be the case. The sciences are against essentialism.

The metaphysician does not do "research." Work is not done in company with others, as happens in a "laboratory." Metaphysics might be part of a university and curriculum, complete with courses and exams and grades, but then metaphysics turns into a philosophy and philosophical specialty, next to other such specialties. A metaphysician has maybe followers but not really "students," in the sense of the cohorts in bureaucratic mass education. The extreme case, Nietzsche, derided those seeking followers as those seeking Zeros and Nullities. Sometimes, as in the ancient world, the sage metaphysician and his devotees share certain communal living arrangements, maybe around a patrimonial household or "academy." The master and his disciples see themselves as the long arm of a destiny or transcendence, not as intellectual workers or even "intellectuals."

Metaphysics does not aim or claim to make any "progress." To the contrary, it suspects or resents progress as the departure from a true origin, authentic life, or essential Being. In Heidegger, this is *Seyn*, as opposed to mere *Sein* and the even lesser *das Seiende*. In Nietzsche, this ultimate Truth is the *Uebermensch*, Zarathustra, and in Hegel and Marx, it is absence of alienation. Unlike any modern science, but much like a religion, metaphysics looks backward, not forward. A metaphysics may have utopian themes to it, but such utopias are often returns also.

Different metaphysics envision the Origin in different ways. It might have the form of a dialectical completion of history, as in Marx, or it might be pre-Socratic Greekhood (Heidegger), the transcendental Ego (Kant, Husserl), or the absolute Idea or Spirit (Plato, Hegel). But that which calls metaphysics into thinking are not solvable problems that disappear once they are solved, to be replaced by future problems (Heidegger, 1938/1977, 1969). Rather, the "problems" of metaphysics are mysteries. Unlike problems, mysteries are perennial and essential. They return forever, as in Nietzsche, though maybe in different guises. Metaphysical mysteries cannot be researched or experimented upon. They are holistic, not analytical, and require not methods but *Wesensschau*.

A metaphysics remains centered and focused on the identity of sages. Their metaphysics is very much *theirs* and difficult to repeat or replicate elsewhere. Even coauthorship does not resonate well with the "spirit" or thrust of metaphysics. Therefore, the death of the sage often means the death of his metaphysics as well. In contrast, a science has no such deep attachments and investments in "personality." It has its prophets and geniuses, but is never *merely* cultish, or for very long. After the metaphysical master's demise, there might be epigones and pupils carrying on the torch, but their work tends to remain derivative and focused the original. A rather late example might be Garfinkel's (1967) *Studies in Ethnomethodology*, which is close to the metaphysics of Husserl and even Heidegger. The epigone's work tends to be confined to commentary, exegesis, or elaboration, without any novel metaphysics emerging in the process. Alternatively, the students of a metaphysical master might enter the universities and transform metaphysics into professional philosophy or research there.

As opposed to science, both metaphysics and *religion* keep remembering their foundations and origins. They do not and do not want or plan to "overcome" their foundations and origins. For, the Truth, with a capital T, is in the beginnings and origins, back when a religion and its First Prophet appeared. The life of metaphysics or religion comes from its source, and that source must be recovered, worshipped, and kept alive. The past is not just studied, as in "historical research," but brought into the present by means of hermeneutics. The passing of time represents a possible danger and threat, not a promise to unlimited progress. The danger comes from forgetting and straying away from the origin.

Both metaphysics and religion believe in essences and universals. They are nothing without "transcendence," although just what is transcendent differs from case to case. No metaphysics or religion could understand itself as just another worldview, system of thought, or ideology. They are not just empirical occurrences, but the origin of all occurrence.

Religions offer and deliver salvation, not knowledge or expertise. Religions do not do "research," although the intellectuals of a church might respond to research in various ways or even do a bit of research themselves, say on sacred texts. Even then, however, research is a subordinate and secondary part of religious and sacred practice, done not to find out something "new" but to affirm and celebrate that which is already True. The truth of a religion lies at its beginnings and ends, in an original state of bliss, and in the eventual recovery of that bliss in the Afterworld. The Truth, again with a capital T, is already known; it may have been forgotten in sin but can be regained by traveling a path to salvation. Religious officials of a church might assist in this quest, due to their special calling and closeness to the sacred.

In sharp contrast, the truth of a science is in its future, not past. Part of that which makes a science scientific is, then, the discarding and overcoming of its past. The past appears as an incomplete version and prehistory of the present. The past is something less than the present and even less than the future. Less was known then than is now or will be known; there was less reason, truth, success, and objectivity in the past. Only the past knowledge that still measures up to what is known now deserves to be preserved and only until it, too, finally becomes obsolete. A science has no developed historical sense, or turns its history into yet another science, such as history of science. A science that goes back to its origins is a dying science, running out of new discoveries to make. When it makes no further progress, a science loses its claim to more support and funds and will rather quickly succumb to the intense competition.

A science is not "foundationalist" in the way religion and metaphysics are. It does research *within* these foundations but not *on* them. This is why Heidegger (1969) suspected that science does not "think"—it does not allow thinking to turn to that which remains unthought as a science goes about its business.

Therefore, science is more "restless" and "homeless" than religion and metaphysics. A science only has the resting points and periods it makes or allows for itself, until it is ready to move on, or is pushed to move on by the competition. The periods of rest are short and idle. A science at rest for a long time is in danger of backwardness and obsolescence. Religions are calmer because salvation can surely be attained, or already has been attained. Whether or not salvation is certain cannot be decided by "research."

In modern times, the sheer tempo of scientific research accelerates spectacularly, up to a level unknown outside of the modern sciences (Price, 1986). Acceleration happens both at the rapidly moving frontiers of a science, as well as through increasing specialization and differentiation. This makes the experts in a science amateurs in most specialties other than their own. The increased speed makes it more and more difficult to "synthesize" scientific knowledge into a comprehensive "worldview." There are still calls for cosilience and unification, but they remain at a very abstract level and are opposed by appeals to emergence and irreducibility. The scientific advances come at a much faster pace than changes in religion or metaphysics. To be sure, changes occur here as well, but no religion or metaphysics is structured so as to make discoveries and advances its regular business.

Solutions to a research puzzle in science become pieces in subsequent puzzles. A science does not come to its natural end, when all the truths converge into the Truth. Grandiose reductions to, say, particle physics are sometimes being envisioned, and this is when a science sounds most "metaphysical," but so far, reduction amounts to little more than promise (Wilson, 1998). There is no end to science, unless it is being destroyed, and there is no "final" theory, as in metaphysics, since a "final" science would put itself out of business—the business of making more progress in the future.

SOME ANTIESSENTIALIST CAUTIONS

Keep in mind that distinctions between science, religion, and metaphysics are empirical and revisable. They do not remain constant and do not refer to any "essences" or natural kinds. Rather, demarcations and distinctions change together with the actual configurations of cultural fields and networks. As the relationships between such cultures change, so do their mutual distinctions and possible insults. Expect that, sometimes, a science will resemble a metaphysics more than at other times. Since not all the sciences are alike, some might be structurally and culturally closer to metaphysics or religion than others. Likewise, some more secular and humanist religions may resonate more strongly with the sciences than more orthodox and traditionalist religions.

For example, a science undergoing major ruptures or revolutions has its own share of prophets, virtuosos, and charismatics. But that science cannot stop there, restricting itself to worship, admiration, or commentary on foundational texts. Rather, a science renormalizes a prophetic vision into a workable and operational research program. As a result, history and systematics become separate.

The densely clustered groups at the frontiers of a science sometimes behave in ways similar to emerging charismatic movements, especially when a novel science comes into being (Mullins, 1972). However, in the course of its institutionalization, charisma becomes routinized and decomposed into procedure. A science worships its heroes and geniuses, but not for their own sake and not because genius represents a link to the transcendental. Rather, "genius" is the way in which a science explains to itself how it makes its most astonishing breakthroughs.

Allow for variation and observe when and why a metaphysics becomes more scientific, or a science more artistic. Demarcations and distinctions are in flux. An ossified religion and a normal science possibly share a degree of bureaucratic routineness in their everyday operations, especially when teaching or instructing large numbers of novices and students in the established truths. There also are some metaphysics closer to science than others, such as Husserl's phenomenology or the antimetaphysics of positivism. As a metaphysics turns into an academic philosophy, it becomes part of an organization and administered in departments. This process gradually renormalizes and assimilates metaphysics into expert philosophical "research."

So the caution is to not treat empirical distinctions as logical criteria and to allow for as much variation as possible, both across social and cultural space and over time.

HOW MUCH OF SCIENCE IS TECHNOLOGY?

Some European philosophers hold that what makes a science scientific is its level of technical control and success, allowing for the manipulation of predictable effects (Mitcham, 1994). When technology is being criticized, this philosophy is called the "critique of instrumental reason." This critique comes in various more or less conservative and romantic versions, but the common theme is that technology means mastery of the world. Mastery becomes possible as the result of mathematical, experimental, and then applied science. Since the origin of science is in metaphysics, it is ultimately this modern metaphysics that allows for mastery and domination of the world.

Modernist metaphysics sees the world and Nature as the object to the Subject's will to power and representation. Correct representations lead to working technologies. How technologies are to be used depends on will and decision. Science and technology provide the will with the power and means of domesticating and disciplining Nature and reified society. Planning and control become the dominant relation to the world, at the expense of other relations, such as poetry or metaphysics.

While science does not "make" or "construct" nature, it does establish such a relation to it that nature appears as raw material, to be decomposed and recombined. In this relation, the world and nature emerge as a lawfully ordered cosmos of observable events. The truth of science is its own truth, and that truth is not the only possible one. In fact, the truths of science are rather shallow and superficial, as opposed to, say, the Truth in a metaphysics or religion, which is deeper, more profound, and longer lasting than mere facts of the matter.

In science, the world appears as such that it can be arranged or rearranged at will and by decision, guided by facts and true theories. Science builds a home for itself in the world by means of technology and the instrumental-*cum*-mathematical reification of the world into things, facts, and their objective relations. This first happens during the Scientific Revolution, with metaphysical assistance and assurance from Descartes, Kant, and the empiricists. After some time, this essentially "modern" way of scientific knowing deems itself the only valid and reliable one. Weber's "unbrotherly aristocracy of rational research" begins its long reign. Whatever knowledge fails to measure up to scientific standards is, from now on, not really knowledge at all.

Since science is cumulative, control and mastery of the world improve over time, with better scientific and social technologies. Progress is possible precisely because science forgets its own metaphysical origins and dimensions. Science cannot even ask the sorts of questions metaphysics or religion ask, let alone transform and renormalize them into soluble puzzles analyzed by the current methods and tools. For science, there is no metaphysics beyond or at the foundation of physics, or else such a metaphysics is sheer nonsense and charlatanry.

This latter insult and assault on metaphysics marks a watershed: Philosophy becomes "scientific philosophy" with Logical Positivism and its analytical heirs. The more thorough and complete this transformation, the more philosophy becomes science's handmaiden, appendix, or popular mouthpiece. Much of this analytical philosophy is philosophy of science, which provides science with cultural rationalizations and myths.

The remaining metaphysics becomes academic philosophy. In the university, philosophy becomes part of the *Betrieb*, which is when metaphysics dissolves. Its organizational form is the cult or charismatic movement, not specialized intellectual administration. From then on, philosophy lives a spooky shadow existence between the humanities and sciences. It loses its identity and becomes uncertain about what philosophy still can do once the sciences move into its territory.

In this European view, science and technology are essentially identical, united by the driving force of instrumental Reason. In this view, what makes a science scientific ultimately is its technical success in bringing about predictable and observable effects. Science works because it is true, and we know it to be true since it works. With this circle, the fact that science is the only way to find out the truth becomes obvious and self-evident.

SOME TROUBLES IN EUROPE

Metaphysics is essentialism and wants to be. In essentialism, there are things-in-themselves, natural kinds, and Being, in addition to empirical and observable Beings. In essentialism, what a science does follows from what it "is," and it is, by its very nature or essence, that which metaphysics believes this essence to be.

Against essentialism, allow for variation and introduce the second-order observer. Sociologically, an essence is not really an essence but an outcome of holding something constant and doing this for a long time, until it becomes habit or institution. An essence emerges as a web of forces and temporarily freezes into a stable and steady *eigenstate*. This is how the observer "philosophy" observes science—at a large distance from where science is actually made, exaggerating its unity, rationality, and logic. Recall that, once an observer moves closer to the sites of science-in-the-making, this essence dissolves into higher complexity.

Empirically, there is little unity or logic to science. Science and technology are related, but loosely so. Citation data suggest that much of the science that gets done leads nowhere and makes little difference to other science or future science (Price, 1986). It has proven terribly difficult to "finalize" research according to preset plans and goals. A technical device that works "follows" more from other devices, those that work already, not from a theory or true representation. There is no direct logical path leading straight from a scientific finding or discovery to a working technical device.

Likewise, metaphysics exaggerates and overestimates technological mastery and effective scientific control. Frequently, control is fragile and prone to breakdowns and failures. This fragility increases with closer coupling and complex interactions (Perrow, 1984). Some sciences, such as those associated with "complex systems," warn against the revenge effects and unplanned consequences of interventions and manipulations. Planning and prediction happen but so do surprises, and surprises often generate still more surprises. The surprises also come at a much faster rate than do the firm and solid solutions. Science and technology are not really that impersonal, cold, or instrumental. There are areas and periods of intense conflict, passion, and drama.

EXPERIMENTAL CONTROLS

The European critics and romantics exaggerate the unity of science and technology, but they do point at a feature that distinguishes science from other ways of relating to reality. This feature is the laboratory, where experiments are being arranged and performed. There might be laboratories and experiments outside of science, but those in science are distinctive in that they try to "entrap" nature by putting it to the test outside of where that nature usually occurs. The displacement of nature inside the laboratory and then again from the laboratory into the world, strengthens control, but this is control over the experimental settings and conditions, not, or at least not yet, control in the sense of technical mastery.

Inside the laboratory, nature is being decomposed and rearranged. This is the sciences' "analytical" approach as opposed to more "holism" in metaphysics and religion. Parts of nature are being subjected to unusual trials and tribulations. Experiments speed up or slow down reactions to "unnatural" levels; they dissect, bombard, and mix up their materials. Laboratories are arranged so that the experiments done can hold constant that which makes a difference to an outcome or effect, but is not currently under investigation.

Experiments focus the attention space on very selective and restricted forces and variables. They separate signals from noise by eliminating backgrounds. It is this analytical zooming-in on isolated signals that makes "cumulation" in a science possible. Progress or cumulation occur when most of the world is taken for granted, including any "presuppositions" research might rely on (Fuchs & Spear, 1999). Cumulation loses its progressive and linear directionality when there is no narrow focus of attention on well-defined puzzles and parameters. Cumulation can occur because experiments "make everything else equal."

Unlike metaphysics, a science does not start anew each day, with the great mysteries of Being. Instead, it operationalizes its problems into soluble puzzles that can be worked on in specialist settings of expertise. In this, one picks up where one left yesterday. In no way does this imply that all the problems a science poses to itself are actually solved in some way. However, the problems that are currently unresolvable will become tractable in the future, when more is known and better instruments are available. A science knows of no "essential" mysteries.

Religion and metaphysics do not "cumulate" or make "advances." They remain textual modes of mental production, restricted to reading and writing. This also restricts their ability to tinker with their materials and equipment. Nonexperimental sciences may have substitutes for experimentation, such as regression analysis and historical comparisons, but these are poor substitutes indeed and remain dependent on verbal and discursive operations.

What makes a science scientific then also is its high instrumental and experimental capacity for progress. Metaphysics does not make and does not want to make any progress. A "progressive" religion turns into a more secular worldview, moving away from the sacred, until the Gods begin to escape altogether or become privatized and personal. In many humanities and the humanistic social sciences the very idea of "progress" has become ideologically suspect.

WHAT WOULD MAKE
SOCIOLOGY SCIENTIFIC?

The prospects for cumulative advances become dimmer still as an intellectual network becomes fragmented into competing ideological positions and movements. Structural fragmentation also fragments the common attention space. A science turns into rival ideological camps when the suspicion hardens that observation is not "disinterested" but driven by unacknowledged standpoints, perspectives, or political biases. Then, a central intellectual strategy is to "reveal" these underlying biases and interests. Science turns into mutual ideological critique and exposure. Theories lose their innocence and are not to be taken at face value. Science becomes ideological politics, driven by the institutional entrenchment of diverse status groups. In the end, science itself becomes ideologically suspect, as an ally of capitalism, imperialism, ethnocentrism, sexism, and so on.

What kinds of work are being done once science fragments into ideological politics? Prominent specimens include textual or "discourse analysis," social theory and philosophy, critical theory, exegesis and commentary, or foundational and epistemological "critique." History gains precedent over systematics. Moral and political advocacy of some "cause" or other becomes acceptable. Debates on the "identity" of a field or discipline run rampant. Very little gets actually solved or resolved, so that old problems and puzzles do not go away but appear and reappear all the time. There is little consensus on even basic matters, such as whether a field "is" a science or even whether it "should" be. The very idea of "progress" comes under attack.

Fields or disciplines where these sorts of work prevail are, in a sense, "metaphysical," not "scientific." A sign of metaphysics is not being able or not wanting to forget the sacred origins and authentic foundations. But this very forgetting is a crucial condition for research and cumulation. These take place when the attention space is very narrowly focused on solvable puzzles for which a protocol of decidability is available. Such protocols do not effectively make sure that a problem or puzzle will, in fact, be resolved, but they do limit which sorts of questions and answers count as a possible solution or step toward solution. No cumulative advances can be made in the presence of manifest uncertainty and controversy over foundational enigmata and mysteries. What makes a science unscientific is its inability to forget its past.

SOME HYPOTHESES

In lieu of a conclusion, here is a hypothetical list of empirical features that distinguish science from metaphysics and religion:

1. A science looks forward and expects to make further progress in the future.
2. A science forgets its origins and brackets its foundations or presuppositions.
3. A science is organized into specialized research professions making continuous advances in highly restricted areas of expertise.
4. Research is done in more or less circumscribed programs or projects for which funding can be obtained.
5. The previous results of a science are the conditions for the current work which generates future results.
6. A science goes to work on relations, not essences.
7. At the uncertain and intensely competitive frontiers of a science, rapid discoveries and innovations are being made. These form the backbone of the reputational structure. High reputations go to discoverers, not sages, priests, or guardians of traditions.
8. Laboratories and equipment allow a science to perform experiments on a select arrangement of variables under controlled conditions.
9. A science institutionalizes nonideological modes of observing, or "objectivity."

REFERENCES

Baecker, D. (Ed.). (1999). *Problems of form.* Stanford, CA: Stanford University Press.
Berger, P., & Luckman, T. (1967). *The social construction of reality.* New York: Doubleday.

Bloor, D. (1976). *Knowledge and social imagery*. London: Routledge.

Cassirer, E. (1969). *Substanzbegriff und Funktionsbegriff: Untersuchungen ueber die Grundfragen der Erkenntnis-kritik*. Darmstadt, Germany: WB.

Collins, H. M. (1988). Public experiments and displays of virtuosity: The core-set revisited. *Social Studies of Science, 18*, 725–748.

Collins, R. (1993). The rationality of avoiding choice. *Rationality and Society, 5*, 58–67.

Daston, L. (1992). Objectivity and the escape from perspective. *Social Studies of Science, 22*, 597–618.

Fleck, L. (1935/1979). *Genesis and development of a scientific fact*. Chicago: University of Chicago Press.

Fuchs, S. (1993). A sociological theory of scientific change. *Social Forces, 71*, 933–953.

Fuchs, S. (1996). The new wars of truth. *Social Science Information, 35*, 307–326.

Fuchs, S. (1997). A sociological theory of objectivity. *Science Studies, 1*, 4–26.

Fuchs, S. (2000). *Against essentialism*. Chicago: University of Chicago Press.

Fuchs, S., & Westervelt, S. (1996). Fraud and trust in science. *Perspectives in Biology and Medicine, 39*, 248–269.

Fuchs, S., & Spear, J. (1999). The social conditions of cumulation. *American Sociologist, 30*, 21–40.

Galison, P. (1997). *Image and logic: A material culture of microphysics*. Chicago: University of Chicago Press.

Garfinkel, H. (1967). *Studies in ethnomethology*. Englewood Cliffs, NJ: Prentice-Hall.

Gilbert, G. N., & Mulkay, M. J. (1984). *Opening Pandora's box*. Cambridge, England: Cambridge University Press.

Hannan, M. T., & Freeman, J. (1989). *Organizational ecology*. Cambridge, MA: Harvard University Press.

Heidegger, M. (1938/1977). *Holzwege* (pp. 75–113). Frankfurt, Germany: Vittorio Klostermann.

Heidegger, M. (1969). *Zur Sache des Denkens*. Tuebingen, Germany: Niemeyer.

Heinich, N. (1996). *The glory of van Gogh: An anthropology of admiration*. Princeton, NJ: Princeton University Press.

Lakatos, I. (1970). Falsification and the methodology of scientific research programmes. In I. Lakatos & A. Musgrave (Eds.), *Criticism and the growth of knowledge* (pp. 91–196). Cambridge, UK: Cambridge University Press.

Latour, B. (1987). *Science in action*. Cambridge, MA: Harvard University Press.

Laudan, L. (1996). *Beyond positivism and relativism*. Boulder, CO: Westview.

Luhmann, N. (1992). *Die Wissenschaft der Gesellschaft*. Frankfurt, Germany: Suhrkamp.

Medawar, P. (1963/1990). *The threat and the glory*. New York: Harper Collins.

Meyer, J. W., & Rowan, B. (1977). Institutionalized organizations: Formal structure as myth and ceremony. *American Journal of Sociology, 83*, 340–363.

Mitcham, C. (1994). *Thinking through technology*. Chicago: University of Chicago Press.

Mullins, N. C. (1972). The development of a scientific specialty: The phage group and the origins of molecular biology. *Minerva, 19*, 52–82.

Mullins, N. C. (1973). *Theories and theory groups in contemporary American sociology*. New York: Harper & Row.

Perrow, C. (1984). *Normal accidents*. New York: Basic Books.

Price, D. J. de Solla. (1986). *Little science, big science … and beyond*. New York: Columbia University Press.

Quine, W. van Ornam. (1964). *From a logical point of view* (pp. 20–46). Cambridge, MA: Harvard University Press.

Rorty, R. (1991). *Objectivity, relativism, and truth* (pp. 21–34). Cambridge, England: Cambridge University Press.

Scheler, M. (1924). Probleme einer Soziologie des Wissens. In M. Scheler (Ed.), *Versuche zu einer Soziologie des Wissens* (pp. 5–146). Munich, Germany: Duncker & Humblot.

Schneider, M. (1993). *Culture and enchantment*. Chicago: University of Chicago Press.

Shapin, S. (1994). *A social history of truth*. Chicago: University of Chicago Press.

Shapin, S. (1995). Here and everywhere: Sociology of scientific knowledge. *Annual Review of Sociology, 21*, 289–321.

Spear, J. H. (1999). *The sociology of reductionism*. PhD Dissertation, Department of Sociology, University of Virginia.

Spengler, O. (1923/1993). *Der Untergang des Abendlandes: Umrisse einer Morphologie der Weltgeschichte*. Munich, Germany: DTV.

Ward, S. (1996). *Reconfiguring truth*. Lanham, MD: Rowman & Littlefield.

Weber, M. (1904/1982). *Gesammelte Aufsatze zur Wissenschaftslehre* (pp. 146–214). Tuebingen, Germany: Mohr.

Weber, M. (1919/1982). *Gesammelte Aufsatze zur Wissenschaftslehre* (pp. 582–613). Tuebingen, Germany: Mohr.

White, H. C. (1992). *Identity and control: A structural theory of social action*. Princeton, NJ: Princeton University Press.

Wilson, E. O. (1998). *Consilience: The unity of knowledge*. New York: Alfred Knopf.

CHAPTER 3

Formal Theory

GUILLERMINA JASSO

INTRODUCTION

We do theory because we want to understand human behavior. The objective of sociology, as of the other human sciences, is to accumulate reliable knowledge about human behavioral and social phenomena. We do theory because of the conviction that theoretical analysis enables swift progress to the goal of understanding human behavior. And we do formal theory because of the conviction that *formal* theory enables *swifter* progress to *deeper* understanding of human behavior.

In this chapter we discuss formal theory. We begin by surveying briefly the entire landscape of sociological analysis in order to locate theory and then formal theory within it. Sociological analysis consists of three kinds of activities: developing a framework, constructing theories, and carrying out empirical work. The framework collects the central questions of the field and the basic building blocks for addressing them. The framework and the theories are linked because the theories address questions posed in the framework and because some of the building blocks in the framework become the assumptions of theories (and others later appear among the predictions of theories).

To characterize formal theory, we address the objective and structure of formal theory, as well as criteria for judging particular formal theories. As will be seen, we discuss two main types of formal theory, plus a hybrid form that combines the two types. The two types are deductive theory and hierarchical theory. Deductive theory, however, is of the first importance, and much of the discussion will pertain to deductive theory only (plus the deductive component of hybrid theories). Indeed, the term "theory" when used alone will always refer to deductive theory, as will the criteria for judging a theory.

Both deductive and hierarchical theory have two-part structures. The first part contains the postulates of the theory; the second part contains the predictions, in the case of deductive theory, and in the case of hierarchical theory, the constructed propositions.

A theory is judged in two ways. First it is judged in terms of theoretical criteria. Theories

This chapter was written in part while the author was a Fellow at the Center for Advanced Study in the Behavioral Sciences, Stanford, California. I gratefully acknowledge the Center's support. I am grateful to Stefan Liebig for many helpful comments and suggestions.

GUILLERMINA JASSO • Department of Sociology, New York University, New York, New York 10003.

Handbook of Sociological Theory, edited by Jonathan H. Turner. Kluwer Academic / Plenum Publishers, New York, 2002.

that survive theoretical scrutiny are then judged by empirical tests of their predictions. The theoretical criteria are simple: The postulates should be mutually logically consistent; there should be a minimum of postulates and a maximum of predictions; and the predictions should include novel predictions, that is, predictions for phenomena or relations not yet observed. Of course, a theory can satisfy all the theoretical criteria and yet be false; empirical evidence is the final arbiter.

Beyond satisfying the criteria by which a theory is judged—and in particular, raising new questions via its novel predictions—a good theory displays one or more of several useful features: the prediction mix includes both intuitive and counterintuitive predictions; the predictions span all levels of analysis; the theory provides a foundation for measurement; and the theory yields a framework for interpretation of rare or nonrecurring events.

To illustrate our discussion of sociological analysis and of formal theory, we draw on the study of the sense of justice. We examine the framework for justice analysis and discuss five theories from the portfolio of theoretical justice analysis. The five theories include deductive, hierarchical, and hybrid theories, and they illustrate somewhat different approaches and tools within the formal theory tradition. As well, they are at different stages of development, ranging from fledgling theories with few predictions to the justice version of comparison theory (hereafter simply "justice-comparison theory"), which is sufficiently well developed that it and its parent theory are described in a separate chapter of this book. The diversity of the theories in the justice portfolio makes them ideally suited for illustrating formal theory. It is likely that a broad range of theories encountered or constructed in social science will resemble in approach, form, content, fruitfulness, or stage of development one or another of these five specimens. Moreover, the five include theories related to each other in ways that exemplify general relations among theories.

This chapter is organized as follows: the second section considers the three main activities of sociological analysis: developing a framework, constructing theories, and carrying out empirical work. In the third section we discuss theory and formal theory. Illustration via the five specimen theories is provided in the fourth section. The chapter concludes with a set of frequently asked questions (FAQs) about formal theory.

THE TRIPTYCH
OF SOCIOLOGICAL ANALYSIS

Sociological analysis consists of everything that sociologists do in order to describe and understand human behavioral and social phenomena.[1] The subject matter of sociological analysis may be any aspect or part of the large set of behavioral and social phenomena, and this topical domain gives its name to the particular analysis that is undertaken. For example, class analysis examines the workings of class-related phenomena; gender analysis investigates gender-related phenomena; justice analysis addresses the operation of the human sense of justice; conversation analysis focuses on conversation-related phenomena; and so on. Indeed, every substantive area in sociology—and every chapter in Part III of this volume—can be thought of as [•] analysis, where [•] is a placeholder for the topical domain. In the same way that the objective of sociological analysis is to describe and understand the whole of human behavioral and social phenomena, the objective of [•] analysis is to describe and understand the [•] subset of human behavioral and social phenomena.

Until recently I held the view that the enterprise of sociological analysis could be usefully

---

[1]Generations of graduate students have begun their doctoral work with a required course titled, "Sociological Analysis." The history of these courses and their content is yet to be written.

subdivided into two main parts—theoretical work and empirical work—and so, too, the enterprise in any domain-specific analysis. That is indeed the inherited and time-tested view. But a newer and perhaps more useful view is that sociological analysis consists of three kinds of activities: not only *theoretical analysis* and *empirical analysis* but also, and even more basic, developing a *framework*.

In the framework, sociologists pose the central questions in a field or subfield and develop the basic building blocks that will be used in both theoretical and empirical work. Theoretical analysis begins with an assumption, and empirical analysis begins with a testable proposition. But these—assumption and testable proposition—have to come from somewhere. That somewhere, I submit, is ultimately and fundamentally the framework. To be sure, as we will discuss below, in the most wonderful kind of theory—deductive theory—the theory yields implications that become the testable propositions of empirical analysis. Yet, in any scholarly adventure, there always are empirical tests of propositions that do not come from theory; that is, there are always inductive explorations. And these tests, these explorations, draw their life from the framework.

Thus, the framework provides building blocks which become the starting assumptions of theories and which also lead immediately to empirical work. It may also happen that relations which arise in the framework later emerge as theoretical predictions. Our emphasis, however, is on the framework as the source of building blocks, and hence we highlight elements of the framework which become the assumptions of theories rather than elements which subsequently appear as theoretical predictions.

Developing a Framework—Justice Analysis

Typically, the building blocks in the framework are formulated by analyzing the basic questions in the field. An example will provide concreteness. In *justice analysis*, whose objective is to describe and understand the operation of the human sense of justice, the framework begins with four questions, which are thought to cover the core issues in the field (Jasso & Wegener, 1997):

1. What do individuals and collectivities think is just, and why?
2. How do ideas of justice shape determination of actual situations?
3. What is the magnitude of the perceived injustice associated with given departures from perfect justice?
4. What are the behavioral and social consequences of perceived injustice?

In the course of thinking about each of these questions, of considering how to address them, the building blocks emerge.

Building Blocks from the First Question

Thinking about the first question—What do individuals and collectivities think is just, and why?—it quickly becomes clear that there is always one fundamental actor: the person who forms ideas of justice and makes judgments about justice and injustice; this actor is called the *observer*. Indeed, the terms "just" and "justice" are always shorthand for "just in the eyes of the observer" and "justice in the eyes of the observer." It also quickly becomes clear that in the distributive-retributive realm there is a second fundamental actor: the recipient of the benefits and burdens that awaken the sense of justice; this actor is called the *rewardee*. The observer forms ideas about the *just reward*, in a particular distributive or retributive domain,

TABLE 3.1. The Just Reward Matrix for N Observers and R Rewardees

$$C = \begin{bmatrix} c_{11} & c_{12} & c_{13} & \cdots & c_{1R} \\ c_{21} & c_{22} & c_{23} & \cdots & c_{2R} \\ c_{31} & c_{32} & c_{33} & \cdots & c_{3R} \\ \vdots & \vdots & \vdots & \ddots & \vdots \\ c_{N1} & c_{N2} & c_{N3} & \cdots & c_{NR} \end{bmatrix}$$

NOTE: In the matrix above, c_{ir} denotes the observer-specific/rewardee-specific just reward, where c denotes the just reward, observers are indexed by i (= 1, ..., N), and rewardees are indexed by r (r = 1, ..., R).

for a set of rewardees (including perhaps him- or herself).[2] The ensuing set of just rewards is called the *observer-specific just reward distribution*; its parameters, such as the mean and inequality, reflect the observer's *principles of macrojustice*. Similarly, the principles that guide each observer's ideas of the just reward for specific rewardees are embodied in the *observer-specific just reward function*, which relates the just reward to characteristics of the rewardees; and the parameters of the just reward function reflect the observer's *principles of microjustice*.

If other observers also form ideas about the just rewards in this domain, all of the *observer-specific/rewardee-specific just rewards* together can be arrayed in a *just reward matrix*. Corresponding to each observer, there is an observer-specific just reward function, just reward distribution, and principles of microjustice and macrojustice. All these are visible in or estimable from the just reward matrix. Table 3.1 presents the just reward matrix, where c denotes the just reward, observers are indexed by i (i = 1, ..., N), and rewardees are indexed by r (r = 1, ..., R). The observer-specific/rewardee-specific just reward is thus denoted c_{ir}.

Of course, individuals form ideas of justice about many things, not only about individuals' rewards, and these produce their own new building blocks. For example, individuals form ideas about the *just mean* and the *just inequality* in a distribution.

In the example of justice analysis, it is the activity of posing the central questions and then thinking about how to address them that quickly leads to a large set of building blocks, of which the ones discussed in the preceding paragraph are a small subset. Note that the building blocks in the framework are ready for use in two ways. First, they are ready for use to construct theories. Second, they are ready for use in empirical work; quantities like the just reward can be measured, and relationships like the just reward function can be estimated.

Two of the five specimen theories used as examples in this chapter—allocation theory and Anselmian theory—use building blocks formulated in addressing the first central question. These building blocks include the just reward and the just inequality.

Building Blocks from the Second Question

In addressing the second question—How do ideas of justice shape determination of actual situations?—a new building block arises immediately, and this is the *actual reward* received by the rewardee, denoted $a_{.r}$. Along with it, there arise an *actual reward function*, an *actual reward distribution*, and, if observers misperceive the actual rewards, an *actual reward matrix*. When misperception occurs, each actual reward is observer-specific as well as rewardee-specific, and the placeholder dot in the subscript becomes the index for the observer, as in a_{ir}. The actual reward function is well known in social stratification, where it appears in various forms, including an earnings function, an occupational attainment function, and an

[2]The term "reward" is used as a convenient shorthand for both goods and bads, benefits and burdens.

educational attainment function. In justice analysis, however, there is an added twist, as the determinants may include, besides the usual factors in these functions, and sometimes instead of them, allocators' ideas of justice.

In some situations, actual rewards are determined by committees or boards whose members in turn rely on their ideas of justice. Of course, the members of such committees or boards may differ in their influence on the actual rewards or on the actual rewards of particular rewardees, producing the *observer-specific/rewardee-specific weight*, denoted w_{ir}. As with the just rewards and actual rewards, the weights can be arrayed in a matrix, called the *weight matrix*.[3] Each rewardee's actual reward is a weighted mean of the just rewards assigned to him or her by all the members of the society.[4] That is, it is a function of the just rewards and the weights attached to all the members in deciding this particular person's actual reward:

$$a_{.r} = \sum_{i=1}^{N} c_{ir} w_{ir} \tag{1}$$

It follows that the actual reward distribution, denoted A, is a linear combination of the N C_i weight distributions:

$$A = \sum_{i=1}^{N} C_i W_i \tag{2}$$

Again, note that these new building blocks are ready for use both to construct theories and in empirical work. We shall see their use in three of the specimen theories: allocation theory, Anselmian theory, and just society theory.

Building Blocks from the Third Question

Thinking about the third central question—What is the magnitude of the perceived injustice associated with given departures from perfect justice?—leads to a new variable, the *justice evaluation*, and a new function, the *justice evaluation function*. The justice evaluation expresses the observer's judgment and sentiment that the rewardee (possibly him- or herself) is justly or unjustly treated, and if unjustly treated, whether overrewarded or underrewarded and to what degree. The justice evaluation is represented by the full set of real numbers, with zero representing the point of perfect justice, negative numbers representing unjust under-reward, and positive numbers representing unjust overreward (panel A, Table 3.2). Thus, a justice evaluation of zero indicates that the observer judges the rewardee to be perfectly justly rewarded. A justice evaluation of -3 and a justice evaluation of -5 both indicate that the observer judges the rewardee to be unjustly underrewarded, with the rewardee associated with the -5 judged to be more underrewarded than the rewardee associated with the -3. Similarly, a justice evaluation of 3 and a justice evaluation of 5 both indicate that the observer judges the rewardee to be unjustly overrewarded, with the rewardee accorded the 5 judged to be more overrewarded than the rewardee accorded the 3.

By the time we reach the third central question, we already have in the set of building blocks the just reward (from analyzing the first question) and the actual reward (from analyzing the second question), and it is thus natural to think of the justice evaluation as arising from the comparison of the actual reward to the just reward. This comparison may be stated as

---

[3]Sometimes the weight matrix is called the power matrix, as each observer's weights in determining the actual rewards may reflect his or her power.

[4]Of course, in the case in which actual rewards are decided by special committees or boards, the weights of most members of society will be zero.

TABLE 3.2. The Justice Evaluation and the Justice Evaluation Function

A. Mathematical Representation of the Justice Evaluation

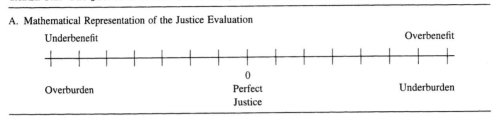

B. The Justice Evaluation Function: General Form

Version 1	Version 2
$J^G = J^G(A,C)$, $\partial J^G/\partial A > 0$, $\partial J^G/\partial C < 0$,	$J = \theta[J(A,C)]$,
$J^B = J^B(A,C)$, $\partial J^B/\partial A < 0$, $\partial J^B/\partial C > 0$,	$\partial J/\partial A > 0$, $\partial J/\partial C < 0$,
	$\theta > 0$ for a good, $\theta < 0$ for a bad,
$J(a_0 = c_0) = 0$,	$J(a_0 = c_0) = 0$,

where J denotes the justice evaluation, A denote the actual reward, C denotes the just reward, the superscripts G and B denote good and bad, respectively, and θ denotes the signature constant; the sign of θ is called the framing coefficient and the absolute value of θ is called the expressiveness coefficient.

C. The Justice Evaluation Function: Logarithmic-Ratio Form

Version 1	Version 2
$J \propto \begin{cases} \ln\left(\dfrac{A}{C}\right), & \text{for a good} \\ \ln\left(\dfrac{C}{A}\right), & \text{for a bad} \end{cases}$	$J = \theta \ln\left(\dfrac{A}{C}\right)$

a general function: The justice evaluation is a function of the actual reward and the just reward, such that, in the case of a good, for example, the justice evaluation increases with the actual reward and decreases with the just reward and such that when the actual reward equals the just reward, the justice evaluation equals zero, the point of perfect justice (panel B, Table 3.2).

Further reasoning about the justice evaluation function, in particular, reasoning about the properties of a desirable functional form, leads to a new specific form, the *logarithmic-ratio specification of the justice evaluation function*.[5] In this form, the justice evaluation varies as the natural logarithm of the ratio of the actual reward to the just reward, in the case of a good, and, in the case of a bad, as the logarithm of the ratio of the just reward to the actual reward (as shown in version 1, panel C, Table 3.2). The logarithmic specification imparts several good properties to the justice evaluation function, including the property that it quantifies the common human experience that deficiency is felt more keenly than comparable excess.

Additionally, there is a parameter called the *signature constant*, which plays two parts. Its sign, called the *framing coefficient*, indicates whether the observer regards the reward under consideration as a good or as a bad (positive for a good, negative for a bad). Its absolute value, called the *expressiveness coefficient*, indicates the observer's style of expression.

The framework distinguishes between the observer's experience of the justice evaluation and his or her expression of the justice evaluation. The *experienced justice evaluation* is written as in version 1 (panel C, Table 3.2), or more simply if the context unambiguously refers to only a good or only a bad. For example, in the case of a good, the experienced justice evaluation is written:

[5] I am here following a logical sequence from general to specific function. In point of fact, the logarithmic-ratio specification of the justice evaluation function was discovered before the general justice evaluation function was formulated.

$$J^* = \ln\left(\frac{A}{C}\right) \tag{3}$$

where A denotes the actual reward, C denotes the just reward, and J^* denotes the experienced justice evaluation.

The observer's style of expression transforms the experienced justice evaluation into the *expressed justice evaluation*. The expressed justice evaluation is thus written as the product of the experienced justice evaluation [as in Eq. (3)] and the expressiveness coefficient (the absolute value of the signature constant). More generally and more simply, for both goods and bads, the expressed justice evaluation is written

$$J = \theta \ln\left(\frac{A}{C}\right) \tag{4}$$

where J denotes the expressed justice evaluation and θ denotes the signature constant.

Like the just rewards, the justice evaluations are both observer-specific and rewardee-specific. They, too, are often arrayed in a matrix, called the *justice evaluation matrix* and denoted J. The justice evaluation matrix is exactly like the just reward matrix in Table 3.1, except that the cell entries are justice evaluations instead of just rewards.

Of course, individuals experience the justice evaluation about other things besides individuals' rewards, and these may include the mean and inequality in a distribution. For example, comparison of an actual inequality with a just inequality yields a justice evaluation about inequality.

It also is useful to have a summary measure of overall injustice in a group or society, and two measures, called *justice indexes*, have been developed for this purpose. The first justice index, *JI1*, is the arithmetic mean of the experienced justice evaluations, and the second justice index, *JI2*, is the mean of the absolute values of the experienced justice evaluations.

More generally, by aggregating the justice evaluation across goods and bads, over time and across persons, many new representations and quantities are obtained, for example: (1) instantaneous J produced by the joint consideration of several goods (bads), (2) the individual's time series of J and its parameters, and (3) the collectivity's instantaneous distribution of J, its parameters, and their time series.

As with the building blocks that emerged from analysis of the first and second central questions, the new building blocks are ready for use in both theoretical work and empirical work. The experienced justice evaluation function can be used immediately as the starting assumption for theories, as can the framing coefficient and the expressiveness coefficient. The expressed justice evaluation function can be used immediately in empirical work.[6] Framing theory and justice-comparison theory, discussed below, begin with the framing coefficient and the experienced justice evaluation function, respectively.

Building Blocks from the Fourth Question

The fourth central question—What are the behavioral and social consequences of perceived injustice?—both plays a prominent part in the predictions of justice-comparison theory and also yields a basic expression, the *justice consequences function*, which can be used immediately in empirical work. The justice consequences function assesses the behavioral and social effects of a large set of terms based on the justice evaluation function, including the

---

[6]Given current measurement technology, empirical work that observes or measures the justice evaluation always must use the expressed justice evaluation; to estimate the experienced justice evaluation, it is necessary to estimate the signature constant and then convert the expressed justice evaluation into the experienced justice evaluation.

individual's justice evaluation, parameters of the individual's set of justice evaluations, parameters of the social distribution of justice evaluations, and so on.

The Framework Collects a Large Set of Building Blocks

Reasoning in this way about all four central questions yields a large set of building blocks, which are now ready for use in both theoretical justice analysis and empirical justice analysis. (Moreover, as already noted, some of the elements in the framework will later appear as the predictions of theories.) The experienced justice evaluation function, for example, is the starting assumption in several justice theories (including justice-comparison theory, one of the specimen theories in this chapter whose generalized version is more fully discussed in Part III of this volume). It proves itself exceedingly fruitful, yielding an abundance of implications for behavioral and social phenomena in far-flung domains, from crime to war to monasteries. The expressed justice evaluation function is a building block in empirical justice analysis. Estimation of the justice evaluation function immediately yields estimates of the signature constant; estimation of a form of the expressed justice evaluation function in which the just reward is unobserved yields, besides the signature constant, estimates of the equation R^2, which in a specified subset of cases has a substantive interpretation (whether actual inequality is greater or lesser than just inequality), and, surprisingly, estimates of the observer-specific/rewardee-specific just rewards, together with estimates of the experienced justice evaluation and the justice indexes. Note that the empirical work just described does not pass through the theoretical work; it does not depend on derivation of theoretical implications.

The Triptych of Justice Analysis

As the foregoing discussion suggests, it has become useful to think of justice analysis as encompassing three branches: framework for justice analysis, theoretical justice analysis, and empirical justice analysis. Justice analysis thus can be represented by a triptych, as illustrated in Figure 3.1. The center panel summarizes the framework, highlighting the four central questions and the set of building blocks. The left panel depicts theoretical work. The right panel depicts empirical work. We have superimposed five arrows to link the panels. Note that, consistent with our discussion so far, three arrows originate in the framework and end in the theoretical and empirical panels. Two of these go to the theoretical panel and one to the empirical panel. In our discussion thus far, we have not yet differentiated between kinds of theories, and thus we leave for a later section further discussion of the two arrows that go from the framework to the theoretical panel (as well as of the two arrows that go directly from the theoretical panel to the empirical panel). The arrow that goes from the framework to the empirical panel, on the other hand, refers precisely to the sorts of empirical work described in the previous paragraph, such as estimation of the just reward function for every observer, estimation of the signature constant for every observer, and so on.

The Triptych of Sociological Analysis and of Other Subfields

In the same way that justice analysis is best represented by a triptych, other subfields of sociology similarly can be represented by a triptych, as can the whole of sociological analysis. For example, the study of inequality—inequality analysis—can be thought of as the triptych of framework, theoretical inequality analysis, and empirical inequality analysis. So, too, can

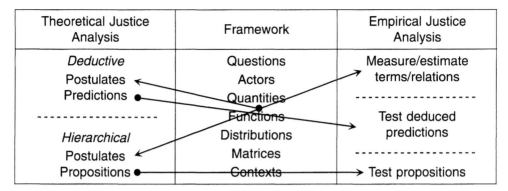

FIGURE 3.1. The triptych of justice analysis.

the study of migration—migration analysis—and the study of race—race analysis. In all these cases, the framework begins with the central questions of the field; as the questions are addressed, the building blocks emerge. Then both theoretical and empirical analysis use the building blocks as the foundation for constructing theories and carrying out empirical work.

As new theoretical and empirical work accumulates and is codified, each domain-specific triptych would grow. Many would be similar to the justice analysis triptych (Fig. 3.1). Examination of the triptych would yield clues as to which fields might be understudied and what may be major gaps in knowledge. A succinct way to summarize the entire discipline is by collapsing the headings of the major triptychs onto a single chart, as in Fig. 3.2.

Before leaving the large landscape of sociological analysis to focus on theory, we pause to notice that the building blocks developed in the framework for justice analysis were born already "formalized." We did not "formalize" them; they simply appeared that way. The justice evaluation variable seemed inherently representable by the real-number line. The set of observer-specific/rewardee-specific just rewards seemed inherently representable by a matrix. The set of rewardee-specific just rewards in the eyes of a single observer seemed inherently representable by a distribution. The relationship between the actual reward, just reward, and justice evaluation seemed inherently representable by a function, as did the relationship between the just reward and the rewardee characteristics.

It is an open question how formal the frameworks will be, initially, in other domains, that is, how much additional work may be required to formalize the basic building blocks. Was justice analysis peculiar in its immediate formalization? Do topical domains vary in the ease with which their central questions yield already-formalized building blocks? My impression is that some domains are almost inherently already formal or already almost-formal. These domains would include inequality analysis, migration analysis, network analysis, and choice analysis. Further thought, however, of the sociology-of-science kind, is required in order to address this question more fully and deeply.

THEORY AND FORMAL THEORY

Preliminaries

A theory begins with an assumption. This assumption, alone or with companion assumptions, illuminates the topical domain. It does so by yielding implications that become, variously, new answers to old questions or unexpected new questions. It yields results that make

Theoretical Justice Analysis	Framework for Justice Analysis	Empirical Justice Analysis
Theoretical Inequality Analysis	Framework for Inequality Analysis	Empirical Inequality Analysis
Theoretical Migration Analysis	Framework for Migration Analysis	Empirical Migration Analysis
Theoretical Norms Analysis	Framework for Norms Analysis	Empirical Norms Analysis
Theoretical Status Analysis	Framework for Status Analysis	Empirical Status Analysis
Theoretical Network Analysis	Framework for Network Analysis	Empirical Network Analysis
Theoretical Emotion Analysis	Framework for Emotion Analysis	Empirical Emotion Analysis
Theoretical Power Analysis	Framework for Power Analysis	Empirical Power Analysis
Theoretical Race Analysis	Framework for Race Analysis	Empirical Race Analysis
Theoretical Class Analysis	Framework for Class Analysis	Empirical Class Analysis
Theoretical Gender Analysis	Framework for Gender Analysis	Empirical Gender Analysis
. .	. .	. .

FIGURE 3.2. The triptychs of sociological analysis.

some relationships necessary and others impossible; it requires some things and forbids others. Theory is like a tree, with all the branches (implications) springing from the same trunk (assumptions). Vast areas of the human experience are linked to a simple and parsimonious set of starting principles.

A theory may be thought of as a list of sentences, including both statements (sentences that can be true or false) and other sentences like definitions and identities. In doing or judging theory, the most fundamental and important habit of thought is to characterize each sentence according to the part it plays in the theory. Is it an assumption or an implication? or something else? The student or theorist who always knows which sentences are assumptions and which are implications has the most formidable defense against confusion, ambiguity, and error. And the theorist who labels the sentences by the part they are playing is doing a service of inestimable value to the discipline; besides guarding against error, he or she is saving others precious time.

It is sometimes said that a theory is general and abstract. What this means, properly understood, is that the *assumptions* of the theory are general and abstract: A theory *begins* at a general and abstract level, but the theory *ends* at the most particular and concrete levels. Of course, it is the generality and abstractness of the assumptions that enable derivation of implications for wide fields of phenomena. The full theory, however, cannot correctly be said to be general and abstract, for if it is a good theory, its implications include observable, particular phenomena and relationships. Part of the great adventure of doing theory is precisely this: great empirical surprises follow from theoretical derivation.

It is sometimes said that a theory is an interrelated set of propositions. Of course, the statements in a theory are "interrelated," but this characterization blurs the great and essential distinction between assumptions and implications and the special way in which assumptions and implications are related to each other.

To achieve precise understanding of the character of the interrelationship among the sentences of a theory, we introduce a distinction between two kinds of theories and as well sharpen our vocabulary. Earlier in the chapter we referred to deductive theory as the most wonderful kind of theory, and our discussion in the previous section about assumptions and implications implicitly took deductive theory as the standard. We turn now to discuss explicitly two main theoretical forms, plus a third, which is a combination of the two main forms.

Types of Theories

There are two main kinds of theories. The first is classical *deductive theory*, which traces its origins to Newton (Toulmin, 1978). In deductive theory, the assumptions are clearly stated, and testable implications are deduced from the assumptions; the usefulness and validity of the assumptions is established by testing the implications. In this first kind of theory, there are two kinds of propositions: propositions in the assumption set and propositions in the prediction set, and the relation between them is one of strict deduction. The second main kind of theory is *hierarchical theory* [in Toulmin's (1953) terminology]. In hierarchical theory, the assumptions are clearly stated, and testable propositions are constructed by linking observable terms with terms in, or produced by, the assumptions. In this second kind of theory, there are two kinds of propositions: propositions in the assumption set and the constructed testable propositions.

In both deductive and hierarchical theory, two things are made explicit: what kind of proposition each proposition is, and the precise nature of the interrelationship among the propositions. Both deductive and hierarchical theory have bipartite structures. Both begin with a set of assumptions.

However, the second part differs radically between deductive theory and hierarchical theory. While in deductive theory the statements in the second part are deduced from the first part, in hierarchical theory the statements in the second part are constructed in a somewhat ad hoc way. That is, while in deductive theory the operation for obtaining the statements in the second part is deduction, in hierarchical theory the operation is a conjecture that one or more observables are related to one or more terms that appear in the assumptions or are produced by the assumptions. Below we shall look at examples, but first it is necessary to sharpen our vocabulary, in particular, to restrict, for clarity, use of the term "proposition."

ASSUMPTION, AXIOM, POSTULATE.   To this point, we have used the term "assumption" for the statements that are assumed in a theory. Assumption is a very general term, however; for example, it is used in empirical work (as in assumptions about the error term in a regression equation) as well as in theoretical work. Other terms that are sometimes used include "axiom," an assumption with the connotation of "self-evident," and "postulate," a term that appears perfectly suited for theoretical work, as it is not often used in empirical work and as well does not carry the "self-evident" connotation of "axiom." In the remainder of this chapter, we will use "postulate" and "assumption" interchangeably.[7]

IMPLICATION, PREDICTION, CONSEQUENCE. The words "implication," "prediction," and "consequence" are often used as synonyms for each other, referring to the propositions deduced from the assumptions in a deductive theory. For clarity, we will use only two of these words, "implication" and "prediction," using them interchangeably.

PROPOSITION. For the rest of this chapter, we reserve use of the term "proposition" for a special kind of proposition, namely, one that is used exclusively in hierarchical theories and exclusively for the statements constructed by linking observables with terms in, or produced by, postulates. We do this only in this chapter and only to simplify the exposition and avoid ambiguity.[8]

Accordingly, the bipartite structure of the two kinds of theories can now be precisely characterized:

DEDUCTIVE THEORY. A deductive theory is a list of sentences that may be divided into two parts, the first part containing the postulates and the second containing testable predictions deduced from the postulates.

HIERARCHICAL THEORY. A hierarchical theory is a list of sentences that may be divided into two parts, the first part containing the postulates and the second containing testable propositions constructed by linking observable terms with terms that appear in, or are produced by, the postulates.

There is a third, mixed form of theory, in which the same postulates are used both to deduce predictions and to construct propositions:

HYBRID DEDUCTIVE-HIERARCHICAL THEORY. A hybrid deductive-hierarchical theory may be divided into two parts, the first part containing the postulates and the second part further subdivided into two parts, one containing predictions deduced from the postulates and the other containing propositions constructed by linking observable terms with terms that appear in, or are produced by, the postulates.

Figure 3.3 depicts the three kinds of theories. Sometimes there is an added twist to the constructed propositions, one not visible in Fig. 3.3. It is this: In a hybrid theory, the propositions may be constructed by linking observable terms with terms that, while certainly produced by the postulates, in fact arrive via the predictions.

Deductive theory is more powerful than hierarchical theory, for it makes explicit the mechanisms by which the observables in the predictions are linked to the postulates. Indeed, one may think of hierarchical theory as a step along the way, perhaps a composite of hunches and empirical evidence lying in wait for a deduction to lay bare the mechanism.

Both deductive and hierarchical theory are as one, however, with respect to two desiderata. The first is that the postulate set should be as small as possible (see Fig. 3.3). The second is that the prediction-proposition set should be as large as possible; that is why the diagrams in Fig. 3.3 have no border at the bottom. A further desideratum is that the prediction-

---

[7]Note again that the assumption set or postulate set of a theory typically includes, besides statements (sentences which can be true or false), other sentences such as definitions and mathematical identities.

[8]Of course, it should be kept in mind that in the larger world outside this chapter, postulates and predictions are themselves propositions, albeit special kinds of propositions with special tasks.

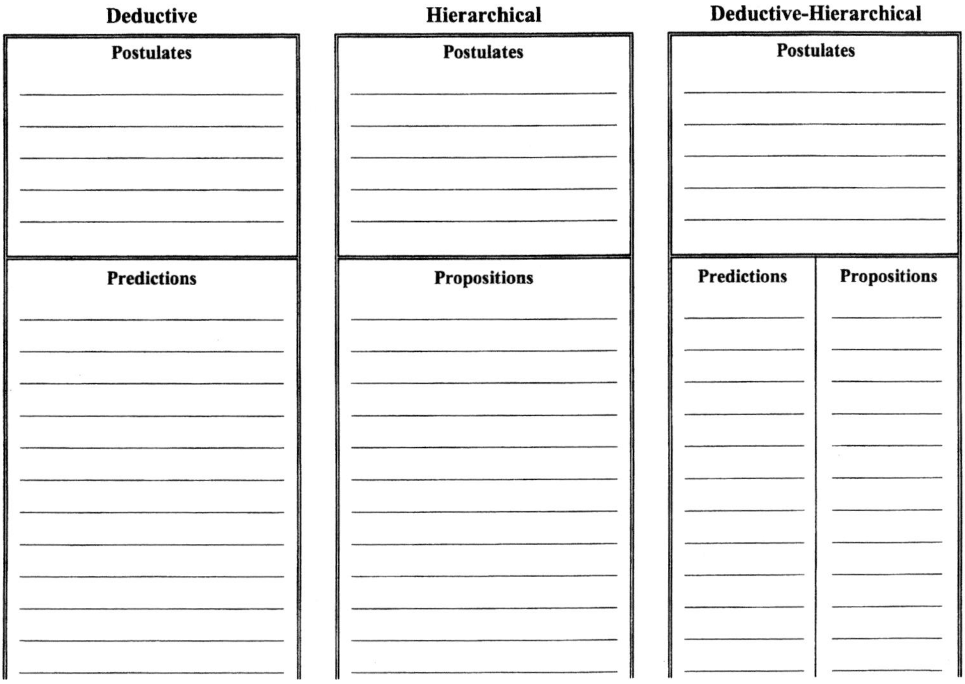

Deductive   **Hierarchical**   **Deductive-Hierarchical**

FIGURE 3.3. Three kinds of theories.

proposition set span wide topical domains and in the case of deductive theory that the prediction set include novel predictions.

Now that deductive theory and hierarchical theory have received precise characterization, we can return to Fig. 3.1. Notice that the theoretical panel is divided by a dashed line into two sections, for deductive and hierarchical theory, respectively. Look at the two arrows that travel leftward from the framework panel to the theoretical panel of the triptych. One arrow goes to deductive theory, the other to hierarchical theory, indicating that building blocks in the framework become the postulates of both kinds of theories.

Now look at the empirical panel. It is divided into three sections, two of which are linked to the theoretical panel. Two arrows originate in the theoretical panel of the triptych and end in the empirical panel. One is an arrow going from deductive theory to theoretical predictions. The second is an arrow traveling from hierarchical theory to propositions in the empirical panel.[9]

Empirical tests are always on the predictions, in the case of deductive theories, and the predictions/propositions, in the case of hierarchical theories. Empirical tests of the predictions/propositions enable assessment of the validity and usefulness of the postulates, leading researchers to revise, refute, or discard one or more of the postulates or to impose boundaries on their scope of operation.

[9]As discussed earlier, the top section of the empirical panel is reached by an arrow that originates in the framework. That is, some empirical work does not pass through the theoretical panel, but is carried out based directly on the framework. To illustrate: Estimation of the just reward or the just reward function requires only the building blocks in the framework; it does not require any theory. On the other hand, a hierarchical theory may test the proposition that the reflexive justice index is related to a country's level of political development.

The big adventure of theoretical analysis is the journey from postulates to predictions and from postulates to propositions. The first, thought of as a theoretical enterprise, leads to what may be called theoretical discovery. The second leads to what may be called empirical discovery. Both bring great surprises. Both also require a modicum of special tools.

In describing the framework for justice analysis, we noted that little of a formal nature had to be explicitly undertaken; the quantities and relations seemed to appear already formalized. Of course, that will not always be the case. But whatever the formalization history of the building blocks that become the postulates of theories, when the time comes to deduce predictions from the postulates, formal things will almost always be done. Formal tools are power tools for extracting from the postulates all the information and insights they contain about wide areas of the human experience.

We now illustrate with five theories from the study of justice.

ILLUSTRATION:
THEORIES FROM THE PORTFOLIO OF
THEORETICAL JUSTICE ANALYSIS

The many building blocks developed in the framework for justice analysis can be used, alone or in combination, as the postulates of theories. Sometimes additional postulates are required before predictions can be deduced. In this section, we briefly describe five theories based on building blocks in the framework for justice analysis. One of these, the justice version of comparison theory is a special case of the larger comparison theory, which receives fuller treatment in chapter 30 in this book. Together, these five theories illustrate all three theoretical structures—deductive, hierarchical, and hybrid—and illustrate as well techniques for deducing predictions and, finally, the great variability across theories in scope and fruitfulness, at least as discernible in theoretical work to date.

Allocation Theory

Allocation theory addresses the process by which ideas of justice shape actual rewards; it thus is a theory addressing the second central question in the study of justice. Allocation theory begins with three building blocks from the framework for justice analysis—the just reward matrix, the weight matrix, and the actual reward.[10]

POSTULATE.   The building blocks are combined into a postulate that states:

- *Postulate (Just Rewards Determine Actual Rewards)*: Actually or metaphorically, actual rewards are produced by aggregation of the observer-specific/rewardee-specific just rewards; the observers, however, may differ in their influence over each rewardee's actual reward.

Formal expressions for all the terms and relations were introduced earlier. To aid in the exposition, we report in Table 3.3 all the basic formulas and matrices used in allocation theory.[11]

---

[10]For an early version of allocation theory, see Jasso (unpublished).

[11]We follow the usual notational conventions. Lowercase letters are used to denote elements of a matrix and uppercase letters to denote the matrix; similarly, lowercase letters are used to denote the values of a variate and uppercase letters to denote the variate or distribution.

Tools for Deducing Predictions in Allocation Theory.   Allocation theory is a young theory in justice analysis. New methods are being developed for deducing predictions from postulates which begin with full matrices; these methods are collectively called the *matrixmodel*. Predictions obtained to date are of two kinds: predictions about the inequality in the actual reward distribution and predictions about the distributional shape of the actual reward distribution. The matrixmodel tools include theorems on weights (Kotz, Johnson, & Read, 1988) and theorems from the study of probability distributions, including theorems on the variance and central limit theorems (Stuart & Ord, 1987), in particular, a version of the central limit theorem owed to Liapunov (1900, 1901), as strengthened by Lindeberg and Feller (Wolfson, 1985).

Predictions of Allocation Theory.   Predictions obtained to date include the following:

1. The larger the number of independent actors involved in an allocation decision, the lower the inequality in the actual reward distribution.
2. The larger the number of independent factions (where each faction exhibits internal consensus on the allocation decision), the lower the inequality in the actual reward distribution.
3. Power concentrations are under certain conditions indistinguishable from consensus processes; a dictatorship is equivalent to a society characterized by complete agreement, a triumvirate is equivalent to a three-faction society, etc.
4. Under certain specified conditions, lack of power has the same effects on inequality in the actual reward distribution as lack of independence of mind.
5. A democracy—defined as a set of equally empowered decision makers—can increase or decrease inequality, depending on the citizens' independence of mind.
6. Dissensus has the effect of reducing inequality.
7. When presidents of democratic nations seek to forge a consensus, they are unwittingly inducing greater inequality.
8. As the number of independent decision makers or of independent decision making factions grows large, the shape of the actual reward distribution tends to normality.
9. If decision making occurs in separate groups, the within-group actual reward distributions may be normal and the overall actual reward distribution nonnormal.

Remarks about Allocation Theory.   Allocation theory is a deductive theory that could become a hybrid theory. It has a single postulate: that just rewards determine actual rewards; this postulate is based on building blocks from the framework for justice analysis. Predictions are deduced by using mathematical tools. The postulate does not describe a feature of human nature but rather a feature of a societal arrangement. Thus, the predictions hold for any situation to which the postulate applies. Accordingly, the predictions may be exciting, perhaps novel, certainly observable, but they are not testable in the usual sense. Indeed, the predictions have more the character of mathematical theorems. What the predictions contribute, however, is a new perspective on the signal importance of two factors (1) societal arrangements and (2) independence of mind. This sets the stage for both inductive exploration of the conditions under which arrangements such as that described in the postulate are instituted, the determinants of variability in the weights of decision makers, and the determinants of independence of mind. Concomitantly, terms in the postulate, such as the weights of decision makers, and new terms produced by the postulate via the predictions, such as independence of mind, can be used to construct propositions for a new hierarchical-theory component. Allocation theory could soon become a hybrid theory.

TABLE **3.3.** **Basic Formulas and Matrices in Allocation Theory**

A. The Just Reward Matrix

$$
C = \begin{bmatrix}
c_{11} & c_{12} & c_{13} & \cdots & c_{1R} \\
c_{21} & c_{22} & c_{23} & \cdots & c_{2R} \\
c_{31} & c_{32} & c_{33} & \cdots & c_{3R} \\
\vdots & \vdots & \vdots & \ddots & \vdots \\
c_{N1} & c_{N2} & c_{N3} & \cdots & c_{NR}
\end{bmatrix}
$$

B. The Weight Matrix

$$
W = \begin{bmatrix}
w_{11} & w_{12} & c_{13} & \cdots & c_{1R} \\
w_{21} & w_{22} & w_{23} & \cdots & w_{2R} \\
w_{31} & w_{32} & w_{33} & \cdots & w_{3R} \\
\vdots & \vdots & \vdots & \ddots & \vdots \\
w_{N1} & w_{N2} & w_{N3} & \cdots & w_{NR}
\end{bmatrix}
$$

C. The Actual Reward and the Actual Reward Vector

$$
a_r = \sum_{i=1}^{N} c_{ir} w_{ir} \qquad\qquad a_r = [a_{.1}\, a_{.2}\, a_{.3} \cdots a_{.R}]
$$

D. The Actual Reward Distribution

$$
A = \sum_{i=1}^{N} C_i W_i
$$

Anselmian Theory

Like allocation theory, Anselmian theory also addresses the second central question in the study of justice—How do ideas of justice shape the actual rewards? Its basic postulate is an idea proposed by St. Anselm of Canterbury, with immediate application to some of the building blocks in the framework for justice analysis, including ideas of justice, the just inequality, the actual reward, and the actual reward distribution. Anselmian theory is a hybrid theory, including both deductive and hierarchical components.[12]

POSTULATE.   The basic postulate is stated:

- *St. Anselm's Postulate (Two Inclinations of the Will)*: Let the will have two inclinations, as proposed by St. Anselm, the *affectio commodi* and the *affectio justitiae*. The *affectio commodi* directs toward the individual's own good, and the *affectio justitiae* directs toward justice, toward the good of society.

TOOLS FOR DEDUCING PREDICTIONS FROM ANSELMIAN THEORY.   The first tool consists of representational devices, including preference orderings and their configuration. For example, to represent the situation in which the two preference orderings are exactly opposite, the tool used is that of conjugate rankings (Kotz, Johnson, & Read, 1982, p. 145). In the application of Anselmian theory to choosing an actual reward distribution, tools are drawn from the study of probability distributions (Stuart & Ord, 1987; Johnson & Kotz, 1970a,b).

PREDICTIONS DEDUCED FROM ANSELMIAN THEORY.   Predictions of Anselmian theory include the following predictions, of which the first five are general and the remainder are from an application of Anselmian theory to choosing an actual reward distribution:

1. In examining behavioral alternatives in a decision-making situation, the individual rank-orders the alternatives according to the Anselmian inclinations, producing two preference orderings.
2. The two preference orderings may be identical, or exactly the reverse of each other,

---

[12]Early work on Anselmian theory is reported in Jasso (1989b).

or neither identical nor exactly opposite. If the two preference orderings are identical, the individual is said to be in the state of harmony; if the two preference orderings are exactly opposite, the individual is said to be in the state of conflict; and if the two preference orderings are neither identical nor exactly opposite, the individual is said to be in the state of ambiguity.

3. If the number of alternatives is two, then the individual is in either the state of harmony or the state of conflict; if the number of alternatives is greater than two, then the individual may be in the state of harmony, conflict, or ambiguity.

4. Individuals in harmony cannot be characterized as being either altruistic or egoistic.

5. Individuals in conflict demonstrate by their decision whether they are altruistic or egoistic.

The remaining predictions are from the application to choosing an income distribution. In this application, persons in harmony are those for whom as own income increases, income inequality decreases; for persons in conflict, own income is an increasing function of income inequality; and for persons in ambiguity, own income is a nonmonotonic function of income inequality. In the special case of an electoral contest between two candidates whose policies would produce particular income distributions, the outcome can sometimes be predicted from the proportions in harmony, conflict, and ambiguity.

6. The proportion of the population in harmony (own income increases as income inequality decreases) can vary greatly; in five distributional families analyzed, it varies from 0.37 to 0.63%.

7. The persons in the state of harmony are the poorest persons in the distribution.

8. While all societies have a segment of their population in harmony (the segment containing the poorest persons), the states of conflict and ambiguity need not both be represented.

9. If the actual reward is Pareto distributed, about 63% of the population are in a state of harmony, and the remaining 37% are in the state of ambiguity; no one is in the state of conflict.

10. If the actual reward is lognormally distributed, half the population is in harmony and half in ambiguity; no one is in the state of conflict.

11. If the actual reward is distributed as a power-function variate, 37% of the population is in the state of harmony, and 63% is in the state of ambiguity; no one is in conflict.

12. If the actual reward is distributed as an exponential variate, 63% of the population is in harmony and 37% in conflict; no one is in ambiguity.

13. If the actual reward is distributed as a quadratic variate, half the population is in harmony and half in conflict; no one is in ambiguity.

14. In an electoral contest between two candidates whose policies would produce Pareto distributions, the candidate associated with the less unequal distribution always wins.

15. In an electoral contest between two candidates whose policies would produce exponential distributions, the candidate associated with the less unequal distribution always wins.

16. In an electoral contest between two candidates whose policies would produce power-function distributions, the outcome can go either way.

17. In an electoral contest between two candidates whose policies would produce income distributions approximated by the lognormal distribution, the outcome is either a draw or otherwise the less unequal wins.

18. In an electoral contest between two candidates whose policies would produce income distributions approximated by the quadratic distribution, the outcome is either a draw or otherwise the less unequal wins.

PROPOSITIONS CONSTRUCTED IN ANSELMIAN THEORY.   Anselmian theory is a hybrid theory, and besides having a deductive component, it also has a hierarchical component. A large number of propositions can be constructed ad hoc by linking observables to the terms produced by the postulate, including terms produced via the predictions. These terms include harmony, conflict, ambiguity, the proportion of the population in each state, the configuration of states, the individual's proportion of time spent in each state, and the society's proportion of time spent in each state or configuration. Obviously, the number of possible ad hoc propositions is virtually limitless. A few such propositions are:

1. Basic personality traits develop in response to the proportion of time an individual spends in each of the three states.
2. The character of civil discourse is determined by the society's history of the population configuration in each of the three states.
3. Saints and heroes are drawn from among individuals in conflict.
4. The literature of *angst* arises among individuals and groups who spend much time in ambiguity.
5. Adam Smith was in the state of conflict when he wrote *The Theory of Moral Sentiments* (1759/1974), but he was in the state of harmony when he wrote *The Wealth of Nations* (1776/1976).
6. The "internal conversation" posited by Peirce and Mead and investigated by Wiley (1994) differs systematically across the states of harmony, conflict, and ambiguity.
7. The propensity to wage war differs systematically by the proportion of the population in the state of harmony.
8. The prevalent ideologies, as well as artistic and cultural products, differ according to the proportions in harmony, conflict, and ambiguity.

REMARKS ABOUT ANSELMIAN THEORY.   Anselmian theory is a hybrid theory, with both deductive and hierarchical components. Its single postulate was proposed by Anselm of Canterbury. Both the postulate and its application to choosing an actual reward distribution use building blocks from the framework for justice analysis. Predictions are deduced using mathematical tools and tools from the study of probability distributions. The postulate is behavioral, and thus the predictions shed light on its validity. The predictions may be rejected empirically, and hence the postulate falsified. Empirical test of the constructed propositions would produce new empirical information.[13]

Framing Theory

The justice evaluation function, which addresses the third central question in the study of justice—What is the magnitude of the perceived injustice associated with given departures from perfect justice?—includes a framing coefficient that represents the observer's idea about whether the thing under consideration is a good or a bad. For example, not all observers regard earnings as a good, and similarly not all observers regard time in prison as a bad. The question thus arises how an individual decides whether to frame a thing as a good or bad.[14] The point of

[13]Note that allocation theory could emulate Anselmian theory and establish a new hierarchical component. In the same way that Anselmian theory includes constructed propositions using terms from the predictions, terms like "proportion in conflict" and "proportion in ambiguity," allocation theory could grow to include propositions using terms from its predictions, terms like "proportion characterized by independence of mind" and "number of factions."

[14]For an early version of framing theory, see Jasso (unpublished).

departure for framing theory is the idea that, whatever may be the ultimate truth about ontological goodness or badness, humans have a basic impulse to judge the goodness or badness of things.[15] The objective of framing theory is to discover the rules by which humans judge the goodness or badness of things, rules that may require or forbid certain combinations of judgments.[16]

POSTULATE. Framing theory takes for its postulate one of the basic building blocks, the justice evaluation function introduced earlier:

- *Postulate (Justice Evaluation Function)*:

$$J = \theta \ln \left(\frac{A}{C}\right) \tag{5}$$

where, as before, J denotes the expressed justice evaluation, A denotes the actual reward, C denotes the just reward, and θ denotes the signature constant, which embodies both the framing coefficient, signum(θ), and the expressiveness coefficient, $|\theta|$.

TOOLS FOR DEDUCING PREDICTIONS FROM FRAMING THEORY. The only tools used are simple algebra and Atkinson's (1970, 1975) measure of inequality. Algebraic manipulation of the justice evaluation function and inspection of the justice index JI1, together with the decomposition of JI1 into a justice evaluation about the mean and a justice evaluation about the inequality (as measured by Atkinson's measure), yield a special relationship between the observer's framing of the reward in the original justice evaluation and the observer's framing of the mean and inequality in the reward's distribution.[17]

PREDICTIONS DEDUCED FROM FRAMING THEORY. Framing theory, as developed to date, yields four main predictions:

1. If an observer regards a thing as a good, then that observer implicitly regards the mean of the thing as a good.
2. If an observer regards a thing as a good, then that observer implicitly regards inequality in the distribution of that thing as a bad.
3. If an observer regards a thing as a bad, then that observer implicitly regards the mean of the thing as a bad.
4. If an observer regards a thing as a bad, then that observer implicitly regards inequality in the distribution of that thing as a good.

The two inequality predictions are sometimes combined into a new statement that is succinct but less rigorous (as it omits the observer): Inequality in the distribution of a good is a bad, and inequality in the distribution of a bad is a good.

REMARKS ABOUT FRAMING THEORY. Framing theory is a young, deductive theory. As developed to date, its scope is limited to individuals who experience the sense of justice. Thus framing theory currently provides only a partial answer in the search for the rules by which humans judge the goodness or badness of things. Moreover, the predictions are based on a particular measure of inequality. It would be desirable to find a more general way to link

[15]As Hamlet put it, "There is nothing either good or bad, but thinking makes it so" (Act II, Scene 2).

[16]As with "justice" and its cognates, the term "good" is always understood as "good in the eyes of the observer," and the term "bad" as "bad in the eyes of the observer."

[17]Atkinson (1970, 1975) proposed a family of measures of inequality, of which one—the measure defined as one minus the ratio of the geometric mean to the arithmetic mean—appears in the decomposition of JI1 (Jasso, 1999).

framing of original things and framing of the mean and inequality in their distribution. Still, this is a useful step in advancing our understanding of framing processes.[18]

Just Society Theory

The first central question asks, What do individuals and collectivities regard as just, and why? This fundamental question has proven itself strongly resistant to formulation of a behavioral postulate. There have been important advances in the empirical estimation of what individuals think is just. However, there is as yet no warrant for postulating a priori what individuals think is just.

Against this backdrop of stubborn resistance, it is remarkable that theories designed to address other justice questions—allocation theory and framing theory—yield results that can be used to construct a theory that predicts what individuals think is just in the domain of institutional distributional arrangements. This new theory is called just society theory.[19]

POSTULATES.   Just society theory has two postulates, one each from the predictions of allocation theory and framing theory:

- *Postulate 1 (Inequality and the Number of Decision Makers)*: Inequality in the distri-bution of a good or bad is a decreasing function of the number of equally weighted, independent-minded decision making units.
- *Postulate 2 (Framing of Inequality)*: If an observer regards a thing as a good, then that observer implicitly regards inequality in the distribution of that thing as a bad; and if an observer regards a thing as a bad, then that observer implicitly regards inequality in the distribution of that thing as a good.

TOOLS FOR DEDUCING PREDICTIONS FROM JUST SOCIETY THEORY.   In the work to date, the derivation has not required any special tools. The results follow immediately from the combination of the postulates.

PREDICTIONS DEDUCED IN JUST SOCIETY THEORY.   The main predictions deduced to date link the just society with the number of decision makers and whether the decision is about a good or a bad:

1. An observer will regard as just a society in which distribution of benefits is by the many (democracy).
2. An observer will regard as just a society in which distribution of burdens is by the few (oligarchy).
3. The just society has a mixed government.

REMARKS ABOUT JUST SOCIETY THEORY.   Just society theory is a fledgling deductive theory. It exemplifies three noteworthy features: First, the predictions follow immediately; there is no need for algebra, or calculus, or probability distributions. Second, the postulates of just society theory are the predictions of other theories (about which, more later). Third, the last prediction echoes the insights of Machiavelli (1532/1950), who saw, but for different reasons, that the just society would have a mixed government.

---

[18]Of course, these results are also a useful step in advancing our understanding of the precise links between inequality and justice.

[19]For an early version of just society theory, see Jasso (unpublished).

Justice Version of Comparison Theory

The justice version of comparison theory addresses the fourth central question in the study of justice, What are the behavioral and social consequences of perceived injustice? Its postulate set begins with an important building block from the framework—the justice evaluation function—supplemented by two individual-level postulates and two postulates based on aggregations of the justice evaluation, one of which—the justice index—also appears in the framework. Justice-comparison theory (as we call it, for simplicity) is a hybrid theory, including both deductive and hierarchical components.[20]

POSTULATES.   As noted, justice-comparison theory has five postulates, which are presented in Table 3.4. Here, in the text, we provide brief description of the postulates.

POSTULATE OF THE LOGARITHMIC SPECIFICATION OF THE JUSTICE EVALUATION FUNCTION.   The first postulate, the reflexive justice evaluation function, provides a mathematical description of the process whereby individuals, reflecting on their holdings of the goods and bads they value (such as beauty, intelligence, or wealth), compare their levels of attributes and amounts of possessions to the amounts or levels they regard as just for themselves, experiencing a fundamental instantaneous magnitude of the justice evaluation J, which captures their sense of being fairly or unfairly treated in the distributions of the natural and social goods. As in the classical literature, this instantaneous experience of being fairly or unfairly treated in the distributions of the natural and social goods is regarded as having the most wide-ranging and diverse consequences for virtually every sphere of human individual and social behavior.[21]

MEASUREMENT RULE FOR HOLDINGS.   The logarithmic specification was initially proposed for cardinal goods; it is easy to measure the actual and just rewards in terms of, say, money or hectares of land. But the literature suggested that goods and bads not susceptible of cardinal measurement (beauty, intelligence, athletic skill) also play important parts in the operation of the sense of justice. Therefore, the second postulate proposes a measurement rule (Jasso, 1980), which states that cardinal things are measured in their own units (the amount denoted by x), while ordinal things are measured by the individual's relative rank $[i/(N+1)]$ within a specially selected comparison group, where i denotes the rank-order statistic in ascending order and N denotes the size of the group or population.

IDENTITY REPRESENTATION OF THE JUST REWARD.   To this point the theory contained a rather large problem: while the actual reward is easily observed, the just reward is not. The very feature that made the theory potentially fruitful—its dynamical character, the same individual capable of manipulating many just rewards for the same good or bad in a short period of time—made it also close to intractable. To deal with this problem, the third postulate proposes an identity representation of the just reward. This new representation, based on the fact that any value in the reward's domain, and hence any just reward, can be expressed as a transformation of the reward's arithmetic mean, expresses the just reward as the product of the mean and an individual-specific parameter ϕ, where ϕ captures everything that is unknown about an individual's just reward. This representation of the just reward possesses the addi-

---

[20]In this chapter, "comparison theory" always refers to the justice version of comparison theory. Chapter 30 provides exposition of the general comparison theory of which the justice version is a special case.

[21]The justice evaluation function in the first postulate of justice-comparison theory is the reflexive justice evaluation function, referring to the individual him- or herself. In contrast, the justice evaluation function in the postulate of framing theory is the general justice evaluation function, describing justice evaluations of others as well as self.

TABLE 3.4. Fundamental Postulates of the Justice Version of Comparison Theory

A. Individual-Level Postulates

    1. Postulate of Logarithmic Specification of the Justice Evaluation Function

$$J = \theta \ln\left(\frac{A}{C}\right)$$

    2. Measurement Rule for Holdings

$$A,C \begin{cases} x, & \text{cardinal good/bad} \\ \dfrac{i}{N+1}, & \text{ordinal good/bad} \end{cases}$$

    3. Identity Representation of Just Reward

$$C = \phi E(A)$$

B. Social-Level Postulates

    4. Social Welfare

$$SW = E(J)$$

    5. Social Cohesiveness

$$\text{Social Cohesiveness} = -GMD(J)$$

NOTES: As described in the text, J denotes the justice evaluation, A the actual reward, and C the just reward. The signature constant θ is positive for goods and negative for bads. For both actual and just rewards, x denotes the amount of a cardinal good or bad, i denotes the rank-order statistics arranged in ascending order, and N denotes the population size. ϕ denotes the individual-specific parameter, $E(\cdot)$ the expected value, and $GMD(\cdot)$ the Gini's mean difference.

tional virtue of enabling theoretical prediction of the effects of the mean's constituent factors, which in the case of a quantity-good are the sum S of the good and the population size N. This postulate, proposed in Jasso (1986), can be traced to early work by Merton and Rossi (1950) and Merton (1957), as discussed in Jasso (2000).

SOCIAL WELFARE POSTULATE.   Social welfare is defined as the arithmetic mean of the instantaneous distribution of justice evaluations in a collectivity.

SOCIAL COHESIVENESS POSTULATE.   Social cohesiveness is defined as the negative of the Gini's mean difference of the distribution of justice evaluations.

TOOLS FOR DEDUCING PREDICTIONS IN JUSTICE-COMPARISON THEORY.   There are two main tools, known as the *micromodel* and the *macromodel*. The micromodel begins with the individual-level justice evaluation and its change across two points in time and uses calculus to deduce predictions. The macromodel begins with the distribution of justice evaluations and uses tools from the study of probability distributions to deduce predictions. Fuller description of these tools appears in Chapter 30 on comparison theory.

PREDICTIONS DEDUCED IN JUSTICE-COMPARISON THEORY.   Justice-comparison theory has been unusually fruitful. Here we present only a small sampling of the predictions obtained to date. For more examples and associated references, see Chapter 30 on comparison theory.

    1. A gift is more valuable to the receiver when the giver is present.
    2. In wartime, the favorite leisure-time activity of soldiers is playing games of chance.
    3. Posttraumatic stress is greater among veterans of wars fought away from home than among veterans of wars fought on home soil.

4. Vocations to the religious life are an increasing function of income inequality.
5. Thieves prefer to steal from fellow group members rather than from outsiders.
6. Informants arise only in cross-group theft, in which case they are members of the thief's group.
7. An immigrant's propensity to learn the language of the host country is an increasing function of the ratio of the origin-country's per capita GNP to the host-country's per capita GNP.
8. In historical periods when wives tend to predecease their husbands (e.g., due to death in childbirth), mothers are mourned more than fathers; but in historical periods when husbands tend to predecease their wives (e.g., due to war), fathers are mourned more than mothers.
9. Parents of nontwin children will spend more of their toy budget at an annual gift-giving occasion rather than at the children's birthdays.
10. If both spouses work full-time, marital cohesiveness increases with the ratio of the smaller to the larger earnings.
11. In a society in which the two-worker couple is the prevailing form of marriage and all husbands earn more than their wives, the societal divorce rate increases with the dispersion in the wives' earnings distribution and with the arithmetic mean of the husbands' earnings distribution and decreases with the dispersion in the husbands' earnings distribution and with the arithmetic mean of the wives' earnings distribution.
12. A society becomes more vulnerable to deficit spending as its wealth increases.
13. Society loses when rich steal from poor.
14. Inequality-reducing schemes arise in societies that value wealth but not in societies that value birth and lineage.
15. In all societies there will arise devices that promote variability in individuals' notions of what is just for themselves.
16. The problem for new groups is to choose the valued goods.
17. Newcomers are more likely to be welcomed by groups that value cardinal goods than by groups that value ordinal goods and more likely to be welcomed by groups that play games of chance than by groups that play games of skill.
18. Among groups whose valued goods are N ordinal goods, the group's longevity is a decreasing function of group size.
19. In a dispute over revealing salary information, the exact preference structure depends on the distributional pattern of the salaries; if this pattern follows the familiar lognormal or Pareto, then the lowest-paid and the highest-paid persons prefer to have the information revealed, forming a coalition against the middle-paid persons.
20. In a materialistic society, the greater the economic inequality, the greater the emigration rate, the more severe the conflict between warring subgroups, and the greater the public benefit conferred by the cloister.
21. In a materialistic society, the overall amount of injustice experienced by the population is an increasing function of economic inequality.

PROPOSITIONS CONSTRUCTED IN JUSTICE-COMPARISON THEORY. Justice-comparison theory is a hybrid theory, and besides having a deductive component, it also has a hierarchical component. A large number of propositions can be constructed ad hoc by linking observables to the terms produced by the postulates. The constructed propositions include:

1. Physical health is a function of the justice evaluation and of properties of the individual's time series of justice evaluations.

2. Mental health is a function of the justice evaluation and of properties of the individual's time series of justice evaluations.
3. Special features of the individual's time series of justice evaluations, for example, the range, the gaps between temporally adjacent justice evaluations, the proportion of time in underrewarded and overrewarded states, govern particular aspects of the individual's emotional and psychological life.
4. The maximum and minimum of the individual's justice evaluations become attenuated over time.
5. Expressiveness varies over the lifecourse.
6. Framing varies over the lifecourse.
7. The proportion of time during which an individual reflects on justice matters is an important marker of his or her personality.
8. The proportions devoted to reflexive and nonreflexive justice evaluations are important markers for political participation.
9. The individual's time series of justice evaluations for any unit of time exhibit self-similarity. This is the individual's signature justice profile.
10. A necessary condition for revolutionary collective movements is the combination of negative reflexive justice evaluations and positive nonreflexive justice evaluations, that is, the twin judgments that self is unjustly underrewarded and others are unjustly overrewarded.
11. The propensity to violent revolutionary conflict varies directly with the absolute magnitude of the lower extreme value of the distribution of justice evaluations.
12. Crime occurs only when the collectivity contains both underrewarded and overrewarded persons and when the absolute magnitude of the lower extreme value is greater than the upper extreme value of the distribution.
13. The crime rate varies directly with the proportion found in that leftmost segment whose upper endpoint is of identical absolute magnitude as the overall distribution's upper extreme value. Such a segment is called a distressed segment.
14. The mean seriousness of all crimes varies directly with the absolute magnitude of the mean of the distressed segment.
15. The mean seriousness of crimes against persons varies directly with the absolute distance between the overall mean and the mean of the distressed segment.
16. The rate of mental illness varies directly with the proportion of negative justice evaluation scores, but excluding the distressed segment, if any.
17. The mean severity of mental illness varies directly with the absolute magnitude of the mean of the unjustly underrewarded segment, again excluding the distressed segment, if any.

REMARKS ABOUT JUSTICE-COMPARISON THEORY. Justice-comparison theory is a hybrid theory, with both deductive and hierarchical components. Its basic postulate, the justice evaluation function, is a behavioral postulate. Predictions are deduced using mathematical tools and tools from the study of probability distributions. The postulate is behavioral, and thus the predictions shed light on its validity. The predictions may be rejected empirically, and hence the postulate falsified. Empirical test of the constructed propositions would produce new empirical information.

Table 3.5 summarizes the five specimen theories used for illustration in this chapter. It provides a convenient way to compare the five theories and to refer to them when they are mentioned in the frequently asked questions in the next section.

TABLE 3.5. Five Theories in the Portfolio of Theoretical Justice Analysis[a]

Theory	Theory type	Postulate(s)	Postulate type	Deduced predictions	Constructed propositions
		Characterization			
Allocation	Deductive	Actual reward is a weighted mean of decision makers' just rewards	Societal	Yes	No
Anselmian	Hybrid	The will is subject to two inclinations, to the own good and to the common good	Behavioral	Yes	Yes
Framing	Deductive	1. Justice evaluation function 2. Justice index	Behavioral	Yes	No
Just society	Deductive	1. Inequality is a decreasing function of the number of independent-minded decision makers 2. Inequality in the distribution of a good is a bad, and inequality in the distribution of a bad is a good	Behavioral Societal	Yes	No
Justice-comparison	Hybrid	1. Justice evaluation function 2. Measurement rule 3. Identity representation of just reward 4. Social welfare function 5. Social cohesivenss function	Behavioral	Yes	Yes

[a]As discussed in the text, a hybrid theory has both deductive and hierarchical components. See also Fig. 3.3.

FREQUENTLY ASKED QUESTIONS

FAQ 1. What Does a Theory Look Like?

A theory is a set of sentences that can be divided into two parts, the first part containing the assumptions, and the second part containing the derived implications, in a deductive theory, or, in a hierarchical theory, the constructed propositions. Thus, a theory has a two-part structure, and looks like the forms in Figure 3.3.

FAQ 2. What Is a Theory About?

A theory is about two things. First, it is about the behavior or process described in the assumptions. Second, it is about the behaviors or processes described in the predictions or in the propositions.

To illustrate, consider justice-comparison theory. The assumptions of justice-comparison theory are about the workings of the sense of justice, in particular, how comparison of an actual reward to one's idea of the just reward produces the justice evaluation. The derived implications and the constructed propositions are about all the things in which justice evaluations play a part, from health and family behavior to religious institutions and international relations. The more basic the behavior or process described in the assumption part of a theory, the more widely-ranging will be the behaviors and processes described in the implication-proposition part.

Justice processes and comparison processes are basic in the sense that they engender behavioral and social phenomena in large topical domains. But they probably are not truly fundamental. Thus, theories whose assumptions describe justice and comparison processes yield implications about large areas of the sociobehavioral life, but not about all areas of the sociobehavioral life. They are not theories about the truly fundamental forces that govern all observed behavioral and social phenomena. It is likely that the starting processes for justice and comparison theories are themselves the product of the joint operation of truly fundamental forces, the kind of forces Newton had in mind for physical nature. Thus, justice and comparison theories lie in the Mertonian middle range.

The Holy Grail in social science is the threefold challenge:

To discover the fundamental forces.
To describe their operation.
To derive their implications.

Social science theories of the future will describe a fundamental force in the postulate part and derive its implications in the prediction part. A special ingredient in understanding observed behavioral and social phenomena will be to examine the clashes in the effects of different forces.

FAQ 3. What Does the Name of a Theory Indicate?

There is no agreed-upon usage; some theories are named for the behavior or process in the assumption part, others for a behavior or process in the prediction part. When a theory is named for the behavior or process in the assumption part, chances are good that it is, or aspires to be, a quite general theory with implications for a variety of topical domains. Examples include rational choice theory and comparison theory.

When a theory is named for a behavior or process in the prediction part, the name provides less information. The theory could be an application of a general theory to one topical domain, or it could be a restricted exploration of the topical domain. Becker's (1973, 1974) theory of marriage is an example of the former; it is an application of the more general economic theory to the topical domain of marriage.

Sometimes the word "theory" is used to refer to a set of theories, and its name refers to a behavior or process that appears in the postulate part of some of the theories and in the prediction part of others. "Justice theory" is an example; justice theory, as has been discussed in this chapter, refers to a set of theories (of which five members were discussed in this chapter). Justice elements may appear in the postulate part, in the prediction part, or in both parts.

FAQ 4. How Is Interpretation of Predictions Related to Types of Assumptions?

An assumption may posit some feature of human nature. Alternatively, it may posit some feature of a societal arrangement or some particular organizational or institutional principle. For example, the justice evaluation function, which is the first postulate of justice-comparison theory, posits that humans make justice evaluations and experience injustice by a process that can be faithfully represented by the logarithm of the ratio of the actual reward to the just reward. Thus, the justice evaluation function posits a feature of human nature. In contrast, the single postulate of allocation theory—that just rewards determine actual rewards—posits a societal arrangement in which the actual rewards are produced by aggregating the members' ideas of the just reward.

In the first case, when a postulate refers to a feature of human nature—we may call these "behavioral" postulates—the empirical fate of the predictions sheds light on human nature. The predictions are logically necessary consequences of the behavioral postulate. If the behavioral postulate correctly describes humans, then the predictions will be observed. If, on the other hand, the predictions are rejected, we learn that human nature does not operate in the way described by the assumption.

In the second case, however, the predictions are logically necessary implications, not of human nature, but rather of a societal arrangement; we may call these "societal" postulates. Whenever that societal arrangement is in place, the predictions will be observed. What is of interest here is not so much testing the predictions as investigating real-world societies to see whether, and how, they may satisfy the assumption. For example, in allocation theory interest centers on societies in which just rewards determine actual rewards and on assessing the extent to which independence of mind is displayed in such societies, together with more general inquiry into the determinants of this type of societal arrangement and of independence of mind.

FAQ 5. How Does Theory Grow?

To answer this question precisely, it is necessary to distinguish between *growth of a theory* and *growth of a theory set*. There are two ways in which a theory can grow: Its postulate set can grow and its prediction set can grow. With respect to the postulate part, in the early phase of a theory's development, the number of postulates may grow until it reaches a size sufficient to facilitate abundant prediction. But, as understanding grows, it may become clear that some of the postulates are unnecessary (for example, being themselves implied by other postulates). And, thus, we may say that the *growth curve of the postulate part of a theory is nonmonotonic, at first increasing, subsequently decreasing.*

In contrast, the prediction part of the theory must increase without limit. Moreover, not only is quantitative growth required but so also is qualitative growth, in particular, the continual derivation of novel predictions, predictions for phenomena and relationships not yet observed. Thus, we may say that the *growth curve of the prediction part of a theory is increasing and so also is the growth curve of the subset containing novel predictions.*

Consider, for example, justice-comparison theory. In the beginning, this theory had a single postulate—the justice evaluation function—and no implications; it was correctly not yet called a theory (Jasso, 1978). Early attempts at derivation indicated that in order to include within the purview of the theory ordinal goods, it would be necessary to introduce a second postulate to describe the measurement rule for cardinal and ordinal things. The first published version of the theory (Jasso, 1980) contains two postulates and includes both derived predictions and constructed propositions. While some of the derived predictions and constructed propositions could have been based on the first postulate alone (those that did not involve ordinal goods), the prediction set was substantially enlarged by incorporation of the second postulate. Similarly, introduction of the third postulate (Jasso, 1986), the identity representation of the comparison holding, produced an explosion of new predictions.

As discussed in the section entitled "Justice Version of Comparison Theory," justice-comparison theory currently has a set of five postulates. Ongoing work is scrutinizing the fifth postulate (social cohesiveness), to see whether it may itself be implied by the other four and to see whether the few predictions that have used it can be derived from the other four. If so, the postulate part of justice-comparison theory would decline from five to four postulates. Meanwhile, the prediction set continues to grow dramatically.

How about growth in a theory set? Growth in a theory set occurs with the introduction of new theories. In the case of the justice theory set, new theories include allocation theory and Anselmian theory, briefly discussed earlier in the chapter. In this case, it is useful to examine how the theories are related and to see whether they can be consolidated, as discussed in the next frequently asked question.

FAQ 6. How Are Theories Related?

Here, we focus on the relations between two deductive theories; in general, it is useful to examine the pairwise relations among all theories in a theory set or, more generally, in a topical or disciplinary domain.

Two theories may be related in one of three ways. First, their postulate sets may share postulates; that is, a postulate may appear as a postulate in both theories. Second, their prediction sets may share predictions; that is, a prediction may appear as a prediction in both theories. Third, a sentence may be a postulate in one theory and a prediction in the other. Fig. 3.4 depicts these relations.

When two theories share a postulate, it is useful to examine whether the two postulate sets can be merged (that is, whether they are fully consistent). If so, the new theory will have fewer postulates than the sum of the two earlier theories, while the new prediction set will equal in size the sum of the two constituent prediction sets. This situation produces a gain in what Heckathorn (1984) calls "theoretical payoff."

When two theories share a prediction, it may mean that, consistent with a multifactor view of empirical reality, the two processes described in the postulate parts of the two theories both play parts in producing the behavior or process described in the prediction. This is very important information for use in empirical estimation and in the interpretation of empirical results.

When a statement appears in the postulate set of one theory and in the prediction set of another, it is useful to investigate whether consolidation may be appropriate. The just society theory summarized earlier in this chapter provides an example of this activity; here the postulate set contains predictions from two theories (allocation theory and framing theory). Current research is assessing whether allocation theory and framing theory can be consoli-

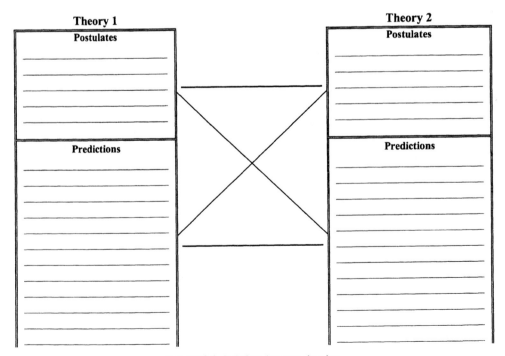

FIGURE 3.4. Relations between theories.

dated, and if so whether, given that framing theory and justice-comparison theory share a postulate (the justice evaluation function), the new theory can be further consolidated with justice-comparison theory. It is not obvious what the results of this assessment will be, in part because the justice evaluation function appears only in reflexive form in justice-comparison theory while it appears in full observer-rewardee form in framing theory.

FAQ 7. How Do We Report the Results of Theoretical Derivation?

A useful way to report the results of theoretical derivation is by means of the Merton chart of theoretical derivation (Table 3.6). The Merton chart is organized as a spreadsheet, with "postulates" as the column designator and "predictions" as the row designator, so that for each prediction one may mark which postulates were used in its derivation. The Merton chart, if fully filled out (as of a given date), would tell at a glance which postulates are "productive" and which not, and which predictions are "expensive" and which not; that is, a postulate's productivity can be gauged by the number of predictions in whose derivation it plays a part. Conversely, a prediction's cost can be gauged by the number of postulates required to derive it. The Merton chart of theoretical derivation was named for Merton who has urged the codification of theoretical results, for example, in Merton (1945).

It is scrutiny of Merton charts for justice-comparison theory that has prompted assessment of the fifth postulate, which, as discussed in the FAQ 5, is a candidate for elimination from the postulate set.

FAQ 8. What Is Theory-Driven Research?

The phrase "theory-driven research" usually refers to two activities: (1) theoretical analysis, and (2) empirical analysis of either (a) predictions derived in deductive theories, or (b) propositions constructed in hierarchical theories. For example, in justice analysis, theory-driven research would encompass derivation of new predictions, empirical testing of predictions derived in deductive theories, and empirical testing of propositions constructed in hierarchical theories. In Fig. 3.1, theory-driven research would include all research in the theoretical panel, and it would include research in the empirical panel which is linked by arrows to the theoretical panel.

There are two other kinds of research represented in Fig. 3.1, both of which are critically important not only for the advancement of a field but also specifically for theoretical development. Yet they cannot be called "theory-driven research" except by a considerable linguistic stretch or by the hope that they will lead to theoretical work.

The first of these two other kinds of research is basic work on the framework for the study of a particular field of phenomena. If we call work on the framework "theory-driven," it is because of the hope that work on the framework will lead to new building blocks for new theories.

What about purely inductive work? Consider, for example, work in the top section of the empirical panel of Fig. 3.1, which is not linked to the theoretical panel, but is linked by an arrow to the framework. Such work cannot truly be said to be "theory-driven," and yet it plays a critically important role in suggesting new ideas for theories. Indeed, the justice evaluation function was discovered via inductive empirical work, and subsequently became the cornerstone of several theories. Put differently, such work is not driven by a theory, yet it can drive a theory. Thus, as with work on the framework, if we call inductive empirical work theory-driven, it is because of the hope that it will lead to new building blocks for new theories.

TABLE 3.6. Merton Chart of Theoretical Derivation

Theory: _____   Date: _____

                                                Page: _____

Predictions	Postulates				

Notes:

FAQ 9. What Do We Test When We Test a Theory?

We carry out tests on the predictions of deductive theories and the propositions of hierarchical theories. These tests shed light on the validity and usefulness of the assumptions in the theories.[22]

FAQ 10. Does Formal Theory Really Enable Swifter Progress to Deeper Understanding of Human Behavior?

You be the judge. Take the postulate or postulates from any of the five specimen theories discussed in the theory section. Think hard about what light the postulate sheds on human behavioral and social phenomena. Think hard about how the postulate may be connected to other areas of the human experience. The key question is: Can thinking hard—by itself—produce the abundance of predictions that formal derivation has produced?

For example, can thinking hard about how individuals experience themselves as unfairly treated if their actual reward differs from what they see as the just reward for themselves yield the predictions listed in the section entitled "Justice Version of Comparison Theory," such predictions as the prediction that whether conflict is more severe when a disadvantaged group constitutes 10% of the population or when a disadvantaged group constitutes 90% of the population depends on the shape of the income distribution?

Similarly, can thinking hard about St. Anselm's idea that the will has two inclinations yield the predictions listed in the section entitled "Aselmian Theory," such predictions as the

<hr>

[22]For analysis of the testing process, see Popper (1935/1959, 1963), Kuhn (1962/1970), and Lakatos (1970), and for brief discussion, Reynolds (1971) and Jasso (1988:3–5, 1989a:139–141, 1993:258–263).

prediction that the proportions of the population in the states of harmony, conflict, and ambiguity depend on the shape of the income distribution?

Can thinking hard about how people form ideas of justice and how they experience injustice lead to predictions about the exact relations between justice and inequality, such predictions as the prediction that when people value wealth, the greater the wealth inequality, the greater the overall amount of perceived injustice?

Look at the postulates. Review in your head how many years the postulates were known. Think about the Anselmian postulate, which captivated Duns Scotus, among others.[23] Think about the basic idea underlying justice-comparison theory, known to the ancients, known to Marx, Durkheim, James. Look at the predictions. And you be the judge.

FAQ 11. How Do I Get Started Doing Formal Theory?

There are two kinds of preparation, remote and proximate. Remote preparation involves building, over a long period of time, a set of habits of mind and a generous toolbox. Proximate preparation involves acquiring a tool that emerges as important in addressing a burning question. Of the two, remote preparation is the more important. It is remote preparation that generates surprises. And theoretical advancement, in the end, is about surprises.

For remote preparation, there are two ingredients. The first is voracious reading in everything connected to human behavior, not only social science but also philosophy, literature, poetry, supplemented by plays, films, television. The second is mathematics. Mathematics is an important tool for reasoning, both directly and indirectly. The direct applications of mathematical tools are obvious. Less obvious, however, is the fact that practice with mathematics improves the ability to think abstractly. It is thinking abstractly that makes it possible for one to see the connections between seemingly unrelated things. Mathematics builds the habits of thought that lead to theoretical surprises.

Proximate preparation has its place. Learning one special tool to address one question gets a job done. But it is no substitute for the lifelong practice of mathematics.

For the young student, there is perhaps no better remote preparation for social science than entering the two worlds—one of mathematics, the other of the literary imagination—now one, now the other. Treat them as ends in themselves, not as means; enter them for the gladness and magic they bring. They will surprise you by setting up links in your mind and creating an entirely new world, a world that seamlessly integrates mathematical and literary insights. It is from this new world in your mind that you will make theories.

REFERENCES

Anselm of Canterbury, Saint. (1070–1109). (1946–1961). *Opera omnia*. F. S. Schmitt (Ed.). O.S.B. Edinburgh: Thomas Nelson and Sons.

Anselm of Canterbury, Saint. (1080–1090) (1967). *Truth, freedom, and evil: Three philosophical dialogues*. J. Hopkins & H. Richardson (Eds. & Trans.). New York: Harper Torchbooks.

Atkinson, A. B. (1970). On the measurement of inequality. *Journal of Economic Theory, 2*, 244–263.

Atkinson, A. B. (1975). *The economics of inequality*. London: Oxford.

Becker, G. S. (1973). A theory of marriage: Part I. *Journal of Political Economy, 81*, 813–846.

Becker, G. S. (1974). A theory of marriage, Part II. *Journal of Political Economy, 82*, S11–S26.

Heckathorn, D. D. (1984). Mathematical theory construction in sociology: Analytic power, scope, and descriptive accuracy as trade-offs. *Journal of Mathematical Sociology, 10*, 77–105.

Jasso, G. (1978). On the justice of earnings: A new specification of the justice evaluation function. *American Journal of Sociology, 83*, 1398–1419.

[23]Duns Scotus (*c.* 1266–1308) found Anselm's idea compelling and used it to develop a new understanding of morality and of the freedom of the will. See Jasso (1989b).

Jasso, G. (1980). A new theory of distributive justice. *American Sociological Review, 45*, 3–32.

Jasso, G. (1986). A new representation of the just term in distributive-justice theory: Its properties and operation in theoretical derivation and empirical estimation. *Journal of Mathematical Sociology, 12*, 251–274.

Jasso, G. (1987). The just society: Three theorems on inequality, justice, and democracy. Revised version of paper presented at the Conference to Honor James S. Coleman, Werner-Reimers Stiftung, Bad Homburg, Germany, October–November 1996.

Jasso, G. (1988). Principles of theoretical analysis. *Sociological Theory, 6*, 1–20.

Jasso, G. (1989a). Notes on the advancement of theoretical sociology (reply to Turner). *Sociological Theory, 7*, 135–144.

Jasso, G. (1989b). Self-interest, distributive justice, and the income distribution: A theoretical fragment based on St. Anselm's postulate. *Social Justice Research, 3*, 251–276.

Jasso, G. (1993). Building the theory of comparison processes: Construction of postulates and derivation of predictions. In J. Berger & M. Zelditch, Jr. (Eds.), *Theoretical research programs: Studies in the growth of theory* (pp. 212–264; references pp. 474–478). Stanford, CA: Stanford University Press.

Jasso, G. (1999). How much injustice is there in the world? Two new justice indexes. *American Sociological Review, 64*, 133–168.

Jasso, G. (2000). Some of Robert K. Merton's contributions to justice theory. *Sociological Theory, 18*, 329–337.

Jasso, G. (unpublished). The just society: Theorems on justice, inequality, and democracy. Paper presented at the Conference in Honor of James. S. Coleman, Reimers Stiftung, Bad Homburg, 31 October–1 November 1996.

Jasso, G., & Wegener, B. (1997). Methods for empirical justice analysis: Part I. Framework, models, and quantities. *Social Justice Research, 10*, 393–430.

Johnson, N. L., & Kotz, S. (1970a). *Distributions in statistics: Continuous univariate distributions—1.* Boston: Houghton Mifflin.

Johnson, N. L., & Kotz, S. (1970b). *Distributions in statistics: Continuous univariate distributions—2.* Boston: Houghton Mifflin.

Kotz, S., Johnson, N. L., & Read, C. B. (1982). Conjugate ranking. In S. Kotz, N. L. Johnson, & C. B. Read (Eds.), *Encyclopedia of statistical sciences*, Vol. 2 (p. 145). New York: Wiley.

Kotz, S., Johnson, N. L., & Read, C. B. (1988). Tukey's inequality for optimal weights. In S. Kotz, N. L. Johnson, & C. B. Read (Eds.), *Encyclopedia of statistical sciences*, Vol. 9 (pp. 361–362). New York: Wiley.

Kuhn, T. S. (1962/1970). *The structure of scientific revolutions*, 2nd ed., enlarged. Chicago: University of Chicago Press.

Lakatos, I. (1970). Falsification and the methodology of scientific research programmes. In I. Lakatos & A. Musgrave (Eds.), *Criticism and the growth of knowledge* (pp. 91–195). Cambridge: Cambridge University Press.

Liapunov, A. M. (1900). Sur une proposition de la théorie des probabilités. *Bulletin Academie Imperiale Sciences St. Petersburg, 13*, 359.

Liapunov, A. M. (1901). Nouvelle forme du théorème sur la limite de probabilité. *Memoire Academie Imperiale Sciences St. Petersburg, 12*, 1.

Machiavelli, N. (1532/1950). *Discourses*. With an introduction and notes by L. J. Walker. Two volumes. New Haven, CT: Yale University Press.

Merton, R. K. (1945). Sociological theory. *American Journal of Sociology, 50*, 462–473.

Merton, R. K. (1949, 1957/1968). *Social theory and social structure*. New York: Free Press.

Merton, R. K. (1957). Continuities in the theory of reference groups and social structure. In R. K. Merton *Social theory and social structure*, 2nd ed., rev. and enlarged (pp. 281–386). New York: Free Press.

Merton, R. K., & Rossi, A. S. (1950). Contributions to the theory of reference group behavior. In R. K. Merton & P. Lazarsfeld (Eds.), *Continuities in social research: Studies in the scope and method of "The American Soldier"* (pp. 40–105). New York: Free Press.

Popper, K. R. (1935/1959). *The logic of scientific discovery*. New York: Basic Books.

Popper, K. R. (1963). *Conjectures and refutations: The growth of scientific knowledge*. New York: Basic Books.

Reynolds, P. D. (1971). *A primer in theory construction*. New York: Macmillan.

Smith, A. (1759/1974). *The theory of moral sentiments*. A. L. Macfie & D. D. Raphael (Eds.). Oxford: Clarendon Press.

Smith, A. (1776/1976). *An inquiry into the nature and causes of the wealth of nations*. R. H. Campbell, A. S. Skinner, & W. B. Todd (Eds.). Oxford: Clarendon Press.

Stuart, A., & Ord, J. K. (1987). *Kendall's advanced theory of statistics. Vol. 1: Distribution theory*, 5th ed. New York: Oxford University Press.

Toulmin, S. (1953). *The philosophy of science: An introduction*. London: Hutchinson.

Toulmin, S. (1978). Science, philosophy of. In *The New Encyclopaedia Britannica, Macropaedia 16*, 15th ed. (pp. 375–393). Chicago: Britannica.

Wiley, N. (1994). *The semiotic self*. Cambridge, England: Polity.

Wolfson, D. (1985). Lindeberg–Feller theorem. In S. Kotz, N. L. Johnson, & C. B. Read (Eds.), *Encyclopedia of statistical sciences*, Vol. 5 (pp. 1–2). New York: Wiley.

CHAPTER 4

Computational Approaches to Sociological Theorizing

Kathleen M. Carley

INTRODUCTION

Sociologists are concerned with explaining and predicting social behavior. Theorists are not concerned with providing a description of society at a particular point in time. Rather, they are in the business of providing insight into how societies change, into the dynamics underlying behavior, into the processes that result in the observed correlations, and into the way in which multiple factors come together to create specific social situation. In other words, the sociological theorizing involves explaining how multiple factors interact in complex, often nonlinear ways to affect social behaviors and in explaining the dynamics by which social agents, groups, teams, organizations, societies, cultures evolve and coevolve. The focus of theory on complex nonlinear and dynamic systems makes computational analysis a natural methodological choice for theorizing.

The use of formal techniques[1] in general and computational analysis in particular is playing an ever-increasingly important role in the development of sociological theory. Computational analysis has been used to theorize about a large number of social behaviors: organizational exploration and exploitation (March, 1996), cooperation (Macy, 1991a,b), coordination (Carley & Prietula, 1994), diffusion and social evolution (Carley, 1991; Kaufer & Carley, 1993), organizational adaptation (Carley & Svoboda, 1996; Levinthal, 1997; Sastry, 1997), change in social networks (Markovsky, 1987) and exchange networks (Yamagishi et al., 1988; Markovsky et al., 1993), collective action (Feinberg & Johnson, 1988, 1990; McPhail & Tucker, 1990), and the fundamental nature of the social agent (Carley & Newell, 1994). One reason for this movement to computational social theory is the growing recognition that social

---

[1]Formal techniques include logic modeling (e.g., Skvoretz & Fararo, 1989, 1994), mathematical modeling (Lave & March), and simulation (Bainbridge et al., 1994; Carley & Prietula, 1994; McKelvey, 1997). In this chapter the focus is on simulation; however, the reader should recognize that these other formal techniques play complementary roles in sociological theorizing.

Kathleen M. Carley • Department of Social and Decision Sciences, Carnegie Mellon University, Pittsburgh, Pennsylvania 15213.

Handbook of Sociological Theory, edited by Jonathan H. Turner. Kluwer Academic / Plenum Publishers, New York, 2002.

processes are complex, dynamic, adaptive, and nonlinear; that social behavior emerges from interactions within and between ecologies of entities (people, groups, technologies, agents, etc.); and that the relationships among these entities are critical constraints on and enablers of individual and social action. Another reason for the movement to formal approaches is the recognition that societies and the groups and institutions within them are inherently computational since they have a need to and the ability to scan and observe their environment, store facts and programs, communicate among members, and transform information by human or automated decision making. In general, the goal of this formal research is to build new concepts, theories, and knowledge about complex systems such as groups, organizations, institutions, and societies. Using formal techniques, theorists search for fundamental social objects, processes, and the mathematical formalism with which to describe their behavior and interactions. Another goal of this research is to discover the most reasonable basis from which, at least in principle, theories of all other processes and behaviors can be derived.

Computational analysis is an ideal way to meet this goal. Indeed, the literature is replete with claims about the value and use of simulation. Fundamentally, these claims rest on the fact that computational analysis enables the theorist to think systematically and thoroughly about systems that are larger, more complex, have more interactions, and have more underlying dynamics than can be thought through without the aid of such automated accounting devices. For example, Markovsky (1992) showed that even very simple models of social interaction across networks were sufficiently complex that researchers are unable to predict their behavior. In a complex process there typically are many interacting objects (e.g., people or procedures in the society or institution), and it is rarely possible to proceed to a complete mathematical solution. Systems in which there are complex processes often exhibit nonlinear behavior and phase changes in behavior and often reach dramatically different end states given only minor changes in initial conditions. Such underlying nonlinearities make it nontrivial to think through the implications of the dynamic processes and multiactor situations. There is a general recognition that the nonlinear dynamics that characterize social systems are not mathematically tractable; hence, simulation is needed. Computational analysis can be used to track and analyze the detailed behavior within and among people, groups, teams, organizations, institutions, and societies. Computational models enable the analysis of groups far larger in size and over longer time periods than can be analyzed in a field or laboratory setting. Computational analysis enables the theorist to address issues of scalability; that is, do behaviors remain the same, do our theories hold, as we move from groups of two or three to thousands? Through simulation, we can gain some insight into whether scale matters to the nonlinear dynamics that underlie fundamental sociological processes such as reciprocity. This is particularly important as we move into a world where technology is making organizations of unprecedented size and distribution possible and giving people unprecedented access to larger numbers of others, ideas, technologies, and resources.

Computational analysis enables the theorist to think through the possible ramifications of complex systems and to develop a series of consistent predictions. Computational models, because they can track and emulate learning, adaptive, and evolutionary behavior are ideally suited to the examination of dynamic systems, to examining emergent behavior, and to suggesting the long-term impacts of new technologies and policies. Consequently, computational models can be and have been used in a normative fashion to generate a series of hypotheses by running virtual experiments. The resultant hypotheses then can be tested in other empirical settings. Other reasons for using computational analysis to do social theorizing include the facts that the resultant analysis can provide sufficiency explanations, can be used to demonstrate gaps in extant verbal theories, and can be used to check the consistency of the predictions made using verbal theories.

In other words, computational models are most useful when there are a large number of variables, substantial nonlinearities, multiple interactions, complex interactions (such as three way or higher interactions, dynamics, and cases where there are more than a small number of actors. As such, simulations are tools for doing theory development. This is not to say that other methods cannot also enable the theorist to reason about complex dynamic systems, but that computational analysis is an important tool in the theorist's toolkit. Computational models, however, are not a panacea. A disadvantage is that such models cannot be used to conclusively demonstrate what people do in novel situations. There are limitations to their usefulness and there are areas where they are more useful than others.

Computational theorizing has led to a new way of thinking about theory and theory building, and four elements of this approach will be described: the model as theory, virtual worlds, empirically grounded theory, and hypotheses generation. After this, some of the major theoretical breakthroughs will be described, then the relation of computational reasoning about social systems to complexity theory.

THE COMPUTER MODEL AS THEORY

One of the first insights of the novice computational social theorist is that the verbal theory is incomplete compared to the level of detail needed in a computer model. Generally, moving from the verbalization to a formal representation, either mathematical or computational, requires the theorist to think through a series of relations among the component processes and entities lying at the core of the theory. This "filling in the detail" is part of the process by which theories are developed. Another part is determining which of these details are irrelevant and which are critical relative to the outcomes of interest. In other words, the computational model becomes the theory.

This same argument underlies the Turing test, a method for testing and validating computational models. Computational models do the task they seek to explain. Consequently, the model itself is substitutable for the entity that is being modeled. For example, if the model is of a human agent, then in principle in an experiment the computational model can substitute for a human or a machine. In this case if recognizable behavior emerges and if the observer cannot discern a relevant difference, then the model passes the Turing test. Turing tests vary in the degree of rigor, use of quantitative data, and use of statistics. Turing tests typically have been employed in simulations of machines or of single humans. Since the computational model does the task it seeks to explain the model itself is the theory.

From a social perspective, however, the Turing test is insufficient. Carley and Newell (1994) suggest that when the computational model is meant to act as a social agent or a group of social agents it is more appropriate to use a revised version of the Turing test that they refer to as the social Turing test. Unlike the classic Turing test, the social Turing test takes the group context into account and expects social not just behavioral responses. To do a social Turing test the researcher follows these three steps:

1. First, a collection of social agents is constructed according to the hypotheses and placed in a social situation, as defined by the hypotheses. Recognizably social behavior should emerge from the computational model.

2. Second, there will be many aspects of the computational model that are not specified by the hypotheses. That is, to create a working computational model one often has to develop the model at a level of detail well beyond that of verbal theorizing. In general, such aspects should be set based on known human data or handled using Monte Carlo techniques.

3. Third, the behaviors that emerge from the computational model can vary widely with such specification, but the behavior should remain recognizably social. The behavior of a computational model is recognizably social if it meets the following criteria. The group's behavior (two or more agents) should take into account social knowledge and the actions and interactions among the agents. Group behavior cannot be generated from the behavior of a single agent. Finally, the behavior of the computational model must match, within some predefined level of fit, the behavior of a human group in terms of qualitatively or quantitatively fitting known data on a human group or fitting a subject matter expert's description of the human group's behavior. When these criteria are met the social Turing test is met.

THE COMPUTER MODEL
AS VIRTUAL WORLD

Virtual worlds are computer-simulated worlds of particular environs, social, or physical. Within a virtual world there is a particular set of physical, temporal, social or cultural laws that must be obeyed. These laws need not match those of earth. For example, in a virtual world agents could have paranormal capabilities, no emotions, or the ability to breathe under water. The worlds are populated by artificial agents. Examples range from game systems such as SimCity to research worlds for understanding the complexities of biological and social life. Virtual worlds become testbeds in which researchers can grow artificial life and communities, develop new procedures and hypotheses, and reason about the impacts of interaction among agents. Virtual worlds also can be used as a learning environment in which the student can engage in solving the problems within the scope of the world described.

One of the earliest examples of a virtual world in sociology is Bainbridge's (1987) sociological laboratory. Bainbridge created worlds in which the student could explore classic theories of social behavior. Within these worlds, the student could run virtual experiments to see the impact of changing norms of social behavior.

Artificial life, or A-life, studies are done within virtual worlds. One example of such a world is Sugarscape (Epstein & Axtell, 1997). In Sugarscape, multiple simple agents engage in social interaction in the process of consuming sugar, moving across planes, giving birth, and dying. Sugarscape is a virtual world where agents can live, eat, die, engage in social interactions, and so forth. In its simplest form the sugarscape world is a torus made by wrapping a grid of 50 by 50 squares such that sugar grows in some of the squares and not others. This world is populated by a number of agents each of whom can move one square on the von Neuman grid (NSEW) each time period as long as they do not occupy a square occupied by another agent or they can consume sugar. Consumed sugar translates into energy. Agents can eat or store sugar. Energy is needed to move, reproduce, and so forth. Without energy the agents die. Agents placed randomly on the grid over time will develop a collective intelligence that moves them toward the fields of sugar. Additional rules, such as inheritance produce more social-like behavior. Indeed, the more factors and rules that are added, the more social behaviors can be explored. For example, introducing a second resource, spice, leads to the emergence of trading and an economic market.

Epstein and Axtell (1997) argue that they are using computers to do "bottom-up" social science. Given a collection of very simple agents with very simple rules, they try and grow complex social behavior. One of the key insights is that complex social outcomes need not have complex causes. Simple behaviors on the part of individual agents can have major social consequences.

The value of virtual worlds is that they enable the researcher and student to reason about social behavior in a controlled setting like a human experiment. However, unlike a human experiment, these worlds can be quite large. Thus issues of scale, emergence, and time varying behavior can be addressed.

THE COMPUTER MODEL AS EMPIRICALLY
GROUNDED THEORY

Computer models can be empirically grounded. A key example here is Heise's affect control theory (Heise, 1986, 1987; Smith-Lovin, 1987). Charles Osgood used semantic differential techniques to identify three dimensions of word meaning: evaluation, potency, and activity. These dimensions became known as the EPA model. Heise, in developing affect control theory, asserts that individuals construct social events to confirm the meanings of social classifications. This is done through a cognitive emotional process in which actors respond to each other at both a sociophysical and affective level. Ongoing interactions lead to alterations both in what the actors know about each other and in how they feel about themselves, the situation, and others. This affective response in turn affects the actors choice of possible actions.

Heise and co-workers have derived a number of mathematical functions to predict how people would rate various combinations of words describing social identities, attributes, actions, and situations and how these ratings would affect the actors choice of words, situations, and actions. These formula have embodied the formulas in the affect control computer model. In addition, Heise and colleagues have gathered substantial EPA data from men and women in various walks of life and in various cultures. Research subjects have provided mean EPA ratings of hundreds of words describing social identities, attributes, actions, and situations. These data also are embedded in the computational model. This empirically grounds the theory and moves the EPA ratings from being theoretical abstractions to concrete and measurable predictions.

Affect control theory, although conceptually straightforward, is sufficiently complex and nonlinear that humans have difficulty determining the full range of implications of the theory. Researchers and students can use the model to reason about the impact of emotions on social outcomes and the effect of actions, situations, and roles on emotions in dynamic situations. Using this model, the researcher can derive hypotheses from the theory to test in the field or laboratory, or can emulate an observed interaction to see whether the behavior observed matches that predicted by the model.

In general, many computational modelers have the desire to develop empirically grounded theory. In many cases, the appropriate data are not amenable to being placed in a large-scale quantitative database. Rather, the type of data needed for empirically grounding the model is ethnographic. In building a model of social and organizational processes, the computational theorist often has a large number of questions of the form "if this happens, then what?" or "what are the space of possible human actions?" Often experimental and survey data have too little detail to answer questions at the depth posed by the modeler, whereas a single protocol or an ethnographic study typically provides the kind of rich detail necessary for addressing the modelers concerns. Although it is ironic to those who view computational theorizing as the most quantitative of the formal theorizing techniques, in actuality the ethnographer is the computational theorists best friend.

THE COMPUTER MODEL
AS HYPOTHESIS GENERATOR

The process of designing, building, and analyzing a computational model is a process of theory building. An important component of this process is hypothesis generation. Computer models can in fact be viewed as hypothesis generation machines. To generate hypotheses the researcher first uses the model to conduct a virtual experiment. A virtual experiment is an experiment in which the data for each cell in the experimental design are generated by running a computer simulation model. In designing this virtual experiment, standard principles of experimental design should be followed.

There are several key ways in which virtual experiments differ from traditional human laboratory experiments. The first of these is scale. That is, it is possible in the simulated environment to run experiments with more subjects (agents), for longer periods of time, without subject fees, and to have the subjects engage in more activities, in larger groups, and so forth. The computer basically mitigates the physical, temporal, coordinating, and monetary constraints. The result is that it is very easy to design too extensive a virtual experiment. That is, it is relatively easy to generate more data than any current statistics package can handle. The constraints on the scale of the virtual experiment are computer storage space, processing speed, and the size constraints of the statistical analysis package.

Another way in which the virtual experiment differs from the traditional human laboratory experiment is in the role of statistical significance. For the human laboratory experiments, access to subjects, monetary and statistical power concerns determine the number of repetitions per cell. In this case, for an outcome variable of interest, such as organizational performance, statistically significant differences in this variable across two or more conditions may signal support for a hypothesis. The lack of a statistically significant difference signals the lack of support. In this case, the fact that there are observable differences is not interesting, whereas the fact that a difference is statistically significant is theoretically interesting and suggests that a real difference has been found. Many virtual experiment have at their core a Monte Carlo experiment, i.e., an experiment in which samples are generated randomly across some parameter space. For virtual experiments, the number of repetitions per cell are influenced by computational processing speed, storage space, and the number of repetitions per cell needed to determine whether an observed difference is statistically significant. When computational storage space and time are not at a premium, the computational theorist will simply run sufficient repetitions to guarantee that observed differences are significant. In this case, the fact that there are observable differences is theoretically interesting, the fact that they are statistically significant differences simply means the theorist had lots of computing power.

This does not mean that statistics does not have a role in analyzing the results of a virtual experiment. Rather, it means that the way in which the statistics are used is different than the way they are used in analyzing the data from a human laboratory experiment. Indeed, a critical step in generating hypotheses from a virtual experiment is to statistically analyze the results. The results of that analysis are the hypotheses that can be examined using data from human laboratory experiments, live simulations, games, field studies, or archival sources. In conducting a virtual experiment and generating a series of hypotheses the followings stages are gone through. First, identify key inputs. Second, explore the input parameter space to determine the values of the key variables that you want to explore. Third, the nonkey inputs, such as control and secondary variables, should be set. These may be set to predefined values or chosen randomly in a Monte Carlo fashion. Fourth, the virtual experiment is conducted, i.e., a number of simulations are to be run. Fifth, to analyze the output a series of statistical analysis should be run. Sixth a number of hypotheses should be generated. This is done by taking the statistical findings and converting them into statements. For example, imagine that when a regression is run related to uncover the relation between two inputs, such as group size and level of turnover, on some outcome such as performance you find that the beta coefficient for size is .2 and for turnover is .4. Then that finding about the relative strength of the regression beta coefficients of two input variables could be converted into a statement of the form turnover has twice the impact of size on performance. These hypotheses can then be tested in other venues.

THEORETICAL BREAKTHROUGHS:
THE NATURE OF THE SOCIAL AGENT

Computational models can be used in a number of ways. Several of these have been discussed: model as theory, model as virtual world, and model as hypothesis generator. Theorists using computational models have used them in these ways and several other ways (e.g., to fine-tune a human experiment). Computational models have a long history in the development of social theory and methodology (Federico & Figliozzi, 1981; Garson, 1987). Results derived from computational models have led to a number of important theoretical breakthroughs that collectively generate a more complete understanding of the social agent.

One of the key uses of computational models is to demonstrate how fundamental behavior can arise from principles other than those taken for granted and to call into question various paradigms. One of the earliest and most profound uses of computational models was to develop the theory of bounded rationality. Prior to the 1960s, most formal theories of social and organizational behavior assumed rational actors with complete information and total insight. Arising out of the Carnegie School, Herb Simon and others argued that humans were boundedly rational, i.e., social structure limits their access to data and human cognition limits their ability to process that information. As a result, decisions are made by satisficing and not by trying to locate the optimal decision. In *A Behavioral Theory of the Firm* (Cyert & March, 1963/1992) and in the garbage can model of organizational choice (Cohen, March, & Olsen, 1972) the authors demonstrate through computational based theorizing that human limitations affect what choices are made when and how. Further, by taking such bounds into account, theoretical propositions better match actual observations. This work was instrumental in revolutionizing theoretical and empirical work on group and organizational behavior. The resulting information processing view is now an integral part of many social theories.

Computer tournaments such as the now-classic "prisoner's dilemma" computer tournament organized by Robert Axelrod (1984) have served to focus the attentions of many researchers on a particular area of behavior, leading to rapid theoretical advancement. The prisoner's dilemma is a game-theoretic problem that explores the conditions under which cooperation may arise between self-interested actors who have the potential to gain in the short run if they violate agreements to cooperate (Rapoport & Chammah, 1965). In a computer tournament, the organizer invites people to submit computational models that do the "task" of the tournament. Results from tournaments demonstrate repeatedly that computational modeling can produce robust and sometimes unexpected results and advance theory. Tournaments enable theories to "compete" with each other, leading to better theoretical understanding of their relative efficacy, common features, and differences. For Axelrod's prisoner's dilemma tournament the programs submitted were models of actors who followed various strategies for playing the iterated prisoner's dilemma game. The "agent" that won was one of the simplest: the agent employing the "tit-for-tat" that cooperated on the first move and then imitated the previous action of its partner. This demonstrated that agents following a simple reciprocity norm could succeed even in an environment that was largely asocial. There were two central theoretical contributions: (1) the primacy of the reciprocity norm, and (2) the recognition that social outcomes are as affected by social interaction as by human cognitive architecture. Today, numerous researchers are using multiagent systems to understand the dynamics and contexts under which cooperation evolves.

Another theoretical breakthrough is in the area of chaos. The notion of deterministic chaos has captured the imagination of scholars and the public (Mandelbrot, 1983; Hao, 1984; Gleick, 1987). Kephart et al. (1992) noted that social behavior can become chaotic. This in itself is not the novel theoretical proposition. However, they ran a series of simulations that demonstrated that intelligent strategies can reduce chaos. The level of chaos in societies is reduced when the intelligent agents in these societies have the capacity to base their actions on beliefs about others' strategies and on the observed behavior of the collection of agents. Mental models, even rudimentary ones, about others and knowledge of the collective behavior are sufficient to generate nonchaotic behavior. This suggests that in order for recognizable social behavior to emerge the content of individual cognition needs to contain mental models of others and knowledge of others actions. One of the key questions here is to what extent does this knowledge need to be of specific others versus the generalized other, and to what extent does this knowledge need to be accurate.

A related breakthrough is in the area of social knowledge. Wegner (1995), using a computer system as a metaphor for human memory, developed the powerful idea of transactive memory. Transactive memory (Wegner, 1987; Wegner et al., 1991) refers to the ability of a group to have a memory system exceeding that of the individuals in the group. The basic idea is that knowledge is stored as much in the connections among individuals as in the individuals. Wegner argues that factors that are relevant in linking computers together such as directory updating, information allocation, and coordination of retrieval also are relevant in linking the individuals' memories together into a group memory. Empirical evidence provides some conformation and suggests that for a group, knowledge of who knows what is as important as knowledge of the task. Transactive knowledge can improve group performance (Moreland, Argote, & Krishnan, 1996). Thus, in order for recognizable social behavior to emerge, part of the content of an individual's mental models needs to be knowledge of who knows what and presumably knowledge of who knows who.

These findings suggest a paradigmatic view in which social agents are information processors and interactors with internal mental models containing a model of self and others (specific and generalized) and others' interaction that can be used to predict others performance, to determine who to interact with, and to select among alternative actions. This model of others and their interaction includes knowledge such as who knows who and who knows what. Norms become rules of behavior that link knowledge of self and other to specific interaction behaviors. An important element of this paradigm is that social behavior realizes social outcomes as the result of changes in interaction among agents and agents who themselves both in their mental models and in their behavior take into account what others know, who they know, and what they are likely to do. This sociocognitive perspective on agents is partially summarized by the Carley–Newell model social agent (1994).

COMPLEXITY AND EMERGENT BEHAVIOR

One of the tremendous values of using computational models is that you can reason about dynamic systems and complex systems. Questions such as what is the impact of learning, socialization, enculturation, and so on can be addressed. Moreover, the coevolution of groups, groups and technology, two cultures, and so on can be addressed. This ability to use computational models to look at change on multiple fronts at once is a very powerful theoretical device.

The ability to use simple computational models to examine dynamics has fired the theoretical imagination leading to a vocabulary and set of tools that can be used for sociological theorizing and collectively referred to as complexity theory. Complexity analysis provides us with a means for rethinking and extending social theories (Axelrod & Cohen, 1999; Morel & Ramanujam, 1999). The vocabulary and tools are deriving in part from advances in biology and physics. Clearly the history of social theory is replete with work on change and on societies as complex, adaptive, evolutionary systems. The work today, however, uses a distinct vocabulary, has a level of formalism not heretofore possible given the ubiquitousness of computing, and has a focus on the pattern of outcomes relative to the pattern of desired outcomes. From a paradigm standpoint there is now an increase of interest in complexity, landscapes, emergence, and coevolution.

Social theory in general and organizational theory in particular has a tradition of looking at societies and organizations as complex systems. A common feature of this work and modern complexity theory is that systems are seen as more complex when there are more parts and more connections among the parts. So, for example, when there are more individuals in the society or more activities in the organization, the system is more complex. Further, when there are more ties among individuals or more constraints among organizational activities then again there is more complexity. To this the formal work on complexity theory would add that complex systems typically have internal change, adaptation, or evolutionary mechanisms that result in behavior that might appear random but that actually has an underlying order (Holland, 1998). The underlying order is attributable to multiple agents, often operating on very simple principles.

The outcomes are complex for two reasons. First, there may be an appearance of randomness. Second, what outcomes are reached can be quite divergent depending on the initial conditions the history of the agents activities (Kauffman, 1995). Complex systems have the ability to self-organize (Bak, 1996). Self-organization means in part that group behavior occurs that is distinct from a simple average of individual agent behaviors. For example, imagine a group of agents moving through a grid. Even though individual agents may only move N, S, E, or W, the group *qua* group can move NE. Moreover, even though individual agents may be trying to optimize their outcome, the overall outcome for the group may be less than optimal. For example, in a group-level repeated dilemma game even though each individual is trying to maximize their return, the overall pattern of cooperation may result in the return to the group being suboptimal. Having a group-level outcome that is less than the optimal can be thought of as a complexity catastrophe (McKelvey, 1999).

The research on complex systems varies in whether or not a time-invariant fitness function is assumed. A fitness function defines the relation of inputs to outputs. A landscape is a graphic depiction of the relation of inputs to the output of concern, of the independent variables to the dependent variable (Levinthal, 1997). In this case there is a known a priori fitness function. The landscape is fixed and features of the landscape may make it harder or easier for individuals and groups to locate the optimum point in this landscape. In contrast, the fitness function may not be known a priori and/or the relation of inputs to outputs is time variant (dancing landscapes). In this case features of the landscape and of the way it changes determine the ease or difficulty of moving about this space. Changes in the landscape are commonly attributable to factors such as learning, innovation, population, turnover, birth and death processes, and so on. Agents and groups move about on this landscape. For some theorists, the agents move about because they are trying optimize their outcomes. For other theorists, the agents are seen as trying to satisfice or to move randomly about on this landscape. While there is growing agreement that social theories need to be dynamic, there is not widespread theoretical agreement about the shape of the underlying landscapes, the nature of the fitness function, whether or not the fitness function is fixed over time, and whether agents optimize or satisfice.

In complex systems things emerge. As previously noted this emergence may take the form of group outcomes that are distinct from individuals, or they make take the form of new procedures, groups, ideas, and so forth. The theoretical issues include what enables new things to emerge, to become stable, to become accepted and whether the history of the system alters what can and does emerge. In Kauffman's models (Kauffman, 1993) emergent structures derived from two sources: (1) forcing functions, and (2) homogeneity bias. When only one input can force a particular outcome state, there is a forcing function. An example here is the relation between age and drug usage. If it is the case that if you have never used drugs by the time you are 35, then you never will use drugs, then there is a forcing function. There will be a resultant structure to the relation between age and drugs that remains fixed across populations and groups such that there will be a larger than chance number of individuals over 35 who do not use drugs. The second factor is a homogeneity bias. Homogeneity biases may be processes or limits on variables that reduce the number of actual outcomes. For example, if the outcome were clothing color and only two dyes were available, that is a stronger homogeneity bias then if the number of dyes were unlimited. Other theorists working with complex systems have noted that learning (Carley, 1990, 1991), mimicry (Macy, 1991a,b), and temporal and physical constraints (Carley & Prietula, 1994) all lead to a certain level of emergent structuration. The basic nature of dynamic systems is that things tend to emerge. Thus the issue is not do patterns emerge, but what patterns emerge when and under what conditions.

The work on organizational adaptation is a classic example. Here, computational theorists have shown that individual learning and strategic choice do enable organizations to adapt. Change, in fact, is pretty much inevitable. Some of those changes are adaptive, i.e., they enable certain outcomes to be maintained or improved. Moreover, this work demonstrates that the emergent patterns are path dependent (history matters) and a complex function of interactions among agents, knowledge, and task. Interdependence among agents and among knowledge and tasks is a fundamental feature of social and organizational systems that affects group and organizational learning, performance, and adaptability (Levinthal, 1997; Sorenson, 1997; Krackhardt & Carley, 1998).

A related argument surrounds the notion of coevolution. Work in the area of ecology led to the view that populations of agents evolve through processes involving Darwinian selection of the fittest and trait propagation. This view was translated to the study of organizations where population ecologists (Hannan & Freeman, 1977, 1989; Hannan & Carroll, 1992), proponents of organizational evolution (Aldrich, 1979; Baum & Singh, 1994b), and economists (Nelson & Winter, 1982) all put forward the view that selectionist processes drive out the less fit firms, leaving "order" to be explained as the consequence of the survival of the more fit firms. Factors such as population density and niche overlap were used, in conjunction with evolutionary principles to explain the varying states populations of firms. Kauffman (1993) suggests that complexity effects may thwart selectionist effects under some circumstances. In particular he argues that the extent of interdependence within and among firms when coupled with regression to the mean can generate order even when the most fit firms do not survive. Kauffman (1993) suggests that *internal* and *external* interdependencies (K and C, respectively) create a level of complexity that can explain order in any world that can be thought of as a multiple groups with linkages within and between the groups. His analysis suggests that aggregate economic order (such as the distribution of size of firms that survive or the distribution of survival times) could be at least as much determined by intrafirm and interfirm dependencies as it might stem from external selection.

These interdependencies ensure that firms coevolve. This line of reasoning, although novel to economics is the familiar social network explanation long part of sociological theorists toolkit. However, from a sociological perspective the core assumptions are obviously nonsocial. For example, a limitation of Kauffman's model from a grounded theory perspective is that it assumes that the number of links within and between groups (or in the example above, within and among organizations) is fixed over time and identical across group members. In other words, the shape of the underlying social network is fixed with uniform centrality per agent. Thus, social order is explained in this work without an appeal to differentiation in the network. In contrast, the Carley (1990, 1991) constructural model, the social network, and the knowledge network coevolve, and initial network differentiation is a key determinant of order.

Not all work in complexity assumes away the importance of the pattern of relations. A parallel line of theorizing, derived from information processing theory and cognitive science, argues that the relations within and among groups evolve over time through a process of individual learning. Moreover, these links are seen as embedding knowledge. In particular, organizational learning theorists (Levinthal, 1997; Carley & Hill, 2001) suggest that even when there is not population-level evolution, organizational learning is sufficient to generate order. In this case, learning determines both the degree of interdependence and the value of that interdependence. For Carley (1990, 1991), the degree of interdependency within and among groups is dynamic and coevolves with the knowledge network (who knows what). Natural leaning and communication processes coupled with barriers to communication and to learning and the advent of new people, technology, and inventions prevent or enable groups from collectively moving toward optimal positions in the landscape and produce order. Coevolution occurs on multiple fronts: individuals coevolve with each other, individuals and groups coevolve, groups coevolve with each other, culture and social structure coevolve, and patterns of individual knowledge and interaction coevolve.

This work has led to a neoinformation-processing perspective in which social outcomes emerge from network dynamics over a set of interlocked networks. Traditional social theory has looked at networks in terms of the relations among people, or at an interorganizational level—the relations among organizations. Linguists and learning theorists have looked at networks in terms of the relations among knowledge and people. Operational researchers at networks as relations among tasks. This can be brought together in a unified metanetwork perspective where the relations within and among agents, knowledge, tasks, and organizations are seen as constraining and enabling social behavior (see Fig. 4.1). Moreover, these networks are seen as coevolving through dynamics such as learning, innovation, and population growth.

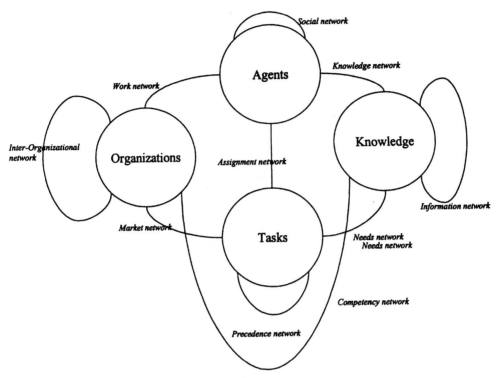

FIGURE 4.1. Embedding social behavior in a metanetwork.

A GLIMPSE OF THE FUTURE

Traditionally there has been a strong tie between the study of machine and human intelligence. For example, mathematical models of human learning (Bush & Mosteller, 1955) were among the first "learning" algorithms used in artificial agents. Advances in cognitive science have come hand-in-hand with advances in computer science. Today, one of the links between social theory and computer science is in the area of machine learning. Machine learning techniques inform and are informed by our understanding of both individual cognition and group or organizational learning. One of the areas of greatest potential for their application is in the area of social agents, another is in the area of organizational theory.

Social agents, such as personalized webbots, avatars, and socially sophisticated data bases are becoming increasingly technologically feasible. Artificial agents can generate and respond to rudimentary emotions, do tasks, and answer questions. As more of these agents are created the issue arises as to how these agents can and should interact with each other and human beings. New questions that need to be addressed include "do these agents need to be social to communicate effectively with humans?" and "will a society of webbots be more or less effective if it follows the same norms of behavior as a human society?" For the social theorists the creation of societies of these agents provides an important opportunity for addressing fundamental questions about the nature and value of socialness and the relation of sociality to other human characteristics such as emotions and cognitive processing.

Computational analysis and theorizing is playing an increasingly important role in the development of social and organizational theory. There is a growing recognition that complex adaptive processes underlie social life. There are three elements to this view. First, social and organizational processes are complex, dynamic, adaptive, and nonlinear. Second, organizational and social behavior emerges from interactions within and between ecologies of agents, resources, knowledge, tasks, and other organizations. Third, the relationships among and within these entities are critical constraints on and enablers of individual and organizational decision making and action. There is a parallel recognition that societies in general and organizations in particular are inherently computational, the reason being that they have a need to scan and observe their environment, store information and procedures, communicate, and transform information through human or artificial agents. Computational theories are providing the social theorist with both a new toolkit for examining social phenomena and new insights into the fundamental nature of the social agent.

ACKNOWLEDGMENTS. This work was supported in part by the Office of Naval Research ONR N00014-97-1-0037 and by the National Science Foundation NSF IRI9633 662.

REFERENCES

Aldrich, H. (1979). *Organizations and environments*. Englewood Cliffs, NJ: Prentice Hall.

Axelrod, R. (1984). *The evolution of cooperation*. New York: Basic Books.

Axelrod, R. M. (1997). *The complexity of cooperation: Agent-based models of competition and collaboration. Princeton studies in complexity*. Princeton, NJ: Princeton University Press.

Axelrod, R. M., & Cohen, M. D. (1999). *Harnessing complexity: Organizational implications of a scientific frontier*. New York: Free Press.

Bainbridge, W. S. (1987). *Sociology laboratory*. Belmont, CA: Wadsworth.

Bainbridge, W., Brent, E., Carley, K., Heise, D., Macy, M., Markovsky, B., & Skvoretz, J. (1994). Artificial social intelligence. *Annual Review of Sociology, 20*, 407–436.

Bak, P. (1996). *How nature works: The science of self-organized criticality*. New York: Copernicus.

Baum, J. A. C., & Singh, J. V. (1994a). Organization-environment coevolution. In J. A. C. Baum & J. V. Singh (Eds.), *Evolutionary dynamics of organizations* (pp. 379–402). New York: Oxford University Press.

Baum, J. A. C., & Singh, J. V. (Eds.). (1994b). *Evolutionary dynamics of organizations*. New York: Oxford University Press.

Bush, R. R., & Mosteller, F. (1955). *Stochastic models for learning*. New York: John Wiley and Sons.

Carley, K. (1990). Group stability: A socio-cognitive approach. In E. Lawler, B. Markovsky, C. Ridgeway, & H. Walker (Eds.), *Advances in group processes: Theory and research*, Vol. VII (pp. 1–44). Greenwich, CT: JAI Press.

Carley, K. (1991). A theory of group stability. *American Sociological Review, 56*(3), 331–354.

Carley, K. (1995). Communication technologies and their effect on cultural homogeneity, consensus, and the diffusion of new ideas. *Sociological Perspectives, 38*(4), 547–571.

Carley, K. M. (1999). On the evolution of social and organizational networks. In S. B. Andrews & D. Knoke (Eds.), *Networks in and around organizations* (pp. 3–30). Stamford, CT: JAI Press.

Carley, K., & Hill, V. (2001). Structural change and learning within organizations. In A. Lomi (Ed.), *Dynamics of organizational societies: Models, theories and methods*. Boston: MIT Press/AAAI Press/Live Oak.

Carley, K., & Newell, A. (1994). The nature of the social agent. *Journal of Mathematical Sociology, 19*(4), 221–262.

Carley, K. & Prietula, M. (1994). ACTS theory: Extending the model of bounded rationality in K. M. Carley and M. Prietula (Eds.), *Computational Organizational Theory* (pp. 55–87). Hillsdale, NJ: Lawrence Erlbaum.

Carley, K. M., & Svoboda, D. M. (1996). Modeling organizational adaptation as a simulated annealing process. *Sociological Methods and Research, 25*(1), 138–168.

Cohen, M. D., March, J. G., & Olsen, J. P. (1972). A garbage can model of organizational choice. *Administrative Sciences Quarterly, 17*(1), 1–25.

Cyert, R., & March, J. G. (1963/1992). *A behavioral theory of the firm*, 2nd ed. Cambridge, MA: Blackwell Publishers.

Epstein, J., & Axtell, R. (1997). *Growing artificial societies*. Boston: MIT Press.

Federico, P., & Figliozzi, P. W. (1981). Computer simulation of social systems. *Sociological Methods and Research, 9,* 513–533.

Feinberg, W. E., & Johnson, N. R. (1988). Outside agitators and crowds: Results from a computer simulation model. *Social Forces, 67,* 398–423.

Feinberg, W. E., & Johnson, N. R. (1990). Radical leaders, moderate followers: Effects of alternative strategies on achieving consensus for action in simulated crowds. *Journal of Mathematical Sociology, 15,* 91–115.

Garson, G. D. (1987). Computer simulation in social science. In *Academic microcomputing* (pp. 110–138). Newbury Park, CA: Sage.

Gleick, J. (1987). *Chaos*. New York: Penguin.

Hannan, M. T., & Carroll, G. R. (1992). *Dynamics of organizational populations*. New York: Oxford University Press.

Hannan, M. T., & Freeman, J. (1977). The population ecology of organizations. *American Journal of Sociology, 83,* 929–984.

Hannan, M. T., & Freeman, J. (1989). *Organizational ecology*. Cambridge, MA: Harvard University Press.

Hao, B. (Ed.). (1984). *Chaos*. Singapore: World Scientific. (NOTE: some libraries list this under Bai-Lin, Hao)

Heise, D. R. (1986). Modeling symbolic interaction. In S. Lindenberg, J. S. Coleman, & S. Nowak (Eds.), *Approaches to sociological theory* (pp. 291–316). New York: Russell Sage Foundation.

Heise, D. R. (1987). Affect control theory. Concepts and model. *Journal of Mathematical Sociology, 13*(1–2), 1–33.

Holland, J. (1998). *Emergence: From chaos to order*. Reading, MA: Perseus Books.

Kaufer, D. S., & Carley, K. M. (1993). *Communication at a distance: The effect of print on socio-cultural organization and change*. Hillsdale, NJ: Lawrence Erlbaum Associates.

Kauffman, S. A. (1993). *The origins of order: Self-organization and selection in evolution*. New York: Oxford University Press.

Kauffman, S. A. (1995). *At home in the universe: The search for laws of self-organization and complexity*. New York: Oxford University Press.

Kephart, J. O., Huberman, B. A., & Hogg, T. (1992). Can predictive agents prevent chaos? In P. Bourgine & B. Walliser (Eds.), *Economics and cognitive science* (pp. 41–55). Oxford: Pergamon Press.

Krackhardt, D. & Carley, K. M. (1998). A PCANS model of structure in organization. In *Proceedings of the 1998 International Symposium on Command and Control Research and Technology* (pp. 113–119). Monterey, CA: EBR.

Lave, C. A., & March, J. G. (1975). *An introduction to models in the social sciences*. New York: Harper and Row.

Levinthal, D. A. (1997). Adaptation on rugged landscapes. *Management Science, 43,* 934–950.

Levinthal, D. A., & March, J. B. G. (1993). The myopia of learning. *Strategic Management Journal, 14,* 95–112.

Macy, M. W. (1991a). Chains of cooperation: Threshold effects in collective action. *American Sociological Review, 56,* 730–747.

Macy, M. W. (1991b). Learning to cooperate: Stochastic and tacit collusion in social exchange. *American Journal of Sociology, 97,* 808–843.

Macy, M., & Skvoretz, J. (1998). The evolution of trust and cooperation between strangers: A computational model. *American Sociological Review, 63*(October), 638–660.

Mandelbrot, B. B. (1983). *The fractal geometry of nature*. San Francisco: W. H. Freeman.

March, J. G. (1996). Exploration and exploitation in organizational learning. In M. D. Cohen & L. S. Sproull (Eds.), *Organizational learning* (pp. 101–123). Thousand Oaks, CA: Sage.

Markovsky, B. (1987). Toward multilevel sociological theories: Simulations of actors and network effects. *Sociological Theory, 5,* 101–117.

Markovsky, B. (1992). Network exchange outcomes: Limits of predictability. *Social Networks, 14,* 267–286.

Markovsky, B., Skvoretz, J., Willer, D., Lovaglia, M. J., & Erger, J. (1993). The seeds of weak power: An extension of network exchange theory. *American Sociological Reviews, 58,* 197–209.

McKelvey, B. (1997). Quasi-natural organization science. *Organization Science, 8,* 351–380.

McKelvey, B. (1999). Avoiding complexity catastrophe in coevolutionary pockets: Strategies for rugged landscapes. *Organization Science, 10,* 294–321.

McPhail, C., & Tucker, C. W. (1990). Purposive collective action. *American Behavioral Scientist, 34,* 81–94.

Morel, B., & Ramanujam, R. (1999). Through the looking glass of complexity: The dynamics of organizations as adaptive and evolving systems. *Organization Science, 10*(3), 278–293.

Moreland, R. L., Argote, L., & Krishnan, R. (1996). Socially shared cognition at work: Transactive memory and group performance. In J. L. Nye & A. M. Brower (Eds.), *What's social about social cognition? Research on socially shared cognition in small groups* (pp. 57–84). Newbury Park, CA: Sage.

Nelson, R. R., & Winter, S. G. (1982). *An evolutionary theory of economic change*. Cambridge, MA: Belknap/Harvard.

Rapoport, A., (1911). *Mathematical models in the social and behavioral sciences*. Translated from the German *Mathematische Methoden in den Sozialwissenschaften*. New York: Wiley.

Rapoport, A., & Chammah, A. M. (1965). *Prisoner's dilemma: A study in conflict and cooperation*. Ann Arbor: University of Michigan Press.

Sastry, M. A. (1997). Problems and paradoxes in a model of punctuated organizational change. *Administrative Science Quarterly*, *42*(2), 237–275.

Skvoretz, J., & Fararo, T. J. (1989). Action structures and sociological action theory. *Journal of Mathematical Sociology*, *14*, 111–137.

Skvoretz, J., & Fararo, T. J. (1994). Adaptive processes, grammars of action and genetic algorithms: Toward a synthesis. In B. Agger (Ed.), *Current perspectives in social theory*, Vol. 14. (pp. 275–299). Greenwich, CT: JAI Press.

Smith-Lovin, L. (1987). Affect control theory: An assessment. *Journal of Mathematical Sociology*, *13*, 171–192.

Sorenson, O. (1997). The complexity catastrophe in the evolution in the computer industry: Interdependence and adaptability in organizational evolution. Unpublished Ph.D. dissertation, Sociology Department, Stanford University, Stanford, CA.

Tuma, N. B., & Hannan, M. T. (1984). *Social dynamics: Models and methods. Quantitative studies in social relations*. Orlando, FL: Academic Press.

Wegner, D. M. (1987). Transactive memory: A contemporary analysis of the group mind. In B. Mullen & G. R. Goethals (Eds.), *Theories of group behavior* (pp. 185–208). New York: Springer-Verlag.

Wegner, D. M. (1995). A computer network model of human transactive memory. *Social Cognition*, *13*(3), 319–339.

Wegner, D. M., Erber, R., & Raymond, P. (1991). Transactive memory in close relationships. *Journal of Personality and Social Psychology*, *61*, 923–929.

Yamagishi, T., Gillmore, M. R., & Cook, K. S. (1988). Network connections and the distribution of power in exchange networks. *American Journal of Sociology*, *93*, 833–851.

CHAPTER 5

The Critical Dimension in Sociological Theory

Craig Calhoun

Human beings "make their own history, but not of their own free will; not under circumstances they themselves have chosen but under the given and inherited circumstances with which they are directly confronted" (Marx & Engels, 1848/1974, p. 103). The implications of this are profound. Human action can change the world. This means that generalization from existing reality does not exhaust social possibility, and thus is a biased basis for science. But human action is shaped by externally imposed or inherited conditions. This means that the range of possible historical developments is not limitless. Nor is human action inexplicably spontaneous. History and action are understandable on the basis of systematic research. Such understanding may never be complete, but it can be improved. Moreover, the making of this understanding is part of the human making of history not external to it.

This is crucial background to critical theory. It is also a challenge to positivism, which would reduce the complexity of social life and history to explanation by a few invariant laws. Equally, it is a challenge to those "postmodernists" who would reduce the struggle for understanding to a struggle for power. Reductionism of either sort does violence to the achievements of social science and to the everyday sociocultural competence of human beings. Invariant laws (or something asymptotically close to them) may be formulated. The pursuit of power (and other interests) certainly does shape knowledge. But neither laws nor interests accounts for the whole of knowledge.

Neither positivism nor relativism will do. Sociology needs systematic empirical research and a struggle to win social facts from the misunderstandings of everyday life, ideology, and previous partial knowledge (Bourdieu, Chambordeon, & Passeron, 1991). Sociology also needs critical awareness of the conditions and limits of knowledge and of social action. Yet, almost since its inception, sociological theory has been divided by a series of partially homologous but consistently problematic oppositions: positivist–critical, empirical–theoretical, objective–subjective, structure–action. The result is that the development of sociological theory is impeded by muddled arguments, unnecessary divisions between research and theory,

CRAIG CALHOUN • Social Science Research Council, and Department of Sociology, New York University, New York, New York 10003.

Handbook of Sociological Theory, edited by Jonathan H. Turner. Kluwer Academic / Plenum Publishers, New York, 2002.

and failures to refine empirical understanding through critical analysis including reflexive analysis of the production of knowledge itself. Attempts at universality falter on weak attention to historical and cultural specificity; conversely, attention to difference degenerates too readily into relativism. Equally, critical theory that is not informed by empirical research must fail in one of its most important tasks: grasping contemporary social reality in relation to historical change (both past and prospective) and in relation to the struggles of human actors to shape it.

In the present chapter my aim is limited to clarifying the nature of the disputes and through this the importance of critique *within* science and critical theory within sociological theory generally. I first provide an introduction to the idea of critical theory, both as it came into sociological currency with the Frankfurt School and as it identifies an approach extending beyond those origins. Next, I identify some misunderstandings built into the split between critical and positivist theory in sociology. In the remainder of the chapter, I explore how three enduring arguments inform the division in sociological theory and the need for critique.

THE IDEA OF CRITICAL THEORY

The idea of "critical theory" came into currency in Germany during the 1920s and 1930s. Initially, it described not so much a new kind of theory as elements common in varying degrees to several existing theories. Marx, Kant, and Hegel were joined with Freud, Nietzsche, and Weber. Rejection of generalization from surface appearances was a common theme. Critical theorists sought to establish underlying conditions of possibility and ask why some possibilities were realized and others not. This was not merely a matter of statistical chances, they argued, but of human projects such as the exercise of power and struggle against it.

At the same time, critical theory combined—unstably—the Hegelian–Marxian concern for historical totality with Nietzsche's, Weber's, and Freud's engagement with the complex play of the irrational and arbitrary amid apparent rationalization. Horkheimer and Adorno (1944/1969) saw the latter as parallel to Marx's focus on the tensions between individual rationality and systemic determinations and crises in capitalism. This informed a critique of instrumental reason and also a critique of the "fetishization" or reification by which the products of living humanity appeared as alien and sometimes opposed forces and even human beings could be approached, by explanatory scientists as much as capitalist employers, as things. Georg Lukacs was an important forebear, bringing neo-Kantianism and Marxism together in his critique of reification. Lukacs (1922) showed among other things that Marx's work could be read against the grain of economic reductionism as a profound inquiry into new kinds of culture and knowledge in the capitalist era, and that aspects of cultural change might be basic to capitalism, not merely superstructural. The critical theorists challenged reductionist marxism just as they challenged the positivist notion of the unity of science, which would apply the same external and ahistorical mode of explanation to human action as to physics. But the critical theorists were not antiscience; they sought to improve empirical research as well as theory, in part by combining the two and in part by approaching each less ideologically.

The key protagonists of early 20th-century critical theory were Max Horkheimer, Theodore Adorno, and a number of colleagues in the Institute for Social Research in Frankfurt. But just as the idea of critique was older, critical theory also would spread beyond the Frankfurt School. The phrase itself drew on a triple meaning. First, there was the Kantian sense of critique as an inquiry into the conditions and limits of knowledge, whether focused on pure reason, practical reason, or judgment. Critique in this sense probed beneath the surface of apparent knowledge to ask how it was that we could know and sought to reconstruct knowledge more securely on the basis of such inquiry. Second, there was the older idea of critique as the public practice of judgment, informed not only by personal taste and intellectual skill but by reasoned argumentation. Critique in this sense was rooted in Socratic dialogues and exemplified by the 18th-century literary public sphere. It also became a part of political life and informed many ideas of science as a kind of public sphere in which reasoned argument and evidence could be evaluated critically by all participants.[1] Third, the idea of critical theory carried the implication of opposition to the established social order. This sense of the word shared with much of our own everyday usage the emphasis on negativity, as criticism suggests objections more than appreciations. But while social critics posed all manner of objections to existing social arrangements and offered fantastic images of what an ideal society might be like, critical theory was disciplined by Marx's rejection of abstract utopianism.[2] Joining normative to empirical theory, it demonstrated that other arrangements were possible, not only preferable. Frankfurt School critique was both "defetishizing" in showing the human and contingent sources of seemingly natural facts and "immanent" in showing how present reality contained the bases and pressures for its supercession.[3]

Max Horkheimer gave a classic formulation to the emerging notion of critical theory in a 1937 essay. Asking "what is theory," he noted the availability of an easy answer:

> for most researchers, it is the sum-total of propositions about a subject, the propositions being so linked with each other that a few are basic and the rest derive from these. The smaller the number of primary principles in comparison with the derivations, the more perfect the theory. (Horkheimer 1937/1972, p. 188)

There was a tendency in the physical sciences for theory to become ever more abstract and distant from the objects of ordinary experience and to be rendered in mathematical form. Ultimately, nonetheless, "the real validity of the theory depends on the derived propositions being consonant with the actual facts" (p. 188). This notion of theory developed primarily with regard to the natural sciences, but was adopted widely in the social sciences. Here Horkheimer (1937/1972) begins to introduce critique, without yet naming it as such; he points out that the social or human sciences follow the natural sciences partly for extraintellectual reasons: "the so-called human studies (*Geisteswissenschaften*) have had but a fluctuating market value and must try to imitate the more prosperous natural sciences whose practical value is beyond question" (p. 191). Knowledge, this reveals, is not simply a reflection of empirical reality; it is a social project.

Horkheimer's essay goes on to elucidate a number of distinctions between "traditional" and "critical" theory. This very first one is basic, though. In a mild and understated form, it raises the point that knowledge is to be explained in part by social conditions (though this does not necessarily invalidate it or render it practically useless). This does not mean that truth

[1]This underwrites such ideas as the necessity of making publicly available the evidence on which scientific fundings are based, and indeed, the general requirement to publish scientific findings. On the public sphere of 18th-century literary criticism and its broader significance, see Hohendahl (1982). More generally, this idea of public communication has informed not only Habermas's (1962/1989, 1997) account of the political public sphere but his (1984, 1988) understanding of science.

[2]Cf. Marx and Engels (1848/1974) and Marx (1845/1975). At the same time, critical theorists have been concerned with the possibility that rationalization and reification eliminated the sources of negativity—of challenging the facticity of actually existing society with recognition of its internal contradictions and instabilities and imagination of how it could be otherwise. Habermas (1989), for example, has worried over a possible "exhaustion of utopian energies" in the contemporary era. See also Marcuse (1964, 1968).

[3]Seyla Benhabib (1986) usefully traces distinct though related strands of immanent and defetishizing critique, both with strong Hegelian roots. On false necessity, see Unger (1987).

claims are to be settled by extrascientific authority (say, institutional power); it does mean that what is known and in what ways knowledge is formed are both shaped by extrascientific factors. Horkheimer's statement also exemplifies a distinctive feature of critical theory. It seeks to advance knowledge in part by identifying the factors that limit or distort the ways in which other existing theories grasp reality. It takes on itself, in other words, not only the task of identifying errors but the task of understanding the implications of different foundations for knowledge, including scientific inquiry, and different conceptual and theoretical approaches. This is the sense of critique that Marx appropriated from German philosophy and put to work in *Capital*, which he subtitled "A Critique of Political Economy." The classical political economists, he argued, had produced impressive economic theory that was nonetheless distorted by their affirmative, uncritical relationship to capitalism. They analyzed processes historically specific to capitalism as though they were universal, presented the commodification of human labor as though it were natural and based simply on freedom rather than a result of coercion, and neglected tendencies to systemic crisis.

Ideally a critical confrontation with other works of social explanation not only establishes the good and bad points of competing perspectives, but shows the reasons behind their blind spots and misunderstandings and demonstrates the capacity to incorporate their insights on stronger foundations. It does this partly by situating the assessment of scientific truth within history, including both the history of transformations and achievements in science and the history of the conditions of social knowledge more generally. Second, seeing theory as critique we also can see the reasons why knowledge advances not simply by the accumulation of truths or the replacement of false understandings by true ones, but by movement from worse to better understandings.[4] In such a view, judgment of what is better is never entirely neutral or free of perspective but necessarily reflects particular formulations of problems for understanding. Finally, with the centrality of critique and judgment in mind we can see why it is important to conceive of science not simply on the model of the individual knowing subject, but in terms of communication among scientists. Improvements in scientific knowledge are achieved not only through observation, analysis, and theorization, but through critical discourse. This is one reason why it is important for scientific works to be publicly accessible and also for the internal organization of science to facilitate open debate and further investigation.

Critique is important, then, as part of the ongoing process of establishing a better, more adequate understanding of the social world. It is not simply a negative effort, a demonstration of weakness, but a direct contribution to better science. It also helps clarify the limits of all specific formulations of scientific knowledge. Neither Marx nor Horkheimer argued that the limitations of specific theoretical systems invalidated all knowledge. Indeed, each thought the modern era had seen terrific progress in knowledge. But each also insisted on the partiality of actually existing systems of knowledge. Indeed, partiality in the sense of incompleteness implied partiality in the sense of bias. The embeddedness of knowledge in history meant not only that it was incomplete until the owl of Minerva flew, but that its achievement was a practical human project. Like all other practical projects, it was pursued in part on the bases of interests (or passions or other motivations) that shaped the specifics of the project (Habermas, 1971).

---

[4]Though implicit in Marx and other 19th-century critical theorists, this argument was developed most clearly in 20th-century hermeneutic philosophy (esp. Gadamer, 1975). From this source Habermas incorporated a version of the insight into his critical theory (1965, 1984) (though see Holub, 1991, on the limits of Habermas's openness to hermeneutics). See discussion of the idea of "epistemic gain" in Taylor (1998) and Calhoun (1995).

This applied as well to critical theory itself. One of the requirements of critical theory is a continual reflexive inquiry into the historical, intellectual, and institutional conditions of the critical theorists' own work. Not surprisingly, Max Horkheimer and his colleagues were generally more perspicacious in identifying the blind spots of others. This should not distract us from the centrality of reflexivity to the more general project of critical theory. Certainly, the founding generation of the Frankfurt School was attentive to the question of what social position and intellectual resources made their own work possible.[5] This dimension of critique, however, has in many ways been developed further by critical theorists outside the Frankfurt School, perhaps most notably Pierre Bourdieu (e.g., 1988, 2000).

The idea of a critique of the conditions and limits of knowledge is basic to scientific reason as such (though not all scientists or even philosophers of science take it up in the same way). In fact, Vienna's logical positivists—Horkheimer's prime antagonists in his 1937 essay—gave primary importance to just this sense of critique, arguing that all knowledge claims are tentative and open to revision through critical analysis as well as empirical test. More distinctive to the critical theory tradition is the critique of "false necessity," though this is closely related. A kind of empiricism (and sometimes positivism) underpins an approach to knowledge based on generalization and verification and claims unity across the natural and the human sciences. This encourages the idea that society could be no other way than as it is, or at least encourages mistaking historical and cultural contingencies for universal processes and mechanisms. This sort of empiricism also serves functionally as a part of "affirmative" theories that offer understanding of existing social arrangements that is always biased toward their maintenance. Simply to generalize from existing social conditions is to miss their location in history, with both a past and a future and usually with internal contradictions and struggles that reflect one and shape the other. Simple generalization does violence not only to historical change and transformation but to human action as a distinctive source of creativity in the world. Yet this is not merely an error of theory but a participation of theory in society and culture at large. Reification—to use Lukacs's category—shapes both the everyday consciousness of workers for whom the commodification of labor seems natural and the scientific consciousness of an era in which corporations seem persons of almost as natural a sort as human beings.

What Horkheimer called "traditional theory" reflected this reification insofar as it regarded human activity from an entirely "objective" vantage point, as a "thing" to be explained by external causes rather than internal reasons. The answer was not a simple inversion, pure subjectivism, but rather a critical inquiry into the conditions that produced the partially false objectification. Traditional theory could not achieve this, however, so long as it failed to locate itself in history and social practice. Ironically, the uncritical objectivism was supported by an uncritical exaltation of the scientific subject as knower. The attempt to find a Cartesian "view from nowhere" was consonant with acceptance of reification. This was reinforced

---

[5]This concern was related to the question of whether Horkheimer, Adorno, and their colleagues could identify a standpoint for social critique that would relate their theoretical work to a possible practical project for social change. Initially, they had shared the Marxist–Lukacsian hope that the standpoint of the proletariat offered such a vantage point, and that the proletariat could become a crucial historical actor. The rise of Nazism dashed such hopes. While some critical theorists vested their hopes in students, the poor, and other possible historical actors, Horkheimer and Adorno became increasingly convinced that none was available. This was basic to their so-called "conservative turn" and to the idea that their theory constituted in part a "message in a bottle" for future generations. This in itself reflected analysis of the limits of the social position from which they could gain intellectual insight but not make it practically efficacious.

by the conception that theory—and science generally—should somehow be understood as properly set apart from the rest of social practice, the province of a group of free-floating intellectuals as Mannheim saw it or simply the province of the individual knower in the tradition of Descartes and Kant.[6]

Horkheimer (1937/1972, p. 197) wrote,

> The traditional idea of theory is based on scientific activity as carried on within the division of labor at a particular stage in the latter's development. It corresponds to the activity of the scholar which takes place alongside all the other activities of a society but in no immediately clear connection with them. In this view of theory, therefore, the real social function of science is not made manifest; it speaks not of what theory means in human life, but only of what it means in the isolated sphere in which for historical reasons it comes into existence.

This view of theory is linked not only to social irresponsibility but to a misleading, if flattering, self-image for theorists: "The latter believe they are acting according to personal determinations, whereas in fact even in their most complicated calculations they but exemplify the working of an incalculable social mechanism" (Horkheimer, 1937/1972, p. 197).[7] The most important result of such a self-misunderstanding, a failure both of reflexivity and of accurate empirical analysis of the conditions of theorizing, is a tendency to treat the existing social conditions as the only conditions that could exist.

If a theorist is unable to see his or her own activity as part of the social world, and especially if he or she simply accepts into theoretical self-awareness the social division of labor with its blinders, this encourages a treatment of the external world as simply fixed and "objective." This obscures the contingency and internal contradictions of the empirical world.

> The whole perceptible world as present to a member of bourgeois society and as interpreted within a traditional world-view which is in continuous interaction with that given world, is seen by the perceiver as a sum-total of facts; it is there and must be accepted. (Horkheimer 1937/1972, p. 199)

The theorist, like most individuals within society, thus fails to see the underlying conditions of social order (or chaos). But this does not necessarily result in a simple objectivism. It is more apt to result in a dualistic splitting of objective and subjective dimensions such that neither corrects the other. The reified view of the external world as mere ensemble of facts is compatible (indeed, perhaps shares an elective affinity) with reliance on a notion of individuals as discrete strategic actors confronting this world. The standpoint of the purposeful individual confers one kind of order on the facticity of the world just as functionalism or systems theory

---

[6]Philosophers are particularly apt to be outraged by nonphilosophical histories of philosophy. These present it as something other than the history of the progress of reason (and thus a transcendence of "ordinary" history). As Bourdieu (2000, p. 42) has argued, "The refusal of thinking about genesis, and above all of thinking about the genesis of thought, is no doubt one of the major principles of the resistance that philosophers put up, more or less universally, against the social sciences, especially when these dare to take as their object the philosophical institution and, by the same token, the philosopher himself, the 'subject' par excellence, and when they refuse him the social extraterritoriality he grants himself and which he means to defend." The reactions of some philosophers to Randall Collins' (1999) recent study of the history of philosophy offer an example; they approach it less as a straightforward empirical project that succeeds to a greater or lesser degree than as a sort of category error, the application of sociological methods where they do not belong.

[7]To treat the individual as an asocial, ahistorical, objective starting point for knowledge, Horkheimer (1937/1972, pp. 210–211) wrote, is "an illusion about the thinking subject, under which idealism has lived since Descartes, is ideology in the strict sense .... Critical thinking is the function neither of the isolated individual nor of a sum-total of individuals. Its subject is rather a definite individual in his real relation to other individuals and groups, in his conflict with a particular class, and, finally, in the resultant web of relationships with the social totality and with nature." See also Bourdieu (1988, 2000) on the scholastic fallacy.

confers another. Individual and social world on such views each appear simply as environment to the other.[8] Not surprisingly, then, many theorists proceed to affirm the treatment of those basic social conditions that cannot readily be understood through purposive rationality, especially those results of human activity that are alienated from the control of conscious human beings, as though they were forces of nature. The products of historical human action are affirmed as unchanging and fixed conditions of human action, and theory cannot articulate the possibility of emancipation from these conditions.

Empirical generalizations are quite useful and of course may be made more precise by use of scope statements; not all are in that sense false universals. But to theorize on the basis of such generalizations alone is to incorporate the conditions of present-day society into theory of society in general. This tends to tie theory to an affirmation of the status quo in which present society appears not only as real but as necessary. Critique helps theory escape this determinism and this diremption from history and human action. This is not only a matter of critically analyzing the internal workings of theory, it is also a matter of approaching actual problems of empirical analysis with attention to the conditions of possibility. That is, we need to ask what sorts of social organization are "objectively" possible and why have some rather than other possibilities become real. The answer may involve the direct exercise of power, or it may turn on more indirect cultural hegemony, or it may be the result of historical accident.[9]

A POORLY FRAMED DEBATE

Horkheimer, Adorno, and other critical theorists engaged in a formative debate with the logical positivists of early 20th-century Vienna. They saw these as intellectually serious but mistaken on two key issues. One was their faith in the unity of science—the Comtean project by which distinctions between the human and natural sciences would vanish as humans came to be understood entirely objectively.[10] Building on Dilthey and Weber, the Frankfurt theorists insisted that such understanding of human actors could never be complete. Moreover, they argued that if pursued without a critical complement that gave greater respect to the distinctiveness of human beings and the importance of action, such positivism would inevitably do violence to humanity. Secondly, they objected to the positivists' notion of science as outside of history and free from social influence. This allowed the illusion of perfect scientific certainty, but that could only be ideological and potentially condone disastrous overconfidence (generally on the lines of being certain enough of ends to claim justification for troubling means, as in various 20th-century projects of social engineering).

These two issues have remained basic to differences between critical theory and so-called positivism but the debate has become muddled. Positivism has become a misleading label

---

[8]A point famously and repeatedly made by Niklas Luhman (e.g., 1998) from the standpoint of systems theory.

[9]One flaw to a good many otherwise important critical analyses is their tendency to rely on more or less explicit conspiracy theories to account for the specific patterns of social or cultural organization. But to show that existing reality could be otherwise and that some people benefit from having it remain as it is does not amount to demonstrating that they have the foresight or power to have determined the actual course of history. As Pierre Bourdieu has many times pointed out, social "games" are set up so that those who are their recurrent beneficiaries may reap rewards from actions that never make their interests explicit.

[10]This project has returned to active discussion following E. O. Wilson's (1998) publication of *Consilience*, drawing its title term from Whewall's 1840 evocation of the project of a unified science. The heirs of Vienna logical positivists (some of whom renamed themselves "logical empiricists") founded an annually extended *International Encyclopedia of Unified Science* as one of their main publications.

because it refers sometimes to a general broad empiricism and sometimes to specific philo-sophical positions and ideas about the progress of science that flourished in the 19th and early 20th centuries. In recent decades, the term "positivism" was kept alive in social science by critics who made it a term of abuse, and then defiantly claimed by advocates of the view that the social sciences should be as much like the natural sciences as possible. Nonetheless, there are important points of disagreement. Consider these core assumptions, offered by one of sociology's leading contemporary advocates of positivist theorizing:

> There is an external universe "out there" which exists independently of our conceptualizations of it; this universe reveals certain timeless, universal, and invariant properties; the goal of sociological theory is to isolate these generic properties and understand their operation. (Turner 1987, p. 165)

Each of the three points Turner makes is important to distinguishing positivism from critical theory.

The critical theorist need not disagree about the existence of the universe, but she or he must question whether it exists "external" to human beings and somehow "out there." Are we not in the midst of this universe? Is human knowledge (and thus conceptualization) not part of it? Likewise, the critical theorist can rejoice at the discovery of "timeless, universal, and invariant properties" to social life. Alas, they are few and appear to account for only a little of social reality as research reveals it. Such knowledge may grow, but the critical theorist will insist on asking recurrently of each ostensible transhistorical invariant, might this in fact be more historically or culturally specific? Even more basically, the critical theorist will point out that the universe does not "reveal" properties, or at least not in any form equivalent to human knowledge of them. Human beings understand those properties only by conceptualizing them—rendering them into language—or in a special sense of the word "understand," by making them objects of effective practical action. Even the properties of the universe that seem most clearly to exist externally to and independently of human beings, say, gravity, are known to human beings only through language or practical orientations to action. Specifically, they are known to theory only through language.

Last but not least, Turner would focus sociological theory on isolating and understanding the transhistorical invariants of social life. The critical theorist will include among the goals of sociological theory the understanding of patterns of difference and change. To be sure, knowing transhistorical invariant laws of social life will be helpful in this, to the extent these may be reliably discerned. But a key goal of critical theory is precisely to be able to locate the present in relation to history, specific patterns of meaning in relation to cultural diversity, and specific institutional forms in relation to other possible ones. Turner's goal reflects the idea of theory as "nomothetic" that came to prominence in the turn of the century *methodenstreit*. Its implicit opposite is the merely "idiographic" particularity of history. But this distinction itself is misleading. It opposes efforts to explain all reality by a small number of universal laws to efforts to account for particular events (either by description or by explanation in a different, noncovering law sense). But there is much to social science that is neither the pursuit of universality by reduction nor the abandonment of general significance to pure particularity.

In the 1950s and 1960s, a famous "positivism dispute" brought the issues to the fore again, at least in German sociology (Adorno et al., 1976). Adorno and then Habermas argued the case for critical theory. Oddly, though, no participant in the debate claimed to represent positivism. Karl Popper was *accused* by Adorno of being positivist, but misleadingly. Pop-per's "critical rationalism" was influenced by logical positivism but broke with it on crucial points. Perhaps most notably, Popper (1934, 1972) replaced the idea of the accumulation of verified truths by the notion of progress through the falsification of erroneous hypotheses. This progressive elimination of error through "conjectures and refutations" underwrote a great deal less certainty than either Comte or the logical positivists had thought science could provide and than the name positivism implied. Neither did Popper try to defend a complete unity of human and natural sciences (though he did hold that each could pursue the kind of objectivity he advocated).

Confusions also have beset the ideas of critique and critical theory. First, the theoretical project of examining the conditions of knowledge is easily confused with simply stating objections to the views of others, regardless of the grounds. Second, the phrase "critical theory" is often used to designate a specific group of theorists (the Frankfurt School) rather than to identify more abstractly and generally an approach to theory. While members of the Frankfurt School have been among the foremost advocates for and developers of critical theory in the 20th century, they neither invented it nor own it.[11] Third, and most problematically, critique is commonly identified with "antiscience" arguments rather than seen as a dimension of science.[12] In the 1960s and 1970s especially, it became common to link the idea of critique to a kind of antiscience perspective, sometimes one rooted in radical subjectivism, and to use the label "positivist" to lump together (and often condemn) all approaches claiming scientific objectivity. The language of objectivity is indeed problematic, but the opposition is simplistic.

In three senses, objectivity is at issue. First, there is the question of what it means to claim that facts are objective. Does it mean that they are external to theory (and more generally, language), or to the mind of the knower? Second, there is the question of whether human beings may be understood as objects in the same sense as physical phenomena or non-language-using animals. Among sociologists, so-called "positivists" are apt to quote Durk-

[11]By means of his writing, his force of personality, and his ability to create an institution, Horkheimer was able to claim the label of critical theory distinctively for the work of his Institute for Social Research. Based in Frankfurt before and after the war, this was an enormously vital and distinctive intellectual enterprise. But no single institution or scholarly group should be granted title over an intellectual approach as broad and as basic as critical theory. As I have argued elsewhere (Calhoun, 1995), this needs to be understood in terms of the several different intellectual streams that flowed together for a time in the work of the Frankfurt theorists; it needs to be seen in the work of a wide range of later thinkers who have shared a critical approach even when they differed substantively from each other and labored at long distances from Frankfurt. The Frankfurt School gave critical theory a name, but the name fits a much wider range of work than that of any one school. Max Horkheimer, Theodore Adorno, Friedrich Pollock, Herbert Marcuse, and other members and associates of the Institute for Social Research produced a variety of specific studies that exemplified critical theory at work on substantive problems (see for discussion Jay, 1975, and Wiggershaus, 1994). These included analyses of state capitalism, the authoritarian personality, mass culture, and the dialectic of enlightenment. All suggest themes that remain important, but critical theory as such needs to be distinguished from any specific set of substantive themes.

[12]Heidegger and some of his followers within both hermeneutic and poststructuralist traditions do argue against science, but such positions are neither the primary nor best parts of critical theory. The antiscience arguments stem largely from a critique of the kind of dualism that radically distinguishes subject and object, and thus alienates mind from matter. Where dualism opposes consciousness to the world, the Heideggerian tradition emphasizes being-in-the-world (the hyphens represent inextricable interconnection). A shift away from Husserl's phenomenology and even Dilthey's hermeneutics, such an approach abandons the project of verifiable or "transitive" knowledge as it has been understood in the tradition of science. Knowledge is not to be understood as an understanding— let alone control—of something external. While many versions of post-Heideggerian philosophy stand simply opposed to empirical science, it may nonetheless make useful contributions to critical theory that does pursue scientific knowledge. Notably in the work of Gadamer it has offered important insights into the operation and limits of dualistic epistemology, and the distance between "truth" and the operations of specific methods for producing knowledge. See Gadamer (1975) and Taylor (1998, Chapter 1). This helps critical theory to challenge mechanistic understandings of how knowledge might be grounded in mental processes and more generally to move beyond the philosophy of consciousness to grasp intersubjectivity (see Habermas's 1984 discussion and the clear summary in 1987).

heim (1895) in both regards. Social facts are external, enduring, and coercive. Social facts should be treated as things.[13] Third, there is the question of how much science (including sociology) should itself be understood in objective or external terms, on the basis of inquiry into its social bases and more or less impersonal processes.

Behind the arguments over objectivity lies the even more basic question, "what is truth?" This is importantly different from asking "what is true?" The latter question may be answered with a variety of "positive" claims about the world: grass is green, groups larger than ten are likely to subdivide, and so forth. Much "everyday positivism" simply stays at this level. The former question, however, demands an account of how we know. This is one source of science's vital self-reflexive inquiry into procedure. It is also one entry point of critique. "Critique" thus refers to examination of the grounds, and thus both the limits and the orientation, of all knowledge. On what basis can we know anything? How can we be sure? What implications do the bases of knowledge have for the character or substance of that knowledge?[14]

None of this means that extrascientific considerations ought to be decisive for assessing the value of truth claims. It does mean that institutional and other extraintellectual factors shape what questions scientists address and how. As a result, while these factors do not determine what is true, they do partially determine what is known. They also influence how "truth" is known: what connections are made among facts, into what contexts they are situated, through what language and concepts, and with what practical orientations they are grasped. None of these various senses of the "construction" of truth amounts to saying that there is no truth, though they do suggest that there is no single, invariant, perfect statement of it.

In order to see what is at stake in the confused arguments between positivism and critical theory, and even more, the unargued assumptions of social scientists on both sides, it is helpful to grasp something of their historical development. Nineteenth-century positivism was indeed influential in these, even though it is not so much the starting point as a false claim about the end point. As Hegel thought the owl of Minerva flew in early 19th-century Prussia, so Comte thought it flew just a few years later in France.

THE CONDITIONS AND LIMITS
OF KNOWLEDGE

In a sense, all modern science started with critique. Tradition was not simply accepted on faith, but examined. The authority of the ecclesiastical hierarchy and even sometimes the Bible itself were challenged by appeals to direct observation and individual reason. Commonplace "truths," like the flatness of the earth, were subjected to empirical and rational tests and rejected unless they could meet standards of internal logic and consistency with observed facts.

On both rationalist and empiricist sides, science staked its claims in terms of the modern

[13]Durkheim was famously inconsistent in following his own methodological advice, and indeed some of his most prominent contributions to sociology would have been impossible on such a strict positivist basis. Alexander (1982) has shown how Durkheim's positions vacillated in this regard as he sought to defend sociology in more or less positivist terms and yet attempted to address questions of subjective consciousness and absorb influences from phenomenology and idealist philosophy.

[14]This is not just a question about bias in the narrow sense of illegitimate intrusions of value or prejudice. Much broader, it joins questions like how does scientific knowledge depend on specific technologies (e.g., microscopes) to those of how it depends on specific conceptual schemes (e.g., atomism).

era's increasingly prominent individualism. Descartes famously exercised doubt of every possible claim to certain knowledge until he came to what he took to be the bedrock, the demonstration of his existence by his thought ("I think therefore I am").[15] Bacon enunciated an increasingly dominant faith in facts and Locke articulated in more detail how these fruits of observation could only be discerned by individuals on the scene to see/hear/feel/taste/smell empirical reality. We should not exaggerate, however, the opposition of rationalism and empiricism in 17th- and 18th-century thought; there was a good deal of agreement among philosophers who claimed opposite first principles. Rationalists and empiricists alike presented science as a critical method in relation to nonscience. But at least from the 18th century, critique also began to be internalized within science, deployed in relation to reason and empirical evidence, and brought to bear on the question of their limits and validity.

Lacking space (or I hope need) to retell the story at length, let me evoke it through one of the decisive points at which the broad agreement faltered. Critique came into clear prominence within science in considering questions about how to relate the claims of empirical evidence to those of reason. This was a development broader than any single individual, but it is usefully represented by attention to the pivotal work of David Hume.

Hume famously questioned an extremely widely held belief about human nature and experience, one taken as axiomatic and indeed obvious by most scientists. Why, he asked, do we believe that every event must have a cause? Indeed, why do we believe that for *any* event we can establish its cause? On what basis do we claim to make inferences from some observed events to other ostensible (but unobserved) causes? For example, we step outside, observe a wet street, and hold that rain that we did not see falling must have caused this state of affairs. Hume's question is not simply whether there might have been some different cause: a firehose, say, instead of rain. His question is about the very status of inference, which is why it goes to the basis of science. What allows us to reason from observed to unobserved phenomena?

Without going into the particulars of Hume's argument, the key is that correlation can never prove cause.[16] He suggests that we may well have developed an impression about the connection of rain to wet streets based on frequent observation, and that this may be accurate but that it still does not amount to establishing causation (in the strict sense of necessary relation). It does not demonstrate a necessary connection but only a contingent one. We can see the conjunction between events, but no matter how frequent that is, it can never amount to observing causality as such.[17] The attribution of cause is introduced by the human mind and not based in any strictly rational fashion on induction from sense impressions (i.e., from empirical data). Indeed, Hume suggested, it turns importantly on the imagination. Accordingly, Hume suggested, the formation of such beliefs needed to be studied as a psychological process not a logical one.[18]

This was a challenge to the notion that beliefs such as those in relations of cause and

[15]To doubt everything was Descartes' basic method, but not to the point of being a full-fledged skeptic. Hence, having discerned a ground for certainty in his own cognition, he proceeded to try to build up a more positive system of knowledge from there, including crucially a proof of the existence of god.

[16]This is why statistical methods based on correlation matrices, such as regression analysis, cannot establish the order in which variables are related; some extra-statistical reason must be adduced.

[17]This becomes particularly important in sociology where relationships are extremely complex and predictions often weak. As Raymond Boudon (1971/1974) put it, we analyze relationships not of strict causality, but of more or less "weak implication."

[18]Hume is often understood simply as a skeptic who completed the negative phase of British empiricism. For the idea that he was in fact offering a more general theory of human nature, see Stroud (1977). Hume's was a critical theory of the relations among reason, passion, knowledge, and morality and as such intended as a contribution to understanding the human predicament, not only a negative argument debunking specious beliefs.

effect could be rational responses to sense data alone. Before Hume, it was easy to hold that human observation worked more or less like a law court. The mind acted as a judge or juror, believing in those things for which there was adequate evidence. The mind could be tricked, but this amounted to an error in observation. What Hume showed was that the belief in cause and effect could never be rational on these empirical grounds. That is, there will be reasons for such belief, but they will not be because experience has rationally determined it. On the contrary, it must be because there is a psychological principle of thought that establishes the link where empirical evidence alone cannot. "If reason determin'd us," Hume (1739–1740/1958, p. 89) wrote, "it wou'd proceed upon that principle, that instances, of which we have had no experience, must resemble those, of which we have had experience, and that the course of nature continues always the same." This principle of the basic continuity of existence (or what Hume called the "principle of union among ideas") is necessary to thought but cannot be justified on purely empirical grounds. More generally, Hume pursued extremely rational reasoning to the conclusion that our most basic beliefs about the world are without rational foundation and must in principle remain so. This does not mean that we must therefore abandon all such beliefs; on the contrary, they remain fundamental but as beliefs supported by experience, practical need, and tradition.

Hume's argument was pivotal to modern philosophy. Contentions about whether it was altogether sound and what its implications are continue to the present day. The point is not to adjudicate these disputes but to grasp the significance of the argument as critical theory. What Hume did was to subject a widespread and basic assumption to critical analysis. His radically skeptical reflection led him to reject the notion of planning progress on the basis of putative rational–scientific laws and instead turn to the study of history, suggesting that knowledge was limited to greater or lesser historical generalization.[19]

Immanuel Kant was impressed by the brilliance of Hume's arguments, which he said woke him from his "dogmatic slumbers." That is, they persuaded him that existing claims to certain knowledge were arbitrary at best. But Kant was unwilling to accept that there could be no rational foundation for thought and moral conviction. He thought skepticism as well as dogmatism needed to be overcome. Famously, therefore, he answered Hume with a further act of critical theory. In his *Critique of Pure Reason*, Kant (1781/1965) agreed that knowledge could hardly be based on sense data alone. Rather, he suggested, knowledge was achievable precisely because the human mind operated with basic categories, including that of causality, that made thinking possible. This indicated (as indeed Hume had argued) that knowledge depended not just on its objects—the things in the world—but on the knower. Kant, however, was prepared to develop a much more elaborate account of what knowers must be like on the basis of the abstractly necessary conditions of knowledge. Some forms of knowledge could be universal and like mathematics known universally with the certainty of pure reason. Others, like ethics, could be known only by judgment and practical reason, and thus were less perfectly universal. In both cases, Kant reminded his readers, knowledge, including science, remained a

---

[19]Indeed, one of the conclusions Hume drew from his argument was that in many regards we should trust the accumulated wisdom of very extended experience and distrust claims to overturn this by means of abstract deductions. This was paradoxical insofar as it was his own very rationalistic explorations that led him to this emphasis on the limits of reason. Nonetheless, it informed his interest in empirical history as a process of learning through experience and a respect for tradition quite different from the more common 18th century attack on it. This also informed Burke and the conservative tradition with its suggestion that there was accumulated wisdom in tradition and established practice that should not be overturned on the grounds of abstract theory, as famously in the French Revolution, which was very much a revolution of rationalism and science against tradition as well as commoners against king.

project. It made no sense to claim dogmatically (in the manner of Leibniz) that scientific knowledge had already attained perfection.[20]

Kant thus formulated an approach to critical theory aimed at establishing the bases for knowledge by reference to the capacities and limits of the knower.[21] Some of his successors would hold that Kant had relied too much on the idea that the human mind was a universal phenomenon, present in principle in each individual, and thus a basis for universal knowledge. Hegel insisted famously on rethinking mind as first social and second historically developing. The latter meant that knowledge could not simply accumulate, but that there was an integral relationship between the development of capacities to know and production of knowledge. Marx introduced a critical analysis of the categories of knowledge (e.g., value) that included attention to how they helped to constitute a specific form of social reality as well as the scientific knowledge tied to it.[22] Along with others, Marx gave more stress to issues of perspective. Kant had acknowledged that in the exercise of judgment it mattered where the individual stood, but argued for overcoming such bias simply by taking a broad view. Marx stressed that the "this-sidedness" of knowledge was not so easily escaped and reflected its embeddedness in practical activity and processes of historical change.[23] His arguments became pivotal, thus, to "ideology critique" as an examination and sometimes unmasking of the ways interests and perspective shape apparently neutral knowledge. Others made the point that individuals never exist except as products of and participants in culture. Knowledge is made possible not just by sense data and mind, but by language, concepts, and dialogue. When such considerations are acknowledged, the critical examination of the conditions of knowledge becomes even more empirically complex but remains vital.

This sort of critique also is basic to substantive scientific theory. Einstein's famous "thought experiments," for example, involved efforts to subject received assumptions (reinforced by everyday culture and experience as well as scientific orthodoxy) to critical examination, theoretically analyzing their necessity, grounds, and significance, not simply adhering to them so long as they were not directly falsified by empirical evidence. Moreover, they turned crucially on the idea that the position and actions of the scientific observer might have an

---

[20]Kant saw his work as superseding the opposition of dogmatism (e.g., Leibniz) and skepticism (e.g., Hume) in previous philosophy. In a sense, positivism and relativism represent a version of the same opposition. Perhaps critical theory is best construed not as offering a claim to transcend the polarity, however, but rather a commitment dialectically to interrelate claims to knowledge and assertions of its limits.

[21]See Goetschel (1994) for a useful discussion of how Kant developed this notion of critique. Of course, he did not invent it *ex nihilo*. His approach was part of a general modern turn to ground knowledge in the individual. This is often symbolized by reference to Descartes, and is indeed marked deeply by the dualistic approach he exemplified, sharply distinguishing mind and body, for example. In any case, Descartes too focused more than invented an approach that was already developing more broadly in his day. It also had ancient forebears—not least among some of the neo-Platonists and in Augustine—though these were concerned mainly with different sorts of knowledge. Future research would probe the specifics of human knowledge further, considering in a way Kant could not the limits of the human eye and other sense organs, the way brains work and cognition develops. Such research has roots in the British empiricists approach to psychology. It only becomes a part of critique when its implications for the project of scientific knowledge itself are considered. At the same time, Kant's approach (and that of most idealism after him) relies heavily on *a priori* reasoning about the nature of mind and knowledge.

[22]Thus "value" is not inherently quantitative. The process of commodification reflects and furthers quantification of value as capitalism develops (Marx, 1867/1977, Chapter 1; Postone, 1993).

[23]This became the basis for innumerable variants of "standpoint theory" and other forms of perspectivism. Some of these focused mainly on the necessary limits of knowledge which must always be "this-sided," while others laid claim to identifying standpoints that offered universal or at least better knowledge. This line of argument has been especially important in legitimating claims to knowledge from subordinated positions. See discussion in Calhoun (1995, Chapter 6).

impact on the knowledge he could achieve[24]; so too in the social sciences. The critical examination of the conditions of knowledge is not something that can be satisfactorily relegated to a sort of philosophical metatheory: to a preparation of the epistemological path for "real" theory. On the contrary, the contributions of critique extend into empirical theory and reach throughout the substantive concerns of social science. This, however, is just what 19th-century positivism tried to deny.

THEORY-LADEN FACTS:
REALISM AND CONSTRUCTIVISM

Two of the great founders of sociology—Henri, Comte de St. Simon, and Auguste Comte (coiner of the very term, "sociology")—also were the founders of "positivism." By this they meant the application of scientific method to all of human existence. They were inspired equally and without clear distinction by two somewhat different understandings of science. The first had been spreading since Francis Bacon and focused on the growth of empirical knowledge; science was the accumulation of demonstrated facts. The second was the somewhat more recent burst of technological innovation that shaped the industrial revolution; here science was the capacity to dominate nature and control the conditions of our lives by the application of knowledge. That St. Simon and Comte did not distinguish these two dimensions made possible a key ambiguity in the idea of "positivism," still evident in different meanings of the word "positive." What made positivism positive was first the certainty granted by empirical knowledge and second the progress offered by technology.

St. Simon and Comte thought that all of human life could be reorganized on positivist principles. Scientists were cast in two roles. First, as researchers they would discover the laws governing all existence. Second, as something close to Platonic Guardians they would use this knowledge to organize society, including family life, politics, and even religion, in the "scientifically" best way possible. Comte presented this notion through what he called the "law" of the three stages. Every individual person, every branch of human knowledge, each society, and ultimately all of humanity must pass through three stages. In the theological stage knowledge is little more than fiction as people represent natural phenomena as results of supernatural agency. In the metaphysical stage, supernatural beings are replaced by abstract forces (natural law, for example, or the Hegelian cunning of history). Finally, in the positive stage, human beings accepted that there was no reality beyond that of this world and the rational laws that organized its observable facts.[25]

St. Simon and Comte had relatively few followers for their religious program, but many more for their scientific one.[26] Comte's theory of progress contributed to the development of

---

[24]Einstein assumed this knower was a "he." Some later critics have suggested that the gender identity of the knower could have a further impact on the knowledge that he or she could achieve, others that Einstein's use of a gendered pronoun was irrelevant.

[25]Foucault (1966) famously redescribed this transition in his account of the movement from classical to modern knowledge, correspondence to causes. According to Foucault, this involved not linear progress but a fundamental shift (a "rupture") in categories of understanding that could not be said simply to be better or worse. The two ages offered different "epistemes," different approaches to relating words and things, creating an image of an orderly world, and indeed creating knowledge.

[26]Indeed, the religious aspect of Comte's positivism did flourish for a while, and in moderated form influenced Durkheim. In Britain, buoyed by the evolutionary current, public figures like Frederic Harrison and Richard Congreve supported Comte's notion of a Church of Humanity, complete with its own positivist humans and pantheon of saints. In the early 20th century services were still being held weekly in London and a few provincial centers. Populism had its greatest public influence in Latin America, where it became an influential political ideology.

evolutionary thought, though under the impetus of biology that rapidly outstripped his own theory. His conception of science as a combination of description and prediction was influential. Perhaps most importantly, their French positivism joined forces with British empiricism to help shape utilitarianism, political economy, and evolutionary theory, notably in the theories of Jeremy Bentham, John Stuart Mill, and Herbert Spencer.

Positivism eventually came unglued, however, over questions about the relationship between theory and facts. Much of the appeal of positivism came (as it still comes) from the notion that its descriptions of the world were neutral accounts of empirical facts and its prescriptions for the world accordingly based on universal scientific knowledge rather than particular social interests. This is precisely what Karl Marx challenged, contending that both the French positivists and the British utilitarians and political economists had produced theories that not only misunderstood the facts of contemporary society but reflected a social interest in affirming key features of existing social arrangements. Marx's (1867/1977) *Capital* opened with a critique of the basic categories of political economy, seeking to show that these do not simply reflect reality but organize perception of it in a problematic way. Moreover, Marx demonstrated that these categories, e.g., work redefined as the quantifiable commodity form of labor, were in important ways constitutive not only of political economy but of capitalism itself. Thus aspects of a historically specific form of social organization were made to appear as though they were transhistorical universals.[27] By uncovering this operation Marx showed that other possibilities were open; existing social conditions were real, but not necessary. The positivist political economists did not see this, Marx contended, partly because their interests lay within the existing political economic system not in its transcendence.

Marx suggested, moreover, that much existing political economy was preoccupied with seeking generalizations about surface facts rather than penetrating to the underlying structure of capitalism. As a result, it merely documented what was going on within capitalism rather than explaining capitalism. Here Marx touched on an issue that was basic to scientific progress of his era. Darwin even more influentially (and perhaps successfully) made a similar move in explaining the origin of species. He argued that underlying processes of generation and inheritance of difference combined with selection through sexual reproduction to explain crucial aspects of evolution. Like Marx's theory of capitalism, Darwin's theory of evolution (or more modestly, of the origin of species) sought to explain observable reality on the basis of unobservable but theoretically coherent phenomena.

This contributed to what came to be called the opposition between realism and instrumentalism (or sometimes constructivism). The most basic issue concerned whether theories were more or less arbitrary tools for examining the world or whether they grasped reality in some more determinate and confirmable way. Realists took the latter view, treating theoretically necessary unobservables as real. Interestingly, for all of positivism's claims for the perfection of knowledge, its most influential 19th-century advocate—John Stuart Mill—was basically an instrumentalist. He attempted to preserve the empiricist notion that all knowledge was based most fundamentally on sensory impressions (and accordingly was dubious about evolutionary theory). Mill made good use of syllogistic deductions, but he insisted on the basic importance of knowledge derived directly from experience. Experience might be aided by techniques and instruments of observation—telescopes or censuses—but it remained the basic stuff of knowledge. Theory was among the instruments; it offered organized ways of

[27]Unmasking this is arguably one of the contributions of dialectic reason to Marx's argument. At a general level, though, the point does not rest on more contentious Hegelian claims to a dialectic logic or approach to science. Marx was much more empirically oriented than Hegel, and critical of Hegel's claims to discern substantive truths on the basis of dialectical reason alone (on Marx as empiricist, see Little, 1998, Chapter 2). Postone (1993) offers a particularly helpful discussion of how Marx's categorical critique opens up the question of historical specificity.

talking about facts.[28] While theory included generalizations, sometimes formulated as laws, these could never be the products of inference from empirical knowledge. All inference, Mill argued, is from particulars to particulars. General laws can only be formulas for making inferences from known to unknown particulars; thus, they may be useful but ought not to be confused with empirical knowledge.

A crucial underlying problem here lay with empiricism itself. Philosophers (and philosophical psychologists) of the 17th and 18th centuries had worked with one or another version of a doubly problematic theory of ideas.[29] First, this suggested that knowledge consisted of a collection of basically discrete items of information in people's heads. Second, it held that these ideas got into people's heads on the basis of sensory impressions. While this theory is old in philosophical terms, it retains a certain currency in common sense and even informs the thinking of some nonphilosophically inclined scientists. Hume improved on this theory by distinguishing ideas from perceptions and adding the possibility that imagination might be an intellectual source, but he was still concerned chiefly with seeking empirical sources for how ideas came to be in people's heads. It was in this pursuit that he arrived at his radical argument concerning the limited empirical basis for certain kinds of ideas, like cause. Mill was the leading representative of this tradition in his day; among the later logical positivists, Mach emphasized the idea that causes are not found as such in nature. Both accepted the importance of theoretical terms such as cause, but held that they (along with other theoretical unobservables) meant that theory was a tool for understanding reality, not precisely a statement of it. "Real" knowledge was that which could be empirically verified.[30]

Although Mill held to the empiricist position, he also contributed to superseding it by turning attention more toward issues of method. Comte had considered experiments primarily as a way to create knowledge; he had not focused on the importance of testing it. Once "truth" was established, Comte expected it to be stable. Mill paid much more attention to the idea of disconfirmation or disproof. In this connection, he shifted the place of empirical data. Mill distinguished the "brute facts" of induction from empirical evidence as it might be deployed in ways that bore specifically on theoretical questions. He remained uncomfortable, however, with the idea that unobservable theoretical entities could be anything more than convenient

---

[28]William James (1907/1995) would later suggest on pragmatist grounds that theories be conceived of as ways of predicting one set of observations from another set of observations. Though they might be helpful, they could not be repositories or guarantors of truth as such, but only as embodied in the practical operation of prediction.

[29]Some of the most basic issues are much older, including the notion that there is a clear and obvious distinction between "mind" and "physical world." The whole epistemological problem to which the theory of ideas and the realist/instrumentalist debate speaks derives from this distinction and the question of how minds can gain knowledge of that which is outside them. The empiricist tradition centers on Locke's assertion of the mind as initially a *tabula rasa* on which sensory objects make impressions; these are the basis of knowledge. While Locke thought that general ideas could be established on this basis (by a stripping away of particulars), Hume challenged precisely this view. Kant's idealism suggested that mind was not a *tabula rasa* but both more active than the metaphor suggested and structured by *a priori* categories of understanding. These last were crucial to the development of general or abstract ideas.

[30]Note that by "verification," Mill (and virtually the entire positivist tradition) meant empirical confirmation of truth. The insistence that knowledge proceeds by falsification which we associate with Karl Popper is not part of positivism, but as noted above actually a break with it based on critique (hence, Popper's name for it, "critical rationalism"). Popper (1958, p. 30) traces the roots of the sort of rationalism he advocates back to the Greek tradition of critical discussion: "the rationalist tradition, the tradition of critical discussion, represents the only practicable way of expanding our knowledge.... There is no way that starts from observation or experiment. In the development of science observations and experiments play only the role of critical arguments.... It is an important role; but the significance of observations and experiments depends *entirely* upon the question of whether or not they may be used to *criticize theories* (original emphases).

fictions. Positivists generally followed Mill in holding that only direct experience could produce empirical evidence and that all factual propositions required empirical verification. In the late 19th century, the prestige of biological evolutionism led many to accept some level of realism. Antirealist hopes for complete empirical grounding of theory were revived, however, with the rise of logical positivism. Anything else was condemned as idealism, intuitionism, or historicism.[31]

The issue was basic to the dispute between the Frankfurt School and the Vienna Circle of logical positivists. As Horkheimer wrote in 1936:

> The view that thought is a means of knowing more about the world than may be directly observed … seems to us entirely mysterious" is the conviction expressed in a work of the Vienna Circle. This principle is particularly significant in a world whose magnificent exterior radiates complete unity and order while panic and distress prevail beneath. Autocrats, cruel colonial governors, and sadistic prison wardens have always wished for visitors with this positivistic mentality.[32]

In fact, some members of the Vienna Circle accepted realist positions; Reichenbach declared himself a "critical realist," a position claimed in the next generation by Bunge (1996). More generally, a minimal version of realism has become widespread in science; unobservable theoretical entities are treated as real, especially under the influence of atomic physics. Realism never means severing all connection to empirical data, to be sure, but it does challenge the straightforward empiricist understanding of truth.[33]

Empirically nonobservable theoretical terms are widely admitted in contemporary science, though there are a range of different "realist" justifications for this (Putnam, 1987). Some realist positions are treated with more skepticism than others. An example is the idea of "real types." Without going into detail, this involves the assertion that in some cases the concepts used to categorize particulars into general classes of objects are not more or less arbitrary features of theory but have an externally verifiable reality. Some scientists claimed that races were real types; few now assert this.[34] More persuasive candidates abound, though, such as the distinction of physical states into gas, liquid, and solid. Even here, typification is at least partially shorthand for a more complex reality. Rational choice theorists similarly wish to

[31]The logical positivists accepted Kant's distinction of analytic and synthetic propositions, and thus granted truth value independent of empirical evidence or experience to mathematics and similar purely formal reasoning. Quine (1953) later attacked precisely this distinction and held that nothing could be known independently of experience.

[32]Horkheimer, "Der neueste Angriff auf die Metaphysik," quoted in Wiggershaus (1994, p. 184). The issue remained current in political terms 40 years later, when Margaret Thatcher famously asserted that society did not exist. This echoed Jeremy Bentham's (1970, p. 12) antirealist remark: "the community is a fictitious body, composed of the individual persons who are considered as constituting as it were its members. The interest of the community then is, what?—the sum of the interests of the several members who compose it." Sociology recurrently faces the challenge of establishing the reality of all manner of collective or emergent phenomena in a culture where the reality of individuals is seen as basic (though in fact, the idea of individual may be just as much a social construction).

[33]Biologists influenced by the success of evolutionary theory were among the first to embrace realist positions; Spencer broke with Mill in this regard. There is irony to this, however, since popular support for science has depended largely on assumption that scientific truth could be defended on empiricist grounds. A gap developed between actual scientific practice and popular and secondary school accounts of science as discovery and empirical confirmation. This has been one source of basic confusions in popular understanding of science, for example, in arguments over evolutionary theory in which "creationists" contend that because evolutionary theory is not true on classical empiricist grounds (or the older sort of positivism) it is merely one speculation among many.

[34]Whether use of genetic markers will animate an effort to restore race to the status "real type" is unclear. Certainly, they seem to suggest this in nonscientific imagination. Arguably, though, they suggest to genetic researchers even less validity to the racial typification both because of the massive genetic commonality of human beings and because of the lines of genetic difference that do not follow plausibly racial lines. Even if "race" is genetically further deconstructed rather than rehabilitated, the idea of explaining human variation by genetics suggests something of how a notion of real types might be persuasive.

assert the value of their simplifying assumptions about human decision processes against those who would argue that this is not how human beings actually think or act.[35]

At the same time, instrumentalism has its heirs. These include pragmatism, Wittgensteinian analysis of theory as a language game, and most poststructuralism. A good deal of work in logic and the philosophy of science has started from a sort of partial or soft instrumentalism, the recognition that there can be no such thing as a direct match between theory and empirical reality. Even strong empiricists acknowledge that all empirical observations are mediated by language.[36] One can work to make language as precise as possible, whether one is a realist or an instrumentalist. One also can see dependence on language as a limit to strict empiricism, as revealing the embeddedness of science in culture (including scientific culture).[37]

The underlying question is something like does science offer us mirrors of nature or only more or less persuasive arguments as to how things work?[38] The first argument amounts to an affirmation of a correspondence theory of truth, precisely what the 19th-century positivists wanted, but now suspect among philosophers and critical analysts of science. Note, however, the problematic implications of the second alternative. If scientific theories are arguments, does this mean that we should judge them by their effectiveness as rhetoric? Or is there a way to judge them by their purchase on "reality?" Note also that the second argument is ironically more strongly "realist" in that it seeks to explain observed reality by theory.

The disputes between realists and instrumentalists have given way to a more general crisis in epistemology. Classical empiricist approaches sought to secure the truth claims of complex theories by building them out of empirically confirmed (or at least confirmable) propositions. This "foundationalism" perpetuates something of the theory of ideas insofar as it suggests that each scientific finding may be independently verified and on this basis become well-founded knowledge. The typical rhetoric of foundationalism is one of accumulating truths and discarding falsehoods. This reveals its roots in inductivist empiricism. It sets up a falsely high standard of perfect knowledge, however, making it relatively easy to attack. Attempts to defend foundational truth have become ever narrower, more abstract, and more distant from actual scientific practice, while challenges too often fall into cynicism in their rejection of all notions of empirical truth.

"Coherentism" offers a corrective, suggesting that the statements in a theory are interdependent and should be judged not just in the separate match between each and external reality but by how well they fit together. This builds on rationalism and idealism. It does not, however, explain how a theory is to be tested against empirical evidence. As Wilfred Sellars (1963, p. 128) phrases the dilemma:

[35]See, for example, the prominence of claims to realism in the arguments of Kiser and Hechter (1998), responding to Somers (1998) who herself claims the realist mantle, albeit with the qualifier "relational realist," which suggests a nod to coherentist rather than foundationalist criteria for judging truth claims. See also my discussion of both and of the nondecisive character of appeals to realism in Calhoun (1998).

[36]Quine (1992), for example, remains thoroughly empiricist even while recognizing that access to observable objects is more than a matter of sensation, and indeed that the role of language is a matter not merely of "observation terms" but of "observation sentences."

[37]The social sciences face more often the added challenge of what Gallie (1967) called "essentially contested concepts." These are scientific terms that are also inescapably terms in ordinary language, any definition of which has potentially prejudicial implications for practical projects. Any clear operationalization of such a concept—like "nation" or "democracy"—will usually grasp only aspects of the more complex whole which is embedded in actual social life and struggles.

[38]The language in which I have posed the question is that of Richard Rorty (1980). Rorty challenges the search for certain knowledge (which animated empiricists and idealists alike) by suggesting that we ought to think of certainty "as a matter of victory in argument rather than of relation to an object known." While Rorty's own views move toward rhetoric and literature, rejection of the "mirror of nature" argument is much more widespread and not limited to those who embrace relativism as openly (or, to his critics, as cynically) as Rorty. Popperian falsificationism and much analytic philosophy also reject the pure correspondence theory of truth.

> One seems forced to choose between the picture of an elephant which rests on a tortoise (What
> supports the tortoise?) and the picture of a great Hegelian serpent of knowledge with its tail in its
> mouth (Where does it begin?). Neither will do.[39]

A simple pragmatic appeal to theory's usefulness does not really help, since it begs the question of usefulness for what.[40] A stronger pragmatist argument follows Peirce's suggestion that what counts as truth at any one time is based on acceptance by the community of scientists. This is less arbitrary than it might seem. Scientists apply rational–critical argumentation and norms of publicness to judge the quality and applicability of observations as well as the coherence of theories. The success of predictions and practical applications can be taken into account alongside inductions. Versions of the Peircean view inform theories as otherwise different as those of Habermas (who conceptualizes science as a special kind of public sphere) and Quine (who approaches science as a specialized speech community).

Partly because it has been posed in extreme terms (opposing perfect truth to perfectly arbitrary statements) the realist–instrumentalist controversy has significantly impeded the integration of critique into the scientific project. Taking unobservable theoretical entities and processes seriously has indeed proved indispensable to science. This is no longer controversial. But the positivist project of perfect truth is. So too is the notion of a continuous accumulation of truths rather than recurrent discontinuous recasting of knowledge.[41] That knowledge—and perforce theory—is incomplete, biased, and implicated in struggles for power does not, however, render it entirely arbitrary.[42] The project of critique assumes the reality of knowledge as well as its imperfection, and also the potential for epistemic gain. It is thus at odds with accusations (more common in the literary versions of "theory" than the sociological) that claims to knowledge are *merely* rhetoric.

THE UNITY OF SCIENCE,
OR DO CULTURE AND AGENCY MATTER?

Critical theory engages knowledge as a product of human action. Like all such products, it is shaped by history and social conditions as well as current choices and perspectives. It is embedded in specific ways of understanding the world—from cultures to ideologies to theories—that enable us to grasp what is going on but do so always in partial and biased ways. This may involve "distortion" but there is no way to contrast this to perfect, undistorted,

---

[39]I have been pointed to the Sellers passage by Haack (1993). Haack herself makes a valiant effort to trace a middle ground and at the same time to restore some confidence that epistemology might, if suitably reconstructed, make valuable critical contributions again.

[40]The "usefulness" of theories (including their capacity to generate acceptance as "true") varies with shifts in practical projects and objects of attention. This need not imply a relativist reduction of truth to taste or power, but it will help to explain why advances in knowledge are not simply and impartially cumulative. Actual historical developments in knowledge are less matters of rejections of the false in favor of the true than of "epistemic gain" offered by one complex package of arguments compared to another. See Gadamer (1975), Taylor (1985, 1989), and discussion in relation to critical social theory in Calhoun (1995, Chapter 2).

[41]This is an aspect of Kuhn's (1970) notion of scientific revolution, though it is less controversial than his stronger claim that because paradigmatic systems of knowledge are incommensurable there can be no way to assess their greater or lesser truth value. Comparing theories, in other words, is radically different from comparing propositions within theoretical frameworks.

[42]As Pierre Bourdieu (1998, p. 26) has written: "In the order of thought, there is, as Nietzsche pointed out, no immaculate conception; but nor is there any original sin—and the discovery that someone who has discovered the truth had an interest in doing so in no way diminishes his discovery. Those who like to believe in the miracle of 'pure' thought must bring themselves to accept that the love of truth or virtue, like any other kind of disposition, necessarily owes something to the conditions in which it was formed, in other words a social position and trajectory."

knowledge. The contrast can only be to other ways of constructing knowledge that grant better purchase is some determinate context (specific project, social field, or cultural orientation). Critical theory thus insists on a middle path between positivism's exaggerated hopes and relativism's exaggerated disappointments.

Following Jeremy Bentham, John Stuart Mill sought to make ethics an "exact science," to reform law and social institutions on the basis of economic, psychological, and sociological science and to direct human conduct in the same way that nature can be controlled through knowledge of its causal laws. "If we knew the person thoroughly," Mill (1843/1986, p. 122) wrote, "and knew all the inducements which are acting upon him, we could foretell his conduct with as much certainty as we can predict any physical event." This basic orientation shaped the "positivist" side in later arguments: the idea that the kind of knowledge we can have of human action and its products is no different in principle from that we can have of the physical world and biological nature.

An important goal of positivism has been to achieve a unity of science in which human life would be understood not only with the precision of physical explanation but as part of the same underlying causal theory. That is, one set of basic theoretical laws should be formulated to account for physics, biology, culture, and social relations. This project challenged traditional humanism in a basic way and indeed helped to produce the division of the humanities from the natural sciences. Philosophers might join the positivist project, redefining their field as a labor of clarification in support of science. When they resisted this, it was commonly, and crucially, in the name of human action. This insistence on the basic and irreducible importance of *action* to the nature of humanity, and thus also to its difference from the rest of nature, led positivists to accuse these philosophers of being metaphysicians or even theologians. Indeed, theology contributed importantly to the understanding of the idea of creative action. So did literature, history, and even versions of linguistics, fields to which nonpositivist philosophy was joined in the notion of the humanities. These disciplines all rejected the notions that problems of meaning could be effectively sidestepped by recourse to external causal explanation and that cultural and historical differences were epiphenomenal to some invariant reality.

The result was a quarrel most famously located in late 19th and early 20th century Germany as the *methodenstreit*. Sociology seems fated to repeat this struggle over and again, usually in a confused way and without much explicit recourse to history. If there is any content associated with the classical "struggle over method" in the minds of most sociologists it is the opposition of "nomothetic" to "idiographic" approaches. Science seeks universal laws, this vague disciplinary memory suggests, while history seeks to account for particular events. A variety of possibilities, however, are obscured by the opposition between idiographic and nomothetic knowledge. Consider, for example, analogies. These are an important form of connection between accounts, generalization of a sort, that fits neither of the allegedly alternative approaches. Indeed, Stinchecombe (1978) has argued that analogies are the basic form of successful reasoning across cases in historical sociology, rather than covering law theories as such.

The opposition of generalizing and particularizing disciplines does not in itself clarify the motivations for the *methodenstreit*. This was a struggle, not simply a convenient division of labor because it turned on commitment to sharply opposed positions about human action. The positivist vision requires that the human production of meaning be epiphenomenal rather than a basic aspect of making the world. It reduces action to behavior (and thus in principle external explanation).[43] The alternative is to see the creative potential of human action as basic not

---

[43]See the classic account and critical analysis by Taylor (1967). Of course, positivist accounts need not reduce action to

merely to human experience but to reality. To understand human beings as actors requires interpretation, recognition that people are themselves interpreting the world and investing it with meaning as they act in it, and thus understanding them in cultural contexts. Cultural contexts, like actors and actions, are necessarily plural. This is why there is an element of particularity, or specification, to the kind of knowledge pursued by the humanities insofar as they take creative action seriously. The link to "particularity" expresses the fact that the human participation in creation of the world produces difference: cultural, historical, personal. It is not simply a matter of events, or detail, or situation within narrative rather than covering law explanation.

A variety of possibilities are obscured by the opposition between idiographic and nomothetic knowledge. Consider, for example, analogies. These are an important form of connection between accounts, generalization of a sort, that fits neither of the allegedly alternative approaches. Stinchecombe (1978) indeed has argued that analogies are the basic form of successful reasoning across cases in historical sociology, rather than covering law theories as such.

The original opposition reflected among other things the interest of Dilthey and other participants in the *methodenstreit* in defining the proper pursuit of the field of history. History, it could be said, was less concerned with generalization than particularization. But even here, history is not solely the history of events but also (as Braudel would later put it) of mentalities and structures. The point was not the virtue of particularity as such (however much historians might tend to prefer particular details in their accounts) and certainly not a refusal of all generalizations. Rather, the points were specificity and difference. Historical analysis required the specification of context, limit, and location, both in space and time. It required the recognition and interpretation of different ways of seeing the world (cultures, knowledges), and it required attention to contingency and action. If history is an account of how the world came to be as it is, then it must acknowledge that the world could have been otherwise.

The social sciences straddle the division between the humanities and the natural sciences. This is not simply a matter of conflicting views about social life that could in principle be resolved by empirical research. Where social scientists stand certainly affects the substantive claims they make, whether they think that the profit motive is natural, for example, or historically and culturally specific. But the issue cannot be kept external. The struggle over methods is not only about technique but about the nature of knowledge itself.[44]

> Whereas the natural and the cultural or hermeneutic sciences are capable of living in a mutually indifferent, albeit more hostile than peaceful, coexistence, the social sciences must bear the tension of divergent approaches under one roof, for in them the very practice of research compels reflection on the relationship between analytic and hermeneutic research methodologies. (Habermas, 1967, p. 3)

---

psychological learning theory; they can reduce it to purely strategic models in which it is the product of interest, context, and cognitive capacity. Intentionality is tricky; some are prepared to accept that it is characteristic of action, though it has proved hard to find a neurophysical process that might account for it. What they cannot allow is that action is fundamentally creative. Perhaps the most emphatic statement of the centrality of creativity to action was made by Hannah Arendt (1965). Hans Joas (1997) recently has pointed out the extent to which even social theory focused on action has failed to do justice to the idea of creativity.

[44]The issue is, in other words, "methodological" in a strong sense. In everyday usage, methodology often refers simply to technical knowledge; the methodologist in a team project is one especially skilled in the application of a technique or possibly one who develops that technique further. But knowledge of method should go beyond this to enable fully informed choice of method. This implies grasping the internal relationship between method and the creation of knowledge. This in turn involves questions about the nature and specific forms of knowledge.

Every objective research method poses challenges of interpretation. At the same time, interpretative research gains its significance as social science by interpreting social life in a way that transcends the individual researcher's personal relation to it.[45]

Within the social sciences, thus, struggle over methods is endemic. It is closely bound to theory and it demands reflexivity. That is, it demands continuous critical consideration about the relationship between the approach to knowledge and the knowledge produced. It is possible, however, to embrace both sides of the division, that is, to learn from both objectifying methods and interpretation. This the founders of the Frankfurt School did, and it remains important to critical theory.[46] Indeed, this is a distinction of critical social theory from some postmodern or poststructuralist or other theories that may claim the label of critical theory. Many of these reject scientific knowledge (or at least its legitimate purchase on human affairs) much as positivism rejects culture and creative action. This, however, is incapacitating for a critical social theory. To refuse the project of disciplining theory by empirical research is to refuse theory a truly practical engagement with the world.

Partly in response to these concerns (though not in a Frankfurt School trajectory), Pierre Bourdieu has pursued simultaneously the objectification of both subjectivist and objectivist perspectives in social science. The polarities of the *methodenstreit* each reflect "scholastic" points of view and also the distinctive sense of honor inculcated in those who succeed in the world of universities and academic disciplines.

> Those who are immersed, in some cases from birth, in scholastic universes resulting from a long process of autonomization are led to forget the exceptional historical and social conditions that make possible a view of the world and of cultural products that is characterized by self-evidence and naturalness. (Bourdieu, 2000, p. 25)

On the one hand there is an exaltation of the individual-as-knower. There is a tendency to idealize the scientist as a distinctive sort of subject, remarkably rational as the artist is held to be aesthetically gifted, and thereby to protect the scientific field from external examination (and indeed internal reflexivity). On the other hand, the ideology of objective facts implies that these are absolute and neutral; they may explain but never need to be explained. Yet there are objective limits to objectivism. Not least, there is no escaping the work of constructing the object, and the responsibility that this entails (Bourdieu, 1988, p. 6).[47] Both depend on what Bourdieu calls the 'autonomization' of the intellectual field, its special historical construction as a quasi-independent realm of the pursuit of (and struggle over) knowledge. The very defenses of this field against outsiders also function as defenses against explanations of either subjectivist or objectivist knowledge as products of historical and social circumstances. Yet, explanations are possible both in terms of the collective history that produces the categories of our thought and the individual histories by which they are inculcated in us (Bourdieu, 2000, p. 9). As the latter clause suggests, the objectification of objective knowledge reveals that it is produced by subjects just as subjective interpretations are shaped by objective conditions.[48]

[45]Hence the joke about what the native said to the postmodernist anthropologist: enough about you, let's talk about me.
[46]Frankfurt School critical theory is often seen as mainly a philosophical project, but this is misleading. The Institute of Social Research was founded precisely to combine empirical inquiries and theoretical development—not least because of the concern Max Horkheimer shared with his colleagues (including their financial backer Felix Weil) that an adequate and practically significant critical analysis of the growing European crisis depended on this.
[47]The enduring debates that pose individual and structure as alternatives (rather than pursuing a relational analysis) reflect these polarities in the scholastic field as well as contrasting substantive perspectives. As Bourdieu (1990, p. 190) writes, "it is easier to treat social facts as things or as people than as relations."
[48]Bourdieu's point applies not only to the pursuit of knowledge but to social life more generally. "The source of historical action, that of the artist, the scientist or the member of government just as much as that of the worker or the

Reflexive inquiry into the nature and conditions of the production of knowledge is not an attack on knowledge but a way of improving it.[49]

Among the most basic of the conditions of knowledge is its constitution in language. Mill (1843/1986) himself began his *System of Logic* with an analysis of language. It remained to later philosophers, however, to develop the conclusion that there is no access to knowledge except through language. Though neither analytic philosophy nor logical positivism is usually considered part of critical theory; in fact, both are based in large part on critique (in the Kantian sense) of how language works to structure knowledge.[50] Linguistic analysis in this sense was closely akin to logic, and with Frege, Russell, and other pioneers it focused on substituting logically clear verbal expressions for misleading or ambiguous ones. Wittgenstein later described this approach to language as a sort of therapy for thought.

However, Wittgenstein also pushed linguistic analysis well beyond this purely clarifying role. His critiques of the solipsism of traditional philosophy, for example, challenged the logical positivists' approach to knowledge as based on a pure relation between knower and experience. Carnap, notably, had argued that all empirical knowledge must be built up out of elementary records or recognitions of experience (what he called "protocol statements"). This notion retains force (without explicit theorization) in much everyday sociological positivism. Complex statements are held to have truth value because they are composed of more basic statements that lead back to "actual data." These data are a secure foundation because they refer to the experience of a researcher directly observing (via sensory relationship) "reality." Wittgenstein does not challenge the existence of such reality (or say much of anything about it), but he challenges the verifiability of any fact recorded in such a way.[51] The problem stems from the implicit individualism of the traditional (including Carnapian) account of observation and cognition (itself embedded in the dualism associated with Descartes). The reliance on direct sensory experience suggests that external reality causes mental states in the observer, hence data. But how does the observer "show" these mental states to others, and thus provide for verification? Indeed, how does she or he identify them as any particular sort of mental states. The answer is generally through language. But, Wittgenstein argued, the language must be social, not private. It is a useful tool for communication because it is shared and it is a skill

---

petty civil servant, is not an active subject confronting society as if society were an object constituted externally. This source resides neither in consciousness nor in things but in the relation between two states of the social, that is, between the history objectified in things, in the form of institutions, and the history incarnated in bodies, in the form of that system of enduring dispositions which I call habitus" (Bourdieu, 1990, p. 190).

[49]Critics recurrently point out that theories ostensibly based purely on facts or on the combination of logic and empirical evidence always also depend on more or less arbitrary assumptions, reflect biases inherent in language and the construction of concepts, and are shaped by interpretations that are necessary to the constitution of any facts. Such criticisms are sometimes answered by assertions that assumptions can be controlled if they are made clear, that biases can be minimized by careful methods, and that interpretation can be checked by measures of reliability. Even more persuasively, many refuse to cede the terrain of argument to such critical questions. "Show me a model that works better," they suggest and they will consider changing their views. While this is an evasion of critical questions that are both legitimate and important, it is not an argument without force. Critical theorists need to respond by participating in the development of better empirical accounts.

[50]Wittgenstein's (1922/1981) *Tractatus*, for example, was "a critique of language designed to reveal the essential structure of the thought which is expressed in language and to discover, through that structure, the limits of thought" (Pears & Kenny, 1994, p. 257).

[51]Positivists and other empiricists have a long tradition of posing arguments against the red herrings of imagined idealists and relativists. They confuse arguments about how we grasp reality or communicate our understanding of reality for arguments that in some sense it does not exist or have material force for us. Thus Berkeley's "immaterialism" is not refuted by kicking a hard object. Neither do advocates of critical science studies who hold that gravity is a concept generally maintain that they would not fall to earth if they leapt from windows.

acquired in social interaction. The use of language involves a practical orientation to action that never reduces to following rules. Thus, the relationship to experience is less direct than initially claimed. Wittgenstein identifies other problems as well, including the tendencies to treat the observer as a disembodied cognitive ego and to treat sensations as objects (rather than responses to objects).

Wittgenstein's inquiries here suggest some of the reasons why critical theory (along with pragmatism and other approaches) has generally challenged "philosophy of the subject."[52] Though this was one of the starting points for modern science, it is also a problem. In its place, and more generally in place of the sharp dualism of internal and external, theorists have developed approaches to intersubjectivity: the mutual interdependence of human subjects as social beings. Empirical data thus involve internal states (experience) that are organized and judged by intersubjective criteria (language and scientific understandings formulated in language).

Wittgenstein's later work here suggests not only a philosophical clarification in regard to science, accordingly, but the importance of anthropological and sociological investigation into culture and the construction of meaning. From the embeddedness of claims to factual knowledge in language, we proceed to the similar embeddedness of all human existence in culture. This is a conclusion also traceable back to the starting point of the "humanistic" side to the *methodenstreit*, the insistence on the creative power of human action. It poses a variety of problems for the project of cross-cultural knowledge, including but not limited to positivist programs pursuing universal truths independent of culture. Following Wittgenstein's approach to languages as "wholes," Winch (1958) argued that translation of notions like "rationality" across cultures may be impossible.[53] This would challenge the very idea of a social science. However, Wittgenstein's notion of language games suggests a different and more promising approach. If we see language in pragmatic terms (and allowing for metapragmatic analysis that does not presume neutral metalanguage), we can see that translation is a poor metaphor for the way cross-cultural understanding actually arises. It develops out of mutual engagement in tasks of practical understanding and action. These encourage change in participants as well as in language and culture and underwrite new possibilities for communication.[54] The positivist idea of a neutral metalanguage into which all empirical observations might be translated may be chimerical, but this does not mean that knowledge—of varying generality—cannot be produced or communicated. One of the tasks of critical theory is to analyze the implications of shifting social foundations, scientific standpoints, and cultural contexts for this knowledge.

At the same time, though, it is crucial to recognize that culture is not merely a means of understanding the physical or even the psychological worlds. It also is constitutive of human reality. The very persons who are observers and knowers and actors exist only as participants in cultural relations. This does not mean that they exist in bounded, internally uniform cultures, since the cultural worlds people inhabit are frequently polyglot, heterogeneous, and shifting. Neither does it mean that persons are passively determined products of culture, fully explicable by it. On the contrary, human beings create culture. But in this as in the making of history generally, people are shaped by great determinations and usually make small changes. Indeed, for the most part, people's participation in the making of culture reproduces it, even when they sometimes make great changes in themselves or their circumstances. Nonetheless,

---

[52]See the opening chapter of Habermas (1987) for a clear account.
[53]See discussion from various vantage points in Wilson (1970).
[54]I have discussed this idea further in Calhoun (1995, Chapter 2).

there are important senses in which the human world is historical precisely because it is the result of human action. It is a world that human beings have made, though not under conditions of their own choosing. At least part of this making moreover involves creation by means of imagination. A whole host of particular practices and relationships exist because human beings were able to imagine them. More basically, though, the very categories through which we give the world form are products of social imagination. Is the world organized into nation-states? Are corporations real? Does a contract bind parties? Is this piece of paper or digital encoding money? As US Supreme Court Justice Marshall wrote in 1819, "a corporation is an artificial being, invisible, intangible, and existing only in contemplation of the law."[55] Many of the realities with which social scientists are appropriately concerned cannot be found in an elemental sensory experience. We need to ask not just of their status as objects of scientific attention, whether realist or instrumentalist, for example, but of their status as material forces in the world. Insisting on the historical creation of the world as *this* sort of world, critical theory reveals that it could be otherwise and seeks to locate the possible and likely directions for change.

CONCLUSION

At this point it would be good to turn from relatively abstract philosophical discussion to more concrete examples of critical theory at work in substantive sociological analysis. Alas, space will not permit this. We must rest content with consideration of the common denominators to a critical theoretical orientation rather than specific theories.

In one sense, this is appropriate. Development of the critical dimension to sociological theory has been impeded by the notion that critical theory is limited to the specific arguments of the Frankfurt School. It is important to see critique in a broader light. In particular, we should recognize that the critique of the conditions and limits of knowledge is important to all science. More specific to the social sciences are the points made by Marx in the passage cited at the beginning of the chapter. To recognize that social life is historical, made by human action, and informed by differences of culture is basic to a critique of false necessity. To recognize conversely that human action is neither unconditioned nor unconstrained is basic to a critique of both voluntarism and the raising of expressive individualism to the status of theory that underwrites relativism.

In a sense, this chapter has remained focused on epistemological or metatheoretical preliminaries. A more substantively sociological critical theory would address the ways in which specific social and cultural formations shape knowledge. It would consider, following the Frankfurt School, how capitalism encourages reification and objectification, instrumental reason, and ideologies that mystify exploitation. It would ask what contradictions may inform struggle and possible directions of change within any social formation. In the essay I discussed in the first section, Max Horkheimer (1937/1972, p. 227) sketched such a theory:

> The critical theory of society is, in its totality, the unfolding of a single existential judgment. To put it in broad terms, the theory says that the basic form of the historically given commodity economy on which modern history rests contains in itself the internal and external tensions of the modern era; it generates these tensions over and over again in an increasingly heightened form; and after a period of progress, development of human powers, and emancipation for the individual, after an enormous extension of human control over nature, it finally hinders further development and drives humanity into a new barbarism.

[55]*Dartmouth v Woodward* 4 Wheat 518 (1819).

I think there is a good deal to this basically Marxist theory, but it is a mistake to present it as *the* critical theory of society. This, like the idea of totality Horkheimer invokes, closes off critical theory where it should be open.[56]

This chapter has presented a more general notion of critical theory and argued that this is appropriately developed alongside and in partnership with empirical explanatory projects, not opposed to them. Indeed, all sociological theory needs (1) to engage in continuous critical examination of the foundations—both intellectual and institutional—on which sociological knowledge rests. At the same time, but distinctly, it needs (2) to approach existing social reality critically, seeing the limits of generalizing from concrete phenomena that are instances of historically conditioned human possibility, not simply universal or unchanging. Finally, it needs (3) to be attentive to the ways in which sociology itself participates in the making of the world, the creation of particular social and even sometimes material conditions in social relationships shaped by sociological knowledge and ways of understanding.

REFERENCES

Adorno, T. W., Albert, H., Daberndorf, R., Habermas, J., Pilot, H., and Popper, K. R. (1976). *The positivist dispute in German sociology.* B. Adey & D. Frisby (Trans.). New York: Harper and Row.

Alexander, J. (1982). *Theoretical logic in sociology*, Volume 2: *The antinomies of classical social thought: Marx and Durkheim.* Berkeley: University of California Press.

Arendt, H. (1965). *The human condition.* Chicago: University of Chicago Press.

Benhabib, S. (1986). *Critique, norm, and utopia.* New York: Columbia University Press.

Bentham, J. (1970). *An introduction to the principles of morals and legislation.* London: Methuen.

Boudon, R. (1971/1974). *The logic of sociological explanation.* London: Penguin.

Bourdieu, P. (1972/1977). *Outline of a theory of practice.* R. Nice (Trans.). Cambridge: Cambridge University Press.

Bourdieu, P. (1988). *Homo academicus.* Stanford, CA: Stanford University Press.

Bourdieu, P. (1990). *In other words: Essays towards a reflexive sociology.* Stanford, CA: Stanford University Press.

Bourdieu, P. (2000). *Pascalian meditations.* Stanford, CA: Stanford University Press.

Bourdieu, P., Chambordeon, J.-C., & Passeron, J.-C. (Eds.). (1991). *The craft of sociology: Epistemological preliminaries.* R. Nice (Trans.). New York and Berlin: Aldine de Gruyter.

Bunge, M. (1996). *Finding philosophy in social science.* New Haven: Yale University Press.

Calhoun, C. (1995). *Critical social theory.* Cambridge, MA: Blackwell.

Calhoun, C. (1998). Explanation in historical sociology: Narrative, general theory, and historically specific theory. *American Journal of Sociology, 108,* 846–871.

Collins, R. (1999). *The sociology of philosophies: A global theory of intellectual change.* Cambridge, MA: Harvard University Press.

Durkheim, E. (1895). *The rules of sociological method.* New York: Free Press.

Foucault, M. (1966). *The order of things: An archaeology of the human sciences.* New York: Random House.

Gadamer, H.-G. (1975). *Truth and method.* New York: Seabury.

Gallie, W. B. (1968). *Philosophy and the historical understanding*, rev. ed. New York: Schocken.

Goetschel, W. (1994). *Constituting critique.* Durham, NC: Duke University Press.

Haack, S. (1993). *Evidence and inquiry.* Cambridge, MA: Blackwell.

Habermas, J. (1962/1989). *The structural transformation of the public sphere.* Cambridge: MIT Press.

Habermas, J. (1967). *On the logic of the social sciences.* Cambridge, MA: MIT Press.

Habermas, J. (1971). *Knowledge and human interests.* Boston: Beacon.

Habermas, J. (1984). *Theory of communicative action*, Vol. 1: *Reason and the rationalization of society.* Boston: Beacon Press.

Habermas, J. (1987). *The philosophical discourse of modernity.* F. Lawrence (Trans.). Cambridge, MA: MIT Press.

Habermas, J. (1988). *Theory of communicative action*, Vol. 2: *Lifeworld and system: A critique of functionalist reason.* Boston: Beacon Press.

---

[56]See Jay (1985) on the theme of totality as it has informed generations of marxist thought. While the Frankfurt School's engagement with Hegel enabled them to expand the critical potential of marxist theory by comparison to their more positivistic marxist predecessors and contemporaries, it encouraged them to see determinate necessity to the social logics they identified.

Habermas, J. (1989). *The new conservatism*. Cambridge, MA: MIT Press.

Habermas, J. (1997). *Between facts and norms*. Cambridge, MA: MIT Press.

Hohendahl, P. U. (1982). *The institution of criticism*. Ithaca, NY: Cornell University Press.

Holub, R. C. (1991). *Jurgen Habermas: Critic in the public sphere*. New York: Routledge.

Horkheimer, M. (1937/1972). *Critical theory: Selected essays*. New York: Continuum.

Horkheimer, M., & Adorno, T. (1944/1969). *Dialectic of enlightenment*. New York: Herder and Herder.

Hume, D. (1739–1740/1958). *A treatise of human nature*. Oxford: Oxford University Press.

James, W. (1907/1995). *Pragmatism*. New York: Dover.

Jay, M. (1974). *The dialectical imagination*. Berkeley: University of California Press.

Jay, M. (1985). *Marxism and totality*. Berkeley: University of California Press.

Joas, H. (1997). *The creativity of action*. Chicago: University of Chicago Press.

Kant, I. (1781/1965). *Critique of pure reason*. N. Kemp Smith (Trans.). New York: St. Martins.

Kiser, E., & Hechter, M. (1998). The debate on historical sociology: Rational choice theory and its critics. *American Journal of Sociology, 104*, 785–816.

Kuhn, T. S. (1970). *The structure of scientific revolutions*, 2nd ed. Chicago: University of Chicago Press.

Little, D. (1998). *Microfoundations, method, and causation: On the philosophy of the social sciences*. New Brunswick, NJ: Transaction Publishers.

Luhmann, N. (1988). *Observations on modernity*. Stanford, CA: Stanford University Press.

Lukacs, G. (1922). *History and class consciousness*. Cambridge, MA: MIT Press.

Marcuse, H. (1964). *One-dimensional man*. Boston: Beacon.

Marcuse, H. (1968). *Negations*. Harmondsworth, England: Penguin.

Marx, K. (1843/1975). On the Jewish question. In *Karl Marx–Friedrich Engels collected works*, Vol. 3 (pp. 146–174). New York: International Publishing Co.

Marx, K. (1852). The 18th Brumaire of Louis Bonaparte. In *Karl Marx and Frederick Engels: Collected Works*, Vol. 11 (pp. 99–197). London: Lawrence and Wishart.

Marx, K. (1867/1977). *Capital*. New York: Viking.

Marx, K., & Engels, F. (1848/1974). Manifesto of the Communist Party. In *Collected Works*, Vol. 6. London: Lawrence and Wishart.

Pears, D., & Kenny, A. (1994). Mill to Wittgenstein. In A. Kenny (Ed.), *The Oxford illustrated history of Western philosophy* (pp. 239–275). Oxford: Oxford University Press.

Popper, K. R. (1934). *Logic of scientific discovery*. London: Hutchinson (Reprinted 1959)

Popper, K. R. (1958). The beginnings of rationalism. In D. Miller (Ed.), *Popper: Selections* (pp. 25–32). Princeton: Princeton University Press. (Reprinted 1985)

Popper, K. R. (1972). *Objective knowledge: An evolutionary approach*. Oxford: Oxford University Press.

Postone, M. (1993). *Time, labor, and social domination*. Cambridge: Cambridge University Press.

Putnam, H. (1987). *The many faces of realism*. Boston: Open Court.

Quine, W. V. O. (1953). *From a logical point of view*. Cambridge, MA: Harvard University Press.

Quine, W. V. O. (1992). *The pursuit of truth*, rev. ed. Cambridge, MA: Harvard University Press.

Rorty, R. (1980). *Philosophy and the mirror of nature*. Princeton, NJ: Princeton University Press.

Sellars, W. (1963). Empiricism and the philosophy of mind. In *Science, perception and reality* (pp. 127–196). London: Routledge and Kegan Paul.

Somers, M. R. (1998). We're no angels: Realism, rational choice, and relationality in social science. *American Journal of Sociology, 104*, 722–784.

Stinchcombe, A. (1978). *Theoretical methods in social history*. New York: Academic Press.

Stroud, B. (1977). *Hume*. London: Routledge and Kegan Paul.

Taylor, C. (1967). *The explanation of behavior*. London: Routledge and Kegan Paul.

Taylor, C. (1985). *Philosophy and the human sciences: Philosophical papers, II*. Cambridge: Cambridge University Press.

Taylor, C. (1989). *Sources of the self*. Cambridge, MA: Harvard University Press.

Taylor, C. (1998). *Philosophical arguments*. Cambridge, MA: Harvard University Press.

Turner, J. H. (1987). Analytical theorizing. In A. Giddens & J. Turner (Eds.), *Social theory today* (pp. 156–194). Stanford, CA: Stanford University Press.

Unger, R. M. (1987). *False necessity*. Cambridge: Cambridge University Press.

Wiggershaus, R. (1994). *The Frankfurt school: Its history, theories, and political significance*. Cambridge, MA: MIT Press.

Wilson, B. (Ed.). (1970). *Rationality*. Oxford: Basil Blackwell.

Wilson, E. O. (1998). *Consilience: The unity of knowledge*. New York: Knopf.

Winch, P. (1958). *The idea of a social science and its relation to philosophy*. London: Routledge.

Wittgenstein, L. (1922/1981). *Tractatus logico-philosophicus*. London: Routledge.

CHAPTER 6

Metatheorizing in Sociology

The Basic Parameters and the Potential Contributions of Postmodernism

GEORGE RITZER, SHANYANG ZHAO, AND JIM MURPHY

The first objective in this chapter is to present an overview of metatheorizing in sociology. To that end, we will delineate four broad philosophical approaches—positivist, hermeneutic, critical, and postmodern—to such metatheoretical work. We also will present a far more concrete typology based on the three different objectives of sociologists (and others) who do metatheoretical work: greater understanding of theory, the production of new theories, and the creation of new metatheories. The second goal is to explore postmodern social theory for a variety of new ideas that might be useful to metatheorists. As we will see, postmodernism is inherently metatheoretical, and as a result it does have a number of fresh and innovative ideas to offer to the metatheorist. The utilization of only a few of these ideas promises to invigorate and alter the nature of metatheorizing in sociology.

WHAT IS METATHEORIZING?

The prefix "meta" connotes "after," "about," and "beyond," and is often used in describing "second-order" studies (McMullin, 1970). Let S denote a given subject of study. The study of S constitutes a first-order study, S_1, and the study of S_1 constitutes a second-order study, S_2. The second-order study, or metastudy, is thus the study of the study, which transcends as well as succeeds the first-order study. Metastudy may involve the continuous monitoring of first-order studies by those doing the studies through self-examination and self-direction. Metastudy also can be undertaken by others interested in examining a study or set of studies. When undertaken by those engaged in first-order studies, metastudy entails a high level of *reflexivity*. Other researchers not involved in the first-order studies also are reflexive, but more about the implications of the first-order studies for the field in which the research is

GEORGE RITZER AND JIM MURPHY • Department of Sociology, University of Maryland, College Park, Maryland 20742. SHANYANG ZHAO • Department of Sociology, Temple University, Philadelphia, Pennsylvania 19122.

Handbook of Sociological Theory, edited by Jonathan H. Turner. Kluwer Academic / Plenum Publishers, New York, 2002.

being undertaken. They cannot be self-reflexive about the first-order studies because they were not involved in them as they were being carried out.

Any first-order study consists of at least the following three elements: purpose, process, and product. The *purpose* of S_1 defines the aim of study or the type of knowledge to be gained through the study; the *process* of S_1 refers to the way in which the goal of study is reached; and the *product* of S_1 includes everything resulting from the study. Whether undertaken by those involved in the research or by others, the examination can entail (1) empirical assessment of the accomplishments (products) of the first-order study and (2) critical evaluation of the appropriateness of the aim of the study (purpose) as well as the effectiveness of the means of study (processes). Bourdieu (1971, p. 181) argues more broadly that this involves "a reflective return to the foundation of science and the making explicit of the hypotheses and operations which make it possible." When done by those doing the studies, the outcome of such examinations serves as the basis for self-direction, e.g., either to continue the ongoing research activities or to make necessary changes. When done by others, metastudy serves to offer future researchers insight into what to do and what not to do.

Metasociology is a subdomain of metastudy and metatheorizing in turn is a form of metasociology that specifically examines the practice of sociological theorizing (Ritzer, 1988, 1990, 1991a,b, 1992). While sociological theorizing attempts to make sense of the social world, metatheorizing in sociology attempts to make sense of sociological theorizing. As is true for sociologists in general, metatheorizing can be practiced by theorists as they do their work and/ or by metatheorists who study the contributions of theorists. As with other forms of metastudy, reflexivity is a crucial component of sociological metatheorizing. While it has other objectives, as we will see, to Bourdieu the reflexive examination of the practice of sociological theorizing is a necessary condition for alerting theorists to and freeing them from the constraints of symbolic struggle in sociology and the social sciences.

A wide variety of specific works can be included under the heading of sociological metatheorizing. What distinguishes work in this area is not so much the process of metatheorizing (it may vary greatly in a variety of ways), but rather the nature of the end products. In our view, there are three varieties of metatheorizing, with each largely defined by differences in its end product. The first type—*metatheorizing as a means of attaining a deeper understanding of theory* (M_u)—involves the study of theory in order to produce a better, a more profound understanding of extant theory. M_u is concerned, more specifically, with the study of theories, theorists, and communities of theorists, as well as with the larger intellectual and social contexts of theories and theorists. The second type—*metatheorizing as a prelude to theory development* (M_p)—entails the study of extant theory in order to produce new sociological theory. The third type—*metatheorizing as a source of overarching theoretical* perspectives (M_o)—is oriented to the goal of producing a perspective, one could say a metatheory, that overarches some part or all of sociological theory. All three types involve the systematic study of sociological theory; they differ mainly in terms of their objectives in that study.

Although metatheorizing takes place in other fields (Connolly, 1973; Radnitzky, 1973; Fiske & Schweder, 1986; Noblit & Hare, 1988), it is particularly characteristic of sociology. The prevalence of metatheorizing in sociology is rooted in the discipline's ontology of the social world. Sociologists deal with a subject matter that is culturally diverse and historically specific (Calhoun, 1992). The human world consists of a multitude of meaningful contexts in which social reality is being defined and redefined by individuals located within different segments of a given social structure. The existence of multiple and contradictory meanings, values, and interests both within and across cultural boundaries invalidates many universal truth claims. Furthermore, the meaning context of a given social structure is not invariant.

Each generation, or each cohort within a generation, reconstructs the complex sociocultural world as its members interact with one another and with the changing historical contingencies in which they find themselves. The mutability of meaning contexts and social practices makes the laws of society inconstant. The persistent failure to discover universal truth and invariant laws in the social world has informed the metatheoretical consciousness of many sociological theorists.

Second, in the realm of sociology, the knower and the known are intricately interconnected. Sociologists are an integral part of the social reality they attempt to theorize. Being encapsulated in a unique cultural tradition, located within a given sociopolitical structure, and affected by various personal interests in the life world, no sociologist is able to escape the grip of certain types of prejudice and bias that come with their situatedness. As a result, theoretical stances taken in sociological discourse are invariably bound up with practical options in life. The clashes of multiple paradigms and grand narratives competing for authenticity and symbolic power in the realm of sociological theorizing create a perfect condition for the emergence of metatheoretical discourse. "The ground for the possibility of metatheory is the multiplicity of theorization in sociology, which permits a second-level theorization about the process of constituting and the form of the theoretical object" (Weinstein & Weinstein, 1992, p. 140).

Third, in sociology not only is the knower related to the known, but theory also is integrated with practice. As the knowledge of a situation affects the decision of an actor, social theory constitutes an essential part of the condition of social action. Social theories do more than explain social reality; they define situations for the members of a society and orient them in action. Thus, "discourse *about* society reflects and engenders discourse *within* society" (Brown, 1992, p. 237), and "accepting a theory can itself transform what that theory bears on" (Taylor, 1985, p. 101). This constitutive power of theory obliges many sociologists to engage in metatheorizing in order to monitor the impact of theory on the social world and to point out the need to change theories in light of changes in that world.

Finally, social theory is embedded not only in the social world of academia but also of the larger society. As a result, there are a series of larger forces that impinge on, even control, social theory. Metatheorizing serves to alert theorists to the existence of these forces as well as to the need to resist them. As Bourdieu puts it,

> it continually turns back onto itself the scientific weapons it produces. It is fundamentally reflexive in that it uses the knowledge it gains of the social determinations that may bear upon it ... in an attempt to master and neutralize their effects. (Bourdieu, in Wacquant, 1996, pp. 226–227)

The coming of age of metatheorizing in American sociology can be traced to the collapse of the dominant sociological paradigm during the 1960s. The social facts paradigm, especially its theoretical component, Parsonsian functionalism, had dominated American sociology for more than two decades before it was seriously challenged by two rival paradigms: the social definition and the social behavior paradigms (Ritzer, 1975). The emergence of a multiparadigmatic structure in sociology in the late 1960s destroyed the unity of the discipline and fragmented sociological research.[1] There was a widespread feeling that a general crisis of sociology was on the horizon (Gouldner, 1970). It was this sense of imminent disciplinary crisis that reinvigorated interest in metastudy. "Thus, only as the discipline discovered its consolidated paradigm—system—in grave difficulty was it tempted to open the Pandora's box that was the sociology of sociology" (Friedrichs, 1970, p. 31).[2]

---

[1] For one effort at a partial reconstruction of a more unified perspective, see Ritzer (1981).

[2] The "sociology of sociology" is an older and largely discredited concept. To distinguish more recent work from the

PHILOSOPHICAL APPROACHES
TO METATHEORIZING IN SOCIOLOGY

Metatheoretical reflections on theoretical practice often take place within a given philosophical orientation. In contemporary sociology, there are four broad approaches to metatheory that differ in their reflections on the purposes, processes, and products of sociological
theorizing (we will relate these four approaches to the three more specific types discussed
above at the close of this section). According to the nature of their philosophical orientation,
these four approaches to metatheory can be labeled *positivist*, *hermeneutic*, *critical*, and
postmodern, respectively, with each advocating a distinctive type of sociological theorizing
(see Table 6.1).[3]

Positivist Metatheorizing

Those who engage in positivist metatheorizing believe that the goal of sociological
theorizing is to discover universal laws of the social. Theory is seen as nothing but a concise
summary of such laws. The following quotations from Zetterberg (1954/1963) best represent
this perspective:

> I want to pursue sociological theory in the sense of systematically organized law-like propositions
> about society and social life. As a reminder that this is a different breed of animal, I shall speak of it
> as "theoretical sociology" rather than "social theory" (p. 5)

> The assumption here is that sociology will eventually discover a small number of propositions that
> are valid in several diverse contexts.... This approach represents what we see as the main task of
> the sociological theorist—that is, the discovery of general propositions. (pp. 8–9)

For positivist metatheorists, therefore, the goal of theorizing is to discover general laws of
human society and to put them together systematically in the form of sociological theories that
are distinguishable from discursive social theories. Positivist metatheorists study extant theories to assess the degree to which they live up to the scientific model.

In recent years a mechanism-based approach to theorizing has emerged as an alternative
to the search for general laws of society. This approach "seeks to explicate the social
mechanisms that generate and explain observed associations between events" (Hedstrom &
Swedberg, 1998, p. 1). Theories of social mechanisms are distinguished from variable-based
statistical analysis on the one hand and narrative accounts of unique events on the other. The
objective of this approach is to discover causal mechanisms capable of explaining a wide
range of social situations. Mechanisms are a special type of causal laws that operate in systems
like biology, machines, and human society (Luhmann, 1995). A mechanism generates a
predictable outcome in a given environment. In the sense that like mechanisms produce like
outcomes in like environments, theories of social mechanisms are nomological in nature.

Positivist metatheorists believe that universal laws of society can be discovered if
theorists employ the correct theoretical methodology. The reason that so few, if any, universal
laws of society have been found is mainly because of sociologists' "ignorance about what

---

atheoretical "navel-gazing" of the sociology of sociology, it is now common to use the concept of metasociology to
refer to more contemporary work of this genre that seeks to overcome some of the early weaknesses of the sociology
of sociology.

[3]Bear in mind that these are "ideal types" and therefore that practicing metatheorists often engage in two or more of
these types simultaneously.

TABLE 6.1. Typology of Philosophical Orienations, Sociological Theories, and Sociological Metatheories

Type of philosophical orientations	Type of first-order sociological theories	Type of metatheoretical reflections on sociological theorizing		
		Purpose	Process	Products
Positivism	Nomological	To discover universal social laws	Methodological codification	Theoretical accumulation
Hermeneutics	Interpretative	To understand intersubjective meanings	Fusion of existential horizons	Enlightenment
Critical	Normative	To seek social justice	Social praxis	Human emancipation
Postmodernism	Relativistic	To construct local narratives	Deconstruction	Delegitimation

scientific knowledge should look like and how it is created" (Reynolds, 1971, p. 163). This belief in scientific methodology led to the launching of a theory construction movement in sociology in the 1950s (Zhao, 1996). The objective of this movement was to codify the procedures of sociological theorizing by imposing on the discipline a verificational approach to theory construction (Merton, 1949/1957/1968). Theories were to be verified by testing the hypotheses derived from them against empirical facts. Although some have declared the movement a failure (Hage, 1994), efforts to look for the proper methodology for discovering the laws of the social continue (Freese, 1980; Turner, 1989).

Positivist metatheorists often seek to evaluate theoretical progress in terms of the accumulation of empirically tested theories. Theoretical accumulation is taken

> to mean that certain fundamental and crucial problems in theory have been resolved or superseded in such a way as to permit more general, sophisticated and systematic theory to develop as the framework for research activity within the sociology community. (Turner, 1989, p. 131)

David Wagner (1984) broadens the criteria of theory assessment to include the following five dimensions of theoretical development: elaboration, variation, proliferation, integration, and competition. Using these criteria, Wagner is able to show that cumulative theoretical growth is not only possible but also occurs frequently in contemporary sociology.

Hermeneutic Metatheorizing

The positivist approach to theorizing (and metatheorizing) has been criticized by hermeneutic metatheorists who argue that the aim of sociological theorizing is not to uncover universal laws of society but to interpret the meanings of human action and to understand the contextualized life world in which human action takes place. As Taylor (1985) put it:

> There is a constant temptation to take natural science theory as a model for social theory: that is, to see theory as offering an account of underlying processes and mechanisms of society, and as providing the basis of a more effective planning of social life. But for all the superficial analogies, social theory can never really occupy this role. (p. 91)

> Social theory is ... concerned with finding a more satisfactory fundamental description of what is happening. The basic question of all social theory is in a sense: what is really going on? (p. 91)

The hermeneutic position on sociological theorizing gives rise to a different methodological approach to theoretical development. Failure of interpretation and inability to understand the life world of others are primarily attributed to the lack of intuitions and to differences in the way of living. As Taylor (1985, p. 5) pointed out, hermeneutic understanding requires a certain measure of insight that is inherently "unformalizable," for the gap in intuitions is a result of "divergent options in politics and life." In order to understand others, one needs to sharpen one's intuitions; but to sharpen one's intuitions, one has to change one's way of life or to live in a way that allows for greater comprehension of others. "Thus, in the sciences of man insofar as they are hermeneutic there can be a valid response to 'I don't understand' which takes the form, not only 'develop your intuitions,' but more radically 'change yourself' " (Taylor, 1985, p. 54). Sociological theorizing is, in this sense, an effort to foster the "fusion of horizons" in social life (Gadamer, 1975).

The criterion used by hermeneutic metatheorists for studying and evaluating theory is not the accumulation of nomological knowledge, but the existential enlightenment derived from an interpretation and the new light an interpretive theory sheds on the understanding of self and society. As understanding is an effort to place oneself "within a process of tradition, in which past and present are constantly fused" (Gadamer, 1975, p. 258), knowing is inherently a historical process. Truth is not the imposition of theorists' interpretation on society, nor is it the removal of theorists' subjective bias in order to let social facts "speak for themselves." Truth is rather defined by the value an interpretation has for the comprehension of the knower's own being in the world (Hoy, 1978). Good sociological theories then should provide people with a type of knowledge that enables them to see a new horizon of life and to advance beyond their current understanding of themselves and their relationships with others. Hermeneutic metatheorists study and assess theory from this point of view.

Critical Metatheorizing

Critical metatheorists differ from both positivist and hermeneutic metatheorists in seeing sociological theorizing as a form of social practice involving an integration of social analysis and political action. Most Marxian and critical metatheorists belong to this camp. For them, sociological theory does not focus on the answer to the question of "What is" but rather "What ought to be." The purpose of sociological theorizing is to articulate and advocate positions for social action. Steven Seidman (1991, p. 132) describes this metatheoretical position in the following way:

> Social theories are typically closely connected to contemporary social conflicts and public debates. These narratives aim not only to clarify an event or a social configuration but also to shape its outcome—perhaps by legitimating one outcome or imbuing certain actors, actions, and institutions with historical importance while attributing to other social forces malicious, demonic qualities. Social theory relates moral tales that have practical significance; they embody the will to shape history.

Instead of searching for the objective and universally valid laws of society, or the intersubjective interpretations of contextualized meanings, critical theorists (and metatheorists) advocate social justice and seek to actualize the advocated theory through praxis.

Critical metatheorists see the processes of theorizing as "enter[ing] constitutively into the world they describe" (Giddens, 1987, p. 20). By advocating "what *ought to* be there," instead of uncovering "what *is* out there," sociological theorizing becomes "a mode of altering reality, not by the direct application of energy to objects, but by the creation of discourse which changes reality through the mediation of thought and action" (Bitzer, 1968, p. 4). Since the aim of theorizing is no longer to make social theory correspond to the social world but to make the social world "conform to" social theory, the success of theorizing is marked by the actualization of what is advocated rather than by the verification of what is uncovered. Sociological theorizing thus becomes a form of social practice, where the emphasis is on the advocacy of reality rather than the discovery of reality, on the actualization of ideas rather than the verification of ideas, on manipulation rather than confirmation.

To the critical metatheorists, the criterion for evaluating the outcomes of theorizing is neither theoretical accumulation nor existential enlightenment, but the degree of emancipation of the oppressed that could be brought about by the theory. The integration of knowing and action in the practice of sociological theorizing renders the positivist approach to theory verification inapplicable. The emphasis on emancipation by ways of changing the object of theorizing rather than on enlightening the knowing subjects also makes the hermeneutic criterion inadequate, for theory as practice can be validated only by the impact the theory produces on practice. "To test the theory in practice means here not to see how well the theory describes the practices as a range of independent entities; but rather to judge how practices fare when informed by the theory" (Taylor, 1985, p. 113). Although social theory alone cannot bring about the success of social practice, social practice cannot succeed without social theory. To test the validity of a social theory is thus to examine the contribution that the theory makes to the outcome of a given social practice.

Postmodern Metatheory

Postmodern metatheorizing marks a major departure from the above three forms of metatheory, which justify their positions on the basis of some kind of "grand narratives." Thus for the positivist the end result of metatheorizing is universal laws; for the hermeneuticist it is intersubjectivity and for the critical theorist the end product is social justice. Postmodern metatheorizing, on the other hand, rejects such grand narratives. It has no ultimate goal. Rather, it is in favor of continually deconstructing grand theories and delegitimating meta-discourses. It may involve the construction of local narratives, but only to be deconstructed once they are created.

Two quotations from Lyotard (1989) illustrate the bases for postmodern metatheorizing:

> I will use the term *modern* to designate any science that legitimates itself with reference to a metadiscourse of this kind making an explicit appeal to some grand narrative, such as the dialectics of Spirit, the hermeneutics of meaning, the emancipation of the rational or working subject, or the creation of wealth. (p. xxiii)

> Simplifying to the extreme, I define *postmodern* as incredulity toward metanarratives.... The narrative function is losing its functions, its great hero, its great dangers, its great voyages, and its great goal. It is being dispersed in clouds of narrative language elements—narrative, but also denotative, prescriptive, descriptive, and so on. Conveyed within each cloud are pragmatic valencies specific to its kind. Each of us lives at the intersection of many of these. However, we do not necessarily establish stable language combinations, and the properties of the ones we do establish are not necessarily communicable. (p. xxiv)

Since the postmodern approach, unlike the other forms of metatheorizing, is relatively new, we devote the bulk of the remainder of this chapter to a discussion of it.

Before we turn to that approach, we need to examine how the four broad philosophical approaches delineated above relate to the three types of metatheorizing discussed earlier. It is clear that each of the first three philosophical types—positivist, hermeneutic, critical—would subsume these three specific types. That is, positivists, hermeneuticists, and critical theorists would all study theory to gain a more profound understanding of it, to produce new theories, and to create new metatheories. However, there would be differences among them in terms of their relative emphasis on the three types and the ways in which they would practice each. For example, while critical theorists would share these three goals, the accomplishment of each would be subordinated to the broader objective of transforming society.

While the first three philosophical approaches fit well with the three more specific types of metatheorizing, the same cannot be said about the fourth, postmodern approach. The three specific types all share a very modern orientation toward progress in understanding theory and metatheory. Postmodernists tend to reject the modern notion of progress in general, as well as in metatheoretical work. Postmodernists who study theory tend to have a very different sense of the objectives of such study. In the next section we will begin to get a sense of those objectives as well as of a variety of specific ideas associated with a postmodern approach.

POSTMODERN METATHEORIZING

As indicated above, this section will be devoted to a discussion of a variety of ideas derived from postmodernism that are of relevance to metatheorizing in sociology. While postmodernists oriented to metatheoretical work will find these of direct relevance, the other types of metatheorists also may well find ideas here that are of utility to them. Specifically, we will focus on such postmodern ideas as text, intertextuality, discourse, and deconstruction (including decentering).

Text

Postmodernists accord great importance to the notion of "texts." This is seemingly not problematic from the point of view of metatheoretical work, since metatheorists would certainly acknowledge that they study theoretical texts. Nevertheless, postmodernists and poststructuralists tend to write about texts in a very specific way. For example, Roland Barthes (1977, pp. 155–164; see also Mowitt, 1992), in his essay "From Work to Text," formulates a seven-point manifesto in which he distinguishes "the work" from "the Text."

First of all, Barthes points out that while other critics posit the ontological reality of the work (see below for a discussion of the work and metatheorist's traditional concern with it) as an object of consumption by the reader, the perspective of textuality consists of a methodological imperative that encourages the role of the active, productive reader. According to Barthes, "the work is a fragment of substance, occupying part of the space of books (in a library, for example), the Text is a methodological field ... or again, *the Text is experienced in an activity of production*" (1977, p. 157; Barthes' emphasis), while "the work is normally the object of a consumption" (1977, p. 161). Metatheorists have tended to consume theoretical works, but this orientation accords the metatheorist (and other readers) a much more active role in the production of the text. In the main this implies that metatheorizing can be a much more active and creative enterprise.

Second, for Barthes "the Text is that which goes to the limit of the rules of enunciation (rationality, readability, etc.) ... the Text tries to place itself very exactly *behind* the limit of the *doxa*" (1977, pp. 157–158; Barthes' emphasis). In other words, embracing textuality entails pushing metatheorizing to the limits of rationality and readability in order to gain a new, often critical, perspective on prevailing opinion. A critical orientation would not be new to metatheoretical work, but pushing the limits of rationality and readability would. Metatheorists, like most social theorists, have tended to be slavish in their efforts to make rational arguments and to put them in as readable a form as possible (at least in comparison to postmodernists). Playing with the limits of rationality and readability might lead to some creative new metatheoretical work.

Third, the Text *plays* with the "*infinity* of the signifier" while "the work closes on a signified" (1977, p. 158; Barthes' emphasis). In this passage, Barthes shifts the emphasis of criticism from the signified, or the idea or concept to which words purportedly refer, to the signifier—the "sound-image" or the word itself. Barthes here opposes the referentiality of the work (and metatheorists traditional analysis of it) to the poetics of textuality. Metatheoretical work has been notably short on such "poetics" and more poetic metatheorizing might be refreshing, to say nothing of offering the possibility of novel insights.

Fourth, according to Barthes, "The Text is plural ... it answers not to an interpretation, not even a liberal one, but to an explosion, a dissemination" (1977, p. 159). Here Barthes argues that in his version of textual criticism the productive activity of the reader and the emphasis on the signifier lead to proliferation of meaning, rather than to a consensus on the essential meaning of a work. This would mark a significant shift for metatheorists who have traditionally been oriented to finding the "essence" of a work or theorist under study, as well as coming to a consensus about that essence. Instead, Barthes' position here implies the search for many different views on the essence or meaning of a text.

Fifth, Barthes contends that his orientation toward the Text deposes the authority of the author in favor of the creativity of the reader. "The author is the reputed father and the owner of his work" while "As for the Text, it reads without the inscription of the Father" (1977, pp. 160–161). This has implications similar to those of Barthes' first point. Metatheorists, as readers, would accord much less importance to what the author of a theoretical text intended and this would serve to free their own interpretive skills.

Sixth, Barthes brings together the above points: "The Text (if only by its frequent 'unreadability') decants the work (the work permitting) from its consumption and gathers it up as play, activity, production, practice" (1977, p. 162). Closely related to previous points, metatheorists are not only freed to do their interpretations, but also to do them more actively, even playfully. Playfulness has been something virtually completely absent from metatheoretical work and freeing the analyst to deal with texts under study more playfully might yield unusual and useful insights.

Finally, Barthes suggests that his orientation toward the Text enables the reader to experience *jouissance*, an erotic enjoyment, both "extreme and disconcerting" (Sturrock, 1979, p. 72). "As for the Text, it is bound to *jouissance*, that is to a pleasure without separation" (1977, p. 164; Barthes' emphasis). It is hard to think of the kinds of texts studied by metatheorists as yielding "erotic enjoyment," but nonetheless metatheorizing that reflects more enjoyment, more pleasure would at least be welcome and perhaps produce some interesting new perspectives.

In short, the Text, as a methodological orientation to reading and writing, rather than an ontological reality, encourages action, productivity, and play, while the work exists as authority, an object of consumption, and of closure. Metatheorists, however, have tended to focus on "works," especially "masterworks"; that is, important pieces authored by specific social thinkers. The latter often leads to metatheoretical work that focuses on specific works and how they relate to the biographical characteristics of the author (see the 25 essays on theorists and their theories in Ritzer, 2000). Thus, one might seek to relate Weber's interest in bureaucracy, Calvinism and the conflict between them to the orientations of his parents and their fundamental disagreements (Mitzman, 1969). This involves an effort to find the fundamental "meaning" or explanation of a work in the essential character and experiences of the author. Postmodernism generally points us away from the idea that a work has an essential meaning. If we take Barthes' notion of Text seriously, this would lead metatheorists to write about sociological theory in a way that would highlight the plurality of the classics, for example. This might provide a fruitful way of pursuing metatheory as a prelude to the development of new theories, or Ritzer's M_p (1991b). In addition, the notion of textuality leads us away from a focus on the author and to the text and its relationship to other texts (*intertextuality*; see below). As Jameson (1991, p. 77) puts it, "the autonomous work ... along with the old autonomous subject or ego— seems to have vanished, to have been volatized." The notion of the Text encourages theorists to view instances of theory as a tissue or woven fabric in which many "quotations without inverted commas" form layers of signification and in which many "influences" interpenetrate (Barthes, 1977, p. 160). In this view, the interweaving of many threads of theory recombines signifiers in such a way that the Text allows for infinite rereading and rewriting.

Intertextuality

While textuality and intertextuality are not new to metatheorists, what is new to them is the idea that they ought *not* to search for the underlying meaning of a work, especially through a greater understanding of the author of that work. After all, virtually all metatheorists have been modernists committed to a search for just such an underlying meaning. A good example of someone who devoted much attention to the thinker as a way of getting at the hidden meaning of a text is Alvin Gouldner (1965, pp. 170–171) who argued, "Some social scientists are interested in studying industrial workers; some study physicians; and still others, drug addicts and prostitutes. I happen to be curious about social theorists, as part of a sociology of social science." More specifically, Gouldner looks at such things as a sociological theorists' training, institutional affiliations, career patterns, and positions within sociology. Gouldner believes that it is important to understand the theorist if we want to understand the theory, since "much of theory-work begins with an effort to make sense of one's experience" (Gouldner, 1970, p. 484). This is the kind of perspective that postmodernists would say is badly in need of "decentering" (see the discussion of decentering below).

Although not to this point done to any great extent by postmodernists, there have been many intertextual analyses in metatheory. Thus, in the volume mentioned above (Ritzer, 2000), the authors also relate theorists' work to their intellectual context, including related works. More generally, some metatheorists (e.g., Sorokin, 1928; Tiryakian, 1979, 1986) have looked at "schools of thought" within social theory and that implies, among other things, a concern with what serves to unify various works associated with specific theoretical approaches as well as what differentiates them as a set from other theoretical schools. Similarly, the various paradigmatic analyses of sociology have tended to focus on commonalities among sets of theoretical works as well as what serves to differentiate one set from other sets of such work. Let us use Ritzer's work on sociology's multiple paradigms (1975) and architectonics (1991b) to illustrate this point.

Ritzer argued that sociology is a multiple paradigm science composed of three major paradigms: social facts, social definition, and social behavior. Each paradigm is characterized by, among other things, a distinctive set of theories. Thus, the social facts paradigm, given its focus on Durkheimian social facts, encompasses structural functionalism, conflict theory, and systems theory. An intertextual analysis of these theories reveals a number of commonalities, especially the fact that they all take social facts as their focal concern. The social definition paradigm encompasses such theories as action theory, symbolic interactionism, phenomenological sociology, and ethnomethodology. Intertextual analysis of these theories indicates that they share a concern for the definition of the situation and resulting action. Finally, the social behavior paradigm focuses on relatively automatic behavior and intertextual analysis reveals that exchange theory and behavioral sociology (and perhaps now rational choice theory) share such an orientation. Thus, intertextual analysis reveals three theory clusters, the components of each of which have a number of important things in common. Furthermore, this intertextual analysis reveals fundamental differences among the three clusters of theory and these differences are at least as consequential as the similarities within clusters.

Similarly, in Ritzer's work on architectonics he sought to outline the six basic elements of one basic architectonic through an intertextual analysis of the work of Marx, Weber, Simmel and Berger, and Luckmann. This revealed a basic underlying commonality in their work. At the same time, it is suggested that there are other architectonics in social theory that serve to distinguish among groups of social theorists. This work on paradigms and architectonics illustrates the point that metatheorists have long been practitioners of intertextual analysis.

However, while metatheorists have done a great deal of intertextual work, it usually is with the objective of finding the deeper meaning underlying the texts being studied. The notions of a paradigm and an architectonic carry with them that sort of implication. In uncovering sociology's basic paradigms, one is seeking to get at some hidden but essential meanings that are crucial to understanding the commonalities among theories and differences between sets of theories. More generally, the overall structure of sociology's paradigms reveals essential characteristics of the field as a whole such as the fact that because there are multiple paradigms, there is no single dominant paradigm and therefore normal science is all but impossible. In getting at the architectonic that undergirds the work of a group of theorists, the metatheorist is similarly getting at the idea that there is a hidden but essential commonality that helps to unify their contributions and to account for similarities in their substantive work.

Discourse

Most scholars associate the analysis of discourse with the work of Michel Foucault. Metatheorists interested in the analysis of discourse would likely find Foucault's (1969/1971/ 1976) ideas quite useful. In *The Arcaeology of Knowledge*, Foucault discusses discourse in many different ways, and eventually settles on a rather cryptic definition: "We shall call discourse a group of statements in so far as they belong to the same discursive formation ... it is made up of a limited number of statements for which a group of conditions of existence can be defined" (1969/1971/1976, p. 117). And again, "the term discourse can be defined as the group of statements that belong to a single system of formation" (1969/1971/1976, p. 107). At another point in the same book, Foucault discusses discourse as a way of organizing concepts, regrouping objects of study, and types of enunciation, the combination of which produces themes or theories, which he also calls "strategies" (1969/1971/1976, p. 64). In contrast to Roland Barthes' ideas about the "Text," the analysis of discourse, while possibly employing the strategies of textuality and intertextuality, raises the level of analysis. The analysis of discourse leads scholars to examine the complex constellations of discourse that emerge under specific social and historical conditions of existence. As such, the analysis of discourse studies "texts" as artifacts and "monuments" (Foucault, 1969/1971/1976) and as evidence of particular historical discursive formations. In other words, Foucault's emphasis was on the "text" as evidence, rather than on the "Text" as the site of "collaboration" between writers and readers (see Barthes, 1977, p. 163).

Foucault's work would lead metatheorists to focus on the statements, relationships among statements, discursive formations and the rules by which they are formed, the contradictions that exist within discursive formations, and the changing nature of discourse (especially its discontinuities) over time. This, of course, leads the metatheorist away from looking at the relationship between author and work and in the direction of looking at theories as social and linguistic formations.

Foucault's later method of genealogy is famously concerned with the relationship between knowledge and power and would clearly lead metatheorists in the direction of a greater concern for the relationship between power in the field of sociology and the fate of paradigms, theories and the like. It also would relate the fate and notoriety of theories to issues of power in the larger society. Thus, for example, Huaco (1986) has linked the rise and fall of structural functionalism to the changing nature of the position of the United States in the world order.

Deconstruction

At bottom, deconstruction, as practiced by Jacques Derrida (1974, 1978) and others (e.g., Paul de Man, Gayatari Spivak), is a form of textual criticism that scrutinizes the ways in which texts are constructed. In other words, one can think of deconstruction as the "reverse engineering" of texts. A deconstructionist critic begins with the finished product, a text or constellation of texts, and proceeds by studying the ways in which various literary devices and strategies of argumentation give the text the impression of working toward a unified coherent whole (as well as working against itself) (Hoy, 1985, p. 44). Several aspects of deconstruction can be linked to metatheorizing[4]:

1. Decentering. The operation known as "decentering" has many fruitful applications in postmodern and poststructuralist thought. First, decentering consists of the effort to dislodge the Cartesian fully conscious, knowable and knowing self from its position of authority in Western thought. "I think, therefore I am" entrenches an autonomous subject as both the center of knowledge and being. Postmodern and poststructuralist theory is only the most recent attempt to decenter the rational, autonomous subject. Derrida, in his lecture "Structure, Sign, and Play in the Discourse of the Human Sciences," sees precursors to his own deconstructionist project in "the Nietzschean critique of metaphysics," "the Freudian critique of self-presence," and "the Heideggerean destruction of metaphysics" (1978, p. 280). To this list others might add Saussure's reformulation of linguistics, which influenced Claude Levi-Strauss's (1966) statement to the effect that "I believe the ultimate goal of the human sciences to be not to constitute, but to dissolve man" (p. 247). Moreover, we can find this theme in other high structuralist texts, such as Roland Barthes's essay "The Death of the Author" (1977, pp. 142–148). "To give a text an Author is to impose a limit on that text, to furnish it with a final signified, to close the writing," but to remove the author as the autonomous subject behind the text is to "liberate what may be called an anti-theological activity, an activity that is truly revolutionary since to refuse to fix meaning is, in the end, to refuse God and his hypostases— reason, science, law" (1977, p. 147). Louis Althusser's structuralist Marxism adopts a some-

---

[4]This list is derived, in part, from Spivak (1974, p. lxxvii).

what similar position. Decentering forces such ultimate *authorities* as God, the Author, Consciousness, and Man into a field of mutually constitutive relationships rather than leaving them at the apex of a hierarchy of knowledge.

Michel Foucault's work elaborates a slightly different type of decentering. In the introduction to Foucault's methodological work, *The Archaeology of Knowledge*, Foucault distinguishes his project from that of previous historians and philosophers by arguing: "A total description draws all phenomena around a single centre—a principle, a meaning, a spirit, a world-view, an overall shape; a general history, on the contrary, would deploy the space of dispersion" (1969/1971/1976, p. 10). Foucault replaces "drawing in to the center" with a "space of dispersion," and in doing so, he initiates a shift of perspective from centers to fields of relationships in which the margins play an important role.

This would lead metatheorists, among other things, to question the centrality of the thinkers most often included in the canon and to seek out important theorists largely if not completely ignored by the discipline. One sees this most commonly among minority groups where there are ongoing efforts to resuscitate thinkers ignored in their time and to this day because of their minority group status. This is especially notable in feminist theory where efforts are being made to make the case for the central importance of such thinkers as Harriet Martineau (Hoecker-Drysdale, 2000), Charlotte Perkins Gilman (Lemert, 2000), and Marianne Weber (Lengermann & Niebrugge-Brantley, 1998). But efforts to reassess the centrality of long-ignored theorists is not restricted to minority group members; one often sees efforts to bring to the fore heretofore ignored white male thinkers. For example, with the increase in interest in the sociology of consumption there is a resurgence of interest in Thorstein Veblen (Ritzer, Murphy, & Wiedenhoft, 2001; Diggins, 1999). All such efforts are useful, if for no other reason than they prevent us from falling into the habit of trotting out the same old theorists and theories on all occasions. Maximally, we often do find that a forgotten thinker really deserves a more detailed second look.

2. Locating the promising marginal text. This is obviously related to the notion of decentering. Traditionally, metatheorists would seek out a *central* text and argue that it best exemplifies the thinking of a theorist or of a school of thought. Thus, one might identify *Economy and Society* (Weber, 1921/1968) or *The Protestant Ethic and the Spirit of Capitalism* (Weber, 1904–1905/1958) as the text that best gets at the essence (a notion postmodernists would reject) of Weber's thinking. However, the logic of deconstructionism would lead the analyst away from such canonical works and in the direction of more marginal works that might prove more revealing. Thus, it might turn out that a letter written by Weber, or a book review, or even a secondary work [say, *The Agrarian Sociology of Ancient Civilizations* (Weber, 1896–1906/1976)] offers unparalleled insights into or unearths contradictions within Weber's *oeuvre*.

Many of the same kinds of things can be done in reinterpreting schools of thought. In any school, there are always key texts that are defined as standing at the core of a given theoretical perspective. A good example is Merton's (1949/1968) essay, "Manifest and Latent Functions," which is usually viewed as the central document in structural–functional theory. However, great dividends, including a better understanding of that theory, might result if a metatheorist looked at less well-known pieces by Merton or better yet positioned Merton's work in a field of discourse or space of dispersion that included the marginal texts and perspectives against which structural functionalism defined itself. Even more might be gained by the study of long-ignored texts in the structural–functional tradition.

And of course, there are the theories that never made it or were central at one time, but have lost their following. Among the latter, as mentioned above, action theory comes to mind as a theory that was of some significance earlier this century but is all but forgotten today. Revisiting that theory and some of the major thinkers associated with it (e.g., Florian Znaniecki) might pay enormous dividends.

This form of decentering also could be practiced more microscopically. Certain passages of specific works often are presented by the authors in such a way that they are made to seem of central importance. Over the years, secondary analysts have tended to emphasize those passages or to enshrine other passages as being of key importance. In this context, deconstructionism leads one away from the familiar passages and into ignored portions of the text or perhaps rarely read footnotes. A similar implication applies to the secondary literature on a theory or theorist. Certain pieces [e.g., Parsons's (1937) *The Structure of Social Action*] achieve their own canonical status and are almost always cited by later analysts. However, the secondary literature on the most important theorists is vast and a systematic search of it may well turn up some interpretive gems in out-of-the-way places. It can also reveal weaknesses and distortions in the canonical interpretive work.

3. Disclosing the undecidable moment. This takes us more into the history of social theory and an analysis of some of the courses taken and, more importantly from the point of view of deconstructionism, *not* taken by social theory. At the microlevel this might lead us into the biographies of specific theorists and why they chose one direction rather than another. For example, we might want to study why Talcott Parsons chose to move in the direction of the macrooriented structural functionalism rather than pursuing the microimplications of his early analysis of the unit act and of action theory. At a more macrolevel we might be led to wonder why symbolic interactionism in the 1930s and 1940s moved in the more interpretive direction championed by Blumer rather than following Mead's propensity toward a more realist orientation. There are clearly many key moments in this history of social theory, and while we may never be able to "decide" issues unequivocally, it is useful to plumb these time periods for insights into directions chosen and perhaps more importantly those not taken.

4. Reversing the resident hierarchy, only to displace it. This idea, as we will see as a specific form of decentering, has at least four implications for metatheoretical work. First, the reversal of hierarchies in theoretical vocabularies can be taken as an ironic intervention in sociological theory in which theorists realize the inadequacy or fatuity of their characterizations (White, 1978, pp. 1–25). Richard Rorty (1989, pp. 73–95), for example, exalts the reversals and negations of the ironist because they lead us to doubt received theoretical vocabularies and they remind us that things can always be seen in different ways. Clearly the leading schools of thought or theoretical vocabularies are not dominant because they are somehow the "best" or most representative of social reality. A great deal of social labor goes into producing a dominant way of theorizing, and the reversals recommended by deconstructionists help us to see that the received hierarchies are in many ways inadequate or distorted.

Second, there is clearly a hierarchy of schools of sociological theory and there is a tendency to devote most attention to the leading schools. This suggests that what metatheorists need to do is focus more attention on the most marginal of schools (this is another version of decentering) for their marginality may tell us a great deal about the theoretical system in which they exist. Furthermore, their very marginality may make them far easier to study than high-ranking theoretical perspectives. This is traceable to the fact that those associated with low-ranking perspectives have little to hide, while thinkers linked with the premier schools have a vested interest in concealing things that may adversely affect their exalted status.

Third, within every school, even those lowest in the hierarchy, there is a hierarchy of thinkers associated with the perspective. Instead of focusing on the leading thinkers associated with such a perspective, the goal would be to devote more attention to the work of those with little or no status in the area (again, a decentering move).

Fourth, and similarly, specific ideas have come to be seen as of central importance in every theoretical perspective. These specific ideas, for example, those associated with Merton's functional paradigm, tend to come to the fore any time a given theory is examined or discussed. However, it is entirely possible that important ideas have been lost and a search for those marginal ideas could pay huge dividends. There is an unfortunate tendency to trot out the same old ideas (and theorists) any time a theoretical perspective is examined. This tendency can be counteracted by a continual effort to unearth ideas that have been shuffled to the bottom of the hierarchy or even lost to history (decentering, yet again).

All of this, as well as much else that involves decentering, relates to the idea of the "strength of the weak" associated with postmodern social theory (Genosko, 1994). This is usually applied to the "social" world (although Baudrillard proclaims the death of the social) and the idea that the masses, while lacking in power, actually exert their strength by luring (albeit not consciously) those in power into self-destructive acts. In de Certeau's (1984) work it involves the view that actors, especially consumers, while seemingly weak, actually have great power. In metatheorizing, this idea can be taken to mean that it is the seemingly weak theorists, theoretical perspectives, or concepts that actually exercise great power in social theory. Perhaps it is they and their weaknesses that play a greater role (in heretofore unexplored ways) in defining theory than obvious, more powerful candidates that always end up the focus of great attention.

However, the search for low-ranking schools, theorists, or ideas should not be turned into a routine or into a new reverse hierarchy. Deconstructionism leads to the idea that all such routines or hierarchies need to be continually displaced. Such an injunction prevents metatheoretical work from settling into any comfortable routines; any new construction immediately must be deconstructed.

It is this aspect of deconstructionism that has the most implications for metatheorizing. As modernists, most metatheorists have implicitly engaged in deconstruction, but almost always with the objective that they and/or those influenced by their work would engage in a process of reconstruction. This could involve the rebuilding of the theory they have just deconstructed or the use of the lessons learned to create an entirely new theoretical perspective. As modernists, most metatheorists would reject the idea of deconstruction in order to further deconstruct. Rather, they would be oriented to the modern view of progress toward the goal of the ultimate theoretical perspective. However, as with all modern notions, this seeks an end or closure of the theoretical "conversation" in the creation of that ultimate theory. The postmodern view is that the goal is not to end the conversation in some ultimate truth (since there is none), but rather to continually deconstruct in order to keep the conversation going (Rorty, 1979). Such an objective makes sense for metatheoretical work; in fact, it may be the *raison d'etre* for such work. One round of metatheoretical work may be seen as merely the basis for the next round of such work and not as aimed at some ultimate and conclusive objective. In these terms metatheorizing may be seen as the exercise *par excellence* in keeping the theoretical conversation going.

5. Dismantling in order to reconstitute what is already inscribed. Since postmodern social theory is inherently poststructuralist, this idea is not meant to imply that the already inscribed idea is the "essence" of a theoretical perspective and once it is uncovered our task as metatheorists is completed. Once that which is already inscribed is reconstituted, the "goal" (if one can think in terms of a "goal" from the point of view of deconstructionism) would be to seek to reconstitute that which is inscribed in what we have recently reconstituted. Again, there is a sense of metatheorizing as a never-ending process of deconstructing that which we have just deconstructed.

This encourages the metatheorist to see to it that the dismantling of a text in the practice of deconstruction leads to novel translations (or reconstitutions) of that text. In other words, it contributes to the poststructuralist view of the reading of texts as a process in which readers actively *construct* meanings rather than simply discover an intended meaning in a text.

The objective in this part of the essay has been to examine postmodern social theory for ideas that are of relevance to postmodern metatheorists and could be used by other metatheorists, as well. While it is possible to look at postmodern theory as a threat to modern forms of theorizing and metatheorizing, it also is possible to see it as offering an array of provocative new ideas that could be used by both. We adopt the latter view toward postmodern theory and see it as offering theorists and all types of metatheorists (and metatheorizing) a set of new ideas and tools that they can use in their work.

CONCLUSION

We have shown that metatheorizing is an integral part of theorizing in sociology. We have delineated four overarching philosophical frameworks within which sociological metatheorizing is practiced. Although positivists, hermeneuticists, and critical theorists would all study theory to gain a more profound understanding of it, to produce new theories, and to create new metatheories, there are differences among them in terms of their relative emphasis on the three specific types of metatheorizing (i.e., M_u, M_p, and M_o) and the ways in which they would practice each. For example, while critical theorists would share these three goals, the accomplishment of each would be subordinated to the broader objective of transforming society.

While the first three philosophical approaches fit well with the three more specific types of metatheorizing, the same cannot be said about the fourth, postmodern approach. The three specific types all share a very modern orientation toward progress in understanding theory and metatheory. Postmodernists tend to reject the modern notion of progress in general, as well as in metatheoretical work. Postmodernists who study theory tend to have a very different sense of the objectives of such study. While it is possible to look at postmodern theory as a threat to modern forms of theorizing and metatheorizing, it is also possible to see it as offering an array of provocative new ideas that could be used by both. In our exposition we have adopted the latter view toward postmodern theory and see it as offering theorists and all types of metatheorists (and metatheorizing) a set of new ideas and tools that can be used in their work.

REFERENCES

Antonio, R. J. (1991). Postmodern storytelling versus pragmatic truth-seeking: The discursive bases of social theory. *Sociological Theory, 9,* 154–163.

Barthes, R. (1977). *Image-music-text.* New York: Hill and Wang.

Bitzer, L. (1968). The rhetorical situation. *Philosophy and Rhetoric, 1,* 1–14.

Blalock, H. M., Jr. (1969). *Theory construction: From verbal to mathematical formulation.* Englewood Cliffs, NJ: Prentice Hall.

Bourdieu, P. (1971). Intellectual field and creative project. In M. F. D. Young (Ed.), *Knowledge and control* (pp. 161–188). London: Collier-Macmillan.

Brewer, J., & Hunter, A. (1989). *Multimethod research: A synthesis of style.* Newbury Park, CA: Sage.

Brown, R. H. (1992). Social science and society as discourse: Toward a sociology for civic competence. In S. Seidman & D. G. Wagner (Eds.), *Postmodernism and social theory* (pp. 223–243). Cambridge, MA: Blackwell.

Calhoun, C. (1992). Culture, history, and the problem of specificity in social theory. In S. Seidman & D. G. Wagner (Eds.), *Postmodernism and social theory* (pp. 244–288). Cambridge, MA: Blackwell.

Collins, R. (1986). Is 1980s sociology in the doldrums? *American Journal of Sociology, 91*, 1336–1355.

Comte, A. (1930/1942/1974). *The positive philosophy*. New York: AMS Press.

Connolly, W. E. (1973). Theoretical self-consciousness. *Polity, 6*, 5–36.

Cooper, H. M. (1984). *The integrative research review: A systematic approach*. Beverly Hills, CA: Sage.

de Certeau, M. (1984). *The practice of everyday life*. Berkeley and Los Angeles: University of California Press.

Derrida, J. (1974). *Of grammatology*. Baltimore: Johns Hopkins University Press.

Derrida, J. (1978). *Writing and difference*. Chicago. University of Chicago Press.

Diggins, J. P. (1999). *Thorstein Veblen: Theorist of the leisure class*. Princeton: Princeton University Press.

Dubin, R. (1969). *Theory building*. New York: The Free Press.

Eckberg, D. L., & Hill, L., Jr. (1979). The paradigm concept and sociology: A critical review. *American Sociological Review, 44*, 925–937.

Effrat, A. (1972). Power to the paradigms: An editorial introduction. *Sociological Inquiry, 42*, 3–33.

Fiske, D. W., & Schweder, R. A. (Eds.). (1986). *Metatheory in social science: Pluralism and subjectivities*. Chicago: University of Chicago Press.

Foucault, M. (1969/1971/1976). *The archaeology of knowledge and the discourse of language*. New York: Harper Colophon.

Foucault, M. (1966/1973). *The order of things: An archaeology of the human sciences*. New York: Vintage.

Freese, L. (Ed.). (1980). *Theoretical methods in sociology*. Pittsburgh: University of Pittsburgh Press.

Friedrichs, R. W. (1970). *A sociology of sociology*. New York: Free Press.

Fuhrman, E. R., & Snizek, W. (1990). Neither proscience nor antiscience: Metasociology as dialogue. *Sociological Forum, 5*, 17–36.

Furfey, P. H. (1965). *The scope and method of sociology: A metasociological treatise*. New York: Cooper Square.

Gadamer, H.-G. (1975). *Truth and method*. New York: Seabury Press.

Gibbs, J. P. (1972). *Sociological theory construction*. Hinsdale, IL: The Dryden Press.

Giddens, A. (1984). *The constitution of society: Outline of the theory of structuration*. Berkeley and Los Angeles: University of California Press.

Giddens, A. (1987). *Social theory and modern sociology*. Stanford, CA: Stanford University Press.

Genosko, G. (1994). *Baudrillard and signs: Signification ablaze*. London: Routledge.

Gouldner, A. (1965). *Enter Plato: Classical Greece and the origins of social theory*. New York: Basic Books.

Gouldner, A. (1970). *The coming crisis of Western sociology*. New York: Basic Books.

Hage, J. (1972). *Techniques and problems of theory construction in sociology*. New York: Wiley.

Hage, J. (Ed.). (1994). *Formal theory in sociology*. Albany, NY: State University of New York Press.

Hedstrom, P., & Swedberg, R. (Eds.). (1998). *Social mechanisms: An analytical approach to social theory*. New York: Cambridge University Press.

Hoecker-Drysdale, S. (2000). Harriet Martineau. In G. Ritzer (Ed.), *The Blackwell companion to major social theorists* (pp. 53–80). Oxford, England and Cambridge, MA: Blackwell.

Hoy, D. C. (1978). *The critical circle*. Berkeley: University of California Press.

Hoy, D. C. (1985). Jacques Derrida. In Q. Skinner (Ed.), *The return of grand theory in the human sciences* (pp. 43–64). Cambridge: Cambridge University Press.

Huaco, G. (1986). Ideology and general theory: The case of sociological functionalism. *Comparative Studies in Society and History, 28*, 34–54.

Hunter, J. E., & Schmidt, F. L. (1989). *Methods of meta-analysis: Correcting error and bias in research findings*. Newbury Park, CA: Sage.

Jameson, F. (1991). *Postmodernism, or, the cultural logic of late capitalism*. Durham, NC: Duke University Press.

Kuhn, T. (1962/1970). *The structure of scientific revolutions*, 2nd ed. Chicago: University of Chicago Press.

Levi-Strauss, C. (1966). *The savage mind*. Chicago: University of Chicago Press.

Lemert, C. (2000). Charlotte Perkins Gilman. In G. Ritzer (Ed.), *The Blackwell companion to major social theorists* (pp. 279–301). Oxford, England and Cambridge, MA: Blackwell.

Lengermann, P. M., & Niebrugge-Brantley, J. (Eds.). (1998). *The women founders: Sociology and social theory, 1830–1930*. New York: McGraw-Hill.

Levine, D. N. (1995). *Visions of the sociological tradition*. Chicago, IL: The University of Chicago Press.

Luhmann, N. (1995). *Social systems*. Stanford, CA: Stanford University Press.

Lzotard, J.-F. (1989). *The postmodern condition: A report on knowledge*. Minneapolis: University of Minnesota Press.

McMullin, E. (1970). The history and philosophy of science: A taxonomy. In R. H. Stuewer (Ed.), *Historical and philosophical perspectives of science* (pp. 12–67). Minneapolis: University of Minneapolis Press.

Merton, R. K. (1949/1957/1968). *Social theory and social structure*. New York: Free Press.

Mitzman, A. (1969). *The iron cage: An historical interpretation of Max Weber*. New York: Grosset and Dunlap.

Mowitt, J. (1992). *Text: The genealogy of an antidisciplinary object*. Durham, NC, and London: Duke University Press.

Mullins, N. C. (1971). *The art of theory construction and use*. New York: Harper & Row.

Noblit, G. W., & Hare, R. D. (1988). *Meta-ethnography: Synthesizing qualitative studies*. Newbury Park, CA: Sage.

Osterberg, D. (1988). *Metasociology: An inquiry into the origins and validity of social thought*. Oslo, Norway: Norwegian University Press.

Parsons, T. (1937). *The structure of social action*. New York: McGraw Hill.

Parsons, T. (1979/1980). On theory and metatheory. *Humboldt Journal of Social Relations, 7*, 5–16.

Radnitzky, G. (1973). *Contemporary schools of metascience*. Chicago: Henry Regnery.

Reynolds, P. D. (1971). *A primer in theory construction*. Indianapolis: Bobbs-Merrill.

Ritzer, G. (1975). *Sociology: A multiple paradigm science*. Boston, MA: Allyn and Bacon.

Ritzer, G. (1981). *Toward an integrated sociological paradigm: The search for an exemplar and an image of the subject matter*. Boston: Allyn and Bacon.

Ritzer, G. (1988). Sociological metatheory: A defense of a subfield by a delineation of its parameters. *Sociological Theory, 6*, 187–200.

Ritzer, G. (1990). Symposium: Metatheory: Its uses and abuses in contemporary sociology. *Sociological Forum, 5*, 1–74.

Ritzer, G. (1991a). Recent explorations in sociological metatheorizing. *Sociological Perspectives, 34*, 237–390.

Ritzer, G. (1991b). *Metatheorizing in sociology*. Lexington, MA: Lexington Books.

Ritzer, G. (Ed.). (1992). *Metatheorizing*. Newbury Park, CA: Sage.

Ritzer, G. (Ed.). (2000). *The Blackwell companion to major social theorists*. Oxford, England and Cambridge, MA: Blackwell.

Ritzer, G., Wiedenhoft, W., & Murphy, J. (2001). Thorstein Veblen in the age of hyperconsumption. In G. Ritzer (Ed.), *Fast food, credit cards and the cathedrals of consumption: Explorations in the sociology of consumption* (pp. 203–221). London: Sage.

Rorty, R. (1979). *Philosophy and the mirror of nature*. Princeton: Princeton University Press.

Rorty, R. (1989). *Contingency, irony, and solidarity*. Cambridge: Cambridge University Press.

Rule, J. B. (1994). Dilemmas of theoretical progress. *Sociological Forum, 9*, 241–257.

Seidman, S. (1991). The end of sociological theory: The postmodern hope. *Sociological Theory, 9*, 131–146.

Skocpol, T. (1986). The dead end of metatheory. *Contemporary Sociology, 16*, 10–12.

Sorokin, P. (1928). *Contemporary sociological theories*. New York: Harper Brothers.

Spivak, G. (1974). Translator's preface. In J. Derrida, *Of grammatology* (pp. ix–lxxxvii). Baltimore: Johns Hopkins University Press.

Stinchcombe, A. L. (1968). *Constructing social theory*. New York: Harcourt Brace Jovanovich.

Sturrock, J. (1979). Roland Barthes. In J. Sturrock, *Structuralism and since* (pp. 52–80). Oxford and New York: Oxford University Press.

Swartz, D. (1997). *Culture and power: The sociology of Pierre Bourdieu*. Chicago: IL: The University of Chicago Press.

Taylor, C. (1985). *Philosophy and the human sciences*: Philosophical papers 2. New York: Cambridge University Press.

Tiryakian, E. (1979). The significance of schools in the development of sociology. In W. Snizek, E. Fuhrman, & M. K. Miller (Eds.), *Contemporary issues in theory and research* (pp. 211–233). Westport, CT: Greenwood Press.

Tiryakian, E. (1986). Hegemonic schools and the development of sociology: Rethinking the history of the discipline. In R. C. Monk (Ed.), *Structures of knowing* (pp. 417–441). Lanham, MD: University Press of America.

Turner, J. (Ed.). (1989). *Theory building in sociology: Assessing theoretical cumulation*. Newbury Park, CA: Sage.

Turner, J. (1991). *The structure of sociological theory*, 5th ed. Belmont, CA: Wadsworth.

Turner, S. P., & Turner, J. H. (1990). *The impossible science: An institutional analysis of American sociology*. Newbury Park, CA: Sage.

Wacquant, L. J. D. (1996). Toward a reflexive sociology: A workshop with Pierre Bourdieu. In S. P. Turner (Ed.), *Social theory and sociology: The classics and beyond* (pp. 213–228). Cambridge, MA: Blackwell.

Wagner, D. G. (1984). *The growth of sociological theories*. Beverly Hills, CA: Sage.

Wallace, W. (1988). Toward a disciplinary matrix in sociology. In N. Smelser (Ed.), *Handbook of sociology* (pp. 1–59). Chicago: Aldive.

Weber, M. (1904–1905/1958). *The Protestant ethic and the spirit of capitalism*. NY: Scribner's.

Weber, M. (1921/1968). *Economy and society*. Totowa, NJ: Bedminster Press.

Weber, M. (1896–1906/1976). *The agrarian sociology of ancient civilizations*. London: New Left Books.

Weinstein, D., & Weinstein, M. A. (1992). The postmodern discourse of metatheory. In G. Ritzer (Ed.), *Metatheorizing* (pp. 135–150). Newbury Park, CA: Sage.

White, H. (1978). *Tropics of discourse*. Baltimore: Johns Hopkins University Press.

Willer, D. (1967). *Scientific sociology: Theory and method*. Englewood Cliffs, NJ: Prentice Hall.

Wolf, F. M. (1986). *Meta-analysis: Quantitative methods for research synthesis*. Beverly Hills, CA: Sage.

Zetterberg, H. L. (1954/1963/1965). *On theory and verification in sociology*. Totowa, NJ: The Bedminster Press.

Zhao, S. (1996). The beginning of the end or the end of the beginning? The theory construction movement revisited. *Sociological Forum, 11*, 305–318.

PART II

THE CULTURAL TURN IN SOCIOLOGICAL THEORIZING

CHAPTER 7

The Strong Program in Cultural Theory

Elements of a Structural Hermeneutics

JEFFREY ALEXANDER AND PHILIP SMITH

Throughout the world, culture has been doggedly pushing its way onto the center stage of debates not only in sociological theory and research but also throughout the human sciences. As with any profound intellectual shift, this has been a process characterized by leads and lags. In Britain, for example, culture has been making headway since the early 1970s. In the United States, the tide began to turn unmistakably only in the mid-1980s. In continental Europe, it is possible to argue that culture never really went away. Despite this ongoing revival of interest, however, there is anything but consensus among sociologists specializing in the area about just what the concept means and how it relates to the discipline as traditionally understood. These differences of opinion can be usefully explained only partly as empirical reflections of geographical, sociopolitical, or national traditions. More importantly, they are manifestations of deeper contradictions relating to axiomatic and foundational logics in the theory of culture. Pivotal to all these disputes is the issue of "cultural autonomy" (Alexander, 1990; Smith, 1998a). In this chapter, we employ the concept of cultural autonomy to explore and evaluate the competing understandings of culture currently available to social theory. We suggest that fundamental flaws characterize most of these models, and we argue for an alternative approach that can be broadly understood as a kind of structural hermeneutics.

Lévi-Strauss (1974) famously wrote that the study of culture should be like the study of geology. According to this dictum, analysis should account for surface variation in terms of deeper generative principles, just as geomorphology explains the distribution of plants, the shape of hills, and the drainage patterns followed by rivers in terms of underlying geology. In this chapter, we intend to apply this principle to the enterprise of contemporary cultural sociology in a way that is both reflexive and diagnostic. Our aim is not so much to review the field and document its diversity, although we will indeed conduct such a review, as to engage

JEFFREY ALEXANDER • Department of Sociology, Yale University, New Haven, Connecticut 06520. PHILIP SMITH • Department of Sociology and Anthropology, Queensland University, Brisbane, Australia.

Handbook of Sociological Theory, edited by Jonathan H. Turner. Kluwer Academic / Plenum Publishers, New York, 2002.

in a seismographic enterprise that will trace a fault line running right through it. Understanding this fault line and its theoretical implications allows us not only to reduce complexity, but also to transcend the kind of purely taxonomic mode of discourse that so often plagues handbook chapters of the present kind. This seismographic principle will provide a powerful tool for getting to the heart of current controversies and understanding the slippages and instabilities that undermine so much of the territory of cultural inquiry. Contra Lévi-Strauss, however, we do not see our structural enquiry as a disinterested scientific exercise. Our discourse here is openly polemical, our language slightly colored. Rather than affecting neutrality, we are going to propose one particular style of theory as offering the best way forward for cultural sociology.

THE FAULT LINE AND ITS CONSEQUENCES

The fault line at the heart of current debates lies between "cultural sociology" and the "sociology of culture."[1] To believe in the possibility of a cultural sociology is to subscribe to the idea that every action, no matter how instrumental, reflexive, or coerced vis-à-vis its external environments (Alexander, 1988), is embedded to some extent in a horizon of affect and meaning. This internal environment is one toward which the actor can never be fully instrumental or reflexive. It is, rather, an ideal resource that partially enables and partially constrains action, providing for both routine and creativity and allowing for the reproduction and transformation of structure (Sewell, 1992). Similarly, a belief in the possibility of a cultural sociology implies that institutions, no matter how impersonal or technocratic, have an ideal foundation that fundamentally shapes their organization and goals and provides the structured context for debates over their legitimation.[2] When described in the folk idiom of positivism, one could say that the more traditional sociology of culture approach treats culture as a dependent variable, whereas in cultural sociology it is an "independent variable" that possesses a relative autonomy in shaping actions and institutions, providing inputs every bit as vital as more material or instrumental forces.

Viewed from a distance, the sociology of culture offers the same kind of landscape as cultural sociology. There is a common conceptual repertoire of terms like values, codes, and discourses. Both traditions argue that culture is something important in society, something that repays careful sociological study. Both speak of the recent "cultural turn" as a pivotal moment in social theory. But these resemblances are only superficial. At the structural level we find deep antinomies. To speak of the sociology of culture is to suggest that culture is something to be explained, by something else entirely separated from the domain of meaning itself. To speak of the sociology of culture is to suggest that explanatory power lies in the study of the "hard" variables of social structure, such that structured sets of meanings become superstructures and ideologies driven by these more "real" and tangible social forces. In this approach, culture becomes defined as a "soft" not really independent variable: it is more or less confined to participating in the reproduction of social relations.

A notion that has emerged from the extraordinary new field of science studies is the

[1]Alexander (1996) posited this dichotomy, and it was further elaborated in Alexander and Smith (1998). The present chapter builds on this earlier work.
[2]Here lies the fundamental difference between a cultural sociology and the more instrumental and pragmatic approach to culture of the new institutionalism, whose emphasis on institutional isomorphism and legitimation would otherwise seem to place it firmly in the cultural tradition. See the forceful critique of this perspective "from within" of Friedland and Alford (1991).

sociologically inspired idea of the "strong program" (e.g., Bloor, 1976; Latour & Woolgar, 1986). The argument here is that scientific ideas are cultural and linguistic conventions as much as they are simply the results of other, more "objective" actions and procedures. Rather than only "findings" that hold up a mirror to nature (Rorty, l979), science is understood as a collective representation, a language game that reflects a prior pattern of sense-making activity. In the context of the sociology of science, the concept of the strong program, in other words, suggests a radical uncoupling of cognitive content from natural determination. We would like to suggest that a strong program also might be emerging in the sociological study of culture. Such an initiative argues for a sharp analytical uncoupling of culture from social structure, which is what we mean by cultural autonomy (Alexander, 1988; Kane, 1992). As compared with the sociology of culture, cultural sociology depends on establishing this autonomy, and it is only via such a strong program that sociologists can illuminate the powerful role that culture plays in shaping social life. By contrast, the sociology of culture offers a "weak program" in which culture is a feeble and ambivalent variable. Borrowing from Basil Bernstein (1971), we might say that the strong program is powered by an elaborated theoretical code, whereas the weak program is limited by a restricted code that reflects the inhibitions and habitus of traditional, institutionally oriented social science.

Commitment to a cultural–sociological theory that recognizes cultural autonomy is the single-most important quality of a strong program. There are, however, two other defining characteristics that must drive any such approach, characteristics that can be described as methodological. One is the commitment to hermeneutically reconstructing social texts in a rich and persuasive way. What is needed here is a Geertzian "thick description" of the codes, narratives, and symbols that create the textured webs of social meaning. The contrast here is to the "thin description" that typically characterizes studies inspired by the weak program, in which meaning is either simply read off from social structure or reduced to abstracted descriptions of reified values, norms, ideology, or fetishism. The weak program fails to fill these empty vessels with the rich wine of symbolic significance. The philosophical principles for this hermeneutic position were articulated by Dilthey (1962), and it seems to us that his powerful methodological injunction to look at the "inner meaning" of social structures has never been surpassed. Rather than inventing a new approach, the deservedly influential cultural analyses of Clifford Geertz can be seen as providing the most powerful contemporary application of Dilthey's ideas.[3]

In methodological terms, the achievement of thick description requires the bracketing out of wider, nonsymbolic social relations. This bracketing out, analogous to Husserl's phenomenological reduction, allows the reconstruction of the pure cultural text, the theoretical and philosophical rationale for which Ricoeur (1971) supplied in his important argument for the necessary linkage between hermeneutics and semiotics. This reconstruction can be thought of as creating, or mapping out, the culture structures (Rambo & Chan, 1990) that form one dimension of social life. It is the notion of the culture structure as a social text that allows the well-developed conceptual resources of literary studies—from Aristotle to such contemporary figures as Frye (1957) and Brooks (1985)—to be brought into social science. Only after the analytical bracketing demanded by hermeneutics has been completed, after the internal pattern of meaning has been reconstructed, should social science move from analytic to concrete autonomy (Kane, 1992). Only after having created the analytically autonomous culture object

---

[3]It is unfortunate that the connection between Geertz and Dilthey has never been understood, since it has made Geertz seem "without a home" philosophically, a position his later anti-theoreticism seems to welcome (see Alexander, 1987, pp. 316–329).

does it become possible to discover in what ways culture intersects with other social forces, such as power and instrumental reason in the concrete social world.

This brings us to the third characteristic of a strong program. Far from being ambiguous or shy about specifying just how culture makes a difference, far from speaking in terms of abstract systemic logics as causal processes (à la Lévi-Strauss), we suggest that a strong program tries to anchor causality in proximate actors and agencies, specifying in detail just how culture interferes with and directs what really happens. By contrast, as Thompson (1978) demonstrated, weak programs typically hedge and stutter on this issue. They tend to develop elaborate and abstract terminological (de)fenses that provide the illusion of specifying concrete mechanisms as well as the illusion of having solved intractable dilemmas of freedom and determination. As they say in the fashion business, however, the quality is in the detail. We would argue that it is only by resolving issues of detail—who says what, why, and to what effect—that cultural analysis can become plausible according to the criteria of a social science. We do not believe, in other words, that hardheaded and skeptical demands for causal clarity should be confined to empiricists or to those who are obsessively concerned with power and social structure.[4] These criteria also apply to a cultural sociology.

The idea of a strong *program* carries with it the suggestions of an agenda. In what follows we discuss this agenda. We look first at the history of social theory, showing how this agenda failed to emerge until the 1960s. We go on to explore several contemporary traditions in the social scientific analysis of culture. We suggest that, despite appearances, each comprises a weak program, failing to meet in one way or another the defining criteria we have set forth here. We conclude by pointing to an emerging tradition of cultural sociology, most of it American, which in our view establishes the parameters of a strong program.

CULTURE IN SOCIAL THEORY: FROM THE CLASSICS TO THE 1960s

For most of its history, sociology, both as theory and method, has suffered from a numbness toward meaning. Culturally unmusical scholars have depicted human action as insipidly or brutally instrumental, as if it were constructed without reference to the internal environments of actions that are established by the moral structures of sacred–good and profane–evil (Brooks, 1985) and by the narrative teleologies that create chronology (White, 1987) and define dramatic meaning (Frye, 1957). Caught up in the ongoing crises of modernity, the classical founders of the discipline believed that epochal historical transformations had emptied the world of meaning. Capitalism, industrialization, secularization, rationalization, anomie, and egoism, these core processes were held to create confused and dominated individuals, to shatter the possibilities of a meaningful telos, to eliminate the ordering power of the sacred and profane. Only occasionally does a glimmer of a strong program come through in this classical period. Weber's (1958) religious sociology, and most particularly his essay "Religious Rejections of the World and Their Directions" (cf. Alexander, 1988) suggested that the quest for salvation was a universal cultural need whose various solutions had forcefully shaped organizational and motivational dynamics in world civilizations. Durkheim's later sociology, as articulated in critical passages from *The Elementary Forms of Religious Life* (1968) and in a posthumously recovered course of lectures (Alexander, 1982), suggested that

---

[4]Smith (1998a) makes this point emphatically in his distinction between American and European versions of cultural sociology.

even contemporary social life had an ineluctable spiritual-*cum*-symbolic component. While plagued by the weak program symptom of causal ambivalence, the young Marx's (1963) writings on species-being also forcefully pointed to the manner in which non-material forces tied humans together in common projects and destinies. This early suggestion that alienation is not only the reflection of material relationships adumbrated the critical chapter in *Capital* (Marx, 1867/1963, pp. 71–83). "The Fetishism of Commodities and the Secret Thereof," which has so often served as an unstable bridge from structural to cultural Marxism in the present day.

The communist and fascist revolutionary upheavals that marked the first half of this century were premised on the same kind of widespread fear that modernity had eroded the possibility of meaningful sociality. Communist and fascist thinkers attempted to alchemize what they saw as the barren codes of bourgeois civil society into new, resacralized forms that could accommodate technology and reason within wider, encompassing spheres of meaning (Smith, 1998c). In the calm that descended on the postwar period, Talcott Parsons and his colleagues, motivated by entirely different ideological ambitions, also began to think that modernity did not have to be understood in such a corrosive way. Beginning from an analytical rather than eschatological premise, Parsons theorized that "values" had to be central to actions and institutions if a society was to be able to function as a coherent enterprise. The result was a theory that of Parsons' modern contemporaries seemed to many to exhibit an idealizing culturalist bias (Lockwood, 1992). We ourselves would suggest an opposite reading.

From a strong program viewpoint, Parsonian functionalism can be taken as insufficiently cultural, as denuded of musicality. In the absence of a musical moment where the social text is reconstructed in its pure form, Parsons' work lacks a powerful hermeneutic dimension. While Parsons theorized that values were important, he did not explain the nature of values them-selves. Instead of engaging in the social imaginary, diving into the febrile codes and narratives that make up a social text, he and his functionalist colleagues observed action from the outside and induced the existence of guiding valuations using categorical frameworks supposedly generated by functional necessity. Without a counterweight of thick description, we are left with a position in which culture has autonomy only in an abstract and analytic sense. When we turn to the empirical world, we find that functionalist logic ties up cultural form with social function and institutional dynamics to such an extent that it is difficult to imagine where culture's autonomy might lie in any concrete setting. The result was an ingenious systems theory that remains too hermeneutically feeble, too distant on the issue of autonomy to offer much to a strong program.

Flawed as the functionalist project was, the alternatives were far worse. The world in the 1960s was a place of conflict and turmoil. When the Cold War turned hot, macrosocial theory shifted toward the analysis of power from a one-sided and anticultural stance. Thinkers with an interest in macrohistorical process approached meaning through its contexts, treating it as a product of some supposedly more "real" social force, when they spoke of it at all. For scholars like Barrington Moore and C. Wright-Mills and later followers such as Charles Tilly, Randall Collins, and Michael Mann culture must be thought of in terms of self-interested ideologies, group process, and networks rather than in terms of texts. Meanwhile, during the same period, microsociology emphasized the radical reflexivity of actors. For such writers as Blumer, Goffman, and Garfinkel, culture forms an external environment in relation to which actors formulate lines of action that are "accountable" or give off a good "impression." We find precious little indication in this tradition of the power of the symbolic to shape interactions from within, as normative precepts or narratives that carry an internalized moral force.

Yet during this same period of the 1960s, at the very moment when the halfway cultural approach of functionalism was disappearing from American sociology, theories that spoke forcefully of a social text began to have enormous influence in France. Through creative misreadings of the structural linguistics of Saussure and Jacobson, and bearing a (carefully hidden) influence from the late Durkheim and Marcel Mauss, thinkers like Lévi-Strauss, Roland Barthes, and the early Michel Foucault created a revolution in the human sciences by insisting on the textuality of institutions and the discursive nature of human action. When viewed from a contemporary strong program perspective, such approaches remain too abstracted; they also typically fail to specify agency and causal dynamics. In these failings they resemble Parsons' functionalism. Nevertheless, in providing hermeneutic and theoretical resources to establish the autonomy of culture, they constituted a turning point for the construction of a strong program. In the next section, we discuss how this project has been derailed by a succession of weak programs that continue to dominate research on culture and society today.

WEAK PROGRAMS IN CONTEMPORARY
CULTURAL THEORY

One of the first research traditions to apply French *nouvelle vague* theorizing outside of the hothouse Parisian environment was the Centre for Contemporary Cultural Studies, also known as the Birmingham School. The masterstroke of the school was to meld ideas about cultural texts onto the neo-Marxist understanding that Gramsci established about the role played by cultural hegemony in maintaining social relations. This allowed exciting new ideas about how culture worked to be applied in a flexible way to a variety of settings, all the while without letting go of comforting old ideas about class domination. The result was a "sociology of culture" analysis, which tied cultural forms to social structure as manifestations of "hegemony" (if the analyst did not like what they saw) or "resistance" (if they did). At its best, this mode of sociology could be brilliantly illuminating. Paul Willis's (1977) ethnographic study of working class school kids was outstanding in its reconstruction of the zeitgeist of the "lads." Stuart Hall et al.'s (1978) classic study of the moral panic over mugging in 1970s Britain, *Policing the Crisis*, managed in its early pages to decode the discourse of urban decay and racism that underpinned an authoritarian crackdown. In these ways, Birmingham work approached a "strong program" in its ability to recreate social texts and lived meanings. Where it fails, however, is in the area of cultural autonomy (Sherwood et al., 1993). Notwithstanding attempts to move beyond the classical Marxist position, neo-Gramscian theorizing exhibits the telltale weak program ambiguities over the role of culture that plague the luminous *Prison Notebooks* (Gramsin, 1971) themselves. Terms like "articulation" and "anchoring" suggest contingency in the play of culture. But this contingency is often reduced to instrumental reason (in the case of elites articulating a discourse for hegemonic purposes) or to some kind of ambiguous systemic or structural causation (in the case of discourses being anchored in relations of power).

Failure to grasp the nettle of cultural autonomy and quit the sociology of culture-driven project of "Western Marxism" (Anderson, 1979) contributed to a fateful ambiguity over the mechanisms through which culture links with social structure and action. There is no clearer example of this latter process than in *Policing the Crisis* (Hall et al., 1978) itself. After building up a detailed picture of the mugging panic and its symbolic resonances, the book lurches into a sequence of insistent claims that the moral panic is linked to the economic logic of capitalism and its proximate demise; that it functions to legitimate law and order politics on streets that harbor latent revolutionary tendencies. Yet the concrete mechanisms through which the inci-pient crisis of capitalism (has it arrived yet?) are translated into the concrete decisions of judges, parliamentarians, newspaper editors, and police officers on the beat are never spelled out. The result is a theory that despite a critical edge and superior hermeneutic capabilities to classical functionalism curiously resembles Parsons in its tendency to invoke abstracted influences and processes as adequate explanation for empirical social actions.

In this respect, by contrast to the Birmingham School the work of Pierre Bourdieu has real merits. While many Birmingham-style analyses seem to lack any clear application of method, Bourdieu's oeuvre is resolutely grounded in middle range empirical research projects of both a qualitative and quantitative nature. His inferences and claims are more modest and less manifestly tendentious. In his best work, moreover, such as the description of a Kabyle house or a French peasant dance (Bourdieu, 1962, 1977), Bourdieu's thick description abilities show that he has the musicality to recognize and decode cultural texts that is at least equal to that of the Birmingham ethnographers. Despite these qualities, Bourdieu's research also can best be described as a weak program dedicated to the sociology of culture rather than cultural sociology. Once they have penetrated the thickets of terminological ambiguity that always mark out a weak program, commentators agree that in Bourdieu's framework culture has a role in ensuring the reproduction of inequality rather than permitting innovation (Alexander, 1995; Honneth, 1986; Sewell, 1992). As a result, culture, working through habitus, operates more as a dependent variable than an independent one. It is a gearbox, not an engine. When it comes to specifying exactly how the process of reproduction takes place, Bourdieu is vague. *Habitus* produces a sense of style, ease, and taste. Yet to know just how these influence stratification something more would be needed: a detailed study of concrete social settings where decisions are made and social reproduction ensured (cf. Lamont, 1992). We need to know more about the thinking of gatekeepers in job interviews and publishing houses, the impact of classroom dynamics on learning, or the logic of the citation process. Without this "missing link," we are left with a theory that points to circumstantial homologies but cannot produce a smoking gun.

Bourdieu's understanding of the links of culture to power also falls short of demanding strong program ideals. For Bourdieu, stratification systems make use of status cultures in competition with each other in various fields. The semantic content of these cultures has little to do with how society is organized. Meaning has no wider impact. While Weber, for example, argued that forms of eschatology have determinate outputs on the way that social life is patterned, for Bourdieu cultural content is arbitrary and without import. In his formulation there always will be systems of stratification defined by class, and all that is important for dominant groups is to have their cultural codes embraced as legitimate. In the final analysis, what we have here is a Veblenesque vision in which culture provides a strategic resource for actors, an external environment of action, rather than a text that shapes the world in an immanent fashion. People use culture, but they do not seem to really care about it.

Michel Foucault's works, and the poststructural and postmodern theoretical program they have initiated, provides the third weak program we discuss here. Despite its brilliance, what we find here, yet again, is a body of work wrought with the tortured contradictions that indicate a failure to grasp the nettle of a strong program. On the one hand, Foucault's (1970, 1972) major theoretical texts, *The Archaeology of Knowledge* and *The Order of Things*, provide important groundwork for a strong program with their assertion that discourses operate in arbitrary ways to classify the world and shape knowledge formation. His empirical applica-tions of this theory also should be praised for assembling rich historical data in a way that approximates to the reconstruction of a social text. So far, so good. Unfortunately, there is another hand at work. The crux of the issue is Foucault's genealogical method; his insistence that power and knowledge are fused in power/knowledge. The result is a reductionist line of reasoning akin to functionalism (Brenner, 1994), where discourses are homologous with institutions, flows of power, and technologies. Contingency is specified at the level of "history," at the level of untheorizable collisions and ruptures, not at the level of the *dispositif*. There is little room for a synchronically arranged contingency that might encompass disjunctures between culture and institutions, between power and its symbolic or textual foundations, between texts and actors interpretations of those texts. This binding of discourse to social structure, in other words, leaves no room for understanding how an autonomous cultural realm hinders or assists actors in judgment, critique, or in the provision of transcendental goals that texture social life. Foucault's world is one where Nietzsche's prison house of language finds its material expression with such force that no room is left for cultural autonomy, and by implication, the autonomy of action. Responding to this sort of criticism, Foucault attempted to theorize self and resistance in his later work. But he did so in an *ad hoc* way, seeing acts of resistance as random dysfunctions (Brenner, 1994, p. 698) or unexplained self-assertions. These late texts do not work through the ways that cultural frames might permit "outsiders" to produce and sustain opposition to power.

In the currently most influential stream of work to come out of the Foucaultian stable, we can see that the latent tension between the Foucault (1972) of the *Archaeology* and Foucault's genealogical avatar has been resolved decisively in favor of an anticultural mode of theory. The proliferating body of work on "governmentality" centers on the control of populations (Miller & Rose, 1990; Rose, 1993), but does so through an elaboration of the role of administrative techniques and expert systems. To be sure, there is acknowledgment that "language" is important, that government has a "discursive character." This sounds promising, but on closer inspection we find that "language" and "discourse" boil down to dry modes of technical communication (graphs, statistics, reports, etc.) that operate as technologies to allow "evaluation, calculation, intervention" at a distance by institutions and bureaucracies (Miller & Rose, 1990, p. 7). There is little work here to recapture the more textual nature of political and administrative discourses. No effort is made to go beyond a "thin description" and identify the broader symbolic patterns, the hot, affective criteria through which policies of control and coordination are appraised by citizens and elites alike. Here the project of governmentality falls short of the standards set by Hall et al. (1978), which at least managed to conjure up the emotive spirit of populism in Heath-era Britain.

Research on the "production and reception of culture" marks the fourth weak program we will identify. Unlike those we have just discussed, it is one that lacks theoretical bravura and charismatic leadership. For the most part, it is characterized by the unsung virtues of intellectual modesty, diligence, clarity, and a studious attention to questions of method. Its numerous proponents make sensible, middle range empirical studies of the circumstances in which "culture" is produced and consumed (for overview, see Crane, 1992). For this reason, it has become particularly powerful in the United States, where these kinds of properties assimilate best to professional norms within sociology. The great strength of this approach is that it offers explicit causal links between culture and social structure, thus avoiding the pitfalls of indeterminacy and obfuscation that have plagued more theoretically ambitious understandings. Unfortunately, this intellectual honesty usually serves only to broadcast a reductionist impulse that remains latent in the other approaches we have examined. The insistent aim of study after study (e.g., Blau, 1989; Peterson, 1985) seems to be to explain away culture as the product of sponsoring institutions, elites, or interests. The quest for profit, power, prestige, or ideological control sits at the core of cultural production. Reception, meanwhile, is relentlessly determined by social location. Audience ethnographies, for example, are undertaken to document the decisive impact of class, race, and gender on the ways that television programs are understood. Here we find the sociology of culture writ large. The aim of analysis is not so much to uncover the impact of meaning on social life and identity formation, but rather to see how social life and identities constrain potential meanings.

While the sociological credentials of such an undertaking are to be applauded, something more is needed if the autonomy of culture is to be recognized, *viz.* a robust understanding of the codes that are at play in the cultural objects under consideration. Only when these are taken into account can cultural products be seen to have internal cultural inputs and constraints. However, in the production of culture approach, such efforts at hermeneutic understanding are rare. All too often meaning remains a sort of black box, with analytical attention centered on the circumstances of cultural production and reception. When meanings and discourses are explored, it is usually in order to talk through some kind of fit between cultural content and the social needs and actions of specific producing and receiving groups. Wendy Griswold (1983), for example, shows how the trickster figure was transformed with the emergence of Restoration drama. In the medieval morality play, the figure of "vice" was evil. He was later to morph into the attractive, quick-thinking "gallant." The new character was one that could appeal to an audience of young, disinherited men who had migrated to the city and had to depend on their wits for social advancement. Similarly, Robert Wuthnow (1989) argues that the ideologies of the Reformation germinated and took root as an appropriate response to a particular set of social circumstances. He persuasively demonstrates that new binary oppositions emerged in theological discourse, for example, those between a corrupt Catholicism and a pure Protestantism. These refracted the politics and social dislocations underlying religious and secular struggles in 16th-century Europe.

We have some concerns about singling such work out for criticism, for they are among the best of the genre and approximate to the sort of thick description we advocate. There can be little doubt that Griswold and Wuthnow correctly understand a need to study meaning in cultural analysis. However, they fail to systematically connect its exploration with the problematic of cultural autonomy. For all their attention to cultural messages and historical continuities, they do little to reduce our fear that there is an underlying reductionism in such analysis. The overall effect is to understand meanings as infinitely malleable in response to social settings. A more satisfying approach to Griswold's data, for example, would recognize the dramatic narratives as inevitably structured by constraining cultural codes relating to plot and character, for it is the combinations between these that make any kind of drama a possibility. Similarly, Wuthnow should have been much more sensitive to the understanding of binary opposition advocated by Saussure: it is a precondition of discourse rather than merely a description of its historically specific form.[5] And so to our reading, such efforts as Griswold's and Wuthnow's represent narrowly lost opportunities for a decisive demonstration cultural autonomy as a product of culture–structure. In the final section of this chapter, we look for signs of a structuralist hermeneutics that can perhaps better accomplish this theoretical goal.

STEPS TOWARD A STRONG PROGRAM

All things considered, the sociological investigation of culture remains dominated by weak programs characterized by some combination of hermeneutic inadequacy, ambivalence

---

[5]It is ironic that in a paper published the year previously to *Communities of Discourse*, Wuthnow (1988) had begun working toward this precise point, suggesting that differences between fundamentalist and liberal religious discourses should be understood as expressions of divergent structural logics rather than as situated ideologies.

over cultural autonomy, and poorly specified, abstract mechanisms for grounding culture in concrete social process. In this final section, we wish to discuss recent trends in cultural sociology where there are signs that a bona fide strong program might finally be emerging.

A first step in the construction of a strong program is the hermeneutic project of "thick description" itself, which we have already invoked in a positive way. Drawing on Paul Ricoeur and Kenneth Burke, Clifford Geertz (1973) has worked harder than any other person to show that culture is a rich and complex text, with a subtle patterning influence on social life. The result is a compelling vision of culture as webs of significance that guide action. Yet while superior to the other approaches we have considered, this position too has its flaws. Nobody could accuse Geertz of hermeneutic inadequacy or of neglecting cultural autonomy, yet on close inspection his enormously influential concept of thick description seems rather elusive. The precise mechanisms through which webs of meaning influence action on the ground are rarely specified with any clarity. Culture seems to take on the qualities of a transcendental actor (Alexander, 1987). So in terms of the third criterion of a strong program that we have specified—causal specificity—the program initiated by Geertz runs into trouble. One reason is the later Geertz's reluctance to connect his interpretive analyses to any kind of general theory. There is a relentless emphasis on the way that the local explains the local. He insists that societies, like texts, contain their own explanation. Writing the local, as a consequence, comes into play as a substitute for theory construction. The focus here is on a novelistic recapitulation of details, with the aim of analysis being to accumulate these and fashion a model of the cultural text within a particular setting. Such a rhetorical turn has made it difficult to draw a line between anthropology and literature, or even travel writing. This in turn has made Geertz's project vulnerable to takeover bids. Most notably, during the 1980s the idea that society could be read like a text was taken over by poststructural writers who argued that culture was little more than contending texts or "representations" (Clifford, 1988) and that ethnography was either allegory, fantasy, or biography. The aim of analysis now shifted to the exposition of professional representations and the techniques and power relations behind them. The resulting program has been one that has told us a good deal about academic writing, ethnographic museum displays, and so on. It helps us to understand the discursive conditions of cultural production but has almost given up on the task of explaining ordinary social life or the possibility of a general understanding. Not surprisingly, Geertz enthusiastically devoted himself to the new cause, writing an eloquent text on the tropes through which anthropologists construct their ethnographic authority (Geertz, 1988). As the text replaces the tribe as the object of analysis, cultural theory begins to look more and more like critical narcissism and less and less like the explanatory discipline that Dilthey so vividly imagined.

Inadequate as it may be, the work of Geertz provides a springboard for a strong program in cultural analysis. It indicates the need for the explication of meaning to be at the center of the intellectual agenda and offers a vigorous affirmation of cultural autonomy. What is missing, however, is a theory of culture that has autonomy built into the very fabric of meaning as well as a more robust understanding of social structure and institutional dynamics. We suggest, following Saussure, that a more structural approach toward culture helps with the first point. In addition, it initiates the movement toward general theory that Geertz avoids. In short, it can recognize the autonomy and the centrality of meaning, but does not develop a hermeneutics of the particular at the expense of a hermeneutics of the universal. We return to the promise of such a structural hermeneutics below.

As the 1980s turned into the 1990s, we saw the revival of "culture" in American sociology and the declining prestige of anticultural forms of macro- and microthought. This strand of work, with its developing strong program characteristics, offers the best hope for a truly cultural sociology finally to emerge as a major research tradition. To be sure, a number of weak programs organized around the sociology of culture remain powerful, perhaps dominant, in the US context. One thinks in particular of studies of the production, consumption, and distribution of culture that (as we have seen) focus on organizational and institutional contexts rather than content and meanings (e.g., Blau, 1989; Peterson, 1985). One also thinks of work inspired by the Western Marxist tradition that attempts to link cultural change to the workings of capital, especially in the context of urban form (e.g., Davis, 1992; Gottdeiner, 1995). The neoinstitutionalists (see DiMaggio & Powell, 1991) see culture as significant, but only as a legitimating constraint, only as an external environment of action, not as a lived text as Geertz might (see Friedland & Alford, 1991). Of course, there are numerous US-based apostles of British Cultural Studies (e.g., Fiske, 1987; Grossberg, Nelson, & Treichler, 1991), who combine virtuoso hermeneutic readings with thin, stratification-oriented forms of quasi-materialist reduction. Yet, it is equally important to recognize that there has emerged a current of work that gives to meaningful and autonomous texts a much more central place (for a sample, see Smith, 1998b). These contemporary sociologists are the "children" of an earlier generation of culturalist thinkers, Geertz, Bellah (1970) (cf. Alexander & Sherwood, forthcoming), Turner (1974), and Sahlins (1976) foremost among them, who wrote against the grain of 1960s and 1970s reductionism and attempted to demonstrate the textuality of social life and the necessary autonomy of cultural forms. In contemporary scholarship, we are seeing efforts to align these two axioms of a strong program with the third imperative of identifying concrete mechanisms through which culture does its work.

Responses to the question of transmission mechanisms have been decisively shaped, in a positive direction, by the American pragmatist and empiricist traditions. The influence of structural linguistics on European scholarship sanctioned a kind of cultural theory that paid little attention to the relationship between culture and action (unless tempered by the dangerously "humanist" discourses of existentialism or phenomenology). Simultaneously, the philosophical *formation* of writers like Althusser and Foucault permitted a dense and tortured kind of writing, where issues of causality and autonomy could be circled around in endless, elusive spirals of words. By contrast, American pragmatism has provided the seedbed for a discourse where clarity is rewarded; where it is believed that complex language games can be reduced to simpler statements; where it is argued that actors have to play some role in translating cultural structures into concrete actions and institutions. While the influence of pragmatism has reached American cultural sociologists in a diffuse way, its most direct inheritance can be seen in the work of Swidler (1986), Sewell (1992), Emirbayer and his collaborators (e.g., Emirbayer & Goodwin, 1996; Emirbayer & Mische, 1998), and Fine (1987), where efforts are made to relate culture to action without recourse to the materialistic reductionism of Bourdieu's praxis theory.

Other forces also have played a role in shaping the emerging strong program in American cultural sociology. Because these are more closely related than the pragmatists to our argument that a structuralist hermeneutics is the best way forward, we will expand on them here. Pivotal to all such work is an effort to understand culture not just as a text (à la Geertz) but rather as a text that is underpinned by signs and symbols that are in patterned relationships to each other. Writing in the first decades of the 20th century, Durkheim and his students such as Hertz and Mauss understood that culture was a classification system consisting of binary oppositions. At the same time Saussure was developing his structural linguistics, arguing that meanings were generated by means of patterned relationships between concepts and sounds. A few decades later, Lévi-Strauss was to pull these linguistic and sociological approaches to classification together in his pioneering studies of myth, kinship, and totemism. The great virtue of this synthesis was that it provided a powerful way for understanding the autonomy of culture. Because meanings are arbitrary and are generated from within the sign system, they enjoy a certain autonomy from social determination, just as the language of a country cannot be predicted from the knowledge that it is capitalist or socialist, industrial or agrarian. Culture now becomes a structure as objective as any more material social fact.

With the thematics of the "autonomy of culture" taking center stage in the 1980s, there was a vigorous appreciation of the work of the late-Durkheim, with his insistence on the cultural as well as functional origins of solidarity (for a review of this literature, see Emirbayer, 1996; Smith & Alexander, 1996). The felicitous but not altogether accidental congruence between Durkheim's opposition of the sacred and the profane and structuralist theories of sign–systems enabled insights from French theory to be translated into a distinctively socio-logical discourse and tradition, much of it concerned with the impact of cultural codes and codings. Numerous studies of boundary maintenance, for example, reflect this trend (for a sample, see Lamont & Fournier, 1993), and it is instructive to contrast them with more reductionist weak program alternatives about processes of "othering." Emerging from this tradition has been a focus on the binary opposition as a key tool for asserting the autonomy of cultural forms (see Alexander & Smith, 1993; Smith, 1991; Edles, 1998; Magnuson, 1997).

Further inspirations for structural hermeneutics within a strong program for cultural theory have come from anthropology. The new breed of symbolic anthropologists, in addition to Geertz, most notably Mary Douglas (1966), Turner (1974), and Marshall Sahlins (1976, 1981), took on board the message of structuralism but tried to move it in new directions. Postmodernisms and poststructuralisms also have played their role but in an optimistic guise. The knot between power and knowledge that has stunted European weak programs has been loosened by American postmodern theorists like Steven Seidman (1988). For postmodern pragmatistic philosophers like Richard Rorty (e.g., 1989), language tends to be seen as a creative force for the social imaginary rather than as Nietzsche's prison house. As a result, discourses and actors are provided with greater autonomy from power in the construction of identities.

These trends are well known, but there also is an interdisciplinary dark horse to which we wish to draw attention. In philosophy and literary studies, there has been growing interest in narrative and genre theory. Cultural sociologists such as Robin Wagner-Pacifici (1986, 1994, 2000; Wagner-Pacifici & Schwartz, 1991), Margaret Somers (1995), Wendy Griswold (1983), Ronald Jacobs (1996, 2000), Agnes Ku (1999), William Gibson (1994), and the authors of this chapter are now reading literary theorists like Northrup Frye, Peter Brooks, and Fredric Jameson, historians like Hayden White, and Aristotelian philosophers like Ricoeur and MacIntyre (cf. Lara, 1998). The appeal of this theory lies partially in its affinity for a textual understanding of social life. The emphasis on teleology carries with it some of the interpretive power of the classical hermeneutic model. This impulse toward reading culture as a text is complemented, in such narrative work, by an interest in developing formal models that can be applied across different comparative and historical cases. In other words, narrative forms such as the morality play or melodrama, tragedy, and comedy can be understood as "types" that carry with them particular implications for social life. The morality play, for example, does not seem to be conducive to compromise (Wagner-Pacifici, 1986, 1994). Tragedy can give rise to fatalism (Jacobs, 1996) and withdrawal from civic engagement, but it also can promote moral responsibility (Alexander, 1995; Eyerman, forthcoming). Comedy and romance, by contrast, generate optimism and social inclusion (Jacobs & Smith, 1997; Smith, 1994). Irony provides a potent tool for the critique of authority and reflexivity about dominant cultural codes, opening space for difference and cultural innovation (Jacobs & Smith, 1997; Smith, 1996).

A further bonus for this narrative approach is that cultural autonomy is assured (e.g., in the analytic sense, see Kane, 1992). If one takes a structuralist approach to narrative (Barthes, 1970), textual forms are seen as interwoven repertoires of characters, plot lines, and moral evaluations whose relationships can be specified in terms of formal models. Narrative theory, like semiotics, thus operates as a bridge between the kind of hermeneutic inquiry advocated by Geertz and the impulse toward general cultural theory. As Northrop Frye recognized, when approached in a structural way narrative allows for the construction of models that can be applied across cases and contexts but at the same time provides a tool for interrogating particularities.

It is important to emphasize that while meaningful texts are central in this American strand of a strong program, wider social contexts are not by any means necessarily ignored. In fact, the objective structures and visceral struggles that characterize the real social world are every bit as important as in work from the weak programs. Notable contributions have been made to areas such as censorship and exclusion (Beisel, 1993), race (Jacobs, 1996), sexuality (Seidman, 1988), violence (Gibson, 1994; Smith, 1991, 1996; Wagner-Pacifici, 1994), and failed sociohistorical projects for radical transformation (Alexander 1995a). These contexts are treated, however, not as forces unto themselves that ultimately determine the content and significance of cultural texts; rather, they are seen as institutions and processes that refract cultural texts in a meaningful way. They are arenas in which cultural forces combine or clash with material conditions and rational interests to produce particular outcomes (Ku, 1999; Smith, 1996). Beyond this they are seen as cultural metatexts themselves, as concrete embodiments of wider ideal currents.

CONCLUSIONS

We have suggested here that structuralism and hermeneutics can be made into fine bedfellows. The former offers possibilities for general theory construction, prediction, and assertions of the autonomy of culture. The latter allows analysis to capture the texture and temper of social life. When complemented by attention to institutions and actors as causal intermediaries, we have the foundations of a robust cultural sociology. The argument we have made here for an emerging strong program has been slightly polemical in tone. This does not mean we disparage efforts to look at culture in other ways. If sociology is to remain healthy as a discipline, it should be able to support a theoretical pluralism and lively debate. There are important research questions, in fields from demography to stratification to economic and political life, to which weak programs can be expected to make significant contributions. But it is equally important to make room for a genuinely cultural sociology. A first step toward this end is to speak out against false idols, to avoid the mistake of confusing reductionist sociology of culture approaches with a genuine strong program. Only in this way can the full promise of a cultural sociology be realized during the coming century.

REFERENCES

Alexander, J. C. (1982). *Theoretical logic on sociology*, Volume 2. Berkeley: University of California Press.
Alexander, J. C. (1987). *Twenty lectures*. New York: Columbia University Press.
Alexander, J. C. (1988). *Action and its environments*. New York: Columbia University Press.
Alexander, J. C. (1990). Introduction: Understanding the "relative autonomy" of culture. In J. Alexander & S.

Seidman (Eds.), *Culture and society: Contemporary debates* (pp. 1–27). Cambridge: Cambridge University Press.

Alexander, J. C. (1995a). Modern, anti, post and neo: How intellectuals have tried to understand the "crisis of our time." *New Left Review, 210,* 63–102.

Alexander, J. C. (1995b). *Fin-de-siecle social theory.* London: Verso.

Alexander, J. C. (1996). Cultural sociology or sociology of culture? *Culture, 10*(3–4), 1–5.

Alexander, J. (2001). On the social construction of moral universalism: The Holocaust from war crime to trauma drama. *European Journal of Social Theory, 4*(4).

Alexander, J. C. (forthcoming). From war crime to holocaust trauma: Progressive and tragic narrations of the Nazi's mass murder of the Jews. In J. Alexander, R. Eyerman, B. Geisen, N. Smelser, & P. Sztompka (Eds.), *Cultural trauma.* Berkeley: University of California Press.

Alexander, J. C., & Sherwood, S. (2001). Mythic gestures: Robert Bellah and the origins of cultural sociology. In R. Madsen, W. M. Sullivan, A. Swidler, & S. M. Tipton (Eds.), *Meaning and modernity: Religion, polity, and the self.* Berkeley: University of California Press.

Alexander, J.,& Smith, P. (1993). The discourse of American civil society: A new proposal for cultural studies. *Theory and Society, 22*(2), 151–207.

Alexander, J. C., & Smith, P. (1998). Sociologie culturelle ou sociologie de la culture? *Sociologie et sociétés, 30*(1), 107–116.

Anderson, P. (1979). *Considerations on Western Marxism.* London: Verso.

Barthes, R. (1970). *S/Z.* Paris: Editions du Seuil.

Beisel, N. (1993). Morals versus art. *American Sociological Review, 58,* 145–162.

Bellah, R. (1970). *Beyond belief.* New York: Harper & Row.

Bernstein, B. (1971). *Class, codes and control.* London: Routledge.

Blau, J. (1989). *The shape of culture.* Cambridge: Cambridge University Press.

Bloor, D. (1976). *Knowledge and social imagery.* London: Routledge.

Bourdieu, P. (1962). Les relations entre les sexes dans la societe paysanne. *Les Temps Modernes, 195,* 307–331.

Bourdieu, P. (1977). *Outline of a theory of practice.* Cambridge: Cambridge University Press.

Brenner, N. (1994). Foucault's new functionalism. *Theory and Society, 23,* 679—709.

Brooks, P. (1985). *The melodramatic imagination.* New York: Columbia University Press.

Clifford, J. (1988). *The predicament of culture.* Cambridge, MA: Harvard University Press.

Crane, D. (1992). *The production of culture.* Newbury Park, CA: Sage.

Davis, M. (1992). *City of quartz.* New York: Vintage Books.

Dilthey, W. (1962). *Pattern and meaning in history.* New York: Harper & Row.

DiMaggio, P., & Powell, W. (1991). *The new institutionalism in organizational analysis.* Chicago: University of Chicago Press.

Douglas, M. (1966). *Purity and danger.* London: Routledge and Kegan Paul.

Durkheim, E. (1915/1968). *The elementary forms of religious life.* London: Allen & Unwin.

Edles, L. (1998). *Symbol and ritual in the new Spain.* Cambridge: Cambridge University Press.

Emirbayer, M. (1996). Useful Durkheim. *Sociological Theory, 14*(2), 109–130.

Emirbayer, M., & Goodwin, J. (1996). Symbols, positions, objects. *History and Theory, 35*(3) 358–374.

Emirbayer, M., & Mische, A. (1998). What is agency? *American Journal of Sociology, 103*(4), 962–1023.

Eyerman, R. (forthcoming). Cultural trauma and the making of African American identity. In J. Alexander, R. Eyerman, B. Geisen, N. Smelser, & P. Sztompka (Eds.), *Cultural trauma.* Berkeley: University of California Press.

Fine, G. A. (1987). *With the boys.* Chicago: University of Chicago Press.

Fiske, J. (1987). *Television culture.* New York: Routledge.

Foucault, M. (1970). *The order of things.* London: Tavistock.

Foucault, M. (1972). *The archaeology of knowledge.* London: Tavistock.

Friedland, R., & Alford, R. (1991). Bringing society back in: Symbols, practices and institutional contradictions. In W. W. Powell & P. DiMaggio (Eds.), *The new institutionalism in organizational analysis* (pp. 232–263). Chicago: University of Chicago Press.

Frye, N. (1957). *Anatomy of criticism.* Princeton, NJ: Princeton University Press.

Geertz, C. (1973). *The interpretation of cultures.* New York: Basic Books.

Geertz, C. (1988). *Works and lives.* Stanford, CA: Stanford University Press.

Gibson, J. W. (1994). *Warrior dreams.* New York. Hill and Wang.

Gottdiener, M. (1995). *Postmodern semiotics.* Blackwell: Oxford.

Gramsin, A. (1971). *Selections from the prison notebooks.* New York: International Publishers.

Griswold, W. (1983). The devil's techniques: Cultural legitimation and social change. *American Sociological Review*, *48*, 668–680.

Grossberg, L., Nelson, C., & Treichler, P. (1991). *Cultural studies*. New York: Routledge.

Hall, S., Critcher, C., Jefferson, T., Clarke, J., & Roberts, B. (1978). *Policing the crisis*. London: Macmillan.

Honneth, A. (1986). The fragmented world of symbolic forms. *Theory, Culture and Society*, *3*, 55–66.

Jacobs, R. (1996). Civil society and crisis: Culture, discourse and the Rodney King beating. *American Journal of Sociology*, *101*(5), 1238–1272.

Jacobs, R. (2000). *Race, media and the crisis of civil society*. Cambridge: Cambridge University Press.

Jacobs, R., & Smith, P. (1997). Romance, irony and solidarity. *Sociological Theory*, *15*(1), 60–80.

Kane, A. (1992). Cultural analysis in historical sociology. *Sociological Theory*, *9*(1), 53–69.

Ku, A. (1999). *Narrative, politics and the public sphere*. Aldershot, UK: Ashgate.

Lamont, M. (1992). *Money, morals and manners*. Chicago: University of Chicago Press.

Lamont, M., & Fournier, P. (1993). *Cultivating differences*. Chicago: University of Chicago Press.

Lara, M. P. (1998). *Moral textures: Feminist narratives of the public sphere*. Berkeley: University of California Press.

Latour, B., & Woolgar, S. (1986). *Laboratory life*. Princeton, NJ: Princeton University Press.

Lévi-Strauss, C. (1974). *Tristes tropiques*. New York: Atheneum.

Lockwood, D. (1992). *Solidarity and schism*. Oxford: Oxford University Press.

Magnuson, E. (1997). Ideological conflict in American political culture. *International Journal of Sociology and Social Policy*, *17*(6), 84–130.

Marx, K. (1963/1867). *Capital*, Vol. 1. Moscow: Foreign Languages Publishing House.

Marx, K. (1963). Economic and philosophical manuscripts. In *K. Marx: Early writings* (pp. 61–220). New York: McGraw-Hill.

Miller, P., & Rose, N. (1990). Governing economic life. *Economy and Society*, *19*(2), 1–31.

Peterson, R. (1985). Six constraints on the production of literary works. *Poetics*, *14*, 45–67.

Rambo, E., & Chan, E. (1990). Text, structure and action in cultural sociology. *Theory and Society*, *19*(5), 635–648.

Ricoeur, P. (1971). The model of a text: Meaningful action considered as a text. *Social Research*, *38*, 529–562.

Rorty, R. (1979). *Philosophy and the mirror of nature*. Princeton, NJ: Princeton University Press.

Rorty, R. (1989). *Contingency, irony, and solidarity*. New York: Cambridge University Press.

Rose, N. (1993). Government, authority and expertise in advanced liberalism. *Economy and Society*, *22*(3), 283–299.

Sahlins, M. (1976). *Culture and practical reason*. Chicago: University of Chicago Press.

Sahlins, M. (1981). *Historical metaphors and mythical realities*. Ann Arbor: University of Michigan Press.

Seidman, S. (1988). Transfiguring sexual identity. *Social Text*, *9*(20), 187–206.

Sewell, W. (1992). A theory of structure: Duality, agency and transformation. *American Journal of Sociology*, *98*(1), 1–30.

Sherwood, S., Smith, P., & Alexander, J. C. (1993). The British are coming. *Contemporary Sociology*, *22*(2), 370–375.

Smith, P. (1991). Codes and conflict. *Theory and Society*, *20*, 103–138.

Smith, P. (1994). The semiotic foundations of media narratives: Saddam and Nasser in the American mass media. *Journal of Narrative and Life History*, *4*,(1–2), 89–118.

Smith, P. (1996). Executing executions: Aesthetics, identity and the problematic narratives of capital punishment ritual. *Theory and Society*, *25*(2), 235–261.

Smith, P. (1998a). The new American cultural sociology. In P. Smith (Ed.), *The new American cultural sociology* (pp. 1–14). Cambridge: Cambridge University Press.

Smith, P. (Ed,). (1998b). *The new American cultural sociology*. Cambridge: Cambridge University Press.

Smith, P. (1998c). Barbarism and civility in the discourses of fascism, communism and democracy. In J. Alexander (Ed.), *Real civil societies* (pp. 115–137). London: Sage.

Smith, P., & Alexander, J. C. (1996). Durkheim's religious revival. *American Journal of Sociology*, *102*(2), 585–592.

Somers, M. (1995). Narrating and naturalizing civil society and citizenship theory. *Sociological Theory*, *13*(3), 229–274.

Swidler, A. (1986). Culture in action: Symbols and strategies. *American Sociological Review*, *51*, 273–286.

Thompson, E. P. (1978). *The poverty of theory*. London: Merlin.

Turner, V. (1974). *Dramas, fields and metaphors*. Ithaca, NY: Cornell University Press.

Wagner-Pacifici, R. (1986). *The moro morality play*. Chicago: University of Chicago Press.

Wagner-Pacifici, R. (1994). *Discourse and destruction*. Chicago: University of Chicago Press.

Wagner-Pacifici, R. (2000). *Theorising the standoff*. Cambridge: Cambridge University Press.

Wagner-Pacifici, R., & Schwartz, B. (1991). The Vietnam veterans memorial. *American Journal of Sociology*, *97*(2), 376–420.

Weber, M. (1915/1958). Religious rejections of the world and their directions. In H. Gerth & C. W. Mills (Eds.), *From Max Weber* (pp. 323–359). New York: Oxford University Press.

White, H. (1987). *The content of the form.* Baltimore: Johns Hopkins University Press.

Willis, P. (1977). *Learning to labour.* Farnborough, UK: Saxon House.

Wuthnow, R. (1988). Religious discourse as public rhetoric. *Communication Research, 15*(3), 318–338.

Wuthnow, R. (1989). *Communities of discourse.* Cambridge, MA: Harvard University Press.

CHAPTER 8

Postmodern Social Theory

GEORGE RITZER AND DOUGLAS GOODMAN

Modernity is already postmodern. The postmodern is not after the modern nor is it opposed to the modern; instead, it is in the modern. We could not, however, call the postmodern the secret heart of modernity. The heart of the modern is its dream of transparency. Its belief that it can, ultimately, know and therefore take control of itself. For social theory, the modern is the belief that the hidden processes of society can be revealed and perhaps even manipulated to bring about a new and better society. Postmodern social theory is *opposed* to, is *after*, this dream of transparency.[1]

Postmodern theory is a recognition of the intractable contingency in modernity—that

---

[1]Postmodernity is "in" the modern in another sense altogether. It is something like the food of the modern, but that part of the food that is indigestible, which cannot be easily incorporated into the system of modernity. Postmodernity is a recognition of the indigestible *contingency* in modernity. It is in modernity, but it is what is left over after the dream of transparency drops away. Perhaps, then, it is appropriate to refer to the postmodern as the *excrement* of modernity.

This is a reference with which many critics of postmodernism can agree, for we often have heard them compare postmodern theory to the excrement of certain barnyard animals. To those familiar with Freudian theory, this scatological analysis explains many sociologists' relation to postmodernism. The relation is determined by that stage, the anal, in which control is the primary issue. To give up the modern dream of transparency is to give up the fantasy of control. As the anonymous revolutionary so succinctly expressed the concept of postmodern contingency, "shit happens," or the Latin variant, "Fex urbis, lex orbis" (Saint Jerome).

Seeing postmodernity as the excrement of modernity also suggests a relation between postmodern theory and the ecological movement. After centuries of ignoring our own refuse, we are finally being forced to deal with it or else be buried in it. This is because our modern civilization has expanded so that there is no longer any place outside of it where our refuse can be safely dumped. Burning, burying, sinking, and transporting only moves it to another location or changes it to another form. There is no outside in which it can be discharged and ignored.

Similarly, the modern has expanded to include our entire consciousness. We can no longer blame archaic traditions or primitive thinking for the failure of modern plans. (Although some now try to blame postmodernism.) There is no outside to modernity, no other place where we can locate the contingency that unsettles our schemes. No matter how we analyze or trace its transformations, contingency remains within the modern. The contingency is internal to modernity and it becomes fully recognizable as modernity expands to its fullest extent. This intractable contingency is the place from which to begin to understand postmodern theory because postmodern theory is what recognizes the contingency in the modern. The postmodern is both the modern to its fullest extent and the failure of the modern dream of transparency.

GEORGE RITZER • Department of Sociology, University of Maryland, College Park, Maryland 20742.   DOUGLAS GOODMAN • Department of Sociology, Wellesley College, Wellesley, Massachusetts 02481.

Handbook of Sociological Theory, edited by Jonathan H. Turner. Kluwer Academic / Plenum Publishers, New York, 2002.

society could be different than it is and that the current situation is the product of a series of historical accidents rather than essential forces. If, in fact, contingency is intractable, there are two ways to deal with this theoretically. On the one hand, theorists can bracket the contingency and focus on what can be determined, even if never completely. They can speak of trends, probabilities, all-things-being-equal. They can make deterministic assumptions and build models that approximate a contingent reality. On the other hand, theorists can focus on the contingency by using theory to show that current formations could be otherwise. Let us call the first approach modern and the second approach postmodern.

For a modern sociology, success is defined by the increased transparency of the social object—the revelation of essential underlying forces and processes. For a postmodern sociology, success is defined by the revelation of society's radical contingency and the opening up of new subject positions and local social projects.

It is not immediately apparent that postmodern sociology can be defined by its focus on contingency, especially since postmodernism is notoriously difficult to define at all. One of the reasons for this difficulty is that few of those we commonly think of as postmodernists (e.g., Foucault, Baudrillard, Virilio) identify themselves as such. Another is that they regularly employ such rhetorical devices as hyperbole, irony, and studied vagueness so that it is difficult to say what one postmodernist believes, let alone what the group as a whole professes. Postmodernism itself is plural as are the interpretations of it. This has led many theorists to simply give up on any attempt at precise definition and equate postmodernism with vagueness, ambiguity, and obscurantism.

Nevertheless, we argue that the characteristics that make postmodern theory (in)famous can be seen as related to a focus on contingency: skepticism toward grand narratives, abandonment of any basis for claiming certainty, rejection of universal standards, playful rhetoric, a subversive approach, and an emphasis on the irrational. All are connected to an attempt to reveal that things could be otherwise. They all proceed from a belief that the objective of theory is not to show why things are as they are, but simply to open up alternatives. However, a common focus on contingency does not establish a set of definitive concepts, nor does it delimit a particular theoretical frame; but it does structure the types of questions that can be fruitfully asked and the key controversies.

Postmodern theories can be approached in two ways that can be themselves categorized as modern and postmodern. A modern approach to postmodern theories would allow for a mapping of postmodern social theories, seeing such a map as useful for providing an overview of possible theoretical tools. A postmodern approach, however, would be skeptical of any attempt to locate, fix, classify, or structure contingency and the theories that attempt to exploit it. Such a postmodern sociology can only work in the margins or perhaps the footnotes of social theory (and this chapter).[2]

[2]Here postmodern theory will not take the form of a critique of modern social theory. We do not intend to produce a postmodern theory of modern theory. Such an attempt can only represent modern theory as something more coherent and rational than it ever has been. Instead, we would like to steal the effects of modern theory.

The effects of modern social theory are not at all tied to its coherence and rationality. The effects appear inconsistently here and there: in the biographical detail of the theorist, in the strangely chosen phrase, in the incongruous metaphor. The force of Weber's Protestant ethics, of Marx's fetishism of commodities, of Durkheim's mechanical solidarity, for example, do not lie at all in their rigorous positivity but in their very ambiguity—Weber's tangled relation to both his mother and his culture, Marx's use of a religious phrase that Freud was to so thoroughly sexualize, Durkheim's argument that social changes associated with the industrial revolution and its mechanization should destroy the society he chose to call mechanical. Postmodern theorists would like to simply appropriate these effects without any pretense to consistency.

After all, what can a postmodern theorist say about modern theory? That it is a myth? a paradox? an

One of the authors of this chapter previously has created a map of postmodern theory (Ritzer, 1997) that focused almost entirely on theorists (other efforts at mapping postmodern theory include Huyssen, 1984; Bertens, 1995; Antonio, 1998; Crook, 2001). In this chapter, we will instead map the *ideas* associated with postmodern social theory. While identifying postmodern ideas can be as difficult and ambiguous as identifying postmodern theorists, we have the advantage that social analysts in a wide variety of fields have selectively recognized and employed these ideas to enrich otherwise modern works. Ritzer (1999), to take one example, has done a very modern analysis of the "new means of consumption" utilizing several concepts that are central to postmodern theory: simulations, implosion, time, and space.

This effort to map postmodern concepts will be divided into three parts. First, we will deal with some of the *epistemological* concepts associated with postmodern social theory. Second, we will deal with a set of critical and ironic *analytical* tools that explore the new world that is emerging with the demise of modernity. In contrast to those who view postmodernists as unrelenting nihilists, we believe that the most useful legacy of postmodern theory may be its creation of a series of critical views of the contemporary world. One of the most important of these critical views is irony. Third, we will look at the relation between postmodern theory and consumer society.

EPISTEMOLOGICAL CONCEPTS

Decentering and Deconstruction

The focus on contingency leads to several postmodern epistemological concepts. First, there is *decentering*, a notion closely associated with Jacques Derrida (1977). Perhaps the most general meaning of decentering involves the surrender of the idea that there is a center, a source, a point of origin that determines subsequent and peripheral phenomena. Modern theory has been characterized by a series of searches for origins, be it Weber's search for the origins of modern capitalism in Calvinism or Durkheim's effort to find the source of mechanical solidarity in the increase in dynamic density. Decentering also involves surrendering the futile search for the "essence" of a social phenomenon as exemplified in modern social theory by Marx's view that the exploitation of the proletariat by the capitalists was the essence of the capitalist system or Wallerstein's neo-Marxist effort to find that essence in the exploitation of peripheral nations in the world system by those that lie at its core. Thus, modernists (e.g., Freudians, structuralists, Marxists) are obsessed by the idea of finding and unraveling the core phenomenon that will end in the discovery of the secret force or event that determines everything else. Postmodernists reject the idea of any such core phenomenon and urge, instead, that observers focus on what is presented as marginal and derivative.

Closely related is the notion, also tied to Derrida, of *deconstruction*. This involves an analysis that demonstrates that phenomena that are presented as marginal and derivative are always necessary for "propping up" what is presented as central and originary. For example,

---

impossibility? As though postmodern theory were not. What is a postmodern theorist to do with modern theory? Perhaps we were given modern theory, but like the borrower in the old joke, we have given it back and now we will admit to nothing: "Jean borrowed a kettle from Karl. Karl accused Jean of damaging the kettle. Jean's reply: first there was no kettle; second, I never borrowed it; and third, it was already damaged when I got it." There never was such a thing as modern theory, and besides, postmodern theory never borrowed it, and finally it was damaged when we got it.

Derrida (1974) is famous for deconstructing the way in which speaking has been presented as original and immediate, while writing has been presented as derivative and indirect. Derrida demonstrates, however, that speaking is better seen as a species of writing. Speaking is a material medium of arbitrary sound marks that is no more immediate and directly interpretable than writing. Presenting speaking as original and immediate allows for a central point from which to derive social rules, as seen from Plato to Garfinkel to Habermas. Once it is realized that all communication proceeds through an arbitrary material medium, the social rules derived from it are revealed as themselves arbitrary and contingent.

Perhaps the key point about deconstruction is what it does *not* involve; postmodernists reject the idea of deconstructing in order to establish a new construction. The latter would be more consistent with a modern approach to disassembling extant theories. Postmodernists reject it because it would simply involve the creation of a new oppressive and hegemonic theory that would in turn need to be deconstructed. The point Derrida makes is not that writing is more central than speaking, but that neither can anchor nonarbitrary social rules. For the postmodernist, deconstruction is to be followed by further deconstructions without end.

This relates to another fundamental difference between postmodern and modern social theory. Modern theory and more generally modern science are about the finding of the answer; the discovery of an underlying truth. Thus, the endless deconstruction of theories cannot be acceptable to modernists because it is of no help in discovering the truth. When they take extant theories apart, modernists only do so as an intermediate step toward the creation of a new theory that offers the answer. The contrary objective of the postmodernists is described by Richard Rorty (1979) as "continuing the conversation" rather than discovering the truth. Only the constant generation of new insights is able to reveal contingency rather than obscure it.

Totalizations and Grand Narratives

Two of the ways that modernists have obscured the contingency of society are through totalizations and grand narratives. *Totalizations* involve an effort to locate an underlying force, experience, or phenomena that explains most, or all, of the social world. Examples are legion in modern social theory and they include Parsons's structural functionalism, Blumer's symbolic interactionism, Luhmann's system theory, Giddens's structuration theory, and Coleman's rational choice theory. *Grand narratives* involve efforts to explain much or all of social history by making social change appear predictable or necessary. Among the modern examples are Weber's rationalization theory, Simmel's tragedy of culture, and various evolutionary theories including those of Comte, Spencer, Parsons, and Luhmann. For postmodernists, totalizations are only useful in order to make "war on totality" (Lyotard, 1993, p. 16) and the only useful grand narrative is "a grand narrative of the decline of the grand narratives" (Lyotard, 1993, p. 29).

Lyotard traces the evils of Nazism and Stalinism to grand theories of the ultimate triumph of the Aryan race and of the proletariat. Thus, totalizations and grand narratives, whether they exist in the social world or in the social sciences, are seen as terroristic and to be avoided at all costs. Wherever they are found they are to be deconstructed.

Overdetermination and Secondary Rationalizations

Postmodern epistemology is often described as *antirepresentational*. All language, including theory, is seen as unable to represent a reality that is external to it. Strangely enough, this is sometimes criticized as a kind of idealism, but far from it; the postmodern theory of language is radically materialist. For the postmodernist, language is not some ideal domain that is privileged over the material; instead, language is itself a material domain with its own history, determinants, and effects. The postmodern argument is that the material history of language has little to do with the history of the natural world. The relationship between language and the world is determined by contingency and pragmatism, it is not a relationship of representation and most especially not a relationship of truth.

Truth cannot possibly describe the relation between language and the world. Only an idealist theory of language can believe that language represents the world in a way that could be described as true. Contrary to the *X Files*, the truth is not out there. Reality is out there (and, for all we know, flying saucers might be out there), but truth is entirely in language. The relation between language and the world can only be useful or not useful. It cannot be true or not true.

This is why postmodernists argue that theories, which are part of language, cannot represent nature. Theories about nature have a contingent relationship with nature because they are different orders of materiality. Language is produced by the manipulation of oral and graphic inscriptions embedded in the historical and social contexts of human interactions. Nature is a separate domain of materiality. To some extent, nature can be made to determine pragmatically our theories about it—this is the point of experiments—but the theory is always underdetermined by the experiments. We can always think of other theories to adequately explain the experiments. We may choose a definitive explanation because it is more elegant or simpler or mathematical, but these have everything to do with the domain of language and nothing to do with nature.

However, this argument does not apply to the relation between society and theories about society. These two are of the same domain. In fact, language and society are so intertwined as to be inseparable. Nevertheless, discussing whether or not a theory about society is true is still seen as an unprofitable topic for a postmodernist. We can certainly discuss whether a theory is able to make accurate predictions about society, but this is not the same as being true. This difference is especially obvious when discussing the moral value of a theory: truth is its own good, while being able to make accurate predictions about human beings can be regarded as objectionable, especially if the prediction is successful because the theory is a reflection of a culturally pervasive domination. It is one thing, for example, to say that rational choice theory makes accurate predictions because it is true. It is another to say that rational choice theory makes accurate predictions because the theoretical assumptions reflect the domination of the capitalist economic system.

Despite the shared domain of language, postmodernists would argue that there is also a contingent relation between theory and society; this time not as a result of underdetermination, but by what Freud called "overdetermination." In dreams, Freud tells us that elements are overdetermined. This does not mean they are strongly determined, but that they can be seen as determined by multiple, contradictory systems. For example, a dream of being chased by a giant hotdog might refer to the dinner one had eaten, as well as a friend we had thought of named Frank, and a dachshund that we had as a child. It is even conceivable that Freud could add some sexual interpretation here.

Similarly, postmodernists would argue that theories about society and the language they are expressed in are overdetermined by the society from which they emerge and that they purport to study. The elements of the theory and the choice of words in which they are expressed are part of multiple contradictory systems. At one and the same time, they can be seen as determined by the biography of the theorist, the contemporary social context, the history of sociological theory, and the contingencies of linguistic, biographical, social, and historical accidents. Postmodernists believe that the force of a theory comes precisely from these overdeterminations.

Furthermore, postmodernists suspect that, like the dream, theory is subject to secondary rationalization. Although the importance of the dream lies in its shocking displacements and juxtapositions, the dreamer begins, soon after awakening, to rearrange the dream into a more rational structure. This tends to obscure the real force of the dream. Postmodernists see something similar happening with theory. The powerful and shocking juxtaposition and combinations of ideas are rationalized and their force is obscured by constructing an explanatory theoretical system. Postmodernists are interested in the original elements' ability to reveal the contingency of the present rather than constructing a secondary rationalization that explains the present and therefore makes it appear inevitable.[3]

Rather than creating a rational system, postmodernists focus on the contingency in language in order to reveal the contingency of the status quo. Postmodernism is interested in the effects of the circulation of overdetermined theoretical elements, but it does not want to rationalize them into a system. In this way, postmodern social theory is just like postmodern architecture, which "randomly and without principle but with gusto" cannibalizes all the styles and theories of the past and combines them "in overstimulating ensembles" (Jameson, 1991, p. 19).

The theoretical effect that postmodernists are most interested in is the creation of new possibilities. But this means that any ideas of theory revealing the true nature of society in the sense of essential underlying laws, forces, or processes must be abandoned. Such a revelation

---

[3]Let us take as an example the very theoretical element we are discussing: the "postmodern." We can understand this word as a contingent overdetermination within a material language system. The prefix "post" is usually taken to mean *after* modern, but this too is overdetermined by multiple linguistic meanings and the choice of any one meaning is contingent. For example, it is also true that the "post" could have the same relationship to the word "modern" that it has to the word "card" in "postcard."

In "postcard," the card carries the message and "post" indicates that it is circulating within a delivery system in which it can be freely read by everyone even if they are not the addressee. Accordingly, postmodern would mean a system that circulates the modern as a message and it would remain "post," i.e., in circulation, as long as it is not delivered to the intended addressee. Postmodern then is the modern that has gotten lost in the mail, is forever circulating, whose delivery is always delayed, and which is always being read by someone who is not the intended addressee. It is, as Baudrillard (1984, p. 25) says, "a game with the vestiges of what has been destroyed.... So we must move in it, as though it were a kind of circular gravity. We can no longer be said to progress."

In addition, postmodernists suspect that the message can never be delivered or else the whole circulating system will collapse. Let us take, for instance, the message that Mannheim circulated within the post system of sociological theory: that all social theories, both ideologies and utopias, are determined by the society from which they emerge. At least implicitly, this message has always circulated within sociology. We cannot imagine sociological theory without it being in circulation, but it can never be finally delivered or else sociology will collapse. What could be said after that message is delivered? What sociologist wants to simply be a mouthpiece for the status quo? Instead of accepting final delivery, we read its message and pretend that we are not the true addressee.

We are not saying that Mannheim, under this definition, was postmodern, but that sociology becomes postmodern so long as it has modern messages circulating within it that can never be delivered. It is these eternally deferred messages that make sociological theory a collection of effects rather than a fully rational system. In this sense, many modern social theories are postmodern in that they have central messages circulating within them that cannot be delivered. For example, exchange theorists look at social actions as a product of reinforcement schedules. The message that never can be delivered is that the theory itself must be a product of reinforcement schedules. If this message is delivered, then debates among the proponents of exchange theory should take the form of an exchange of food pellets or whatever passes as reinforcement. Rational debate would be a performative contradiction.

Of course, this meaning of "post"-modern makes a mockery of almost all criticisms of postmodernism. Every critic without exception has misunderstood the denotative meaning as a connotative meaning. "Post" does not mean after, but postal. We might say that, with this definition, postmodern theory has gone postal and the critics are among its victims.

(assuming it was a possibility) would place limits on what can be done. Instead, postmodernists believe that the essential nature of society is contingency and the role of theory is to reveal that. Theory should not tell us what *is to be* done but what *can be* done. Totalizing theoretical systems obscure the first brilliant flashes of new possibilities.

Theoretical Pluralism

Since theories are used as tools for revealing possibilities rather than for revealing essential underlying forces, postmodernists may juggle several descriptions of the same event without asking which one is correct. Instead of theoretical consistency, postmodernists ask whether the use of a particular theory gets in the way of our use of other theories. If Marxist macro theory and ethnomethodology make contradictory predictions, that is no reason not to use them together, so long as their conjunction opens up new possibilities.

A charge of relativism is simply irrelevant here. The relativism of the present society is precisely the goal of postmodern theory. Rather than revealing deep forces, postmodern theory reveals the contingency of present configurations by making comparisons with other attempts at social organization, both historical and utopian.[4]

The Subject

Postmodern contingency even invades the core of modern epistemological thought, the subject. Modern social theory has notoriously taken the subject, the human actor, as its assumed foundation. This is manifest in such diverse approaches as Freudian theory with its focus on the ego, Marxian theory and its central concern with species being and the proletariat, and Giddens's structuration theory with its focus on the empowered actor. Postmodern social theory, on the other hand, is rife with examples of subversions of the subject.

Foucault (1976, p. 16), for example, sought to create "a method of analysis purged of all anthropologism." He saw the focus on humans as subjects and objects as a relatively recent (18th century) development in the human sciences. For Foucault, modernity is precisely that era that produced the subject that is also an object. Under Foucault's definition, modernity began when human nature was seen as constituted by a social history. Rather than studying the

---

[4]In fact, most of the criticisms of postmodern theory, such as being contradictory and embracing relativism, are simply the projection of disputes that are internal to modern theory. What modern sociologist does not already use an array of contradictory theories? The charge of relativism assumes that there is an agreed upon foundation, but what foundation have modern theorists agreed on? Modern theory requires that the messages of sociology's intractable contradictions and always deferred foundation never be delivered. These circulate as post elements within the modern system. Each sociologist reads the message, uses the information, but never acknowledges receipt.

Postmodern theory does not create the contradictions, the relativism, or the contingency; it merely points them out. This is what the critics of postmodernism find most objectionable; like the man who came in to his doctor complaining of constantly farting, although they were at least silent and did not smell.

"In fact," said the patient, "since I've been here, I've farted no less than 20 times." The doctor gave him pills and instructed him to return next week. When the man returned, however, he was livid.

"I don't know what was in those pills, but the problem is worse! I'm farting just as much, and they're still soundless, but now they smell terrible! What do you have to say for yourself?"

"Calm down," said the doctor soothingly. "Now that we've fixed your sinuses, we'll work on your hearing."

Postmodern theory simply attempts to use theoretical effects to reveal the stench of contingency in the contemporary situation. It does this by focusing on the always deferred messages, the shocking juxtapositions, the overdeterminations, while trying to avoid any secondary rationalizations.

social history *of* human nature, it became necessary to understand human nature *as* social history. History and society were not something that happened to us, but something that we were. It was this change in perspective that made sociology possible.

Not only did human nature become a historical and social object of study, it also was fragmented into different specialized objects. Human nature existed within a biological organism of unfathomable complexity, at the center of an economic system whose products weighed upon it (him or her), embedded in a social system to which it (he or she) never agreed, lodged in a language whose history shaped its (his or her) thoughts. Each aspect required its own specific study. Rather than there being a unified human subject, there was the possibility of multiple human objects in different epistemic locations. The economic, linguistic, biological, historical, and social location of human nature were studied by different specialized sciences.

Modernity could no longer believe in a pure, direct apperception of the self. The knowledge of our fragmented self could only be secured through our very finitude. We can know the history of our being because we are historical beings; we can know society because we are social; and we can know biology because we are biological. Each of these positive forms in which one can learn that she is finite is given to her only against the background of her own finitude.

In what Foucault calls the classical age, one could believe in Descartes' simple equation of "I think" and "I am." In the modern age, the very language in which this is expressed becomes a problem. The words are seen as having a sociohistorical position, an indexicality, without which they are meaningless. The knowledge of ourselves is not given to us in the form of a pure language. The self's being and thinking are constituted by a social history that precedes that self and escapes any attempt to grasp it as a totality. In modernity, there is no guarantee that the "I" that thinks and the "I" that is are the same "I." In fact, the modern concept of the unconscious argues that they are not. The use of the same word to refer to both these selves is historically contingent. Consequently, the manifest philosophical truth that founded Descartes' system depends on a linguistic accident that is subject to change.

According to Foucault (1970, p. 316), the modern view of the subject creates an "interminable to and fro of a double system of reference." In the sciences that study humanity, humans appear as both the determined object of study and the free subject that knows. On the one hand, humans create history, society and language; on the other hand, we are produced by them and can only know ourselves through them and possibly we can only know them. From the second paragraph of Marx's (1926) *Eighteenth Brumaire* to Giddens' concept of structuration, modern sociology has never found a way to resolve this basic paradox, only clever ways to restate it.

In sociology, human nature appears both as a socially determined object and as a freely chosen project. This paradox threatens to undermine any sociological analysis, since the analysis itself may be the determined product of a social ideology. The paradox can be avoided only if the subject matter for sociological study is delimited ahead of time so that it excludes a self-reference to the theory being used. This is why sociologists cling so desperately to their traditional areas of study, for example, class, inequality, and production. A sociological analysis that is allowed to go outside these limited areas threatens to be self-refuting because sociology itself could be seen as a socially determined ideology.[5]

---

[5]These problems with the modern subject are projected onto postmodernism, which is criticized for suggesting that the subject is contingent. But the impossible place of the subject is a modern problem. Postmodernism is not concerned with the true nature of the subject, only with the way in which the subject circulates within a system that cannot

Modern sociology's solution to the impossible position of the subject has been an exhortation to get on with the important work of sociology. "Don't look behind the curtain," we have been told. That little object, who is also the wizardly subject, is of no importance. But the work we would get on with depends on which side of the ambivalent view of the self we use.

Beyond Positivism and Eschatology

In keeping with this double reference, we see two kinds of analysis in sociology: (1) a positivism that views human beings as determined objects; and (2) a political eschatology that sees human nature as a project of freedom. Modern sociology has been divided into positivists, surveyors, and economic historians on the one side and humanists Marxists, liberals, feminists, and multiculturalists on the other. While it may seem as if these two are alternatives, they really operate as a "fluctuation" (Foucault, 1970). Positivists have always nourished a hidden political eschatology and humanists have always reached for empiricism. A discourse attempting to be both empirical and critical must be both positivist and eschatological. Without both of these, modern sociologists lose their motivation to do sociology.

Postmodernism is usually supposed to be on the side of political eschatology, since its focus on contingency can be seen as preparing the ground for a new regime of human freedom. However, modern political projects usually take the form of totalizing theories that are based on assumptions about human nature that postmodernism would question. In this one sense, postmodernists show a certain humility. They do not believe that any theory can provide the motivation for social change. This must come from the local situation. Theory can only reveal the contingency of the present and the multiple possibilities of the future.[6]

---

deliver its message without collapsing: the positions it (he or she) can assume, the rules for its (his or her) circulation, the symptoms caused by its (his or her) nondelivery. For the postmodernist, the goal of this analysis is not to understand the subject, but to understand what can come after the subject.

In the circulating system of modern sociology, the self functions as a postmodern element. A central tenet of modern sociology is that the subject is a socially determined object, a social fact. This, however, is a message that can never be finally delivered to at least one set of subjects, that is, to sociologists. Sociologists can only believe in the importance of what they do if they can pretend that the message is not addressed to them. Otherwise, if the sociologist is herself a socially determined object, what can she say that is not simply a reflection of her social position? This constant circulation of the always deferred message makes for peculiar symptoms in sociology's depiction of the human subject. As Dennis Wrong (1961) pointed out, the sociological subject always seems "oversocialized."

[6]Conversely, postmodernists are usually supposed to be against positivism. However, in a strange way, postmodernists and positivists seem to need each other. Both are marginal to sociology but each feels compelled to present the other as dominant. Nevertheless, despite the rhetorical flights of animosity, postmodernism is not *necessarily* opposed to positivism.

Positivism can be defined in two ways. First, it can be defined, as Habermas (1971) does, as an aversion to reflexivity. Second, it could be defined, as Turner (1992) does, as a focus on invariant laws. Postmodernism, with its focus on contingency, would reject the first and be skeptical but interested in the second.

It is easy to see why Habermas would define positivism as an aversion to reflexivity. Not only do positivists not engage in reflexivity, but they go to great rhetorical lengths to dismiss it as navel gazing, solipsism, unresolvable metatheorizing, German idealism, French foolishness, American pseudorevolutionary ranting, and so forth. In many ways, positivism seems to be structured around an attempt to evade the paradox of the modern subject. There is a complete lack of consideration of what it means if the invariant laws discovered by the sociologist also apply to the sociologist. This is precisely what the positivist wants to dismiss as navel gazing. For the postmodernist, these sorts of paradoxes are a primary source of contingency, and therefore they are to be studied and elaborated on, rather than dismissed with catchwords.

On the other hand, anyone concerned with revealing contingency must also be interested in what is not

There are many other important epistemological ideas associated with postmodern social theory—*essentialism, difference, genealogy, intertextuality, representation, text, difference, alterity*, to name just a few—but we lack the space here to deal with more of them. The essential point is that the postmodernists have developed a wide array of epistemological concepts that lead them to take a very different approach to social theory than the modernists.

ANALYTIC CONCEPTS

In this section, we will look at a second set of the most important postmodern concepts: those concepts that can be used to critically analyze social phenomena in order to reveal their contingency. Modern sociological concepts are often compared to a set of analytic tools. These are used to investigate epiphenomena in order to reveal underlying forces and categories. Postmodern concepts can be seen as a set of "special effects" used to reveal the contingency of the phenomena. As in cinematic special effects, the audience is not asked to believe in the reality of the effect, but on the contrary to suspend belief in reality.

The difference between the two can be illustrated in the film that many consider to be the epitome of postmodernism, *Blade Runner*. *Blade Runner* is about discerning the difference between true humans and the manufactured simulations called replicants. This is a life and death difference, since the job of the hero of the film is to "retire," or murder, the replicants. In the film, the difference is established by an analytical tool that supposedly magnifies the eye of the subject in order to examine emotional responses to a set of preselected questions. However, when we watch the movie closely, we notice that the eye being examined is not so much magnified as simulated. Even when different eyes are being tested, their simulation on the screen of the analytical tool is always the same and the color of the simulated eye does not match the eye of the subject.

The eye as the site of analysis for revealing the underlying truth is one of the central themes of the movie. We see the factory where the replicants' eyes are manufactured; the "father" of the replicants (their primary designer and founder of the manufacturing company) is killed by putting out his eyes; and the final emotional appeal from the dying replicant is in terms of what his eyes have seen. But most importantly, the entire enterprise of distinguishing between humans and replicants is subverted. By the end of the movie, we know that the replicants are more human than the originals.

If modern sociologists appeared in this movie, we could imagine them refining the analytical test, improving the preselected questions, and perfecting the eye's simulation, but the sociologists would not notice the inescapable contingency of the distinction that they are investigating. The distinction between humans and their simulation is a brutal contingency with fatal consequences for those on the wrong side of the historical accident. Any search for an underlying force used to distinguish between the real and the simulation simply serves to

---

contingent. Positivism's invariant laws would indicate both those social elements that cannot be contingent and the framework for increasing contingency for the rest. Nevertheless, it is difficult not to be skeptical about this goal. After over a century of pursuing it, sociological positivism has yet to produce one nontrival, generally accepted, invariant sociological law. By its own criteria, it has failed.

The problem for positivist might be called the $n+1$ dilemma. It is easy enough for positivists to propose n laws that seem to govern the local situation, but their hope is always to find the $n+1$ rule that governs the application of the n rules, and therefore is invariant. Postmodernists also believe in an $n+1$ rule, but for them it functions like Lecercle (1990, p. 93) describes the rules of grammar. For any natural language, there are n rules that describe correct language use and there is always an $n+1$ rule that "allows any or all of the n rules to be broken." In other words, the invariant law that the positivists search for is contingency.

justify the contingency and its brutality. The application of this insight to such staples of sociological investigations as race, gender, and class should be obvious. While a modern analysis takes these as independent variables and investigates their consequences, a postmodern analysis reveals the contingency of the categories.

Genealogy

This, for example, is the point of Foucault's use of *genealogy*. Genealogy is opposed to the search for origins, for the real, for the hidden truth. According to the genealogist, there is no essential secret behind history, except the secret that there is no essence, "or that the essence was fabricated in piecemeal fashion from alien forms" (Foucault, 1984, p. 78). Genealogy traces this piecemeal fabrication and shows historical change to be as contingent as the relation between generations in a family. This is not to say that the present inherits nothing from the past, but that the relation is as likely to be a reactionary reversal, or a mythical recreation as a straightforward adaptation.

In his analyses of punishment (Foucault, 1979) and sexuality (Foucault, 1980), Foucault's genealogies never reveal the truth of punishment or sex but rather their contingency. His history of sexuality, for instance, does not aim to locate the true nature of sex and then analyze its repression; instead, he reveals the historical contingency of our present notions of sex in order to open up the possibilities for new configurations of pleasures.

Hegemonic Articulations

Ernesto Laclau and Chantal Mouffe stress the contingency of constructing political identity. They see this as happening through a process of hegemony within a project of radical democracy. This concept of hegemony goes back to Gramsci's (1988) ambivalent definition. It is, as commonly recognized, a tool of the dominant class, but it is also the process through which diverse subaltern interests are brought together to construct a revolutionary class. In the hands of Laclau and Mouffe, hegemony becomes the solution to the problem of postmodern identity and totalizations. They take from Derrida (1972) the idea that all identity is an effect of systems of differences that are inherently unstable and decentered. And they take from Jacques Lacan (1977) the idea that human beings are essentially defined by a lack which they struggle to cover over. Identity then is not something that we have, but something that is cobbled together out of the multiplicity of subject positions that can be found within the systems of differences that make up society. Hegemonic practices provide a temporary and ultimately impossible center that allows us to construct an identity within a differential system.

Hidden hegemonic practices have been used to maintain the traditional belief in an essential identity and a totalized social field despite personal and social fragmentation. These hegemonic practices, once freed from their secret servitude to an essentialist logic, exhibit the nature of social reality as irreducibly plural and diverse. Sociological analysis can acknowledge and privilege this difference without making it an essential characteristic of individuals. This approach rejects both "the abstract Enlightenment universalism of an undifferentiated human nature" (Laclau & Mouffe, 1985, p. 36) and the Romantic celebration of individual diversity. It sees the plurality of subject positions as a product of a diversity of discourses.

Discourse comprises everything (including material objects) that is "meaningful" in a system of differences in which meaning for any particular element is given by temporarily and partially fixing a center for that system. It is, according to Laclau (1988, p. 71), "coterminous with the 'social.' Because every social action has a meaning, it is constituted in the form of discursive sequences that articulate linguistic and extralinguistic elements." Michéle Barrett (1991, pp. 65–66) points out that the

> ... definition of discourse by Laclau and Mouffe does not, as has been immediately concluded by several materialists, represent a vertiginous leap into idealism. The concept of discourse in their hands is a materialist one that enables them to rethink the analysis of social and historical phenomena in a different framework.

Most significantly, material social structures and their meanings can be seen as linked through hegemonic practices rather than a natural and immutable relationship.

Irony and Fatal Strategies

Even genealogy and hegemonic articulations, however, are too modern for some postmodernists, since they seem to ignore the contingency of the analysis itself and are presented as the basis for a triumphant progression toward greater freedom of the subject. Instead, the most important conceptual conceits for many postmodernists is irony and many of the concepts and categories proposed by postmodernists must be understood in terms of this.

Baudrillard, for example, unable to hold onto his former Marxist hope for a revolutionary subject, instead ironically reverses the Marxist division between revolutionary subjects and the ideologically controlled masses. He assigns a revolutionary role to the masses and their fatal strategies (Baudrillard, 1990). While the masses do not want to be liberated, their silence and ability to absorb everything that is done to them makes it possible for them to drag "power down to its fall" (Baudrillard, 1990, p. 95). Such strategies are fatal because the masses respond of their own accord and it is impossible to escape from those responses. The victory of the masses will not be a dazzling revolution, "but obscure and ironic; it won't be dialectical, it will be fatal" (Baudrillard, 1990, p. 96). To attain such a revolution, fatal objects like the masses cannot take direct, conscious action. Rather, they must aim "to the side, beyond, off center"; in this way, "duplicity is strategic and fatal" (Baudrillard, 1990, pp. 77, 78).

Baudrillard's ironic conceptions mirror the irony of the contemporary world. For some, there is no other way to approach a postmodern world. This is also the basis for Lyotard's (1984) *paralogy*, which continually undermines itself through such devices as seeking out or inventing counterexamples, looking for paradoxes, and aiming at dissensus.

Simulation, Simulacra, and Hyperreality

For many, the postmodern world is associated with a type of unreality that Jean Baudrillard (1994) has labeled *simulation*. The increasingly widespread existence of simulations erodes many crucial modern distinctions such as those between the real and the fake, the true and the false, the original and the copy. As we live more and more of our lives in simulated settings, we will increasingly lack a basis for making these kinds of distinctions. Thus, if we are born and raised in Disney's town of Celebration, or one of the many communities throughout the United States that are its clones, we will be increasingly unable to distinguish Las Vegas casino-hotels like Paris, the Venetian, and Mandalay Bay from the real thing.

Simulacra (Baudrillard, 1994) is a particularly important form of simulation. Here we have a simulation of a simulation with no actual original.[7] For example, the concept of traditional family values used in politics today is a simulation that has its original in the type of families that existed in television programs such as *Father Knows Best*. It is thus a simulation of a simulation with little relation to actual traditional families.

With the concept of the *hyperreal*, Baudrillard argues that these simulations have become more real than real and truer than true. It is little wonder, then, that people increasingly come to prefer simulated hyperreality to the real thing. Disneyland (and Celebration) is far cleaner than the world outside its gates and the personnel under the simulated Eiffel tower in Las Vegas are far friendlier than those in France. In the hyperreal world, *Father Knows Best* becomes the basis according to which we measure our family, Las Vegas's simulations are the model for judging the authenticity of other cultures, and pornography is the standard for real sex.

Dromology

For Paul Virilio, the move to the hyperreal allows for the emergence of high-speed, global, virtual systems that are at war with reality. Pushed by technology, especially in the service of war, superspeeded virtual systems replace the slower intersubjectivity necessary for traditional political, economic, and ethical decisions. This makes all traditional sociological analysis obsolete and in need of replacement by what Virilio (1986) calls *dromology*, an analysis of the critical role played by brakes and accelerators. What is important for contemporary society is not a study of the differences between periphery and core or between urban and rural, but of the brakes and accelerators connecting the flow of images and information between the different regions.

Of special importance for this analysis is what Virilio calls vectors, those interconnections along which information and images flow. These vectors delocalize events, making distant public actions appear as private dramas. Spatial proximity becomes irrelevant and instead the speed of transmission is crucial. The tendency of vectors is toward increasing velocity, flexibility, and interconnection.

Virtual Geography

According to McKenzie Wark (1994, p. vii), this hyperreal, dromological virtual reality creates a virtual geography that "doubles, troubles and generally permeates our experience of the space we experience first-hand." In fact, the virtual reality is so much a part of our everyday life that now the real only emerges in times of extreme weirdness. For example, the stock market is now a virtual reality where crucial economic decisions are made by machines because of the amount of available information that must be processed and the premium placed on speed. We can only understand the market by looking at such times of weirdness as the crash of 1987, when there are extreme movements with no apparent basis in reality.

At those times of weirdness, we see that movements in the stock market are increasingly in response to high-speed changes in virtual representations rather than any change in the underlying reality of concrete firms. The exponential increases in the amount of information and the speed of transmission do not result in greater transparency but in a system that no

---

[7]Baudrillard is not consistent in this distinction between simulations and simulacra and often uses the two interchangeably.

human being can possibly understand. The high-speed virtual representations of the market become a third reality that is autonomous from the second reality of the market and almost wholly removed from the first reality of actual businesses. Since this virtual market on computer screens is everywhere and never sleeps, smart investors study the movements of the more accessible virtual market rather than trying to determine the reality beneath the representation. Increasingly, the economic well-being of the individual is as tied to the virtual reality of the market represented on their computer screens as it is to the actual business he or she may work for.

CONSUMER SOCIETY

One of the central figures of postmodernism is consumer society and it is especially here that postmodern theory begins to theorize its own condition of possibility. The postmodernism of endlessly circulating, always deferred messages is not simply an intellectual fantasy. It finds its roots in the everyday life of consumer culture where messages are overproduced and overdetermined. Advertising becomes precisely the type of "post" system that we have been discussing when the target audience takes up the ironic position of the nonaddressee of the message. Who really believes that "Coke is it" or that Nike wants you to "just do it" or that you can "have it your way?" These messages simply circulate within the system and are never delivered as modern messages to anyone.

In the ideal consumer culture, consumption does not use things up; instead, it keeps things in circulation. Commodities are taken up on whim and passed off as soon as their instant gratification begins to fade. Items are not worn out; they go out of fashion so that they can later be recirculated as nostalgia.

This creates what Baudrillard (1993) describes as a fashion system. First, capitalism transforms all objects into commodities where qualitative differences are transformed into the interchangeable quantitative differences of a monetary system. Then a similar thing happens to messages where meaningful differences between messages are transformed into an interchangeable fashion message. To wear the scarf of the *intifada* or a French beret is a fashion choice rather than a message about identity. A white bridal dress no longer indicates that one has maintained the "purity" demanded by a religious affiliation. The choice of ethnic foods has little to do with one's own background. All of these become simply another expression of fashion.

The message of fashion refers only to its own circulation. Communication is replaced by play. Changes in fashion do not represent any change in an underlying reality. This year's model refers to last year's model and the creative novelties added to it, or to last decade's model, and the ironic attitude with which it is reappropriated. The rhetoric of new and improved replaces actual change.

A fashion system makes a mockery of any attempt to analyze underlying forces. Fashion has no deep meaning and it revels in its superficiality. Analyses of class, gender, or racial determinations are likely to find themselves entering the fashion system as the latest element. Feminist critiques of fashion produced feminist fashions and then postfeminist fashions, which are actually ironic prefeminist fashions.

Baudrillard's argument is that all of our serious codes—politics, morality, sexuality, economics, science—are being transformed into a fashion system. Gore is the new and improved Clinton; Bush is the new and improved Bush. Differences between candidates have more to do with style than substance.[8]

Resistance and Irony

Talk of resisting the hyperreal fashion system of consumer culture is part of the game. Resistance is already built into consumer culture in the ironic detachment that is part of its pleasure. We buy music to reflect our revolutionary pretensions, cars to escape the rat race, toilet paper to save the environment, and scented soap to enrich the Third world.

The critique of consumer culture cannot emerge from an analysis that reveals the underlying truth of advertising and consumption. The falsity of consumer culture does not lie in the difference between its facade and any underlying reality. In consumer culture, there is nothing but facade and everyone knows it for what it is. Consumers already know that advertising is not true and that fashions are superficial and they turn their same ironic attention to the ideology critiques of sociologists.

The falsity of consumer culture lies in the idea that there is something outside of the fashion system, just as the falsity of Las Vegas lies in the idea that there is an authentic Eiffel tower that is not just a tourist gimmick and the falsity of pornography lies in the idea that there is an authentic sexual encounter where bodies are no longer objectified. Modern social theorists cling to the fading hope that their revelation of underlying reality is something different from an advertisement, something that will finally be taken seriously by the ironic consumer. What can the social theorist tell consumers about their culture that they do not already know? What idea can theorists produce that will not be turned into an advertising slogan? The critical force of consumer culture emerges not from a comparison of its surface mendacity to its underlying reality. Instead, it comes from what consumer culture reveals about modernity: that modernity is an endlessly circulating advertising slogan to be taken ironically.

All the criticisms of consumer culture are true. It has lost its connection to any objective reality. It wastes energy in the pursuit of impossible fantasies. It absorbs and co-opts its own

---

[8]We see this even in the intellectual world where buzzwords and catchphrases are used to sell books and attract students. Foremost among these are the terms "modernism" and "modernity." There is a constantly increasing list of books and articles that discuss modernity or modernism despite the fact that no one seems quite sure what the words mean. Most definitions are hopelessly vague and often inconsistent with each other. Modernism is, in the words of Ernst Gellner (1992, p. 22), "a contemporary movement. It is strong and fashionable. Over and above this it is not altogether clear what the devil it is." Even its supporters admit to its lack of meaning. "I have the impression that it is applied today to anything the users of the term happen to like" (Eco, 1989, p. 65). Dick Hebdige (1986, p. 78) complains that the term "modern" can be applied to "the decor of a room, the design of a building, the diegesis of a film, the construction of a record, or a 'scratch' video, a TV commercial, or an arts documentary, or the 'intertextual' relations between them, the layout of a page in a fashion magazine or a critical journal...." In a full-page sentence, he goes on to note that there are modern philosophies, modern music, modern subjects, modern styles, modern crises, modern narratives, modern technologies, modern nations, modern ages. When it becomes possible to describe all these things as modern, he concludes, "then it's clear we are in the presence of a buzzword."

In their infamously ironic style, these modernists and their tongue-in-cheek critics use the term postmodern rather than modern in the above quotes, but it is clear that the postmodern is actually the truth of the modern. The meaning of the modern itself is always post, always lost in the mail, eternally deferred, and constantly circulating. There really is no such thing as the modern, only a postmodern; but nevertheless, it is useful to retain the term "modern" to designate the deferred messages circulating within postmodernity.

criticisms. But what the critics must pretend not to see is that their own visions of modernity have these same defects circulating within them as undelivered messages. Modern social theory also has trends and fads, it has also entered the fashion system. For this year's model, we see an updated Parsonsian garb (fashionable now that it is passé), accessorized with frills derived from ethnomethodology and exchange theory and, for that daring touch, a hint of postmodern decadence.

It is not the frivolous contingency of consumer culture versus the serious truth of modernity. If that is it, how can we explain why consumer culture is increasingly dominant, except with a fatalistic theory of ideological dupes? Instead, it is the frivolous, playful, ironic contingency of consumer culture against the serious contingency of modernity. The truth is that most people prefer the former. Perhaps sociological theorists prefer the seriousness of modernity because theirs is already such a frivolous profession that they feel they must prove their seriousness.

Even sociological theorists should consider shopping for a new and improved social theory. Ask yourself this: Don't you deserve a brand new social theory? Haven't you worked hard for it? You owe it to yourself! You owe it to your friends and loved ones! Hurry down and see our new models!

FUTURE PROSPECTS

Postmodernists have had a profound impact on contemporary social theory. It is difficult to do social theory today without at least knowing the basics of postmodern theory. While many use it as a negative touchstone in their own work, a not insignificant number of social theorists are employing postmodern ideas in the development of their theories and others are making unique contributions to postmodern social theory. Some forms of social theory—symbolic interactionism, critical theory, globalization theory—have proven very receptive to postmodern ideas, but others—exchange theory, rational choice theory—have been highly resistant. Others, most notably feminist theory, have been very ambivalent about postmodern social theory, with some like Judith Butler (1990) (Clough, 2000) and Donna Haraway (1990) making important contributions of their own to the theory, while other feminists (e.g., Harding, 1990) have been highly critical of theory because it undercuts some of the goals and aspirations of feminist theory. For example, while at least some feminist theorists have sought to develop a general theory of women in the contemporary world, postmodernists are seen as rejecting the very idea of a general theory. Overall, there is a very uneasy relationship between feminist and postmodern social theory.

Not only is the impact of postmodern social theory uneven across the range of theoretical perspectives, it also varies geographically. European theorists were much quicker than their American counterparts to understand the importance of postmodern social theory, to address its basic ideas in their own work, and to make positive contributions to that theory. Indeed, to this day postmodern social theory is dominated by European thinkers. There has been much more resistance to postmodern ideas in American social theory and their impact was felt much later in this country. Even when it was felt, it had far less impact on American theorists than on their European counterparts and many Americans remain unalterably opposed to postmodern theory, even if they know relatively little about it. What they know of it seems to them both baffling and threatening.

Interestingly, while postmodern social theory retains the aura of being something new in American social theory, it seems passe to many Europeans. After all, many of the most important works in postmodern social theory (e.g., by Derrida, Lyotard, Foucault, and Baudrillard) were published decades ago and many of today's European theorists read them while they were graduate students or relatively new professors. The public uproar over postmodern ideas has long since passed and European theorists in varying ways have made their peace with them. Thus, from the European perspective, the situation in the United States seems incomprehensible. Many European theorists wonder why so much heat is being generated in the United States today over a set of ideas that is "old business" as far as they are concerned.

More extremely, many European theorists have gone beyond postmodernism to create what is known as "post-postmodernism." Thinkers associated with this perspective (e.g., Lipovetsky, 1994; Ferry & Renaut, 1990; Lilla, 1994) are well-steeped in postmodern ideas, but they are uncomfortable with many of them. They often take the position that the postmodernists went too far in rejecting various ideas associated with modern social theory—the human subject, individualism, universal rational norms, human rights, liberalism, democracy—and they seek to resurrect such ideas and give them their rightful place at the heart of social theory.

While some social theorists are just now learning the basics of postmodern social theory and others have moved beyond it, basic works in postmodern social theory continue to appear. While Foucault is dead and Baudrillard is long past his prime, Zygmunt Bauman (now in his late 70s) continues to produce works that develop his unique perspective that represents a fusion of modern and postmodern ideas. In his most recent books, *Globalization* (Bauman, 1998) and *Liquid Modernity* (Bauman, 2000), he describes a postmodern world in which the "solidity" of early modernity and the later efforts at reforming those solid structures and replacing them with new and improved ones have both passed from the scene. They have been displaced by a new form of modernity that is defined by its liquidity rather than its solidity. It is increasingly difficult for people to understand and deal with the fluidity that exists everywhere from global relations, interpersonal relationships, and even the self. This new, highly fluid world can be thought of as postmodern and in need of being conceptualized from the perspective of postmodern social theory.

While Bauman has an ambiguous relationship to postmodern social theory, Paul Virilio is more clearly associated with postmodern social theory and he, too, remains active and productive. Among his most recent books are *Open Sky* (Virilio, 1997) and *The Information Bomb* (Virilio, 2000). In these works Virilio continues his analysis of the increasing importance of speed in the contemporary world, but he brings it more up-to-date by dealing with the Internet, cyberspace, and the new information technologies.

However, the real problem facing postmodern social theory is whether it will be able to produce a second-generation of postmodern theorists who will pick up and develop the ideas created by the founding generation of Derrida, Lyotard, Foucault, Baudrillard, and Virilio. At the moment, the prospects do not appear bright; no younger theorist has emerged as the leader of the next generation of postmodern social theorists. It may be that the first generation was so idiosyncratic and their ideas so unique that they defy efforts by others to build upon them. The parallel in more mainstream American social theory is Erving Goffman whose ideas were so brilliant and idiosyncratic that no thinker ever emerged to carry forth and extend his perspective. In fact, it may be that this entire idea of building on one's predecessors is far too modern for the postmodernists; it implies some sort of grand and positive trajectory for the development of social theory. It also implies, in the ultramodern terms of Thomas Kuhn (1996), some sort of "normal science" following the "revolutionary" breakthroughs of the first generation of postmodern theorists. It may be, however, that we are more likely to see, given the postmodern perspective, another revolutionary breakthrough with only a genealogical relation to the previous one.

The future is always murky, especially using a postmodern optic; but it is clear that social theory will never be the same in the aftermath of the postmodern revolution.

REFERENCES

Antonio, R. (1998). Mapping postmodern social theory. In A. Sica (Ed.), *What is social theory: The philosophical debates* (pp. 22–75). Malden, MA: Blackwell.
Barrett, M. (1991). *The politics of truth: From Marx to Foucault*. Stanford, CA: Stanford University Press.
Baudrillard, J. (1984). Game with vestiges. *On the Beach, 5*, 19–25.
Baudrillard, J. (1990). *Fatal strategies*. New York: Semiotext(e).
Baudrillard, J. (1993). *Symbolic exchange and death*. London: Sage.
Baudrillard, J. (1994). *Simulacra and simulation*. Ann Arbor, MI: University of Michigan Press.
Bauman, Z. (1998). *Globalization: The human consequences*. New York: Columbia University Press.
Bauman, Z. (2000). *Liquid modernity*. Cambridge, England: Polity Press.
Bertens, H. (1995). *The idea of the postmodern: A history*. New York: Routledge.
Butler, J. (1990). *Gender trouble: Feminism and subversion of identity*. New York: Routledge.
Clough, P. (2000). Judith Butler. In G. Ritzer (Ed.), *The Blackwell companion to major social theorists* (pp. 754–773). Malden, MA.: Blackwell.
Crook, S. (2001). Social theory and the postmodern. In G. Ritzer & B. Smart, (Eds.), *Handbook of social theory* (pp. 308–323). London: Sage.
Derrida, J. (1974). *Of grammatology*. Baltimore: Johns Hopkins University Press.
Derrida, J. (1977). Structure, sign and play in the discourse of the human sciences. In R. Macksey & E. Donato (Eds.), *The structuralist controversy: The languages of criticism and the sciences of man* (pp. 247–272). Baltimore: Johns Hopkins University Press.
Eco, U. (1989). Postscript. In *The name of the rose* (pp. 501–536). New York: Harcourt Brace Jovanovich.
Ferry, L., & Renaut, A. (1990). *French philosophy of the sixties: An essay on antihumanism*. Amherst: University of Massachusetts Press.
Foucault, M. (1970). *The order of things*. New York: Vintage Books.
Foucault, M. (1976). *The archaeology of knowledge and the discourse of language*. New York: Harper Colophon.
Foucault, M. (1979). *Discipline and punish*. New York: Vintage.
Foucault, M. (1980). *History of sexuality*. New York: Vintage.
Foucault, M. (1984). *Power-knowledge: Selected interviews and other writings, 1972–1977*. New York: Pantheon.
Gellner, E. (1992). *Postmodernism, reason, and religion*. London: Routledge.
Gramsci, A. (1988). *A Gramsci reader: Selected writings, 1916–1935*. London: Lawrence and Wishart.
Habermas, J. (1971). *Knowledge and human interests*. Boston: Beacon Press.
Haraway, D. (1990). A manifesto for cyborgs: Science, technology, and socialist feminism in the 1980s. In L. Nicholson (Ed.), *Feminism/postmodernism* (pp. 190–233). London: Routledge.
Harding, S. (1990). Feminism, science and the anti-enlightenment critiques. In L. Nicholson (Ed.), *Feminism/postmodernism* (pp. 83–106). London: Routledge.
Hebdige, D. (1986). Postmodernism and "the other side." *Journal of Communication Inquiry, 10*(2), 78–98.
Huyssen, A. (1984). Mapping the postmodern. *New German Critique, 33*, 5–52.
Jameson, F. (1991). *Postmodernism, or the cultural logic of later capitalism*. Durham, NC: Duke University Press.
Kuhn, T. (1996). *The structure of scientific revolutions*, 3rd ed. Chicago: University of Chicago Press.
Lacap, J. (1977). *Écrits: A selection*. New York: Norton.
Laclau, E. (1988). Politics and the limits of modernity. In A. Ross (Ed.), *Universal abandon? The politics of postmodernism*. Minneapolis: University of Minnesota Press.
Laclau, E., & Mouffe, C. (1985). *Hegemony and socialist strategy: Towards a radical democratic politics*. New York: Verso.
Lecercle, J.-J. (1990). Postmodernism and language. In R. Boyne & A. Rattansi (Eds.), *Postmodernism and society* (pp. 76–96). New York: St. Martin's Press.
Lilla, M. (1994). *New French thought: Political philosophy*. Princeton: Princeton University Press.
Lipovetsky, G. (1994). *The empire of fashion: Dressing modern democracy*. Princeton: Princeton University Press.
Lyotard, J.-F. (1984). *The postmodern condition*. Minneapolis: University of Minnesota Press.
Lyotard, J.-F. (1993). *The postmodern explained*. Minneapolis: University of Minnesota Press.
Ritzer, G. (1997). *Postmodern social theory*. New York: McGraw-Hill.

Ritzer, G. (1999). *Enchanting a disenchanted world: Revolutionizing the means of consumption*. London: Sage.

Rorty, R. (1979). *Philosophy and the mirror of nature*. Princeton, NJ: Princeton University Press.

Turner, J. (1992). The promise of positivism. In S. Seidman & D. Wagner (Eds.), *Postmodernism and social theory* (pp. 156–178). Malden, MA: Blackwell.

Virilio, P. (1986). *Speed and politics*. New York: Semiotext(e).

Virilio, P. (1997). *Open sky*. New York: Verso.

Virilio, P. (2000). *The information bomb*. New York: Verso.

Wark, M. (1994). *Virtual geography: Living with global media events*. Bloomington, IN: Indiana University Press.

Wrong, D. (1961). The oversocialized conception of man in modern sociology. *American Sociological Review, 26*(2), 183–193.

CHAPTER 9

Culture and Identity

Michèle Lamont

In line with the charge given to the contributors to this volume by its editor, instead of providing a broad theoretical discussion of cultural theory and identity, I spell out my own contribution to the study of culture and identity. I will concentrate primarily on themes central to my most recent book, *The Dignity of Working Men* (Lamont, 2000a). I will also refer to my edited books, *Rethinking Comparative Cultural Sociology* (Lamont & Thévenot, 2000) and *The Cultural Territories of Race* (Lamont, 1999), and to recent papers. I will emphasize theoretical and empirical contributions. Within space constraints, I also will locate my work within the literature and discuss future challenges and research directions.

I share the widely held view that the constitution of personal and collective identity is relational in nature. I analyze this relational process by studying inductively boundary work, i.e., on how people define "us" and "them." Whereas the literature opposes primordial–essentialist and constructivist (or modern and postmodern) conceptions of identity, I position myself in between: My research suggests that identity is constructed but bounded by the cultural repertoires to which people have access and the structural context in which they live. My work largely consists in analyzing the meaning-making process by which groups create boundaries between "us" and "them"; I demonstrate how the meanings given to boundaries vary across class, race, nations, and so forth, depending on the cultural and structural contexts that shape these groups' lives. This focus on meaning-making in the drawing of boundaries across groups leads to new empirical insights in comparative sociology and the sociology of inequality that eschew flattening out differences in definitions of status and in the criteria of evaluation used across groups. It also leads to new theoretical insights by bringing to light a range of questions that speaks to issues of cultural membership and commensuration processes.

The discussion will revolve around (1) identity and symbolic boundaries; (2) comparative sociology and collective/national identity; (3) self, inequality, and resistance; and (4) boundaries and racism. I will conclude with a reflection on future research agendas.

An early version of this chapter was presented at the plenary session on "Cultural Identity" at the Conference "The Culture Society: A New Place for the Arts in the Twenty-first Century" organized by the International Sociological Association Research Committee for the Sociology of the Arts, the Spanish Association for the Sociology of Culture and the Arts, and the European Sociological Association Network of the Sociology of the Arts, July 6–8, 2000.

MICHÈLE LAMONT • Department of Sociology, Princeton University, Princeton, New Jersey 08540.

Handbook of Sociological Theory, edited by Jonathan H. Turner. Kluwer Academic / Plenum Publishers, New York, 2002.

IDENTITY AND SYMBOLIC BOUNDARIES

Symbolic boundaries are the lines that define some people, groups, and things while excluding others (Epstein, 1992, p. 232). These distinctions can be expressed through normative interdictions (taboos), cultural identities, attitudes and practices, and more generally through patterns of likes and dislikes.[1] They play a central role in the definition of identity. Indeed, Freud, Lacan, and other classical theorists of identity understand it as defined relationally, in opposition to other meanings, against which identities take on their own significance. References to this relational process also are present in much of the contemporary literature on identity in the social sciences and in cultural studies.[2] While contemporary social psychologists also understand the relational process as a universal tendency,[3] my own work is concerned with analyzing how boundary work is accomplished and more specifically with what kinds of typification systems or inferences concerning similarities and differences groups mobilize to define who they are. This is one of the loci where cultural sociologists can make a contribution to the literature on identity: by studying meaning-making processes and categories through which group boundaries are constructed and how they are shaped by available cultural repertoires and the structural conditions in which people live.

My approach to the study of categorization has been largely inductive: Through in-depth interviews, I have asked individuals to describe the types of people they feel are superior and inferior to them, or similar and different, and how they define worthy people more generally.[4] This inductive approach, which avoids imposing a priori definitions of identity onto my subject,[5] is supplemented by the use of survey data that allow me to identify patterns across groups and to generalize, within limits, about group differences.

In my earlier book, *Money, Morals, and Manners* (Lamont, 1992), I was specifically interested in analyzing how professionals and managers define worthy people and how they use these criteria to draw class boundaries. This book documented the relative salience of cultural, socioeconomic, and moral boundaries and the criteria used to draw these boundaries across contexts (e.g., in France vs. the United States, in cultural centers vs. cultural peripheries, among social and cultural specialists vs. for-profit workers). It provided a grounded critique of Bourdieu's (1984) most influential book, *Distinction*, by examining the importance of cultural boundaries relative to other types of boundaries and by questioning some of its meta-theoretical assumptions.

[1]For reviews of the social science literature on symbolic boundaries, see Lamont (forthcoming) and Molnár and Lamont (forthcoming).

[2]For instance, sociologist Richard Jenkins (1996) views collective identity as constituted by a dialectic interplay of processes of internal and external definition. On the one hand, individuals must be able to differentiate themselves from others by drawing on criteria of community and a sense of shared belonging within their subgroup. On the other hand, this internal identification process must be recognized by outsiders for an objectified collective identity to emerge. On this relational dimension of identity, see Calhoun (1994), who offers an excellent comparison of identity theory in sociology, poststructuralism, postmodernism, feminism, and literary criticism. From a cultural studies perspective, see Grossberg (1996).

[3]Social psychologists working on group categorization have analyzed the segmentation between "us" and "them." Brewer's (1986, p. 21) social identity theory suggests that "pressures to evaluate ones' own group positively through in-group/out-group comparison lead social groups to attempt to differentiate themselves from each other." This process of differentiation aims "to maintain and achieve superiority over an out-group on some dimension" (Tajfel & Turner, 1985, pp. 16–17).

[4]I take for granted that this categorization process has a cognitive and an emotional dimension and that it is shaped by past relations and their projection into the future. On this last dimension of the self, see Wiley (1994, p. 218). Concerning emotional categorizing, see Berezin (1997, pp. 19–30) on "hierarchies of felt identity."

[5]This is where my work differs most from Bourdieu's (1984). For a critique, see Lamont (1992, Chapter 7).

The Dignity of Working Men (Lamont, 2000a) is more ambitious in scope in that it does not focus on class alone: it explores how various criteria are used to draw symbolic boundaries by French and American workers against different groups, particularly racial minorities and immigrants, in addition to the poor and the wealthy. I compare the boundaries drawn by white and black workers in the United States and those drawn by native whites and North African immigrants in France.

The inductive approach allows for an empirical assessment of postmodern theories of identity. My findings support the postmodernist view of identity as constructed, as opposed to "primordial," essential and fixed in time. In particular, I suggest that French and American workers define who they are in opposition to different "others"—the straightforward workers versus the snotty professionals, for instance. However, my findings also undermine common postmodernist theoretical assumptions. Following Derrida, postmodernists/poststructuralists often assert that the relational principle functions in an undifferentiated manner across settings, and that identity is multiple, problematic, fluid, self-reflexive, "plural," and "decentered."[6] Instead of asserting this principle and/or illustrating it with anecdotal evidence, I systematically compare the different types of arguments that groups (e.g., white and black workers in the United States) use to define self and "other." Also, instead of positing that this process is open and fluid, I show that it is tied to the cultural resources workers have access to and to the conditions in which they live. For instance, I show that French workers are less likely than American workers to define themselves in opposition to the poor in part because socialism, republicanism, and Catholicism put at their disposal a discourse on solidarity and because institutional arrangements such as the quasi-absence of means-tested social benefits makes it less likely that they emphasize the boundary between workers and the poor (Lamont, 2000a, p. 237). In other words, I establish empirically that some patterns of self-identification and boundaries are more likely in one context than in another. This is not to deny the importance of individual agency or to flatten out intragroup differences and situational variations, but to show that boundary work is framed by the *differentially structured* contexts in which people live.

I should stress that my work on identity overlaps with poststructuralist and some postmodern approaches in its emphasis that exclusion is intrinsic to the constitution of identity. However, whereas authors as diverse as Pierre Bourdieu (1984), Judith Butler (1990), Stuart Hall (Hall & Du Gay, 1996) and Ernesto Laclau and Chantal Mouffe (1984) posit that identification always proceeds through exclusion, *Money, Morals and Manners* (Lamont, 1992) takes into consideration the strength of boundaries. For instance, this book compares the degree of boundedness of French and American upper-middle-class cultures, showing that classification systems mobilized by French professionals and managers are more tightly bounded and less permeable than those of their tolerant American counterparts (Lamont, 1992, Chapter 4).[7] Hence, I consider empirical variations in degree of exclusion that postmodern theories ignore and I propose analytical devices to make sense of them. Similarly, in *The Dignity of Working Men* (Lamont, 2000a), I consider the *bridging* of boundaries (e.g., the discursive inclusion of the poor and blacks among "people like us" in France) as well as exclusion, instead of positing that boundary work is everywhere and always "at work." I show

---

[6]Drawing on Rorty's antifoundational pragmatism and on Derrida's understanding of signification as unstable and shifting, postmodern cultural studies is concerned with the fixity/fluidity of dimensions of identity and the extent to which they presume foundational artifice that allows dominant groups to make universal statements (Lash, 1990, p. 14).

[7]Along these lines, see also Peterson and Kern (1996), Bryson (1996), and Barnett and Allen (2000).

the importance of looking at the definition of identity in connection with both the bridging and creation of boundaries, and with institutionalized definitions of social membership.

To state the obvious, I should also add that my approach to identity also contradicts the basic premises of rational action theory (RAT). While RAT in principle recognizes the importance of culture by positing the centrality of individual orientations, it also ignores it by assuming the principle of rational pursuit of goals. In contrast, my work demonstrates the multiplicity of cultural orientations across groups and considers rational action to be a distinct narrative privileged by specific groups. Giving rational action an a priori privileged status as a normative orientation would flatten out the cultural diversity revealed by my interviews, and thus proves to be theoretically unproductive, at very least for the kinds of questions that I am pursuing (Lamont, 1992, Chapter 7).

Other sociologists and anthropologists have been interested in analyzing boundary work by looking at self-definitions of ordinary people, while paying particular attention to the salience of racial and class groups in boundary work.[8] Just to take a few examples, Newman (1999) analyzes how poor fast-food workers define themselves in opposition to the unemployed poor. Lichterman (1999) explores how volunteers define their bonds and boundaries of solidarity by examining how they articulate their identity in relation to various groups. He argues that these mappings translate into different kinds of group responsibility, in "constraining and enabling what members can say and do together" (p. 7). Binder (1999) analyzes boundaries that proponents of Afrocentrism and multiculturalism build in relation to one another in conflict within the educational system. Becker (1999) studies how religious communities build boundaries between themselves and "the public." Finally, Gamson (1992) shows that identity, and especially "us" and "them" oppositions, serves as a source of mobilization and shapes the injustice frames that people use in defining their position on various political issues. While my work shares much with these studies,[9] it also has a systematic comparative dimension that distinguishes it from other contributions, which I now describe.

COMPARATIVE SOCIOLOGY AND COLLECTIVE/NATIONAL IDENTITY

The Dignity of Working Men (Lamont, 2000a) offers a multifaceted theory of status that centers on the relationship between various standards of evaluation of the self—for instance, morality and socioeconomic status—within national repertoires. It also shows that racial and class divides are articulated differently across national contexts and that specific groups attach different meanings to the various attributes they use to define their own positioning and that of others in a hierarchy of worth, instead of positing a consensus about who is "up" and "down" and of flattening cultural differences in evaluation of status (Lamont, 2000a, p. 116). Thus, the study provides a comparative sociology of group boundaries and of ordinary models of definition of community while offering a dynamic and complex picture the fundamental aspects of inequality. The long-term theoretical stake is to develop a more sophisticated understanding of processes by which cultural membership is defined and equivalencies are established between different categories of people, in line with recent studies of commensuration processes (Espeland & Stevens, 1998; Boltanski & Thévenot, 1991).

[8]See in particular the activities of the members of the symbolic boundaries network of the culture section of the American Sociological Association.

[9]In contrast to this literature, recent studies in cognitive sociology (e.g., Zerubavel, 1997) tends to focus on classification systems and are not concerned with group boundaries and inequality.

   This section briefly sketches what this comparative sociology of group boundaries looks like in the case of French and American workers, how it leads to an analysis of national boundary patterns (as part of processes of definition of national identity), and how my explanation for these patterns differs from traditional culturalist explanations by focusing on the different cultural repertoires available across contexts. It also suggests that a focus on "cultural structures" offers a way out of the unproductive culture–structure dichotomy in comparative sociology and elsewhere.

   Drawing on 150 in-depth interviews, *The Dignity of Working Men* (Lamont, 2000a) shows that in the United States white workers draw strong boundaries against blacks and the poor on the basis of specific moral criteria having to do with work ethic and self-reliance. Most are indifferent toward immigrants, or they are accepting of them if they perceive them to be in the pursuit of the American dream. In France, by contrast, white workers define the poor and blacks as "part of us," using the widely available discourse of class solidarity. They accept these groups but reject North African immigrants, who, they say, lack civility, violate the principles of republicanism, and are culturally incompatible with the French. Yet, amid laments concerning the decline of working class culture in France, French workers continue to draw on the language of class struggle to define their relationship with the upper half, whom they view as exploitative and dehumanizing. Even more than American workers, they adopt alternative definitions of success centered on personal integrity and the quality of their interpersonal relationships to locate themselves above or next to "people above." This permits them to guard their own self-worth and dignity, even though most of the men I talked to fare poorly on traditional measures of success.

   This study reveals that group boundaries are organized very differently across two national contexts, and that ordinary definitions of cultural membership—of what makes a worthy person—vary as well. These definitions imply distinct views about collective identity: how "us" is different from "them." They also imply different types of imagined communities and distinct definitions of national identity (Anderson, 1983/1991). For instance, while compared to American workers, French workers downplay material success in their definitions of worth; they also draw boundaries against Americans for their materialism, defining what they view as France's distinctiveness and sacred values (e.g., solidarity) against Americans' perceived cold-bloodedness.[10] In the context of accelerated globalization, it will be important to assess whether such national boundary work is being replaced by a cosmopolitan logic that downplays the place of the nation in definitions of collective identity and in new forms of collective memory.[11] *The Dignity of Working Men* (Lamont, 2000a) suggests that patterns of boundary work remain localized and highly differentiated across national groups (Lamont, 2000b).

   The explanatory framework I deploy to account for national patterns of boundary work can be contrasted with the standard framework used to study national cultural differences— the "modal personality" and "national character" frameworks—which stress psychological traits shared by all members of a society (Crozier, 1964; Inkeles, 1979).[12] Whereas this approach accounts for cultural orientations by childhood socialization, as indicated above, I account for French and American patterns of boundaries toward blacks, immigrants, the upper half, and the poor by available cultural repertoires (such as a prominent discourse on solidarity) and structural conditions in which workers live (such as the availability of welfare

---

[10]Lamont (1995) dubbed this process "national boundary work." See Saguy (forthcoming) for another analysis of the place of boundary work in the construction of national identity.

[11]On the conflict between nationally based models and cosmopolitan ones, see Beck (2000).

[12]For a critique, see Lamont (1992, Chapter 5).

benefits). I understand these patterns of boundary work not as essentialized individual or national characteristics, but as cultural structures, that is, institutionalized cultural repertoires or publicly available categorization systems.[13] This framework can explain intranational variance that is ignored by culturalist approaches. Indeed, it accounts for patterns of boundaries across groups within a nation, as well as for patterns across nations; for instance, African Americans draw weaker boundaries toward the poor than white Americans in part because their experience with racism makes them more likely to dissociate moral worth from socioeconomic success (Lamont, 2000a, p. 144). Also, the mainstream black religious tradition historically has made available to blacks a ready-made discourse about the need for collective solidarity that is less readily available to whites (Lamont, 2000a, p. 50). Finally, unlike culturalist approaches, this framework takes into consideration, and can account for, cross-national similarities, such as the weak boundaries that white French workers and African-American workers draw toward the poor.[14]

Rethinking Comparative Cultural Sociology (Lamont & Thévenot, 2000) complements *The Dignity of Working Men* (Lamont, 2000a) in that it provides a comparison of the salience of criteria of evaluation in France and the United States. Here again, the focus is on relatively stable schemas of evaluation that are used in varying proportions across contexts.[15] The analysis draws on eight case studies conducted by 11 French and American researchers who have worked together over a period of 4 years toward developing systematic comparisons.[16] Together, these case studies reveal that each nation makes more readily available to its members specific sets of tools which means that members of different national communities are not equally likely to draw on the same cultural tools to construct and assess the world that surrounds them. Hence, like *The Dignity of Working Men* (Lamont, 2000a), these case studies show that elements of repertoires are present across geographic units such as nations or regions, but in varying proportions. For instance, the cultural repertoires prevailing in the United States make market references more readily available to Americans and enable them to resort to such references in a wider range of situations (e.g., the assessment of literary and artistic value, the critique of sexual harassment, the meaning of voluntary activities, and so forth). In contrast, the French repertoires make principles of solidarity more salient and enable a larger number of French people to resort to them across situations and often precisely in

---

[13]On cultural structures and institutionalized cultural repertoires, see Sewell (1992), Wuthnow (1987), Dobbin (1994), and Jepperson (1991).

[14]Because cultural repertoires, like structural conditions, change, the patterns of boundaries that I have documented should be regarded as historically contingent. A dramatic increase in the number of blacks in France could lead to a strengthening of antiblack boundaries, especially if combined with other structural and cultural changes (for instance, a sharp decline of the left and a greater availability of neoliberal ideas that would make solidarity less salient).

[15]They are also defined as "cultural environment(s) and the material contained therein ... the socially constructed, readily available cultural materials of a society—the archetypes, the myths, the epigrams and adages, the morals, the means–end chains, the evaluation criteria, the categorization schemas, all of the materials of shared "tool-kits" (Corse, 1997, p. 156).

[16]The cases bear on how French and American workers assess racial inequality; how French and American activists and intellectuals appraise what constitutes sexual harassment; how identity politics shape what is valued in literary studies in French and American academia; how publishers in Paris and New York understand the market and literary value of books; what kind of rhetoric the French and American publics use to evaluate contemporary art; how journalists (including Communists in France and the Religious Right in the United States) evaluate the legitimate boundary between personal commitments and professional roles; how participants in environmental conflicts in California and the South of France define their positions and evaluate those of others; and how French and American Rotary Club members understand their voluntary activity in terms of particular professional self-interest and universal humanitarian purposes.

situations in which Americans would resort to market principles (in the elaboration of an anti-racist discourse, the defense of the environment, etc.). However, this does not mean that market criteria of evaluation are absent from the French repertoires, but only that they are used in a small number of situations by a smaller number of people (Lamont, 1992, Chapter 3).

This cultural refocusing is a significant contribution to comparative sociology. Indeed, despite important changes, as is the case in comparative historical sociology, this field tends to privilege macroeconomic, political, and institutional differences. Despite the influential writings of Pierre Bourdieu, Michel Foucault, and others, in some quarters cultural "factors" continue to be thought of as "superstructural" (i.e., relatively insignificant) and cultural explanations as inherently conservative (for their idealism or because they allegedly involve "blaming the victim").[17] This is at odds with developments in cultural sociology and other fields where the unproductive dichotomy between "culture" and "structure" is being displaced by a new focus on "cultural structures" (Sewell, 1992) to stress both how resources are meaning-laden and how taken-for-granted definitions of reality act as structures.[18] Conceptual tools such as "cultural repertoires" make it possible to move beyond the psychologism, naturalism, and essentialism that characterized much of the comparative cultural analysis of the 1960s.[19]

SELF, INEQUALITY, AND RESISTANCE

The intersection between culture and inequality has been one of the fastest growing subfields of cultural sociology over the last 15 years. Pierre Bourdieu (1984) and his collaborators (e.g., Bourdieu & Passeron, 1970/1977) have given the impetus to sociologists as diverse as Bryson (1996), DiMaggio (1987), Erikson (1996), Hall (1992), Halle (1993), and Peterson and Kern (1996), who have followed with significant theoretical and substantive developments. Most recently, important work has focused on the ways in which inequality shapes the self. For instance, Newman (1999) reveals in poignant terms how the working poor construct selves that go beyond the limits of their immediate environment while hanging on to minimum wage jobs. Waller (1999) analyzes how unmarried poor men understand their role as fathers and the emotional and material contributions they make to the lives of their children. Lareau (2000) shows important differences in childhood socialization across social classes, with upper-middle-class parents being involved in "concerted cultivation" of the self, whereas working-class people encourage "natural growth." Kefelas (forthcoming) analyzes how white working-class people define and defend their selves in what they perceive to be an imperiled world, through the care with which they keep their home clean, cultivate their gardens, maintain their property, defend the neighborhoods, and celebrate the nation. Like *The Dignity*

---

[17]Rueschemeyer (1999) describes some of these perspectives in his work in progress.

[18]Worldviews structure people's lives to the extent that they limit and facilitate their action. In Durkheim's words, "the power attached to sacred things conducts men with the same degree of necessity as physical force." (1911/1965, p. 260).

[19]Other recent research that refocuses on the cultural dimensions of comparative sociology, using conceptual tools recently developed by cultural sociologists, include Corse (1997) on the American and Canadian national identity and their literary canons, Spillman (1997) on the celebration of bicentennials in Australia and the United States (which shows that national identity creation is a continuous process that requires elaboration and reinforcement, but also loss and innovation in national representations), Griswold (2000) on the worlds of the Nigerian novel in England and Nigeria, and Saguy (forthcoming) on the meanings of sexual harassment in France and the United States. This new literature complements the very influential phenomenological comparative research on the rationalization of the world system carried by John Meyer, John Boli, Francisco Ramirez, David Strang, and others (e.g., Meyer & Jepperson, 2000).

of Working Men (Lamont, 2000a) these four studies demonstrate how meaning making, particularly at the level of the self, is an essential dimension of inequality and hint at a vast research area that remains unexplored. Together, they illustrate that the structural analysis of inequality, which largely defines the field of stratification, needs to be complemented by systematic empirically based research centering on the cultural dimensions of inequality. The latter should examine questions such as: (1) how inequality shapes the self (either today or historically, à la Elias (1982)); (2) how cultural practices are segmented across groups; (3) how various groups perceive racial, class, and gender differences; and (4) what is the impact of the media and various cultural institutions in shaping these group representations. Some of these topics already have been the object of several studies while others remain largely neglected. My book in progress, *Culture and Inequality* (Lamont, in progress) will provide an integrated framework for understanding these questions and a synthesis of available knowledge.

With the explosive growth of cultural studies since the 1970s, considerable attention has also been given to the study of cultural domination and of resistance among subaltern groups. These also are topics to which *The Dignity of Working Men* (Lamont, 2000a) contributes by focusing on group differences in standards of evaluation and on how these shape subjective group boundaries. For instance, it shows that white American workers emphasize moral standards related to "the disciplined self" (e.g., work ethic, perseverance, self-reliance) to distinguish between "people like us" and others: they distance themselves from the upper half, who lack integrity and straightforwardness, and from blacks and "people below," who are lazy and hold immoral values. Similarly, the moral standards privileged by African Americans, who emphasize "the caring self," overlap with the criteria they use to evaluate all whites, who are domineering and lack human compassion, and the white upper half in particular, who are exploitative and lack solidarity. Moreover, although each group takes their moral values to be universal, each privileges very different aspects of morality, with regard to which they judge the other group to be deficient. Both groups draw strong boundaries toward the other, but on the basis of very different criteria, with whites being better able to institutionalize their own criteria ("the disciplined self") as hegemonic (Lamont, 1997).[20] This illustrates how a focus on the content of moral criteria enriches the understanding of the process of constitution of strong symbolic intergroup boundaries.

To turn to the issue of resistance, I find that both in France and the United States workers put themselves above the "upper half" because they perceive themselves to be more moral and to have more personal integrity. Whereas most analysts view the development of alternative codes of honor and the rejection of mainstream norms of resistance as an explicit goal and act of resistance (e.g., Willis, 1977), my study suggests that resistance is often the unintended consequence of workers' search for respect and alternative spheres of worth; by defending their dignity, they defend distinct criteria of evaluation that allow them to locate themselves above the dominant group.

Social psychologists have shown that groups that are in positions of dependency or limited access to power often value morality and/or collective over individualistic aspects of morality. This is the case not only of blacks as compared with whites, but also of workers as compared with professionals and of women as compared with men (see Lamont, 2000a, p. 246). This may point toward a more general theory of boundary work among groups in

---

[20]The "struggle for recognition" is a central theme in the literature on identity. The term refers to collective public struggles for legitimacy that calls upon other people or groups to respond (Calhoun, 1994, p. 20). My work speaks to this topic to the extent that the groups I study promote criteria that allow them to locate themselves above others (see also Bourdieu, 1984). However, my focus is on everyday narratives about identity and self-understandings, as opposed to identity struggles enacted in social or political movements.

subordinated positions.[21] However, instead of understanding the relationship between morality, self-worth, and hierarchical position in terms of the universal disposition of all low-status individuals, as social psychologists tend to do, I stress the relationship between these agents' emphasis on morality and the context in which they live. I explore how conceptions of self-worth are shaped by the broader context of political and social relationships and by institutionalized definitions of cultural membership that people have access to, a topic rarely visited by social psychologists working on the self and identity.[22] I also historicize patterns of inclusion and exclusion by analyzing how these conceptions of morality are shaped by changing political traditions (such as the ideology of republicanism in France, which is central to the inclusion of the poor and blacks among "people like us").

A last point concerning the place of class identity in contemporary societies: Postmodern writings have asserted the declining significance of class as a basis of identity (Pakulski & Waters, 1996).[23] In contrast, my research suggests that it remains an important basis for collective identity among workers: *The Dignity of Working Men* (Lamont, 2000a) shows that many workers define who they are in opposition to hierarchically defined groups ("people above" and "people below" broadly defined) and that they identify with people who share similar living conditions ("nothing is easy for people like us") and similar cultural definitions of "who we are not." In fact, like the professionals and managers analyzed in *Money, Morals, and Manners* (Lamont, 1992), these working men use a rhetoric of class to talk about differences between "our kind of people" and others. Their definitions of social membership are one of the cultural roots of inequality because, like racial identity, class identity is expressed and tied to the criteria that workers use to evaluate others. The study thus confirms that we should study class consciousness by focusing not only on taste, on explicit class conflict, or on positions in the system of production.[24] We also need to look at workers' sense of *worth* and more broadly at their social identification and group categorization as workers. Hence, the greater radicalism of French workers, as opposed to American workers, is best understood in the context of their wider moral worldview, which stresses solidarity and which plays an important role in making this radicalism possible. As Grusky and Sorensen (1998) imply, if the concept of class is to be salvaged, through occupational location, for instance, it will be because sociologists pay heed to the identity and lifestyle dimensions of inequality, as well as to its structural dimensions.

BOUNDARIES AND RACISM

The concept of boundary is central in the study of race and ethnicity. Indeed, the relational process involved in the definition of collective identity ("us" vs. "them") often has been emphasized in the literature on these topics. The work of Barth (1969) and Horowitz (1985), for instance, concerns objective group boundaries and self-ascription and how feelings of communality are defined in opposition to the perceived identity of other racial and ethnic groups. More recently, Bobo and Hutchings (1996) analyzed racism as resulting from threats to group positioning. They follow Blumer (1958), who advocates

---

[21]Along these lines, Bobo (1991, p. 80) finds that individuals who tend to emphasize social responsibility over individualism in survey tend to be individuals with low-status characteristics, namely, blacks and low-income and -education whites.

[22]For a review of social psychological approaches to the self and identity, see Gecas and Burke (1995).

[23]For a critique of the postmodern stance on this issue, see Wright (1996).

[24]This confirms the findings of Halle (1984, p. 219).

shift[ing] study and analysis from a preoccupation with feelings as lodged in individuals to a concern with the relationships of racial groups ... [and with] the collective process by which a racial group comes to define and redefine another racial group. (p. 3) (see also Hechter, 1975)

Racial boundaries are also a central concern in *The Dignity of Working Men* (Lamont, 2000a). My goal in this book was to explore uncharted territory in the area of racism and racial differences by focusing on boundaries and meaning making, again bringing together cultural sociology and the study of inequality. Whereas studies of racism tend to focus on racism per se (e.g., Feagin & Vera, 1995; Wellman, 1993), I believe that we need to gain purchase on the broad cultural frameworks that facilitate it and on those used to respond to it. Hence, *The Dignity of Working Men* (Lamont, 2000a) contributes to the sociology of racism by analyzing it in the context of individuals' broad moral worldviews and bringing to light their inner logic through comparative lenses. For instance, the study shows that the concern white workers have for providing for their families helps us understand the centrality of self-reliance in the boundaries they draw against blacks. It also documents inductively which norms the majority group perceives the minority group to violate (e.g., traditional morality, but not straightfor-wardness), and thus, complements the literature on symbolic racism, which posits that the majority group rejects blacks because they are viewed as not respecting ideal American values such as individualism.

The Dignity of Working Men (Lamont, 2000a) also bring together cultural sociology and the study of racial boundaries by analyzing how ordinary white Americans and French men think about the issue of racial equality, i.e., about what makes people equal or commensurate. Interviews reveal that whites American workers offer less evidence of racial equality than of their equality with "people above," focusing, for instance, on the fact that money makes people equal. In contrast, African Americans point to a wider range of evidence to demonstrate racial equality, including the color of blood, our common human destiny, our common origin as children of God, and so forth. Moreover, the most popular forms of antiracist discourse found in academia, which center on multiculturalism and cultural relativism, find little resonance among the black and white American working men I talked to. Instead, these groups more often ground their understanding of racial equality in their everyday experience, epito-mized by the notion that there are good and bad people in all races. Finally, the study analyzes how ordinary blacks represent whites and understand racial differences: blacks challenge dominant white representations of blacks as morally lacking when they emphasize their own greater generosity and caring. Hence, the research informs our understanding of the cultural frameworks through which minority and majority groups alike understand restricted and open definitions of cultural membership.

Several studies assembled in *The Cultural Territories of Race* (Lamont, 1999) also analyze the subjective experience of race and on racial and ethnic identity construction. For instance, Waters (1999a) examines the repertoires of cultures and identity that West Indian immigrants bring to the United States as well as their strategies of self-presentation and the ethnic and racial boundaries they find most salient (p. 12). The goal is to move beyond the simple "politicized dichotomies of structure and culture" (Waters, 1999b) that characterized as much the "culture of poverty" debate as traditional Marxist and network-analytic frame-works. It is also to unveil meaning-making processes that are at work in all aspects of immigration and race relations. Along similar lines, Alford Young, Jr.'s (1999) work on the understandings of mobility and racial constraints developed by "rags-to-riches" young black men dissects the "mental maps" and "models for" living [to use Geertz's (1973, pp. 93–94 and 220) expression] found in various corners of American society. These studies are often informed by the analytic tools central to cultural sociologists, such as "repertoires of strategies of action," "symbolic boundaries," "cognitive classification," and "scripts of personhood." They herald what cultural sociology has to contribute to the study of race, ethnicity, and immigration: new analytical frames and concepts that can be used to identify neglected questions and that have the potential to broaden these fields' intellectual agendas.

Moving in another direction, drawing on Richard Jenkins (1996) who distinguishes between group identification and social categorization as essential dimensions of racial identity, Lamont and Molnár (2001) interviewed African-American marketing specialists to understand how they shape the collective identity of blacks in the United States. More specifically, we examined: (1) how African-American marketing specialists, considered as cultural producers, understand the images of the "black consumer" they diffuse, thus providing African Americans with resources for defining their collective identities; (2) how these marketing specialists provide blacks with models and recipes about how to achieve full social membership, through consumption, for instance; (3) how they believe blacks use consumption to signal aspiration to membership in symbolic communities (as citizens, middle-class people, etc.); and (4) how they believe black consumers perform, affirm, and transform the social meaning attributed to them.

CHALLENGES AND FUTURE QUESTIONS

Although the contributions described speak to a range of substantive issues, they nevertheless converge around the fundamental social processes involved in the construction of commonalties and differences. The drawing and bridging of racial, national, and class boundaries and their relationship with definitions of identity and the self are at the center of my research agenda and they revolve around whether and how individuals think of "us" as similar, equivalent, commensurate, or compatible with "them." Perhaps the added value of these contributions is to be found less in specific theoretical propositions than in their pointing to ways of capturing old problems through different lenses, which I hope will have become apparent to the reader.

Several new challenges emerge from this research agenda. First, we need a synthesis of the various strands of work that speak to boundary issues across substantive areas. Second, we need a better understanding of the relationship between subjective and objective boundaries. Third, we need a better grasp of boundary work not connected to networks. Finally, we need comparative studies of the drawing and bridging of boundaries and of the place of universalism and particularism in these processes.

1. The concept of boundaries is playing an increasingly important role in a wide range of literatures beyond those discussed above. For instance, in the study of nationalism, citizenship, and immigration, scholars have used the idea to discuss criteria of membership and group closure within imagined communities (Brubaker, 1992; Baubeck, 1992; Zolberg & Long, 1998). Gender and sexual boundaries also are coming under more intense scrutiny (e.g., Epstein, 1992; Gerson & Peiss, 1985; Stein, 1997). Because these literatures deal with the same social process—boundary work—it may be appropriate at this point to begin moving toward a general theory of boundaries which, for instance, would analyze similarities and differences between boundaries drawn in various realms: moral, cultural, class, racial, ethnic, gender, and national boundaries.[25] This synthesis could be accomplished by focusing on a number of

---

[25]Tilly (1997) moves in this direction. He argues that dichotomous categories such as "male" and "female" (but also "white" and "black") are used by dominant groups to marginalize other groups and block their access to resources.

formal features and characteristics of boundaries, such as their visibility, permeability, bound-edness, fluidity, and rigidity. We may also want to compare embedded and transportable boundaries, explicit and taken-for-granted boundaries, positive and negative boundaries, and the relationship between representations of boundaries and context. Social scientists also should think more seriously about how different types of boundaries (e.g., moral and aesthetic boundaries) combine with one another across local and national contexts (Lamont & Thévenot, 2000).

2. Students of objective boundaries have focused on topics such as the relative impor-tance of educational endogamy versus racial endogamy among the college educated (Kalmijn, 1991), racial hiring and firing (Silver & Zwerling, 1992), the extent of residential racial segregation (Massey & Denton, 1993), and the relative permeability of class boundaries (Wright & Cho, 1992). I have argued that symbolic boundaries are a necessary but insufficient condition for the creation of objective boundaries (Lamont, 1992, Chapter 7). More empirical work is needed on the process by which the former transmutes into the latter. It also would be important to produce a more detailed analysis of the ways in which institutional forces, history, and material factors shape boundaries. We also need to analyze more closely the process of institutionalization of symbolic boundaries, i.e., how workers come to take them for granted and give them objective reality.

3. More work is needed on collective definitions of cultural membership as locus for "identity work," which does not require that individuals be connected through networks and engage in face-to-face contacts (Cerulo, 1997). Such boundary work can operate either at the level of bounded subcultures or at the level of widely shared cultural structures, of "hidden codes that make individuals and groups predictable and dependable social actors" (Melucci, 1996, p. 8) that exist beyond the enactment of specific interpersonal ties.[26]

4. More work is needed on the bridging of boundaries across groups. In particular, we know very little about how individuals produce universalism and promote forms of cosmopol-itanism in different settings: at work, in the public sphere, in neighborhoods, in kinship net-works, and so forth. We need to study the extent to which professionals and workers consider it natural to first help "their own kind" and how they reconcile meritocratic norms in the workplace with clientelistic practices (Lamont, 2000c). While in recent years, political philos-ophers have given considerable attention to questions of community boundaries, by discussing tribalism (Barber, 1995), patriotism–cosmopolitanism (Nussbaum, 1994, 1996a,b), and particularism–universalism (Walzer, 1997), much work needs to be done before we can understand how ordinary citizens conceptualize these questions as well as widely shared, institutionalized views on these crucial issues.

REFERENCES

Anderson, B. (1983/1991). *Imagined communities: Reflections on the origin and spread of nationalism*. London: Verso.
Barber, B. (1995). *Jihad vs. McWorld*. New York: Ballantine.
Barnett, L. A., & Allen, M. P. (2000). Social class, cultural repertoires, and popular culture: The case of film. *Sociological Forum, 15*, 145–164.

He points to various mechanisms by which this is accomplished, such as exploitation and opportunity hoarding. He asserts that durable inequality most often results from cumulative, individual, and often unnoticed organizational processes.

[26]For more network-bound approaches to identity, see Emirbayer and Goodwin (1994), Somers and Gibson (1994), Tilly (1997), and White (1992).

Barth, F. (1969). Introduction. In F. Barth (Ed.), *Ethnic groups and boundaries: The social organization of culture difference* (pp. 9–38). London: George Allen and Unwin.

Baubeck, R. (1992). *Immigration and the boundaries of citizenship*. Coventry: Monograph in Ethnic Relations No. 4, Center for Research in Ethnic Relations, University of Warwick.

Beck, U. (2000). The cosmopolitan perspective: Sociology of the second age of modernity. *British Journal of Sociology, 51,* 79–106.

Becker, P. (1999). *Congregations in conflict: Cultural models of local religious life*. New York: Cambridge University Press.

Berezin, M. (1997). *Making the fascist self: The political culture of inter-war Italy*. Ithaca, NY: Cornell University Press.

Binder, A. (1999). Friend and foe: Boundary work and collective identity in the Afrocentric and multicultural curriculum movements in American public education. In M. Lamont (Ed.), *The Cultural territories of race: Black and white boundaries* (pp. 221–248). Chicago: University of Chicago Press and New York: Russell Sage Foundation.

Blumer, H. (1958). Race prejudice as a sense of group position. *Pacific Sociological Review, 1,* 3–7.

Bobo, L. (1991). Social responsibility, individualism, and redistributive policies. *Sociological Forum, 6,* 71–92.

Bobo, L., & Hutchings V. L. (1996). Perceptions of racial group competition: Extending Blumer's theory of group position to a multiracial social context. *American Sociological Review, 61,* 951–972.

Boltanski, L., & Thévenot, L. (1991). *De la justification. Les économies de la grandeur*. Paris: Gallimard.

Bourdieu, P. (1984). *Distinction: A social critique of the judgment of taste*. Cambridge, MA: Harvard University Press.

Bourdieu, P., & Passeron, J.-C. (1970/1977). *Reproduction in education, society, and culture*. Beverly Hills: Sage.

Brewer, M. B. (1986). The role of ethnocentrism in intergroup conflict. In S. Worchel & W. G. Austin (Eds.), *Psychology of intergroup relations* (pp. 88–102). Chicago: Nelson-Hall Publishers.

Brubaker, R. (1992). *Citizenship and nationhood in France and Germany*. Cambridge, MA: Harvard University Press.

Bryson, B. (1996). "Anything but heavy metal": Symbolic exclusion and musical dislikes. *American Sociological Review, 61,* 884–899.

Butler, J. (1990). *Gender trouble*. London: Routledge.

Calhoun, C. (1994). Social theory and the politics of identity. In C. Calhoun (Ed.), *Social theory and the politics of identity* (pp. 9–36). New York: Blackwell.

Cerulo, K. A. (1997). Identity construction: New issues, new direction. *Annual Review of Sociology, 23,* 385–409.

Cornell, S., & Hartman, D. (1997). *Ethnicity and race. Making identity in a changing world*. Thousand Oaks, CA: Pine Fore Press.

Corse, S. (1997). *Nationalism and literature: The politics of culture in Canada and the United States*. Cambridge: Cambridge University Press.

Crozier, M. (1964). *The bureaucratic phenomenon*. Chicago: University of Chicago Press.

DiMaggio, P. (1987). Classification in art. *American Sociological Review, 52,* 440–455.

Dobbin, F. (1994). Cultural models of organization: The social construction of rational organizing principles. In D. Crane (Ed.), *The sociology of culture: Emerging theoretical perspectives* (pp. 117–142). New York: Blackwell.

Durkheim, E. (1911/1965). *The elementary forms of religious life*. New York: Free Press.

Elias, N. (1982). *The civilizing process*. New York: Blackwell.

Emirbayer, M., & Goodwin, J. (1994). Network analysis, culture, and the problem of agency. *American Journal of Sociology, 99,* 1411–1454.

Epstein, C. F. (1992). Tinker-bells and pinups: The construction and reconstruction of gender boundaries at work. In M. Lamont & M. Fournier (Eds.), *Cultivating differences: Symbolic boundaries and the making of inequality* (pp. 232–256). Chicago: University of Chicago Press.

Erickson, B. (1996). Culture, class, and connections. *American Journal of Sociology, 102,* 217–251.

Espeland, W. N., & Stevens, M. L. (1998). Commensuration as a social process. *Annual Review of Sociology, 24,* 313–343.

Feagin, J. R., & Vera, H. (1995). *White racism: The basics*. New York: Routledge.

Gamson, W. (1992). *Talking politics*. New York: Cambridge University Press.

Gecas, V., & Burke, P. J. (1995). Self and identity. In K. S. Cook, G. A. Fine, and J. S. House (Eds.), *Sociological perspectives on social psychology* (pp. 41–67). Boston: Allyn and Bacon.

Geertz, C. (1973). *The interpretation of culture*. New York: Basic Books.

Gerson, J. M., & Peiss, K. (1985). Boundaries, negotiation, consciousness: Reconceptualizing gender relations. *Social Problems, 32,* 317–331.

Griswold, W. (2000). *Bearing witness: Writers, readers and the novel in Nigeria*. Princeton: Princeton University Press.

Grossberg, L. (1996). Identity and cultural studies: Is that all there is? In S. Hall & P. Du Gay (Eds.), *Questions of cultural identity* (pp. 87–107). Thousand Oaks: Sage.

Grusky, D. B., & Sorensen, J. B. (1998). Can class analysis be salvaged? *American Journal of Sociology, 103*, 1187–1234.

Hall, J. R. (1992). The capital(s) of cultures: A nonholistic approach to status situations, class, gender, and ethnicity. In M. Lamont & M. Fournier (Eds.), *Cultivating differences: Symbolic boundaries and the making of inequality* (pp. 257–288). Chicago: University of Chicago Press.

Hall, S., & Du Gay, P. (Eds.). (1996). *Questions of cultural identity*. London: Sage.

Halle, D. (1984). *America's working man: Work, home and politics among blue-collar property owners*. Chicago: University of Chicago Press.

Halle, D. (1993). *Inside culture. Art and class in the American home*. Chicago: University of Chicago Press.

Hechter, M. (1975). *Internal colonialism: The Celtic fringe in British national development, 1536–1966*. Berkeley: University of California Press.

Horowitz, D. L. (1985). *Ethnic groups in conflict*. Berkeley: University of California Press.

Inkeles, A. (1979). Continuity and change in the American national character. In S. M. Lipset (Ed.), *The third century: America as a post-industrial society* (pp. 390–453). Stanford, CA: Stanford University Press.

Jenkins, R. (1996). *Social identity*. London: Routledge.

Jepperson, R. (1991). Institutions, institutional effects, and institutionalism. In W. W. Powell & P. J. DiMaggio (Eds.), *The new institutionalism in organizational analysis* (pp. 143–163). Chicago: University of Chicago Press.

Kalmijn, M. (1991). Status homogamy in the United States. *American Journal of Sociology, 97*, 496–523.

Kefalas, M. (forthcoming). *The last garden: Culture and place in a white working class Chicago neighborhood*. Berkeley: University of California Press.

Laclau, E. (1994). *The making of political identities*. London: Verso.

Laclau, E., & Mouffe, C. (1984). *Hegemony and socialist strategy*. London: Verso.

Lamont, M. (1992). *Money, morals, and manners: The culture of the French and American upper-middle class*. Chicago: University of Chicago Press.

Lamont, M. (1995). National identity and national boundary patterns in France and the United States. *French Historical Studies, 19*, 349–365.

Lamont, M. (1997). The meaning of class and race: French and American workers discuss differences. In J. Hall (Ed.), *Reworking class* (pp. 193–220). Ithaca, NY: Cornell University Press.

Lamont, M. (Ed.). (1999). *The cultural territories of race: Black and white boundaries*. Chicago: University of Chicago Press and New York: Russell Sage Foundation.

Lamont, M. (2000a). *The dignity of working men: Morality and the boundaries of race, class, and immigration*. Cambridge, MA: Harvard University Press and New York: Russell Sage Foundation.

Lamont, M. (2000b). Defining cultural membership: Enduring national models among French and American workers. Paper presented at the interdisciplinary workshop on "Re-Mapping Europe: Territories, Membership, and Identity in a Supra-National Age." Center for European Studies, New York University, April 7.

Lamont, M. (2000c). Ordinary cosmopolitanisms: Strategies for bridging boundaries among non-college educated workers. Working paper WPTC-2K-03, Transnational Communities Programme, Oxford University.

Lamont, M. (forthcoming). Symbolic boundaries. In N. J. Smelser & P. B. Baltes (Eds.), *International encyclopedia of the social and behavioral sciences*. London: Pergamon Press.

Lamont, M. (in progress). *Culture and inequality*. New York: W. W. Norton.

Lamont, M., & Molnár, V. (2001). How blacks use consumption to shape their collective identity: Evidence from marketing specialists. *Journal of Consumer Culture, 1*, 31–45.

Lamont, M., & Thévenot, L. (Eds.). (2000). *Rethinking comparative cultural sociology: Repertoires of evaluation in France and the United States*. New York: Cambridge University Press and Paris: Presses de la Maison des Sciences de l'Homme.

Lareau, A. (2000). Contours of childhood: Social class differences in children's daily lives. Working Paper, Center for Working Families, University of California, Berkeley.

Lash, S. (1990). *Sociology of postmodernism*. London: Routledge.

Lichterman, P. (1999). Civic culture meets welfare reform: Religious volunteers reaching out. Paper presented at the Annual Meetings of the American Sociological Association, Chicago, August.

Massey, D., & Denton, N. A. (1993). *American apartheid: Segregation and the making of the underclass*. Cambridge: Cambridge University Press.

Melluci, A. (1996). *Challenging codes: Collective action in the information age*. Cambridge: Cambridge University Press.

Meyer, J. W., & Jepperson, R. J. (2000). The "actors" of modern society: The cultural construction of social agency. *Sociological Theory, 18*, 100–120.

Molnár, V., & Lamont, M. (forthcoming). The study of boundaries in the social sciences. *Annual Review of Sociology*.

Newman, K. (1999). *No shame in my game. The working poor in the inner city.* New York: Knopf and New York: Russell Sage Foundation.

Nussbaum, M. (1996). *For love of country.* Boston: Beacon Press.

Nussbaum, M. (1996). Patriotism and cosmopolitanism. In J. Cohen (Ed.), *For love of country. Debating the limits of patriotism* (pp. 2–20). Boston: Beacon Press.

Pakulski, J., & Waters, M. (1996). The reshaping and dissolution of social class in advanced society. *Theory and Society, 25,* 667–691.

Peterson R. A., & Kern, R. (1996). Changing highbrow taste: From snob to omnivore. *American Sociological Review, 61,* 900–907.

Rueschemeyer, D. (1999). Reflections on cultural explanation in macrosociology. Paper presented in the Department of Sociology, University of California at Los Angeles.

Saguy, A. (forthcoming). *Defining sexual harassment in France and the United States.* Berkeley: University of California Press.

Sewell, W. H., Jr. (1992). A theory of structure: Duality, agency, and transformation. *American Journal of Sociology, 98,* 1–29.

Silver, H., & Zwerling, C. (1992). Race and job dismissals in a federal bureaucracy. *American Sociological Review, 57,* 651–660.

Somers, M. R., & Gibson, G. D. (1994). Reclaiming the epistemological "other": Narrative and the social constitution of identity. In C. Calhoun (Ed.), *Social theory and the politics of identity* (pp. 37–99). Cambridge, MA: Blackwell Publishers.

Spillman, L. (1997). *Nation and commemoration. Creating national identities in the United States and Australia.* Cambridge: Cambridge University Press.

Stein, A. (1997). *Sex and sensibility: Stories of a lesbian generation.* Berkeley: University of California Press.

Tajfel, H., & Turner, J. C. (1985). The social identity theory of intergroup behavior. In S. Worchel & W. G. Austin (Eds.), *Psychology of intergroup relations* (pp. 7–24). Chicago: Nelson-Hall.

Tilly, C. (1997). *Durable inequality.* Cambridge: Harvard University Press.

Waller, M. (1999). Meanings and motive in new family stories: The separation of reproduction and marriage among low-income black and white parents. In M. Lamont (Ed.), *The cultural territories of race: Black and white boundaries* (pp. 182–220). Chicago: University of Chicago Press and New York: Russell Sage Foundation.

Walzer, M. (1997). *On toleration.* New Haven, CT: Yale University Press.

Waters, M. C. (1999a). Explaining the comfort factor: West Indian immigrants confront American race relations. In M. Lamont (Ed.), *The cultural territories of race: Black and white boundaries* (pp. 63–97). Chicago: University of Chicago Press and New York: Russell Sage Foundation.

Waters, M. C. (1999b). *Black identities. West Indian immigrant dreams and American realities.* New York: Russell Sage Foundation and Cambridge, MA: Harvard University Press.

Wellman, D. (1993). *Portraits of white racism,* 2nd ed. New York: Cambridge University Press.

Wiley, N. (1994). *The semiotic self.* Chicago: University of Chicago Press.

White, H. (1992). *Identity and control. A structural theory of social action.* Princeton: Princeton University Press.

Willis, P. (1977). *Learning to labour: How working class kids get working class jobs.* New York: Columbia University Press.

Wilson, J., & Musick, M. (1997). Who cares? Toward an integrated theory of volunteer work. *American Sociological Review, 62,* 694–713.

Wright, E. O. (1996). The continuing relevance of class analysis. Comments. *Theory and Society, 25,* 693–716.

Wright, E. O., & Cho, D. (1992). The relative permeability of class boundaries to cross-class friendships: A comparative study of the United States, Canada, Sweden, and Norway. *American Sociological Review, 57,* 85–102.

Wuthnow, R. (1987). *Meaning and moral order: Explorations in cultural analysis.* Berkeley: University of California Press.

Young, A., Jr. (1999). Navigating race: Getting ahead in the lives of "rags to riches" young black men. In M. Lamont (Ed.), *The cultural territories of race: Black and white boundaries* (pp. 30–62). Chicago: University of Chicago Press and New York: Russell Sage Foundation.

Zerubavel, E. (1997). *Social mindscapes: An invitation to cognitive sociology.* Cambridge, MA: Harvard University Press.

Zolberg, A. R., & Litt. L. Wong Long, (1990). Why Islam is like Spanish: Cultural incorporation in Europe and the United States. *Politics and Society, 27,* 5–38.

CHAPTER 10

Alley Art

Can We ... See ... at Last, the End of Ontology?

JUDITH R. BLAU

Last year our village's Downtown Council commissioned an artist, Michael Brown, to paint a mural on the full wall of one of the buildings adjoining a narrow alleyway just off the main street. The wall is roughly the length of an ordinary Manhattan apartment building that faces either north or south, which makes the mural nearly half the length of an uptown–downtown Manhattan block. Cream and black on a gray wall, the mural that Brown designed and painted, along with his apprentice and local school children, depicts the *joie de vivre* of a procession, whose participants are towners and gowners, from the past and the present. Its catalogue name for the purpose of town records is Mural #12, but villagers call it "Parade."

Most of the academicians are puffed up with cheerful pomposity, just as some shop-keepers give the air of great importance. But, really, the whole town is there: political activists, clergy, football players, cheerleaders, cops, firefighters, city officials, kids (some with spiked hair; others with baseball mitts; one with a violin), dads with strollers, homeless regulars, and students—blacks, whites, Latinos, Asians. It is an affirmative monument to the villagers, but I also detect some irony: that our unity is more apparent than real and our pluralism stands up only at public ceremonies.

Do we know that it is art, that is, in the sense that art is an institution? In the lower corner of "Parade," at the end furthest from the main street is a drawing of a sink, an old double sink, dating from about the 1920s. As the casual passer-by might say, "This mural has everything *and* the kitchen sink!" On the sink is painted, "R. Mutt," the signature that Duchamp sprawled on his 1917 urinal (*Fountain*). Although I was pleased with myself that I recognized this reference—a credit to my art history professors—I missed others, including one to Judy Chicago, prominent feminist artist and craftsperson. (She is in drag, so to speak.) The giveaway, Brown told me, is that she wears a baseball shirt with a Cubs logo, suggesting perhaps that public roles and public display trump conviction; or if the allusion is to Andy Warhol's Marilyn Monroe it might suggest that feminists are more authentic than commer-cialized sex goddesses. (Whatever. The joke provokes.)

JUDITH R. BLAU • Department of Sociology, University of North Carolina, Chapel Hill, North Carolina 27599.

Handbook of Sociological Theory, edited by Jonathan H. Turner. Kluwer Academic / Plenum Publishers, New York, 2002.

Figure 10.1. Wall mural, *Parade*, by Michael Brown (Chapel Hill, North Carolina) (photograph by Lisa M. Collard).

Figure 10.2. Detail of wall mural, *Parade*, by Michael Brown (Chapel Hill, North Carolina) (photograph by Lisa M. Collard).

For all of the mural's populist themes—provincialism, theatricality, and satire—it *is* art. It cites some of Western art's memorable notations and uses art's institutionalized vocabularies, such as composition and framing. It also plays with themes that preoccupy contemporary artists, notably publicness, the deconstruction of durable structures, and historical memory. Yet it is not art in the Kantian sense of the term. The Kantian tradition of *art pour l'art* rests on the assumption that an artwork exists in its own autonomous realm. In the late 19th century, this came to mean autonomy from capitalism, industrialism, and bourgeois values, and then, in the United States, as autonomy from all values other than art's own. According to this tradition, art is sovereign only onto itself.

Like many contemporary public art works, "Parade" both invades and appropriates its context. It has no presumptions of its own autonomy. It celebrates its contemporary and historical subjects and enjoins them to commingle among themselves and engage those who pass them by. By the same token it makes no moral claim that it relates to universal aesthetic values, as the Kantian tradition would insist. Brown does not demand assent, but instead invites our reactions and comments, while he rebukes us. Nor does Brown assume much about the nature of the subjectivity that viewers ought bring to the experiencing of the work—something of importance in Western aesthetics—as signaled by, for example, the imperative of stylistic unity as a criterion for evaluation and appreciation (Adorno, 1984). In my view, "Parade," like other contemporary public art works, is part of a quiet revolution in aesthetics that has great significance for the social sciences.

Postontological art rejects the distinction between the "I" and the "You," and the "Us" and the "Them," and the correlative distinction between "the subjective" and the "objective." As I will argue, contemporary artworks are about "betweenness"; between, for example, groups, races, genders, nations, generations, and historical periods (Blau, 2000). The starting point for "betweenness" involves "introductions all round," which are required for artworks whose details about particular places, people, and history may be obscure to outsiders. Museums and galleries now often provide detailed narratives printed on cards off to the side of an artwork to help make these introductions. Contemporary artworks often exist in interstitial social spaces (and sometimes, interstitial geographical spaces; see Harris, 1999) and do not recognize or grant privilege to any.

THE CENTRAL PROBLEM

The reason why I use the hulky terms, "ontology" and "postontology," is that I want to refer to an historical divide of consciousness, between considering that the self is uniquely and autonomously constituted and the view of a plural self that exists in terms of many codependencies. In Kantian aesthetics, a corollary of ontology is the imperative of a universal standard of beauty, namely, that a person judges an artwork in a "disintererested" way, which leads to sound judgment. The Kantian "I" who sought cognitive understanding in science was not so different from the "I" who sought subjective pleasure from art, and it is roughly in these terms that we can see the origins of utilitarianism, capitalism, consumerism, taste, rationality, and reason. This conception of the "I" is very different from the current conception of the Self that is uncentered, underdetermined, pluralistic, and who struggles with multiple identities, or is preoccupied with a master identity. The brilliance of Kant's aesthetic philosophy is attested to by its long-standing usefulness; it lasted from the end of the 18th century through nearly the whole of the 20th century and helped to sustain European avant-gardes as well as America's

Abstract Expressionism, even though ostensibly, as I will suggest, they were rooted in quite different art traditions.

It is useful to expand a bit on Kantian aesthetics to show that both reason and aesthetic judgments were situated with individuals and that both involved principles to which individuals refer. He contrasts reason (from his *Critique of Pure Reason*) with aesthetic evaluations in *Critique of Judgment* (1790):

> These concepts (the categories) call for a Deduction, and such was supplied in the Critique of Pure Reason.... This problem had, accordingly, to do with the *a priori* principles of pure understanding and its theoretical judgments. [But in contrast] ... there arises a judgment which is aesthetic and not cognitive.... How are judgments of taste possible? This problem, therefore, is concerned with *a priori* principles of pure judgment in *aesthetic* judgments, i.e., not those in which (as in theoretical judgments) it has merely to subsume under objective concepts of understanding, and in which it comes under a law, but rather those in which it is itself, subjectively, object as well as law.... All that it [aesthetic judgment] holds out for is that we are justified in presupposing that the same conditions of judgment which we find in ourselves are universally present in every man. (Kant 1790/1952, pp. 143–145)

Taste, thus, is enlightened judgment and derives its imperativeness from being universal. Moreover, it is the artist, as creative genius, who gives the "rule to art," namely, dictates the standards that becomes universally accepted (Kant, 1790/1952, p. 168). This view survived more or less intact through Hume, Wittgenstein, Hegel, Nietzsche, Trotsky, and Derrida. However, it just barely survived Derrida, and did not at all survive Foucault.

We have come to understand that contemporary conditions—a multiplicity of social worlds, of worldviews—pose different challenges for aesthetic theory, art making, and evaluating art. The conception of the decentered, underdetermined, or the pluralistic self has particular significance in understanding contemporary art. To begin with we might provisionally consider an artwork to be something like a link involving the artist, viewers, groups, and meanings. This argument snips at the heels of the Kantian assumptions about genius, individual subjectivity, and universal standards of judgment. One answer, which I consider too easy as a way out, is to consider contemporary art as merely another expression of cultural and social pluralism. Such a relativist perspective denies art its institutional character, and by posing that art simply mirrors social life, undermines its moral power.

THE DISTINCTIVE CLAIMS OF AESTHETICS

I approach the topic of aesthetics as being worthy in its own right, rather than to reiterate the view that art is a component of culture (for example, Williams, 1961; Halle, 1993) or the view that art traditions survive because they shore up class boundaries (Bourdieu, 1984; Gans, 1999; DiMaggio, 1982) and help to legitimize political elites (Mukerji, 1997). These approaches have been extremely useful, and not, in my view, at all wrong. Most importantly, they have challenged the high–low distinction and demonstrated the extent to which the rich have relied on High Art to define class lines. However, a consequence has been that social scientists have marginalized the power of aesthetic theory and quite inadvertently trivialized what artists do and what they say they do.

Art, whether it is rooted in the aesthetics of a craft convention, a religious or cultural tradition, or a self-conscious canon, is bracketed in its own terms, as an expression of sensuousness and imaginative performance. Art forms establish a world for which meaningfulness is a given, but the given is the occasion of considerable critical and interpretive analysis (Wood, 1999). When I use the term "aesthetics," I mean it in the sense of any self-conscious critical and interpretive tradition, for which there are exemplary cases: the way the horns on the mask must be carved, a particular Corot landscape, Duchamp's urinal, or the manner of depicting the rain god Tlaloc.

There are four reasons why aesthetics may be of interest to social theorists. First, aesthetics, to the extent that it is a specialty of moral philosophy, deals with questions of human values and meaning, something with which contemporary social scientists grapple, as there is growing concern about social justice and human rights. Second, as aesthetics veers from philosophy to criticism and advocacy, it requires a practical concern with ethics, a field underdeveloped in the social sciences, but which may accompany our newfound interest in social justice and human rights. Third, critical traditions in the arts are not vexed by the splits with which sociologists contend involving positivism, interpretation, and historical study. Finally, aesthetics takes representation as a central problem, and because representation is in constant flux, aesthetics is routinely in a crisis mode, as it might be said of social theory in contemporary times.

Given the problems of comparability among the performing, visual, and musical arts, art theory has traditionally been about the visual arts, and this too will be my focus. However, I will suggest at the close of my chapter that this tight specialization is bound to change as artists create works that are not easily contained within museum walls. Owing to digitalization and other technologies (see Virilio, 1994), artists are able to transgress traditional boundaries in the arts. In the meantime, it is possible to draw on aesthetics as it is currently configured around art practices and suppose that there will always be aesthetic principles just as there will always be institutional frameworks for the application and development of these principles.

WHAT IS ART?

A reference point for any aesthetics is a conception of art practice, and the most generous of conceptions gives wide berth to others while containing the kernel of one's own version of what the morrow might bring. Here I draw broadly from contemporary art theory, the striking tone of which highlights pluralism and the dialogical qualities of art. It is useful to start with some major dimensions of art that I believe are not all that controversial within contemporary aesthetics.

First, art *defines a real world of its own*. Art—folk, commercial, abstract, figurative, tribal—is mimetic (inauthentic), although people reference artworks in terms of what they take to be real at the time and in their context. What museum-going Americans in around 1970 may have taken as an exemplary statement involving emancipation and freedom, say, a Rothko painting exhibited at the Museum of Modern Art is now in some permanent collection and viewed by the public as an icon of an earlier time. The African mask loses its magic, although not its beauty, on the wall in a collector's home. Yet then, what is more "real," the thing itself or the representation of the thing? Is it possible to greatly marvel at a water lily in a pond after seeing one of Monet's paintings of water lilies? Can your lover hold a candle to any Greek sculpture? Yet in another sense, the artwork takes power and agency from what it represents and gives it to the viewer. The lion is tamed by the photographer and images of gods give redemption to pilgrims. Brown's mural is congenial, but it rebukes its subjects, as its subjects; we, the viewers, are aware. Thereby, second, art is *subversive and critical*.

Third, in apparent contradiction to its mimetic and its fleeting character and its subversive and critical capacity, art is *affirmative* as it represents a feeling or conception (Langer, 1957). Thus, artworks, at least many of those that are very interesting, shape a dialectic between

subversiveness and affirmation. Cezanne subverted space to affirm the compositional principles on which space depends. Goya's mannerisms mocked his royal subjects. Picasso's
"Guernica" depicts evil but affirms painterly expression. Maya Ying Lin's Veterans Memorial
subverts ostentatious monumentality, long considered as only appropriate for public com-
memorative statutes.

Fourth, art is a *reference point* for trans-local meaning and communication, and thereby
expands both knowledge and understanding across great boundaries involving language,
culture, and other differences. Artworks mediate and thereby weakly tie together different
reference points and identities, potentially bringing about a sense of mutual awareness. The
diffusion of an art style and the absorption of many others mark the genius of Islam between
about 750 to the 12th century, Christianity later, and likewise the Romans even earlier, but the
contemporary challenge is to achieve intermingling without mangling what already exists.
Crossovers between African, Caribbean, and Latin music retain qualities from each original
source. Official attempts to lace Peking opera productions with Western components have
been lamentable failures. It seems to work the more casual it is.

Fifth, artworks are part of a *historically dynamic institution*, which in turn relates in
complex ways to other institutions, such as the political economy, religion, and the nation-
state (for example, Corse, 1997). The avant-garde, even with its pretense of autonomy, was no
exception to this. Sixth, the artwork–public (viewer) nexus is made in the terms of an
enigmatic link that involves meaning, which may or may not be informed by theory. We can
call this enigmatic link *interpretation*. This can be formalized as criticism (Shrum, 1996), but
interpretation rightfully belongs to those who view the artwork, just as the right to experience
and evaluate live music is that of the listener's. Something of this enigmatic link between the
viewer and artwork may be hardwired in human beings, but still we can describe it in
experiential terms, as the capacity to "feel" or "know" beauty, delight, tranquility, or terror.

My approach is to ignore the conventional distinctions in aesthetics, those that relate to
experiencing art (Dewey, 1934/1958; Gadamer, 1975), evaluating art (Dickie, 1988; Hume,
1757/1998), and the character of aesthetic objects (Gombrich, 1971), but I attempt to select
puzzles in art theory that suggest parallels to social theory, namely, art's criticality and social
affirmative functions, as spanning local meaning, as an institution, and as mediation.

Another convergence between aesthetics and social theory might be considered in the
following terms. As Alexander (1995, p. 11) points out, modernism in sociology was articulated in the following ideal typical terms: coherently organized systems; progressive evolution
from traditional to modern (individualistic, democratic, capitalistic, universalistic, and secular); and functional interdependence. Modern art, or at least American Abstract Expressionism, was nicely compatible with this modernist conception. It relied, as Bernstein (1992)
argues, on a sharp differentiation between morality and beauty and on the mythic conception
of the individual (the creative artist). Modernism in art, at least in the United States, as
Abstract Expressionism, also disavowed any political agenda. It was antiparticularistic (that
is, anti-Kitsch), elitist, and defended as nonideological and universalistic. Its very principled
nonfigurativeness and abstractness were presumably testimony to its transcendence over
political and cultural differences.

Contemporary art is different now than it was in the 1950s and 1960s, as our understanding of social worlds is also different. Now social theorists consider that social life is weakly
organized through networks, local practices, and social cooperation instead of by ordered
systems (Misztal, 2000). Aesthetic theorists suggest that we consider how meaning and value
are also weakly organized by thematic interpretations that have significance for linking
traditions, affirming local practices, and for helping to achieve awareness of codependencies.

Art has a particular advantage in this, and there are "things" that mediate transactions, namely, performances, dances, murals, videos, exhibits, sculptures, paintings, and events.

AN ACCOUNT OF THE MODERN

To illustrate that art is self-consciously distinct from culture and that at least for the past century in Europe many artists participated in movements that were explicitly ideological, I provide a listing in Table 10.1 of major 20th-century art movements. They are identified as either avowing a political ideology or not, and for those that were ideological, I label them as either having a Left or Right agenda. The primary source used is Harrison and Wood (1992) and I explain later why I end the series about 1975. Dates of formation are not always clear, but I use dates of manifestos or major first exhibits given by Harrison and Wood. Political orientations are usually clear enough. The futurists are listed twice—1912 and 1922—because they began as a left-oriented radical movement, but many of the artists later sided with Mussolini. The formation of the Artists' Union in the Soviet Union on April 23, 1932, was the effective end of artistic diversity and dissent in the Soviet Union until toward the end of the Cold War. Other movements are described as having a right agenda, including US Regional-ism (c. 1935), owing to an appeal to nationalism, absolutism, and social purification. The main point is to show how very early art movements self-consciously evolved in terms of "art for art's sake," and subsequent movements became increasingly involved in geopolitical align-ments, until Abstract Expressionism in the United States (ostensibly) abandoned the partisan-ship of such alignments.

By 1900, the revolution against the academy and traditional constraints was considered to have been successful. The Impressionists, and then the Postimpressionists, had completely overturned conventions about style, technique, and training. Court and official patronage had come to an end. The early 20th-century movements—Divisionism, Symbolists, Synthetism, Metaphysics, Jugendstil, Fauves, Orphism, Suprematism, Cubism, Purism, and the German Expressionist movements (Brücke and Der Blaue Reiter)—centered on controversies dealing with painterly values—line, color, shapes, and form. During this early period art styles were defended by their respective publicists in terms of their psychological appeal and often justified in terms of Freudian theory. For example, Benedetto Croce (1913/1965) described Symbolism as epitomizing "intuition"; the Postimpressionists, such as Gauguin, were consid-ered by Roger Fry (1909/1924) to be drawing from "deep, instinctual primitivism"; Hermann Bahr (1916/1925) stressed the "life-giving" qualities of German Expressionism; and, it was "purity" that Guillaume Apollinaire (1913/1949) found in Cubist works. Early modernism in art, in short, was something of an escape from the ordeals of the brutalizing conditions in cities and factories, but at the same time signaled a rather precocious appeal to universal values and an international order. Artworks related to personal, subjective identities and emotional needs, something Abstract Expressionism would later draw upon.

Paradoxically, these early movements that dominated the first two and a half decades of the century became a negative frame of reference for most subsequent European avant-gardists, although they were appropriated by American avant-gardists. A somewhat sim-plified, but largely correct interpretation, is that American Abstract Expressionism was rooted in a denial of heterodoxy and of vexing global problems, and instead was preoccupied with the relationship between individual expression and what was considered to be a baseline universal aesthetic (Crane, 1987). Ignoring philosophical movements in Europe, such as Existentialism as well as the Marxist debates that fueled European art movements, US critics appropriated

TABLE 10.1. Art Movements 1900–1975, Classified as: Exclusive Claim as Art for Art's Sake, or Not, and If Not, as Politically Progressive Agenda (Left) or a Politically Right Preservationist Agenda (Right), with Approximate Founding Dates, and Representative Artists[a]

	Art for art's sake	Left agenda	Right agenda
Divisionism, c. 1900 (Paul Signac)	A		
Symbolism, c. 1900 (Paul Gaugin)	A		
Jugendstil, c. 1900 (August Endell)	A		
Brücke, c. 1905 (Ludwig Kirchner)	A		
Synthetism, c. 1910 (Paul Cezanne)	A		
Fauve, c. 1910 (Henri Matisse)	A		
Metaphyiscal School, c. 1910 (Giorgio di Chirico)			R
Futurism, c. 1912 (Filippo Tommaso Marinetti)		L	
Orphism, 1912 (Robert Delauney)	A		
Theosophy, c. 1914 (Wassily Kandinsky)	A		
Vortex, c. 1914 (Percy Wyndham Lewis)			R
Suprematism, 1915 (Kasimir Malevich)		L	
Neo-Primitivism, c. 1915 (Alexander Shevchenko)		L	
Der Blaue Reiter, c. 1915 (August Macke)	A		
Neo-Plasticism, c. 1915 (Piet Mondrian)	A		
Cubism, c. 1915 (Pablo Picasso)	A		
De Stijl, c. 1917 (Theo van Doesburg)	A		
Novembergruppe, 1918 (Max Peckstein)		L	
Bauhaus, c. 1919 (Walter Gropius)		L	
KOMFUT, c. 1919 (Vladimir Tatlin)		L	
Arbeitstrat für Kunst, c. 1919 (Bruno Tat)		L	

TABLE 10.1. (*Continued*)

	Art for art's sake	Left agenda	Right agenda
Purism, 1920 (Charles Edouard Jenneret)	A		
Dada, c. 1920 (Man Ray)		L	
Constructivists, 1920 (Alexander Rodchenko)		L	
L'Esprit Nouveau, 1921 (Juan Gris)			R
Opposition to Novembergruppe, c. 1921 (Otto Dix)		L	
Futurism (Novecento), c. 1922 (Mario Sironi)			R
Unism, c. 1922 (Wladyslaw Strzeminski)		L	
Syndicate of Technical Workers Painter and Scultors, c. 1922 (David A. Siqueros)			R
UNOVIS, c. 1923 (El Lissitsky)		L	
Left Front for the Arts (LEF), c. 1923 (Leon Trotsky)		L	
Surrealism, c. 1924 (Andre Breton)		L	
AkhRR, c. 1924 (early Socialist Realism)			R
Red Group, c. 1924 (Georg Grosz)		L	
ARBKD (Asso), c. 1928 (Otto Nagel)		L	
October, 1928 (Alexander Rodchenko)		L	
Combat League for German Culture, 1929 (Alfred Rosenberg)			R
Ash Can School, c. 1930 (Reginald Marsh)		L	
Harlem Renaissance, c. 1930 (Sargent Johnson)		L	
Artists' Union, c. 1932 (official Stalinist art)			R
[b]Early American modernism, 1932 (Hans Hoffman)	A		
Association Abstraction-Création, c. 1932 (Hans Arp)	A		
Artists' Union, US, c. 1935 (Stuart Davis)		L	

continued

TABLE 10.1. (*Continued*)

	Art for art's sake	Left agenda	Right agenda
Regionalism, c. 1935 (Grant Wood)			R
Artists' International Association, c. 1935 (Henry Moore)		L	
New Realism, c. 1936 (Fernand Léger)		L	
American Abstract Artists Association, c. 1936 (Ibram Lassaw)	A		
Constructivism, c. 1937 (Naum Gabo)	A		
Independent Federation, c. 1938 (Diego Rivera)		L	
^cNew York School, 1945 (Adolph Gottlieb)	A		
Art Brut, 1948 (Jean Dubuffet)		L	
Cobra, 1948 (Karl Appel)		L	
Spatialism, c. 1946 (Lucio Fontana)	A		
Independent Group, c. 1952 (Brit., Pop Art; Richard Hamilton)		L	
Situationists, c. 1957 (Guy Debord)		L	
Nouveaux Réalistes, c. 1959 (Yves Klein)	A		
The New Realists, c. 1960 (Paris—Jean Tinguely)		L	
Happening, 1960 (Allan Kaprow)		L	
Pop Art, c. 1962 (US, Claes Oldenbrg)		L	
Post-Painterly Abstraction, 1962 (Barnett Newman)	A		
Socialism ou Barbarie, c. 1965 (Jean-François Lyotard)		L	
Conceptual art, c. 1967 (Sol LeWitt)	A		
Arte Povera, 1967 (Giovanni Anselmo)	A		
Art & Language, 1968) (Brit., Terry Atkinson)	A		
Society for Theoretical Art and Analysis, c. 1969 (Brit., Ian Burn)	A		

TABLE 10.1. (*Continued*)

	Art for art's sake	Left agenda	Right agenda
Minimalists, 1970 (US, Donald Judd)	A		
Earth projects, c. 1970 (Robert Smithson)		L	
Flexus, c. 1970 (Joseph Beuys)		L	
Art Workers Coalition, c. 1970 (US, Carl Andre)		L	
Art Meeting for Cultural Exchange, c. 1975 (United States and United Kingdom, Mel Ramsden)		L	

[a]Political labels apply only within their context; for example, Leninist and Trotskyite art movements are classified as Left and Stalinist art movements are classified as Right. Compared with other German art movements, Bauhaus might not be considered to be Left-wing, but it self-identified as a social visionary movement. This summary should not be used as a primary source because it is not based on sufficient examination of original documents. National identity is not indicated except to distinguish some of the differences between the United States and Britain.
[b]Not an art movement, but indicated to clarify early source of Abstract Expressionism.
[c]See text.

the language of early modernism from the initial decades of the 20th century. It is somewhat ironic that if a 1960s Ad Reinhardt work were to be placed next to Malevich's 1915 "Black Square," it would be difficult to tell the difference. Oddly enough, early innovative Russian works—for example, by Malevich, Gabo, Pevsner, and Kandinsky—were canonized by US critics and museums during the Cold War, while contemporary Soviet works (Socialist Realism) were banned from public exhibit in the United States (though not in Canada, which is where interested Americans traveled to see them).

Throughout the Cold War period there existed a three-way split: Socialist Realism, European avant-garde movements, and Abstract Expressionism. The first was virtually isolated after the 1936 Moscow show trials under Stalin, and European artists launched alternative art movements that resonated with Marxism. A widely circulated paper by André Breton, Diego Rivera, and Leon Trotsky (1938) signaled the irrevocable break between Latin American and European art and Soviet art. European avant-garde movements nevertheless engaged socialist themes and were for the most part anticapitalist. Throughout this period in Europe, it was not only art theorists and critics who wrote about art, but also people who we nowadays consider as social theorists or social philosophers. These included George Lukács, Francis Klingender, Walter Benjamin, Georges Battille, Jean Paul Sartre, Guy Dubord, Theodor Adorno, Max Horkheimer, Louis Althusser, Walter Kracauer, and Jürgen Habermas. In contrast, American intellectuals were not involved in the arts, except in the never-ending debate about the problem of the massification of tastes. When the House Committee on Un-American Activities denounced "realists," such as Ben Shahn and Willem De Kooning (along with authors Langston Hughes and Arthur Miller), most American academicians remained silent. The conventional account of this period is that the Left was intimidated, while "innocents" were bought off. The CIA put up front money to support artists through the American Committee for Cultural Freedom, an anticommunist effort supported by the Museum of Modern Art and many prominent artists (see Guilbaut, 1983; Saunders, 1999). Leaders in the official art world, such as Alfred H. Barr, Jr., who spoke out against painters such as Shahn, defended *art pour l'art* and denounced realistic tendencies as communist (see Harrison & Wood, 1992, pp. 654–668). Another interpretation of the failure of academicians to respond is that there were too few intellectuals in the United States, compared with Europe, who had ties with artists or who cared enough about art to understand what the issues were.

The time series in Table 10.1 stops at 1975. The events around 1968 politicized the avant-garde in the United States and elsewhere, and there was a growing hiatus between theory and practice. Generally, new questions began to challenge the conventional understanding about the relationships involving what was represented, the significance of what was represented, and how what was represented was received. More specifically, semiotic structuralists, such as Barthes and Eco, suggested there were oppositions involving what is expressed (written or painted), what is believed (myth and ideology), and what is experienced/seen. This perspective, codified in somewhat overly scientific terms, as sign, signifier, and signified, was taken up in architectural theory by Charles Jencks (1973), and greatly helped liberate US architects from the formal pretensions that had dominated Modernism in American architecture (see Blau, 1980). In museum art, as Pop Art, semiotics achieved a genuine coup against Abstract Expressionism, followed by a rapid succession of movements that centered on similar theoretical concerns: Conceptual Art, Minimalist Art, Photorealism, and "text art."

As Danto (1981) proposed (although not explicitly in the language of semiotics, namely, sign, signifier, and signified), an artwork is what is merely titled—labeled—an artwork. In other words, it is the institution of art that gives credentials to an artwork and there is nothing inherent in any work that makes it special (see Becker, 1982). But it was Foucault who drove the last nail in the Kantian, Modernist coffin, not only by arguing somewhat along the same lines, but concluding that originality was an ideological construction (see Foucault, 1973/1982; Krauss, 1986). The artist, the poet, the author, the creator were all "dead." There was a growing consensus in the mid-1980s in both Europe and the United States that all avant-gardes had come to an end (for a summary in sociology, see Blau, 1995). At the conclusion of this chapter, I will speculate about the emerging issues in contemporary art. However, I think it is useful to look more closely at Abstract Expressionism; for one thing, it dominates major US museums' current permanent collections; and for another, it is likely to remain an important reference for any art movement because of its prominence during the middle decades of the 20th century.

AMERICAN MODERN

Although its defenders traced the origins of Abstract Expressionism back to Kandinsky's abstractions done in the first decades of the century and claimed dominance over all other styles, Abstract Expressionism itself was a short-lived affair, from the early 1940s to the early 1970s, and mostly confined to the United States. We could say that American modernism appeared around 1943 with the opening of Pollock's first exhibit in New York and an exhibition in New York of the Federation of Modern Painters and Sculptors, which included Gottlieb, Rothko, and Newman. By the 1950s, it was claimed by American art critics that Modernism—Abstract Expressionism and American architecture—comprised the "International Style."

Its appeal lay with its abolition of content by color and its denial of history, ideology, particularity, identity, oppression, and struggle. Is most ardent defender, Clement Greenberg, argued

> It has been the search of the absolute that the avant-garde has arrived at "abstract" or "nonobjec-
> tive" art ... [the] artist tries in effect to imitate God by creating something valid solely on its own
> terms.... Something *given*, increate, independent of meanings, similars or originals. (Greenberg,
> 1939, p. 36; italics in original)

Such a defense was echoed about two decades later by the artist Ad Reinhardt, toward the end of Abstract Expressionism: "The one standard in art is oneness and fineness, rightness and purity, abstractness and evanescence. The One thing to say about art is its breathlessness, lifelessness, deathlessness, contentlessness, formlessness, spacelessness, and timelessness" (Reinhardt, 1962/1992, p. 809). One American dissenter, Harold Rosenberg, described American modernism in these terms: "In this parody of vanguardism, which revives the academic idea of art as a separate 'realm,' art can make revolutionary strikes without causing a ripple in the streets or in the mind of the collector" (Rosenberg, 1967, p. 91).

Later, Jameson (1981) noted that its philosophical premises—the dominance of style over substance and its centered subject—could not withstand the fragmented, decentered, postmodern consciousness (see also Larson, 1993, on this point). As disillusionment set in regarding America's claims as the innocent defender of democracy around the globe, the idea of Abstract Expressionism receded. It had been defended in the terms of individualism *and* universalism, choice *and* evolutionary determinism—the very stuff of claims about free markets and capitalist democracy but the antithesis of substantive politics and authentic identities. As noted, the CIA and the Defense Department considered Abstract Expressionism to be a perfect weapon in the Cold War precisely because artworks exemplified nonspecific, abstract freedoms (Guilbaut, 1983; Saunders, 1999). The conclusion would be that art is never agnostic, as we may have thought it was.

MEANINGS IN ART

Lest this account be interpreted to imply that artists work entirely along lines dictated by theory and closely tied to their historical context, I discuss two works to illustrate the point that styles and labels tell us little about individual works of art, although any artwork nevertheless exists within an institutionalized domain (Bürger & Bürger, 1992).

"Power"

Figures 10.3 and 10.4 are different views of *Power*, an anodized, bright-dipped aluminum sculpture. Its 192 strips, alternating bronze and silver, were cut from 354 feet of metal. Its weight—259 pounds—is carried by a 4 × 18 × 18 inches piece of solid transparent Plexiglas, atop a brick base that is about 3 feet tall. A contemporary observer might think about its similarity with modernist works, such as Mondrian, say, owing to its formality, proportionality, and also its affinities with early industrial design and the technological precision of early Russian Constructivism. "Power" was designed and constructed by Dan Murphy for a specific location, namely, in our courtyard, just adjacent to a large Imperial azalea, which for about 2 weeks a year backdrops the stark metal with the softest of white blossoms. "Power" is shaded during the summer by a drooping wax myrtle and tall oak trees. The environment and the sculpture interact, so as the sun and clouds move through the sky and the light filters through the oak branches, the surface of the sculpture reflects patterns of motion.

FIGURE 10.3. Top view of *Power*, sculpture by Dan Murphy (photograph by Lisa M. Collard).

In 1920, Mondrian wrote about formal structure as plasticity:

> Logic demands that art be the *plastic expression of our whole being*: therefore, it must be equally the plastic appearance of the *nonindividual*, the absolute and annihilating opposition of subjective sensations. That is, it must also be the *direct expression of the universal in us*—which is the *exact appearance of the universal outside us*. (Mondrian, 1920/1992, p. 287, italics in original)

Yet the sculpture's continual interaction with its environment reminds us that this is not, as Mondrian conceived art, as an object that is self-contained for a self-referential experience. Much later, environmental artist Smithson wrote, "I am for an art that takes into account the direct effect of the elements as they exist from day to day apart from representation" (Smithson, 1979, p. 133). A point I make is that the beauty of Murphy's "Power" is self-contained in the way that a Mondrian painting is, but "Power" is also a work of the late 20th century and derives some of its meaning from contemporary environmentalism. In this sense individual works affirm continuities within institutional traditions of art, while they also exhibit the conditions of their own origins.

FIGURE 10.4. Side view of *Power*, anodized aluminum sculpture by Dan Murphy (photograph by Lisa M. Collard).

"Thirsty Traveler"

Betty Bell's "Thirsty Traveler" (Fig. 10.5) is a painting of a homeless man. He is resting on a stone wall, being accommodated by the wall, or perhaps better put, he shapes it with his body and weight. The cats and birds around him seem both curious and consoling. Someone has brought him a glass of water and it is placed just near him, on the street. The colors, textures, and shapes give the piece an expressive quality, but the affinities between animate and inanimate objects, between nature and man, are also reminiscent of symbolist works, by Gauguin, perhaps. That is, there is something here that suggests a transcendent unity, perhaps a divine one, but probably a more animistic idea than a Christian one, which is that consciousness is possessed in their being and becoming by all living things. Aside from these speculative possibilities, the most obvious point about this painting is its strikingly humanistic quality. Though homeless, we are assured that the man is comfortable, sheltered by the trees and protected by the animals. He has a glass of water, which Bell explains, "Was all that he wanted when he was asked." Although Bell's painting is contemporary and resonates with a general

FIGURE 10.5. *The Thirsty Traveler*, painting (oil on canvas) by Betty Bell (photograph by Lisa M. Collard).

return of humanism in the arts in about 1995, it also recalls the writings of Sartre and works by Giacometti, one of his favorite artists (see Sartre, 1948).

In other words, like Brown's mural, "Parade," "Thirsty Traveler" draws its meaning from a vast storehouse of tradition, technique, and material possibilities and in so doing disallows singular interpretations. At the risk of belaboring the metaphor, I, as a viewer and member of the community in which this homeless man may still be living, can pull from my own memory bank the closest matches I know—Giacometti—as I consider the puzzles it raises. Why a wall? If walls are boundaries, why does this one accommodate a man without a home? Are walls for transgression? This is precisely how an artwork's own premises elude theory.

ART INSTITUTIONS VIS-À-VIS
OTHER INSTITUTIONS

Although the crisis in modernism within the social sciences was not evident until later, it began in the arts in the late 1960s as events cascaded and dissent erupted in America and Europe. These events centered on Civil Rights, the Vietnamese war, the Cultural Revolution in China, the Cuban missile crisis, Czech Spring. The most evident manifestations of this crisis appeared most clearly in architecture, which was profoundly influenced by Italian and French semiotic theory and then by postmodernist conceptions of narrative, language, and discourse. In my view art became more inaccessible to the public than ever before. Buildings that looked like ducks or paintings of flags were incomprehensible outside of an institutional matrix, and that matrix was distinctly High Art in the United States in the 1970s. Yet, High Art is not the only institution that can dominate art. Religion did in the United States throughout much of the 19th century and a conception of language attempted to at the 20th century. I would like to briefly explain.

Art and Religion

There are strong indications that the reason American art sharply diverged from European art beginning in about 1830 was due to the domination in the United States of evangelical religion over art after the Second Great Awakening. Besides portraiture, only representational artworks of nature were allowed the American artist, as landscapes alone was considered to do justice to God's designs. Artists who insisted on painting or drawing mythical, allegorical, or historical works, in the tradition of their English and European contemporaries, were shunned by critics and collectors. Already early in the century, English and French artists had started to experiment with nonfigurative approaches and depict scenes from ordinary life. American artists could only depict themes that were congruent with religious values, whereas many English and French artists had already adopted a critical and realistic approach to topics relating to class relations and ownership (see Antal, 1966, p. 183). Virtually all those whom we now consider the finest 19th-century American artists fled the United States to work abroad. They included John Copley, John Trumbull, Samuel Morse, Thomas Cole, Thomas Eakins, Mary Cassatt, James Whistler, and John Singer Sargent.

It was not so much that the clergy kept a tight rein on artists (although some did), but rather than institutionalized religion was inimical to artworks except for landscapes that reflected the manifestation of the Divine. As I have documented in much greater detail elsewhere (Blau, 1996), the suppression of artistic creativity lasted well into the 1870s, until Boston's and New York's elites were swayed by arguments, especially by those presented by Matthew Arnold, that art had more to do with refined taste and distinctions of learning and social class than with spiritual values. Once there was a fissure opened between Sectarianism and the arts, revolutionary transformation in the arts was rapid; in 1896, Santayana (1896/1955) provided the secular language for the autonomy of the arts. The Armory Show in New York in 1913 was the self-defining moment when avant-gardists in America could join Europeans in exhibiting works by Cubists, early Surrealists, and Expressionists. In short, American Protestants were intolerant of all art that did not encode religious values. By 1880, Americans were well on their way to becoming artistic snobs.

Art and Language

One way of considering what has been termed the "Post-Aesthetic" is precisely in the terms of the positioning of art along with another institution, namely language. Mike Sutton's drawing, "*Ceci n'est pas un chien,*" in Fig. 10.6, is in the spirit of one by Rene Magritte, which later became an occasion for an essay by Foucault (1973/1982). Magritte's work is a careful replica of a pipe, under which he wrote in cursive script, "*Ceci n'est pas une pipe*" ("This is not a pipe"). Surrealist Magritte may have had a political intention, but Foucault used it to

Ceci n'est pas un chien.

FIGURE 10.6. Illustration by Mike Sutton (India ink on paper), after Rene Magritte.

make a point about representation and language, no doubt more subversive than Magritte originally intended.

Foucault notes that its strangeness is not the contradiction between the image ("a pipe") and the text ("this is not a pipe"), because, he argues, contradiction can exist only between two statements or within one statement, not, in other words, between the sign and what is signified. In short, he denies the premise of the traditional European avant-garde that pitted ideology against a material reality. "What misleads," Foucault states, is "the impossibility of defining a perspective that would let us say that the assertion is true, false or contradictory" (Foucault, 1973/1982, p. 19). Clearly among the many things problematized by Foucault is the European avant-garde's taken-for-granted contradiction between objective conditions and consciousness. In the context of my discussion about art, Foucaultian assumptions about language undermine the ontological independence of artist, viewer, work, and critic. They also undermine the premise of the European avant-garde, say starting from Novembergruppe in 1918 to Socialism ou Barbarie in about 1965. Foucault had a somewhat different impact on American scholars (Kurzweil, 1980), and I suspect on American artists and theorists as well. Without a vital political avant-garde tradition, Foucault's influence in US art circles was to challenge the notion of the creative artist, an important component of Abstract Expressionism. Yet, in an important way, Foucault was the intellectual heir of structuralism. The problems about art, history, and language had been addressed earlier by Umberto Eco and Roland Barthes who challenged the taken-for-granted relations among sign, signifier, and signified, and by Derrida who questioned the idea about stable historical interpretations (see Bernstein, 1992).

AESTHETICS LOST AND REGAINED

Aesthetics is always at the center of any philosophical crisis. The choir members sang at the funeral: "The Museum Is Dead" (Crimp, 1983), "Metaphysics Is Dead" (Dziemidok, 1985), "Epistimology Is Dead" (Vattimo, 1985), "The Audience Is Dead" (Gopnik, 1992), "Art Is Disenfranchised from Philosophy" (Danto, 1985), and "No more narrative ... subject ... object.... No more representation" (Owens, 1983, p. 66). The death sentence created an interesting predicament, but the situation was not viewed as such dire straits by everyone, and as it turns out it was a premature warrant.

Lyotard's (1988/1992) argument was that art and representation are not the problem, as Foucault had insisted, but rather the public is. He contended the central problem for artists was *Öffentlichkeit*, "finding a public." He writes: "Artists and writers must be made to return to the fold of the community; or at least, if the community is deemed to be ailing, they must be given the responsibility of healing it" (Lyotard, 1992, p. 4). Additionally he focused attention on practice; artists must be their own philosophers, creating the works that make the rules for *"what will have been made"* (Lyotard, 1992, p. 15; italics in the original). The inference I draw from his argument is that collectively artists will appeal to pluralities of publics and that addressing publics will lead to particularized and localized "solutions" *and* to practices that prevail over universalistic and supremacy claims. Art in the 1990s increasingly became configured less in terms of art movements, but more idiosyncratic and localized.

Major issues in contemporary art are not that dissimilar to those in contemporary social sciences: the representation of particularized locales and contexts and mediation. If there is a philosophical counterpart (for art) to Foucault these days it might be Emmanuel Levinas (1998; also see Cambell & Shapiro, 1999). Levinis is especially helpful in this context; he is an ethicist or moral philosopher, and art always advances an ethical or moral claim with which aesthetic theorists must grapple. It is in these terms that I have already contrasted the European avant-gardes that denounced, on ethical grounds, class domination and capitalism and the American avant-garde that made moral claims for individualism.

Levinas states the challenge as being responsible for the Other; it must be the totalizing concern with the Other that annihilates the self-interest of the I. That is, in contrast to Kant's ontology involving the "I" and its own subjectivity, the loci of consciousness and practice are interstitial spaces within pluralities. In social theory terms, these are clarified by concepts such as symmetry of power, networks of mediation, places of participation, and distributions of rights and resources, hybridization, and commons. In art we can think of this as "between-ness," as Lyotard suggested in his discussion about the artist "finding" the public. The "Thirsty Traveler" serves as my example. It evokes the responsibility and sense of caring—the You—the stranger—who brought the homeless man the glass of water, the metaphorical wall or barrier that softens to accommodate his shape, the trees that provide shade, and the cats and birds that are the sentries, as he might be theirs. (One recalls the contrasting premise in Manet's Olympia, in which a black cat stands guard to protect Olympia and her black companion against You, the prurient viewer.) Such considerations as these suggest the difference between ontology and postontology. They also suggest that "betweenness" is a useful conceptual companion to contemporary social theory's "decentered self."

CAN THE ARTS SURVIVE CULTURE?

Let us assume that pluralism is on the ascent in art practices and that the boundaries between performance, the visual arts, and music are diminishing. Let us also assume, along with aestheticians, such as Krauss (1986), that the notion of creative genius was a myth that sustained the avant-garde and it bifurcated canonical judgments of art from the experiencing of art. We also might imagine that there will be a growing interest in public art, for it uniquely addresses concerns about inclusion, public life, and shared use of the commons. Public arts are currently defined extremely broadly: parks, sculpture, fountains, sand castles, parades, the Chicago cows, street theater, outdoor video displays, decorated cars, murals, monuments, decorated benches, and pyrotechnic displays (see Senie & Webster, 1992). Public art is craft. But is it art?

Lyotard (1992, pp. 4–5) argued that the modernists fostered allusions for the presentable, whereas postmodern art is based on what is conceivable but not presentable. It is then consistent with Levinas to consider that art, public art especially, now focuses on how the conceivable invokes the Other—"betweenness"—as an ethical project. Sociologists should be wary about calling artworks "cultural productions" lest they strike down their philosophical premises. This is to argue that art remains practice with an ethical bite, which is an invitation to sociologists to consider that as artists struggle with a utopian project—engaging publics to consider what is imaginatively conceivable—that we struggle to understand what is socially conceivable.

ACKNOWLEDGMENTS: The Spencer Foundation is gratefully acknowledged. I would like to especially thank the members of the arts committee of the Social Science Research Committee and Ellen Perecman for inviting me to participate in their discussions. Initial work on this paper began as I prepared comments for a meeting of the Center for Arts and Culture, Washington, DC. I am very grateful to Carolyn Wood of the Ackland Museum, University of North Carolina, who by providing support for classes also provides support for interloping social scientists.

REFERENCES

Adorno, T. W. (1984). *Aesthetic theory*. London: Routledge & Kegan Paul.
Alexander, J. C. (1995). *Fin de siècle social theory*. London: Verso.
Antal, F. (1966). *Classicism and romanticism*. New York: Basic Books.
Apollinaire, G. (1913/1949). *The Cubist painters*. New York: Schultz Wittenborn.
Bahr, H. (1916/1925). *Expressionism*. London: F. Henderson.
Becker, H. S. (1982). *Art worlds*. Berkeley: University of California Press.
Bernstein, J. M. (1992). *The fate of art*. University Park: Pennsylvania University Press.
Blau, J. R. (1980). A framework of meaning in architecture. In G. Broadbent, R. Bunt, & C. Jencks (Eds.), *Signs, symbols, and architecture* (pp. 333–368). New York: Wiley.
Blau. J. R. (1995). Art museums. In G. R. Carroll & M. T. Hannan (Eds.), *Organizations in industry* (pp. 87–114). New York: Oxford University Press.

Blau, J. R. (1996). The toggle switch of institutions: Religion and art in the US in the nineteenth and early twentieth centuries. *Social Forces, 74,* 1159–1177.

Blau, J. R. (2000). Bringing in codependency. In J. Blau (Ed.), *Companion to sociology.* Malden, MA: Blackwell.

Bourdieu, P. (1984). *Distinction.* Cambridge, MA: Harvard University Press.

Breton, A. B., Rivera, D., & Trotsky, L. (1938). Towards a free revolutionary art. *Partisan Review, 4*(1), 49–53.

Bürger, P., & Bürger, C. (Eds.). (1992). *The institutions of art.* Lincoln: University of Nebraska Press.

Campbell, D., & Shapiro, M. J. (Eds.). (1999). *Moral spaces: Rethinking ethics and world politics.* Minneapolis: University of Minnesota Press.

Corse, S. M. (1997). *Nationalism and literature.* Cambridge: Cambridge University Press.

Crane, D. (1987). *The transformation of the avant-garde.* Chicago: University of Chicago Press.

Crimp, D. (1983). On the museum's ruins. In H. Foster (Ed.), *The anti-aesthetic* (pp. 43–56). Port Townsend, WA: Bay Press.

Croce, B. (1913/1965). *Guide to aesthetics.* Indianapolis: Bobbs-Merrill.

Danto, A. C. (1981). *The transfiguration of the commonplace.* Cambridge, MA: Harvard University Press.

Danto, A. C. (1985). The philosophical disenfranchisement of art. In P. J. McCormick (Ed.), *The reasons of art/L'art a ses raisons* (pp. 11–22). Ottawa: University of Ottawa Press.

Danto, A. C. (1997). *After the end of art.* Princeton, NJ: Princeton University Press.

Dewey, J. (1934/1958). *Art as experience.* New York: Capricorn Books.

Dickie, G. (1988). *Evaluating art.* Philadelphia: Temple University Press.

DiMaggio, P. J. (1982). Cultural entrepreneurship in nineteenth-century Boston. *Media, Culture and Society, 4,* 33–50.

Dziemidok, B. (1985). On aesthetic and artistic evaluations of the work of art. In *The reasons of art/L'art a ses raisons* (pp. 295–396). Ottawa: University of Ottawa Press.

Foucault, M. (1973/1982). *This is not a pipe.* With illustrations and letters by Rene Magritte. Berkeley: University of California Press.

Fry, R. (1909/1924). An essay in aesthetics. In *Vision and design.* New York: Brentano's.

Gadamer, H.-G. (1975). *Truth and method.* London: Sheed and Ward Ltd.

Gans, H. J. (1999). *Popular culture and high culture.* New York: Basic Books.

Gombrich, E. H. (1971). *Norm and form,* 2nd ed. London: Phaidon.

Gopnik, A. (1992). The death of an audience. *The New Yorker, 68,* 141–146.

Greenberg, C. (1939). Avant-garde and kitsch. *Partisan Review, 6,* 39–49.

Guilbaut, S. (1983). *How New York stole the idea of modern art.* Chicago: University of Chicago Press.

Halle, D. (1993). *Inside culture.* Chicago: University of Chicago Press.

Harris, M. D. (1999). *Transatlantic dialogue: Contemporary art in and out of Africa.* Ackland Art Museum, University of North Carolina at Chapel Hill.

Harrison, C., & Wood, P. (1992). *Art in theory: 1900–1990.* Oxford: Blackwell.

Hume, D. (1757/1998). On the standard of taste. In C. Korsmeyer (Ed.), *Aesthetics: The big questions* (pp. 137–149). Oxford: Blackwell.

Jameson, F. (1981). *The political unconscious.* Ithaca, NY: Cornell University Press.

Jencks, C. (1973). *Modern movements in architecture.* Garden City, NY: Anchor.

Kant, I. (1790/1952). *The critique of judgement.* Oxford: Clarendon Press.

Krauss, R. (1986). *The originality of the avant-garde and other modernist myths.* Cambridge, MA: MIT Press.

Kurzweil, E. (1980). *The age of structuralism.* New York: Columbia University Press.

Langer, S. K. (1957). *Problems of art.* New York: Scribner's.

Larson, M. S. (1993). *Behind the postmodern façade.* Berkeley: University of California Press.

Levinas, E. (1998). *Entre nous: On thinking of the other.* New York: Columbia University Press.

Lyotard, J.-F. (1992). *The postmodern explained.* Minneapolis: University of Minnesota Press.

Misztal, B. A. (2000). *Informality.* London: Routledge.

Mondrian, P. (1920/1992). Neo-plasticism: The general principle of plastic equivalence. In C. M. Harrison & P. Wood (Eds.), *Art in theory 1900–1920* (pp. 287–290). Oxford: Blackwell.

Mukerji, C. (1997). *Territorial ambitions and the gardens of Versailles.* Cambridge: Cambridge University Press.

Owens, C. (1983). The discourse of others. In H. Foster (Ed.), *The anti-aesthetic* (pp. 57–82). Port Townsend, WA: Bay Press.

Reinhardt, A. (1962/1992). Art as art. In C. Harrison & P. Wood (Eds.), *Art in theory, 1900–1990* (pp. 806–809). Oxford: Blackwell.

Rosenberg, H. (1967). Collective, ideological, combative. In T. B. Hess & J. Ashbery (Eds.), *Avant-garde art* (pp. 81–92). London: Collier-Macmillan.

Santayana, G. (1896/1955). *The sense of beauty.* New York: The Modern Library.

Sartre, J.-P. (1948). *Existentialism and humanism*. London: Methuen.

Saunders, F. S. (1999). *Who paid the piper?* London: Granta Books.

Senie, H. F., & Webster, S. (Eds.). (1992). *Critical issues in public art*. Washington, DC: Smithsonian Institution Press.

Shrum, W. M., Jr. (1996). *Fringe and fortune*. Princeton, NJ: Princeton University Press.

Smithson, R. (1979). Cultural confinement, In N. Holt (Ed.), *The writings of Robert Smithson* (pp. 132–133). New York: New York University Press.

Vattimo, G. (1985). Aesthetics and the end of epistemology. In P. J. McCormick (Eds.), *The reasons of art/L'art a ses raisons* (pp. 287–295). Ottawa: University of Ottawa Press.

Virilio, P. (1994). *The vision machine*. Bloomington: Indiana University Press.

Williams, R. (1961). *The long revolution*. New York: Columbia University Press.

Wood, R. E. (1999). *Placing aesthetics*. Athens: Ohio University.

PART III
THEORIZING INTERACTION PROCESSES

CHAPTER 11

Traditional Symbolic Interactionism, Role Theory, and Structural Symbolic Interactionism

The Road to Identity Theory

SHELDON STRYKER

INTRODUCTION AND OVERVIEW

The major claim of this chapter is that a social structural version of symbolic interactionism is a potentially fruitful source of empirically testable theories of social behavior important to the discipline of sociology. The chapter focuses on identity theory, a theory of role-choice behavior, and related ideas to illustrate this potential. The structural symbolic interactionist frame incorporates in modified form ideas that on the one hand stress the possibility for openness and fluidity of social interaction, self-direction, and human agency inherent in the symbolic capabilities of human beings and on the other hand stress constraints on that openness, fluidity, self-direction, and agency inherent in the fact that persons are members of society (Stryker, 1980; Stryker & Statham, 1985). For purposes relating to the first emphasis, it makes use of symbolic interactionism as it developed from the 18th to mid-20th century and carried into the present with little change. For purposes relating to the second, it turns to role theory. While this presentation of the frame draws on prior writings of the author (especially Stryker, 1980, 1988, 1994, 1996; Stryker & Statham, 1985), it incorporates ideas from the literature of sociology and social psychology over (roughly) the past 50 years, perhaps especially the writings of Ralph Turner (1962, 1978), George McCall and J. T. Simmons (1966), Peter Burke (Burke, 1980; Burke & Reitzes, 1981; Stryker & Burke, 2000), and Morris Rosenberg (1979).

Implied in the foregoing are several considerations important to this chapter:

1. There is no symbolic interactionist orthodoxy. Those working with that frame agree that an adequate account of social behavior must incorporate the perspectives of participants in

SHELDON STRYKER • Department of Sociology, Indiana University, Bloomington, Indiana 47405.

Handbook of Sociological Theory, edited by Jonathan H. Turner. Kluwer Academic / Plenum Publishers, New York, 2002.

interaction; both self- and social organization emerge from social interaction; and self mediates the relations of social structure and interaction (Stryker, 1988). They disagree, however, on a variety of issues of objectives, contents, and methods of analyses (Stryker, 2000). Most disagreements relate to the possibility of achieving the aspiration of a structural symbolic interactionism, namely, incorporating the conceptual and methodological insights of traditional symbolic interactionism and role theory's sense that persons' locations in social structures constrain their behavior in a frame that produces theories of social behavior subject to rigorous test within the conventions of science as commonly understood.

2. For some (e.g., Blumer, 1969), symbolic interactionism is an approach to sociology. As seen here, symbolic interactionism is one of three major approaches to sociological social psychology (the others are a group processes and a social structure–personality approach; see Stryker, 2001). The responsibility of sociological social psychology is to contribute to sociology by examining ways in which social structures impact persons and interaction and the reciprocal impact of persons and interaction on social structures; this statement of responsibility reasserts the concurrent emphases on agency and constraint defining structural symbolic interactionism.

3. Conventional sociological use of the term "theory" often ignores an important distinction. If "theory" intends a proposes explanation of social phenomena that can be evaluated through empirical evidence, neither symbolic interaction nor role theory meets the test. Both offer perspectives on social life and concepts pointing to what the perspectives deem important to explaining social life. To label them frameworks does not devalue them. Perspectives and concepts are tools theorists use to build theories by translating perspectives and concepts into an empirically testable account of why specified social phenomena occur. Effective theory building is not likely absent a persuasive perspective and prescient concepts. The distinction is especially important in thinking about symbolic interactionism. For many, its central ideas are assumed true and the derivation of testable theories unnecessary. Too, for some symbolic interactionists the very idea of testable general theoretical arguments is misbegotten. There also are symbolic interactionists who believe it possible to work with symbolic interactionist ideas *and* accept the charge of formulating general theoretical explanations of human social behavior subject to reasonably rigorous empirical examination and test.

As noted, the structural symbolic interactionist frame incorporates aspects of traditional symbolic interactionism and role theory, more of the former. The second section of this chapter reviews as much of these two intellectual streams as seems useful for understanding their contributions to the frame. The third section reviews and appraises critiques of traditional symbolic interactionism and role theory to provide insight into the motivation for merging them, then presents the structural symbolic interactionist frame. In the fourth section, attention shifts to theories emergent from this frame taken from the author's work. These are intended only to serve as illustrations of the frame's capacity to generate theories. One, a theory of role-choice behavior, has received a fair number of tests. A second offers an extension of identity theory addressing the broad question of the social circumstances contributing to relative freedom of action. The fifth section provides a brief coda.

SOURCES OF THE STRUCTURAL
SYMBOLIC INTERACTIONIST FRAME

Traditional Symbolic Interactionism

The most significant precursors of this frame are the Scottish moral philosophers of the 18th century and American pragmatic philosophers of the late 19th and early 20th centuries, especially William James and John Dewey. The psychologist James Mark Baldwin, the sociologists Charles Horton Cooley and William Isaac Thomas, and beyond any other the philosopher and psychologist George Herbert Mead contributed more directly to its evolution, whose further development and promulgation was largely although not exclusively tied to Herbert Blumer and other University of Chicago sociologists and their students in the period after World War I.

THE PERSPECTIVE OF TRADITIONAL SYMBOLIC INTERACTIONISM. There is considerable variation among the forerunners and formulators of traditional symbolic interactionism. However, they tend to share an imagery of human beings, society, the relation of society and human beings, and the nature of human action and interaction. Society is a web of communication or interaction, the reciprocal influence of persons taking each other into account as they act. Interaction is symbolic, proceeding in terms of meanings developed in interaction itself. The environment of action and interaction of humans is symbolically defined. Persons use symbols developed in their interaction and they act through the communication of these symbols. Society is a summary of such interaction. In this image, social life is a thoroughly dynamic process. Society does not exist as a static entity; it is continuously being created and recreated as persons act toward one another. Social reality is a flow of events involving multiple persons. Just as society derives from the social process, so do persons: Both take on meanings that emerge in and through social interaction. Since both derive from the social process, neither society nor the individual possess a reality that is prior to or takes precedence over the other. Society, as a web of interaction, creates persons; but the actions of persons create, through interaction, society. Society and person are two sides of the same coin; neither exists except as they relate to one another.

The symbolic capacity of humans implies they have minds and think, i.e., manipulate symbols internally. They can think about themselves—respond reflexively to themselves—and in so doing come to have a self both shaped by the social process and entering into the social process. Thinking occurs in the form of internal conversation making use of symbols that develop out of the social process. Mind and self arise in response to interruptions in the flow of activities, or problems, and involve formulating and selecting among possible courses of action to resolve the problems. Choice is part of the human condition; its content contained in the subjective experience of the person emerging in and through the social process. Consequently, in order to comprehend human behavior, sociology must come to terms with the subjective experience of persons studied and incorporate that experience into accounts of their behavior. Part of that subjective experience, important for choices made, is the experience of self.

Contained in the imagery is the idea that, individually and collectively, humans are active and creative, not only responders to external environmental forces. The environments in which they act and interact are symbolic environments; the symbols attaching to human and nonhuman environments are produced in interaction and can be manipulated in the course of interaction; thought can be used to anticipate the effectiveness of alternatives for action intended to resolve problems; and choice among alternative courses of action is a feature of social conduct. Thus, human social behavior is indeterminate; as a matter of principle (and not incomplete knowledge) neither the course nor the outcomes of social interaction can be predicted from factors and conditions that precede that interaction.

EARLY PRECURSORS. This exposition of the forerunners of symbolic interactionism begins with the Scottish moral philosophers. The start point has a rationale: these thinkers were important in establishing an empirical basis for the study of persons and society and they directly influenced early American sociology (Bryson, 1945). They were committed to inductions from empirical observation as the road to useful knowledge. Observing their everyday experience, they theorized by reference to principles found by understanding human nature via introspections informing them of the fundamentals of human mind. Most important to an emergent symbolic interactionism, they agreed that as the science of man, psychology is basic to understanding society, but the facts of human association are basic to understanding human psychology.

Links between these philosophers and the symbolic interactionist frame appear in the former's emphases on communication, sympathy, habit, convention, and imitation, all placing persons in social relationships and most emphasizing mindedness. These links are seen in ideas propounded in the work of Adam Smith, David Hume, and Adam Ferguson. Most likely known as key in shaping classical economics, Smith (1759) argued that society is a network of interpersonal communication through which persons are controlled by the approval, disapproval, desires, and evaluations of others, and that sympathy is a universal human characteristic allowing putting ourselves in other's places to see the world through their eyes. Anticipating Cooley (1902), Smith offers the figure of society as a mirror through which persons view and judge their own behavior. Hume (1888) sees persons as weak and defective alone, society as compensating for these deficiencies, the interests of person and society as inextricably tied to one another, noting that sympathy permits the development of fellow feeling and concern for society and a sense of benefits that can be expected from society. Ferguson (1792), espousing an instinct doctrine, stressed that behavior also results from habit acquired through association with others and their indications about what is and what is not acceptable conduct.

Many of these ideas reappear in the work of American pragmatic philosophers, finding their way into symbolic interactionism through William James, John Dewey, and James M. Baldwin. James' (1890) import is through his treatment of consciousness and the "self" that emerges as a consequence of consciousness. For James, self is everything that persons call theirs; implied is that humans respond to themselves as to any object in the external world. More, how they respond to self impacts how they act with reference to both themselves and external objects (including others). Elaborating four types of self—material, spiritual, social, and pure ego—what is said about social self is most relevant: The source of the social self is recognition given to a person by others; while persons have as many social selves as individual others who recognize them, as a practical matter they have as many social selves as distinct groups of others about whose judgments they care. For Dewey (1930), personality organization is largely a matter of habit and social organization largely a matter of collective habit or custom. The intimate relation of custom and habit means there is an intimate relation of society and person. Since everyone is born into society, habit reflects prior social order. Custom and habit are requisite to thinking; thinking is instrumental, allowing persons to adapt to their environments. Humans define objects in their world (Dewey, 1896), rehearse in thought possible actions with respect to those objects, and choose those actions facilitating adaptation. Baldwin (1906) modifies James' concept of self, insisting that all self is a product of person–other relationships. The relationship of social and personal, society and mind, evolves through three stages of development: a projective stage when children are aware of others, distinguish others from objects, and differentiate among others; a subjective stage when self-consciousness emerges through imitating others and learning there are feelings associated with those imitations; and an ejective stage when children become aware, by associating feelings with conceptions of persons, that others also have feelings just as they do. This last stage "provides a foundation on which Cooley's method of sympathetic introspection and Mead's theory of role taking rest" (Meltzer, Petras, & Reynolds, 1975, p. 12).

Cooley (1902) moves these ideas in a phenomenological direction. According to Cooley, the special concern of sociology is the mental and subjective because these are distinctively social. Persons exist in the personal idea, society is a relation among personal ideas, and the solid facts of society are imaginations persons have of one another. Thus, the business of sociology is to observe imaginations ultimately accessible only to those experiencing them. Cooley rejected Cartesian introspection as the method of sociology, privileging "sympathetic introspection," a process of imagining the life of others through intimate involvement with them, then recalling and describing those imaginations. He saw individual and society as the distributive and collective aspects of the same human life. Consequently, he saw self as inextricably bound up with others, a social product defined and developed in social interaction, specifically through a "looking-glass self" process in which persons imagine how they appear to others, imaging other's judgment of how they appear, and react with affect (e.g., pride or shame) to those judgments. This conception of self reinforces ideas in the symbolic interactionist stream: there is no individuality outside of social order; individual personality is a development from extant social life and the state of communication among persons sharing that social life; and central to the development of personality are expectations of others.

W. I. Thomas' (1931) import lies in his joint emphases on the methodological and substantive significance for sociological theory of subjective facts of how persons and groups define situations they are in *and* objective, verifiable facts of situations. Sociology's purpose is analyses of processes of adjustment of people and groups to other people and groups. Adjustments occur in situations as responses to objective circumstances in which persons and groups are embedded. However, definitions of the situation intervene between objective circumstances and adjustments; they are necessary parts of explanations because the same objective situation does not lead to identical behavior. To capture persons' definitions of situations, Thomas looked to personal documents: case studies, life histories, autobiographies, letters are the principal sources through which the meaning of the situation from the point of view of a participant is revealed and the principal sources revealing important variables affecting behavior, suggesting hypotheses to account for how these variables affected that behavior, and aiding in the interpretation of mass data. He recognized, however, that personal documents in themselves could not test hypotheses. For this purpose, Thomas opted for statistical research.

GEORGE HERBERT MEAD AND HERBERT BLUMER.   Mead (1934) is the most important influence shaping symbolic interactionism, whether traditional or structural, and Herbert Blumer is the most important voice articulating a symbolic interaction to which the structural version is a reaction. Mead's basic social psychological dictum—begin social psychological analysis with the social process—is his answer to the philosophical problem he set himself: derive mind and self from society without assuming a preexistent self. It follows from the evolutionary principles undergirding his philosophy and psychology: essential to human survival is communication; communication about solutions to problems related to survival is made possible by symbols held in common by those whose survival is at stake; and symbols emerge in and develop through interaction, the social process. Mind, self, and society are concurrent emergents from the social process. Mead, like Dewey, insists on the active nature of human behavior, asserting that things become stimuli as they take on meaning, and they take on meaning when defined as relevant to completing acts initiated by the person. This holds for acts relating persons to their physical environments and for acts implicating other humans. Since other humans are actors, meanings they take on are developed in interaction, the social process made possible by communication.

Self develops via the same social process; it exists in viewing oneself reflexively by adopting the standpoint of others to attach meanings to self. Thus, self emerges from inter-action; it is a social product. According to Mead, it is necessary to understand the critical role of self to understand human behavior. He specifies two parts to self: the "me," or organized attitudes of others with reference to the person, and the "I," or the person's responses to these attitudes of others. Behavior is a product of an internal conversation in which the "I" responds to the "me" responds to the "I," and so forth. The "I" represents spontaneity and creativity; characteristically, Mead sees these as occurring within the social process. He sees behavior as self-controlled but takes social control to be necessary for self-control. He suggests that self develops in stages along with a child's language competence. In play, the child takes the role of particular others (e.g., playing "mommy"); in the game, the child learns to respond to an intricate pattern of organized behaviors of multiple others (e.g., to play baseball, a player must anticipate the responses of a diverse set of team members, opponents, and umpires in order to play the game well). In brief, self-development presupposes the prior existence of organized patterns of multiple persons' actions; self-development presupposes society. But society presupposes self; just as society shapes self, the self (through the I–me dialectic) shapes society. Society continuously undergoes recreation; it is a continuous construction. Social order and social change are aspects of the larger social process. As the society shapes self-argument, self must be continuously under construction; personal order and personal change are aspects of the larger social process as well.

Blumer's influence on traditional symbolic interactionism is greater than that of anyone since Mead. He is especially significant to a structural symbolic interactionism: his writings serve as a negative model with respect to the aspiration for a symbolic interactionist frame permitting adherence to canons of science, while not abandoning essentials of the position found in Mead. Importantly, his polemical writings persuaded succeeding generations of symbolic interactionists who reject the possibility of reasonably meeting that goal. He defines symbolic interactionism (he invented the term) by strongly contrasting it to conventional sociology. Symbolic interactionism recognizes the obdurate fact of humans as defining, interpreting, and indicating creatures who have selves through which they construct actions to deal with their worlds. Conventional sociology sees social behavior as resulting from values, norms, expectations, role requirements, and so on, a practice inconsistent with these obdurate facts. Social organization has little impact in modern societies, since there are few situations to be dealt with through standardized actions. Even established forms of action have to be continuously renewed through interpretation and designation, and social organization enters only to the extent it shapes situations and provides the symbols used in interpreting situations. From this viewpoint, society is not organization or structure; it is the sum of the actions of persons occurring in situations constructed and reconstructed by those persons through interpreting the situations, identifying and assessing things that have to be taken into account in the situations, and acting on the basis of these assessments (Blumer, 1962).

That vision leads Blumer (1954, 1956) to assert methodological principles and positions contra conventional understandings of science. Sociologists should avoid initiating research with "definitive concepts," prescriptions for what to see blinding them to what would really enable understanding the situations they investigate; they should begin their research with "sensitizing concepts" that only suggest directions in which to look. For similar reasons, he argues against initiating research with hypotheses based on prior theory or extant literature, and that there is no point to measuring variables or seeking relationships among variables as part of a scientific sociological inquiry (because anything that is defined can be redefined, thus is without the qualitative constancy or stability required of variables).

Role Theory

There are two role theories, structural and interactional (Stryker & Statham, 1985), the latter drawing heavily on symbolic interactionism. Treatment here focuses on structural role theory.

THE PERSPECTIVE OF STRUCTURAL ROLE THEORY.   The theater is the major metaphor of structural role theory: the vision is of actors playing parts in scripts written by culture and shaped by evolutionary adaptation. The parts are written to restore the play to its original form should improvisation threaten its fundamentals. Analysis of a part is in terms of how its relationship to other parts meets survival needs of the larger system. Society is a system with functional substructures having their own substructures; the group is the structural context of most social interaction. Groups are systems of cooperating actors with common goals, recognized membership, and recognized interdependency. Persons enter groups as parts that are action systems of members, and behaviors toward group members are guided by subjective meanings and by evaluations using normative standards. Repeated interactions develop expectations of proper behavior among the persons involved. Norms applying to one relationship need not apply to others, nor are norms the same for all parties to relationships. Behaviors of interrelated pairs are likely mutually reinforcing and satisfactory, an image reflecting the conceptualization of groups as cooperative, goal-seeking systems and the assumption that parts are functional for the system as a whole.

Visualizing groups as made up of actors behaving in varying, interrelated ways makes necessary a language describing the variation. Structural role theory uses "status" for parts of organized groups and "role" for basically fixed behaviors expected of persons occupying a status. Underlying roles are moral norms rooted in culture. Roles exist prior to interaction of persons occupying statuses. They derive from the accumulated experience of past occupants of statuses, shaped slowly as past generations adapt to environmental requirements. Socialization is the process by which norms are transmitted, how persons learn expectations for others and for themselves that attach to statuses. For persons in social relations, these expectations tend to develop into moral imperatives that, if society works properly, fit well together. When persons in relationships conform to complementary expectations, they gain approval from others occupying related statuses and playing related roles; that approval reinforces conformity.

SHAPERS OF STRUCTURAL ROLE THEORY.   Deeply embedded in sociological thought from the 19th century on is the premise that persons are systematically influenced by positions they occupy in society. That premise is embodied in the conceptions of exteriority and constraint Durkheim used to define a social fact and is basic to his accounts of moral behavior (Durkheim, 1950) and anomie (Durkheim, 1960). It is developed in Weber's (1946, 1947) discussions of bureaucratic structure, a point of reference for a role theory of organizations, as well as his use of the concept of calling, or vocation, as critical in relating social structure and person. His methodological argument (Weber, 1949) that sociology must grasp the subjective motivation of actors in order to explain their behaviors is a bridge between role theory and symbolic interactionism. Simmel (1950) also made use of the concept of vocation. Raising the Hobbesian question of how society is possible, he answers that society, as the minded association of persons, becomes possible when persons are in part "generalized." To be members of a group, persons must be both more and less than individual personalities. They enter society by foregoing aspects of individuality for the generality of parts played as members of social units.

Society appears to persons as a set of vocations that can be filled by anyone. Persons move into vocations partly as a consequence of an inner call and are motivated to accept the requirements of the vocations they enter. Simmel and Weber both emphasize that social structures contain differentiated positions. Role theory joins this emphasis to Sumner's (1906) types of norms that place variable demands on members of society to arrive at the conception of role as understood in structural role theory. That is, differentiated norms are assembled into sets of expectations applicable to persons occupying specific positions in organized social units, and those expectations define a role.

This conception of role was given currency by the work of Park (1926), Moreno (1934), and others, and the idea that group members' performances are affected by group norms is exploited by early small group researchers using various theoretical perspectives (e.g., Festinger, Back, Schacter, Kelley & Thibaut, 1950; Sherif, 1936; Bales, 1950). However, structural role theory developed mainly through Ralph Linton (1936) and Talcott Parsons (1951) who focused on societies as functional units. For Linton, society is composed of persons whose adaptation and organization are required for survival. A division of labor, elaborated and stabilized over time, makes individual conduct predictable and cooperation among individuals complete and effective. Adaptations are perpetuated through continuous training guided by ideal patterns, positively valued ideas transmitted across generations through imitation and instruction, which also guide behaviors in situations for which persons are not specifically trained. Never completely realized, ideal patterns strongly influence behavior. Linton sees every culture as having ideal patterns for social relationships, the essence of which is reciprocity, creating circles of rights and duties. Persons occupy polar statuses in reciprocal ideal patterns. Roles are the dynamic aspect of statuses, their associated rights and duties in action. Conflicting duties and obligations within the same or among different persons are rare; otherwise, society could not function. Persons have a general role, summarizing particular roles, determining what they do for society and what they can expect in return. Status and role bring ideal patterns to the level of the person; a smoothly functioning society reflects the adjustment of persons to their statuses and roles. Critical to functioning of society, general roles (e.g., age and sex) tend to be ascribed without regard to individual differences; other roles are open to achievement. Most of these are escapes for individuals or baits for socially acceptable behavior.

While functionality of parts vis-à-vis social systems as wholes and complementarity of role expectations are not among its necessary features, there is an empirical tie between structural role theory and the structural–functional perspective in sociology reflecting the fact that many influential role theorists (e.g., Davis, 1949; Parsons, 1951) worked from a structural–functional perspective. Parsons, recognizing that perfect integration of parts of society is likely empirically impossible, used this special case as a start point for analyzing conformity to societal expectations, suggesting this is induced through actors gratifying one another's needs, acting in ways useful to each other's attainment of goals, feelings of gratification accompanying conformity to legitimate expectations and the demands of others when shared values are internalized, and approval and esteem received for conformity to others' expectations that results from sensitivity to others' attitude. Structures of social systems are made up of interactional systems relating individual actors and the status-role is the most convenient unit for the analysis of these systems. Roles are what people in statuses do as constrained by normative expectations, institutionally defined and regulated parts of relationships shaped by shared values and internalized norms made part of actors' personalities. Conformity to role expectations is rewarded, failure to conform sanctioned, and an equilibrium of interpersonal interactions is maintained. The larger systems of interaction developing in society are modeled on the interpersonal system. Thus, roles are complementary and various inducements lead persons to conform to their roles. Persons, according to Parsons, choose their courses of action in concrete situations. In principle arrived at through freely expressed preferences or the demands of personality, choices are basically understood as defined by the culture in which roles are institutionalized.

Linton and Parsons focused their theoretical work on total societies; Robert Merton's (1949) argument for the development of theories of middle range led to a shift in focus of role theorists to communities, associations, and groups that link paired interaction to total societies. Otherwise, the major themes in Linton and Parsons permeate the newer role theoretic emphasis: roles are the main mechanisms linking persons to social structures, and persons are under continuous and heavy pressure from both outside and inside themselves to conform to social expectations.

STRUCTURAL SYMBOLIC INTERACTIONISM

Reviewing critical appraisals of traditional symbolic interactionism and structural role theory sets the stage for discussion of the structural symbolic interactionist frame and theory based on the frame. In particular, doing so can illuminate the motivation behind that frame.

Criticisms of Traditional Symbolic Interactionism and Role Theory

An early and trenchant critique of traditional symbolic interactionist ideas is Mead's (1930) comment on the solipsism inherent in Cooley's conception of society. In the intervening years, critiques have been offered by persons who work within the frame (Meltzer, 1959; Kuhn, 1964; Stryker, 1980; Stryker & Statham, 1985; Reynolds, 1990) and others whose perspectives fall outside the frame (Gouldner, 1970; Collins, 1975; Huber, 1973). These cover a wide gamut of intertwined ideological, theoretical, methodological, and substantive issues. Interest here lies in only those to which a structural symbolic interactionism sought to be responsive: those directed to the scientific adequacy of the frame, and those directed to the failure to take social structure sufficiently seriously.

The first set of criticisms asserts that traditional symbolic interactionism does not provide clear and precise concepts necessary for developing theory subject to rigorous empirical test. If concepts are neither clear nor precise, they cannot be used in rigorous research. Two basic interactionist concepts—self and situation—illustrate these criticisms. With regard to situation, sociologists have long complained there exists no satisfactory understanding of its referents. Volkart (1951) argues, in spite of the centrality of the term in Thomas' work, it was never defined with sufficient precision to make it a useful descriptive or analytic tool. Years later, the same conclusion is reached (Stryker, 1964). After another 30 years, Seeman (1997) initiates his attempt, harking back to his analyses of alienation, to solve the problem of conceptualizing a situation by iterating this conclusion. With respect to the concept of self, while defining self as that which is an object to itself, i.e., by the reflexive responses of persons to themselves as objects, is evocative, the precision required for theory and test of theory is absent. This is particularly true when the attempt to give content to that conception of self has largely followed James' (1890) tack by asserting that self includes anything to which the personal pronouns I, me, or mine can be attached, thereby rendering self in a virtually limitless way.

Criticisms claiming the scientific inadequacy of traditional symbolic interactionism go beyond such relatively narrow methodological matters to broad epistemological issues. These hold that the extreme process imagery of the frame, arguing social life is continuously under construction through actors' interpretive processes and that interpretations themselves are continuously reformulated in the context of situated activity, means that society and self—and all intervening concepts implying some degree of organization or structure—exist in the moment and have no reasonable applicability beyond the moment. That implication itself asserts that seeking the development of general, testable theories of social life applicable beyond the momentary is a false aspiration, not in accord with the essential character of human behavior: We can hope to achieve post hoc understandings of what happened but we cannot hope to achieve theoretical accounts of what will or is most likely to happen. In short, critics argue, science is defeated a priori. Too, science is defeated a priori for those who view it as presupposing a deterministic universe: The emergence that underwrites a view of social life as indeterminate rules out the possibility of predictive theory

A methodological principle underlying denial of the possibility of science, according to critics of traditional symbolic interactionism, is the demand that accounts of human behavior be based on the points of view of actors involved in interaction studied. That principle and implications of an emphasis on process also are said by critics to deny the import of social structure for social behavior. That is, the demand that the interpretations of actors be central to accounts of social behavior, the correlative emphasis on definitional processes organizing ongoing interaction, the focus on immediate situations of interaction, and a view of social structure as a temporary emergent from ongoing interaction, all serve to minimize or trivialize the importance for social behavior of social structure on any level beyond the immediate situation of interaction. This methodological demand and the resultant foci of attention mean the perspective or frame cannot deal with the relations among societies or with large-scale features of societies such as the differential distribution of wealth, social class, or power structures; in effect, the charge is that social structural realities are dissolved in a universal solvent of definitions of the situation. On these grounds, traditional symbolic interactionism is accused of ideological bias in favor of the status quo (Gouldner, 1970; Kanter, 1972). Huber (1973), on different grounds, comes to the same conclusion. The charge of ideological bias also has been leveled against traditional symbolic interactionism as a consequence of its emphases on communication and the development of shared meanings and on cooperation as the necessary means for evolutionary survival, the charge being that these emphases lead to a neglect of the fact and functions of conflict in social life. Presumably contributing to this neglect is Mead's view that evolutionary processes favor the ultimate arrival of a universe of discourse coterminous with humanity.

Structural role theory has also been charged with ideological bias (Gouldner, 1970). In good part as a result of its link to structural functionalism, role theory has been criticized as promulgating a one-sided view of social behavior emphasizing consensus, cooperation, and continuity in social life at the expense of disagreement, conflict, and change, and as rationalizing the subservience of persons to the social order. A related, more value neutral criticism is that structural role theory has an oversocialized conception of man (Wrong, 1961), solving the Hobbesian problem of social order by denying or explaining away any impact of individual human beings in the social process. Persons are visualized as automatons who simply accept and reflect social norms they have been socialized to adopt. Their motivations are the result of internalizing norms via socialization and conformity to these norms that come from self-esteem derived from the positive feedback from others for conformity.

Just as structural role theory implicitly is a critique of traditional symbolic interactionism, so too is the latter a critique of structural role theory through its insistence that human beings are actors who through self creatively construct their actions with reference to others as well as through other themes in Blumer's work reviewed earlier. Aaron Cicourel (1972), whose "cognitive sociology" shares the premise of traditional symbolic interactionism privileging the interpretations of the actor, asserts it is not clear that concepts like status and role have much relevance for how people negotiate everyday behavior, and that the structural frame of status and role presupposes agreement on their content and takes for granted that their content is known and clear, while in reality these are problematic.

Appraising the Criticisms

Some criticisms reviewed may not be as applicable as critics believe and some may apply only to a segment of the frame criticized. For example, the criticism of traditional symbolic interactionism's concepts as vague and imprecise has general validity. However, the claim of some critics that this frame stands in opposition to the goal of formulating general theoretical accounts of social life and testing these using any available social science method depends on accepting Blumer's (1969, pp. 1–2) contention that his methodological dicta are made necessary by defining premises of symbolic interactionism (Stryker, 1988). Blumer infers from these premises that general, predictive sociological theory makes no sense, since preexistent concepts cannot match emergent interpretations of actors constructing their lines of social interaction.

Consequently, research initiated by a priori theory anticipating behavioral outcomes through hypotheses deduced from such theory is futile; methods that fail to directly examine interpretations in the process of emergence (e.g., experimentation, surveys) lack validity and the capacity to generate meaningful data; mathematical manipulations of numerical data produce findings bereft of meaning. However, the fundamental ideas of the symbolic interactionist frame do not necessarily lead to the metatheoretical and methodological conclusions Blumer reaches. Actors' interpretations, demonstrably important to the course and content of interaction, are not unconstrained. Meanings that are possible for actors to invoke in defining situations and those they are likely to invoke from among those possible are not random events. Too, there is stability over time to most meanings persons attach to objects; these meanings do not change greatly from moment to moment in ways that call for radical change in behavior. Indeed, if considerable stability in meanings did not exist, even over years, social life could not and would not have the predictability that enables persons to live their lives as they do. In short, that meanings can change greatly and precipitously does not say they do change either greatly or precipitously. If this is a reasonable assertion, theoretical propositions offering explanations of empirical generalizations going beyond individual phenomenology are possible and not subject to a priori rejection whatever may be their fate on meeting empirical evidence. That social life is constructed and there are few limits on what constructions are possible does not require sociology to forego predictions of future behaviors or force sociologists to believe predictions of social behavior must lack validity. Nor does acceptance of a social construction position mean that sociologists cannot recognize that the social process often crystallizes in a manner allowing the use of abstract concepts like self, role, and social structure in general theoretical arguments seeing that to which these concepts refer as effectively constraining and limiting the possibilities for emergence in social life and operating to change possibility to probability.

Implicit in the last paragraph is another assertion: To accept a principled indeterminacy in social life does not require sociologists to reject aspiring to generalized theoretical knowledge based on the degree to which empirical evidence supports theory-based explanatory claims, and it does not require rejecting conventional science as a model for work sociologists do. A deterministic universe is not needed to justify science, only that there is some regularity in behavior of interest; given such regularity, the task of a science is to describe and explain it. Nor does adequate explanation require accounting for every one of a class of cases for which it is argued to hold. Science seeks explanations of classes of behaviors, not particular behaviors, and all particular behaviors differ in some way. Sociology draws its data from the everyday world of social interaction, the number of variables entering so great that each instance of interaction must in some ways be unique. The search for general patterns of social behavior and general explanations for observed patterns must ignore that which may be idiosyncratic about but nonetheless crucial for some instances of social interaction. Consequently, some instances of interaction develop in ways contrary to what holds for most cases and so exist as exceptions to general explanations. Aspiring to explanations that hold for every concrete social behavior is unrealistic is implied. Stated alternatively and more positively, all empirical generalizations and explanations of these in sociology and social psychology are probabilistic in form.

Again, some criticisms may not be as valid as critics offering them believe. The charge that an interactionist framework, traditional or structural, does not incorporate macrolevel variables or does not provide for relations of macrolevel units, e.g., nation-states (Reynolds, 1990) is damning only if the frame is offered as a general frame for sociology as a whole. While some present a symbolic interactionist frame in that way; others present it as restricted in scope to social psychology or even more restricted to a sociological social psychology. Any frame, to be useful, must be partial in pointing up a selected set of concepts deemed of special import for illuminating problems with which the frame is concerned. By virtue of pointing up particular concepts a frame must, at least relatively, downplay others. However, limiting a frame's claims to issues important to a sociological social psychology does not absolve it from providing conceptual means for articulating social cognitive and interactional processes and social structures impinging on those processes, nor from providing for articulating links between those impinging social structures and more macrostructures that impinge on these. Indeed, the meaning of a sociological social psychology requires that such matters be attended to. Since the structural symbolic interactionism frame is explicitly pointed to a sociological social psychology (Stryker, 1980, 2001), this issue will be discussed further.

Sociologists have a penchant for "either–or" dichotomies: social behavior is either completely determined by location in social structure or is free of external constraints; social life is either process or structure; subjective definitions or interpretations either underlie human behavior or do not matter; the human is either actor or reactor. In the present context, this penchant is expressed by either accepting or rejecting in their entirety traditional symbolic interactionism or structural role theory, but neither the criticisms offered of these frames nor the frames themselves need be fully accepted or fully rejected. As Wrong (1961) long ago observed, the image of human beings as thoroughly socialized creatures contained in structural role theory has its purposes so long as it is not taken as the whole truth about human beings. Similarly, as W. I. Thomas claimed, definitions of the situation are important to human behavior but so are the realities of the situations themselves. More generally, cooperation and stability are readily observable in social life and so are conflict and change. An adequate frame intended for use in the analysis of social life must include conceptual means for dealing with both cooperation and conflict, stability and change. Put in other terms, the process emphasis of traditional symbolic interactionism *and* the structure emphasis of structural role theory are both needed.

The either–or propensity also can be problematic by obscuring useful aspects of a frame to which there otherwise may be legitimate objections. While the overall emphasis of structural role theory may well be one-sided in its view of social life as based on consensus, cooperation, and the contribution of parts of a social system to the stability of the whole, the structural role theoretic frame also provides resources for visualizing dissensus and conflict as normal in social life. It does so by making explicit what is implicit in a conception of social groups as structures of differentiated statuses and roles, namely, that persons are typically involved in multiple groups and so occupy multiple positions tied to multiple roles. While this may mean persons carry norms of a group to others and so minimize conflict among groups, it also means that conflicting norms can be introduced into persons and the groups of which they are a part, affecting the behavior of both. The insight that multiple role involvements can result in intrapersonal, interpersonal, and intragroup conflicts as well as the obverse of these owes much to the work of structural role theorists such as Merton (1957) and Goode (1960).

Building a conceptual frame capable of underpinning empirically testable theories of social behavior and make a contribution to the larger sociological enterprise is a worthy goal for sociologists who do social psychology. Summarizing the argument thus far: meeting this goal is more likely if appropriate elements in structural role theory are joined to appropriate elements in symbolic interactionism, and achieving the goal requires working within the framework of science.

A Social Structural Version of Symbolic Interactionism

Since structural symbolic interactionism builds on a recombination of elements contained in traditional symbolic interactionism and structural role theory, to describe it as the latter two frames were described would involve considerable redundancy. To avoid this repetitiveness, the structural frame is described in a different way, by first drawing on an essay (Stryker, 1996) written in response to the question: What is the message of social psychology? The essay answered that question from the point of view of a sociologist whose special interests are in social psychology; in so doing, it provides the metatheoretical and conceptual underpinnings of the structural symbolic interactionist frame. Then it presents a statement of the frame drawing on and elaborating an earlier discussion (Stryker, 1980).

Once self and society emerge in interaction, they exist in a recursive system: their relations are reciprocal. That reciprocity, however, does not preclude recognizing that every historical human being is born into and cannot survive outside the context of already-existing organized social relationships and social interactions, which themselves are embedded in larger systems of relationships and interactions. This recognition underwrites assigning priority to "society" in the metatheoretical starting point of the structural symbolic interactionism frame, the assertion "in the beginning, there is society."

This aphorism, a sociological response to the question of how best to conceptualize the relation of person and society asserts that social psychological inquiry taking the isolated individual as its start point and then asking how individual experience and behavior is affected by others will misunderstand many social psychological issues, and treatments of the social as simply setting for individual experience and behavior will be similarly deficient. In short, it accepts Mead's argument that the most fruitful way of conceptualizing the relation of person and society requires recognizing that society is built into the mind and self of the individual. There is no individuality outside of society, yet there is no society except through persons' actions. Society and individual are indeed constitutive of one another. Nevertheless, for purposes of investigating the society–person(s) relationship, society is assigned causal priority.

The implications of the preceding paragraph provides the metatheoretical context of a structural symbolic interactionist frame:

1. *Human experience is socially organized.* Mead prepares for this assertion by arguing that the organization and content of self reflect persons' participation in society. However, Mead's image of society does not reflect the complexity of contemporary society in which members occupy multiple positions in multiple social structures. Contemporary societies are not particularly unitary or coherent; they incorporate diverse congeries of organized role relationships, groups, social networks, institutions, strata, some isolated and some not, some overlapping and some not, some conflicting and some not. Persons' experience is importantly shaped by what relationships, groups, networks, institutions, and strata they enter or leave and by how these structures relate to each other. Experience is not random but is strongly impacted by persons' locations in social structures. Social structures define boundaries, some permeable, others less so. The boundaries serve as barriers to or facilitators of interaction, the barriers inhibiting or precluding interactions with others, the facilitators encouraging or requiring interaction with others. Social structures, then, are likely to bring only certain people together to interact over particular topics with particular instrumental and symbolic resources; alternatively, they are likely to keep certain people out of particular interactions. Who persons interact with and who they do not is critical to their life chances generally to the kinds of situations they have opportunities to enter; to the resources, symbolic and otherwise, they have available to define situations they do enter; to the kinds of self they can and are likely to develop; and so on. Again, human experience is socially organized; who and what persons are and can do, while not determined, reflects that fact.

2. *Social life is constructed.* The forms and the content of social life are not fixed by nature; they are products of collective activities of persons as they develop solutions to problems in their lives. To say that social forms and content are constructions is to say they are results of human action and interaction, and that reconstruction of and even radical change in these forms and content are possible. These assertions, however, do not imply there is no objective social world or that the objective world does not limit and constrain the structures and cultures constructed. Nor do they imply that social constructions are ephemeral, incapable of limiting the probability of reconstruction or radical change.

3. *Human beings are actors.* As noted, sociologists sometimes have presented a view of individuals as socialized automatons, as merely reactors. Symbolic interactionist thought says otherwise, asserting that mind and self, the symbolic and reflexive capacities of humans, permit actors to formulate, anticipate outcomes of, select from alternative lines of action, and revise actions as information is returned in the course of the action itself. Its social constructionism develops from viewing humans as active agents. This view does not deny the impact of normative demands on persons to enact roles as scripted, nor does it deny the impact of conditioning on human behavior; it simply asserts that humans can and sometimes do have significant impact over what happens to them. We can expect most if not all social behavior to reflect a blend of action and reaction, the blend in given cases a matter of empirical investigation, as is the question of the circumstances under which behavior reflects primarily (or even totally) prior conditioning or normative demands and the circumstances under which behavior reflects the initiative of actors. Implied in this conception of humans is that social psychology has the obligation of investigating both processes of social production and change as well as processes of social reproduction and stability, conformity and creativity, constraint and autonomy.

4. *The subjective and the symbolic are central in social life.* Restating the import of

persons' definitions and interpretations for behavior, the assertion does not imply there is no reality outside of definitions and interpretations: that undefined and uninterpreted aspects of the world have no impact on person: definitions denying the existence of social class does not eliminate the impact of class on those holding such definitions, nor do interpretations attributing disease to the devil lessen the effect of germs. What the assertion does imply is that actors' definitions and interpretations are consequential for how they construct their own behavior and how they interact with others; thus, explanations of social interaction must take into account interactants' definitions and interpretations.

5. *Self mediates the relation of society to social behavior and social behavior to society.* How persons define themselves reflects response to them of coparticipants in ongoing interactions and social relationships. Once defined, selves interact dialectically with others' responses to produce emergent selves that organize and guide persons' behavior. Thus, built into self are processes of social control and self-control, means to account theoretically for the impact of society on person and person on society.

6. *There is both constraint and freedom in personal and social life.* Persons are constrained in what they are, can become, and do as a consequence of membership in society. Yet, they have some freedom of action. In many ways, the most interesting and important questions of sociology and of social psychology are contained within this apparent paradox.

7. *The concept of role facilitates the articulation of symbolic interactionist and role theory ideas.* The fundamental referent of this concept is the expectations impinging on persons in their interaction with others. These expectations are used as a basic building brick by symbolic interactionists (who do not necessarily use the language of role) to build "down" to the social person in pursuing their interest in issues relating to personal organization and disorganization, socialization and interaction processes themselves. Role theorists use these expectations to build "up" to larger and more complex social units in pursuing their interest in issues of social organization and change, the functioning of groups and larger units of social organization. A satisfactory framework for a sociological social psychology must bridge structure and person, allow movement from the level of the person to the level of larger-scale social structures and back again. A common theme of interactionist thought is that social structure creates social persons who (re)create social structures ad infinitum. Basic to understanding social life, that insight is both trite and trivial unless it leads to research specifying variations in social structures and variations in social persons and the connections of these variations. Getting to that research requires a conceptual frame facilitating movement bridging person and social structure.

A brief and highly generalized version of the structural symbolic interactionist frame follows (see Stryker, 1980, for an expanded statement).

Behavior depends on a named or classified world providing the ends toward which human activity is directed and the means by which these ends are (or are not) achieved. That world represents opportunities for action, conditions that enhance or defeat success, and makes more or less probable contact with others with whom persons cooperate or conflict as they act. Names or class terms attached to the physical and social environment carry meanings: shared behavioral expectations growing out of social interaction. One learns from interaction how to classify objects and in that process learns the expectations for behavior with reference to those objects. Among the class terms learned are symbols used to designate positions, relatively stable morphological components of social structures, and the kinds of persons it is possible to be in a society. Attached to positions are the shared behavioral expectations conventionally called roles. Roles, necessarily social in derivation and in that all roles at least implicitly reference counterroles, vary in ways important to interaction: they may carry strong norms or not; require specific behaviors or be couched in nonspecific terms; be clear in demands made or vague and uncertain; apply to few interactions or across a large range of interactions, and so on.

Persons acting in the context of social structures recognize and label one another as occupants of positions. Doing so, they invoke expectations for behavior. They also name themselves. These reflexively applied positional designations become part of the self, creating internalized expectations with regard to persons' own behavior. Such selves may develop in response to contingencies in immediate situations of interaction; they also may enter into different and new situations. When entering an interactive situation, persons define that situation by applying names to it, themselves, other participants, and particular features in the situation, and use these to organize their own behavior in the situation. Others engage in the same process. Interactions with others can validate and often challenge definitions, including self-definitions; they are venues of conflict among competing definitions. Indeed, interactions are often battles of varying intensity over whose definitions will organize the interaction. Early definitions constrain the possibilities for alternative definitions to emerge, but behavior is not determined by early definitions. Behavior is the product of role-making (Turner, 1962) beginning with expectations invoked in the process of defining situations but continuing through a tentative, probing, sometimes extremely subtle interchange among interacting persons that shapes the form and content of the interaction. The degree to which roles are simply played or are made and the elements entering the construction of roles depend on the larger social structures in which interactive situations are embedded. Every structure limits the kinds of definitions available to call into play, and thus limits possibilities for interaction. Nonetheless, some structures are relatively open to creativity and innovation in roles and in role performances. Changes can occur in content of definitions, in names and class terms used in those definitions, and in the possibilities for interaction, depending on the degree to which roles are made rather than played. Such changes can lead to changes in social structures within which interactions take place.

The structural symbolic interactionist frame holds a view, consistent with the imagery of contemporary sociology, of society as a complex, differentiated but organized mosaic of relatively durable interactions and relationships embedded in an array of groups, organizations, communities, and institutions intersected by encompassing structures of age, gender, class, ethnicity, religion, and more. Persons live and act in relatively small and specialized networks of social relationships, largely doing so through roles underwriting their participation in these networks. The networks themselves are embedded in larger units of social structure that constitute boundaries affecting the probability of persons entering those networks, consequently interacting with the particular kinds of others also in those networks rather than other kinds of persons, and developing shared meanings constrained by the constitution of those networks.

IDENTITY THEORY AND RELATED IDEAS

If a framework can be tested, it is by its fertility, i.e., by the theories it generates that can be examined empirically. The claim here is that structural symbolic interactionism is a fruitful source of theories of social behavior important to sociology. Attention now turns to work developing from the symbolic interactionist frame that can be characterized and judged as theory. In particular, an account of role-choice behavior called "identity theory" and related ideas was selected for the most obvious reason: these have been the central preoccupation of this essay's author for the past 35-plus years.

Identity theory seeks to explain why, where choice is possible, one role-related behavioral choice is made rather than another. It is a minimal but potentially useful theory applicable to a particular kind of social behavior that examines a small set of variables representing part of the heritage of Mead, somewhat amended, to see how far they can serve to explain behavior of interest. Derived from structural symbolic interactionism, the theory shares assumptions of that frame: humans are actors as well as reactors; social interaction and social structures constrain human action; action and interaction are shaped by definitions or interpretations of situations based on shared meanings developed through interaction with others; self-conceptions are critical to producing action and interaction and are shaped in part by others' responses to persons. This last premise is often stated as self reflects society; it, together with the third premise, underwrite the standard formula of symbolic interactionism, a formula that insists on the reciprocity of its parts: society shapes self and self shapes social behavior.

Identity theory builds on refinements of traditional symbolic interactionism and specifications of that formula. It adopts a view of society consistent with the imagery of contemporary sociology that is contained in a structural symbolic interactionism.

Arguing the priority of society on grounds suggested earlier, the point of departure in developing the theory is specifying what it seeks to explain. Specification is required because, clearly, social behavior is much too general a category to be researchable; i.e., one cannot hope to develop and test a theory of social behavior in general both because it is impossible to observe social behavior in general and because the category includes too varied content to be subject to the same explanatory account. Identity theory elects to focus on role choice behavior as worthy of social psychological and sociological attention. It is central to many interesting and important questions about social life. Why does a man devote time and effort in one arena of his life—say, work—to the neglect of other social relationships—say, family? What underwrites radical change in careers or in lifestyle more generally? Why do some members of a social movement engage in dangerous activities in the interests of the movement while others will not do so? What are the consequences of role choices made for ongoing interaction and social relationships?

While the relationship is not deterministic—social constraints on choice obviously are limiting factors—the interactionist formula and identity theory suggest that role-choice is a product of self. However, self also requires specification. If in the beginning there is society, self must reflect society; and if contemporary selves reflect contemporary society, an image of self emerges that reflects the complexities of contemporary society. That vision sees self as highly differentiated but organized, made up of multiple parts reflecting the multiple structures of various kinds that exist within society, as well as the multiple ways these structures relate to one another: overlapping, isolated, cooperative, conflicting. The theory accepts James' (1890) idea that persons have as many selves as groups of persons with which they interact and, using the term "identity" to refer to each group based on self, asserts that persons have as many identities as distinct sets of social relations in which they occupy a position and play a role. Since roles are expectations attached to positions in networks of relationships, identities are internalized role expectations. The theory holds, reflecting the import of hierarchy as an organizational principle in society, that identities are organized in a salience hierarchy. Identities are understood as cognitive schema (Markus, 1977; Markus & Zajonc, 1985), internally stored information and meanings; as schema, they are cognitive bases for defining situations and they result in greater sensitivity to external and internal behavioral cues matching in some way the schema. As cognitive schema, they carry across situations in which persons find themselves. The salience of an identity is defined as the probability an identity will be invoked in and across situations (alternatively, as the differential probability across persons that an identity will be invoked in a given situation). Identity theory hypothesizes that the higher the salience of an identity relative to other identities in into the self, the higher the likelihood of behavioral choices corresponding to expectations attached to that identity.

Building identity theory also required specification of the third term in Mead's formula—society—and accomplishes that specification through the concept of "commitment." As noted earlier, persons live and act in relatively small, specialized networks of social relationships. Commitment concerns ties to networks and refers to the degree persons relations to others in networks depend on having particular identities and playing particular roles, measured by the costs of foregoing meaningful relations with others should the identity and role be foregone. The hypothesis is that the salience of an identity reflects commitment to the role relationships requiring that identity. Identity theory's specification of Mead's formula arrived at with this step is: commitment shapes identity salience shapes role choice behavior.

This is not the place for a detailed discussion of the research examining identity theory hypotheses, either by the author and colleagues or others. Two observations about that research are, however, pertinent. First, while research confirms the linkages indicated in this specification (see Stryker & Burke, 2000); it also suggests the need for refining and amplifying the conceptual resources of identity theory to expand its explanatory power. Stryker (1987) believes that master statuses (e.g., ethnicity, gender) can be incorporated into the theory by recognizing that both at times have the characteristics of role identities and that often they serve as modifiers of role identities (as in female lawyer). Serpe (1987) demonstrates that commitment has two partially independent components—affect and interaction—and that introducing this distinction in research clarifies relationships of commitment to identity salience and identity salience to role behaviors. Stryker and Serpe (1994) show that introducing the psychological centrality (Rosenberg, 1979) of identities along with identity salience adds to the understanding of how commitment links to role choices. Ervin and Stryker (2001) propose incorporating self-esteem into the identity theory model to expand the scope of that model considerably. Stryker and Burke (2000) offer a consolidation of their respective identity theory emphases, the former's focus on the ways in which social structures link to identities and the latter's on internal processes of self-verification, which promises a more complete understanding of the reciprocal relation of self and society. Second, this research evidences the capacity of identity theory to sustain a programmatic (rather than a scattershot) approach to research on issues of identity.

Earlier, it was said a paradox of freedom and constraint poses interesting and important social psychological questions. An extended identity theory can deal with these questions provided freedom and constraint are defined to allow direct or indirect observation. Conceptualizing freedom as the degree to which persons exercise choice, constraint as the degree to which choice cannot be exercised meets this proviso. But persons can choose only among available options. So conceived, freedom can be measured by the range of realistic alternatives open to actors; constraint by limitations on this range. This conceptualization permits the question: What expands or contracts action alternatives available to actors? Consider what expands alternatives. To exist and have reasonable probability of enactment, alternatives must be symbolically present in thought: we cannot choose what we can or do not conceive of doing. To be viable, alternatives must attach to self; we are not likely to choose what we can or do not conceive we can or would do. To be probable, alternatives must relate to salient identities; if not, they are unlikely to emerge in a situation. For identities to be salient, they must link to networks of relationships to which persons are highly committed. For a given alternative to have high probability of being chosen, some networks must be organized around that set of actions. Otherwise, little social support in existing networks is likely available, making the actions unattractive. For social networks to support action alternatives in some degree oppositional, the networks must be independent of one another. If not, they are likely to evolve equivalent norms and remove alternatives. To support oppositional alternative actions, networks must be relatively open. If not, persons' access to multiple identities with attached varying and oppositional alternatives will be restricted. For networks to be open yet independent, society must have crosscutting boundaries and mobility across boundaries. Otherwise, networks will consist of persons sharing the same characteristics or persons will be unable to resist conformity pressures from networks they cannot escape. The same elements (with different values) account for constraint. Societies with few independent networks and little social mobility are unlikely to permit or support multiple independent identities calling for alternative, especially oppositional actions. When not symbolically present, attached to salient identities, or supported by networks to which persons are highly committed, alternatives have low likelihood of being chosen.

CODA

The story of identity theory's development illustrates what is needed to move from the level of frame to the level of theory derived from a frame. In so doing, it suggests the challenge that faces those sociologists who believe the ideas reviewed in this chapter are worthy of their serious consideration and that serious consideration must involve translating the ideas into testable theory made to confront empirical evidence. Identity theory per se is a small theory applicable to a restricted albeit important social psychological issue; expanding the theory's explanatory scope requires expanding its repertory of concepts. However, its potential is wide, as illustrated by the theoretical attempt to deal with the broad issue of freedom and constraint in social life. A framework is a heuristic, and heuristics change as the questions of persons using them shift. That humans live in a historical social world guarantees new questions will be asked, existing concepts of a framework reformulated, and new concepts introduced. This chapter has been written in the belief that the sociological traditions of symbolic interactionism provide a strong and lasting basis for such further development .

REFERENCES

Baldwin, J. M. (1906). *Mental development in the child and the race*. New York: Macmillan.

Bales, R. F. (1950). *Interaction process analysis*. Reading, MA: Addison-Wesley.

Blumer, H. (1954). What is wrong with social theory? *American Sociological Review, 19*, 3–10.

Blumer, H. (1956). Sociological analysis and the variable. *American Sociological Review, 22*, 683–690.

Blumer, H. (1962). Human society as symbolic interaction. In A. M. Rose (Ed.), *Human behavior and social process* (pp. 179–192). Boston: Houghton Mifflin.

Blumer, H. (1969). *Symbolic interactionism: Perspective and method*. Engelwood Cliffs, NJ: Prentice-Hall.

Bryson, G. (1945). *Man and society: The Scottish inquiry of the eighteenth century*. Princeton, NJ: Princeton University Press.

Burke, P. J. (1980). The self: Measurement requirements from an interactional perspective. *Sociometry, 43*, 18–29.

Burke, P. J., & Reitzes, D. (1981). The link between identity and role performance. *Social Psychology Quarterly, 43*, 83–92.

Cicourel, A. (1972). *Cognitive sociology*. Middlesex, England: Penguin.

Collins, R. (1975). *Conflict sociology*. New York: Academic Press.

Cooley, C. H. (1902). *Human nature and the social order.* New York: Scribner's.

Davis, K. (1949). *Human society.* New York: Macmillan.

Dewey, J. (1896). The reflex arc in psychology. *Psychological Review, 3,* 357–370.

Dewey, J. (1930). *Human nature and conduct.* New York: Modern Library.

Durkheim, E. (1950). *The rules of sociological method.* Glencoe, IL: Free Press.

Durkheim, E. (1960). *The division of labor in society.* Glencoe, IL: Free Press.

Ervin, L., & Stryker, S. (2001). What does self-esteem have to do with it? Theorizing the relationships between self-esteem and identity theory. In T. Owens, S. Stryker, & N. Goodman (Eds.), *Extending self-esteem theory and research* (pp. 2955). New York: Cambridge University Press.

Ferguson, A. (1792). *Principles of moral and political science.* Edinburgh, Scotland: Printed for W. Creech.

Festinger, L., Back, K., Schacter, S., Kelley, H. H., & Thibaut, J. (1950). *Theory and experiment in social communication.* Ann Arbor, MI: Research Center for Group Dynamics, Institute for Social Research.

Goode, W. J. (1960). Norm commitment and conformity to role-status obligations. *American Journal of Sociology, 66,* 246–258.

Gouldner, A. W. (1970). *The coming crisis in western sociology.* New York: Basic Books.

Huber, J. (1973). Symbolic interactionism as a pragmatic perspective: The bias of emergent theory. *American Sociological Review, 38,* 278–284.

Hume, D. (1888/1739). *A treatise on human nature.* Oxford: Clarendon Press.

James, W. (1890). *The principles of psychology.* New York: Holt.

Kantor, R. M. (1972). Symbolic interactionism and politics in systematic perspective. *Sociological Perspective, 42,* 7–92.

Kuhn, M. H. (1964). Major trends in symbolic interaction theory in the past twenty-five years. *Sociological Quarterly, 5,* 61–84.

Linton, R. (1936) *The study of man.* New York: Appleton-Century.

Markus, H. (1977). Self-schemas and processing information about the self. *Journal of Personality and Social Psychology, 35,* 67–78.

Markus, H., & Zajonc, R. B. (1985). In G. Lindzey & E. Aronson (Eds.). *The Handbook of Social Psychology,* Vol. I, 3rd ed. (pp. 137–230). New York: Random House.

McCall, G. & Simmons, J. T. (1966). *Identities and interaction.* New York: Free Press.

Mead, G. H. (1930). Cooley's contribution to American social thought. *American Journal of Sociology, 35,* 693–706.

Mead, G. H. (1934). *Mind, self, and society.* Chicago: University of Chicago Press

Meltzer, B. M. (1959). *The social psychology of George Herbert Mead.* Kalamazoo, MI: Center for Sociological Research.

Meltzer, B. M., Petras, J. W., & Reynolds, L. T. (1975). *Symbolic interactionism: Genesis, varieties, and criticism.* London: Routledge.

Merton, R. K. (1957). *Social theory and social structure.* Glencoe, IL: Free Press.

Moreno, J. L. (1934). *Who shall survive?* Washington, DC: Nervous and Mental Disease Publication.

Park, R. E. (1926). Behind our masks. *Survey, 56,* 135–139.

Parsons, T. (1951). *The social system.* Glencoe, IL: Free Press.

Reynolds, L. T. (1990). *Interactionism: Exposition and critique,* 2nd ed. Dix Hills, NY: General Hall.

Rosenberg, M. (1979). *Conceiving the self.* New York: Basic Books.

Seeman, M. (1997). The elusive situation in social psychology. *Social Psychology Quarterly, 60,* 4–13.

Serpe, R. T. (1987). Stability and change in self: A structural symbolic interactionist explanation. *Social Psychology Quarterly, 50,* 44–55.

Sherif, M. (1936). *The psychology of social norms.* New York: Harper.

Simmel, G. (1950). *The sociology of Georg Simmel.* Glencoe, IL: Free Press.

Smith, A. (1759). *A theory of moral sentiments.* London.

Stryker, S. (1964). The interactional and situational approaches. In H. T. Christensen (Ed.), *Handbook of marriage and the family* (pp. 125–170). Chicago: Rand McNally.

Stryker, S. (1980). *Symbolic interactionism: A social structural version.* Menlo Park, CA: Benjamin/Cummings.

Stryker, S. (1987). Identity theory: Developments and extensions. In K. Yardley & T. Honess (Eds.), *Self and identity: Psychosocial perspectives* (pp. 89–103). London: John Wiley.

Stryker, S. (1988). Substance and style: An appraisal of the sociological legacy of Herbert Blumer. *Symbolic Interaction, 11,* 33–42.

Stryker, S. (1989). Further developments in identity theory: Singularity versus multiplicity of self. In J. Berger, M, Zelditch, Jr., & B. Anderson (Eds.), *Sociological theories in progress* (pp. 35–57). Newbury Park, CA: Sage.

Stryker, S. (1994). Freedom and constraint in social and personal life: Toward resolving the paradox of self. In G. Platt & C. Gordon (Eds.), *Self, collective behavior and society: Essays honoring the contribution of Ralph H. Turner* (pp. 119–138). Greenwich, CT: JAI Press.

Stryker, S. (1996). In the beginning there is society: Lessons from a sociological social psychology. In C. McGarty & S. A. Hastam (Eds.), *The message of social psychology* (pp. 315–327). London: Blackwell.

Stryker, S. (2000). Symbolic interaction theory. In E. F. Borgatta & R. J. V. Montgomery (Eds.), *Encyclopedia of sociology*, rev. ed. (Vol. 5, pp. 3095–3102). New York: Macmillan.

Stryker, S. (2001). Social psychology, sociological. In N. J. Smelser & P. B. Baltes (Eds.), *International encyclopedia of the social and behavioral sciences*. Oxford: Elsevier Science.

Stryker, S., & Burke, P. J. (2000). The past, present, and future of identity theory. *Social Psychology Quarterly, 63*, 284–297.

Stryker, S., & Serpe, R. T. (1994). Identity salience and psychological centrality: Equivalent, overlapping, or complementary concepts? *Social Psychology Quarterly, 57*, 16–35.

Stryker, S., & Statham, A. (1985). Symbolic interaction and role theory. In G. Lindzey & E. Aronson (Eds.), *Handbook of social psychology*, Vol. I, 3rd ed. (pp. 311–378). New York: Random House.

Sumner, W. G. (1906). *Folkways*. Boston: Ginn.

Thomas, W. I. (1931). The relation of research to the social process. In W. F. G. Swann, W. W. Cook, C. A. Beard, J. M. Clark, K. N. Llewellyn, A. M. Schlesinger, W. F. Ogburn, & W. I. Thomas (Eds.), *Essays on research in the social sciences* (pp. 174–194). Washington, DC: The Brookings Institution.

Turner, R. H. (1962). Role-taking: Process vs. conformity? In A. M. Rose, (Ed.), *Human behavior and social processes* (pp. 20–40). Boston: Houghton Mifflin.

Turner, R. H. (1978). The role and the person. *American Journal of Sociology, 84*, 1–23.

Volkart, E. H. (Ed.). (1951). *Social behavior and personality: Contributions of W. I. Thomas to theory and research.* New York: Social Science Research Council.

Weber, M. (1946). *From Max Weber: Essays in sociology.* H. Gerth & C. W. Mills (Eds.). New York: Oxford University Press.

Weber, M. (1947). *The theory of social and economic organization.* A. M. Henderson & T. Parsons (trans.). New York: Oxford University Press.

Weber, M. (1949). *The methodology of the social sciences.* New York: Free Press.

Wrong, D. (1961). The oversocialized conception of man. *American Sociological Review, 26*, 184–193.

CHAPTER 12

Role Theory

RALPH H. TURNER

Role theory deals with the organization of social behavior at both the individual and the collective levels. Individual behavior in social contexts is organized and acquires meaning in terms of roles. Work responsibilities in organizations are organized into roles, as is participation in groups and in society. Consequently, role theory is one key element in understanding the relationships among the micro-, macro-, and intermediate levels of society. At the individual level the concept of role begins, by analogy to the stage, with two observations: that (1) a given individual may act and even feel quite differently in different situations or positions; and (2) otherwise different individuals may behave quite similarly in similar relationships. At the various collective levels, groups, organizations, and societies function by differentiating sets of tasks, each of which is assigned to or assumed by particular individuals. At both levels, it is important to understand that role refers to a *cluster* of behaviors and attitudes that are thought to belong together, so that an individual is viewed as acting consistently when performing the various components of a single role and inconsistently when failing to do so.

Versions of role theory that begin at the collective level are referred to as *structural* theories. Ralph Linton (1936) defined role as the dynamic aspect of status, contending that every status in society has an attached role and that every role is attached to a status. While Linton defined status as a collection of rights and duties, subsequent usage came to view status as position and role as the expected set of rights and duties. Attempts to enumerate the duties attached to particular statuses soon led Newcomb (1950) and Dahrendorf (1973) and others to distinguish between expected *obligatory* and *optional* behaviors and *forbidden* behaviors for persons occupying specific positions in social structures. Recognizing that some of these structural approaches were overly deterministic and static, Merton (1957) and Gross, Mason, and MacEachern (1958) offered more dynamic theories in which roles are viewed as the foci of often conflicting expectations from the various *alter* roles with which they interact. Merton went so far as to propose that the occupant of a position played a *set* of roles (*role set*), each corresponding to an alter role, and offered a theory of how an occupant reconciled or otherwise dealt with these conflicting expectations. The essential dynamic of all these structural theories

RALPH H. TURNER • Department of Sociology, University of California, Los Angeles, California 90095.

Handbook of Sociological Theory, edited by Jonathan H. Turner. Kluwer Academic / Plenum Publishers, New York, 2002.

is that role players are guided by a set of *expectations* that are either internalized or experienced from external sources, or both, and are judged and judge themselves according to how well they conform to the expectations. An important research question becomes: When and under what circumstances do people comply with what others expect of them (Biddle, 1979)?

In contrast to the various structural theories, *interactional* role theory starts from the patterning of social interaction among individuals and groups of individuals. Most structural theorizing starts with the implicit assumption that the status or position antedates the role and that the role is in some sense imposed on the individual. This assumption is an often useful partial truth when the origins of roles and statuses are not at issue. But interactional theorizing assumes that the patterning of behavior that constitutes roles arises initially and recurrently out of the dynamics of interaction and that statuses and positions arise to place roles in a social organizational framework. This interactional approach involves casting the net wider than most structural approaches do, defining role as a comprehensive pattern for behavior and attitude that is linked to an identity, is socially identified more or less clearly as an entity, and is subject to being played recognizably by different individuals. Four broad types of roles are included in this definition. The most inclusive are *basic roles* (Banton, 1965) such as those associated with gender, age, and social class identities. They are basic, both in the wide range of situations to which they apply and in the ways in which they modify the content and control access to other kinds of roles. *Position* or *status roles* are linked to positions in organizations and formally organized groups. Occupational and family roles are typical examples. Position or status roles, along with basic roles, are the standard fare of structural theories. *Functional group roles* (Benne & Sheats, 1948) are the unformalized behavior patterns that emerge spontaneously as individuals acquire situational identities during sustained interaction in a group setting. They include such roles as "leader," "follower," "counselor," "mediator," and "devils advocate." *Value roles*, like functional group roles, emerge spontaneously but are attached to very positively or negatively valued identities. "Hero," "saint," and "villain" are common examples. Interactionists see the dynamics of functional group roles and value roles as fundamental to understanding more structurally grounded roles.

Interactionist theory attempts to deal with at least four questions that often have been neglected by structural theorists: (1) What are the dynamics of disvalued roles? Under the structuralists' expectation–conformity–social approval formula, it is difficult to understand deviant roles except in the context of a deviant subculture. Is there a formulation that will explain disvalued and valued role dynamics equally well? (2) How can a theory of roles apply equally well to roles that are and are not formalized in organizational structures? (3) How and when do roles change, as we know that even such formalized roles as the police role, the teacher role, and the Christian churches' ministerial role have done in the last century or two? (4) How are we to account for creativity in role-playing, especially creativity that turns out to be appreciated by others?

ASSUMPTIONS

1. Interactionist theory begins by postulating a tendency to create and modify conceptions of self and other roles as a key orienting process in social interaction. While roles viewed as clear sets of identity-related expectations exist only in varying degrees of concreteness and consistency, the critical observation is that people behave *as if* there were roles. Role is a sort of ideal folk conception that constrains people to render any interaction situation into more or less explicit collections of interacting roles. In attempting from time to time to make aspects of

the roles explicit the actor is creating and modifying roles as well as merely bringing them to light; the process is not only role-taking and role-playing, but *role-making* (Turner, 1962).

Even roles in such authoritarian settings as military, police, and corporate organizations turn out, in critical situations, to leave a great deal to individual discretion. Stephen Ambrose's (1997) intimate account of battlefield behavior during World War II documents the prevalence of role-making in even so authoritarian an organization as the army. Police and many other occupational groups have held conferences in more or less vain attempts to specify their roles more concretely. When subjects are asked to describe roles such as those of mother, father, attorney, or teacher, they more often do so in terms of broad goals and sentiments than in terms of very specific behaviors. Mother loves and cares for her child, but just how remains vague or a matter of controversy. Jerald Hage and Charles Powers (1992) point out that there are often alternative designs for particular role relationships: "Many stable configurations are possible. Interestingly, the number of family and work forms has increased rather dramatically in recent years" (p. 114). Only in a stagnant bureaucracy is the functionary who does everything strictly "according to the book" greatly admired. Recognition more often goes to the creative role player.

2. George Herbert Mead's (1934) discussion of "taking the role of the other" identifies another fundamental premise of interactionist role theory. Actors choose their own actions by imagining the roles of those with whom they are interacting. Rather than playing the role mechanically, they shape their own roles so as to interact effectively with the role they attribute to the relevant others. Sometimes this is a matter of conforming to expectations, but more fundamentally it is a matter of collaboration, opposition, or any of many other possible relationships. This interrelationship goes beyond simply acting in response to the other's actions or expected actions, because roles are patterned clusters of actions. Taking the role of the other involves understanding a cluster of actions into which any given action fits and which supplies a basis for assigning meaning to the action in question.

3. Most social roles exist in pairs or sets. There could be no teacher role without a student role, no leader role without a follower role. Social roles that are not part of a pair or set involve interaction with other incumbents of the same role. For example, the role of friend presumes a friend to interact with. Thus roles are linked through distinctive *role relationships*.

4. Role-taking presumes some prior familiarity with the role of the relevant other. This understanding may come partially out of projection, i.e., imagining what I would do if I were in the other's position. But it requires some learning of a more generalized role conception. Such generalized role conceptions may be specified organizationally, conveyed in the culture, and formed from accumulated past experience.

5. The prevalence of role-making is balanced by a tendency for the broad outline of roles and sometimes quite specific role elements to become normative. This tendency has at least two roots. First, because of the linkage of roles through role relationships, changes in a focal role threaten the stability of relationships and force some change in relevant alter roles. The general principle is that when alter's behavior is dependent on a particular pattern of behavior in the focal role, alter will feel that the focal role incumbent is obligated to continue the relevant behavior. Second, a basic level of predictability is essential for social relationships to continue in any group, organization, community, or society. Abrupt or radical changes in roles undermine predictability and provoke anxiety. Hence there is a general tendency to assume that established role structures constitute the framework within which social life ought to be carried on. This observation does not mean that gradual change is not common, nor that abrupt and radical role change cannot be forced on a populace. But it does mean that many people will continue to view such changes as morally or ethically wrong.

ROLE DIFFERENTIATION

An interactional theory, which assumes that roles are continuously being remade in relation to relevant other roles, must begin by identifying the bases on which roles are differentiated. The tendency for actions and sentiments to be differentiated into roles is the most fundamental observation underlying role theory and should be the foundation on which any theory is built. Differentiation means sorting out and separating different actions and sentiments and combining them into separate roles. Differentiation also means the *accretion* of behaviors and sentiments as they are added to particular roles. I will suggest three principles that explain the manner in which differentiation into roles takes place. I call these principles *functionality*, *representationality*, and *tenability*. Their relative importance will vary from role to role and setting to setting (Turner & Colomy, 1988).

Functionality

The functional principle is clearest when roles are understood as a division of labor by which some collaborative goal is to be achieved. Tasks are initially divided up so that everybody is not trying to do everything. A baseball team without players assigned to individual positions would be chaotic. But there are more and less effective and efficient ways to divide up tasks. The division of responsibilities between, for example, shortstop and second baseman often has been tested and adjusted for greater effectiveness. Over the years, football teams have reorganized players' roles so as to win more games. There are three chief bases for making role differentiation functional, namely (1) differentiation by associated skills, knowledge, and dispositions; (2) differentiation according to the diversity of actual or potential incumbent characteristics; and (3) differentiation to minimize incompatibility of goals and means.

The simplest and most rational basis for clustering activities into particular roles is the *association principle*. It is obvious that there should be differentiated physician and attorney roles because the same underlying knowledge of the human body is necessary for a variety of medical tasks and a fundamental understanding of law is needed for a variety of legal tasks. As the underlying body of knowledge and skills grows, further differentiation is functional, so the physician role becomes differentiated into orthopedists, rheumatologists, and other specialists. Then the orthopedist role breaks down into spinal specialists, foot and ankle specialists, and more. Likewise, the differentiation between physician and patient and between attorney and client assumes a different level of specialized knowledge and a distinction between giving and receiving orientations.

The association of activities also may be based on location. Traditional differentiation between husband and wife roles may have been substantially based on grouping activities performed in and near the home as the wife role and activities performed away from home as the husband role.

The second *principle of functional differentiation* takes account of the variability in the talents and dispositions of potential recruits to the role system. If the population varies in levels of literacy, relevant roles are likely to be differentiated according to the level of literacy expected or required of role incumbents. If the population varies in such personal dispositions as aggressiveness and submissiveness, coarseness and gentleness, insensitivity and empathy, the clustering of activities by roles will tend to take account of these dispositions.

In considering functional role differentiation according to variable talents and dispositions it is important not to fall into the trap of assuming an Adam Smith form of "invisible hand" at work. Keeping in mind the tentative and testing nature of social interaction, we may safely assume that human intelligence often will recognize or discover more effective ways to utilize the diversity of talents and resources among potential role incumbents, and that the more effective differentiations will become customary and transmitted in the relevant culture. But there are two important limitations to role differentiation on this basis. First, differentiation is primarily based on what interaction participants believe are the talents and resources of different categories of people, which are not often reality tested. During World War II when it was necessary to assign unprecedented leadership responsibilities to young military and naval officers and equally unprecedented factory jobs to women, it often was noted with surprise how satisfactorily young officers and women mechanics could perform their roles. Second, existing patterns of role differentiation often create or perpetuate the putative differences in talents and resources on which functional differentiation is based. This observation applies especially to basic roles such as gender, age, race, and ethnicity. For example, beliefs about the limited capacity of women to master mechanical tasks were reflected in early school socialization patterns that provided woodshop courses only for boys and cooking classes only for girls. Since the more formally institutionalized position roles typically involve preliminary stages of selection and role socialization, assumptions about differential capabilities are typically made real by differential role allocation.

To be functional, the clustering of goals, activities, and sentiments to form a role must maximize mutually reinforcing elements and minimize contradictory effects. If two different activities contribute to the same goal, they are candidates for inclusion in a single role. If two activities have opposite effects, they are likely to be split off into separate roles. The latter observation finds formal legal recognition in the *conflict of interest principle*. In order to avoid conflict of interest, the roles of judge and prosecutor must be sharply separated, as must referee and coach in sporting events and advocate and mediator or arbitrator in labor disputes.

The most important contribution toward understanding nonobvious functional role differentiation comes from studies of emerging functional group roles. Bales (1953) and Bales and Slater (1955) advanced the hypothesis that, in task-oriented groups, two distinct leadership roles will emerge. A task or instrumental leader assumes principal responsibility for seeing that group tasks are performed and that goals are reached. The task leader has to override conflicting ideas about how to achieve goals and must pressure group members to concentrate on group goals. In doing so, the task leader is likely to ruffle some feathers and stir up antagonisms that, if they become serious enough, could undermine the leader's efforts. As a result there often emerges an expressive or social–emotional leader role. The expressive leader works gently to soothe hurt feelings and resolve interpersonal hostilities in the group so that members can concentrate more effectively on group goals. Task leaders are unlikely to be able to incorporate these expressive functions into their role because they are seen as insensitive in their pursuit of group goals. While this hypothesis arose out of laboratory studies of small task-oriented group interaction, the principle extends to leadership roles in many large formal organizations. The CEO role is task leader and a personnel officer, industrial relations officer, or other high-level functionary is responsible for uncovering and dealing with employee dissatisfactions. Often in universities the teaching assistant (TA) role incorporates expressive leadership, since students are more willing to express anxieties and dissatisfactions about a course to the TA than to the professor (as task leader).

The hypothesis of task and expressive role differentiation has been offered as an explanation for traditional differentiation between father and mother roles and extended to the more basic gender role differentiation. However, cultural change and widespread cultural and individual differences have called the explanatory value of this hypothesis in relation to gender roles into question.

Further research into emerging leadership roles in small groups produced an important qualification to the leadership role differentiation hypothesis. Later experimental work with small task groups revealed that in many instances a single leader was able to perform both leadership functions. When cases were compared, it turned out that the differentiation of leadership roles occurred most often when group members had only a weak commitment to group goals. When there was strong member commitment to group goals there was little if any need for a separate expressive leader. Hence the limited utility of this theory for explaining family roles and roles in many voluntary groups (Burke, 1968).

There are more broadly applicable limitations to functional differentiation to minimize conflicting effects. First, conflict of interest is much in the eye of the beholder, so that there is wide cultural variation in what is viewed as a conflict of interest. For example, in many societies there is no felt need to separate prosecutor and judge roles. Similarly, in contemporary Western societies the combination of these two functions in the parent role is not seen as a conflict of interest. Second, in a highly stratified society or organization, conflict of interest is unlikely to become an issue so long as it chiefly affects the rights of subordinate classes.

Representationality

William F. Whyte (1955), in his pioneering and classic study of Boston's "street corner boys," reports that at election time the boys stuffed ballot boxes and in other illegal ways tried to influence the outcome of balloting. Seeking to maintain his rapport with the group, Whyte joined in some of these activities. But he found that the "boys" were surprised and even disconcerted by his participation. Whyte then realized that in his role as a trusted observer of the "boys," he need not have participated in their illegal behavior. Here was a pattern of understood and accepted role differentiation based not on functionality but on what the roles represented. The point is that a role may incorporate an image and the components of the role are selected for consistency with that image.

The clearest examples of representational differentiation are value roles. A paraphrased dictionary definition of "hero" is a person of distinguished courage or ability, admired for brave deeds. But there is much more than bravery and ability to being a hero. As many people fitting this definition have learned, much is expected of a hero. In the United States the hero is expected to accept and appreciate public adulation, do good deeds to reflect a heroic disposition, and display great wisdom in realms unrelated to the initial heroic act. The putative hero who shuns public adulation or eschews good deeds quickly loses the heroic identity, as some astronauts and sports stars have learned. The point, again, is that a conception of the role of hero is conveyed in the culture. The hero role is differentiated out in terms of an image: what the hero represents.

Deviant roles are similarly differentiated so as to concentrate negatively valued characteristics. The murderer, the thief, the rapist are imagined also to be unfriendly neighbors and unfaithful husbands and parents. Encounter with a known murderer who appears to be a "nice person" is likely to be disorienting; how, indeed, does one engage in small talk at a Boy Scouts parents meeting with a father who was recently reported in blazing headlines as having attempted to kill his wife and mother-in-law? One may view these images as merely stereotypes, but as role conceptions they make it difficult for the deviant to participate normally in a range of social settings.

While some roles appear to be differentiated primarily on representational grounds, it is far more common that roles that are basically differentiated functionally acquire an overlay of representationality. The young husband, while hanging out washing to dry, who calls out to his (male) neighbor, "I'm doing it but I don't believe in it!" expresses a representational aspect of a traditional husband role. The differentiation of work roles between head and hand work, clean and dirty work, dignified and menial work, light and heavy work, or sacred and profane work is as much or more representational than functional.

It is a plausible hypothesis that representationally differentiated roles are more resistant to change than functionally differentiated roles. Although the fact that change in any functionally differentiated role requires complementary changes in relevant alter roles is a source of resistance to change, constructive adaptation to conditions under which roles are played surely will win out when functional considerations are paramount. But the way in which a role is viewed both from outside and by role incumbents is usually quite slow to change. As a result, a functionally differentiated role that has been heavily overlayed with representationality may become quite dysfunctional yet still endure with little change.

Several conditions contribute to the overlaying of functionally differentiated roles with representational elements. The need to find concrete embodiment of both strongly positive and strongly negative values in human behavior is the most widely applicable basis for representational differentiation, whether as functional role overlay or as the primary basis for role differentiation. To the religious person, the minister or pastor role can be an inspiration to godly behavior. What the President of the United States represents as a public symbol was paramount in the impeachment trial of President Clinton in 1998.

When role incumbents have been recruited from distinctive populations, the role conception tends to become imbued with an imagery that reflects the way the relevant population is viewed. Popular conceptions of the role of farm worker in the US Southwest are inextricably merged with local stereotypes of Mexicans, as were the cotton-picker role and stereotypes of blacks in the old South.

Roles tend to acquire representational overlays when closely associated alter roles are strongly representational. Lawyers' roles are differentiated according to the evaluation of their clientele, so that lawyers who handle petty criminal cases have less prestige and fewer privileges than corporation lawyers. It is accepted as natural that the university professor is paid more and has greater freedom than the elementary school teacher, at least partly because of whom they teach. When particular roles come into a protracted relationship of conflict or competition that becomes of concern to the larger community, there also is a tendency to enhance their differences representationally.

Representational differentiation also occurs when *role interchangeability* is marked. Interchangeability refers to the fact that the same behavior enacted as part of different roles can have quite different meanings. Giving advice can be part of a helping role or of a domineering role. The very similarity of behavior in two roles to which the appropriate response is quite different calls for a pattern of imagery that makes them seem more different than they are (Turner & Shosid, 1976).

Tenability

In speaking of functionality and representationality we are addressing primarily the relationship between a focal role and relevant alter roles. But regardless of how functional a role might be or how clear and even admirable the image it projects, a role must have incumbents who are able and willing to play it. Tenability is a matter of the balance and nature of benefits and costs to the role incumbent, always in relationship to viable alternatives. Tenability contributes to the character of a role through tendencies to add or enhance benefits and to minimize or offset costs. To understand tenability we must distinguish between consensually and nonconsensually valued benefits and costs. Pain and suffering are illustrative of consensual costs, while a good income, prestige, and respect are consensual benefits that may come with a role. But even with these examples, the relative importance and threshold levels will vary by individuals and by groups of individuals, so they are not perfectly consensual.

When rewards and costs of a role are consensually valued, a *power principle* and a *compensatory accretion principle* govern the pattern of tenability-based role differentiation. The power principle is simply that individuals and groups with more power are able to construct roles with a more favorable balance of benefits and costs than are the less powerful. Once again, this principle underlines the significance of the population from which role incumbents are drawn. The articulation with a system of social stratification works in both directions: Roles that recruit from lower social strata have fewer benefits to balance higher costs, because role incumbents have few alternatives; reciprocally, roles with a relatively unfavorable balance of benefits to costs can only recruit from disadvantaged populations. While in some versions of exchange theory there should be an almost automatic balancing of benefits and costs, the observed tendency is for roles to accumulate a disproportionate range of benefits or of costs, depending on the population from which the role recruits incumbents.

Compensatory accretion works in part to offset an unfavorable balance of benefits to costs. When lack of alternatives locks incumbents into a disadvantageous role, they often devise ways to enhance their control and seek to cultivate potential but normally unappreciated gratifications in the role. For example, part of the lore of the naval enlisted personnel is an accumulation of folk wisdom about how to get favors from officers and how to avoid compliance with their orders or escape punishment after noncompliance. It is well known that slaves often have understood their masters better than masters understood slaves and have used this understanding to improve their role benefits-to-cost ratio. There may be truth in the popular belief in "women's intuition," as learned and transmitted skills enabling women in their traditionally subordinate positions to offset to some degree the unequal power men exercised over them by understanding men better than they are understood and by transmitting their understanding to their daughters.

Among the socially most important role benefits are *prestige* and *esteem*. Kingsley Davis (1949) distinguished between the prestige that is derived from mere incumbency in a highly respected role and esteem based on the adequacy with which the role is performed. One may have considerable prestige as a physician, a corporation CEO, or even a university professor, but be accorded little esteem as a "quack doctor," Dilbert's boss, or a dull teacher. In some situations there is a balancing of prestige and esteem, so that a superior carpenter or creative electrician may win more respect than a doctor whose medical knowledge and skills are out of date. Emphasis on esteem is an important compensatory benefit that is often savored and exploited in low-ranking roles, as when the legendary John Henry becomes a folk hero and role model.

Role-incumbent populations often differ in their evaluation of particular benefits and costs. The difference may be so great that what is a benefit to one population may be a cost to another and vice versa. Risk, for example, may be a cost to most elderly, while it is often a benefit to young people. The governing principle of tenability in case of nonconsensually valued benefits and costs is the *fit* between role and personal dispositions. In most instances this means the extent to which a role affords opportunities for incumbents to affirm or enhance their self-conceptions, though it can also be a matter of talent, ability, and resources needed in order to play a role successfully.

The relationship between role and self-conception is reciprocal. On the one hand, social roles provide the principal organizing framework for the self-conception. In spite of what others might regard as excessive costs, incumbents whose work roles constitute careers may find identification with the career a sufficient offsetting benefit, bolstered by an enhancing career mythology. But lower status or ephemeral work roles may provide little anchorage for the self-conception, in which case more consensual assessments of benefits and costs are usually paramount.

On the other hand, when social structural and other conditions foster role–person merger (Turner, 1978; and below), any discrepancies between role and self-conception cause a strain to reconstruct roles into fuller congruity with self-conceptions. In lowly occupations there often have been organized movements to identify the occupations as professions or take on responsibilities ordinarily assigned to a role accorded higher status.

It is clear from this discussion that there is a close relationship between tenability and representational aspects of role differentiation, especially when role–person merger is high. With regard to consensually valued benefits and costs, high self-esteem and status consciousness motivate people to seek identification with prestigious representations, while those with low self-esteem more readily settle for less prestigious roles. With respect to nonconsensually valued benefits and costs, such self-conceived qualities as toughness or gentleness or intellectuality or nurturance dispose people to choose congruently representational roles for strongest identification.

Similarly, tenability is related to functionality. For most people, and especially for those whose self-conceptions emphasize personal effectiveness, high functionality makes a role more tenable. In teaching, for example, evidence that students are learning becomes an important role benefit, while negative evidence becomes a cost. These are but limited illustrations of the complex interrelationships among functionality, representationality, and tenability in the shaping of roles by redifferentiation and accretion.

It is important to note that these three processes work both idiosyncratically, as each individual engages in personal role-making and collectively as groups or populations of recruits and potential recruits combine forces to create and recreate culturally based role conceptions.

Role Persistence

There is a tendency for role structures, once more or less stabilized, to persist in spite of changes in the actors who play the roles. This tendency arises out of the complementary nature of the roles in any group or organization. If a fairly stable pattern of interaction or division of labor has developed in which each role has a recognized set of functions, the group comes to depend on having someone perform each role's functions. Less modification of the relevant alters' roles is required if the same role is refilled than if the functions were absorbed somehow into other roles. A polarized group may need someone to play a mediator role; any group may come to depend on a jokester role to lessen potentially disruptive tensions.

Role persistence is also observed in cases where *role appropriation* occurs. Perry, Silber, and Block (1956) applied this term in their study of family responses to disaster. In some instances, when a parent became disorganized and assumed a childlike role of dependency, a child suddenly blossomed into responsibility and took over the responsible parent role.

ROLE ALLOCATION

Complementary to role differentiation is *role allocation*: the attachment of individuals and categories of individuals to particular roles. In Linton's (1936) structural role formulation, he emphasized a distinction between *ascribed* and *achieved* statuses. The individual has no choice with respect to ascribed statuses such as male or female, white or black, youth or elder, and occupation in caste societies, and is expected to play the roles appropriate to these statuses. Achieved statuses in more modern societies, such as occupations, must in some way be chosen and earned by potential incumbents. Linton and others have noted that in most of the world's societies, throughout most of history, most statuses with their attached roles have been ascribed. Only in recent history and in more developed societies has a vast range of statuses and roles been open to achievement.

While acknowledging the usefulness of the ascription–achievement distinction, interactionists understand role allocation as more often a process of negotiation between potential role incumbents and relevant alters. Allocation processes work from two directions, with the potential incumbent choosing and working toward a particular role allocation, while relevant others affirm or impede the choice and often seek to assign the individual to a particular role. In the case of functional group roles and value roles in particular, behavior intended as performance of one role may be interpreted by others so as to cast the individual into quite a different role than intended. For example, the would-be group leader can be cast by associates into the role of disrupter and the would-be helper can be cast into a domineering role (Turner & Shosid, 1976). Weinstein and Deutschburger (1963) have suggested a concept of *altercasting* to identify a process whereby the incumbent of one role attempts to play his or her role in such a way as to force alter into a particular role that may not be of the latter's choosing.

When strangers interact there is an initial, sometimes frantic, mutual effort at role allocation. Until this is accomplished, the meanings of all but the most trivial and conventional exchanges are difficult to interpret. The comment, "I don't know what to make of him!" expresses the frustration of unsuccessful efforts at role allocation. Role allocation is not fully accomplished until relevant alters interact with the focal person on the basis of the same role that he or she is performing.

We have observed earlier that role structures tend to persist. Similarly, role allocations tend to become stable and often difficult to change. In a discussion group someone may be allocated the role of intellectual and will then be called on to clarify difficult issues whenever they arise. Someone who has been allocated the mediator role will be expected to start the reconciliation process whenever dispute becomes intense. Someone who has been allocated a troublemaker role will find even constructive remarks and actions misinterpreted as efforts to cause trouble.

The same principles of functionality, representationality, and tenability that govern differentiation help to explain how role allocation occurs. The role incumbent must be able to perform the role adequately (functionality). The image, however stereotyped, of an individual or category of individuals must be consistent with the representational image of the role. As always, the more powerful or otherwise favored individuals and populations achieve the most desirable roles (tenability).

ROLES IN ORGANIZATIONS

Placement of a role in an organization supplies direction and constraint to the principles and processes of role differentiation and allocation and brings them into more complex relationships. We are now talking about position or status roles, each of which is linked to a defined position. Because organizations have goals and the component roles exist for the benefit of the organization, all role processes must contribute, directly or indirectly, toward organizational aims.

Because organizational goals are paramount and because of the complex division of labor in large organizations, role prescriptions are more normative than in less formalized relationships. Individuals typically have less discretion in the execution of their roles. The special function of defining roles becomes important and is either explicitly a part of certain management roles or becomes a role in itself. *Legitimate role definers*, often far removed from those who play the targeted roles and their immediate alters, specify what role incumbents are and are not to do and the criteria by which role adequacy is to be evaluated. While this formalization of roles makes individual actors predictable and facilitates the organization's work, it also limits creativity and often prevents or delays needed changes in the way the organization functions.

Working Roles

There always are discrepancies between role conceptions and role behavior. When these discrepancies are widespread, the role conceptions may change to correspond more closely to customary performance of the role. Such discrepancies are particularly prevalent with respect to organizational roles because of the formalization, the separation between role definers and role incumbents, and the organizational rigidity that resists prompt adaptive change. As a result, role incumbents typically develop what might be called an informal or working role that differs significantly from the formal role. The working role is not an example of individual deviance. It is a set of shared understandings among role incumbents about how the role is to be performed that differ in important respects from the formal role specification. When workers and their employers are in a markedly antagonistic relationship, the informal role is often developed so as to subvert the aims or regulations built into the formal role. Early studies of informal organizational structures documented informal worker alliances to restrict factory output (Roethlisberger & Dickson, 1947). Opportunities to enhance role tenability also can lead to a working role that fosters corruption. Barker (1977, p. 364) writes:

> The police occupation per se provides its members with numerous opportunities for corrupt acts and other forms of deviance. In some police departments there is a social setting where this inherent occupational structure is combined with peer group support and tolerance for certain patterns of corruption. The peer group indoctrinates and socializes the rookie into patterns of acceptable corrupt activities, sanctions deviations outside these boundaries, and sanctions officers who do not engage in any corrupt acts.

More recent exposure of scandal in the Los Angeles Police Department reveals that such antiorganizational worker roles still are not uncommon.

In contrast to these antiorganizational examples, as Edward Gross (1953) showed, informal structures probably more often facilitate organizational aims. The working role typically enhances the functionality, representationality, and tenability of a role when the formal role definition is deficient in these respects. Functionally, formal roles are incomplete and vague with respect to details of role performance and they fail to take account of changes in significant alter roles. For example, formal definitions of the physician's role leave vague the criteria by which a physician decides to allow a terminally ill patient to die. Similarly, the formal rules that define the policeman's role often provide imprecise guidance in individual situations. The individual physician or police officer is then likely to look to peers for a consensus on how to proceed. Role incumbents often find better ways to perform their responsibilities than those specified in the formal role and are quicker to recognize and by general agreement adapt to change in the execution of relevant alter roles. In the late 1960s, for example, police found little guidance in their formal roles for dealing with a citizenry increasingly losing respect for police and disposed to confront rather than to cooperate with them. Police had to turn to their fellow officers to develop informal guidelines for dealing with these newly developing situations.

Legitimate role definers are likely to overlook entirely the representational aspect of a role. It then falls to the incumbents to incorporate into the working role elements that project a clearer image of the role.

Perhaps the most important contributions to a working role come from the tenability deficiencies in most formal role definitions. Manuals and organizational charts seldom address the sensitive relationships between the role and those who will play it. For roles performed under critical supervisory evaluation, the problem for the incumbent is to have a clear sense of what is expected and of how well he or she is doing. When the formal role is vague, role incumbents typically develop informally shared ideas of what they should be doing on an hour-by-hour and day-by-day basis and criteria for deciding when they have done their jobs. For example, a police lieutenant in charge of traffic officers in a large city commented that officers shared the belief that they were expected to give a certain number of traffic tickets on a regular basis, though there was no departmental policy to that effect. The official dictum that they would be judged by their success in reducing automobile accidents within their jurisdictions, regardless of whether they gave any citations or not, left the role too vague and the attainability of the goal too uncertain. By agreeing among their fellows on what constituted a good day's work and making their duties more specific and more fully under their control, they made the traffic police role more tenable.

Intrarole Conflict

While even highly formalized role prescriptions remain vague in critical respects and especially in unanticipated situations, the formalizations often are internally contradictory. The very complexity and hierarchical nature of organizations insures intrarole conflict. On the one hand, each differentiated role in an organization conveys responsibility for performing functions and the skills relevant to their performance. On the other hand, organizations are hierarchical and each specialist, no matter how competent, is subject to authority from above. Should the author of an important policy report modify the recommendations at the behest of a superior who commissioned the report? The conflict between expertness and hierarchy is nowhere clearer than in the case of the US Navy disbursing officer who is held fiscally responsible by the General Accounting Office but is expected to respect the authority of officers of higher rank. If a particular payment sought by a commanding officer is deemed illegal, higher authority is likely to expect the disbursing officer to find a way to make the payment—to be "a can-do paymaster" (Turner, 1947).

The complexity of organization also contributes to intrarole conflict because the focal role involves interactions with multiple alter roles, each of which incorporates a somewhat different understanding of the focal role, reflecting their respective interests and values (Merton, 1957). The elementary school teacher, for example, must respond to often conflicting expectations from students, parents, and supervisors. Intrarole conflict also occurs because roles often incorporate multiple functions. While limited time and resources often preclude equal attention to all functions, the effective performance of one function may undermine the performance of another function, requiring ideally a delicate balance in executing the role. This is the case when both task and expressive leadership, as discussed earlier, are vested in a single leader role. The teacher who should both maintain high academic standards and maintain student interest and enthusiasm often finds it difficult to achieve the right balance.

Intrarole conflict is another potent source for formal role-working role separation. Incumbents share experiences and often reach peer understandings of how to handle such conflicts, whether by agreeing to emphasize one function at the expense of another, denigrating the expectations of certain relevant alters, or dealing with the hierarchy-expert dilemma. We shall say more about how intrarole conflicts are resolved in a later section.

Office and Role

Everett Hughes (1937) observed that some organizational roles control behavior outside of the organization to which they apply. The house painter or carpenter or receptionist is seldom under critical organizational scrutiny when off the job. The role applies only to organizationally relevant behavior: to the *office*. But the competence and trustworthiness of a banker or physician or Christian minister who gambles on a day off from work or who dresses in a sloppy fashion may be questioned. A nominee for US Supreme Court Justice was described, somewhat derisively, in the newspaper as driving an "unwashed Volkswagen Beetle," something that contradicted the dignity of this high judicial post. This tendency for the role to be applied beyond the limits of the office is related to the importance of the representational aspect of a role. Representational aspects of a role assume greatest importance when relevant alters must place special trust in the focal role incumbent and when the focal role is responsible for protecting or promoting an important value.

ROLES IN SOCIETY

Functional group roles are anchored in particular groups and may have no carryover to other groups or larger settings. Position roles are anchored in particular organizations and may have limited if any carryover to different settings. But basic roles and value roles tend to apply across all group and organizational boundaries. Consequently, we say that they are anchored in society at large. The tendency for gender roles, for example, to affect participation in organizations and informal groups is illustrated by the frequency with which women are assigned responsibility for preparing minutes or serving coffee. While someone often may be able to escape from an uncongenial role by changing groups or organizations, the basic or value role is carried with one from setting to setting.

There appears to be some tendency for similar roles in different contexts to become merged and identified as a single role recurring in different relationships. For example, when we hear that someone becomes CEO of a corporation, we have at least an orienting idea of what is expected of him or her, based on the responsibilities of CEOs in other companies. Furthermore, roles in situations of limited generality and social significance tend to be shaped in accordance with roles in situations of greater generality and social significance.

Allocation Consistency and Interrole Conflict

Individuals play several roles, and this raises the question of consistency or inconsistency among the roles they play. When a person plays roles that call for contradictory kinds of action, such as kindness versus aggressiveness, openness versus scheming, or impartial judgment versus friendly or familial bias, we speak of *interrole conflict*. To a considerable extent, contradictory roles played by the same individual do not come into conflict because society is compartmentalized. The jurist who is committed to be "tough on crime and criminals" in court can be forgiving of her children's offenses within the family. The "tight-fisted" business man can be "generous to a fault" toward his friends. Role incumbents are unlikely to experience any sense of contradiction between roles thus compartmentalized. Furthermore, there is a tendency for individuals to be allocated to compatible roles. For example, the jurist noted for his impartial judgment will be called on to preside over potentially controversial discussions in his club or church.

Deviant Roles

Deviance is of two kinds, namely, socially disapproved behavior (moral deviance) and physical or mental deficiencies that affect ability to perform roles in the usual way. Occasional minor morally deviant behavior may be reflected in evaluations of lowered role adequacy but seldom leads to deviant role allocation. But single acts of severe deviancy, such as murder, armed robbery, or an episode of insanity, or repetitive acts of minor deviance typically lead to deviant role allocation. As we have mentioned earlier, the specific deviance is generalized to a more comprehensive pattern of deviance, met with distrust, social avoidance or ostracism, and more punitive responses from the community. While the community conceives of these responses as steps toward reforming the deviant, they more typically have the effect of isolating the deviant who is forced into the company of other deviants, making reform more difficult, as labeling theorists have pointed out (Lemert, 1951) The representational aspect of the role becomes dominant to alters, while escaping the role or making it tenable becomes a dominant concern of the role incumbent.

When the individual is altercast into a deviant role revolving about competence rather than moral failure, such as the blind, the cripple, or the limited intelligence role, social expectations and pressures tend to force the incumbent into a limited pattern of activity. Robert Scott (1969) has shown how social agencies formulated a blind role into which the blind person must fit in order to receive necessary services and resources. Many individuals resist this altercasting, employing a variety of tactics of deviance disavowal (Davis, 1961), ranging from the blind person refusing to carry a white cane to much more assertive claims to normality.

From the point of view of tenability, there are benefits as well as costs to deviant roles, even though the latter usually outweigh the former. The principal benefit is freedom from many of the responsibilities of "normal" people. In such cases there may be a pattern of deviance avowal (Turner, 1972). Deviance avowal may be practiced to neutralize a personal commitment to conventional values, as well as to resist demands from alters. Willard Waller's (1930) interviews with divorced persons who had been raised to view divorce as an unthinkable sin revealed some telling examples. In one case the divorcee had reportedly attempted to overcome guilt by deliberately frequenting prostitutes and in other ways violating his own moral standards so as to neutralize his commitment to his own moral outlook.

Talcott Parsons (1951) formulated the concept of a sick role as a temporary role that grants the incumbent freedom from many usual responsibilities. The privileges of the sick role include exemption from social responsibilities and the right to expect to be taken care of and otherwise helped by family members, close friends, and the medical establishment. But these privileges are contingent on the incumbent's performance of the role obligations to want to get well and to seek medical advice and cooperate with medical experts. The specific nature of these privileges and obligations and the specific procedures and criteria by which the individual is "certified" as eligible for the sick role are culturally quite variable (Gordon, 1966). The idea of a sick role can be generalized to a class of such exemptive roles, including a bereavement role, a drunken role (MacAndrew & Edgerton, 1969), and in some societies a "stress role" (Hogan, 1984). In all these exemptive roles the privileges are withdrawn after what is considered a reasonable period for recovery. In this respect they differ from disabled roles, which carry a lifetime insulation from selected responsibilities.

ROLE AND PERSON

While roles can be viewed organizationally and societally as at least vague frameworks for individual action, real persons must learn and hold role conceptions and enact roles, including dealing with both intrarole and interole conflict.

Role Learning

The idea of roles is learned by small children as they observe how different people act toward them and each other and discover the different privileges and obligations accorded boys and girls and younger and older children. Much of the actual learning of roles begins as very young children play at being mother, father, and baby, and children correct each other when they stray from an imagined script. But the critical observation is that roles are learned in pairs or sets. In order to play the role of a child one must develop at least a rudimentary conception of the roles of mother, father, older sibling, and others with whom one interacts frequently. The principle that one learns the most relevant alter roles in the process of learning one's own role continues throughout life. In school, students learn a great deal about the role of teacher as that role relates to students. The key to such learning is discovering what works in dealing with the teacher and what kinds of responses to expect to behavior in the focal role. This learning facilitates *role transitions*, as from child to parent, student to teacher, and employee to employer. This learning is not complete, since it supplies little guidance to relationships with the parent, teacher, or employer's other important alters. But it is an important first step in role learning.

The early learning of roles has more to do with representationality and tenability than with functionality. Children's play sharpens the role images: who is good and who is naughty, who has the right to give orders and who must comply with orders, who is interesting and who is dull. Awareness of tenability comes early as children compete to play at the "best" roles. Functionality comes later as the learners enact roles purposely with real consequences and begin to discover whether their playtime role conceptions work in real interaction.

Early and throughout the learning process the learner finds role models whose patterns of behavior are unwittingly or deliberately incorporated into one's own role conceptions and behavior. Parents, elder siblings, prestigious peers, popular heroes, and figures from books and other media are common examples.

Thornton and Nardi (1975) proposed that role learning takes place in a sequence of four steps. The *anticipatory* step takes place before role incumbency through media depictions and familiarity with people who play the role. Anticipatory learning tends to be stereotypical. The *formal* step comes with the start of role incumbency, involving prescriptions for behavior more than attitudes. The formal step is followed by an *informal* step, marked by a loosening up and recognition of the range of variability with which a role may be played. As the incumbent becomes more competent and comfortable in the role there comes a *personal* stage in which one develops an idiosyncratic version of the role that suits the individual's unique disposition. Thus role learning proceeds from being fitted into a preestablished social mold to making a version of the role that is comfortably and expressively ones own.

Role learning has implications for the broader process of socialization, since most learning of values and norms takes place initially in the context of particular roles. As a result, there is no automatic carryover of values learned in one context to other contexts; hence, what we often call hypocrisy. A further stage of learning is required for values and norms to be generalized beyond the roles in which they are first learned.

Role and Person Merger

Because people play different roles in different contexts, roles have sometimes been regarded as only superficial clues to individual identity or personality. Roles often can be put on and taken off like work clothes and play clothes. The confidence man is a prototypical example of one who assumes and sheds roles at will according to shifting self-interest. An extreme view held by some scholars is that as persons we are no more one of our roles than any other; that we are as many distinct selves as we have different roles.

The more generally accepted approach is to recognize that roles vary in their depth and superficiality. For each individual, roles are arranged in a loose hierarchy from those most important to the individual's identity or self to those that matter relatively little to the role player. For roles high in one's hierarchy, performing at a high level of role adequacy is important, while poor performance of roles low in the hierarchy is not greatly disturbing to the incumbent. According to identity theory (Stryker, 1968), roles most closely linked to personal identity are most predictive of individual behavior.

In a different but compatible approach, Turner (1978) has offered a theory of *role–person merger*. Merger is indicated by three criteria, namely: (1) resistance to abandoning a role when it would seem reasonable to do so; (2) acquisition and internalization of attitudes and beliefs appropriate to the role; and (3) failure of role compartmentalization, with special emphasis on the latter. There are social structural constraints on role–person merger, chief among which is the identification of certain roles, such as the occupational role, as master roles, which are viewed as prima facie evidence of who the person is. Besides such structural constraints, role–person merger is propelled interactively by a sort of negotiation between the way others view the individual and the way the individual seeks to identify him- or herself. Three interactive principles guide the way others view the individual. The *appearance principle* states that, in the absence of contradictory cues, people tend to accept each other as they appear. The *effect principle* is that the greater the potential effect of someone's role on ourselves, the more we conceive that someone on the basis of the role being played. The *consistency principle* is that people tend to identify a person with a given role on the basis of consistency with observations of behavior in other settings. The individual tends to merge self with given roles on the basis of three principles: (1) the consensus principle is a tendency for us to view ourselves as others view us: the looking-glass self; (2) an autonomy and favorable evaluation principle is that we seek to identify most strongly with those roles in which we experience autonomy and favorable evaluations; and (3) the investment principle is that we tend to identify most strongly with those roles in which we have made the greatest investment, which often means those for which we have made great sacrifices.

Complementary to role–person merger is role distancing (Goffman, 1961). Role distancing consists of mechanisms for demonstrating that one does not take the role being played seriously or overseriously. Goffman described adults clowning while riding a merry-go-round so as to show any spectators that they were not taking the apparent role seriously. The childish role was incompatible with their self-conceptions as adults who were beyond such amusements. Goffman also described the surgeon who made flippant remarks to accompanying staff while completing a serious operation. In this case the point of role distancing was to signal that he was more than just a surgeon; that he had human qualities in addition to surgical proficiency.

Role Strain

The enactment of roles often involves anxiety, tension, and frustration, which can be summarized as an experience of role strain (Goode, 1960). Role strain can result from performance or fear of performance at a low level of adequacy, from role overload, or from interrole or intrarole conflict. Role strain will be most intense when it stems from roles that are merged with the person.

Low role adequacy can result from deficiencies of skill, talent, or motivation, lack of resources, or competitive disadvantage. The novice role incumbent often performs poorly until experience is gained. People often assume or are altercast into roles for which they lack sufficient training or ability. According to the Peter Principle (Peter & Hull, 1969), people in organizations tend to be promoted on the basis of good role performance until they reach their level of incompetence where they remain, which explains why organizations often do not function well and why role strain is a widespread organizational problem. A role incumbent may identify strongly with a role but have little motivation for performing the chore aspects of the role. For example, the enthusiastic teacher may find grading students unpleasant, or the strongly identified policeman may find the filing of reports difficult and unpleasant. In both cases, poor performance of the disdained aspect of the role often can affect relevant alters' judgment of overall role adequacy and provoke role strain in the incumbent. Competitive relationships raise the standards of role adequacy above what might otherwise be completely satisfying levels of performance. Deficiency in resources leading to low role adequacy and almost inevitable role strain can be illustrated by the physician without access to a well-equipped hospital, a research scientist without a laboratory or research grant, and a homeless or impoverished parent.

In all these cases of role strain both functional and tenability considerations push for some resolution. The obvious solution in many instances is to seek further training or make extraordinary efforts to secure needed resources. But the alternate solutions are to abandon the role or to lower personal identification (merger) with the role. The good teacher–poor administrator may choose or be pushed to return to the classroom, thereby solving both the functionality and tenability problems. Shifting personal identification to other roles so that low role adequacy matters less to the incumbent can relieve the tenability problem without solving the functionality problem. This is not an uncommon way of relieving role strain, as when workers start counting the years, months, and weeks toward retirement.

Role overload is a common condition when people play more different roles than they have time, energy, or resources for. For both men and especially women (in American culture), a career role often must contend with a parent role for time and energy. But the stress of multiple roles is often moderated because of the multiple benefits that come with multiple roles and the possibility that compatible duties of different roles can sometimes be combined, according to a principle of *role accumulation* (Sieber, 1974). Most recent research has provided support for the role accumulation principle in the case of career and mother role combinations. In the tradition of Robert Park's (1928) early suggestion that highly creative persons usually have been "marginal men," caught between two cultures, Rose Coser (1991) argues that participation in multiple and complex relationships fosters reflection. Alienation in the workplace, she says, occurs principally at the lower organizational levels where workers do not have complex and multiple relationships.

Some kind of choice between or among contending roles may relieve role strain from role overload when there is insufficient accumulation. The obvious choice is to devote more time and energy to the role with which the incumbent is most strongly identified. But the choice does not always go in this direction, because a less fully merged role, such as the occupation or even a recreational role, may provide the resources necessary to support a more strongly identified family role. Also, at given moments, a choice in a less strongly merged role may be irrevocable, as when failure to attend a meeting will end chances for occupational promotion, so performance of the occupational role will be placed ahead of the family role (e.g., being home for daughter's birthday) regardless of the relative identification with occupational and family roles.

Interrole and intrarole conflict go beyond role overload in demanding behavior in one role that violates the values in another role. The scholar–politician who must withhold judgment until there is sufficient evidence but also must take early, clear, and forceful stands on controversial issues faces intense interrole conflict. The parent seeking to teach a child strict honesty and integrity who works as a salesperson and must make unsupportable claims for the superiority of the product being sold is likewise in an interrole conflict situation. The school principal who must convey often contradictory messages to the superintendent, teachers, and parents is in intrarole conflict. We have mentioned already that role compartmentalization can alleviate role strain and even awareness of conflict in many instances, until a crisis arises when compartmentalization is breached. When compartmentalization fails because relevant alters come into communication or because the individual's value system has been generalized beyond the boundaries of particular roles, much the same kind of choice situation arises as in the case of role overload.

Role Transitions

Throughout life, people give up roles and are allocated new ones. This is especially notable with the succession of age roles and in occupational life with promotions, demotions, and job changes. *Role transitions* (Allen & van de Vliert, 1982), even to more advantageous roles, are seldom as uncomplicated as they at first seem. Two overarching considerations are the foundation for a theory of role transitions. First, the change involves both internal and external transitions. The incumbent must make appropriate changes in behavior and attitude (internal) and relevant alters must change their behavior and attitudes toward the focal person (external) unless the changer can find a new social world in which to claim the new role. Second, role transition involves both adopting and being accepted into a new role and abandoning and no longer being viewed in the old role.

Subjectively, role transition may be facilitated or impeded if, as usual, it means leaving a role that is played reasonably successfully and comfortably (functionally and tenably) for a role that requires new learning and gaining new recognition. Transition may be similarly affected because it always involves some change in relevant alters. For example, graduating from high school to college and from college to a profession mean weakening or abandoning old friendships and establishing new ones. Even the security of a practiced deviant role with familiar companions may be preferred to a less familiar socially acceptable role and the need to cultivate new and different friends.

Externally, support or nonsupport by others for the role transition is critical to its course. In the United States Navy, for example, the practice when an enlisted man is commissioned has been to transfer him to a different unit where he is not remembered and not likely to be treated as a peer or viewed with jealousy by former peers. Ambiguity of either role definition or role allocation is likewise an impediment to smooth transition. Transition is facilitated when it is formalized through rites of passage (van Gennep, 1909) such as graduation ceremonies, marriage ceremonies, and funerals and memorial services (for the survivors).

In cases where there is widespread ambiguity over role reallocation, patterns emerge that almost constitute transition roles. Thus the ambiguity in the United States over the transition from childhood to adulthood has led to considerable agreement on an adolescent role, marked by alternating independence and dependence behaviors and other unpredictable and often antisocial actions. In a revealing study of widows, divorcees, ex-nuns, ex-prostitutes, and other transitionists, Helen Ebaugh (1988) notes that "People in society are conscious of ex-statuses and place an individual in a social structure not on the basis of current role occupancy alone but also on the basis of who the individual used to be." Likewise, "Exs tend to retain role residual or some kind of 'hangover identity' from a previous role as they move into new social roles" (1988, p. 5). Thus we tend to know people as widows, divorcees, and ex-convicts in many situations.

ROLE CHANGE

Beyond the continuous role-making by individuals and the more or less stable accommodations between official and working roles, major changes in roles have taken place historically and continue to occur. Historical changes in gender roles, age roles, and religious leadership roles and professionalization of a variety of occupational roles are examples. Role change is always a complex matter because it means a change in role relationships with two or more roles necessarily changing in some kind of reciprocity Thus changes in student roles forced a change in teacher roles and changes in patient roles are forcing a change in physician roles. A model for role change suggests a separation between conditions creating an impetus to change and conditions facilitating or impeding the implementation of role change (Turner, 1990).

The impetus to role change begins with a change in cultural values attached to the role or its functions, altered demand for role services, changing social support, increased or decreased availability of needed resources, demographic changes in the number or personal characteristics of potential role recruits, or technological changes. Jerald Hage and Charles Powers (1992) attribute revolutionary changes in work and family roles to the transition from industrial to postindustrial society. Any of these conditions may mean changes in the networks that support the focal role, or in the most relevant alter roles, as when the societywide rise of democratic values changed women's roles and thereby forced compensating changes in men's roles, or when more assertive children's roles forced accommodative changes in parents' and teachers' roles. In some cases the resulting dysfunctionality, unacceptable representationality, or untenability of the role is handled by role reallocation, as when factories are moved to economically poorer areas that have been less affected by the relevant cultural and social structural shifts and where workers are less demanding. Role reallocation is a then a substitute for role change, which is thereby aborted.

Implementation of role change requires a period of negotiation, leading to a more or less stable accommodation, but not necessarily consensus, about a revised pattern of role relations. Whether role change is completed or aborted by collective resignation to the old pattern depends on several factors. These factors include (1) whether there appears to be a realistically achievable role pattern whose benefit–cost ratio is more favorable than the old pattern; (2) the extent of structural autonomy of the role setting, the extent of freedom from close observation, or the weakening of normative controls over role performance; (3) the extent to which role incumbents are unified in their desire for role change and mobilized to promote change; (4) the extent to which there is mobilized "client" demand for the services this role provides or would provide under a new pattern; (5) the cultural credibility of the new role pattern; and (6) success in gaining institutional support for the new pattern, including in many cases legal and judicial action. (Turner, 1990, p. 107). Role changes that involve taking something away from one role and giving it to the other, such as transfer of the right to perform general medical services from pharmacists to physicians (Kronus, 1987) and the widespread diffusion of authority associated with democratization, often lead to fierce competition until outcomes are determined by a redistribution of power.

CONCLUSIONS

Networks of social roles constitute frameworks into which activities in society, organizations, and groups are organized and acquire meaning and by which individuals organize and understand the meaning of their own behavior and the actions of others. According to interactional role theory, roles are cultural resources but are typically vague, though people act as if they were real and relatively precise. Roles are continuously constructed and reconstructed as individuals engage in role-making in the course of interaction with incumbents of alter roles, or as legitimate role definers specify and respecify the organization of activity. When role definitions become ossified through formal organizational definition or strongly normative cultural tradition, or are too vague or internally or externally conflicting to supply a basis for action, the continuous process of role redefinition leads to the development of informal or working roles that deviate in significant ways from the formally recognized role definitions.

The dynamic reconstruction and role-making and the resolution of role conflicts are governed by three principles of functionality, representationality, and tenability. Roles are constantly modified for greater apparent effectiveness (functionality), limited by the understandings and misunderstandings of incumbents and legitimate role definers. Roles become vehicles for conveying certain images (representationality) and are framed and reframed in relation to what they are seen to represent. Roles are subject to continuous tension to supply a tenable balance of benefits to costs for role incumbents, limited by the power and resources of those incumbents.

REFERENCES

Allen, V. L., & van de Vliert, E. (Eds.). (1982). *Role transitions: Explorations and explanations*. New York: Plenum Press.

Ambrose, S. E. (1997). *Citizen soldiers: The U.S. Army from the Normandy beaches to the Bulge to the surrender of Germany.* New York: Simon and Schuster.

Bales, R. F. (1953). The equilibrium problem in small groups. In T. Parsons & R. F. Bales (Eds.), *Working papers in the theory of action* (pp. 111–116). Glencoe, IL: Free Press.

Bales, R. F., & Slater, P. E. (1955). Role differentiation in small decision-making groups. In T. Parsons & R. F. Bales (Eds.), *Family, socialization, and interaction process* (pp. 259–306). Glencoe, IL: Free Press.

Banton, M. (1965). *Roles: An introduction to the study of social relations.* New York: Basic Books.

Barker, T. (1977). Peer group support for police occupational deviance. *Criminology, 15,* 353–366.

Benne, K. D., & Sheats, P. (1948). Functional roles of group members. *Journal of Social Issues, 4,* 41–49.

Biddle, B. J. (1979). *Role theory: Expectations, identities, and behavior.* New York: Academic Press.

Burke, P. J. (1968). Role differentiation and the legitimation of task activity. *Sociometry, 31,* 404–411.

Coser, R. L. (1991). *In defense of modernity: Role complexity and individual autonomy.* Stanford, CA: Stanford University Press.

Dahrendorf, R. (1973). *Homo sociologicus.* London: Routledge & Kegan Paul.

Davis, F. (1961). Deviance disavowal: The management of strained interaction by the visibly handicapped. *Social Problems, 9,* 120–32.

Davis, K. (1949). *Human society.* New York: Macmillan

Ebaugh, H. R. F. (1988). *Becoming an ex: The process of role exit.* Chicago: University of Chicago Press.

Goffman, E. (1961). *Encounters: Two studies in the sociology of interaction.* Indianapolis: Bobbs-Merrill.

Goode, W. J. (1960). A theory of role strain. *American Sociological Review, 25,* 483–496.

Gordon, G. (1966). *Role theory and illness: A sociological perspective.* New Haven, CT: College and University Press.

Gross, E. (1953). Some functional consequences of primary controls in formal work organizations. *American Sociological Review, 18,* 368–73.

Gross, N., Mason, W. S., & MacEachern, A. W. (1958). *Explorations in role analysis: Studies of the school superintendency role.* New York: Wiley.

Hage, J., & Powers, C. H. (1992). *Post-industrial lives: Roles and relationships in the 21st century.* Newbury Park, CA: Sage Publications.

Hogan, R. R. (1984). The stress role. *Sociological Quarterly, 25,* 567–579.

Hughes, E. C. (1937). Institutional office and the person. *American Journal of Sociology, 43,* 404–413.

Kronus, C. L. (1987). The evolution of occupational power: An historical study of task boundaries between physicians and pharmacists. *Sociology of Work and Occupations, 3,* 3-37.

Lemert, E. M. (1951). *Social pathology: A systematic approach to the theory of sociopathic behavior.* New York: McGraw-Hill.

Linton, R. (1936). *The study of man: An introduction.* New York: D. Appleton-Century.

MacAndrew, C., & Edgerton, R. B. (1969). *Drunken comportment: A social explanation.* New York: Aldine De Gruyter.

Mead, G. H. (1934). *Mind, self, and society.* Chicago: University of Chicago Press.

Merton, R. M. (1957). The role set. *British Journal of Sociology, 8,* 106–120.

Newcomb, T. M. (1950). *Social psychology.* New York: Henry Holt.

Park, R. E. (1928) Human migration and the marginal man. *American Journal of Sociology, 33,* 881–893.

Parsons, T. (1951). *The social system.* Glencoe, IL: Free Press.

Peter, L. J., & Hull, R.(1969). *The Peter principle.* New York: W. Morrow.

Scott, R. A. (1969). *The making of blind men.* New York: Russell Sage Foundation.

Perry, S. E., Silber, E., & Block, D. (1956). *The child and his family in disaster.* Washington, DC: National Academy of Sciences-National Research Council

Roethlisberger, F. J., & Dickson, W. J. (1947). *Management and the worker.* Cambridge, MA: Harvard University Press.

Sieber, S. (1974) Toward a theory of role accumulation. *American Sociological Review, 39,* 567–578.

Stryker, S. (1968). Identity salience and role performance. *Journal of Marriage and the Family, 30,* 558–564.

Thornton, R., & Nardi, P. M. (1975). The dynamics of role acquisition. *American Journal of Sociology, 80,* 870–885.

Turner, R H. (1947). The Navy disbursing officer as a bureaucrat. *American Sociological Review, 12,* 342–348.

Turner, R. H. (1962). Role taking: Process versus conformity. In A. Rose (Ed.), *Human behavior and social processes* (pp. 20–40). Boston: Houghton-Mifflin.

Turner, R. H. (1972). Deviance avowal as neutralization of commitment. *Social Problems, 19,* 308–321.

Turner, R. H. (1978). The role and the person. *American Journal of Sociology, 84,* 1–23.

Turner, R. H. (1990). Role change. *Annual Review of Sociology, 16,* 87–110.

Turner, R. H., & Colomy, C. (1988). Role differentiation: Orienting principles. In E. Lawler (Ed.), *Advances in group processes: A research annual,* Vol. 5 (pp. 1–27). Greenwich, CT: JAI Press.

Turner, R. H., & Shosid, N. (1976). Ambiguity and interchangeability in role attribution. *American Sociological Review*, *41*, 993–1006

van Gennep, A. (1909). *Les rites de passage*. Paris: Ferme.

Waller, W. (1930). *The old love and the new: Divorce and readjustment*. New York: Horace Liveright.

Weinstein, E., & Deutschberger, P. (1963). Some dimensions of altercasting. *Sociometry*, *26*, 454–466.

Whyte, W. F. (1955). *Street corner society: The social structure of an Italian slum*, enlarged ed. Chicago: University of Chicago Press.

CHAPTER 13

The Emotional/Relational World

Shame and the Social Bond

Thomas J. Scheff

Emotions and relationships have long been recognized in sociology as crucially important, but most references to them lack specificity and therefore are vague. This chapter proposes that shame and the social bond are key components of social connectedness, the dimension of solidarity–alienation. It furthermore is proposed that connectedness, together with power, make up the basic dimensions of social structure.

The emotional/relational (e/r) world is important in classical sociological theory, but contemporary sociology focuses mainly on ramifications of power. I consider contributions by six sociologists to a theory of the e/r world: Georg Simmel, Charles Cooley, Norbert Elias, Helen Lynd, Erving Goffman, Richard Sennett, and Helen Lewis, a psychologist–psychoanalyst. Cooley and Lynd, particularly, contributed to a theory of connectedness. I show that Lewis's idea that shame arises from threats to the bond integrates the contributions of the sociologists. A comprehensive theory of social integration would require attention to both power and connectedness.

ALIENATION IN MARX, DURKHEIM, AND WEBER

Marx believed that most human conduct was a product of political–economic interests, that is, of power. In Marx's analysis of capitalism, power struggles, particularly between social classes, were the dominant forces. Later Marxians, especially Communist theoreticians, elevated this crude proposition to the central core of their theory.

However, Marx himself qualified the proposition. First of all, he allowed that certain middle-class intellectuals, like himself, would forsake their class interests to become the vanguard of the proletariat. What force could bring these intellectuals to forsake their class interests?

Thomas J. Scheff • Department of Sociology, Santa Barbara, California 93106.

Handbook of Sociological Theory, edited by Jonathan H. Turner. Kluwer Academic / Plenum Publishers, New York, 2002.

Marx's theory of alienation implies such a force. It suggests that in addition to economic and political causes of class conflict, there are relational and emotional ones. The middle-class intellectuals who formed the vanguard had presumably become alienated from their class. More generally, Marx proposed that persons in capitalist societies become alienated not only from the means of production, but from others and from self. That is, that capitalism reflects and generates disturbances in social relationships and in the self. In his review of empirical studies of alienation, Seeman (1975) found evidence of both kinds of alienation: alienation from others and from self (Seeman referred to the latter as "self-estrangement"). In the discussion below, I call these two forms of alienation isolation (from others) and engulfment [alienation from self: to be loyal to the others(s), one gives up parts of one's self (Scheff, 1990, 1997)].

Marx went on to implicate the emotions that accompany alienation. He proposed that it gave rise to feelings of "impotence" (shame) and "indignation" (anger) (Marx, in Tucker, 1978, pp. 133–134). Marx's theory of alienation proposes that the causes of class conflict are not only political and economic, but also relational and emotional.

Although Marx supplemented his theory of the political–economic causes of class conflict with a theory of emotional–relational causes, there is a great disparity in his development of the two theories. The political–economic theory is lavishly elaborated. The bulk of his commentary on alienation takes place in his early work. Even there, as in later works, formulation of theory of alienation is brief and casual. It is easy to understand why Marx's followers have also made it secondary to material interests.

Suicide, perhaps Durkheim's (1905) most important study, strongly implied that power and connectedness were the basic dimensions of social integration. The dichotomy between anomie and fatalism involves power: a society can under- or overregulate individuals to the point that they commit suicide. But the dichotomy egoism–altruism involves connectedness: individuals in a society may be under- or overconnected, Durkheim's version of the isolation and engulfment forms of alienation.

Weber, the last of the three major theoreticians of classic sociology, also implied that power and connectedness were the basic dimensions of social integration. These dimensions can be found in most of his formulations. For example, the distinction he makes between power and authority implies a dimension of connectedness that is distinct from power. Authority involves the legitimate use of power, that is, subjects feel connected with the state, the chief user of power.

The direction of Weber's thought that most clearly invokes connectedness is his insistence on a *verstehende soziologie*, a sociology that focused on the subjective orientation of actors, not just on their power positions. His idea that real understanding of human action requires empathic understanding implies that societies exist to the point that their members understand each other. This idea links Weber to the tradition of intersubjective understanding manifested in the work of Cooley and Mead, to be discussed below.

I have been unable to find any indication in Weber's work, however, that he proposed the continuum of social integration that I am calling isolation–solidarity–engulfment. This continuum is implied in Marx and Durkheim, as discussed above, and many other sociological theories, but may be absent from Weber. But all three theorists pointed toward connectedness and power as the core dimensions of social structure. Modern sociological theory, however, has focused on the power dimension, since the idea of connectedness has received little further attention. For this reason, this essay will focus on connectedness, the e–r world, arguing that a complete theory of social integration would require that the two dimensions be given parity.

In modern societies, the emotional–relational world is all but invisible, compared to obvious manifestations of power. I propose that studies of shame in social structure and process would make manifest the state of social bonds in relationships and in societies.

EMOTIONS IN CLASSICAL THEORY

Many theorists have at least implied that emotions are a powerful force in social process. Although Weber did not refer to emotions directly, his emphasis on values implies it, since values are emotionally charged beliefs. Especially in his later works, Durkheim proposed that collective sentiments created social solidarity through moral community. G. H. Mead proposed emotion as an important ingredient in his social psychology. For Parsons it a component of social action in his adaptation, goal, attainment, integration, latent pattern maintenance (AGIL) scheme (Parsons & Shils, 1951).

Marx implicated emotions in class tensions in the solidarity of rebelling classes. Durkheim proposed that "... what holds a society together-the 'glue' of solidarity—and [Marx implied that] what mobilizes conflict—the energy of mobilized groups—are emotions" (Collins, 1990, p. 27–57).

WHY SPECIFIC EMOTIONS ARE
NECESSARY FOR THEORY AND RESEARCH

The inclusion of emotions in classical sociology was abstract and therefore virtually meaningless. Generalized emotions have only ambiguous reference. Our knowledge of emotions is not generalized, but particular. For example, we all know a great deal about anger. No doubt some of what we think we know may not be the case. But much of what we know is probably accurate or at least accurate enough to often be able to understand each other. About anger we know or believe we know sources from which it arises, different forms and gradations it can take, and some of the outcomes that it can lead to. We also have similar kinds of knowledge and beliefs about other primary emotions, such as fear, grief, shame, contempt, disgust, love, and joy.

Our knowledge about emotions held in common allows us to communicate with each other on this topic and restrains flights of fancy. The different emotions may have several underlying similarities, but what is much more obvious is the great differences in origins, appearance, and trajectories. It is for this reason that general statements about emotions in the abstract have so little meaning. Some of what Durkheim, Mead, and Parsons said about emotions might appear plausible when applied to one emotion, say anger or fear, but not to most of the others. The sources, appearance, and consequences of anger and fear are so different as to forbid lumping them together.

Treating all emotions together under a single heading amounts to a kind of dismissal. A current parallel can be found in rational choice theory, which divides behavior into the rational and the nonrational. In this theory, attention is given only to rational behavior. As in classical theory, the nonrational, the irrational, and emotional behavior is simply dismissed.

In any case, even the theorists who dealt with emotions explicitly, Durkheim, Mead, and Parsons, did not develop concepts of emotion, investigate their actual occurrence in real life, or collect data that might bear on propositions about the role of emotions in human conduct. Their discussions of emotion, therefore, have not borne fruit.

The researchers whose work I review took the step of investigating a specific and therefore concrete emotion. In their various studies that I will describe, they did not always emphasize the name of the emotion. Sennett and Cobb (1972), for example, in *The Hidden Injuries of Class*, made no move to develop a concept of shame and named it infrequently, but their findings and many of their interpretations clearly imply it. As it turns out, the act of explicitly naming and defining is an important part of investigation. Before turning to these

authors, however, I review the treatment of shame by psychoanalytic authors, in order to show
the problem that the sociologists and Lewis solved.

SHAME AND THE SOCIAL BOND
IN PSYCHOANALYTIC THEORY

The treatment of shame in most psychoanalytic writing is problematic because it leaves
out the social matrix. Psychoanalysis predicates individuals rather than relationships. Like
most psychological theory, Freud's formulations concern emotions in isolated individuals,
ignoring the social context. Individualistic formulations give rise to what might be called the
inside–outside problem. If one ignores the context in which emotions arise, it will inevitably
be difficult to understand their place in human behavior. Freud's solution to the inside–outside
problem was to ignore the outside.

Although in his later work Freud also ignored shame, it had an important role in his first
book. In *Studies on Hysteria*, Freud and Breuer (1895) stated early on (p. 40) that hysteria is
caused by hidden affects, and named the emotion of shame as one of these affects. Near the end
of the book, this idea is urged more strongly: "[The ideas that were being repressed] were all of
a distressing nature, calculated to arouse the affects of shame, self-reproach and of psychical
pain and the feeling of being harmed" (p. 313).

Note that all of the affects mentioned can be considered to be shame derivatives or
cognates. Self-reproach is a specific shame cognate, the feeling of being harmed (as in rejection) somewhat broader, and finally the quite abstract phrase "psychical pain," which, like
"hurt" or "emotional arousal" can be applied to any emotion. In this passage and several
others, shame is given a central role in the causation of psychopathology. Freud and Breuer
also proposed that shame is the inhibiting emotion that leads to repression, therefore giving it a
central role in the development and maintenance of psychopathology. The idea that it is shame
that causes repression also would give shame the leading role in the causation of all mental
illness, not just hysteria, if Freud had stayed with it.

However, in 1905, with the publication of *The Interpretation of Dreams*, Freud permanently renounced his earlier formulation in favor of drive theory, especially the sexual drive. In
Freud's thinking, shame was replaced by anxiety and guilt, the appropriate emotions for
responsible adults, especially male adults. By this time, Freud had become biased about
shame. He thought that it was regressive emotion, seen only in children, women, and savages.
His rejection of his earlier work on shame can be seen as a lapse into the ethnocentric and
sexist attitudes that prevailed at the time, as well as being psychologistic.

Since 1905, shame has been largely ignored in orthodox psychoanalytic formulations.
Although several psychoanalysts made crucially important contributions to shame knowledge,
these contributions helped make them marginal to psychoanalysis. Shame also goes unnamed
and/or undefined even in these marginal analysts. Alfred Adler, Abraham Kardiner, Karen
Horney, and Erik Erikson provide examples.

Adler's formulation of the core position of prestige seeking in human behavior, and his
concept of the inferiority complex are clearly shame based ideas. To make the search for
prestige and honor a central human motive is to focus on the pride–shame axis, as Cooley did.
Similarly, the concept of an inferiority complex can be seen as a formulation about chronic low
self-esteem, or the put it more bluntly, chronic shame.

Yet Adler never used the concept of shame to integrate the various dimensions of his work, as he might have. His theory of personality was that children deprived of love at key periods in their development would become adults with either a drive for power or an inferiority complex. This theory can be restated succinctly in terms of a theory of shame and the social bond: children without the requisite secure bonds will likely become adults whose affects are predominately bypassed (drive for power) or overt shame (inferiority complex) (Lewis, 1971).

Like Adler, Karen Horney (1950) did not name the emotion of shame, but her formulations clearly implied it. Her theory of personality was based on what she called "the pride system." Most of her central propositions imply that pride and shame are the keys to understanding both neurotic and normal behavior. Her concept of the "vindictive personality" seems to imply shame–anger sequences as the emotional basis for vengeful behavior.

Abraham Kardiner was an anthropologist who applied psychoanalytic ideas to his studies of small traditional societies. In *The Individual and His Society* (1939), he offered an extensive analysis of the role of shame in four traditional societies. Unlike Adler and Horney, he named the emotion of shame clearly, and stated directly, like Freud and Breuer, that shame is the emotion that leads to repression. Like Adler, he also gave prominence to prestige as a fundamental human motive. Going further than Adler or Freud, he named shame as the principal component of the superego, that is, of conscience.

Like Kardiner, Erik Erikson (1950) also named shame directly, in his analysis of the relationship between shame and guilt. In his investigation of these emotions, he proposed, again contra Freud, that shame was the most fundamental emotion and that it had a vital role in the developmental stages through which all children must pass. His analysis of shame was an important source for Helen Lynd's work on shame; reading Erikson might have been the beginning of Lynd's interest in shame. Like most theorists who discuss shame, neither Kardiner nor Erikson tried to define it.

The work on shame by these four analysts was not recognized by the psychoanalytic establishment. Both Adler and Horney were excluded for their deviationism. Although neither Kardiner nor Erikson were excluded, there was no response to their contributions on shame, with the exception of Helen Lynd to Erikson. It also is of interest that among the disciples of Adler and of Horney that there was also no response to their work on shame.

Although there has been a reawakening of interest in shame by current psychoanalysts, still only a small minority of analysts are involved. Even in this group, converting from drive theory to shame language is a struggle. The work of Lansky (1992, 1995) on shame preserves drive theory. Morrison (1989) has translated drive theoretic formulations into shame dynamics, trying to bridge the two worlds. Broucek (1991) has rebelled against drive theory, but does not attempt a social formulation of shame. Only Lewis (1971) has succeeded in throwing off drive theory, recasting shame in social terms. I return to her work after considering sociological contributions to the study of shame and the bond.

SEVEN PIONEERS IN THE STUDY
OF SOCIAL SHAME

Five of the six sociologists I review acted independently of each other. In the case of Elias and Sennett, their discovery of shame seems forced on them by their data. Neither Simmel nor Cooley define what they mean by shame. Goffman only partially defined embarrassment. The exception is Helen Lynd, who was self-conscious about shame as a concept. Lynd's book on shame was contemporaneous with Goffman's first writings on embarrassment and realized their main point: facework meant avoiding embarrassment and shame.

Helen Lewis's (1971) empirical work on shame was strongly influenced by Lynd's book. She also was sophisticated in formulating a concept of shame and in using systematic methods to study it. Sennett's work involved slight outside influence. He approvingly cited the Lynd book on shame in *The Hidden Injuries of Class* (Sennett & Cobb, 1972) and his *Authority* (Sennett, 1980) has a chapter on shame. All six sociologists advanced a theory of shame and the bond, even though all but Lynd focused only on shame.

Simmel: Shame and Fashion

Shame plays a significant part in only one of Simmel's (1904) essays, on fashion.[1] People want variation and change, he argued, but they also anticipate shame if they stray from the behavior and appearance of others. Fashion is the solution to this problem, since one can change along with others, avoiding being isolated, and therefore shame (Simmel, 1904, p. 553). Simmel's idea about fashion implies conformity in thought and behavior among one group in a society—the fashionable ones—and distance from another—those who do not follow fashion—relating shame to social bonds.

There is a quality to Simmel's treatment of shame that is somewhat difficult to describe but needs description, since it characterizes most of the other sociological treatments reviewed here. Simmel's use of shame is casual and un-self conscious. His analysis of the shame component in fashion occurs in a single long paragraph. Shame is not mentioned before or after. He does not conceptualize shame or define it, seeming to assume that the reader will know the meaning of the term. Similar problems are prominent in Cooley, Elias, Sennett, and Goffman. Lynd and Lewis are exceptions, since they both attempted to define shame and locate it with respect to other emotions.

Cooley: Shame and the Looking Glass Self

Cooley (1922), like Simmel, was direct in naming shame. For Cooley, shame and pride both arose from self-monitoring, the process that was at the center of his social psychology. His concept of "the looking glass self," which implies the social nature of the self, refers directly and exclusively to pride and shame, but he made no attempt to define either emotion. Instead, he used the vernacular words as if they were self-explanatory.

To give just one example of the ensuing confusion: In English and other European languages, the word "pride" used without qualification usually has an inflection of arrogance or hubris (pride goeth before the fall). In current usage, in order to refer to the kind of pride implied in Cooley's analysis, the opposite of shame, one must add a qualifier like *justified* or *genuine*. Using undefined emotion words is confusing.

However, Cooley's analysis of self-monitoring suggests that pride and shame are the basic social emotions. His formulation of the social basis of shame in self-monitoring can be used to amend Mead's social psychology. Perhaps the combined Mead–Cooley formulation can solve the inside–outside problem that plagues psychoanalytic and other psychological approaches to shame, as I suggest below.

[1] I am indebted to Eduardo Bericat for calling this essay to my attention.

Elias: Shame in the Civilizing Process

Elias (1994) undertook a ambitious historical analysis of what he calls the "civilizing process." He traced changes in the development of personality and social norms from the 15th century to the present. Like Weber, he gave prominence to the development of rationality. Unlike Weber, however, he gave equal prominence to emotional change, particularly to changes in the threshold of shame: "No less characteristic of a civilizing process than "rationalization" is the peculiar molding of the drive economy that we call "shame" and "repugnance" or "embarrassment" (Elias, 1982, p. 297).

Using excerpts from advice manuals, Elias outlined a theory of modernity. By examining advice concerning etiquette, especially table manners, body functions, sexuality, and anger, he suggests that a key aspect of modernity involved a veritable explosion of shame. I will cite only one of many advice excerpts used by Elias. He first presents a lengthy excerpt from a 19th century advice book, *The Education of Girls* (von Raumer, 1857), that advises mothers how to answer sexual questions. In response to the question, "Where do babies come from," Von Raumer suggests, "Children should be left as long as possible in the belief that an angel brings the mother her little children." If the issue comes up again, the child is to be sternly warned: "It is not good for you to know such a thing, and you should take care not to listen to anything said about it." Von Raumer concludes this passage with advice that both shames the mother and advises her to shame the daughter: "A truly well-brought-up girl will from then on feel shame at hearing things of this kind spoken of" (p. 49).

This advise suggests three different puzzles:

1. Why is the author, von Raumer, offering the mother such absurd advice?
2. Why does the mother follow his advice (as most did, and still do)?
3. Why do the daughters follow their mothers' advice (as most did, and still do)?

Modern feminist theory might respond to the first question that von Raumer's advice arises from his position of power: He sought to continue male supremacy, by advising the mother to act in a way that is consonant with the role of women as subordinate to that of men. That is, he was promulgating the woman's role as "Kirche, Kueche, Kinder" (church, kitchen, children). Keeping women ignorant of sexuality and reproduction would help to continue this system.

This formulation is probably part of a complete answer, but it does not attend to the other two questions. Why do mothers and daughters submit to ignorance and shame? Elias's formulation provides an answer to all three questions, without contradicting the feminist answer. Each of these persons, the man and the two hypothetical readers, the mother and the daughter, is too embarrassed about sexuality to think clearly about it. It could be true that von Raumer's advice is part of his male chauvinist position and also true that he is too embarrassed to think about the meaning of his advice. Thoughts and emotions are both parts of a causal chain.

Elias's study suggests a way of understanding the social transmission of a *taboo* on shame. The adult, the author von Raumer in this case, is not only ashamed of sex, but he is ashamed of being ashamed and probably ashamed of the shame that he will arouse in his reader. The mother responding to von Raumer's text, in turn, will probably react in a similar way, being ashamed, and being ashamed of being ashamed, and being ashamed of causing further shame in the daughter. Von Raumer's advice is part of a social system in which attempts at civilized delicacy result in an endless chain reaction of unacknowledged shame. The chain reaction is both within persons and between them, three spirals (one spiral within each party and one between them). The spiral idea integrates social and psychological processes and suggests a solution to the usual separation of inside and outside, as I suggest at the end of this chapter.

Elias showed that there was much less shame about manners and emotions in the early part of the period he studied than there was in the 19th century. In the 18th century, a change began occurring in advice on manners. What was said openly and directly earlier begins only to be hinted at or left unsaid entirely. Moreover, justifications are offered less. One is mannerly because it is the *right* thing to do. Any decent person will be courteous; the intimation is that bad manners are not only wrong but also unspeakable, the beginning of repression.

The change that Elias documents is gradual but relentless; by a continuing succession of small decrements, etiquette books fall silent about the reliance of manners, style, and identity on respect, honor, and pride, and avoidance of shame and embarrassment. By the end of the 18th century, the social basis of decorum and decency had become virtually unspeakable. Unlike Freud or anyone else, Elias documents, step by step, the sequence of events that led to the repression of emotions in modern civilization.

By the 19th century, Elias proposed, manners are inculcated no longer by way of adult to adult verbal discourse, in which justifications are offered. Socialization shifts from slow and conscious changes by adults over centuries to swift and silent indoctrination of children in their earliest years. No justification is offered to most children; courtesy has become absolute. Moreover, any really decent person would not have to be told. In modern societies, socialization *automatically* inculcates and represses shame.

Richard Sennett: Is Shame the Hidden Injury of Class?

Although *The Hidden Injuries of Class* (Sennett & Cobb, 1972) carries a powerful message, it is not easy to summarize. The narrative concerns quotes from interviews and the authors' brief interpretations. They do not devise a conceptual scheme and a systematic method. For this reason, readers are required to devise their own conceptual scheme, as I do here. The book is based on participant–observation in communities, schools, clubs and bars, and 150 interviews with white working-class males, mostly of Italian or Jewish background, in Boston for one year beginning in July of 1969 (pp. 40–41).

The hidden injuries that Sennett and Cobb discovered might be paraphrased: their working-class men felt that first, because of their class position, they were not accorded the *respect* that they should have gotten from others, particularly from their teachers, bosses, and even from their own children. That is, these men have many complaints about their status. Second, these men also felt that their class position was at least partly their own fault. Sennett and Cobb imply that social class is responsible for both injuries. They believe that their working men did not get the respect they deserved because of their social class, and that the second injury, lack of self-respect, also is the fault of class, rather than the men's own fault, as most of them thought.

Sennett and Cobb argue that in American society, respect is largely based on individual achievement, the extent that one's accomplishments provide a unique identity that stands out from the mass of others. The role of public schools in the development of abilities forms a central part of Sennett and Cobb's argument. Their informants lacked self-respect, the authors thought, because the schooling of working-class boys did not develop their individual talents in a way that would allow them to stand out from the mass as adults. In the language of emotions, they carry a burden of feelings of rejection and inadequacy, which is to say chronic low self-esteem (shame).

From their observations of schools, Sennett and Cobb argue that teachers single out for attention and praise only a small percentage of the students, usually those who are talented or closest to middle class. This praise and attention allows the singled-out students to develop their potential for achievement. The large majority of the boys, however, are ignored and in subtle ways rejected.

There are a few working-class boys who achieve their potential through academic or athletic talent. But the large mass does not. For them, rather than opening up the world, public schools close it off. Education rather than becoming a source of growth provides only shame and rejection. For the majority of students, surviving school means running a gauntlet of shame. These students learn by the second or third grade that is better to be silent in class than risk humiliation of a wrong answer. Even students with the right answers must deal with having the wrong accent, clothing, or physical appearance. For most students, schooling is a vale of shame.

Helen Lynd: Shame and Identity

During her lifetime, Helen Lynd was a well-known sociologist. With her husband, Robert, she published the first American community studies, *Middletown* and *Middletown in Transition*. But Lynd was also profoundly interested in developing an interdisciplinary approach to social science. In her study *On Shame and the Search for Identify* (1958), she dealt with both the social and psychological sides of shame. She also clearly named the emotion of shame and its cognates and located her study within previous scholarship, especially psychoanalytic studies. But Lynd also modified and extended the study of shame by developing a concept and by integrating its social and psychological components.

In the first two chapters, Lynd introduced the concept of shame, using examples from literature to clarify each point. In the next section, she critiques mainstream approaches in psychology and the social sciences. She then introduces ideas from lesser-known approaches, showing how they might resolve some of the difficulties. Finally, she has an extended discussion of the concept of identity, suggesting that it might serve to unify the study of persons by integrating the concepts of self, ego, and social role under the larger idea of identity.

Lynd's approach to shame is much more analytical and self-conscious than the other sociologists reviewed here. They treated shame as a vernacular word. For them, shame sprung out of their data, unavoidable. But Lynd encounters shame deliberately, as part of her exploration of identity.

Lynd explains that shame and its cognates get left out because they are deeply hidden but at the same time pervasive. She makes this point in many ways, particularly in the way she carefully distinguishes shame from guilt.

One idea that Lynd develops is profoundly important for a social theory of shame and the bond, that sharing one's shame with another can strengthen the relationship: "The very fact that shame is an isolating experience also means that ... sharing and communicating it ... can bring about particular closeness with other persons" (Lynd, 1958, p. 66). In another place, Lynd went on to connect the process of risking the communication of shame with the kind of role-taking that Cooley and Mead had described: "communicating shame can be an experience of ... entering into the mind and feelings of another person" (p. 249). Lynd's idea about the effects of communicating and not communicating shame was pivotal for Lewis's (1971) concepts of acknowledged and unacknowledged shame and their relationship to the state of the social bond, as outlined below.

Goffman: Embarrassment and Shame in Everyday Life

Although shame goes largely unnamed in Goffman's early work, embarrassment and avoidance of embarrassment is the central thread. Goffman's "everyperson" is always desperately worried about his image in the eyes of the other, trying to present herself with her best foot forward to avoid shame. This work elaborates and indeed fleshes out Cooley's abstract idea of the way in which the looking glass self leads directly to pride or shame.

Interaction Ritual (Goffman, 1967) made two specific contributions to shame studies. In his study of facework, Goffman states what may be seen as a model of "face" as the avoidance of embarrassment and losing face as suffering embarrassment. This is an advance, because it offers readily observable markers for empirical studies of face. The importance of this idea is recognized, all too briefly, at the beginning of Brown and Levinson's (1987) study of politeness behavior.

Goffman's (1967) second contribution to the study of shame was made in a concise essay on the role of embarrassment in social interaction. Unlike any of the other shame pioneers in sociology, he begins the essay with an attempt at definition. His definition is a definite advance, but it also foretells a limitation of the entire essay, since it is behavioral and physiological, ignoring inner experience. Framing his analysis in what he thought of as purely sociological mode, Goffman omitted feelings and thoughts. His solution to the inside–outside problem was to ignore most of inner experience, just as Freud ignored most of outside events.

However, Goffman (1967) affirms Cooley's point on the centrality of the emotions of shame and pride in normal, everyday social relationships.

> One assumes that embarrassment is a normal part of normal social life, the individual becoming uneasy not because he is personally maladjusted but rather because he is not ... embarrassment is not an irrational impulse breaking through social prescribed behavior, but part of this orderly behavior itself. (p. 109 and 111)

Even Goffman's partial definition of the state of embarrassment represents an advance. One of the most serious limitations of current contributions to the sociology of emotions is the lack of definitions of the emotions under discussion. Much like Cooley, Elias, and Sennett, Kemper (1978) offers no definitions of emotions, assuming that they go without say. Hochschild (1983) attempts to conceptualize various emotions in an appendix, but does not go as far as to give concrete definitions of emotional states. Only in Retzinger (1991, 1995) can conceptual and operational definitions of the emotions of shame and anger be found.

Lewis's Discovery of Unacknowledged Shame

Helen Lewis's (1971) book on shame involved an analysis of verbatim transcripts of hundreds of psychotherapy sessions. She encountered shame because she used a systematic method for identifying emotions, the Gottschalk–Gleser method (Gottschalk, 1995; Gottschalk & Gleser, 1969), which involves use of long lists of key words that are correlated with specific emotions.

Lewis found that anger, fear, grief, and anxiety cues showed up from time to time in some of the transcripts. She was surprised by the massive frequency of shame cues. Her most relevant findings:

1. *Prevalence*: Lewis found a high frequency of shame markers in all the sessions, far outranking markers of all other emotions combined.
2. *Lack of awareness*: Lewis noted that patient or therapist almost never referred to

shame or its near cognates. Even the word "embarrassment" was seldom used. In analyzing the context in which shame markers occurred, Lewis identified a specific context: situations in which the patient seemed to feel distant from, rejected, criticized, or exposed by the therapist.

However, the patients showed two different seemingly opposite responses in the shame context. In one, the patient seemed to be suffering psychological pain but failed to identify it as shame. Lewis called this form "overt, undifferentiated" shame. In a second kind of response, the patient seemed not to be in pain, revealing an emotional response only by rapid, obsessional speech on topics that seemed somewhat removed from the dialogue. Lewis called this second response "bypassed" shame.

3. *Shame, anger, and conflict*: In her transcripts, Lewis found many episodes of shame that extended over long periods of time. Since emotions are commonly understood to be brief signals (a few seconds) that alert us for action, the existence of long-lasting emotions is something of a puzzle. Lewis's solution to this puzzle may be of great interest in the social sciences, since it provides an emotional basis for long-standing hostility, withdrawal, or alienation.

She argued that her subjects often seemed to have emotional reactions to their emotions, and that this loop may extend indefinitely. She called these reactions "feeling traps." The trap that arose most frequently in her data involved shame and anger. A patient interprets an expression by the therapist as hostile, rejecting, or critical, and responds with shame or embarrassment. However, the patient instantaneously masks the shame with anger, then is ashamed of being angry. Apparently each emotion in the sequence is brief, but the loop can go on forever. This proposal suggests a new source of protracted conflict and alienation, one hinted at in Simmel's treatment of conflict.

Although Lewis did not discuss other kinds of spirals, there is one that may be as important as the shame–anger loop. If one is ashamed of being ashamed, it is possible to enter into a shame–shame loop that leads to silence and withdrawal. Elias's work on modesty implies this kind of loop.

4. *Shame and the social bond*: Finally, Lewis interpreted her findings in explicitly social terms. She proposed that shame arises when there is a threat to the social bond, as was the case in all of the shame episodes she discovered in the transcripts. Every person, she argued, fears social disconnection from others.

Lewis's solution to the outside–inside problem parallels and advances the Darwin–Mead–Cooley definition of the social context of shame. She proposed that shame is a bodily and/or mental response to the threat of disconnection from the other. Shame, she argued, can occur in response to threats to the bond from the other, but it also can occur in response to actions in the "inner theater," in the interior monologue in which we see ourselves from the point of view of others. Her reasoning fits Cooley's formulation of shame dynamics and also Mead's (1934) more general framework: the self is a social construction, a process constructed from both external and internal social interaction, in role-playing and role-taking.

SHAME AS THE SOCIAL EMOTION

Drawing on the work of these pioneers, it is possible to take further steps toward defining shame. By shame I mean a large family of emotions that includes many cognates and variants, most notably embarrassment, humiliation, and related feelings such as shyness, that involve reactions to rejection or feelings of failure or inadequacy. What unites all these cognates is that they involve the feeling of a *threat to the social bond*. That is, I use a sociological definition of shame, rather than the more common psychological one (perception of a discrepancy between ideal and actual self). If one postulates that shame is generated by a threat to the bond, no matter how slight, then a wide rage of cognates and variants follow: not only embarrassment, shyness, and modesty, but also feelings of rejection or failure and heightened self-consciousness of any kind. Note that this definition usually subsumes the psychological one, since most ideals are social, rather than individual.

If, as proposed here, shame is a result of threat to the bond, shame would be the most social of the basic emotions. Fear is a signal of danger to the body, anger a signal of frustration, and so on. The sources of fear and anger, unlike shame, are not uniquely social. Grief also has a social origin, since it signals the loss of a bond. But bond loss is not a frequent event. Shame on the other hand, following Goffman, since it involves even a slight threat to the bond, is pervasive in virtually all social interaction. As Goffman's work suggests, all human beings are extremely sensitive to the exact amount of deference they are accorded. Even slight discrepancies generate shame or embarrassment. As Darwin (1872) noted, the discrepancy even can be in the positive direction; too much deference can generate the embarrassment of heightened self-consciousness.

Especially important for social control is a positive variant, a *sense of shame*. That is, shame figures in most social interaction because members may feel shame only occasionally, but they are constantly anticipating it, as Goffman implied. Goffman's treatment points to the slightness of threats to the bond that lead to anticipation of shame. For that reason, my use of the term "shame" is much broader than its vernacular use. In common parlance, shame is an intensely negative, crisis emotion closely connected with disgrace. But this is much too narrow if we expect shame to be generated by even the slightest threat to the bond.

An obvious question arises from my description of the zigzag progress of shame studies described above. What gives rise to the slipperiness of the concept of shame? Why did Elias, Sennett, Goffman, and others make fundamental contributions to shame knowledge, yet fail to explicitly name and define the emotion they studied as shame or ignore it in their later work? Why did Mead and Dewey ignore the obvious importance of shame in Cooley? Why did Brown and Levinson recognize the importance of Goffman's concept of face as the avoidance of embarrassment but fail to utilize it in their empirical studies? My description of the history of shame studies by psychoanalysts suggests many similar questions, particularly Freud's early discovery of shame and his later disavowal.

My explanation derives from Elias's idea of the advance of the shame threshold and Lewis's work on unacknowledged shame. Elias's response to his data led him to an analysis of the underlying process in our civilization that was too advanced for his audience. In Western societies, as Elias pointed out, the threshold for shame has been decreasing for hundreds of years but at the same time awareness of this emotion has been declining. As his own analysis could have predicted, in our era the level of awareness of shame is so low that only those trained to detect unacknowledged shame could understand the point that Elias was making. Because Retzinger and I were guided by Lewis's (1971) work, we were responsive to Elias's shame analysis. Within psychology and psychoanalysis, Lewis's work is widely acclaimed but seldom used.

The development of a concept of shame, which includes both analytical and operational definitions of shame, is crucially important for the scientific study of shame. It would appear that subjects' testimony about shame states and indeed the presence or absence of any other emotion may not be valid. Perhaps most emotional states are disavowed or exaggerated.

Following Lewis it would appear that most shame states are not experienced in consciousness but are either unconscious or misnamed [bypassed or overt, undifferentiated shame, in Lewis's (1971) terminology]. For this reason studies that rely on testimony of subjects rather than analysis of their behavior and their discourse are apt to leave out most shame. It also is not clear that subject's reports of their own shame and that of others are accurate. Studies are needed to test the validity of subjective reports of shame. In my view, such a test would mean validating standardized shame measures against analysis of discourse.

To develop a comprehensive theory of social integration, to complement theories of power, the sociology and psychology of emotions should follow up the leads offered by the authors reviewed here. If we could agree on a method for studying shame that would be reliable and valid, we might start by testing the key hypotheses on collective shame Elias stated: shame is increasing in modern societies, but at the same time awareness of shame is decreasing. Another hypothesis, following Sennett and Cobb, is that members of the working and lower classes are shamed by their status. Even though shame is usually unacknowledged, still cues to shame are much more visible than other markers of the state of the bond. A reliable analysis of shame cues could lead to studies of alienation–solidarity in social interaction.

One direction that might take concerns the dynamics of racial, gender, ethnic, and class relationships. In her chapter "Honor and Shame," Howard (1995) proposes that women and blacks are likely to be ashamed of themselves. She suggests that they are dishonored, that their status is consistently derogated. To coordinate their actions in a white male-dominated society, women and blacks must take the role of white males, which leads to seeing themselves as they are seen. She supports this idea by pointing to the amount of "self-mutilation" that women and blacks undergo in attempting to fit themselves into the male or white ideal. She argues that women's sustained attempts to be slender and have small waists and feet, to the point of self-starvation, suggest shame in these women. Similarly, she proposes that hair straightening and the high status of light skin among blacks has the same implication.

Howard's analysis of shame and honor in race and gender relations is suggestive but is only a first step. If her formulation is accurate, it would mean that there is an emotional–relational structure that sustains the domination of white males, in addition to legal, political, and economic causes. In order to test this idea, however, shame would need to be investigated so that its presence or absence in women and blacks could be documented. Retzinger's (1991) theory of conflict and my application of it to collective conflict (Scheff, 1994) suggest that protracted and intense hatred, resentment, and envy derive from unacknowledged shame. Research on gender, race, ethnic, and class emotional tensions and alienation could be inspired by this idea.

CONCLUSION

The classic sociologists believed that emotions and the social bond are crucially involved in the structure and change of whole societies. The authors reviewed here suggest that shame is the premier social emotion. Lynd's work particularly suggests how acknowledgment of shame can strengthen bonds and by implication lack of acknowledgment can create alienation. This idea was developed by Lewis into a theory of shame and social bond, with both conceptual and operational definitions. Lewis's work further suggests how shame–anger loops can create perpetual hostility and alienation. If shame and the bond are the key components of social integration, then acknowledged shame would be the glue that holds relationships and societies together and unacknowledged shame the force that drives them apart.

REFERENCES

Broucek, F. (1991). *Shame and the* self. New York: Guilford.

Brown, P., & Levinson, S. (1987). *Politeness: Some universals in language usage.* Cambridge: Cambridge University Press.

Collins, R. (1990). Stratification, emotional energy, and the transient emotions. In T. D. Kemper (Ed.), *Research agendas in the sociology of emotions* (pp. 27–57). Albany: State University of New York Press.

Cooley, C. H. (1922). *Human nature and the social order.* New York: Scribner's

Darwin, C. (1872). *The expression of emotion in men and animals.* London: John Murray.

Durkheim, E. (1905/1952). *Suicide.* London Routledge.

Elias, N. (1978). *The civilizing processes,* Vol. 1. New York: Pantheon.

Erikson, E. (1950). *Childhood and society.* New York: Norton

Freud, S. (1994). *The interpretation of dreams.* New York: Modern Library.

Freud, S., & Breur, J. (1895/1966). *Studies on hysteria.* New York: Avon.

Goffman, E. (1967). *Interaction ritual.* New York: Anchor.

Gottschalk, L. (1995). *Content analysis of verbal behavior.* Hillsdale, NJ: Lawrence Erlbaum Associates.

Gottschalk, L., Winget, C., & Gleser, G. (1969). *Manual of instruction for using the Gottschalk–Gleser Content Analysis Scales.* Berkeley: University of California Press.

Hochshild, A. (1983). *The managed heart.* Berkeley: University of California Press.

Horney, K. (1950). *Neurosis and human growth.* New York: Norton

Howard, R. E. (1995). *Human rights and the search for community.* Boulder, CO: Westview.

Kardiner, A. (1939). *The individual and his society.* New York: Columbia University Press.

Kemper, T. (1978). *A social interactional theory of emotions.* New York: Wiley.

Lansky, M. (1992). *Fathers who fail: Shame and psychopathology in the family system.* Hillsdale, NJ: Analytic Press.

Lansky, M. (1995). *Posttraumatic nightmares.* Hillsdale, NJ: Analytic Press.

Lewis, H. B. (1971). *Shame and guilt in neurosis.* New York: International Universities Press.

Lynd, H. M. (1961). *On shame and the search for identity.* New York: Science Editions.

Mead, G. H. (1934). *Mind, self, and society.* Chicago: University of Chicago Press.

Morrison, A. (1989). *Shame: The underside of narcissism.* Hillsdale, NJ: Analytic Press.

Parsons, T., & Shils, E. (1951). *Toward a general theory of action.* Cambridge: Harvard University Press.

Retzinger, S. (1991). *Violent emotions.* Newbury Park, CA: Sage.

Retzinger, S. (1995). Identifying shame and anger in discourse. *American Behavioral Scientist, 38,* 1104–1113.

Scheff, T. (1990). *Microsociology.* Chicago: University of Chicago Press.

Scheff, T. (1994). *Bloody revenge: Nationalism, war, and emotion.* Boulder, CO: Westview Press.

Scheff, T. (1997). *Emotions, the social bond, and human reality.* Cambridge: Cambridge University Press.

Seeman, M. (1975). Alienation studies. *Annual Review of Sociology, 1,* 91–124.

Sennett, R. (1980). *Authority.* New York: Alfred Knopf.

Sennett, R., & Cobb, J. (1972). *The hidden injuries of class.* New York: Vintage Books.

Simmel, G. (1904). Fashion. *International Quarterly, X,* 130–155. (Reprinted in the *American Journal of Sociology, 62,* 541–559)

Tucker, R. C. (1978). *The Marx–Engels Reader.* New York: Norton.

Von Raumer, W. (1857). *Education of girls.* (Cited in Elias, 1978)

CHAPTER 14

Action Theory

HANS JOAS AND JENS BECKERT

INTRODUCTION

The concept of "action" has played a prominent role in sociology ever since the institutional-ization of the field as an academic discipline in the late 19th century. For example, Max Weber's (1968) best-known theoretical work, *Economy and Society*, opens with a set of influential definitions regarding the conceptualization of action and its distinction from the notion of behavior. Weber's fourfold typology of action provides the foundational categories for his approach to sociology. But Weber is by far not the only sociologist who developed his theoretical conceptualizations from the notion of action. One generation after Weber, Talcott Parsons synthesized the theoretical achievements of the "founding fathers" of sociology and the utilitarian tradition in an action–theoretical framework that takes the "unit act" as its basic component. His masterpiece of 1937, *The Structure of Social Action*, still has to be seen as the most important such attempt at theoretical synthesis in the middle of the 20th century. The unit act, which stands at the core of the "voluntaristic" approach of Parsons' sociology, gives special emphasis to the role of ultimate values and normative orientations in actions and to "effort" as a category for depicting the active involvement of actors. Other sociologists who stand for the centrality of action theory in the discipline can easily be named. Among them are George Herbert Mead and Alfred Schutz. More recently Jürgen Habermas and Anthony Giddens have based their approaches on theories of action that follow the sociological tradition but make use also of theories of action that have been developed in other disciplines like psychology and philosophy.

This already indicates that the centrality of the concept of action is by far not an exclusive feature of sociology. Most importantly, the discipline of economics developed along a specific model of action that stands in the utilitarian tradition and claims that actors' decisions can be understood from their motivation to optimize their utility. Disputes in economics address the question whether the optimizing assumption is meant as an empirical description of action or as a normative recommendation as to how actors should act. But it is uncontroversial that

---

Since the task of this chapter is the presentation of a specific action–theoretic approach developed much more extensively in books and articles by the two authors, we rely in a few passages on earlier formulations of our position.

HANS JOAS AND JENS BECKERT • Department of Sociology, Free University of Berlin, 14195 Berlin, Germany.

Handbook of Sociological Theory, edited by Jonathan H. Turner. Kluwer Academic / Plenum Publishers, New York, 2002.

economic processes should be analyzed on the basis of a particular notion of action. In psychology the cognitive turn during the last decades has increasingly opened up the perspective of founding psychology on a theory of action instead of behavior. In philosophy there are again separate traditions of theorizing about human action, e.g., in analytical philosophy, pragmatism, and some versions of Marxism.

Despite the diversity of the concept of action in the social sciences and in philosophy the debate on action in sociology tends to focus primarily on rational choice theory on the one hand and normative theories of action on the other. Rational choice theories have gained importance in sociology since the 1960s, a development that can be understood as a reaction to the dominance of normative theories during the two preceding decades. This has not silenced, however, normative theories and their critique of the rational actor model. But arguments between the two sides have been exchanged so often now that further theoretical gains are hardly to be expected from the continuation of this controversy. Instead, it would be more fruitful to take advantage of the existing diversity of action theories in the other disciplines for the development of new theoretical insights in sociology. This has been the approach, for instance, of Anthony Giddens (1984) who incorporated findings from developmental psychology and phenomenology into his structuration theory. Giddens emphasizes the role of cognitive rules and routines but also the developmental preconditions of identity formation. However, the alternative that reaches even further beyond the routinized exchanges between rationalist and normativist theories of action seems to us an action–theoretic conceptualization that focuses on the notion of the *creativity* of human action. Such a theory can be based primarily on the tradition of American pragmatism that originated in philosophy and psychology but also has a significant sociological tradition. The central thesis of such an approach is the claim that a third model of action can be added to the two predominant models of action—rational and normatively oriented action—namely, a model that emphasizes the creative character of human action. The intention of such a theory expands to the claim that this third model overarches both of the others. It does not simply draw attention to an additional type of action, relatively neglected to date, but rather asserts that there is a creative dimension to all human action, a dimension that is only inadequately expressed in the models of rational and normatively oriented action.

This proposition will structure our presentation of action theory in this chapter. After a brief outline of the rational actor model and the normative model of action, we will discuss key concepts of such a theory of the creativity of action as it has been developed more extensively in a book of one of us before (Joas, 1996). Subsequently, we will summarize the main results of the debate about Parsons' action frame of reference and develop the agenda for the further elaboration of a theory of the creativity of action. In the last part, we shall apply the outlined theoretical concepts to the understanding of two economic action situations: cooperation and innovation. Here, too, the argument is based on a more extensive elaboration (Beckert, 2002). This will help to clarify the significance of the theory of creativity of action for the understanding of action in one concrete social arena.

THE RATIONALITY OF ACTION
AND ITS TACIT ASSUMPTIONS

Within the social sciences the utilitarian rational actor model rose to prominence primarily in economics where it achieved a paradigmatic status for the discipline. In its basic form it assumes that actors enter a situation with preferences between different bundles of goods and choose the bundle that maximizes their utility. This choice takes place under constraints, most importantly the limitation of goods that an actor owns and therefore can exchange. Sociology has not been unaffected by this model of action. It entered Max Weber's typology of action under the name of "purposively rational action," though it took on some additional meaning in Weber's work as a whole, and has had an increased significance in sociology and political science since the 1960s mainly under the heading of "rational choice theory." The peak of this development was undoubtedly the publication of James Coleman's masterpiece *Foundations of Social Theory* in 1990.

The increased significance of the rational actor model in sociology, however, cannot distract from the fact that this understanding of action has been judged by many sociologists as alien to sociological thinking proper. The competition between economics and sociology is largely founded on radically opposed action theories. The most influential sociological alternative to rational actor theory has been the normative model of action. In it, action is not seen as based on individual preferences but analyzed as being anchored in normative orientations that contribute to the constitution of action goals and to the selection of means. Actors have a shared normative orientation that allows them to coordinate their acts. For Durkheim, but also for Parsons, the stability of social order was only possible because of such common normative action orientations.

The clear-cut opposition of rational actor theory on the one hand and the normative theory of action on the other easily leads to the failure of recognition of a common deficiency that both theories share. Both theories proceed from a notion of rationality and place all action that does not suit the model into a residual category of nonrational action. In economics rational action is contrasted with irrational action which is defined as the deviation from the optimal decision strategy. Vilfredo Pareto distinguished between logical action and nonlogical action, reserving the latter category for all action that did not fit into the first category. Even Max Weber's more differentiated typology of action follows a logic of gradual abandonment. While purposively rational action satisfies completely the conditions for rationality, the three other types are defined by their deficiencies judged from the standard provided by the first type: in value–rational action, consideration of the consequences of action is omitted; in affectual action, consideration of values; and in traditional action, consideration even of ends. The ideal remains an action that rationalizes ends, values, and consequences of action. This holds true independently of the exact determination of the notion of rationality, but the same dilemma can be found in normative theories of action. When we conceive of rationality as morally reflective behavior, this type will be called rational by normatively oriented theories. In opposition to theories that see utility maximization as the norm of rationality, such amoral orientations toward one's own interests are now put into the category of nonrationality.[1]

Defining action theory from a notion of rationality and contrasting the privileged concept of rationality with residual categories of nonrationality dramatizes discussions in action theory as a choice between different notions of rationality. Utilitarian and normative theories of action thus find a common discursive ground. For the theoretical understanding of action, however, the fixation on different concepts of rationality might omit more than it reveals. At the very least, it leaves unquestioned those presuppositions on which the utilitarian and the normative notion of rational action are based alike. Theories that proceed from a type of rational action

---

[1]Even Habermas (1984/1987), whose communicative notion of rationality certainly is the boldest and most promising new approach in the field of a comprehensive understanding of rationality, develops his types of action out of his types of rationality, and this leads to a rather poor version of *action* theory (see Joas, 1993, pp. 125–153). While we feel quite close to Habermas' theory of rationality, our views on action theory deviate sharply from Habermas' approach.

assume at least three things, whether they have a narrow or a comprehensive, a utilitarian or a normativist understanding of rationality. First, they assume the actor as being able to act in a purposeful manner. Second, they assume the actor as being able to control, to dominate, or to instrumentalize his or her own body. Third, they assume the autonomy of the individual actor toward his or her fellow actors and toward the environment.

While utilitarian and normative theories can admit that these presuppositions do not always hold, this does not have any consequences for their theoretical understanding of action. If an actor cannot clearly define the goals of his or her course of action, if bodily control is lost, or if autonomy cannot be maintained, the chances for rational decisions decrease. But this restricted empirical validity of the theory is attributed to a deficiency of the actor that can be ignored for theory construction because it does not affect the notion of rationality. An illustration of this can be found in the way rationalist theories react to the fact that human beings are not rational actors from the beginning of their lives on, but have to learn over many years how to act in order to enhance utility or to make moral judgments. Instead of incorporating these genetic processes as informative for the theoretical understanding of action, they are vastly ignored because they do not add anything to the predefined rational model of action.

We maintain that the fixation on the notion of rationality constitutes a crucial limitation of both utilitarian and normative theories of action. While these theories can be fruitful analytical tools if the tacit assumptions on which they are based are fulfilled, they remain partial theories of action because they do not systematically integrate the theoretical consequences that derive from the fact that in many instances the tacit assumptions are not fulfilled. By choosing the path of a genetic reconstruction of the three tacit assumptions, within the idea of rational action the central role that the creativity of action plays for the understanding of action and its coordination has to be demonstrated. This can here be done, of course, only in a summary way.

Intentionality

The rational actor model is based on an analytical action frame that focuses on means and ends as its central categories. It assumes that actors possess goals and apply means to achieve these goals while they take constraints on their possible courses of action into account. In this sense goals can be viewed as the causes of action. This teleological perspective on action not only has been the basis for utilitarian theories but has been advocated by classical sociologists such as Weber and Parsons as well. Sociological accounts within the teleological tradition typically take norms and values into consideration as well but otherwise subscribe to the same model of action.

Despite its dominant role in much of sociological theory the teleological model of action has not remained unquestioned within sociology. In modern sociological theory the most refined critique of it can be found in a book entitled *The Notion of Purpose and the Rationality of Systems* written by German sociologist Niklas Luhmann (1968).[2] On the basis of a critical assessment of Weber's theory of bureaucracy Luhmann rejects the idea that goals can provide sufficient explanation for the selection of means. The reason for this is that the complexity of social situations does not allow for the identification of the multiple causes and their interrelations, which lead to an outcome. It would be impossible for actors to analyze a situation fully enough to understand means–ends relationships accurately. Luhmann proposes instead to see

[2]Niklas Luhmann (1968), *Zweckbegriff und Systemrationalität*. Unfortunately, this book has never been translated into English. In American sociology it is not Luhmann's pathbreaking book but the development of the new institutionalism which caused a similar reorientation (see Powell & DiMaggio, 1991).

goal-setting from a functionalist perspective as a means to reduce the complexity of the situation. By setting a goal, the fluidity of human interaction is interrupted through "systematizing the experiential and behavioral potentialities that manifest themselves in natural experience and interpreting them in such a way that they become available for the purposes of comparison and thus accessible to rationalization" (Luhmann, 1968, p. 29; our translation). With regard to the model of ends and means, Luhmann sees it as fulfilling the selective function of perceiving and evaluating the consequences of actions.

Luhmann's critique of the means–ends scheme is usually read as an early step toward his radically functionalist systems theory. In this reading the critique of the teleological model of action provides reasons for leaving action theory altogether behind. Though this is undoubtedly a correct interpretation of Luhmann's further theoretical development, the reading tends to overlook at the same time that his critique of the teleological interpretation of action is based on phenomenological concepts and especially on the pragmatist theory of action as developed by John Dewey. Luhmann and Dewey drew radically different consequences for possible theory development, but they did so based on a fairly similar critique of the teleological model of action. In clear distinction from Luhmann, Dewey used the critique of the means–ends scheme for a radical reformulation of action theory. This opens a path for maintaining action theory in spite of the critique of its teleological version. This path is followed in the theory of the creativity of action.

Dewey's alternative to the teleological understanding of action sets out from the point that ends are not simply anticipations of future conditions that actors bring into being. In the radically "presentistic" metaphysics of pragmatism (Dewey, 1958 [1925]; Mead, 1932) goals belong to the present. Only as such they can become part of the action situation. The central notion Dewey introduces to express the role of goals for the organization of action is the concept of "ends-in-view." By this he refers to the fact that goals are not externally set but emerge in the action process itself in a reciprocal interaction between means and goals. At the beginning of an action process goals are frequently unspecific and only vaguely understood. They become clearer once the actor has a better understanding of the possible means to achieve the ends; even new goals will arise on the basis of newly available means. The more concrete understanding of goals or their change makes in turn a new perspective on available means possible. This reciprocal process between means and ends structures action. It anchors the notion of goals firmly in the action process itself and argues against the external setting of goals as advocated in teleological theories of action. This allows one to perceive perception and cognition not as acts preceding action but as part of the action process that is inherently connected to the situational context. Goal-setting does not take place as a cognitive act prior to action but is based on prereflective aspirations that are operative in the action situation. The aspirations are located in our bodies. The body's capabilities, habits, and ways of relating to the environment form the background to conscious goal-setting, i.e., to intentionality.

If this nonteleological understanding of intentionality provides the basis for a viable theory of action, it radically changes our picture of perception, the regulation of action, the setting of motives and plans, and the creation of goals. Perception now can be interpreted as an action-related phenomenon. The world exists not simply as an external counterpart to our internal self but is structured by our capacities for and experiences of action. It exists in the form of possible actions. Our perception is directed toward the situational context of what we perceive. Since the basic forms of our capacity for action lie in the intentional movement of our body in connection with locomotion, object manipulation, and communication, our world is initially structured according to these dimensions. In our perception we divide the world into categories such as accessible and inaccessible, familiar and unfamiliar, controllable and uncontrollable, responsive and unresponsive. Only if these action-related expectations are not met, the world transpires to be inaccessible and unfamiliar, uncontrollable or unresponsive for us. In such a situation it becomes an external object. This is, however, an exceptional situation. The typical relationship to the world is characterized by a familiarity that is anchored in our capacity for action.

A second change of our understanding of action due to the introduction of the nonteleological concept of intentionality affects the account of the regulation of action. The fact that every action takes place in a situation plays a role for the teleological theory of action only to the extent that an actor has to take into account the contingent conditions of the situation. These are the available means, the unalterable conditions, but also prevailing norms and values. For the theory of creativity of action the significance of the situation is far greater: Action is not only *contingent* on the structure of the situation but the situation is *constitutive* of action. This means that the situation is not simply a neutral field that actors enter with preset goals; instead, the situation itself exercises a regulative role for our responses in a specific action context. The ability to act presupposes that the actor judges the kind of situation he or she is in; thus, a judgment of the situation entails a judgment about the appropriateness of possible responses. A very accurate term for the conceptualization of the relationship between the actor and the situation has been introduced by Dietrich Böhler (1985), who speaks of a "quasi-dialogical" relationship. Quasi-dialogical means that actions can be understood as responses to demands by the situation. This shall not imply any kind of behavioral determinism of action. Actors do enter situations with goals, but, as the concept of ends-in-view suggests, action plans get changed and reformulated as a result of the confrontation with the situation.

This leads us to the third change in the understanding of action, namely, to the altered role of motives and plans for action. According to the teleological model of action, motives appear to be the cause of action and plans are seen as the anticipation of the course of action to reach the goal that is only put into practice in the actual action process. From the perspective of the theory of creativity of action, action can never be explained solely from the motives and the plans of the actor. The reason for this is that though plans and motives may place us in situations, they do not provide complete answers to the challenges actors confront in the situation. If action is based on our prereflective, practical ways of relating to the situation, the concrete course even of purely individual action can never fully be traced back to some specific intentions. Moreover, even designing a plan or formulating motives must be seen as products of prereflective aspirations and not as the factual causes of action.

This touches already on the fourth change in the understanding of action, namely, at the image we have of the very act of setting and creating goals. According to the teleological view actors design their goals independently from influences of the outside world. Talcott Parsons (1937) has stressed this point in his critique of utilitarianism and answered it by referring to the role of ultimate values for the socially coordinated setting of ends. As Harold Garfinkel (1984) has argued, this, however, is not a satisfactory answer because norms and values could only steer action if they would provide unequivocal answers on how to act in a situation. Garfinkel has persuasively argued, based on his microsociological experiments on social coordination, that this is not the case. An adequate theoretical understanding of values in human action has to conceptualize instead the interaction between the values embodied in prereflective aspirations and the situation where we establish which course of action accords with our values. This concretization or specification of values is an exercise in the creativity of action. In contrast to the teleological or the normative interpretation of action, goal-setting is understood as such a creative concretization of values. This refers again to a dialogical process between the actor and the situation.

Corporeality

Although the expositions on the first tacit assumption of teleological action theories would gain from further elaboration (but see Joas, 1996, pp. 148–167), we will now turn to the instrumentality of the body as the second tacit assumption. In rational actor theory, but also in Parsons' early version of action theory, the body plays only a marginal role as the locus of cognitive or evaluative mental processes. It is seen as a technical instrument for the processing and expression of information, intentions, and calculations. Otherwise it is simply assumed that the actor exercises an effective disciplinary control over his or her body. One can speak of a sort of theoretical prudishness in much of action theory (Turner, 1984). The anthropologies of Norbert Elias and Michel Foucault contributed to an analysis of the historical processes in which bodily control became a dominant aspect of modern culture and identity (Honneth & Joas, 1988). But it seems a fair criticism of these authors to say that they overgeneralize the findings of their historical research and overlook contradicting developments in the civilization process. A similar claim can be made with regard to action theories that ignore the unstable balances of instrumental and noninstrumental relationships to our bodies.

The type of phenomena we have in mind when we speak of a noninstrumental relationship to our body have been expressed in the theory of creativity of action (Joas, 1996, pp. 167–184) in the notions of "passive intentionality" and "meaningful loss of intentionality." They refer to the possibility of loosening the discipline over the body either as an intentional act or as a nonintentional response to a situation. An example for passive intentionality is the process of falling asleep. To repeat the thought, "I want to fall asleep now," again and again, after not having been able to fall asleep for several hours, is not only likely to create the opposite effect but also can be seen as a demonstration of the limits of active intentionality. We can, however, very well intentionally attempt to release control by accepting and sponsoring the prereflective intentions of our body and thereby reach the intended result: falling asleep. Examples from creative problem solving to sexuality can easily be added. "Meaningful loss of intentionality" is the term used for those forms of action in which we lose the ability to act rationally, because the ambiguity of a situation or its emotional quality are so overwhelming that the actor loses his distance to the situation and disciplinary control over his or her own actions. Laughing and weeping are examples for the meaningful loss of intentionality.

While these remarks give reason for the necessity of an anthropological basis for the theory of action, it also must be clarified *how* the role of the body shall be integrated into action theory. The first point here is that the body becomes part of our intentionality via the development of a "body image." This term refers to the way in which an actor experiences his or her body subjectively. The actor has a consciousness about the morphological structure of the body, its parts and its attitudes, its movements, and its boundaries. In the theory of creativity of action it is maintained that the body image is the result of an intersubjective process. Based on writings by Maurice Merleau-Ponty (1982) and George Herbert Mead, it is argued that the instrumental relationship to one's body presupposes the constitution of the "permanent object" and that the permanent object presupposes elementary abilities of role-taking (Joas, 1985). It implies that the formation of a body image is connected to the development of the communicative abilities of the child. This goes beyond theories of the body image that emphasized neurological mechanisms, psychological representations, or as in the case of Merleau-Ponty mostly tried to integrate the cognitive and the affectual dimensions of the body image.

The theory of creativity of action maintains that the relationship between actors and their bodies is shaped by the structures of interaction in which an actor develops. We can respond to bodily signals sensitively but we also can treat our bodies like an instrument that we attempt to subdue to our cognitive intentions. If the actor's body is not immediately given, but only via a body image, and if this body image is the result of an intersubjective process, then we find sociality right in the core of human agency. The term used to describe this aspect is "primary sociality," which means that sociality in this sense is not the result of conscious interaction but precedes the ability to act as an individual.

Sociality

This refers to the third tacit assumption of the rational action models. It is the least tacit of the three assumptions insofar as critical voices on this point always have been quite frequent and in a certain sense even constitutive for the discipline of sociology. For socialization research the question of the social conditions for the genesis of the self, of autonomous individuality, are crucial. Only the narrow versions of rational action simply presuppose the autonomy of individual actors and ignore the problem of the constitution of their autonomy. The normativist models are connected to a theory of the internalization of norms, and the theory of communicative action itself aims at a notion of primary intersubjectivity. This point will not be developed here in any detail (but see Joas, 1985, 1996, pp. 184–195). Only one possible objection against the thesis of primary sociality shall be discussed briefly. The objection is that sociality is only a genetic but not a structural precondition of human action. To refute this objection one has to face the eruptive forms of sociality in which the boundaries of the self are shattered. There are two main approaches to conceptualize the self-transcending experiences or primary sociality in mature persons. One goes back to romantic speculations about the possibility of a return to Dionysus and of the Dionysian as an evasion from the cultural *aporiae* of the modern age. This found its most stimulating expression in Nietzsche whose passionate interest in the self-enhancement of the creative personality sensitized him to the tension between creativity and the exclusionary mechanisms of a self that depends on closure and the maintenance of consistency. Nietzsche was willing to sacrifice identity for the sake of creativity, or, to put it better, to consider creative self-enhancement as a liberation from the coercion to be a determinate, that is, restricted individual. The other version allowed for an integration of creativity and the formation of a consistent self and considered Dionysian experiences as a form of the religious experience that collectivities need for their revitalization. Within sociology, this found its classical form in Durkheim's analysis of the elementary forms of religious life. Durkheim's analyses of collective effervescence and of the origins of the sacred do not refer to the genesis of obligatory rules or norms, but to the genesis of values and world constitutive ideals. The birth of the religious idea for Durkheim lies in the experience of a loss of self-identity. For him the experience of self-transcendence is not a primitive or irrational marginal phenomenon of sociality but the constitutive basis for any affectual social attachment to other individuals, collectivities, or values. From this attachment flow our deepest motives and the cohesion of our personalities. Hence, we have never reached action ability once and forever, but can feel the permanent necessity to reconstruct our identity faced with the unanticipated events of life.

THE "ACTION FRAME OF REFERENCE"
AND ITS ELABORATION

This brief summary of an attempt to genetically reconstruct the three tacit dimensions in both the rational and the normatively oriented approaches can answer only a few questions arising in the context of a systematic elaboration of the alternative conception. While such a full elaboration of the theory of creativity of action goes beyond the goals of this chapter, it is at least possible to present some of the main tasks on this agenda. This can be achieved by recalling the questions that arose in the long and rich debate about possible deficiencies of Parsons' action frame of reference (see Camic, 1989; Levine, 1980). For two related reasons, Parsons' (1937) *The Structure of Social Action* represents the appropriate reference point in action theory for measuring the advances made by the presented theoretical conceptualization. First, Parsons provided a definite critique of utilitarian theories of action and thereby achieved a crucial advancement within action theory. Second, the action frame of reference represents the most important systematic statement of action theory and as such has structured much of the later sociological theorizing about action in the 20th century. This significance of Parsons for the framing of later debates allows one to assess the achievements of the theory of creativity of action from its capability to address the systematic problems that have been identified in Parsons' early theorizing and have provided starting points for alternative conceptualizations in action theory. We do not have in mind here the intricate interpretive questions with respect to Parsons' interpretations of sociological classics or regarding the omission of other figures from his attempt at theoretical synthesis. It is exclusively the systematic aspect that is of importance for the further development of action theory.

The debate about the action frame of reference in Parsons' theory, which contained the actor, the situation of action, i.e., conditions and means, the goals of action, norms, and values, produced at least six major unsolved problems for future theory construction: (1) What is the appropriate place of the consequences of action? (2) How can the relationship between actors be integrated into the action frame? (3) How can the cognitive dimension become part of the action frame? (4) What are the limits of the means–end scheme for the analysis of action? (5) How are norms and values being specified in order to serve as orientations in concrete action situations? (6) How do norms emerge and values arise? This list of problems brings together the most relevant elements in the critiques of authors like Niklas Luhmann, Alfred Schutz, Stephen Warner, Harold Garfinkel, Anthony Giddens, and Alain Touraine. These authors quite often went beyond mere criticism and developed their own solutions of the problems or weak spots they had detected in Parsons' theory.

1. The first-mentioned problem had even been addressed in the Parsonian camp itself. In the much neglected chapter on Pareto in Parsons' (1937) *Structure of Social Action*, Parsons himself had important things to say about unintended consequences of action, but he did not really integrate these insights into the action frame of reference at this point of his intellectual development. This changed later on when Parsons and Robert Merton found in the role of unintended consequences of action major support for their plea in favor of functionalism. The epistemological critique of the logic of functionalist reasoning, however, led to a rediscovery of this topic as the point of departure for nonfunctionalist social theories, e.g., in the work of Anthony Giddens.

2. Parsons' action frame contains only one singular actor. It has been argued that the systematic reason for Parsons' omission of Simmel lay in the difficulties he had with the alternative assumption of taking social relationships as the point of departure. A similar point

could be made regarding the only partial integration of George Herbert Mead's achievements and the neglect of symbolic interactionism in the Parsonian school. The followers of Simmel and Mead and, in our days, Jürgen Habermas with his emphasis on communicative action have developed this point much farther.

3. The third question had already been raised in Alfred Schutz's phenomenological critique of Parsons with its emphasis on the subjective perspective of actors. Steven Warner (1978) wrote an important article in which he claimed that paying the cognitive element its due is one of the most pressing problems of action theory. In his last phase, Parsons seemed to take this suggestion seriously and began to incorporate Jean Piaget's cognitive psychology into his own theoretical approach. But again, mostly authors outside the immediate Parsonian tradition went further in this direction. On the basis of the phenomenological literature, Anthony Giddens introduced the important distinction between recognized and unrecognized conditions of action into the action frame of reference.

4. While Parsons stuck closely to the means–end scheme in his first major book and even chose a pertinent quotation from Max Weber for the motto of this work, in his later writings he came closer to integrating an expressivist model of action into his theory (Staubmann, 1995). As has been demonstrated above, the critique of the means–end scheme is crucial both for Luhmann's radicalization of Parsons' functionalism and for the pragmatist alternative.

5. The problem of how norms and values relate to concrete situations of action, whether we can simply assume this relationship to be one of "application" or whether we should rather see it as a creative process of ever risky specification became the crucial dividing line between Harold Garfinkel's "ethnomethodology" and Parsonianism in a narrower sense. Garfinkel had, of course, been influenced by phenomenology; he also could have found inspiration in the pragmatist writings. Ethnomethodology since the 1960s has produced an enormous amount of empirical microsociological findings on these processes of specification; it is an important task for action–theoretical work today to relate these findings back to the systematic elaboration of the action frame of reference.

6. The only authors who early on posed the question of the genesis of values in the context of debates about Parsons' action frame of reference were Alain Touraine, writing outside of the Parsonian school, and Shmuel Eisenstadt, arguing from within. In Touraine's case, the objection that Parsons could not explain the genesis of values was intimately bound up with a version of the ethnomethodological critique, which is directed at the problem of the situation-specific application of values. In his sociological research on industry Touraine had gained the experience that decisions mostly cannot be interpreted as merely applications of general principles to certain situations, but are rather the result of transactions between actors with heterogeneous interests and divergent power potentials (Touraine, 1964). While Touraine was initially in danger of regarding culture as a mere resource in power struggles, he increasingly moved away from this viewpoint and understands culture as intrinsically diverse and conflictual.

If we cannot put culture into a transcendental realm of values (or cognitions), we have to understand how it is not only effective in action but also how it arises from actions and the experiences they entail. Of all Parsons' successors, Shmuel Eisenstadt has placed the most emphasis on the problem of the genesis of values as a subject of research. His background in Martin Buber's philosophy of creativity provided him with the vantage point from which he could perceive such shortcomings in Parsons' work (Eisenstadt, 1995). This point is related to the objections mostly raised by cultural anthropologists and historians: that in his work Parsons does not ascertain "values" through deep hermeneutic penetration into cultures, nor does he represent them in terms of a "thick description" (Clifford Geertz) of their nature. For

Parsons, "values" are analytic constructs abstracted from a culture as a whole and then designated as responsible for concrete actions. This objection has been taken up within the Parsonian tradition by sociologists like Robert Bellah and Jeffrey Alexander. In our opinion, the problem of the genesis of values had already been addressed very forcefully in the pragmatist tradition, mostly in the writings on religion by William James and John Dewey. They derived their solution of this problem from an analysis of the experience of self-transcendence, which had also been so crucial for Durkheim's sociology of religion.

The pragmatist theory of action sketched above in its present form already has taken a number of the problems on this list into consideration. The pragmatist approach clearly goes beyond the means–end scheme and integrates the cognitive dimension. It introduces creativity into its analysis of the specification of norms and values. At least in its Meadian version, the concept of "primary sociality" allows one to avoid a monological concept of action from the outset. The interplay between intentions and the experience of unintended consequences of action also is crucial for the pragmatist model. In a book on the "genesis of values" problem, the pragmatist idea that values originate in experiences of self-transcendence has been elaborated in greater detail (Joas, 2000a). But instead of providing more details about these areas or going deeper into this agenda of the ongoing theoretical project to develop a theory of the creativity of action (see also Camic, 1998; Straub, 1999; Touraine, 1999), we will now illustrate the usefulness of such a pragmatist revision of action theory in a specific area of social theorizing, an area moreover that is usually considered to be a sphere of rational action so that rational action models may seem to be ideally suited for its analysis.

AN EMPIRICAL APPLICATION: COOPERATION AND CREATIVITY IN ECONOMIC ACTION

The paradigmatic status of rational actor theory in economics has made it the privileged starting point for the investigation of economic phenomena. The sociological critique, which has accompanied economic reasoning since the formation of sociology as an academic discipline, chose mostly the path of developing normative countermodels to the assumption of utility maximization. According to this reasoning, economic action cannot be understood as the maximization of individual utility but reflects social norms and values. At the very least the notion of utility maximization has to be understood not as a natural propensity but from its social origin.

The almost ritualized opposition between utilitarian and normative theories of action in understanding economic processes and structures makes it difficult for any alternative conceptualization of action to find recognition. That such an alternative is desirable becomes apparent from the realization that teleological action theories are ill-suited to address crucial problems that become relevant in economic decision-making contexts: Modern economic settings usually are characterized by a high complexity of parameters that determine the causal structure of the situation but cannot be grasped comprehensively through rational calculation. This creates uncertainty for actors with regard to choosing the optimal strategy, a problem that exists independently from the question of which goal to pursue. In complex situations the goal of utility maximization cannot be translated into an optimizing strategy (Beckert, 1996, 2002). The issue becomes even more difficult if goals can only be described vaguely, not for normative but for logical reasons, as it is the case in innovative activities, which are concerned with the "not yet known." The intentionality of actors cannot be guided by goals, i.e., the telos of action cannot be its cause, if means–ends relationships cannot be recognized at the beginning of the action process.

This takes up Luhmann's critique of the rational actor theory, which has been presented at the beginning of this chapter. The nonteleological theory of intentionality provides concepts for understanding this crucial action problem in economic contexts because the notion of intentionality it advocates is firmly rooted in the dynamic interplay between the goals actors pursue and the evolving features of the situation. To give proof to the claim that the theory of the creativity of action can be fruitfully applied to the understanding of core economic processes, it is useful not to analyze economic action as such but to investigate the problems actors confront in concrete settings. Two such settings, which have created large amounts of research from the rational actor perspective, are cooperation and innovation.

Rational actor theory explains cooperation with reference to rational calculation. In game theory actors choose the strategy that gives them the highest payoff, given their tolerance for risk. This leads to the well-known paradox that under certain conditions cooperation will not take place, though both actors would benefit from it. Responses to this paradox from within the rational actor model refer either to iteration, i.e., that the relation between the players will continue over many rounds of the game, or to the modification of external conditions. Threats or gratification, the investment into the inducement of norms or the installation of control mechanisms change the payoff matrix for players and give rational reasons to cooperate in situations where actors would otherwise not cooperate. Normative critiques of these models explain cooperation not based on utility maximizing but based on social norms that actors have internalized and follow even if it would be in their individual interest not to do so. Though this is a possible explanation for cooperation in situations where rational actor theory fails, it is based on the problematic assumption that actors willingly transcend their individual interests and that their partners will do so as well. Especially in the context of modern market economies this assumption is quite heroic, since it is immediately confronted with the free-rider problem.

But the rational actor model is likewise based on assumptions that are difficult to maintain in real-world situations. Here, it is not the morality of actors but their calculative capabilities that are systematically overestimated. To illustrate this point we turn to some of the calculative demands that are presupposed by the theory. Computer models show that cooperation in prisoner dilemma situations increases if the game is iterated. The rationale behind this is that actors do not defect if they expect higher gains from future cooperation which they will forgo if they cheat their partner now. To make a rational decision whether to cooperate or to defect, however, depends on how many rounds the game will actually be played. There has to be at least knowledge about the expectations that each player has with regard to the length of the game. Otherwise, players follow strategies where they either cooperate too long or not long enough for attaining optimal payoffs. Moreover, to play a strategy successfully depends on the visibility of the moves the other players make. If the other players can hide their moves, a rational reaction is impossible, as Robert Axelrod (1984, p. 100) has noted: "An individual must not be able to get away with defecting without the other individuals being able to retaliate effectively. The response requires that the defecting individual not be lost in a sea of anonymous others."

Hence, to make rational decisions is much more difficult than suggested by clear-cut textbook models. While the mentioned problems can, at least in part, be overcome in labora-tory experiments through simplification of the modeled situations and sheer computational capacity, it is quite unlikely that an actor in a real situation will indeed understand all the parameters proper to make a rational decision. While the pragmatist approach to cooperation maintains that actors may well have the intention to increase their welfare, it proceeds from the concrete action situation and advocates a fundamentally different approach as to how actors reach decisions. In a very condensed formulation it is the interpretation of the situation in acts of role-taking that explains cooperation.

The situation consists of reciprocal expectations that actors hold with regard to their mutual intentions, needs, motives, goals, and strategies. According to Mead's concept of the self, it is the ability of the actor to take the role of the other and to form expectations about his attitudes (Mead, 1934; see also Joas, 1993, pp. 217–237, 2000b). Action can only be reciprocally oriented because of the ability of role-taking. To conceive of action as intersubjectively constituted in role-taking offers an explanation for the anthropological presuppositions for coordinated social acts. But it does in addition to this also shed light on the question of how a person comes to believe that his cooperative move will not be exploited. This is the core problem of prisoner dilemma type situations.

In the process of role-taking it is not the case that an individual consciousness contemplates monologically on the possible reactions of an external object world (be it material or social) from which it is otherwise divorced. Instead, the dialogical processes through which the actor makes the world intelligible are themselves socially shaped by the representation of expectations from other actors. This is reflected in Mead's notion of social control which states that the reaction of an actor is guided by his reflection on the attitude of the group (Mead, 1964, p. 290). In this perspective, goals but also strategies have their origin not in the isolated individual consciousness but reflect the individual's interpretation of expectations of the group. These expectations form "constitutive expectancies" for actors that pattern a cognitive and practical background for decisions. Constitutive expectancies are created and reinforced in social action and supply a basis on which actors can increasingly generalize the expectation of reciprocity of action. The "rules of the game" or the "generalized other" refer to a common basis in the situation that makes cooperation partly independent from intimate knowledge of the person we cooperate with. The expectations are anchored in culturally or institutionally rooted understandings but also in power asymmetries between actors. In fact, economic theory itself can be seen as an important part of this social horizon, shaping expectations and actions of actors in economic contexts (see Callon, 1998). The generalized expectations predispose the decision on cooperation from a social horizon without assuming the elimination of contingency inherent in the situation. It remains always possible for an actor to also disappoint expectations. The freedom to choose a noncooperative strategy creates a fragility in cooperative relations, which makes their implosion an ever-present possibility. Though the fluidity of the situation is limited by the structuring impact of social rules, including legal regulations and reputation, the maintenance of desirable constitutive expectations of other actors remains, from a pragmatist perspective, a continuous task for actors for whose fulfillment they must rely on participation and communication with actors who are relevant for the cooperative act.

In the realm of the economy this communicative reinforcement of cooperation can be easily observed, for instance, in the extended marketing activities of firms. The cooperative problem can be described as a principal agent situation in which the company (agent) holds information about the product that is usually unavailable to the customer. To prevent the breakdown of the market the company has to convince potential customers that it does not take advantage of the asymmetric distribution of information. Banks, for instance, communicate especially the topic of trust to reassure their customers of the security of their investments and prevent a meltdown through panic withdrawal of assets. Even product recalls, although they are costly for companies, provide an opportunity to communicate the company's concern for the safety of its customers. Communicative reinforcement of cooperative relationships also takes place through performative self-portrayal "on stage" (Goffman). As Giddens (1991, p. 85) has pointed out, expert systems signal trustworthiness through communicative performances of their representatives at entrance points. Lawyers show confidence for winning the case for their client in personal conversations as do flight attendants before takeoff through the performance of ritualized routines. This anchors the willingness to cooperate firmly in the communicative structure of the situation itself. While the pragmatist understanding of cooperation allows one to explain cooperative moves in situations where rational actor theory would expect defection, at the same time it makes the fragility of cooperation apparent. It rejects a model of action that sees decisions on cooperation as a calculative contemplation or as the application of internalized values. In an important theoretical contribution to economic sociology Neil Fligstein (1997, pp. 33*ff*) has identified the ability to induce cooperation as the crucial social skill of strategic actors and as an important prerequisite for the emergence of stable social fields.

The significance of innovation for the economic growth of modern capitalist societies is self-evident. For those not familiar with the history of economics it might be surprising that the integration of endogenic change into economic theory has been one of the most puzzling problems for economics in the 20th century. These problems can ultimately be traced to a specific paradox of innovation: Optimal strategies for innovative activities could only be devised if we would know at the outset what the innovation is. But if we know the innovation, there is no need for innovation anymore. The two principal questions relating to innovation are first the determination of optimal levels of investments for innovations and second the actual understanding of processes of innovative activities. With regard to the latter question, which will be discussed here, there are answers based on both variants of the teleological understanding of action: the rational actor model and normative theories.

Conceptualizations that proceed from the background of the rational actor model see innovative processes as starting with the setting of goals that provide a comparative standard for the evaluation of different means, i.e., the suggested solutions to the problem. One crucial methodological instrument is the phase-model, which portrays innovative processes as based on a plan that is structured in several independent phases and guides the activities of the innovator. There are, of course, more or less sophisticated phase models, but they all come together in subscribing to a teleological interpretation of innovative processes, in which the cognitively recognized end-stage directs the intentional activity of the designer.

Normative theories of innovation are not very widespread, but one attempt has been made by Talcott Parsons and Neil Smelser (1956) in their book *Economy and Society*. According to them the motivation to innovate is rooted in the personality system of actors that has been socialized for an efficient use of resources. Innovative processes start out of a conflict between the personality system and the integrative system of the economy, i.e., the organization of the labor process. The conflict emerges if resources are used inefficiently and is resolved through efficiency-increasing innovations.

The teleological understanding of innovation has been criticized on the basis of empirical studies of actual design processes. The interpretation of innovation as an optimizing problem would presuppose that the task of innovation could be articulated as a well-formed instrumental problem. This is not the case, however, because "design processes are inherently ill-defined, and as such possess poorly specified initial conditions, allowable operations and goals" (Eckersley, 1988, p. 87). As a consequence of this, ends can only stand in an unspecified and unclear way at the beginning of an innovative process. Empirical studies indicate even that ends are developed in the process of invention and become entirely clear only when the innovation process has been completed. As Donald Schön (1983, p. 68) has argued: The designer "does not keep means and ends separate, but defines them interactively as he frames the problematic situation. He does not separate thinking from doing, ratiocinating his way to the decision which he must later convert to action." This finding, which has been confirmed in numerous empirical studies on technological innovations coincides with John Dewey's concept of "ends-in-view," which was presented here in the context of a non-teleological concept of intentionality. According to this concept ends are loosely defined action plans that structure current action on the basis of the perception of the situation.

The correspondence between empirical design studies and the theory of creativity of action becomes apparent also in the description of the research process itself. Donald Schön (1983) summarized the formation and clarification of goals for innovation as a "dialogue" between the designer and the situation in which at the beginning only vaguely understood problems and solutions become clearer until a solution has been reached. This constitutive situation relatedness of innovation finds theoretical backing in Mead's discussion of instrumental action. For Mead the way of appropriation of physical objects is not so distinct from communication with other actors. As in social interaction, the relationship to physical objects demands the actor to take the role of that object. The designer has to indicate to himself expected characteristics of the object, for example, that a brick has a certain weight. By indicating these expectations he takes the role of the object and anticipates its "reaction." The actual lifting of the brick will either confirm the expectation or create a surprise if it is much lighter or much heavier than expected. Then the relationship to the physical object will change. The discrepancy between the perception of a problem in a situation and routines blocks the unreflected continuation of action. The routinized action flow will be interrupted and designers are forced into what Schön (1983) has termed "reflection-in-action," a reflective mode that corresponds to the pragmatist notion of reconstruction. This reflective mode leads actors into an experimental "conversation" with the indicated physical objects ("the situation") until the inquiry has led to a new line of action: a solution to the problem. If one understands innovations as taking place in complex situations, the process of reflection-in-action cannot be depicted as a rational deliberation about means based on known ends. Instead, the "conversation" with the situation is based on the meaning given to objects in interpretations. For this the designer takes the role of the object. At the same time he perceives the characteristics and possible applications of the physical object on the background of the representation of the generalized other. The generalized other can be seen as a frame through which the situation is simultaneously conceived and structured. This includes not only general knowledge on the characteristics of physical objects but also value judgments. It is this expectational background that structures the situation for the innovator. He or she can experiment with the problem until a discovery has been made that qualifies as a solution. In pragmatist terms this solution is intersubjectively created since the generalized other, i.e., the expectational background, is always socially constituted.

CONCLUSION

Whereas models of rational action apply normative preconditions to the study of action, this is not the case with a theory of the creativity of action. The models of rational action, unless they do not pretend to be merely normative, inevitably force phenomena of action to fit the concepts found in the model, or else they must distinguish one concrete, rational kind of action from the other concrete, less rational types of action. By contrast, a reconstructive introduction of the tacit assumptions found in models of rational action that is informed by the overarching idea of creativity from the beginning is aimed at discovering the specific characteristics of *all* human action. Such a revised theory is concerned not just with one specific type of creative action, but with the creativity of human action as such. This, of course, does not imply that all human actions are said to contain the same degree of creativity in contrast to routines and habits. This cannot be so for the simple reason that every action theory that takes basic pragmatist ideas as its point of departure must assume that creatively found solutions to an action problem will be absorbed into new "beliefs," or more precisely into altered routines. This means that even acts of the utmost creativity assume the preexistence of a bedrock of underlying routine actions and external conditions that are simply taken as given (see Camic, 1986). There are naturally large differences between various acts and actors with regard to creativity; however, an empirical, differential psychology and sociology of creativity is a completely different matter. This, too, would have to start with a general theory of action in order to examine concrete types of creative action, and here we are asserting that such a general theory should regard creativity as a dimension that is present in all human action and should interpret routine as a result of creativity. Consequently, such a general action theory does not contain value judgments on concrete instances of creativity. From this perspective, creativity in itself is neither good nor bad; there are many reasons why routine could be considered praiseworthy, and many a vision of permanent aesthetic or political creativity is a vision of terror that would overtax human capabilities. Whether a particular creative act is good or bad can only be settled in a discourse. Yet the search for a normative agency to justify validity claims is not the same as the search for a model to describe in empirical terms how new validity claims arise.

The advantages of revising action theory in this way extend far beyond the immediate bounds of action theory itself. This has been elaborated in this chapter with regard to cooperation and innovation as two crucial activities in economic contexts. In addition to this, organizations could be analyzed independently of the rational actor model in order to explore the unlikely and highly contingent character of the rational type. In the theory of social movements we also find examples of the consequences of rationalist prejudice, such as the widespread idea that clear goals held by individual actors or the group as a whole are the driving force behind the movements. The theory of the creativity of action would proceed from a radically different starting point. And finally, in a theory of history and the analysis of present-day society, rational models of action theory show an affinity to those interpretations that consider historical developments to be more or less linear "processes of rationalization." What tends to be forgotten here is that, even when trends toward rationality can be empirically observed, they should not be universalized, as there will always be spheres of life and some actors who do not passively submit to the rationalization process. Their resistance sparks countermovements, which may end up prevailing over the tendencies toward rationality (Joas, 2000c). These arenas of research hint at the fact that, contrary to a widespread assumption, action theory is not only suitable for the analysis of microsociological phenomena; it also can serve as the basis for the development of a macrosociological theory liberated from the fallacies of functionalism and evolutionism.

REFERENCES

Axelrod, R. (1984). *The evolution of cooperation.* New York: Basic Books.

Beckert, J. (1996). What is sociological about economic sociology? Uncertainty and the embeddedness of economic action. *Theory and Society, 25,* 803–840.

Beckert, J. (2002). *Beyond the market. The social foundations of economic efficiency.* Princeton, NJ: Princeton University Press. (In German: Campus Verlag, 1997)

Böhler, D. (1985). *Rekonstruktive Pragmatik. Von der Bewußtseinsphilosophie zur Kommunikationsreflexion: Neubegründung der praktischen Wissenschaften und Philosophie.* Frankfurt: Suhrkamp Verlag.

Callon, M. (1998). Introduction: The embeddedness of economic markets in economics. In M. Callon (Ed.), *The laws of the market* (pp. 1–57). Oxford: Blackwell Publishers.

Camic, C. (1986). The matter of habit. *American Journal of Sociology, 91,* 1039–1087.

Camic, C. (1989). "Structure" after 50 years: The anatomy of a charter. *American Journal of Sociology, 95,* 38–107.

Camic, C. (1998). Restructuring the theory of action. *Sociological Theory, 16,* 284–291.

Coleman, J. (1990). *Foundations of social theory.* Cambridge, MA: Harvard University Press.

Dewey, J. (1958). *Experience and nature.* London: Open Court.

Eckersley, M. (1988). The form of design processes: A protocol analysis study. *Design Studies, 9,* 86–94.

Eisenstadt, S. (1995). *Power, trust, and meaning. Essays in sociological theory and analysis.* Chicago: University of Chicago Press.

Fligstein, N. (1997). *Fields, power, and social skill: A critical analysis of the new institutionalism.* Unpublished paper, Berkeley, University of California.

Garfinkel, H. (1984). *Studies in ethnomethodology.* Cambridge: Polity Press.

Giddens, A. (1984). *The constitution of society.* Cambridge: Polity Press.

Giddens, A. (1991). *Modernity and self-identity.* Stanford, CA: Stanford University Press.

Habermas, J. (1984/1987). *Theory of communicative action.* T. McCarthy (Trans.). Boston: Beacon Press.

Honneth, A., & Joas, H. (1988). *Social action and human nature.* R. Meyer (Trans.). Cambridge: Cambridge University Press.

Joas, H. (1985). *G. H. Mead. A contemporary re-examination of his thought.* Cambridge, MA: MIT Press.

Joas, H. (1993). *Pragmatism and social theory.* Chicago: University of Chicago Press.

Joas, H. (1996). *The creativity of action.* Chicago: University of Chicago Press.

Joas, H. (2000a). *The genesis of values.* Cambridge: Polity Press.

Joas, H. (2000b). The emergence of the new: Mead's theory and its contemporary potential. In G. Ritzer & B. Smart (Eds.), *Handbook of social theory* (pp. 89–99). London: Sage.

Joas, H. (2000c). *Kriege und Werte. Studien zur Gewaltgeschichte des 20. Jahrhunderts.* Weilerswist: Velbrück. (English translation in preparation)

Levine, D. (1980). *Simmel and Parsons.* New York: Arno.

Luhmann, N. (1968). *Zweckbegriff und Systemrationalität.* Frankfurt/Main: Suhrkamp.

Mead, G. H. (1932). *Philosophy of the present.* La Salle, IL: Open Court.

Mead, G. H. (1964). The genesis of the self and social control. In A. J. Reck (Ed.), *George Herbert Mead: Selected Writings* (pp. 267–293). Chicago and London: University of Chicago Press.

Mead, G. H. (1934). *Mind, self, and society.* Chicago: University of Chicago Press.

Merleau-Ponty, M. (1982). *Phenomenology of perception,* C. Smith (Trans.). London: Routledge.

Parsons, T. (1937). *The structure of social action.* New York: McGraw Hill.

Parsons, T., & Smelser, N. (1956). *Economy and society. A study in the integration of economic and social theory.* Glencoe, IL: Free Press.

Powell, W., & DiMaggio, P. (Eds.). (1991). *The new institutionalism in organizational analysis.* Chicago: University of Chicago Press.

Schön, D. (1983). *The reflective practitioner. How professionals think in action.* New York: Basic Books.

Staubmann, H. (1995). *Die Kommunikation von Gefühlen. Ein Beitrag zur Soziologie der Ästhetik auf Grundlage von Talcott Parsons' Allgemeiner Theorie des Handelns.* Berlin: Duncker und Humblot.

Straub, J. (1999). *Handlung, Interpretation, Kritik. Grundzüge eienr textwissenschaftlichen Handlungs- und Kulturpsychologie.* Berlin: de Gruyter.

Touraine, A. (1964). *Production de la societé.* Paris: Éditions du Seuil.

Touraine, A. (1999). Preface to the French translation of H. Joas, *The creativity of action* (pp. I–VII). Paris: du Cerf.

Turner, B. (1984). *The body and society. Explorations in social theory.* Oxford, England: Blackwell.

Warner, S. (1978). Toward a redefinition of action theory: Paying the cognitive element its due. *American Journal of Sociology, 83,* 1317–1349.

Weber, M. (1968). Basic sociological categories. In M. Weber, *Economy and society.* G. Roth & C. Wittich (Trans.). New York: Bedminster Press.

CHAPTER 15

Accounts of Conduct in Interaction

Interruption, Overlap, and Turn-Taking

EMANUEL A. SCHEGLOFF

INTRODUCTION

The opening sentences of Max Weber's (1978, p. 4) *Economy and Society*, it may be recalled, read as follows:

> Sociology ... is a science concerning itself with the interpretive understanding of social action and thereby with a causal explanation of its course and consequences. We shall speak of "action" insofar as the acting individual attaches a subjective meaning to his behavior—be it overt or covert, omission or acquiescence. Action is "social" insofar as its subjective meaning takes account of the behavior of others and is thereby oriented in its course.

Weber illustrated the point of these discriminations by the case of two cyclists who might be imagined as approaching an intersection at right angles to one another with a building blocking mutual visual access. The collision which results, Weber said, was not a "social action" in the sense he was concerned to establish, though the aftermath of recriminations which followed it almost certainly were. What Weber (1978, p. 23) wrote was:

> Not every type of contact of human beings has a social character; this is rather confined to cases where the actor's behavior is meaningfully oriented to that of others. For example, a mere collision of two cyclists may be compared to a natural event. On the other hand, their attempt to avoid hitting each other, or whatever insults, blows, or friendly discussion might follow the collision, would constitute "social action."

For all practical purposes, that is the last we hear of social action at that primordial level of direct interaction between societal members in *Economy and Society*; thereafter, the focus shifts to bureaucracy, legitimation formulae, administrative staffs, systems of law, rational foundations of music, religious worldviews, patriachalism and patrimonialism, political and hierocratic domination, the city, and the like. What happened to the two cyclists?

EMANUEL A. SCHEGLOFF • Department of Sociology, University of California, Los Angeles, California 90095.

Handbook of Sociological Theory, edited by Jonathan H. Turner. Kluwer Academic / Plenum Publishers, New York, 2002.

A moment's reflection suggests that, if indeed "sociology ... is a science concerning itself with the interpretive understanding of social action," and "action is 'social' insofar as its subjective meaning takes account of the behavior of others and is thereby oriented in its course" (Weber, 1978, p. 4) then the discipline should be sustainedly preoccupied with settings on a scale at which analysts can address actors engaged in action which "takes account of the behavior of others and is thereby oriented in its course" (p. 4). Direct interaction between persons is the most obvious site for such inquiry, as Weber's own example suggests.

So why did Weber not pursue it? Perhaps it involved (in addition to his own prior preparation, commitments, and scholarship, which led in other directions) his recognition that serious work along such lines could not survive for long and thrive by *imagining* how people conduct themselves, or by relying on consensually stipulated recollections of scenes one had observed casually or been party to oneself. These days, however, the development of technology has made it possible to record many such scenes of interaction and to document at a level of detail that Weber might well not have imagined how a participant's action "takes account of the behavior of others and is thereby oriented in its course" (p. 4). The literature of conversation analysis (CA) is full of such demonstrations.

Consider, for example, Goodwin's (1979) analysis of the production of a single sentence at the dinner table. John begins to announce that he has stopped smoking, but as his gaze traverses the table, he finds neither of the two adults who are the dinner guests looking at him and thereby embodying themselves as aligned recipients of his talk. His wife *is* so aligned, but for her it is not news that he has stopped smoking and therefore that is not an appropriate "sayable." John then modifies his utterance in the course of its production by adding "one week ago today, actually," making the turn into the sort of utterance (registering an "anniversary") that might be news, and thus properly sayable, to the only person present who is an aligned recipient for it. Goodwin's analysis is considerably more detailed than this and is grounded in repeatedly observable videotape of the scene, in which can be tracked moment by moment where John is gazing, what he sees, what the import is for his utterance-to-that-point, how the utterance is changed "on the fly," where he looks next, what he sees, and so on. Surely this is an exemplification precisely of Weber's (1978) proposed focus on action which "takes account of the behavior of others and is thereby oriented in its course" (p. 4). The topic of the present chapter—"interruption"—offers another exemplification even more resonant with Weber's own anecdotal example.

The empirical arena examined here takes Weber's illustration of the collision of bicycle riders, extracts its key formal and defining feature—the circumstance of more than one person trying to occupy a "position" that can accommodate only one—and pursues its study in a setting where it is vastly recurrent, structurally endemic, and potentially profoundly consequential because the setting is one through which all the institutions of society get much of their work done, namely, talk-in-interaction and especially conversation, which I take to be the primordial site of sociality. This is an arena and a phenomenon within it that has been explored by social scientists working within mainstream paradigms as a strategic site in which to investigate the operation in interaction of features of larger-scale social organization such as power, status, hierarchy, gender, and the like, often in experimental or quasi-experimental investigations (see the following section). For such interests, what is promised is an account of an interactional mechanism by which the effects otherwise represented by conceptual linkages or statistical associations might observably be produced by the participants, and this outcome exemplifies a more general implication for accounts of actual conduct in sociological and other social scientific research enterprises. But his promise is best reserved for the end of the chapter, after its substance has been explicated.

INTERRUPTION

"Interruption," often considered part of the relatively superficial species of normative regulation and violation we term "etiquette," was moved into a position of greater seriousness by the initiative taken by West and Zimmerman in the mid-to-late 1970s (West, 1979; West & Zimmerman, 1983; Zimmerman & West, 1975). In an effort to bring the resources of conversation analysis to bear on topics of greater visibility and already established concern to a broader audience, they undertook a series of studies examining interruption in the context of dyadic interactions of varying gender composition, an initiative of interest to a broad sociological and social scientific constituency, not to mention a feminist one, and a more general, extra-academic one (as witnessed by coverage in the popular magazine *Psychology Today*). The upshot taken from this work can be put most roughly as, "men interrupt women much more than women interrupt men."

In the years that followed (the mid-to-late 1980s), this line of inquiry and its results engendered (if I may put it that way) a range of contrary stances and reported findings (e.g., the series of publications by Murray and his colleagues, inter alia; cf. Murray, 1985, 1988; Murray & Covelli, 1988). The upshot of many of these reports, largely in the context of preoccupations with gender relations, whether from a feminist point of view or other, can be put most roughly as "No they don't," and/or "That's not the way to look at it, study it, interpret it, etc."

At the same time, other investigators extended the effort to relate interruption to aspects of social structure and social organization in other directions. For example, taking interruption as an indicator and instrument of hierarchy and dominance relationships, they deployed it in studies of small groups of various sorts to explore such topics as whether dominance relationships were fundamentally grounded in gender categories or whether gender was itself simply (or not so simply) an index of or proxy for status and power relationships (e.g., Kollock, Blumstein, & Schwartz, 1985; Smith-Loven & Brody, 1989, inter alia). The upshot taken from this work can be put most roughly as, "It depends." The upshot of a review of this entire domain of literature and its variants in the mid-1990s (James & Clarke, 1993) roughly can be characterized as "indeterminate," that is, that few conclusions can be said to be supported other than that men do not interrupt more and that not all interruptions are disruptive or dominating. This chapter undertakes to revisit the topic of "interruption" under conversation-analytic and ethnomethodological auspices,[1] to clarify how interruption figures in a technical account of conversational interaction, and to reconsider and (re-)assess its status as an analytic tool for more traditional and mainstream sociological concerns.[2]

---

[1]At the time this line of work was being launched, conversation analysis and ethnomethodology, although already somewhat drifting apart, were rather more kindred undertakings than they have since become. Furthermore, some recent publications (e.g., Lynch, 1993) have characterized the work of the 1960s and 1970s as a kind of proto-ethnomethodology or precursor to more contemporary work, which in this view is "echt" ethnomethodology. I use the term "ethnomethodology" here to refer to work from the 1960s and 1970s, and in particular one line of work developed by my late colleague Harvey Sacks concerning "membership categorization devices," which was at the time still and even especially valued by ethnomethodologists as an important element of that program of studies.

[2]The preceding three paragraphs include citations to treatments of interruption from very different points of view, with varied theoretical, methodological, and disciplinary commitments, not to mention political ones. The early work of West and Zimmerman, for example, represented its authors' efforts to bring their understanding of then-current work in conversation analysis to bear on gender relations, using interruption as a kind of indicator or case-in-point. Much of the literature critical of their work distanced itself from that resource, out of either problematic understanding, disagreement, or both. Still other streams of literature did not treat the connection to conversation analysis as relevant. It is neither possible nor in my judgment necessary to incorporate in the present discussion a differentiated comparative treatment of this literature or these literatures. References to "the literature" in the remainder of the

"Interruption" is ordinarily (that is, vernacularly) used to mean a starting up of an intervention by one person while some undertaking by another is in progress. And it often is used to mean not only a *starting up* of an intervention, but also, as we say, "not letting them finish," a "full-fledged interruption" we might call it, what some of the literature in this area refers to as "successful interruption." The *Oxford English Dictionary* codifies both components when it offers as its account of "interrupt": "to break in upon (a person) while doing something, esp. speaking, to hinder or cause to stop..."

There are, of course, various sorts of units that occur in "speaking" by which and into which "speaking" is organized. Children who have successfully learned to avoid "interrupting" by not talking while someone else *is* may find themselves bewildered to be hushed up upon starting to talk when the room is quiet and to be told nonetheless "not to interrupt." Yet they encounter this contingency if they have not yet learned to analyze the organization of storytelling in conversation and to recognize when a storytelling was "over." So also do they encounter this contingency if they have not yet sufficiently grasped the practices of topic-talk in conversation so as to recognize when some current topic has been brought to possible closure or so as to know how to segue step-by-step from where the talk currently is to what one means to talk about. So stories, topics, and other structured activities that can be pursued in talk-in-interaction (for example, list-making), are vulnerable to "interruption" in the sense conveyed by the *Oxford English Dictionary* as is any structured conduct that has a trajectory, one that other events or courses of conduct can intersect before they have reached a recognizable (or plausibly claimable) ending. It is notable, then, that virtually the only unit of talk-in-interaction that has been discriminably targeted in the voluminous literature on interruption is the "turn," that is, the basic unit of talking (in interaction) per se. Although interrupting another may gain its sharpest profile when a story or other such unit is in progress, there is little in the literature that discriminates such interruption from other instances of "break[ing] in upon (a person) while doing something, esp. speaking, to hinder or cause to stop..." (*Oxford English Dictionary*). It is to the turn, then, that we must turn and to its deployment and disposition in talk-in-interaction as organized by systems of turn-taking, for it is by reference to the turn—and its rights and obligations—that "interruption" gets its import.

POINT OF DEPARTURE:
INTERRUPTION OR OVERLAP

The occasion for much of the literature on interruption (and the analytic leverage for the West–Zimmerman work) was one of the central points in the 1974 paper by Sacks, Schegloff, and Jefferson (henceforth SSJ) on the turn-taking organization for conversation, namely, that a key design feature for turn-taking in conversation is an orientation to one party speaking at a time; that is, no more than one at a time and no less than one at a time. Among the most common reactions to this claim was the search for counterexamples, and the most common counterexample put forth by critics was that of "interruption" as the most obvious departure from "no more than one at a time;" given all the occurrences of interruption, the argument went, how can one take seriously the claim that people talk one-at-a-time.

There is much that is incorrect in this line of critique, most importantly that failures of

---

chapter for the most part concern usages, such as the term "interruption" itself, common across otherwise divergent stances. Where I have inadvertently thereby slighted intraliterature differences critical to the field and/or offensive to authors, I regret having done so.

some organized set of practices or operations to work as designed, even on many occasions, is not evidence that it was not designed to work that way or that it does work that way (Schegloff, 2000, pp. 2–3). But for present purposes the key observation should be that, technically speaking, the potential problematic event of this sort for the SSJ account of turn-taking is "more than one talking at a time," and the occurrence in the world that embodies that is not in the first instance "interruption" but "overlap," which is precisely "more than one party talking at a time." The question posed by the occurrence of such events in conversation (and other talk-in-interaction) is: how is overlap dealt with when it occurs in conversation? If nothing special happens, if no note is taken of it, if its occurrence engenders no consequences in the talk or other conduct in the interaction that follows, then there are strong grounds for arguing that the claims of SSJ's account of the turn-taking organization are wrong. If overlap does engender consequences, and in particular consequences designed to eliminate it, then there are grounds for arguing that the SSJ account is correct and describes the operative orientations of parties to conversation.

The Practices of Talking in Overlap

The matter of how overlap is dealt with in conversation and its implications is dealt with in a companion paper to this chapter on overlap management and resolution (Schegloff, 2000). Because its results are germane to the topic of this chapter, I summarize them below in a series of points; in the companion paper they are developed in substantially greater detail, with data (which is sharply limited here because of space constraints) and with analysis that makes explicit how conduct while talking simultaneously embodies the features of social action insisted on by Weber in his explication of social action. In the following section, I take up the question of how the findings about overlap resolution, as well as ones about overlap onset, relate to interruption and the literature about it:

1. Several classes of overlapping talk do appear to be treated nonproblematically in conversation and are not apt subjects for an account of "overlap management" or "overlap resolution" (Schegloff, 2000, pp. 4–6 for matters treated in this paragraph). Overlapping talk from separate conversations is, of course, not a departure from a constraint to have "one speaker at a time in a single conversation." But four configurations of simultaneous talk also are in the first instance beside the point for an overlap resolution device. These are (1) "terminal overlaps" (in which a next speaker starts a next turn by virtue of a current speaker's incipient finishing, but overlaps a bit of its end; (2) "continuers" (such as "uh huh"), which pass an opportunity to take a full turn, while they display an understanding that current speaker is producing an extended turn or discourse unit that is not yet complete; (3) various forms of "conditional access to the turn," in which the intervention of a recipient of a not-yet-complete turn is accommodated within the turn's space as long as that talk furthers the project of the turn-in-progress, for example, by offering a try at a word search or by collaboratively completing and thereby actively coconstructing the turn-in-progress; and (4) various "choral" phenomena, which are either mandated or allowed to be produced in concert rather than seriatim, such as laughter, collective greetings or congratulations, and so on. None of these are ordinarily treated as problematic events interactionally, which warrant deployment of the resources afforded by an overlap resolution device to deal with them (although on particular occasions, any one can be so treated).

2. Overwhelmingly in conversation, "more than one" speaking at a time involves two

speaking at a time, invariant to the number of participants in the interaction. For various reasons, the key configuration of this talk is the one in which the simultaneous speakers are addressing one another [again invariant to number of participants, although obviously in two-person interaction there is no alternative to this configuration (Schegloff, 2000, pp. 7–10)].

3. Most overlaps are over very quickly, although some persist to great length. Many are characterized by hitches and perturbations in their production. An account of the organized set of practices by which overlapping talk is managed and resolved by its participants—an "overlap resolution device"—should provide for and explicate the production of these features (Schegloff, 2000, pp. 10–11).

4. Such a device appears to be composed of three elements: a set of resources for overlap-oriented turn production; a set of places where these resources are deployed; and an interactional "logic" that has those resources in those places constitute "moves" of a describable sort in a competitive sequential topography.

4.1. The resources are deflections or discontinuities of various sorts in the production of the talk: The talk can get suddenly markedly (1) louder in volume, (2) higher in pitch, or (3) faster or slower in pace, depending on where in the overlapping talk it occurs. The talk-in-progress may be (4) suddenly cut off, most commonly with what linguists call a glottal, labial, dental, or some other oral stop; or (5) some next sound may be markedly prolonged or stretched out, or (6) a just prior element may be repeated. Several of these deflections from the "normal" course of production may be combined, as when a speaker repeatedly cuts off a word or phrase in progress and then repeats it, only to cut off the repeat at the same point and redo the entire operation, resulting in a sort of spinning-of-one's-wheels in getting on with it (Schegloff, 2000, pp. 11–15).

4.2. The places can be characterized as phases through which an overlap may develop. Among the most important are preonset and postonset (just before the actual start of simultaneous talk and just after it) and preresolution and postresolution (just before the projectable end of the overlap, e.g., by virtue of the hearable incipient end of one or the other of the simultaneous turns, and just after the resolution, as one turn emerges into the clear). The consequentiality of these phases is observable in their effect on the deployment of the previously mentioned resources. For example, in trying to head off incipient overlap onset (i.e., in the preonset phase), a current speaker may vary the pace of the talk by speeding up; if the overlap has already begun (in the postonset phase), pace change takes the form of slowing down (Schegloff, 2000, pp. 15–19). These are situated actions, not mere arbitrary variations in talking.

4.3. A more finely grained set of places, composed of the successive "beats" (roughly, syllables) of the talk's production, provides the locus for the interactive logic through which the competition for the turn space is worked out. After the first beat of simultaneous talk, each party to it must take up a stance toward the overlap in progress: withdraw (by stopping talking); continue in "solo production" mode; or upgrade to competitive production by deploying one or more of the "resources" described above. The stance each party is taking is displayed in the next beat. At that point each party can assess the stance the other is taking and must react in the next beat by dropping out, continuing (despite the other's tack), or upgrading (or counterupgrading) by use of competitive resources, and so on (Schegloff, 2000, pp. 19–22), until the overlap is resolved by one or both parties coming to the end of their turn in the overlap or withdrawing before reaching it.

5. There are several major outcomes of such competitions. First, many overlaps are resolved after a single beat by the withdrawal of one or both parties at the first evidence that simultaneous talk is in progress. Second, of overlaps that survive the first beat, a great many

end within one beat after one of the speakers upgrades the talk to competitive production, the resolution being implemented by a cutoff by the recipient of the upgrade. Often, the first move to competitive production occurs in the second or third beat of the overlap. A consequence of these observations is that, by the third beat, the vast majority of overlaps have been resolved to a single speaker. Many such episodes represent turn-taking "miscues," involving little interactional investment by the parties. However, overlaps can be extended to considerable length if neither party drops out despite the stances taken by the other, and these invite treatment (both by cointeractants and by investigators) as involving some sort of greater interactional moment or investment for the parties, either proximately interactional (such as needing for various reasons to get something said in that turn position) or representing more distal and even symbolic matters, such as ones of deference, standing, and so forth (Schegloff, 2000, pp. 22–24).

6. The upshot then is that resolution of overlap is an outcome worked out by the parties in a step-by-step, or beat-by-beat, interaction, at each step of which there are options available for responding to the just preceding conduct of the other. Although one cannot predict the outcome, or even how on any given occasion some participant (or class of participants) will conduct themselves (not even the participant can predict this), the organization of practices itself is relatively straightforward (and formal) and allows the parties to negotiate the impasse at just that moment, for just those participants, and for just that juncture of topic and/or action on just that occasion, given who they respectively are—relevantly are—at that moment (Schegloff, 2000, pp. 25–29).

7. There are other criteria of "success" to which parties may be oriented in dealing with an overlap in which they find themselves implicated besides competition to "win" the floor. Among these are talking one's turn to completion, or to a point at which its thrust or upshot is accessible to interlocutors, or so conducting oneself that the ensuing talk in the interaction is addressed to one's own talk in the overlap rather than to that of the other party who is speaking. Orientation to the last of these success criteria in particular may make relevant conduct in the overlap quite different from conduct seeking to win the turn space (Schegloff, 2000, pp. 29–32).

Interruption and Overlap: Onset and Resolution

What is the bearing of this account of overlap management and resolution on "interruption"? Can we simply plug in "interruption" where "overlap" appears? Not really. At most, "overlap" and "interruption" are partially overlapping sets. On the one hand, overlapping talk does not necessarily involve interruption. For example, simultaneous starts by two speakers, neither of whom has special rights to the turn by virtue of preceding talk, can produce overlapping talk without constituting interruption (although, if one of them was the addressee of a question, interruption may be involved, as in footnote 3 below). On the other hand, "interruption" (as the term has been employed) without overlap can occur when the newly entering stream of talk is designed by its speaker to be in continuity and complementarity with the talk already in progress and does not embody the conventional sense of aggression or hostility associated with the term "interruption," what Lerner (1991, 1996) termed "anticipatory completion" and Sacks (1992, Vol. 1) termed "collaborative constructions" (see also Tannen, 1983). To make this much explicit already may be a gain in clarity, and it helps to focus our attention on that intersection at which there is overlapping talk in an environment arguably involving a startup of talk by a new speaker intervening in (and possibly interdicting completion of) an as yet not-possibly-complete turn.

"Overlap," as we have already seen, refers to the sheer fact of more than one person talking at a time. "Interruption," as noted earlier, is ordinarily used to mean a starting up of some intervention by one person while another's turn is in progress, often including "not letting them finish," what some of the literature in this area refers to as "successful interruption." An analytical interest in "interruption" as an interactional event might then be expected to be pursued along two lines. "Starting to talk while another is already talking" directs attention to overlap onset—the start of the talking-at-once. The second aspect of "interruption"— "continuing to talk until prior speaker stops"—directs attention to what happens after the simultaneous talk has already started: the conduct of persons talking simultaneously and its outcome.

THE OUTCOME.   Once put that way, of course, it quickly becomes clear that simultaneous talk does not invariably result in the new speaker preventing the prior speaker from completing what they were saying, and we are invited to see the resolution of such simultaneous talk as a contingent outcome. What it is the contingent outcome *of* and how to describe the organization of overlap resolution in an analytically compelling way and one that gets at the orientations of the participants has constituted the principal interest and result of the companion paper partially summarized above (Schegloff, 2000). The line that has been pursued there takes the outcome of overlap to be, in the first instance, a contingent outcome of the conduct of the parties (rather than, for example, the identities of the parties or any particular aspect thereof), and that paper offers an empirically grounded account of the organization of that conduct and its relationship to other elements of the distribution of opportunities to talk in conversation (and other talk-in-interaction), that is, to the organization of turn-taking.

Of course, the domain of occurrences we have been addressing includes episodes in which the outcome "someone stopping before finishing" was *not* the product of another having invaded their already-ongoing talk, which is another key element of "interruption." This is because the domain that has been under examination and many of the exemplars that have been discussed included overlapping talk in which the speakers started simultaneously.[3]

---

[3]It should be noted, though, that some simultaneous starts also involve interruption, as when two speakers simultaneously start an answer to a question that was addressed to one of them, the other's talk then being a possible interruption—of the sequence, not the turn, and often so delivered and received interactionally. For example:

```
[US, 123:10-31]
 1   MIKE:   →  =Joe,
 2                (0.7)
 3   CAROL:     A ha[ssock
 4   MIKE:   →      [Whatsa di[ffrence b'tween a hassock en 'n ottoman.
 5   VIC:                     [No difference.
 6   JOE:    → [I think it's the shape.
 7   VIC:    → [De difference between a sofa enna cou[ch.
 8   CAROL:                                          [A hassock
 9               [is square like that one you [did befaw.
10   MIKE:   → [Waidaminnit I didn' ask you, [
11   VIC:                     [Oh:. Wul [uh-
12   JOE:                                [I think it's the shape
13                (0.8)
14   MIKE:     The shape?
15   JOE:      Yeh. (The) hassock is usually round, sits onna floh wit'
16               no legs. [Where en ottoman,
17   CAROL:              [A hassock [is square wid[out [legs.
18   MIKE:                          [Okay.       Now-[
```

Still, the organization of conduct we have described can be applied to the more narrowly circumscribed domain in which "interruption" is plausibly claimable.

The outcome, however, is to render this sense or criterion of "interruption"—"causing to stop," as the *Oxford English Dictionary* put it—problematic, and with it the notion of "successful interruption" employed in some of the social scientific literature. If there is an interaction between the parties throughout the simultaneous talk along the lines that have been described, then the unidirectional attribution of efficacy to the interruptor (when one speaker has intersected the ongoing talk of another) misses the real-time heart of the phenomenon. This component of the vernacular sense of interruption and the *Oxford English Dictionary's* account of it conveys a misleading and in fact an inapplicable sense of what actually transpires when more than one is talking at a time. "Causing to stop" is not a unilateral action but an interactional achievement; each party constitutes both agent and patient; either can end up "stopping."[4]

THE ONSET.   The other component of the vernacular "interruption"—starting while another is already talking—is no more straightforward. On the one hand, in a literal sense, it is not required; when another starts talking during an analyzable pause in a current speaker's not-yet-possibly-complete turn, it does not lose its interruptive potential by virtue of the "current speaker" happening not to be literally talking at that moment. On the other hand, such starting is not necessarily interruptive; recall the various incomings that are normative (laughter, greetings) or mobilized (orchestrated co-saying). But these are neither the most common nor the most telling locus of this key element.

The first component of "interruption"—overlap onset—has been systematically described by Jefferson (1984) who has much to tell about where—and by implication how—a

---

19   VIC: [Waid[aminnit.
20   MIKE: [Is- dz a
21   [hassock actually open up so yih c'n throw] shoes innit? hnhh hih hih!
22   VIC: [Ken I ask you dis, what's this.] ((taps object))

Here Mike, who works in a used furniture store, has asked Joe, its owner, what the difference is between an "ottoman" and a "hassock" (two versions of footstools). Actually, he already has asked this of Joe just before, only to have Vic, who hangs out in the store, offer an answer. So the extract represents a second try at asking Joe. Note then that Joe and Vic start to respond simultaneously. Yet at line 10, Mike treats Vic's response to be an interruption, and without being cued again, Joe again delivers his answer, this time in the clear.

[4]Although readers committed to the "interruption as domination" view may find this similar to Anatole France's observation that, under capitalism, all are free to sleep under bridges, the rich as well as the poor, the positions are quite different. Unless hierarchical relationships are invariably and exclusively relevant determinants of interactional conduct and invariably result in a "subordinate" yielding to a "superordinate," then something other than the sheer hierarchical positioning is involved, and the conduct in interaction is a prime candidate for relevant consequentiality. [In this regard, recall West's (1979) finding that after onset, there are no gender differences in resolution-relevant practices or outcomes.] That the playing field is not level (when it is not level, when it is relevantly not level) does not entail that the action on the field is irrelevant.

The related notion of "successful interruption" is a problematic usage on other grounds as well, for it appears to be based in the premise that "interruptions" have "forcing the other out" as their goal, so that the other's stopping makes the interruption "successful" (and presumably the other's not stopping makes it unsuccessful, whatever the interruptor has succeeded in saying). It thereby excludes, without making it explicit, those "interruptions" aimed, for example, at coarticulating what another is saying, in which the "interruptor's" saying, rather than the prior speaker's stopping, is the criterion of success (cf. the data extracts in notes 11 and 12). It excludes as well the other success criteria sketched above for overlap; it thereby makes of interruption (and of overlap) a zero-sum game. Insofar as participants do not invariably do so, this terminological move—"successful interruption"—can contribute to the misapprehension of the phenomena involved. Often this is related to a presupposition that interruption is exclusively an indicator and instrument of "domination," a view that the usage "successful interruption" covertly underwrites.

great many overlaps get started. One upshot of her work is that many instances of overlapping talk that present themselves initially to investigators as "interruptions," that is, as invasive social actions, can be quite differently understood and may have been quite differently understood by the participants.

Jefferson formulates three types or categories of overlap onset, each describing an environment in which such onsets occur in terms which embody an orientation by a "recipient–next speaker" to ongoing talk by a current speaker:

1. By reference to one of these orientations, a recipient–possible next speaker monitors the talk-in-progress for its possible completion and "transition-relevance," and launches a next turn's start by reference to this feature of the talk-in-progress. This strategic locus in the organization of turn-taking was termed in Sacks et al. "the transition place" (in contrast to "transition point," cf. Sacks et al., 1974, pp. 705–706, fn. 15) to provide for a range of positions at which transition to a next turn may be relevant and appropriate. Jefferson (1984, pp. 2–18) describes a number of such positions. Some of them embody "terminal overlaps" — of various sorts, of differing degrees of extensiveness, composed differently in their course, and arrived at by various routes—in which a recipient–next speaker starts up a bit before, and in anticipation of, imminent possible completion of the ongoing talk (what Jefferson terms "reasonable turn incursion"). About these instances Jefferson (1984, p. 6) remarks that

> ... at the point of overlap onset the recipient/now-starting next speaker is doing something perfectly proper, perfectly within his rights and obligations as a recipient/next speaker. He is not doing what we commonly understand to be "interrupting"—roughly, starting up "in the midst of" another's turn at talk, not letting the other finish. On the other hand, the current speaker is also doing something perfectly proper. He is producing a single turn at talk which happens to have multiple components in it.

But these "transition-related" overlap onsets include as well instances in which recipient–next speakers start up after a possible completion in the ongoing talk which is followed by a rapid continuation by that speaker (i.e., the prior speaker) starting a new turn unit in the beat of silence ordinarily allowed by a next speaker to pass before starting a next turn (a "rush-through" in the usage of Schegloff, 1982). Here Jefferson (1984, p. 9) observes that much talk that initially presents itself as interruptive "because it start up after a current speaker has shown himself to be producing further talk," and thus appears to be "starting up 'in the midst' of another's talk," otherwise can be understood as positioned by reference to the other's (the prior speaker's) having come to possible completion and transition place—just the place at which it is proper to start a next turn.[5]

2. A second environment for overlap onset can be formulated by reference to another orientation that recipient–possible next speaker brings to the monitoring of talk-in-progress, namely an orientation to what is getting said or done in that talk. At some point in the production of the ongoing talk, recipient–possible next speaker can recognize what is being said or what is being done by that talk: its thrust or upshot. The point at which the ongoing turn-so-far permits recognition of its designed upshot is another environment for overlap onset, what Jefferson (1984) terms "recognitional onset." Such onset is more likely to occur remote from possible completion and transition-relevance of the ongoing talk or the moments just before and after it. It therefore is more vulnerable to being taken by prior speaker (and by

---

[5]This may apply differentially to subsequent analysts of the tape or transcript, seeing/hearing "interruption" in the retrospective view of the outcome on the one hand and on the other the operating-in-real-time participants, monitoring and projecting the trajectory of the ongoing talk, and acting on the basis of its progressively unfolding elements and their understanding. This disparity can overpromote the post hoc analysis of "interruption."

professional analysts) as interruptive and in that respect problematic and may be oriented to as such by the recipient–next speaker in the very manner of its production.

3. In addition to monitoring "on-line" for possible completion of the turn-constructional units out of which talk is fashioned and for the action, upshot, or thrust of what is being done through that talk, recipient–possible next speaker is oriented as well (and this is a third orientation) to the "progressivity" of the talk in its course. That is, each next moment should deliver something recognizable as furthering the course and trajectory of the talk, and the sorts of occurrence termed earlier in this chapter (and elsewhere, e.g., Schegloff, 1979) "hitches" and "perturbations" can serve to indicate and embody problems with that progress. Such troubles in the talk's progressivity—some embodied in silence or "silence fillers" that are not at possible completions, others by "mid-utterance 'stuttering' "—turn out to be another environment in which overlap onsets occur: a third type that Jefferson (1984) terms "progressional." As she points out, these may variously be seen as invasive and exploiting a "weakness" in the ongoing talk, or as " 'neutral' materials 'drawn' by ... a 'hitch' " (p. 37)[6]

UPSHOT.   What is the upshot of this analysis? On the one hand, there is Jefferson's (1984, p. 37) claim that"... *in principle there is no point in an utterance which is proof from systematically-accountable (if not interactionally legitimate) overlap*" (emphasis in original). That is, on this account, taking the several environments that she has described together, in principle, overlap onsets may be found virtually anywhere in an utterance. Some of these overlaps are "by-products" and others represent various degrees of "turn incursion":

> These variously generated onsets can be seen to be at least systematic, if not perfectly "proper," reasonable, legitimate, rightful, etcetera. And with these orderlinesses a mass of overlapping talk is lifted from the realm of nonsystematic, perhaps unaccountable, perhaps only interactionally motivated/accountable "interruption." (Jefferson, 1984, p. 28).

We have here, then, a systematic array of accounts of the onset of overlap (by reference to turn-transition, by reference to early or "premature" recognition of upshot, and by reference to retarded progressivity) that are potentially alternative to an interactionally motivated account formulating the occurrences as "interruption." Yet this treatment does not exclude "interruption" and allows juxtaposition of its formulations with "interruption."

At the very least, it is no longer analytically defensible to treat any startup of overlapping talk (whatever the categorical membership of the participants) as "interruption"—with all the commonsense inferences supported (and invited) by that term—without subjecting the interactional environment of the overlap's onset to inspection by reference to these demonstrably relevant systematic possibilities. The result of such examination is less likely to yield the analysis that "interruption" has occurred where none was suspected than it is to yield the analysis that the finding of "interruption" is called into question by the details of the relationship of the incoming talk to the already ongoing talk. Based on detailed examination of the talk, then, particular instances are apt to slip *out of* the category of "interruption" and not *into* it and *not out of* the category of overlapping talk.

What we have, then, is that neither the starting of a second speaker while a first is already

[6]It is worth underscoring that Jefferson (1984) has examined a substantial collection of overlap onsets and sorted out environments in which they specially appear to occur. Places with trouble in the progressivity of a turn are such an environment. It does not follow that places of compromised progressivity invite overlap onset, etc., for Jefferson has not examined a collection of such places/occurrences to establish the sorts of things that happen at them and has not found that overlap onset is specially recurrent in them. Her paper reports on orderliness of overlap onset, not orderliness (other orderliness) of the environments in which overlap onset occurs. For a discussion of some problems of progressivity which do appear to invite "interruption" see Schegloff (1979, pp. 272–280).

speaking nor the stopping of a first speaker by virtue of a second having started is a reliable indicator of "interruption," in the ordinary vernacular sense of that term. Both the onset and the offset, taken by themselves, are problematic criteria, and in a fashion that does not lend itself readily to straightforward or formulaic solutions.[7] Whatever its vernacular usage may be, talking while another is talking is not a reliable indicator or embodiment of what it has been taken for in intendedly disciplined inquiry.

In the first instance, of course, whether or not some newly starting talk is interruptive or not is the parties' issue, not an academic one; it is engaged on a case-by-case basis, or rather as an occurrence within its immediate context (rather than as "one-overlap-out-of-a-collection"); and it appears that a variety of elements enter into the parties' determination. What follows is a sketch of some, perhaps many, of those elements and their import for the understanding of interruption as an interactional occurrence and of "interruption" as an object of inquiry and topic of empirical–analytic discourse.

WHAT MAKES FOR INTERRUPTION: THE ROLE OF COMPLAINABILITY

First, it appears that adequate analysis of an overlap as a possible "interruption" in principle cannot be independent of the character and details of the talk already ongoing (if there is any)[8] and exactly where in that talk new talk by another gets started. That is, the "turn-so-far" in its incremental development must be taken to figure centrally, both with respect to its detailed composition and with respect to the position in it at which the intervention occurs. Almost certainly we do not yet know the full range of facets of the turn-so-far that in any particular instance can have a bearing on the matter. But, as noted, the "first possible place" at which what is being said or done can be recognized has been shown by Jefferson (1984) to be a place where new and overlapping turns are begun and where new turns designed to do certain actions (such as showing prior knowledge) should begin (Jefferson, 1973). On the other hand, agreement tokens interpolated before that point in a turn-so-far at which what is being said is recognizable are likely to convey that the "agreer" is rushing the turn's completion, the more quickly to begin their own next turn. Lerner (1991) shows that certain "compound" grammatical constructions can promote the occurrence of "anticipatory completion" by another party and powerfully shape just where that undertaking should begin (just after the construction's "preliminary component"), with intervention elsewhere presumably having quite a different "interruption" potential. The points at which turns-so-far convey what they are saying/doing, of course, will vary instance by instance-in-context and by virtue of their turn design[9] and will be parsed for "possible interruptivity" by the parties for that particular instance-in-context.

---

[7]As, for example, West's (1979) proposal to treat next-turn starts that overlap more than two syllables (or any number, for that matter) as interruptive; or the suggestion of Wells and Macfarlane (1998) that positioning before the "TRP-projecting accent" (in combination with features of the incoming talk) is key to constitution of an overlap as interruptive, on which see below.

[8]The parenthetical qualification here is meant to allow for overlapping talk in which the speakers started simultaneously and with comparable entitlement and in which therefore there was no "talk already ongoing."

[9]It seems most likely that prosodic features such as the "tonic syllable" proposed as criterial in an early version of Wells and Macfarlane (1998) ordinarily derive their criteriality by virtue of their serving to index and embody such features of turn design, such as "upcoming possible completion" (Schegloff, 1996a, 1998). A wholly different sense of the relevance of "turn design" may be sought in the consequences of the grammatical characteristics of the language, for example, what is grammatically favored for placement early or late in a clause; cf. Schegloff et al. (1996, pp. 28–32).

Second, it appears that the parties' analysis of an overlap as a possible "interruption" in principle cannot be independent of the character and details of the incoming talk, specifically:

1. Issues related to its addressee: Is it addressed to current speaker? To the targeted current addressee of the ongoing talk? To one of a set of possible addressees of the ongoing talk? To none of these? In which case is it then even a candidate for the status "interruption" or is it more properly understood as schism-launching (Sacks et al., 1974, pp. 713–714; Egbert, 1997)?[10]

2. Its displayed relationship to the already ongoing talk: such as (a) an unrelated "side involvement" (as in a request for salt at the dinner table), (b) an aligning utterance (such as continuer, agreement, aligned assessment, anticipatory completion,[11] celebratory uptake,[12] etc.); (c) a misaligned or agonistic stance toward the already ongoing

---

[10]By "schism-launching" I mean to register the following possibility. In an interaction with four or more participants in which A is addressing B, an utterance addressed by C to D may be understood (depending, of course, on its composition) as potentially initiating a separate, "breakaway" conversation between C and D. In that case, if taken up, the result is two conversations, each with a single speaker, and neither overlap nor interruption would end up having been heard to occur.

[11]Although anticipatory completions are ordinarily designed (by both parties) to be said in the clear, the originating speaker may end up producing the final component as well, and the two articulated completions may not be identically composed, even they are designed to deliver the same completion. for example, in the following exchange Bee is telling Ava about the courses she is taking and comes to the course in modern art:

```
[TG, 8:19-9:02]
  1  BEE:    I'nna tell you on:e course.
  2          (0.5)
  3  AVA:    [(      ).]
  4  BEE:    [The mah- ] the mah:dern art. The twunnieth century a:rt
  5          there's about eight books,
  6  AVA:    Mm [hm,
  7  BEE:       [En I wentuh buy a book the other day I [went ] ˙hh went=
  8  AVA:                                               [(mm)]
  9  BEE:    =downtuh N.Y.U. tuh get it becuz it's the only place thet
 10          car[ries the book.
 11  AVA:       [Mmm
 12  AVA:    Mmh
 13  BEE:    Tch! En it wz twun::ty do::lliz.
 14  AVA:    Oh my god.
 15          (0.4)
 16  BEE:    Yeuh he- ez he wz handing me the book en 'e tol' me twunny
 17          dolliz I almos' dro(h)pped i(h) [t ˙hh ˙hh
 18  AVA:                                    [hhunh.
 19  BEE:→   ˙hhh I said but fer twunny dollars I bettuh hh ˙hh yihknow,
 20          (0.2)
 21  BEE:→   ˙hh h[hold o:nto i(h)hh] huhh huh] ˙hh!
 22  AVA:→        [not  drop  it. ] huhh huh]
 23          (0.2)
 24  BEE:    Ih wz, (0.2) y'know (fun)...
```

At line 22 Ava (it becomes clear over the course of her talk's production) means to align with Bee by collaborating on the production of this turn. As it happens, Bee completes it herself, with the same upshot but different composition.

[12]As in the following exchange, in which Nancy, a woman of some years, is reporting to Emma on having met a really nice, eligible, man:

```
[NB:II:4:16]
  1  NANCY:  He's jist a ri:l sweet GU:y. .h .t [.hhhh
```

talk (such as disagreement, challenge, repair initiation or correction, etc.); (d) a reparative relation to preceding talk by the same speaker that might bear on the ongoing talk.[13]

3. What its manner of production is: such as muted (e.g., whispered) side-involvement or by-play (Goffman, 1981; Goodwin, 1997), turn-competitive incoming (French & Local, 1983; see also Wells & Macfarlane, 1998), and so forth.

4. What its construction is designed to reveal at the very start about the talk being launched, relative to the turn-so-far into which it is introduced (if any), and how it reveals itself over the course of its progressive real time display.

Third, to the focus on the onset of the overlap featured in the preceding points we must add that adequate analysis of an overlap as an "interruption" will need to consult the character and details of the conduct of the parties to the overlap subsequent to its onset, both during its developmental course and in its "aftermath" position.

Academic focus on these aspects of overlaps that invite attention as "candidate interruptions" or "possible interruptions"[14] may render many apparent "interruptions" equivocal and

---

```
2   EMMA:                                    [WONderful.
3   NANCY:      So: we w'r [sitting in
4   EMMA:    →              [YER LIFE is CHANG[ing
5   NANCY:                                    [EEYE::A:H
```

Emma's utterance at line 4 is what I refer to in the text by "celebratory uptake" in raising the issue of the bearing of its character on its treatment as interruption or not. But treating it as an "interruption" could in such a case register not a negative feature of it but the eager supportiveness of what it was doing. My thanks to Paul Drew for having brought the issue and the extract to my attention.

[13]The most common occurrences in this regard are transition space repairs which intersect an already begun next turn. These may be "self-induced," as in:

```
[Heritage:1:5:3–4]
1   DOROTHY:     But (0.4) uh::m (0.9) uh-:: (.) if:: .h.h uhw he won't do
2               whatchu want him tuh do: t- .h twice a week with you'n twice
3               a wee:k with me.
4   EDGERTON:   We:ll we[: we-
5   DOROTHY:  →          [Uh twice a:, a month.
6   EDGERTON:   Well we've got to we've gotta talk to him about it. I haven'
7               mention'it to him yet.
```

Or they may be prompted by a co-present third person who is not party to the conversation, as in:

```
[MDE:60-1, 1:23–29]
1   MARSHA:     What time did'e get on the pla:ne.
2   TONY:       Uh::: (0.2) I: do:n't know exactly I think ih wz arou:nd
3               three uh'clo:ck or something a' that sort.
4                   (0.2)
5   MARSHA:     Oh: maybe he g[o t s ' m]
6   TONY:    →               [He took it] et fou:r. Hilda says.
```

In both instances, a speaker introduces repair (in both instances, self-correction) in talk that intersects another's responsive next turn, which allows that next turn to be responsive to the corrected version. Here again I am indebted to Paul Drew.

[14]For the way in which the usage "possible X" is deployed technically in conversation-analytic work, see Schegloff (1996, pp. 116–17, n.8), reproduced here in part:

The usage is not meant as a token of analytic uncertainty or hedging. Its analytic locus is not in the first instance the world of the author and reader, but the world of the parties to the interaction. To describe some utterance, for example, as "a possible invitation" (Sacks, 1992, pp. I:300–302; Schegloff, 1992b, pp. xxvi–xxvii) or "a possible complaint" (Schegloff, 1988, pp. 120–122) is to claim that there is a describable practice of talk-in-interaction which is usable to do recognizable

possibly "joint productions." But in addition to the actual features of conduct that compose the onset of simultaneous talk and its preceding context, the trajectory of its development to resolution, and its postresolution aftermath, another quite different ingredient figures in its assessment as an interruption as well.

"Interruption" is in the first instance a vernacular term; a term of vernacular description in the practical activity of ordinary talk. Unlike "overlap," it is not designed to do the work of "mere description," nor is it well-designed to serve as a tool for "disciplined" analysis. It is a term of complaint, and its invocation can ordinarily serve to implement the action of complaining. Because the terms "overlap" and "interruption" are part of such contrastive domains, the relationship of "interruption" to overlapping talk is equivocal over and above the sources of equivocality already mentioned.[15] Furthermore, to the several dimensions of analysis by the parties that may inform the stance they take up to the treatment of an overlap as an interruption there is the practical matter of its "complainability" for those parties, at that moment, with those overlapping utterances, and so forth.[16]

"Compainability" appears to be an ingredient of analysis quite differentially accessible to parties to the interaction on the one hand and to external analysts on the other. The former have a direct interactional interest in the matter, practically relevant grounds for assessing it, and the prospect of immediate interactional consequences of acting on it, all of which served to inform, to constrain, and to discipline their treatment of an overlap/candidate interruption. What "standing" (as it is put in the legal system) external analysts have, on what basis they make such assessments, what interests they have in them, and what constrains and disciplines their judgments and the complaints that may issue from them in the absence of proximate interactional consequences remains to be clarified.[17]

But what is the relevance of introducing the observation that "interruption" is not only an analysis of its target occurrence but a complaint about it? That it is *so*, is a matter quite apart from its relevance, after all. Here is one relevance.

If it were the case that the status of some incoming talk as an "interruption" could be assessed by juxtaposing its features (including its relationship to the talk that it intersected and the features of that talk) with formulable criteria, even if fuzzy and sometimes indeterminate ones, then a party-to-conversation could plausibly undertake in principle to avoid "violations" to avoid being found to have interrupted by talking in such a way as to not satisfy the criteria. Avoid the conduct in question and avoid the label entailed by that conduct. But if what is

---

invitations or complaints (a claim which can be documented by exemplars of exchanges in which such utterances were so recognized by their recipients), and that the utterance now being described can be understood to have been produced by such a practice, and is thus analyzable as an invitation or as a complaint. This claim is made, and can be defended, independent of whether the actual recipient on this occasion has treated it as an invitation or not, and independent of whether the speaker can be shown to have produced it for recognition as such on this occasion. Such an analytic stance is required to provide resources for accounts of "failures" to recognize an utterance as an invitation or complaint, for in order to claim that a recipient failed to recognize it as such or respond to it as such, one must be able to show that it was recognizable as such, i.e., that it was "a possible X"—for the participants (Schegloff, 1995, 1996b). The analyst's treatment of an utterance as "a possible X" is then grounded in a claim about its having such a status for the participants.

[15]A similar point is made in Bennett (1981).
[16]See the related point in Murray (1985).
[17]It should be clear that I mean here to be calling under review not the commitments or craftsmanship of particular investigators who have worked in this area, often with great skill and dedication, but the analytic terrain to which operating with the notion "interruption" inescapably commits any investigation, given its irremediable semantic loadings and their origin in vernacular discourse and the contingencies of practical action interaction.

involved is complaining, then this is a less plausible tack. In principle, one cannot avoid complaints by avoiding complainables; for virtually anything can be made into a complainable.

For example, a party can turn themselves into an aggrieved party—an "interrupted party"—although the complaint target does nothing "wrong." Even when there is in the first instance no overlap at all, a turn-transfer can be reconfigured to make of it a "candidate interruption." Consider Extract (01):

```
[(01) TG, 14:36–43]
 1   BEE:      t! We:ll, uhd-yihknow I-I don' wanna make any- thing
 2             definite because I-yihknow I jis:: I jis::t thinking:g
 3       →     tihday all day riding on th'trai:ns hhuh-uh
 4             'hh[h!
 5   AVA:      [Well there's nothing else t'do.<I wz
 6             thingin[g of taking the car anyway.] ·hh
 7   BEE:→     [that I would go into the ss-uh-]=I would go
 8             into the city but I don't know,
```

Ava has been trying to entice Bee to join her the next day when she travels from Long Island into Manhattan to the college that she attends and that Bee once attended as well, before transferring to another school. Bee has been resisting and is resisting again at lines 1–4, being in the course of retracting the possible plan of going "into the city" that has elicited Ava's efforts. It had appeared by line 4 that Bee had possibly finished her turn. To be sure, the turn-so-far was not grammatically complete, but given the laugh tokens at the end of that line displaying and projecting the stance she is taking up, the turn-so-far allows analysis by its recipient (and by us) as a "trailoff" (a form virtually definable by its possible completion through grammatically incomplete). But when Ava starts to talk (at line 5), displayedly in response to what preceded, Bee starts up again. The talk that she produces here ("… that I would go into the city") is designed from the outset to show itself to be *not* a new turn (which might be taken as "an interruption" of Ava) but "a continuation" of her own prior talk (the so-called "complement" of the verb "was thinking"), thereby rendering Ava's intervening talk interruptive of Bee's now retroactively reconstituted "incomplete" talk and shifting the burden of "possible interruption" from herself to the other.

A similar outcome can be produced without benefit of the claimable ambiguity of the trailoff. A next speaker can start a next turn after a prior speaker has brought a turn-so-far to apparent completion grammatically, prosodically, and pragmatically (Ford & Thompson, 1996) and can do so after allowing the normative beat of silence to pass after the possible completion of the prior talk before staring a next turn. Still, the prior speaker can start up after a next speaker has begun a next turn and add an increment to the prior otherwise complete turn which can render the subsequent start to have been a possible "interruption."[18] This happens twice in the following episode from a conversation between four undergraduate students in a dormitory room in the mid-1970s:

```
[(02) SN-4 12:35-13:35]
 1             (1.2)
 2   MARK:     That's about it hell I haven't been doing anything but-
 3             (·) s- (Well,) (0.2) going out [a c t u ]ally.
 4   ?KAR:                                    [mmh ]
 5             (0.7)
```

---

[18]Not to mention claims that the prior speaker had some other, larger unit under construction—a story, a topic, etc.—which was not yet complete.

```
 6   MARK:    I 'aftuh start studying no:w
 7            (0.7)
 8   KAR:     Yeah I shou[ l d  °t  o  o]
 9   MARK:              [nI've got a pap]er t'write after
10            (0.7)
11   MARK:→  'haftuh wait until Friday.(·) t'see the last films.
12            (0.8)
13   KAR:  →  Y'[d never know I had a] paper due Wednesday, wouldju.
14   MARK:     [in  that  film  class.]
15            (·)
16   MARK:    N[(h)o] hhh=
17   ?RUT:     [(    )]
18   (??)     =h[hhh        ((through nose?))
19   ?RUT:      [°hmhh
20            (0.4)
21   RUTH:    [I h've one] due Thu:rsday
22   MARK:    [(        )]
23            (0.9)
24   RUTH:→  Have one due tih≠morrow.too:.=
25   SHER:    =mmh [ h m h ]
26   KAR:  →  [Isn't it] f[un ta:lking about] it?
27   RUTH:→          [B't it's  finished]
28   RUTH:    Yeah I a[m.
29   ?SHE:            [(h(h)uhh]
30            (0.6)
31   SHER:    It's more fun ta:lking about it then wri:ting them
32   (??)     hh
33            (1.6)
34   MARK:→  Hev en English takehome I 'aftuh do over the weekend, 'n-
35            (0.7)
36   MARK:→  study on Sunday °n Monday,
37            (·)
38   ?RUT:→  (°Oh: I'm s:[:-  (0.2)  ((sn]eeze)))
39   MARK:→          ['r that e:con test. ]
40            (2.0)
41   SHER:    Howijuh like t'do our dishes.
```

Mark's recounting of a series of recent exploits is brought to a close after a longish silence at line 1, and the talk turns to pressing school work. Mark is the first to start detailing his obligations (line 9) and seems to be finished (at least with this particular assignment) at line 11. Despite the apparently full-fledged closure of this turn and·the longer-than-normal gap of silence following it, when Karen begins a next turn (at line 13) in which she will recount her own current "fix," she has no sooner started than Mark is talking again (at line 14), with talk that shows itself from its outset to be an increment to his prior talk. That prior talk of Mark's is thereby rendered retroactively claimably incomplete, which in turn renders Karen's start-up claimably (and complainably) "interruptive." Moments later, Mark starts another installment of course work that awaits him (line 34), which by the end of line 36 appears to have come to completion, but when Ruthie starts up a next turn after a slightly overlong interim silence, Mark's resumption (at line 39) again renders the newly started turn suspect of "interruption." Nor is this a distinctively male practice; Ruthie and Karen's exchange at lines 24–27 embodies the same trajectory.

In none of these instances, it may be noted, is a complaint about interruption actually articulated; indeed, such voiced complaints are extremely rare in ordinary conversation.[19] Still, in each instance we may note the sort of deflection of "solo production," which suggests movement into competitive production and thereby an orientation to overlapping talk as possibly problematic.[20]

[19]For readers consulting their own personal experience this may appear an odd claim; it may appear that such complaints are not uncommon. But recall that such complaints, encountered either as agent or as target, are "eventful" and thereby memorable, whereas the nonoccurrence of complaints is not. For those who examine a great deal of data of talk-in-interaction as the material of empirical inquiry, these events and occasions for expecting their relevant occurrence appear differently. So examined, complaints about interruption are relatively rare events; cf. Schegloff (1993).

[20]More generally, there are resources by which a party—any party—can register an orientation to intersecting talk as problematic without explicitly complaining about it or formulating it as an "interruption," including the manner of their withdrawal from he overlap and in particular their conduct in what is described in Schegloff (2000, pp. 32–41) as "overlap aftermath," in which parties can display "... how the overlap figured for them in the interactional dynamic of the moment" (p. 41).

That the issue is "complainability" and not complaints can be seen in the conduct of persons whose talk is vulnerable to being taken as "interruptive" who end their utterance with an apology token such as "sorry" or a registering of their talk as complainable as they surrender the turn, as in the following extract (in which the transfer of some tickets is being arranged), brought to my attention by Paul Drew (and reproduced here from Schegloff, 2000, p. 55):

```
      [Holt corpus]
    1   LESLEY:    ... he dzn't normally go on a Fri:day see it's just c'z these
    2              Italian: fellows've come ovah .hh[h an'
    3   HAL:                                        [Oh ee Have the"y.=
    4   LESLEY:    =iYe[:s.
    5   HAL:           [Yeh
    6   LESLEY:→  .hhh And so that's why we're [a bit-
    7   HAL:     →                             [(But)-
    8              (0.3)
    9   LESLEY:    -hh
   10   HAL:     → Ah- (0.2) Oh interrruptin' you I wz g'nna say you could ↓leave
   11              it'n I mean if you wanted to come you could j's pay me when
   12              you ca:me.
```

Or the following exchange (called to my attention by John Heritage) taken from an encounter between broadcast news interviewer Dan Rather an then-vice-President George Bush during the 1988 primary campaign of the Republican nomination for the presidency, an encounter that was transformed from an interview into what was termed a "confrontation":

```
      [Bush/Rather]
    1   GB:    =.hh Mister Buckley, (.) uh: heard about Mister Buckley being
    2          tor:tured tuh death. later admitted (as a) CIA chief. .hh so
    3          if I erred, I erred on thuh side of tryin' tuh get those
    4        → hostages outta there.
    5   DR:→  Mis[ter Vice President, you set the::]=
    6   GB:      [an thuh who:le story 'ez been  ] [told to thuh congress.    ]
    7   DR:                                        [you set thuh rules fer this]::
    8        →   this talk here.=I didn' mean to step on your line there, .hhh
    9            but you insisted thet this be li::ve, an' you
   10            [know that we have a limited amount of time.]
   11   GB:    [Exactly.      That's      why       I- ] that's why I wanta
   12          g[et m]y share in here [on     something] OTHer than what you=
   13   DR:    [Now-]                 [Thuh President-]
   14   GB:    =wanta [talk about.]
```

Note that Bush appears to have come to possible completion of his turn at line 4, after which Rather begins a next

The upshot is that a "charge" of "interruption" is a type of complaint that has an ostensible criterial target, but occurrences of that target only infrequently prompt production of the complaint on the occasion and within that interaction. Furthermore, parties to interaction have practices by which they in effect can "lure" co-participants into conduct that can be transformed into an instance of the complainable, though they do not then complain about it. One conclusion might be then that "complaining about interruption" is an activity substantially disengagable from actual instances of the complainable—some clearly recognizable, interactionally motivated conduct. The complaints may well occur subsequently, in other venues, in other interactions, with other co-participants (for example, among others, in the literature on the topic).[21] But "interruption" does not appear as an actionable complainable in interaction very much. Or it is registered in other ways on the occasion, largely body behavioral—winces, eye aversion, mutual gaze (of a "knowing" sort) between victims and sympathizers (co-class or otherwise). But these can be used to mark registering of and stances toward a variety of conversational doings, of which "candidate interruption" is only one.

I have tried to argue that:

1. Examination of overlap onsets suggests that many that may look (to nonparticipant observers) like interruptions are/were not, in fact, invasive.
2. That does not mean that it is all arbitrary, that all incomings are equivalent with respect to their interruptiveness.
3. For example, conjecturally, the greater the separation of a "recognition point" (Jefferson, 1973, 1984) or problematic progressivity from the transition-space, the more vulnerable an overlap onset there is to being heard as interruptive. But "more vulnerable" is not equivalent to "being" an interruption. That requires the additional ingredient of complainability. On the other hand, some "incomers" clearly recognize that the onset of their talk could be heard as "interruptive" and begin by marking it as such ("Excuse me;" "waitaminnit," etc.).
4. Nor does "making original speaker stop" supply a compelling criterion of interruption. It is demonstrably an interactionally achieved product in which either party to overlapping talk may emerge with the turn or end up setting the terms for the immediately ensuing talk.
5. But why does it matter in the first instance whether some overlap is an interruption? Because whereas "overlap" is a characterization of mere description, "interruption" is not. Calling something an "interruption" implements a further action—a complaint.
6. So assigning to some overlap-event the characterization "interruption" implicates not only the features of that target event and whether it meets some criteria for assignment to the category "interruption,"[22] but implicates as well the features and contingencies

---

turn (line 5), only to find that Bush has added additional talk (at line 6), designed as a continuation of his preceding turn. In the course of the ensuing contest for the turn position, Rather acknowledges his commission of an apparent complainable. [On the Bush/Rather confrontation, cf. Clayman & Whalen (1988/89); Schegloff (1988/89).] In these episodes, one of the parties articulates an orientation to the complainability of some prior conduct, but such an orientation can inform and linger on in episodes in which it is not articulated, such as data extracts 1 and 2 in the text, in which a prior speaker adds an increment to their otherwise possibly complete turn after another has started a next turn, even though there is in those extracts no demonstrable orientation to complainability.

[21]Apropos the observation that "... complaints are voiced, if at all, after the fact to a party other than the alleged offender," Don Zimmerman (personal communication) reports, "I have heard such 'testimony' from a number of women about male interruptions on various occasions, including the classroom, where the Z[immerman] & W[est] studies were discussed."

[22]Although some contributors to the literature on interruption decry the use of "objective" criteria of interruption

of "complaining" as a kind of action and the ensuing trajectories of action that it can sequentially implicate. It can embody a moral assessment of the action being characterized and of its agent.

7. These exigencies of "complaining" are very different for parties and for outside analysts. It appears that parties rarely formulate the characterization "interruption" (any more than they do of other actions, but they do for some actions), whereas outside commentators do.

8. In any case, although some configurations of talk, when examined by reference to the relevant features in context, are clearly vulnerable to being termed "interruptions," and although so terming them constitutes a complaint whether done in the same interaction, in another interaction, or in writing about it, neither the features of the characterized event nor the contingencies of characterizing it, i.e., the contingencies of complaining, seem to exhaust what is implicated in discussions of "interruption." What else is involved?

9. An additional ingredient in assessments and charges of interruption seems to be a characterization of the parties composing the overlapping talk.[23] Having earlier disattended as "social organizational" the focus on categories of participant so as to attend more closely to the actions that constitute "interrupting," we now return to those categories. This turning is prompted by the observation that, at least for this-action-so-characterized, its production cannot be described by reference to practices of talking alone, followed by an examination of the particularized deployment and distribution of those practices across contexts and participants. Rather, the constitution of "interruption" implicates a characterization of the participants in the first instance.

INTERRUPTION AS A CATEGORY-BOUND ACTIVITY: A CONJECTURE

An interactional event formulated as "an interruption" is above all a complainable. To ask whether something "*is*" an interruption is to ask whether it is a complainable, but that rests

---

(e.g., Bennett, 1981; Murray, 1985), their shortcomings entail problems of various sorts. To mention only one, such "objective criteria" might allow us to register in an analytically defensible way that someone has been "interrupted" even in the absence of their complaining about it or showing any "resistance" to it. Sacks (1992, pp. I:637–638) suggested one basis for not complaining about interruption, namely, that the complaint could itself be treated as a complainable, thereby engendering a sequence on that matter, thereby further subverting the interrupted party's chances of bringing the interrupted talk to completion (or prosecuting the complaint about the interruption to completion, for that matter). Surely there are other bases for "not complaining." As with issues of understanding/misunderstanding, where external analysts must develop an independent account of what some utterance was doing in order to be able to warrant the claim that some interlocutor had possibly misunderstood it and its speaker had let the misunderstanding pass (Schegloff, 1996c, p. 173n), so also with "interruption." In order to be able to argue cogently that someone had been interrupted but was somehow stopped from contesting the violation, one would need an independent analysis of the occurrence—one independent of overt complaint or resistance *in* the occasion, which is, after all, just what is being analyzed. For this undertaking and for the possibility of showing that some complaints of interruption are unwarranted and strategic "moves," "objective criteria" are critical resources. This is so not only where the analyst wishes to claim that there was interruption even though the parties appear not to have registered it (Bennett, 1981; Tannen, 1989), but also when the possibility being entertained is that there was not interruption, even though others might claim that there was (Edelsky, 1981).

[23]In the literature, for example, one does not find much research characterizing the parties to "overlap" by categories such as gender, hierarchy, or by any categories, for that matter.

on more than where exactly it started in the talk of another or how it was prosecuted once started. Not that that is not a relevant category for members–participants and one that they "experience," but that does not make it a first-order category usable for professional analysis. Rather than being employed in professional analysis, it is better treated as a target category for professional analysis.

A substantial literature over the last 20 years or so has used "interruption" as a first-order category of analysis. Some combination of onset plus further prosecution of simultaneous talk constitutes an event as an "interruption," independent of who the parties are, and so on. Then one can count the numbers of such events for different combinations of parties (and classes of parties) such as male–male, female–female, male–female, high–low power, and so on. Proceeding in this not implausible way takes as independent matters who the parties are or how they are to be characterized, on the one hand, and how the event is to be characterized or formulated, on the other. The result is as an empirical finding: men interrupt women (West & Zimmerman, 1983) or they do not (Murray & Covelli, 1988); professionals interrupt clients (West, 1984) or they do not (West, 1984); superordinates interrupt subordinates (Kollock et al., 1985); and so forth.

There are two issues to be raised here, which may turn out themselves not to be independent. One concerns how the category set "men–women" (or any other category set for that matter) is to be grounded as a warrantable way to formulate the participants. This is an issue independent of whether it is implicated in the formulation of the object of inquiry as "an interruption." But the second issue (to be explored below) is this: is it not the case that the very formulation of an event as "interruption" may incorporate, or implicate, the category membership of its participants? If so, we need to understand a finding like "men interrupt women" or "doctors interrupt patients" rather differently.

Membership Categorization Devices

As noted earlier, a substantial part of the literature on interruption is focused specifically on its relationship to gender. Much of this work concerns cross-gender relationships, starting with the West and Zimmerman work on male–female interruption disparities (West, 1979; West & Zimmerman, 1983; Zimmerman & West, 1975; and the review in James & Clarke, 1993), while other work focuses on gender-distinctive conduct with respect to talk and simultaneous talk (often with a specific focus on women's talk, for example, Coates, 1988; Coates & Cameron, 1988; Tannen, 1989). In all this literature a key issue that is rarely addressed explicitly concerns the characterization of the participants. The issue may be most suitably explicated here by reference to a central element of Sacks' early work.

The relevant work of Sacks (1972a, b, 1992) was centered on what he termed "membership categorization devices." Among the resources employed for talking in ordinary interaction and in commonsense understanding of the world, persons may be identified, described, referred to and transparently grasped by reference to terms that name categories of persons: [man–woman]; [adult–chid]; [doctor–patient]; [protestant–catholic–jew–muslim]; and so on. These categories compose collections of categories; they are bracketed in such collections in the preceding sentence. That bracketing is an empirical claim about an element of a culture and can be wrong; [man–woman–catholic] would be wrong, for example, as these categories are not parts of a single collection or "categorization device" in American vernacular culture (or any other of which I am aware). Together with some rules for bringing these collections of categories to bear on actual occasions of referring to persons, as well as seeing, hearing, grasping, formulating, and so forth, the world by reference to persons, these collections constitute "membership categorization devices" (or MCDs).[24]

The importance of these category terms (and their organization) goes far beyond the role they play in persons' practices for referring to other persons (Schegloff, 1996d), important though that be. The categories of these collections are one major repository, perhaps the major repository, for commonsense knowledge of the society by members of the society *as* members of the society. "Knowledge" of what different "sorts" of people are like, what they do, how they behave, and so on—one key element of what is often termed "culture"—is organized and stored by reference to these categories (Sacks, 1992, I:40–49). Among the mechanisms of the organization of such commonsense knowledge is what Sacks (1972, 1992, pp. I:179–181, 236–266; 578–590) termed "category-bound activities."

Within the organization of vernacular or common-sense knowledge, some sorts of activities are "bound" to certain categories of persons.[25] One might be able to convey that someone was a member of some category by attributing such an activity to them (Sacks, 1972, 1992, pp. I:301). One could provide a transparent account for someone having done some action or behaved in some way by involving their membership in that category, for example, by referring to them with a reference form—a "category label" (Moerman, 1988)—which names a "sort" of person who does that sort of thing. Indeed, one could figure who had done some action, especially a problematic one, by seeking out persons who were members of a category to which actions of that sort were bound, who were "known" to do "things like that." As Sacks put it in his initial discussion of this matter in an early one of his lectures (1992, p. I:180).

> The fact that some activities are bound to some categories is used, then, in a tremendous variety of ways, and if somebody knows an activity has been done, and there is a category to which it is bound, they can damn well propose that it's been done by such a one who is a member of that category.
> What's important, in part, is that it's not the case that deviant activities are especially problematic, but there are categories of persons who do deviant activities and you've got a solution to a deviant activity if you've got a member of a category which is known to do this.

Referring to someone by such a category term or seeing/hearing them as a member of a category provides for bringing to bear a stock of commonsense knowledge on that person by virtue of that categorical membership (Sacks, 1992, I:40–49). The import of these resonances of category terms is not restricted to conversational contexts but is pervasive in the deployment of language and other symbolic resources in cultural expression. We will return to the bearing of category-bound activities to the present concerns in a moment, but it is first in point to draw out one major consequence of the operation of MCDs that Sacks described.

Because at least two of these MCDs (for example, age and sex) can categorize any person at all, there always will be more than one category term that can be used to refer correctly to any person. Anyone who is female also will be adult or child. Of course, there are many, many other correct category terms that can be used to refer to any person and to inform one's auditory or visual grasp of them. The consequence is that one cannot account for referring to someone as an "adult" because they are, in fact, an adult; they are, in fact, many other things as well. So that way of referring to them, of categorizing them, is profoundly equivocal.

[24]Subsequent work undertaking to exploit and develop these initiatives of Sacks may be found in Jayyusi (1984) and Hester and Eglin (1997).

[25]A similar point is explored in relating activities to settings in Levinson (1979). The notion of forms of conduct that index social types is pursued in Ochs (1992) and in Brown and Levinson (1979).

Without some grounding of the relevance of that categorization—of *any* categorization—it lacks a compelling warrant, for its correctness by itself does not warrant its invocation on any particular occasion. Given the centrality of the categories in organizing vernacular cultural "knowledge," this equivocality can be profoundly consequential, for which category is employed will carry with it the invocation of commonsense knowledge about that category of person and bring it to bear on the person referred to on some occasion, rather than bringing to bear the knowledge implicated with another category of which the person being referred to is equally a member.

There does not seem to be any general method for establishing the exclusive relevance of any particular category or any particular categorization device. Anyone who is a female is lots of other things as well, as is anyone who is a male. In interaction, selection among the alternatives is grounded in relevance rules, recipient design, the activity being done, and so forth and is accessible to interactional accountability—challenging, convergence between participants, and so on. The same logic applies to noninteractional venues, like writing, research, and so forth (although not necessarily the same accountability).

Without some explicit grounding of the relevance of characterizing the parties to the events being described as "male" and "female," as "doctor" and "patient," as "manager" and "worker," then the claims in the literature on interruption, in common with those of the rest of social science that has proceeded in this way, are profoundly equivocal. This has been aggravated in the case of the literature with which we are concerned here because (1) the events being treated—formulated as they were as "interruption," i.e., a complainable action—were being directed at a category or categories of persons, and (2) the argument has strongly implied, if it has not said so explicitly, that the "interruptors" (whether "male," "professional," "higher status/power," etc.) were doing what they were doing to the "interuptees" by virtue of being themselves male and the others being female, being themselves managers and the others being employees, and so forth, i.e., that these categories informed the parties to those interactions, on the occasion of these actions, as the relevant capacities (or among the relevant capacities) in which conduct was being produced and understood. (This has been as true of the writings in the literature which have contested these findings, or which have sought to characterize the distinctive conduct of some interactants by reference to such categories, e.g., how women talk by virtue of being women.) This surely is the way in which the categories as repositories of commonsense knowledge work. The unproblematicalness with which this presupposition has been put forth, on which the interest of the findings has rested in substantial measure, stands in startling contrast with Sack' demonstration of its profound equivocality. However, raising this issue has at times been treated as antifeminist; even proposing that analysis was required to establish that gender categories were in fact demonstrably relevant to the parties on the interactional occasion of an interruption has often seemed to be taken as offensive.

In what follows, I want to understand both the initial and persistent appeal to plausibility and believability of the findings concerning categorical bases of interruption and the treatment of the questioning of the categories' relevance as offensive. What I think we will find is that the two types of issue that I have raised—about the characterization of the events as "interruption" and of the participants as "male–female" or other such categories—are reflexively connected. Explicating their sources and their connection, however, serves not only to explicate the implicit critique and ground it, but may contribute to rehabilitating the very findings that were being opened to question, or at least allowing a recasting and reappreciation of their import.

Interruption as a Category-Bound Activity

Perhaps I can introduce the conjecture in the following way. Commonly the participants to interaction where interruption figures are not understood or described in such anonymous and activity-specific terms as candidate-interruptor or interrupted. Rather, they are as a matter of cultural practice (both putatively on their part qua participants, and on the part of observers) understood to be members of deeply grounded categories of societal membership, the categories composing the membership categorization devices, but those categories reconfigured in a particular way. In this configuration, the categories come in coordinate pairs, as in: candidate–interruptor is male, candidate–interruptee is female; candidate–interruptor is employer, candidate–interruptee is employee; candidate–interruptor is teacher, candidate–interruptee is student; candidate–interruptor is professional, candidate–interruptee is client; and, generically, candidate–interrutor is *super*ordinate (in power, status, class, income, wealth, knowledge, skill, prestige, legal entitlement, etc.), candidate–interruptee is *sub*ordinate (in the same resource)[26]

The relevant practice can be formulated this way: Confronted with some action that can be taken as an "infliction," if the action is one bound to members of one category as the doer–agent and to members of another category as the victim–patient, and on a given occasion the actual agent and patient are members of the appropriate categories,[27] then "see it that way." [I use here the format of Sacks' (1972a) "viewers' rules," which I will call "observer's rules" to include more than just visual perception.] Then, treating "interruption" as a category-bound action—done by "employers" to "employees," by "men" to "women," and so on—such occurrences get their character as actions—as "interruptions"—via the membership categories of which the involved parties are members, as they in turn reflexively get their relevant identity and characterization (as male–female, professional–client, etc.) via the parsable action that it makes "transparently" graspable.[28] This reflexive practice thereby constitutes a

[26]Indeed, when Smith-Lovin and Brody (1989, p. 425) characterize the literature in this area, the categories they find are exclusively those of putative hierarchy. They write, "Earlier studies have found that men interrupt women, adults interrupt children, doctors interrupt patients (except when the doctor is a 'lady'), the more powerful spouse interrupts the less powerful one, and those with masculine identities interrupt those with more feminine self-images." For the point being discussed in the text, it matters less that the aggregate finding on male–female interruption appears to be inconclusive (cf. the review by James and Clarke, 1993) than that there is a nearly exclusive focus on these categories of inquiry. It is striking to have the finding that "adults interrupt children," with no report about children interrupting adults, or the finding about doctors interrupting patients, juxtaposed with the observation of Paul Drew (personal communication) regarding doctor/patient interaction: "In many cases instances of overlap in which doctors begin speaking whilst patients are already talking are identified—and vilified—as 'interruption.' ... However, points where patients begin speaking whist doctors are still doing so (much more frequent in my experience) are not so treated." Indeed, it is striking that the whole enterprise revolves around categories of person altogether, whether by reference to gender, occupation, place in hierarchy, cultural membership, etc., rather than being focused on the conduct together by which outcomes get interactionally produced. Although some complain about the "inevitability" of references to the West and Zimmerman work which they criticize (Talbot, 1988, p. 113; Murray, 1988, p. 115), what is even more striking is the invocation of categories of members of the society as the decisive way of formulating the character of their conduct. This resonates deeply with the mundane operation of the categories of membership categorization devices and with the workings of category-bound activities in particular.

[27]That is, if they can be mapped into the appropriate categories such that the one who intruded on ongoing talk is a member of a superordinate category and the one intruded upon is a member of not merely a subordinate category, but of such a subordinate category as is paired with the category of which the intruder is a member.

[28]Another such reflexive codetermination of action and participants is described by Sacks (1992, pp. I:594–596) in showing how a veiled move to end a therapy session gets its recognizable import as that action by reference to its having been articulated by "the therapist," i.e., by an individual whose formulation as "therapist" is made relevant

solution to the equivocality problem in formulating/referring to persons; it serves as a relevance rule by which a particular way of grasping and formulating the participants in a scene can be grounded and preferred over others.

This way of proceeding can be proposed to be that used by members in situ as a vernacular interpretive procedure, or not. If it demonstrably is, it can be (and should be) so described by professional analysts. But it is far from clear that it should be adopted by professional analysts as a first-order orientation in their own right to yield analyses of how interaction is coconstructed by parties in its course.[29]

Again, then: Seeing the events as "interruption" in such instances[30] is category-bound not to a discrete MCD or a particular category in an MCD but to a variety of paired category terms that share the feature of relative super/subordinacy.[31] There thus is a reflexive cograsping of the nature and character of the event/action that has occurred and the relevant identities

---

by an utterance which, if articulated by "therapist," signals the ending of the session (with subsequently implicated consequences for the copresent others), but which would not do so if articulated by anyone else, i.e., by any of the other bodies in the room or by anybody not formulated as "therapist."

[29]The issue here is the unproblematized incorporation by professional analysts of vernacular "knowledge" as an unexplicated component of their own analyses. For a more detailed explication of the problem here, cf. Schegloff (1992, pp. xli–xlii).

Several collegial readers of a draft of this chapter have alerted me to a possible misconstrual of what I am suggesting here, namely (as one put it) that I am "charging that researchers are biased (or blinded) by their reliance on commonsense knowledge of such matters. It usually is the case that 'interruption' is given an operational definition, and assuming competent execution of such operations, a classification of events emerges which could show that women interrupt more or that there is no difference (as has been shown by some studies)." Let me be clear: (1) The issue is *not* operationalization and scrupulous observance of appropriate coding procedures in deciding which cases should be counted as "interruption." (2) There is an issue about the relationship between the judgments made by following such a procedure scrupulously and the judgments made by the parties to the interaction in situ. For the type of inquiry at issue here, it is how the participants understand some overlapping utterance—as interruption or not—not the treatment of it by external analysts, no matter how impeccable, that matters, and that must be located in the data of the interaction, not the coding procedures of the investigators. But even that is not the crux of the issue being raised here. (3) Even if each coding decision about overlapping utterances were then reinforced by data analyses grounding the result in the observable conduct of the participants, there would still be the issue of the formulation of the participants as "male" and/or "female," or any other of the categories recurrently employed in the literature. Those too need to be grounded in the observable conduct of the parties. To warrant employment of those categories, it would need to be shown that the parties were oriented, just when the putative interruption occurred, to the category assignments in question in order to ground the investigator's decision to employ those categories rather than any of the other ones available in the cultural inventory of the participants. (On some ways this might be approached, see the second paragraph of note 37.).

This is clearly not how the investigators came to employ these categories. How do they come to use the categories and category sets they do? They might well point to the theoretical or analytical resources of their disciplines. For most of the social sciences, these converge to a substantial degree with the categories provided by the vernacular or commonsense culture, but in an aggregate or generic fashion, not as prompted by the particularities of situations as they arise. It is here that the claims of the text find their point: how inquiries come to be couched in the terms they are, not only with respect to the target event or dependent variable (here "interruption") but in terms of the universe of discourse by which and in which a solution is to be found. That is how Smith-Lovin and Brody (1989) could find (cf. note 26) only the categories they did in their survey of the literature, with no reports of children interrupting adults, of patients interrupting doctors, or more compellingly of any reports couched in terms of categories that are not hierarchically positioned. Further discussion of these issues may be found in Schegloff (1997a) (which, as it happens, deals with an instance of overlap/interruption and its relationship to gender) and in several rounds of exchange with Billig about this chapter (Billig, 1999a,b; Schegloff, 1999a,b).

[30]Obviously not all instances of "interruption" are constituted or construed in this way, or even all those involving participants who can be identified with the relevant category terms.

[31]This is not the MCD (referred to as "R") in which paired-category terms figured in Sacks (1972a). Those were paired relational terms as a locus of obligation, terms of kinship and relationship. These are terms of paired hierarchy.

of the parties engaged in it for observers (which has been the point of departure for the discussion here), but also potentially for the participants as constituting observers of their own interaction. Indeed, such a grasping by observers is on behalf of the participants.

What lends the character of interruption to the events in the talk is the categorical membership of the parties and their distribution of participation or "mapping" in the action (male as interruptor, etc.). What makes male–female self-evidently the relevant set of category terms is the action, once it is formulated as "interruption." Indeed, the categories and category-bound activities can come to figure not only in the interpretation and parsing of the conduct but in its production. The action comes to be seen as a way of "doing being male–female," of "doing gender" (West & Zimmerman, 1987; see also Ochs, 1992).[32] Hence, the irritation that can arise with challenges to provide empirically grounded analysis to establish the relevance of these otherwise equivocal (if ungrounded) categorical identifications. The result is "irritation" or "outrage" because the request for demonstration ipso facto constitutes a nonparticipation by the questioner or critic in the cultural practice which renders the linkage of action-type to membership category transparent via the operation of the "category-bound activity."[33]

This "divergence of perspective" is at the level of the academy and social science. But it also may be a divergence among the primary interactants. There has been much discussion of events that reveal that "whites" see some action as indifferent to race (e.g., a merit denial of "an employee," the prosecution of "a celebrity" for murder) at the same time that "African Americans" see it transparently as informed by considerations of race. This is sometimes attributed to a kind of "omnirelevance of race" for African Americans. A similar omnirelevance of gender is also sometimes invoked, in the same bifurcated way: a stance and vision transparent for women, occluded for men.[34]

The conjecture here raises a related but less broad possibility. Instead of omnirelevance, we may entertain the possibility of divergent or variant ties of category-boundedness, which provide under restricted conditions for differing grasps of "what" has happened and "who" has participated in it. Not everything is a candidate for these divergences. Rather, the right configuration of witnessed event—candidate-characterizable as an instance of action X, together with participants appropriately implicated in its occurrence—candidate-characterizable by categories Y and Z, can get grasped as a *gestalt* by those who have that way of seeing which provides for "such a person" doing "such an action" to "such an other person," and will not be so seen by those who do not have that way of seeing/hearing.[35]

---

[32]There is a resonance here with the view that treats so-called "women's language" not as some sort of biological inheritance but as a practice for the embodiment of a social identity. It seems more cogent to distinguish (if they can indeed be distinguished, which is by no means assured) different practices of talking without at the same time identifying them with categories like gender categories—call them type A and type B—and then specifying differential distribution of these practices among relevant social categories, if any. It might then turn out that some configuration of practices (e.g., the familiar hesitant, self-effacing, etc.) is both treated as specially affiliated to women (either productionally or indexically) and is specially vulnerable to intervention by others (e.g., by way of the overlap onset characterized by Jefferson (1984) as "progressional," i.e., attracted by the retarded progressivity of the talk marked by multiple self-interruption and restart (and see Schegloff, 1979). A great deal of work remains to be done before such a view could be supported with confidence. I am indebted to Celia Kitzinger for suggesting that this connection be made explicit here.

[33]It may be, in this respect, akin to the reactions of some of those unknowingly co-opted into participation in Garfinkel's demonstrations regarding the operation of commonsense knowledge (Garfinkel, 1967, pp. 35–75).

[34]For further discussion of omni-relevance and gender, cf. Schegloff (1992, I:xlviii–l, liii–liv).

[35]Recall here Sacks' (1992, pp. II:184–187) in some respects similar discussion of whites and blacks seeing "cops on a scene with trouble," whites seeing them as the fixers of it, blacks seeing them as the causes of it.

The upshot of this discussion is not that there is no such thing, no such studyable and describable category of events, as "interruption." Nor that it is "uninteresting" (in a scholarly/scientific sense) to study it. Nor that it is not worth studying it by reference to gender. Instead, I have tried to review a variety of elements of conduct that contribute to the eligibility or vulnerability or candidacy of an occurrence in conversation to being taken by a party (or the parties) to it as "interruption," the makings of "possible interruption," which is to treat "interruption" not as a transparent tool of analysis but as a problematic component of the object of analysis. The elements have included many familiar features of the already ongoing talk and of the newly starting talk and perhaps some that are less familiar. To these I have tried to add quite a different sort of ingredient that may figure in the treatment of a spate of overlapping talk as an "interruption": the vernacular origin of the notion "interruption" and its associated action import of "complaint." I have tried to add another different sort of ingredient: the on-occasion inseparable relevance[36] of the mapping of actual participants into hierarchical category pairs, on the one hand, to the constitution/recognition of an occurrence of an "incoming" as an "interruption," on the other—the category-boundedness of the activity and the activity-triggered relevance of the membership categories.[37] "Interruption" is a real

---

[36]By this term I mean to note both that not all casting of incoming talk as "interruption" is so constituted (the "on-occasion" part) but that on the occasions that work this way, the mappings of the participants into membership categories and of the event into the action category "interruption" are inseparable.

[37]Elsewhere (Schegloff, 1997a, pp. 180–182) I take up another instance in which an activity implemented in the talk prompts the introduction of a category term (also a gender category) that has not (ostensibly) otherwise figured in the activity of the moment. A young man at the dinner table, being passed the butter that he has requested, rejects, or mock-rejects, the requests for it of two other diners and then adds, "ladies last," thereby introducing a category that, however correctly and differentially it formulates its referents, is on the face of it not relevant to the activity at hand and that has not otherwise figured in the preceding talk. How the talk engenders the invocation of the category is taken up there and is not relevant here, but the episode reinforces the conjecture that activities can trigger the relevance of categories, even ones that may not otherwise be implicated in the setting at the moment.

But need there be explicit mention of a category (as in "ladies last") in order to show the parties to be oriented to it? How otherwise can it be shown? This question takes on some urgency for those interested in category-related treatments of conduct, who take seriously the need to ground the relevance of the categories in the displayed orientation of the participants in the interaction (cf. note 29). It is not a question that has an established answer that can be simply delivered; it is an issue for a projected line of research that will have to be developed by those committed to pursuing it. I can suggest a promising starting point, however, and that is what is termed in conversation analysis the practice of recipient design [Sacks, 1992; Schegloff, 1972 (where it is referred to as "membership analysis"); Sacks & Schegloff, 1979)]. This refers to the many ways in which talk (and other conduct) is designed to be suited to the recipient to whom it is directed (sometimes specified to a particular known individual, sometimes categorical in character), a practice that then can be consulted for what it reveals about the speaker's orientation to the recipient. I offer here only three sketchy cases in point as illustrations. (1) While shopping once at the local farmer's market, I was complimented by the woman selling pistachio nuts on the boldly patterned shirt I was wearing. When I thanked her, she went on to inform me that it was Thai in origin. I replied that I knew that, and as I walked away, I remarked to my wife that she had offered that information to me as a man; she would not have volunteered it to a woman. The recipient design involved here involves what men as compared to women are taken to know (here about clothing). (2) Some years ago, my colleague Gene Lerner, examining my collection of other-initiated repair sequences (Schegloff, 1997b) happened to examine the instances then already partially analyzed in which women were the speakers of the so-called "trouble-sources" and men were the initiators of repair. The result was described by Heritage (1995, p. 405) as follows: "Or again, in a technical demonstration of a computer program for working with conversational materials, Lerner and Schegloff (personal communication) ran a cross-tabulation linking repair initiation by males on female talk with the content of the repair and found a larger than expected number of cases where the object of the repair initiation was an unusual color term. Here might be an empirical lead on the claim by Lakoff (1975) and others that women use more unusual color terms than men. And still more intriguingly, it opens up an opportunity to explore the possibility that these repair initiations are a vehicle through which males can assert a masculine identity and thereby 'do gender' in interaction" (West & Zimmerman, 1987). (3) Gail Jefferson has an unpublished paper (1997) on the recipient design of laughter by putative "Tarzans" for putative

category of event of members of the society; it is socially situated by them in particular ways; it is not for students of the society to affirm it or deny the category or how it is situated. It is for students of the society to get a handle on how it works and it should not surprise us when that is different from the vernacular grasp of it, and indeed takes the vernacular grasp of it as a major part of what is to be understood.

In the end, it appears that "interruption" is the wrong level of granularity (Schegloff, 2000b) to capture the dynamics of what is going on at the appropriate level of detail, in an appropriately "technical" way, that is, as a matter of technique, of "practice." As a matter of practice, talking-in-interaction relative to others' talk, whether in overlap or not, has to do with where/when to come in under relevantly calibrated and formulated analyses of the state of the talk and positions in it, what to do beat by beat, and so forth. "Interruption" is a vernacular gloss for what it treats as "an event," whose design is precisely to submerge and lose the "technical" (or "technique-al") details in favor of the "upshot" vernacular interactional import. The two takes are alternatives, perhaps irreconcilable alternatives, because the "details" call attention to themselves and lead analysis down their path, which is disabling for parsing-for-interaction, for which the interactional upshot is the critical focus. There is very likely no formula for converting one to the other. The "upshot" is designed to avoid just this attention to technique-al detail and to have the upshot level of granularity be the thing focally analyzed for its import for the interaction. This is the interface between action-as-product and practice-as-method.

DISCUSSION

The central contribution of this chapter and its companion (Schegloff, 2000) has been a detailed analysis of a recurrent contingency of talk-in-interaction—more than one person talking at a time—and its management and an incorporation of the resulting account into an expanded formulation of the organization of turn-taking for conversation. The line that has emerged from these undertakings then has been juxtaposed to prior treatments of a closely related but importantly different phenomenon—interruption—in an effort to clarify some of the issues posed by the literature on that highly visible topic. Before concluding, it may be useful to elaborate some the work developed here for traditional sociological and social psychological interests in power and status as these are played out in the arena of "interruption" in talk-in-interaction, even though conversation-analytic interests in these topics will be quite different.[38]

"Janes," with consequent responsive laughter or its withholding. In such instances, there is no overt reference to gender categories, and yet gender-relevant orientations are displayed. The same resource, I might add can be used for other categories and MCDs as well. (My thanks to Celia Kitzinger for suggesting that I address this matter here.)
[38]And in many instances incompatible. For example, in the remainder of this section I continue to discuss "successful interruption," even though I have earlier found this notion problematic on a number of grounds: (1) The dropping out of one party to an overlap is a contingent product of conduct in the overlap, conduct which is variously motivated. (2) This conduct is a property of overlapping talk, not interruption per se. (3) "Successful interruption" presupposes that intervention is designed to drive the other out and more particularly for the new speaker to drive the prior speaker out, but (a) that is often not what the intervention is for (as in aligning coconstruction), and (b) when it is the "goal," it can be the goal for either party, but only one direction of forcing out is counted as "success." (4) The correlative presupposition is that "dropping out" is "losing" or "failure," but (as shown in Schegloff, 2000, pp. 31–32), it can be a move in an alternative and "larger" success strategy, i.e., to shape the immediately following course of the talk. The upshot, to my mind, is that "successful interruption" is a deeply flawed analytic tool, even if it has a prima facie vernacular resonance. This last feature may prompt social psychologists to incorporate "successful

One payoff promised by this work is an (the) interactional mechanism by which the effects otherwise represented by statistical associations are produced by the participants. Finding a relationship between status/power and interruption or "successful" interruption [whether in contexts meant to approximate the work place a la Smith-Lovin and Brody (1989), or long-term personal relationships a la Kollock et al. (1985)] is analogous to finding an association between smoking and cancer: The association may seem robust, but lacking the mechanism by which it is produced, the phenomenon remains less than fully understood. To be sure, Kollock et al. (1985) make a compelling case for their disentangling of gender per se and power relations in the conduct of interaction. Smith-Lovin and Brody effectively sort out the claimed effects of gender, power, and the sex composition of the interaction. What is lacking is the "cellular biology" that "closes the connection," which explicates the mechanism linking the outcomes being studied, initiating interruptions and "succeeding" with them, and the variables which assertedly engender these outcomes.

If it were just the greater status or power of one of the parties (in whatever context made such factors efficacious), then the outcome would be determined by the onset; all lesser power/ status speakers would stop right after interruption by a higher status/power interruptor. But not all interruptions are "successful" in driving the prior speaker out and many that are successful are successful only after a stretch of talking at once. So something more apparently is involved than status and power in the abstract and in principle. Several sorts of "something more" invite consideration.

One is this. In order to establish the effects of high status or power, researchers pro- cedurally "remove" other effects, varying them or holding them constant by experimental design or statistical manipulation, and so forth. They are treated as "confounding effects" that need to be filtered out so as to establish the robustness of the relationships being studied. But for the participants in the real world, those effects are co-present; it is the "natural" operation of the real world that put them there for experimenters and analysts to control. It is the multiplicity of category memberships, identities, situational contingencies, proximate inter- ests, and projects in the interaction, what is discussed elsewhere (Schegloff, 2000) under the rubric "investments," which inform any person at any moment that is at issue. How do the parties achieve the relevance of their relative power and status (among all other features and projects of the setting) in some here-and-now (if indeed they do so)? How is that activated (if it is) so as to have the effects that researchers claim them to have? Is it exclusively by some anterior, cognitively processed and affectively informed orientation to one another? Or do the parties do things that engender others' orientations to the features in question, features such as their relative power or status? And how? That is what conduct in the overlap can be about: activating whatever features can be found to make it relevant for the parties. For the objec- tively factual higher power of one of them, or their gender, remains to have its relevance activated at some here-and-now, and when it is not made relevant, perhaps the higher status/ power member of the interaction does not start in the course of another's talk, or having started does not press the matter to "success" (or is committed to a different criterion of success).

More lies down this path: once this issue is taken seriously, how the status/power of the parties is made relevant, at a determinate moment, out of the range of identities and other features of the interaction that have a claim on the next increment of conduct, it is not only the instances in which the high-power party's interruption is, for example, not successful that

interruption" in further inquiry nonetheless, and I include it in this section of the chapter for that reason. Similar grounds inform other instances in which this section appears to revive notions seriously called into question in earlier sections.

invites review. Even if the "power differential" has been made relevant, it does not follow that it—or it alone—accounts for an overlap/interruption's outcome. All instances invite reexamination to elucidate what social and interactional process a particular successful interruption exemplifies and illuminates.

Features other than power/status aside, a second sense of the "something more" to be pursued may be couched as a question: how does the activation of those features, whether status or power or gender per se, come to have the effects which it does? How does higher status "lead to" overlap onset? How does it lead to "successful" interruption, i.e., to the dropping out of the prior speaker? As noted earlier, if what was relevant was just the fact of differentials in status or power, the "lower status/power" interrupted party would "fold" at the first hint of overlap. This is another thing then: explicating in detail the "translation" of the relevant "factors" into their moment-to-moment import for the conduct of the parties—*both* of them—and how contingent outcomes (sometimes "success" for the interruptor, sometimes not) are produced by the consequent conduct in interaction.

Smith-Lovin and Body (1989, p. 432), for example, write that

> ... interruptions are more likely to succeed against women than against men (especially when interruptions are disruptive and negative in character). men, on the other hand, are more able to fend off potential disruptions, especially when directed at them by women (... especially ... with neutral interruptions).

But how are these successes and "fendings off" achieved? How do they vary by tenor of interruption (i.e., "disruptive," "negative," "neutral")? If status and power make a difference, it not only is by "recipient design," that is, by the design of conduct by reference to the identity of the recipient, whether categorical, relational, or personal, it also is by step-by-step working out in the interaction what the outcome of the overlap—*this* overlap—is to be. For the most part, Smith-Lovin and Brody's account is conceptual, categorical, psychological, and conjectural. But some empirically specifiable mechanisms are involved.

Similarly, Kollock et al. (1985, p. 40) report that "interruptions are clearly a sign of conversational dominance"; but, noting that in more than half the cases the interrupted party did not yield the floor, they go on to suggest that "Perhaps ... it is better to think of interruptions as *attempts* at conversational control. Successful interruptions, then, become a more sensitive measure of *actual* dominance." But what then—interactionally, behaviorally— makes of an "interruption" a "successful interruption?" Whether or not this "success" in indicative of dominance or of something else, how is what it achieves achieved?

Indeed, perhaps the "something more" that invites inclusion in these accounts is the very locus, the very mechanism, by which power and status are brought to bear, are embodied, are parceled out in limited or unlimited commitments. The operation of this mechanism is directly observable and describable—it is the overlap resolution device described in the companion to this paper, or some subsequent, more sophisticated version of it. Whatever conceptual intermediaries are invoked or hypothesized to account for the observed results (Kollock et al., 1985, pp. 42–45; Smith-Lovin & Brody, 1989, pp. 432–434), surely the conduct through which the effects are achieved must play a central role in the account. In the end, it is that conduct that closes the connection between gender–status–power and interactional outcome.

Again, let me be clear. I am not here arguing the position that interruptions or "successful" interruptions, in the vernacular import of those terms, are not a matter of status, power, dominance, gender, and so forth; only that, if that is so, some sort of linkage—in conduct, not in concept—needs to be shown.[39] Studies too often disengage an outcome, such as the

---

[39]Nor am I arguing for further experimental studies to do the showing. It is in the analysis of the raw materials of interaction that the showing is to be done, preferably in naturally occurring interactions of the participants' ordinary

occurrence of, or success of, an interruption, from the behavioral and contextual elements in which it was embedded and by reference to which it was produced by the participants; they aggregate such disengaged outcomes and relate them, instead of to their real life context in the round, to disengaged elements of the investigator's preferred analytical commitments. That may not necessarily yield problematic outcomes within the investigator's own frame of reference, but it does replace statistical and conceptual representations disengaged from their empirical counterparts for the robust and textured configuration of elements (or rather, the preserved detailed records of them) in which the outcomes of interaction were formed up.[40] Where the understanding of an empirical process is in question this is not desirable, and it is not necessary. The work reported earlier in this chapter and its companion may provide resources for enriching work in this genre in this respect.

CONCLUSION

Having elsewhere provided an account of the practices by which overlapping talk is resolved in conversation and other forms of talk-in-interaction (Schegloff, 2000), I have tried here to work out the implications of this aspect of the organization of turn-taking for a proper understanding of interruption, which over the last 30 years of social science inquiry has received the bulk of the attention accorded this entire domain. One upshot has been that the conventional understanding of interruption, grounded in its onset and its outcome, does not fare well when juxtaposed with the data of what actually happens in the talk, and that social scientific work based on this notion is problematic. How then has it come to have the shape and character it has?

One possibility is that the unanalyzed incorporation of the vernacular action category "interruption" has imported into the proposed analyses a moral component that resonates with what early ethnomethodology termed "practical theorizing" and "commonsense knowledge," but which is incompatible with the "mere description" that conversation analytic inquiry aims at. The conjecture pursued here has been that the action category "interruption" has implicated associated categories of actors—agents and patients—who have populated and dominated the literature in this area. As a consequence, that literature has featured the social structural scaffolding for conduct rather more prominently than that "social action," with its "subjective meaning tak[ing] account of the behavior of others and ... thereby oriented in its course," which Weber (1978, p. 4) envisioned as being at the heart of sociology. The discipline that Weber envisioned but did not in fact pursue may now in fact be possible, whether it will be called "sociology" or something else.[41] Whatever contribution it may make in its own right, it may be useful to ask how much of the sociology of the past 100 years is to be understood, or reunderstood, by reference to the absence of appropriate resources for the study of social action in its most immediate contexts of occurrence and its consequent displacement to more distal categories of social structure. Has the time come to review the consequent, attenuated, indexical connections between social structure and social interaction?

The broader possibility embodied in this work invites collegial reflection. A very great

---

lives where real "investments" may be mobilized at particular junctures in the talk, but if not there, in the talk already collected for such past studies as have talk-in-interaction that defensibly bears on these issues. Working with such materials may, however, make the alternative terms of analysis introduced here and in Schegloff (2000) more attractive.

[40]For another locus of this problem in social science, see Suchman and Jordan (1990).

[41]How ironic it would be if the delivery of "verstehende Soziologie" were to come from the once-despised "hippie sociology from California" (Gellner, 1975).

range of sociological theories and analytical stances takes the conduct held to compose the world of social life as the point of departure and return for their mandate and are grounded either explicitly or implicitly in some view of what that conduct is, in what terms it should be understood, what is or is not relevant in and about it, and what shapes and drives it. At bottom, almost all such views of what the conduct is are derived from the vernacular culture of the society and are assessed (if they are assessed at all) not by repeatable, direct, and detailed observation of such naturally occurring conduct, but by tighter or looser derivation of inferences which are then compared with data that are largely grounded in those same vernacular presuppositions.

Work of the sort presented here and especially in the companion paper on which this chapter draws offers the possibility of an alternative. Our notions of how social conduct is composed, shaped, driven, and so forth can now be made accessible to the constraint of direct observation. Some will not survive the challenge of meeting the constraint; some will be enhanced and specified by it. Much will have to be reformulated and recalibrated once significant numbers of workers begin to look—at this relevant level of detail—at the occurrences that compose most directly the observable stuff of the society.

ACKNOWLEDGMENTS: This chapter is a companion piece to Schegloff (2000). Originally written as a single paper, considerations of length and thematic diversity prompted a reconfiguration into two separate papers. What is now the "other companion" paper is an empirically grounded analysis and explication of the practices deployed by participants in interaction who find themselves talking simultaneously, complemented by digitized sound files of the supporting data, accessible on the worldwide web. The details of that analysis are not irrelevant to the examination of "interruption" in the present chapter, but are necessarily barely glossed in the summary review of the companion paper in this one. Full appreciation of the present chapter would be greatly enhanced by (ideally prior) reading of the other.

I have benefited over the years from comments from many students and colleagues on both the larger work and the separate parts into which it has been deconstructed, most recently Rogers Brubaker, Steve Clayman, Paul Drew, John Heritage, Celia Kitzinger, Gene Lerner, Candace West, Tom Wilson, and Don Zimmerman; where their contributions have been appropriated, it mostly has been without further notice.

I was able to pursue work on this project while I was the grateful beneficiary (during the 1998–1999 academic year) of a Guggenheim Fellowship and a Fellowship in Residence at the Center for Advanced Study in the Behavioral Sciences, Stanford, California, under support provided to the Center by the National Science Foundation through Grant # SBR-9022192. Parts of this work also have benefited from research on other-initiated repair supported by the National Science Foundation under Grant No. BNS-87-20388.

REFERENCES

Bennett, A. (1981). Interruptions and the interpretation of conversation. *Discourse Processes, 4,* 171–188.
Billig, M. (1999a). Whose terms? Whose ordinariness? Rhetoric and ideology in conversation analysis. *Discourse & Society, 10,* 543–558.
Billig, M. (1999b). Conversation analysis and the claims of naivete. *Discourse & Society, 10,* 572–576.
Brown, P., & Levinson, S. (1979). Social structure, groups and interaction. In K. Scherer & H. Giles (Eds.), *Social markers of speech* (pp. 292–341). Cambridge: Cambridge University Press.
Clayman, S. E., & Whalen, J. (1988/1989). When the medium becomes the message: The case of the Rather–Bush appointment. *Research on Language and Social Interaction, 22,* 241–272.

Coates, J. (1988). Gossip revisited: Language in all-female groups. In J. Coates & D. Cameron (Eds.), *Women in their speech communities: New perspectives on language and sex* (pp. 94–122). London, New York: Longman.

Coates, J., & Cameron, D. (Ed.). (1988). *Women in their speech communities: New perspectives on language and sex.* London, New York: Longman.

Edelsky, C. (1981). Who's got the floor? *Language in Society, 10*, 383–421.

Egbert, M. (1997). Schisming: The collaborative transformation from a single conversation to multiple conversations. *Research on Language and Social Interaction, 30*, 1–51.

Ford, C. E., & Thompson, S. A. (1996). Interactional units in conversation: syntactic, intonational, and pragmatic resources of the management of turns. In E. Ochs, E. A. Schegloff, & S. A. Thompson (Eds.), *Interaction and grammar* (pp. 134–184). Cambridge: Cambridge University Press.

French, P., & Local, J. K. (1983). Turn-competitive incomings. *Journal of Pragmatics, 7*, 17–38.

Garfinkel, H. (1967). *Studies in ethnomethodology.* Englewood Cliffs, NJ: Prentice-Hall.

Gellner, E. (1975). Ethnomethodology: The re-enchantment industry or a Californian way of subjectivity. *Philosophy of the Social Sciences, 5*, 431–450.

Goffman, E. (1981). *Forms of talk.* Philadelphia: University of Pennsylvania Press.

Goodwin, C. (1979). The interactive construction of a sentence in natural conversation. In G. Psathas (Ed.), *Everyday language: Studies in ethnomethodology* (pp. 97–121). New York: Irvington Publishers.

Goodwin, M. H. (1997). By-play: Negotiating evaluation in story-telling. In G. R. Guy, C. Feagin, D. Schiffrin, & J. Baugh (Eds.), *Towards a social science of language: Papers in honor of William Labov, Volume 2: Social interaction and discourse structures* (pp. 77–102). Amsterdam/Philadelphia: John Benjamins.

Heritage, J. C. (1995). Conversation analysis: Methodological aspects. In U. M. Quasthoff (Ed.), *Aspects of oral communication* (pp. 391–418). Berlin: De Gruyter.

Hester, S., & Eglin, P. (Ed.). (1997). *Culture in action: Studies in membership categorization analysis.* Washington, DC: University Press of America.

James, D., & Clarke, S. (1993). Women, men, and interruptions: A critical review. In D. Tannen (Ed.), *Gender and conversation interaction* (p. 231–280). New York: Oxford University Press.

Jayyusi, L. (1984). *Categorization and the moral order.* Boston: Routledge & K. Paul.

Jefferson, G. (1973). A case of precision timing in ordinary conversation: overlapped tag-positioned address terms in closing sequences. *Semiotica, 9*, 47–96.

Jefferson, G. (1984). Notes on some orderlinesses of overlap onset. In V. D'urso & P. Leonardi (Eds.), *Discourse analysis and natural rhetorics* (pp. 11–38). Padova, Italy: CLEUP Editore.

Jefferson, G. (1997). A note on laughter in "male-female" interaction. Paper delivered at the annual Conference of the Center for Language, Interaction and Culture (CLIC), UCLA, Los Angeles, CA.

Kollock, P., Blumstein, P., & Schwartz, P. (1985). Sex and power in interaction: Conversational privileges and duties. *American Sociological Review, 50*, 24–46.

Lakoff, R. (1975). *Language and women's place.* New York: Harper.

Lerner, G. H. (1991). On the syntax of sentences-in-progress. *Language in society, 20*, 441–458.

Lerner, G. H. (1996). On the "semi-permeable" character of grammatical units in conversation: Conditional entry into the turn space of another speaker. In E. Ochs, E. A. Schegloff, & S. A. Thompson (Eds.), *Interaction and grammar* (pp. 238–276). Cambridge: Cambridge University Press.

Levinson, S. (1979). Activity types and language. *Linguistics, 17*, 365–399.

Lynch, M. (1993). *Scientific practice and ordinary action: Ethnomethodology and social studies of science.* Cambridge: Cambridge University Press.

Moerman, M. (1988). *Talking culture: Ethnography and conversation analysis.* Philadelphia: University of Pennsylvania Press.

Murray, S. O. (1985). Toward a model of members' methods for recognizing interruptions. *Language in Society, 13*, 31–41.

Murray, S. O. (1988). The sound of simultaneous speech, the meaning of interruption: A rejoinder. *Journal of Pragmatics, 12*, 115–116.

Murray, S. O., & Covelli, L. H. (1988). Women and men speaking at the same time. *Journal of Pragmatics, 12*, 103–111.

Ochs, E. (1992). Indexing gender. In A. Duranti & C. Goodwin (Eds.), *Rethinking context: Language as an interactive phenomenon* (pp. 335–358). Cambridge: Cambridge University Press.

Sacks, H. (1972a). An initial investigation of the usability of conversational materials for doing sociology. In D. N. Sudnow (Ed.), *Studies in social interaction* (pp. 31–74). New York: Free Press.

Sacks, H. (1972b). On the analyzability of stories by children. In J. J. Gumperz & D. Hymes (Eds.), *Directions in sociolinguistics: The ethnography of communication* (pp. 325–345). New York: Holt, Rinehart and Winston.

Sacks, H. (1992). *Lectures on conversation*, 2 volumes, G. Jefferson (Ed.). Oxford, England: Blackwell.

Sacks, H., & Schegloff, E. A. (1979). Two preferences in the organization of reference to persons and their interaction.

In G. Psathas (Ed.), *Everyday language: Studies in ethnomethodology* (pp. 15–21). New York: Irvington Publishers.

Sacks, H., Schegloff, E. A., & Jefferson, G. (1974). A simplest systematics for the organization of turn-taking for conversation. *Language, 50*, 696–735.

Schegloff, E. A. (1972). Notes on a conversational practice: Formulating place. In D. N. Sudnow (Ed.), *Studies in social interaction* (pp. 75–119). New York: Free Press.

Schegloff, E. A. (1979). The relevance of repair for syntax-for-conversation. In T. Givon (Ed.), *Syntax and semantics 12: Discourse and syntax* (pp. 261–288). New York: Academic Press.

Schegloff, E. A. (1982). Discourse as an interactional achievement: Some uses of "uh huh" and other things that come between sentences. In D. Tannen (Ed.), *Georgetown University roundtable on languages and linguistics 1981; Analyzing discourse: Text and talk* (pp. 71–93). Washington, DC: Georgetown University Press.

Schegloff, E. A. (1988). Goffman and the analysis of conversation. In P. Drew & A. Wootton (Eds.), *Erving Goffman: Exploring the interaction order* (pp. 89–135). Cambridge, England: Polity Press.

Schegloff, E. A. (1988/1989). From interview to confrontation: Observations on the Bush/Rather encounter. *Research on Language and Social Interaction, 22*, 215–240.

Schegloff, E. A. (1992). Introduction, Volume 1. In G. Jefferson (Ed.), *Harvey Sacks: Lectures on conversation* (pp. ix–lxii). Oxford, England: Blackwell.

Schegloff, E. A. (1993). Reflections on quantification in the study of conversation. *Research on Language and Social Interaction, 26*, 99–128.

Schegloff, E. A. (1995). Discourse as an interactional achievement III: The omnirelevance of action. *Research on Language and Social Interaction, 28*, 185–211.

Schegloff, E. A. (1996a). Turn organization: One intersection of grammar and interaction. In E. Ochs, E. A. Schegloff, & S. A. Thompson (Eds.), *Interaction and grammar* (pp. 52–133). Cambridge, England: Cambridge University Press.

Schegloff, E. A. (1996b). Issues of relevance for discourse analysis: Contingency in action, interaction and co-participant context. In E. H. Hovy & D. Scott (Eds.), *Computational and conversational discourse: Burning issues—An interdisciplinary account* (pp. 3–38). Heidelberg: Springer Verlag.

Schegloff, E. A. (1996c). Confirming allusions: Toward an empirical account of action. *American Journal of Sociology, 104*, 161–216.

Schegloff, E. A. (1996d). Some practices for referring to persons in talk-in-interaction: A partial sketch of a systematics. In B. A. Fox (Ed.), *Studies in anaphora* (pp. 437–485). Amsterdam: John Benjamins.

Schegloff, E. A. (1997a). Whose text? Whose context? *Discourse & Society, 8*, 165–187.

Schegloff, E. A. (1997b). Practices and actions: Boundary cases of other-initiated repair. *Discourse Processes, 23*, 499–545.

Schegloff, E. A. (1998). Reflections on studying prosody in talk-in-interaction. *Language and Speech, 41*, 235–263.

Schegloff, E. A. (1999a). "Schegloff's Texts" as "Billig's Data": A critical reply to Billig. *Discourse & Society, 10*, 558–571.

Schegloff, E. A. (1999b). Naivete vs. sophistication or discipline vs. self-indulgence: A rejoinder to Billig. *Discourse & Society, 10*, 577–582.

Schegloff, E. A. (2000a). Overlapping talk and the organization of turn-taking for conversation. *Language in Society, 29*, 1–63.

Schegloff, E. A. (2000b). On granularity. *Annual Review of Sociology, 26*, 715–720.

Schegloff, E. A., Ochs, E., & Thompson, S. A. (1996). Introduction. In E. Ochs, E. A. Schegloff, & S. A. Thompson (Eds.), *Interaction and grammar* (pp. 1–51). Cambridge, England: Cambridge University Press.

Smith-Lovin, L., & Brody, C. (1989). Interruptions in group discussions: The effects of gender and group composition. *American Sociological Review, 54*, 424–435.

Suchman, L. A., & Jordan, B. (1990). Interactional troubles in face-to-face survey interviews. *Journal of the American Statistical Association, 85*, 232–241.

Talbot, M. (1988). The operation was a success; unfortunately the patient died: A common on "Women and Men Speaking at the Same Time," by Murray and Covelli. *Journal of Pragmatics, 12*, 113–114.

Tannen, D. (1983). When is an overlap not an interruption? One component of conversational style. In R. J. Dipietro, W. Frawley, & A. Wedel (Eds.), *The first Delaware symposium on language studies* (pp. 119–129). Newark: University of Delaware Press.

Tannen, D. (1989). Interpreting interruption in conversation. In *Papers from the 25th annual regional meeting of the Chicago Linguistics Society* (pp. 266–287). Chicago: Chicago Linguistic Society.

Weber, M. (1978). *Economy and society: An outline of interpretive sociology* (Guenther Roth & Claus Wittich, Trans.). Berkeley and Los Angeles: University of California Press.

Wells, B., & Macfarlane, S. (1998). Prosody as an interactional resource; Turn-projection and overlap. *Language and Speech, 41*, 265–294.

West, C. (1979). Against our will: Male interruptions of females in cross-sex conversation. *Annals of the New York Academy of Sciences, 327,* 81–97.

West, C. (1984). when the doctor is a "lady": Power, status and gender in physician–patient exchanges. *Symbolic Interaction, 7,* 87–106.

West, C., & Zimmerman, D. H. (1983). Small insults: A study of interruptions in cross-sex conversations between unacquainted persons. In B. Thorne, C. Kramarae, & N. Henley (Eds.), *Language, gender and society* (pp. 102–117). Rowley, MA: Newbury House.

West, C., & Zimmerman, D. H. (1987). Doing gender. *Gender & Society, 1,* 125–151.

Zimmerman, D. H., & West, C. (1975). Sex roles, interruptions and silences in conversation. In B. Thorne & N. Henley (Eds.), *Language and sex: Difference and dominance* (pp. 105–129). Rowley, MA: Newbury House.

CHAPTER 16

Inequality, Status, and the Construction of Status Beliefs

CECILIA L. RIDGEWAY

As Weber (1922/1968) observed, status is a fundamental dimension of social inequality in complex societies, along with wealth and power. Status inequality is based on evaluative rankings in terms of social honor, esteem, and prestige. Compared to wealth and power, the organization and consequences of inequality based on status is relatively undertheorized in contemporary American sociology, at least as a large-scale social process. Part of the difficulty in developing comprehensive analyses of status inequality derives from the multilevel nature of status processes. Status involves evaluative relations between social groups, such as occupations, ethnic groups, or genders. It also involves hierarchies of esteem and influence among actors.

In his analysis, Weber focused on the status honor attached to groups of people who recognize each other as equals and share a "style of life." The status honor of groups, he argued, is a dimension of social cleavage and inequality that, while correlated with wealth and power, cannot be simply reduced to them. Weber's insight about the importance of group status survives in contemporary studies of social stratification in a relatively truncated and undertheorized form. It is typically reduced to measures of occupational prestige and educational attainment.

A different tradition of American sociology, on the other hand, has devoted decades to studying status processes. Furthermore, it has developed systematic theories and evidence in regard to them (Balkwell, 1991; Berger & Zelditch, 1998; Berger, Conner, & Fisek, 1974; Berger, Fisek, Norman, & Zelditch, 1977; Fisek, Berger, & Norman, 1991; Goffman, 1956, 1970; Lovaglia, Lucas, Houser, Thye, & Markovsky, 1998; Ridgeway & Walker, 1995; Skvoretz & Fararo, 1996; Troyer & Younts, 1997; Webster & Foschi, 1988). This tradition, however, approaches status as a hierarchy of influence, deference, and esteem that emerges from interaction among actors.

To better understand the role of status in social inequality, we need to understand the relationship between status between groups and status hierarchies among actors. There are two reasons why it would be valuable to achieve such a more comprehensive account of status

CECILIA L. RIDGEWAY • Department of Sociology, Stanford University, Stanford, California 94305.

Handbook of Sociological Theory, edited by Jonathan H. Turner. Kluwer Academic / Plenum Publishers, New York, 2002.

inequality. First, even casual observation of human affairs suggests that the social esteem in which people are held is a powerful motivating factor in their behavior and consequently in the organization of social life. Teenagers risk physical harm for "respect" in the streets. Athletes turn down lucrative financial offers because they feel the offer does not show them the respect they deserve. Executives jockey for influence on the board. Academics struggle for esteemed reputations.

In addition, status processes are a process through which one type of social "closure" and exclusion occurs (Giddens, 1973). This, of course, was Weber's point. Stratification theorists emphasize the importance of social, cultural, and institutional exclusionary mechanisms that effectively channel people toward positions of power and wealth that are consistent with their social background and away from those that are inconsistent with that background. Interactional status processes have been shown to bias the perceived competence, performance, and influence of people in manner consistent with their social background. This, in turn, affects those people's opportunity to achieve positions of power, wealth, and social honor (Lovaglia et al., 1998; Ridgeway, 1997; Webster & Foschi, 1988). This can be viewed as a closure and exclusion process that contributes to inequality on the basis of status valued social distinctions such as occupation, race, gender, and education.

The task of building a systematic account of status inequality that links status between groups with status hierarchies among actors is complex. The systematic theory and knowledge that has accumulated in regard to status hierarchies among actors, however, provides a useful theoretical platform from which to approach the problem. This body of knowledge directs our attention to the linking concept of status beliefs. Status beliefs are widely shared cultural beliefs that people in one social group (professionals, men, whites) are more esteemed and competent than people in another social group (service workers, women, people of color) (Berger et al., 1977; Ridgeway & Walker, 1995). Status beliefs can be held as people's perceptions of what "most others" believe or as what people themselves believe. As their definition suggests, status beliefs are cultural representations of the evaluative relationship between social groups or categories of people in a society.

Status beliefs construct and justify inequality between social groups by asserting differences between them in social worth and competence. By so doing, status beliefs affirm the significance of the group distinction for social relations in a society. As a variety of researchers have observed, in virtually all societies the social distinctions among people that are most important for organizing social relations (e.g., gender, ethnicity, age, education, and occupation) are also status-valued distinctions (Sidanius & Pratto, 1988; Jackman, 1994). Perhaps not surprisingly, then, research on status hierarchies among individuals has repeatedly demonstrated that these hierarchies are largely organized by the way people's distinguishing attributes evoke status beliefs about the social groups to which they belong (see Webster & Foschi, 1988, for a review). Status beliefs tell people "who" they are dealing with.

Although status beliefs are a key linking mechanism between group-level status distinctions in a society and status hierarchies among individuals, we have surprisingly little knowledge about the social processes by which status beliefs emerge, are maintained, or change. A systematic account of multilevel status processes will remain out of reach until we gain a greater understanding of the social determinants of status beliefs.

Status construction theory is a recent effort to describe one (although not the only) set of processes through which status beliefs arise or change in a population (Ridgeway, 1991, 1997, 2000; Ridgeway & Balkwell, 1997; Ridgeway, Boyle, Kuipers, & Robinson, 1998; Webster & Hysom, 1998). Status construction theory is built on the theoretical platform of expectation states theory. Expectation states theory, in turn, is the dominant and empirically best-documented account of the organization of status hierarchies among actors (see Wagner & Berger, 1993, for a review). Thus, status construction theory builds on what is known about microlevel status processes and attempts to formulate initial links between these processes and group-level status dynamics. This chapter reviews status construction theory and research that addresses it. In order to do so, it begins with a brief review of the evidence in regard to microlevel status processes and expectation states theory's account of these processes.

INTERACTIONAL STATUS HIERARCHIES

When people interact in regard to a shared, collective goal or task, inequalities quickly emerge among them in how much they participate, the attention and evaluation they receive from others, and the influence they achieve over group decisions (Bales, 1970; Fisek et al., 1991; Fisek & Ofshe, 1970; Strodtbeck, James, & Hawkins, 1957). Expectation states theory calls this interactional status hierarchy a power and prestige order and explains it in terms of the implicit performance expectations group members form for themselves compared to each other member of the group (Berger et al., 1974, 1977; Wagner & Berger, 1993). Performance expectations, which are often unconscious, are members' guesses about the likely usefulness of their own contributions to the group task or goal compared the contributions of another. The lower an actor's expectations for her own contributions compared to another's, the more likely she is to hesitate in presenting her own ideas, to ask the other for suggestions, to react positively to ideas the other presents, and to accept influence from the other. In this self-fulfilling manner, each member's expectation disadvantage (or advantage) compared to others shapes her participation, evaluation, attention, and influence, creating a behavioral power and prestige order. A large body of evidence supports this account of status in goal-oriented encounters (see Wagner & Berger, 1993; Ridgeway & Walker, 1995, for reviews). Note that this account reveals interactional status hierarchies to be a ranking of members in terms of expected competence in the situation and in status-marking behaviors such as assertion, deference, and influence.

Since members' expectations for one another's competence in the situation drives the behavioral power and prestige order, expectation states theory devotes its attention to predicting how social factors shape the formation of these expectations. Research has shown that differences in the social rewards or resources, such as pay, that actors possess tend to create corresponding expectations about competence and therefore influence and deference in the situation (Cook, 1975; Harrod, 1980; Stewart & Moore, 1992). Actors' assertive or hesitant behaviors in themselves also tend to create self-fulfilling expectations for differences in competence (Berger et al., 1974; Fisek et al., 1991). However, among the most pervasive and powerful factors that shape competence expectations and power and prestige in a setting are social distinctions such as gender, race, education, or occupation that carry status value in society.

Extensive research has shown that when a status-valued social distinction becomes salient in a situation, either because actors differ on the distinction (e.g., gender in a mixed sex context) or it is relevant to the situation (gender in a gender-linked situation), status beliefs about the distinction are evoked and shape the expectations actors form for one another's competence in the local situation. Through this implicit, usually unconscious process, people who belong to more honored social groups (men, whites, professionals) expect themselves and are expected by others to be more competent than people in the situation from less-honored social groups (women, nonwhites, service workers). As a consequence, those from more honored groups are emboldened to act more assertively, are given more opportunities to perform, are perceived as performing better, are attributed more underlying ability, and may actually perform better, given their greater opportunities, compared to those from less-honored social groups (see Webster & Foschi, 1988; Foschi, 1998, for reviews; see Lovaglia et al., 1998; Troyer & Younts, 1997, for recent developments).

Interactional processes in schools, job interviews, and workplaces mediate many of the processes by which people are directed toward or away from positions of power, material rewards, and social honor. Consequently, the implicit status processes that organize these interactions act as social closure processes that subtly but persistently channel people from higher-status groups toward more valued social outcomes than those that people from lower status groups are channeled toward.

The decades of systematic theorizing and research about status processes at the micro-level have demonstrated that cultural status beliefs about the evaluative standing of social groups are persistently at play in goal-oriented interactional contexts. Status construction theory takes this basic finding as its initial point of departure. The theory reasons that, if status beliefs are continually at play in interaction, then encounters among people, especially across social difference boundaries, are likely to be a potent forum for the creation, spread, mainte-nance, and change of status beliefs about those social differences (Ridgeway, 1991, 2000; Ridgeway & Balkwell, 1997; Ridgeway & Erickson, 2000; Ridgeway et al., 1998).

STATUS CONSTRUCTION THEORY

Status construction theory argues that when people on opposite sides of a social differ-ence boundary regularly interact in regard to shared goals, the terms on which they interact, which will be shaped by structural conditions such as resources differences, affect the hierarchies of influence and esteem that emerge in the encounters. The repeated association between people's social difference categories and their influence and esteem in encounters induces participants to form shared status beliefs about the social difference. People carry these status beliefs to subsequent encounters with individuals from the other category and by acting on the beliefs induce some of those others to take on the status beliefs as well. This creates a diffusion process that under some structural conditions will create roughly consen-sual (i.e., widely shared) status beliefs. In effect, status construction theory argues that inter-actional contexts "bootstrap" the formation of consensual status beliefs about social groups or categories by creating powerful local realities for people that embody for them and appear to presume a given status belief before the belief is widely accepted in actuality.

As this brief summary implies, status construction theory applies to the development, maintenance, and change of status beliefs about socially distinguished groups or categories of people who are cooperatively interdependent in that they must regularly interact to achieve mutual goals. The theory does not argue that the processes it describes are the only means by which status beliefs develop in such populations. However, if the processes described by status construction theory can be shown to be sufficient to produce status beliefs and if they are plausibly present in society in regard to a socially salient distinction such as gender or race, then they are likely to be important for maintaining or changing status beliefs about that distinction. These processes can contribute or undermine current status beliefs about a social distinction whether or not they played a role in the actual historical origin of those beliefs.

The social distinction that provides the group boundary around which status beliefs form can be marked by anything from lifestyle to behavioral or physical attributes. The theory assumes that the distinction is relatively salient in that it is easily recognized among the population. Since the more salient a social attribute is, the more susceptible it is to acquire status value, the theory assumes that the distinction in question is not systematically correlated with distinguishing attributes (other than resources) that are more salient than it is. Of course, the social demarcation of a difference and the development of status beliefs about it are likely to shape one another in a reciprocal process. Simply to provide a logical starting point, the theory assumes that a social distinction exists that is easily recognized in the population but has not yet acquired a status evaluation that is widely shared in the population. In that sense, it is a nominal (i.e., unordered) distinction among people in the society.

There is substantial evidence that the simple creation of a difference boundary of any sort between people is enough to create evaluative favoritism in them for their own group or category (Brewer & Brown, 1998; Messick & Mackie, 1989; Dovidio & Gaertner, 1993; Turner, 1987). It is important to keep in mind, however, that there is a difference between this simple in-group favoritism and the formation of status beliefs. With the development of status beliefs, groups on both sides of a difference boundary agree, or at least concede, that one group is socially recognized as more esteemed and more competent than the other group. Thus it is the beliefs of those who are disadvantaged by status beliefs that distinguish such beliefs from the in-group bias created by difference alone. For status beliefs to emerge, such people must overcome their tendency to prefer their own group and come to believe that, as a matter of social reality, the other group is more socially respected and competent than their own.

As this discussion implies, status beliefs are beliefs about what "most people" think. The presumption that "most people" would accept a given status belief gives that belief a social validity that allows it to constrain people's behavior (Ridgeway, 2000). It makes the belief seem to be a "social fact" that the person must deal with whether she likes it or not. Status construction theory argues that interactional contexts create powerful local realities for their participants that give them the sense that most people would accept a given status belief. In this way, interactional contexts persuade people to take on status beliefs even when those beliefs disadvantage their own group.

To explain how interactional processes create widely shared status beliefs in a population, status construction theory offers arguments that proceed on two levels. At the macrolevel, that theory considers how structural conditions affect the rate of encounters across the group boundary (say, between As and Bs) and the terms on which these encounters occur. Principal among the structural conditions that shape the terms of encounters are inequalities between the groups in the distribution of material resources or other factors, such as the control of technology, that would systematically bias the development of influence hierarchies in inter-group (i.e., A/B) encounters. At the microlevel, the theory offers an account of the processes by which intergroup encounters induce their participants to form and spread status beliefs about the group distinction. The two levels of arguments come together in the consideration of whether status beliefs acquired in local encounters have the potential to spread widely in society or whether they are likely to dissipate in a meaningless sea of conflicting beliefs about the group distinction. I will first describe the theory's microlevel arguments about interaction and the formation of status beliefs, along with empirical tests of these arguments. These microlevel arguments build on the platform of accumulated theory and evidence about interactional status processes. Then I will return to the theory's macrolevel arguments about the structural conditions in which these belief formation processes are embedded and describe how these conditions shape the likelihood that widely shared status beliefs will emerge. The macrolevel arguments draw on an insight from Weber's observations about status distinctions between groups.

Interaction and the Formation of Status Beliefs

The core of status construction theory is a deceptively simple set of assumptions abut how interactional contexts induce people to form and spread status beliefs. Expectation states research has demonstrated that interactional status hierarchies in goal-oriented contexts can be understood as observable orders of power and prestige, or status-marking behaviors (e.g., influence, opportunities to participate, evaluation, and participation) that are driven by actors' underling assumptions about each other's relative competence in the situation. Status construction theory argues that these implicit assumptions about particular actors' competence and esteem in the situation can provide the seeds out which those actors form beliefs about whole categories of actors.

When actors come together in a goal-oriented encounter, an influence hierarchy quickly develops. When the actors also differ on a salient group distinction, the formation of an influence hierarchy between them creates a local reality in which a person from one group (say, an A) is active, influential, and apparently more competent. The person from the other group (a B) finds herself cast in the role of reacting to the first person. Because such hierarchies develop implicitly, through multiple small behaviors and reactions, actors rarely closely scrutinize what is happening. Instead, they simply find it revealed to them, through the unfolding of events, that the A is more competent and assertive and the B is more reactive and apparently less competent. Since both the A and the B participate in these unfolding events, the social validity of what they apparently reveal becomes difficult for them deny. Since the actual origin of the influence hierarchy is obscure for them but their group difference is salient, both the A and the B may associate their standing in the hierarchy with their group difference. They may form a fledgling status belief that As are more competent and status worthy than Bs.

The A may hold this self-flattering belief as a matter of personal conviction as well as a reality most others would accept. The B may simply concede that "most others" would assume that As are more competent than Bs. Either way, however, the belief constructs an apparent reality that both will have to take into account in their future A/B encounters. If subsequent encounters repeat the association between As and Bs and the enactment of influence and esteem, then the fledgling status belief will be strengthened. Encounters that contradict that association will undermine the belief.

All other things being equal, however, future encounters are more likely to confirm a believing A or B's initial status belief than to contradict it. Expectation states research has shown that when actors modify their expectations for a category of social actors in one goal-oriented encounter, they transfer those modified expectations to future encounters with such actors and treat those actors according to the modified expectations (Markovsky, Smith & Berger, 1984; Pugh & Wahrman, 1983). As other research shows, the result is often a self-fulfilling prophecy (Fisek et al., 1991; Moore, 1985; Skvoretz & Fararo, 1996). Other things equal, when an actor treats another assertively, assuming the other to be less competent and status worthy, or deferentially, because "most people" would presume the other to be more competent, a corresponding influence hierarchy emerges between them that confirms the first actor's assumptions. Thus status beliefs fostered in an initial encounter may be strengthened in future encounters through their self-fulfilling effects on those encounters.

When a believing A or B treats a nonbeliever according to the belief in an A/B encounter and creates a corresponding influence hierarchy between them, a second effect occurs as well. The believer creates an experience for the nonbeliever that may cause the nonbeliever to take on the believer's status belief as well. This effect is also important for status construction theory. Due to her status belief, say, an A presumes that the B in this situation will have less to offer than she herself does. So A speaks up confidently, offering suggestions for accomplishing their shared goal. B sees a display of confidence and assertiveness that is usually associated with status and competence. When B offers her own suggestions, A disagrees with them, implicitly assuming that they are less likely to be helpful. In the face of A's confident disagreement, B hesitates and A's ideas come to dominate their collective decisions. Through the belief formation processes described earlier, there is a chance that this experience will cause B to form a status belief favoring As as well. As a result, status construction theory argues that status beliefs not only can be created but also spread through intergroup encounters, creating a diffusion process that makes widely shared status beliefs possible.

These arguments are summarized in the theory's belief formation assumptions (Ridgeway, 2000). A few definitions will make these assumptions clearer. Status beliefs are corresponding when the nominal state (i.e., group or category) that is associated with more valued status markers and greater expected competence in the situation also is associated in the status belief with more positive social evaluation and greater competence compared to the other nominal state. Following Weber (1922/1968) and Zelditch and colleagues (Zelditch & Walker, 1984; Zelditch & Floyd, 1998), such a correspondence is socially valid for an actor when the actor expects others to accept the correspondence in the situation. When such a correspondence appears consensual in a situation in that it is not openly challenged, it appears to be mutually accepted and therefore socially valid (see Ridgeway, 2000, for a discussion). Status markers include the assertion, influence, and deference behaviors by which the behavioral power and prestige order is enacted.

1. Given a situation in which there is a socially valid correspondence between individuals' differing states of a nominal (i.e., unordered) distinction and their differentiated status markers and expected competence, then there is a likelihood that actors in the situation will form corresponding status beliefs about the nominal distinction.
2. Actors transfer expectations about categories of actors formed in one setting to future encounters with actors that also differ in those categories.
3. Subsequent encounters with others who differ on the nominal distinction that confirm an actor's newly formed status belief strengthen that belief while inconsistent, disconfirming experiences undermine it.

These microlevel assumptions about the creation and spread of status beliefs in intergroup encounters are at the core of status construction theory's larger argument about the emergence and maintenance of widely shared status beliefs. As a result, the theory turns on their empirical plausibility. What is the evidence that interaction can create and spread status beliefs?

Evidence that Interaction Can Create and Spread Status Beliefs.   As I mentioned, there is existing empirical support for the second assumption. Experiments show that when interactional experiences modify actors' expectations for categories of people such as men and women, actors transfer their modified expectations to future encounters with people of those categories (Markovsky et al., 1984; Pugh & Wahrman, 1983). However, the impact of their modified expectations weakens with each transfer unless it is strengthened by subsequent confirming experiences (Markovsky et al., 1984). The latter point offers partial support for the third assumption.

What is the evidence for the crucial first assumption about belief formation? Two recent experiments support its plausibility. In the first experiment, Ridgeway and Erickson (2000, study 1) created a nominal distinction between subjects and their partners by giving them a test purportedly of "personal response style" that classified people into two types: S2s and Q2s. Then subjects and partners worked as two-person teams on a group decision-making task. The partner was actually a confederate who interacted with the subject in either an assertive, confident manner or a hesitant, deferential manner. As expectation theory predicts, this produced clear influence hierarchies between the confederate and subject that favored the subject when the confederate was deferential and favored the confederate when the confederate was assertive. Subjects then worked on another round of the decision task with a new partner, also a confederate, who also was nominally different from the subject and who again acted assertively or deferentially, creating a second influence hierarchy similar to the first. Thus the subjects experienced two goal-oriented encounters where those from the other nominal group consistently differed from the subjects in influence.

After these two encounters, subjects were asked how "most people" rate the typical S2 and the typical Q2. Subjects who were influential over their nominally different partners thought that their own group is seen as more respected, higher status, more powerful, more competent, but not as socially considerate as the other group. Even more important for the theory, subjects who were less influential than their partners thought that most people consider their own group to be less respected, competent, powerful, and lower status but more socially considerate than their partner's group. Thus subjects formed clear status beliefs about the nominal distinction from their interactional experiences. They formed these beliefs even when the beliefs disadvantaged their own group.

Note the interesting compensatory relationship in these results between the secondary "social considerateness" factor compared to the dominant status and competence factors. Studies of a variety of existing status beliefs about occupations, gender, and general social status show a similar structure (Conway, Pizzamiglio, & Mount, 1996). That this structure also was represented in the beliefs that subjects formed in this experiment further supports our conclusion that genuine status beliefs developed.

This experiment supports two aspects of status construction theory's argument about the creation and spread of status beliefs, both of which are captured in the first belief formation assumption. First, it demonstrates that a socially valid (i.e., uncontested) correspondence between influence and esteem in goal-oriented encounters and a previously unordered group difference, at least if repeated, does induce those in the encounter to form status beliefs about the difference. Second, it supports the idea that those who held status beliefs can spread them to others by treating those others in accord with the beliefs so that a corresponding influence hierarchy develops between them. In effect, the confederates in this experiment, by acting assertively or deferentially, treated the subjects as if they held status beliefs about the group difference. By creating influence hierarchies between the confederates and subjects, this treatment effectively "taught" the status belief to the subjects. Thus this experiment also demonstrates that status beliefs can be spread through interaction by treating others in accord with them.

How powerful is the process by which interaction spreads status beliefs to others? In Ridgeway and Erickson's (2000, study 1) experiment, encounters were dyadic. What if others were involved as well? Would they acquire the status belief from seeing someone different from them repeatedly either assert influence over or defer to someone like themselves? The logic of the first assumption seems to suggest that they should. After all, these bystander participants also experience the enactment of a socially valid correspondence between actors' nominal categories and their influence and esteem in the situation. A second experiment examined this question.

Ridgeway and Erickson (2000, study 2) told subjects that they would be part of three-person decision-making teams. Based on the purported test of response style described earlier, subjects found they were similar to one teammate but different from the other. The teammates were actually taped confederate–subject interactions from the first experiment. The live subject was always the opposite response style from the taped confederate. In half the conditions, subjects heard the confederate defer to the influence of someone like them. In the other half of the conditions, subjects heard the confederate assert influence over a teammate like them. Subjects listened to their teammates' discussion before all three made a combined team choice on each task trial. In round two of the experiment, subjects worked on a second team under identical circumstances as in the first round. Thus round two repeated round one with different taped teammates.

The results showed that subjects did indeed take on status beliefs from repeatedly witnessing a different other accept influence from or assert influence over someone like them. Again, subjects who heard people like them deferred to by different others thought that their own group is seen as higher status, more competent, but less considerate than the other group. Those who observed people from another group repeatedly assert influence over those like them conceded that most would view their own group as lower status and less competent, although more considerate, than the other group. Once again, subjects formed clear status beliefs about the group distinction even when those beliefs disadvantaged their own group.

Taken together, these experiments offer clear support for status construction theory's claim that interactional experiences can cause people to form status beliefs about social distinctions. Furthermore, those who acquire status beliefs about a social distinction can "teach" those beliefs to others by acting on the beliefs in subsequent encounters with others who differ on the distinction. Yes, the status beliefs participants formed in these studies are relatively artificial in that they pertain to a made up social distinction. Yet, if people are willing to form strongly differentiated beliefs about minor differences from relatively unimportant interactions in an experiment, are they likely to form any weaker beliefs about real social distinctions from their much more powerful and involving experiences in real interaction? That seems unlikely.

A question remains, however, about the significance of such local-level individual beliefs for the development of consensual status beliefs that are part of the culture of the society as a whole. On the basis of chance alone, As will become more influential in some A/B encounters, while Bs will be more influential in other such encounters. As a result, some people will emerge from A/B encounters with status beliefs favoring As, while others will form beliefs favoring Bs. At the macrolevel, the aggregate result of such conflicting beliefs could just be cultural "noise." Furthermore, when as many people form beliefs favoring Bs as As from A/B encounters, participants are likely to find their fledgling beliefs contradicted and undermined in their subsequent A/B encounters. In this situation, widely shared status beliefs about the A/B distinction will not emerge even though interactional experiences induce local level beliefs.

Status construction theory argues, however, that interactional processes will lead to widely shared status beliefs if some "tipping" or biasing factor is present that gives people from one group (either As or Bs) a systematic advantage in gaining influence over those from the other group in A/B encounters. It is for this reason that the theory focuses on the structural conditions within which A/B encounters are embedded in the society. These conditions govern the terms on which As and Bs encounter one another in the society and thus the advantages they have in gaining influence in those encounters. Structural conditions affect as well the frequency with which As and Bs encounter one another and therefore, the opportunities that exist for interactional processes to induce and spread status beliefs.

Structural Conditions and the Terms of Encounters

Many, including Max Weber (1922/1968), have observed that one group's acquisition of superior material resources compared to another group is a common precondition for the emergence of status beliefs favoring the resource advantaged group. This observation posits that the development of a particular structural condition in society, an inequality in the distribution of material resources between As and Bs, leads to the development of shared status beliefs about the A/B distinction. Status construction theory was initially formulated to explain this common observation (Ridgeway, 1991). It sought to specify how interactional processes could transform a structural inequality in resources (say 60% of As are rich but only 40% of Bs are similarly rich) into widely shared beliefs that As are more worthy and competent than Bs are even when Bs equal As in resources.

The theory argues that an inequality in the distribution of resources between As and Bs provides a "tipping" factor that causes microlevel belief formation processes to yield macro-level cultural beliefs. Several expectation states studies have shown that in goal-oriented encounters differences in actors' resources or rewards (e.g., pay level) lead them to infer corresponding differences in their competence in the situation (Cook, 1975; Harrod, 1980; Stewart & Moore, 1992). As a result, resource-advantaged actors tend to assert themselves more confidently in the situation, while the resource-disadvantaged hesitate and defer, creating influence hierarchies favoring the resource-advantaged actors. In effect, resource differences, by biasing the development of influence hierarchies, constrain the terms on which people encounter one another. If more As are resource rich than Bs in society, then more As than Bs will have a systematic advantage in gaining influence in A/B encounters. As a result, A/B encounters in the society will more often induce status beliefs favoring As than Bs.

Subsequent developments in status construction theory by Webster and Hysom (1998) and Mark (1999) have suggested that there should be, on a logical basis, a general group of "tipping factors" in addition to resource inequalities that also cause interactional processes to create widely shared status beliefs. For clarity, however, I will follow through with the example of resource inequalities to illustrate the theory's macrolevel arguments about struc-tural conditions and "tipping" factors.

The theory argues that structural conditions have two types of macrolevel effects that are important for the emergence of status beliefs. First, structural conditions affect the rate of A/B encounters in the population and thus the opportunities for interactional processes to create and spread status beliefs. Second, structural conditions shape the terms on which these encounters occur by affecting the likelihood that As and Bs in an encounter differ in resources, and if they do, the likelihood that one group rather than the other will have the resource advantage in the encounter.

To specify how structural conditions in a society affect the rate and terms of A/B encounters in the population, status construction borrows arguments from Blau's structural theory of association. Blau (1977) (Blau & Schwartz, 1984) argues that rates of intergroup contact can be calculated from the way people's effective preferences for associating with similar others are constrained by the availability of similar and different others in the population. Blau's formulation alerts us to several structural parameters that affect the rate of encounters in the population between As and Bs and the terms of these encounters based on resource similarities or differences. The distribution of the population across categories of the A/B distinction (i.e., the ratio of As to Bs in the population) and across resource categories (i.e., the ratio of rich to poor in population) will affect the frequency with which As and Bs interact as well as the likelihood that they are similar or different in resource level. The strength of the correlation between resources and the A/B distinction also shapes the proportion of encounters between As and Bs that are "doubly dissimilar" in that the As and Bs also differ in resources. The correlation particularly affects the percentage of doubly dissimilar encounters in which As rather than Bs are resource advantaged. Finally, the effective strengths of people's preferences (if any) for associating with similar others on either the A/B dimension or the resource dimension further constrain the rate of A/B encounters, especially those that are "doubly dissimilar" encounters.[1] Skvoretz (1983) provides a formalization of Blau's argument that allows us to calculate the likelihood of encounters of various types (e.g., between rich As and poor Bs or rich As and rich Bs) under different assumptions about the structural conditions that prevail in the population within which the encounters occur. Ridgeway and Balkwell (1997) draw on this logic to create computer simulations of the processes described by status construction theory. These simulations suggest that if interactional processes do induce people to form and spread status beliefs as the theory suggests, then widely shared status beliefs are a logical outcome under many structural conditions.

DOUBLY DISSIMILAR ENCOUNTERS AND WIDELY SPREAD BELIEFS.   To see why this might be so, let us trace through the process by which a correlation between resources and the A/B distinction leads to widely shared beliefs that As are more status worthy and competent than Bs. As we saw earlier, the key to the development of status beliefs that are widely shared rather than local and contradictory is the operation of some "tipping" factor that systematically biases the development of influence hierarchies in encounters between As and Bs. Following this logic, the theory singles out those encounters between As and Bs where the participants also differ in resources as the primary engines behind the development of widely shared beliefs. Since when actors differ in resources, the resource-advantaged actor tends to become more influential, these "doubly dissimilar" encounters induce their participants to form status beliefs that favor the social group of the advantaged actor.

Some doubly dissimilar encounters will be between rich As and poor Bs; others will involve rich Bs and poor As. Thus, like other A/B encounters, doubly dissimilar encounters will produce some contradictory beliefs that are likely to undermine each other and dissipate.[2] However, because of the correlation between resources and the A/B distinction, there will always be more doubly dissimilar encounters between rich As and poor Bs than rich Bs and poor As. As a result, in the population as a whole, ongoing doubly dissimilar encounters will produce a continual surplus of status beliefs favoring As.

The surplus of status beliefs favoring As produced in doubly dissimilar encounters has the potential to spread widely in the population because other types of encounters either produce no status beliefs about the A/B distinction (because they are not intergroup encounters) or produce a random mix of contradictory beliefs. As actors carry the status beliefs formed in doubly dissimilar encounters to other A/B encounters and act on them there, they spread their beliefs to at least some others. At the same time, actors in the population are continually circulating in and out of doubly dissimilar encounters. This disproportionately fosters the dominant status belief favoring As and disproportionately reinforces the beliefs of those who have already acquired the dominant status belief. Of course, actors with any form of the status belief may encounter another who challenges and undermines that belief. Yet, due to the correlation, disconfirming encounters always will be more likely for those who hold status

[1]Effective preference refers to the strength with which persons seek out or avoid associates that are similar or different from them on a particular dimension, given the countervailing constraints they face, such as their degree of interdependence with those others for the attainment of valued goals.

[2]This will occur as long as the correlation between the group (e.g., A/B) distinction and resources is less than perfect.

beliefs favoring Bs than those who hold the dominant belief favoring As. As a result, actors who acquire the dominant belief favoring As will be more likely to hold those beliefs longer and to spread them successfully to more others. In this way, the small advantage for status beliefs favoring As that flows out from doubly dissimilar encounters gradually intensifies, allowing those beliefs to spread throughout the population in a classic diffusion process.

Do Doubly Dissimilar Encounters Create Status Beliefs?   Clearly, the capacity of doubly dissimilar encounters to induce status beliefs that favor the resource advantaged is essential to status construction theory's argument. It is plausible to assume that such encounters do create such beliefs based on existing evidence that resources differences create influence differences (Cook, 1975; Harrod, 1980; Stewart & Moore, 1992) and that the correspondence between influence and group differences in encounters creates status beliefs (Ridgeway & Erickson, 2000). There is more direct evidence, however, that doubly dissimilar encounters do induce participants to form status beliefs favoring the resource-advantaged group.

Ridgeway et al. (1998) created doubly dissimilar decision-making teams with procedures similar to those in the other experiments I have described. Subjects completed a brief background information questionnaire and a test of personal response style in preparation for working with a partner on a team decision-making task. Subjects were then told that based on the information the laboratory has about them they had been assigned to one pay level (either $8 or $11) and their partner had been assigned to another pay level ($11 or $8), creating a resource difference between all subjects and partners. Subjects also found that they differed from their partners in personal response style, creating a nominal distinction between them.

Subjects and partners then worked as a two-person team on the task. The partner was a confederate who acted confidently and assertively when better paid than the subject, as research suggests people tend to do (Stewart & Moore, 1992). The confederate acted more hesitantly when less well paid than the subject. This behavioral dynamic created influence hierarchies in the teams that favored the pay-advantaged member. According to the theory, this is the condition under which doubly dissimilar encounters should crate status beliefs favoring the resource-advantaged group. As in the previous experiments, subjects then participated in a second round of the experiment that replicated the first with a different partner.

After participating in two consistent doubly dissimilar encounters, subjects formed beliefs that "most people" see the typical person from the nominal group that was better paid in the encounters as higher status and more competent but not as considerate as they see the typical person from the lower paid group to be (Ridgeway et al., 1998). Even subjects who were themselves lower paid formed such beliefs. They reported that the typical person in their own group is viewed by most as lower status and less competent than the typical person from their better paid partner's group. Thus, doubly dissimilar encounters induced participants to form status beliefs favoring the resource advantaged group even when these beliefs personally disadvantaged the participants.

Other Intergroup Encounters and the Spread of Status Beliefs.   Doubly dissimilar encounters are the engine that drives the formation of widely shared beliefs. Such encounters, however, always will be a relatively small proportion of encounters in society, given people's general preferences for associating with similar others. The engine of doubly dissimilar encounters is only sufficient to create widely shared beliefs because its effects are intensified in more common encounters between As and Bs who are similar in resources. As we saw, there is experimental evidence that in encounters among resource similar As and Bs, a believer who treats people from the other group in a status-evaluated way can "teach" the status belief to all who are present in the group (Ridgeway & Erickson, 2000). Due to this effect, simulations indicate that A/B encounters of three to six people become social dynamos that manufacture believers, greatly speeding the diffusion process (Ridgeway & Balkwell, 1997). These simulations show that, because of the power of encounters to teach and spread status beliefs, even a modest correlation between the group distinction and resources (or another tipping factor) is sufficient to create roughly consensual status beliefs under most structural conditions.

The process of teaching and spreading status beliefs in encounters between As and Bs who are similar in resources is important in another way as well. It is only through such encounters that people who are "off diagonal" from the correlation (e.g., poor As and rich Bs) acquire the dominant status belief favoring As. Their own doubly dissimilar encounters do not foster the dominant status belief, but their more frequent encounters with resource-similar others who hold the dominant belief can pressure them into adopting that belief as well. Rich women, for instance, do not learn that it is low status to be a woman from their encounters with poor men. They learn it from the treatment they receive in their more common encounters with rich men.

There is some evidence that off-diagonal people indeed can acquire the dominant status belief from being treated according to that belief by nominally different but resource-similar others. As part of their larger experiment, Ridgeway and Erickson (2000, study 1) included a set of conditions where subjects, like their nominally distinct partners, were well paid but where they saw evidence that others in the study from their own nominal group had been less well paid than they were. These subjects were in the position of the rich women described above. Their similarly well-paid partners treated them assertively, creating influence hierarchies that disadvantaged the subjects. From these experiences, these off-diagonal subjects, despite being better paid than most in their group and equal in resources to their partner, still formed beliefs that the partner's nominal group was higher status and more competent in the eyes of most people than their own group was.

TIPPING FACTORS OTHER THAN RESOURCES.   This extended description of how interactional processes transform a structural inequality in resources into widely shared status beliefs illustrates status construction theory's main arguments about the emergence of status beliefs from macrolevel conditions and microlevel experiences. This particular story shows us how the Weberian observation that riches precede group status could come about. On the other hand, the transformation of wealth to status is not the only story that the theory offers. As Webster and Hysom (1998) point out, the theory implies that an inequality in the distribution between nominal groups of any factor that systematically biases the development of influence hierarchies in intergroup encounters will foster the development of status beliefs favoring the advantaged group. Thus, differences between groups in technology or computer literacy or other such factors that give people from one group a systematic edge in gaining influence in intergroup encounters also would foster status beliefs favoring the advantaged group. Webster and Hysom (1998) use this implication of status construction theory to provide an account for how differences in the moral evaluations attached to heterosexuals and homosexuals could be transformed by interactional processes into widely shared status beliefs that heterosexuals not only are more worthy but more competent than homosexuals.

Mark (1999) has observed that it is logically possible for chance processes alone to occasionally act as the tipping factor that fosters status beliefs about a group difference. Even in the absence of an inequality between the groups in some biasing factor like resources or technology, initial encounters between As and Bs just by chance might come out dispropor-tionately one way. As a series of coin flips occasionally can produce a string of "heads," initial encounters might result in a string of hierarchies favoring Bs. Through the intensifying, "booster" processes described above, the initial preponderance of status beliefs favoring Bs that result from these early encounters could spread and grow until beliefs favoring Bs become widely shared. Note, however, that if status beliefs develop through chance processes, it cannot be predicted in advance which nominal group will end up high status. The development of status beliefs through such chance path-dependent processes is most likely to occur when nominal groups do not differ on a systematic biasing factor such as resources and are just beginning to regularly interact together on a cooperative basis for the first time.

Applying Status Construction Theory

For purposes of logical clarity, status construction theory is phrased as an account of the emergence of status beliefs about nominal groups or categories of people who must regularly interact to achieve mutual goals. It is important to recognize, however, that the structure of the argument as an account of the initial development of status beliefs is a logical convenience only. In fact, the theory describes a set of reciprocal effects between structural conditions and interactional events that are ongoing (see Ridgeway, 1991). As a result, the theory can be applied to the maintenance or erosion of status beliefs about social groups as much as to the emergence of these beliefs. The theory, for instance, may offer some help in understanding the emergence of new status beliefs about the so-called digital divide between the computer knowledgeable and the computer ignorant. At the same time, it also can offer insights about the way differences in computer literacy are refreshing and fortifying existing status beliefs based on gender and race.

Indeed, one of the more useful applications of status construction theory may be to the problem of understanding how status beliefs about social groups are sometimes maintained in society despite major transformations in the material conditions that appear to maintain them. Gender status beliefs in Western societies, for instance, are sufficiently ancient that we can speculate only about their precise origin. We cannot say whether the processes described by status construction theory were implicated in the origin of gender status beliefs. We can say, however, that these processes are likely to have been and continue to be a factor in the maintenance of gender status beliefs. Men as a group have had and continue to have a larger share of material resources than women in Western societies. This factor alone constrains interaction between men and women in such a fashion as to continually reproduce widely shared beliefs that men are more worthy and competent than women. Even if the original sources of gender status beliefs disappear or lose significance, status construction theory predicts that existing resource differences between men and women are sufficient to continu-ally construct gender status beliefs.

Gender status beliefs in fact have been preserved in Western societies despite profound socioeconomic transformations such as industrialization and the more recent entry of women into the paid labor force. Interactional status processes such as those described by expectation states and status construction theories arguably have played a significant part in these preser-vation process (Ridgeway, 1997).

Consider a situation where widespread structural changes in society, such as economic, technological, or social organization changes, cause a decline in existing distributional in-equalities between men and women in material resources (or another factor that biases influence in encounters). In these circumstances, interactional experiences that disconfirm people's gender status beliefs will become more frequent. There will be more mixed sex encounters where, for instance, a woman has sufficient resource advantages to override her gender status so that she becomes men's actual superior in situational power and prestige (Pugh & Wahrman, 1983; Wagner & Berger, 1997).

Unless structural change produces a rapid outright reversal in the distributional inequalities so that the inequalities now favor women, however, the rate of reversal interactions that result may not confront enough people with enough disconfirming experiences to permanently undermine gender status beliefs except over a long period. Once status beliefs are established as part of the taken-for-granted consensual culture, evidence suggests that repeated disconfirmations are necessary to erode them (Hewstone, 1994; Rothbart & John, 1985). This is partly because such beliefs tend to have self-fulfilling effects on perceptions and because those who benefit from the beliefs tend to be cognitively resistant to disconfirming information (Fiske & Neuberg, 1990)[3] As a consequence, change in the evaluative content and consensuality of gender status beliefs is likely to substantially lag behind changes in the distributional inequalities that maintain them (Ridgeway, 1997).

This lag in the change of gender beliefs creates a transitional interval during which, even as societal changes mitigate the former distributional inequality, gender status beliefs continue to shape most mixed-sex encounters. As they do, these beliefs frame the interactional contexts through which new or different resources are allocated and opportunities in emerging organizational forms are distributed. In this way, gender status is rewritten into newly developing economic and organizational forms. Men effectively retain their advantage over women in power and resources within these new forms, although their degree of advantage may be altered in some way. The new forms of distributional inequalities thus created between men and women in turn conserve the basic evaluative order of gender status beliefs that favors men despite the social change that has occurred (Ridgeway, 1997).

CONCLUSION

Cultural beliefs about the evaluative standing of social groups in society are probably both created and maintained by a variety of macrolevel and microlevel social processes, not all of which are mediated by interaction among individuals. Status construction theory focuses exclusively on one path by which status beliefs develop and change: that of interaction between people from different but interdependent social groups that is constrained by the structural conditions that affect those groups. The point of the theory, however, is that even if other factors also may produce widely shared status beliefs, the processes described by status construction theory are sufficient in themselves to create such beliefs. As a result, they must be taken into account in understanding how status beliefs develop and change in society. Status beliefs, after all, have life histories. It used to be low status to be Irish in the United States, but this belief has dissipated as Irishness has been folded into "whiteness." New status beliefs develop, as may be happening currently with computer literacy.

The processes described by status construction theory reveal an intimate and ongoing mutual determination between macrolevel status beliefs about the evaluation of social groups

---

[3]Such evidence suggests that there is an asymmetry between the relative pliability of status beliefs in the initial period when an individual first acquires them and later when an individual not only takes the beliefs for granted personally but presumes that the larger culture does as well.

and microlevel hierarchies of esteem and influence among actors. As expectation states theory has long demonstrated, status beliefs about social groups powerfully shape hierarchies of esteem and influence among actors (Berger et al., 1977; Webster & Foschi, 1988). Status construction theory, in turn, argues that these hierarchies have the power to construct and reconstruct status beliefs about social groups. The local constructions of reality that emerge in intergroup encounters create powerfully persuasive experiences for participants that induce them to form and act on status beliefs about the social groups to which they belong. This occurs even when these status beliefs disadvantage participants' own groups.

When a structural condition such as an inequality in resources systematically constrains the terms on which intergroup encounters occur, the interactional experiences that result transform that structural condition into widely held status beliefs favoring the resource-advantaged group. Once established, such status beliefs benefit individual members of that group even when those members do not personally command superior resources. Thus, although status beliefs are created out of a structural inequality, once they become widely held in society, they define an independent status distinction that creates social cleavages that are not fully reducible to economic or other differences.

Status construction theory has the benefit of offering a systematic account of the emergence and change of status beliefs where few such theories have yet been proposed. By describing some of the ways that status relations between groups and status hierarchies among individuals interconnect, the theory takes a step toward the larger goal of developing a comprehensive account of inequality based on status. If we are to develop a comprehensive understanding of status as a fundamental dimension of inequality and social cleavage in complex societies, we will require many more such theoretical steps.

REFERENCES

Bales, R. F. (1970). *Personality and interpersonal behavior*. New York: Holt, Rinehart, and Winston.

Balkwell, J. W. (1991). From expectations to behavior: An improved postulate for expectation states theory. *American Sociological Review, 56*, 355–369.

Berger, J., & Zelditch, M., Jr. (1998). *Status, power, and legitimacy: Strategies and theories*. New Brunswick, NJ: Transaction Press.

Berber, J., Conner, T. L., & Fisek, M. H. (1974). *Expectation states theory: A theoretical research program*. Cambridge, MA: Winthrop.

Berber, J., Fisek, H., Norman, R., & Zelditch, M. (1977). *Status characteristics and social interaction*. New York: Elsevier.

Blau, P. (1977). *Inequality and heterogeneity: A primitive theory of social structure*. New York: Free Press.

Blau, P., & Schwartz, J. E. (1984). *Crosscutting social circles: Testing a macrostructural theory of intergroup relations*. New York: Academic Press.

Brewer, M. B., & Brown, R. J. (1998). Intergroup relations. In D. T. Gilbert, S. T. Fiske, & G. Lindzey (Eds.), *The handbook of social psychology*, 4th Ed. (vol. 2, pp. 554–594). New York: McGraw-Hill.

Conway, M., Pizzamiglio, M. T., & Mount, L. (1996). Status, communality, and agency: Implications for stereotypes of gender and other groups. *Journal of Personality and Social Psychology, 71*, 25–38.

Cook, K. S. (1975). Expectations, evaluations, and equity. *American Sociological Review, 40*, 373–388.

Dovidio, J. F., & Gaertner, S. L. (1993). Stereotypes and evaluative intergroup bias. In D. M. Mackie & D. L. Hamilton (Eds.), *Affect, cognition, and stereotyping* (pp. 167–194). New York: Academic Press.

Fisek, M. H., & Ofshe, R. (1970). The process of status evolution. *Sociometry, 33*, 327–346.

Fisek, M. H., Berger, J., & Norman, R. Z. (1991). Participation in heterogeneous and homogeneous groups: A theoretical integration. *American Journal of Sociology, 97*, 114–142.

Fiske, S., & Neuberg, S. (1990). A continuum of impression formation, from category-based to individuating processes: Influences of information and motivation on attention and interpretation. In M. Zanna (Ed.), *Advances in experimental social psychology* (pp. 1–73). New York: Academic.

Foschi, M. (1998). Double standards: Types, conditions, and consequences. In J. Skvoretz & J. Szmatka (Eds.), *Advances in group processes* (Vol. 15, pp. 59–80). Stamford, CT: JAI Press.

Goffman, E. (1956). The nature of deference and demeanor. *American Anthropologist, 58,* 473–502.

Goffman, E. (1970). *Strategic interaction.* Oxford, England: Blackwell.

Giddens, A. (1973). *The class structure of the advanced societies.* London: Hutchinson.

Harrod, W. J. (1980). Expectations from unequal rewards. *Social Psychology Quarterly, 43,* 126–130.

Hewstone, M. (1994). Revision and change of stereotypic beliefs: In search of the elusive subtyping model. In W. Stroebe & M. Hewstone (Eds.), *European review of social psychology* (Vol. 5, pp. 69–109). Chichester, England: Wiley.

Jackman, M. R. (1994). *The velvet glove: Paternalism and conflict in gender, class, and race relations.* Berkeley: University of California Press.

Lovaglia, M., Lucas, J. W., Houser, J. A., Thye, S. R., & Markovsky, B. (1998). Status processes and mental ability test scores. *American Journal of Sociology, 104,* 195–228.

Mark, N. (1999). The emergence of status inequality. Paper presented at the annual meeting of the American Sociological Association, Chicago, August 1999.

Markovsky, B., Smith, L. F., & Berger, J. (1984). Do status interventions persist? *American Sociological Review, 49,* 373–382.

Messick, D. M., & Mackie, D. (1989). Intergroup relations. *Annual Review of Psychology, 40,* 45–81.

Moore, J. C. (1985). Role enactment and self identity: An expectations states approach. In J. Berger & M. Zelditch (Eds.), *Status, rewards, and influence: How expectations organize behavior* (pp. 262–316). San Francisco: Jossey-Bass.

Pugh, M., & Wahrman, R. (1983). Neutralizing sexism in mixed-sex groups: Do women have to be better than men? *American Journal of Sociology, 88,* 746–762.

Ridgeway, C. L. (1991). The social construction of status value: Gender and other nominal characteristics. *Social Forces, 70,* 367–386.

Ridgeway, C. L. (1997). Interaction and the conservation of gender inequality: Considering employment. *American Sociological Review, 62,* 218–235.

Ridgeway, C. L. (2000). The formation of status beliefs: Improving status construction theory. *Advances in Group Processes, 17,* 77–102.

Ridgeway, C. L., & Balkwell, J. (1997). Group processes and the diffusion of status beliefs. *Social Psychology Quarterly, 60,* 14–31.

Ridgeway, C. L., & Erickson, K. G. (2000). Creating and spreading status beliefs. *American Journal of Sociology, 106,* 579–615.

Ridgeway, C. L., & Walker, H. (1995). Status structures. In K. Cook, G. Fine, & J. House (Eds.), *Sociological perspectives on social psychology* (pp. 281–310). New York: Allyn and Beacon.

Ridgeway, C. L., Boyle, E. H., Kuipers, K., & Robinson, D. (1998). How do status beliefs develop? The role of resources and interaction. *American Sociological Review, 63,* 331–350.

Rothbart, M., & John, O. (1985). Social categorization and behavioral episodes: A cognitive analysis of the effects of intergroup contact. *Journal of Social Issues, 41,* 81–104.

Sidanius, J., & Pratto, F. (1999). *Social dominance: An integroup theory of social hierarchy and oppression.* New York: Cambridge University Press.

Skvoretz, J. (1983). Salience, heterogeneity, and consolidation of parameters: Civilizing Blau's primitive theory. *American Sociological Review, 48,* 360–375.

Skvoretz, J., & Fararo, T. (1996). Status and participation in task groups: A dynamic network model. *American Journal of Sociology, 101,* 1366–1414.

Stewart, P. A., & Moore, J. C. (1992). Wage disparities and performance expectations. *Social Psychology Quarterly, 55,* 78–85.

Strodtbeck, F. L., James, R. M., & Hawkins, C. (1957). Social status in jury deliberations. *American Sociological Review, 22,* 713–719.

Troyer, L., & Younts, C. W. (1997). Whose expectations matter? The relative power of first-order and second-order expectations in determining social influence. *American Journal of Sociology, 103,* 692–732.

Turner, J. C. (1987). *Rediscovering the social group: A self-categorization theory.* New York: Basil Blackwell.

Wagner, D. G., & Berger, J. (1993). Status characteristics theory: The growth of a program. In J. Berger & M. Zelditch (Eds.), *Theoretical research programs: Studies in the growth of theory* (pp. 23–63). Stanford, CA: Stanford University Press.

Wagner, D., & Berger, J. (1997). Gender and interpersonal task behaviors: Status expectation accounts. *Sociological Perspectives, 40,* 1–32.

Weber, M. (1922/1968). *Economy and society.* Berkeley: University of California Press.

Webster, M., & Foschi, M. (1988). *Status generalization: New theory and research.* Stanford, CA: Stanford University Press.

Webster, M., & Hysom, S. J. (1998). Creating status characteristics. *American Sociological Review, 63,* 351–379.

Zelditch, M., & Floyd, A. S. (1998). Consensus, dissensus, and justification. In J. Berger & M. Zelditch (Eds.), *Status, power, and legitimacy: Strategies and theories* (pp. 339–368). New Brunswick, NJ: Transaction Press.

Zelditch, M., Jr., & Walker, H. A. (1984). Legitimacy and the stability of authority. In E. J. Lawler (Ed.), *Advances in group processes* (Vol. 1, pp. 1–25). Greenwich, CT: JAI Press.

PART IV

THEORIZING FROM THE SYSTEMIC AND MACROLEVEL

CHAPTER 17

Macrostructural Theory

PETER M. BLAU

The introduction summarizes the views of two philosophers of science on the method of theorizing. The main section has two parts: the first deals with the effect of size differences on intergroup relations, and the second presents the macrostructural theory. I conclude with a synopsis of test results of the research on the theory's implications and a brief summary of the most interesting findings.

METHODOLOGICAL INTRODUCTION

Karl Popper is the most prominent 20th-century representative of logical deductionism. His major publication, *The Logic of Scientific Discovery*, (1935/1968) has become the model of deductionism in this century. Two persons who have influenced his work were Bertrand Russell and Ludwig Wittgenstein. Russell was a mathematician and philosopher, whose widely influential book was *Principles of Mathematics* (1903/1938). Wittgenstein's major publication, *Tractatus Logico-Philosophicus* (1921/1933), on the relationship between logic and language, inspired the positivism of the Vienna Circle, through Wittgenstein rejected their positivism in preference of more refined deductionism.

In his classic book on deductive theory, Popper distinguished universal and existential statements. As a strict logician, Popper emphasizes that the more general universal (his term for theoretical) statements cannot be affected by the less general existential (his term for empirical) statements. This raises an important question: If a theory cannot be rejected by a single empirical implication that the data prove to be wrong, does it not make it impossible to falsify any theory?

Popper gives an ingenious negative answer to this question. As a consistent logician and yet without making all theories infallible, he starts by agreeing that the narrower existential data cannot influence a theory's universal propositions. He remains a strict logician, even at the cost of having to admit that one of his universal statements may not be universal. To be sure, a less general empirical proposition cannot influence a more general theoretical proposition. However, the logical deductions from a theory's universal proposition must be correct.

PETER M. BLAU • Department of Sociology, University of North Carolina, Chapel Hill, North Carolina 27599.

Handbook of Sociological Theory, edited by Jonathan H. Turner. Kluwer Academic / Plenum Publishers, New York, 2002.

A single false deduction from a theory's universal propositions shows one or more of them cannot be correct, and this inadequacy of its predictions, not the empirical data, require the theory to be rejected. (This sounds like sophistry, but is it not what scientists do when they accept test data and reject a theory failing to predict them?) Popper concludes that deductive theories can be tested, possibly falsified, and if not falsified in repeated tests they may be considered to be corroborated and provisionally accepted. [This is not very different from Cohen and Nagel's (1934/1951) criterion of accepting a theory on the basis of probable inference from repeated tests, which Popper dismisses as illogical.]

I was fascinated by Popper's deductive theory and his clever method of testing it. Having my sabbatical and being invited to spend the year at Netherlands Institute for Advanced Study (NIAS) in 1975–1976, I decided to take advantage of this opportunity and try to construct a macrostructural theory following Popper's model and simultaneously Braithwaite's, also a deductive theory. Whereas Popper acknowledges the significance of empirical research for testing theories and shows how to derive from a theory its empirical implications to test it, he dismisses any suggestion that logic may contribute indirectly to developing theories as illogical.

Maybe so, but this merely shows the limitations of logic for the advancement of science and does not help the working scientist. (It also contradicts the implicit claim of Popper's book, titled *The Logic of Scientific Discovery*.) The word *discovery* implies he would give hints about how to discover or at least construct theory.

Of course, one cannot logically derive a more general from a less general statement, but that does not mean that it cannot indirectly help in deriving one, perhaps by inference from research findings. Inference is not logical deduction, and one has no idea whether an inferred theory is correct. But whatever means for creating a new theory are used—imagination, other theories, remarks made in discussions with colleagues—none gives assurance or even realistic hope that the theory is valid *before* it has been tested.

Impressed as I am with Popper—as illustrated by the deductive character of the theory presented below—I am disappointed that he fails to discuss anything about constructing theory. I also disagree with his criterion for theoretical statements that they must be universal statements, for I consider the distinction between theoretical and empirical propositions more profound than that between 100% and 99%, or even 90%. But I am in full agreement with his implicit claim that theories should be logical models. Maybe his and my Viennese roots made us susceptible of the positivism of the Vienna Circle, for deductivism is surely a positivistic approach.

Lakatos (1970) distinguished sophisticated falsificationism from its naive form, claiming loyally that the former was already implicit in Popper's writings. His basic point is that theories should be neither rejected nor accepted on the basis of a single test result, because either may be happenstance. He stressed that complex theories have applications in diverse fields, and they are considered to be corroborated only when numerous tests have confirmed their empirical implications in several different fields. By the same token, a single negative outcome, or a few, should not lead to the rejection of a theory widely accepted and supported by many scientists, but inadequate procedures or failings of investigators should be held responsible for the failed results. Only repeated research findings disconfirming a theory should arouse suspicions of it, leading to attempts to improve it or discover a better one. Even then, a theory should only be rejected, Lakatos concluded, after a new superior theory has been discovered, one that has a wider range of implications that do not fail empirical tests.

Braithwaite's (1953/1955) scientific theorizing is, like Popper's, a deductive theory tested by its logical implications, but there are interesting differences. Braithwaite made an interesting suggestion for inferring theories, which is one reason, but not the only one, for my great admiration for him and my sorrow that he and his work seems to have been forgotten. Perhaps the most important difference from Popper is that Braithwaite also stresses the significance of empirical data, not only for testing, as Popper does, but also for deriving theory, which Popper dismisses as illogical. He also differs from Popper in the defining criterion of theoretical propositions: Popper's criterion for theoretical statements is that they are universal, but Braithwaite's criterion is that they must explain empirical data and specifically should be *abstract* explanations of them.

Granted that logic cannot be used directly to produce theories, for doing so requires imagination as well as logic, logic can help. Braithwaite stresses the empirical grounding of theory, which is largely neglected by Popper, and he treats empirical data as essential not only for testing theory, as does Popper, but also for creating theories, inasmuch as explaining empirical generalizations is the very purpose of theoretical generalizations.

But what is an explanation? According to Braithwaite (1953/1955), it is "an answer to a 'Why?' question that gives some intellectual satisfaction" (pp. 348–349). This is surely too vague; and indeed he specifies with an ingenious clue for developing theory:

> To explain a law [empirical generalization] is to exhibit and establish a set of hypotheses from which the law follows. It is not necessary for these higher-level hypotheses to be established independently of the law which they explain; all that is required for them to provide an explanation is that they should be regarded as established and that the law should logically follow from them. (p. 343)

This statement has been much criticized by humanistic social scientists who prefer interpretive meaningful theories and criticize theories that attempt to be rigorous and logical as attempts to mimic natural sciences.

I, however, find this conception of theory congenial, particularly because I am very impressed by Braithwaite's sophisticated elaboration of his conception of theories and their construction. I also think that social scientists can do worse than taking theories in the natural sciences as their model. Braithwaite's criterion for distinguishing theoretical from empirical generalizations is that the former are abstract, which itself is a more abstract criterion for theory than Popper's criterion of universalism, which I above criticized.

To explain several abstract propositions, one must infer a more abstract proposition that implies, and therefore explains, all of them. Such multilevel abstractions exist in physics and probably in other natural sciences but not in social science, and Popper's model enabled me only to produce a one-level abstraction, as shown in the next section. This may be the result of my limitations, those of social science, or a combination of the two.

Richard Braithwaite influenced my thinking very much and so did Georg Simmel (1923/1965). The task of theoretical sociology, according to Simmel, is to analyze the social forms themselves, abstracted from their contents. Whereas abstractions are not empirical facts and abstract forms cannot be observed to test abstract theories, their diverse empirical manifestations can provide such tests. Despite my having long admired Simmel, I had not realized that the parameter concept in my theory is akin to Simmel's concept of social forms. (Similar but not identical, since Simmel's forms refer to social processes, whereas my parameters are dimensions of social structure.) Neither had I realized, when I came to admire Braithwaite's abstract model of theorizing, that Simmel's idea of social forms had provided a sociological procedure for theoretical abstraction, thereby, so to speak, anticipating Braithwaite's insight of the importance of abstraction in theory.

THE THEORY IN TWO PARTS

Size and Interpersonal Relations

The central concern of macrostructural theory is how the structural conditions in a community or population affect people's social life. To be sure, the structural conditions themselves were produced by people—who had children and educated them, built and maintained houses and churches, and established local traditions—but these were members of previous generations. Whereas influences of preceding generations on the changing social structure are of great importance, it is largely studied by historians and historical sociologists. Most sociologists' interests center on the influences of existing social conditions on people's social life, and for structural sociologists this means the effects of structural conditions.

The study of the influences of social structure on people's interpersonal relations analyzes how population distributions among positions along various lines affect human relations. My definition of social structure is a multidimensional space of social positions among which people are distributed by their characteristics, such as age or income. The term "social position" is used broadly to refer not only to various group affiliations, like that of a soldier or salesman, but also differences not yet categorized, such as living on the upper west side of Manhattan or being intelligent. In short, all social differences among people that may affect their social relations are considered differences in social positions. The differences may be a dichotomy, like sex, or have multiple categories, like occupation, or be continuous variable, like age.

Another triple-categories scheme, used in the theory to be presented, entails three types of population distributions: heterogeneity, equality, and multiplicity. Heterogeneity refers to diversity in categorical variables, such as occupation. Inequality entails differences in a continuous variable, like income. Multiplicity refers to the number of dimensions of human differences being considered in an analysis. The total number is very large and unknown. Limited numbers are used in any analysis. Most often two dimensions are being compared, such as race and income. (The negative correlation between being black and income level is a blemish on our democracy.)

Intergroup relations (this dichotomy will be used so often that the abbreviation, IR, will be used for it in the rest of the chapter) are more interesting than in-group relations, if only because IR are less frequent, as many studies have shown. (It makes actually little difference which rate is reported, because either reveals the other, the two being complementary.) An additional reason of their significance is that in-group relations strengthen solidarity and social support but engender group barriers, making IR essentially important for the social cohesion of communities and larger collectivities, notably in entire nations. The dichotomy in-group–IR is misleading, because it seems to imply one in-group and one outgroup (IR) relation. But every person has many characteristics and every social relation involves simultaneously numerous ingroup and IR.

In presenting a synopsis of the theory, I shall not confine myself to the abstract theorems but will illustrate how these abstract theoretical propositions imply empirical predictions with which the theory can be tested. In the book in which I originally presented the theory, I was eager to show how widely it was applicable to different subject matters. I ended up with more than 180 propositions (Blau, 1977). Only later, after having read and admired Braithwaite as well as Popper, I revised the theory, using only three major terms: heterogeneity, inequality, and multiplicity. These three are used in the major abstract theorems, which I shall present with illustrations of their empirical applications. The theorems meet Braithwaite's criterion that theorems are abstract, through I was not able to infer them from empirical data, nor was I able to conceptualize multiple levels of abstraction. I do not know whether this is my fault or is due to an intrinsic difference between the social and natural sciences These three abstract terms do not strictly imply, but they can be used to derive empirical implications, which furnish tests of the theory and are so used when presenting the theory below.

The initial spark of an idea that stimulated my theory on the influences of various social differences in relations among people was to distinguish sociology from psychology. To do so, I asked myself which attributes of a population are not based on the attributes of its individual members, like mean earnings or death rates. I could think of two: the differences among group members and the intergroup relations between all pairs of them.

Knowing of the prevailing in-group preferences that often have been documented, I considered the study of IR of greater interest. Then it occurred to me that the size of groups is an objective condition of all groups that affects individual members' likelihood of associating with members of other groups. This probably occurred to me because I had found in earlier studies of formal organizations that their size exerts a strong influence on their characteristics. Although my theory does not include the implications of size differences, I am presenting them and their important practical implications here as an introduction to the theory.

To start thinking how size differences might influence IR, I first simplified matters by considering only two groups of different size. For only two groups, the number of persons engaged in dyadic group IR (spelled out for emphasis) must be the same, since each pair must consists of one from each group. The difference in the rates of IR of the two groups, therefore, depends only on their difference in size. The members of the smaller group must participate more (more often or more of them) in IR than those of the larger. The average is the mean rate, but it does not indicate whether there are great or very little differences in rates within groups, particularly in the smaller, who are constrained to have a higher IR rate than the larger.

Without knowing whether all members have higher rates or a subset of them has particularly high rates, it is impossible to infer from the rates of individual members. We can only infer that the mean IR in smaller groups is larger than that in larger groups, but one cannot predict the rates of specific members or even how much they vary. The mean size of both groups provides the probable IR of both groups' members. This suffices for drawing practical implications.

It implies that members of minority groups have much higher rates of intergroup contacts than those of the dominant majority, which in turn implies that blacks and Hispanics, the two largest ethnic minorities in the United States, have much higher rates of contacts with the members of the white majority than whites have with them. Hence blacks and Hispanics know more whites and undoubtedly have a better understanding of whites than whites know and can understand blacks. The same could be said for other minority–majority differences, such as Jews and Christians in the United States, though not in Israel.

MACROSTRUCTURAL THEORY

The macrostructural theory's fundamental substantive assumption is that the probability of social relations depends on opportunities for contact. This may sound like a tautology, since both terms—social contacts and social relations—are sometimes used for the actual associations between persons. Opportunity for contact refers here, however, not to actual social interaction between persons but to being in the same location, not only living in the same place but also working in the same shop or office, belonging to the same club, shopping regularly in the same supermarket, or frequenting the same bar. Even if the two words do not literally mean the same, however, one may ask whether it is not quite obvious that people are more likely to associate if they have opportunities to do so than if they have never seen one another. In a sense it is, if we mean by obvious that it is so likely to happen or that it could occur by sheer chance.

The assumption is essentially a reflection of the mathematical law of probability: the closer people are in space, the greater the likelihood that they meet, which in turn increases the chance or probability that they will start to associate. But if reference is to established relations that are not mere fleeting acquaintances, probability suffices to make the case far from obvious, notably for IR. People do not tend to become friendly with just anybody they encounter on a street or a bus.

Chance encounters, however, often turn into acquaintances, and these sometimes grow into personal relations. A few personal relations ripen into lasting friendships and close friendships between members of the opposite sex often become love relations. Not all lovers get married, of course, but most marriages, optimists hope, are based on love, not on convenience. Most chance meetings do not become marriages, of course, but many if not most marriages started as chance meetings, less likely on the street than in private homes, in schools, or on jobs in factories and offices.

The main dimensions of social differences in my theory are heterogeneity, inequality, and multiplicity. They make it possible to draw parsimonious distinctions about the fundamental and generic differences among people. Definitions of the differentiation parameters and a single assumption suffice for deriving theorems.

The degree of heterogeneity in a population depends on the number of different groups and how irregular the population's distribution among them is. But a more precise definition is required for theorems to imply predictions about heterogeneity that can be measured. This precise definition specifies that heterogeneity is the chance expectation that any two persons in the population differ in a given dimension.

Inequality refers to differences in degree, from an abstract maximum of infinity and minimum of zero (I do not consider minus infinity a meaningful term). Realistically, differences in inequality must be set by empirical maxima and minima, although even these are often difficult strictly to determine. Many people consider Bill Gates the richest person in United States, and possibly in the world, but I do not think anybody has an idea who of the many very poor people is the very poorest. But wealth is not the only difference in degree. Athletic contests establish world records in many fields. Nevertheless, inequality in income and standard of living is very important. If a small minority is very rich and a large proportion of the population is quite poor, it is a serious flaw for any country and a particularly grave one for a democracy.

Multiplicity refers to the number of differences in a population. This number is, of course, not known, and even the number of known differences would be virtually innumerable. Realistically, multiplicity (multiple, for short) refers to the number of known differences a given investigator takes into account. These are most often two, or the means of several pairs.

However, for multiple continuous variables, means and other statistical measures easily can be combined for comparisons of large populations. For example, the income of all college graduates for a certain year (or decade) in different states or regions can be compared, and so can the income differences in the same occupations between blacks and whites, as well as those between women and men. For specific multiple continuous differences, there are terms to indicate how independent or interdependent they are. The former—degree of independence— is called "intersection" and the latter—degree of dependence—is called "consolidation." Intersection and consolidation are complementary; either reveals the other ($X + Y = 1.00$).

The heterogeneity theorem is the first illustration of my theory. If heterogeneity is defined by the probability that any two member of a population belong to different groups, and if social relations are assumed to depend on contact opportunities, it follows that the chance of encounters of two members of different groups increases with the population's heterogeneity. To be sure, most casual meetings are soon forgotten, but no new associations could ever develop if two strangers were never to meet and no new friendships could if acquaintances were never to lead to closer ties. Some chance meetings lead to brief associations, some of these ripen into closer relations, and a few may become friendships or even intimate ties. Our strongest relations, except those with our families, frequently originate in casual encounters, such as a few words exchanged after an introduction by a common friend.

The theorem is formulated in abstract terms, for heterogeneity is a social form devoid of substantive content that gives it meaning. The general proposition implies specific empirical statements that supply substance and meaning. The theorem's empirical expressions provide tests of it. Failure of any test, of course, implies the theory is falsified, according to Popper and at least is made questionable, according to Lakatos. Of eight tests made, all except one, race (in two versions: a dichotomy and multiple categories), shoed that the degree of heterogeneity increased intermarriage (Blau & Schwartz, 1997, p. 44).

The inequality theorem's implications derived from its definition and the assumptions are surprising. I had thought greater inequality between two persons makes their association less likely, and I said so in a book (Blau, 1977, p. 55). Although the statement for two persons is correct, it is not correct to infer from this the average inequality in the population. (Contrary to my structural perspective that structure effects individuals, I made an inference from what happens between individuals to a population, instead of starting with the population.)

The greater the inequality in a population, the greater is the average status difference between the individuals composing it. The difference between an individual's wealth or income, height or weight, is the average negative difference from those above and the average positive difference from those below her or him, and these will discourage the alters or him from associating. The total difference in the social structure, which is the mean difference between all possible pairs, becomes the common standard and departures from this standard are experienced as being richer or poorer, for example.

A final and important dimension of differences is multiplicity, the number of distinct differences. This number is, of course, very large and unknown. For continuous variables, averages for entire populations can be compared. Examples are the differences in high school seniors' SAT scores in different states or the average income in various occupations. The degree of independence is termed "intersection" and the degree of correlation "consolidation"; the two are complementary and either indicates the other $(X + Y = 1.00)$.

There are many dimensions of social differences in a population. People have many characteristics in different combinations, and the strength of the relationships between attributes in various dimensions governs their effect, such as how strongly race is related to income. The consolidation of one dimension of social differences with another enhances their negative effect on IR, thus strengthening in-group ties.

In contrast, a high degree of intersection of two or more dimensions of differences reduces their negative effect on intergroup ties, thus weakening in-group boundaries. The substantial correlation between being white and being rich enhances the social distance between rich whites and poor blacks to an extreme. (There are subtle modifications, however. The very security of their superior social status of rich upper-class whites compared to their upper-middle-class brethren may make it more important for the less rich to keep their distance from poorer people than for the richest.)

In abstract terms, consolidation promotes in-group relations and intersection IR. The two actually refer to the same relationship of two or more dimensions of social differences from opposite perspectives. In other words, the two are complementary: consolidation refers to the strength of relationships between two or more attributes of persons, intersection, to the degree of independence of two or more attributes (how close to being orthogonal they are). The positive influence of intersection is the same as the negative influence of consolidation. The positive correlation of education with income is reflected in the negative correlation between high school dropout and upward social mobility.

The general conclusion of the effects of intersection on IR has interesting practical implications. Pronounced intersection implies great diversity in a population. The more pronounced the intersection of two attributes of people, the greater is the social distance between two groups. Once slavery ended, of course, what happened was not a "happy ending." Pronounced intersection between white landlords and black sharecroppers continued to divide the population in the South for more than half-a-century, and it is still reflected in the consolidation of race and income.

Pronounced intersection exerts considerable structural constraints on IR. This bold assertion may appear in conflict with free will. People are indeed free to associate with anybody, including anybody who is not in any of their in-groups in various dimensions. This freedom to choose associates like oneself in any respect, however, does not imply being free to choose associates like oneself in every respect. Indeed, this is impossible. People have many attributes, particularly in complex societies like ours, and we cannot avoid associating with others who differ from us in some ways. To be sure, we all have free will, but it hardly implies freedom to choose any combination of characteristics of others in one's environment.

Of course, we can only choose persons that exist in our environment, but this is not a serious limitation, at least not in cities, given their great diversity. Our multigroup affiliations necessitate that we make in-group choices sequentially, starting to look for an associate characterized by our most important preference, continuing with the second and adding others step by step until we run out of degrees of freedom, so to speak.

To explicate: the multigroup affiliations in complex societies imply that individuals have many ingroup preferences that greatly vary in importance to them; it also implies that different persons have different combinations of them. People establish rank orders of their in-group preferences, particularly for close or intimate ones, seeking to satisfy as many top-ranking in-group preferences as possible. [A final caveat must be entered here: for our most important choices—love and marriage—the first choice for most of us is a gender out-group one (IR).]

Intensive intersection restricts the ability to satisfy many of these preferences, however. Once we have made our most important in-group choices, we cannot easily find someone who still has another group affiliation or attribute in common with us. The combination of a structure's intersection and a person's satisfying one preference after another increasingly restricts her or his remaining options until one is forced to associate with others who, though sharing several of our affiliations or attributes, are unlike us in still others. Indeed, much intersection implies that any in-group choice in one dimension involves out-group relations (IR) in some others, for increasing intersection involves more and more restrictions on the number of ingroup preferences that can be satisfied.

Social structures exert constraints, yet individuals also have free will. They are free to make choices but not any combination of choices, because social conditions limit opportunities, hence the choices we make limit our further choices. With respect to social relations, people are free to satisfy their important in-group preferences, but their satisfying some increasingly restricts their further choices. The greater the intersection, the greater are structural constraints to establish relations with persons who, though satisfying our in-group preferences in some respects, differ from us in others. In sum, intersection limits people's freedom to choose associates who satisfy all their preferences, but it does not preclude their choosing associates with the characteristics they value most. Preferences for in-group choices prevail, as indicated by their being observed always in excess of chance expectations. Even in-group choices that are rare, like occupational homogamy, occur more often than chance.

TESTS

A theory's validity must be tested. This theoretical chapter is not the place to report in detail testing procedures (see Blau & Schwartz, 1997, pp. 16–27.) The tests were originally conducted for an earlier study of the 125 largest metropolitan areas in the United States in 1970 (all those with a population of more than 250,000) (see Blau & Duncan, 1967). The independent variable in this empirical study was the ethnic diversity in a metropolitan area. The dependent variable was intermarriage, which is for most people their most intimate social relation, thus constituting a very severe test of the theory.

In the early tests without controls, five of six forms of heterogeneity were correlated with intermarriage, as the theory implies, but one did not. Specifically a Standard Metropolitan Statistical Area's (SMSA) heterogeneity is correlated with its intermarriage rate in respect to national origin, birth region, industry, major occupation, and detailed occupation (logit), but not with respect to race (whether measured by a dichotomous or a multiple variable). The reason is that race is highly correlated with socioeconomic status (SES), which, as noted earlier, distorts its effect on intermarriage. If SES is controlled, racial heterogeneity and intermarriage are significantly related.

An SMSA's mean inequality in education is correlated with a couples' differences in years of education and so are its socioeconomic inequality and a couples' difference in the SES of their parents (but this correlation is not independent of education's). No correlations for intersection's influences are presented, because its influences require controlling the parallel one of heterogeneity or inequality in regression analysis.

As just noted, the parallel effects of intersection with differentiation require that intersection and heterogeneity or inequality are both entered in the regressions of various forms of intermarriage (for a table of results, see Blau, 1994, p. 71). No intersection measure of detailed occupation's heterogeneity is available, owing to excessive costs of constructing one for each of the 444 occupational categories.

Four of five forms of heterogeneity and intersection exert cumulative positive effects on intermarriage, with other structural influences controlled, and so do educational inequality and intersection under controls. Specifically, intersection and heterogeneity in race, nativity, birth region, and industry exert independent influences on the likelihood of intermarriage and so do intersection and inequality in education. But only the intersection of *major* occupational with other differences significantly influences intermarriage; heterogeneity of major occupational groups does not.

In sum, only 1 of 13 tests—that for the effect of heterogeneity in major occupations—failed to support the theory's empirical implications. The theory must be considered falsified by Popper's strict criterion, but in terms of Lakatos' less strict criterion that a single test failing to support a theory supported by other tests need not require a rejection; pending future tests, which I like to think of as sophisticated falsificationism, it could be tentatively accepted. The greater the heterogeneity in a population, the greater are the chances that marriages involve partners who differ in categorical characteristics.

CONCLUSIONS

I conclude by calling attention only to the findings I find most interesting. These are the distinctions between the seemingly identical differences of every individual with all others and the structural differences between all possible pairs in the population.

The greater the heterogeneity among people, the greater are the chances that two people meeting will differ. But the greater the structural heterogeneity in a population, which is the mean difference between all possible pairs, the more likely are two people who differ to have any relation with one another, including marriage [Empirical tests confirm this for seven of eight differences, all but that in race (two versions of it: a dichotomous and multiple one)].

Inequality between a people decreases the likelihood of friendships. But the degree of inequality in a social structure, based on the differences between all possible pairs, increases the likelihood of status different relations of all kinds, including marriages.

REFERENCES

Blau, P. M. (1977). *Inequality and heterogeneity*. New York: Free Press.

Blau, P. M. (1994). *Structural contexts of opportunities*. Chicago: University of Chicago Press.

Blau, P. M., & Duncan, O. D. (1967). *The American occupational structure*. New York: Wiley.

Blau, P. M., & Schwartz, J. (1997). *Crosscutting social circles*. New Brunswick, NJ: Transaction Press.

Braithwaite, R. B. (1953/1955). *Scientific explanation*. Cambridge, England: Cambridge University Press.

Cohen, M. R., & Nagel, E. (1934/1951). *An introduction to logic and scientific method*. New York: Harcourt, Brace and Company.

Lakatos, I. (1970). Falsification and the methodology of scientific research programmes. In I. Lakatos & A. Musgrave (Eds.), *Criticism and the growth of knowledge* (pp. 91–196). Cambridge: Cambridge University Press.

Popper, K. R. (1935/1968). *The logic of scientific discovery*, New York: Basic Books.

Russell, B. (1903/1938). *Principles of mathematics*. New York: W. W. Norton.

Simmel, G. (1923/1965). *Soziologie*. Muenchen and Leipzig: Dunker & Humblot.

Wittgenstein, L. J. J. (1921/1933). *Tractatus logico-philosophicus*. New York: Harcourt, Brace.

CHAPTER 18

The Return of Grand Theory

JONATHAN H. TURNER AND DAVID E. BOYNS

Something happened to sociological theory in the last half of the 20th century. Those who practice science have become specialists and those who present grander visions of the social universe have become antiscience. Among theorists committed to the epistemology of science, a new timidity is evident; and despite the high quality of their specialized work, it lacks a big vision about big processes that cut across big amounts of time. Obviously, we are overstating the case, because there have been some interesting efforts at grand theory, but still the term "grand theory" now carries negative connotations as something that failed scholars like Talcott Parsons once did, a half century ago. Yet, despite this fact, sociological theory continues to worship the graves of Max Weber, Karl Marx, and Émile Durkheim, who thought big and who presented sociology with grand theories. Thus, it appears that we like our early masters to be grand theorists, but in the age of specialization, we stand in their shadows rather than on their shoulders.

In this chapter, we argue for a return of grand theory. It is time to consolidate specialized theories and recapture the vision of the last century where everyone—from Comte and Spencer, through Marx, Weber, and Simmel to Pareto and even Mead—was concerned with explaining big processes with grand theories.

CONNECTING THE MICRO AND MACRO

Theory is "grand" when it seeks to explain a large social landscape, or in a more contemporary vocabulary it tries to link macro- and micro levels of reality. Much sociological commentary over the last few decades has been concerned with the "gap" between the micro and macro, with only a few really trying very hard to fill this gap theoretically (Alexander et al., 1986). Indeed, for all their antiscience and critical rhetoric, postmodern theorists have been more grand than those committed to the epistemology of science. They are more in tune with the vision of the early masters, but unfortunately, they often poison their own soup with a vocabulary to choke on, with antiscience rhetoric, with relativism, and with critique. Still, at least someone is thinking big. Grand theory, therefore, must be about a full range of social

JONATHAN H. TURNER AND DAVID E. BOYNS • Department of Sociology, University of California, Riverside, California 92521.

Handbook of Sociological Theory, edited by Jonathan H. Turner. Kluwer Academic / Plenum Publishers, New York, 2002.

353

forces operating at all levels of social reality. The more of reality to be examined, the more "grand" is the theory.

Strategies for Linking Micro and Macro

Before presenting our vision of how to cut across all levels of reality, let us briefly examine how others have sought to make the connection between micro and macro. Here we can get a sense, perhaps, for where sociological theory went wrong in recent decades. It is our contention that eight different theoretical approaches to resolving the micro–macro problem can be discerned in sociological theory (Turner, 1983). We refer to these approaches as (1) microchauvinism, (2) macrochauvinism, (3) middle-range theory, (4) action-to-structure model building, (5) formal–network sociology, (6) deductive reductionism, (7) agency–structure duality, and (8) multidimensional approaches. Although there is some overlap in these seven categories, they capture the range of efforts used to reconcile the micro–macro theory-building strategies.

MICROCHAUVINISM.   While microchauvinism is expressed in many different forms, there is a common core to these approaches. First, most microchauvinist approaches assert that sociological conceptualizations of social structure are reifications (Berger & Luckmann, 1967), since the only empirically observable processes are individuals moving in space, engaging in symbolic and ritualized interaction, and actively adapting and adjusting their responses to one another. The "emergent properties" of social structures are seen as primarily the symbolic constructions not only of sociologists, but also of laypersons who use the folk concepts of social structure as one of the many symbolic components guiding their interpretation of a situation (Garfinkel, 1967). Second, microchauvinist approaches contend that sociological analysis must be initiated through an investigation of the process of interaction among individuals in a face-to-face context (e.g., Blumer, 1969; Collins, 1981). That is, theoretical efforts must be made to understand the basic processes by which gestures are emitted, received, and interpreted in human interaction.

Despite these points of commonality, there is variety in microchauvinist strategies. Some, such as Herbert Blumer (1969) and most of the Chicago school symbolic interactionists (Turner, 1998), deny that sociology can emulate the natural sciences. At best, these approaches argue, sociologists can develop interpretive understandings through the use of "sensitizing concepts" (Blumer, 1969) with which tentative and ephemeral patterns of "joint action" among individuals can be understood and described. Others (e.g., Collins, 1975, 1981, 1988) take a more positivist position, arguing that sociological theory can develop invariant, abstract laws of human interaction by examining how microencounters are "chained" together to form larger, more complex, and more enduring social structures. Still others, such as those working within ethnomethodology (Garfinkel, 1967), suggest that social reality is primarily a social construction and that individuals are not "judgmental dopes" of social structures. In this way, ethnomethodologists argue that it is the "folk methods" through which individuals construct their social world and their sense of social structure that is real the basis for sociological investigation and theoretical development.

It is obvious that the theoretical approaches of microchauvinists vary, depending on their conceptualization of the dynamics of action and interaction. At one extreme is Blumer's interpretive approach and at the other extreme is Collins' sociological positivism that seeks to explain the existence of a nonreified social structure as the epiphenomenon of micro-level interaction rituals. Both extremes, however, are surrounded by considerable skepticism about their conceptualizations of meso- and macrorealities and their ability to explain the stable, enduring, and often constraining nature of social structures.

MACROCHAUVINISM. Proponents of macrochauvinism argue that the fundamental unit of analysis of sociological investigations is "social structure," loosely conceptualized as regularized and persistent patterns of social interaction among individuals and corporate units. From this point of view individual subjectivity and the interpersonal dynamics of social interaction are irrelevant to the analysis of the emergent properties of social structures. Instead, these microprocesses as taken as "givens" and are simply "bracketed out" of the analysis. As a result, macrochauvinist perspectives emphasize concepts that reflect more macro aspects of social reality, such as spatial, temporal, and hierarchical differentiation; population size, density, and demographic composition; levels of technology and resource mobilization; rates of social mobility; distributions of power and material inequality; network relationships; roles of interaction; and other emergent aspects of social structures.

These approaches are illustrated by Parsons' (1951) structural functionalism, as well as Dahrendorf's (1959) conflict theory in its emphasis on "imperatively coordinated association." Mayhew's (1974, 1980a,b, 1984) baseline model strategy, however, is probably the most extreme within this macrotradition. Mayhew argues that variables such as population size and density circumscribe and delimit opportunities for interaction, and hence, explain high proportions of variance in human social systems. In essence, people are pushed and pulled around by such basic parameters of existence that the process of interaction can be ignored; in fact, it can often be conceptualized as a "random process" (Mayhew, 1981a,b). Less extreme is Blau's (1977) macrostructural approach in which the rate of interaction is considered a salient variable rather than the process of interaction itself.

While macrochauvinism eliminates from theoretical consideration the processes that are central to microchauvinist approaches, most of these macroapproaches are consistent in their belief that sociological theory should emphasize the development of abstract, timeless, and invariant social laws, and thereby produce more positivist models of sociological theory. This further distinguishes the macrochauvinists from the microchauvinists who are often critical of positivism.

MIDDLE-RANGE THEORY. Robert Merton's (1968) call for theories of the middle range emerged not only as a criticism of Parsonsian and Marxian grand theory, but also as a strategy to narrow the gap between abstract theory and empirical research. The unintended consequence of Merton's call was to elevate empirical generalizations in substantive areas to the status of theoretical principles or laws. For example, the middle-range strategy produced a vast array of theories of deviance and crime, gender inequality, ethnic antagonism, organizational growth and change, social movements, power and status competition, group dynamics, marriage and family, economic development, social institutions, and world systems, just to name a few.

While Merton did not envision his middle-range theory resolving the micro–macro gap, his strategy nonetheless has had important implications for bridging the micro and macro levels of social reality. Because tests of middle-range theories often employ the use of questionnaires, the theories are more about people's attitudes and perceptions of actions, emotions, interactions, culture, and social structure. Aggregated responses to questionnaires, however, can hardly capture the subtle dynamics of gestures, emotions, subjective deliberations, and group context, nor can they be adequate proxies for macrostructures like stratification systems.

ACTION-TO-STRUCTURE MODEL BUILDING.   Perhaps the earliest and most self-conscious attempts to bridge the micro–macro gap are those that begin with an analysis of social action and interaction and then shift to how these more microprocesses become regularized and institutionalized to generate emergent meso- and macrostructures. This micro–macro strategy is best exemplified in the works of George Herbert Mead and Talcott Parsons. Mead (1934) argues that the structures of society are essentially composed of the symbolic exchanges that occur among individuals. These interactions form the basis of human social organization and the emergent properties of social structure. In addition, Mead suggests that this process is recursive, whereby social structures, in the form of institutions and generalized others, come to shape and guide the development of self, social action, and interaction. In this respect, Mead's work also may be seen as a structure-to-action model-building strategy. Parsons' theory of action, on the other hand, is perhaps the most ambitious of these approaches. Building on Weber's (1968) conceptualization of action, Parsons' (1937) voluntaristic theory of action begins with an analysis of the unit act and moves to an analysis of how mutually oriented actors form larger, more complex social systems (Parsons, 1951) governed by four functional requisites (Parsons, Bales, & Shils, 1953). While Mead's work is often criticized for its inability to thoroughly conceptualize macro-level reality (Turner, 1999), Parsons' work quickly moves beyond its microfoundation to a macroreality that pays scant attention to action or interaction (Scott, 1963).

FORMAL SOCIOLOGY.   Simmel's (1950) analysis of the forms of sociation has generated unique approaches to the simultaneous examination of micro- and macroprocesses. Simmel's formal sociology has emphasized the form of social relationships over their content, making the actual unit of analysis a secondary concern. In this way, theorists adopting this strategy have been able to develop statements asserting the isomorphism between both individual and collective forms of social relations. Some exchange theorists (Emerson, 1972; Blau, 1966) and more recently network theorists provide the most conspicuous examples of this approach. For example, in Blau's (1966) early exchange theory four basic processes—attraction, competition, differentiation, and strains toward integration and opposition—typify the exchange processes between both individuals and collective units. Similarly, Emerson's (1972) approach develops structural theorems about generic social forms where the units of analysis are less important than the formal structures of their interrelations. Network theorists (e.g., Wellman, 1983; Burt, 1982) have formalized these approaches asserting that the formal structures of the interrelations of both individuals and collectivities reflect similar formal principles, such as the number, strength, density, transitivity, and reciprocity of ties. Here, what is important is not the contents of the social relations but instead their formal structure.

Yet, while formal sociology offers a unique solution to the micro–macro problem, its utility is limited. The approaches of formal sociology tend to obscure the actual processes emphasized by both micro- and macrochauvinist strategies, bracketing out their fundamental differences, in lieu of an assertion of their structural uniformity. Although it is often the case that interrelations between individuals and corporate units do reveal isomorphic tendencies, it is questionable that their differences can be ignored in building a micro-to-macro link. Still, formal sociology does open new avenues for addressing the micro–macro problem. The primary issue raised by this strategy is not the "linkage" between the micro and macro levels, but instead the isomorphism and divergence between them. This strategy allows the micro–macro problem to be addressed in a novel way, emphasizing the similarities and differences among social relations at distinct levels and in diverse contexts. Yet, if the larger networks can be determined to be constructed out of smaller ones, then the problems of conceptualizing "linkage" reemerges.

DEDUCTIVE REDUCTIONISM. George Homans' (1974) behaviorism is the most conspicuous example of deductive reductionism. His basic argument is that the "laws" of social structure can be systematically deduced from those of individual behavior. In this way, the link between micro and macro levels lies in the logic of deductive theory, with the elemental units described by more general laws, and the structures that emerge from them established through theoretical deduction from axioms about microprocesses to propositions about meso- and macro-processes.

This strategy represents a technically elegant solution to the micro–macro debate in that it encourages the articulation of micro- and macrotheoretical principles and their reconciliation through the logic of deductive theory. As Homans (1974) argued, sociological theory would worry less about whether or not its theoretical laws are reducible to those of behaviorist psychology if it had some laws in the first place. While there is merit to this approach, it is difficult to assess the utility of Homans' and more recent examples of this approach, since little theoretical work has been done toward the logical deduction of the laws of social structure from those of psychology. Even if such a reconciliation through deduction can be carried out, it does not encourage a search for those principles on different domains of the social universe that are to be deduced from axioms about psychological processes.

AGENCY AND STRUCTURE DUALITY. While the micro–macro problem is theoretically distinct from the agency–structure debate within sociology, several influential attempts examining the question of agency versus structure can shed light on the micro–macro debate. Generally, these approaches deny ontologically superiority to either the micro or macro levels and suggest that the micro–macro problem is best resolved, or in some cases completely obviated, by an attempt to reconcile the agency–structure dilemma within sociological theory. These approaches are best exemplified by the works of Giddens (1981, 1984) and Bourdieu (1977, 1980). While a distinctive vocabulary and rhetorical style largely differentiates these theorists, their collective strategy is one that attempts to wrestle both microprocesses and macrostructures from their separate domains and produce a theory that reflects a synthesis of what are perceived as needless oppositions.

Giddens' (1981, 1984) structuration theory is one of the most conspicuous illustrations of this strategy. For Giddens, the constitutions of both individual agents and collective structures are intertwined, producing what he calls a "duality" of agency and structure. Here, actors employ the "rules and resources" of structures in their everyday practice, and in doing so alter or sustain these rules and resources and inevitably the social structures that they reflect. These practices when extended over both time and space become instantiated as social institutions and social systems. Despite terminological differences, Giddens' approach is conceptually quite similar to Bourdieu's. The key concept in Bourdieu's scheme is "habitus," which is a set of class-based and internalized dispositions, tastes, and practices that individuals utilize in their engagement in the social world. For Bourdieu, the habitus is embodied within individuals and is both a "structuring structure" as well as a "structured structure." It is a means by which individuals internalize the structure and culture of their social world and simultaneously modify and reproduce it. In addition, Bourdieu suggests that individual agents employ their habitus in their engagement in different fields of activity—like art, science, or academics—whereby the utilize habitus-based "strategies" in their attempt to acquire various forms of capital and as a result reproduce the structural and cultural arrangements of their social world.

While these approaches have developed highly influential theoretical systems, their chief weakness is that they do not adequately resolve the micro–macro problem. Instead, they are highly metaphorical and rather vague because they fail to specify in any detail linkages between either agents and structures or micro- and macroprocesses. Rather, they simply assert that they are linked but offer few conceptual details.

MULTIDIMENSIONAL APPROACHES.   Given the diversity of approaches to the micro–macro problem, several prospects have been developed for a multidimensional resolution to the issue. These approaches attempt to integrate a diverse set of theoretical approaches at different levels of analysis, drawing together the theory and research pertaining to the dynamics of social interaction, the structure of formal organizations, the constraining impact of culture, and the processes by which reality is socially constructed.

The most conspicuous of these multidimensional strategies is that proposed by Ritzer (1981, 1990, 2000). In these models Ritzer attempts to develop what he calls an "integrated paradigm" that will help to reconcile the micro and the macro. He asserts that the approaches to the study of the social world can be categorized along two crosscutting continua. The first is the macroscopic–microscopic continuum, and the second is a objective–subjective continuum. From these continua Ritzer builds a model that has four quadrants: the macroobjective, the macrosubjective, the microobjective, and the microsubjective. On the macro side, the macroobjective reflects the more institutionalized features of society—law, bureaucracies, material technology, and language; while, the macrosubjective, on the other hand, comprises the social dimensions that are more explicitly cultural, including norms, values, and beliefs. On the micro side, the microobjective dimension is that which emphasizes the process of action and interaction, while the microsubjective focuses on social perceptions and the practical routines by which individuals construct their sense of reality.

Although Ritzer sees his approach as embedded in an ongoing process over time and has subjected his model to empirical investigation (1995), it is difficult to see how this scheme can be used to develop formal propositions about the links between the micro and macro. Its primary weakness is that it categorizes but does not explain, and it offers little in the way of integration among the four different dimensions.

In sum, the current strategies of generating grand theories that conceptually connect the micro and macro all reveal problems. Yet we should not give up on the problem but perhaps take a new tack in resolving it. Below, we propose an alternative strategy for resolving the micro–macro link, one that we hope resolves many of the limitations embodied in the preceding discussion.

An Alternative Strategy for Linking Micro and Macro

For many theorists, distinctions among micro-, meso-, and macroreality are merely analytical. Some are chauvinists, as we have pointed out, arguing that one level is *the only really real* reality. Our view is radical: the social universe actually unfolds along micro, meso, and macro levels; and while we develop analytical concepts to denote and describe the processes of each of these levels, these levels are more than analytical conveniences. *They are reality*. Understanding of any one level will not be adequate to a grand theory; a grand theory must somehow connect them together conceptually, seeing the dynamics of one level as embedded in and affecting the dynamics of the other two levels. This has been, of course, the challenge of various efforts to fill the micro–macro gap; our goal is to carry this effort a step further by presenting an outline of what is involved in micro–meso–macro linkages.

One way to link the micro, meso, and macro is to change our angle of vision on the social universe. Sociologists talk loosely about structures and processes, but in our view we need to be more precise. We require a vision of reality as governed by social forces. We have in mind something very similar to what Comte and Spencer saw as the paradigmatic force in physics of their time—gravity. Gravity is a force that structures some dimensions of the physical universe, obviously along with other forces. We can conceive of the social universe in much the same way: as governed by forces that drive behavior, interaction, and organization in certain directions. The substantive topics that occupy sociologists' attention thus are to be conceptualized as manifestations of the operation of underlying forces. We need laws of such forces; and with these laws, we can explain virtually any substantive social phenomenon at any place and time. Thus, the goal of grand theory is to (1) denote the key forces that are always operative when humans behave, interact, and organize; (2) uncover the dynamics of these forces; and (3) explain their relationship to each other. For us, there are distinctive forces operating at the micro, meso, and macro levels of reality; in fact, this is what makes these levels distinctive. We can, of course, have separate micro-, macro-, and mesotheories; these theories would be about the forces governing these realms of the universe. But a grand theory seeks to explain the relationships among these forces; while a full theory is beyond the scope of a single chapter, we will, as noted above, offer a minimal conceptual scheme for talking about these forces and their relations.

THE FORCES OF THE SOCIAL UNIVERSE

Macro-Level Forces

The macro level of the social universe encompasses the organization of larger numbers of people in space and over time. The macro level ultimately deals with how populations as a whole are organized in environments, both the biophysical environment as well as the environment created by patterns of social organization. And, try as we might, analysis of the macro level pulls us into the issues raised by functional sociology and anthropology. Functionalism—from Spencer through Durkheim, Radcliffe-Brown and Malinowski to Talcott Parsons—all emphasized that patterns of social organization reflect, to some degree, efforts on the part of actors to deal with fundamental needs or requisites that had to be met if a population is to remain viable in its environment. The problems of this approach are well documented and need not be reviewed here, but functionalism emphasized something that we cannot sweep under the rug: human populations are always adapting to environments, both external and internal; this fact of existence must be part of a theory of the macro level. But how are we to conceptualize what functionalists emphasized without being pulled into the quagmire that can emerge when we see theory as finding the need or requisite served by a social phenomenon? Our answer is to reconceptualize the notion of requisites in terms of the forces of the macro level.

What are these forces? For us, there are five: (1) population, (2) production, (3) reproduction, (4) distribution, and (5) regulation. Rather than visualize these as functional needs or requisites, it is better to see them as forces that drive humans to organize themselves in their environments. Moreover, the goal of explanation is not so much to cross-tabulate structures with one of these forces, but to develop laws explaining the operation of these forces and how they structure the organization of a population (see Turner, 1995, for one effort to articulate "laws" of these forces).

POPULATION.   We typically view population as a demographic variable, which it is, but it also is a force because it drives patterns of social organization. The size of a population, its rate of growth, its characteristics, and its distribution in space push for certain kinds of cultural and social arrangements, thereby making it one of the most powerful forces in the social universe. In general, as the population grows, it sets into motion pressures that increase the values for other macro-level forces. Production must expand to sustain the larger population; new forms of reproduction beyond simple species procreation generally emerge; distribution becomes more extensive; and regulation through consolidation of power will increase. Early functional theorists like Herbert Spencer (1874–1896) and Émile Durkheim (1893) tended to see population size and growth as a kind of master force, setting into motion the process of social differentiation; while this emphasis is not misplaced, we do better to see population as one of five forces that both drives other forces, while at the same time responds to the dynamics of the other four forces.

PRODUCTION.   To survive, humans must secure resources from the environment and convert them into usable goods. Whether simple gathering and hunting or complex industrialism service industries, production is one of the powerful driving forces of human organization. The organization of a population is determined, to a very great extent, by how production is carried out. Several conditions influence production: (1) the level of technology or knowledge about how to manipulate the environment, (2) physical capital used in gathering resources; (3) human capital or labor power and skill; (4) property systems for allocating rights to control technology and capital; and (5) entrepreneurship or the ways of organizing technology, capital, property for gather, and converting resources. The higher the values of these five elements, the higher will be the level of production, and vice versa.

REPRODUCTION.   Humans, like all life, replicate themselves biologically; this force drives the way in which humans are organized. But, humans also must pass on more than genetic material; they also must reproduce culture, social structures, and social beings who are motivated to occupy positions and play roles in existing social structures, who are willing to abide by cultural scripts, and who have the relevant interpersonal skills to sustain social relationships. Indeed, human genetic reproduction is not possible without social reproduction, and the larger and more complex the structure and culture of a population, the more its organization is shaped by reproductive structures.

DISTRIBUTION.   Humans must distribute the goods and commodities of production and reproduction. There are two essential mechanisms of distribution: (1) infrastructural, and (2) exchange. Humans are driven to develop systems for moving resources, goods, people, and information about space, and these systems can be seen as the infrastructure of distribution. Humans also are likely to engage in exchanges of resources with each other, and once exchange is initiated, marketlike forces are set into motion. The necessity of creating a distributive infrastructure and of developing the exchange systems are two of the most important forces driving the organization of a population.

REGULATION.   Activities of people and the collective units of their organization need to be regulated and coordinated. Two aspects of power are critical (Turner, 1995): (1) consolidation of power whereby the respective bases of power—coercive, administrative, symbolic, and material incentives—are mobilized into various configurations, and (2) centralization of power whereby the bases of power are concentrated in proportionately fewer actors. When populations are small, centralization and concentration of power to regulate and coordinate activity are typically absent, but as populations become larger and relations among actors more complex, power becomes ever-more evident as a driving force organizing a population. Without the concentration and centralization of power, other macro level forces cannot be coordinated and directed.

These five forces—population, production, reproduction, distribution, and regulation—determine the organization of populations and the cultural systems that they develop and use. When these forces are not active, a population cannot sustain itself in its environment. We could conceptualize these as functional needs or requisites, but we best not do so. Rather, it is better to convert the idea of requisites into forces that push actors, whether individuals or collectivities, to engage in certain lines of action to sustain themselves. In general, the larger the population, the more complex are the structures and cultural symbols devoted to production, reproduction, distribution, and regulation. Thus, for our purposes, a theory of macrostructure will revolve around principles explaining the operative dynamics of these five forces (Turner, 1995). The structures and cultural complexes that are generated by these driving forces are what sociologists term "social institutions." For us, these institutional systems set parameters for all other forces operating at the meso and micro levels of reality, and reciprocally these systems are structured from and sustained by the forces operating at the meso and micro levels. But we need to do more here than simply recognize that the macro, meso, and micro levels of reality are embedded in each other; we will need to indicate how this embeddedness operates and what its dynamics are.

We take what initially may seem like a macrochauvinist position: the effects of the macro on meso- and microprocesses are more constraining than the reverse. No one microevent or mesoaction can influence or change an institutional system, but the existence of one institutional system can constrain many sets of mesostructures and microencounters. There is an aggregation problem in micro-to-macro analysis: It takes many micro-level events, iterated among large numbers of individual people over longer time frames to change an institutional system; it takes fewer mesoevents to do so, but nonetheless it requires iterated changes in the structure of many sets of mesostructures to change institutional systems. Thus, even though in some ultimate sense the macro is built from micro- as well as mesostructures and processes, for any given moment of analysis the effects of macro on both the meso and micro will be more dramatic; we will understand much more about the meso and micro by analyzing their embeddedness in macroinstitutional systems than we will by studying micro- and mesoevents in order to gain an understanding of the macro level of reality. True, if we understand the structure and culture of mesostructures that make up an institutional system, we can learn more about the macro level, but if we rely only on meso-level analysis, we will not see the forest for the trees. The reason for this is that the macrorealm has its own distinct forces that cannot be reduced to or explained by those forces operating at the meso and micro levels. Thus, we are macrochauvinists to this extent: we will almost always learn more about the meso- or microevent by examining their embeddedness in an institutional system than vice versa. This is not to say, however, that the macro determines the meso and micro. These two levels of reality reveal their own dynamic forces, which, while constrained by those operating at the macro level, are distinctive to each level of reality. Moreover, as we will also emphasize, micro- and macroprocesses can change the operation of the macro-level dynamics driving the organization of institutional systems.

Meso-Level Forces

The meso level of reality consists of the dynamics creating, sustaining, and changing structures that are, on the one side, the units from which institutional systems are built and, on the other side, the units within which microencounters of face-to-face interaction occur. Meso-units, however, cannot explain the dynamics of either the micro or macro levels of reality because they in turn are constrained by the forces operating at the macro and micro levels. Institutional systems constrain the number, nature, and dynamics of mesounits, whereas meso-units ultimately are built from strings or chains of microencounters. This fact of social reality might tempt us to become microchauvinists, as so many have become, since the macro level of reality is built from meso and the meso is constructed from the micro. But, when we try to make this reduction, we distort the very nature of social reality.

There are, we argue, two basic forces operating at the meso level of human organization standing between macroinstitutional systems and microencounters of face-to-face interaction: (1) differentiation of (a) corporate and (b) categorical units; and (2) integration within and between corporate and categorical units.

DIFFERENTIATION.   The notion of social differentiation is as old as sociology, gaining prominence with Auguste Comte and then becoming the center points in the functional theories developed by Herbert Spencer and Émile Durkheim, or more recently by Niklas Luhmann. Differentiation can occur at all levels of reality. Institutional systems differentiate at the macro level as do status and roles at the micro level, but the key locus of differentiation is, we believe, at the meso level. What, then, differentiates at this level? Amos Hawley (1986) has captured the essence of two types of generic structures that exists at this level of reality: (1) corporate unit in which activities are organized for the pursuit of ends or goals, and (2) categorical units which distinguish individuals in terms of certain characteristics.

Corporate units can be of many types, ranging from complex organizations, kinship systems, towns and larger communities, and even groups (as distinct from micro-level encounters). All that is necessary for a corporate unit to exist is a division of labor coordinated to some end. At the most general level, corporate units vary along several important dimensions: (1) the size of the unit, (2) the integrity of the unit's external boundaries differentiating it from other units as well as partitions within the unit, (3) the formality of structure, (4) the explicitness and extensiveness of the horizontal division of labor, and (5) the explicitness and extensiveness of the vertical division of labor. Any corporate unit can have a particular configuration among these dimensions, but size is perhaps the most determinative. The larger the size, the more likely are the values for the other four dimensions to be high, although big differences among corporate units can still exist as is illustrated by the obvious variations between a large business corporation and a city. A theory of corporate units, we contend, will revolve around principles stating the dynamics of and between these five dimensions; such theoretical principles will be a significant part of a general theory of mesodynamics. Indeed, these principles already exist, for the most part, in the large literature on complex organizations.

Categorical units are structures created when individuals are placed into distinct categories and then differentially responded to by virtue of this placement. Examples of categorical units include age, gender, ethnicity, and social class. These are categorical units because they do not reveal a division of labor in pursuit of ends, although at times members of categorical units do become organized into corporate units to pursue an end, such as civil rights. But, categorical units are masses of people distinguished by characteristics that make a difference in terms of their behaviors and how others respond to them. Like corporate units, categorical units vary along five dimensions: (1) the degree of homogeneity or heterogeneity of members in a categorical unit, (2) the clarity and discreteness of the markers that distinguish a categorical unit, (3) inequalities or rank-ordering of categorical units in terms of some standard of differential evaluation (e.g., prestige, money), (4) correlation among or superimpositions of memberships in different categorical units (e.g., lower-class blacks), and (5) correlation of categorical units with the structure of corporate units (e.g., all women in a business are secretaries). A theory of the dynamics of categorical units then will explain processes of each dimension as well as the relationships among them; like a theory of corporate units, principles on the dynamics of categorical units will go a long way to explaining mesolevel social reality.

Differentiation of corporate and categorical units is a driving force of mesoreality. When humans organize activities, they do so along two basic lines of differentiation: formation of corporate and categorical units. They are driven to do so by the very nature of social reality because once it becomes necessary to coordinate the activities, corporate units are formed; it is built into our biology to make categorical distinctions, at least along age and sex considerations. But as populations get larger or as migrations of peoples occur, new distinctions are made along the lines of social class, ethnicity, region of origin, religion, and other markers of difference. These differentiating dynamics are inevitable, and they drive the nature of human social organization.

INTEGRATION.   When corporate and categorical units are created, forces are activated to order relations between and within them. For integration within corporate units, these forces revolve around (1) the structural and cultural constraints imposed by the institutional domain in which the corporate unit operates, and (2) the dynamics inhering in administrative structures used to coordinate and control the division of labor. Perhaps more interesting for a grand theory are the integrative dynamics among and between corporate units at the meso level (Turner, 1996): (1) structural interdependence, (2) structural inclusion, (3) structural overlap, (4) structural mobility, (5) structural segregation, and (6) structural domination. With differentiation of corporate units, some combination of these forces is activated; and as Table 18.1 summarizes, these forces have integrative and disintegrative effects. Thus, the forces of integration also contain the seeds for disintegration.

For categorical units, integrating forces revolve around (1) the degree to which the structure and culture of institutional domains and corporate units within these domains define distinctions and sustain them through their divisions of labor, (2) the extent to which the distributional processes, especially exchange, differentially allocate material and cultural resources so that members of categorical units have common shares, (3) the degree to which these differences in shares are defined as legitimate by members of categorical units, and (4) the rates and patterns of intra- and intercategory interaction. Table 18.2 outlines the integrative and disintegrative effects of these forces.

As is emphasized in Tables 18.1 and 18.2, integration does not imply either "good" or "bad." Oftentimes, integration sustains inequalities within corporate units or between categorical units, and these can generate conflict and tension. The only point that needs to be emphasized is that differentiation forces generating corporate and categorical units will set into motion integration forces that will work to order relations within and between these units.

TABLE 18.1. Integrative Dynamics among Corporate Units

1. Structural interdependence, or the exchange of valued resources among differentiated units	Regularizes interrelations among units in terms of normative expectations for resources, norms of fairness in exchange of resources, and mutual dependence for resources	Increases inequalities and conflict group mobilization by resource disadvantaged in exchanges
	Encourages market forces to develop that increase (1) the number and scope of interdependencies among units in terms of the volume, variety, and velocity of resource exchanges, (2) the use of common measures of value in transactions, (3) the use of generalized media like money that mitigate against particularistic media, and (4) the correspondence between individual preferences and resources available for consumption	Increases cyclical oscillations in prosperity, and hence, sense of deprivate among those affected by such oscillations
		Increases opportunities for fraud, corruption, and misrepresentation
		Increases overspeculation in metamarkets that can lead to collapse of higher-order markets, thereby escalating deprivations and conflict group formation
2. Structural inclusion, or the embedding of smaller units or congeries in larger ones	Specifies boundaries and delimits the range of resources used in exchanges among units	Creates rigidities and conservatism across arrays of embedded units
	Provides rules and media for exchanges of resources among units	Reinforces hierarchies of power and potentially raises the conflict potential in such hierarchies
3. Structural overlap, or the extent to which a population's members are incumbent in diverse positions of corporate and categorical units	Promotes crosscutting affiliations and weak-tie bridges that reduce the particularizing effects of consolidated parameters	Potentially creates larger sets of structures, thereby ratcheting up the size of units, and hence, the intensity of conflict when it emerges
4. Structural mobility, or movement of population members across boundaries of corporate	Extends networks across corporate units and decreases the density of networks, thereby reducing particularism associated with categorical unit differentiation	Can increase relative deprivation among those who are less movile, especially if mobility is correlated with inequalities
5. Structural segregation, or the partitioning of potentially conflictual and incompatible activities of corporate units in time or space	Reduces opportunities for conflict, at least in the short run	Reduces integrative effects of mobility and crosscutting affiliations
	Reduces tensions associated with reconciling incompatible activities	Promotes particularism of segregated corporate units
		Aggravates conflict-producing inequalities when segregation is correlated with inequalities in resource distribution

Integration dynamics are perhaps the most volatile because full order within and between units is rarely complete; differences almost always generate tensions, especially when structured around inequalities. Thus, we need not fall into the trap of seeing integration as a functional need or requisites; rather, it is a force that is only set into motion with differentiation but which is never an end state. Sometimes integrative forces sustain corporate and categorical units for a long time; at other times, these forces never take hold and generate tension, conflict, and

TABLE 18.1. (*Continued*)

6. Structural domination, or the use of coercion, material incentives, symbols, and administrative apparatuses to control, and regulate	Promotes control and coordination of actions and transactions between corporate units when balances among the coercive, material, symbolic, and administrative bases of power are maintained, with the cooptive use of material incentives dispensed through a moderately centralized administrative system that is legitimated by widely accepted evaluational symbols and that only strategically and episodically relies on coercion	When coercive base is overused, resentments over tight regulation accumulate and their control escalates the costs of administration and coercion (to repress conflict group mobilization) which, in turn, increase inequalities, drain resources, and discourage innovation
	Can promote control and coordination, even when bases of power are skewed, especially when supply of resources can be sustained and not be consumed by the costs of monitoring, administrating, and coercing as well as when consensus over legitimating symbols can be maintained	When the symbolic based is overused, contradictions between the ideals of evaluative symbols and the realities of regulation and control are exposed and escalate resentments and potential conflict group mobilization
		When the material incentive base is overused, questions and resentments over the fairness, equity, and efficiency of resource distribution can initiate conflict group mobilization and erode the symbolic base of power
		When the administrative base is overused, resentments over close monitoring, and regulation of actions and transactions mount, often leading to conflict group mobilization, which only escalates administrative costs and typically invites the overuse of the coercive base of power as well

change. Indeed, if we examine social reality at all levels, the most volatile dynamics—ethnic and class conflict, mobilizations of social movements, revolutions, and the like—are all dynamics inhering in differentiation and integration dynamics driving the meso level.

Micro-Level Forces

The micro level of reality consists of face-to-face interaction among individuals. Following Erving Goffman (1961, 1983), we visualize the most fundamental unit of the micro realm as the encounter, both focused and unfocused. In focused encounters, individuals face each other in an ecological huddle and generally have a common focus of attention and mood, whereas in unfocused interaction individuals avoid direct face-to-face contact, while monitoring each

TABLE 18.2. Integrative Dynamics among Categoric Units

	Integrative effects	Disintegrative effects
1. Institutional domains define categorical units	Attaches categories to highly salient structures critical to maintenance of population, thereby giving them legitimacy	Generates hostilities and potential conflict to the extent that categories defined by domain are differentially evaluated by cultural symbols, differentially rewarded by material well-being, and differentially available to members of a population
2. Corporate units division of labor defines categorical units	Attaches categories to highly salient activities in structures, thereby making them seem legitimate	Generates hostilities and potential conflicts to the extent that categories defined are differentially evaluated by cultural symbols, differentially rewarded by material well-being, and differentially available to members of a population
3. Exchange system defines categorical units	Attaches resource levels to those at common location for distributional system, thereby creating homophily in experiences in lifestyle	Generates hostility and potential conflict to the extent that (1) homophily promotes discrimination and (2) inequalities are not seen as legitimate
4. Rates of endogamy define categorical units	High rates of intracategory interaction and reproduction promote common culture for members	Generates hostility and potential conflict with other categorical units to the extent that endogamy promotes inequalities that are not defined as legitimate
5. Rates of exogamy define relations among categorical units	High rates of interaction with, and mobility to and from, categorical units loosens common culture and thereby increases tolerance and understanding among members of different categorical units	Generates a sense of threat as common culture is weakened, while undermining the control exerted by common culture

other's movements in space. The smallest corporate mesounit is a group, and the largest micro-unit is the encounter, although the line between groups and encounters can be fuzzy. Yet, groups will often break down into constituent encounters; moreover, groups tend to have more permanent structure than encounters, although again there is a fine line here. As a distinctive level of reality, encounters are driven by distinctive forces, and the most important of these forces are (Turner, 1999, 2000): (1) emotions, (2) transactional needs, (3) symbols, (4) roles, and (5) status. That is, the flow of face-to-face interaction in encounters is pushed along by the force of emotions, need states, cultural symbols, roles, and status; while these forces are constrained by the corporate and categorical units in which they are embedded (Turner, 2000) and by extension the institutional systems in which these mesostructures are embedded, they operate as an independent set of forces in face-to-face interaction (Turner, 2000, 2002).

EMOTIONS. All interaction is structured by the flow of emotions, revolving around variants and combinations of at least four primary emotions: satisfaction–happiness, assertion–anger, aversion–fear, disappointment–sadness (Turner, 1999, 2000, 2002). Emotions are aroused by expectations that individuals have for what will and should transpire in an encounter, and critical to emotional arousal is the extent to which expectations are realized. When expectations are met or exceeded, individuals experience variants and combinations of satisfaction–happiness; when they go unmet, variants and combinations of the three negative emotions—anger, fear, or sadness—are aroused. Moreover, combinations of these negative emotions produce important emotional states like guilt and shame. Shame is generated by sadness, anger at self, and fear of the consequences to self for not having met expectations for competent behavior, whereas guilt is produced by sadness, fear of the consequences, and anger at self for failing to realize expectations inhering in moral codes. Attribution processes become a critical process in the flow of these negative emotions. When individuals blame themselves for the failure to realize expectations, they experience sadness, and if they also are angry at self and fearful of the consequences, they also will experience shame as well as guilt if moral codes are invoked. When individuals blame others, they will experience and express anger at these others, but if others fight back or are powerful, persons also will experience fear and as a result displace their anger onto the corporate and/or categorical units in which an encounter is embedded. Alternatively, a person may displace anger onto those with less power, and in extreme cases repress the anger, which will produce sadness and depression punctuated by episodes of anger as well as fear if this latter emotion was also repressed.

NEEDS.   Human behavior and interaction are motivated by need states that are activated any time that individuals enter into encounters. When these need states are realized, individuals feel satisfied, and when they are not met, they experience negative emotions. There are, we believe, five such need states (Turner, 1987, 1988, 2000, 2002): (1) needs for self-confirmation and verification, (2) needs for positive exchange payoffs, (3) needs for predictability and trust, (4) needs for facticity, and (5) needs for group inclusion. These can be visualized as "transactional needs," since they are activated when face-to-face interaction begins and their state of activation and fulfillment shapes the flow of interaction.

Needs for self-confirmation operate at several levels. At the deepest emotional level of self, individuals possess core self-feelings about themselves as persons; these are transsituational core self-conceptions, and when they are salient, powerful emotional forces can be unleashed. At another level of self are subidentities, which are conceptions of self usually within a particular institutional domain of activity, such as economy, family, school, and the like. A third level of self is the role identities that individuals seek to fulfill as they make roles for themselves. In general, the more core self is salient, the more emotional loadings in an interaction, especially when expectations for core self are not realized. Needs for positive exchange payoffs are aroused in all encounters, usually around intrinsic reinforcers but at times extrinsic ones as well. Individuals enter encounters with expectations for payoffs, given the costs and investments they have incurred measured against standards of justice and compared to the costs and investments of others. When expectations are realized or exceeded, positive emotions ensue, whereas when they are not realized, negative emotions are aroused in accordance with the pattern described earlier. Needs for predictability and trust revolve around individuals' desire to feel that the behaviors of others are predictable, that others are in rhythmic synchronization with self, that others are being sincere, and that self is being treated with respect. When these needs are met, individuals feel satisfied, and when they are not, people become angry at others. Needs for facticity drive individuals to feel that, for the purposes of the interaction, all participants in an encounter share common experiences, that things are as they appear, and that the situation constitutes an obdurate reality. When individuals accomplish this sense of facticity, they reveal low-key satisfaction, but when they do not, anger is easily aroused. Needs for group inclusion push individuals to achieve a sense that they are part of the ongoing flow of interaction. Individuals do not need to experience high solidarity with a group to feel inclusion; all that is essential is their sense that they are not excluded from an encounter. When they feel this sense of inclusion, persons are satisfied; when they do not, they experience sadness and at times anger and fear as well.

SYMBOLS.   All interactions are guided by cultural forces. For any interaction, we believe there is a process of normatization in which expectations along a number of dimensions are activated (Turner, 2000, 2002): (1) categorization, (2) frames, (3) forms of communication, (4) rituals, and (5) emotions.

Categorization is the process of typifying others as representatives of a category, as persons or as intimates and situations in terms of the relative amounts of work-practical, ceremonial, and social content expected. Framing is the process of indicating what is to be included or excluded during the course of interaction with respect to relevant values and ideologies, persons, props and stages, bodies and biographies, and corporate and/or categorical unit memberships. Forms of communication are expectations about how talk along the auditory channel and how visual signaling are to be carried out. Ritualizing revolves around expectations for the emission of stereotyped sequences of gestures used to open, close, form, and repair breaches in the flow of interaction. Feeling rules signal the appropriate type and intensity of emotions that can be expressed in an encounter. These normatizing processes are all interconnected, with any one influencing the others. In general, individuals categorize situations initially; on the basis of this categorization, they impose frames and forms of talk which are then enacted ritually and regulated by norms dictating the emotions to be expressed, but should emotions, rituals, frames, or talk suddenly shift, then categorization and other normatizing dynamics will have to be readjusted. Thus, interaction always involves a dynamic interplay among the norms that allow individuals to categorize, frame, decide on forms of communication, use rituals, and express feelings.

ROLES.   The key mechanism of all interaction is role taking (Mead, 1934), whereby individuals read gestures in order to assume each other's perspective and likely dispositions to act. At the same time, all individuals role make (R. Turner, 1962) by emitting gestures signaling their role. A role is a sequence of gestures marking a course of action; while roles are often attached to specific status positions (see below) and regulated by norms, the process is much more robust. Humans carry, we believe, extensive and rather fine-grained conceptions of different roles in their stocks of knowledge; in role taking and role making they draw on these stocks. Individuals are driven by their transactional needs and probably by gestalt tendencies built into the neurology of the human brain to see patterns and consistency among elements; because roles are so critical to the flow of interaction, people assume implicitly that the gestures of others reveal a pattern signaling an underlying role. There are several different kinds of roles carried in people's stocks of knowledge, and these organize how individuals role take and role make.

One kind of role is what can be termed a "preassembled role" in that the sequences and patterns of gestures denoting the role are well known to all (e.g., mother). Another type is what might be seen as a "combinational role" in which several preassembled roles are put together into a new role (e.g., host of family gathering). Still another type is a "generalized role," which are sequences of gestures that can be used in specific roles, typically marking expressive and stylistic content (e.g., aggressive, shy, upbeat, serious). Finally, there is a "trans-situational role," which is often related to categorical unit membership (e.g., gender, ethnicity, age, class positions) and is displayed in all situations, or nearly all. Thus, as individuals role take and role make, they are utilizing complicated stores of information about these four types of roles. It is rather rare for a person to emit an entirely original role because even a novel role generally will carry elements of older preassembled roles and most certainly elements of generalized and trans-situational roles.

When individuals successfully role take and role make, they experience and express positive emotions, but when roles are not successfully made and when role taking leaves individuals uncertain of the role being played by another, negative emotions are aroused. These negative emotions will follow the dynamics on emotions and transactional needs outlined earlier, especially as they are driven by attribution processes (see Turner, 2000, 2002, for details).

STATUS. Not only do individuals role take in interaction, they also "position take" or "status take." For an interaction to proceed smoothly, people need to know each other's positions relative to self and to others in the situation. By virtue of recognizing status, role taking and making are facilitated, but equally important, the relevant norms and other expectations become more clear-cut and it becomes easier to know how transactional needs can be met.

Status positions reveal a number of critical properties. Among the most important are the (1) relative clarity of status, (2) the network properties of status, and (3) the inequalities of status. When position are discrete and clear, individuals are more likely to enter interaction with realistic expectations, meet their transactional needs, normatize the situation, and role take and role make with greater ease. Conversely, when the respective status of individuals is not clear, individuals will have to work at sustaining the interactive flow because they will be actively role and status taking as they try to discern each other's expectations, emotional moods, and need states, while trying to normatize the encounter. Status positions all reveal network properties revolving around the density (or lack thereof) of connections among positions and around the equivalence of positions. When individuals are in dense networks of positions or structurally equivalent positions, the interaction will proceed more smoothly than is the case when positions are not connected to each other or are equivalent. When positions are connected, interactions likely will have been iterated in the past, and as a result individuals will have some experience at establishing expectations, meeting each other's transactional needs, normatizing the situation, and role making/taking. Similarly, when they occupy equivalent positions, even if these are not connected, they will have had similar experiences, thereby making it much easier to meet needs, normatize, role take, and role make. Inequalities of positions in terms of their power–authority and honor–prestige are an important dynamic in interaction. When positions are unequal, they generate expectation states for performance that tend to sustain the system of inequality; as long as individuals meet or abide by these expectation states, the interaction proceeds smoothly. When expectations are not met, however, negative emotions are aroused because there has been a challenge to the status order; while this dynamic exists for the other properties of status, e.g., clarity and network, it is particularly powerful when inequalities of status are challenged or contested.

THE EMBEDDEDNESS OF REALITY

These forces driving encounters—emotions, need states, norms, roles, and status—exert independent effects on the flow of face-to-face interaction. Virtually all encounters are embedded in corporate and categorical units of the meso level of reality, and as a result they are constrained by the structure and culture of the meso level. In turn, corporate and categorical units are embedded in an institutional domain of the macro level, and hence, influenced by the structure and culture of this domain and often by the broader culture of the society or system of societies. As noted earlier, it takes many iterated encounters among large numbers of individuals to change mesostructures and their cultures, to say nothing of an institutional domain. Even at the meso level, no one structure can define an institutional domain, except in the simplest hunting-and-gathering societies. Thus, at a given time, the embeddedness appears to work top-down or from macro to ever-more micro, but over longer periods of time, change can move from encounters to meso- and macrostructures. But these changes take time; no one encounter will cause much dramatic change. Only when iterations and aggregations of encounters change mesostructures, which in turn change macrostructures, will the micro change the macro. Thus, in theorizing about the micro level of reality, it is much easier to see how the meso constrains the forces operating at the level of the encounter than vice versa.

Thus, grand theory will reveal a top-down, big-unit-to-small-unit bias, but as we will see, this does not obviate small-to-big processes. But, it does suggest that we will get more payoff by viewing how the embeddedness of the meso in macro and micro in meso constrains the forces operating at these two levels. True, in some ultimate sense, the macro is composed of meso- and microstructures, and we will need to theorize about this fact, but initially, we will get more explanatory payoff by exploring macro- to meso- and meso- to macroconnections. Figure 18.1 outlines these lines of influence among the three levels of reality.

Figure 18.1 represents a skeletal outline of what we believe a grand theory should address. The properties of each force and their dynamic relations should be the topics of theorizing. A grand theory thus would be a set or series of abstract theoretical principles on the dynamics of each force; if this strategy were pursued, sociology would be a science of the underlying forces operating in all of the very diverse substantive fields of the discipline. Indeed, we might have introductory texts organized around the principles for each level rather than the current

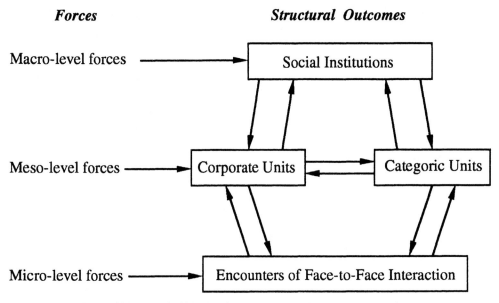

FIGURE 18.1 The embeddedness of macro-, meso- and micro-level social forces.

hodgepodge of topics, cartoons, and boxes that authors think students find interesting. Much of the theoretical work actually has been done; what is needed is an effort to consolidate these into more abstract and parsimonious sets of principles that would be the "laws" of sociology. True, this all sounds naive and too grandiose, even for a grand theory, but if sociology does not pursue this kind of strategy, it will never be a highly respected guest at the table of science.

Moreover, many of the principles will address the relationships among forces within and across each level of reality, as is denoted by the arrows in Figure 18.1. In fact, these will be among the most interesting principles, and of course they will be what makes the theory grand. Where, then, do we begin? We cannot fill in all of the details, but the senior author has tried to do some of the work (see Turner, 1984, 1988, 1995, 2000, 2002, for theoretical principles developed for each level), and others have also made significant progress in stating principles at various levels. Here, let us simply sketch in more detail how we might approach an integrated grand theory.

Cultural Embeddedness

At the most general level, a society or system of societies reveals several different types of symbol systems: technologies or information about how to manipulate the environment, values and evaluational symbols about what is right–wrong, good–bad, appropriate–inappropriate, and texts of lore, aesthetics, philosophy, history, and other symbolically stored information. This last element of culture, of course, is a bit of a residual category, but sufficient for our purposes. These elements of societal culture are generated by macro-, meso-, and microdynamics, but perhaps more significantly, they constrain what occurs in institutional domains, corporate and categorical units, and encounters.

In Fig. 18.2, we have outlined the key ways in which broader cultural systems are translated into the culture of institutional domains, corporate and categorical units, and the normatizing processes of encounters. All institutional domains, whatever the underlying force generating them, develop systems of symbols that become part of the broader culture of the entire society; once present, actors in institutional domains draw on, perhaps elaborate, and even change symbol systems as new problems are confronted. The key point is that culture is used by actors along several dimensions: applications of value orientations to a domain (e.g., economy or kinship), translations of values to ideologies about what should occur in a domain, use of particular technologies for a domain, elaboration of texts for the domain, and development of general institutional norms for a domain. Within an institutional domain, these cultural contents are further translated, applied, used, and perhaps changed in the culture of corporate units. These cultural materials from institutional domains and corporate units also can become the standards and criteria by which categorical units are defined. Normatization of episodes of face-to-face interaction are very much constrained by the culture of the corporate and categorical units in which an encounter is embedded; in this way, the culture of an institutional domain, as it filters through the culture of corporate and categorical units, constrains how individuals categorize each other and the situation, how they frame the interaction, how they communicate, how they use rituals, and how they express emotions.

Thus, at the most micro level—the encounter—culture reaches participants through successive filtering, alterations, and elaborations of the culture from more macro levels of social organization. Talcott Parsons' theory of culture and the cybernetic hierarchy of control was not too far off the mark on this score; while cultural sociology has gone in many different directions in recent years, the dynamics of culture as outlined in Fig. 18.2 have not been

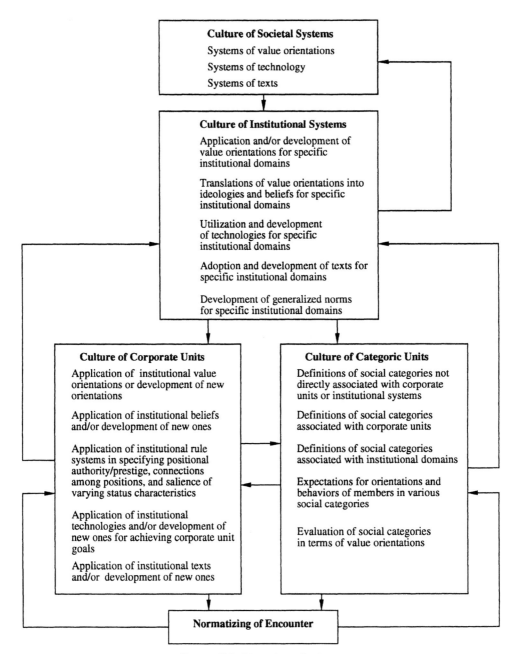

FIGURE 18.2. Dimensions of culture.

obviated because they are fundamental to human social organization. If these lines of constraint did not exist, interaction at the micro level would be exhausting, constantly breached,
and incessantly renormatized, while corporate and categorical units would not hold together in
any coherent form. Thus, there is enormous opportunity for a new cultural sociology that looks
somewhat like old functionalist cultural analysis, but this time around, the emphasis will be on

how to express these dynamics in elementary theoretical principles. The problem with the old grand theory of Parsons was not its grandness, but its inability to generate explanatory laws and principles.

Structural Embeddedness

At the macro level, the forces generating institutional domains are interrelated, each setting values for the others (see Turner, 1995, 2002, for formal laws demonstrating this). Thus, each institution is interrelated with the others, a fact that Talcott Parsons and Neil J. Smelser (1956) tried to demonstrate for the economy and as the senior author (Turner, 1972, 1997) has sought to do for other institutional domains. Thus, institutional systems are embedded in each, constraining the forces generating institutional systems.

At the meso level of reality, corporate units are almost always embedded in an institutional domain, drawing on its culture and using this culture as blueprints for structuring a corporate unit in this domain. True, there are dynamics operating purely at the meso level that drive corporate unit formation, but the structural profile of a corporate unit is very much constrained by culture and structure of an institutional domain. For example, economic organizations in a capitalist economy look very similar because they operate in a particular type of institutional system, and the same is true for corporate structures in other institutions.

Similarly, categorical units are highly constrained by both the institutional sphere and the division of labor of corporate units of this domain. For example, the social categories of worker and father are different because they come from positions in different kinds of corporate units in different institutional arenas. Similarly, one's social class is very much a reflection of the resources secured in the markets of an economy, although here other institutions such as the polity and education may also be involved. Other categorical distinction, however, are less explicitly tied to particular institutional sphere. Age, gender, and ethnicity need not be explicitly tied to a domain, although it would not be difficult to see the influence of family on definitions of age, economy and polity on gender distinctions, and economy or religion on ethnicity. Thus, most categorical distinctions are embedded to some degree in an institutional arena and the corporate units in this sphere.

At the micro level, most encounters are embedded in corporate and categorical units, which in turn indirectly embeds them in institutional domains (see Turner, 2000, 2002, for specific theoretical principles on the dynamics of this embeddedness). Encounters frequently involve people in different categorical units and at varying places in the division of labor of corporate units, and the dynamics of the encounter—that is, emotional, transactional needs, norms, roles, and status—will be greatly affected by this embeddedness. Indeed, a person's expectations for what will occur, relative status, role-making efforts, perceptions of how to meet transactional needs, categorization of self, others, and situation, frames, modes of communication, use of rituals, and emotional displays will almost always be highly constrained by the structure and culture of corporate and categorical units in which the encounter is embedded.

Micro-to-Meso-to-Macro Embedding

As we have emphasized, many of the theoretical principles of a grand theory will revolve around delineating the dynamics of the forces operating at each level and on the top-down embeddedness of the meso in macro and the micro in the meso. Still, bottom-up changes do occur. Strategic encounters can alter meso structures, and changes of meso structures will ultimately alter the structure and culture of institutional domains. The question is: How can we theorize these bottom-up forms of embeddedness? Below we offer some suggestions.

While there is a long history in sociology of the investigation of the external and constraining aspects of macro and meso social forces, we follow those who assert that this social constraint does not imply deterministic control. Human beings reject authoritarian control and resist their caged confinement within social structures that are too rigid and limit individual autonomy (Maryanski & Turner, 1992). Although individuals can act to restructure the social encounters that impose too much constraint, these changes typically will not be reflected on more macro or even meso levels. However, individual action can be effective in creating social change and transforming higher-level social structures under certain conditions. We propose that there are seven general conditions under which change in the dynamics of encounters can have important ramifications for altering the structure and culture of corporate and categorical units and ultimately social institutions. These conditions are (1) the power and status of individuals occupying corporate and categorical units, (2) the centrality, density, and embeddedness of the encounter within networks of encounters, (3) the nature of the institutional structure in which the encounter is embedded, (4) the number of iterations of the encounter, (5) the size of the encounter, (6) the visibility of the encounter, and (7) the level of emotional energy produced by the encounter.

POWER AND STATUS DYNAMICS.   The power and status of individuals in a social encounter can have an enormous impact on the potential of an encounter to have effects for the larger cultures and structures in which they are embedded. In this way, the greater the power and status of individuals within relevant corporate or categorical units, the more likely are their actions to affect the macro- and mesostructures that circumscribe an encounter in which they are involved. High-ranking members of corporate units and highly prominent members of categorical units will be much more likely to capture attention, enforce their authority, and have an opportunity to be heard than those members who are more low ranking. This is especially true for individuals who possess high levels of charismatic authority in corporate units and who are prominent members of highly evaluated categorical units. In general, the more membership in categorical units serves as a vehicle for the creation of corporate units, the more likely will change in encounters among members of a categorical unit have effects on changing the culture and structure of larger structures.

CENTRALITY, DENSITY, AND NETWORK EMBEDDEDNESS.   The more an encounter is centrally embedded within networks of social relations, the more likely is that encounter to produce change at more meso and ultimately macro levels. This effect is compounded as the density of the network structure increases, facilitating the flow of resources, lines of communication and authority, and in some cases increases in structural interdependence. Moreover, if an encounter is highly embedded in the division of labor in a corporate unit or is crucial to the maintenance of categorical distinctions, then this encounter is more likely to influence other encounters and mesostructures. When change emerges in a single, highly embedded and centralized encounter, it can have a cascading effect on other nodes in the network. This conclusion runs counter to the image of change as coming from outside of a social system, but it is our view that most change occurs within established systems of network relations. External sources of change will be mostly likely to be effective when they penetrate and alter encounters critical to the maintenance of existing networks of corporate and categorical units.

Thus, external sources of change often must become internal to the system if they are to be effective.

THE INSTITUTIONAL CONTEXT OF THE ENCOUNTER.   Another condition that produces micro- to macrochange is the nature of the institutional system in which an encounter is embedded. When a corporate or categorical unit is embedded in what Amos Hawley (1986) has called a "key function" institutional domain, the changes initiated at the level of the encounter will have a greater impact not only on the mesostructure and culture but also on the institutional domain. Such key function domains are institutional systems that engage in interchanges with the external environment of a society. For example, changes in corporate units, like those in the economy and polity, that mediate interrelations between a population and its environment, like the economy and polity, will tend to have more of an impact than units, such as those involved in reproduction, religion, or socialization, that operate internally. Thus, changes at the level of the encounter within the corporate and categorical units of "key" institutional domains will have the potentially greater impact on meso- and macrostructures than those encounters embedded within other corporate and categorical units.

THE ITERATIONS OF AN ENCOUNTER.   A single encounter will effectively change a corporate unit or institutional system only under rare conditions. Instead, it takes repetition of change-oriented encounters to have an effect on mesostructures and by extension institutional domains. The greater the number of iterations of an encounter, the more likely will it change the corporate and categorical units in which it is embedded, especially if other conditions enumerated above prevail.

THE SIZE OF THE ENCOUNTER.   The number of individuals engaged in an encounter is another important source of change. The greater the number of individuals with sustained attention in an encounter, the more likely is the encounter to have effects on other corporate and categorical units in which it is embedded. While sheer numbers alone certainly increase the immediate visibility of an encounter, the impact of a large encounter spreads when members disperse to new encounters. Participation in encounters thus becomes a form of cultural capital that is disseminated throughout corporate and categorical units as the participants of the encounter separate and talk about their experiences with nonparticipants.

THE VISIBILITY OF THE ENCOUNTER.   As mentioned above, the greater the visibility of an encounter, the more likely is the encounter to affect change in more inclusive corporate and categorical units. As Collins' (1998) research has suggested, successful interaction rituals energize an encounter and allow it and its participants to capture more "attention space." Such encounters become more highly visible and are more likely to have an impact on subsequent encounters. Modern communications technology has greatly extended this process through technologically mediated mass dissemination and reproduction. It is for this reason that efforts to introduce changes at the level of the encounter are almost always staged as "media events" in order to influence the largest number of people.

EMOTIONAL ENERGY AND THE ENCOUNTER.   A final condition affecting the potential for social encounters to generate change is the level of emotional energy aroused in an encounter. Encounters that generate high levels of emotional energy, either positive or negative, will be much more likely to initiate change in corporate and categorical units. It is for this reason that encounters specifically oriented toward change are often orchestrated by social rituals in order to accelerate the level of emotional energy that they produce. When an encounter produces high levels of positive emotional energy, the participants are energized and are likely to spread this energy to other encounters, although this energy is more likely to reinforce existing corporate and categorical units than change them. In contrast, when the emotional energy generated is negative, reacting against existing corporate and categorical units, individuals will be much more likely to push for change in these structural arrangements. Thus, the more negative emotional energy aroused in an encounter and the more that this encounter is embedded in networks of other encounters manifesting the same negative emotional energy, the greater is the potential for change in corporate or categorical units. This tendency is increased when facilitators of collective action tap into the negative emotions directed toward corporate or categorical units, with arousal of positive emotions about the direction that change can take.

CONCLUSIONS

It is not possible, of course, to present a fully developed theory in one chapter, but we hope that the general direction that grand theory might take is clear. Grand theory must resolve the micro–meso–macro linkage problem with more than metaphors and vague pronouncements. Our suggestion is to visualize each level of reality as revealing forces that drive the culture and structure of micro-, meso-, and macrounits. The forces for these levels differ and they produce varying types of structures. Yet, each level of reality is embedded in the other, and so the goal is to develop abstract theoretical principles that explain not only the dynamics of each level but the relations among these levels.

Embedded is a more powerful force working from the macro through meso to micro, and so we will gain more theoretical payoff focusing on this chain. Still, in some ultimate sense, the macro is composed of the meso and the meso of the micro, forcing us to develop theoretical principles to explain how the micro influences the structure and culture of more inclusive structures. Whether working in either direction, the key to grand theory is to be more precise than previous theorizing. It is essential that specific principles be articulated for (1) each force operating at a given level and (2) patterns of embedding across levels. When concern is with developing principles rather than metaphors, such as habitus, structuration, chains of rituals, and the like, sociology will make more progress in building grand theory.

Some would suggest that sociology avoid grand theory altogether, or at least until it has more well-developed specialized theories, but we have seen the results of this advocacy: the proliferation of over-specialized theories. There are now so many different theories that it seems impossible to gain a vision of the social universe as a whole; rather, our theories have chopped up reality in so many arbitrary ways that it is difficult to see the forest through the trees. In contrast to current trends toward specialization, both inside and outside of theorizing proper, we argue that specialized theories are best developed within a more encompassing vision of how the social universe unfolds. Only grand theory can provide this vision.

Finally, grand theory has been stigmatized, we believe, not so much because previous theories were grand but they were not theoretical. Most involved elaborating conceptual schemes to the point of excluding propositions. Our approach suggests the opposite: a very minimal conceptual scheme with the weight of the theory coming from abstract principles about the dynamics specified in the scheme. We have not presented formal principles, but they are being developed, and we encourage others to follow this approach.

REFERENCES

Alexander, J., Giessen, B., Munch, R., & Smelser, N. J. (Eds.). (1986). *The micro–macro link*. Berkeley: University of California Press.

Berger, P., & Luckmann, T. (1967). *The social construction of reality*. New York: Doubleday.

Blau, P. (1966). *Exchange and power in social life*. New York: Wiley.

Blau, P. (1977). *Inequality and heterogeneity: A primitive theory of social structure*. New York: Free Press.

Blumer, H. (1969). *Symbolic interactionism*. Englewood Cliffs, NJ: Prentice-Hall.

Bourdieu, P. (1977). *Outline of a theory of practice*. New York: Cambridge University Press.

Bourdieu, P. (1980). *The logic of practice*. New York: Cambridge University Press.

Burt, R. (1982). *Towards a structural theory of action*. New York: Academic Press.

Collins, R. (1975). *Conflict sociology: Toward an explanatory science*. New York: Academic Press.

Collins, R. (1981). On the microfoundations of macrosociology. *American Journal of Sociology*, 86, 984–1014.

Collins, R. (1988). *Theoretical sociology*. New York: Harcourt Brace Jovanovich.

Collins, R. (1998). *The sociology of philosophies*. Cambridge, MA: The Belknap Press of Harvard University Press.

Dahrendorf, R. (1959). *Class and class conflict in industrial society*. Stanford, CA: Stanford University Press.

Durkheim, E. (1893). *The division of labor in society*. New York: Free Press.

Emerson, R. (1972). Exchange theory: Part II. In J. Berger, M. Zelditch, & B. Anderson (Eds.), *Sociological theories in progress*, Volume II (pp. 38–87). Boston: Houghton-Mifflin.

Garfinkel, H. (1967). *Studies in ethnomethodology*. Englewood Cliffs, NJ: Prentice-Hall.

Giddens, A. (1981). *Central problems in social theory*. Berkeley: University of California Press.

Giddens, A. (1984). *The constitution of society*. Berkeley: University of California Press.

Goffman, E. (1961). *Encounters: Two studies of the sociology of interaction*. Indianapolis, IN: Bobbs-Merrill.

Goffman, E. (1983). The interaction order. *American Sociological Review*, 48, 1–17.

Hawley, A. (1986). *A theory of human ecology*. Chicago, IL: University of Chicago Press.

Homans, G. (1974). *Social behavior: Its elementary forms*. New York: Harcourt Brace Jonavonich.

Maryanski, A., & Turner, J. H. (1992). *The social cage: Human nature and the evolution of society*. Stanford, CA: Stanford University Press.

Mayhew, B. (1974). Baseline models of system structure. *American Sociological Review*, 39, 137–143.

Mayhew, B. N. (1981a). Structuralism versus individualism: Part I, Shadowboxing in the dark. *Social Forces*, 59, 335–375.

Mayhew, B. N. (1981b). Structuralism versus individualism: Part II, Ideological and other obfuscations. *Social Forces*, 59, 627–648.

Mayhew, B. (1984). Baseline models of sociological phenomena. *Journal of Mathematical Sociology*, 9(4), 259–281.

Mead, G. H. (1934). *Mind, self and society*. Chicago, IL: University of Chicago Press.

Merton, R. (1968). *Social theory and social structure*. New York: Free Press.

Parsons, T. (1937). *The structure of social action*. New York: McGraw-Hill.

Parsons, T. (1951). *The social system*. New York: Free Press.

Parsons, T., & Smelser, N. J. (1956). *Economy and society*. New York: Free Press.

Parsons, T., Bales, R. F., & Shils, E. (1953). *Working papers in the theory of action*. Glencoe, IL: Free Press.

Ritzer, G. (1981). *Toward an integrated sociological paradigm: The search for and exemplar and an image of the subject matter*. Boston: Allyn and Bacon.

Ritzer, G. (1990). Micro–macro linkage in sociological theory: Applying a metatheoretical tool. In G. Ritzer (Ed.), *Frontiers of sociological theory: The new syntheses* (pp. 1–30). New York: Columbia University Press.

Ritzer, G. (1995). *Expressing America: A critique of the global credit card society*. Thousand Oaks, CA: Pine Forge Press.

Ritzer, G. (2000). *Modern sociological theory*, 5th Edition. Boston: McGraw Hill.

Scott, J. F. (1963). The changing foundations of the Parsonian action scheme. *American Sociological Review*, 28, 716–735.

Simmel, G. (1950). *The sociology of Georg Simmel*. K. Wolff (Trans.). Glencoe, IL: Free Press.

Spencer, H. (1874–1896). *The principles of sociology*, 3 vols. New York: Appleton-Century.

Turner, J. H. (1972). *Patterns of social organization*. New York: McGraw-Hill.

Turner, J. H. (1983). Theoretical strategies of linking micro and macro processes: An evaluation of seven approaches. *Western Sociological Review*, 14(1), 4–16.

Turner, J. H. (1984). *Societal stratification: A theoretical analysis*. New York: Columbia University Press.

Turner, J. H. (1987). Toward a sociological theory of Motivation. *American Sociological Review*, 52, 15–27.

Turner, J. H. (1988). *A theory of social interaction*. Stanford, CA: Stanford University Press.

Turner, J. H. (1995). *Macrodynamics: Toward a theory of the organization of human populations*. New Brunswick, NJ: Rutgers University Press.

Turner, J. H. (1996). A macro-level functional theory of societal disintegration. *International Journal of Sociology and Social Policy, 16,* 5–36.

Turner, J. H. (1997). *The institutional order*. London: Longman.

Turner, J. H. (1998). *The structure of sociological theory*, 6th Edition. New York: Wadsworth.

Turner, J. H. (1999). Toward a general sociological theory of emotions. *Journal for the Theory of Social Behavior, 29,* 133–162.

Turner, J. H. (2000). A theory of embedded encounters. *Advances in Group Processes, 17,* 285–322.

Turner, J. H. (2002). Face-to-face: Towards a sociological theory of interpersonal behavior. Stanford, CA: Stanford University Press.

Turner, R. H. (1962). Role-taking: Process versus conformity. In A. Rose (Ed.), *Human behavior and social processes* (pp. 20–40). Boston: Houghton-Mifflin.

Weber, M. (1968). *Economy and society*. G. Roth (Trans.). New York: Bedminister Press.

Wellman, B. (1983). Network analysis: Some basic principles. *Sociological Theory, 1,* 155–200.

CHAPTER 19

Systems Theory

Kenneth D. Bailey

A system is a bounded set of interrelated components. Systems theory is somewhat of a paradox within sociological theory. It is venerable, yet continues to arise in new forms such as complexity theory or second-order sociocybernetics. It was considered by many to be the backbone of 1950s macrotheory, but remains largely unknown or an enigma to the newest cohort of sociologists. A number of theorists who are not traditionally labeled as systems theorists use the term "system" quite extensively in their work (Coleman, 1964, 1990; Giddens, 1979). It is somewhat ironic that an approach that on the one hand is so current and so well-accepted on a superficial level (how many words are more familiar than "system" or even "social system"), is so scorned and misunderstood on a deeper level (Lillienfeld, 1978). There are a number of possible reasons for this paradox. It may be that its mere aging, and the fact that it was widely espoused by such 19th-century social theorists as Spencer (1892) and Pareto (1935) reinforces the notion that systems theory is obsolete, scientistic, or overly conservative (Collins, 1975).

INDICATORS FOR A SYSTEMS APPROACH

There are instances in sociological scholarship where a systems approach is indicated (or even mandated) and times when it appears less useful or is perhaps even contraindicated. Systems theory often is unnecessary when the goal is to correlate two or more variables for a single individual (for example, examining the correlation between education and income), which constitutes the bulk of current sociological research. Such studies using a random sample of individuals have little need for systems theory. This format roughly corresponds to Merton's (1949) "middle-range theory" in which the scholar formulates a theory that is sufficiently complex to yield explanatory power (but not so complex as to impede empirical investigation), and then formulates a research project to test this theory, usually with the individual as the unit of analysis.

Middle-range studies wed theory and data and they have the advantage of having a relatively high probability of successful completion. Such micro- and middle-range theories are necessary for sociological advancement but hardly sufficient. The studies are often rather

Kenneth D. Bailey • Department of Sociology, University of California, Los Angeles, California 90095.

Handbook of Sociological Theory, edited by Jonathan H. Turner. Kluwer Academic / Plenum Publishers, New York, 2002.

specialized (even "piecemeal" from a systems perspective) and include a variety of familiar forms, such as case studies, various descriptive studies, ethnography, focus groups, surveys, experiments, and so forth. As important as these familiar modes of analysis are, they must be augmented with (but not supplanted by) modes of analysis that can be best described as global, integrative, large scale, comprehensive, complex, "grand theory," macro, and so forth.

The reason that the smaller studies are not sufficient as a mode of sociological analysis, even when aggregated, is because they can routinely exhibit a number of anomalies of various sorts (Kuhn, 1962). Writ large, we may define an anomaly as any unexpected or unsatisfactory result. This includes contradictory findings, inexplicable findings, unexpected findings, and disappointing findings, such as findings that fail to support hypotheses (for example, correlations that are not statistically significant). Such anomalous findings are not necessarily the result of flawed theory or flawed research design, but may occur with a valid theory and a well-designed research project if the scope of the project is simply too narrow and does not encompass the degree of complexity necessary to study such a complex phenomenon as society.

If anomalies or disappointing results of any sort are encountered during the course of the research, this may be an indication that the degree of complexity encompassed by the research design is simply insufficient. This may mean that the research design has to be expanded in as many as six or more ways, including increasing: (1) the number of individuals, (2) the number of variables, (3) the number of relationships among individuals (both linear and nonlinear), (4) the number of relationships among variables (both linear and nonlinear), (5) the number of macroconcepts, (such as societal integration, society–environment relationships, division of labor, and so forth), and (6) the number of instances when the focus of the study is the society *sui generis*.

Another point is that the dominant mode of contemporary sociological research, such as a small-scale survey or ethnographic study, is hardly the unique domain of sociologists. In fact, scholars from a variety of disciplines utilize this familiar research mode, including anthropology, social psychology, social welfare, geography, public health, political science, history, business, public policy, urban planning, market research, and other disciplines. While there is nothing wrong with sociologists working in this crowded arena, it does not justify their almost total exclusion of studies of a more complex nature as just described. In fact, a harsh critic might almost describe the paucity of studies of social complexity as sociological malfeasance, as sociologists are eschewing the area of research where they are seen to have the most expertise of any scholars (if not a unique mandate) and are engaging instead in the crowded arena of small- or midrange research, with the individual not only as the basic research unit but as the focus of ultimate interest.

Why is there such a reluctance on the part of sociologists to study the society *sui generis*, as advocated so long ago by Durkheim (1951)? Some of it is probably simple force of habit: doing that they have always done. Some of it is surely convenience and conformity. The "mainstream" study is safe, rewarding, and has a fairly high probability of completion. Some of it is undoubtedly the lack of a role model. How, indeed, does one study a whole society? How likely is it that such a study can be successfully completed? What tools are needed? What are the rewards for such research? Probably many contemporary sociologists are rather unsure about the answers to such questions.

Introductory sociology texts (see Gregory & Bidgood, 1939)) were much more comprehensive decades ago, when the society being studied was less complex. Newer introductory texts are considerably less complex, now that the society is more complex. What is the sense of this? Until sociologists utilize complex modes of analysis to study complex societies, their work is open to criticism that it is superficial, tangential, piecemeal, and incomplete. Macrotheory offers the chief hope for the adequate study of complexity, and a macro social systems model is well-suited to the study of contemporary societal complexity.

My assessment of sociology is harsh. I do not believe that sociology can permanently defend a practice of limiting its work largely to the study of surveys done on a random sample of individuals. Nor do I believe that it is adequate to view society chiefly as a cultural phenomenon emanating from the interaction of individuals. I think that at some point it is inevitable that sociology must confront the need to allocate at least a portion of its resources to the analysis of the complex modern society *sui generis* (Durkheim, 1933, 1951), even if this task seems daunting, is prone to failure, and is devoid of an easy pathway to success.

This is not to say that all microsociologists must be transformed into macrosociologists, but only that in addition to its legions of hyperspecialists, sociology must count among its numbers some scholars who are willing and able to study holistically the complex modern society, all of its parts, all of its internal relations among its parts, and all of its external relations with other complex societies. Until this is done, sociology cannot claim to be the study of society, only the study of some parts of society.

Some might see this as a plea for theory rather than survey research, or for structure rather than agency. In reality, it is merely a suggestion that sociology, while continuing its current emphases on specialized studies, agency, culture, and other phenomena, also should reconsider the analysis of some long-neglected macrosociological topics such as complexity, societal differentiation, societal integration, the division of labor, technology, information processing, energy processing, and so forth.

In 1949, middle-range theory was perhaps an appropriate prescription for the ills of sociology. Many sociologists felt caught between the extremes of small-scale descriptive studies and grand theories. There was no good intermediate approach, and so middle-range theory was appropriate. It was the time for specialized studies. Now some 50 years later, specialized studies threaten to choke sociology with fragmentation. The challenge now is to study the complexity of modern society. I will first lay out the challenges that confront us and that specialized or middle-range theories are ill-suited for. These include the study of internal and external linkages, both vertical and horizontal, as well as the explication of boundary problems (including the insider–outsider dilemma), and an array of other epistemological issues. I will next review the extant sociological systems theories and will close with a recommendation for the future.

THE TASK AT HAND:
THE CHALLENGE OF COMPLEXITY

The complex society is a multilevel system, with layers of both vertical and horizontal internal subsystems, and is subject to both vertical and horizontal internal differentiation and integration, all occurring within systems boundaries. In addition to nested vertical differentiation such as individuals, groups, and organizations, a society contains varied degrees of horizontal differentiation, with links among the various entities. For example, each group must relate horizontally to other groups, and individuals must relate horizontally to other individuals. In addition, entities at each level relate vertically to entities at other levels (e.g., individuals deal with groups, and groups with organizations). Thus, I am proposing that sociologists need to study the stuff of society—individuals, groups, organizations, and so forth—not separately, piecemeal, or even sequentially, nor in a specialized fashion, but rather in terms of all their possible interrelations (both vertical and horizontal, internal and external) with each other. Sociological systems theory has attempted to deal with these broad issues, but unfortunately past efforts made some mistakes that led to intense criticisms.

Past Mistakes

Sociological systems theory had its roots in 19th-century thermodynamics (Clausius, 1879) and was introduced into sociology by Spencer (1892), Pareto (1935), and others and subsequently was widely adopted by Parsons (1951) and others. Unfortunately, while systems theory was popular (at least in some circles) for almost 100 years, it endured a great deal of criticism in a number of areas.

EQUILIBRIUM.   The notion that a social system was routinely in equilibrium unless disturbed by external forces and would return to equilibrium after a brief period was popularized by Pareto (1935). He said that societies that were the victims of external disturbances such as earthquakes or short wars in rich countries would return quickly to equilibrium (assuming that the forces that caused equilibrium in the first place remained intact). The concept of social equilibrium evinced strong criticism within sociology. Critics charged that equilibrium models favored the status quo, so that social change was seen basically as an aberration (Lockwood, 1956; Gouldner, 1970). Thus, critics charged that systems models were inadequate for the study of social change. Parsons (1961) and others reacted to their critics by attempting to defend and repair equilibrium models. Repairs were attempted by substituting some allied concept such as moving equilibrium, homeostasis, or steady state, but ultimately none of these mechanisms were able to satisfy critics (Bailey, 1990).

The reality was that as a physics concept, the concept of equilibrium was simply applied inappropriately in sociology. Thermodynamic equilibrium does not constitute a desirous state of social equilibrium at all, but rather is a state of maximum entropy (dissolution, or system death), as Spencer (Duncan, 1908) learned to his chagrin many years ago. Further, even if the equilibrium concept were appropriate, it was never adequately defined or operationalized in mathematical terms in sociology (Russett, 1966). In retrospect, from the standpoint of a pure systems perspective, the social equilibrium concept proved to be a giant red herring and an embarrassment. As applied in sociology, it was never appropriate, never successful, and in the end, never necessary. Modern systems theory does not rely on an equilibrium model.

IDEOLOGY.   The emphasis on equilibrium favored the status quo. This, among other things, led to the criticism that not only is systems theory conservative by nature but that systems theorists themselves are politically conservative (Collins, 1975). Modern nonequilibrium systems theories do not have the same emphasis on integration that equilibrium theory had and are quite conducive to the study of social change (Rhee, 1982). Modern systems theorists span the range of political ideology, from liberal to conservative.

ABSTRACTION.   Social systems models, along with other "grand theory," have been criticized for being overly abstract or for neglecting the study of human activity, as evidenced by Homans' (1964) famous plea for "Bringing Men Back In." It seems that the pendulum has swung sufficiently to justify the reverse plea and issue a call to "bring society back in."

DIFFICULTY IN TESTING.   A fourth criticism is that systems theory often is insufficiently tested. Again, this is a more general critique that can often be applied to macrotheory as a whole and not just to systems theory. It is true that as one gets above the limits of "middle-range" theory that testability does become more difficult. The goal for macrosystems theorists is to design theory with testability in mind to generate testable hypotheses (Bailey, 1994; Miller, 1978) and to resist the temptation to draw a discrete demarcation line between "theory" "and research."

THE UNIT OF ANALYSIS.   A legitimate debate arises over the proper unit or "component" for systems analysis. While many see the concrete human individual as the logical unit of systems analysis, others see the "act" or social role (Parsons, 1951) or the communication (Luhmann, 1986) as the proper unit. In reality, there is no one correct unit. It is possible to choose different units in different instances, as long as one realizes that these can define radically different systems. For example, Parsons (1979) recognized that the concrete individual is the "ultimate" systems unit but rejected the individual as the unit of the social system in favor of the role.

Other criticisms could probably be made, but these are some of the principal ones. In retrospect, it is clear that none of these are fatal flaws or even particularly damning for modern complex social systems theory. Some of these flaws are generic to "grand theory," and thus are applicable to most macrotheories. Clearly there are trade-offs with microtheory. Macro-theories (including systems theories) have flaws such as lack of manageability and lack of testability, are expensive and time consuming to conduct, and perhaps have uncertain probabilities of success. On the other hand, microtheories have their own flaws. They may be insufficiently complex, sometimes deal with simplistic issues, may be fraught with anomalies, or may simply leave critics with a general feeling of inadequacy. The obvious answer is to work with both micro- and macrotheories and to emphasize their integration (Alexander, Giesen, Munch, & Smelser, 1987).

THE COMPLEX SOCIETAL SYSTEM

The basic definition of a system is a (bounded) set of interrelated components, such that change in one component of the system initiates change in other components of the system. The exact nature of the subsequent changes is determined by the particular nature of the relationship, such as its strength of relationship, whether it is linear or nonlinear, and so forth. While the internal components of the system are highly interrelated, they are less related (or even uncorrelated) with the environment outside the systems boundaries.

The system may be a closed system that is entirely shut off to flows from the environment, or alternatively can be an open system that is open to flows of information and energy from the environment. In classic structural–functional systems theory, each internal component (sub-system) had a function that it performed to ensure the survival of the system (society) as a whole. If the subsystem failed to perform its function and if this function were not then subsequently picked up by another subsystem, the equilibrium and stability of the entire system, or perhaps even its very survival, would be at stake.

Systems exist at many levels, so the first task in social systems analysis is to decide what is the basic system that we wish to study. If one has a micro-orientation, the basic system of interest could be the individual, dyad, small group, and so forth. For our purposes, we consider it axiomatic that the basic system of interest for sociology is the holistic society *sui generis*, generally operationalized as a politically bounded nation. The society is a fundamental unit. It has a certain degree of systemic autonomy, yet it has relations with other systems. In addition to this external focus, involving relations with other societies or even with smaller external units (such as corporations) or larger global units (such as the United Nations), there also is an internal focus of interest. This internal focus reveals a wealth of complexity in a large contemporary society such as the United States.

The internal complexity of a large society like the United States is so great that the systems model is the clear choice for analyzing it. Any narrower or more-specialized model quickly gives short shrift to the analysis of all salient internal societal features. Even with a far-reaching model such as the systems model, the researcher generally will be unable to simultaneously analyze all the salient internal features of the society, and thus will be forced to be selective and make some difficult choices as to how to frame these internal components. One alternative is to simply omit entire sections of the society from the analysis. We will reject this alternative as a distinctly "unsystemic" approach that would quickly lead us to the sort of narrow, piecemeal model that we are trying to avoid. If we seek comprehensiveness, we dare not leave portions of the society out of our analysis. The best alternative is to frame the whole of the internal society, but to delete some precision from the analysis (if we find that the fully comprehensive systems analysis is simple unmanageable).

Vertical Levels

For example, assume that we examine the vertical structure within a given society and identify (following Miller & Miller, 1992) the following levels: the societal level, the community level, the organizational level, the group level, and the individual level. The traditional (nonsystems) sociological approach is to study each level separately, in a piecemeal fashion. That is, one sociologist specializes in organizational analysis, while another studies small groups, and yet another conducts surveys on individuals. While we could give lip service to integrating these disparate studies at some point in time, the reality of this occurring successfully seems quite low.

The systems alternative to this problem is quite different. Rather than making the analysis manageable by limiting it to one narrow (but isolated) specialty, we prefer to frame the model so that it encompasses (and has the potential for recognizing) all these internal vertical levels, including even those that we might not yet be aware of. This is done by simply drawing wide boundaries for our model. Then, after all the levels are specified, the researcher can analyze them in the greatest degree of complexity that he or she can manage, given constraints of time, funding, and so on. For example, for our purposes here, we will focus on the internal vertical levels of the individual, group, and organization. The other levels remain in the model and we can return to them as needed.

Horizontal Links and Boundaries

In addition to the vertical levels, the complex society is replete with horizontally bounded entities within each level. The bounding for most of these entities is rather straightforward. For example, a business can be legally defined as an operating entity and also can have a spatial location that provides boundaries. Thus, "Roy's Bakery," with a total of seven employees, is a clearly delineated group comprising the seven persons who work daily in a set physical location. Such entities can grow by division (starting another branch at a different location) or by aggregation (hiring another employee).

A more difficult group-bounding problem for systems theory (and really, for sociology as a whole) is the problem of deciding who the members of social groups or institutions are. The problem is basically a tautology: a group member is a person who is a member of the group. That is, groups would like to define themselves totally in terms of what they are, but this is basically tautologous (Luhmann, 1986). What is a scientist? That is a person who studies science. But what is science? That is what a scientist studies. So, groups must clarify their identity by defining themselves not only in terms of what they are but also in terms of what they are not (Luhmann, 1989). Thus, science is defined not only by what it is but also by what it is not. Members (scientists) are adamant about labeling aspiring members such as astrologers as nonscientists (and thus nonmembers).

Among the institutions that are very sensitive about protecting their boundaries are key institutions such as law, medicine, science, religion, education, and so forth. All these subsystems are vigilant in protecting their membership. Luhmann (1986) refers to such institutions as "differentiated function systems." This terminology indicates that the subsystem has matured to the degree that it exhibits functional autonomy, although operating with the context of the larger society.

In Luhmann's (1989) theory, binary coding plays a key role in boundary establishment and maintenance. Since the group cannot define itself in terms of itself, as this is tautologous, it must establish binary categories (a member and a nonmember). While pervasive in society, these dichotomies are themselves logically inadequate, as they result in a paradox. "A member is a person who is a member" is a tautology. But, "A member is not a nonmember" is a paradox, because a member cannot exist without a nonmember to define it and a nonmember cannot exist without a member to define it. The problems of tautology and paradox are illustrated by self-reference theory and are represented by the huge volume of binary coding in complex society.

Thus, the complex society is seen to be composed of many subsystems that can be identified both vertically and horizontally. The potential number of internal links is simply the number of links between all subsystems, both among and within levels, and is a very large (but finite number). In addition, all internal entities have potential links, both vertical and horizontal, with a large number of other external systems (societies) and with all of their internal components.

These links, whether vertical or horizontal, external or internal, are chiefly conduits of energy or information, or both. In previous centuries, the emphasis was on the challenge of successfully moving large energy sources, such as raw materials for industry. The successful movement of raw materials fostered the industrial revolution. In contemporary complex society, emphasis has shifted to the development of technology for information transmission and storage. Information links are increasing rapidly, not only in number, but also in speed of transmission. This revolution means that impacts, particularly global financial impacts, now can be almost instantaneous. Thus, if one country in a region suffers a financial calamity such as a currency devaluation, its neighbors best have their own financial houses in order, for the vast array of external and internal information links, both vertical and horizontal, means that the speed of the external impact on their own internal financial affairs leaves little time for extensive planning.

SOCIETAL BOUNDARIES.   Why are societies increasingly vulnerable to external impacts, such as financial crises? Is it because their boundaries are more easily penetrated by new information-processing technology, or simply that their boundaries have always been vulnerable but the extreme speed of new technology exposes boundary weaknesses? Obviously, both are true to some extent. The analysis of societal boundaries incorporates much of the analysis of group boundaries just discussed but requires some additional discussion as well. A social system boundary is a demarcation that distinguishes the system from its environment. If a system were indistinguishable from its environment, then boundary placement would be purely arbitrary. Generally, however, a boundary represents a break (perhaps a sharp break) in entropy levels, with entropy being higher externally (outside the system, or in the environment) than it is in the system. This is an example and of course is not always the case, as this depends to a certain extent on the location of the observer.

Entropy is the degree of disorder in the system. Humans fix societal boundaries in a reflexive manner (Bailey, 1990, 1994). They post a boundary (sometimes for an important reason, but sometimes arbitrarily or out of convenience or necessity) and then reflexively react over time in a way that will lower the internal entropy within the system, as via the process of autopoiesis (Luhmann, 1986). The system defines the boundary and then the boundary subsequently defines the system. After a boundary is fixed and defended, the internal order is developed within the system through work, which consists of the expenditure of energy. This expenditure of energy must be increasingly guided by information in complex society, so that the outcome of the work is nonrandom (orderly). Random work conducted through ignorance (and without guidance by the most current information available) will not result in an optimal reduction of system entropy.

The best way to determine the existence of a system boundary is to compute entropy levels on both sides of the boundary. Since a boundary is by definition an entropy break, the entropy levels will be significantly different on different sides of the boundary. If entropy measurement cannot be done, then the easiest clue to the existence of a boundary is to look for breaks in energy and information flows, such as security measures. A similar clue is in coding, as in the 128-bit encryption used in computer security to protect financial information on the Internet. Any time a significant system boundary is crossed, it is necessary to recode a certain amount of information (e. g., money, language). Another clue to the existence of a boundary is the identity of persons on opposing sides of the boundary. If persons refer to themselves as insiders (us) and other persons as outsiders (them), then a boundary exists.

After determining the societal boundaries, the next step is to recognize the existence of a vast array of potential links (relationships), both within and between levels and internal and external. A given subsystem, be it an individual, group, corporation, or government entity, can have four basic kinds of links: internal–horizontal (e.g., a link between two corporations within the same society), internal–vertical (e.g., a link between a corporation and an individual within the same society), external–horizontal (e.g., a link between a corporation in one system [society] and another corporation in another system [another society], and external–vertical (e.g., a link between a corporation in one society and an individual in another society).

EPISTEMOLOGY

If one only considers the number of internal links (both vertical and horizontal) within a contemporary society, the degree of complexity is staggering, comprising perhaps billions of potential relationships. This challenging arena is the unique purview of sociology, as no other academic discipline has laid claim to it (although some other discipline may claim adverse possession if sociology fails to act). Why have sociologists practically abandoned the study of societal complexity? There obviously are many reasons, some already discussed. One chief factor is that adoption of such a complex model represents a dramatic epistemological departure from the model of research extant in contemporary sociology.

The extant model, discussed previously, deals largely with a sample of individuals. Sociologists are accustomed to analyzing models to discover their underlying assumptions. Rarely do they examine carefully the consequences of a particular model. The current sociological model, with the individual as the chief unit of analysis, has one salient sequiter: it mandates the locus of power within the human individual rather than within some larger (macro) unit. For example, consider the typical sort of study, where a sociologist examines a random sample of individuals and finds a correlation between education and income. The locus of control is the individual. One conclusion is that if an individual wishes to increase his or her income, he or she will pursue additional education. The individual is assumed to have the power to alter his or her income (at least to some degree) in this situation.

A subtler exigency is that the extant sociological model demands not only individual power but also individual explanatory power. That is, a sociologist seeking an explanation of his or her findings can "fill in" an anomalous or incomplete explanation (e.g., can explain away a low correlation coefficient) by involving personal knowledge or experiences about individual-level affairs. Thus, one might find a sociologist studying "empty nesters" and "boomerang kids" (adult children who return to live with their parents) beginning with a sophisticated statistical analysis, but ending by repairing anomalies with homilies or by invoking his or her personal knowledge about "what teenagers are like," or "I know in my case, my son wanted to return home," and so on.

Epistemologically, the solution is much different for the mode of analysis in complex social systems theory. Here, the chief unit of analysis is the society *sui generis* (in all its holistic complexity). A chief sequiter from the model is that the individual does not have much control over the social complexity represented by billions of potential internal links that are processing energy and information. While some might find this model dehumanizing, I would say that it represents reality. It shows that individuals do exercise control, but only within the context posed by a high degree of societal complexity. Therborn (2000, p. 155) states the issue as a question. Is the world a system that directs the actors in it, or is it a stage upon which they act? I would of course answer that it is both, and Therborn (2000, p. 157) seems to reach basically the same conclusion.

A key component here is the role of the observer. The observer is an important element in reflexive sociology (Giddens, 1979, 1984; Luhmann, 1986, 1989; Bailey, 1997a). Systems theory has emphasized the role of the observer (Geyer & van der Zouwen, 1978; Marturana & Varela, 1980). Of particular importance is the second-order cybernetics focus on "observing the observer" (Luhmann, 1986). The role of the observer (including the researcher) is key to studying a system (or any social group). The observer not only has a role in the objectivity–subjectivity debate but also helps fix insider–outsider designations, fixes systems boundaries, and distinguishes the system from the nonsystem (environment), which often is a difficult thing for the system itself or its insider members to do.

We mentioned earlier the issues of tautology and paradox stemming from self-reference. Luhmann (1986) sees second-order cybernetics, as discussed below, as the greatest hope for resolving these issues in sociological systems theory. An internal observer that is observing or defining himself or herself (an insider) is in a very different position from an external observer who is observing the same system (an outsider), or is observing another observer in the process of observing his or her own system, and so on. Of course, second-order observation is only one link in an infinite chain, and n-order observation just as easily can be envisioned (Bailey, 1997a, 1998).

Insider–Outsider

While some scholars might view the insider–outsider issue as merely a facet of the group membership issue discussed previously, I see it as a deeper epistemological issue and so I decided to explore it here. It is not simply a boundary issue or a membership–nonmembership issue but involves vertical power relations and dominance issues as well. The insider–outsider issue is epistemologically difficult for sociology, partially because the extant middle-range formulations are ill-suited for dealing with the origins of the insider–outsider dilemma. Small-scale studies in homogeneous societies can largely skirt this issue, as can holistic or global studies. It is primarily middle-range studies that leave themselves most open to the vagaries of insider–outsider claims.

The insider–outsider dilemma stems from the ubiquitous practice of closed binary coding in the complex society, as discussed previously. I think that the only solution is to formulate multichotomies (within the context of the complex system), rather than relying on perpetually inadequate dichotomies. The dyadic member–nonmember distinction is internally closed, as will be discussed later. Dichotomous boundary formulation (member–nonmember) is deceptive, as it is so familiar that it can appear to be "natural" when it is really being imposed (perhaps arbitrarily) by a dominant insider.

For example, many Americans would probably accept the familiar "heterosexual–homosexual" distinction as a "natural" dichotomy of sexual preference. Unfortunately, this distinction is quickly seen to be anomalous, as it does not provide a category for the increasingly visible designation of "bisexual." Adherents of the heterosexual–homosexual dichotomy face a crisis in the form of a bisexual liberation movement, as they fear that their dichotomy will be deposed by the equally "natural" (but not so familiar) unisexual–bisexual dichotomy. In this new dichotomy, the distinction between heterosexuality and homosexuality has disappeared (as indeed these concepts have disappeared) as both are merged into "unisexual." This effectively usurps power from the previously dominant heterosexual group. Thus, some people (both heterosexual and homosexual) may take defensive measures, such as claiming that bisexuality does not really exist.

The only way that the anomalies of tautology (posed by unichotomous group membership definition) or paradox (posed by dichotomous group membership definition, and now standard) can be removed is by shifting the scope of the research to the society as the basic unit of analysis. Then, by analyzing the group as a subsystem within the larger context of the complex society, we allow for the analysis of multichotomous categories. Now, the locus of analysis rests not on the insider individual but on the society, so that the plurality of all social groups can be analyzed without contradiction and without the need to deny the existence of one or more groups (such as bisexuals or multiracial persons).

The insider–outsider dilemma is a classic example of an anomaly that is ill-treated with a middle-range formulation. Other examples of common anomalies in overly narrow sociological models often can be found by searching for unresolved debates or controversial issues. These often can be identified by looking for dichotomies with connecting terms such as "versus" or "or." Some common examples include the debates over free will versus determinism, structure or process, synchronic versus diachronic, agency or structure, abstract versus concrete, and so forth. The central problem with all these is that they are formulated as dichotomies. For example, the insider–outsider distinction is hardly a dichotomy in a pluralistic society. There may be one insider (you) but hundreds of outsiders representing the plurality of groups within the larger society. In reality, complex societies have many insiders as well as many outsiders. Middle-range studies have difficulty representing them all, but complex systems theory comes much closer to providing a realistic rubric for their analysis.

Indeed, with a mere shift of scope from the individual or the middle-range study to the complex model, the entire insider–outsider anomaly largely (but not entirely) disappears. If the entire complex society (rather than the individual) is taken as the basic unit of analysis, then individual researchers (as well as individual research subjects) are all insiders as well as outsiders. That is, at the system level, all individuals are insiders, as they all reside within the system. At the subsystem level, as observed from the larger perspective of the society, all individuals are dual insiders and outsiders, as they reside within one subsystem and outside of another subsystem.

In our complex model the research focus is not on individuals and their study by either outsiders or insiders, but rather on the society as a whole as a research arena. That is, the focus is on the analysis of a huge amount of data conducted by countless researchers and stored in a computer in a fashion to be subsequently aggregated so as to effect macrological conclusions concerning the holistic complex society. Not only is complex systems theory sociology's best hope for avoiding self-destructive solipsism, it also is the best hope for avoiding not only legions of anomalies (such as those mentioned above), but also for avoiding the kind of unwitting change of scope (or Durkheimian fallacy, or ecological fallacy, see Bailey, 1990, 1994) that long has plagued sociology.

CONTEMPORARY SYSTEMS APPROACHES

Now that I have sketched some of the criticisms of past systems theorists and have examined in some detail the high degree of complexity that any systems model of the complex society must deal with, it is time to briefly review some of the extant systems approaches. Readers who have not kept abreast of the field may be surprised by the depth and breadth of contemporary approaches, such as soft systems theory, critical systems theory, world systems theory, functionalism, neofunctionalism, autopoietic theory, sociocybernetics, complexity and chaos theory, living systems theory, social entropy theory, and others. This list is not complete and obviously a full review is impossible here. We must be content with a brief sketch of the major features of some of the major approaches. The most visible approach has been functionalism. It is important for students of sociological systems theory to be familiar with structural–functionalism, but also to recognize that most of the contemporary approaches are not functionalist approaches. Since we already have discussed briefly functionalism in our review of the critiques of earlier systems models, we shall consider it again only very briefly in our discussion of contemporary approaches.

Functionalism

The most visible social systems theory has been the approach known broadly as structural–functionalism. This approach and its variants have been presented by a large number of scholars, most notably Parsons (1951, 1961), Merton (1949), and others (see Buckley,

1967, 1968, 1998). This approach continues to be visible in sociology in the form of neofunctionalism (Alexander & Colomy, 1990). Since neofunctionalism is represented in this volume and functional systems theory has been discussed and analyzed at great length (see Turner & Maryanski, 1979; Bailey, 1982, 1984, 1990, 1994), it is unnecessary to discuss it here in much detail.

Since there are many variants and applications of functionalism, it is difficult to summarize them all. However, from the standpoint of systems theory, the main points are clear. Functionalism emphasizes part–whole relationships. The social system is seen as a whole that incorporates a set of interrelated subsystems, such as institutions (education, religion, science, law, etc.). A central notion (as discussed earlier) is that the interrelated internal parts interact over time (function) in a manner that ensures the survival of the system. Systems can be classified as either open (allowing exchanges with the environment) or closed (not allowing such changes). Social systems are said to be open systems.

While functionalists in reaction to their critics stressed that the social system is adaptable and amenable to change, nevertheless the bias toward integration and stability was clear. The function of each subsystem separately (and in concert) was to ensure the survival of the society. If one subsystem was impaired, since all were interrelated the others would react to compensate for the loss of function in the ailing subsystem. Thus, the internal cohesion of the system was maintained over time. This coherence was variously represented by equilibrium, homeostasis, or a steady state (Bailey, 1990, 1994). If equilibrium were disturbed (usually by external forces), it would be restored through the internal changes of the interrelated subsystems, usually within a short period of time. That is, as long as the original forces that achieved equilibrium remained, external disturbances would soon be rectified (Pareto, 1935).

As discussed previously, writers soon decried the inability of the system to respond to change, since equilibrium presumed a return to the status quo. There were charges of conservatism and a bias toward integration, with deemphasis on societies that were undergoing a revolution or societies that had disappeared altogether. Further, critics said that equilibrium was a physics concept that was inappropriately applied to sociology and that equilibrium was vague, not properly operationalized, and not subject to empirical test (see Russett, 1966).

While the bulk of the criticism of functionalism came from critics who were not systems theorists, some systems theorists also were unhappy with some of the tenets of functionalism. In particular, Luhmann (1986) was critical of the part-whole emphasis and with the overly simplistic closed–open systems model. While his own subsequent systems approach (Luhmann, 1995) dealt with both parts and wholes, it dealt with them in a much different way. Luhmann (1986) did acknowledge of course the relation between parts (differentiated function subsystems) and the whole society, but he focused primarily on the boundary and relations with its environment. This approach was rather unique in systems theory in terms of the amount of emphasis he placed not only on system–environment relations, but also on subsystem–environment relations. This protects the autonomy of the subsystems and emphasizes their role in dealing with the environment in a manner that is not only distinct from but different from system–environment relations.

Functionalism did systems theory (and sociology) a great service by emphasizing the holistic analysis of the social system. As the dominant theoretical paradigm of the 1950s and 1960s, functionalism was invaluable in keeping sociology focused on macrotheory. Its limitations were that it depended too heavily on the 19th-century equilibrium model of Pareto (1935), which was based largely on the study of isolated (closed) systems in thermodynamics. If systems theory is to be successful, it cannot continue to look inward to such an extent that internal relations are emphasized at the expense of internal-external relations. In order to get from the model of equilibrium-based classical functionalism to the externally-directed model of social complexity, sociological systems theory must make three main shifts away from classic functionalism:

1. Nonequilibrium. Analysis of social system internals must shift from an equilibrium model to a nonequilibrium model.
2. Control. There must be a shift toward explication of decision making and control, as in Miller's (1978) emphasis on the decider as the most important subsystem. Classic functionalism relied so heavily on equilibrium that return to the status quo was considered almost automatic, and this precluded the necessity to explicate how and where decisions regarding system control are made. It is very important to acknowledge and analyze the exercise of power (at all levels, individual, corporate, governmental, etc.) within the complex social system.
3. Internal–external relations. There must be a shift away from the overly simplistic open–closed dichotomy and toward a more sophisticated model detailing the complex interplay between internal systems components (at all levels) and the external environment.

Fortunately, recent trends in sociological systems theory have approximated these needed shifts. This is fortuitous, as these shifts have occurred without the guidance of an overarching paradigm to replace functionalism and in the context of waning interest in sociological systems theory. With so few sociologists currently identifying themselves as systems theorists (particularly in North America), it is amazing that the field continues to advance as it does. However, progress has proceeded apace in a number of areas. Although space precludes extended analysis, we can briefly discuss some of the chief areas of contemporary systems emphasis relevant to sociology.

General Systems Theory

The general systems theory (GST) movement (von Bertalanffy, 1956) has itself waned since its apex in the 1950s and 1960s (roughly corresponding with the height of systems popularity in sociology) and ironically also has faced fragmentation in the form of a number of competing associations and internal specialization within associations. Nevertheless, there are still a number of associations like the International Society for Systems Science (ISSS) that do continue to foster the aims of integrative scholarship. GST seeks to identify commonalities across disciplines, so that generic systems principles can be identified, redundant or contradictory efforts can be minimized, and integrative systems research can follow. GST has been perhaps the most visible force for countering the increasing fragmentation and hyperspecialization that if carried to an extreme could trivialize research in many disciplines (not just sociology). In addition to carrying the symbolic banner of academic integration, GST has been notable for a number of other achievements. Space precludes extended discussion of all of these, so I will focus on the first recent trend noted above: the shift from equilibrium to nonequilibrium models.

While sociology clung strongly to its emphasis on equilibrium (Parsons, 1951) in spite of mounting criticisms and evidence that the application in sociology was inconsistent with the concept of equilibrium in thermodynamics, GST was instrumental in adopting entropy rather than equilibrium as the basis for a systems model applicable to social science and biology. GST faced a dilemma in attempting to integrate social science and thermodynamics, as the second law of thermodynamics dictates that in an isolated system, entropy will increase over time until it reaches a maximum (equilibrium). But equilibrium is essentially a state of dissolution rather than its opposite—a state of maximum cohesion or integration—as envisioned by equilibrium theorists in sociology. It was clear that social systems such as bureaucracies did not fit the second law, as they tended to grow increasingly complex (orderly) over time rather than more disorderly. Was it possible that the second law was incorrect? This loomed as a major anomaly until Prigogine (Prigogine, 1955; Prigogine & Stengers, 1984; see also von Bertalanffy, 1956) demonstrated that while entropy increases inexorably in a closed system (such as the isolated heat bath studied in thermodynamics), in an open system the exchanges with the environment can result in decreasing entropy that is sufficient to compensate for the internal increase of entropy. This explains how vast bureaucracies can arise in apparent contradiction of the second law.

Another development that has contributed to our first trend (the shift from equilibrium to nonequilibrium models) is synergetics (Haken, 1983; Weidlich & Haag, 1983). Although Haken does not seem to identify himself too closely with GST, synergetics does contribute to the trend of emphasizing entropy rather than equilibrium. Haken moves from entropy analysis in isolated thermodynamic systems to entropy analysis in self-organizing systems that may be far from equilibrium, such as biological or social systems.

While synergetics is quite quantitative, another development within the grand rubric of GST is so-called "soft systems theory." This is an approach to organizational analysis that is decidedly less quantitative than many systems approaches. It was developed in England by Checkland (1994). The existence of soft systems theory, as well as critical systems theory (Flood & Jackson, 1991), is probably a surprise to many sociologists who stereotype the systems approach as being positivistic, conservative, or even "scientistic."

Still another notable development within GST is living systems theory (LST), as developed over a number of years by an interdisciplinary group led by Miller (1978; Miller & Miller, 1992). Miller provided much of the detailed concrete analysis of systems internals that can aid in the analysis of the processes of control and decision making. Miller (1978; Miller & Miller, 1992) specified eight levels of living systems analysis (cell, organ, organism, group, organization, community, society, and supranational). He also specified 20 subsystems that process either matter–energy or information, or both. The reproducer and the boundary are dual subsystems that process both matter–energy and information. The eight matter–energy-processing subsystems are the ingestor, distributor, converter, producer, matter–energy storage, extruder, motor, and supporter. The ten information-processing subsystems are the input transducer, internal transducer, channel and net, timer, decoder, associator, memory, decider, encoder, and output transducer.

Miller's schema provides for the comprehensive analysis of all 20 subsystems at all eight levels. In particular, it provides for the detailed analysis of information processing. By presenting a framework for analyzing the complex network of energy and information flows, LST sets the stage for developing a modern theory of systems complexity. LST is notable for choosing the concrete individual as the basic system unit (a concrete systems in Miller's terminology) rather than the social role (an abstracted system in Miller's terminology) as did Parsons. Parsons continues to oppose Miller on this even in one of his last publications before his death (Parsons, 1979), contending that concrete systems analysis was insufficient for the study of the social system.

Among the latest developments of a general systems nature are chaos theory and complexity theory (although some of their proponents may strongly resist any association with the old GST model). Complexity theory shares some of the same goals as earlier systems movements, except that it is more quantitative and seems somewhat less general. Its activities are centered largely (but not exclusively) around the Santa Fe Institute and many of its adherents are from scientific fields such as physics, biology, or mathematics (but with some interest from sociologists and others; see Eve, Horsfall, & Lee, 1997). A chief concept in complexity theory is the notion of the complex adaptive system (CAS). Somewhat ironically, one of the earlier publications on this topic was by a sociologist (Buckley, 1968, 1998).

Gell-Mann (1994a) defines a complex adaptive system, such as a society, as a system that acquires information about the environment and its own interaction with it. It further identifies regularities in this information, condenses these regularities into a "schema" or guide model, and uses this information to guide its activities in the real world. Complexity theory contributes to the first shift (from equilibrium to nonequilibrium models) by emphasizing entropy. It also contributes toward the third shift (toward the analysis of system–environment relations) by focusing on the manner in which the system adapts to its environment through information processing. For further discussion, see Bailey (1997b), Gell-Mann (1994a,b), Casti (1994), Holland (1995), Gleick (1987), and Goerner (1994).

The second necessary shift in sociological systems theory is toward increased specification of internal decision making, power, and control processes. We saw that LST (Miller, 1978) contributed significantly toward this trend through its careful analysis of information processing and its emphasis on the decider as the most important systems component. A second contribution has come from sociocybernetics, or the "new cybernetics" (Geyer & van der Zouwen, 1978, 1986). Growth in this area is significant, as evidenced by the fact that in 1998 the International Sociological Association (ISA) recognized "sociocybernetics" as research group 51.

As originally developed by Wiener (1948) and others, cybernetics was seen by many sociologists largely as a mechanical or "engineering" analysis of control systems such as thermostats, with limited applicability to sociology. Classic thermodynamics was responsible for disseminating a number of terms that are now commonly used not only in sociology, but in the larger lay language. These include "feedback loop" and "steady state." Unfortunately, these terms have been widely misapplied. The term "negative feedback" is certainly familiar to every American, but unfortunately is consistently misused. In cybernetics, a negative feedback (signified by a minus sign) in a loop serves to rectify a positive feedback (signified by a plus sign), leading to an overall steady state (equilibrium analogue) in the system. In common parlance it is used to indicate disagreement with a speaker's previous comment.

Recent developments are more fortuitous for sociological systems theory. Sociological systems theorists such as Geyer and van der Zouwen (1978, 1986), and Aulin (1986) have developed cogent sociological analyses based on cybernetics. This new sociocybernetics moves beyond the machine imagery of early cybernetics to an actor-oriented approach somewhat reminiscent of the earlier work of Buckley (1967, 1968) and Parsons (1951). The new cybernetics emphasizes control, often denoted by the term "steering." One characteristic of the new sociocybernetics is that it views information as constructed and reconstructed by an individual interacting with the environment (the parallels with complex adaptive systems within complexity theory are striking). This provides an epistemological foundation for systems theory by viewing it as observer dependent. An important concept is second-order cybernetics, which essentially deals with "observing the observer" and has parallels with sociological work of a recursive or reflexive nature by Giddens (1979, 1984), Luhmann (1986, 1995), and others (see Bailey, 1997a, 1998). The work of Aulin (1986) also is important for an understanding of control issues within the social system. He makes the distinction between partial steering of the system from the external environment (power) and human self-steering action, which emanates internally.

The third major shift mentioned above deals with boundary relations. In particular, the shift must be from the simple open–closed dichotomy to a more sophisticated analysis of the relationship between internal system components and the external environment. A major recent development in systems theory that has contributed to boundary analysis is autopoiesis (Maturana & Varela, 1980; Luhmann, 1986, 1989, 1995). Autopoietic systems are self-reproducing and self-organizing. Self-reproduction means that they possess internally the means for their own reproduction, or that the system produces the processes that produce the system. This theory was developed chiefly by Maturana and Varela (1980) for cellular self-reproduction, and there is widespread consensus that the theory holds at the level of the cell.

However, there is a continuing debate over whether social systems are autopoietic. Maturana and Varela themselves leave the situation unresolved, saying that humans are autopoietic and so human society forms the context for autopoiesis (and has autopoietic components), but they stop short of saying that the social system itself is autopoietic. Some scholars such as Mingers (1995) are rather adamant in stating that social systems are not autopoietic, while others such as Robb (1989) say that they are. For further discussion, see Bailey (1994, 1998). This debate centers largely around a prior debate over the proper unit of systems analysis. Mingers (1995) argues that the unit of the social system is the human individual and that humans reproduce themselves, not social systems. In contrast, Luhmann (1986) rejects the individual, the act, and the role and designates the communication as the basic system unit. He says that societies are definitely autopoietic, as communication does self-reproduce continuously. An utterance immediately disappears as soon as it is uttered and must be continually self-reproduced by the society.

A key feature of autopoietic theory is that the system is simultaneously both closed and open. That is, it is organizationally closed, in the sense that the internal self-reproductive loop is autonomous, but it is open to exchanges with the environment and with other systems. An important concept here is structural coupling, which refers to the relations between the autopoietic system and its medium (environment), which allows the system to maintain its autopoiesis. That is, through structural coupling the system selects those exchanges that foster internal reproduction and rejects those that would lead to internal disintegration (Maturana, 1978; Maturana & Varela, 1980). The role of the observer also is very important in autopoietic theory, with the observer able to operate as if he or she were external to the circumstances in which he or she finds himself or herself (Marturana, 1978, p. 31).

Luhmann (1986, 1989, 1995) has applied autopoiesis to sociology. He studied briefly with Parsons, and his theory still shows the functional influence, as in his discussion of the theory of functional–system differentiation (Luhmann, 1989, pp. 34–35). Luhmann's systems theory is extremely well-developed and extremely valuable. It clearly shows the value of mature systems theory for sociology and goes far beyond Parsonian functionalism. Unfortunately, it is not very accessible, particularly for scholars who do not read German. However, quite apart from the language, the theory is very dense and abstract and requires substantial effort on the part of the reader. Those willing to invest the considerable amount of time required to understand Luhmann's theory will find it very rewarding and to be time well spent.

Luhmann's systems theory is too massive, comprehensive, and cogent to present here without doing it a major injustice. For more discussion, see Bailey (1994, 1997a, 1998). I consider Luhmann's systems theory to be a masterful contribution, but it does have critics (see Mingers, 1995), particularly with regard to the choice of communication as the unit of analysis of the social system and the contention that social systems are autopoietic. The contributions are many but are not all well understood. This is probably due partially to the relative unpopularity of systems theory at the moment (particularly in North America) and the difficulty that readers have in mastering Luhmann's theory. Rather than attempt to discuss all these contributions in the short space available, I will focus on the contributions to the third theoretical shift discussed above: boundary relations (although it is clear that Luhmann contributed to the literature on all three theoretical shifts).

Luhmann is best known for his work on social autopoiesis, with the communication as the unit of analysis. But even this internal analysis is set in the context of his abiding interest in system–environment relations. He says that society is environmentally open but operatively closed, with communication being its sole mode of observation. The environment cannot communicate with the society, as communication is an exclusively social operation. The environment can only make itself noticed through communicative disturbances (Luhmann, 1989, p. 79). Luhmann (1989, p. 12) poses the question, "How can a restrictedly complex society exist in a much more complex environment and reproduce itself?" The answer is greater system complexity. Greater system complexity is seen in the internal development of differentiated function systems. These differentiated function systems within the society (law, science, medicine, etc.) are reciprocally dependent: "Functional differentiation generates interdependence and an integration of the entire system because every function system must assume that other functions have to be fulfilled elsewhere. This is the precise purpose of the binary code" (Luhmann, 1989, p. 42).

Binary coding is critical in Luhmann's theory. Indeed, the code and the program for the code make possible the combination of closure and openness in the same system (Luhmann, 1989, p. 40). The internal code is always closed. That is, in binary coding, with two codes X and Y, X only refers to Y, and Y only to X, and no other values exist in the closed system. But the programming of the system brings in external data (Luhmann, 1989, p. 40).

A contemporary example of this is the recent development of public key infrastructure (PKI) technology for Internet security. This is a coding system (for example, with 128-bit encryption) that uses both a private key and a public key. The private key is in the individual computer user's system, which remains internally closed even during interaction with external parties. However, through interaction between the internal system and the external environment, through coding and recoding (encryption), and through dual use of the private and public keys, secure communication takes place, thus protecting information such as credit card numbers. An external party can communicate with you only by accessing the public key.

This example not only illustrates Luhmann's assertion that systems can be simultaneously closed and open but also illustrates a key to the continued development of the Internet. Unless individuals can be convinced that their internal closed communications regarding private data such as credit card numbers can remain secure, they will be unwilling to purchase over the Internet, thus stifling its further development. This is a classic example of the role of structural coupling in the maintenance of internal autopoiesis. The autopoietic system will allow those external interactions (such as encrypted interactions), which preserve its internal autopoiesis, but will reject those external interactions (such as interactions lacking PKI), which may threaten internal autopiesis by revealing internal financial information to non-authorized users.

As noted, much more attention has been paid to Luhmann's discussion of autopoiesis than to his discussion of coding. But coding is really the key to it all—communication, autopoiesis, boundary determination, and openness–closure—so students of Luhmann should pay particular attention to coding.

Social Entropy Theory

Functionalism performed a great service for sociology and for systems theory. It counter-acted (temporarily) hyperspecialization, it emphasized macrotheory, and it delimited important part–whole relationships. But its weaknesses were evident, and eventually led to its demise. However, it is important that in critiquing functionalism we do not throw out the systems baby with the functionalist bath water. It was not systems theory (which in its skeletal form is quite general) that was flawed, but only specific features of functionalism (such as equilibrium). The idea is not to abandon systems theory but simply to construct a systems theory without the flaws of functionalism (which can be done). The critical decision has to be whether functionalism can be merely repaired, or whether we should abandon it for a new model. In developing social entropy theory (SET), I made the decision to construct a new model (Bailey, 1990, 1994). I felt that the negative legacy of functionalism was so entrenched in sociology that any revision of it probably would be viewed with a persisting bias. It seems difficult to get some sociologists even today to realize that not all sociological systems theory is functionalism.

SET roughly uses the model of the complex society sketched above. I started with a search for the bare essentials of the social system (society). I began with the population (P) and the spatial (S) environment that the population occupies. Within this space, the society must use energy (as derived both from its internal resource base and from external exchanges) to do work, so as to maintain or improve its level of living (L). The society accomplishes useful work by organizing (O) itself in a manner that is efficacious for using the technology (T) and information (I) available to it.

These are the six key macrosocietal variables (PILOTS or PISTOL). They are all recipro- cally interrelated, so that at a given time any one can be seen alternatively as a dependent variable (with the other five as independent variables), or as one of the five independent variables (see Bailey, 1990, 1994). If the social system can effectively organize within its boundaries to efficiently use its technology and information, then it can raise or maintain its level of living and can offset the inexorable increase of internal entropy. If the society does not do this, then entropy will increase.

GLOBALS, MUTABLES, AND IMMUTABLES.   The PILOTS variables are considered to be global variables in SET, or purely macrosocietal variables, meaning that (with the exception of P) they can be measured with little or no information about characteristics of individuals. Thus, they are characteristics of the society *sui generis*, as distinct from societal characteristics that can only be computed by aggregating information about individuals. In contrast to the globals, we also can delimit some uniquely microproperties of individuals, such as race, sex, and age (birthdate). These are termed "immutable variables," as they generally (with a few exceptions) cannot be changed during the individual's lifetime.

In between the purely macrovariables (globals) and the purely microvariables (immut- ables) are the mesovariables (mutables). The mutables are a micro–macro link having essen- tially a dual micro–macro character. They can be measured at the microlevel as mutable properties of individuals that are amenable to change in value over the course of the individ- ual's lifetime. Mutable variables are roughly equivalent to achieved variables, while immut- ables are roughly equivalent to ascribed variables. Common examples of mutable micro- characteristics of individuals (and their corresponding PILOT representations) are occupation (O), education (I), income (L), residence (S), and technological (T) proficiency licenses, such as a pilot's license.

In addition to the micromutable level, we can discover a macromutable level. The macro- variables are derived by distributing the population (P) across the other five global variables (ILOTS) to form five mutable distributions. These five mutable distributions are macroproper- ties, but they are analytically distinct from the macroglobal properties, as the mutables are aggregated from individual data, while the globals are not. Some examples of macromutable distribution measures would be measures of the occupational division of labor in a society (O), measures of the percentage of households with computers (T), measures of the mean income (L), and measures of the mean educational level (I).

Each individual is born with a particular set of immutable characteristics (sex, race, birthdate) and a particular position in the five-dimensional mutable space [family residence (S), family occupation (O), family income (L), family education (I), and family technological skills (T)]. Social mobility is achieved by changing one's position in one or more of these five mutable dimensions.

Consider a person wishing to change his or her position in the occupational mutable structure (O) by applying for a new job. This involves initiating a relationship between the prospective employer and the prospective employee. Each of these individuals has an initial perception of the other person. The relationship could be initiated through a personal visit (interview), and in this case the first impression would be achieved through direct observation of each other, and precedence would likely be given to important easily observed immutable characteristics such as age, sex, and race. Alternatively, the job search could be initiated, for example, over the Internet. The applicant could send his or her resume electronically. Here, the initial emphasis would likely be on the mutable characteristics emphasized in the resume, such as education (I), residence (S), prior organizational affiliations (O), and licenses (T).

The individual's locus of control can vary widely in complex society. A 19th-century farmer in the midwestern United States perhaps was substantially a subsistence farmer, having only minimal contact with other individuals. He or she was most interested in energy flows (as if a stream bringing water into his or her property was diverted by neighbors) and had few if any external links with entities outside the United States and relatively few internal vertical links. In contrast, the President of the United States now has a locus of control that involves directly (or indirectly through delegation of authority) millions of internal and external links, both vertical (mostly vertical within the United States) and horizontal (links with other countries).

Each individual acts within the social context provided internally within the society by the six global variables [the country's population size (P), wealth (L), educational level (I), etc.], the five-dimensional mutable distributions, and his or her salient immutable characteristics. Thus, while the six globals may be constant at a given moment for all residents of the United States, the various individuals living within the context provided by these six globals still have different social contexts and different mobility chances, due to their different positions in the five mutable distributions and their particular configuration of immutables.

For example, consider two persons at the same position in the five-dimensional structure (same residential neighborhood, same income, same occupation, etc.) but with different immutable configurations. Imagine that one is a young black female and one is an elderly white male. These two persons would have different social contexts, as would two persons with the same immutable configurations, but with radically different positions in the five-dimensional mutable structure. While different individual actors within the complex society have different specific configurations of immutables and mutables, all work (by processing energy and information) to accomplish their goals within a certain global structure (population size, etc.). The aggregate effects of all of these situated individual efforts, of all persons in the population, must be sufficiently orderly (as guided by the globals, mutables, and immutables) to ensure that internal entropy does not rise to unacceptable levels.

CONCLUDING REMARKS

Our discussion to this point has established a number of important facts. It has become abundantly clear that while the development of specialized approaches via middle-range theory was desirous in 1949, by the same token, in 2000 we clearly again need an alternative to this extant model. We cannot stay stuck in the middle range while global complexity is exploding all around us. It is increasingly clear that the approaches of mid-20th-century sociology (including not only middle-range theory, but also equilibrium-based systems approaches) will no longer suffice. The goal is not to eliminate or even supplant existing approaches such as middle-range theories or even equilibrium models. Indeed, SET does not preclude the analysis of equilibrium when this is warranted, but does not rely on it (Bailey, 1990, 1994).

It is clear that narrow specialties have not adequately dealt with important issues such as boundary problems, the insider–outsider anomaly, information-processing across group boundaries, and so forth. Our brief review of contemporary systems approaches shows that they certainly have not solved all the problems of analyzing complex society. In fairness, they have barely begun the task. But to their credit they have at least been dealing with the issue of complexity, something that middle-range theories have largely failed to do and indeed are ill-equipped to do.

Ironically, while some sociologists might see a resurgence in sociological systems theory as a return to the past, a strong case can be made that to the contrary it is really a major step toward the future. Our example of the job search within the global, mutable, and immutable context shows that the complex systems model is a boon and not a bane for individual-level analysis. The complex systems model also will prove to be a viable framework for the synthesis of a number of important but isolated topics within sociology, such as the insider–outsider distinction and globalization. Globalization is an important (but undeveloped) concept that can benefit from the grounding provided by the complex systems model of society, as adequate grounding of this concept requires careful analysis of vertical and horizontal links, internal as well as external.

The world systems literature on globalization (Wallerstein, 2000) refutes the notion that systems theory is inherently conservative, as the world systems approach hardly has the reputation of being conservative. Further, as the article by Mato (2000) illustrates, indigenous people are currently recoding their external communications to include global terms such as biosphere, biodiversity, ecology, and so forth, so that they may foster viable external–vertical links of the type discussed above. The reason that an indigenous representative uses recoded neutral global jargon in external links is not through a wish to have his or her indigenous culture merged into a global "melting pot" culture, but the opposite—to save his or her indigenous lifestyle from the external invaders.

Mato (2000) noted that an indigenous leader of the Embera people of Panama had incorporated these expressions into his vocabulary through exchanges with representatives of nongovernmental organizations (NGOs) from both Panama (internal–vertical links in my terminology) and abroad (external–vertical links in my terminology). By adopting this external global "eco-jargon," the indigenous representative can use such language in the public sphere (the equivalent of the public key in PKI), while safeguarding the internal security and autopoesis (insider status) of all internal tribal communications. Tribal communications remain in the tribal (Embera) language (the equivalent of the private key in PKI), and thus are permanently closed to outsiders.

In addition to safeguarding the internal autopoiesis of Embera society, the act of recoding into the public eco-jargon provides acceptable meaning of Embera activities to Panamanian and foreign governmental and nongovernmental entities (internal– and external–vertical links). As this illustration shows, the complex social systems model is not inherently conservative or a hindrance to the understanding of such topics as insider–outsider relations and the inclusion of indigenous peoples, but can in fact be a valuable tool in the analysis of such phenomena.

This sort of coding and recoding occurs billions of times a day in the complex society and can be observed at virtually every group boundary within the complex society. The understanding of this coding phenomenon, as well as of other boundary phenomenon, is crucial to the analysis of the complex society. In fact, I would go so far as to say that until we understand how private (insider) keys and public (outsider) keys are linked through recoding or through various forms of symbolic encryption, we will not fully comprehend how groups can retain their identity within the complex society, or how the complex society itself operates. However, this boundary recoding is widely neglected in sociology, despite its obvious importance. This is simply because most specialized studies do not cross boundaries and so tend to miss the crucial coding and recoding phenomenon that occurs at the boundary.

Not every sociologist should be a systems theorist, but not all should neglect systems theory either. The complex society is too important, too intellectually inviting, and too encompassing for sociology to neglect. Although specialized studies of a small portion of the whole society are familiar and perhaps have a higher probability of success, we neglect study of the complex society *sui generis* (and its relations with other societies) at our peril. If we can find a way to aggregate piecemeal specialized studies of the type that are common in sociology today into a unified portrayal of the social whole, then this approach should be pursued.

I for one am skeptical of the success of this endeavor for a variety of reasons. The most obvious reason that the aggregation of specialized sociological approaches cannot succeed is because, as we have just discussed, each specialty is coded into its own unique jargon for consumption by its insiders. Aggregation would require the adoption of a public key in the form of an external jargon accessible to all specialized approaches. Such an external jargon does not exist. Its creation would require either the adoption of the jargon of one specialty by all specialties (probably an impossibility) or the invention of a new neutral language that all specialties would be willing to adopt (probably also an impossibility).

Similarly, if one could find an alternative to the systems framework that is adequate for the holistic study of the complex society *sui generis*, then this approach also should be pursued. However, a realistic view is that at the present time, viable forms of both alternatives are lacking. Thus, I invite you to join me in the systems analysis of complex society, not by default and not as an alternative to microsociology, but as a viable complement to the other extant variations of contemporary sociological theorizing.

REFERENCES

Alexander, J., & Colomy, P. (1990). Neofunctionalism today: Reconstructing a theoretical tradition. In G. Ritzer (Ed.), *Frontiers of social theory: The new synthesis* (pp. 33–67). New York: Columbia University Press.

Alexander, J., Giesen, B., Munch, R., & Smelser, N. (Eds.). (1987). *The macro–micro link.* Berkeley: University of California Press.

Aulin, A. (1986). Notes on the concept of self-steering. In R. F. Geyer & J. van der Zouwen (Eds.), *Sociocybernetic paradoxes: Observation, control, and evolution of self-steering systems* (pp. 100–118). London: Sage.

Bailey, K. (1982). Post-functional social systems analysis. *Sociological Quarterly, 23,* 18–35.

Bailey, K. (1984). Beyond functionalism: Toward a nonequilibrium analysis of complex social systems. *British Journal of Sociology, 35,* 1–18.

Bailey, K. (1990). *Social entropy theory.* Albany: State University of New York Press.

Bailey, K. (1994). *Sociology and the new systems theory: Toward a theoretical synthesis.* Albany: State University of New York Press.

Bailey, K. (1997a). The autopoiesis of social systems: Assessing Luhmann's theory of self-reference. *Systems Research and Behavioral Science, 14,* 83–100.

Bailey, K. (1997b). System entropy analysis. *Kybernetes, 26,* 674–688.

Bailey, K. (1998). Structure, structuration, and autopoiesis: The emerging significance of recursive theory. *Current Perspectives in Social Theory*, *18*, 131–154.

Buckley, W. (1967). *Sociology and modern systems theory*. Englewood Cliffs, NJ: Prentice Hall.

Buckley, W. (Ed.) (1968). *Modern systems research for the behavioral sciences*. Chicago: Aldine.

Buckley, W. (1998). *Society—A complex adaptive system: Essays in social theory*. Luxembourg: Gordon and Breach.

Casti, J. L. (1994). *Complexification*. New York: HarperCollins.

Checkland, P. B. (1994). *Systems thinking, systems practice*. Chichester, England: Wiley.

Clausius, R. (1879). *The mechanical theory of heat*, R. Browne (Trans.). London: Macmillan.

Coleman, J. S. (1964). *Introduction to mathematical sociology*. New York: Free Press.

Coleman, J. S. (1990). *Foundations of social theory*. Cambridge, MA: The Belknap Press of Harvard University Press.

Collins, R. (1975). *Conflict sociology: Toward an explanatory approach*. New York: Academic Press.

Duncan, D. (1908). *Life and letters of Herbert Spencer*, 2 volumes. New York: Appleton.

Durkheim, E. (1933). *The division of labor in society*. New York: Macmillan.

Durkheim, E. (1951). *Suicide*. Glencoe, IL: Free Press.

Eve, R. A., Horsfall, S., & Lee, M. E. (Eds.). (1997). *Chaos, complexity, and sociology: Myths, models, and theories*. Thousand Oaks, CA: Sage.

Flood, R. L., & Jackson, M. C. (Eds.) (1991). *Critical systems thinking: Directed readings*. Chichester, England: Wiley.

Gell-Mann, M. (1994a). *The quark and the jaguar: Adventures in the simple and complex*. New York: Freeman.

Gell-Mann, M. (1994b). Complex adaptive systems. In G. A. Cowan, D. Pines, & D. Meltzer (Eds.), *Complexity: Metaphors, models, and reality* (pp. 17–45). New York: Addison-Wesley.

Geyer, R. F., & van der Zouwen, J. (Eds.). (1978). *Sociocybernetics: An actor-oriented social systems approach*, Volume 2. Leiden, Holland: Martinus Nijhoff.

Geyer, R. F., & van der Zouwen, J. (Eds.). (1986). *Sociocybernetic paradoxes: Control and evolution of self-steering systems*. London: Sage.

Giddens, A. (1979). *Central problems in social theory: Action, structure and contradiction in social analysis*. Berkeley: University of California Press.

Giddens, A. (1984). *The constitution of society: Outline of the theory of structuration*. Berkeley: University of California Press.

Gleick, J. (1987). *Chaos: Making a new science*. New York: Penquin.

Goerner, S. J. (1994). *Chaos and the evolving ecological universe*. Luxembourg: Gordon and Breach.

Gouldner, A. (1970). *The coming crisis of Western sociology*. New York: Basic Books.

Gregory, E. W., & Bidgood, L. (1939). *Introductory sociology*. New York: Prentice Hall.

Haken, H. (1983). *Synergetics: An introduction*. New York: Springer-Verlag.

Holland, J. H. (1995). *Hidden order: How adaptation builds complexity*. Reading, PA: Addison-Wesley.

Homans, G. C. (1964). Bringing men back in. *American Sociological Review*, *29*, 809–818.

Kuhn, T. (1962). *The structure of scientific revolutions*. Chicago: University of Chicago Press.

Lillienfeld, R. (1978). *The rise of systems theory: An ideological analysis*. New York: Wiley Interscience.

Lockwood, C. (1956). Some remarks on the "social system." *British Journal of Sociology*, *7*, 134–146.

Luhmann, N. (1986). The autopoiesis of social systems. In R. R. Geyer & J. van der Zouwen (Eds.), *Sociocybernetic paradoxes: Observation, control, and evolution of self-steering systems* (pp. 172–192), London: Sage.

Luhmann, N. (1989). *Ecological communication*. Cambridge, England: Polity Press.

Luhmann, N. (1995). *Social systems*, J. Bednarz, Jr. (Trans.). Stanford, CA: Stanford University Press.

Mato, D. (2000). Transnational networking and the social production of representations of identities by indigenous peoples' organizations of Latin America. *International Sociology*, *15*, 343–360.

Maturana, H. (1978). Biology of language: The epistemology of reality. In G. Miller & E. Lenneberg (Eds.), *Psychology and biology of language and thought: Essays in honour of Eric Lenneberg* (pp. 27–63). New York: Academic Press.

Maturana H., & Varela, F. G. (1980). *Autopoiesis and cognition: The realization of the living*. Dordrecht: Reidel.

Merton, R. (1949). *Social theory and social structure*. Glencoe, IL: Free Press.

Miller, J. G. (1978). *Living systems*. New York: McGraw-Hill.

Miller, J. L., & Miller, J. G. (1992). Greater than the sum of its parts I. Subsystems which process both matter–energy and information. *Behavioral Science*, *37*, 1–38.

Mingers, J. (1995). *Self-producing systems: Implications and applications of autopoiesis*. New York: Plenum Press.

Pareto, V. (1935). *The mind and society*, Volume 4. New York: Harcourt, Brace.

Parsons, T. (1951). *The social system*. Glencoe, IL: The Free Press.

Parsons, T. (1961). The point of view of the author. In M. Black (Ed.), *The social theories of Talcott Parsons* (pp. 311–363). Englewood Cliffs, NJ: Prentice Hall.

Parsons, T. (1979). Concrete systems and "abstracted systems." *Contemporary Sociology, 8*, 696–705.

Prigogine, I. (1955). *Introduction to thermodynamics of irreversible processes.* Springfield, IL: Charles C. Thomas.

Prigogine, I., & Stengers, I. (1984). *Order out of chaos.* New York: Bantam Books.

Rhee, Y. P. (1982). *The breakdown of authority structure in Korea in 1960: A systems approach.* Seoul: Seoul National University Press.

Robb, F. (1989). Cybernetics and supra human autopoietic systems. *Systems Practice, 2*, 47–74.

Russett, C. E. (1966). *The concept of equilibrium in American social thought.* New Haven, CT: Yale University Press.

Spencer, H. (1892). *First principles.* New York: Appleton.

Therborn, G. (2000). Globalizations: Dimensions, historical waves, regional effects, normative governance. *International Sociology, 15*, 151–179.

Turner, J., & Maryanski, A. (1979). *Functionalism.* Menlo Park, CA: Benjamin/Cummings.

von Bertalanffy, L. (1956). *General system theory.* New York: George Braziller.

Wallerstein, I. (2000). Globalization or the age of transition? A long-term view of the trajectory of the world system. *International Sociology, 15*, 249–265.

Weidlich, W., & Haag, G. (1983). *Concepts and models of a quantitative sociology: The dynamics of interacting populations.* New York: Springer-Verlag.

Wiener, N. (1948). *Cybernetics.* New York: Wiley.

PART V
NEW DIRECTIONS IN EVOLUTIONARY THEORIZING

CHAPTER 20

Sociobiological Theorizing

Evolutionary Sociology

JOSEPH LOPREATO

INTRODUCTION

To theorize in sociobiological terms is to theorize in the evolutionary terms of the "modern synthesis" (Huxley, 1942) and its extensions of the last seven decades. Hence, a sociobiologically informed sociology is ipso facto evolutionary sociology, although it is appropriately located within those reaches of sociobiology that stress sociocultural factors in the explanation of human behavior. This, however, may seem an overreaching way of expressing the affinity between sociobiology and evolutionary sociology. Further clarification, therefore, is desirable. According to a recent, highly informative essay, sociology pursues an evolutionary logic along the following fronts:

> (1) the "ecological" approach where Darwin's notions of competition and selection are emphasized; (2) the stage evolutionary approach where sequences of societal development are delineated; (3) the "instinct" approach where basic and presumably biological needs or drives of humans are postulated; and (4) the sociobiological or genic approach where human behavior is seen under the control of selfish genes which seek only to maximize their reproductive success. (Maryanski, 1998, p. 2).

There certainly is some basis in practice for such distinctions, which in addition have the virtue of tracing the somewhat jagged lines that encompass evolutionary spaces in the discipline. In basic terms, however, the present chapter presumes to comprise three of the four distinctions. Thus, the focus on competition and natural selection is the sine qua non of all Darwinian sciences, though perhaps more decisively of some than of others. In fact, a capital deed of sociobiology is to have redeemed Malthus' and Darwin's own stress on competition or "struggle" as the behavioral "basis" of natural selection. It is true, however, that, at least as practiced in biology, ecology may be granted a degree of programmatic primacy by virtue of the fact that the parameters of modern population biology, which give rise to sociobiology, constitute the natural focus of evolutionary ecology (Wilson, 1975, p. 5, Fig. 1.1).

JOSEPH LOPREATO • Austin, Texas 78701.

Joseph Lopreato is now retired. He has taught sociology at various American and European universities.

Handbook of Sociological Theory, edited by Jonathan H. Turner. Kluwer Academic / Plenum Publishers, New York, 2002.

The modern concepts of human needs and drives refer to what are typically termed predispositions or psychological adaptations within the core of human sociobiology, namely the theory of human nature. Moreover, while sociobiologists refer to genes metaphorically as "selfish" agents (e.g., Dawkins, 1976), they do not hold that organisms seek only to maximize their reproductive success. Through the synthesis of protein (the only direct action of genes), genes do much of what their bearers do. Self-reproduction is their "ultimate aim" in the special sense in which this locution is employed in scientific language. At issue here, as we shall see, is the fundamental principle of sociobiology (of all evolutionary behavioral science), whose stress on reproductive success is only a bottom-line epistemological strategy.

With regard to the "stage evolutionary" approach, my own view is that at the present it is more developmental than evolutionary, and for the near future at least it represents the most formidable challenge facing evolutionary sociology. Some of the most promising work in this area belongs to Sanderson (1992, 1994). The effort, however, departs from the classical evolutionary position that in order to speak of evolution it is necessary to specify a uniform mechanism, such as natural selection in biology. Sanderson's claim, probably correct, is that there is no such thing; many material conditions—e.g., technology, the economy, various ecological pressures—can act as mechanisms and agents of social evolution, which, moreover, may take place in all types and sizes of social organizations. An enormous challenge faces this exceedingly enterprising area of study. Evolution has come to signify something special, namely a form of transformation in a given entity that is given "direction" and "order" by a universally applicable and uniform mechanism, whatever and however many the actual agents of change may be.

It is likely, as another student of social evolution has argued (Freese, 1997), that societies do not evolve in this technical sense. Evolution, according this scholar, takes place in ecosystems, otherwise termed "biosociocultural systems," and he buttresses his argument with the Lotka Principle, also known as Volterra's Law, according to which natural selection favors those populations that, on the proviso of the availability of energy, are most adept at converting and controlling energy forms (Lotka, 1925). Accordingly, he arrives at the following proposition:

> Instead of assuming evolution by natural selection for biosociocultural systems, we shall here assume evolution by self-organization. We take selection to contribute to order-production by means of Lotka's Law, which we shall take as the force law that drives evolution in biosociocultural regimes. (Freese, 1997, p. 130)

It is to be hoped that this admittedly incomplete argument bodes well for a biosocial theory of evolution, though its central statement appears to turn Lotka on his head, and it is not clear how exactly natural selection and Lotka processes can cooperate to produce evolution by self-organization, an echo of sorts of the old idea in physiology of a *vis medicatrix naturae* (the self-healing of nature). In a sense, all evolution is self-organizing; the point is to reveal the forces behind this otherwise theoretically vacuous process. The fundamental problem with this and analogous, exceedingly demanding, endeavors is that understandably they offer no explicit conception of evolution. The stumbling block is the difficulty, if not impossibility, of fruitfully specifying some unit-of-heredity analogue, though some feeble attempts are not lacking [e.g., Dawkins (1976) on the "meme," Lopreato (1984) on the "variant," and Lumsden and Wilson (1981) on the "culturgen."] Without some such metric, how do we know at what point enough "mutations" have occurred in a given system whereby we can say that the analogue of speciation has taken place? What we may be left with is indefinite theories of change.

One other set of comments had best be disposed of at the outset. Not long before Carl Sagan returned into his beloved cosmos, he and his wife (Sagan & Druyan, 1992) published the results of another brilliant adventure in a volume titled, *Shadows of Forgotten Ancestors: A Search for Who We Are*. Debuting as a study of "the political and emotional roots of the nuclear arms race," the venture led, through a series of inquiries ranging from mythology to astronomy, back to our hunting and gathering ancestors. It is almost sad to experience the authors' feverish hunger for knowledge: "We humans are like a newborn baby left on a doorstep" without identification. "We long to see the orphan's file" (Sagan & Druyan, 1992, p. 5). By the time this volume will go to the publisher, the hunger of many a restless mind will have been partly sated by the publication of a first draft of the 46-volume encyclopedia that is encoded in the human genome. Nothing in human history can compare even remotely with the revolutionary import of that event. It would be most unfortunate if sociologists were to show less hunger for it.

A grasp of the fundamentals of human sociobiology is a first step toward reading the contents of the orphan's file. This chapter therefore comprises a practical aim. There is a pervasive, though certainly not universal, feeling that sociology is in a long-standing crisis that may be getting worse rather than better (e.g., Cole, 2000; Collins, 1990; Davis, 1994; Lieberson, 1992; Lopreato & Crippen, 1999; Turner, 1996a). The following is a partial list of the alleged signs and/or causes. We bicker a great deal, often on banal grounds, and fail to recognize that an argument may have some validity even in the absence of supporting data. Our concepts are too often what have been termed "panchrestons," namely, words referring with differing meanings to a wide range of facts; accordingly, they are rarely unambiguously operationalized. The defect then spills over into our research statements, which are seldom subject to falsification. There is thus a babble of mutually exclusive vocabularies accompanied by a grievous dispersion of fact and theory. Fragmentation and disorientation are reflected in an excessive dose of politically correct behavior that results in, or threatens, "intellectual lynchings." Political correctness bars "controversial" contributions from our journals and defines the search for "foundations" as a "malicious" quest for power. With few exceptions, our texts are boring and aim at mediocrity. Like much of classroom instruction, they belabor the obvious and are better at declaring how important sociology is than at actually demonstrating its utility. Thus, sociology is sometimes described as consisting of "bombastic banalities." Little wonder, some point out, that everywhere sociologists have lost reputation, having been superseded by philosophers and political scientists as leaders of public opinion and even by economists and psychologists in the areas of market surveys and related types of professional activity. Some ask in desperation, Why do we put up with this state of affairs? Others wonder in equal measure of distress whether we really need sociologists, for litterateurs and philosophers (not to mention pundits) often do better theory than our "qualitative" theorists, while any reasonably equipped bureau can perform the statistical analyses of prepackaged data that fuel much of sociological activity. Still others fear that the most pressing problems of our age (e.g., the origins of war, ecological problems, societal breakdowns) escape the sociological imagination. At the basis of the crisis are a disjunction of theory and method, an absence of laws properly speaking, and hence a lack of systematic, cumulative knowledge to further guide organized research and theorizing.

There may be both excess and denial in the above diagnosis, depending in part on one's idea of what sociology should be, one's awareness of the expectations facing would-be sciences, and one's aptitude for neophilia or its antithesis, neophobia. My own view is that, however defined, the crisis is real, grave, and deepening. As an evolutionary sociologist, furthermore, I would state the case a little differently. Eminently sociological research areas are increasingly being appropriated by a multiplying number of "schools" and "centers" (e.g., social work, business, criminal justice, urban studies). More ominously for our continuing academic survival, sociology is being cannibalized by more prestigious disciplines, including several branches of evolutionary biology as well as anthropology and psychology, both of which are effecting sturdy links to the extraordinary revolution currently going on in biological science, largely in our own direction. Sociology is like that famous invalid whose illness was exacerbated by starvation, as his neighbors were a good deal fond of his provisions. The predation is facilitated by sociologists' obstinate isolation from biological science, urged by the addiction to the assumption, now more than ever implausible, that human behavior is solely the result of socialization, or that it can at least be adequately explained on this assumption alone. As a natural issue of this condition, most sociologists are unaware of the formidable challenge being posed from without.

Reduced to the common denominator, the crisis and the challenge lie in the fact that we have failed to discover a single general principle or law to guide systematic, cumulative research and discovery. Without such a tool, science is not possible. Thus the diagnosis. The prescription is simply to do as others before us have done and borrow from the established natural science closest to us in subject matter. Now that the orphan's file is about to be read, there is hardly a doubt as to the identity of our scientific neighbor. The aim of this chapter is to introduce us to the neighbor who, incidentally, is eager to meet us, too.

EVOLUTION BY NATURAL SELECTION

We must begin with Charles Darwin's theory of evolution by natural selection. It is now almost part of folklore that on December 27, 1832, Darwin, then barely 23 years of age, embarked on a sea voyage around the globe that lasted nearly 4 years. His mission was what he would make of it as companion to the skipper of the now famous *Beagle* and as budding naturalist. And he made very much indeed. His epochal feat was to establish to an almost inconceivably methodic degree the fact that species are mutable entities, and thus in the course of time give rise to new, related species. In the Amazon forests and the rocky barrens of Patagonia, among other places, he observed firsthand an amazing diversity of life in both living and fossil forms. Endowed with a naturally keen eye, he was quick to notice the subtle features of anatomy and behavior that distinguished various species of animals and plants. Change the environment, e.g., the type and availability of foodstuffs, nature seemed to be saying, and more or less gradually you will also see changes in the organisms subject to those changes. Organisms "adapt" to their environment through their "variations" (subsequently termed "genes"), but they are not bearers of identical variations; nor are these equally adapted to the same changes. As a result, he reasoned, some organisms are more likely than others to survive, reproduce, and convey their adaptations to the next generation. A species' pool of variations thus changes from one generation to another, and the various species go through a process of "descent with modification," Darwin's expression for "evolution."

This basic idea occurred to Darwin fairly early in the course of his observations. One field experience, however, was particularly poignant. During a 5-week visit to the Galápagos Islands, some 600 miles off the coast of Equador, Darwin was faced with abundant examples of descent with modification. For example, focusing on certain groupings of birds ("Darwin's finches"), it was transparent enough that, while they constituted different species, they were also kindred to varying degrees, some species differing from others only to Darwin's now trained eye. Just as clearly, they were related to species he had witnessed on the mainland.

What could account for this conjunction of similarities and differences? Chances were good that the island species had originated on the mainland. But in the course of time, as the birds distributed themselves across the islands under the pressure of competition for resources, enough changes in variations accumulated among the migrants' descendants to produce related species. Thus we encounter the essentials of Darwin's concept of "natural selection," though this capital idea did not really dawn on him, as we shall presently see, until the fall of 1838.

There was, however, no longer any question about the reality of evolution. With characteristic thoroughness, Darwin (1958, pp. 376–377) later wrote:

> The most striking and important fact for us is the affinity of the species which inhabit islands to those of the nearest mainland, without being actually the same .... the close affinity of most of these birds to American species is manifest in every character, in their habits, gestures and tones of voice.

He proceeds to remark that in geology, climate, and other conditions of life, the Galápagos were considerably more similar, say, to the Cape Verde Islands than to the South American coast. Yet "what an entire and absolute difference in their inhabitants! The inhabitants of the Cape Verde Islands are related to those of Africa, like those of the Galápagos to America. Facts such as these," he added doubtless with some trepidation, "admit of no ... explanation on the ordinary view of independent creation."

We should now make a point of noting that Darwin could have identified a multiplicity of mechanisms of evolution in his exceedingly rich set of data. As a natural scientist, however, he sought a universally applicable and uniform mechanism. The issue deserves a moment of special notice. I recall a statement written by Stephen Hawking in defense of Albert Einstein, *Time*'s Man of the Century, concerning his role in the production of the atom bomb. Blaming Einstein for it, as some have done, wrote Hawking, is "like blaming Newton for the gravity that causes airplanes to crash." No one would hold that Hawking has no awareness of the multiplicity of causes involved in airplane crashes: faulty engineering, weather conditions, human errors, and so forth. Cognizant of the beauty and the economy of the Occam path to explanation, however, he went straight to the bottom line: gravity. This is science's way.

As was suggested above, the idea of natural selection, though fairly simple in retrospect, did not come easily to Darwin. Fortunately, he was not averse to learning from others, including social scientists. Among the ideas that guided Darwin to the discovery of his famous mechanism, none were so influential as Malthus' 1798 argument that, absent certain checks, population tends to increase at a much faster rate than the resources required for its survival. Until Malthus' vision of scarcity and struggle rang Darwin's bell, Darwin "had not been able to identify an agent for natural selection" (Gould, 1977, p. 22). He himself writes in his autobiography:

> In October 1838 I happened to read for amusement Malthus on *Population*, and ... the struggle for existence ... it at once struck me that under these circumstances favourable variations would tend to be preserved and unfavourable ones to be destroyed. The result of this would be the formation of new species.

In *The Origin of Species*, Darwin (1958, p. 75) puts it more fully as follows:

> ... as more individuals are produced than can possibly survive, there must in every case be a struggle for existence, either one individual with another of the same species, or with individuals of distinct species, or with the physical conditions of life. It is the doctrine of Malthus applied with manifold force to the whole animal and vegetable kingdoms; for in this case there can be no artificial increase of food, and no prudential restraint from marriage.

The effect of the struggle for existence is differential survival and reproduction, and thus differential inheritance of variations through the generations: "This preservation of favourable individual differences and variations, and the destruction of those which are injurious," Darwin concluded, "I have called Natural Selection" (1958, p. 88) (by contrast to the then well-known practice of artificial selection). For convenience sake, many Darwinian scholars refer to natural selection simply as "differential reproduction."

Darwin's basic but fuller argument, updated to an extent in order to account for some later developments, may now be conveniently represented with a series of sentences as follows:

1. Reproduction in the various populations, e.g., species, takes place at a faster rate than the expansion of the resources needed to sustain all those born into them.
2. The resulting scarcity stimulates competition within and between species: the struggle for existence.
3. Individuals differ in terms of the variations required for success in the struggle.
4. Those bearing the better-adapted variations are more likely to succeed, survive, and reproduce, thus conveying them to their descendants.
5. This differential reproduction and survival of variations is termed "natural selection."
6. The transformation of species through this process of natural selection eventually results in the "transmutation" of one species into another or others: in evolution, or descent with modification.

This theory was complete in 1838 but was not published until 21 years later, and then only because Darwin was about to be scooped by Alfred Russell Wallace, the codiscoverer of natural selection. In the meantime, of course, Darwin was busy classifying detailed information on numerous species, but in his autobiography he doubted "whether the work was worth the consumption of so much time." What troubled Darwin was the fact that his theory was at odds with the foundations of creationism: the fixity of species, independent creation, and at bottom the idea that humans were created in God's own image. Less theologically, his work committed the heresy of philosophical materialism, according to which mental phenomena are by-products, not causes, of the material conditions of the existence. Little wonder that Marx was a self-styled "sincere admirer" of Darwin and that at Marx's graveside Engels (1978, p. 681) eulogized by comparing Marx's work to Darwin's own. Darwin must have been aware that Copernicus had postponed the full version of his *De Revolutionibus* from 1514 to the year of his death in 1543, and that Galileo had had a grave brush with heresy nearly a century later. By the same token, it is not difficult to understand why so many sociologists, while privately favorable to an opening toward evolutionary biology, are nevertheless reluctant to take the plunge for fear of ostracism by their colleagues and students. It is an open secret that in many sociological spaces the atmosphere is stifling.

We should finally note that, in the strictest sense, Darwin's theory is not a theory of evolution. Evolution requires three processes working concurrently, namely natural selection, heredity, and mutation (as novelty in the genetics or DNA of a species). The latter plays no formal role in Darwin's work and he had at best only a vague conception of it (Mayr, 1982, p. 400). In the absence of mutations, existing DNA can undergo shuffling and reshuffling (recombination), including some deletion, but no change in the materia prima of evolution. I have been led to point out this blemish in Darwin's theory by the recollection of sociologists' penchant for destructive criticism, even on far less significant defects. Theories need not be perfect, especially when they are first conceived (e.g., Lieberson, 1992). Nor do they need to be exactly what they claim to be. Certainly, biologists have wasted little time worrying whether Darwin's is a full-fledged theory of evolution. In time they have effected modifications and integrations that have stimulated a scientific revolution whose prodigious catalytic processes are still accelerating today. A 1999 special publication of *Scientific American* features 12 revolutions; half concern various branches of evolutionary biology. Sociology's fate is very probably tied to this extraordinary development.

THE MODERN SYNTHESIS

Darwin's theory was hardly an immediate and universal success. The probability of zealous controversy was built into its challenge to the Book of Genesis and the corollary of the pre-Copernican assumption of geocentrism, namely anthropocentrism, which continues to be the bewitcher of the sociological organ. Partly the problem lay with the early Darwinians. They were too timid in dismissing Darwin's own equation of natural selection with Spencer's "survival of the fittest," which did much to celebrate capitalist ideology under the totally wrong label of "social Darwinism" (Badcock, 1994). Furthermore, for nearly three quarters of a century, the early Darwinians occupied themselves with such uninspiring activities as looking for fossils, establishing cases of natural selection, constructing phylogenetic trees, and applying certain tools of comparative anatomy and physiology, such as homology and recapitulation.

Missing was the other essential wing of evolutionary biology: population genetics. This had been launched by Gregor Mendel with an 1866 paper on "experiments in plant hybridization." The paper contains the "fundamental theory of heredity, from which a whole new branch of science, genetics, would develop" (Dobzhansky, Ayala, Stebbins, & Valentine, 1977, p. 482). The theory consists of two laws of inheritance and numerous implications. They have played an elemental role in clarifying the workings of natural selection and in the eventual emergence of basic concepts of sociobiology. Generalized to species relying on diploid sex determination (two parents), the basics of Mendel's theory state: (1) For each feature in an organism, e.g., hair color, there is a pair of genes, one from each parent; (2) each pair segregates at random during meiosis and each gamete receives only one of the genes; (3) each gene in the pair has a 0.50 probability of appearing in the gamete. Thus, parents and their children, for example, are related at this 50% level.

Unfortunately, Mendel's work went at once into eclipse and had little if any influence on biology until it was rediscovered in 1900. Even so, most geneticists of the next three decades were not naturalists and, misunderstanding Darwinian adaptation, they disowned the theory of natural selection (Mayr, 1978, p. 52). Or they were typologists focused exclusively on mutation and rejected Darwin's alleged "gradualism" in favor of "stepwise mutational changes of large extent" (Huxley, 1958, p. xii), an idea that in somewhat different form recurred recently in so-called "punctuated equilibrium" theory (e.g., Eldredge & Gould, 1972; Stanley, 1981). Then around 1930, a number of great minds (recalling, in the English-speaking world, such names a R. A. Fisher, J. B. S. Haldane, and S. Wright) succeeded in spanning the two wings with what was later termed the "synthetic theory" or "modern synthesis" (Huxley, 1942). Subsequent waves of evolutionists (e.g., Dobzhansky, 1937; Mayr, 1942; Simpson, 1944) elaborated the synthesis, paving the way to such dramatic stages as Watson and Crick's 1953 discovery of the DNA molecule structure and, some 40 years later, to the "genome project": the mapping of the human DNA molecule, or the orphan's file.

The modern synthesis comprises rich theory in scores of disciplines. Dobzhansky et al. (1977, p. 18) have so encapsulated the pervading idea: "All biological organization, down to the level of molecules, has evolved as a result of natural selection acting on genetic variation." This causal interpretation of natural selection, still common today (e.g., Alexander, 1990, p. 244; Trivers, 1985, p. 9), may reflect a bit of "political" compromise—or perhaps just the convenience of metaphors. *Stricto sensu*, however, natural selection does not "act" on genetics. The agents of evolution may be identified in a nutshell in what has been termed the "interaction principle," according to which any aspect of phenotype (anatomic, physiological, behavioral) is the result of the interaction between genotype and environment (Barash, 1982, p. 29; see also Simpson, 1967). Human beings, for instance, are born genetically wired with the capacity for language and then learn it by means of the practices provided by their environment.

Natural selection is a demographic process that in the course of the generations orders genetic transformations and their by-products, the functional organismic designs. Darwin (1958, p. 88) himself rejected the conception of natural selection as an agent of genetic variation: "Some have even imagined," he complained, "that natural selection induces variability, whereas it implies only the preservation of such variations as arise and are beneficial to the being under its conditions of life." Indeed, as early as 1860 he regretted not having used "natural preservation" instead, and A. R. Wallace expressed grave concerns about the misconceptions arising from "Darwin's metaphor." It bears stressing, however, that evolutionists have wasted little or no time arguing over the issue. Mayr (1980, p. 1; emphasis provided) has furnished the following clarification:

> The term "evolutionary synthesis" was introduced by Julian Huxley ... to designate the general acceptance of two conclusions: gradual evolution can be explained in terms of small genetic changes ("mutations") and recombinations, and the *ordering* of this genetic variation *by natural selection*; and the observed evolutionary phenomena, particularly macroevolutionary processes and speciation, can be *explained* in a manner that is consistent with known *genetic mechanisms*.

It bears noting moreover that the blemish of the earlier statement is the bearer of a most revealing saving grace. The cornucopia of laws in physical science has been epitomized by the general proposition that the universe is a system of matter in motion obeying immanent, natural laws (Kuhn, 1957). The general proposition of the modern synthesis is but a corollary of this statement. The logical kindredness can be readily apprehended if, without doing harm to logical structure, we translate the latter to read as follows: The universe (of biological organizations) is a system of (genetic) matter in motion obeying (the) immanent, natural laws (of natural selection and genetic variation). It is a most remarkable case of scientific immanence. There are others in the development of behavioral science. Sociobiology will act as a major catalyst.

HUMAN SOCIOBIOLOGY

By the early 1970s, numerous researchers and four zoologists in particular (W. D. Hamilton, R. Trivers, G. Williams, E. O. Wilson) could dispose of a vast amount of information on the organization and behavior of various social species. A number of lessons seemed to come across with particular clarity. All species were unique in some respects, but in keeping with Darwin's notion of cross-species kindredness they also reflected striking similarities. Moreover, the more similar they were anatomically, the closer they also were in behavior and social organization, so that studies in primatology, for instance, implied a certain urgency toward human–nonhuman comparative analyses. Further, in the midst of all this "animal sociology," as some early scholars called it, a central idea emerged with compelling proof that, across a multiplicity of animal taxa, organisms direct a large portion of their behavior toward enhancing their chances of reproductive success and/or the success of their blood kin. In short, organisms engage in all sorts of behaviors, but in the last analysis they appear to behave, to the varying degrees demanded by the logic of natural selection, as if their ultimate goal in life were to convey the maximum possible portion of their genes (genotype) to the future generations. This idea, inherent in Darwin's concept of the struggle for existence, may at another level be accepted as an inference from the fundamental biochemical property of the cell, namely self-replication. It is on this latter basis that scholars sometimes refer to the gene as the "immortal replicator" and to the organisms as a "temporary vehicle" of genes (Wilson, 1975, p. 3) or as a "survival machine" acting at the service of "selfish genes" (Dawkins, 1976).

Then, in 1975, entomologist E. O. Wilson published a hugely influential work that creatively codified much of the evolutionary knowledge on animal social behavior and formally launched the "new synthesis," or sociobiology (a coinage dating back to the mid-1940s), which constitutes, along with neurophysiology, today's main branches of behavioral biology. Students of evolution and behavior have barely scratched its vast and towering theoretical program, which stresses issues of social organization and emergent properties; the centrality of various properties of demography; the multiplier effect and its companion concept of hypertrophy; the importance of ecological pressures; the relevant principles of population biology, such as genetic variation, r and K selection, and density dependence; the question of group selection; the determinants of group size; learning and socialization; culture and innovation; and, among many others, the problems of territoriality, communication, and dominance orders (Wilson, 1975, Parts I–II).

The human dimension that appears in this volume and subsequent work by many scholars in various disciplines has inspired two major lines of inquiry. One concerns the quest for a theory of biocultural evolution. As noted earlier, this has not proven so far to be a promising trail, although science certainly has a splendid way of surprising even on the most improbable conceptions.

The Fitness Principle

The second, far more promising, line of inquiry refers to the quest for a theory of human nature, thus nudging sociologists toward one of the fundamental concerns of all our founders: what are the natural forces driving human beings and how are they expressed in group living? Directing this endeavor, more or less explicitly, is something we touched on just above. Sometimes referred to as the "maximization principle" or the "fitness principle," it may be stated as follows: *Organisms tend to behave so as to maximize their inclusive fitness.* This is the general law or principle of sociobiology. It is fair to add at once that the principle marks a major development in evolutionary biology. The traditional focus on natural selection tends to conflate the *how* with the *why* of phenomena because, as we have seen, natural selection is a demographic process, not a cause. This blending may be unavoidable or even necessary for many problems. However, Darwin's own causative focus was not on natural selection but on the struggle for existence on which, as he (1958, Chapter 3) put it, natural selection "depends." Sociobiology thus restores Darwin's etiologic focus and establishes itself as the core of behavioral Darwinism, while in the process it provides an explicitly nomothetic bridge between evolutionary biology and the social sciences.

A few clarifications are now in order about the fitness principle. First, the term "fitness" refers exclusively to a measure of differential reproductive success. Therefore, it is an error to question the principle because of, say, the fact of infanticide. Where there are four mouths to feed and food for two, the gene is thoroughly lacking in sentimentality. Second, the adjective "inclusive" is intended to account for the fact that one's fitness is a sum of one's own reproductive success and the net reproductive success of one's genetic relatives. Third, the principle should not be understood in rationalistic terms; what it implies is that observable organisms are the descendants of organisms that were more reproductively successful than others, and as their genetic heirs they are "designed" for competition to achieve analogous success. This extremely important notion of "functional design" is most thoroughly elaborated in Dawkins' (1986) delightful book, *The Blind Watchmaker*.

Fourth, the principle is a probability statement. It follows that it is faulty to accuse sociobiologists of holding that all behavior is optimally adaptive (e.g., Lewontin, 1979), as an earlier critic finally admitted by reference to Darwinian adaptation in general (Popper, 1978). The probabilistic nature of the principle, however, is unnecessarily excessive, and on that account it is susceptible of constructive criticism. General laws are most productive when stated as "theoretical idealizations" (Lopreato & Alston, 1970) or at least as propositions true in view of certain specified conditions. Some work in this direction is available and the context strongly hints at special promise of sociological input. The specified conditions are: (1) "creature comforts," which are singularly compelling in view of the low fertility rates in modern society, though all of human evolution flaunts the pleasure principle; (2) "self-deception," as when we substitute salvation of the soul for salvation of the gene; and (3) "autonomization," or the common tendency for behavioral predispositions (e.g., the quest for resources) to persist as ends in themselves—divorced, or autonomized, from their original adaptive value, e.g., the modern quest for riches (Lopreato, 1989; see also Crippen, 1994; Lopreato & Crippen, 1999; Maryanski, 1998).

Fifth, the fitness principle does not imply that the enhancement of fitness is organisms' sole aim in life. In fact, across innumerable species they engage in a great variety of behaviors, some of great complexity and subtlety by any standard. Moreover, culture has placed severe constraints on biology. What the principle does is to underscore the bottom line, the ultimate, irreducible cause of animal behavior. As we have noted, this is established practice in the mature sciences.

The accent on fitness also may be viewed as a focus on remote concepts. In sociology we are uncomfortable with remote concepts and are often accused of thrashing over the commonplace or pursuing "the wisdom of the *hoi polloi*," as a critic wrote about one of our departed leaders (Black, 1961, pp. 279–280). It is as if we were Newton and stuck on the idea that when the apple ripens it falls, instead of trying to conceptualize the force of gravity, which yielded the law of universal gravitation. Perhaps the discovery of culture as a scientific concept was more affliction than glory, after all. We have become too involuted, less inquisitive, more domestic, perhaps even too nosy. Richard Machalek (1999) recently has argued that if sociologists are serious about Durkheim's injunction to study "social facts" or emergent properties, they have chosen the wrong species, in effect applying the hoi polloi method. Human social facts are contaminated by biography and history; hence, studying purely social species, such as eusocial insects, probably would be more productive, at least at the elementary level.

Avoidance of remote concepts is engendered by many factors. One stands fairly well for all: Sociologists are prejudiced against reductionist explanation—against the search for comprehensive propositions that comprise less general ones. But reduction is the ultimate aim of science. In the April 1950 issue of *Scientific American*, Albert Einstein was quoted as giving two reasons for the desire to expand existing theory. One responds to the need to cover facts not explained by existing theory. The "more subtle motive" is "the striving toward unification and simplification of the premises of the theory as a whole," that is, the reduction of existing propositions to more comprehensive ones. Science may be termed the art of "regressing" the why. That is why cosmologists, for example, feel unfulfilled with the "big bang theory." As Guth (1997, p. 2) has noted, the theory assumes that all the matter now in the universe was present from the start and then "describes the aftermath of the bang, but makes no attempt to describe ... what caused it to 'bang.'" Closer to us, human biologists, having produced a fairly detailed map of the brain, now turn to an old philosophical question: What is the mind?

It should be stressed that to reduce to more general propositions is not necessarily to jettison the lower-level ones. As Wilson (1998, p. 55) has noted, "at each level of organization, especially at the living cell and above, phenomena exist that require new laws and principles, which still cannot be predicted from those at more general levels." Less general propositions help to account for significant details of phenomena. They are useless for constructing bridges between one another, and they are very poor for constructing large orders of knowledge, such as those produced by interdisciplinary research. "One of sociobiology's great virtues," writes sociologist A. Maryanski (1994, pp. 380–381), "is its clear methodological protocol which addresses broad and basic questions in terms of one set of coherent concepts. As a result, investigators follow a systematic research procedure which, in turn, allows scholars from diverse fields to converge upon a common set of issues." It also is a good feeling to discover in the process that what had appeared to be disparate, disconnected observations often turn out to belong to the same class of phenomena and to share an identical theoretical anchorage point. Following is a partial list of topics that are comprised at least partly under the theoretical umbrella of the fitness principle: social conflict, including ethnic and religious strife; prejudice and discrimination; mating patterns; mating preferences; "the battle of the sexes"; abortion and infanticide; generational conflict; inequality and exploitation; differences in communication styles between the genders; play activity; the ambiguity of fatherhood; cooperation, altruism, and various aspects of morality; child abuse; child adoption; harems; despotism; intrafamily favoritism; alliances and associations; mate jealousy and mate guarding; deception of self and others; friendship; sense of distributive justice; incest, incest avoidance, and incest taboo; homogamy and heterogamy; polygamy; hunting and fishing as sports; and, among numerous others, various aspects of deviant–criminal behavior.

Sociology's extreme emphasis on culture, socialization processes, and social structure as explanatory devices creates grave disabilities. It is one thing, for instance, to say that boys learn deviant behavior from one another; it is quite another to consider the origin of the common learning and to explain why the fact is universal and heavily concentrated in the years of maximum reproductive power. Furthermore, it hardly seems likely that we have nothing to learn from the fact that socialization is widespread in the animal kingdom. Careful observers have noted that in many respects chimpanzee youth are barely different from their human counterparts (e.g., Goodall, 1986; see Sagan & Druyan, 1992, Chapters 16–19, for an informative survey of the "human" qualities of many of our primate cousins). In some species of mobbing birds, the socialization effects are so intense that under special circumstances individuals can be taught to mob even nonpredators (Gould & Marler, 1987). If young songbirds are isolated from adult males during the critical period of the "subsong," they fail to develop their species song. Bees must learn to distinguish between nectar-bearing flowers and void ones. They "learn by instinct," favoring a hierarchy of cues that corresponds to adaptive behavior: odor, color, and shape in this declining order of reliability (Gould & Marler, 1987, p. 77).

It is well known that culture has different effects on the sexes. Less readily allowed is the fact that such differences are often rooted in deeply evolutionary causes. Modern women, for example, have a longevity advantage over men, and the fact is typically explained in cultural terms. But the reverse was true until only decades ago, and that complicates matters.

Previously, at childbirth death had long taken a heavy toll as a result of the interaction of various environmental factors (e.g., poor hygiene and nutrition) and the ancient risk produced by bipedalism, which reduced the pelvic inlet even as the size of the fetus' cranium was on the rise. Environmental factors have greatly improved and in the process attenuated the ancient risk. The male Achilles' heel always has been the competition for mates (sexual selection), a topic to be encountered presently, and modern culture has acted differently on the survival of males by putting at their disposal more efficient weapons with which to harm themselves and one another. Death by trauma, especially during the young reproductive years, is much higher among males than among females. Hygiene, drinking, smoking, driving too fast, staying close to mother, and numberless other proximate factors enter the scenario as stimulators or mitigators of far more constant forces hidden deeply in our evolutionary past (Carey & Lopreato, 1995).

Elements of Human Nature Theory

The fitness principle is the anchorage point of human nature theory. Some writers, preeminently the exceedingly active and publicity diligent "evolutionary psychologists," have accused zoologists and "Darwinian anthropologists" of allegedly using the principle as an all-purpose, "domain-general" tool, arguing in favor of "many, domain-specific, specialized mechanisms" or adaptations (Symons, 1992). The stricture is thoroughly misguided. As zoologist R. D. Alexander (1990) has pointed out, virtually every biologist or evolution-minded social scientist adheres to such position, and also would expect that a more nearly complete theory of human nature will eventually reveal a hierarchical structure of such adaptations. The point, then, is not how many or how few they are; rather it is the form that they will take as constituents of a theory. Darwinian logic aside, they hardly can be imagined to achieve a coherent structure apart from some organizing general principle. Evolutionary psychologists, in short, apparently continue to have insufficient regard for the role of general laws in research. Such a stance is a bit mystifying when one notes that their research studies—whether on mate preferences, child abuse, or even rape—are faithfully anchored to the fitness principle. One study shows, for example, that the violence of stepfathers attains its highest peak by far among the youngest (Daly & Wilson, 1988), namely the innocents who of course send a signal to the brutes' mind that mother is currently nonreproductive or at any rate otherwise occupied (see also, e.g., Buss, 1989).

Evolutionary psychologists further argue that, since our species spent 99% of its evolutionary history as hunter–gatherers in the Pleistocene, a period that comprises 2.5 million years up to 5000 BP, this must be our environment of evolutionary adaptation (EEA), and our "cognitive mechanisms" should be adapted to it, not to the present environment (Cosmides, 1989, 194n; Symons, 1992). Why psychologists would wish to practice both sociobiology (though they abhor this biology-inspired coinage) and at the same time an unqualified paleoanthropological psychology is not very easy to divine. Be it what it may, one would find it difficult to deny current human adaptation in the face of a global explosion of population. However young or old our numerous adaptations may be, it appears that, in keeping with Darwinian and Mendelian calculi, they are fairly flexible, though to varying degrees (Lopreato & Crippen, 1999, pp. 126–131; see also Maryanski & Turner, 1992).

Research into human nature is aided by a variety of related theoretical tools, including, as we shall see, those that are proposed by certain aspects of physioanatomy. The elements of the theory of human nature are typically referred to as "epigenetic rules," "behavioral predispositions," and "psychological adaptations," with the latter terminology having the greater currency. Psychological adaptations may be conceived of as fundamental forces forged in the mind, perhaps especially during the last 2–3 million years of evolutionary history. They may be conveniently divided into a specieswide class and one comprising sex-specialized ones. The former are distinctively relevant to such subjects as economic, ethnic, and cooperative behaviors, while the latter are specialized for behavior along sex lines. We turn first to the former.

KIN SELECTION AND ALTRUISM.   Central under this rubric is the theory of altruism, a term that is often used synonymously with "cooperation" and is closely related to the concepts of sociality and morality. Altruism theory offers an evolutionary answer to the perennial question of social thought and moral philosophy: For whose benefit does the individual behave? Social thinkers have lacked a well-defined and generally useful metric with which to answer the question to their mutual satisfaction. The result has been an endless and inconclusive debate, though most thinkers have favored a view of human nature that in extreme form is exemplified by Hobbes' formula of an original nasty, brutish, and short life. The softer view recalls the fable of the wolf who, having promised the crane a rich reward for ridding him of the bone in his throat, then admonishes that it is reward enough to have escaped a wolf's jaws. Sociobiologists have been luckier. The Mendelian metric has allowed a law-based definition of altruism, namely genetically "self-destructive behavior performed for the benefit of others" (Wilson, 1975, p. 578).

As with many other evolutionary problems, the question of altruism has its beginning in problems of Darwin's theory. Recall that Darwin's struggle for existence was a little too focused on organismic survival, though reproductive success nearly always lurked behind this concept. How then to explain the huge tail of the peacock, the alarm calls of birds, and the huge antlers of certain species, among numberless other like facts (Darwin, 1871)? Such "secondary sexual characters" reduce motility or call the predator's attention, and thus tend to reduce the probability of survival. Or, inasmuch as the bottom line is reproduction, how about the case of eusocial insects, such as ants, among which the vast majority of individuals do not reproduce?

Darwin was not entirely in the dark about such problems. But the real breakthrough did not take place until 1964 in connection with studies of such insects by a young British geneticist (Hamilton, 1964). It turns out that ants, like other eusocial insects, have a rather odd system of reproduction and sex determination known as *haplodiploidy*. The queen lays two kinds of eggs. One, typically three quarters of the total, is diploid or fertilized and yields females: the famous "workers." The other type is unfertilized and gives rise to males, the fatherless drones. The arithmetic of haplodiploidy results in some very odd facts. The coefficients of relatedness (r) do not correspond fully to those in diploid species, such as the mammals. For the task at hand, we need focus only on the r between worker and niece. In diploid species, it is on average one half of the r between parent and offspring, namely .25. Not so in haplodiploid species, where it is .375. The explanation, briefly, is as follows. Workers have in common, on average, .25 of their mother's genotype. But since their father derived from a meiotic cell, all of them had to receive the entirety of his genotype in order to achieve diploidy, that is, a full half of their own genotype. Add .25 to .50 and the result is .75 rather than the .50 that obtains in diploid species. It follows further that the r between nonreproductive ants and the next queen, their niece, is .375 rather than .25. In short, these little animals have foregone direct reproduction, but they redeem at least part of their loss in fitness through genetic kinship, what has come to be known as *kin selection*. We may note, parenthetically, that this is the context for the concept of inclusive fitness in the fitness principle. Another degree of fitness is gained by being extremely diligent in catering to the needs of the queen, the young, and the colony as a whole. That is why eusocial insects are so labeled.

Through a series of studies and articles, Hamilton concluded that altruistic or cooperative acts are favored by natural selection as the r between benefactor and beneficiary increases and as the benefit enjoyed by the beneficiary is greater than the cost incurred by the benefactor. In short, the higher the fitness payoff deriving from kin selection and the lower the cost, the greater the probability of altruistic behavior. But is this altruism in view of the above definition? The sociobiologist's "altruism" is a misnomer. What it really refers to is behavior that redounds to one's own benefit, in this case to nepotistic favoritism. Hence, Wilson's definition might better be restated as behavior that benefits other(s) without necessary prejudice to one's own fitness.

We now should consider briefly a seeming superfluity in this question of the relationship between altruism and kinship. As the reader is aware, one often encounters statements to the effect that humans and their cousins the chimpanzees are genetically related at something like the 98% level. Why, then, all this talk of kin altruism and 50% coefficients of relatedness if we are related to one another at a much higher rate than that? The quick answer is that there must be something in Mendelian heredity that makes a difference insofar as the selection of altruism-predisposed genes are concerned. Nondescendant estimates of genetic similarity consider the genotype as a whole, namely all the gene-bearing loci on the various chromosomes. Kinship theory conversely holds that there are special loci that code for altruism, and these, Hamilton's work has shown, are favored by natural selection. At these loci kin by descent are more closely related than mere conspecifics. Some small differences in genotype do matter, especially, it appears, on the question of tribal behavior.

RECIPROCAL ALTRUISM.   The mitigation of kin selection is the defining evolutionary event of the last 10,000 years. It is hardly an accident that reciprocity or exchange theory and related topics, e.g., incest avoidance and taboo, are among the oldest and enduring topics in sociocultural science (e.g., Blau, 1964; Homans, 1961; Lévi-Strauss, 1969; Mauss, 1954; see Turner, 1998, Part IV, for an excellent treatment of this topic). Recent numbers of sociology journals are heavy on the topic, though, with very rare exceptions, the authors steer away from the evolutionary channel. The topic is central to sociobiological theory and the principal figure here is Robert Trivers (1971, 1985). His hugely influential theory of "reciprocal altruism" is broad enough to encompass reciprocally beneficent behavior even between members of different species. An astounding example is provided by cleaning symbioses among certain species of the sea. These, including several species of shrimp, perform tasks reminiscent of services performed in the dentist's office. They enter the mouth and gills of fish and rid them of parasites. The technicians even have been observed to take up rather permanent cleaning stations, while their patients queue up in order to obtain service. In the exchange, one gets a meal, while the other receives medical attention and sometimes even protects the benefactor from would-be predators.

Social scientists rarely if ever inquire into the evolution of reciprocity, typically approaching the fact by way of its functions or just taking it as given. For evolutionists reduction is unavoidable. Aside from the inevitable appointment with natural selection and fitness theory, Trivers argues in favor of six essentially sociological parameters: longevity, low migration, the need for mutual dependence and defense against predators, prolonged parental care, a weak dominance order, and exposure to combat situations. All these suggest high frequency of interaction, high expectation of reciprocation, and thus mutual benefit accruing from acts of beneficence. Trivers' theory further argues that wherever there is opportunity for gain, some will reciprocate more faithfully than others, although natural selection tends to get rid of "gross cheaters." "Subtle cheaters," on the other hand, are harder to detect. Nevertheless, precisely because reciprocal altruism is vulnerable to cheating, its evolution had to be accompanied in fairly close synchrony by the evolution of some defense system. Trivers discusses such adaptations as moralistic aggression, a sense of justice, gratitude, sympathy, friendship, and so forth. The human mind necessarily includes inferential procedures that facilitate detection of cheating in social contracts (Cosmides, 1989). At least in the small ancestral communities that survived until recent times, it is probably true also that genes favoring reciprocal altruism were at an evolutionary advantage (Cosmides & Tooby, 1989).

Reciprocal systems and attendant defense systems almost certainly have played a large part in the independent evolution of society in many thousands of animal species. The proof is provided by probability theory as well as numerous field observations. Consider schools of fish and flocks of birds. The members of both rely on the odds of mass aggregation for their defense against predators; it is the laggards and the individualists that are the most vulnerable to predation. Sometimes, grouping provides even the courage to attack, or to "mob," the predator, proof of the apothegm honored on the American nickel: *e pluribus unum*. Baboons turn very aggressive upon sighting leopards and even certain species of deer bark menacingly at them. Mobbing takes the danger home to the predator. The peregrine falcon is a formidable hunter endowed with lethal talons and wings that facilitate exceptional speed in diving. But such finely tuned machine is also a sort of life policy for the conformist prey. Diving into a tight-knit group is a very dangerous business. The meal must come from the individual who cannot keep pace or from the rover, usually a young male.

In their classic on game theory, John von Neumann and Oskar Morgenstern made an exceedingly useful distinction between zero-sum games, in which if one party wins, the other loses, and non-zero-sum games in which the gain of one is not necessarily the loss of the other. A football game is an example of the former, and the sport understandably evokes the battlefield. Cooperative hunting, as among lions and wolves, the sharing of food in certain species of bats, mutual aid societies, and international coalitions are essentially cases of non-zero-sum games. The evolution of society has spawned a rich repertoire of cooperation strategies (Axelrod, 1984).

There is some danger in stressing questions of reciprocity and cooperation. In sociology the practice has invited criticism on the part of "conflict theorists." It is a virtue of evolutionary theory that it immunizes against the susceptibility to "consensus theory" by stressing the self-serving nature of social behavior. Consensus and conflict are but two sides of the same coin. Such a touch of cynicism might be all to the good in sociology. Across "schools of thought," too many sociologists are single-mindedly committed to the position that human transgressions (theft, deception, homicide, ethnic cleansing, genocide, etc.) are the effects of faulty socialization. We should be equally attentive to the causes of the defective training. Primatologists find analogous forms of evil in our close relatives (e.g., de Waal, 1982; Goodall, 1986). An informed analysis of primate evolution by two sociologists leaves little doubt that hominoid evolution has tended toward low-density networks, low sociality, and strong individualism (Maryanski & Turner, 1992). Maryanski (1998, p. 39) has challenged "some long held beliefs in sociology about humans' needs for extended kinship, intimate ties, collectivism, and solidarity," arguing that human nature is in fact "predisposed towards freedom, autonomy, restricted kinship networks, weak ties, and mobility in space." Little wonder, she adds, for the structure of the hunter–gatherer society resembled so closely the troop of chimpanzees, anthropoids with whom we share a common ancestor as recently as 4 million years BP.

Of course, it is unlikely that elsewhere in the creation there are individuals capable of committing suicide out of shame for disgracing their community, though there are plenty who do it in defense of the community. Human sociality is more finely tuned by morality. Turner (1996b–d) has argued that, as our distant ancestors shifted to savanna living, natural selection favored greater compactness as a means of securing provisions and defense against predators. This quantitative departure from the Great Ape template was probably facilitated by, or occurred concomitantly with, the expansion of the neuroanatomy toward greater cortical control of the emotional centers. The limbic and hypothalamus system yielded some of its authority to the more rational neocortex. We became less willful, more social, more reciprocally altruistic, almost certainly more subtle cheaters and smoother hypocrites, in short, far more adapt at constructing "flexible and more tight-knit social bonds built on emotions" (Turner, 1998, p. 444). In keeping with the logic of the interaction principle, Turner argues that the selection pressures were sociological in nature and resulted in greater emotional capacity for the mobilization of energy, the attunement of responses, moral sanctioning and coding, pricing exchanges, and decision making.

Something else almost certainly happened as "the snake gave way to the dove." As Dickens' Pip put it, "all other swindlers upon earth are nothing to self-swindlers." Self-deception is perhaps the most unique feature of the human mind and an essential ingredient of our social condition. "Since the mind recreates reality from the abstractions of sense impressions, it can equally well simulate reality by recall and fantasy" (Wilson, 1978, p. 75; see also Trivers, 1985, Chapter 16). As neuroanatomy came to govern more and more the ancient emotional centers, consciousness increased and the mind created a rich repertoire of mischievous tricks. Introspection revealed that the evil without was also within. Toward the end of the *Homo erectus* reign, some 300,000 years BP, self-judgment probably gave rise to a fiction, the *soul*, that mimicked the fundamental feature of the gene: the quest for immortality. The specific mechanisms that gave birth to the idea of the soul will probably remain forever a mystery. Part of the riddle, however, transpires from Spencer's work on dreams and from Mead's discussion of the social self. Dreams, a dimension of the conscious mind, return the dearly departed to us, and thus invite the idea of a life of the spirit following the death of the body. The social self, in turn, suggests that the person is a mosaic of bits and pieces of our "significant others." Their departure, therefore, creates a crisis in the mind, at once maiming it and with the help of dreams prodding it to deny eternal death: "Thus the emergence of the soul was probably a sort of moral echo of the gene, a sublimation of a portion of pure genetic activity into moral, altruistic activity" (Lopreato, 1984, pp. 227; see also Lopreato, 1981).

The soul is a universal dimension of the human mind. Universal, too, is the human endeavor to save the soul (Brandon, 1962). Furthermore, its definition bears an uncanny resemblance to the basic properties of the gene. Both are "animating principles." Both refer to the individual's "characteristic skills, motives, and capacities." In many societies, the soul, like the gene, has been regarded as existing prior to the formation of the body and surviving the decomposition of the body. Again, almost universally in preagrarian society the soul mimics heredity by undergoing reincarnation. Above all perhaps, in a symbolic bow to the fitness principle, a central feature of all religious systems includes behavior intended to save the eternal soul.

Sociobiologists deny the existence of true altruism or behavior that acts negatively on one's own genetic fitness. The rationale is that by definition such behavior is quickly weeded out of the gene pool. But how to account for the Mother Teresas and the monks who forego reproduction and shy away from kin favoritism? The answer to true, "ascetic" altruism need not make appeal to altruistic genes. Given the evolution of self-deception and the idea of the soul, "it is entirely possible to have genuinely altruistic behavior WITHOUT altruistic genes" (Lopreato, 1984, p. 233). There probably is no better example of a cultural bridle on biology, although certain changes had to occur in our biology before the harnessing could take place.

KIN SELECTION THEORY AND ETHNIC CONFLICT.   If the last 10,000 years are marked by the alleviation of kin selection, the ages before then made a fetish of it. Despite the rising control of cortical activity over the limbic system, the brain's roots were stuck in the clan, and in consequence the imperative orientation to humanity leaned heavily on the side of clannishness. To an unsuspected degree, that is still true today. Sociologists have been overly influenced by the Industrial Revolution and the "class struggles" that it stimulated. But it would be helpful to bear in mind that ethnic struggles are much older and more persistent phenomena. Human evolution is to an odious extent a history of competition, often violent, for scarce resources along clan or kin group divisions. A general theory of ethnicity is impossible without earnest allowance of this fact, and hence of kin selection theory (van den Berghe, 1981; Lopreato & Crippen, 1999).

Tentative steps in this direction were fairly common at one time. They appeared out of Max Weber's argument that status groups, unlike classes, constitute communities characterized by consciousness of kind. They were more resolute in Weber's view (1968, p. 389) of ethnic members as individuals who "entertain a subjective belief in their common descent because of similarities of physical type or customs or both, or because of memories of colonization and migration." Pareto (1963, Section 1022) made a closer approach to an explicitly evolutionary conception in his critique of the then lively theories of group formation:

> But there is [another] hypothesis that explains the known facts much better. It considers the groups as natural formations growing up about a nucleus which is generally the family, with appendages of one sort or another, and the permanence of such groups in time engenders or strengthens certain sentiments that, in their turn, render the groups more compact, more stable, better able to endure.

Sumner's (1906) discussion of in-groups, out-groups, and the ethnocentrism promoted by the "exigencies of war" is still more to the point and too well known to require more than a passing mention here. There were later promising attempts, too, especially those of Park and Burgess (1921) and Gordon (1964).

On the whole, however, subsequent generations of sociologists of ethnicity have highlighted factors specific to given times and places, with a heavy emphasis on the making of the American mosaic. On occasion we have even been tempted to descry the disappearance of ethnicity, only to be restored to unpleasant reality by seemingly capricious eruptions of ethnic hostility. The temptation then is to suppose that something new has happened (e.g., Glazer & Moynihan, 1975). That may be correct, in a passing sense. But the awakenings can be awfully embarrassing and reinforce the suspicion that sociology is yet to demonstrate its utility. As the Soviet Union, for instance, was approaching its final entropy, we should have been better prepared for its fragmentation into an awesome array of warring groups that had long borne a dictated kindredness. Even the tragedy of the Balkans caught us essentially by surprise. And yet, across the globe, one of the most salient facts of history has been the periodic disruption of ethnic mosaics. Today, wherever we look in the "global village" we find mixtures of peoples who have an awfully difficult time living together in peace, rather discrediting Plutarch's temperate dictum of some 2000 years ago that "what all peoples honor is the maintenance of their own ways."

In some measure, the failure to focus on the universal is an effect of the sociologist's commitment, theoretical and personal, to cultural pluralism: the celebration of cultural diversity. As private predilection, few things are more commendable. As theoretical strategy, it is problematic on more than the question of efficiency. One wonders whether the engrossment with cultural diversity may not have the unintended effect of perpetuating, if not altogether kindling, the prejudice and ethnocentrism that in the ancient brain are unconsciously entangled with cultural diversity. In this respect, one advantage of evolutionary theory transpires from the knowledge that genetic diversities in the species are not only minute. Rushton's (1995) racial "findings" notwithstanding, they are also found almost entirely *within*, not between, populations (Cavalli-Sforza & Cavalli-Sforza, 1995). Science is simply more efficient than "patronage" in disclosing sham and wrecking ancient barriers. It does make us freer.

Evolutionary sociology does not propose that we disregard facts specific to given times and places. It holds that universal and persistent phenomena demand universal explanations. People hardly need sociologists to show, for example, that attributions of blame for socio-economic disadvantage are not as fixed as late-1960s data suggest (Schuman & Krysan, 1999). Little if anything is really fixed. Our journals are laden with such well-meaning and in many respects exemplary studies. But the governor's office and countless other public and private bureaus can do just as well, and they compete fiercely. Likewise, morning-after analyses of ethnic strife, a fair record in sociology, can be done quite nicely by journalists, who inform without befuddling correlations. Historians are better trained to underscore the unique facts of each case. A general theory of ethnic conflict requires attention to unique factors filtered through the wide-angle lens of kin selection, among other theoretical tools.

Our hominid ancestors lived in kin groups of 25–40 souls on average. There were alliances among clans, for, born geneticists that they were, our ancestors "knew" to avoid the "inbreeding depression" of incestuous relations and preferentially practiced exogamous cross-cousin marriage. But the enemy was rarely far off and alliances were oftentimes but shifting arrangements. Given the exigencies of war, kin selection stimulated the evolution of adaptations that cemented the in-group with sentiments of suspicion, fear, and hatred of the out-group. We know why, then, human infants develop close bonds with those who care for them and then, at about the age of 7 months, begin to show signs of xenophobia, which peaks in the subsequent year, in step with a deeper attachment to kin and nurturer (Freedman, 1974).

Violent spasms of ethnic hostility, hardly a specialty of human beings (e.g., Goodall, 1986, pp. 525–528), have been of all times and places in our species. Preagricultural peoples have hunted one another as they have hunted wild animals (e.g., Chagnon, 1988; Davie, 1929; Eibl-Eibesfeldt, 1989). The fortunes of the Jews, the Kurds, the Amerindian populations, the "Indios," among many other persecuted peoples, continue to grip our tutored memory. But there is no widespread awareness in sociology that in the 1990s there were at least 50 ethnic wars throughout the world. Millions, including totally defenseless women and children, were sacrificed to ethnic hatred and many more were forced to wander hungry, sick, cold, and destitute. Judging by the evidence from ethnography, tribal warfare has taken a horrendous toll throughout hominid evolution. One of the more credible hypotheses on the disappearance of *Homo sapiens neanderthalensis* some 28,000 years BP is that *Homo sapiens sapiens* did away with them, just as, with the discovery of the New World, we did our best to annihilate countless "heathen" peoples and currently we are making it hard in the extreme for other organisms to share this good earth with us.

Human beings today are ethnocentric and frequently violent against "outsiders" ultimately because we are the descendants of individuals whose natural selection favored the forging of intense nepotistic favoritism within a context of group competition. Hence, to say that ethnic hatred is rooted in kin selection is to assert that, at least in the environment in which it evolved, it had adaptive significance. Within a Malthusian–Darwinian environment, natural selection favored those who were most efficient in aggressing their conspecifics outside the inner circle of kinfolk. The fact was not just a case of the best defense being a vigorous offense. It also was an application of the Lotka Law.

The fitness principle predicts that social organisms are inclined toward "heterologous contraposition" and conversely toward "homologous affiliation," namely a "genetically based inclination to favor alliances ... with others in direct proportion to one's degree of kinship and/or phenotypical similarity to these" (Lopreato, 1984, p. 304). Of course, the trick is to distinguish between "us" and "them" In the ancestral society, it was hardly a problem. Clan members were related by blood or ties of marriage, and lived their lives in close proximity. The problem is dramatically different in today's society. The agricultural revolution stimulated population explosion, recurrent resettlements, and ever-growing political coalitions across various groups of prior strangers. As a result, the mind, still roaming the ancient brain, has had to artificially expand the boundaries that separate us from them.

Ethnic Conflict in the Megasociety.   We are literally out of place in the megasociety. The evidence from genetics and paleoanthropology is that the basic forces behind kin selection have not altered: that our brain is still in the clan. But the clannish whispers—"Who am I?" "Who are mine?" "Who are the others?"—these do not find the easy answers of times past. We therefore must rely on proxies, often a mere "bag of tricks" (van den Berghe, 1981), that signify or at least echo a degree of "weness." We strain to detect "ethnic markers." They include such features as commonality of historical experience, a common name and/or language, a shared cuisine, a "genetically transmitted phenotype," such as skin color, and among others the indications of common descent, however tenuous, inherent in patterns of assortative mating (van den Berghe, 1981, pp. 28–29).

In conclusion of this section, the intention has not been to argue that ethnic conflict is the effect solely of kin selection and kin favoritism. Like other facts, the phenomenon results from a complex of factors—in evolutionary terminology, from the interaction of genotypical and environmental forces. The typical sociological focus on unique factors of time and place may amount to good historiography but not to mature science. The intensity of prejudice against the "outsider" shifts from time to time, depending on many environmental factors. A few years ago, for instance, when employment in the United States was precarious, "Hardhat Joe" became awfully intolerant of "foreigners" and black Americans. But reactions of this sort would be inconceivable in the absence of kin selection, just as birds may learn to mob nonpredators, but they would mob no one if mobbing were not an evolutionary adaptation in the first place.

Kin selection is rhythmic in the intensity of its expression, but it is of all times and places. The interaction between the ultimate and the proximate may be conveniently expressed by the following "central tenet of biocultural science": "Fitness-enhancing sociocultural behaviors are favorably selected, and then react on natural selection by influencing the distribution of genetic material and the distribution of sociocultural behaviors that are associated with it" (Lopreato, 1984, p. 107). There has been a complex concatenation of feedback effects between genetic and sociocultural forces. Natural selection has favored those individuals who more successfully have met the exigencies of the struggle for existence, through ethnic aggression, *inter alia.* The strategies and means of aggression, in turn, have been transmitted through the generations and acted in favor of their more zealous practitioners. Such has been the old order. Such, alas, is likely to be the new, unless we learn the why; then we may learn the how of attenuating forces. At the end of the Cold War, hopes were high that a period of universal peace would ensue. Instead, its demise was immediately followed by scads of little hot wars fueled by old ethnic hatreds that had been held in check by the giant's rivalry. The history of our species has been, and in all probability will continue to be, a history of ethnic assortments, ethnic collisions, and ethnic disarrays, despite the mitigation of kin selection.

Anisogamy, Differential Parental Investment, and Sexual Selection.   The sex-differentiated part of human nature theory has had a faster and richer course, thanks in part to a basic diversity in physioanatomy and a seminal paper by the zoologist Trivers (1972) on "relative parental investment." Throughout the creation, there is a fundamental difference between males and females that harbors numberless implications for a fuller understanding of maleness and femaleness. *Anisogamy*, the name given to it, refers to the difference in size and structure between female and male gametes (sex cells). The latter are minuscule, contribute only genes to the offspring, and in sexually mature individuals are produced continuously in huge quantities. Hence, men (like other males) could in principle father thousands of offspring and some have done so (Betzig, 1986).

By contrast, eggs are much larger and far fewer. They are also formed only once, in the embryo, and are subject to daily wear an tear, so that by menarche the typical woman is left with roughly one third of the original 2 million oocytes and may expect no more than 450 ovulations at most during the rest of her life. Moreover, given gestation, lactation, and the other constraints on fecundity, only a very small number of eggs can possibly be promoted into offspring. When we consider the common discomforts of pregnancy, the dangers of childbirth and postpartum complications, lactation, and the protracted nursing of the children, it becomes clear that females make both a greater initial investment in the offspring and a greater subsequent investment. Furthermore, precisely because of the huge expenditure in each child, a mistake—an unwanted pregnancy, mating with an uncaring and resource-poor individual, and so forth—can be genetically very costly.

The basic implications of anisogamy and differential parental investment have been drawn by Trivers. But these, in a nutshell, are the basic facts that our ancestors were subject to as far as their reproductive activity was concerned. Certain things, e.g., childbirth risk, have changed considerably in recent times. But since the human brain, which contains the neuro-endocrinology of anisogamy, was not forged in recent times, the old implications cannot have disappeared altogether. Subject to different reproductive constraints, the two sexes have entered the modern world with different reproductive strategies. For convenience sake and with an eye to the typical case, evolutionists refer to female and male reproductive strategies with such terms as "choosy" and "philandering," respectively. In short, males have evolved to stress quantity. Females are more keen to quality. More broadly, what has been termed the "law of anisogamy" states that "the two sexes are by nature endowed with different reproductive strategies, and their behaviors reflect that difference in direct proportion to their relevance to it" (Lopreato, 1992, p. 1998).

The focus on anisogamy also has clarified to an extent a central aspect of Darwin's theory, which we can now report briefly here. The reference is to what Darwin called "sexual selection." We may recall that his concept of survival was focused a bit too much on the organism. Accordingly, certain facts did not fit neatly in his conception of the struggle for survival. Why, for instance, the splashy feathers of certain birds, the huge antlers, the "instrumental music," the extraordinary size of the peacock's tail, and endless other such "secondary characters" that tend to undermine survival through "pugnacity," reduced motility, enhanced visibility to the predator, and so forth? In keeping with fitness theory, Darwin was led to conclude that, if a given characteristic enhances an individual's ability to reproduce, it is likely to be favorably selected, whatever the handicaps. In view of the focus on sexual characteristics, he coined the concept of sexual selection to comprise the "odd" observations (Darwin, 1958, p. 94).

The coinage is a bit unfortunate owing to the implication of an alternative to natural selection, whereas sexual selection refers to a form of agonistic behavior that is inherent in anisogamy and constitutes a major cause of natural selection (Dobzhansky et al., 1977, p. 118). Viewed as competition for mates, as Darwin certainly intended it, sexual selection has become a critical theoretical tool in the study of evolution and behavior. It suggests, in keeping with the fitness principle, that much animal behavior is adapted not so much to the problem of organismic survival as to the task of genetic survival through securing reproductive mates.

Darwin (1871, p. 916) distinguished between two major types of sexual selection. In one, the "sexual struggle" is

> between individuals of the same sex, generally the males, in order to drive away or kill their rivals ... whilst in the other, the struggle is likewise between the individuals of the same sex, in order to excite or charm those of the opposite sex, generally the females, which ... select the more agreeable partners.

Evolutionists commonly refer to the first type as "intrasexual selection" and distinguish between male–male and female–female subtypes, with Darwin's own emphasis on the former. The second type is referred to as "intersexual selection" or, more generally, as "female choice." In either case, the focus is on behavior that is inherent in the fact of anisogamy. This feature of the organism—the enormous imbalance in reproductive potential between the sexes—results in scarcity of females, and hence in avid and often rough male sexual selection or competition for females. Differential parental investment and sexual selection, therefore, may be viewed both as corollaries of the law of anisogamy. Combining the two concepts, Trivers (1972, p. 140) has stated the following important proposition:

> Individuals of the sex investing less will compete among themselves to breed with members of the sex investing more, since an individual of the former can increase its reproductive success by investing successfully in the offspring of several members of the limiting sex.

On this tendency, species of course vary. I also may add in passing that a fuller treatment of sexual selection could show that, along with the "struggle" in general, the concept is fundamental to a general theory of social stratification (Lopreato & Crippen, 1999, Chapter 8).

Anisogamy: Of Women and Men.   Any reasonable person reading Trivers' statement above is likely to react a little incredulously, for it hardly seems applicable to our species. Nevertheless, it would be desirable to at least view it as a primate characterization and then proceed from there to assess the extent to which our primate species has departed from this rule, or conversely to discover whatever residue of it may still linger in our ranks. At any rate, we have nothing to gain from a continuing alienation from anisogamy theory. At worst, we may lose what we are bound to lose anyway. A fair perusal of our journals reveals that, like the famous Red Queen, we have been running in place, powerless amid a mass of "facts" that are rediscovered and factiously "explained" anew every few years. Much of our theory seems to ape the metaphysics of postmodernist philosophers and litterateurs or to be guided by "revolutionary criteria" for "another science: the sciences and politics of interpretation, translation, stuttering ... a critical vision" (Haraway, 1988, pp. 589–590; see also Oakley, 1997). "Foundational" sociology is alleged to be under the spell of "malicious forces" working at the service of a privileged club (e.g., Hill, 1996; Seidman, 1991).

Such thinking, predating the faculties that jailed Galileo and for 21 years delayed publication of Darwin's *Origin*, is common in feminist studies (but see Turner, 1998, Chapters 18, 43, for helpful distinctions between gender studies); and yet few if any sociological areas can be better enriched by evolutionary theory. Consider the issue of patriarchy, the theoretical bottom line of most gender studies. Patriarchy is alleged to cause sex-differentiated disparities that result in female submission. There is truth in this view, but it is no more than an assertion. "*Why*," Sarah Hrdy (1997, p. 8) has rightly asked, "should males seek to control females?" Indeed, we might add, why is it not the other way around? The absence of such questions suggests a degree of theoretical timidity that verges on paralysis. Surely it is incumbent upon us to try to explain the rise of patriarchy in the first place. The phenomenon is very old and in its fundamentals virtually universal in the entire mammalian class. The sexes have evolved under the pressures of differential parental investment and sexual selection. Males have competed for access to the "limiting sex" and females have aided and abetted the dominant males through their preference for them. This is the basic meaning of "female choice." In short, the pickle that many, women and men alike, find distasteful was not prepared by males alone.

What is perhaps more remarkable is that female "collusion" persists to this very day. In "pursuing their material and reproductive interests, women often engage in behaviors that promote male resource control and male control over female sexuality," *inter alia* (Smuts, 1995, p. 18). One result of this sexual selection has been a greater variation in reproductive success in men than in women (e.g., Betzig, 1986), and the fact persists in modern society (e.g., Lindquist Forsberg & Tullberg, 1995). The disparity attains extraordinary degrees in some species, where only a small minority of males are ever reproductive. Little wonder that hypergyny is far more common than hypogamy and that throughout the world researchers discover a recurrent theme: Women more than men value in their prospective mates status characteristics that reveal or show promise of the rich resources needed to raise successful children, whereas men are significantly more likely to emphasize aspects of physical appearance—e.g., youth and good looks—that presumably imply high reproductive value (e.g., Buss, 1989). The uniformity is observable in innumerable contexts, including the famous "Personals." A careful analysis shows that "lonely hearts" personals reflect sexually dimorphic mating strategies along the above lines (Thiessen, Young, & Burroughs, 1993). Furthermore, women's concern for man's status escalates as emotional commitment increases (Townsend & Levy, 1990).

Of course, most sociologists are quick to argue that women have been socialized to behave this way. The simple fact, however, is that the physical "sex dimorphisms" arising from anisogamy are inextricably associated with all sorts of dimorphic strategies, and none as accentuated as those pertaining to gender behavior. The vigorous commitment to socialization, which entails a rather dismal view of the female sense of personal integrity, neglects the fact that dimorphic socialization is universal in the entire mammalian class. It also can lead to truly absurd positions. Many feminists still accept an old argument to the effect that the universal sexual division of labor is a result of learned behavior; in their respective relationships with mother, girls learn a mothering identification, whereas boys develop so as to behave as males (Chadorow, 1978). Leaving aside the question as to why the universality of such socialization, this theorizing seems to assume that in principle we could raise boys to behave like girls and vice versa, at least in reproductively irrelevant contexts.

Generally, assumptions are as good as their hypotheses. From the socialization premise we should be able to predict that, for example, as sex roles approach greater equality, sex stereotypes proceed to weaken. This was the problem posed by three sociologists (Lueptow, Garovich, & Lueptow, 1995), and they have found, on the basis of data collected in sociology courses during 1974 to 1991, that despite remarkable changes in sex-related attitudes during this period, gender stereotypes on various personality traits remained stable and in some cases increased, even on the self-ratings. Among the traits commonly scored as most masculine were competitive, authoritative, aggressive, adventurous, and ambitious, while obedient, affectionate, romantic, talkative, and sympathetic were least accentuated. The very reverse was true for feminine traits. There is nothing in these findings to cheer the boys, should one wish to inject a moral judgment. The authors concluded that so-called stereotypes were not stereotypes at all, but "reflect the perceptions of real personality differences between women and men, based to some undetermined degree on innate differences between the sexes" (Lueptow et al., 1995, p. 526).

There is a paradox of sorts in findings of this nature. One scholar has expressed it as follows: "where behavior choice is broad and opportunities are egalitarian, biological variables, reflecting natural differences in behavioral predispositions, explain increasing variation in behavior" (Udry, 1996, p. 335). There may be a prophecy hidden in here: Further cultural development will facilitate, not impede, an opening to biology in social science, with or without sociological participation.

In domestic matters, the predictions from evolutionary theory amount to a rich and growing harvest. The following are a few examples. According to a set of findings in sociology, husbands place greater emphasis than wives on youth and physical appearance; as a result, they are the first to get tired of sex in the wedded nest. Not infrequently, the next stop is divorce. As usual, the various explanations beg the question, some more flagrantly than others. In general, the recourse is, as expected, to culture, as in the assertion that "people's sexual preferences result from an elaborate normative superstructure that informs perceptions and gives meaning to the things we do" (Margolin & White, 1987, p. 22). This normative emphasis is unnecessarily excessive. Differential parental investment and sexual selection predict that, given the opportunities, males are more likely than females to seek them out. Loss or reduction of sexual interest in the present partner is but a symptom of this tendency. Opportunity is certainly a good stimulator.

The question of opportunity outside the nest is the subject of another sizable and closely related set of research endeavors. According to one of the better studies, "women's labor force participation may increase *married men's* propensity to seek a divorce by increasing the probability that men will find a more attractive alternative to their current wife." Further theorizing then "anchors the study of marital dissolution in … social structure" (South & Lloyd, 1995, p. 33; emphasis in the original). Sociology is drunk on social structure. We need to consider seriously that structural variables can never be anything more than intervening factors in explanation. Can you imagine a physicist arguing that the artificial light in his laboratory is caused by the switch on the wall? Increased opportunities play a role in marital instability. That is hardly deniable. But anisogamy suggests that, at least once the brood is complete, husbands are more impelled than wives to undo the social structure. This consideration does not enter the authors' reasoning and the upshot is very gauche. The broader claim of the study is that "the risk of marital disruption is greater when *either* husbands or wives encounter a relatively sizable quantity of alternatives to their current spouse" (South & Lloyd, 1995, p. 31; emphasis added). To an equal degree? Consider: Before women's participation in the labor force constituted a "sizable quantity of alternatives" for married men, working men certainly represented quite a quantity of alternatives for married women. That was the case, say, in the 1950s. Were women then as diligent in falling prey to "social structure" as men have more recently turned out to be? Beyond that, the question hangs: *Why* should alternatives be more attractive to one's spouse? Why do socialization and experience have so little value within the nest? Old proverbs often hit the nail on the head: Doesn't the old hen make the best broth?

The number of sociological discoveries is probably staggering, although severed from an organizing principle and thus disconnected from one another, they constitute theoretical noise more than reliable knowledge. Ironically, the vast majority most likely conform to evolution-ary theory, and there is some hope in that for the future of sociology. Sociologists find, for instance, that husbands have more sexual partners than wives; males are more likely to fantasize about numerous sexual partners; they have sex earlier and are more likely to have it with a stranger; they have a higher rate of infidelity in courting and cohabiting as well as in marital relationships; they are more likely to abuse spouses and children; they are far more dangerous as stepparents, especially toward infants; they are more violently jealous; they commit more homicides and other crimes, especially in "the flower" of their youth; and on and on along a very long trail leading straight to evolutionary theory (e.g., Daly & Wilson, 1988; Laumann, Michael, Michaels, & Gagnon, 1994; Lopreato & Crippen, 1999).

Certain recent events have tempted many sociologists to proclaim the breakdown of the family as an institution. In this attitude, we are inspired by what we have known of advanced agricultural society up to a few decades ago. In fact, monogamy and fidelity, the points of reference, were a historical novelty, to the extent that they really existed. The sanctity of the marriage bond is not a hominid feature, certainly not as far as males are concerned. Polygamy has been allowed in the vast majority of human societies, but the guess of informed scholars is that the desire for novelty has been satisfied far more frequently through adultery. Rising opportunities due to greater desegregation of the sexes have facilitated the flourishing of ancient forces, especially among males, as is predictable from evolutionary theory. The recent changes in family structure are far more "natural" than is generally believed. The typical family unit of human evolution consisted of a small group of kin in which mother, aunt, grandmother, and older siblings were the major figures. Men were essentially irrelevant. The father was often away, hunting animals or human heads when he was not himself a trophy head. The family structure of the inner city, far from being the social pathology that it often is portrayed to be, probably is the closest thing to the "natural" family of our evolutionary past. It may be prelude as well.

At least until a few years ago, there was a very lively debate on whether today's father is a "new father," that is, a man who in an extreme version of his depiction is so nurturing, "expressive and intimate ... with his children" that he verges on the "unmasculine" (Ro-tundo, 1985, p. 17). The opposite version held in effect that the "culture of fatherhood" has changed much more than the "conduct of fatherhood"; what we really have is a "technically present but functionally absent father" (LaRossa, 1988, pp. 451–452). The details of the controversy are very complex and as usual nothing conclusive has been accomplished. It is safe to say, however, that there is partial validity in both points of view. The interaction principle predicts that the culture of fatherhood has had to have some effect on the conduct of fatherhood. But evolutionary theory also predicts that the effect cannot be so great as to cancel millions of years of endocrinal activity and natural selection. Proximate explanations are far too often either–or debates. Fathers as a category have evolved along the primate model, though the neuroendocrinal vicissitudes of our species must have facilitated an increase in the intensity of the father–child relationship as part of the evolution toward greater sociality. But in mammals, child care has in general been the responsibility of mothers and their female surrogates (Murdock, 1967; Maryanski & Turner, 1992). Childhood is also the time in which intense emotional ties are forged for the duration.

Differential parental investment aside, there is another, complementary reason why the father–child tie is typically more tenuous than the mother–child tie. And here it is particularly important to follow the logic of natural selection, and thus to avoid interpreting statements in rationalistic, teleological terms. The subject was well known to the ancients. In evolutionary science it is known as "paternal uncertainty." *Pater semper incertus*, the practical Romans used to say. Earlier, according to Homer, when Telemachus was asked by Athena whether Odysseus was his father, he replied aptly enough: "My mother saith that he is my father; for myself I know it not, for no man knoweth who hath begotten him." Paternal uncertainty is an effect of internal insemination and is wired deeply in the male brain. Its effects, often associated with those of differential parental investment, may seem extremely far-fetched. According to a recent study, the "most caring" of the grandparents is the maternal grandmother. She is followed not by the paternal grandmother, as common sense would have it, but by her husband. The paternal grandfather comes last (Euler & Weitzel, 1996).

CONCLUSION

Sociology was born in the family of sciences, a creature of the culture of reason and progress spawned by the Age of Enlightenment (Bury, 1955). The Founders were without exception polymaths intent on creating a science of society based on what Comte (1896, Volume 1, pp. 5–6) called, with a touch of excess, "invariable natural laws" analogous to "the doctrine of Gravitation." The 19th century, moreover, was the "evolutionary century," and all the great sociologists up to the first quarter of the 20th century partook of the evolutionary inspiration, though to varying degrees of explicitness and success. It may help to note that Durkheim, who almost invariably is viewed as the quintessential "emergentist," was nevertheless motivated by a deeper scholarship. "Most sociologists," Durkheim (1958, pp. 89–97) complained, "think they have accounted for phenomena once they have shown how they are useful, what role they play..... But this method confuses two very different questions. To show how a fact is useful is not to explain how it originated or why it is what it is ... it is proper, in general, to treat the [cause] before the [utility]," though a fact must "be useful in order that it may maintain itself.... [Else] the budget of the organism would have a deficit"—else the fact would be maladaptive. Lest there be doubt about the Darwinian intention here, there is no dearth of corroborating evidence. "If work," for instance, Durkheim (1933, p. 266) argues elsewhere, "becomes divided more as societies become more voluminous and denser, it is ... because the struggle for existence is more acute." Indeed, if interpreted in the light of modern evolutionary theory, his first classic turns out to be a compelling attempt at a theory of evolution from a kin-selected basis of sociality to one relying increasingly on reciprocal altruism (Lopreato, 1990; Lopreato & Crippen, 1999, pp. 15–16). Durkheim (1965, p. 15) in effect concludes his brilliant career with the admonition that the explanation of social facts lies in the origin of their elementary forms: "Every time that we undertake to explain something human, taken at a given moment in history ... it is necessary to commence by going back to its most primitive and simple form, to try to account for ... how it became that which it is at the moment in question." This is reductionism pure and simple.

It is very likely that subsequent generations of sociologists have been deceived by the mountains of debris heaped on elementary facts by the vertiginous acceleration of socio-cultural change. Driven by the multiplier effect, cause of Spencer's (1972) famous law of evolution, sociology has become mired in a jungle of structural ramifications and in the process in a veritable forest of words as well. Structural variables by themselves tend to hide information. If we wish to get at the forces holding the edifices together, it is essential that we practice some social archaeology. Little in sociology makes lasting sense at too great a distance from the fundamentals of our evolution; it is these that hold the key to our general principles.

No general laws or principles, no science. This, then, is the primary cause of the crisis in sociology: the absence of a statement of theory about the fundamentals of the human condition whose inherent logical program encompasses a number of other propositions to account for the accretions upon the elementary facts. Wanting such a tool, we lack also a recognizable body of systematic, cumulative knowledge. In this state of affairs, a community of scholars, however keen their wits, are bound to perpetuate the impairing condition. We should do as other disciplines before us have done and borrow the law, however imperfect, from the established science closest to us in subject matter. Our kin is evolutionary biology, as many in psychology and anthropology already have concluded in view of their own like affliction. If we give these disciplines too much of a head start, they will burn the bridges behind them. Ours is a problem of survival. This chapter has provided a modest depiction of relevant particulars of our scientific neighbor. I believe that, to put it in Nietzsche's famous words, they can help "to compose into one and bring together what is fragment and riddle."

General principles perform various essential functions. They provide the logic for denotative and generally applicable concepts, for their operationalization, for their combination into testable and falsifiable hypotheses, for the linking of discoveries and explanations in a coherent whole, for the discovery of further statements of theory, and for a hierarchical organization of propositions into what is properly termed a scientific theory. In short, they are focal points of research leading to a systematic, cumulative body of knowledge. In the process, the borrowing discipline may very well adjust the debt according to its own special needs and even pay it back by contributing in turn.

Human sociobiology or evolutionary sociology holds special promise for two major types of enterprise. One is to hypothesize about the origins of such phenomena as ethnocentrism, sexism, inequality, violence, reproductive strategies, and related family facts and to theoretically organize discoveries into classes of behavior. The other suggests hypotheses about the variable persistence of human facts. The discipline already can claim a small but growing number of sociologists who have taken the plunge (see Maryanski, 1998, for a partial but very useful critical survey). Others may have done equally well by decrying what Davis (1994, p. 189) has termed our "doctrinaire denial of any biological influence on human behavior."

We should be under no illusion, however, about a quick solution of our crisis. George Eliot begins her superb *Daniel Deronda* with the following dictum: "Men can do nothing without the make-believe of a beginning." It may be that sociology has still some make-believe to do. Or rather it may be suffering from the quandary of the convalescent patient. According to an interesting story, Walter de la Mare was slowly recovering from a grave illness when one day his younger daughter asked him if there was anything that she could get for him: "some fruit or flowers?" "No, no, my dear," replied he, "it's too late for fruit, too soon for flowers."

Yet there are possibilities. One of these may seem naive if not entirely objectionable, but it probably would give us the remedy within 10–15 years at the most. Why not do everything possible to attract students to our graduate programs who have at least a minor in biological science? At the same time, our own majors could be required to minor in that area and more generally to leave college with a much enhanced education. There are two good reasons why such a strategy could work. One, our students would enter their professional career better prepared to engage evolutionary science. Two, while in training they would challenge their instructors to broaden their horizons and at the same time provide them with the cover needed against the "doctrinaires." Then sociologists would be able to grant each other genuine academic freedom, for as long as the doctrinaires rule, science is vile and free speech is hazardous.

REFERENCES

Alexander, R. D. (1990). Epigenetic rules and Darwinian algorithms: The adaptive study of learning and development. *Ethology and Sociobiology, 11*, 241–303.

Axelrod, R. (1984). *The evolution of cooperation.* New York: Basic Books.

Badcock, C. (1994). *PsychoDarwinism: The new synthesis of Darwin and Freud.* London: Harper Collins.

Barash, D. P. (1982). *Sociobiology and behavior.* New York: Elsevier.

Betzig, L. L. (1986). *Despotism and differential reproduction: A Darwinian view of history.* New York: Aldine.

Black, M. (1961). Some questions about Parsons' theories. In M. Black (Ed.), *The social theories of Talcott Parsons: A critical examination* (pp. 268–288). Englewood Cliffs, NJ: Prentice-Hall.

Blau, P. M. (1964). *Exchange and power in social life.* New York: Wiley.

Brandon, G. S. F. (1962). *Man and his destiny in the great religions.* Manchester, England: Manchester University Press.

Bury, J. B. (1955). *The idea of progress.* New York: Dover. (Original publication 1932)

Buss, D. M. (1989). Sex differences in human mate preferences: Evolutionary hypotheses tested in 37 cultures (with commentary). *Behavioral and Brain Sciences, 12*, 1–49.

Carey, A. D., & Lopreato, J. (1995). The biocultural evolution of the male–female mortality differential. *The Mankind Quarterly, 36*, 3–28.

Cavalli-Sforza, L. L., & Cavalli-Sforza, F. (1995). *The great human diasporas: The history of diversity and evolution.* Reading, MA: Addison-Wesley.

Chadorow, N. (1978). *The reproduction of mothering: Psychoanalysis and the sociology of gender.* Berkeley: University of California Press.

Chagnon, N. A. (1988). Life histories, blood revenge, and warfare in a tribal population. *Science, 239*, 985–992.

Cole, S. (Ed.). (2000). *What's wrong with sociology?* New Brunswick, NJ: Transaction.

Collins, R. (1990). The organizational politics of the ASA. *American Sociologist, 21*, 311.

Comte, A. (1896). *The positive philosophy of Auguste Comte,* 3 volumes, H. Martineau (Trans. and Abridger). London: Bell.

Cosmides, L. (1989). The logic of social exchange: Has natural selection shaped how humans reason? Studies with the Wason selection task. *Cognition, 31*, 187–276.

Cosmides, L., & Tooby, J. (1989). Evolutionary psychology and the generation of culture, Part II. Case study: A computational theory of social exchange. *Ethology and Sociobiology, 10*, 51–97.

Crippen, T. (1994). Toward a neo-Darwinian sociology: Its nomological principles and some illustrative applications. *Sociological Perspectives, 37*, 309–335.

Daly, M., & Wilson, M. (1988). *Homicide.* New York: Aldine de Gruyter.

Darwin, C. (1958). *The origin of species.* New York: New American Library, Mentor Books. (Original publication 1859)

Darwin, C. (1871). *The origin of species and the descent of man and selection in relation to sex.* New York: Random House. (Undated collection)

Davie, M. R. (1929). *The evolution of war: A study of its role in early societies.* New Haven: Yale University Press.

Davis, J. A. (1994). What's wrong with sociology? *Sociological Forum, 9*, 179–197.

Dawkins, R. (1976). *The selfish gene.* Oxford, England: Oxford University Press.

Dawkins, R. (1986). *The blind watchmaker.* New York: Norton.

de Waal, F. B. M. (1982). *Chimpanzee politics.* New York: Harper & Row.

Dobzhansky, T. (1937). *Genetics and the origin of species.* New York: Columbia University Press.

Dobzhansky, T., Ayala, F. J., Stebbins, G. L., & Valentine, J. W. (1977). *Evolution.* San Francisco: Freeman.

Durkheim, E. (1933). *The division of labor in society.* New York: Macmillan. (Original publication 1893)

Durkheim, E. (1958). *The rules of sociological method.* Glencoe, IL: Free Press. (Original publication 1895)

Durkheim, E. (1965). *The elementary forms of the religious life.* New York: Free Press. (Original publication 1912)

Eibl-Eibesfeldt, L. (1989). *Human ethology.* New York: Aldine de Gruyter.

Eldredge, N., & Gould, S. J. (1972). Punctuated equilibrium: An alternative to gradualism. In T. J. M. Schoph (Ed.), *Models in paleobiology* (pp. 82–115). San Francisco: Freeman, Copper.

Engels, F. (1978). Speech at the graveside of Karl Marx. In R. C. Tucker (Ed.), *The Marx–Engels reader* (pp. 681–682), 2nd ed. New York: Norton. (Original publication 1883)

Euler, H. A., & Weitzel, B. (1996). Discriminative grandparental solicitude as reproductive strategy. *Human Nature, 7*, 39–59.

Freedman, D. G. (1974). *Human infancy: An evolutionary perspective.* Hillsdale, NJ: Lawrence Erlbaum.

Freese, L. (1997). *Evolutionary connections.* Greenwich, CT: JAI Press.

Glazer, N., & Moynihan, D. P. (Eds.). (1975). *Ethnicity: Theory and experience*. Cambridge, MA: Harvard University Press.

Goodall, J. (1986). *Chimpanzees of Gombe*. Cambridge, MA: Harvard University Press.

Gordon, M. M. (1964). *Assimilation in American life*. Oxford: Oxford University Press.

Gould, S. J. (1977). *Ever since Darwin: Reflections in natural history*. New York: Norton.

Gould, J. L., & Marler, P. (1987). Learning by instinct. *Scientific American, 256*, 74–85.

Guth, A. H. (1997). *The inflationary universe: The quest for a new theory of cosmic origins*. Reading, MA: Addison-Wesley.

Hamilton, W. D. (1964). The genetical theory of social behaviour: I and II. *Journal of Theoretical Biology, 7*, 1–52.

Haraway, D. (1988). Situated knowledges: The science question in feminism and the privilege of partial perspective. *Feminist Studies, 14*, 575–599.

Hill, M. R. (1996). Joan Huber, Irving Louis Horowitz, and the ideological future of objectivity in American sociology. *Sociological Imagination, 33*, 228–239.

Homans, G. C. (1961). *Social behavior: Its elementary forms*. New York: Harcourt, Brace & World.

Hrdy, S. B. (1997). Raising Darwin's consciousness: Female sexuality and the prehominid origins of patriarchy. *Human Nature, 8*, 1–49.

Huxley, J. (1942). *Evolution: The modern synthesis*. New York: Harper.

Huxley, J. (1958). Introduction to the Mentor edition. In C. Darwin (1859), *The origin of species* (pp. ix–xv). New York: Mentor Books.

Kuhn, T. S. (1957). *The Copernican revolution*. Cambridge, MA: Harvard University Press.

LaRossa, R. (1988). Fatherhood and social change. *Family Relations, 37*, 451–457.

Laumann, E., Michael, R., Michaels, S., & Gagnon, J. (1994). *The social organization of sexuality*. Chicago: University of Chicago Press.

Lévi-Strauss, C. (1969). *The elementary structures of kinship*. Boston: Beacon Press. (Original publication 1949)

Lewontin, R. C. (1979). Sociobiology as an adaptationist program. *Behavioral Science, 24*, 5–14.

Lieberson, S. (1992). Einstein, Renoir, and Greeley: Some thoughts about evidence in sociology. *American Sociological Review, 57*, 1–15.

Lindquist Forsberg, A. J., & Tullberg, B. S. (1995). The relationship between cumulative number of cohabiting partners and number of children for men and women in modern Sweden. *Ethology and Sociobiology, 16*, 221–232.

Lopreato, J. (1981). Toward a theory of genuine altruism in *Homo sapiens*. *Ethology and Sociobiology, 2*, 113–126.

Lopreato, J. (1984). *Human nature and biocultural evolution*. London: Allen & Unwin.

Lopreato, J. (1989). The maximization principle: A cause in search of conditions. In R. W. Bell & N. J. Bell (Eds.), *Sociobiology and the social sciences* (pp. 119–130). Lubbock: Texas Tech University Press.

Lopreato, J. (1990). From social evolutionism to biocultural evolutionism. *Sociological Forum, 5*, 187–212.

Lopreato, J. (1992). Sociobiology. In E. F. Borgatta (Ed.), *Encyclopedia of sociology* (pp. 1995–2000). New York: Macmillan.

Lopreato, J., & Alston, L. (1970). Ideal types and the idealization strategy. *American Sociological Review, 35*, 88–96.

Lopreato, J., & Crippen, T. (1999). *Crisis in sociology: The need for Darwin*. New Brunswick, NJ: Transaction.

Lotka, A. (1925). *Elements of physical biology*. Baltimore, MD: Williams & Wilkins.

Lueptow, L. B., Garovich, L., & Lueptow, M. B. (1995). The persistence of gender stereotypes in the face of changing sex roles: Evidence contrary to the sociocultural model. *Ethology and Sociobiology, 16*, 509–530.

Lumsden, C. J., & Wilson, E. O. (1981). *Genes, mind, and culture: The coevolutionary process*. Cambridge, MA: Harvard University Press.

Machalek, R. (1999). Elementary social facts: Emergence in nonhuman societies. *Advances in Human Ecology, 8*, 33–64.

Margolin, L., & White, L. (1987). The continuing role of physical attractiveness in marriage. *Journal of Marriage and the Family, 49*, 21–27.

Maryanski, A. (1994). The pursuit of human nature in sociobiology and evolutionary sociology. *Sociological Perspectives, 37*, 375–389.

Maryanski, A. (1998). Evolutionary sociology. *Advances in Human Ecology, 7*, 1–56.

Maryanski, A., & Turner, J. H. (1992). *The social cage: Human nature and the evolution of society*. Stanford, CA: Stanford University Press.

Mauss, M. (1954). *The gift*. London: Cohen & West. (Original publication 1925)

Mayr, E. (1942). *Systematics and the origin of species*. New York: Columbia University Press.

Mayr, E. (1978). Evolution. *Scientific American, 239*, 47–55.

Mayr, E. (1980). Prologue: Some thoughts on the history of the evolutionary synthesis. In E. Mayr & W. Provine (Eds.), *The evolutionary synthesis: Perspectives on the unification of biology* (pp. 1–48). Cambridge, MA: Harvard University Press.

Mayr, E. (1982). *The growth of biological thought: Diversity, evolution, and inheritance.* Cambridge, MA: Harvard University Press.

Murdock, G. P. (1967). *Ethnographic atlas.* Pittsburgh, PA: University of Pittsburgh Press.

Oakley, A. (1997). A brief history of gender. In A. Oakley & J. Mitchell (Eds.), *Who's afraid of feminism?* (pp. 29–55). New York: New Press.

Pareto, V. (1963). *Treatise on general sociology* (also known as *The mind and society*), 4 vols. New York: Dover. (Original publication 1916)

Park, R. E., & Burgess, E. W. (1921). *Introduction to the science of sociology.* Chicago: University of Chicago Press.

Popper, K. R. (1978). Natural selection and the emergence of mind. *Dialectica, 32,* 339–358.

Rotundo, A. (1985). American fatherhood: A historical perspective. *American Behavioral Scientist, 29,* 7–25.

Rushton, J. P. (1995). *Race, evolution, and behavior.* New Brunswick, NJ: Transaction.

Sagan, C., & Druyan, A. (1992). *Shadows of forgotten ancestors: A search for who we are.* New York: Random House.

Sanderson, S. (1992). *Social evolutionism: A critical history.* Cambridge, England: Blackwell.

Sanderson, S. (1994). Evolutionary materialism: A theoretical strategy for the study of social evolution. *Sociological Perspectives, 37,* 47–73.

Schuman, H., & Krysan, M. (1999). A historical note on whites' beliefs about racial inequality. *American Sociological Review, 64,* 847–855.

Seidman, S. (1991). The end of sociological theory: The postmodern hope. *Sociological Theory, 9,* 131–146.

Simpson, G. G. (1944). *Tempo and mode in evolution.* New York: Columbia University Press.

Simpson, G. G. (1967). *The meaning of evolution.* New Haven, CT: Yale University Press. (Original publication 1949)

Smuts, B. B. (1995). The evolutionary origins of patriarchy. *Human Nature, 6,* 1–32.

South, S. J., & Lloyd, K. M. (1995). Spousal alternatives and marital dissolution. *American Sociological Review, 60,* 21–35.

Spencer, H. (1972). Population and progress. In J. D. Y. Peel (Ed.), *Herbert Spencer on social evolution* (pp. 33–37). Chicago: University of Chicago Press. (Original publication 1852)

Stanley, S. M. (1981). *The new evolutionary time table.* New York: Basic Books.

Sumner, W. G. (1906). *Folkways.* New York: Ginn.

Symons, D. (1992). On the use and misuse of Darwinism in the study of human behavior. In J. H. Barkow, L. Cosmides, & J. Tooby (Eds.), *The adapted mind* (pp. 137–159). New York: Oxford University Press.

Thiessen, D. D., Young, R. K., & Burroughs, R. (1993). Lonely hearts advertisements reflect sexually dimorphic mating strategies. *Ethology and Sociobiology, 14,* 209–229.

Townsend, J. M., & Levy, G. D. (1990). Effects of potential partners' physical attractiveness and socioeconomic status on sexuality and partner selection. *Archives of Sexual Behavior, 19,* 149–164.

Trivers, R. L. (1971). The evolution of reciprocal altruism. *Quarterly Review of Biology, 46,* 35–47.

Trivers, R. L. (1972). Parental investment and sexual selection. In B. H. Campbell (Ed.), *Sexual selection and the descent of man, 1871–1971* (pp. 136–179). Chicago: Aldine.

Trivers, R. L. (1985). *Social evolution.* Menlo Park, CA: Benjamin/Cummings.

Turner, J. H. (1996a). American sociology: Can what was never coherently composed be decomposed? *Sociological Imagination, 33,* 191–201.

Turner, J. H. (1996b). The evolution of emotions: A Darwinian–Durkheimian analysis. *Journal for the Theory of Social Behavior, 26,* 1–33.

Turner, J. H. (1996c). The evolution of emotions: The nonverbal basis of human organization. In U. Segerstrale & P. Molnar (Eds.), *Biology with a human face: Nonverbal communication and social interaction* (pp. 300–318). New York: Lawrence Erlbaum.

Turner, J. H. (1996d). The nature and dynamics of the social among humans. In J. D. Greenwood (Ed.), *The mark of the social* (pp. 105–133). New York: Roman and Littlefield.

Turner, J. H. (1998). *The structure of sociological theory.* Belmont, CA: Wadsworth.

Udry, J. R. (1996). Sociology and biology: What biology do sociologists need to know? *Social Forces, 73,* 1267–1277.

van den Berghe, P. L. (1981). *The ethnic phenomenon.* New York: Elsevier.

Weber, M. (1968). *Economy and society,* 3 volumes. New York: Bedminster Press. (Original publication 1921–1922)

Wilson, E. O. (1975). *Sociobiology: The new synthesis.* Cambridge, MA: Harvard University Press.

Wilson, E. O. (1978). *On human nature.* Cambridge, MA: Harvard University Press.

Wilson, E. O. (1998). *Consilience: The unity of knowledge.* New York: Knopf.

CHAPTER 21

Evolutionary Theorizing

Stephen K. Sanderson

SOCIAL EVOLUTIONISM AND ITS CRITICS

Social evolutionary theories have held a prominent place in the history of the social sciences. Although there are many kinds of evolutionary theories, the essential element that they hold in common is their assumption that history is more than just a lot of noise signifying nothing— more, in other words, than a series of particular and unique events revealing no noteworthy patterns. On the contrary, the evolutionist assumption is that history reveals a certain directionality in the sense that there are similar processes occurring at similar times at various points throughout the globe. As theories, evolutionary analyses of human society do not limit themselves to simply describing directional patterns, but go on to provide causal explanations for the observed sequence or sequences.

Elsewhere, I (Sanderson, 1990) have written a detailed history of evolutionary theories, but a brief synopsis may be presented here. Evolutionary theorizing goes back to the beginning of both sociology and anthropology as disciplines in the middle of the 19th century. Indeed, sociology and anthropology were both born evolutionary. In anthropology the two most important evolutionary theorists were Lewis Henry Morgan (1974) and Edward Burnett Tylor (1871), both among the most important founding fathers of that discipline. Morgan identified three stages of social evolution, which he called savagery, barbarism, and civilization. Societies in the stage of savagery are technologically rudimentary and survive mostly by hunting and gathering. The transition to barbarism is marked by the invention of pottery and the domestication of plants and animals. For Morgan, the stage of civilization was achieved with the invention of the phonetic alphabet and writing. Tylor employed the same three stages used by Morgan, but he was more interested in the evolution of the ideational rather than the material dimensions of culture, especially with the development of language, myth, and religion. In sociology the leading evolutionist of this time was Herbert Spencer (1972) (cf. Peel, 1971; Turner, 1985), whose evolutionism is very familiar to sociologists even today. Spencer set forth a famous law of evolution that he thought governed not only changes in society, but changes in all of nature. Like all phenomena, societies had a tendency to change from a highly undifferentiated to a highly differentiated state, thus becoming more complex

Stephen K. Sanderson • Department of Sociology, Indiana University of Pennsylvania, Indiana, Pennsylvania 15705.

Handbook of Sociological Theory, edited by Jonathan H. Turner. Kluwer Academic / Plenum Publishers, New York, 2002.

and more functionally integrated. At a more concrete level, Spencer spoke of the evolution of the institutions of societies, especially their economic and political institutions, and he identified such factors as population pressure and warfare as primary determinants of evolutionary change. There were many other evolutionists in both disciplines during this period, and even thinkers whose main contributions are not usually thought of as evolutionary commonly held deep and often implicit evolutionary assumptions. I think especially of Durkheim. Anyone familiar with his *The Division of Labor in Society* (Durkheim, 1933) cannot help but notice his strong and completely unquestioned evolutionary assumptions about the world historical shift from mechanical to organic solidarity. He even explained the shift from mechanical to organic solidarity in Darwinian natural selectionist terms.

By the last decade of the 19th century evolutionary theorizing had waned and social science, anthropology in particular, fell under the spell of an "antievolutionary reaction" (Harris, 1968; Sanderson, 1990). In anthropology, evolutionism became virtually disreputable at the hands of Franz Boas (1932, 1940) and his disciples, who dominated anthropological thinking, at least in the United States, until the 1930s. Boas thought that evolutionism was flawed in many ways. He was an extreme historical particularist who argued that neither history nor cultures had any patterns at all. Every culture was just a polyglot of shreds and patches put together largely by culture contact and diffusion. Each culture had its own unique structure and its own unique history. Generalizing about either history or culture was foolhardy in the extreme, if not utterly impossible. However, despite Boas's enormous influence, evolutionary thinking during this period by no means disappeared entirely. Indeed, it was embraced by such prominent scholars as William Graham Sumner and his disciples (Sumner & Keller, 1927), L. T. Hobhouse (Hobhouse, Wheeler, & Ginsburg, 1965), and a number of other thinkers. But evolutionary thinking had acquired a bad reputation among many of the intellectual leaders of the social sciences, and the students of these leaders realized that to think evolutionarily was to place one's intellectual career at risk.

And yet, evolutionism revived. The first stirrings of this revival came in the 1930s in the work of V. Gordon Childe (1936, 1951, 1954), an Australian archaeologist living and working in Scotland. Childe argued that history seemed to reveal few patterns if we look at it close up or in minute detail; but if we stand back and view it from a very long-term perspective, patterns begin to reveal themselves. Childe thought of himself as a kind of Marxist and gave technological change the primary role as a prime mover of social evolution. He identified two great evolutionary transformations in human history and prehistory, what he called the Neolithic and Urban revolutions. The former was associated with the development of agriculture and animal husbandry, along with settled village life, whereas the latter was associated with the rise of civilization and the state and all their accoutrements. Childe was followed in the 1940s by two other anthropologists friendly to evolutionary theory, Leslie White (1943, 1945, 1949, 1959) and Julian Steward (1949, 1955). White was a maverick who had been taught by the Boasians but who rebelled against them when he actually began to read the works of the evolutionists, Morgan's in particular. By the 1930s, he had become a vigorous evolutionist, a position that he defended the rest of his life. Like Childe, White emphasized the causal role of technological change. He formulated his own evolutionary law, which stated that culture developed according to the amount of energy harnessed per capita per year. Julian Steward was more cautious than either Childe or White in reviving evolutionary thinking, insisting that for the most part evolution was multilinear rather than unilinear. Although an overall line of evolution could be traced, culture also developed along many different lines and it was these divergent lines that most interested Steward. Like Childe and White, Steward was a materialist, but he emphasized the role of ecological rather than technological factors as causal forces.

Along with Childe and Steward, White not only resurrected evolutionary theory, but played a major role in bringing about what I have called the second generation of the evolutionary revival (Sanderson, 1990). By the 1950s, and especially by the 1960s, evolutionism became not only respectable again in anthropology but actually a perspective of major significance. The most important evolutionists in this period were, in anthropology, Marvin Harris (1968, 1977, 1979), Robert Carneiro (1970, 1973), Marshall Sahlins (1958, 1960, 1963), and Elman Service (1960, 1962, 1975), all students of either White, Steward, or both. Harris, Carneiro, and Sahlins were all materialists who gave primacy to such factors as technology, demography, and ecology as prime movers, although Sahlins was eventually to abandon and reject both evolutionism and materialism altogether. In his *Cannibals and Kings: The Origins of Cultures* (1977), Harris, the most important evolutionist of the period, attempted to explain social evolution over the past 10,000 years by emphasizing a continuing cycle of environmental depletion and intensification. We all would have remained hunter–gatherers if such groups had been able to achieve zero population growth. But they could not do so, and the resulting population growth and population pressure depleted hunter–gatherer environments and necessitated the shift to agriculture. As population continued to grow (now even faster), new depletions of the environment had to be followed by various forms of the intensification of agricultural production in order to maintain the standard of living, until eventually we were brought to the doorstep of the Industrial Revolution. Societies thus have grown larger and more technologically sophisticated and their institutions have been remade again and again, as a result of the constant pressure of numbers.

In sociology, which by this time had become almost hermetically sealed off from anthropology, these ideas had little influence—indeed, were probably largely unknown—but evolutionism was revived there by such thinkers as Gerhard Lenski (1966, 1970) and Talcott Parsons (1966, 1971). Lenski was actually one of the few sociologists to be strongly influenced by anthropology, and the evolutionary model he formulated in his major work on stratification, *Power and Privilege* (1966), and in his textbook, *Human Societies* (1970), was very similar to White's. Lenski took over White's basic causal model—technological change leads to changes in social systems, which in turn produce changes in ideologies—but produced a more adequate typology of evolutionary stages, distinguishing between hunter–gatherers, simple horticulturalists, advanced horticulturalists, agrarian societies, and industrial societies. With Parsons the situation was quite different. Stung by the criticism that his structural–functional model was incapable of dealing with social change, Parsons responded by formulating an extremely ambitious evolutionary interpretation of the past 5000 years of human history. This theory was strikingly different from the evolutionary theories dominant in anthropology at this time, as well as from Lenski's. It was a highly idealist and by all appearances teleological type of evolutionism that retained the functionalist assumptions for which Parsons was so well known (Sanderson, 1990). In many ways it was highly Spencerian. Societies changed by a process of increasing differentiation, and as they became more complex and more functionally integrated their "adaptive capacity" was enhanced.

The second generation of the evolutionary revival had begun to burn out by the late 1970s in both anthropology and sociology, and today antievolutionism has become rampant again in both fields. Both disciplines seem to be beating a hasty retreat to a modern version of Boasian historicism, arguing that history reveals few if any directional patterns and that we must be extremely cautious about generalizations. In sociology, Weberians like Randall Collins (1986) and Michael Mann (1986) are suspicious of evolutionary thinking, as are most Weberians, but they are hardly alone. In anthropology the situation in some respects is even worse. But what is it exactly that modern critics of evolutionism object to in this form of social theory? Let me take up and respond to six different criticisms (for a much more detailed analysis of these criticisms, see Sanderson, 1990):

1. It frequently has been charged that evolutionary theories are illegitimate because they explain history and social change teleologically, thus conceiving history as nothing but the unfolding of predetermined patterns toward some ultimate goal. My own reading of evolutionary theories is that this criticism, while not entirely wrong, grossly overstates its case. The classical evolutionists of the second half of the 19th century often seemed to employ this kind of model of change, but I think it has largely disappeared since that time. Virtually all forms of evolutionism in the 20th century have abandoned such thinking in favor of looking at social evolution as the outcome of particular conditions operating at particular times in the lives of particular individuals. (The most striking exception may be Parsons's version of evolutionism.) In other words, evolutionists attempt to explain social evolution in terms of simple causal models.

2. It often is asserted that evolutionary theories have a strong endogenous bias, i.e., that they look at evolutionary events as occurring entirely within societies and fail to consider the role of various external influences, such as diffusion or political conquest. Leslie White took up this criticism in the 1940s with respect to the evolutionism of Morgan and Tylor and showed it to be manifestly false: both Morgan and Tylor, in fact, gave diffusion an important role in the evolutionary process itself. More recent versions of evolutionism, while perhaps more endogenist than exogenist, usually leave plenty of room for the role of external factors.

3. Critics of evolutionary theories such as Giddens (1981, 1984) and Irving Zeitlin (1973) have objected to them on the grounds that they employ a specious concept of adaptation. This objection seems to be rooted in the notion that the concept of adaptation is incurably functionalist, and since both thinkers object to functionalism, this makes evolutionary versions of functionalism highly suspect. It must be conceded that some versions of evolutionism do employ a functionalist notion of adaptation. This is most apparent in Parsonian evolutionism, whereby it is societies that do the adapting, and in which societies evolve toward continually higher degrees of "adaptive capacity." But the concept of adaptation can be reformulated so that it is individuals rather than societies that do the adapting, and so that notions of evolution as producing increasing adaptive capacity are cut away. In fact, there are current evolutionary theories that do precisely that.

4. Many critics also object to evolutionary theories for being inherently progressivist, i.e., for assuming that social evolution is tantamount to one or another form of improvement in the human condition. In fact, the vast majority of evolutionary theories *are* progressivist, some of them strongly so. The question then remains as to whether progressivism is justified by the actual historical record. My view is that this is an extremely complicated question that permits no easy or simple answer. History really is a mixed bag in which some things have gotten better and others gotten worse. The answer also depends on whether you are looking at social evolution over its entire course or simply at some phases of it (cf. Sanderson, 1995, 1999b, pp. 336–357). For example, it matters a great deal whether one is talking about social evolution before the rise of capitalism in the 16th century or social evolution since that time. But the real issue is whether evolutionary theories are inherently progressivist, i.e., whether or not they must be such. The answer to this question is no; there is no inherent association between evolution and progress. The best example of this is the work of the anthropologist Marvin Harris, who has formulated an evolutionary theory that, while viewing history as a mixed bag, often is antiprogressivist, and his antiprogressivism is supported by striking empirical data. I have developed my own version of evolutionism directly on the basis of Harris's model (see below).

5. Anthony Giddens (1981, 1984), one of the leading antievolutionists in sociology today, has made a special point of criticizing evolutionary theories for their lack of any concept of human agency, which for Giddens completely invalidates any social theory. In Giddens's view, evolutionary theories are hard forms of determinism that see individuals as just the playthings of blind social forces. My reading of evolutionism, or at least of the best current evolutionism, is quite different. I see the best current evolutionary theories as clearly implicating the individual and his or her choices in social evolution. For example, what was going on in the first great evolutionary transformation, the Neolithic Revolution, which brought agriculture and agricultural communities into the world? My answer, based on the work of many anthropologists and archaeologists, is that individuals were making choices about shifting toward a new mode of production in terms of their various interests: the standard of living they wanted to enjoy, the amount of time and effort they wanted to expend in making a living, and so on. The Neolithic Revolution was a human creation, just as later evolutionary transitions were. No one was reacting blindly to unseen social forces. Agency and structure were intertwined. Now, of course, the notion of agency I am employing here is one that sees individuals as making choices within the context of a set of constraints, and thus these choices are not truly voluntaristic, which may cause Giddens to object that this is no real concept of agency at all. But to my mind it is. It is just what Marx was talking about when he declared that men make history, but not just as they please.

6. Perhaps the biggest objection to evolutionary theories today, especially among sociologists, is that they impute far too much directionality to the flow of history. Weberian sociologists like Collins (1986) and Mann (1986), for example, see history in terms of particularity and the general absence of definable patterns. This is perhaps the most difficult of all the criticisms of evolutionism to answer. In his famous critique of evolutionism written over 30 years ago, Robert Nisbet (1969) claimed that the detection of historical pattern is not a property of history itself, but simply is in the eye of the beholder. To a large extent this is correct, but Nisbet refuses to play fairly. He claims that pattern is in the eye of the beholder, but that the absence of pattern apparently is not; it is just the way things are. But how can that be so? I would argue that both pattern in the form of directionality and historical uniqueness are fundamental parts of the historical record. Some scholars seem more attuned to one, others more attuned to the other, for reasons that are not very well understood. This seems to be like one of those Gestalt drawings where first you see a woman's face, then you see a candlestick rather than the face, and then you see the face again. My point is simply this: Why not play it both ways and recognize that pattern and unique event are there to be observed? Why deny the one in order to embrace the other? Evolutionists do not deny the existence or the importance of historical uniqueness and divergence, but simply try to discern directional patterns that may be, in all candor, a lot more difficult to pick out.[1]

---

[1]It is interesting to see how critics of evolutionism sometimes become, *malgré eux*, evolutionists of a sort. In his famous book, *The Sources of Social Power*, Michael Mann (1986) argues against evolutionary interpretations of history, at least with respect to the last 5000 years. However, one of the major points his book establishes is the steady concentration of power over time, or increasing "power capacity," as he prefers to call it, and he spends a lot of time talking about how this has come to be so. That looks very much like a type of evolutionary argument to me. Consider Anthony Giddens, an even more severe critic of evolutionism. Giddens's (1981, 1984) own alternative to evolutionism is a theory of what he calls increasing time-space distanciation. If this theory is not a theory of directional social change, and thus a version of evolutionism, I am at a loss to know how to describe it. The reason that Giddens thinks it is nonevolutionary (or possibly even antievolutionary) is because he has a very narrow and restricted conception of what an evolutionary theory actually is (cf. Sanderson, 1990).

A COMPREHENSIVE MODEL
OF SOCIAL EVOLUTION:
EVOLUTIONARY MATERIALISM

Recently I have developed my own comprehensive model of social evolution largely by formalizing and extending Harris's materialist model (Sanderson, 1994, 1995, 1999b). I call my model "evolutionary materialism." An abbreviated version of evolutionary materialism is presented below (for the full model, see Sanderson, 1994, 1995, 1999b, pp. 3–16):

1. World history displays social transformations and directional trends of sufficient generality such that typologies of social forms may be usefully constructed. Social evolutionists concentrate on general and repeatable patterns of social evolution, but at the same time take note of the unique and nonrecurrent. They also take note of social stasis, devolution, and extinction. A proper theory of social evolution must explain all of these phenomena.

2. Social evolution is not a teleological process somehow operating "behind the backs" or "over the heads" of individuals. Rather, it is the accumulation of the acts of individuals in concrete circumstances responding to their biological, psychological, and social needs and aims.

3. Social evolution occurs at all levels of social life, i.e., from simple dyads to world systems, but macrolevel evolution is simply the aggregation of microlevel evolution.

4. Increasing social differentiation is an important evolutionary process, but it is neither the only nor the most important evolutionary process. Much social evolution has little to do with differentiation.

5. Social evolution is both similar to and different from biological evolution. It is similar in that both forms of evolution involve adaptational processes and both are characterized by specific as well as general forms of change. However, social evolution differs from biological evolution in that (1) biological evolution is largely divergent, whereas social evolution is largely parallel and convergent; (2) biological evolution depends on random variations (genetic mutations), whereas social evolution results largely from variations that are deliberate and purposive; (3) social evolution is much more rapid; and (4) natural selection is not a sufficient explanation of social evolution. Because of these differences, social evolution must be studied as a process (or set of processes) it its (their) own right rather than simply by way of analogy with biological evolution

6. The principal causal factors in social evolution are the material conditions of human existence, i.e., demographic, ecological, technological, and economic forces. These factors operate probabilistically, i.e., in the long run and over the majority of cases; they have the significance they do because they relate to the most basic of human needs, i.e., those concerning production and reproduction.

7. Which of the material conditions (or which combination of conditions) is of greatest causal importance varies from one historical period or evolutionary stage to another. Thus, different types of societies in different historical epochs have different "evolutionary logics." There is no universal cause of social evolution.

8. Much of social evolution results from adaptational processes. *Adaptation* must be sharply distinguished from *adaptedness*. Adaptation is the process whereby individuals create social patterns intended to meet their needs and desires. Adaptedness involves the extent to which a social pattern arising as an adaptation actually meets

the needs and desires of individuals. All adaptations must originally lead to adaptedness, but in the long run the original adaptedness may be lost (or even turn into maladaptedness).

9. The extent to which adaptations lead to adaptedness can vary dramatically from one set of individuals or from one time period to another. The greater the level of differentiation of a society, the more this is likely to be the case. For example, what is adaptive for dominant groups may well be maladaptive for subordinate groups.

10. Adaptation is a process pertaining to individuals rather than to groups or societies. Only concrete individuals can be adaptational units because only they have needs and wants.

11. Adaptedness is not a process that necessarily increases or improves throughout social evolution. New social patterns are adaptations to local conditions only and lead to adaptedness only relative to those conditions. Social evolution is not necessarily progressive.

12. Individuals are egoistic beings who give priority to the satisfaction of their own needs and desires. They behave adaptively by attempting to maximize the net benefits of any given course of action. This egoistic behavior is the proper starting point for evolutionary analysis.

13. Individuals acting egoistically create social systems that are frequently constituted in ways those individuals never intended. Social evolution is driven by purposive human action, but it is often an unintended process.

14. The social systems that individuals create act as new sets of constraints acting on both themselves and their progeny. Social evolution is the result of the continuous interplay between individual agency and social structure.

15. Social evolution is the result of both endogenous and exogenous forces, i.e., forces operating within societies on the one hand and on the other hand forces operating within the framework of intersocietal networks or "world systems."

16. Social evolution varies in its pace, becoming more rapid at later stages. However, like biological evolution it is a "gradualist" process, i.e., one that occurs as the result of relatively small, step-by-step changes.

In formulating evolutionary materialism, I have attempted to eliminate the most objectionable features of evolutionary theories (more or less epitomized by the Parsonian functionalist evolutionary model). Evolutionary materialism reconceptualizes adaptation as the striving of individuals to reach their goals and satisfy their interests, and there is no suggestion that societies achieve higher levels of adaptive capacity as they evolve. The model is explicit in its claim that imputing progress to social evolution is always problematic; whether progress or regression is occurring is always an empirical question that must consider the historical time period and the particular dimension of social life. Most importantly, evolutionary materialism is explicitly antiteleological; evolution is simply the response of particular individuals located at particular points in time and space to the conditions that they face. Evolution over the longest periods of time is the sum total of these responses. A great deal of room is allowed for a variety of evolutionary responses, i.e., no assumption is being made that social evolution is a unitary, purely unilinear process. It involves not only parallel lines of change undergone by different societies, but divergent lines of change as well.

I have reviewed in great detail elsewhere the evidence supporting my evolutionary materialist model (Sanderson, 1995, 1999b). I find it impossible to see how the broad features of human history can be viewed in anything except evolutionary terms. There were three great social transformations in world history and prehistory: the Neolithic Revolution, beginning some 10,000 years ago; the evolution of civilization and the state, beginning some 5,000 years ago; and the transition to the modern capitalist world, beginning some 500 years ago. The Neolithic Revolution occurred in at least six (and probably eight) different parts of the world at remarkably similar times and the social outcomes were strikingly similar in each case. The rise of civilization and the state was another instance of remarkable parallel evolution on a world scale. The modern capitalist world can be dated to about AD 1500 and was to a large extent a European phenomenon, although Japan provides a strikingly parallel case (Sanderson, 1994), and in fact much of the world was evolving in a more capitalistic direction after about AD 1000 (McNeill, 1982; Modelski & Thompson, 1996). Nor should we overlook the long time period between about 3000 BC and AD 1500. All over the world during this time we find striking directional trends in the form of population growth, technological change, increasing commercialization, increases in the size and scope of political empires, and even ideological changes associated with the rise of Greek philosophy and the major world religions (Sanderson, 2000). These changes, which to me are highly deserving of the name evolutionary, were fundamental in setting the stage for the events after AD 1500 (Sanderson, 1994, 1995, 1999b). With the Industrial Revolution and the rise of industrial capitalism, we see remarkably parallel changes throughout the societies of Western Europe, North America, and Japan. For the past century or more these societies have been evolving very similar divisions of labor, forms of social stratification, political systems, systems of mass education, and have placed very similar emphases on large-scale scientific and technological development (Sanderson, 1995, 1999b).

FROM EVOLUTIONARY MATERIALISM
TO DARWINIAN CONFLICT THEORY

Evolutionary materialism as I have formulated it was about 20 years in the making. During that time I struggled to see how biological evolution—not the evolution of species per se, but rather human nature as conceived by sociobiology—fit together with it, or even could become part of it. In the last 5 years or so my thoughts have crystallized along these lines. As a result I have come to see that evolutionary materialism can be made part of a more general and abstract theory, one that I call Darwinian conflict theory (previously called synthetic materialism—see Sanderson, 1998, 1999b). Darwinian conflict theory is a synthesis of the economic and ecological materialism and conflict theory stemming from Marx and Marvin Harris and the biological materialism of Darwin. Evolutionary materialism now may be regarded as a subtype of Darwinian conflict theory especially intended for explaining evolutionary phenomena; Darwinian conflict theory itself is assumed to be applicable to explaining all social phenomena, not just sequences of social evolution.

The basic principle of sociobiology is that many features of human behavior have evolved as adaptations designed to promote an individual's reproductive success (Daly & Wilson, 1978; Alexander, 1979; Symons, 1979; Lopreato & Crippen, 1999). In a sense, sociobiology is the ultimate form of sociological materialism and conflict theory, and economic and ecological forms of materialism and conflict theory must be grounded in it. Sociobiology establishes essential "first principles" for social theory. Many sociologists will question this attempt to synthesize sociobiology with Marxian conflict theory and Harris's cultural materialism. Both Harris and the Marxists have been extremely critical of sociobiology (cf. Harris, 1979, pp. 119–140, 1999, pp. 99–109). But a connection is there. Darwinian natural selection is, after all, a conflict theory of nature and society that actually predicts many of the phenomena observed by Marx, but explains them differently and at a deeper level (cf. Barkow, 1989; Betzig, 1986). As for Harris, his most important theoretical principles are not only compatible with sociobiology, but make sense only in light of it (van den Berghe, 1991; Alexander, 1987). As Richard Alexander (1987) has pointed out, Harris explains many phenomena (as do the Marxists) in terms of the search for wealth and power, but he fails to see that this proximate goal is intimately linked to a deeper ultimate goal, that of achieving reproductive success. On many occasions Harris has spoken of the importance of the modes of production and reproduction in social life without appearing to realize the full implications of his assertion. Many of Harris's explanations are not so much wrong as simply incomplete.

In a forthcoming work, I (Sanderson, 2001) present the principles of Darwinian conflict theory in full, along with a detailed summary of evidence that I believe supports its principles. Here I will provide a somewhat truncated version of the theory.

Principles Concerning the Deep Wellsprings of Human Action

1. Like all other species, humans are organisms that have been built by millions of years of biological evolution, both in their anatomy/physiology and their behavioral predispositions. This means that theories of social life must take into consideration the basic features of human nature that are the products of human evolution.
2. The resources that humans struggle for, which allow them to survive and reproduce, are in short supply. This means that humans are caught up in a struggle for survival and reproduction with their fellow humans. This struggle is inevitable and unceasing.
3. In the struggle for survival and reproduction, humans give overwhelming priority to their own selfish interests and to those of their kin, especially their close kin.
4. Human social life is the complex product of this ceaseless struggle for survival and reproduction.
5. Humans have evolved strong behavioral predispositions that facilitate their success in the struggle for survival and reproduction. The most important of these predispositions are as follows:
   - Humans are highly sexed and are oriented mostly toward heterosexual sex. This predisposition has evolved because it is necessary for the promotion of humans' reproductive interests, i.e., their inclusive fitness. Males compete for females and for sex and females compete for males as resource providers.
   - Humans are highly predisposed to perform effective parental behavior and the female desire to nurture is stronger than the male desire. Effective parental behavior has evolved because it promotes reproductive success in a species like humans. The family as a social institution rests on a natural foundation.
   - Humans are naturally competitive and highly predisposed toward status competition. Status competition is ultimately oriented toward the securing of resources, which promotes reproductive success. Because of sexual selection, the predisposition toward status competition is greater in males than in females.
   - Because of the natural competition for resources, humans are economic animals. They are strongly oriented toward achieving economic satisfaction and well-being, an achievement that promotes reproductive success.
   - In their pursuit of resources and closely related activities, humans, like other species, have evolved to maximize efficiency. Other things being equal, they prefer to carry out activities by minimizing the amount of time and energy they devote to

these activities. A law of least effort governs human behavior, especially those forms of behavior that individuals find burdensome or at least not rewarding in and of themselves. The law of least effort places major limits on the behavior of humans everywhere; much behavior can be explained satisfactorily only by taking it into account.

6. None of the tendencies identified above are rigid. Rather, they are behavioral predispositions that move along certain lines rather than others but that interact in various ways with the total physical and sociocultural environment. The behavioral predispositions tend to win out in the long run, but they can be diminished or even negated by certain environmental arrangements. At the same time, other environments can amplify these tendencies, pushing them to increasingly higher levels.

7. From the above it follows that humans' most important interests and concerns are reproductive, economic, and political. Political life is primarily a struggle to acquire and defend economic resources and economic life is primarily a matter of using resources to promote reproductive success. However, at the experiential level, individuals have no conscious recognition that their behaviors are driven by these motives. People often experience economic and political behaviors as valuable in themselves and are often highly motivated to continue and elaborate such behaviors in their own right.

8. Many, probably most, of the features of human social life are the adaptive consequences of people struggling to satisfy their interests. The following provisos concerning the notion of adaptation are in effect (deleted here, but these are essentially the same as principles 8-11 of evolutionary materialism).

Principles Concerning Group Relations

1. Individuals pursuing their interests are the core of social life. The pursuit of interests leads to both highly cooperative and highly conflictive social arrangements.

2. Many cooperative forms of behavior exist at the level of social groups or entire societies. Cooperative social relations exist because they are the relations that will best promote each individual's selfish interests, not because they promote the well-being of the group or society as a whole. The selection of cooperative social forms occurs at the level of the individual, not the group or society.

3. Cooperative forms of interaction are found most extensively among individuals who share reproductive interests in common, i.e., among kin and especially close kin. This is the basis for the family as a fundamental social institution.

4. Outside of kinship and family life, cooperative relations are most likely to be found among individuals who depend heavily on each other for the satisfaction of their basic interests.

5. When conflictive behavior will more satisfactorily promote individual interests, cooperative relations will decline in favor of conflictive relations.

6. People are unequally endowed to compete in the social struggle (i.e., some are bigger, more intelligent, more aggressive or ambitious, more clever, more deceitful, etc.), and as a result social domination and subordination often appear as basic features of social life.

7. Members of dominant groups benefit disproportionately from their social position, and frequently they are able to make use of subordinate individuals to advance their

interests. Their use of these individuals frequently takes the form of economic exploitation or social exclusion.

8. Because they benefit from their situation, members of dominant groups are highly motivated to structure society so that their superior social position can be preserved or enhanced.

9. Social life therefore is disproportionately influenced by the interests and actions of the members of dominant groups.

10. The primary forms of social domination and subordination in human social life relate to gender, ethnicity, social class, and politics, although other forms of domination and subordination occur as well. These forms of domination and subordination are most basic because they stem directly from the deep wellsprings of human action.

Principles Concerning Systemic Relations within Societies

1. Human societies consist of four basic subunits:
   * Individuals themselves as biological organisms, which we may call the "biostructure."
   * The basic natural phenomena and social forms that are essential to human biological reproduction and economic production, i.e., the ecological, demographic, technological, and economic structures essential for survival and well-being; this we may call the "ecostructure."
   * The institutionalized patterns of behavior shared by individuals, especially the patterns of marriage, kinship, and family life; the egalitarian or inegalitarian structuring of the society along the lines of class, ethnicity, race, or gender; its mode of political life; and its mode or modes of socializing and educating the next generation; these patterns may be identified as the "structure."
   * The primary forms of mental life and feeling shared by the members of the society, i.e., its beliefs, values, preferences, and norms as these are expressed in such things as religion, art, literature, myth, legend, philosophy, art, music, and science; these we may refer to as the "superstructure."

2. These four components of societies are related such that the flow of causation is primarily from the biostructure to the ecostructure, then from the ecostructure to the structure, and finally from the structure to the superstructure; the flow may sometimes occur in the reverse manner, or in some other manner, but these causal dynamics occur much less frequently.

3. According to the logic of second principle, it is clear that the forces within the biostructure and the ecostructure are the principal causal forces in human social life; the biostructure structures social life both indirectly, i.e., through its action on the ecostructure (which then acts on the structure and superstructure) and through its direct effect on some of the elements of the structure and superstructure. It follows, then, that the ideas and feelings within the superstructure have the least causal impact on the patterns of social life.

4. The components of societies are related as they are because such causal dynamics flow from the deep wellsprings of human action. The biostructure and the ecostructure have a logical causal priority because they concern vital human needs and interests relating to production and reproduction.

5. Once structures and superstructures have been built by biostructures and ecostruc-

tures, they may come to acquire a certain autonomy. New needs and new interests may arise therefrom, and these new needs and interests, along with reproductive, economic, and political interests, may form part of the human preference and value structure characteristic of the members of a society.

Modes of Darwinian Conflict Explanation

1. As is obvious from the principles stated in the preceding section, Darwinian conflict explanations are materialist in nature; these explanations may take any or all of three forms: biomaterialist, ecomaterialist, or polimaterialist.
2. Biomaterialist explanations explain a social form by direct reference to a basic feature of the human biogram. That is to say, an explanation is biomaterialist if it links a social form to the human biogram without reference to any mediation of the causal relationship by some other social form. Example: Polygyny is a widespread feature of human societies because it springs from an innate desire of males for sexual variety and from the tendency of females to be attracted to resource-rich males.
3. Ecomaterialist explanations explain a social form by linking it directly to the influence of ecological, technological, demographic, or economic forces, and thus only indirectly to a feature of the human biogram. Example: Hunter–gatherer societies frequently display intensive sharing and cooperation because these are behaviors that promote individuals' interests within the configuration of hunter–gatherer techno-economic systems and natural environments.
4. Polimaterialist explanations explain a social form by linking it directly to the political interests or situations of the participants. Political interests or situations ordinarily spring from the participants' economic interests, which in turn are ultimately derived from the character of the human biogram. Examples: Democratic forms of government emerged earliest in those Western societies with the largest and most politically organized working classes. Third World revolutions occur most frequently in societies where the state is highly vulnerable to a revolutionary coalition.

In my forthcoming book (Sanderson, 2001), I have developed Darwinian conflict theory and the background to it at much greater length and have applied it to several of the dimensions of social life of primary concern to sociologists: reproductive behavior; human sexuality; sex and gender; marriage, kinship, and family patterns; economic behavior and economic systems; social hierarchies; and politics and war. Here space permits only a brief discussion of one of these substantive phenomena as understood by Darwinian conflict theory, social hierarchies.

DARWINIAN CONFLICT THEORY APPLIED AND ILLUSTRATED: THE CASE OF SOCIAL HIERARCHIES

Social hierarchies are a universal feature of the human condition, although their nature and extent vary greatly from one society to another. At one end of the continuum, marked by hunter–gatherer and simple horticultural societies, we find few or no differences in wealth or power between individuals and only differences of social esteem or rank. At the other end, marked by agrarian and industrial societies, we find highly stratified societies with major differences in wealth and power between relatively distinct social strata or classes (Lenski, 1966; Sanderson, 1999a). My argument is that social hierarchies have to be explained by all three modes of Darwinian conflict explanation, i.e., bio-, eco-, and polimaterialistically. Social hierarchies are biologically rooted but elaborated by a range of social and cultural conditions, especially those relating to economic and political organization.

A number of social scientists have stressed that hierarchies are biologically rooted. Somit and Peterson (1997) have noted that all human languages contain words referring to distinctions of honor and status. James Woodburn (1982) and Elizabeth Cashdan (1980) point out that, whereas there are a number of societies that have been able to maintain very high levels of social and economic equality, this equality seems to be constantly challenged. In order for it to be maintained, people must be ever vigilant and constantly enforce the tendency of individuals to seek dominance over others. Joseph Lopreato (1984) claims that humans have an innate desire for creature comforts, and Jerome Barkow (1989) argues that there is a natural human hunger for prestige that dominates much human behavior. Why should such innate human motivations exist? The answer is that competition for status and resources, not only in the human world but throughout the animal world as well, is essential for mating and thus the promotion of an individual's reproductive success. Hundreds of studies show that social rank and reproductive success are highly correlated among mammals, humans included (Ellis, 1995; Betzig, 1986). However, it should not be assumed in the human case that people seek status and resources only to reproduce. At the proximate level of human experience, humans seek status and privilege for their own sake and find achieving them inherently pleasurable (Green, 1994). Nonetheless, the human brain has evolved for status and resource seeking because throughout hominid evolution those individuals who displayed such behavior (especially those who displayed it most vigorously) left more offspring than those who did not.

Alice Rossi (1977, 1984) has argued that a pattern of human behavior can be assumed to have a biological basis if two or more of four conditions are met: the behavior is universal or at least widespread in human societies; the behavior is widely found among other animals, especially nonhuman primates and other mammals; the behavior is found in young children prior to major socialization influences or emerges at puberty; the behavior is closely associated with anatomical or physiological attributes. In the case of hierarchy formation, all four of Rossi's criteria are met. In terms of the second condition, Pierre van den Berghe (1978) is only one of many scholars who have pointed to the virtual universality of hierarchy among primates. Van den Berghe notes that some primate societies display only minimal hierarchies, but among terrestrial primates, from whom humans are descended, strongly hierarchical societies are the rule.

As already noted, hierarchies are universally found in human societies (Rossi's first condition), and in terms of Rossi's third condition dominance- and rank-oriented behavior appears to be characteristic of infants and young children, as shown by a variety of ethological studies (Bakeman & Brownlee, 1982; Missakian, 1980; Strayer & Trudel, 1984; Russon & Waite, 1991; Omark & Edelman, 1975; Weisfeld, Omark, & Cronin, 1980). Most of these studies have been of children in American society, but an important cross-cultural study has been carried out by Barbara Hold (1980). She looked at the behavior of German and Japanese kindergarten students and children of comparable age from the G/wi San, hunter–gatherers from southern Africa. The children established dominance hierarchies in all three societies. In all cases, there were children who sought the limelight. Those children who became the center of attention were much more likely to initiate activities than lower-status children and the lower-status children frequently imitated the behavior of the dominants. The G/wi children, however, were distinctive in two ways: They did not try to dominate or manipulate other children and their hierarchy seemed to be less rigid than those of the German and Japanese children. These are differences that likely spring from the more greatly enforced egalitarianism characteristic of G/wi society, an egalitarianism that stems from their economic situation.

There are also ample data to show that Rossi's fourth condition also is well met. Height is a widespread and possibly universal indicator of social status. In a well-known study (reported in Freedman, 1979), ostensible job recruiters were asked to choose between two applicants for a position, one of whom was much shorter than the other. The vast majority of the recruiters chose the taller applicant. In presidential elections throughout the history of the United States, the taller candidate nearly always has won the election. In Africa, shorter tribes have been dominated by taller tribes. In many horticultural societies, the highest-ranking man in a village is often called by a word that literally means "big man" (Hogbin, 1964; Harris, 1974, 1977; Brown & Chia-yun, 1993). In Russia and England higher-status individuals have tended to be much taller than those of lower status (Freedman, 1979). A common expression of submission throughout the world is bowing or crouching (van den Berghe, 1974). It is not likely that the correlation between height and social status can be explained simply by the better nutrition of high-status individuals, an explanation apt to be favored by most sociologists. Even in societies where there are no significant differences in nutritional intake, higher-status individuals tend to be taller. Furthermore, many studies show that most of the variance in human height results from genetic rather than social factors (Ellis, 1994), and thus it would appear that individuals acquire high status because they are tall rather than the reverse.

If human anatomy is related to status, is physiology as well? The answer appears to be yes. The best candidate for a neurochemical substrate of status-seeking behavior is the neurotransmitter serotonin. Research showing that serotonin and dominance-seeking are related in vervet monkeys (McGuire, 1982; McGuire, Raleigh, & Johnson, 1983) has been replicated for humans (Madsen, 1985, 1986, 1994). In one of the most recent studies, Douglas Madsen (1994) examined the relationship between blood serotonin levels, social rank, and aggressiveness in the context of a game-playing situation. He found that the serotonin levels of the participants who played the game nonagressively declined as their perceived social status rose. By contrast, the serotonin levels of the participants who played the game in an aggressive fashion increased as their perceived social status climbed. Moreover, serotonin is known to play a major role in the regulation of mood, with low brain serotonin levels being associated with depression. Many individuals who have been treated for depression with fluoxetine (trade name, Prozac) have not only seen their mood improve, but also have experienced personality changes in the direction of less shyness or reticence and more confidence and boldness (Kramer, 1993). Confidence or boldness are very likely correlated with status-seeking behavior.

How does this natural status- and resource-seeking behavior of humans get translated into the actual systems of inequality and stratification that we observe in human societies? It seems to be the case that where societies are small, simple in scale, technologically rudimentary, and incapable of producing economic surpluses, hierarchies are minimally developed because there is no real wealth that can be contested, and thus no basis for the formation of classes (Lenski, 1966). In these kinds of societies no one is in a position to compel others to work for them and create wealth. Moreover, where people live only or primarily by hunting and gathering, intensive cooperation and sharing seem to derive from a sensible strategy of variance reduction (Wiessner, 1982; Cashdan, 1985; Winterhalder, 1986a,b; cf. Kelly, 1995). Hunting success varies greatly from time to time and place to place, and thus by sharing with others when you have resources others will share their resources with you when you are in need. In fact, this may be the reason why egalitarianism is so strongly policed in most hunter–gatherer societies: It is in everyone's long-term self-interest. But when societies evolve in size and scale, become more technologically advanced, and become capable of producing large economic surpluses, competition and conflict begin to replace cooperation at the level of the wider society because now there are resources that individuals deem it useful to compete for (Lenski, 1966). Inequalities of esteem or status not only get magnified, but come to be accompanied by differences in wealth that develop a rigidly hereditary character. Also critical to this process seem to be changes in political relations that allow some people to be in a position to compel others to produce the economic surpluses that more advanced technology makes possible, i.e., surpluses are usually only potential rather than actual until someone can coerce someone else to work harder and longer to produce them (Sanderson, 1999a, 2001). As technological, economic, and political evolution continue, stratification systems become more elaborate and extreme.

A close examination of hunter–gatherer societies will show that they seldom extend hierarchies beyond the level of status differences, and often these differences are minimal. Yet we know that the tendency toward stratification is there because under certain conditions hunter–gatherer societies have become stratified, sometimes markedly. One of these conditions is the presence of an environment or economy sufficiently productive to allow people to accumulate and store foodstuffs. Alain Testart (1982) has divided hunter–gatherer societies into two types: those who store food and those who do not. Upon examining a sample of contemporary hunter–gatherers ($N = 40$), he found that the vast majority who stored food had genuine class stratification compared to only a small handful of the nonstorers. One of the most ethnographically famous of all societies is the Kwakiutl of the Northwest Coast region of North America. The Kwakiutl were hunter–gatherers who lived in one of the most bountiful societies on earth, with seemingly endless supplies of fish, berries, and other food substances. They were storing hunter–gatherers par excellence, and as a result had developed a highly stratified society led by ruling chiefs who ranted about their own prestige and displayed it by giving away resources to neighboring chiefs.

In simple horticultural societies the technological and economic base usually is not sufficient to allow for the creation of stratification, but because such groups depend much more on cultivation than on hunting or gathering the need for variance reduction is considerably lessened. Therefore, the desire of some individuals for high status and even deference from others can be given freer rein. These societies are often characterized by status-seeking men known in the local language as "big men" (Harris, 1974, 1997; Brown & Chia-yun, 1993). Big men are village leaders and economic organizers. They push people to work harder and produce more food so they can hold feasts and distribute this food widely, certainly to all the members of their own village but usually to some of the members of other villages as well. Big men are greatly admired and often given considerable praise and deference. One sees individuals like this among hunter–gatherers only seldom.

Compared to simple horticultural societies, advanced or intensive horticultural societies cultivate the land more intensively and more permanently, squeezing more out of it, and thus are more economically productive. These societies often are divided into social strata or classes that have a highly hereditary or self-perpetuating character. A common pattern is a division into three main social strata, consisting of chiefs, subchiefs, and commoners, respectively (Lenski, 1966). These strata are distinguished by differences in social status, political power, dress and ornamentation, consumption patterns, the extent of direct involvement in subsistence production, and styles of life. Many African horticultural societies in recent centuries have had stratification systems of this type, as have a number of Polynesian societies. Precontact Hawaii, for example, had a hierarchy consisting of a paramount chief and his family at the top, regional or village subchiefs in the middle, and a large class of commoners at the bottom (Sahlins, 1958). The paramount chief and subchiefs organized and administered economic production, which was carried out by the commoner class. The paramount chief was considered divine and many taboos existed concerning contact with him, such as prohibitions on touching anything he used.

Agrarian societies have been devoted to the cultivation of large fields with the use of the plow and traction animals. As a result, they have been far more economically productive than horticultural societies, with their gardens and hand tools. Agrarian stratification systems have been the most extreme of any found in human history and they contained numerous social classes (Lenski, 1966). However, the most important of these classes, those that related to the primary axis of economy activity, were the political–economic elite and the peasantry. Lenski (1966) has divided the elite class into two segments: the ruler and the governing class. The ruler was the official political leader of society, and he (or she) surrounded himself (or herself) with an administrative apparatus of government. What Lenski calls the governing class might be more accurately called the landlord class, since its members were the major owners of land. The political–economic elite as a whole usually consisted of no more than 1 or 2% of the population but controlled perhaps as much as half to two-thirds of the total wealth. Wealth was created by imposing rent and taxation on the peasantry, or perhaps by exploiting slave labor, and thus was skimmed off as an economic surplus. It also was created by plundering other societies and incorporating their land, peasants, slaves, and other economic resources and by receiving economic tribute from them (Snooks, 1997). Elites in most agrarian societies created an elaborate status culture that distinguished them sharply from the rest of society. For example, among the Chinese gentry emphasis was placed on the idle and highly cultivated man, and extremely long fingernails were worn in order to indicate a detachment from physical labor. The gentry developed a "high culture" of arts, cuisine, architecture, and furnishings (Annett & Collins, 1975).

As Lenski (1966) has noted, in the transition from agrarian to industrial societies after the Industrial Revolution of the last two centuries, there occurred something of a reversal in the relationship between the level of stratification and the degree of technological development. In many respects, modern industrial societies are less stratified than their agrarian predecessors. Agrarian elites controlled much more wealth than do elites in modern industrial societies, and industrial societies also have witnessed a much greater diffusion of income and wealth throughout the large mass of the population. However, industrial societies still exhibit very high levels of stratification. Kevin Phillips (1990) has reported levels of income inequality for several industrial societies expressed as the ratio of income of the top income quintile to the bottom quintile. The figures, which are for the late 1970s and early 1980s, are United States, 12:1; France, 9:1; Canada, 9:1; Britain, 8:1; West Germany, 5:1; Sweden, 5:1; the Netherlands, 5:1; and Japan, 4:1. The level of inequality in the distribution of wealth rather than income— total assets minus total liabilities—is much greater than this.

Another major change in the nature of stratification in the transition to industrial societies is the decline in status and deference cultures and the emergence of a widely accepted ideology of egalitarianism, especially in the United States (Annett & Collins, 1975). This decline, along with the greater economic equality of industrial societies, might be thought to undermine biologically oriented theories of society, such as Darwinian conflict theory. But this is not the case. Once again it is a matter of biological tendencies interacting with a wide array of social conditions. These changes in industrial stratification systems can be linked to the emergence of mass consumer capitalism and the rise of democratic forms of government (Annett & Collins, 1975; Lenski, 1966). Democratic governments, themselves the result largely of the rise of large and powerful working classes (Rueschemeyer, Stephens, & Stephens, 1992), allowed the many to combine against the few in order to restructure society more in their favor. The rise of mass consumer capitalism led to the disintegration of the old patterns of status and deference for several reasons, but especially because increases in the financial resources of the working and middle classes have allowed them to maintain a lifestyle closer to that of the upper classes (Annett & Collins, 1975). In the end, status distinctions have shrunk not because society dominates biology, but because of the very existence of natural status desires on the part of the large mass of the population. It has been through their status-seeking behavior that the status gap between themselves and the old elite has been reduced.

The industrial societies we have discussed have been industrial capitalist societies. So-called state socialist societies emerged earlier in the 20th century as an alternative form of society that would eventually become highly industrialized and attempt to equal or surpass the capitalist societies in the standard of living and the quality of life. The Soviet Union, of course, was the primary exemplar of this type of society. One of its official aims was to create a "classless" society and it attempted to accomplish this by means of socializing the means of production. This was rooted in the Marxian assertion that social classes could not exist if there was no private ownership of the means of production. However, despite these changes in the economic system a classless society did not emerge; what developed instead was a new type of class society. Broadly speaking, the most privileged social class was the so-called white-collar intelligentsia, which comprised some 20% of the population and consisted primarily of top Communist party bureaucrats, managers of state-owned companies, and learned professionals (Parkin, 1971). This class received higher incomes than the rest of society, but also had access to a range of special privileges unavailable to others. A small segment of this class, consisting of full-time, high-level party bureaucrats and known most often as the *apparatchiki* or *nomen-klatura*, constituted a ruling class virtually in the Marxist sense of the term. Milovan Djilas (1957) called this class a "new class" and claimed that it was the most powerful class known to history. These developments, occurring as they did in the face of an official policy of classlessness, strongly suggest that biological realities were at work under the surface and behind the scenes, realities that would make a mockery of public declarations.

It also is highly instructive to see what has happened in Russia since the collapse of Communism in the Soviet Union in 1991. Increasing privization has created far greater economic inequalities that probably will expand even further, perhaps much further, in the years to come. The old *nomenklatura* has been broken up, with the careers of many of its members virtually ruined, but other members of this ruling elite, often fortuitously, have found themselves in a position to benefit from the economic changes. They seem to be forming a new class of private entrepreneurs and have become extremely wealthy, often displaying their wealth in the most garish and ostentatious ways (Zaslavsky, 1995). These changes of the last decade are also strong evidence for a human primal urge for status seeking and resource accumulation. Although this urge was always present in the old Soviet Union, privatization of the economy has given it much freer rein and the results are apparent to all.

CONCLUSION

Let me conclude this chapter by connecting the discussion of social hierarchies back to the earlier discussion of long-term social evolution. One of the most striking features of this evolution is the existence of parallel trends all over the world. What we see are remarkably similar patterns of increasing inequality and stratification everywhere as societies have grown in size and scale and changed their technological foundations, their modes of economic ownership, and their types of political organization. This growth of increasing inequality and stratification surely must be explained in ecomaterialist and polimaterialist terms. But we cannot stop there, because there is no major exception to the trend of increasing hierarchy, at least among preindustrial societies. In no part of the world do we find societies changing their technological and economic foundations and maintaining old patterns of hierarchy, let alone regressing to some earlier form of hierarchy. It is true, of course, that with the transition to modern industrial societies the extreme differences in status, lifestyle, and standard of living characteristic of agrarian societies were reduced, but industrial societies have remained strikingly hierarchical nonetheless. All this can only mean that long-term social evolution, like many other features of social life, has been subject to strong biological constraints. If this were not the case, then we should see much more variation than we do in the historical and prehistorical record of the world's societies. We have now come full circle. Social evolution, though quite different as a process from biological evolution, has been underlain by biological evolution in the sense of being constrained by the biological nature of humans as a species. The quest to understand in much greater detail how this nature exerts its impact on social life and the major changes therein seems to me one of the most fruitful lines of investigation that sociologists should be pursuing in the years ahead.

REFERENCES

Alexander, R. D. (1979). *Darwinism and human affairs.* Seattle: University of Washington Press.

Alexander, R. D. (1987). *The biology of moral systems.* Hawthorne, NY: Aldine de Gruyter.

Annett, J., & Collins, R. (1975). A short history of deference and demeanor. In R. Collins, *Conflict sociology: Toward an explanatory science* (pp. 161–224). New York: Academic Press.

Bakeman, R., & Brownlee, J. R. (1982). Social rules governing object conflicts in toddlers and preschoolers. In K. H. Rubin & H. S. Ross (Eds.), *Peer relationships and social skills in childhood* (pp. 99–111). New York: Springer-Verlag.

Barkow, J. H. (1989). *Darwin, sex, and status.* Toronto: University of Toronto Press.

Betzig, L. L. (1986). *Despotism and differential reproduction.* Hawthorne, NY: Aldine de Gruyter.

Boas, F. (1932). The aims of anthropological research. *Science, 76,* 605–613.

Boas, F. (1940). *Race, language, and culture.* New York: Macmillan.

Brown, D. E., & Chia-yun, Y. (1993). "Big man" in universalistic perspective. Manuscript, University of California at Santa Barbara.

Carneiro, R. L. (1970). A theory of the origin of the state. *Science, 169,* 733–738.

Carneiro, R. L. (1973). The four faces of evolution. In J. J. Honigmann (Ed.), *Handbook of social and cultural anthropology* (pp. 89–110). Chicago: Rand McNally.

Childe, V. G. (1936). *Man makes himself.* London: Watts & Co.

Childe, V. G. (1951). *Social evolution.* London: Watts & Co.

Childe, V. G. (1954). *What happened in history.* Harmondsworth, England: Penguin Books. (Original publication 1942)

Cashdan, E. A. (1980). Egalitarianism among hunters and gatherers. *American Anthropologist, 82,* 116–120.

Cashdan, E. A. (1985). Coping with risk: Reciprocity among the Basarwa of northern Botswana. *Man, 20,* 454–474.

Collins, R. (1986). *Weberian sociological theory.* New York: Cambridge University Press.

Daly, M., & Wilson, M. (1978). *Sex, evolution and behavior.* North Scituate, MA: Duxbury Press.

Durkheim, E. (1933). *The division of labor in society.* George Simpson (Trans.). Glencoe, IL: Free Press. (Originally published 1893)

Djilas, M. (1957). *The new class.* New York: Praeger.

Ellis, L. (1994). The high and the mighty among man and beast: How universal is the relationship between height (or body size) and social status? In L. Ellis (Ed.), *Social stratification and socioeconomic inequality,* Volume 2 (pp. 93–111). Westport, CT: Praeger.

Ellis, L. (1995). Dominance and reproductive success among nonhuman animals: A cross-species comparison. *Ethology and Sociobiology, 16,* 257–333.

Freedman, D. G. (1979). *Human sociobiology*. New York: Free Press.

Giddens, A. (1981). A *contemporary critique of historical materialism*. Berkeley: University of California Press.

Giddens, A. (1984). *The constitution of society: Outline of the theory of structuration*. Berkeley: University of California Press.

Green, P. A. (1994). Toward a biocultural theory of class circulation: An application of Joseph Lopeato's sociology. *Revue Européenne des Sciences Sociales, 32*, 195–214.

Harris, M. (1968). *The rise of anthropological theory*. New York: Crowell.

Harris, M. (1974). *Cows, pigs, wars, and witches: The riddles of culture*. New York: Random House.

Harris, M. (1977). *Cannibals and kings: The origins of cultures*. New York: Random House.

Harris, M. (1979). *Cultural materialism: The struggle for a science of culture*. New York: Random House.

Harris, M. (1999). *Theories of culture in postmodern times*. Walnut Creek, CA: AltaMira Press.

Hobhouse, L. T., Wheeler, G. C., & Ginsburg, M. (1965). *The material culture and social institutions of the simpler peoples*. London: Routledge & Kegan Paul. (Original publication 1915)

Hogbin, H. I. (1964). *A Guadalcanal society: The Kaoka speakers*. New York: Holt, Rinehart, and Winston.

Hold, B. C. L. (1980). Attention structure and behavior in G/wi San children. *Ethology and Sociobiology, 1*, 275–290.

Kelly, R. L. (1995). *The foraging spectrum: Diversity in hunter–gatherer lifeways*. Washington, DC: Smithsonian Institution Press.

Kramer, P. D. (1993). *Listening to Prozac*. New York: Penguin.

Lenski, G. E. (1966). *Power and privilege: A theory of social stratification*. New York: McGraw-Hill.

Lenski, G. E. (1970). *Human societies: An introduction to macro-level sociology*. New York: McGraw-Hill.

Lopreato, J. (1984). *Human nature and biocultural evolution*. Winchester, MA: Allen and Unwin.

Lopreato, J., & Crippen, T. (1999). *Crisis in sociology: The need for Darwin*. New Brunswick, NJ: Transaction Publishers.

McGuire, M. T. (1982). Social dominance relationships in male vervet monkeys. *International Political Science Review, 3*, 11–32.

McGuire, M. T., Raleigh, M., & Johnson, C. (1983). Social dominance in adult male vervet monkeys II: Behavior-biochemical relationships. *Social Science Information, 22*, 311–328.

McNeill, W. H. (1982). *The pursuit of power*. Chicago: University of Chicago Press.

Madsen, D. (1985). A biochemical property relating to power seeking in humans. *American Political Science Review, 79*, 448–457.

Madsen, D. (1986). Power seekers are different: Further biochemical evidence. *American Political Science Review, 80*, 261–269.

Madsen, D. (1994). Serotonin and social rank among human males. In R. D. Masters & M. T. McGuire (Eds.), *The neurotransmitter revolution* (pp. 146–158). Carbondale: Southern Illinois University Press.

Mann, M. (1986). *The sources of social power*. Volume 1: *A history of power from the beginning to AD 1760*. Cambridge, England: Cambridge University Press.

Missakian, E. (1980). Gender differences in agonistic behavior and dominance relations of Synanon communally reared children. In D. R. Omark, F. F. Strayer, & D. G. Freedman (Eds.), *Dominance relations: An ethological view of human conflict and social interaction* (pp. 397–413). New York: Garland.

Modelski, G., & Thompson, W. R. (1996). *Leading sectors and world powers: The coevolution of global economics and politics*. Columbia: University of South Carolina Press.

Morgan, L. H. (1974). *Ancient society, or researches in the lines of human progress from savagery through barbarism to civilization*. Gloucester, MA: Peter Smith. (Original publication 1877)

Nisbet, R. A. (1969). *Social change and history: Aspects of the Western theory of development*. New York: Oxford University Press.

Omark, D. R., & Edelman, M. S. (1975). A comparison of status hierarchies in young children: An ethological approach. *Social Science Information, 14*, 87–107.

Parkin, F. (1971). *Class inequality and political order: Social stratification in capitalist and communist societies*. New York: Holt, Rinehart, and Winston.

Parsons, T. (1966). *Societies: Evolutionary and comparative perspectives*. Englewood Cliffs, NJ: Prentice-Hall.

Parsons, T. (1971). *The system of modern societies*. Englewood Cliffs, NJ: Prentice-Hall.

Peel, J. D. Y. (1971). *Herbert Spencer: The evolution of a sociologist*. New York: Basic Books.

Phillips, K. (1990). *The politics of rich and poor*. New York: Random House.

Rossi, A. S. (1977). A biosocial perspective on parenting. *Daedalus, 106*, 1–31.

Rossi, A. S. (1984). Gender and parenthood. *American Sociological Review, 49*, 1–19.

Rueschemeyer, D., Stephens, E. H., & Stephens, J. D., (1992). *Capitalist development and democracy*. Chicago: University of Chicago Press.

Russon, A. E., & Waite, B. E. (1991). Patterns of dominance and imitation in an infant peer group. *Ethology and sociobiology, 13*, 55–73.

Sahlins, M. D. (1958). *Social stratification in Polynesia.* Seattle: University of Washington Press.

Sahlins, M. D. (1960). Evolution: specific and general. In M. D. Sahlins & E. R. Service (Eds.), *Evolution and culture* (pp. 12–44). Ann Arbor: University of Michigan Press.

Sahlins, M. D. (1963). Poor man, rich man, big man, chief: Political types in Melanesia and Polynesia. *Comparative Studies in Society and History, 5*, 285–303.

Sanderson, S. K. (1990). *Social evolutionism: A critical history.* Oxford, England: Blackwell.

Sanderson, S. K. (1991). The evolution of societies and world-systems. In Christopher Chase-Dunn & Thomas D. Hall (Eds.), *Core/periphery relations in precapitalist worlds* (pp. 167–192). Boulder, CO: Westview Press.

Sanderson, S. K. (1994). The transition from feudalism to capitalism: The theoretical significance of the Japanese case. *Review, 17*, 15–55.

Sanderson, S. K. (1995). *Social transformations: A general theory of historical development.* Oxford, England: Blackwell.

Sanderson, S. K. (1998). Synthetic materialism: An integrated theory of human society. Paper presented at the annual meetings of the American Sociological Association, San Francisco, August 21–25, 1998.

Sanderson, S. K. (1999a). *Macrosociology: An introduction to human societies,* 4th edition. New York: Longman.

Sanderson, S. K. (1999b). *Social transformations: A general theory of historical development,* Updated edition. Lanham, MD: Rowman & Littlefield.

Sanderson, S. K. (2000). World systems and social change in agrarian societies, 3000 BC–AD 1500. In R. A. Denemark, J. Friedman, B. K. Gills, & G. Modelski (Eds.), *World system history: The social science of long-term change* (pp. 185–197). New York: Routledge.

Sanderson, S. K. (2001). *The evolution of human sociality: A Darwinian conflict perspective.* Lanham, MD: Rowman & Littlefield.

Service, E. R. (1960). The law of evolutionary potential. In M. D. Sahlins & E. R. Service (Eds.), *Evolution and culture* (pp. 93–122). Ann Arbor: University of Michigan Press.

Service, E. R. (1962). *Primitive social organization: An evolutionary perspective.* New York: Random House.

Service, E. R. (1975). *Origins of the state and civilization.* New York: Norton.

Snooks, G. D. (1997). *The ephemeral civilization: Exploding the myth of social evolution.* London: Routledge.

Somit, A., & Peterson, S. A. (1997). *Darwinism, dominance, and democracy: The biological bases of authoritarianism.* Westport, CT: Praeger.

Spencer, H. (1972). *Herbert Spencer on social evolution,* J. D. Y. Peel (Ed.). Chicago: University of Chicago Press.

Steward, J. H. (1949). Cultural causality and law: A trial formulation of the development of early civilizations. *American Anthropologist, 51*, 1–27.

Steward, J. H. (1955). *Theory of culture change.* Urbana: University of Illinois Press.

Sumner, W. G., & Keller, A. G. (1927). *The science of society,* 4 volumes. New Haven, CT: Yale University Press.

Strayer, F. F., & Trudel, M. (1984). Developmental changes in the nature and function of social dominance among preschool children. *Ethology and Sociobiology, 5*, 279–295.

Symons, D. (1979). *The evolution of human sexuality.* New York: Oxford University Press.

Testart, A. (1982). The significance of food storage among hunter–gatherers: Residence patterns, population densities, and social inequalities. *Current Anthropology, 23*, 523–537.

Turner, J. H. (1985). *Herbert Spencer: A renewed appreciation.* Beverly Hills, CA: Sage.

Tylor, E. B. (1871). *Primitive culture: Researches into the development of mythology, philosophy, religion, language, art, and custom,* 2 volumes. London: John Murray.

van den Berghe, P. L. (1974). Bringing beasts back in: Toward a biosocial theory of aggression. *American Sociological Review, 39*, 777–788.

van den Berghe, P. L. (1978). *Man in society: A biosocial view,* 2nd edition. New York: Elsevier.

van den Berghe, P. L. (1991). Sociology. In M. Maxwell (Ed.), *The sociobiological imagination* (pp. 269–282). Albany: State University of New York Press.

Weisfeld, G. E., Omark, D. R., & Cronin, C. L. (1980). A longitudinal and cross-sectional study of dominance in boys. In D. R. Omark, F. F. Strayer, & D. G. Freedman (Eds.), *Dominance relations: An ethological view of human conflict and social interaction* (pp. 205–216). New York: Garland.

White, L. A. (1943). Energy and the evolution of culture. *American Anthropologist, 45*, 335–356.

White, L. A. (1945). History, evolutionism, and functionalism: Three types of interpretation of culture. *Southwestern Journal of Anthropology, 1*, 221–248.

White, L. A. (1949). *The science of culture.* New York: Grove Press.

White, L. A. (1959). *The evolution of culture.* New York: McGraw-Hill.

Wiessner, P. (1982). Risk, reciprocity, and social influences on !Kung San economics. In E. Leacock & R. Lee (Eds.), *Politics and history in band societies* (pp. 61–84). New York: Cambridge University Press.

Winterhalder, B. (1986a). Diet choice, risk, and food sharing in a stochastic environment. *Journal of Anthropological Archaeology, 5,* 369–392.

Winterhalder, B. (1986b). Optimal foraging: Simulation studies of diet choice in a stochastic environment. *Journal of Ethnobiology, 6,* 205–223.

Woodburn, J. (1982). Egalitarian societies. *Man, 27,* 431–451.

Zaslavsky, V. (1995). From redistribution to marketization: Social and attitudinal change in post-Soviet Russia. In G. W. Lapidus (Ed.), *The new Russia: Troubled transformation* (pp. 115–142). Boulder, CO: Westview Press.

Zeitlin, I. (1973). *Rethinking sociology: A critique of contemporary theory.* Englewood Cliffs, NJ: Prentice-Hall.

PART VI

THEORIZING ON POWER, CONFLICT, AND CHANGE

CHAPTER 22

Sociological Marxism

Michael Burawoy and Erik Olin Wright

Discussions of Marxism as a social theory typically adopt one of four basic stances:

1. *Propagating Marxism.* Marxism is a comprehensive worldview for understanding the social world. It provides the theoretical weapons needed to attack the mystifications of capitalism and the vision needed to mobilize the masses for struggle. The central task for Marxist intellectuals is to articulate the revolutionary core of Marxism in such a way that its influence increases, particularly within oppressed classes. Often this has taken the form of dogmatic enunciations of Marxism as a doctrine, but making Marxism an effective ideology need not imply rigid, dogmatic beliefs. The central issue is that Marxism must be made accessible and internalized as a subjectively salient belief system.

2. *Burying Marxism.* Marxism is a doctrine with virtually no ideas of relevance for serious social inquiry. The historical durability of Marxism is entirely due to its role as a mobilizing ideology linked to political parties, social movements, and states, not the scientific credibility of its arguments. The demise of Marxist-inspired political regimes may at last signal the long overdue death of this antiquated and often pernicious doctrine. It is time to bury the corpse.

3. *Using Marxism.* Marxism is a source of interesting and suggestive ideas, many of which remain useful for contemporary social scientific analysis. Some Marxist ideas may have been deeply flawed from the beginning and others may have lost relevance for understanding contemporary societies, but still the Marxist tradition contains many useful insights and arguments, and these should be preserved as an enduring legacy. Much of what goes under the rubric of "Marxist Sociology" has this character—selectively using particular concepts and themes in the Marxist tradition to understand specific empirical problems. But one does not have to be a "Marxist" to use Marxism in this way.

4. *Building Marxism.* Marxism is an analytically powerful tradition of social theory of vital importance for scientifically understanding the dilemmas and possibilities of social change and social reproduction in contemporary society. Particularly if one wants to change the world in egalitarian and emancipatory ways, Marxism is indispensable. This does not mean, however, that every element within Marxism as it currently exists is sustainable. If

MICHAEL BURAWOY • Department of Sociology, University of California, Berkeley, California 94720. ERIK OLIN WRIGHT • Department of Sociology, University of Wisconsin, Madison, Wisconsin 53706.

Handbook of Sociological Theory, edited by Jonathan H. Turner. Kluwer Academic / Plenum Publishers, New York, 2002.

Marxism aspires to be a social scientific theory, it must be continually subjected to challenge and transformation. Building Marxism thus also means reconstructing Marxism. Marxism is not a doctrine, a definitively established body of truths. But neither is Marxism simply a disjointed catalogue of interesting insights. If the goal is to enhance our ability to understand the world in order to change it, building Marxism is a pivotal task.[1]

The first two of these stances both treat Marxism primarily as an ideology: a system of beliefs to which people adhere and which provides interpretations of the world and motivations for action. Both are in tension with the aspiration of Marxism to be a social science: the first stance because it is concerned with Marxism's power to persuade rather than its validity per se and the second because it views Marxism as either unequivocally false or morally and politically pernicious.

Sociology, at least as it is currently practiced in the United States, has mainly engaged Marxism in the third of these modes. There are, of course, instances of calls to bury Marxism by sociologists, and certainly there were periods in American sociology in which Marxist ideas were almost completely marginalized.[2] In some times and places, building Marxism has been an important intellectual current within sociology. But mostly, American sociology has simply accepted Marxism as one of the sources of the "sociological imagination." Courses in sociological theory typically include respectful discussions of Marx, Weber, and Durkheim as "founding fathers" of central currents in the history of sociology. Durkheim is identified with norms and problems of social integration, Weber with rationalization and the cultural sociology of meaningful action, and Marx with class and conflict. Studies of politics and the state routinely borrow from the Marxist tradition a concern with business influence, economic constraints on state action, and the class bases of political parties and political mobilization. Discussions of the world economy typically talk about the globalization of capital, the power of large multinational corporation, and the ways international markets impinge on local conditions, long-standing Marxist themes going back to Marx. Discussions of work frequently talk about the labor process, the problem of extracting effort from workers, and the impact of technology on skills. Discussions of social change talk about contradictions. Perhaps above all, discussions of social conflict are influenced by the core Marxist idea that conflicts are generated by structurally based social cleavages, not simply subjective identities. Often the Marxist pedigree of these themes and ideas gets completely lost. Instead of using Marxism as Marxism, these ideas are simply absorbed into the diffuse mainstream of sociology. But using

---

[1]The term "Marxism" is in some ways a liability of the project of "building" for it suggests that the theoretical structure in question is primarily defined by the writings of its foundational theorists. Marxism often degenerates into Marxology. This is the equivalent of calling evolutionary biology "Darwinism," a term used primarily by Creationists in an effort to suggest that evolutionary theory is an ideology rather than a scientific theory. Engels proposed the term "scientific socialism" for the theoretical tradition launched by Marx, and Marx himself once declared "je ne suis pas un Marxist." Nevertheless, since the tradition that we are discussing is called "Marxism," we will continue to use this label here.

[2]Until the era of the Cold War, American sociology largely ignored Marx and Marxism. This was as true of the Chicago School, which saw Marxism as propaganda unrelated to social science, as it was of structural functionalism, which saw Marx as a utilitarian whose ideas had little relevance beyond the 19th century. The Cold War brought forth Marxism as calumniated other. Political sociology, in particular, defined itself in opposition to Marxism, understood as communist ideology. Ironically, this attempt to bury Marxism gave it space and recognition—a recognition that was taken up in the 1960s by those who saw the reigning paradigms as out of touch with reality. This rejuvenated Marxism turned Marx's early writings against the American order but also against communist totalitarianism. Today there are renewed attempts to bury Marxism by those who argue that class is no longer relevant for the analysis of contemporary societies. In this chapter we set ourselves against this perspective, arguing the opposite, namely that class continues to be at the core of the dynamics and reproduction of capitalism.

Marxism also can be a self-conscious practice of deploying these ideas in ways that affirm the continuing relevance of the Marxist tradition for sociological scholarship.

Building Marxism is the most ambitious stance toward the Marxist tradition, going beyond simply deploying Marxist categories explicitly or implicitly to tackle a range of sociological problems. Here the goal is to contribute to the development of Marxism as a coherent theoretical structure by understanding its shortcomings and reconstructing its arguments. In practice, this engagement with Marxism involves strong normative commitments, not simply beliefs in the scientific virtues of Marxist ideas. Without a serious normative commitment to the radical critique of capitalist institutions and to the political vision of an egalitarian, emancipatory alternative to capitalism there would be little incentive to struggle with the demanding intellectual task of building and reconstructing Marxism as a coherent theoretical structure.[3] Building Marxism as an intellectual project thus is deeply connected with the political project of challenging capitalism as a social order.[4]

In this chapter we primarily will elaborate the basic contours of this fourth stance toward Marxism. We begin in the next section by outlining the central components of the traditional Marxist theory of capitalism, the point of departure for building what we will call sociological Marxism.

SETTING THE STAGE: THE CENTRAL COMPONENTS OF MARXIST THEORY

While there is little consensus, either among Marxists themselves or among non-Marxist commentators on Marxism, over what constitutes the essential elements of Marxism, most commentators would agree that whatever else it is, the centerpiece of Marxism is a theory of capitalism as a particular kind of class society.[5] This is the aspect of Marxist theory that is most intimately linked to the Marxist political project of radically challenging capitalism. It is on this aspect of Marxism that we will focus.

The central arguments of the theory of capitalism within the Marxist tradition fall under three theoretical clusters: (1) A theory of the trajectory and destiny of capitalism, (2) a theory of the contradictory reproduction of capitalism, and (3) a emancipatory theory of socialism and communism as the alternative to capitalism. While each of these theoretical clusters is interconnected with the others, they nevertheless have considerable autonomy, and at different times in the history of Marxism one or another of these has been given greater prominence.

In Marx's own work, the most elaborated and systematic theoretical arguments were in

---

[3]One can, of course, endorse the Marxist political and normative project of the egalitarian critique of capitalism and still reject the theoretical project of building Marxism on the ground that the flaws within the Marxist tradition make this task hopeless.

[4]Building Marxism does not imply a commitment to the view that Marxism should aspire to be a grand theory of everything, or even that it alone can provide a complete theoretical foundation for emancipatory social change. The broad project of developing theoretical resources for emancipatory social change also requires building feminism and building critical cultural theory among other things. Building Marxism and building feminism are complementary, not inherently competing, tasks.

[5]Because there are many Marxisms, it often makes sense to speak of "the Marxist tradition" rather than "Marxism" as such. Alvin Gouldner (1980, 1985), for example, argues that while there are two Marxisms (critical and scientific), they form a "speech community," a terrain of debate, a culture of critical discourse, rather than a unified theory. Perry Anderson (1976) also argues that there are two Marxisms—classical and Western—but that the latter is a diversion from the true path of the former, reflecting the defeat of revolutionary movements. But he too constitutes an internal dialogue which gives an internal coherence to Marxism as a whole.

462 MICHAEL BURAWOY AND ERIK OLIN WRIGHT

the first of these three clusters. The central achievement of Marx's work in political economy was an account of the "laws of motion" of capitalism and how these propelled capitalist development along a trajectory toward a particular kind of destination. Marx devoted very little energy to elaborating a real theory of the destination itself—socialism—either in terms of the normative principles that socialism should embody or the problem of what institutional designs would render socialism feasible and sustainable. Instead, the normative dimension of Marx's writing primarily took the form of the critique of capitalism as a social order characterized by alienation, exploitation, fetishism, mystification, degradation, immiseration, the anarchy of the market, and so on. The transcendence of capitalism by socialism and eventually communism was then posited as the simple negation of these features, an implicit unelaborated theoretical utopia that eliminated all the moral deficits of capitalism: a society without alienation, without exploitation, without fetishism, and so on. While there are brief places in Marx's work in which a more positive discussion of socialism is engaged—some passages in the *Critique of the Gotha Program* broach issues of normative principles and the writings on the Paris commune are evocative of some possible design principles for socialist institutions—nowhere are these issues given sustained, theoretical consideration.

Marx gave more attention to the problem of the contradictory social reproduction of capitalism as it moved along its historical trajectory of development. There are important, suggestive discussions of the role of the state and ideology in reproducing class relations, most notably perhaps in the bold programmatic statement about base and superstructure in *The Preface to a Contribution to a Critique of Political Economy*,[6] and a few places where the contradictory quality of this reproduction is touched on.[7] More significantly, Marx elaborates significant elements of a theory of social reproduction within capitalist production itself in his analyses of the labor process and commodity fetishism.[8] Still, taken as a whole, the theory of the contradictory reproduction of capitalist relations remains extremely underdeveloped within Marx's own work: there is no real theory of the state, only fragments of a theory of ideology, and only the beginnings of a theory of the reproduction of class relations within production itself.

Twentieth-century Western Marxism, confronting the enduring failure of revolutionary movements in the West, became much more focused on the problem of the social reproduction of capitalism. Gramsci is the most significant early contributor to these discussions, particularly in his writings on hegemony and the problem of the material basis for consent.[9] The theme of social reproduction was further developed, in especially functionalist ways, by

[6]G. A. Cohen (1978, 1988) presents the most analytically rigorous exploration of the implications of Marx's brief statement in the preface for a general theory of the reproduction of capitalism.
[7]In *The German Ideology*, Marx and Engels (1970) refer to the ruling ideas in every epoch being the ideas of the ruling class. In *The Communist Manifesto* they refer to the executive of the modern state as the committee for managing the common affairs of the whole bourgeoisie. These are the more functionalist understandings of state and ideology, whereas in *The Eighteenth Brumaire* (Marx, 1963) and *The Class Struggles in France* (Marx, 1964) Marx is at pains to show the ways in which the expansion of democracy challenges capitalism, how universal suffrage unchains class struggle.
[8]See, *Capital*, Volume I (Marx, 1967a), especially parts I and VII.
[9]There is an enormous literature inspired by Antonio Gramsci's (1971) prison writings, not only by his signature concept of hegemony, but also by his understanding of state and civil society, his theory of ideology and intellectuals, of common sense and good sense, his reconceptualization of class struggle as war of position and war of movement, his development of the now influential notion of passive revolution, his treatment of political parties and trade unions, as well as his comparative sociology of Fascism, Fordism and Soviet communism. He provides the foundations, if in a relatively fragmentary form, of a sociological Marxism.

Frankfurt School critical theorists in the middle third of the century.[10] But it really was only in the Marxist revival of the 1960s and 1970s that the problem of the contradictory reproduction of capitalism became the widespread subject of theoretical and empirical debate among Marxists. The problem of the normative theory of socialism also grew in importance, first in the context of the fierce political debates among Marxists over the character of the Soviet Union and later in the less impassioned attempts at diagnosing the causes of stagnation and eventual collapse of the attempts at building state socialism. Still, as in Marx's own work, much of the normative dimension of Western Marxism, particularly in the work of the Frankfurt school, took the form of the negative critique of capitalism rather than the positive elaboration of an emancipatory alternative. In the context of the collapse of Communist regimes and the apparent triumph of capitalism, the development of a serious positive normative theory of socialism has become even more pressing.

In what follows we will first lay out the central theses in the traditional Marxist theory of the destiny of capitalism and examine why we feel these theses are unsatisfactory. We then turn to the theory of the contradictory reproduction of capitalism which we will argue constitutes the foundation of sociological Marxism. Finally we will discuss the problem of developing a theory of Marxism's emancipatory project.

THE CLASSICAL MARXIST THEORY
OF THE TRAJECTORY AND DESTINY
OF CAPITALISM

The traditional Marxist theory of the trajectory and destiny of capitalism was grounded in three fundamental theses:

1. *The long-term nonsustainability of capitalism thesis.* In the long-run capitalism is an unsustainable social order. Capitalism does not have an indefinite future; its internal dynamics ("laws of motion") will eventually destroy the conditions of its own reproducibility. This means that capitalism is not merely characterized by episodes of crisis and decay, but that these episodes have an inherent tendency to intensify over time in ways which make the survival of capitalism increasingly problematic.

2. *The intensification of anticapitalist class struggle thesis.* As the sustainability of capitalism declines (thesis 1), the class forces arrayed against capitalism increase in numbers and capacity to challenge capitalism.[11] Eventually the social forces arrayed against capitalism will be sufficiently strong and capitalism itself sufficiently weak that capitalism can be over-

---

[10]While not as sociologically rich as Gramsci, classics such as Georg Lukacs's (1971) *History and Class Consciousness,* Horkheimer and Adorno's (1972), *Dialectic of Enlightenment,* and Marcuse's *One Dimensional Man* (1964) and *Eros and Civilization* (1955) all pointed to the ubiquity of capitalist domination. They stressed the way the mass media, consumer culture lured the popular classes into acceptance of capitalism, generating psychological processes that obliterated all forms of resistance. Their prognoses were either profoundly pessimistic or sort out imaginary utopias.

[11]The locus classicus of the argument for the intensification of class struggle is *The Communist Manifesto* where Marx and Engels (1998) show how capitalism sows the seeds of its own destruction by creating its own grave digger—the proletariat whose struggles develop from scattered attacks on capital, to the development of trade unions and from there the constitution of national political parties to represent the working class against the state. In "Socialism: Utopian and Scientific," Engels (1978) writes of the coincidence of deepening economic crises and the intensification of class struggle until finally the "proletariat seizes state power."

thrown.[12] Two additional claims are often attached to this thesis: (1) that the destruction of capitalism must be ruptural rather than incremental (i.e., that the destruction takes place in a temporally condensed historical episode), and (2) that the rupture requires violent overthrow of the state rather than democratic capture. Neither of these claims, however, are inherent in the intensification of anticapitalist class struggle thesis itself and should be regarded as historically contextual propositions rather than fundamental theses of Marxism.

3. *The natural transition to socialism thesis.* Given the ultimate nonsustainability of capitalism (thesis 1), and the interests and capacities of the social actors arrayed against capitalism, in the aftermath of the destruction of capitalism through intensified class struggle (thesis 2), socialism is its most likely successor (or in an even stronger version of the thesis: its inevitable successor). Partially this is because capitalism itself creates some of the institutional groundwork for socialism: concentration of ownership through trusts, massive increases in productivity liberating people from the necessity of long hours of work, increasing interdependence among workers, the removal of the capitalist as an active entrepreneur in production through the joint-stock company, and so on. But mainly socialism emerges in the aftermath of capitalism's demise because the working class would gain tremendously from socialism and it has the power to create it. There are occasional places where classical Marxism entertained some other fate for capitalism than socialism, as in Luxembourg's famous formula of "socialism or barbarism," but nowhere is a nonsocialist postcapitalist future given any theoretical precision.

These theses were meant to embody real predictions based on an understanding of the causal mechanisms at work in the social world, not simply expressions of wishful thinking or philosophical speculation. The predictions are derived from an account of two causal processes that are seen as imparting the fundamental logic to the dynamics of capitalist economic systems: exploitation of workers by capitalists, and competition among capitalists in various kinds of markets. These two processes generate the causal streams that provide the fundamental explanations for the theses about the destiny of capitalism.

Exploitation of workers and competition among capitalists are the fundamental causes of the most salient properties of capitalist development: the steady increase in its productive capacity, the expansion of its global scope, the increasing concentration and centralization of capitalist production. This development dynamic, however, contains internal contradictions, contradictions that mean that capitalism has inherent tendencies to generate periodic, intensifying economic crises. Traditional Marxist crisis theory is complex and there are many different kinds of causal processes in play in explaining the disruptions of capitalist accumulation. The two most important of these for the eventual fate of capitalism in classical Marxism are the long term tendency for the aggregate rate of profit to fall and, particularly as argued by Engels, the tendency for capital accumulation to lead to ever more serious crises of overproduction.[13]

---

[12]The intensification of class struggle thesis does not imply that revolution is only possible at the point when capitalism becomes completely moribund and unsustainable. Since the relevant anticapitalist forces come to know that capitalism is moving toward unsustainability, they have the possibility of organizing to overthrow before it reaches the point of complete internal collapse. Unsustainability is still important in this revolutionary transformation for two reasons: first, the apparatuses that defend capitalism are weakened by the intensifying crises of capitalism even before complete unsustainability has been reached, and second, the knowledge of the eventual demise of capitalism plays a significant role in mobilizing people against capitalism.

[13]In Volume III of *Capital* (Part III) Marx (1976) argues that competition drives capitalists to innovate, especially through the introduction of new technology, which simultaneously brings down the rate of profit and generates crises of overproduction. In "Socialism: Utopian and Scientific" Engels (1978) argues that the pursuit of profit

The argument that capitalist crisis tendencies have an inherent long-term tendency to intensify means that as capitalism becomes more and more developed, more and more global, it ultimately becomes harder and harder to maintain the aggregate rate of profit or to find new markets—the necessary condition for continued capital accumulation and innovation—and this, in turn, means that capitalism becomes less and less sustainable, eventually reaching limits for its own material reproduction. To use another classical Marxist formulation: the relations of production become fetters on the development of the forces of production.[14] The first causal stream generated by the two interconnected generative processes of capitalism, then, leads to the strong prediction of thesis 1: in the long-run capitalism will become an unreproducible economic system. It cannot last forever.

The long-term fragility and problematic reproducibility of capitalism, however, does not in and of itself say much about what kind of social order would emerge in its place. Here the important issue is the effects of capitalism on class structure and class formation: capitalism not only develops the productive forces and expands into a worldwide system of capitalist markets and competition, it also creates social agents—the working class—with a specific set of interests opposed to capitalism and a set of capacities that enable them to challenge capitalism. Workers have interests opposed to capitalism for a variety of reasons. Most fundamentally, they are exploited in capitalism. But capitalism also renders the lives of workers insecure, subject to unemployment, work degradation, and other hazards. Workers' material interests thus would be advanced if the social relations of production could be transformed from relations based on private ownership of the means of production—capitalism—to relations based on democratic, egalitarian control over the organization of production, or what came to be called "socialism."[15]

Having a class with anticapitalist interests, however, still is not enough for the natural transition to socialism thesis. That class must also have a capacity to challenge capitalism. Capitalism as an economic system may be increasingly crisis-ridden and irrational, but capitalist societies also contain an elaborate array of institutions to defend and reproduce capitalist class relations (see the discussion of social reproduction below). These institutions develop in tandem with capitalism in response to class struggles and other threats to capitalist reproduc-

---

through innovation leads to ever-deepening crises of overproduction, which leads to the concentration of capital, and eventually the state itself becomes a capitalist—capitalism is brought to a head and once brought to a head it topples over.

[14]This formulation is part of the larger, more abstract theory of historical trajectory in historical materialism. In historical materialism the bold thesis is advanced that it is a property of every class-based system of production relations that (1) within each type of class relations there is a limit to the possible development of the forces of production, (2) that the forces of production will eventually develop to reach those limits, (3) when those limits are reached—when the relations fetter the further development of the forces—the relations will become increasingly unstable, and (4) eventually this instability will lead to a transformation of the relations of production, enabling the forces of production to develop further. It is this "dialectic" between forces and relations of production that provides the basic dynamics for the theory of historical trajectory and gives it a specific kind of directionality. For a systematic exploration of the logic of this theoretical structure, see Cohen (1978).

[15]Like many Marxist terms, the term "socialism" has many competing meanings. Often socialism is identified with a specific institutional design, such as centralized state ownership of the means of production and central planning. State ownership, however, is not an inherent feature of the concept understood as the "socializing" private ownership. The pivot is rendering social relations of production egalitarian and democratic. Many possible institutional forms could accomplish this. Capitalism as well comes in many different institutional forms: family firms, joint ventures, large multidivision corporations, worker codetermination firms, state-regulated firms, and so forth. Socialism—understood as an egalitarian, democratic control over production—can also be envisioned in many institutional varieties: centralized state ownership, centralized ownership with decentralized control, market socialism, and workers co-ops.

tion. While classical Marxism did not systematically theorize these flanking institutions, nevertheless Marx recognized that the transformation of capitalism depends on the increasing capacity of opponents of capitalism to mobilize effective challenges against capitalism.

In classical Marxist theory, the dynamics of capitalist development were thought to enhance working-class capacity for such challenge for a variety of reasons: the working class becomes more numerous; it becomes concentrated in ever-larger units of production; communications and interdependencies among workers improve; internal differentiation among workers declines under the pressures of deskilling and other homogenizing forces; the organizational competence increases. Many of these developments in capitalism not only increase the capacity of workers to struggle, but also create some of the economic conditions for socialism itself: the concentration of capitalist ownership and the emergence of the joint-stock corporation make the person of the capitalist increasingly superfluous; the greater interdependency among workers make production evermore social in character. As Marxists were fond of saying, the conditions for socialism are created "in the womb of capitalism." Eventually the working class becomes a revolutionary class both in the sense of having revolutionary socialist objectives and of having the capacity to make a revolution against capitalism (thesis 2) and to create the institutions of socialism (thesis 3).

Taking these arguments together generates the fundamental predictions of classical Marxism about the destiny of capitalism: capitalism has an inherent tendency to create the conditions both for its own destruction and for the triumph of socialism as an alternative. As the economic reproduction of capitalism becomes more and more problematic and precarious, agents with an interest in transforming capitalism increasingly have the capacity to effectively struggle against capitalism. In such a context there was little need to speculate on the institutional design of this alternative. Given the interests and capacities of the relevant social actors, socialism would be invented through a process of pragmatic, creative, collective experimentalism when it became an "historical necessity."

This is an elegant social theory, enormously attractive to people committed to the moral and political agenda of an egalitarian, democratic, socialist future. Since struggles for social change are always arduous affairs, particularly if one aspires to fundamental transformations of social structures, having the confidence that the "forces of history" are on one's side and that eventually the system against which one is fighting will be unsustainable, provides enormous encouragement.[16] The belief in the truth of this classical theory arguably is one of the things that helped sustain communist struggles in the face of such overwhelming obstacles.

Unfortunately, there is little evidence for the scientific validity of the theory of the destiny of capitalism as formulated. While Marx's theory of capitalist dynamics and development contains many penetrating insights about the inner workings of capitalism in the period of unregulated early industrial capitalism with its sharp polarizations and chaotic crisis tendencies, the actual trajectory of capitalism in the 20th century does not support the pivotal claims of the theory.

First, the nonsustainability of capitalism thesis: While capitalism does contain inherent crisis tendencies, there is no empirical evidence that these crises have any long-term tendency for intensification. Furthermore, there are serious flaws in the principle theoretical arguments advanced by Marx that capitalism has inherent limits to its own sustainability. In particular,

---

[16]It might seem that the determinism of this prediction of the demise of capitalism would lead people to ask, "Why should I engage in struggle since capitalism is doomed by the laws of history whether or not I do so?" In fact, since one of the main impediments to people's participation in struggle is the fear that sacrifices will be pointless, having confidence in the ultimate victory of one's cause can help motivate people for action, making that victory more likely.

the most systematic argument for his predictions, the theory of the tendency of the falling rate of profit, is unsatisfactory. Marx believed on the basis of the labor theory of value that aggregate profits are generated exclusively by the labor of workers currently using the means of production (what he called "living labor"). Since capital intensity (or what Marx called "the organic composition of capital") tends to increase with the development of capitalism, and thus the costs of capital relative to labor increases over time, the profit-generating capacity of capitalism declines as a proportion of total costs and thus the rate of profit will tend to decline. This theoretical argument has been shown repeatedly to be unsatisfactory, both because of flaws in the labor theory of value on which it is based and because of specific flaws in its argument about the impact of capital intensity on the rate of profit. The other main idea within classical Marxism for a tendency for crises to intensify in capitalism—the problem of overproduction—also does not yield any inherent intensification of crisis once it is recognized that the state and other innovative institutions are capable of generating increased demand to absorb excess production. The first fundamental thesis of the classical Marxist theory of the trajectory of capitalism—the thesis that there is an inherent tendency for capitalism to eventually become unreproducible—therefore cannot be sustained.[17]

Second, the intensification of anticapitalist class struggles thesis and the natural socialist transition thesis: The theory of class formation and class struggle that underpins the arguments that socialism is the future of capitalism is also problematic. There is little evidence to support the classical Marxist view of an overriding tendency for structurally determined classes to become organized as collective actors around class interests, and for the articulated class interests of workers so organized to become increasingly anticapitalist. Instead of becoming simplified and more polarized, class structures in capitalist societies are becoming more complex and differentiated. Even within the working class, instead of material conditions of life becoming more precarious and more homogeneous, heterogeneity has increased on many dimensions in many parts of the world. Furthermore, even apart from the failures in its predictions about how the trajectory of capitalist development would affect the class structure, as we shall see below, classical Marxism did not anticipate that the various institutions of social reproduction that develop within capitalism would be so robust, flexible, and effective.[18] As a result, there appears to be much more contingency and indeterminacy in the relationship between class structure, class formation and class struggle, even in the long run, then was countenanced in the classical theory.

If capitalism has no inherent tendency to become progressively weakened and eventually unsustainable and if the class forces arrayed against capitalism have no inherent tendency to become collectively stronger and more able to challenge capitalism, then there are no solid grounds for predicting, even in the long run, that socialism is the probable future of capitalism. This does not, of course, imply the converse—that socialism is not a possible future for capi-

---

[17]This does not, of course, imply that evidence exists for the converse counterthesis that capitalism is indefinitely reproducible. It also does no imply that there are no other possible arguments for the long-term nonsustainability of capitalism. Arguments of environmental limits to the sustainability of capitalism may well have persuasive force, and these environmental limits may be reached by virtue of the internal dynamics of capitalism: because of the tendency of capitalist firms to ignore negative externalities and for capitalist markets to encourage very short time horizons capitalism may destroy its ecological conditions of existence. All that is being claimed here is that there are no convincing theoretical arguments of the distinctively Marxist variety of the nonsustainability thesis.

[18]The theory of the "superstructure" was quite underdeveloped in classical Marxism, which generally regarded superstructures as rigid, largely repressive apparatuses, incapable of flexible adaptation and transformation in response to changing demands of social reproduction. The very use of an architectural metaphor to capture the mechanisms of social reproduction suggest this rigidity. The centerpiece of sociological Marxism is understanding how such institutions function, adapt, and change.

talism, or even that it is an improbable future—but simply that the traditional theory provides no firm basis for any predictions about the likelihood of this outcome.

If one rejects the historical destiny theses of the traditional theory, one might well ask: What's left of Marxism? Perhaps all that is left are some scattered, if still valuable, insights of a Marxist legacy, as suggested by the "Using Marxism" stance. We will argue to the contrary that there remains a conceptual core to Marxism that can provide the foundation on which Marxism can be (re)built. There are two basic directions this reconstruction can take. First, one can try to reconstruct the theory of the dynamics of capitalist development, freeing it from its traditional commitment to uncovering an immanent trajectory toward an ultimate destination. Recent work by Giovanni Arrighi (1994) would be an example of this kind of reconstruction. Alternatively, one can turn to the second cluster of traditional Marxist theses, the theory of the contradictory reproduction of capitalist class relations, and try to build a sociological Marxism on this basis. This is the strategy we will adopt here. This involves identifying salient causal processes within capitalist society that have broad ramifications for the nature of institutions in such societies and the prospects for emancipatory social change, but it will not identify an inherent dynamic process that propels such societies toward a specific emancipatory destination. The problem of challenging capitalism will remain a central anchor to this proposed sociological Marxism, but socialism will no longer be viewed as an historical necessity but as the potential outcome of strategy, constraint and contingency.[19] Let us now turn to the core concepts that constitute the foundation of this reconstructed sociological Marxism.

SOCIOLOGICAL MARXISM:
CONCEPTUAL FOUNDATIONS

Complex scientific theories often can be captured by simple conceptual phrases that define the foundational core of the theory. Thus, for example, the core of the Darwinian theory of biological evolution is encapsulated by the concept "natural selection" and the proposition "biological evolution is broadly explained by natural selection through reproductive fitness." Of course, modern evolutionary biology contains a vast array of additional concepts and complex propositions. No one would reduce the theory to this simple core. Ideas such as genetic drift, for example, do not exactly fit this proposition. Nevertheless, this does constitute a kind of bottom line that unifies the theoretical framework. Or take another example: neoclassical economics. The simple concept at the core of neoclassical economics is the idea of "rational utility maximization under constraints" and the accompanying proposition would be something like "market outcomes are broadly explained by interactions among constrained rational utility maximizers." Again, the actual elaboration of the theory contains much more than this. There is a recognition, for example, that information imperfections can interfere with the rationality assumption in all sorts of ways. Nevertheless, the neoclassical paradigm in economics has at its core these elements.

What, then, is the core of sociological Marxism? We believe that the core concept of sociological Marxism is "class as exploitation" and the accompanying proposition is "the dilemmas and dynamics of the reproduction and transformation of capitalist institutions are broadly explained by class." As in the case of Darwinian biology and neoclassical economics,

[19]Ultimately, of course, these two strands of theoretical development need to be joined, since a fully reconstructed Marxism would systematically link an account of capitalist dynamics to an account of its contradictory reproduction. Here, however, we pursue the more limited aim of giving some precision to the conceptual foundations of sociological Marxism.

this does not imply that the reproduction and transformation of capitalism can be reduced to class. There are many complications and many situations in which other causal processes play an important role. Rather the claim is that class as exploitation identifies the bottom line of sociological Marxism that provides coherence to its explanations.

In the next section we will elaborate the implications of this claim for the theory of the contradictory reproduction of capitalist social relations. In this section we will explicate more systematically the idea of class as exploitation itself. The discussion will involve clarifying six conceptual issues: (1) the concept of social relations of production; (2) the complementary concept of social relations in production; (3) the idea of class as a specific form of relations of production; (4) the problem of the forms of variation of class relations; (5) exploitation and domination as central processes within class relations; and (6) the conceptual shift from an abstract analysis class relations to a concrete analysis of class structure.

Relations of Production

Any system of production requires the deployment of a range of assets or resources or factors of production: tools, machines, land, raw materials, labor power, skills, information, and so forth. This deployment can be described in technical terms as a production function: so many inputs of different kinds are combined in a specific process to produce an output of a specific kind. The deployment also can be described in social relational terms: the individual actors that participate in production have different kinds of rights and powers over the use of the inputs and over the results of their use. Rights and powers over resources, of course, are attributes of social relations, not descriptions of the relationship of people to things as such: to have rights and powers with respect to land defines one's social relationship to other people with respect to the use of the land and the appropriation of the fruits of using the land productively. The sum total of these rights and powers constitute the "social relations of production."

Relations in Production

The social relations of production—the relations within which rights and powers over productive assets are distributed—do not exhaust the social relations that take place within systems of production. There are also social relations of cooperation, coordination, and control among actors within the labor process. Whenever there is a division of labor, different actors need to cooperate with each other and their activities need to be coordinated in order to get things done. The social relations within which such cooperative–coordinating interactions take place can be called social relations in production.[20]

[20]In effect we are replacing the couple "forces of production–relations of production" with the couple "relations in production–relations of production." There are several implications. First, we remove the teleology associated with the expansion of the forces of production that conventionally drive history forward from one mode of production to another. We now open up both the internal dynamics of modes of production and the transition from one mode to another. Second, by underlining the relational moment of the "forces of production" we pose the question not only of innovation of new techniques but of the reproduction of the relations of work, which thereby offers a more nuanced understanding of domination. Third, it compels the recognition of political and ideological apparatuses of production (responsible for guaranteeing the reproduction of the relations in production) and thus brings politics into production—the politics of production (see Burawoy, 1985).

The social relations in production are not autonomous from the relations of production. In particular, the relations of production directly shape one particularly salient aspect of the social relations in production: workplace domination—the relations within which one set of actors controls the activities of another set of actors. When a manager tells a worker what to do this action both involves exercising delegated rights and powers over resources derived from the relations of production (the manger can fire the worker for noncompliance) and providing coordinating information so that cooperation within a division of labor can take place. Domination can be organized in various ways: in strict, authoritarian hierarchies where workers activity is closely monitored and noncompliance swiftly sanctioned; in more relaxed systems of control where considerable individual autonomy is allowed; through the creation of collectively supervised teams with high levels of internal mutual monitoring; in governance structures where workers have a variety of rights as "industrial citizens." In all these cases, the relations in production constitute specific ways in which the social relations of production are translated into concrete power relations within organization of work.

Class Relations as a Form of Relations of Production

When the rights and powers of people over productive resources are unequally distributed—when some people have greater rights/powers with respect to specific kinds of productive resources than do others—these relations can be described as class relations.[21] The classic contrast in capitalist societies is between owners of means of production and owners of labor power, since "owning" is a description of rights and powers with respect to a resource deployed in production.

Let us be quite precise here: The rights and powers in question are not defined with respect to the ownership or control of things in general, but only of resources or assets insofar as they are deployed in production. A capitalist is not someone who owns machines, but someone who owns machines, deploys those machines in a production process, hires owners of labor power to use them, and appropriates the profits from the use of those machines. A collector of machines is not, by virtue of owning those machines, a capitalist. To count as a class relation it therefore is not sufficient that there be unequal rights and powers over the sheer physical use of a resource. There also must be unequal rights and powers over the appropriation of the results of that use. In general this implies appropriating income generated by the deployment of the resource in question.

Variations in Class Relations

Different kinds of class relations are defined by the kinds of rights and powers that are embodied in the relations of production. For example, in some systems of production people are allowed to own the labor power of other people. When the rights accompanying such ownership are absolute, the class relation is called "slavery." When the rights and powers over labor power are jointly owned by the laborer and someone else, the class relation is called "feudalism."[22] In capitalist societies, in contrast, such absolute or shared ownership of other people is prohibited.

[21]"Powers" refer to the effective capacity of people to control the use of means of production, including the capacity to appropriate the results of that use; "rights" refer to the legal enforcement by third parties of those powers.
[22]This may not seem to be the standard definition of feudalism as a class structure. Typically feudalism is defined as

Class, Exploitation, and Domination

What makes class analysis distinctively Marxist is the account of specific mechanisms embedded in class relations. Here the pivotal concept is exploitation, although domination plays an important role as well.

Exploitation is a complex and challenging concept. It is meant to designate a particular form of interdependence of the material interests of people, namely a situation which satisfies three criteria:[23]

1. *The inverse interdependent welfare principle.* The material welfare of exploiters causally depends on the material deprivations of the exploited.
2. *The exclusion principle.* This inverse interdependence of welfare of exploiters and exploited depends on the exclusion of the exploited from access to certain productive resources.
3. *The appropriation principle.* Exclusion generates material advantage to exploiters because it enables them to appropriate the labor effort of the exploited.

Exploitation thus is a diagnosis of the process through which the inequalities in incomes are generated by inequalities in rights and powers over productive resources: the inequalities occur, in part at least, through the ways in which exploiters, by virtue of their exclusionary rights and powers over resources, are able to appropriate surplus generated by the effort of the exploited. If the first two of these principles are present but not the third, economic oppression may exist but not exploitation. The crucial difference is that in nonexploitative economic oppression, the privileged social category does not itself need the excluded category. While their welfare does depend on the exclusion, there is no ongoing interdependence of their activities. In the case of exploitation, the exploiters actively need the exploited: exploiters depend on the effort of the exploited for their own welfare.[24]

This deep interdependence makes exploitation a particularly explosive form of social relation for two reasons: First, exploitation constitutes a social relation that simultaneously pits the interests of one group against another and requires their ongoing interactions; and second, it confers on the disadvantaged group a real form of power with which to challenge the interests of exploiters. This is an important point. Exploitation depends on the appropriation of labor effort. Because human beings are conscious agents, not robots, they always retain

---

a class system within which extraeconomic coercion is used to force serfs to perform labor for lords, either in the form of direct labor dues or in the form of rents. Here I am treating "direct economic coercion" as an expression of a property right of the lord in the labor power of the serf. This is reflected in the fact that the serf is not free to leave the land of the lord. This is equivalent to the claim that the flight of a serf from the land is a form of theft—stealing labor power partially owned by the lord. For a discussion of this conceptualization of feudalism, see Wright (1985, Chapter 3).

[23]For a more extensive discussion of these three principles, see Wright (1997, pp. 9–19).

[24]The fate of indigenous people in North America and South Africa reflects this contrast between nonexploitative economic oppression and exploitation. In both cases indigenous people were excluded from access to the pivotal resource of their economies: land. And in both cases, by virtue of this exclusion the material welfare of European settlers was advanced at the expense of the indigenous people. The crucial difference between the two settings was that in North America, Native Americans were generally not exploited, whereas in Southern Africa indigenous people were. The result was that genocide was an effective, if morally abhorrent, strategy for dealing with Native American resistance: the white settlers did not need the Native Americans and thus they could simply be eliminated. Such a strategy is not possible where indigenous people are exploited. Mona Younis (2000) has used this distinction to explain the different trajectories of the Palestinian Liberation Organization and the African National Congress. Because Palestinians were largely excluded from the Israeli economy, they did not have the leverage power of the large African working class in South Africa.

significant levels of real control over their expenditure of effort. The extraction of effort within exploitative relations thus to a greater or lesser extent always is problematic and precarious, requiring active institutional devices for its reproduction. Such devices can become quite costly to exploiters in the form of the costs of supervision, surveillance, sanctions, and so forth. The ability to impose such costs constitutes a form of power among the exploited.

Domination is a simpler idea. It identifies one dimension of the interdependence of the activities within production itself—what we have called the relations in production—rather than simply the interdependence of material interests generated by those activities. Here the issue is that by virtue of the relations into which people enter as a result of their rights and powers they have over productive resources some people are in a position to control the activities of others, to direct them, to boss them, to monitor their activities, and to hire and fire them. Since the powers embodied in domination are directly derived from the social relations of production, domination also can be understood as an aspect of class relations. Class relations therefore imply not simply that some people have the fruits of their laboring effort appropriated by others, but that significant portions of their lives are controlled by others, directed by people outside of their own control. In traditional Marxist terms this latter condition is called alienation.[25]

From Abstract Class Relations to Concrete Class Structures

The concept of class relations so far discussed is defined at a very high level of abstraction. The relations are perfectly polarized between exploiters and exploited, dominators and dominated. Actual class structures within which people live and work are much more complex than this in all sorts of ways:

- Varieties of different forms of exploitation coexist: actual class structures can combine aspects of capitalist relations, feudal relations, and even various forms of postcapitalist relations of production.
- Exploitation and domination do not perfectly correspond to each other: managers, for example, may dominate workers and yet themselves be exploited by capitalists.
- The rights and powers associated with the relations of production are not perfectly polarized: all sorts of state regulations may deprive capitalists of having unfettered rights and powers over the use of their means of production; institutional arrangements like works committees or worker co-determination may give workers certain kinds of rights and powers over the organization of production.
- Individuals can have multiple, possible inconsistent, relations to the system of production: ordinary workers in capitalist production can also own stocks, either in their own firms (e.g., employee stock ownership programs) or more broadly; families may contain people occupying different locations within the relations of production, thus indirectly linking each person to the class structure in multiple ways.

---

[25]The idea of alienation is also often used to describe a situation in which one's life is controlled by impersonal forces, such as "the market," rather than simply by the agency of other people. In this broader sense, one can say that while they are not exploited, capitalists, not just workers, are alienated in capitalism: their lives, like those of workers, may be controlled by "alien" forces: the market, competitive pressures, inflation, and so forth. The idea of alienation also is not exclusively linked to class relations: one can have one's life controlled by forces outside of one's control not simply because of how one is situated within the relations of production, but also because of one's relationship to the state, because of gender relations, and so forth.

While we will not discuss the various strategies for conceptualizing these complications here, one of the important issues in sociological Marxism is elaborating a repertoire of class structure concepts at different levels of abstraction in order to coherently understand this complexity.[26]

SOCIOLOGICAL MARXISM:
THE THEORY OF THE CONTRADICTORY
REPRODUCTION OF CLASS RELATIONS

Let us recall what we have said so far. We began by claiming that it is worthwhile to build Marxism, rather than simply use it (let alone bury it), because of its importance for understanding the obstacles and possibilities for egalitarian, emancipatory social change. This normative, political agenda provides the central motivation for worrying about these issues. We then reviewed classical Marxist theory, focusing on the part of the theory of history that tries to explain the trajectory of capitalism toward its ultimate demise and transcendence by socialism. We argued that while this theory provides a compelling vision, it is unsatisfactory as an explanatory theory. Marxism, however, also contains a theory of the contradictory reproduction of class relations. At the core of this theory is the concept of class as exploitation. We now want to show how this concept is deployed within the Marxist theory of social reproduction and how this can form the foundation for developing sociological Marxism.

The Marxist theory of the contradictory reproduction of capitalist class relations is based on three fundamental theses:

1. *The social reproduction of class relations thesis.* By virtue of their exploitative character, class structures are inherently unstable forms of social relations and require active institutional arrangements for their reproduction. Where class relations exist, therefore, it is predicted that various forms of political and ideological institutions will develop to defend and reproduce them. In classical Marxism these were typically referred to as political and ideological superstructures which reproduced the economic base.[27]

2. *The contradictions of capitalism thesis.* The institutional solutions to the problems of social reproduction of capitalist class relations at any point in time have a systematic tendency to erode and become less functional over time. This is so for two principle reasons: First, the dynamics of capitalist development generate changes in technology, the labor process, class structure, markets, and other aspects of capitalist relations, and these changes continually pose new problems of social reproduction. In general, earlier institutional solutions will cease to be optimal under such changed conditions. Second, class actors adapt their strategies in order to take advantages of weaknesses in existing institutional arrangements. Over time, these adaptive strategies tend to erode the ability of institutions of social reproduction to effectively regulate and contain class struggles.

3. *Institutional crisis and renovation thesis.* Because of the continual need for institu-

---

[26]For a discussion of the issues involved in coherently incorporating complexity into a concept of class structure, see Wright (1997), and Wright et al. (1989).

[27]The standard argument was that superstructures, particularly the state and ideology, existed to protect the economic base from challenge. Typically this argument took the form of a strong functional explanation in which the form of the superstructure was explained by functional requirement of reproducing the base. We are avoiding the use of the term "superstructure" here because of the tendency for this term to suggest too high a level of integration and coherence among those institutions involved in social reproduction, as well as an image of functional efficiency, which we believe is unjustified. For an important discussion of the explanatory logic of the concept of superstructure, see Cohen (1978, 1988, pp. 155–179).

tions of social reproduction (thesis 1) and the tendency for the reproductive capacity of given institutional arrangements to erode over time (thesis 2), institutions of social reproduction in capitalist societies will tend to be periodically renovated. The typical circumstance for such renovation will be institutional crisis, a situation in which organized social actors, particularly class actors, come to experience the institutional supports as unsatisfactory, often because they cease to be able to contain class conflicts within tolerable limits. These institutional renovations can be piecemeal or may involve dramatic institutional reconfigurations. There is no implication here either that the new institutional solutions will be optimal or that capitalism will collapse in the face of suboptimal arrangements. What is claimed is that capitalist development will be marked by a sequence of institutional renovation episodes in response to the contradictions in the reproduction of capitalist relations.

These three theses provide the core framework that anchors the agenda of sociological Marxism. As with the theory of capitalism's destiny, they are not meant to be simply an interpretative discourse but to identify real mechanisms that exist in real institutions.

The Social Reproduction of Class Relations Thesis

In a fundamental sense, the issue of social reproduction applies to all types of social relations. No type of social relation, whether friendship relations, authority relations within organizations, gender relations, or class relations, simply continues to exist in a given form by sheer inertia; there always is some kind of practice involved in maintaining the social relation in question. But equally, those practices are themselves structured by social relations; they are not simply the unconstrained acts of voluntaristically acting persons. This is a fundamental metatheoretical idea that sociological Marxism shares with many other currents of sociological theory: social relations are reproduced (and transformed) by social practices that are themselves structured by social relations. Here we will focus on the issues of reproducing class relations; in the next section we will examine their transformation.

While social reproduction is an issue for all social relations, different sorts of social relations pose different kinds of problems for social reproduction. Class relations, by virtue of their exploitative character, are an example of a kind of social relation for which social reproduction is a particularly complex and problematic business, requiring the deployment of considerable resources, social energy, and institutional devices. This is so for two reasons: First, exploitative class are relations in which real harms are imposed on some people for the benefit of others. Social relations within which antagonistic interests are generated will have an inherent tendency to generate conflicts in which those who are harmed will try to change the relation in question.[28] The fact that there will be a tendency for active efforts at changing such relations to occur imposes greater burdens on the practices of reproducing those relations; social reproduction does not simply need to counter tendencies for relations to decay or drift over time, but active forms of challenge and resistance. Second, exploitation confers important

---

[28]There are some difficult (and murky) metatheoretical issues invoked by the claim that exploitation generates "antagonistic interests," and such interests in turn have a tendency to create conflict. The implication of the statement is that the hypothesized antagonism of interests is objectively given irrespective of the subjective understandings of the actors. Many people reject the idea that interests can be in any meaningful sense "objective." The relations themselves may be objectively describable, bt the interests of actors only exist as subjective meanings. In any case, the claim here is not that antagonistic interests automatically generate conflict but simply that there is a tendency for antagonistic interests to generate conflict. It is not clear that this is substantively different from saying that there is a tendency for exploitative relations to generate subjectively antagonistic interests, which in turn have a tendency to generate conflicts.

forms of power on the exploited. Since exploitation rests on the extraction of labor effort and since people always retain some measure of control over their own effort, they always confront their exploiters with at least some capacities to resist exploitation.[29] Thus, not only do we have a social relation that breeds antagonisms of interests, but the disadvantaged within these relations have inherent sources of power to resist their exploitation.

Given these features of exploitative class relations, the first fundamental sociological thesis of Marxism predicts that where capitalist class relations are stable, an array of complex institutional devices will exist to reproduce those relations. The conditional form of this prediction is important. The claim is not that capitalist class relations always will be stable, but simply that such stability, where it occurs, requires active institutional supports. Thus, there is a kind of quasifunctionalist reasoning at work here, since class systems are seen as posing significant problems of their own reproduction, problems that will tend to provoke the construction of solutions. However, there is no homeostatic assumption that effective functional solutions are always forthcoming. Indeed, one of the central concerns of a sociological Marxist exploration of the problem of social reproduction is precisely studying the ways in which social reproduction is itself challenged, undermined, contradictory.

These institutional mechanisms of social reproduction of class relations exist both in the microsettings of class relations and the macroinstitutional supports of capitalism. At the microlevel the pivotal problem is understanding the ways in which consent and coercion are articulated within everyday practices, particularly in the labor process. At the macrolevel, the central problem is the way various apparatuses—the state, the media, education—contribute to the stabilization of class structures.

Much of the theoretical and empirical work in neo-Marxism from the 1960s to the 1980s explored this issue of social reproduction. To give just a few examples: Bowles and Gintis' (1976) analysis of education analyzed the functional correspondence between schooling practices and class destinations of children. They argued that schools attended predominantly by working-class children engaged in pedagogical practices revolving around discipline and obedience, thus facilitating the future roles of these children as exploited labor within production, whereas schools for more middle-class or elite children inculcated autonomy and creativity, thus enabling them to better fulfill the roles of domination and direction of production. Schooling helps solve a problem of reproducing class relations: to enable children from different class origins to function effectively in their class destinations. Paul Willis (1977) also explores the ways in which schools constitute a context for reproducing class relations, but in his case the analysis centers on the ways in which forms of resistance contribute to the reproduction of places in the class structure. Burawoy (1979) in his work on "manufacturing consent" among factory workers argues that the organization of work together with the political regime of production generate consent to managerial domination while obscuring capitalist exploitation. Przeworski and Sprague (1986) study the way electoral rules of capitalist democracies channels working-class politics, which might potentially threaten capitalist interests, into practices that are consistent with the reproduction of capitalism, creating the conditions for a hegemonic form of rule. In each case there is a problem for the reproduction of class relations posed by the potential for resistance to capitalist exploitation and domination. The institutional solutions do not eliminate this potential altogether, but when successful they do contain that resistance within acceptable limits.

[29]It is important to note that one need not accept the normative implications of the concept of "exploitation" to recognize the salience of the problem of the "extraction of labor effort" and the ways in which this generates conflicts and capacities of resistance. This is one of the central themes in discussions of principal/agent problems in transaction costs approaches to organizations. For a discussion of class and exploitation specifically in terms of principal/agent issues, see Bowles and Gintis (1990).

The Contradictions of Capitalism Thesis

If sociological Marxism was simply a theory of the social reproduction of class relations, it could easily devolve into a variety of functionalism. Indeed, Marxist analyses often are accused (sometimes correctly) of this: treating all social institutions as functional, perhaps even optimal, for the stability of capitalism and the securing of the interests of the capitalist class. Much of the debate over the influential work of Louis Althusser (1971) on ideology and of Nicos Poulantzas (1973) on the capitalist state, for example, centered on the extent to which their arguments had an overly functionalist cast.[30]

The contradictions of capitalism thesis avoids this kind of functionalism. It argues that the social reproduction of class relations is inherently unstable and problematic, both because of the ways in which the institutions of reproduction themselves become objects of challenge and because of the ways in which capitalist development continually disrupts would-be functional solutions.

The tendency for institutions of social reproduction to erode over time also has been the subject of considerable research and theorizing. O'Connor's (1973) work on the fiscal crisis of the state argues that patterns of state spending that arise in an effort to neutralize certain crisis tendencies in capitalism and to contain class conflict are internally contradictory so that eventually they provoke a fiscal crisis that requires some sort of institutional transformation. Abraham's (1981) work on Weimar Germany argues that the adaptive strategies of different class actors taking advantages of the institutional opportunities in the Weimar Republic eventually made the creation of a stable hegemonic block capable of reproducing German capitalism impossible under the existing constitutional framework. Schwartzman's (1989) study of the First Portuguese Republic shows the disarticulating effects of the global economy, making impossible the consolidation of a united dominant class that eventually succumbs to dictatorship. Claus Offe's (1984) analysis of the "crisis of crisis management" explores how the forms of rationality developed within state institutions to handle social tensions around redistribution become dysfunctional when the state needs to intervene more deeply into production in order to stabilize the conditions for capitalist reproduction. Writers in the French Regulation School (Aglietta, 1979; Lipietz, 1987; Boyer, 1990) and the American Social Structures of Accumulation School (Gordon, Edwards & Reich, 1982; Bowles, Gordon & Weisskopf, 1990) have argued that in the immediate post-World War II period an institutional configuration called "Fordism" was consolidated that combined a specific form of state activity with a pattern of capitalist production and class compromise. This institutional arrangement facilitated a stable, sustained reproduction of conditions favorable for capitalist accumulation. The capitalist development spurred by this configuration, however, ultimately empowered workers in ways that undermined the capacity of the institutions to maintain these reproductive conditions, eventually leading to a "crisis of Fordism."

The Institutional Crisis and Renovation Thesis

The final core thesis of sociological Marxism is that the erosion of the effectiveness of institutions of social reproduction will tend to provoke episodes of institutional renovation, typically in response to situations of felt crisis. The prediction is that these institutional renova-

---

[30]For detailed discussions of the problem of functional explanations within Marxism, see Cohen (1978) and Elster (1985).

tions will tend to secure the basic interests of the capitalist class, but there is no prediction that the resolution will always be optimal for capitalists and certainly not that capitalists will never be forced to make significant compromises in order to consolidate new institutions.

Some of the most interesting research in sociological Marxism centers on the problem of the process through which new institutional solutions to the problem of the social reproduction of class relations are generated. David James (1988) examines how in the aftermath of the Civil War and the destruction of slavery, the Southern planter class faced a serious problem in the reproduction of its class power. He shows how the creation of the radicalized state in the American South in the post-Reconstruction era made possible the reproduction of particularly repressive forms of labor effort extraction in sharecropping. He then demonstrates how the eventual elimination of sharecropping by the middle of the 20th century set the stage for a successful challenge to the racial state. Edwards (1979) shows how new institutional arrangements for the control of labor are created in response to the pressures generated by new technologies and changes in the labor process. Much of the research of social democracy and neocorporatism can be viewed as an analysis of how new forms of "class compromise" are institutionalized to resolve problems of class conflict and social reproduction in the face of economic crisis (Przeworski, 1985; Pontusson, 1992; Heller, 1999).

Taken together with the contradictions of capitalism thesis, the institutional crisis and renovation thesis does argue that capitalist societies are characterized by an inherent dynamic of change. In this way it is like the theory of capitalism's trajectory and destiny. But unlike the ambitious theory of history in classical Marxism, there is no claim here that the "punctuated equilibria" of institutional change is moving toward some predictable destination. What is predicted is a pattern of episodic reorganizations of capitalism and its support institutions in the face of the erosion of processes of social reproduction, but not that cumulatively these episodes have a tendency to increase the probability of socialism.[31]

TOWARD AN EMANCIPATORY THEORY
OF SOCIALISM

If the theory of capitalism's destiny developed by Marx were valid, then there would be less need for an elaborate theory of socialism. If we had good reason to believe (1) that capitalism will eventually become unsustainable, (2) that as capitalism becomes less unsustainable, the institutional supports that reproduce capitalism will tend to become more fragile, (3) that as sustainability declines, the class forces opposed to capitalism will become stronger and stronger, and (4) that the class location of people within the anticapitalist forces meant that they would overwhelmingly benefit from an egalitarian and democratic reorganization of production, then it might be reasonable to suppose that through some sort of pragmatic, creative trial-and-error process some kind of viable socialism could be constructed. Where there is a will there is a way; necessity is the parent of invention. So, if the claims of the

---

[31]In a sense sociological Marxism is more, rather than less, like a form of "evolutionary" theory than is historical materialism (the theory of history in classical Marxism). In the theory of biological evolution there is no inherent tendency for biological history to move toward some destiny. *Homo sapiens* are not the inherent destiny of single-celled creatures 3 billion years ago. Rather, the actual trajectory of the development of species is a function of various kinds of dynamic processes combined with contingent events. Historical materialism, in predicting a general tendency for the trajectory of history to follow a particular course, thus is more like a theory of the development of an organism from embryo to adulthood than it is like evolutionary theory. For a discussion of the relationship between the logic of social change in historical materialism and evolutionary theory, see Wright, Sober, and Levine (1992).

classical Marxist theory of capitalism's destiny were true, perhaps there would be less need for a positive theory of socialism, a theory that clarified its normative foundations and institutional principles. Once we drop the optimistic predictions of historical materialism, however, there is no longer a theoretical grounding for bracketing these issues.

One option, of course, would be to continue the tradition of the Frankfurt School and other important currents of Western Marxism in which the emancipatory dimension of Marxism is developed primarily as the critique of capitalism. Socialism, then, is the idealized negation of the oppressions of capitalism.

While this may provide us with a valuable moral anchor, it will not do as a normative model of alternatives to existing institutions. We have witnessed several historical experiments of trying to build socialism in the aftermath of anticapitalist revolutions that relied heavily on moral visions combined with "where there is a will there is a way" and "necessity is the parent of invention." The problem, of course, is that what was invented with this will was not an egalitarian, democratic organization of production. If we have learned anything from the history of revolutionary struggles against capitalism it is that anticapitalism is an insufficient basis on which to construct a socialist alternative. In addition to a sociological Marxism that explores the contradictory reproduction of class relations in capitalism we therefore need a theory that illuminates the nature of the emancipatory project itself and its institutional dilemmas. The development of this emancipatory theory is one of the essential tasks for Marxism in the 21st century.

As we see it, the development of a theory of socialism would have two principle concerns. First, emancipatory Marxism must thoroughly understand the dilemmas and dynamics of the historical attempts at creating socialist relations. This concerns, above all, understanding the development and unraveling of authoritarian state socialisms since, for better or worse, these constitute the main empirical cases for attempts at putting Marxist-inspired socialist ideas into practice. Partially the purpose of such investigations is to avoid repeating the same mistakes in the future, but more fundamentally the purpose is to enrich our general understanding of the institutional requirements for feasible emancipatory alternatives.

Second, emancipatory Marxism must take more seriously the problem of theoretically elaborating institutional designs embodying emancipatory principles. This does not imply the fantasy of developing fine-grained social blueprints that could be taken off the shelf and instituted through some massive project of social engineering. Marx rightly thought that such blueprints for socialism were implausible. But it does mean elaborating much more systematically the principles that would animate the pragmatic development of real institutions. This involves both thinking through the abstract design principles for realizing particular emancipatory ideals and studying empirical cases where some of these design principles may have been put into practice. We refer to this effort as "envisioning real utopias."

Understanding State Socialism

For those who desire to bury Marxism, state socialism, especially its Soviet variety, becomes its dirge. For them, Soviet communism demonstrates the bankruptcy and totalitarian danger of Marxism. There is nothing to be learned or recovered. For those who wish to propagate Marxism, given the widespread disrepute into which it has fallen, state socialism is something to be avoided. Or at least the propaganda must be that state socialism has nothing to do with Marxist socialism. Even those who use Marxism have no use for state socialism except as a negative case, perhaps an expression of degenerate Marxism. They too want to dissociate themselves from the deceased body. Only those who seek to build Marxism, and not all of them, are likely to do a serious postmortem and extract the lessons to be learned, the positive and the negative, in the one enduring example of socialism.

What has the history of state socialism to contribute to building an emancipatory theory of socialism? Ironically, perhaps, modifications of the three theses of classical Marxism concerning the destiny of capitalism may help us understand the trajectory of state socialism: the nonsustainability of state socialism; the intensification of antisocialist challenges, and the transition to an alternative society, in this case some form of capitalism.

State socialism involved the central redistribution of surplus, appropriated by a class of "planners" from a class of "direct producers." Its appropriation was palpable and therefore had to be legitimized in the name of the superior knowledge of the planner about the needs of the people (Konrád & Szelényi, 1979). This worked fairly effectively when the central task of state planning was mobilizing resources for basic industrialization against the backdrop of an underdeveloped agrarian economy; it encountered increasing contradictions when the central task became enhancing productivity within the industrial economy.

Central appropriation and planning led to a shortage economy in which the bottleneck was from the side of supply (Kornai, 1980, 1992). If all that was required of the economic system was simple reproduction—the allocation of given inputs to produce a given array of outputs—then central planning was quite feasible and the supply-side bottlenecks could be overcome by various institutional innovations. In and of itself, this failure in state socialism was no more pathological than the chronic problem of market failure in capitalism with its excess production, the bottleneck of demand. Just as capitalism could counter the problem of demand failures in the market through various forms of state-generated demand, state social-ism could counter the supply failures of state planning through various forms of quasimarket mechanisms.[32]

Where state socialism had deeper problems, problems that it was unable to overcome, was in its dynamic properties, particularly the inability to innovate on a systematic basis. Bureaucratic competition for resources, unlike market competition, did not have the effect of generating sustained innovation. Relative to the capitalist world beyond, state socialist rela-tions of production impeded the development of its forces of production. The result over time was deepening stagnation and increasingly problematic sustainability of state socialism.

There also seems to have been a tendency for state socialism to inspire challenges to its continuity. Because legitimacy was so central to its stability, state socialism was vulnerable to an imminent critique in which the ruling ideology that permeated the day to day practices was turned against the ruling class, the party state, for failing to realize its proclaimed ideals (Burawoy and Lukács, 1992). In other words, because under the banner of Marxism these were proclaimed to be workers' states, it was not surprising that workers would take up struggle against them in the face of their failure to live up to their ideals (Berlin, 1953; Poland and Hungary, 1956; Czechoslovakia, 1968; Poland, 1980–1981; Russian miners, 1989, 1991). In the end, the failure of state socialism was so dramatic that the ruling class lost confidence in all possible reforms, so that the only alternative was capitalism. With the discrediting of all forms of socialism and the demise of state socialism, a transition to some kind of capitalism became the "natural" solution.

Capitalism, of course, also had its crises, sometimes very deep crises, but this did not lead

[32]There is an extensive literature on the way marketlike practices—the so-called "second" or "black" economy—emerge to solve supply-side problems in state socialism. See, for example, Berliner (1957) and Lewin (1985) for the Soviet Union and Stark (1986) and Szelényi (1988) for Hungary. One of the best overall assessments of the Soviet type economy is Nove (1983).

to its collapse, because, we argue, following Gramsci, it developed an expanded state and a vibrant civil society. Robust institutions of social reproduction were elaborated that could flexibly absorb challenges and respond through a process of iterated institutional renovation. While there were clearly embryonic beginnings of and aspirations for such an institutional complex in state socialism—think of *perestroika* that aspired to a vibrant civil society, solidarity, which sought to create participatory institutions, and Hungary, which created a significant second economy—institutions of social reproduction never developed into fully fledged superstructures. These experiments never came to fruition, they never stabilized, but they held within them the seeds of a democratic socialism. In other words, centrally directed state socialism spawned a range of alternative socialisms of a democratic character that at different times captured the imagination of subordinated classes.

Perhaps if state socialism had occurred in a more benign global environment, it might have avoided the extreme forms of authoritarianism that characterized these regimes, and thus have allowed for a more vibrant and open associational life in civil society. This in turn might have created the conditions, which in the face of the failures of central planning might have generated more coherent counterhegemonic visions of socialism. Just as the internal contradictions of early capitalism led to an organized capitalism with its flanking institutions, under more propitious circumstances, state socialism might have given way to democratic socialism rather than capitalism.

The posing of a qualitative alternative to state socialism—capitalism—occurred in the context of a pervasive belief that state socialism had exhausted any capacity for renewal or development. Virtually no one believes in capitalism's immanent demise. It therefore seems unlikely that visions of radical egalitarian alternatives to capitalism will be spontaneously generated by struggles within capitalism. When capitalism runs into difficulties, the spontaneous impulse is to try to perfect it rather than dismantle it. If Marxism is to render alternatives to capitalism credible therefore it is necessary for alternatives to be given coherent and compelling theoretical force. Part of building Marxism in these conditions involves formulating "real utopias," utopias that are rooted in real practices, and embody feasible institutional designs that point beyond capitalism.

Envisioning Real Utopias

Marxists traditionally have been skeptical at best, and often sharply hostile to anything that smacked to utopian thinking. Marx criticized "utopian socialists" who thought they could build emancipatory enclaves within capitalism rather than struggle for the revolutionary transformation of capitalism itself. Yet, as we have argued, building Marxism needs to go beyond a vision of the critical negation of capitalism toward the exploration of alternative models. Such models should be "utopian" insofar as they try to embody in a serious way the central values of traditional emancipatory projects of social change—radical equality, deep democracy, caring community, individual self-realization, and freedom. But they also should be "real," insofar as what is envisioned are not fantasies or purely moral constructions, but feasible institutional designs capable of contributing to real human progress.

To flesh out this idea, let us consider in some detail one such real utopian idea: unconditional universal basic income grants. The idea of universal basic income has a long pedigree, but recently has been revived (Van der Veen & Van Parijs, 1986; Purdy, 1994; Van Parijs, 1992; Cohen & Rogers, 2000). The proposal has come under a variety of names: universal basic income, demogrant, citizen dividend. While the details may vary, the basic idea is quite simple: Every citizen receives a monthly living stipend sufficient to live at a culturally defined respectable standard of living, say 125% of the "poverty line." The grant is unconditional on the performance of any labor or other form of contribution and it is universal—everyone receives the grant as a matter of citizenship right. Grants go to individuals, not families. Parents are the custodians of minority children's grants.

With universal basic income in place, most other redistributive transfers are eliminated—general welfare, family allowances, unemployment insurance, tax-based old age pensions—since the basic income grant is sufficient to provide everyone a decent subsistence. This means that in welfare systems that already provide generous antipoverty income support through a patchwork of specialized programs, the net increase in costs represented by universal unconditional basic income would not be extraordinary, particularly since administrative overhead costs would be so reduced (since universal basic income systems do not require significant information gathering and close monitoring of the behavior of recipients). Special needs subsidies of various sorts would continue, for example, for people with disabilities, but they are likely to be smaller than under current arrangements. Minimum wage rules would be relaxed or eliminated: there would be little need to legally prohibit below-subsistence wages if all earnings, in effect, generated discretionary income.

Universal basic income has a number of very attractive features from the point of view of radical egalitarianism. First, it significantly reduces one of the central coercive aspects of capitalism. When Marxists analyze the process of "proletarianization of labor," they emphasize the "double separation" of "free wage labor": workers are separated from the means of production, and by virtue of this are separated from the means of subsistence. The conjoining of these two separations is what forces workers to sell their labor power on a labor market in order to obtain subsistence. In this sense, proletarianized labor is fundamentally unfree. Unconditional, universal basic income breaks this identity of separations: workers remain separated from the means of production (these are still owned by capitalists), but they are no longer separated from the means of subsistence (this is provided through the redistributive basic income grant). The decision to work for a wage therefore becomes much more voluntary. Capitalism between consenting adults is much less objectionable than capitalism between employers and workers with little choice but to work for wages. By increasing the capacity of workers to refuse employment, basic income generates a much more egalitarian distribution of real freedom than ordinary capitalism.

Second, universal basic income is likely to generate greater egalitarianism within labor markets. If workers are more able to refuse employment, wages for crummy work are likely to increase relative to wages for highly enjoyable work. The wage structure in labor markets therefore will begin to more systematically reflect the relative disutility of different kinds of labor rather than simply the relative scarcity of different kinds of labor power. This in turn will generate an incentive structure for employers to seek technical innovations that eliminate unpleasant work. Technical change therefore would not simply have a labor-saving bias, but a labor-humanizing bias.

Third, universal basic income directly and massively eliminates poverty without creating the pathologies of means-tested antipoverty transfers. There is no stigmatization, since everyone gets the grant. There is no well-defined boundary between net beneficiaries and net contributors, since many people and families will freely move back and forth across this boundary over time. Thus, it is less likely that stable majority coalitions against redistribution will form once basic income has been in place for some length of time. There also are no "poverty traps" caused by threshold effects for eligibility for transfers. Everyone gets the transfers unconditionally. If you work and earn wages, the additional income is of course taxed, but the tax rate is progressive, and thus there is no disincentive for a person to enter the labor market if they want discretionary income.

Fourth, unconditional universal basic income is one way of valorizing a range of decommodified caregiving activities that are badly provided by markets, particularly caregiving labor within families, but also caregiving labor within broader communities. While universal income by itself would not transform the gendered character of such labor, it would counteract some of the inegalitarian consequences of the fact that such unpaid labor is characteristically performed by women. In effect, universal basic income could be considered an indirect mechanism for accomplishing the objective of the "wages for housework" proposals by some feminists: recognizing that caregiving work is socially valuable and productive and deserving of financial support. The effects of basic income on democracy and community are less clear, but to the extent that basic income facilitates the expansion of unpaid, voluntary activity of all sorts, this would have the potential of enhancing democratic participation and solidarity-enhancing activities within communities.

There are, of course, significant questions about the practical feasibility of universal basic income grants. Two issues are typically raised by skeptics: the problem of labor supply and the problem of capital flight.

A universal basic income is only feasible if a sufficient number of people continue to work for wages with sufficient effort to generate the production and taxes needed to fund the universal grant. If too many people are happy to live just on the grant (either because they long to be couch potatoes and/or simply because they have such strong preferences for nonincome-generating activities over discretionary income) or if the marginal tax rates were so high as seriously dampen incentives to work, then the whole system would collapse. Let us define a "sustainable basic income grant" as a level of the grant that if it were instituted would stabley generate a sufficient labor supply to provide the necessary taxes for the grant. The highest level of such grants therefore could be called the "maximally sustainable basic income grant." The empirical question, then, is whether this maximally sustainable level is high enough to provide for the virtuous effects listed above. If the maximally sustainable grant was 25% of the poverty line, for example, then it would hardly have the effect of rendering paid labor a noncoercive, voluntary act and probably not dramatically reduce poverty. If, on the other hand, the maximally sustainable grant was 150% of the poverty level, then a universal basic income would significantly advance the egalitarian normative agenda. Whether or not this would in fact happen is, of course, a difficult-to-study empirical question and depends on the distribution of work preferences and productivity in an economy.

Apart from the labor supply problem, universal basic income also is vulnerable to the problem of capital flight. If a high universal basic income grant significantly increases the bargaining power labor, if capital bears a significant part of the tax burden for funding the grant, and if tight labor markets dramatically drive up wages and thus costs of production without commensurate rises in productivity, then it could well be the case that a universal basic income would precipitate significant disinvestment and capital flight. It is for this reason that Marxists have traditionally argued that a real and sustainable deproletarianization labor power is impossible within capitalism. In effect, the necessary condition for sustainable high-level universal basic income may be significant politically imposed constraints over capital, especially over the flow of investments. Some form of socialism then may be a requirement for a normatively attractive form of basic income. But it also may be the case that in rich, highly productive capitalism, a reasonably high basic income could be compatible with capitalist reproduction. Particularly in generous welfare states, the increased taxes for funding a basic income might not be excessive and the technological and infrastructural reasons why capital invests in developed capitalist economies may mean that massive capital flight is unlikely. Maybe.

Universal basic income is not the full realization of the emancipatory vision of Marxism. It does not create democratic control over society's productive capacity; it does not produce radical egalitarianism; it does not eliminate domination in production; it does not eliminate capitalist exploitation, although it may render it less morally objectionable. Nevertheless, it is a feasible institutional design with many normatively attractive features that advance some of the core goals of the socialist project.

Universal basic income is only one example of a model envisioning real utopias. Other examples would include John Roemer's (1994, 1996) proposal for an institutionally feasible form of market socialism; various innovative ideas about ways of deepening democratic governance through a new articulation of the state and secondary associations (Cohen & Rogers, 1995) or through the elaboration of new forms of empowered deliberative participation of citizens in political decision making (Fung, 2001; Fung & Wright, 2001); and proposals to create egalitarian market institutions through sustained redistribution of assets (Bowles & Gintis, 1998).

All these proposals in various ways challenge the prevailing idea that there is no alternative to capitalism. If people generally believed that capitalism was inevitably doomed within their lifetimes, then this itself would undercut the notion that there was no alternative. But if this belief is dropped, then articulating alternatives is a necessary condition for putting alternatives on the historical agenda.

Envisioning real utopias, however, is meant to be more than just an ideological strategy for challenging fatalism. Because of the contradictory quality of social reproduction in capitalism, under certain political conditions, aspects of these institutional designs can potentially become part of pragmatic projects of social reform even within capitalist society. There are many possible capitalisms with many different institutional arrangements for social reproduction. One crucial issue for emancipatory Marxism is the extent to which it is possible to introduce and sustain significant aspects of emancipatory institutional arrangements in some varieties of capitalism. Although the arguments of sociological Marxism suggest that the constraints of social reproduction of class relations necessarily make any emancipatory project within capitalism difficult, this does not imply that elements of emancipatory alternatives cannot be prefigured within the contradictory reality of capitalism.[33] Envisioning real utopias thus is ultimately part of an active agenda of social change within capitalism rather than simply a vision of a destiny beyond capitalism.

In other words, a sociological Marxism is a Marxism without guarantees (Hall, 1983). It substitutes the working out of real utopias for the "end-of-capitalism" certainties of classical Marxism. At the center of sociological Marxism's agenda is the articulation and dissemination of alternatives, alternatives that already exist in embryonic form within capitalism. Sociological Marxism does not depend on inevitable laws of motion that will automatically bring forth a socialist world but instead must actively propagate real utopias that will capture a popular

---

[33]The idea that emancipatory principles can be prefigured within institutions in capitalism runs counter to the more functionalist versions of sociological Marxism. In the more functionalist versions, all significant, sustainable institutional innovations in capitalist society are viewed as in some sense contributing to stabilizing and securing class relations. While some institutional changes in the state, for example, may make life easier for ordinary people, these are at best palliatives that make capitalism more acceptable, and thus more stable. Reforms have the appearance of being more radical, of posing significant alternatives to capitalism, are either illusions or are quickly undermined and neutralized. If this strongly functionalist view of institutional possibilities is accepted, there is little room for emancipatory ideals to be embodied even prefiguratively in the institutions of capitalist society.

imagination. In this case building Marxism as a coherent scientific research program has to be combined with propagating Marxism, challenging capitalism's capacity to absorb or ridicule alternatives to itself, and providing the grounds for a prefigurative politics. Thus, a sociological Marxism has to be not only science but also ideology—ideology in Gramsci's sense that embeds real utopia in a concrete fantasy that will move people to collective action.[34]

CONCLUSION

We have argued in this chapter that the main theoretical ideas of Marxism can be grouped into three broad clusters: a theory of dynamics and destiny of capitalism—historical materialism; a theory of the contradictory reproduction of capitalism—sociological Marxism; and a theory of emancipatory alternatives.

Classical Marxism developed during the early phases of industrial capitalism. It brilliantly captured the historical dynamics of that period—the extraordinary power of capitalism to transform the world, to destroy preexisting class relations and forms of society, but also its inherent tendency to crisis and self-destruction. This dynamic self-destructive logic of capitalism was given theoretical coherence by historical materialism.

Sociological Marxism was present in embryonic form within classical Marxism, but only later did it become an elaborate, developed theoretical framework for understanding the new array of institutions built up around capitalism, counteracting its tendency toward self-destruction. Historical materialism and sociological Marxism complemented each other—one explaining the trajectory and ultimate destiny of capitalism and the other the impediments toward movement along that trajectory. Together they provided a grounding for Marxist-inspired political parties who saw their mission to be overcoming these impediments, particularly those embodied in the state, and thus hastening the arrival at the destiny.

So long as historical materialism was accepted, there was little need for sociological Marxism to embrace an emancipatory theory that went much beyond the critique of capitalism. If we abandon the pivotal theses of historical materialism—the nonsustainability of capitalism thesis and the intensification of class struggle thesis—then developing an emancipatory theory becomes critical for building Marxism. Sociological Marxism demands that we now pay close attention to developing alternatives to capitalism, since the end of capitalism no longer is given as an inherent tendency and the attempts at socialism have not been successful. The emancipatory theory of a reconstructed Marxism must examine state socialism for the lessons as to what should be avoided and imagination of what might have been. But even more important are developing real utopias based on real institutions of capitalism and exploring the idea that those flanking institutions themselves potentially contain seeds of alternative societies.

Sociological Marxism without emancipatory Marxism degenerates into cynical, pessimistic critiques of capitalism, ultimately encouraging passivity in the face of capitalism's enormous capacity for reproduction. Emancipatory Marxism without sociological Marxism falls into an unanchored utopianism that is ungrounded in the real contradictions of capitalism and is unable to capture the imagination of people. Only by building Marxism with a combination of the two can the apparent naturalness and inevitability of capitalism be prevented from turning all alternatives into far-fetched impossibilities.

[34]Gramsci (1971, pp. 125–126) spoke of the power of political ideology "expressed neither in the form of a cold utopia nor as learned theorizing, but rather by a creation of concrete fantasy which acts on a dispersed and shattered people to arouse and organize its collective will."

REFERENCES

Abraham, D. (1981). *The collapse of the Weimer Republic*. Princeton, NJ: Princeton University Press.

Aglietta, M. (1979). *A Theory of Capitalist Regulation*. London: New Left Books.

Althusser, L. (1971). Ideology and ideological state apparatuses. In *Lenin and philosophy and other essays* (pp. 127–186). London: New Left Books.

Anderson, P. (1976). *Considerations on Western Marxism*. London: New Left Books.

Arrighi, G. (1994). *The long twentieth century*. London: Verso.

Berliner, J. (1957). *Factory and manager in the USSR*. Cambridge, MA: Harvard University Press.

Bowles, S., & Gintis, H. (1990). Contested exchange: New micro-foundations for the political economy of capitalism. *Politics and Society, 18*(2), 165–222.

Bowles, S., & Gintis, H. (1976) *Schooling in capitalist America*. New York: Basic Books.

Bowles, S., & Gintis, H. (1998). *Recasting egalitarianism: New rules for communities, states and markets*. Volume III, *Real utopias project*, E. O. Wright (Ed.). London: Verso.

Bowles, S., Gordon, D. M., & Weisskopf, T. E. (1990). *After the wasteland*. New York: M. E. Sharp.

Boyer, R. (1990). *The regulation school: A critical introduction*. New York: Columbia University Press.

Burawoy, M. (1979). *Manufacturing consent*. Chicago: Chicago University Press.

Burawoy, M. (1985). *The politics of production*. London: New Left Books.

Burawoy, M., & Lukács, J. (1992). *The radiant past*. Chicago: University of Chicago Press.

Cohen, G. A. (1978). *Karl Marx's theory of history: A defence*. Princeton, NJ: Princeton University Press.

Cohen, G. A. (1988). *History, labour, and freedom*. Oxford, England: Clarendon Press.

Cohen, J., & Rogers, J. (1995). *Associations and democracy*, Volume I, *Real utopias project*, E. O. Wright (Ed.). London: Verso.

Cohen, J., & Rogers, J. (Eds.). (2000). *Delivering basic incomes*. Special issue of *The Boston Review, 25*(5), October–November.

Edwards, R. (1979). *Contested terrain*. New York: Basic Books.

Elster, J. (1985). *Making sense of Marx*. Cambridge, England: Cambridge University Press.

Engels, F. (1978). Socialism: Utopian and scientific. In R. Tucker (Ed.), *The Marx–Engels reader* (pp. 683–717). New York: W. W. Norton.

Engels, F. (1988). *History, labour and freedom*. Oxford, England: Oxford University Press.

Fung, A. (2001). Deliberative democracy, Chicago style. *Politics and Society, 29*(1), 73–103.

Fung, A. & Wright, E. O. (2001). Experiments in empowered deliberative democracy. *Politics and Society, 29*(1), 5–41.

Gordon, D., Edwards, R., & Reich, M. (1982). *Segmented work, divided workers*. New York: Cambridge University Press.

Gouldner, A. (1980). *The two Marxisms: Contradictions and anomalies in the development of theory*. New York: Seabury Press.

Gouldner, A. (1985). *Against fragmentation: The origins of Marxism and the sociology of intellectuals*. Oxford, England: Oxford University Press.

Gramsci, A. (1971). *Selections from the prison notebooks of Antonio Gramsci*, Q. Hoare & G. N. Smith (Eds./Trans.). New York: International Publishers.

Hall, S. (1983). The problem of ideology: Marxism without guarantees. In B. Mathews (Ed.), *Marx: 100 years on* (pp. 57–84). London: Lawrence and Wishart.

Heller, P. (1999). *The labor of development*. Ithaca, NY: Cornell University Press.

Horkheimer, M., & Adorno, T. W. (1972). *Dialectic of enlightenment*. New York: Seabury Press.

James, D. (1988). The transformation of the southern racial state: Class and race determinants of local–state structures. *American Sociological Review, 53*, 191–208.

Konrád, G., & Szelény, I. (1979). *The intellectuals on the road to class power*. New York: Harcourt Brace Jovanovich.

Kornai, J. (1980). *The Economics of shortage*, 2 volumes. Amsterdam: North Holland Publishing Company.

Kornai, J. (1992). *The socialist system*. Princeton, NJ: Princeton University Press.

Lewin, M. (1985). *The making of the Soviet system*. New York: Pantheon Books.

Lewin, M. (1992). *The socialist system*. Princeton, NJ: Princeton University Press.

Lipietz, A. (1987). *Mirages and miracles: The crisis in global Fordism*, D. Macey (Trans.). London: Verso.

Lukács, G. (1971). *History and class consciousness*. Cambridge, MA: MIT Press.

Marcuse, H. (1955). *Eros and civilization*. Boston: Beacon Press.

Marcuse, H. (1964). *One-dimensional man*. Boston: Beacon Press.

Marx, K. (1963). *The eighteenth brumaire of Louis Bonaparte*. New York: International Publishers.

Marx, K. (1964). *Class struggles in France (1848–1850)*. New York: International Publishers.

Marx, K. (1967a). *Capital, Volume I*. New York: International Publishers.

Marx, K. (1967b). *Capital, Volume III*. New York: International Publishers.

Marx, K., & Engels, F. (1970). *The German ideology*. New York: International Publishers.

Marx, K., & Engels, F. (1998). *The communist manifesto*. London: Verso.

Nove, A. (1983). *The economics of feasible socialism*. London: George Allen & Unwin.

O'Connor, J. (1973). *The fiscal crisis of the state*. New York: St. Martin's Press.

Offe, C. (1984). *The contradictions of the welfare state*. Cambridge, MA: MIT Press.

Pontusson, J. (1992). *The limits of social democracy*. Ithaca, NY: Cornell University Press.

Poulantzas, N. (1973). *Political power and social classes*. London: New Left Books.

Przeworski, A. (1985). *Capitalism and social democracy*. Cambridge and New York: Cambridge University Press.

Przeworski, A., & Sprague, J. (1986). *Paper stones*. Chicago: University of Chicago Press.

Purdy, D. (1994). Citizenship, basic income and the state. *New Left Review, 208*, 30–48.

Roemer, J. E. (1994). *A future for socialism*. Cambridge, MA: Harvard University Press.

Roemer, J. E. (1996). *Equal shares: Making market socialism work*, Volume II, *Real utopias project*, E. O. Wright (Ed.). London: Verso.

Schwartzman, K. (1989). *The social origins of democratic collapse*. Lawrence: University of Kansas Press.

Stark, D. (1986). Rethinking internal labor markets: New insights from a comparative perspective. *American Sociological Review, 51*, 492–504.

Szelényi, I. (1988). *Socialist entrepreneurs*. Madison: University of Wisconsin Press.

Van der Veen, R., & van Parijs, P. (1986). A capitalist road to communism. *Theory and Society, 15*(5), 635–655.

Van Parijs, P. (Ed.). (1992). *Arguing for basic income*. London: Verso.

Willis, P. (1977). *Learning to labour*. Farnborough, England: Saxon House.

Wright, E. O. (1985). *Classes*. London: Verso.

Wright, E. O. (1997). *Class counts*. Cambridge and New York: Cambridge University Press.

Wright, E. O., Becker, U., Brenner, J., Burawoy, M., Burris, V., Carchedi, G., Marshall, G., Meiskins, P. F., Rose, D., Stinchcombe, A., Van Parijs, P. (1989). *The debate on classes*. London and New York: Verso.

Wright, E. O., Levine, A., & Sober, E. (1992). *Reconstructing Marxism*. London and New York: Verso.

Younis, M. (2000). *Liberation and democratization: The South African and Palestinian national movements*. Minneapolis: University of Minnesota Press.

CHAPTER 23

Weberian Theory Today

The Public Face

ALAN SICA

A protracted debate has occurred within the social sciences during the last 25 years, particularly in scholarly circles whose primary goal is the elaboration of social theory. The question at stake, "Who among the 'holy trinity' of classical theorists will most forcefully propel social analysis into the 21st century?" seems finally to be settled, at least for the foreseeable future. Marx has been consigned by most laypersons and many scholars, perhaps only temporarily, to the same "dustbin of history" he eloquently invoked when criticizing his theoretical forbears or contemporary enemies. The Marxist star was most firmly hitched, properly or not, to the political fortunes of the Soviet Union and its Eastern Bloc satellites. As they failed to construct a workable communist social order and were dragged unwillingly into the capitalist world system, the relevance of Marxist social analysis seemed, especially to the theoretically uninformed, to have disappeared as quickly as did statues of Stalin and Lenin from the streets of Moscow. Marx's uniquely astute analysis of how capitalist accumulation occurs on the corporate or global level will likely regain its pertinence during the next major economic downturn. For the inevitable price of uncontrolled global capitalism, environmentally and otherwise, will require a "rethinking" once the current so-called "boom" has exhausted itself, especially in the West, where such "booms" are politically defined for mass consumption. But for now, without a major national government using his name for the purposes of political legitimation, the kind of intellectual supremacy Marx's ideas enjoyed between the mid-1960s and late 1970s, especially in those countries where social sciences flourish, is difficult to foresee.

The case of Durkheim, of course, is entirely different, since his ideas were never overtly attached to government policies beyond the reach of French pedagogical practices. Yet it is probably fair to say that Durkheim's most general ideas have so thoroughly saturated analysis common to the social sciences that it is difficult to speak in any tongue but his, especially regarding the related phenomena of deviance, the division of labor, and religious practices. Oddly, though, even given the ubiquity of "the Durkheimian perspective" or "a Durkheimian conceptualization," his works themselves, when reread carefully, seem increas-

ALAN SICA • Department of Sociology, Pennsylvania State University, University Park, Pennsylvania 16802.

Handbook of Sociological Theory, edited by Jonathan H. Turner. Kluwer Academic / Plenum Publishers, New York, 2002.

ingly musty and time-bound. Leading today's novices through *Elementary Forms of the Religious Life* (Durkheim, 1912/1915) or even *Division of Labor* (Durkheim, 1893/1933) with any real hermeneutic care becomes ever more an exercise in identifying antiquated debates and forgotten scholars than is the case even with Marx's work, despite its having been written 30 or 40 years prior to Durkheim's. The latter's pronounced moralism and his dedication to the cause of making civility into a religion (to borrow from Robert Bellah) will always suit certain mindsets and political situations. Yet his role in the postmodern intellectual environment seems more like that of the visiting uncle from deep within the underdeveloped countryside than as a viable family member whose daily advice is prized for its enduring applicability to modern life. Arguments that there is indeed a "postmodern Durkheim," no matter how creatively posed, do little to ward off the suspicion that he truly is of another era. His principal theoretical concerns, it now seems, spoke more immediately to modes of social organization and the worldviews that sprang from them, which have weakened in form and force since World War I, a catastrophe, it should be remembered, that killed not only Durkheim's only son but his own spirit to live. Increasingly, I suspect, his works themselves will assume a role in social analysis not unlike that of Hobbes' (1651/1962) *Leviathan* in political thought: always cited, seldom read.

One therefore could argue with some confidence that it is Weber who remains the towering figure from the classical period, whose work and person continue to inspire endless emulation, commentary, critique, and utility in empirical or "theory-driven" studies, as well as in less lofty forms of published work where normally the names of social theorists seldom appear. His language is quoted, without irony or embarrassment, by everyone from newspaper columnists to philosophers of religion; his principal theoretical and substantive concerns are those that continue to inspire ever-growing bodies of scholarship internationally; his theories and corporeal self seem as much at home in today's cultural and intellectual environment as those of his historical peers do not. There is a distinctly Weberian approach, an almost "Weberian mood," as it pertains to various features of the contemporary social scene for which no apology or second-guessing is required and which still bears as much analytic power as did Marxism only 20 years ago or as Durkheim continues to do when applied to more restricted zones of social life.

I make these somewhat contentious observations not out of vague impressions based on haphazard reading but rather from an "empirical study" of my own devising that has been in process for a decade. Years ago I was asked to answer in book form what then seemed a simple enough question: "To what extent and in what ways does Weber continue to influence contemporary thought and research?" or, to mimic Croce's (1907/1915) wonderful title regarding Hegel in 1907, *What Is Living and What Is Dead in the Theorizing of Max Weber*? What began as a casual study of major sources has become over time an obsessive search for materials that speak in Weberian diction, which examine his own works in homage or critique, or somehow enlarge on themes he introduced during his relatively short professional heyday between 1904 and early 1920. What I have learned from this bibliographical study has proved endlessly interesting, not only because so many of Weber's ideas continue to lead researchers into passionate and diverse courses of study, but also due to what has *not* been pursued owing to his implied or explicit directives. Weber's mind and writings become all the more interesting after one recognizes how his particular viewpoint and language necessarily curtailed study that might otherwise have occurred. (My own study of Weber's difficulty with the "problem of irrationality" is one example among an increasing number that look for and try to repair specifiable lapses in his thinking, few though they may have been; Sica, 1988). Some of his metaphors ("the iron cage" is the most famous) and many concepts, like "charisma," are still much with us, as are heated arguments over whether, for example, the "Protestant Ethic thesis" applies to historical formations all the way from Korea to Namibia. Yet as with any supremely talented thinker, "lacunae" are almost as informative as the research topics for which he had a ready affinity and left behind detailed analyses. Thus, his forgetfulness, as it were, becomes ours, just as his enthusiasms infect and inform our own.

In a short chapter it is impossible more than to hint at the vast range of scholarly and subscholarly works in English over the last 80 years that clearly bear the Weberian stamp. The bibliography I have assembled currently numbers 3400 published items (nearly all of it in scholarly as opposed to journalistic outlets) and 410 dissertations, plus hundreds of book reviews directly addressing products of "the Weber industry." There also are 90 individually published English translations of Weber's own writing, with more appearing all the time. In Germany the monumental collected works in German (the *Gesamtausgabe*) moves slowly toward its eventual goal of publishing 33 thick, annotated volumes of Weber materials, much of it, particularly the letters, currently unknown. Out of this cornucopia, of course, even more and improved translations will surely be made into all the major languages. (Weber has a particularly strong following in Japan, for example.) Although it would be facile, therefore, to summarize under a few simple topic headings everything that is going on today under the Weberian bigtop, there are noticeable tendencies that have differentiated themselves to some extent from those that held the attention of scholars in preceding decades.

Very unlike his peers, Durkheim and Simmel, Weber's works had not been deemed worthy of attention by English language translators until well into the century. Finally in the 1930s, Weber gained some currency in the anglophone world, but even then he was generally misclassified as an unusually broad-gauged historian of socio-economic change, since only his *General Economic History* (1927) and *The Protestant Ethic and the Spirit of Capitalism* (1930) were the only extant translations for many years after his death. As is well known, the former work was assembled posthumously from sets of student notes taken in a course called "Outlines of Universal Social and Economic History," which Weber gave at Munich in the winter term of 1919–1920, materials he never imagined to constitute a finished work. He offered this course due to student demand and to counter the perceived aridity of his previous lectures on "conceptual foundations" of social science (which apparently drove away students en masse) and were later issued as Part One of *Economy and Society* (1968). *The Protestant Ethic and the Spirit of Capitalism* (1930), the much more famous piece, came from revised and augmented versions of two essays Weber published as journal articles in 1904–1905, and the voluminous debates they inspired until about 1910 when Weber publicly retired from the argument. To these materials was added a 1920 introduction written for another purpose, plus a "Forward" by R. H. Tawney, a noted British economic historian. Not until the late 1940s were what became the two warhorses of Weber scholarship available to readers of English, *From Max Weber* (1946) and *The Theory of Social and Economic Organization* (Part I of *Economy and Society*) (1947), which have remained in print continuously ever since. During the 1950s, many more Weber works appeared, most notably his comparative studies of world religions, some of his methodological essays, his sociology of law, and the fragmentary sociology of music.

It was at this point that Reinhard Bendix (1960) published his *Max Weber: An Intellectual Portrait*, a book that more than any other shaped learned opinion across disciplines about Weber's sociological and political theorizing and served as a surrogate for those thousands of social scientists for whom the original or translated works themselves proved too much of a burden to absorb. Although a few reviewers, like C. Wright Mills, found Bendix's version of Weber objectionably "bloodless," for the great majority Bendix's interpretation became dogma and remained so until at least the early 1980s when specialist monographs (there are now dozens) and a few full-scale treatments began to appear that were intentionally constructed around more "nuanced" approaches to Weber's complicated life and work (e.g., Käsler, 1988).

In short, the "Weber industry" has imitated the Dow Jones average during the last 20 years, so that what was still in the 1960s and 1970s a more or less tractable accumulation of scholarship, either generally inspired by Weber's ideas or directly attentive to his own work, has since then become a mountain too high for any one scholar to climb without losing consciousness. What I want to do in this chapter is give a topographical description of part of this comprehensive, embracing Weberian terrain as seen from an airplane overhead, rather than digging into specific debates at ground level, some of which are so intricate as almost to defy solution (e.g., the precise relationship between Weber's writings and those of the greatest German writer, Goethe; or how exactly was Weber's greatest work, *Economy and Society*, constructed into book form after his death; or in what ways does the Protestant Ethic thesis apply to farming communities in Wisconsin in the mid-19th century).

WEBER AND HIS IMAGE
IN TODAY'S POPULAR PRESS

The formerly sharp demarcation between "serious" thought and the discourse of mass media, particularly of the printed form, has lately become blurred at points almost beyond distinction, following closely Marshall McLuhan's (1964) predictions of 40 years ago. So before attending, however briefly, to the mountain of scholarly contributions that are clearly Weberian in nature, it might be useful to consider, as a micro-case study in the sociology of public knowledge, how Weber's name and reputation are currently exploited in the mass media. Put another way, why has the descriptor "Weberian" begun to be recognized among ever larger numbers of readers with the same facility that "Freudian" has been known since the 1930s? (I speak here only of English language cultures, since his name has long been better known in Europe for a variety of reasons, partly to do with a different division of labor there between academics and journalists.) It is fair to say that prior to the 1980s or so, his name was scarcely known to journalists, but as the cadré of "public intellectuals" or quasi-intellectuals themselves became more widely educated as a group, and as the labor market for their talents pushed them out of universities and into magazine or newspaper production, Weber became not only an historically recognizable and intriguing person, but an icon of sorts.

Probably the most important sign that Weber had crossed from the seminar room into public discourse was his central importance in Allan Bloom's (1987) *The Closing of the American Mind*, a semi-scholarly polemic that sold in the hundreds of thousands and was serialized in daily newspapers (e.g., the *Kansas City Star*). By using a caricatured argument first put forth by his beloved teacher, Leo Strauss (1953, pp. 36–78), Bloom's international bestseller argued somewhat preposterously that Nietzsche and Weber, in a combined assault upon so-called "Western cultural values," had themselves led the "youth movement" of the 1960s down the road of axiological nihilism. This dire development, Bloom argued forcefully, had in turn helped cause a Spengler-like "decline" in civility, educational standards, sexual morality, and associated features of cultural decomposition. This extraordinary contention was widely reported, reproduced, and apparently accepted by numbers of readers whose familiarity with Weber's own works seemed to go no further than Bloom's misuse of them.

In another book, while eulogizing Strauss, Bloom observed that "Strauss recognized the seriousness and nobility of Max Weber's mind, but he showed that he was a derivative thinker, standing somewhere between modern science and Nietzsche, unable to resolve their tensions" (Bloom, 1990, p. 238). There is no room here to investigate the flourishing debate over the strengths and weaknesses of Strauss's rationalist political philosophy. But it is important only to note that the joint effect of Strauss having declared that Weber's thought was "derivative," stranded between scientism and nihilism, plus Bloom's broadcasting this view to the world at large (very few ordinary readers ever having heard of Leo Strauss) established in "popular consciousness" a straw man of Weber, and one that only recently has begun to diminish in the mass media. For the record, Weber never claimed for an instant to be an "original thinker." His modesty, however, did not prevent one of Germany's most original philosophers of the 20th century, Karl Jaspers, from characterizing Weber as "the greatest German of our era" (Jaspers, 1989, p. 31), an epithet that has become famous since he wrote it in 1958. But that aside, if there is any truth to Whitehead's (1938) claim that "In Western literature there are four great thinkers.... These men are Plato, Aristotle, Leibniz, and William James" (p. 2), or, as he is often quoted, "Western philosophy is a footnote to Plato," then being "derivative" seems a universal fate. The real question, one could argue, is which writers are "more or less" derivative.

The more important issue is Bloom's charge that Weber's cultural influence has been pernicious, an accusation that still remains in place among literate nontheorists, largely owing to Bloom's posthumous influence and that of his imitators and students. One way of answering Bloom, though too briefly, is to remind his believing readers that Weber never held a brief for a particular set of values, epistemological or otherwise, unless he was writing an explicitly political tract. He simply reported what he uncovered using historical and contemporary data, in the most objective and value-free terms he could muster. And what he saw within Western culture at the fin-de-siècle provoked in him grave forebodings about the future of Europe and all those countries which imitated its general model of social organization. Now needless to say, these misgivings were fully borne out in the 45 years following Weber's unforgettable imagery at the close of the two essays (1904–1905) which became known in English as the *Protestant Ethic and the Spirit of Capitalism*:

> In [Richard] Baxter's view the care for external goods should only lie on the shoulders of the "saint like a light cloak, which can be thrown aside at any moment." But fate decreed that the cloak should become an iron cage.
>
> Since asceticism undertook to remodel the world and to work out its ideals in the world, material goods have gained an increasing and finally an inexorable power over the lives of men as at no previous period in history.... In the field of its highest development, in the United States, the pursuit of wealth, stripped of its religious and ethical meaning, tends to become associated with purely mundane passions, which often actually give it the character of sport.
>
> No one knows who will live in this cage in the future, or whether at the end of this tremendous development entirely new prophets will arise.... For of the last stage of this cultural development, it might well be truly said: "Specialists without spirit, sensualists without heart; this nullity imagines that it has attained a level of civilization never before achieved." (Weber, 1930, pp. 181–182; for the possible origin of the famous final quotation, see Sica, 1985)

I do not repeat these honored passages from Weber's most quotable book because they are unknown, but because they recently have come under reexamination for reasons Weber would never have imagined. This is one of Weber's charms, if I may put it that way.

He crafted the final paragraphs of his book with a burst of uncharacteristic rhetoric, a flurry of human sentiment, which he normally excluded from his "scientific" writing. The reason his words proved prescient and, if correctly read today, illustrate the inaccuracy of Bloom's charges against Weber (conflated somewhat with Nietzsche) is because his hopes for human liberation in the 20th century lay not with regimentation and "rationalization processes," but with their opposite. He never renounced the national-liberal tradition in which he was reared, never underestimated the significance of the nation–state in global politics, or the necessary harshness of *Realpolitik*. But he believed, as did Leo Strauss, that certain, definable human values were preservative of global society and others wholly destructive. The difference between them, and therefore with Bloom, lay in Weber's highly skeptical view of modernity, in his unwillingness to believe that the machinery of bureaucratized production and government would relinquish its iron grip on well-meaning individuals and allow them to pursue the philosophically virtuous lives that Strauss and Bloom recommended. Weber's "sin" does not lie in promoting destructive values for the 20th century but in believing that the era of individual righteousness had ended for macrostructural reasons—with the invention of the machinegun, barbed wire, poison gas, and high explosives (my own expression and not Weber's).

Bloom's student, friend, and beneficiary, Francis Fukuyama, exploded onto the highbrow popular culture scene in 1992, with *The End of History and the Last Man*, the first of three books that borrowed heavily from "serious" social and political theory and applied these ideas to contemporary concerns. Most recently he addressed the "literate middle class" in one of their favorite organs, *The Atlantic Monthly*, with a cover story designed to encourage Americans who had wearied of the social initiatives begun in the 1960s and now shown, so he claims, to be at the root of today's major forms of social disorganization (Fukuyama, 1999a). Once again Weber's name appears in multiple contexts, but usually under the same general theme: the dark, brooding, Germanic presence whose dread of modernity's apparent direction seems unduly fearsome to more optimistic spirits, like Fukuyama. It is unnecessary to recount the main argument to his first book, or the subsequent two of the series (Fukuyama, 1995, 1999b), other than to say that their general proclamation of "glad tidings" plays very well among victims of a shaken world order, yet would have been given short shrift by Weber, I suspect. The very virtues that Karl Jaspers saw in Weber—incorrigible honesty and acute insight, realism, and a refusal to indulge in mystical escape from painful truths—are missing or highly diluted in books like Fukuyama's. Part of being a Weberian lies in the responsibility to bear up under the weight of bad news without being rendered helpless by it, and this central ingredient of Weber's worldview seems always to be lacking in popularizations purporting to solve world problems through inspirational rhetoric. In short, "New Age" philosophy and Weberian thinking are antonymous.

Weber's name and his image, of the hyperserious, brooding Teuton, are appearing more regularly in the popular press than ever before, according to the data that have come my way. In a *New York Times* review of John Diggins' (1996) *Max Weber*, the political theorist Alan Ryan concludes his remarks by observing

> [The book's] purpose is an essentially uncomfortable one. It is to get readers to take Weber's distaste for the brashness, vulgarity and general foolishness of modern democratic societies as seriously as he, John Patrick Diggins, takes it. In that he is rather successful, not in showing that Weber's distaste was right, but in demonstrating that Weber made a case that needs to be answered—and today, surely, more urgently than ever. (Ryan, 1996, p. 14)

Ryan, as a renowned political philosopher, speaks with considerable authority, while other writers usually refer to Weber (far more often than actually quoting him) to validate some broad generalization they seek to make. But occasionally a truly interesting connection to Weber's influence is made, as in another recent *Atlantic Monthly* piece about today's reevaluation of Confucius: "Zhang Binglin used the cultural–evolutionary theories of Weber and Herbert Spencer to recast Kongzi ["Master Kong," i.e., Confucius] as a secular quasi-modern, China's first rationalizer of a superstitious indigenous tradition" (Allen, 1999, p. 83). This quotation manages to include a range of Weberian concerns: the role of the traditional intelligentsia in either promoting or retarding "modernization" ("rationalization") processes, the importance of charisma in a cultural or political leader, and the routine redefinition of cultural heritages in the face of societal evolution. In fact, the author might well have had a difficult time even conceptualizing the quoted sentence without an awareness of the Weberian viewpoint regarding Confucian ethics and its role in Chinese economic history (as explained in Weber, 1951).

Numerous other citations to Weber's ideas or his person have become available in subscholarly publications during the recent past. A few examples might give the general flavor of uses to which the Weberian heritage is now being put, for good or otherwise. Restricting ourselves to the last 3 years, one can find an abundance of references to Weber from the global press, not all of them mere grace notes to a given text's larger theme. Andrew Porter in the *New York Times Book Review*, evaluating a major book by the historian David Landes, observes:

> Landes's list of false prophets with misguided diagnoses is long. It includes dependency theorists; the new economic historians, who neglect older findings and dismiss any such thing as the Industrial Revolution; econometricians in pursuit of numbers, however unreal; multiculturalists irrelevantly quibbling over the terminology of European "discovery" of the rest of the world; ethnologists denying that there are grounds for criticizing or detecting weaknesses in another culture. By contrast, he admires the champion of the Protestant ethic Max Weber, and Karl Wittfogel, the outstanding student of what he calls "Oriental despotism." "If we learn anything from the history of economic development, it is that cultures makes all the difference," Landes says. (Porter, 1998, p. 15)

This use of Weber, particularly as a polemical weapon, is important in this context since Landes is a distinguished historian (especially of Egyptian economic history and of time-pieces), and the enclaves he is attacking by means of Weber have been for some time in the seat of academic power, especially in the United States. It is instructive that the reviewer is British. That Weber is made out to be "the champion" of the Protestant Ethic, of course, is a distorting simplification, as clearly indicated by the quotation above from the closing pages of that essential book. But his identification with that ever-growing stream of research on the relationship between religious impulses and socioeconomic action in some ways resembles Freud's connection in the "popular mind" with "id, ego, and superego," terms that in his own work are far from crystalline.

Mortimer Zuckerman, Editor-in-Chief of *U.S. News and World Report*, called upon Weber similarly in the context of "Creators of Our Prosperity," a paean to Bill Gates:

> However, the predominant view of entrepreneurs is pejorative, and the vocabulary is one of selfishness, greed, and self-interest. As George Gilder has written, it is as if "our wealth springs from some Faustian pact: a deal with the devil by which we gain material benefits in exchange for succumbing to the sin of avarice," while millions of worthy poor go hungry. Such a negative perception goes back a long way. Max Weber commented on it in the *Protestant Ethic and the Spirit of Capitalism*: "A flood of mistrust, sometimes of hatred, above all of moral indignation, regularly opposed itself to the fist innovator." (Zuckerman, 1998, p. 64; quotation is from Weber, 1930, p. 69)

Linking Gilder and Weber falls under the heading of journalistic license, but the quotation from *Protestant Ethic* is a good one and not often seen, even in the scholarly literature. Zuckerman claims that "American capitalism" managed to "confirm Weber's insight" by employing innovative trade practices and invention rather than hiding behind trade tariffs. The fact that this seriously distorts not only the record of American innovation proper, but also Weber's intensely nationalist appreciation for German trade barriers does not detract overmuch from the good use made here of his major ideas. Along with Lester Thurow, Weber is the only scholar named in Zuckerman's strongly worded endorsement of Gates' entrepreneurial "spirit." Thus, when an opinion-maker of high visibility such as Zuckerman chooses to speak of capitalist creativity, he turns without many alternatives (Sombart now being forgotten) to Weber.

This is only one step lower on the intellectual ladder from theologian Michael Novak's apologias for capitalist "ethics," including *The Spirit of Democratic Capitalism*, *The Catholic Ethic and the Spirit of Capitalism*, and *Business as a Calling: Work and the Examined Life*, all of them clearly imitating Weber's conceptual lead. As a winner of the lucrative Templeton Prize, Novak became an official spokesperson for what might be called "Christian business practices," if such a phrase were not at base oxymoronic. He, too, often quotes Weber, while trying to legitimate worldwide predatory capitalist practices (e.g., Novak, 1996, pp. 80–81, 119–120). That Weber would almost surely regard Novak's "casuistry"—precisely that right word for Novak's thinking, and one which Weber applied even to himself—as subtle capitalist propaganda does not detract from the fact that without Weber's ideas, writers like Novak would be able to construct a much less coherent argument. The same can be said for a British columnist who begins an op-ed piece in *The Guardian* (London) thus: "Passivity and fatalism used to be regarded as oriental failings by Rudyard Kipling and his like. These characteristics were often attributed, no doubt falsely, to the influence of oriental religions compared with the capitalist-oriented Protestantism celebrated by Max Weber" (Holtham, 1998, p. 17). This smattering of learning is typical in the higher echelons of the British press, once again setting up a straw man to which is attached the label "Max Weber."

A staff writer from the European office of *The Wall Street Journal* took another route down the Weberian linguistic path while reviewing a philosophy book: "… illegitimate application of scientific reasoning tends to shrink our world, to 'disenchant' it, in Max Weber's famous term" (Pollock, 1998). The German term, *Entzauberung*, means literally to remove magic, to "demagicalize," for which "disenchantment" is not a wholly satisfactory translation, particularly given the cultural background to Weber's particular use of the word. Nevertheless, it has become a readily recognizable term in the Weberian language of cultural criticism, though one whose prominence today would probably surprise and annoy Weber, since it seems to make of him an epigone of Nietzsche (reminiscent of Bloom's accusation). Still another Weberianism (if I may coin a term) appears in a review of Daniel P. Moynihan's *Secrecy*: "As noted by historian Richard Gid Powers in his trenchant introduction, Moynihan's most formidable insight (borrowed from Max Weber) is that secrecy is a form of regulation in which bureaucrats hoard secrets like assets" (Kirkus Reviews, 1998). It is interesting that this rather minor point in Weber's definitive analysis of bureaucratic behavior, as intriguing as it is given today's post-Watergate political culture, should be "Moynihan's most formidable insight," apparently rediscovered by the senator 90 years after Weber first made it part of his encompassing theory of organizational functioning. Yet as is so often the case, the anonymous reviewer nodded toward Weber primarily in order to indicate that Moynihan's analysis of Washington's political life is more "serious" and "theoretically grounded" than the run-of-the-mill Washington, DC, memoir.

Within a month of Holtham's piece in *The Guardian*, a columnist for *The Wall Street Journal* made use of still another chestnut from the Weber lexicon:

> Death and enemies drive dictators from power, but notable democratic leaders have fallen time and again at the hands of electorates whose gratitude has worn thin under the grind of politics; sociologist Max Weber called this phenomenon "routinization of charisma." Weber held that a leader can keep his job only by repeatedly demonstrating his specialness. (Steinmetz, 1998, p. 1)

It becomes clear, then, that as one proceeds through a range of more or less highbrow organs of mass culture, a briskly formed familiarity with Weber's ideas becomes discernible, as key phrases appear regularly: Protestant Ethic thesis, iron cage of bureaucratized life, transformations of charismatic authority to fit modern politics, and so on. What is lacking, of course, is any contextual or elaborated understanding of what exactly Weber intended by these terms and to which historical configurations he intended them to be applied. Still another gambit, particularly popular since 1989, is to announce that "Max Weber has triumphed over Karl Marx" (MacShane, 1998). Given that during Weber's first year of teaching, he took a class through Marx's *Das Kapital* with painstaking thoroughness, and that his comments on Marx's work were invariably respectful, remarks of this order substitute the crass political symbols "Marx" and "Weber" for the scholars known by the same names.

The most amusing popular use of Weber during 1998 appeared in *The Observer*, where Simon Caulkin (1998) described him under the rubric of the "Guru Guide" of the week, apparently a regular feature of the paper. Scanning the formulaic categories "Age," "Claim to fame," "Biography," "Achievement," and "Said," the busy modern reader can "get the gist" of Weberian theory in only 276 words. One of his alleged "claims to fame" is "co-draughtsman of the constitution of the Weimar Republic," an odd and insupportable remark when the details of the case are studied carefully; in fact, Weber's most cherished ideas and suggestions were jettisoned by the constitution's real author, Hugo Preuss (Mommsen, 1984, pp. 332–389; Halperin, 1946, pp. 154–167). Caulkin (1998, p. 8) admirably captures what I referred to above as "the Weberian mood":

> Although Weber is ridiculed [by whom?] for his description of the ideal bureaucracy as "the most rational means of carrying out imperative control over human beings," history has the last, and darker, laugh. Today's call-centres and fast-food outlets do nothing to dispel Weber's thesis of a society increasingly alienated by formal rationality; nor his insight that formal rationality often has irrational consequences (such as the dehumanisation of work). Weber also wrote tellingly about hierarchy, leadership and authority. Neo-Weberians, of which there are many, sometimes suggest that Scott Adams, creator of Dilbert, is their man in disguise.

I do not know any neo-Weberians who have made the connection in print between Dilbert and Weber's theorizing—perhaps because it is too obvious to merit mention—through for years I have indeed pointed to this confluence in my lectures to undergraduates. What is most intriguing about Caulkin's précis of Weber's ideas is that it appears on the "Observer Work Page," presumably for the edification of the busy executive who might want to know the serious background to Dilbert's black humor.

The final entry of popularized Weberianism from 1998 is a brief but dense article in the less ordinary venue, *Management Today*. Borrowing from a 1967 polemic against psychological theory by Arthur Koestler, the author entitles his comment "The Ghost in the Machine." Stuart Crainer quotes lightly from Parsons's 1947 translation of *Wirtschaft und Gesellschaft* (Part One), arguing that "The man saddled with the reputation of being the founding father of the mechanistic world view is Max Weber." The bureaucratic "machine" was to work efficiently, as Weber described it, and human "needs" (of the kind Marx wrote about) became irrelevant:

> But this does not mean that Weber advocated the bureaucratic system. He simply described it.... In many ways the bureaucratic world mapped out by Weber is similar to Orwell's *1984*: a nightmare scenario rather than a prediction. In some respects, the nightmare has come to pass. Henry Ford echoed many of Weber's thoughts in his faith in strict demarcations and a fervently mechanistic approach to business. Ford preferred science to art. "How come when I want a pair of hands, I get a human being as well?" he lamented. (Crainer, 1998, p. 87)

While linking Orwell and Weber has become a standard ploy among cultural critics, the tie with Ford is less plausible, since his unapologetic, aggressive capitalism shared very little with Weber's humanistic values. Though granting that the machine "metaphor" (here falsely attributed to Weber) now has been replaced with those of "fractals and amoebas—elusive and ever-changing rather than efficient and static," Crainer ends his piece in a way that has become standard fare for journalists who exploit Weber's larger ideas: "Even so, Max Weber remains important.... Weber's bureaucratic model stands as a constant reminder of what could be. Aspects of the bureaucratic model remain alive in many organisations. Weber's world lives on and not only in our nightmares" (Crainer, 1998, p. 87).

Weber's name, often attached to some of his best-known ideas, continued to appear in the mass media dozens of times in 1999 and 2000. There is no room here to analyze carefully even the most provocative samples of this peculiar, relatively new form of transplantation—moving material from texts of the most densely systematic social thought into those that suit the facile needs of everyday journalism. A dozen items from 1999 exhibit an even wider range of usages than those from the preceding year. From the subcontinent, a letter to *The Statesman* quotes Weber's "insightful" *Religion of India* in order to buttress a subtle argument regarding today's caste system (Sarbadhikari, 1999). Another uses Ritzer's "McDonalisation thesis," as an extension of Weber's rationalization theory, to explain why modern tourism has become "a version of being at home" (Boddy, 1999). A feature story in *Lingua Franca* characterizes Roberto Unger's recent utopianism as "a fusion of Christian romanticism, Max Weber, and the Marquis de Sade," surely an improbable amalgam, and one that would probably have perplexed even Weber (Press, 1999). At the other extreme, a British historian nominates Weber as an "overrated author" in the *Sunday Telegraph* (London):

> It is a sign of a truly overblown reputation when one is referred to rather than actually read. Weber's theory that the industrious culture of capitalism evolved from the ascetic culture of Puritanism is well known. But who has actually waded through the *Protestant Ethic*.... Anyone who bothers will be dismayed by the discrepancy between Weber's huge assertions and the tiny empirical basis on which they rest.... There is no denying that Weber had big ideas. (Ferguson, 1999, p. 15)

This is a standard dismissal, particularly from Catholic writers, but given that no fewer than three new English translations of the *Protestant Ethic* are soon slated for publication, and that serious reanalysis of Weber's "thesis" continues apace, assertions like those of Ferguson's seem futile. In fact, the opposite viewpoint was expressed within several months in *The Daily Telegraph* (London) under the heading "Weber was Right":

> Max Weber's theory about the correlation between Protestantism and progress may be discredited by many of your readers (letters, July 3), but it is alive and thriving in South America. During the past two decades, many South Americans have abandoned "Marxist" Catholicism for the un-ashamedly capitalist fervour of the growing evangelical Protestant churches throughout Brazil, Argentina, and Mexico. In Brazil the evangelical Protestants are transforming the urban poor into a new entrepreneurial class. They have formed a separate political group in parliament and are doing for Brazil what Methodism did for Britain during the early stages of the industrial revolution (O'Grady, 1999, p. 25)

The use of Weber's name as a cultural "icon" further illustrates that even for those millions who will never "wade through" the *Protestant Ethic* or *Economy and Society* , his larger ideas—or the popularized surrogates for the actual ideas themselves—somehow "resonate" with today's cultural themes. In one whimsical article, Max Weber is claimed to form a so-called "mondegreen" (i.e., the mishearing of popular song lyrics, slogans, or sayings) for the words "Las Vegas" (Carroll, 1999). In another, serious article from *The New York Times* about software and human thought, the puzzling observation is made that "Academic critics echo the arguments made by Max Weber and Marshall McLuhan ("the medium is the message") that form has a critical impact on content" (Zuckerman, 1999, pp. 4–5 of online edition). Linking Weber and McLuhan might be feasible in some contexts, but this instance is ingenuous, first, because the observation attributed to both men is a platitude, and second, because to my knowledge Weber never wrote anything about this general topic. At a higher level, but in the same zone of rhetorical impertinence, a reviewer of a scholarly book about ancient Athens begins with, "To possess the capacity to be amazed by the world, Max Weber wrote, is a prerequisite of all unbiased inquiry. The Classical Athenians had this capacity in abundance ..." (Stace, 1999, p. 3). Here it is enough, so the reviewer apparently believes, to invoke Weber's name in order to set the correct tone of high seriousness for what follows. With less solemnity, *The Independent* (London) offered this "Thought for the Day": "The experience of the irrationality of the world has been the driving force of all religious revolution," attributed to "Max Weber, German sociologist" (*The Independent*, 2000, p. 3). One wonders what the newspaper's readers made of this decontextualized observation since Weber specialists are still debating its precise meaning.

Weber's name seems to spark imaginations across the globe, at least in the higher reaches of print journalism, especially as a handy device for grabbing the reader's attention. Closer to home, a reviewer in *The Washington Post* opens an essay with

> It was the roaring '90s—the 1690s—and British investors were swept up in a passion for new technologies, emerging markets and new theories of the discounted value of future earnings. Initial pubic offerings were the rage, new financial derivatives were invented, and ordinary citizens invested as never before. Centuries later, the era's commercial zeal was even elevated to philosophical heights *by no less* than Max Weber, who declared the robust capitalism of the age an extension of the Enlightenment and evidence of the triumph of rationalism. (Mufson, 1999, p. X06; emphases added)

That this is almost entirely wrong regarding Weber's ideas—*not* the Enlightenment but the Reformation, not "rationalism" but "rational action"—is beside the point. What matters in this context is that the words "Max Weber" when used in concert have become part of the lingua franca of "civilized discourse," a shorthand notation covering a range of sociocultural concerns that even a decade ago would not have seemed plausible. When a Scottish journalist writes, "Take away or undervalue these things [cultural values] and we reduce teachers to what Max Weber called specialists without spirit, soulless technicians constructing machines rather than forming persons," he efficiently situates his argument in a proud polemical lineage against the mediocre and overly rationalized (Reilly, 1999, p. 15). Other recent linkages to Weber were forged regarding the St. Louis Exposition of 1904, which Weber attended (Tolson, 1999), the relationship of Hans Kelsen, the great legal theorist, to Weber as explained by a celebrated German novelist and jurist (Schlink, 1999), and Mother Teresa's "indefinable quality that Max Weber called charisma" (Johnson, 2000).

During the first part of 2000, Weber has been used even for academic humor: "Refusing to be hemmed in with a 'career,' Ralf Gothoni, the Finnish pianist–conductor, echoes Max Weber, the German founder of modern sociology, who once complained, 'I do not have a field because I am not a donkey' " (Binaghi, 2000, p. 24). It seems that Weber's sentiments are now entering the realm of the apocryphal. Competition between journalists to cite Weber even hints at mild plagiarism, e.g., an editorial from *The Economist* begins "Max Weber once described politics as a struggle between bureaucracy and charisma" (*Economist*, 2000), when from India only 4 weeks later a similar piece opens thus: "Max Weber once described politics as a struggle between charisma and bureaucracy" (Pande, 2000). Other works within the same few months allude to Weber's distinction in "Politics as a Vocation" between those who live "for politics" versus "from politics" (Martinez-Saenz, 2000, p. 17), or Weber's ideas about how historical causality should be established (Mclynn, 2000). In the opening pages of a popular book, *Bobos in Paradise*, about today's nouveaux riches, the author comments, "Finally, a word about the tone of this book. There aren't a lot of statistics in these pages. There's not much theory. Max Weber has nothing to worry about from me" (Brooks, 2000, p. 3). Of all the names Brooks could have chosen to distinguish his chatty social analysis from "theory" proper, Weber's apparently seemed to him the most austere or authoritative.

The most important recent comparison between Weber and another social analyst has occurred in the British press, where Manuel Castells' latest, essentially cheery pronouncements about globalization and the internet-driven economy have been pointedly compared to the otherwise unrivaled Weber. For example, "Castells will be ranked by future generations as comparable in breadth and stature to Max Weber or Emile Durkheim" (Taylor, 2000, p. 12), or "[Castells' book] *The Information Age: Economy, Society, and Culture* [is] a work which, in one admiring view, does for the internet economy what Max Weber's the *Protestant Ethic* ... did for the industrial age a century. Like Weber, Castells is European.... He is also a social theorist." The author later wisely observes that "Castell's internet is also a deeply unsentimental place, as underdeveloped socially as it is overdeveloped technologically. Weber would recognise it at once. Thus it excludes unwanted elements as ruthlessly as it embraces what's valued" (Caulkin, 2000, p. 9). A comparison of Castells' work with Weber's along the lines suggested here will likely be carried out by some enterprising graduate student eventually, but one wonders what exactly such a study would yield. In a way, of course, Castells' 1000-page "three decker" is precisely not what the "global libertarian hacker culture" needs or wants from its social theorists—to the extent this "culture" (essentially young males) is aware that such work even exists. If Castells is right about the socially "underdeveloped" nature of globalized electronic "culture," the role of literacy-based social theory of the kind Weber and Durkheim pioneered is thrown entirely into question, in much the same way that classical music has been ousted from the hearts of ordinary people by popular forms ever since World War II. Who can now believe that the Metropolitan Opera radio broadcasts of the 1930s and 1940s were then considered "popular culture"? The reason that Caulkin's premonition about Castells' eventual status as a rival to Weber in the realm of social theory seems far-fetched has less to do with Castells' abilities than with the nature of reasoned social analysis in a postliterate, image-driven society. Weber chose from an abundance of texts to analyze and the specific historical groups who tried to live by them. What materials can Castells draw on of comparable intellectual density? And even if they could be shown to exist, to have been created by analogously self-conscious social entities—in ways that resemble the role of Richard Baxter's or John Calvin's writings as part of the Protestant transformation of Europe and the United States—where is an audience of the kind who have been studying the *Protestant Ethic* unremittingly for nearly a century?

Last, from the plethora of popular references to Weber, several verge on the absurd: a popular book called *Charisma: Seven Keys to Developing the Magnetism That Leads to Success* (Alessandra, 1998), the advertisement for which reads "Now Tony Alessandra explores the most crucial element in gaining success in every phase of your life. It's the power, mysterious, unstoppable force called ... *Charisma*.... Breaking down charisma into its key ingredients—the ability to talk, to adapt, to listen, to speak, and to persuade ... Using self-quizzes and power examples of charisma in action, Tony offers you a step-by-step program of 'charisma basics'." Presumably Jesus, Confucius, Luther, Mao Zedong, and others of that ilk would have done even better in their "careers" had they studied this book before "deciding" to become charismatic. A full-page magazine ad for a line of bedding called "Charisma" features a "headshot" of Marilyn Monroe at her most photogenic, with the caption "Some People are Born with Charisma; Others Just Buy It." The Mendel Group, part of "BioMed Management Systems," offered online in 1997 something called the "Rationalization Grid," a term that they copyrighted, that "applies a matrix-based approach to the standard licensing process. Products are selected based on more objective, customized criteria that incorporate rapid screening, classification, and priority ranking of in-licensing candidates based on preset parameters." The language is ersatz Weberian, but the aim seems to revolve around the selection of medical treatments based on a "multidimensional matrix" of "preset criteria." But surely the most charming "use" of Weber's theoretical insight comes from the cattle-breeding industry. In 1998, a bull named Foreplay, at 2345 pounds, with suitable scores on both "Frame" and "Scrotal," was described as having fathered calves that brought large prices, from $6,000 to $22,000 each: "These calves reflect Foreplay's extreme thickness, moderate frame, whistle front, uncanny style, and *abundance of charisma*. Foreplay has been used successfully on heifers due to the light birth weight of his calves" (SEK Genetics, 1998). Perhaps his owners read Alessandra's book on "how to become charismatic" to the bull when he was young.

It could be argued, and not facetiously, that the proliferating appearances of Weber's name and ideas in the printed mass media are much more important as a contribution to "globalization" than is his perennial popularity among academic scholars. It often is claimed that one defining quality of cross-cultural postmodern culture is the breakdown of barriers between regions, religions, and the finer distinctions of quality that previously held sway. If this is true, then one knowing reference to Weber's ideas, say, about the rationalization process in *The Economist* or *The Washington Post* is surely "worth" a hundred articles in "refereed journals" with readership numbering in the hundreds rather than hundreds of thousands or millions. Though impossible to analyze adequately here, it would seem that this fairly new phenomenon—the "popularization of Weberianism"—will probably itself become a subfield within the "Weber industry" or the sociology of culture in the not too distant future.

ACADEMIC DIRECTIONS
OF WEBERIAN SCHOLARSHIP

A distinction could be made, and probably should be, between so-called "substantive" works that are explicitly inspired by one or another of Weber's "big ideas" (e.g., the charismatic nature of the "founders" of the American Republic) and theoretically motivated writings that probe, expand upon, or truncate an idea or set of notions which Weber offered the social science community during his most fertile creative period. The comprehensive bibliography I have assembled naturally contains far more works of the former type than of the latter. This is because—as evidenced in the journalistic literature—it has become *de rigueur* for scholars of all kinds to invoke Weber's concepts in order to lend luster to their work or to clarify a thorny point that crops up in their data that seems otherwise intractable. Yet the number of theorists who have come to know Weber's work thoroughly enough and with sufficient subtlety to expand upon it, or to clarify some notion of his that appears insufficiently lucid in the original, has remained relatively small. Such so-called "hard-core Weberians," despite their pedantic tendencies, play a vital role in clarifying the original texts from semiphilological or purely conceptual points of view. Selected works by Roth (2000), Roth and Schluchter (1979), Mommsen (2000), Hennis (1988), Scaff (1989), Kalberg (1994, 1997a), Oakes (1988), or Burger (1976/1987) typify this sort of work, which is as indispensable to a precise understanding of Weber as it is generally unknown to most other researchers who simply utilize one or another of Weber's ideas as it suits their projects.

Yet Weber's ideas have come to "infect" and affect so many realms of scholarship that it would be difficult even to list them all. To take but one typical example, a serious battle of wits has consumed the energies of historians for some time in trying to ascertain the validity of "the Protestant ethic thesis" (in addition to other Weberian notions) when applied to Colonial and Federalist America. Applications of Weber's ideas within the context of American history are as various as his substantive and theoretical innovations were far-flung. The notable aversion many historians feel for the "merely theoretical" (see Burke, 1992, pp. 1–11, for an enlightened discussion of this condition) has not prevented them from plundering Weber's ideas when it suited them, though it is clear that many more could have strengthened their studies had they known more about his methods and ideas (for an exception, see Jäger, 1991). The uniquely high quality of Weber's theorizing probably reflects the fact that his generalizations always grew directly from contact with historical data and his unswerving desire to solve substantive problems by means of theoretical innovation.

Popular uses of his ideas among historians have included treatments of presidents and other leaders who either exhibited "charisma" (Lincoln, both Roosevelts, Kennedy; see particularly Schwartz, 1987, on Washington, and Schwartz, 2000, on Lincoln) or who lacked this mysterious power over their followers (most of the remaining ones). The church historian, Rudolf Sohm, supplied Weber with a scholarly use of charisma ("gift of grace"), but Weber characteristically broadened it to include forms of political, military, or religious leadership that draw on "irrational" sources of attraction to inflame followers. Hundreds of studies have put to use Weber's explanation of "charismatic domination" (the *locus classicus* for which is in his *Economy and Society*, pp. 1111–1114 and 1141–1142), including those by Lindholm (1990), Spencer (1980), Peacock (1989), and Schweitzer (1984). No one has argued that this relatively small part of Weber's oeuvre can be viewed as an unassailable analytic device, yet its widespread use among historians and other social scientists, even in diluted form, suggests its fundamental strength as a way of interpreting macropolitical events.

The "Protestant ethic thesis" is a perennial favorite with which historians love to do battle, often with carefully documented caveats. The debate has by now occasioned several thousand publications in international scholarship. It is unnecessary to recount Weber's argument here, other than to note that its subtleties are very often missed, perhaps because most of the data are buried in forbidding endnotes that make up over half the printed text. Briefly, he held that in northern Europe, Britain, and the United States, attitudes toward work, savings, and a prohibition against conspicuous consumption (to use Veblen's term, coined in 1900; see Diggins, 1999, pp. 111ff, for a comparison of Weber's and Veblen's theories of capitalist development) all conspired to establish fertile ground in which capitalism could flourish. Southern European (hence, Catholic) countries, as well as those in Asia, did not inculcate their citizens with the requisite virtues of thrift, punctuality, rational accounting, and a fear of luxurious living, necessarily attached to ideas of predestination, that Weber identified as essential for capitalist processes and economic organization. It is important to note that Weber did not argue that sharp business practices had never existed, say, in China, India, or Italy. Rather, capital accumulation and rational accounting procedures had never found so suitable an ideological basis as that provided by Reformation theology, much of which can be summarized in the unique German concept of *Beruf* (God-given work).

One need not look very far in American religious texts to find documentation of this attitude. It was well summarized by Thomas Chalkley, an American Quaker:

We not only have Liberty to labour in Moderation, but … it is our duty so to do. The Farmer, the Tradesman, and the Merchant do not understand by our Lord's doctrine, that they must neglect their Calling, or grow idle in their Business, but must certainly work, and be industrious in their Calling (Tolles, 1948, p. 56)

Needless to say, his arguments about this issue, particularly because he used Benjamin Franklin's *Autobiography* (see *inter alia*, Axelrad, 1978; Bier, 1970), Richard Baxter's devotional literature (see Cooke, 1994), and other familiar writings as hallmarks of "the Protestant ethic," have been scrutinized in extraordinary detail. Not surprisingly, when particular cases have been considered [e.g., the merchants of 17th century Boston (Bailyn, 1955)], what is taken to be Weber's general prescription for capitalist growth has not always held (see Henretta, 1991, pp. 35–70; also Buck, 1993; Johnson, 1971; Kolbenschlag, 1976; for a sharp critique, see Kolko, 1961; for an intriguing extension concerning presidential rhetoric, see Falk, 1980). Part of this is the result of misinterpretation of what Weber actually claimed (for thorough documentation, see Lehmann & Roth, 1993; also Hudson, 1988), and partly it is because even as good as he was in handling historical data, he could not possibly anticipate every "anomalous case" that researchers would subsequently be able to identify, e.g., "The Business Ideology of Benjamin Franklin and Japanese Values of the 18th Century" (Watanabe, 1988).

James Henretta (1991) has examined the Weber thesis carefully in terms of the Colonial American case, and overall finds considerable support for the argument, even if modifications must be made to accommodate peculiarities of place and time. First of all, it is childsplay to find quotations from early Americans, especially in Quaker Philadelphia or Puritan Massachusetts, who wrote testaments of faith that clearly support Weber's portrait of the prototypical capitalist "mentality." As Weber put it, dedication to a calling originated in "rational planning of the whole of one's life in accordance with God's will" (Weber, 1930, p. 153). Bailyn had already demonstrated the persuasiveness of Weber's view in an early work, by quoting sources like Joshua Scottow of Boston, who, after moving to Maine, declared in 1691 that mercantile Boston had become "a lost Town … We must cry out" and admit "our Leanness, our Apostasy" (Bailyn, 1955, pp. 122–123). Scottow knew that unbridled capitalist activity would spell the end of religious devotion, even as devout practices enlarged capitalist fortunes. Perry Miller (1953) and Frederick Tolles (1948) were early students of this phenomenon, and recognized that "the lives of such Puritans and Quakers were not easy, for this religious doctrine created a major tension in their lives" (Henretta, 1991, p. 38). As their fortunes grew, the strain within their religiosity and that of their children naturally began to tell. Existential contradictions of this type were studied by later historians of the phenomenon, such as Foster (1971) and Ziff (1973), and even though certain clarifications of Weber's claims had to be made, the edifice of his argument held.

The most important alteration sprang from the insight that independent entrepreneurial activity generated substantial friction when set opposite the needs of community, a problem that surfaced very early, as most famously documented in *The Apologia of Robert Keayne* (Bailyn, 1965). Keayne, a successful merchant, was punitively fined in 1639 for having practiced what we now call "price-gouging," but his ornate self-defense celebrates the virtues of his business practices as part and parcel of his religious devoutness. Joyce Appleby (1984, 1993), Jack P. Greene (1988), Karl Hertz (1991), Daniel Howe (1972), Rex Lucas (1971), Gary Nash (1984), and Michael Walzer (1963) have elaborated this modification of the Weberian picture, highlighting the economic communalism that was practiced in early American society as opposed to ruthless capitalist practices of the ideal type. Bruce Mann (1980, 1987) extended this stream of argument from the familiar case of Boston to a Connecticut village, with particular attention to the ways "community norms of equity" controlled profit-making (Henretta, 1991, p. 68). Yet even with all such qualifications duly registered, Henretta summarizes his survey with this observation: "The ambiguities of the 'Protestant ethic' carried to New England by John Hull, Joshua Scottow, and John Higginson had achieved a clear definition in the 'capitalist spirit' of the founders of Waltham and Lowell, their religious and biological descendants" (Henretta, 1991, p. 70). Thus, considering early American history without utilizing Weber's ideas seems at this point in scholarly developments almost inconceivable.

A number of tangent scholarly streams can be connected to the Protestant ethic debate. In a recent publication, Dorothy Ross has shown that

> Another kind of new history emerged from efforts to use modernization theory as the narrative and analytical spine of American historiography. Modernization theory descends from ideas of liberal progress that have been powerful since the eighteenth century and from the sociological theories of Ferdinand Tönnies and Max Weber (Ross, 1998, p. 93)

She enlarges the argument by pointing out that modernization theory served broad American political interests during the Cold War as an antidote to revolutionary Marxism, "casting economic development as the prime motor of progress, to which were linked changes in personality and politics ... it tended to view modernization as an integrated, deterministic process but allowed for failure, particularly through the semiautonomous sphere of politics" (1998, p. 93). Although historians were "wary of it from the start," modernization theory had a strong impact on American foreign policy and theories of global economic life, much of which owes its fundamental notions to Weber's work in his magnum opus, *Economy and Society*. Just as an understanding of imperialism as an economic or political policy is impossible to understand with reference to Marx's work, so too modernization theory must necessarily be tied to Weber's conceptualization of the global market and the violent struggles that typically occur when "traditional" societies are confronted by those committed to "rational action," particularly along economic lines. An important contribution to this neo-Weberian research was Robert Wiebe's (1967) *The Search for Order, 1877–1920* , in which "island communities" were shown over time to be unwillingly amalgamated into a nation-state built on capitalist foundations. Wiebe's version of what happened undercuts naive views of bureaucratization as being seamless, untroubled processes, for in fact, "separate bureaucracies, barely joined in some areas, openly in conflict elsewhere" were more the norm than the exception as the United States was being shaped into the mid-century powerhouse it later became (Wiebe, 1967, p. 300).

The range of historiography regarding US culture, from its colonial beginnings to its postmodern incarnation, which has benefited from Weber's ideas, is obviously too broad and deep to canvass here in any detail. But a sense of its scope might be gained by mentioning a few other studies of the sort that now make up the Weberian canon. General statements that highlight Weber's utility to historiographical method include William Green (1993) and H. Stuart Hughes (1960). Earl Hamilton (1929) long ago used a Weberian perspective in showing how riches plundered from the Americas buttressed capitalist development in Europe. One of many such works, Ronen Shamir (1993) contrasted "formal" versus "substantive" rationalization in American legal history, two Weberian notions that are as central to the history and sociology of law as "charisma" has become to studies of leadership. Fresh additions to this vast literature include those of Kennedy (2000), Marsh (2000), and Joerges (2000). There also is a body of work that connects Weber as a political actor or researcher with actual US conditions during his lifetime, including Eileen Leonard's (1975) prescient dissertation, and Jonathan Imber's (1996) more recent reflections. The history of political theory and practice in the United States also can be easily linked with Weber's work, e.g., in Stephen Kalberg's (1997b) studies. John King's (1983) *The Iron of Melancholy* illustrates how a more psycho-historical vantage point can be tied fruitfully to old-fashioned concerns with conversion processes and religious activity. Such studies are the tip of an iceberg that has not yet been thoroughly analyzed, either by American historians or by Weber scholars.

In addition to issues of charisma and the Protestant ethic, American historians have been concerned at least since the days of Charles Beard with questions surrounding objectivity in the transmission of historical knowledge. Weber, of course, wrote the seminal works in this regard, delivered as two speeches to large, unsympathetic audiences, "Science as a Vocation" (1917) and "Politics as a Vocation" (1919) (both in *From Max Weber*, 1946, pp. 77–156). His contentious argument insisted that the scholar's job is to tell the truth, no matter what the social costs, and that the politician's is to further the goals of his or her platform, once duly elected. Thus, they cannot be one in the same person, and he who conflates the two roles risks destroying the efficacy of both. Weber's beliefs in this regard have been subjected to endless critique, most recently by Haskell (1998, pp. 15–19, 337–345, *passim*) and Novick (1988). Yet in any analysis of the political uses to which social knowledge is put, Weber's essays form the bedrock of all subsequent discussion. The same can be said—and has been with increasing frequency during the last 30 years—for nearly all Weber's theoretical work in its relation to the most ambitious forms of historical writing and thinking now being carried out, here and abroad.

What this excursus on Weberian inroads into American historiography suggests is this: using my bibliography as a database, one could surely continue along the lines I have begun here, with the rather tidy example of American history, and divide the bulk of empirical or substantive studies into a range of plausible categories. These might include topics such as power, legitimation, cross-cultural assessments of the Protestant ethic thesis, ideal types and related methodological problems, rationalization processes considered historically and comparatively, changes in bureaucratic organization and procedure, the role of the press, the sociology of music, 20th-century German politics, global geopolitics, the Russian revolutions of 1905 and 1917, and changes in the nature of charismatic domination after Weber's death, to name a very few. But such an undertaking must await another occasion. Meanwhile, it is enough to observe that Weber's significance seems to grow daily, as scholars attempt to understand the contemporary socioeconomic and political world by means of analytic devices and categories he devised more than 80 years ago.

REFERENCES

Selected Works by Max Weber in English translation

Weber, Max (1927). *General Economic History*, tr. Frank Knight. London: Allen and Unwin. (Reissued in 1981 by Transaction Publishers).

Weber, Max. (1930). *The Protestant Ethic and the Spirit of Capitalism*, tr. Talcott Parsons. London: Allen and Unwin. (Reissued in 1995 by Roxbury Publishing Co.)

Weber, Max. (1946). *From Max Weber: Essays in Sociology*, tr., ed., and intro. by Hans H. Gerth & C. Wright Mills. New York: Oxford University Press.

Weber, Max. (1947). *The Theory of Social and Economic Organization*, tr. A. M. and Talcott Parsons, ed. and intro. Talcott Parsons. New York: Oxford University Press.

Weber, Max. (1951). *Religion of China: Confucianism and Taoism*, tr. and ed. Hans H. Gerth. Glencoe, IL: Free Press.

Weber, Max. (1952). *Ancient Judaism*, tr. and ed. by Hans H. Gerth & Don Martindale. Glencoe, IL: Free Press.

Weber, Max. (1968). *Economy and Society: An Outline of Interpretive Sociology*, 3 vols., ed. Guenther Roth & Claus Wittich. New York: Bedminster Press. (Reissued in 1978 in 2 volumes by the University of California Press.)

Weber, Max. (1976). *The Agrarian Sociology of Ancient Civilizations*, tr. R. I. Frank. London: NLB.

Weber, Max. (1994). *Weber: Political Writings*, ed. Peter Lassman & Ronald Speirs. New York: Cambridge University Press.

Weber, Max. (1995). *The Russian Revolutions*, tr. Gordon C. Wells & Peter Baehr. Oxford: Polity Press.

Works about Weber or Using His Ideas

Alessandra, Tony (1998). *Charisma: Seven Keys to Developing the Magnetism that Leads to Success*. New York: Warner Books.

Allen, Charlotte (1999). Confucius and the Scholars. *Atlantic Monthly, 283*(4), 78–83.

Appleby, Joyce (1984). "Value and Society." In Jack P. Greene & J. R. Pole (Eds.), *Colonial British America: Essays in the New History of the Early Modern Era* (pp. 291ff.). Baltimore: Johns Hopkins University Press.

Appleby, Joyce (1993). "New Cultural Heroes in the Early National Period." In Thomas L. Haskell & Richard F. Teichgraeber III (Eds.), *The Culture of the Market: Historical Essays* (pp. 163–188). Cambridge, UK: Cambridge University Press.

Axelrad, Allan M. (1978). The Protagonist of the Protestant Ethic: Max Weber's Benjamin Franklin. *Rendezvous, 13*(2), 45–59.

Bailyn, Bernard (1955). *The New England Merchants in the Seventeenth Century*. Cambridge, MA: Harvard University Press.

Bailyn, Bernard (Ed.) (1965). *The Apologia of Robert Keayne: The Last Will and Testament of Me, Robert Keayne, All of It Written With My Own Hands and Began by Me, MO: 6: I: 1653, Commonly Called August*. New York: Harper & Row.

Bendix, Reinhard (1960). *Max Weber: An Intellectual Portrait*. New York: Doubleday. (Reissued in 1998, London: Routledge.)

Bier, Jesse (1970). Weberism, Franklin, and the Transcendental Style. *New England Quarterly, 43*(2), 179–192.

Binaghi, Claudia (2000). Dark Horse Likes to Gallop Free [Letter to the Editor]. *Financial Times* (London), May 15, p. 24.

Bloom, Allan (1987). *The Closing of the American Mind*. New York: Simon and Schuster.

Bloom, Allan (1990). *Giants and Dwarfs: Essays 1960–1990*. New York: Simon and Schuster.

Boddy, Kasia (1999). Travelling as a Version of Being at Home. *The Independent* (London), February 26, p. 7.

Brooks, David (2000). *Bobos in Paradise: The New Upper Class and How They Got There*. New York: Simon and Schuster.

Buck, Robert Enoch (1993). Protestantism and Industrialization: An Examination of Three Alternative Models of the Relationship between Religion and Capitalism. *Review of Religious Research, 34*(3), 210–224.

Burger, Thomas (1987). *Max Weber's Theory of Concept Formation: History, Laws, and Ideal Types*, expanded edition. Durham, NC: Duke University Press.

Burke, Peter (1992). *History and Social Theory*. Ithaca, NY: Cornell University Press.

Carroll, Jon (1999). More, Yes, More of Mondegreens. *San Francisco Chronicle*, April 13, p. B10.

Caulkin, Simon (1998). Guru Guide: Max Weber. *The Observer* (London), October 4, p. 8 (The Observer Work Page).

Caulkin, Simon (2000). Seer of Cyberspace Symbols. *The Observer* (London), June 18, p. 9 (The Observer Business Pages).

Cooke, Timothy R. (1994). Uncommon Earnestness and Earthly Toils: Moderate Puritan Richard Baxter's Devotional Writings. *Anglican and Episcopal History, 63*(1), 51–72.

Crainer, Stuart (1998). The Ghost in the Machine. *Management Today*, December, p. 87.

Croce, Benedetto (1907/1915). *What Is Living and What Is Dead in the Philosophy of Hehel*, trans. Douglas Ainslie. London, Macmillan.

Diggins, John Patrick (1996). *Max Weber: Politics and the Spirit of Tragedy*. New York: Basic Books.

Diggins, John Patrick (1999). Thorstein Veblen: Theorist of the Leisure Class. Princeton, NJ: Princeton University Press. (Originally published as *The Bard of Savagery: Thorstein Veblen and Modern Social Theory*, Seabury Press, 1978)

The Economist (2000). Striking Back at the Empire. February 26.

Falk, Gerhard (1980). "Old Calvin Never Died: Puritanical Rhetoric by Four American Presidents Concerning Public Welfare." In Milton Plesur (Ed.), *An American Historian: Essays to Honor Selig Adler* (pp. 183–190). Buffalo: State University of New York Press.

Ferguson, Niall (1999). Millennium Reputations: Which Are the Most Overrated Authors, or Books, of the Past 1,000 Years? *Sunday Telegraph* (London), March 14, p. 15.

Foster, Stephen (1971). *Their Solitary Way: The Puritan Social Ethic in the First Century of Settlement in New England*. New Haven, CT: Yale University Press.

Fukuyama, Francis (1992). *The End of History and the Last Man*. New York: Free Press.

Fukuyama, Francis (1995). *Trust: Social Virtues and the Creation of Prosperity*. New York: Free Press.

Fukuyama, Francis (1999a, May). The Great Disruption. *Atlantic Monthly, 283*(5), 55–80.

Fukuyama, Francis (1999b). *The Great Disruption: Human Nature and the Reconstruction of the Social Order*. New York: Free Press.

Green, William A. (1993). *History, Historians, and the Dynamics of Change*. Westport, CT: Praeger.

Greene, Jack P. (1988). *Pursuits of Happiness: The Social Development of Early Modern British Colonies and the Formation of American Culture*. Chapel Hill: University of North Carolina Press.

Halperin, S. William (1946). *Germany Tried Democracy: A Political History of the Reich from 1918 to 1933*. Chicago: University of Chicago Press.

Hamilton, Earl J. (1929). American Treasure and the Rise of Capitalism (1500-1700). *Economica, 9*(27), 338–357.

Haskell, Thomas L. (1998). *Objectivity is Not Neutrality: Explanatory Schemes in History*. Baltimore: Johns Hopkins University Press.

Hennis, Wilhelm (1988). *Max Weber: Essays in Reconstruction*, tr. Keith Tribe. London: Allen and Unwin.

Henretta, John A. (1991). The Weber Thesis Revisited: The Protestant Ethic and the Reality of Capitalism. In John A. Henretta (Ed.), *The Origins of American Capitalism: Collected Essays* (pp. 35–70). Boston: Northeastern University Press.

Hertz, Karl H. (1991). "Max Weber and American Puritanism." In Peter Hamilton (Ed.), *Max Weber: Critical Assessments 2* (pp. 86–102). London: Routledge.

Holtham, Gerald (1998). Debate: Lie Back, Think of South Korea. *The Guardian* (London), August 3, p. 17.

Howe, Daniel Walker (1972). "The Decline of Calvinism: An Approach to Its Study." *Comparative Studies in Society and History 14*, 317ff.

Hudson, Winthrop S. (1988). The Weber Thesis Reexamined. *Church History 57* (Suppl.), 56–67.

Hughes. H. Stuart (1960). "The Historian and the Social Scientist." *American Historical Review, 66*(1), 20–46.

Imber, Jonathan (1996). "Incredible Goings-On": Max Weber in Pennsylvania. *American Sociologist, 27*(4), 3–6.

The Independent (London) (2000). Thought for the Day. January 14, p. 3.

Jäger, Friedrich (1991). Culture or Society? The Significance of Max Weber's Thought for Modern Cultural History. *History and Memory, 2*(2), 115–140.

Jaspers, Karl (1989:). *On Max Weber*, ed. John Dreijmanis. New York: Paragon House.

Joerges, Christian (2000). Rationalization of Law and Bureaucratic Rationality in the EU: Legitimacy Problems of European Governance in the Light of Weberian Concepts. Presented at the Economy and Society: Max Weber in 2000 conference, Madison, Wisconsin, September 22–24.

Johnson, Benton (1971). Max Weber and American Protestantism. *Sociological Quarterly, 12*(4), 473–485.

Johnson, Daniel (2000). Mother to the Unborn Child. *The Daily Telegraph* (London), February 19, p. 24.

Kalberg, Stephen (1994). *Max Weber's Comparative-Historical Sociology*. Oxford: Polity Press.

Kalberg, Stephen (1997a). Max Weber's Sociology: Research Strategies and Modes of Analyses. In Charles Camic (ed.), *Reclaiming the Sociological Classics: The State of Scholarship* (pp. 208–241). Malden, MA: Blackwell.

Kalberg, Stephen (1997b). Tocqueville and Weber on the Sociological Origins of Citizenship: The Political Culture of American Democracy. *Citizenship Studies, 1*(2), 199–222.

Käsler, Dirk (1988). *Max Weber: An Introduction to His Life and Work*, tr. Philippa Hurd. Oxford: Polity Press.

Kennedy, Duncan (2000). Weber's "Logically Formal Rationality": A Genealogy and an Assessment of Current Status. Paper presented at the Economy and Society: Max Weber in 2000 conference, Madison, Wisconsin, September 22–24.

King, John Owen, III (1983). *The Iron of Melancholy: Structures of Spiritual Conversion in America from the Puritan Conscience to Victorian Neurosis*. Middletown, CT: Wesleyan University Press.

Kirkus Service (1998). Review of Daniel Patrick Moynihan, *Secrecy: The American Experience*. July 1, 1998.

Kolbenschlag, Madonna Claire (1976). The Protestant Ethic and Evangelical Capitalism: The Weberian Thesis Revisited. *Southern Quarterly, 14*(4), 287–306.

Kolko, Gabriel (1961) Max Weber on America: Theory and Evidence. *History and Theory, 1*(3), 243–260.

Lehmann, Hartmut, and Guenther Roth (Eds.) (1993). *Weber's Protestant Ethic: Origins, Evidence, Contexts*. Cambridge, England: Cambridge University Press/German Historical Institute.

Leonard, Eileen (1975). Max Weber and America: A Study in Elective Affinity. Unpublished Doctoral Dissertation (Sociology). New York: Fordham University; 511 leaves.

Lindholm, Charles (1990). *Charisma*. Cambridge, MA: Blackwell.

Lucas, Rex A. (1971). "A Specification of the Weber Thesis: Plymouth Colony." *History and Theory, 10*(3), 318–346.

McLuhan, Marshall (1964). *Understanding Media: The Extensions of Man*. New York: McGraw-Hill.

MacShane, Denis (1998). Can We Adapt to the Third Way? [a review of Anthony Giddens' *The Third Way*] *The Independent* (London), September 16, p. 5.

Mann, Bruce H. (1980). "Rationality, Legal Change, and Community in Connecticut, 1690–1740." *Law and Society Review, 14*, 196ff.

Mann, Bruce H. (1987). *Neighbors and Strangers: Law and Community in Early Connecticut*. Chapel Hill: University of North Carolina Press.

Martinez-Saenz, Miguel (2000). "Whose Interests are Being Represented?" *The Tampa Tribune*, March 25, p. 17.

Marsh, Robert (2000). Weber's Misunderstanding of Traditional Chinese Law. Paper presented at the Economy and Society: Max Weber in 2000 conference, Madison, Wisconsin, September 22–23.

Mclynn, Frank (2000). When the Past Changes Direction. *The Independent* (London), June 3, p. 10.

Miller, Perry (1953). *The New England Mind: From Colony to Province*. Boston: Beacon Press.

Mommsen, Wolfgang J. (1984). *Max Weber and German Politics, 1890–1920*, tr. Michael Steinberg. Chicago: University of Chicago Press.

Mommsen, Wolfgang J. (2000). Max Weber's "Grand Sociology:" The Origins and Composition of *Wirtschaft und Gesellschaft*, Sociology. Paper presented at the Economy and Society: Max Weber in 2000 conference, Madison, Wisconsin, September 22–24.

Moynihan, Daniel Patrick (1998). *Secrecy: The American Experience*. New Haven, CT: Yale University Press.

Mufson, Steven (1999). "Great Expectations" [review of Edward Chancellor, *Devil Take the Hindmost: A History of Financial Speculation*]. *The Washington Post*, September 12, Book World, p. X06.

Nash, Gary (1984). "Social Development." In Jack P. Greene and J. R. Pole (Eds.), *Colonial British America: Essays in the New History of the Early Modern Era* (pp. 236ff). Baltimore: Johns Hopkins University Press.

Novak, Michael (1982). The Spirit of Democratic Capitalism. New York: Simon and Schuster.

Novak, Michael (1993). *The Catholic Ethic and the Spirit of Capitalism*. New York: Free Press.

Novak, Michael (1996). *Business as a Calling: Work and the Examined Life*. New York: Free Press.

Novick, Peter (1988). *That Noble Dream: The "Objectivity Question" and the American Historical Profession*. Cambridge, UK: Cambridge University Press.

Oakes, Guy (1988). *Weber and Rickert*. Cambridge, MA: MIT Press.

O'Grady, Bernard (1999). "Weber Was Right." *The Daily Telegraph* (London), July 6, p. 25.

Pande, Mrinal (2000). "Budget Talks and Ballot Boxes." *The Hindu*, March 19.

Peacock, James L. (1989). "Calvinism, Community, and Charisma: Ethnographic Notes." *Comparative Social Research, 11*, 227–238.

Pollock, Robert L. (1998). "Bookshelf: Review of Robert Scruton," *An Intelligent Person's Guide to Philosophy. Wall Street Journal*, June 29.

Porter, Andrew (1998). The Gap [review of David S. Landes, *The Wealth and Poverty of Nations*, W. W. Norton]. *New York Times Book Review*, March 15, p. 15.

Press, Eyal (1999). The Passion of Roberto Unger. *Lingua Franca*, March, 44–54.

Reilly, Patrick (1999). Why You Might as Well Look for God Through a Telescope. *The Herald* (Glasgow), November 29, p. 15.

Ross, Dorothy (1998). The New and Newer Histories: Social Theory and Historiography in an American Key. In Anthony Molho & Gordon S. Wood (eds.), *Imagined Histories: American Historians Interpret the Past* (pp. 85–106). Princeton, NJ: Princeton University Press.

Roth, Guenther (2000). Max Weber's Anglo-German Family History. [Translated extract from *Max Weber's Anglo-German Family History*, Tübingen: Mohr Siebeck, 2001 (in German)]. Paper presented at the Economy and Society: Max Weber in 2000 conference, Madison, Wisconsin, September 22–24, 2000.

Roth, Guenther, & Wolfgang Schluchter (1979). *Max Weber's Vision of History*. Berkeley: University of California Press.

Ryan, Alan (1996). Review of John P. Diggins, *Max Weber: Politics and the Spirit of Tragedy*, New York: Basic Books, 1996. *New York Times Book Review*, August 4, p. 14.

Sarbadhikari, Atanu (1999). Dalit and Conversion (Letter to the Editor). *The Statesman* (India), February 20.

Scaff, Lawrence (1989). *Fleeing the Iron Cage: Culture, Politics, and Modernity in the Thought of Max Weber*. Berkeley: University of California Press.

Schlink, Bernhard (1999). Best Lawyer, Pure Law [Hans Kelsen]. *New York Times Magazine*, April 18, Section 6, p. 100.

Schwartz, Barry (1987). *George Washington: The Making of an American Symbol*. New York: Free Press.

Schwartz, Barry (2000). *Abraham Lincoln and the Forge of National Memory*. Chicago: University of Chicago Press.

Schweitzer, Arthur (1984). *The Age of Charisma*. Chicago: Nelson-Hall.

SEK Genetics (1998). Website advertisement for the breeding bull, "Foreplay": http://www.pitton.com/~sekgen/w14.htm.

Shamir, Ronen (1993). Formal and Substantive Rationality in American Law: A Weberian Perspective. *Social and Legal Studies, 2*, 45–72.

Sica, Alan (1985). Reasonable Science, Unreasonable Life: The Happy Fictions of Marx, Weber, and Social Theory. In Robert Antonio & Ronald Glassman (eds.), *A Weber–Marx Dialogue* (pp. 68–88). Lawrence: University Press of Kansas.

Sica, Alan (1988). *Weber, Irrationality, and Social Order*. Berkeley: University of California Press.

Spencer, Olin (1980). The Oneida Community and the Instability of Charismatic Authority. *Journal of American History, 67*(2), 285–300.

Stace, Christopher (1999). Goodbye to Sepulchral Bury [review of Christian Meier, *Athens*]. *The Daily Telegraph* (London), July 3, p. 3.

Steinmetz, Greg (1998). Democracies Bestow a Fleeting Blessing on History's Greats. *The Wall Street Journal*, September 2, Section A, p. 1.

Strauss, Leo (1953). *Natural Right and History*. Chicago: University of Chicago Press.

Taylor, Robert (2000). A Dream in Reach: Sociology Has Fallen on Hard Times Until It Was Revived by the Dynamic Insights of a Pioneering Spanish Academic. *Financial Times* (London), June 15, p. 12.

Tolles, Frederick B. (1948). *Meeting House and Counting House: The Quaker Merchants of Colonial Philadelphia, 1682–1763*. New York: Norton; Chapel Hill: University of North Carolina Press.

Tolson, Jay (1999). A Meeting of Minds, with a Nod to Yesterday. *U.S. News and World Report*, June 28, p. 61.

Walzer, Michael (1963). Puritanism as a Revolutionary Idea. *History and Theory, 3*, 59–90.

Watanabe, Kishichi (1988). The Business Ideology of Benjamin Franklin and Japanese Values of the 18th Century. *Business and Economic History, 17*, 79–90.

Weber, Marianne (1975). *Max Weber: A Biography*, tr. Harry Zohn. New York: Wiley. (Reissued in 1988 with a new introduction by Guenther Roth. New Brunswick, NJ: Transaction Publishers)

Whitehead, Alfred North (1938). *Modes of Thought*. New York: Macmillan.

Wiebe, Robert (1967). *The Search for Order, 1877–1920*. New York: Hill & Wang.

Ziff, Larzer (1973). *Puritanism in America: New Culture in a New World*. New York: Viking Press.

Zuckerman, Laurence (1999). Words Go Right to the Brain, but Can They Stir the Heart? *New York Times*, April 17, p. 4 in online edition.

Zuckerman, Mortimer (1998). Creators of Our Prosperity: We Should Thank Capitalists Like Bill Gates, Not Scapegoat Them. *U.S. News and World Report*, June 8, p. 64.

Additional References

Durkheim, Émile. *Elementary Forms of the Religious Life* (Paris, 1912; first translated into English by Joseph Ward Swain, London: Allen and Unwin, 1915).

Durkheim, Émile. *The Division of Labor in Society* (Paris, 1893; first translated into English by George Simpson. New York: Macmillan, 1933).

Hobbes, Thomas. *Leviathan, Or the Matter, Forme, and Power of a Commonwealth Ecclesiasticall and Civil* (London, 1651; edited by Michael Oakeshott, selected and with an introduction by Robert S. Peters. New York: Collier Books, 1962).

CHAPTER 24

Conflict Theory and Interaction Rituals

The Microfoundations of Conflict Theory

Jörg Rössel and Randall Collins

THE PROBLEM OF MICRO–MACRO

The focus of this chapter is a conflict theory solution to the micro–macro problem in sociology. In conflict theory micro and macro do not stand for separate areas of social reality, as illustrated by opposing concepts such as actor and system or agency and structure, but they represent segments of the spatiotemporal continuum of social reality. This spatiotemporal continuum extends from very small entities such as nonverbal communication, as in eye contact in interaction situations, to very large entities such as economic world systems (Collins, 1988a, p. 386). The continuum is constituted by three variables: time, space, and number of persons/situations.

Conflict theory takes as its starting point the insights of ethology and ethnomethodology. Its primary focus lies in observable behavior. Empirical studies and observations are always situated in small spatiotemporal locations. Human experiences and actions take place in microsocial reality: for example, sitting at desks, reading documents, driving vehicles, having arguments, or even conducting questionnaire surveys in a plant (Collins, 1981a, pp. 262–264, 1981c, pp. 83–86, 1988b, p. 244). Second, conflict theory relies on the ethnomethodological concept of indifference or bracketing. This notion precludes observers of a situation from explaining the behavior of the participants by referring to their privileged versions of social structure or social norms that are not observable in the situation (Heritage, 1987, p. 231). Microconflict theory therefore regards the social norms and rules postulated by a number of sociological theories as unfounded macrosociological presuppositions; at best they describe empirical regularities of behavior but do not explain them; norms are descriptions masquerading as explanations (Collins, 1981c, pp. 90–91). Valid empirical studies and sociological

Jörg Rössel • Department of Science of Culture, Universitat Leipzig, Leipzig, Germany.   Randall Collins • Department of Sociology, University of Pennsylvania, Philadelphia, Pennsylvania 19104.

Handbook of Sociological Theory, edited by Jonathan H. Turner. Kluwer Academic / Plenum Publishers, New York, 2002.

explanations based on the methodological rule of ethnomethodological indifference can be formulated only in concepts that refer to observable phenomena in interaction situations. Therefore, the three variables—time, space, and number of persons/situations—that constitute the spatiotemporal continuum of the social are the only three pure macrovariables in conflict theory.

The aim of this approach is an explanatory theory that uses only concepts that refer directly to observable features of interaction situations. Macrosociological statements should deal only with the distribution of certain types of interactions with particular features in time and space. All other notions or variables on the macrolevel, like the autonomy of the state or the openness of a social structure, are only metaphoric expressions or typified concepts, which relate in a relatively unfocused way to aggregations of different types of microsituations. This does not mean macrosociology is an impossible endeavor. It is a necessary part of sociological research, and it has produced some good results in the form of comparative historical sociology. However, its results have to be founded in microsociological concepts, which means that macrosociological notions and structures have to be translated, as far as possible, into their microsociological elements (Collins, 1988b, pp. 246–247). Of course, this kind of microtranslation cannot become usual practice because then every macrosociological study would take up a great deal of time and would have to deal with continually repeating unchanging microsituations. Therefore, in macrosociology it is necessary to typify and to refer to aggregates of microsituations:

> An extreme, all-or-nothing empiricism is impossible; but a flexible empiricism, working with imprecisions and intuitive concepts where necessary, and making a great deal of room for theoretical work that ties things together, is a central part of science. One needs to work non-positivistically, so to speak, to be a successful positivist. (Collins, 1989e, pp. 128–129).

In this connection macrosociological studies have to rely on one hand on a strategy of controlling their results through comparative research and on the other hand by showing their validity by demonstrating the consistency with results of analyses taken from lower levels of the spatiotemporal continuum of social reality (Collins, 1989e, p. 132). For example, macrosociological studies of political conflict and change in comparative perspective can rely on research on power struggles in organizations, the mobilization of social movements, or bargaining networks.

The ideal strategy of the microfoundation of macrosociological relationships starts from a theoretically generalized description of the typical microsituations that underlie the analyzed structures (Collins, 1983, p. 194). We then present the ties between different microsituations, their interdependencies in organizations, networks, or markets. The actual subject of macrosociology is the complex configuration of organizations, networks, and markets in space and time (Collins, 1968). What is most important for conflict theory is not the description of microsociological counterparts of macrosociological terms but the connection of macrosociological theoretical generalizations with microsociological theories founded on the analysis of observable behavior in natural interaction situations (Collins, 1988b, p. 246). Corresponding to the premise that time, space, and the number of persons/situations are the only true macrovariables, spatiotemporal relationships and population sizes have a central explanatory role in macrosociological conflict theory; thus, the power of the state is conceived of geopolitically, in terms of the shifting extension and contraction of controls over territory.

The linkage between micro and macro is a problem of order of magnitude. Such an approach stands in sharp contrast to the systematic efforts, which were undertaken for example by James Coleman (1990) in his "Foundations of Social Theory" to derive macro- or system features from people's interests, resources, and interdependencies, such as the emergence of norms and the different types of collective behavior. We present several criticisms. First, Coleman does not reach the relevant microlevel of situated interactions but concentrates on the relatively persistent attributes of persons through medium periods of time (Collins, 1988a, p. 389, 1996). Second, the macro–micro link in Coleman's model attempts something impossible according to the concept of microtranslation because macrofeatures cannot directly influence the behavior in situations, they are only an interlinked aggregate of microsituations. Third, Coleman concentrates on a rather modest system-level in his macroanalysises. Therefore, it is possible for him to derive what we might call macrofeatures from relatively persistent individual attributes. In analyzing larger systems he has to refer to typifications of individuals as well as their attributes too. However, Coleman presents a systematic analysis of interdependencies of actions and shows that the mere aggregation of actions, respectively, interaction situations in time and space, is not sufficient for an adequate explanatory conceptualization of the relationship between micro and macro. Therefore, the analysis of these interdependencies is an indispensable aspect of the conceptualization of the micro–macro problem.

Conflict theory attempts to take up this idea by focusing on the interlinkages or connections between interaction situations. Macrosociological concepts do not refer to the simple aggregation of different types of microsituations in time and space but to spatiotemporally situated configurations and interlinkages of microsituations. These interlinkages can be conceptualized in three ways: First, in the life histories of individuals there is an accumulation of microsituations as they are composed of chains of microsituations.[1] Second, actors are able to compare possible interaction situations and therefore create interlinkages between them.[2] Furthermore, they are constrained in this comparison by the availability of different types of situations in their life-histories, and so by the actual spatiotemporal distribution of situation types. Third, actors themselves use typifying concepts symbolizing complex social entities such as organizations or nations that are made up of complex configurations of a multitude of interaction situations.[3] The actual existence of such entities is of course independent of this kind of verbal or emotional reference. These three concepts of interlinkages are the fundamental building blocks of the conflict theory analysis of the spatiotemporal connections between microsituations. Even the concepts of interdependence, as they were developed in rational choice theory could be microtranslated into these types of interlinkage. Of course, all macrosociological notions are necessarily relatively fuzzy and typified labels for such configurations of interlinkages of microsituations in space and time.

MICROTHEORY:
THEORY OF INTERACTION RITUALS

Foundations of the Theory

Empirically grounded in the concept of microtranslation, microconflict theory takes a naturalistic perspective on human action resembling animal ethology. It starts with the

---

[1]For example: "The more one gives orders, the more one is proud, self-assured, and formal and identifies with organizational ideals in whose names one justifies the orders" (Collins, 1981, p. 96).

[2]For example: "The more unique and irreplaceable a conversational exchange, the closer the personal tie among individuals who can carry it out" (Collins, 1981c, p. 97–98).

[3]For example: "The more one gives orders in the name of an organization, the more one identifies with the organization" (Collins, 1981, p. 87).

assumption that social organization is not specific to human beings, but exists on the sub-human level as well. Hence, the higher cognitive capacities of humans cannot be the basis of their social life (Collins, 1975, pp. 91–92). This thesis is supported by a number of micro-sociological studies showing that human beings in natural interaction situations have only a limited capacity for rational decision making, have cognitive restrictions, and show ritualistic or routinized types of behavior. Research in ethnomethodology, symbolic interactionism, and conversation analysis has argued that social scientific theories explaining actions by referring to social norms or rational decisions are inadequate to the process of interaction. These theories reduce social action to the application of norms or the unfolding of rational decisions and omit the actual process of interaction; in contrast, the foregoing microsociological traditions have shown in empirical detail how actors negotiate and stabilize the actual meaning and emotional mood of ongoing streams of actions (Heritage, 1987, pp. 238–239; Joas, 1987). This process of muddling through interaction situations goes beyond the mere application of norms or rational decision making and requires the flexible utilization of interpretation routines (Cicourel, 1973), mutual trust in the meaningful action of alter and ego (Garfinkel, 1967), the readiness for corrective behavior in the case of faux pas (Goffman, 1963), and the employment of nonverbalized and often subliminal forms of knowledge and action routines (Collins, 1981b, 1993c; Polanyi, 1967).

On the basis of the research results of these microsociological traditions and in keeping with the subhuman evolution of social life, it can be argued that complex processes of action cannot be explained by referring to control via specific social rules and norms. In fact, actors use norms or rules only to describe and make sense of their past actions (Collins, 1981b). This indicates that these phenomena are cognitive constructs, like the social typifications used by actors themselves in concrete interaction situations that do not really explain human behavior but are used for retrospective rationalizations. In a similar way conflict theory makes a number of well-known points of criticism against rational action theory: the prevalence of routinized rather than calculating action; the difficulty in choosing among a large number of goals to be maximized; and above all the unsolved problem of a common denominator of utility for different goals. Conflict theory regards the research results of the microsociological traditions as an alternative and better point of departure, which allows for a richer and empirically more adequate description and explanation of interaction processes (Collins, 1993b, 1996).

Conflict theory develops an affective theory of social action, rather than rationalistic or normativistic models. It takes as the most important results of the microsociological research traditions, that social situations and interaction processes operate through the mutual coordination of people on the basis of taken-for-granted definitions of situations and routines of action (Garfinkel, 1967; Goffman, 1967; Heritage, 1987). However, certain aspects of microsociology are not really suited for a microconflict theory because of their cognitivistic bias and their rather exclusive focus on language and thinking. What is central for human interaction is the dynamic of emotions that make up the subhuman basis of social reality. This starting point in ethological and Darwinian notions can be connected to the ideas of the sociological classics, especially the theories of Emile Durkheim. His idea of precontractual solidarity as the foundation of social cohesion as well as the possibility of the social division of labor and the existence of markets and contracts, can be interpreted in terms of emotional or affective bonds (Collins, 1982, pp. 3–29, 1985a, pp. 149–152; Collins & Makowsky, 1972, pp. 82–84). This interpretation differs sharply from Talcott Parsons' functionalist reading of Durkheim in terms of social norms and cultural values. The multitude of cultural symbols, social classifications, and ideological systems are based on the emotional dynamic, which is the foundation for every kind of social life. The decisive breakthrough to this understanding of the role of affective bonds can be found in Emile Durkheim's study on the "Elementary Forms of Religious Life" (Durkheim, 1965). In this work Durkheim shows that social rituals are the mechanisms that produce social solidarity in the form of collective emotions and their symbolic objectivations. Crucial for the development of a conflict theoretic microapproach is the microsociological turn of the notion of rituals proposed by Erving Goffman. Goffman himself referred in his article "On Deference and Demeanor" to the analyses of Durkheim and pointed out that rituals can be performed on single individuals: "the person in our urban secular world is allotted a kind of sacredness that is displayed and confirmed by symbolic acts (Goffman, 1967, p. 47). Goffman's idea of analyzing everyday interactions as rituals in which the sacral character of individuals is produced and stabilized is, along with the radical empiricism of ethnomethodology, the central reference point of microconflict theory (Collins, 1981, pp. 227–238, 1988a, pp. 203–208).

Interaction Rituals, Emotions, and Cultural Capital

The theory of interaction rituals is the attempt to provide an adequate microsociological theory for conflict sociology (Collins, 1990b, p. 72). It starts with the distinction between two types of rituals: intentional rituals and natural rituals. The type of social interaction labeled intentional rituals corresponds to the common usage of the term ritual, like religious ceremonies or patriotic festivals. These are rituals that intend to have a certain effect, whereas natural rituals are not consciously intended to have effects. These are the types of rituals that were called interaction or interpersonal rituals by Erving Goffman (1967). The basic elements of an interaction ritual are present to a varying extent in every interaction situation; accordingly, every kind of interaction has to a certain degree the effect of changing the moods and emotions of the involved actors and along with this producing and reproducing their affective bonds to certain cultural symbols. Obviously not all interactions have these effects to the same extent; their variations may be predicted by the strength of the following three conditions:

1. At least two persons must be assembled as their physical presence is a central foundation of interactions rituals; the number of assembled human beings is one determinant of the intensity of ritual outcomes.
2. There must be a common focus of attention on a certain object, like a religious emblem, a national flag, or a certain conversation topic. The decisive point is not any intrinsic quality of the object but the existence of a common focus of attention and the actors' mutual awareness of this common focus.

    As in condition 1, this determinant of ritual outcomes can vary in its strength. The higher the commonality of the focus, the higher the intensity of the ritual outcomes. Since interactional situations are chained receptively in time, a buildup on ritual solidarity occurs as the preexisting cultural homogeneity of the ritual participants, resulting from past rituals, increases the chances for a common focus of attention.
3. A further condition of socially successful interaction rituals is the arousal of a common mood among the participants as they enter the situation and the further intensification of this shared emotion during the interaction process. The more homogenous the mood, the stronger the ritual outcomes.

Conditions 2 and 3 tend to interact, hence a common mood furthers a common focus and vice versa. If the intensity rises high enough, the object of the common focus becomes a symbol of community, a membership symbol that is affectively charged according to the degree of rituality achieved in the interaction. These emotionally charged symbols extend from religious symbols to social classifications and systems of ideas (Hammond, 1984). Violation or pollution of such membership symbols provoke negative reactions by the group members or ritual participants, because their ritually engendered emotions are tied to the symbol. The intensity of possible reactions varies by the intensity of the involvement. To divert a dinner party conversation from its constituting topic produces usually no or only slight anger, but to distract a heated discussion from its topic leads to much sharper reactions, and to violate or pollute a national flag can evoke a sense of outrage.

Very much like Durkheim, microconflict theory views interaction rituals as a source of energy that strengthens social bonds and produces new affective ties. Just how much emotion and affective bonding occurs depends on the degree to which the three determinants of interaction rituals outlined above are met. Since every social interaction can be described as somewhere along the continuum of variation of these three conditions, the theory of inter-action rituals is not a special theory designed for a particular kind of interaction but claims instead to be a general theory of interaction (Collins, 1993b, p. 208). Conversations, which make up a good deal of our everyday interactions, are a good illustration of this assertion. In conversations participants focus on a common topic of talk, they use nearly the same symbol system, and mutually coordinate their mood and indeed their entire nonverbal pattern. Even in everyday conversations participants coordinate and harmonize their emotions and gestures as measured by harmonization of voice pitches, bodily (especially eye) movements, and rhythms of speech (Collins, 1988a, pp. 201–203, 1998, pp. 6–7). The degree of solidarity generated in such everyday interactions, and hence the degree of interpersonal influence, varies in a pattern that can be predicted from the intensity of the process depicted in interaction ritual theory.

The decisive connections in the theory of interactions rituals are between interaction rituals one the one hand and the production of emotions and affectively charged cultural symbols on the other hand. These two outcomes of interaction rituals are called resources (Collins, 1981b). In the language of interaction ritual theory these two resources, which actors can accumulate in chains of interaction rituals are known as first, cultural capital and second, as emotional energy. Cultural capital can be differentiated into two types:

1. Generalized cultural capital consists of membership symbols widely charged with shared significance for large groups or social categories, including social manners, topics of conversation, styles and tastes, and so forth. Generalized cultural capital is equivalent to what Bourdieu (1984) calls "habitus."
2. Particularized cultural capital refers to specific persons and situations. It consists of memories of names, personal habits, and social positions of specific other persons. Whereas generalized cultural capital is primarily transmitted through long-distance media and formal organizations, particularized cultural capital is specific to local networks of personal contact

Whereas generalized cultural capital can be universally utilized, particular cultural capital can be employed only in the presence of or in reference to specific persons. A person's reputation is a special form of particular cultural capital, which can have an important role in conversations independent of the presence of those specific persons being discussed in the interaction situation, especially in the form of gossip.

The second type of resource, emotional energy, is in the current development of conflict theory rather fuzzily defined. Emotional energy refers to a dimension of a person's emotional state that extends from a state of high self-confidence, enthusiasm, and good mood to depression, loss of motivation, and negative emotions on the opposite side of the spectrum. The dynamic of emotional energy is basic for social interactions. Emotions are the driving force for interactions and the common denominator of the things people seek in interactions. It is not the maximization of economic utility that determines the course and directions of interactions but the attempt to maximize one's own emotional energy (Collins, 1993b).

These two types of resources have a central explanatory role in the theory of interaction rituals, but in the current development of the theory, their definitions remain imprecise. Disparate things are included in the notion of cultural capital, like religious symbols, cultural values, worlds, or nonverbal signs of social status. Finally, every kind of everyday conversation topic can become part of a person's cultural capital. A starting point for a further differentiation of the notion of cultural capital could be Pierre Bourdieu's definition and analysis of this concept. He distinguishes between three types of cultural capital: first, the institutionalized type of cultural capital consisting of credentials and titles provided by the educational system; second, the incorporated type, which refers to a person's bodily and psychologically incorporated cognitive, esthetic, and social competencies; and third, the objectified type, which refers to the ensemble of socially existing cultural assets. Furthermore, Bourdieu (1984) analyzes the processes of acquisition of each type of cultural capital, their specific features and their exchangeability with other types of capital (social and economic capital). Bourdieu's classification remains too much at the mesolevel to be useful in a theory of interaction rituals focusing on spatially situated interactions in short spans of time, but it could be a starting point for the further differentiation of the notion of cultural capital in interaction ritual theory.

The same applies to the notion of emotional energy. There are a wide variety of emotions in everyday and scientific usage, in contrast to which the continuum of emotional energy gives a rather bare single dimension. The claim of microconflict theory is that emotional energy is central to motivating social interactions and attachment to social symbols, but more work is needed to connect this dimension to the varieties of emotions that are subjectively experienced and socially expressed. The further development of a differentiated notion of emotional energy can be linked to work in the sociology of emotions (Kemper, 1978, 1990; Thoits, 1989). Scheff (1990) has developed a model of interaction, also based on the Durkheimian solidarity of successful microinteractions, in which the master emotions are pride, arising from intact social bonds (high solidarity), and shame, arising from the breaking or refusal of social bonds. Scheff's continuum of pride and shame may be regarded as the equivalent of high and low emotional energy, viewed from the perspective of a favorable or unfavorable self. The work of Scheff and Retzinger (1991) is rich in microempirical observations of pride and shame, using as indicators both verbal content, paralinguistic behavior (intonational and rhythmic aspects of talk), and bodily expressions and postures. Such work provides good empirical indicators by which the dynamics of high and low emotional energy may be further studied. Sharpening the concepts of cultural capital and emotional energy, and studying their dynamics by systematically comparing a variety of microsituations should be central topics in the further development of interaction ritual theory.

Resources accumulated in interaction rituals, up to any given moment in time, shape an individual's progress through further interaction rituals. Cultural capital and emotional energy determine which kind of interaction rituals a person seeks, restrictions on access for certain interactions for the particular person, which part a person can play in an interaction situation, and above all which definitions of situation and courses of actions can be negotiated in future interaction rituals. The dynamic of emotional energy and cultural capital based on the mechanisms of interaction rituals is the explanatory core of the theory of interaction rituals. The dynamic of emotional energy determines the importance of specific symbols and classification systems, whereas cultural capital affects the content of actions, conversations, and thinking (Collins, 1989a, 1998).

> This model of emotional energy-seeking in the local market for IRs [interaction rituals] also implies a theory of individual thinking. The symbols with which the most conscious cognition takes place are for the most part circulated in the conversational market. Thinking is above all internalized conversations. The symbols which come most readily to mind in a given situation are those which are charged by the individual's trajectory of experiences in their personal chain of IRs. One thinks with symbols which are emblems of the group in which one has the strongest emotional resonance. (Collins, 1966, p. 334)

This theory of thinking has been developed further into a sociology of intellectuals as exemplified by philosophers and utilized to explain the trajectory of philosophical debate in different world civilizations (Collins, 1998). In general, emotional energy is the most important resource a person will seek in interaction situations. On the microlevel the world does not revolve around material wealth or the maximization of utility but around emotional energy and acquiring the cultural capital which resonates with it (Collins, 1993b). Material things are valued for their emotional significance in interactional ritual situations.

The question that remains is how to deal with common resources like goods, money, credentials, or weapons in this microtheory based on the dynamic of emotions. Four points are relevant to the theory of interaction rituals: (1) Material resources are fundamental for carrying out interactions (Collins, 1993b, pp. 214–216). Without the adequate equipment like drinks, food, and the relevant entertainment technology a party could not take place; analogously, religious ceremonies and political rallies all require their material bases. Here conflict theory of rituals blends Marx and Engels with Durkheim. (2) Furthermore, the development of interaction rituals is partly determined by its physical setting. This finding was above all developed in the microsociological research of Erving Goffman (1969). The spatial ordering of people in a lecture hall for example places the person on the platform directly in the focus of attention of all participants in this social situation. The capacity to idealize frontstage settings, or alternatively, to bond a group behind closed doors, depends on material resources; thus inequalities in the material bases of ritual performances result in inequalities in ritual outcomes. (3) Certain material things can themselves become objects of emotional bonds if they are, in specific situations, the focused object of attention, such as money in economic transactions or certain clothes in specific social groups (Collins, 1993b, p. 219). (4) In this way a person can develop claims to specific resources, and this constitutes the institution of property. However, property is not only based on situationally present emotions; a person claiming a certain object as property can call on the vigorous support of others, whose definition of the situation includes the duty of protecting objects defined as the property of particular people. These relationships between people, based on networks of chains of interaction rituals, can be called enforcement coalitions (Collins, 1987b, 1988a, pp. 404–405).

How, finally, do material objects enter into the motivational side of the theory of interaction rituals? The line of argument is that there must be a common denominator if persons are able to make choices among disparate kinds of payoffs for their actions; otherwise, they would be unable to decide between material rewards and emotional or symbolic rewards (or for that matter, between different kinds of material rewards such as food or sexual pleasure) (Collins, 1993b). The argument of microconflict theory is that all interaction rituals pay off in a certain level of emotional energy, which is the personal or subjective side of the Durkheimian collective effervescence built up in that situation; and emotional energy from past interaction rituals charges up the symbols that go through people's minds and attracts them toward creating new interaction rituals in future encounters; since any situation at all can be categorized as an interaction ritual with stronger or weaker level of appeal for persons with a given history of interaction ritual chains, we can use emotional energy as the common denominator of all choices. But this leaves us with the question of explaining how people can become motivated to seek such mundane, nonemotional rewards like eating, which happens to be necessary for them to stay alive.

The argument is that people are emotional energy seekers and that they gravitate toward situations in which they can get the most Durkheimian effervescence. But as we have seen, rituals also need material inputs: places to meet, costumes to wear, all sorts of material conditions that make it possible for people to assemble and to display certain symbolic markers to each other. Among these material conditions are that the participants must have enough food, shelter, and other necessities so that they stay alive and healthy enough to participate. Thus one way the theory derives people's motivations for material goods is by their need for them in order to take part in rituals. The first point of the argument, then, is that people work for money for food and other necessities, because they are excluded from rituals if they do not have them. This is tantamount to saying that people go to church, or to entertainment events or parties, or whatever turns them on until they run out of money; they have to do work so that they can come back to what gives motivation to their lives. The argument is akin to Weber's claim that religious motivation is what puts people to work; without this (as in pre-Protestant religions, in Weber's view) people work as little as they can in between festivals. People do not have unlimited or even constant material desires; it is the expense of rituals they participate in that makes some of them more willing to work for material things than others. This version of conflict theory is not a material interest theory; material interests enter only in a roundabout way.

There is a second pathway by which material things acquire value to people: the ritual itself focuses on them and makes them sacred objects, emblems of membership in the group. Eating luxury food or owning a house with a swimming pool are valued by certain groups of people because these have become status symbols; the process by which this occurs can be shown by the kinds of interaction rituals those persons take part in. The advantage of this way of theorizing is that it is no longer a mystery why some people are blatant "materialists" seeking luxury goods, while others value a Bohemian lifestyle and still others are ascetic monks; in all these cases, the same kind of mechanism operates, making a certain kind of relationship to material good a symbolic value. Thus the value of the swimming pool or the gourmet meal is not in the materials itself, but only in the symbolic value of the materials. In a twist on Weber's conception of capitalist motivation, we can say that "materialists" are motivated by the secular–religious significance of the objects they endlessly seek. Relatedly, for some persons, the interaction ritual situations that give them the biggest emotional energy payoffs are their work situations, because they have jobs that give them prestige, excitement, or the experience of being in the focus of group attention. They become "workaholics," for whom the process of working is of more value to them than anything extraneous payoff that comes from it. Thus it is the stratification of interaction ritual situations among persons, giving some of the emotional energy payoffs in their work, others in religious participation, intellectual life, mass entertainment, or elsewhere, or indeed depriving them of most ritual payoffs, which determine the range of symbolic objects that various people value. In short, the opportunity structure of interaction rituals determines the stratification of cultural values.

Interaction Ritual Chains, Power, and Status

Until this point only the way that interaction rituals engender emotions and affectively charged symbols or emotional energy and cultural capital have been presented. The next step in the microfoundations of conflict theory is to explain the differing distributions of these resources to various persons. In the course of their life histories individuals pass through a multitude of successive interaction rituals that can be called an "interaction ritual chain." The acquisition of resources in passing through this chain is above all determined by the restriction of access to certain types of interaction rituals for particular people and the specific power and status position of individuals in certain interaction rituals. The two key concepts are first the notion of the accessibility of a certain ritual and second the notions of power and status rituals.

Interaction rituals vary in how open they are to those individuals willing to participate. The first determinants of the accessibility of interaction situations is their spatiotemporal context. Availability of interaction partners usually depends on their ecological or spatiotemporal location in buildings or other places, technological processes, and orderings in workplaces, on one hand, and on the availability of media of transport and communication on the other (Collins, 1975, pp. 132–133, 1988a, pp. 358–360). For example, many people find their marriage partner within walking distance. These background conditions are an important structuring precondition for interaction rituals. Persons who control these spatial and material background conditions are in a position of controlling the course of interactions. Someone who controls a highly ritualized interaction has the possibility of focusing the attention of the participants onto his or her own person and therefore gaining a certain power of defining the situation and reputation. In certain technological orderings the individuals in charge can use their control over the course of action to gain power and prestige.

Besides the spatial restrictions of access to interaction rituals, the second important determinant of accessibility is the individual's resources. Assuming that an individual has a certain necessary amount of emotional energy, it is above all the person's cultural capital that determines whether he or she gets access to a particular interaction. Only in some specific situations does the question of access involve a kind of conscious decision process, as in the necessity to have certain credentials to be invited to a job interview. In most everyday interactions individuals feel by themselves, on the basis of their emotional energy and cultural capital, whether they should and whether they want to enter a particular interaction ritual. Especially in informal conversations and interactions it can be expected that a high incongruity in the cultural capital of the participating individuals lowers the pleasure of participation and therefore the expected gain in emotional energy and relevant cultural capital. For those people with interest in action and excitement, a conversation with a highbrow cultural academic may be viewed as relatively boring and not as a chance to gain new and interesting cultural capital (Schulze, 1992). Also, those people known for repeating the same gossip again and again are relatively uninteresting as conversation partners, whereas those whose knowledge is always up to date are sought after as interaction participants. This remains the same in neighborhood gossip and in gossip in economic or academic networks. However, in modern societies the spatiotemporal distribution of cultural capital has a structure that lowers the chances for informal meetings of people with widely differing cultural capital (Collins, 1975, p. 214).

Hence, the chances for getting access to particular rituals are determined by the amount of cultural capital an individual possesses and the spatiotemporal distribution of possible interaction situations. Here it is possible to speak of a market for interaction rituals that varies in openness according to the relevant spatiotemporal preconditions and that offers each participant differing options according to this or her resource endowment.

Besides the accessibility of rituals, the second ingredient for explaining the distribution of resources throughout the population are the dimensions of power and status in rituals. As shown by the empirical results of a diverse array of fields of research, the dimensions of power and status are, along with the instrumental conditions, the most important determinants of action (Kemper & Collins, 1990). Power rituals are defined as interactions in which one person can make another person display a certain kind of behavior. Status rituals, in contrast, are characterized by voluntary recognition and sympathy, thus by a formally egalitarian relationship between the interacting people (although one person may be more in the center of attention than the other). The two dimensions must not be reified; as in real interactions they can coincide and intersect. It is possible to measure the power and status dimension of interaction rituals by the relative amount of emotional energy and cultural capital the interaction participants have at their disposal. What is crucial are the following two mechanisms: whereas in power rituals the dominant person gains an increase in emotional energy while the subordinate person loses emotional energy, status rituals are characterized by the feature of being able to provide all interaction participants with increases in emotional energy. These two principles help to explain some further aspects of social life, for example, the fact thay people develop affective ties to certain values and symbols in whose name they give orders, and thus carry out successful power rituals.

Over a period of time, by passing through chains of interaction rituals characterized by certain kinds of power and status relationships, a person's emotional energy tends to find a particular long-term level, a kind of stable background feeling; short-term fluctuations caused by single interaction rituals result only in specific short-term emotions (Collins, 1989d). Thus people who usually dominate in interaction rituals are able to accumulate high levels of emotional energy and usually are not thrown back by short-term deviations from their normal emotional state. They can enter new interaction rituals with high motivation and self-confidence. The feedback between accumulated reserves of emotional energy and cultural capital and success in entering or dominating further power and status rituals tends to produce recurrent patterns that observers often reify as "personality." This analysis may be related to the differentiated theory of the emergence of different emotions along the concepts of power and status worked out by Theodore Kemper (1978).

Empirical operationalization of the theory of interaction rituals points to new directions that are far from the dominant practice of survey research. In contrast to trends in rational choice theory or the normativist approach, asking individuals about the intentions, motivations, and normative reasons for their actions is rendered by the theory of interaction rituals as nearly meaningless; at best it describes the ideological surface of everyday life, not its deeper structures. The empirical foundations and hypothesises of this theory have to be tested by using methods developed in the sociology and psychology of emotions or in biosociology, such as the systematic coding of facial expressions, research into voice pitch and frequencies, and the measurement of physiological quantities used to trace the level and dynamic of emotional energies of certain persons. Furthermore, conversation analysis offers a crucial method in analyzing the cultural capital people store and use in interaction rituals because it records verbal symbols in its natural setting and reconstructs them with painstaking exactness. Following the classification of speech codes by Basil Bernstein, for example, the systematic use of different types of cultural capital in natural interaction situations may be analyzed (Collins, 1983, pp. 197–200, 1989d, pp. 50–51).

The most systematic empirical treatment of a related theoretical approach was provided by Theodore Kemper. He has covered the empirical studies on the relationship between the participation in power and status rituals and the level of testosterone in human bodies. The results confirmed the proposed theory to a high degree. Not only was the level of testosterone in the blood raised by successful participation in power and status rituals, but the test subjects entered the following interaction rituals with a higher degree of emotional energy (Kemper, 1990.

The different emotional states of human beings are determined not only by the location of an interaction ritual on the dimensions of power and status, but also by certain nonsocial conditions. As indicated, microconflict theory begins with an ethological perspective on human behavior and social structures. Thus the effects of interaction rituals are dependent on certain biological conditions. Conflict theory has above all dealt with two areas of research: first the human body's potential for sexual excitement and second its physical vulnerability. The first condition is fundamental for explaining the relations between the sexes and the historical geopolitics of family and kinship relationships (Collins, 1971b, 1985b, 1992a). The second condition is basic for the connection between the affective arousal caused by military violence and the dynamics of political legitimation based on this emotional dynamic (Collins, 1986, 1989b).

Having sketched the relatively parsimonious principles of interaction ritual theory, which remain to be developed further in a more differentiated way, we turn now to the meso- and macrolevels of conflict theory.

MESO- AND MACROLEVEL: ORGANIZATIONS, NETWORKS, AND MARKETS

In macrosociological investigations the analyst necessarily aggregates repeated chains of interaction rituals and uses macrosociological typifying names for these aggregates, such as nation or society. Conflict sociology focuses above all on the mesolevel of social life, i.e., on the level of organizations, networks, and markets, which are of crucial importance for the description of relationships between interaction rituals. Conflict theory is skeptical about postulating unified social entities on the macrosociological level, such as "societies," and therefore tends to focus on the intersection of interaction rituals on a mesolevel. Above all, research in historical sociology has shown that "societies" cannot be treated as systemic entities with consistent boundaries or self-determining linear pathways in time. The "entity called society" should not be treated as a "thing apart" (Tilly, 1984, pp. 20–26) but as a certain configuration of status groups, organizations, and networks, with differing spatiotemporal extensions (Gerhards & Rössel, 1999). The systemness or unity of this configuration can be only empirically established (Collins, 1968, pp. 48–51). The notion of society should be used only as an abbreviated name for more complex descriptions of the configuration of social networks and organizations in a certain spatiotemporal area. This skepticism about the notion of macrosociological entities leads quite naturally to a focus on the mesolevel, to which we shall now turn.

Sociology of Organizations and the Theory of Interaction Rituals

The sociology of organizations is a crucial specialty in the social sciences, first, because the principles of organizations explain a diverse array of topics in sociology ranging from military structures to the networks and schools of scientists and philosophers, and second, especially in the contemporary era, organizations are one of the most important structuring features of our daily lives, in which social classes and status relationships are formed, individuals are socialized, and cultural symbols are produced. The invention of organizations may be regarded as the discovery of a kind of special instrument of the macrocoordination of microsituations (Collins, 1988a, p. 450).

The starting point for a sociology of organizations from a conflict theory point of view is Max Weber's research on bureaucracies and organizations. However, conflict theory does not take Weber as a theorist of ongoing rationalization, but as a conflict theorist explaining organizational structures and arrangements by struggles of interests and material resources (Collins, 1986). Conflict sociology views organizations as an arena for conflicting interests where the members of an organization use whatever strategies of control and avoidance are made possible by their respective resources to further their own interests. People on top of an organizational structure try to arrange their subordinates in certain structures so as to control their behavior and obtain an optimal output:

> The "organization" is only people attempting to get certain things for themselves and using other people as a means; what many such statements mean empirically is what leaders or owners of an organization, in trying to get their subordinates to do certain things, will end in arranging them in a certain way. Even this is not quite accurate, because "organizational structure" is only a way of referring to how people behave repetitively toward each other; no individual can unilaterally decide how large numbers of people will interact, and any pattern is the result of bargaining among many parties. (Collins, 1975, pp. 315–316).

The structures of organizations are networks of interactions in which strategies of control and avoidance are used; for example, people in the higher ranks of the administrative hierarchy of organizations are those holding resources to coordinate the microbehavior of individuals on lower ranks.

A good starting point for the analysis of structures of control in organizations is Amitai Etzioni's model of types of control and sanctions. He differentiates between three types of control and their respective types of sanction: first, control by physical coercion; second, control by material rewards; and third, control by normative integration (Etzioni, 1975). These types of organizational control lead to specific types of motivation and avoidance behavior: people controlled by physical coercion will react with resistance, if it is possible, and if not, with alienation and passivity; control through material rewards leads to acquisitive and calculative behavior; internalization of organizational goals and norms produces intrinsic motivations of organization members to work for the organizational goals. These different types of control can be used only under certain conditions. Coercive control is only useful in controlling crude physical labor that needs very little initiative and motivation; monetary control is suitable for controlling steady, routinized processes of production, as in classical mass production industries; activities needing a certain amount of initiative and intrinsic motivation can only be controlled by a kind of normative integration.

These different conditions can be partly inferred from the theory of interaction rituals. Take, for example, the conditions of the successful application of normative control strategies. Following the theory of interaction rituals, the preconditions for normative control are successful social rituals that engender an affective tie to the organizational goals, norms, and symbols in the participants. However, it is only possible to achieve these results when these interaction rituals are relatively low in the power dimension and high in the status dimension. Therefore, successful normative control is possible only in organizations where the subordinates share power and authority or the persons on top permit the emergence of strong communities among their subordinates, which would allow for the carrying out of successful status rituals. For people who are under supervision or isolated in their work activities, it is nearly impossible to participate successfully in organizational interaction rituals and to achieve an affective tie to the organizations' goals or symbols that would promote intrinsic motivation. Hence, normative integration is found primarily within the higher ranks of the hierarchy. In these positions the conditions for successful status rituals are supported by the high restrictions on admittance in the professional and academic occupations. Requirements of higher educational credentials produce homogeneity of cultural capital among the members of a specific occupation and increase their opportunities for successful status rituals (Collins, 1971a, 1979). Those people who during their occupational life in organizations and in the labor market have no opportunities of participating in successful interaction rituals according to the theory of interaction rituals will have only a weak emotional tie to their work or to the particular organization that is their place of work. Their motivation for participating in work-related interaction rituals is only founded in the necessity of acquiring material goods, which are resources necessary for carrying out interaction rituals in other areas of social life, such as family and leisure (Collins, 1993b, p. 220).

All types of sanctions exist in any organization in different mixtures, as in the end the weaker kinds of control are based on the stronger ones. The notion of enforcement coalition noted above can be exemplified in this context. References to other interaction rituals are present in every interaction ritual. These references can be mobilized if a conflict ensues:

> The foreman has authority over his employees because he can always call on his superior to fire someone, the superior in turn can call on the police to eject him if he does not leave, and the police can call on other police and ultimately on the army to reinforce him against resistance. (Collins, 1975, p. 291)

Organizations would obviously not be very efficient if enforcement coalitions had to be mobilized every time to enforce particular directives or orders. In everyday encounters the enforcement of authority relies on effective presentation by superiors and their ability to create a suitable definition of the situation in interaction rituals based on their superior level of cultural capital and emotional energy. Erving Goffman (1969) has hinted at the fact that this presentation of one's own power and ability to direct is not shown through verbal discourse but through nonverbal signs. Research in different social areas has shown that facial expressions, bodily posture, and certain kinds of behavior function as a powerful representation of an individual's social position that are recognized by other interaction participants as signs of power and authority. An interesting example is given in Ulrich Mueller and Alan Mazur's (1996) study on the connection between facial expression and military careers that shows that the degree of dominance in the facial expression of a West Point graduate was a strong predictor of his later military career. That means that those with a certain kind of facial expression are perceived as powerful and successful in military organizations and therefore are more successful (see also Bourdieu, 1984, on the incorporation of the cultural habitus in the body types of different social classes).

Control is not employed only and directly in interaction rituals. The sociology of organizations discusses a wide range of different kinds of indirect types of control (surveillance, checking output, rules, control of information, control through technical structures) and the conditions for their usage (Collins, 1975, pp. 297–314, 1988a, pp. 450–464); it would lead too far from the central concerns of this essay to discuss the relationship of these types of control to the theory of interaction rituals and conflict theory.

Microconflict theory systematize the organizational conditions that lead to certain types of organizational structures and hierarchies. The administrative hierarchy of an organization is a device for the macrocoordination of microsituations, consisting of people who control the activities of other people who are on lower levels of the hierarchy. The development of specific administrative structures thereby is determined by three general features of the organizational microactivities; first, the degree of uncertainty in each activity; second, the degree of uncertainty in the connections between activities, depending foremost on the number of activities to be coordinated; and third, the strength of coupling between the activities, i.e., the degree in which the practical unfolding of processes have to follow a certain strongly structured sequence (Collins, 1988a, pp. 473–476; compare Perrow, 1986). Different combinations of these three dimensions determine different organizational structures. For instance, employees whose work involves high task uncertainty control relatively autonomous work places, making for a decentralized organization, whereas in enterprises with high coupling, low uncertainty of coordination, and low task uncertainty, all activities can be rigidly controlled by a centralized administrative hierarchy. Inside the administrative hierarchy itself, control over strategic areas of task uncertainty, for example, unique access to social networks connecting with financial institutions, is a strong power resource (Fligstein, 1987; Scott, 1992). However, because conflict theory does not view organizations as a kind of unitary social entity, but rather as a specific configuration of interaction situations, interaction rituals on all levels of the administrative or organizational hierarchy can be influenced by extraorganizational networks, like the typical educational career of certain types of employees and their respective resources (Collins, 1979; Maurice, 1986; Sorge & Warner, 1986).

Besides control over areas of technological uncertainty, conflict theory emphasizes the spatiotemporal structures of organizations under given technologies of transport and communication because these are the basis for carrying out successful interaction rituals. Thus, people with similar work activities have fewer opportunities of developing a common identity if they are spatially dispersed, because of their restricted possibility of carrying out successful status rituals. The practical characteristics of technological processes and the emerging spatiotemporal dispersion of people are central determinants of workplace solidarity and therefore organizational power relations (Welskopp, 1994). In summary, these types of organizational structures and the control strategies employed within them determine to a high degree the interests of those within an organization as well as their behavior and the resources they are able to command during organizational conflicts (Collins, 1988a, p. 466). Microconflict theory is congruent with developments in organizational sociology which emphasize the distribution of resources, conflicts, and power in order to explain organizational structures (Fligstein, 1987; Perrow, 1986; Pfeffer, 1982). The theoretical principles involved in this kind of organizational sociology can be derived from the microtheory of interaction rituals, as, for example, in the distribution of power in organizations, the strategies of control employed, and the role of technology. This microtheoretically founded theory of organizations has a wide range of application, from the analysis of military organizations, the diverging organization of different sciences, to the role of schools in the history of philosophy (Collins, 1975, pp. 350–362, 1987a, 1989c, 1992b, 1998).

Markets and Networks

Besides organizations, markets and networks are the most important sociological concepts at the mesolevel. We already have noted that interdependencies between interaction rituals have certain marketlike features. With a particular endowment of resources an individual is able to enter only into certain interaction rituals, because access is restricted to those with specific types of cultural capital. On the other hand individuals seek those interaction rituals that they expect to provide them with the most gain in emotional energy and cultural capital and avoid some accessible interactions simply because they are not interesting enough for them. The connections among interaction rituals can be described as a market or opportunity structure. And the ensuing configurations between chains of interaction rituals engender a networklike structure between people who engage in repetitive interactions. Contrary to the analytical approach of mainstream microeconomics, the market or opportunity structure of individuals is not taken as homogeneous but is shaped by differing degrees of embeddedness in social networks; for instance, many of one's possible future interaction partners also will have been one's past interaction partners. Networks of affective ties are a restriction on the similarity of the structure of interaction rituals within a market. The explanatory principles of the theory of interaction rituals allows for the formulation of statements about the importance of network structure for certain types of markets, an important topic of economic sociology (Burt, 1983; Granovetter, 1985; White, 1981). People's behavior in market structures is a dynamic element of social structure and change. The institutionalization of markets results in their social and spatial expansion, in their development of an organizational and economic dynamic, and in the production of new layers of markets. Moreover, in the long run markets tend toward crises, with booms entering finally into periods of depression (Collins, 1990a). This can be exemplified in the upswing of the medieval economy, the ensuing development of rational bureaucracies, and the dramatic growth of universities and their final collapse in the late middle ages (Collins, 1981a, pp. 191–215.

The theory of interaction rituals focuses not only on conventional economic markets for goods and services, but on several types of historically important markets: first, kinship markets, where the sexual property in women was the foremost mode of appropriation; second, slave markets, where above all war prisoners were traded; third, agrarian coercive markets based on control over land and its attached labor; and fourth, capitalist markets for the exchange of all manner of goods and labor (Collins, 1990a). This typology of markets does not involve a linear sequence of evolution as in classic historical materialism. The notion of market is used as a convenient device for analyzing and explaining the long-term dynamics in certain areas of societies, although it is not in the "last instance determinant" of the society's development. In a study of kinship markets, for example, the importance of kinship networks and markets for the development of stateless societies has been shown (Collins, 1992; Lévi-Strauss, 1949; Searle, 1988). In such societies investment in kinship alliances is simultaneously an investment in military and political alliances, and therefore, the right long-term investments in kinship alliances can pay off in the form of large-scale military alliances that provide the investing family with large power resources. Emergence of an elite of alliance-rich families was a crucial step toward state formation. An interesting empirical example for such kinds of alliance building within markets is Padgett and Ansells (1993) analysis of the rise of the Medici family. The Medicis created a complex support network by combining marriage alliances with the old aristocracy of Florence and economic alliances with the "nouveau riche." This powerful combination of support networks enabled the Medici family to occupy and remodel the Florentine state.

Social networks are an important result of the overlapping and intersection of chains of interaction rituals. An individual's position in particular social networks is determined as a result of the series of interaction rituals accessible for this individual. Second, network position determines the resources a person can mobilize, his or her worldview, emotional state, and the amount and types of cultural capital he or she can command (Collins, 1988a, pp. 416–418). For example, the denser a particular person's networks are, i.e., the longer and more exclusively an individual is physically present in a certain group of people, the more he or she will identify with the cultural symbols of this group and behave in conformity to these symbols, as well as enforce conformity to these symbols on others. This statement summarizes the cumulative effect of a succession of interaction rituals on the thinking of a particular person. Finally, the theory of interaction rituals combines the notion of action and the notion of structure. On one hand it explains the emergence of certain types of structures, like networks and markets, as specific distributions of interaction rituals in time and space, while on the other hand, these structures or the implied configuration of actual and possible interaction rituals determine the individuals' actions and thinking.

Societies as Overlapping Networks in Space and Time

Research in network analysis is relevant not only for connections among interaction rituals at the mesolevel of social life, but also for the analysis of the macrolevel. At this level societies or social configurations can be described as complex networks of organizations, lower-level networks, social classes, and status groups (Collins, 1968, p. 51). However, macrosociological research has to obey the microsociological caveats formulated above. Its description can be taken only as approximations of empirical reality that involve the typification of certain types of network structures and interaction rituals, even though a full-scale microtranslation of macrosociological patterns is impractical. The task of macrosociology is to prove the consistency of its findings with the research results of meso- and microsociology, because coherence of principles on the theoretical level gives us reason to be confident that macrosociological principles operate by real social mechanisms.

The macrosociological model best suited for conflict theory is Michael Mann's model of social networks of power. He differentiates four dimensions of power and therefore types of power networks: military/geopolitical, political, economical, and cultural/ideological power (Mann, 1986, 1993). Social networks exist in all four kinds of power dimensions, but with varying shapes and spatial extension. The notion of society as a bounded unit (in practice, a reification of the nationalist notion of the nation-state) is abandoned and replaced by a concept of historically specific, spatially located overlapping power networks. The question of the primacy of one of the networks can be answered in the same way. Under varying historical and spatial conditions different networks of power will emerge as the leading sectors of social change.

This model not only is suited for the description of macrosociological entities, but it is capable of formulating explanatory principles for the development of these overlapping power networks. Historical sociology has been successful in proving explanations for macrosocial developments primarily from a conflict theory point of view, from question in political sociology, like state breakdowns and revolutions (Goldstone, 1991; Skocpol, 1979), the development of democracy (Rüschemeyer, Stephens, & Stephens, 1992), the determinants of industrial conflict (Franzosi, 1995), long-term patterns of intellectual change (Collins, 1998), and the determinants of ideologies and worldviews (Wuthnow, 1993). All these focus on conflicts of interest, relations of power between social groups and organizations, and changes in resources in order to explain political and social change. Five concepts are of special importance for conflict explanations of macrosociological change:

1. Macrosociology can borrow central explanatory models from the sociology of organizations. For example, the structure of military organizations is of primary importance in the explanation of premodern forms of political rule (Andreski, 1968; Collins, 1975, pp. 350–362). In such diverse areas as in the explanation of the mobilization of power resources by contending groups or the conflict dynamic of rival schools in the long-term development of philosophical thinking, organizations and their structures are of crucial importance (Collins, 1998; Rössel, 1998).

2. The theory of interaction rituals and the sociology of organizations provide explanatory mechanisms for the analysis of the development and structure of stratification in society. The structure of societal stratification determines the basic interests that shape individuals into categories such as classes or status groups. These interests are of primary importance in the explanation of political and social developments, as, for example, Rüschemeyer et al. (1992) have shown in their historical comparative analysis of the emergence of democracy in capitalist societies. Analysis of structures of stratification is closely connected to the notion of markets because markets and their developments determine the distribution and scarcity of resources.

3. Explanations in conflict theory refer to the mobilization of power resources by contending actors. On one hand this implies the analysis of the development of social movements and the organization of social classes in explaining the power basis of subordinate groups in society, while on the other hand this includes the analysis of networks, institutions, and status cultures of powerful and ruling classes in order to explain their social dominance (Collins, 1979; Jenkins, 1983; Katznelson & Zolberg, 1986; Korpi, 1983; Lachmann, 1989; Tilly, 1978). The analysis of collective action remains to be theoretically integrated into the explanatory principles of the theory of interaction rituals; a sketch of this is attempted along the lines of social movements as conflicts among rival movements over a space of emotional attention (Collins, 2000).

4. As implied by the model of overlapping networks, conflict theory does not treat societies as sharply delimited and isolated entities. Instead, rivalry and mutual influence among states and other global centers of power and organization are key factors in political and social change (Collins, 1968, pp. 57–61; 1990b, pp. 77–78). Whereas the dependency and world system schools of analysis have advanced the analysis of exogenous economic relationships, conflict theory argues against the sole primacy of economic structures and stresses the influence of geopolitics and military power relationships on the long-term development of state power and internal politics (Collins, 1978, 1986, pp. 186–209). The analysis of geopolitics does not imply that spatial relationships between contending centers of military power are the sole determinants of the structure and development of states and societies. Of equal importance in explaining the origins and outcomes of conflicts between power contenders is their respective bases in economic resources and the technology of communication and transport.

5. The last point returns to the argument that the only empirically existing macrovariables are time, space, and the number of persons/interactions involved. The fact that social life consists essentially of nothing more than repetitive interactions between individuals scattered in space and time calls attention to the way in which social structures are determined by historically available means of transport and communication. These determine the possible social integration of social entities across time and space and therefore are a crucial factor for the spatial extension and structuration of particular states and societies (Giddens, 1981, 1984; Mann, 1986, 1993). A related insight refers to the importance of the development and sizes of populations under given ecological conditions. This connection between ecological circumstances (climate, soil, natural catastrophes, plagues), the development of populations, and the resulting economic, social, and political consequences was discovered at an early date in the historical sciences, notably by Wilhelm Abel (1980), and was developed further by the French historical school of the Annales (Braudel, 1982–1984; Le Roy Ladurie, 1971, 1974). In the social sciences, Jack Goldstone (1991), for example, has shown the fruitfulness of such an approach in his comparative analysis of the connections between population growth, inflation, state budgetary crises, and thence state breakdowns and revolutions (see also Collins, 1993a).

CONCLUSION

The primary concern of this chapter has been to sketch the central theoretical notions of conflict sociology. We have concentrated here on the concept of microtranslation and the theory of interaction rituals rather than listing particular results of conflict theory research on the meso- and macrolevel. This has enabled us to emphasize the microfoundation of the key points of conflict theory notions on the meso- and macrolevels.

The microtheoretical core of conflict theory—the theory of interaction rituals—was developed by broadening Emile Durkheim's analysis of religious rituals and Goffman's research on everyday interaction rituals. It attempts to explain the emergence of affective ties between people and the charging of cultural symbols with membership significance for particular groups. The analysis of markets of interaction rituals and the accumulation of resources in chains of interaction rituals and of power and status rituals show how principles of interaction ritual theory explain the emergence of resource divergences, stratification, and conflict. Insofar as it explains both social conflict and social integration, this approach claims the central analytical ground in social theory.

The crucial claim of the theory of interaction rituals is founded in the concept of microtranslation as a strategy for solving the micro–macro problem. This concept is based on the radical empiricism of ethnomethodology and implies that empirical observations are only possible in the microrealm of social life, i.e., human interaction in situations. More complex macrosociological notions, like state or social class, refer to entities that are not empirically observable. All macrosociological concepts should be understood as referring to particular distributions of interaction rituals across time and space. The only true macrosociological variables are time, space, and the number of situations/persons. All macrosociological concepts can be translated into the distribution of microsociological entities in time and space. However, this kind of radical empiricism and microtranslation can be only partly realized; thus macrosociological concepts have to be used in a pragmatic way. Nevertheless, macrosociological theories still have to be compatible and in general reducible to micro- and mesosociological concepts and explanatory principles. The principal explanatory link between the micro- and macrolevel is to be found in the principles of the theory of interaction rituals, which can be connected to the emergence and structures of organizations, markets, and networks as social entities on the mesolevel. In the explanation of domination and control strategies in organizations, for example, it became evidence that the theory of interaction rituals is able to specify the conditions for particular forms of social integration and control more exactly than a mesolevel sociology of organizations. A current shortcoming of the theory of interaction rituals is the lack of an explicit connection to theories of collective action and social mobilization. This is of crucial importance because the interests and power of collective actors are of primary importance in explanations in historical sociology.

The theory of interaction rituals contains some gaps that need to be filled and some fuzzy concepts that need to be differentiated. The notions of cultural capital and emotional energy especially need a further specification. Explanations of particular forms of behavior are formulated on the basis of specific information about the cultural capital and the level of emotional energy of interacting individuals. Therefore, it is necessary to develop differentiated concepts for a more fine-graded explanation of human interactions. A particular gap in the theory of interaction ritual is its treatment of material goods and resources and their relation to the level of emotional energy. The question how the fulfillment of basic needs with resources enters into the level of emotional energy has to be answered.

The theory of interaction rituals is a comprehensive attempt to provide a microtheoretical core for the conflict theoretic tradition in sociology. The considerable accumulation of explan-atory results of conflict theory in historical sociology increases the need for an adequate microfoundation of meso- and macrosociological principles. Interaction ritual theory inte-grates a wide range of empirical studies and specialized theories of numerous social phenom-ena. Of crucial importance is the ability of the theory of interaction rituals to explain both the emergence of competition and conflict on one hand and affective ties and solidarity on the other. Theory of interaction rituals can be connected in diverse directions with other fruitful branches of thinking in the human sciences. On the one hand it can be connected to research in biosociology because of its foundation in human emotions and to geography and history because of the crucial importance of spatiotemporal relations in this theory (Barchas & Mendoza, 1984a,b; Bolin & Bolin, 1984; Kemper, 1990). On the other it can be related to diverse fields of sociological thinking, from social stratification, to political sociology, mili-tary conflict, and the sociology of science and thinking.

Microconflict theory developed as an attempt at integration of many strands of sociology. It holds that the classic theories of Marx, Weber, and Durkheim are mutually coherent and mutually reinforcing, provided that we see their overlapping core as an explanation of how groups struggle over power, while shaped and constrained by resources. Conflict is intimately connected with solidarity, because the key microprocess that constitutes groups, as well as energizes individuals and gives them a symbolic repertoire in terms of which to frame the world, is Durkheimian ritual. We are able to understand social solidarity and shared culture and at the same time maintain a realistic picture of conflict and domination by seeing how pockets of solidarity and culture are generated on the microlevel in an endlessly shifting process, instead of assuming that there are fixed macroentities called "societies" (or any other identities or meaning systems) which by definition are characterized by a common solidarity and culture.

Microconflict theory, as set forth in the mid-1970s (Collins, 1975), attempted to integrate not only the major theoretical traditions, but the patterns found in empirical research. One claim that microconflict theory can make, in contrast to other contemporary theories, is that it integrates generally theory with empirical research and that it does so across the board. Microconflict theory embraces the most militant versions of microempiricism in the study of situations of interaction, but goes on to tie this to middle-sized structural patterns such as networks, organizations, and markets and these to large-scale patterns of political, economic, and cultural change. There are no excluded empirical areas in microconflict theory. Thus it works to make isolated areas of research significant in their relation to the whole, and like the strands of a spider web to transmit the strength of successful areas of research from one part of sociology to another.

REFERENCES

Abel, W. (1980). *Agricultural fluctuations in Europe from the thirteenth to the twentieth centuries.* New York: St. Martin's Press.

Andreski, S. (1968). *Military organization and society.* London: Routledge & Kegan Paul.

Barchas, P. R., & Mendoza, S. P. (Eds.). (1984a). *Social cohesion. Essays toward a sociophysiological perspective.* Westport, CT: Greenwood Press.

Barchas, P. R., & Mendoza, S. P. (Eds.) (1984b). *Social hierarchies. Essays toward a sociophysiological perspective.* Westport, CT: Greenwood Press.

Bolin, R., & Bolin, S. B. (1984). Sociobiology and sociology: Issues in applicability. In P. R. Barchas & S. P. Mendoza (Eds.), *Social hierarchies. Essays toward a sociophysiological perspective* (pp. 3–22). Westport, CT: Green-wood Press.

Bourdieu, P. (1984). *Distinction: A social critique of the judgement of taste*. Cambridge, MA: Harvard University Press.

Braudel, F. (1982–1984). *Civilization and capitalism, 15th to 18th century*. New York: Harper & Row.

Burt, R. S. (1983). *Corporate profits and cooperation. Networks of market constraints and directorate ties in the American economy*. New York: Academic Press.

Cicourel, A. V. (1973). *Cognitive sociology: Language and meaning in social interaction*. Harmondsworth: Penguin.

Coleman, J. S. (1990). *Foundations of social theory*. Cambridge, MA: Belknap Press.

Collins, R. (1968). A comparative approach to political sociology. In R. Bendix (Ed.), *State and society* (pp. 42–67). Boston: Little.

Collins, R. (1971a). Functional and conflict theories of educational stratification. *American Sociological Review, 36*, 1002–1019.

Collins, R. (1971b). A conflict theory of sexual stratification. *Social Problems, 19* 3–21.

Collins, R. (1975). *Conflict sociology. Towards an explanatory science*. New York: Academic Press.

Collins, R. (1978). Some principles of long-term social change. The territorial power of states. *Research in Social Movements, Conflict and Change, 1*, 1–34.

Collins, R. (1979). *The credential society. An historical sociology of education and stratification*. New York: Academic Press.

Collins, R. (1981a). *Sociology since midcentry: Essays in theory cumulation*. New York: Academic Press.

Collins, R. (1981b). On the micro-foundations of macro-sociology. *American Journal of Sociology, 86*, 984–1014.

Collins, R. (1981c). Micro-translation as a theory-building strategy. In K. Knorr-Cetina & A. V. Cicourel (Eds.), *Advances in social theory and methodology. Towards an integration of micro- and macro-sociology* (pp. 81–108). London: Routledge and Kegan Paul.

Collins, R. (1982). *Sociological insight. An introduction to non-obvious sociology*. New York: Oxford University Press.

Collins, R. (1983). Micromethods and macrosociology. *Urban Life, 12*, 184–202.

Collins, R. (1985a). *Three sociological traditions*. New York: Oxford University Press.

Collins, R. (1985b). *Sociology of marriage and the family: Gender, love and property*. Chicago: Nelson Hall.

Collins, R. (1986). *Weberian sociological theory*. Cambridge and New York: Cambridge University Press.

Collins, R. (1987a). A micro-macro theory of creativity in intellectual careers. The case of German idealist philosophy. *Sociological Theory, 5*, 47–69.

Collins, R. (1987b). Interaction ritual chains, power and property. In J. Alexander, B. Giesen, R. Münch & N. J. Smelser (Eds.), *The micro–macro link* (pp. 193–206). Berkeley: University of California Press.

Collins, R. (1988a). *Theoretical sociology*. San Diego: Harcourt, Brace, Jovanovich.

Collins, R. (1988b). The micro contribution to macro sociology. *Sociological Theory, 6*, 242–253.

Collins, R. (1989a). Towards a neo-Meadian sociology of mind. *Symbolic Interaction, 12*, 1–31.

Collins, R. (1989b). Sociological theory, disaster research, and war. In G. Kreps (Ed.), *Social structure and disaster. Conception and measurement* (pp. 365–385). Newark: University of Delaware Press.

Collins, R. (1989c). Toward a theory of intellectual change. The social causes of philosophies. *Science, Technology and Human Values, 14*, 107–140.

Collins, R. (1989d). Stratification, emotional energy, and the transient emotions. In T. Kemper (Ed.), *Research agendas in the sociology of emotions* (pp. 27–57). Albany: SUNY Press.

Collins, R. (1989e). Sociology: Pro-science or anti-science. *American Sociological Review, 53, 121*–139.

Collins, R. (1990a). Market dynamics as the engine of historical change. *Sociological Theory, 8*, 111–135.

Collins, R. (1990b). Conflict theory and the advance of macro-historical sociology. In G. Ritzer (Ed.), *Frontiers of social theory* (pp. 68–87). New York: Columbia University Press.

Collins, R. (1992a). The geopolitical and economic world systems of kinship-based and agrarian coercive societies. *Review, 15*, 373–388.

Collins, R. (1992b). On the sociology of intellectual stagnation. The late 20th century in perspective. *Theory, Cultural and Society, 9*, 73–96.

Collins, R. (1993a). Maturation of the state-centered theory of revolution and ideology. *Sociological Theory, 11*, 117–128.

Collins, R. (1993b). Emotional energy as the common denominator of rational action. *Rationality and Society, 5*, 203–230.

Collins, R. (1993c). The rationality of avoiding choice. *Rationality and Society, 5*, 58–67.

Collins, R. (1996). Can rational action theory unify future social science? In J. Clark (Ed.), *James S. Coleman* (pp. 329–342). London: Falmer Press.

Collins, R. (1998). *The sociology of philosophies: A global theory of intellectual change*. Cambridge, MA: Belknap Press.

Collins, R. (2000). *Social movements and the focus of emotional attention*. Manuscript.

Collins, R., & Hanneman, R. (1998). Modelling interaction ritual theory of solidarity. *Journal of Mathematical Sociology*, Manuscript.

Collins, R., & Makowsky, B. (1972). *The discovery of society*. New York: Random House.

Durkheim, E. (1965). *The elementary forms of religious life*. New York: Free Press.

Etzioni, A. (1975). *A comparative analysis of complex organizations: On power, involvement and their correlates*. New York: Free Press.

Fligstein, N. (1987). The intraorganizational power struggle. Rise of finance personnel to top leadership. *American Sociological Review, 52*, 44–58.

Franzosi, R. (1995). *The puzzle of strikes: Class and state strategies in postwar Italy*. Cambridge, England: Cambridge University Press.

Garfinkel, H. (1967). *Studies in ethnomethodology*. Englewood Cliffs, NJ: Prentice Hall.

Gerhards, J., & Rössel, J. (1999). Zur Transnationalisierung der Gesellschaft der Bundesrepublik. Entwicklungen, Ursachen und mögliche Folgen für die europäische Integration. *Zeitschrift für Soziologie, 28*, 325–344.

Giddens, A. (1981). *A contemporary critique of historical materialism*, Volume 1. London: Macmillan.

Giddens, A. (1984). *The constitution of society. Outline of a theory of structuration*. Cambridge: Polity Press.

Goffman, E. (1963). *Behavior in public places. Notes on the social organization of gatherings*. New York: Free Press.

Goffman, E. (1967). *Interaction ritual. Essays on face-to-face behavior*. Garden City, NY: Doubleday.

Goffman, E. (1969). *The presentation of self in everyday life*. London: Allen Lane.

Goldstone, J. (1991). *Revolution and rebellion in the early modern world.*. Berkeley: University of California Press.

Granovetter, M. (1985). Economic action and social structure. The problem of embeddedness. *American Journal of Sociology, 91*, 481–510.

Hammond, M. (1984). Affectivity and stratification in the work of Emile Durkheim. In P. R. Barchas & S. P. Mendoza (Eds.), *Social cohesion: Essays toward a sociophysiological perspective* (pp. 121–138). Westport, CT: Greenwood Press.

Heritage, J. (1987). Ethnomethodology. In A. Giddens & J. Turner (Eds.), *Social theory today* (pp. 224–272). Cambridge, England: Polity Press.

Jenkins, C. (1983). Resource mobilization theory and the study of social movements. *Annual Review of Sociology, 9*, 527–553.

Joas, H. (1987). Symbolic interactionism. In A. Giddens & J. Turner (Eds.), *Social theory today* (pp. 82–115). Cambridge, England: Polity Press.

Katznelson, I., & Zolberg, A. (Eds.). (1986). *Working class formation: Nineteenth century patterns in western Europe and the United States*. Princeton, NJ: Princeton University Press.

Kemper, T. (1978). *A social interactional theory of emotions*. New York: Wiley.

Kemper, T. (1990). *Social structure and testosterone. Explorations of the socio-bio-social chain*. New Brunswick, NJ: Rutgers University Press.

Kemper, T., & Collins, R. (1990). Dimensions of microinteraction. *American Journal of Sociology, 96*, 32–68.

Korpi, W. (1983). *The democratic class struggle*. London: Routledge & Kegan Paul.

Lachmann, R. (1989). Elite conflict and state formation in 16th and 17th century England and France. *American Sociological Review, 54, 141–162*.

Le Roy Ladurie, E. (1971). *Times of feast, times of famine. A history of climate since the year 1000*. Garden City, NY: Doubleday.

Le Roy Ladurie, E. (1974). *The peasants of Languedoc*. Urbana: University of Illinois Press.

Lévi-Strauss, C. (1949). *Les structures élémentaires de la parenté*. Paris: Presse Universitaire de France.

Mann, M. (1986). *The sources of social power*. Volume 1: *A history of power from the beginning to AD 1760*. Cambridge, England: Cambridge University Press.

Mann, M. (1993). *The sources of social power*. Volume 2: *The rise of classes and nation-states, 1760–1914*. Cambridge, England: Cambridge University Press.

Maurice, M. (1986). *The social foundations of industrial power: A comparison of France and Germany*. Cambridge, MA: MIT Press.

Mueller, U., & Mazur, A. (1996). Facial dominance of West Point cadets as a predictor of later military rank. *Social Forces, 74*, 823–850.

Padgett, J. F., & Ansell, C. K. (1993). Robust action and the rise of the Medici, 1400–1434. *American Journal of Sociology, 98*, 1259–1319.

Perrow, C. (1986). *Complex organizations. A critical essay*. New York: McGraw-Hill.

Pfeffer, J. (1982). *Organizations and organization theory*. Boston: Pitman.

Polanyi, M. (1967). *The tacit dimension*. Garden City, NY: Doubleday.

Rössel, J. (1998). Der Effekt der Organisation. Mobilisierung und Erfolg von Challenging Groups am Beispiel amerikanischer Kohlenbergarbeiterstreiks 1881–1894. *Politische Vierteljahresschrift, 39*, 28–54.

Rüschemeyer, D., Stephens, E. H., & Stephens, J. D. (1992). *Capitalist development and democracy.* Cambridge, England: Polity Press.

Scheff, T. (1990). *Micro-sociology: Discourse, emotion and social structure.* Chicago: University of Chicago Press.

Scheff, T. J., & Retzinger, S. (1991). *Emotions and violence: Shame and rage in destructive conflicts.* Lexington, MA: Lexington Books.

Schulze, G. (1992). *Die Erlebnisgesellschaft. Kultursoziologie der Gegenwart.* Frankfurt: Campus.

Scott, W. R. (1992). *Organizations: Rational, natural, and open systems.* Englewood Cliffs, NJ: Prentice Hall.

Searle, E. (1988). *Predatory kinship and the creation of Norman power, 840–1066.* Berkeley: University of California Press.

Skocpol, T. (1979. *States and social revolutions.* New York: Cambridge University Press.

Sorge, A., & Warner, M. (1986). *Comparative factory organization: An Anglo-German comparison of manufacturing, management and manpower.* Aldershot, England: Gower.

Tilly, C. (1978). *From mobilization to revolution.* Reading, MA: Addison-Wesley.

Tilly, C. (1984). *Big structures, large processes, huge comparisons.* New York: Russel Sage Foundation.

Thoits, P. A. (1989). The sociology of emotions. *Annual Review of Sociology, 15,* 317–342.

Welskopp, T. (1994). *Macht und Arbeit im Hüttenwerk: Arbeits- und industrielle Beziehungen in der deutschen und amerikanischen Eisen- und Stahlindustrie von 1860er bis zu den 1930er Jahren.* Bonn: Dietz.

White, H. (1981). Where do markets come from? *American Journal of Sociology, 87,* 517–547.

Wuthnow, R. (1993). *Communities of discourse. Ideology and social structure in the Reformation, the Enlightenment and European socialism.* Cambridge: Harvard University Press.

CHAPTER 25

The Enduring Vitality
of the Resource Mobilization
Theory of Social Movements

JOHN D. MCCARTHY AND MAYER N. ZALD

It is now just over three decades since the initiation of the research and writing that came to be called resource mobilization theory (RMT). Developed during a period of heightened activism and social movement participation, it grew out of our sense that the then extant theories and approaches did not well explain the levels of mobilization and the trends that were occurring in an affluent American society. One line of those earlier theories focused on the role of grievances and deprivation in triggering social movements. But should not the level of grievances and deprivation and consequently the number of social movements be going down as society becomes more affluent? Nor did others of the available theories do very well at explaining the large number of movements and high level of mobilization of the period.

Beginning as an attempt to provide a set of answers to that seeming paradox, we developed a fairly general but partial theory of social movement growth and decline and the relationship of growth and decline to movement structure and differentiation. The intellectual roots of RMT lie in our own background in the then current organizational and economic theories that critiqued simple notions of rationality and made it clear that self-interest alone was an inadequate basis to account for the contribution of effort to the pursuit of the collective goods that social movements seemed to be involved in. The theory took an entrepreneurial–organizational approach to movements and generated a set of topics, propositions, and hypotheses that had been little investigated in prior research and certainly had not been organized in that way before. Although the theory was stated in fairly general terms, as if it could be applied to most societies, especially industrialized societies, it was in fact designed to focus on the dynamics and trends of social movements in contemporary American society. Stated another way, the scope conditions were not well articulated.

We thank Pat Gillham, Debra Minkoff, and Jackie Smith for providing useful comments on earlier drafts.

JOHN D. MCCARTHY • Department of Sociology, Pennsylvania State University, University Park, Pennsylvania 16802. MAYER N. ZALD • Department of Sociology, University of Michigan, Ann Arbor, Michigan 48109.

Handbook of Sociological Theory, edited by Jonathan H. Turner. Kluwer Academic / Plenum Publishers, New York, 2002.

RMT developed as one among several related attempts to understand collective action and social movements that shared problematics and broke with earlier traditions. Anthony Oberschall, Charles Tilly, William Gamson, Pam Oliver, Gerald Marwell, and others, though differing with each other in important ways, also shared some common assumptions. They differed, for instance, in how much they focused on the conditions for individual mobilization and participation, the extent to which they took an organizational or political process approach, how much they focused on the Olsonian problem of the provision of collective goods, and so on. As is evidenced in the essays in Zald and McCarthy (1979), the results of a conference held in 1977, on the one hand, there already was an awareness that a new paradigm or approach (which came to be called the resource mobilization/collective action program) was developing, and on the other there were substantial differences within the program. (The political process approach associated with Charles Tilly came to be called RMI, while our entrepreneurial/organizational approach was called RMII.) Jenkins (1985) provides a systematic account of the differences between these two variants of RMT.

Over this 30-year period, there has been a vast flowering of research on social movements and collective action. Some substantial portion of that research, especially that conducted by sociologists and political scientists, has drawn on the formulations of RMT scholars as it attempted to "test" these formulations or use them to explain phenomena of interest in specific movements, collective action events or event sequences. For instance, we have identified more than 150 doctoral dissertations that make explicit reference to resource mobilization in their abstracts. (It is not always clear from the abstracts which variant or combination of variants of RMT they are using.) We have identified more than 600 articles that make reference just to the foundational articles (McCarthy & Zald, 1973, 1977) of RMII. Most of the publications are in sociology or political science, but one also finds work in journals related to specific social movements and/or professions (e.g., public health, natural resources and environmental studies, gender studies). Some of these works confirm original hypotheses or expectations and others criticize RMT or combine it with other perspectives or theoretical approaches, for instance new social movement theory. Some attempt to adjudicate among variants. Moreover, as we have continued writing and doing research and as we have listened to the critics of RMT, we have changed our position on many of our original assumptions or ways of thinking. But we have never attempted to restate the theory or to directly respond to the criticisms of the theory that have emerged. Restricting ourselves to our own formulation of the RM program, this chapter summarizes the original theory and core assumptions, examines the analytical and conceptual problems that emerged, and assesses the trends in research and research findings that bear on the main hypotheses. In no way a complete summary of research, it will allow us to isolate some important problems that deserve future attention. The next section states the background assumptions, the implicit scope conditions, and the core assumptions and propositions of the original theory. The second section directly addresses conceptual criticisms and reviews research as it bears upon major components of the theory. The third section locates RMII in its relationship to complementary and competitive approaches.

ASSUMPTIONS, SCOPE CONDITIONS, AND ORIENTING PROPOSITIONS

Social movements can be defined as mobilized or activated (effective) demand (preferences) for change in society. This definition is not fully accepted in the larger community of scholars, or even among the community of scholars that constitute the RMT community. Nevertheless, it is useful for RMII because it focuses on how and why demands are generated and how social movement organizations (SMOs), whether small and informal or large and more formal, are generated and organized. Central to RMII is some notion of increasing or decreasing demand for movement activity and social change and some notion of SMO stimulation of demand, organizational growth, decline, and adaptation as demand increases or decreases. [Effective demand is different from grievances or preferences in that it focuses on resources available to pursue (purchase, extend effort) wants, rather than on grievances or preferences alone.] Moreover, as demand increases and as the overall movement meets with responses from the larger society and polity, the possibilities for SMO differentiation increases. All the SMOs relating to a SM can be thought of as an industry (SMI), with attendant goal and tactical differentiation and internal competition and conflict. There may be few or many SMs and SMIs in a society at any one point in time. All the SMs and SMIs may be considered a social movement sector (SMS). One important issue is what accounts for the size and orientation(s) of the SMS (Garner & Zald, 1985).

Background Assumptions and Scope Conditions

Four background assumptions or contrasts set off RMT from earlier traditions or approaches in social movement theory. (1) Contrasted with theories that attempted to predict mobilization levels directly from "frustration" or deprivation, RMT argues that the amount of mobilization or movement participation cannot be predicted directly from the level of deprivation or grievances. Participation involves expenditures of time, energy, and money and populations with few resources are less able to act on grievances or perceived injustices. (2) Some earlier theories had argued that participation in movements was a form of irrational and pathological behavior: at the individual level it was an expression of personal alienation and/or pathology; at the societal level, a result of isolated, uprooted, and unattached behavior. RMT treats social movement participation as normal behavior, emerging out of biographical circumstances, social supports, and immediate life situations. (3) Most prior theories located the resources that were mobilized largely or completely within the aggrieved or beneficiary constituency. RMT locates resources in the larger society, including governmental and religious institutions, and in conscience constituencies, groups that support the movement's goals, even though its members do not receive the direct output of the policy/political changes that the movement advocates. (4) Prior theories of social movements focus largely on the interaction of movement and authorities, with the movement attempting to raise the costs to authorities or drawing attention to the legitimacy of their claims. RMT draws attention to the role of the media in mediating between the movement and bystander publics. Thus, movement and authorities are both caught in a larger contest for support of bystander publics and reference elites.

SCOPE CONDITIONS. RMT grew out of an empirical stocktaking of trends in the dynamics of social movements in the United States. Although it was stated in quite general terms, seemingly applicable to social movements in any society, it had implicit and explicit scope conditions that limited its "untranslated" applicability. Among the most important of these scope conditions are the following: (1) Societies have voluntary association traditions. Individuals can choose to affiliate and participate in voluntary associations and knowledge of how to organize them is fairly widespread. (2) Freedom of speech and freedom of assembly are normatively accepted, even if not universally applied. (3) There is a mass media and it is fairly open to reporting grievances and protest. (4) The electoral system is so structured that small groups have little chance of gaining legislative office. Thus, mobilization and action outside of the electoral system is encouraged.

RMT can and has been applied in situations where these conditions do not hold. For instance, RMT has been used to analyze social movements in authoritarian regimes and in societies without voluntary association traditions. Other versions of RMT (Oberschall, Tilly) are not dependent on these scope conditions. Yet, it is clear that our version was formulated with these conditions in mind and the propositions we developed and the objects of analysis that were chosen took these scope conditions as shaping the parameters in which analysis took place.

ORIENTING PROPOSITIONS. RMT is a middle-ranged theory that develops propositions about the interrelationship between demands for change (i.e., sentiments, preferences, tastes, values, grievances), costs and benefits of attempting to realize those demands, SMOs and technologies of mobilization and protest, SMIs, and the SMS. Here we present the core concepts of the theory and selected propositions.

Demands, Costs and Benefits, and Resources.   SMs draw on the sentiment/preference pool in the larger society. Sentiment or preference pools vary in the number of people who share the grievance or sentiment and the intensity with which those sentiments for change are held. Over time the size and intensity of the preference pool changes as issues and problems succeed each other on the public agenda. Of course, for some parts of the population, the preference structure may be relatively stable, even while the size of the sentiment pool in the rest of the society may fluctuate. (For example, the grievances and preferences of the African-American community may be relatively stable on civil rights issues, even while the rest of the society may have fluctuations in the level of concern.) Issue entrepreneurs (politicians, journalists, ministers, SMO leaders, public intellectuals, and so on) attempt to define the issues for specific and general audiences. If they are successful, they enlarge and intensify the sentiment pool,[1] that is, they increase the number of people committed to a demand/preference for change and intensify the commitment to the issue of those who already share that preference.

Having a preference for change, or having a grievance or sense of injustice, does not automatically translate into action to rectify the grievance. Action occurs in the context of the life situation of the potential participant and in the context of competing commitments, social supports, costs, and resources. Competing commitments may include commitments to work, to family, and to educational goals that may inhibit participation. Individuals differ in the resources that they command relevant to a movement's tasks and the extent to which those resources (skills, money, time, and status) can be put in the service of the movement. Individuals with discretionary time and money, for whatever reason, and with few competing commitments, are more likely to act on their preferences to participate in movement activities. Similarly, if others in ones life space share values and grievances and participate in movement-related activities, social costs of participation are lowered. Conversely, if there are few supports for participation, we would expect lower rates of acting on preferences.

The resources social movements draw on come from many sources. Specific resources, such as labor, facilities, and money, may be supplied by individuals who are part of the presumed beneficiary base of the movement—members of the group whose claims of injustice or deprivation are to be rectified. Or they may come from conscience constituencies—others in the society who believe in the rightness of the cause, even though they themselves and their friends and relatives will not directly benefit from the changes advocated. Monies, labor, and

---

[1]RMT originally included notions of issue entrepreneurship in the definition of grievances and the proffering of solutions and pathways of action. But we did not have available the language of framing to examine the ways in which symbols were used to package diagnoses and prognoses as was later developed by Snow and Benford (1988, 1992).

facilities also may be made available through institutional channels, such as church bodies, philanthropic foundations, and government programs. There also are general infrastructural resources that may be available to movements that effect their ability to mobilize. The development of the mass media, of cheaper and more rapid transportation means, of postal systems, and of electronic communication systems (faxes, internet) affect mobilization costs.

Social Movement Organizations: Structure, Technologies, and Professionalization. SMOs are relatively formal organizations that develop to manage the interdependencies of adherents and activists committed to the movement. If a movement effort endures beyond a single event and links several networks of adherents and activists, a more or less formal organization (at a minimum a mailing list, a name, and a set of controllers of the mailing list and attendant resources) is likely to develop. Although many SMOs may be relatively small, enduring movements with substantial number of adherents may develop larger SMOs that link adherents in different locales and even countries.[2]

Activists, acting on their own, as members of networks, or as self-identified agents of SMOs, attempt to transform bystander publics into sympathizers and sympathizers into adherents (contributors of money and labor). Cadre, the activists who devote the most time, money, and energy to the organization, are drawn from the ranks of adherents to an SM. They also may be drawn from the ranks of cadre and adherents of previous movements and ideologically related activities. Thus, as a new focused movement emerges, it can draw on adherents of prior movements or ideologies that are less active and "hot" at the present time.

As SMOs grow larger and command larger resource flows, they are likely to develop cadre and staff that devote considerable amounts of time to the SMO. Indeed, professionalization may occur in that cadre may develop skills specific to leading and managing SMOs such that careers in a specific SMI or related organizations and industries may develop. A number of structural/institutional problems also may emerge as SMOs become larger and less transient. These include the relationship of cadre to adherents and how choices are made about programs, tactics, and goals, the relationships of central offices to chapters or local groups, and the extent to which SMOs operate in conformance with accounting and other standards that constrain organizations in general and the nonprofit/social movement sector.

SMOs combine resources to attempt to accomplish social change. Thus, two interlinked sets of repertoires or technologies can be thought to be employed. Technologies of mobilization include techniques for recruiting adherents—members who contribute money through direct mail and telephone campaigns, participants in demonstrations and marches, and recruits to cells for illegal and terroristic activities. Technologies of protest range from relatively peaceful and legal activities, such as speaking to public gatherings, marches and demonstrations, and lobbying efforts. They extend further to such activities that may be legal or illegal, such as boycotts, sit-ins, and other blockades of "normal" civil activity, to illegal activity such as property damage, murder, arson, and theft. The two kinds of technologies may be interlinked in that the protest or change activity, when visible, affects bystanders' and sympathizers' readiness to become adherents. On the other side, the kinds of mobilization technologies that are utilized may bring in adherents with different kinds of commitments to protest activities, shaping the tactical repertoires of SMOs.

[2]Zald and Ash (1966) first introduced the acronym of SMO in 1966. Their analysis had used an organization–environment framework, which then was current in organizational theory, to explicate the dynamics of organizational adaptation. In particular they asked how and when SMOs were able to avoid the tendencies to bureaucratization and conservatism that had been predicted by Michels and Weber. RMT tended to assume their analysis and did not pay much attention to organizational dynamics.

In modern societies, which are usually large with dispersed communities, the conditions and injustices that SMs wish to rectify are not directly experienced or perceived by bystanders. Similarly, bystander publics do not directly perceive the actions of SMOs and SM activists. Instead, mass media (print, television, and radio) filter perceptions through their reporting routines and the images that they convey. The amount, substantive content, and biases of media coverage is a complex resultant of the range of events and newsworthy stories in the larger society, the competitive situation of the media, and the professional commitments and expectations of media staff. Since enlarging sentiment pools depends at least in part on this indirect filtering, SMOs and SM cadre are dependent on and strategically attempt to shape the amount and nature of media coverage of the movement. Reference elites and authorities, too, are affected by filtered perceptions of the movement and its causes. And authorities may also attempt to shape and limit media coverage.

Social Movement Industry (SMI) and Social Movement Sector. As the sentiment pool expands, as more people support the movement, and as more resources are available for mobilization, the number of SMOs increase and they differentiate in terms of ideological/ constituency constellation and in terms of the functional niche that they occupy. If the sentiment pool was fully homogeneous, fewer SMOs might be founded, but SMOs are created to gather up the resources of segments of the pool that differ in the extremity of their diagnoses and in their commitments to different kinds of tactics and program. In turn, those SMOs encourage the segmenting and fragmenting of the sentiment pool.

All of the SMOs that share a general movement goal can be thought of as an industry. SMOs within an industry cooperate, compete, and conflict with one another. They come together for some shared purposes either of protest or of collective representation, they compete for resources from sympathizers and adherents, and they conflict over leadership of the movement as a whole, over who should represent the movement to authorities and the larger public. Moreover, as more resources are available, specialization of function may occur. Some SMOs may become information-gathering organizations, provide legal services, or lobbying services to other SMOs committed to the broad general goals.

There may be several social movements at varying degrees of mobilization at any one time in a society, or there may be none. Societies differ in the extent to which they encourage and facilitate social movements. All the SMIs in a society can be conceived as the social movement sector. The size and orientation of the SMS is a function of the amount of resources devoted to social change (whatever its substantive focus, either left or right), the associational supports provided by the larger society, the pluralistic or authoritarian orientation of the state, and the relationship of the movement sector to the political party space. The size and shape of the SMS varies between nation-states and over time within them.

These are the core conceptual components of RMII. Over the past 20 years RMII has been used in several ways. Sometimes it has been used to provide a recipe list of topics to be examined as scholars studied the growth and transformation of specific movements, for instance, studies of the environmental movement, or of specific conflicts, for instance, the battle over North American Free Trade Association (NAFTA). Sometimes it has been used to point to topics that had not been studied in earlier approaches. This has been especially the case with studies of the relationship of external funding to movement growth and directions, but also to studies of professionalization and mobilization technologies. In still other cases, there has been a direct attempt to test specific hypotheses stated in the 1977 article by McCarthy and Zald. RMII has been subjected to substantial critique and also has been used in conjunction with other theoretical formulations. In the next section we attempt to summarize our current understanding of the status of the theory and of the research surrounding it.

TOWARD A REFORMULATION
OF RESOURCE MOBILIZATION II:
A SELECTIVE REVIEW
OF RESEARCH AND CRITICISM

Over the last 25 years a substantial number of theoretical critiques and a vast number of empirical studies have appeared that bear on central issues posed by the RM approach. It is beyond the scope of this chapter to systematically review this extensive body of scholarship. What we wish to accomplish is more modest. We will revisit several of the central questions posed by the RMII approach and consider them in the light of subsequent criticism and research.

Six key questions that are central to the original RMII focus will help us structure our review of several main lines of critique and subsequent research bearing on issues they raised. These are: (1) what are the main explanatory elements of the micromobilization of SMO activism; (2) what resources are important for SMOs, where do those resources come from (internal or external sources), and what role do they play in organizational dynamics; (3) what are sentiment pools, what accounts for changes in their size, and are SMO and SMI recruitment dynamics more or less important than sentiment pool size in accounting for rates of micromobilization, SMO founding rates, and SMO, SMI, and SMS growth; (4) what is the impact of SMO capacity (density) on protest extent, form, and likelihood of disruptiveness; (5) what are the historically specific and universal patterns of SMO life cycles and SMO population dynamics and how can they be accounted for; and (6) what are the key dynamics of SMIs and the SMSs and how can they be accounted for?

The ratios of theoretical criticism, systematic research attention, and theoretical elaboration to one another in subsequent work addressed to the six questions have varied considerably. We attempt to honor those ratios in our discussion. A number of critiques of RMII have emphasized our blind spots and omissions.[3] We will return to those in the conclusion to this section.

As we have implied a core assumption of RMII is that understanding SMO processes is a key to accounting for social movement ebbs and flows. Central to such understanding is to know how SMOs are formed and how their leaders think strategically about how to establish stable resource flows in order to survive. These organizations are not committed to making a profit to survive but pursuing public goods. Nevertheless, many of them find it necessary to confront the dilemmas of establishing stable resource flows in order to maintain themselves. We made a number of claims about these processes. But we were mostly speaking out of ignorance about their empirical scope conditions because we did not possess anything like a census of SMOs that would allow us to describe their demography, although we did make strong claims about the increasing number of professionalized ones. We now can specify more clearly the demography of the US SMS. We being by doing so in order that we can nest our discussion of our six key questions more securely.

Toward a Demography of the US SMS

SMI AND SMS SIZE.   It has been only recently that researchers began to document in fuller detail the size and shape of segments of the US SMS. While the task of completing an adequate census of SMOs for any SMI and therefore the entire sector is fraught with obstacles,[4] we now

---

[3]The most important of these are that we deemphasize political and cultural processes.

[4]SMOs are a subset of nonprofit organizations in the United States, but are not required to register with the IRS unless they seek special tax status as formal nonprofits. As a consequence, many, especially small local, SMOs do not

have a number of very useful SMI wide estimates of the number of SMOs (Mitchell et al., 1992). For instance, based on Internal Revenue Service (IRS) 990 registrations, Brulle (1996, 2000) estimates that in 1990 there were more than 15,000 US environmental organizations. This is surely an underestimate, since many local volunteer-led social movement groups do not register with the IRS.[5] A group of researchers led by Collwell and Bond (1994) estimated that the US peace movement consisted of at least 7,700 organizations in 1988 (Edwards & Marullo, 1995; Edwards, 1994; Marullo, Pagnucco, & Smith, 1996) and an independent estimate by Lofland (1993) put the number at 8,000. Both estimates are especially helpful because they are not confined to SMOs of large size and broad geographic scope and therefore can demonstrate that as for economic organizations (as with firms, sole proprietorships, and partnerships) most SMOs are small and local. We do not have such well-documented estimates for other US SMIs.[6] But if these numbers are at all indicative of other well-established SMIs, including victim's rights, antitoxic, community empowerment, gay and lesbian, racial and ethnic, prolife and prochoice and animal rights SMIs, it is not difficult to suggest that there are at least several hundred thousand US SMOs.[7] This is an enormous number of organizations seeking social change.[8]

SMS Demography.   Based on these attempts to provide a census of two important SMIs, what can we say about the demography of the SMS? There are four theoretically important dimensions along which distinct SMOs can vary. These main SMO demographic variables are: (1) the extent to which the leadership is volunteer or is paid; (2) the geographic scope of operations (local versus state and/or national); (3) whether the SMO has any members and if so whether the members are individuals or other organizations (or some combination of the two); and (4) whether the SMO is a stand alone or is affiliated in any way with a network of groups.

The vast majority of SMOs rely on volunteer leaders, are small and locally based, and are what Lofland and Jamison (1985) call association locals. Most are independent groups, although some are linked to broader umbrella organizations. The evidence presented by Edwards (1994) indicated that about half of the local peace groups were affiliated with other groups. A surprisingly large proportion of small local associations are led by paid staff, if the peace movement SMI is any indication: about one third of the local peace groups had reported paid staff. At the local level there also are many service/advocacy organizations (e.g., health clinics and shelters) closely associated with broader movements such as the women's[9] and gay rights movements. These are nowhere near as numerous as associations and are typically led by paid staff. Nor are the associations that are organizations of organizations, such as the many congregation-based community organizations, as numerous as association locals (Delgado,

---

register. Methods for finding these unregistered groups are costly and unreliable (see McCarthy & Castelli, 2000). Until recently, the IRS nonprofit information system as well has not been easily accessible.

[5]Edwards (1994) provides evidence for SMOs in the peace movement in 1988 that about 20% of the groups identified were not registered. See also McCarthy, Britt, and Wolfson (1991) and D. H. Smith (1997).

[6]See also Rucht (1989) on the German and French environmental SMIs and Kriesi (1996) on the French, German, Dutch, and Swiss new social movement SMIs.

[7]This compares with estimates of the total number of religious congregations in the United States of 300,000 and the total number of about 20 million economic organizations, and one million formally registered nonprofit organizations, an unknown subset of which are SMOs (Hodgkinson and Weitzman, 1996).

[8]Note that we have not included patriot groups, radical right-wing groups, fundamentalist religious groups, or right-to-bear-arms groups. Social movement scholars have, in general, ignored such groups, instead focusing the bulk of their research attention upon SMOs with which they sympathize.

[9]Martin (1990) calls attention to this class of SMOs noting that they have been ignored for the most part both by organizational and social movement analysts. See also, Ferree and Martin (1995).

1994)[10] but they may be more common than most analysts have assumed. One sample of local SMOs seeking to empower poor communities found, for instance, that about 10% of them were based on a membership made up primarily of other organizations, while another 10% included both individual and organizational members (McCarthy & Castelli, 1994). Minkoff (personal communication) reports that 21% of the white women's SMOs she has analyzed elsewhere (1995) are composed of organizational members. The census of SMOs in the peace movement showed that only about 25% of the small, mostly local groups, relied exclusively on individual rather than other organizations as members (Edwards, 1994).

The minority of SMOs whose geographic scope of operations is broader than local communities typically have larger annual budgets than locally based ones and are far more likely to be led by paid staff (Edwards, 1994). Some of them include other organizations as well as individuals as members, some have exclusively organizational members, and some have no individual members. Walker's (1991) evidence for Washington-based citizens groups with members shows that while a slim majority rely exclusively on individual members, the rest rely wholly or in part on organizational members. His data also show that a subset of these nonlocal organizations has state and/or local affiliates in some federated arrangement and that citizens' groups are more likely than other Washington-based groups to have state or local chapters. Finally, that evidence shows that those SMOs derive only about a third of their resources from membership dues of any kind, while about another third of their aggregate revenue flow comes from grant sources (individual, foundation, and government).

CHANGING SM SECTORAL DEMOGRAPHY.   What can we say about the changing demography of the sector? We know more about the nonlocal part of the sector than the local part. There is evidence of high mortality rates among local associations, but the majority of them appear able to survive downturns in movement fortunes (Edwards & Marullo, 1995). Some of the forms that have received attention, for example, feminist service organizations and congregation-based organizations, appear to have grown in numbers over recent decades and to have established stable resource bases (e.g., Martin, 1990; Rogers, 1990). Because of the difficulties of enumerating this part of the SMS to which we have already alluded, it is not possible to develop credible estimates of its trajectory. This is evident, for instance, in Robert Putnam's (2000) difficulty in accounting trends in the SMS that are consistent with his broader claims of a decline of local association participation in the United States in recent decades.

Trends in the size and demography of the national-level SMS are more easily documented.[11] Beginning in the 1960s, the national SMS grew at a vigorous pace, faster than other national noneconomic organizational sectors (Walker, 1983, 1991) and has continued to grow at such a pace into the 1990s (Baumgartner & Leech, 1998; Berry, 1999). The size of the SMS at the state level appears to have stabilized in recent years (Gray & Lowrey, 1996). Minkoff's (1995) analyses of racial–ethnic and women's SMOs show a trend toward a greater proportion of national-level groups being advocacy groups as a result of both the founding of new groups and the adoption of an advocacy strategy by formerly service groups.

THE TRANSNATIONAL SOCIAL MOVEMENT SECTOR.   Finally, a number of scholars (J. Smith, 1997; Smith et al., 1994, 1998; Young, 1992; Young et al., 1998) have begun to estimate

---

[10]There are other local forms that have received attention, such as communes and what Lofland and Jamison (1985) call cell locals and sect locals, but these are quite rare ones in most movements. The affinity group form, however, plays an important role in the emergent anti-globalization movement (Gillham & Marx, 2000; Smith, 2001).

[11]We assume that most of the citizen's groups studied by Walker (1991) and most of the advocacy groups included in Minkoff's (1995) analyses are SMOs.

the size and demography of transnational social movement organizational (TSMO) sector. This work shows that rapid growth has occurred in the sector since the 1970s, led by a proliferation of environmental TSMOs. TSMOs are more likely to enroll organizational than individual members than is the case for equivalent national level SMOs, and, in the case of the environmental movement, trend evidence suggests that the growth of the transnational sector led growth in national SMIs (Frank et al., 1999).

Micromobilization: Explaining Activism

The broader collective action research program, of which RM can be considered a part, has maintained a central focus on understanding the conditions surrounding individual mobilization.[12] Among a population of sympathizers who share the concerns of a movement, why do some participate while others do not? Our approach to this question was embedded in the empirical puzzle we had identified, namely that while individual participation appeared to be declining, the vitality of social movement groups appeared to be increasing.[13] This paradox led in two theoretical directions: the exploration of both organizational processes and individual processes that might help to resolve it.

RMII stressed the supply side far more than had our RMI compatriots—how extensive and active are the mobilizing vehicles whose aim it is to turn bystanders into adherents and adherents into organizational constituents—in contrast to the demand side—what are the conditions that motivate individuals to respond positively to organized attempts to engage them in social change efforts.[14] The supply of opportunities for activism depends first on the vitality of mobilization efforts. Are sympathizers asked by SMO representatives to do anything? But it also depends on what potential activists are asked to do, where and when they are asked to do it, and what sort of mobilizing vehicle asks them to do it. Much more attention subsequently has been focused on the demand side of this equation than the supply side. We first take up the supply side in order that we can put the overemphasis on the demand side and our own conceptualization of it into theoretical and empirical context. Subsequent research has reinforced the importance of the supply of opportunities for explaining the extent of activism and specified the dimensions of activism with more clarity.

SUPPLY OF ACTIVIST OPPORTUNITIES.   As mundane as it may first appear, one of the most important predictors of collective action by individuals is whether or not adherents are *asked* to participate (Oliver & Marwell, 1992) by joining an SMO (Snow et al., 1980) and/or by taking part in a protest event (Brady et al., 1995; Klandermans & Oegema, 1987). SMOs provide such opportunities for activism by structuring collective action.[15] It follows, then, that the more SMOs that are attempting to engage adherents in collective action by supplying them opportunities to do so the more of it can be expected to take place, other things being equal.

---

[12]Indeed, Lofland (1996) claims that studies of individual mobilization make up the largest segment of collective action research in recent years.

[13]Robert Putnam's assessment of the decline of social capital in the United States echoes our original statement of the puzzle. Our approach, unlike his, did not lament the conclusion that the rise of new, less participatory forms of SMOs could account for the paradox. This is the result of the fact that our approach was animated by a concern for purposive, mostly political outcomes. See Edwards and Foley (1997).

[14]This distinction between demand and supply remained implicit in our early statements, but has been subsequently more clearly articulated by Finke and others (Finke & Stark, 1992; Finke et al., 1996; Warner, 1993) for religious groups and Klandermans (1998) for social movements.

[15]Some collective action emerges, of course, with little or no such organized leadership. See Useem (1998).

The kinds of things that adherents are asked to do—*the forms of activism*—vary considerably in their duration and the amount of effort they require. Giving money and signing a petition require little effort and imply no long term involvement, while both membership and leadership in SMOs implies longer involvement, the latter requiring greater effort. Civil disobedience may require great effort for a very short period of time. Klandermans (1997) persuasively argues that different explanations are required to account for why individuals are more or less likely to engage in each of these forms of activism. SMO leaders' mobilization calculations depend on understandings of the organizational strategies necessary to supply opportunities for these various forms of activism (Oliver & Marwell, 1992). We will come back to this issue below when we visit issues of organizational processes and dynamics.

ADHERENT DEMAND FOR PARTICIPATION.   In attempting to account for variable levels of rank and file activism the RMII approach emphasized primarily what has come to be called biographical availability (McAdam, 1988). This concept focuses on how conditions of work, family, and schooling make classes of potential participants more or less available to invest time and more or less capable of investing material resources in social movement activity. Availability was stressed over motivation (the purposive incentive) or the social benefits of participation (solidary incentives). In addition we suggested that significant amounts of SMO participation took the form of paid employment.

We acknowledged the important link between broader organizational participation and social movement activism, which has been consistently reaffirmed by subsequent research (e.g., Verba et al., 1995). Subsequent research (e.g., Snow et al., 1980), however, has shown the crucial importance of social network connections between activists and potential activists in accounting for the likelihood of opportunities for participation.

The general RM program, including our version of it, has been roundly criticized for adopting the unrealistic social psychological assumptions of rational choice theory in explaining social movement activism (Turner, 1981; Ferree & Miller, 1985; Ferree, 1992; Perrow, 1979; Buechler, 1993). We did subsequently take Mancur Olson's theory of public goods seriously as we continued to attempt to make sense of organizational and social movement activism trends, although we were not aware of his work when we completed our original formulation. In thinking about material incentives we began and remain convinced that it is more useful to focus on how the costs of activism inhibit it (ranging from the kind we mentioned above through state repression) rather than how selective incentives facilitate it. We saw an important role for solidarity incentives in understanding especially the ongoing volunteer participation of small cadres of activists. But we are not now and never have been orthodox rational choice theorists.

There is, however, a sense in which the approach was nested in a concept of rational action, one that has rarely been recognized by critics and therefore not been the subject of critique.[16] In addition to accounting for individual activist participation, the approach requires an account of organizational emergence as well as of strategic decision making by SMO leaders and cadre. We drew on Stinchcombe's (1965) ideas about the emergence of new organizational populations, but were almost silent, at least theoretically, on the issue of strategic decision making. In fact, we took for granted Herbert Simon's (1947; March & Simon, 1958) then-predominant formulation of the concept of bounded rationality. Along with Simon we assumed that organizational decision makers attempt to make rational decisions among a

---

[16]Ralph Turner (1981) both recognizes the utility of Simonian concepts of bounded rationality and satisficing for the RMI approach and criticizes us for not explicitly and sufficiently deploying them.

limited set of available choices while being constrained by a narrow set of assumptions about how things can be accomplished as well as assumptions about logic of chains of means/ends rationality. Our lack of systematic attention to a theoretical logic of strategic decision making by SMOs represented a serious lacunae in RMII, but one that has begun to be filled as a younger generation of SM scholars have engaged in ongoing dialogue with theorists of complex organizations. We return to these developments below.

The lines of critique that have been more telling in demonstrating the shortcomings of the approach are those that emphasize the collective nature of collective action participation. RMII ignored the jointness of social movement participation, as well as perceptions of its jointness. One line of this analysis has yielded a vigorous research literature based on formal modeling of collective action. Pam Oliver (1993) summarizes its main patterns:

> First, models with quite different assumptions about individual decision processes and quite different assumptions about interdependence and coordination mechanisms all tend to yield predictions of thresholds and discontinuities, and predictions of internal divisions of labor within collectivities. Something like "critical mass" phenomena seem endemic to collective action. Second, the degree of group heterogeneity always changes results, but its effects vary: Sometimes it promotes action and sometimes it inhibits it. (pp. 292–293)

Another strand of this line of critique is based on empirical studies of collective action participation draws on "expectancy theory." Bert Klandermans (1997) summarizes its conclusions when he says:

> [O]rganizers of protest movements cannot assume that success expectations will arise spontaneously; such expectations must be constructed socially, in interactions among potential participants. Hence, these expectations are in a sense self-fulfilling: the greater the number of individuals who believe collective action will be successful, the more likely it is that mass action will materialize and that authorities will have to respond. If no one person believes collective action will be successful, mass action becomes impossible. (p. 28)

This line of criticism and the research it has inspired make an important contribution to both expanding the understanding the condition of individual participation as well as the logic of SMO strategic decision making.

In conclusion let us recall our brief description of the demography of the SMS in the United States along with Klandermans' argument that different accounts of different kinds of participation are needed. First, it seems increasingly clear that significant numbers of SMO leaders and cadre are paid for their efforts. No special theory of collective action participation appears necessary to explain this. Second, a significant number of SMOs have other organizations as members. We need a theory of organizational decision making to account for organizational participation, not a theory of individual activism. Third, many SMOs have no members and do not deploy adherents in collective action. As a consequence, a theory of micromobilization is irrelevant to many, increasingly important, domains of collective action.

Resources: What Are They? What Role Do They Play?

We began by pointing to the importance of material resources, labor, and legitimacy as key factors in understanding how social movement organizations use them to turn preference pools or solidary groups into challenging groups and then how the more general availability of resources figure in efforts by groups to pursue challenges. A number of critics have emphasized how little attention we paid to thinking about the concept of resources beyond the three we named and especially our emphasis on material over human resources (Cress & Snow, 1996; Oliver & Marwell, 1992; Turner, 1981). Gamson (1987) called this inattention the "soft underbelly of the theory" (p. 1), noting that our attention was instead devoted to how resources were used. We were indeed almost silent on the key concept of resources. We had been deeply influenced by William Gamson's (1968) *Power and Discontent* where he developed a convincing brief for assessing the power of groups through their control of slack resources. We followed him [as did Charles Tilly (1978) in *From Mobilization to Revolution*] by emphasizing the use of resources rather than developing a more sophisticated conception of kinds of resources, which groups control which kinds, and their fungibility and transferability.

RMII emphasized instances of the transfer of resources from advantaged to disadvantaged groups, suggested that such transfers were not uncommon, and argued that they are central to modern resource mobilization processes. In this we differed from our RM compatriots. Most focused primarily on the mobilization of resources within solidary groups and how such groups use resources in attempting to exert influence. Or they have ignored the issue of the source of resources. Thinking about resource transfers across group boundaries leads directly to the need for a typology of kinds of resources, their fungibility, the symmetry of their fungibility, and the legitimacy of their transfer. Subsequent SM analysts have devoted relatively little attention to the conceptualization of categories of resources. Tilly (1978), for instance, appropriates the standard categories used by economists, "land, labor and capital" (p. 69). A few analysts, however, have attempted to more clearly articulate kinds of resources. Oliver and Marwell (1992) focus their attention primarily on money, labor, and what they call action technologies. These come in two varieties: production technologies (aimed at goal achievement) and mobilization technologies (aimed at mobilizing resources). Cress and Snow (1996) developed a typology of kinds of resources generated out of a thick description of the mobilization of resources by local homeless insurgent groups. The four resource types they identify include moral (equivalent to the loan of legitimacy), material (including many in-kind resources), human (equivalent to labor for Oliver and Marwell), and informational (close to Oliver and Marwell's action technologies). With minor exceptions (e.g., Oliver & Marwell, 1992), no systematic attention has been paid by SM analysts to questions of resource fungibility.[17]

MOBILIZING LABOR AND MONEY.   Resources may be controlled by individuals, networks, organizations, and states. We think of money as the most fungible of resources, although Zelizer (1994) shows that even its fungibility is in many instances socially constrained. So money can be converted to labor, land, and maybe even under the right circumstances human, cultural, and social capital. But labor may not, in the short run, be convertible into human capital, as when an SMO needs an accountant, but only high school volunteers are available

---

[17]There have been important developments in other parts of the discipline toward the conceptualization of a more sophisticated range of resource types (Shanahan & Tuma, 1994; Tilly, 1998). Beyond land labor and capital, we now have rich conceptualizations available and measurement armies working to specify the distribution of human capital, social capital and cultural capital across, and even more specific subtypes of each, e.g., "civic skills" as a form of human capital (Verba et al., 1995). There are technological resources, which are independent of the others, those most familiar to SM analysts being protect and organizational repertoires. It appears that there are enough giants' shoulders to stand on now in order to develop a typology of kinds of resources. Christian Lahusen's (1996) analysis of the combination of financial resources and celebrity in the production of cause music concerts goes some way in specifying a typology of resources broader than land, labor, and capital. Other useful discussions of social movement resources include Gamson et al. (1982); Jenkins and Perrow (1977); Knoke (1989, 1990); and Lofland (1996).

for work.[18] On the other hand, congregation-based Industrial Areas Foundation groups seem to be successful in turning the paid labor of organizers through a long process, employing a widely available social technology, into social capital (Rogers, 1990).

Thinking of labor as a resource is the flip side of thinking about the supply of activism. At the local, grass-roots level of associations led by volunteers, labor is a key social movement resource (McCarthy & Wolfson, 1996). As the scope of SMO foci expand beyond local communities, material resources become more important, and SMO labor is more likely to be purchased than to be volunteer (McCarthy, 1997). Groups with money can buy specialized labor. Mobilizing labor is labor intensive and so is supervising it. The control of some kinds of resources is inherently more exclusive, such as money and land, than it is of others, such as resource aggregation technologies like direct mail techniques.

MOBILIZATION OF EXOGENOUS RESOURCES. In general, there has been little criticism of our claims about the importance of resources for understanding collective action by formally organized social movement actors. Cress and Snow (1996), for instance, suggest that these claims are now pretty much taken for granted. Subsequent research has provided us with more evidence about the flow of types of exogenous resources to SMOs and the timing of those flows, though there has been little attention to the causes of variability in the flows. We know most systematically about the flow of money to national-level SMOs and the least about the transfer of information and moral legitimacy. The mobilization of exogenous human resources by SMOs is captured by our concept of conscience constituents and remains common, especially for movements aimed at changing the conditions of the most impoverished.[19]

National SMOs are highly likely to have received financial support from institutional sources such as foundations, governmental agencies, and other citizens groups (Walker, 1991). National SMOs are highly likely to receive a significant proportion of financial support from such sources and at the same time remain dependent on their original supporters that provided start-up support. Wealthy individuals are an important source of start-up support for national citizen's groups, a pattern that Walker (1991) interprets as suggesting that individuals are more likely to make risky investments in new national SMOs, while institutional supporters are inclined to provide support for established, more legitimate ones.

We do have some systematic empirical work on the transfer of resources through the money provided by foundations for social change efforts. Craig Jenkins has been tracking these patterns over the last five decades (Jenkins & Halci, 1999). That evidence demonstrates an increasing flow of financial resources to SMOs from foundations, the early manifestations of which were a central hinge to the original RMII articulation. As well, this evidence shows major shifts in which of the SMIs are most privileged by the flow of foundation material resources. The early dominance of the civil rights SMI in the 1960s has been eclipsed by the environmental and local community organizational SMIs by the 1980s.

It is clear that there exists a large flow of informational resources to SMOs from sources specializing in information dissemination. Among movement leaders such resource transfers are commonly known as "technical assistance." For instance, reports by the leaders of a sample of local groups working to empower poor communities (McCarthy & Castelli, 1994) indicate that more than two thirds of them used some technical assistance in a typical year.

---

[18]Oliver and Marwell (1992) offer a cogent discussion of the question of the question of fungibility of labor and money in the social movement context.

[19]McAdam's (1988) study of northern, white college students participation in Freedom Summer dramatically illustrates this process.

These included professional services such as accounting and grant writing, advice about recruiting, help in assessing organizational effectiveness, and substantive issue research. These informational resources were supplied, some gratis and some paid for, but typically at deep discounts by governmental agencies, religious organizations, foundations, and organizations established specifically to provide technical assistance to particular SMIs. Morris (1984) described several such organizations that provided assistance for civil rights SMOs. Similar institutions exist in many other SMIs (Edwards & McCarthy, 1992). Little systematic attention has been paid to the transfer of such informational resources, unfortunately, since they can be expected to be consequential in shaping SMO structure and process thereby homogenizing SMS fields.

EVIDENCE ON THE TIMING AND DIRECTION OF RESOURCE FLOWS.   We were interpreted as having made strong claims about the consequences of the timing of outside financial resource to the dynamics of the southern civil rights movement (SCRM; McAdam, 1982, p. 124). We had implied that the vitality of the SCRM was the result of exogenous resources, especially financial ones from foundations. Subsequent research has shown that foundation resource flows to civil rights SMOs, which started to become plentiful in the 1960s, were inspired by the vitality of the indigenous elements of the movement, rather than having initially facilitated them (Jenkins & Eckert, 1986). Later work (Jenkins & Halci, 1999) suggests as well that the same pattern holds in the United States for peace movements of the 1960s and 1970s, the women's movement, and the environmental movement: increases in the flow of foundation support followed spikes of indigenous protest. The pattern does not hold, however, for the consumer rights/government accountability movement, one that has staged very little public protest. The bulk of foundation support has been directed toward the most professionalized advocacy organizations, by 1990 more than three quarters of the 88 million dollars that was supplied to the SMS (Jenkins & Halci, 1999). Susan Ostrander (1995, 1999) has provided thick descriptions of the tensions inherent in such resource relationships between foundations and SMOs.

The pattern of the timing and direction of resource flows from the US federal government to SMOs of the movement against drunk driving and the antismoking movement suggests a somewhat different, more clearly interactive, process. Following the emergence of a few fledgling groups of local anti-drunk-driving activists, the National Highway Safety Transportation Agency, and later the National Organization of Victim Assistance encouraged the formation and supported the ongoing operations of the many small local SMOs through technical assistance and grants (Ross, 1992; McCarthy & Harvey, 1989). Weed (1995) calls NOVA (National Organization of Victim Assistance) a centralized resource agency, facilitating a common frame of reference through conferences and flow of support for local victim services, and the National Victim Center he calls a meshing organization aimed at networking the more than 3500 local victim groups. The 1984 VOCA (Victims of Crimes Act) provided block grant funds for local victim assistance, some of which found their way to local victim advocacy groups, including anti-drunk-driving groups.

A similar pattern is seen in the efforts of a number of US federal health agencies by indirectly supporting professional advocacy antismoking SMOs and also aggressively attempting to form local citizens groups with a series of grants funneled through university public health departments (Wolfson, 2000). The national level antismoking groups were highly professionalized, as were state level efforts. Wolfson suggests that, similar to the pattern seen in other SMIs for foundations, the government resources were allocated to the least confrontational SMOs. (See also Bennett & DiLorenzo, 1985.)

COMMUNITY RESOURCES AND MOBILIZATION.   We also made strong claims that linked the general availability of community resources with the likelihood that SMOs would be mobilized, other things being equal. Subsequent research bears on those claims suggesting that resource availability does facilitate collective action, but that the processes are more complicated than we had suggested. For instance, the research of Snow et al. (2000) shows that homeless protest activity is strongly related to the level of United Way contributions and total transfer payments in a community. Research reported by Khawaja (1994) shows that under certain conditions protest activity over time on the West Bank is related to variations in GDP per capita—increases in indigenous resources are related to higher rates of protest. Other research (McCarthy et al., 1988) shows that the wealthier a US county, the earlier a local anti-drunk-driving activist group appeared. Debra Minkoff's (1999) time series analysis of nonlocal women's and racial ethnic SMOs, however, suggests a more complicated dynamic. There the level of societal resource availability (per capita income) is shown to be more important in accounting for the ongoing vitality of SMOs than it is in explaining rates of the founding of new SMOs (Minkoff, 1999). Amenta and Zylan (1991) show, on the other hand, that the lower a state's per capita income the greater the number of local Townsend Movement groups per capita.

ORGANIZATIONAL RESOURCES AND SURVIVAL.   Given the increasing dependence of many national SMOs on resources of the federal government, the Reagan presidency provided a natural experiment in how the instability of material resources can affect SMO operations since it took office committed to defunding what it perceived as "leftist" SMOs. Two studies provide us insight on this process.

The first is that of Jack Walker (1991). Surveys of Washington-based citizens groups in 1980 and 1985 allow a comparison of how that category of groups responded to the decline in governmental support of their activities. First, almost none of the groups went out of existence. The aggregate response was to seek more diverse sources of funding. The groups most heavily dependent on government funds were forced to reduce their staff size, inevitably creating an impact on their ability to advocate. At the same time they stepped up their efforts to generate support from constituents through membership dues.

The second relevant study is Doug Imig's (1996) case study of six national antipoverty advocacy groups. He examined their ability to maintain stable levels of funding during the early Reagan period when federal grant funds available to such organizations fell by 58%. The three groups dependent mostly on government funds lost support and it severely affected their ability to devote resources to advocacy, but they each diversified their lines of financial support rather quickly, in the process redefining their strategic approach. The three privately funded groups expanded their resource base as well as their advocacy efforts during the period, as the period saw a 75% increase in available grant funds.

A study of mortality among peace movement SMOs (Edwards & Marullo, 1995) is consistent with this pattern. It shows that, with other relevant factors taken into account, neither the size of an organization's budget nor its membership size was related to its likelihood of going out of existence between 1988 and 1992. This was true for both small local as well as large national peace groups. In contrast, for both local and national groups indications of an SMO being granted wide legitimacy by the actions of other groups, indicated by entering into alliances with them, was one of the strongest predictors of a group's survival. J. Smith (1997) reports a similar pattern for the transnational SMOs she investigated. While the resource of organizational legitimacy is substantially more difficult to assess than those of labor and money, these results suggest that the legitimation of organizations by other organizations acts a resource and is quite common (as was also shown in Snow and Cress's study of local homeless SMOs (Cress & Snow, 2000)). Increased empirical and theoretical attention needs to be paid to legitimation as an organizational resource.

Sentiment Pools

We employed the concept of sentiment pools to refer to reservoirs of support for changes in the structure of society (Zald & McCarthy, 1987). Our use is parallel to the use of the concepts of taste and preference by economists, and like them we took sentiment structures mostly as given. We focused our attention instead on the tasks confronting SMO activists of turning bystanders into adherents and adherents into constituents, or as these processes are now widely called, consensus mobilization and action mobilization (Klandermans, 1997).

Our approach did not conceive of the availability of sufficient preferences for change as problematic, and hence, outside the scope of the theory. More problematic we thought was how to make sense of the variable rates at which such preferences result in action mobilization given the fact that those rates are almost always incredibly low. The resulting shift in focus of attention away from the factors shaping the size and substantive content of sentiment pools remains at the same time one of the great strengths of RMII, but also one of its most important limitations. This element of the approach has not in itself drawn much sustained criticism other than as part of broader attacks on its pervasive economistic assumptions (e.g., Turner, 1981; Perrow, 1979; Ferree, 1992). By ignoring how sentiment pools come about and change, they remain detached from historical, cultural, and political processes. As a result the theory remains blind to the broader structural processes that produce the raw material of sentiment structures that provide the mobilization opportunity structure to SMO activists at any particular historical time and place. Our attention to the efforts of SMO activists to expand their own pools of supporters, while aimed at understanding the role of one important factor in explaining their size, does not substantially undermine the strength of this line of criticism.

One of us (Zald, 2000) recently has argued that the concept of ideologically structured action (Dalton, 1994) can be usefully deployed to generate an account of the structure and processes of change within and among clusters of societal preferences for social change. Ideologically structured action is behavior shaped by ideological charged beliefs, factual and evaluative, about both the ends of action and the means of action. Ideology, in turn, is generated out of a complex process of cultural and historical development. A focus on the ideological basis of sentiment pools has several advantages. Ideology ties to culture and discourse (Steinberg, 1999) and therefore sentiments and sentiment pools would no longer be treated as isolated from processes of cultural and discourse change. Moreover, since ideologies are learned and transmitted, it is possible to study the socialization processes through which sentiments are learned, adopted, and reinforced (Sherkat, 1998; Sherkat & Blocker, 1994), rather than focusing just on the sentiment preferences of already-socialized late adolescents and adults.

Subsequent research has stressed more strongly than we did that the social organization of sentiment pools is as important as their size and intensity in understanding the likelihood of their implicit aggregate social change demand resulting in collective action (e.g., McAdam, 1982; McCarthy, 1987; McAdam et al., 1988). Such work, however, has not typically developed accounts of the shifting nature of the sentiments that cohere within social infrastructures. As a consequence this line of analysis does little to blunt the force of the line of criticism we have described.

In the end, however, even if an adequate approach is developed to understanding the nature and evolution of sentiment structures, the question still remains whether the approach is very useful in accounting for the size, shape, and evolution of particular SMIs and/or the SMS. One of our boldest claims was to suggest the possibility that it would not be very helpful. The basic argument in support of the claim, which we did not articulate very clearly, includes three assertions. First, the supply side is more important than the demand side in explaining collective action. Second, accounting for the evolution of the population of organizations that make up particular SMIs and the SMS is necessary in order to explain the vigor of the supply side. Third, those explanations depend on organizational logics that are not very directly coupled with the nature of citizen demand for social change. While very difficult to test directly, we remain convinced that organizational logic is more important in explaining the dynamics of the population of lead organizations in the SMS—the fortune 500 of SMOs— than are the size of the sentiment pools.

Organizational Processes and Dynamics

In spite of RMIIs being widely seen as characterized primarily by a focus on organizational dynamics (Jenkins, 1983), our inattention to these dynamics, as we concentrated on how SMOs gather resources and longer run trends in MO transformation, was an important weakness of the original statements. While a comprehensive statement of SMO change processes remains to be accomplished, many colleagues have made the dynamics of organizational adaptation a central focus of their work, thereby strengthening this strand of a RM approach. These newer strands of research are in dialogue with current theoretical debates among organizational researchers and generally adopt one or another variant of an "open-systems" perspective that stresses the crucial importance of environmental factors on organizational transformation (Scott, 1998).

Both neo-institutional (DiMaggio, 1991; Fligstein, 1990) and ecology (Carroll et al., 1988) theorists of organizations emphasize the role of the surrounding environment of political, economic, and professional organizations in understanding the dynamics of organizational populations. And, movement researchers have begun to employ the concept of "organizational fields," for instance, to analyze the structure of inter-organizational networks within SMIs. For instance, Brulle and Caniglia (1999) show how the flows of foundation funds to environmental SMOs shapes the ongoing relationships among them.

We had, of course, stressed the increasing professionalization of social movement activism. This process characterizes the nature of SMO work in that it has become increasingly organized into career forms with apprenticeships and hierarchies of expertise and skill. The process seems dependent on the availability of stable employment in the SMS, which has clearly increased dramatically over the last three decades, but is by no means an inevitable product of the expansion of paid positions. While this process has not drawn systematic research attention, strong examples of the process continue to present themselves. For instance, the Industrial Areas Foundation (IAF), the direct progeny of Saul Alinsky's community-organizing efforts, in recent years has structured the work of its paid staff organizers into a stable career form. Potential organizers are hired for probationary terms, are trained in apprenticeship situations, and their work is closely evaluated. A candidate who survives the probationary period then begins a career of organizing with an established hierarchy of positions that can be achieved through seniority and performance. As well, regular employees become eligible for standard group health coverage and participation in a group retirement plan. The National Organizers Alliance, a group that has begun to bring together activists doing work similar to that of the IAF organizers, now offers health and retirement plans to their members in an effort to make career employment a more attractive alternative.

As activist labor becomes professionalized, it can be expected to affect both who is hired to lead an SMO as well as its internal operations. Swanson (1996) has shown that when local anti-drunk-driving groups began to hire paid staff—by 1989 more than 25% of the groups had done so—they were more likely to hire people based on their professional credentials than on their victim status that had been one of the key status requirements for the original founders of chapters. Similarly, Weed (1995) shows in the results of a survey of paid activists in the crime victim advocacy movements that more than one third of them have professional degrees and that advertisements for new victim advocate positions are likely to include requirements for professional degrees. He says:

> Victim advocacy or providing victim services has become a paid career, partly because of the development of stable formal-participatory agencies. These occupational positions allow for the development of specialized skills that go along with the commitment to the moral ideals of the movement. (Weed, 1995, p. 117)

Another key form of organizational adaptation that has received research attention includes features of internal structure. First is the ongoing concern with the classic dimension of the oligarchization of SMOs. The little work of which we are aware on the question pretty much reinforces the general conclusions of the earlier paper by Zald and Ash (1966). Both Minkoff (1999), in her study of the changing nature of the population of racial–ethnic and women's SMOs in the United States, and Rucht (1999), in his study of the evolution of dissident groups in Berlin during the transition to reunification, are consistent. They show no inevitable shift toward conservatism of goals or tactics through time and suggest that the patterns of change they uncover are in important part contingent on environmental factors.

A second important dimension is the level of formalization of organizational structure. Some movement scholars have continued to insist that movement groups are less highly structured than other group forms (e.g., Rothschild-Whitt, 1979). This may still be so in the aggregate, but there is strong evidence that many SMOs are quite highly structured and that the tendency toward being formalized is associated with finances and formal registration with the state. Edwards (1994) shows, for instance, that for peace movement organizations, having a large budget, being formally incorporated, and being registered as a federally approved nonprofit organization are each strongly related to whether or not the SMO has in place formal operating procedures. It has been shown elsewhere (McCarthy et al., 1991; Cress, 1997) that registration as a nonprofit and being incorporated are very common across a range of small local SMIs.

These studies are based on cross-sectional evidence, but it seems reasonable to assume that as an SMO increases the size of its budget it is increasingly likely to become formalized and professionalized. In her rich case study of the SMOs of the prochoice movement, Staggenborg (1988, 1991) has described this process in detail. In the face of prolife mobilization following *Roe v. Wade*,

> On the national level, movement leadership began to become more professionalized and movement organizations began to formalize their structures. Paid staff, rather than volunteer activists, slowly began to assume leadership of pro-choice movement organizations. As they did so, the movement organizations gradually developed more formal divisions of labor and operating procedures. (1991, p. 63)

These transformations of the national level organizations, however, allowed one of the groups to direct extensive resources toward successful grass-roots mobilization of local chapters.

A third important dimension of organizational structure relevant for an important subset of SMOs is represented by the formal relationship between local groups and state or national umbrella groups. The variety and consequences of these relationships have not been the focus of much research, but it is clear that certain structures that tie local with non-local SMOs may create great tension and conflict between them (Oliver & Furman, 1989), may make them dependent and less likely to survive (Weed, 1991), and may facilitate their ability to mobilize local adherents (McCarthy & Wolfson, 1996).

SMOs may also adapt their strategic repertoires over time. Minkoff's (1995, 1999) examination of such change among ethnic–racial and women's SMOs over recent decades and her results also challenge the image that formalized, bureaucratized SMOs are lethargic. In fact, the older, larger, and more professionalized SMOs are the most likely to make major changes in their strategic repertoires, even though such changes are relatively uncommon.

Social Movement Industry and Sector

We defined a social movement industry as all of the SMOs that have as their goal the attainment of the broadest preferences of a social movement, and the social movement sector as the aggregate of all the SMIs in a society. We did so with the intention of moving the focus of analysis away from individual organizations and their transformations, which had been the traditional focus of SMO studies, and toward the dynamics of organizational populations. We assumed that one of the important environmental elements that shape the structure and processes of individual SMOs will be their natural organizational competitors as well as the broader social change organizational field within which they operate. Garner and Zald (1985) later sketched out in greater detail the potential of such a theoretical approach. This strand of RMII remains in our view one of its potentially most theoretical useful ones, yet it has attracted almost no criticism and has not been the focus of much subsequent research attention. Della Porta and Rucht (1995) come closest in their discussion of the family of left-libertarian SMIs in Germany and Italy, 1965–1990; however, they were not interested in mapping the total SMS.

As we noted in our discussion above, a number of scholars have attempted to map particular national SMIs (e.g., Kriesi, 1996), but we have as yet no very comprehensive map of a national SMS. This incomplete picture is the result of the difficulties of developing a comprehensive census of SMOs in a society that we discussed above, as well as the relative neglect by social movement scholars of reactionary movements. For instance, the US prolife movement, one of the most vital and variegated ones to have mobilized over recent decades, has drawn very little systematic research attention by social movement scholars (but, see Meyer & Staggenborg, 1996, for an exception). Debra Minkoff (1998, forthcoming) has devoted the most systematic attention to both deepening the conceptualization of the US SMS and designing an attempt to survey all of its national level SMOs.

Several key questions that should animate a research agenda on SMIs and in aggregate the SMS are first their size as well as how diverse they are along the key demographic dimensions we introduced earlier. Ultimately, the more interesting questions concern the transformation of industries and sectors and their impacts on other societal domains. Subsequent research and theoretical debate among organizational sociologists has provided useful tools for pursuing these questions. First is the idea of a population of organizations (e.g., Hannan & Freeman, 1982) that are directly analogous to SMIs. Organizational ecologists have been looking at very diverse populations of organization and in the process developing both theories about how their composition changes as well as methods for analyzing such changes.

They stress the importance of patterns of the formation of new organizations (births) and patterns of organizational demise (deaths and mergers) on the changing composition of organizational populations. Following Stinchcombe (1965), they tend to assume that organizations, once founded, establish standard ways of operating and are quite resistant to structural change and goal transformation. Such an assumption, of course, contradicts the classic emphasis on goal transformation in SMOs, but it provides a powerful alternative account of how populations of SMOs may be transformed over time. Institutional analysts generally (e.g., DiMaggio & Powell, 1983) and institutional analysts of SMO structures in particular (e.g., Clemens, 1996, 1997) in contrast stress environmentally driven mechanisms of organizational change, assuming that organizations are quite adaptable. As far as we know, only Debra Minkoff's (1999) work on the transformation the national ethnic–racial and women's movement organizations in the United States provides a systematic effort to assess these two accounts of SMI transformation. That research suggests that the pattern of organizational births and deaths among the SMOs of these SMIs is far more important in accounting for its general transformation away from services toward advocacy than are processes of organization change. The 1955 to 1985 period was one of rapid organizational formation in these SMIs, as Minkoff notes, and consistent with other attempts to map the population of citizens movement groups (Walker, 1991). As a result, we might expect that as such populations stabilize in size, as analyses of other kinds of organizational populations indicate inevitably happens, the relative importance of organizational change in contrast to patterns of SMO birth and death in explaining population transformation might be altered.

Several studies provide comparisons of a number of "new social movement" SMIs across European nations, thereby providing us a systematic look at differences in size and organizational diversity. These efforts (Kriesi, 1996; Rucht, 1989, 1996) look at a variety of SMIs, including women, environmental, peace, and gay rights, across some subset of France, Germany, the Netherlands, and Switzerland. The general picture that emerges is that the total mobilization of the new social movement SMIs can vary dramatically in size across nations. For instance, in general the rate of mobilization in France is quite low. Second, the relative mix of mobilization among SMIs can vary dramatically across countries. For instance, the gay rights movement is weakly mobilized in Switzerland. Third, while the range of organizational forms represented in each SMI may be roughly equivalent across nations, the relative mix of organizational forms within each SMI can vary dramatically across nations, especially the variable strength of grass-roots local groups and national level SMOs.

Research on the US civil rights movement (McAdam, 1982; Morris, 1984; Haines, 1988) has provided us with very thick descriptions of its organizational diversity and provided us with several strong hypotheses. The first, consistent with what we have called a supply side argument, is that the more SMOs there are and the more diverse the mix of organizational forms, the greater the rate at which the SMOs of a movement will be able to mobilize adherents. Staggenborg's (1991) work on mobilization within the prochoice movement also is consistent with these expectations. The second is that in addition the more diverse a movement is in the tactics and goals that animate its SMOs the greater the rate at which adherents will be mobilized. As well, diversity of goals and tactics within an SMI may increase the impact of the less confrontational SMOs that seek less radical social change.[20]

Techniques for analyzing hypotheses like these concerning the transformation of populations of SMOs are now available (Minkoff, forthcoming). What we lack to make much

---

[20]Gamson's (1975) findings for a sample of national SMOs from across the SMS is consistent with this argument, although it is based only on a set of less confrontational SMOs from a variety of SMIs.

research progress are widely available sources of information that will allow is to characterize such populations through time. The lack of such evidence has clearly hindered thinking about transformation processes across SMIs and the comparisons of SMSs across nations.

The Impact of Organizational Capacity on Protest

Public protest is an important tactical form widely utilized by social movement activists. While our original focus on protest participation emphasized the demand side, especially through the heightened availability of some groups such as Students for Mobilization, the approach clearly led to expectations about the relationship between organizational growth and protest. The greater the organizational capacity of an SMI, the more able it will be to generate large-scale and as well as sustained campaigns of protest events. Piven and Cloward (1977) have strenuously challenged this implication of the theoretical approach, arguing that SMOs get in the way of the wildfire spread of protest rather than facilitate it and water down the tactics and demands of participants. For them, SMOs only normalize protest. On the other hand, many scholars have accepted the proposition. The claim is especially difficult to assess directly since it requires evidence of variable protest intensity, assessments of the extent to which protest events are staged by SMOs, and movement or adherent organizational capacity either over time or across communities.

Some research bears on the claim, but no study includes all of the relevant variables that would allow a strong test of it. Koopmans' (1995) evidence on German protest between 1965 and 1989 shows that about one half of them involved no SMO sponsor. On the other hand, McCarthy and colleagues found that more than 75% of the large protests held in Washington, DC, in 1982 and 1991, had an official SMO sponsor. Khawaja (1994) found, in his time series study of protest by Palestinians on the West Bank between 1976 and 1985, that the presence of organizational sponsors of protest events increased their intensity.

The staging of large public protests by SMOs, however, is not simply a process where organizations mobilize individuals, both their members and sympathizers. Much of the time it is more a process of what Gerhards and Rucht (1992) have called "mesomobilization." They carefully monitored the staging of two large multiissue protest events in Berlin, demonstrating that the organizational capacity of various sympathetic. SMIs was an important indicator of the makeup of the organizational structure of the large coalition that mobilized individuals for the events.

Given a number of the trends in SMO form and operation we have described above, there is good reason to expect that protest events staged by SMOs will be less confrontational over time in the United States and that the increasing professionalization of the SMS will serve to routinize public protest (McCarthy & McPhail, 1998; Meyer & Tarrow, 1998). However, the emerging wave of anti-globalization protests suggests that the late 20th century détente between authorities and protest groups in the United States may be a short-lived one (Gillham & Marx, 2000; Smith, 2001). Koopmans' (1995) German data suggest that protest mounted by formal SMOs are far less confrontational and violent, and that the same pattern holds for Dutch protest between 1975 and 1989. Low levels of organization among the protesters marked the more violent and confrontational protests.

In the most rigorous test of the claim, Minkoff (1997) examined the impact of women's and ethnic-racial SMO capacity, what she has subsequently called "organizational potential" (Minkoff, forthcoming), on the level of protest around women's and racial–ethnic issues. Her results are consistent with the claim: increases in protest potential are associated with later increases in protest.

Underemphasis on Cultural and Political Processes

A BLINDNESS[21] TO THE ROLE OF CULTURE IN SOCIAL MOVEMENT PROCESSES.   Critics have taken our silence about culture as what in fact was an unintended lack of appreciation of its role. RM has taken probably the greatest amount of criticism for this silence. Beginning with Turner's (1981) measured brief that a balanced theoretical approach to understanding social movements not abandon the concept of ideology, through those of recent critics (e.g., Jasper, 1997; Buechler, 1993, 2000) inspired by the broader cultural turn who have argued that cultural processes be privileged over the material and organizational, the refrain has continued. Part of the explanation of our silence was strategic. By ignoring cultural processes, we were able to put in the foreground organizational and macroenvironmental processes.

But we had been steeped in the "social construction of social problems" theoretical tradition (Schneider, 1985) and we took it for granted, which also was important in explaining our silence. We assumed that the processes of the social construction of grievances, loyalty, and partisanship were central to understanding the mobilization of solidary groups. Those approaches include the role of agency and depend on contests between social actors and are the direct theoretical ancestors of the strategic framing approach. We will return to how RM articulates with strategic framing in the next section.

Our blind spot was more in what Rucht (1996) calls the cultural context. RMT, like much of sociology before Geertz, before Foucault, and before structuration and practice theory treats social structure and social relations as somehow analytically separable from culture. The intellectual strategy was to treat patterns of social relations and social organization as some-how separate from the meanings and rhetorics that constituted, defined, and symbolized them. In explaining movements, aspects of culture were treated as parameters or as ad hoc scope conditions, rather than as constitutive of the forms of social organization and tactics of protest. Tilly's (1979) concept of a repertoire of contention is an important milestone in the beginning of RMT to recognize cultural processes. Repertoires are invented, learned, and diffused. As they spread across populations within a nation or culture and between nations and cultures, they are adapted to local contexts and are assimilated to cultural understandings. Social movements are embedded in a larger cultural context of the appropriateness and meaning of forms of mobilization and of protest expression. How the shift to a more integrated view of culture and social structure works out in the case of RMT is yet to be fully determined (but see Polletta, 1999; Sherkat, 1998).

AN UNDERDEVELOPED ANALYSIS OF THE ROLE OF POLITICAL OPPORTUNITY.   Starting with Chick Perrow's (1979) early and trenchant critique of us through Herb Kitschelt's (1991) more recent one, a number of critics have pointed out that our early statements, for the most part, ignored the role of political processes. This was in contrast to the more central role they were accorded in the early statements of Tilly (1978), Oberschall (1973), and Gamson (1975). Of course, we took the thrust of the statements of our theoretical RM compatriots seriously, and our early statements made clear that we believed that a comprehensive theory of move-

---

[21]Gamson (1987) called culture a blind spot in the RMII approach.

ment processes would include a strong element of political process. Their muscular, emergent sketches of the political process approach also were a taken-for-granted backdrop to our early statements. Anyone who knew Zald's work on the political economy of organizations would have appreciated the centrality of political process background meta-assumptions for what we were about. [The Epilogue to the Vanderbilt Conference volume (Zald & McCarthy, 1979), for instance, claimed that RM approaches brought the study of social movements back into the mainstream of political sociology.]

Political process approaches have become increasingly influential in movement scholarship, providing the dominant image for thinking about movement emergence and trajectories in the last decade. Its leading scholars have pioneered a research methodology—protest event analysis—that has become a major force in the empirical study of movement processes. In the next section we attempt to nest RM and RMII in this broader trend of theoretical and research development.

THE PLACE OF RMII
IN THE CONSTELLATION
OF SOCIAL MOVEMENT RESEARCH

It is clear that RMII developed a set of concepts and research questions that have been useful to a generation of scholars. It has been subject to lively debate and criticism, has suggested research questions and hypotheses, and has led to more nuanced and complex views of the social movement world. During this period complementary and supplementary frameworks have been proposed that either offered alternative accounts of social movement activity, were useful additions, or posed fundamental challenges to the framework. Here we briefly examine three lines of theoretical development that have been extremely important for the contemporary study of social movements: political process and opportunity models, framing and culture, and new social movement theory. It is impossible for us to give a full sense of the development of each of these approaches or theories; rather, we focus on what we see as their distinctive contributions and on their relationships to RMII.

Political Process Models (PPM)

As we noted in the first section of the chapter, a political process or political opportunity variant of the RM/CA program already was being articulated when the program was first coming together. Implicit in the early work of Gamson but explicitly developed by Tilly, Jenkins, Perrow, and later McAdam, the political process model differs from RMII. It takes as its focal concerns the ways in which state actions and the possibility of influencing state action provide opening or closing for social movement action. State policies and actions directly threaten or benefit specific groups in society. State action facilitates or discourages groups and the organized claimants that speak for groups or causes. Changes in regimes through electoral or other means, changes in potential coalitions, and changes in the governmental agenda—executive, legislative and judicial—lead SMOs, activists, and others to perceive the possibility of new opportunities for action or new threats to their well-being. Moreover, different kinds of political structures are more or less open to organized political action.

It may well be the case that the political process approach has become the more prominent of the variants spawned by the RM/CA approach. Much research and writing has taken place that critiques, builds on, and tests political process assumptions. McAdam (1996) provides a consolidated statement of the status of the concept of political opportunity and structure, and Tarrow (1998) provides an overview of social movement theory and research through the lens of a political process point of view. In 1999, *Sociological Forum* published a number of critiques of political process approaches and concepts, as well as replies to those critiques.

From our point of view, the central difference of political process approaches from RMII is that they properly locate a central role of the state and political action as the source of both collective and individual costs and benefits and the threat or promise of future costs and benefits. Thus, changes in political opportunities lead to changes in the perception of risk/ reward ratios for activists. Such changes lead to perceptions of hope that encourage action or despair that discourages action. They lead to a sense of outrage that sharpens the sense of grievance and the reward/righteousness of acting in behalf of a cause. In our view, this is a correct and important specification of RM/CA for the very large category of political movements. It deserves the attention it has received.

There are other differences between RMII and PPM that to us seem less central. For instance, it is the case that RMII has focused more on the role of money and its mobilization and on techniques of mobilization by SMOs. PPM theorists have focused on the role of interpersonal networks as the base of mobilization. RMII has more to say about movements in the doldrums and in decline than PPM. Yet, these differences are not integral to the approaches and reflect the personal tastes, intuitions, and bets of the scholars associated with each of the approaches, rather than we think a fundamental disagreement about assumptions or concepts.

Framing and Culture

RMII arose partially as a reaction to grievance- or deprivation-based approaches. Both as a rhetorical strategy of distinguishing RMII from these approaches and as a way of sharpening the focus on mobilization both grievances and their articulation were largely ignored. In the long run, this distancing could not hold. First, it is clear that sharp changes in "objective" conditions and their purported connection to social policies and governmental relations shift perceptions in the costs and benefits of social arrangements and the readiness of populations to respond to demands for change. So, on an empirical basis, RMII overstated its case: grievances matter; the question is when and how do they matter? Second, it is clear that SMO leaders, issue entrepreneurs, and cadres spend a good deal of time attempting to define the issues, to define what is wrong with the system, and what kinds of policies would rectify the grievances. Moreover, they do this in a competitive context where other SMOs, issue entrepreneurs, and cadre are competing for attention.

Drawing on developments in cognitive psychology that focused on how individuals develop metaphors and packages of related cognitive elements to interpret the world they live in, William Gamson and his collaborators developed a form of script analysis to examine how people come to understand social issues on the public agenda. But Gamson's approach was not especially focused on how SMOs and their leaders attempted to use scripts and metaphors to mobilize resources. David Snow, Robert Benford, and their collaborators took this as a central problematic. Starting from Goffman's gestalt-related notion of a "frame," Snow and Benford examined how SMOs and their leaders used diagnostic frames as techniques for mobilizing resources, especially from individuals, and how they framed courses of action for the movement. In the process they developed a number of subsidiary concepts, such as frame resonance and frame amplification to account for the ways in which frames did or did not appeal to different population and the ways in which frames could change over time. (A number of papers on framing processes and a critique of the research tradition can be found in a special issue of *Sociological Quarterly*, 1998.)

Framing processes are used to mobilize new recruits to a movement, to sustain and motivate current adherents, and to appeal for change in the larger society. They compete for attention. Consisting of root metaphors and elaborated rationales, they can be thought of as symbolic resources. They are employed by leaders to mobilize other resources, to appeal to bystanders, and to attempt to convince authorities. But, as noted in our discussion of the problem of defining resources, frames as resources have special problems. Nevertheless, in our view, framing processes are a central component of the strategic action of SMOs and their leaders.

Frames are largely symbolic and draw on a larger cultural stock of symbols and their meanings. Part of culture and developing culture, frames may be more or less embedded in historical ideologies. The analysis of frames and of scripts owed more to social and cognitive psychology than they did to the analysis of culture. The study of social movements has had an opening to cultural approaches. Clearly, the larger culture provides the pool of symbols and cultural assumptions that movement members share; moreover, movements develop their own cultures and the symbols and assumptions developed within movements feed back on the cultural stock of the larger society. What is not yet clear is how cultural analysis complements RMT. Or does it supplant and contain it? (See Polletta, 1999; Adams, 1999, for a discussion of relevant issues in how cultural analysis reveals problems in structuralist and rational choice type approaches.)

New Social Movement Theory

Many of the specific movements that developed in advanced industrial nations as well as elsewhere in the world in the late 1960s and 1970s, such as gay rights, peace, women's, and environmental movements, seemed different from earlier movements in at least two ways. First, they were not easily arrayed or contained in a left–right continuum as earlier movements could be, nor did they align with established political parties arrayed on that continuum. Second, and especially relevant to discussions about the choice of concepts and analytic focus of social movement theory, the new social movements (NSMs) seemed to be much more about the development of personal and collective identities, the development of lifestyles, holistic ideologies, and personal consciousness. This is in contrast to earlier movements that were about the achievement of well-articulated goals that could be shown to grow out of well-defined interests. Stated another way, both PPM and RMII largely assumed interests and identities; movements were about realizing the goals that stemmed from identities and interests. The new social movements seemed to be operating at a different level—defining identities, developing collective awareness and solidarity, formulating and developing ways of life to go with the new identities.

Of course, many of the NSMs had parallels in earlier movements. After all, peace movements often have emerged as wars were threatened. Yet, recent peace movements went beyond critiquing specific war threats to developing antisystemic ideologies of the nation-state and capitalism that focused on a different worldview. So, too, at least part of the environmental movement developed a holistic ideology challenging the consumption orientation of modern society and developing an environmentalist ideology and identity that argued for a transformed way of living.

Scholars in Western Europe such as Alain Touraine and Alberto Melucci made the transformation of meaning, worldview, and identity central to their analysis of contemporary movements.[22] Melucci especially raised the possibility that NSMs reflected a transformation of advanced industrial societies that somehow permits and encourages a focus on lifestyle definition and identity that was not possible at earlier stages of industrialization and modernization.

From our point of view, NSMs are not truly different from earlier movements. After all, NSMs all engage in political action and all face problems of resource mobilization and of using and coming to grips with political opportunity structures. Nevertheless, NSM theory points to a set of issues that were largely outside of the purview of RMT: collective interests presume collective identity and individual identity. Older social movements, the ones related to class, economic position, and race, for instance, may appear to have clear interests and unproblematic collective identities. But in their own histories, the making of those identities, the forging of a sense of solidarity and the definition of interests in relationship to those identities has been problematic. Class identities and collective programs were emergent, not automatically realized.

If identity formation, consciousness raising, and solidarity occurred outside of the purview of movement mobilization and political action, there would be a better case for treating NSM theory as a separate kind of theory. However, we would argue that at least in part identity formation and solidarity emerge in struggle. As Mary Bernstein (1997) has shown for the case of the gay and lesbian rights movement the aspects of identity that are emphasized in the movement are at least in part shaped by the vicissitudes of movement mobilization and political dialogue.

Although standing in different relationship to RMII, NSM theory, framing, and culture, and PPM together with RMII raise an interrelated set of research questions that vastly expand the original agenda of the RMT program of research. At this time, even though some attempts have been made to bring these streams of research and theorizing together (McAdam, McCarthy, & Zald, 1996; Melucci, 1996; Tarrow, 1998; Della Porta & Diani, 1999), a concise and widely accepted comprehensive paradigmatic formulation has yet to emerge. But a lively set of debates and research questions remain.

SUMMARY AND CONCLUSION

In *Opening Pandora's Box*, Gilbert and Mulkay (1984) trace the process by which a new and provocative theory in chemistry that has few supporters becomes widely accepted and acclaimed, even while the reasons for its acceptance and acclaim are seen variously by different chemists. RMII was once a new and provocative theory of social movements. In the intervening years, it has led to a substantial body of research, has been very useful in the framing of specific research questions and guiding research programs, and has been subjected to substantial criticism. It is no longer that brash and provocative theory. In some cases it has been found inadequate, some would even say wrong in its emphases.

---

[22]Initially, scholars in the United States were less likely to see the new movements as different in kind from earlier movements in part, we suspect, because the United States has provided fertile ground for a plethora of movements relatively unconnected to the left–right continuum. As a result, their novelty was less apparent.

In this chapter we have summarized the original assumptions, core concepts, and orienting propositions of RMII. We then attempted to summarize the state of research and theorization that has followed on the original statement. There remains a substantial agenda suggested by RMII that deserves attention. There are great domains of research questions that have been barely explored.

Nevertheless, RMII is no longer setting the agenda for many younger scholars. In some cases, RMII has become the routine grounds of a research tradition that barely recognizes its own routine grounds. In other cases, the lessons of RMII are ignored. We believe that scholars who ignore those lessons will recreate the errors of earlier theories. Resources matter, they are variable, they come from a variety of sources, and this variety creates problems and contradictions for organizations. SMOs matter and SMOs must be analyzed as entities and as components of SMIs. Societies differ in their support of movements and movement like activities. That seems to us to be enough for one paradigm.

REFERENCES

Adams, J. (1999). Culture in rational-choice theories of state formation. In G. Steinmetz (Ed.), *State/culture: State formation after the cultural turn* (pp. 98–122). Ithaca, NY: Cornell University Press.

Amenta, E., & Zylan, Y. (1991). It happened here: Political opportunity, the new institutionalism, and the Towsend movement. *American Sociological Review, 56*, 250–265.

Baumgartner, F. R., & Leech, B. L. (1998). *Basic interests: The importance of groups in politics and in political science.* Princeton, NJ: Princeton University Press.

Bennett, J. T., & DiLorenzo, T. J. (1985). *Destroying democracy: How government funds partisan politics.* Washington, DC: Cato Institute.

Bernstein, M. (1997). Celebration and suppression: The strategic uses of identity by the lesbian and gay movement. *American Journal of Sociology, 103*, 531–565.

Berry, J. M. (1999). *The new liberalism: The rising power of citizen groups.* Washington, DC: The Brookings Institution.

Brady, H. E., Verba, S., & Lehman Scholzman, K. (1995). Beyond SES: A resource model of political participation. *American Political Science Review, 89*, 271–294.

Brulle, R. J. (1996). Environmental discourse and social movement organizations: A historical and rhetorical perspective on the development of U.S. environmental organizations. *Sociological Inquiry, 65*, 58–83.

Brulle, R. J. (2000). *Agency, democracy and nature: The U.S. environmental movement from a critical theory perspective.* Cambridge, MA: MIT Press.

Brulle, R. J., & Schafer Caniglia, B. (1999). Money for nature: A network analysis of foundations and environmental groups. Paper presented at the Annual Meetings of the American Sociological Association. Chicago, IL.

Buechler, S. M. (1993). Beyond resource mobilization theory? Emerging trends in social movement theory. *The Sociological Quarterly, 34*, 217–235.

Buechler, S. M. (2000). *Social movements in advanced capitalism: The political economy and cultural construction of social activism.* New York: Oxford University Press.

Carroll, G. R., Delacroix, J., & Goodstein, J. (1988). The political environments of organizations: An ecological view. *Research on Organizational Behavior, 10*, 359–392.

Clemens, E. S. (1996). Organizational form as frame: Collective identity and political strategy in the American labor movement, 1880–1920. In D. McAdam, J. D. McCarthy, & M. N. Zald (Eds.), *Comparative perspectives on social movements: Political opportunities, mobilizing structures, and cultural framings* (pp. 25–226). Cambridge, England: Cambridge University Press.

Clemens, E. (1997). *The people's lobby: Organizational innovation and the rise of interest group politics in the United States, 1890–1925.* Chicago: University of Chicago Press.

Collwell, M. A., & Bond, D. (1994). *Peace movement organizations: The 1988 and 1992 surveys.* San Francisco: Institute for Nonprofit Management, University of San Francisco.

Cress, D. M. (1997). Nonprofit incorporation among movements of the poor: Pathways and consequences for homeless social movement organizations. *The Sociological Quarterly, 38*, 343–360.

Cress, D. M., & Snow, D. A. (1996). Mobilization at the margins: Resources, benefactors, and the viability of homeless social movement organizations. *American Sociological Review, 61*, 1089–1109.

Cress, D. M., & Snow, D. (2000). The outcomes of homeless mobilization: The influence of organization, disruption, political mediation, and framing. *American Journal of Sociology, 105*, 1065–1104.

Dalton, R. J. (1994). *The green rainbow: Environmental groups in Western Europe.* New Haven, CT: Yale University Press.

Delgado, G. (1994). *Beyond the politics of place: New directions in community organizing in the 1990s.* Oakland, CA: Applied Research Center.

Della Porta, D., & Rucht, D. (1995). Social movement sectors in context: A comparison of Italy and West Germany, 1965–90. In J. C. Jenkins & B. Klandermans (Eds.), *The politics of social protest* (pp. 229–272). Minneapolis: University of Minnesota Press.

Della Porta, D., & Diani, M. (1999). *Social movements: An introduction.* Malden, MA: Blackwell.

DiMaggio, P. J. (1991). Constructing an organizational field as a professional project: U.S. art museums, 1920–1940. In W. W. Powell & P. J. DiMaggio (Eds.), *The new institutionalism in organizational analysis* (pp. 267–292). Chicago: University of Chicago Press.

DiMaggio, P. J., & Powell, W. W. (1983). The iron cage revisited: Institutional isomorphism and collective rationality in organization fields. *American Sociological Review, 48*, 147–160.

Edwards, B. (1994). Semiformal organizational structure among social movement organizations: An analysis of the U.S. peace movement. *Nonprofit and Voluntary Sector Quarterly, 23*, 309–333.

Edwards, B., & Foley, M. W. (1997). Social capital and the political economy of our discontent. *American Behavioral Scientist, 40*, 669–678.

Edwards, B., & Marullo, S. (1995). Organizational mortality in a declining social movement: The demise of peace movement organizations in the end of the cold war. *American Sociological Review, 60*, 908–927.

Edwards, B., & McCarthy, J. D. (1992). Social movement schools. *Sociological Forum, 7*, 541–550.

Ferree, M. M. (1992). The political context of rationality: Rational choice theory and resource mobilization. In A. Morris & C. McClurg Mueller (Eds.), *Frontiers of social movement theory* (pp. 29–52). New Haven, CT: Yale University Press.

Ferree, M. M., & Miller, F. (1985). Mobilization and meaning: Toward an integration of social psychological and resource perspectives on social movements. *Sociological Inquiry, 55*, 38–61.

Ferree, M. M., & Yancey Martin, P. (1995). *Feminist organizations: Harvest of the new women's movement.* Philadelphia: Temple University Press.

Finke, R., & Starke, R. (1992). *The churching of America, 1776–1990: Winners and losers in our religious economy.* New Brunswick, NJ: Rutgers University Press.

Finke, R., Guest, A. M., & Stark, R. (1996). Mobilizing local religious markets: Religious pluralism in the empire state, 1855 to 1865. *American Sociological Review, 61*, 203–218.

Fligstein, N. (1990). *The transformation of corporate control.* Cambridge, MA: Harvard University Press.

Frank, D. J., Hironaka, A., Meyer, J., Schofer, E., & Tuma, N. B. (1999). Rationalization and organization of nature in world culture. In J. Boli & G. M. Thomas (Eds.), *Constructing world culture: International nongovernmental organization since 1875* (pp. 81–99). Stanford, CA: Stanford University Press.

Gamson, W. A. (1968). *Power and discontent.* Homewood, IL: Dorsey Press.

Gamson, W. A. (1975). *The strategy of social protest.* Homewood, IL: Dorsey Press.

Gamson, W. A. (1987). Introduction. In M. N. Zald & J. D. McCarthy (Eds.), *Social movements in an organizational society* (pp. 1–14). New Brunswick, NJ: Transaction Books.

Gamson, W. A., Fireman, B., & Rytina, S. (1982). *Encounters with unjust authorities.* Homewood, IL: Dorsey Press.

Garner, R., & Zald, M. (1985). The political economy of social movement sectors. In G. D. Suttles & M. N. Zald (Eds.), *The challenge of social control: Citizenship and institution building in modern society* (pp. 119–145). Norwood, NJ: Ablex.

Gerhards, J., & Rucht, D. (1992). Mesomobilization: Organizing and framing in two protest campaigns in West Germany. *American Journal of Sociology, 98*, 555–595.

Gilbert, G. N., & Mulkay, M. (1984). *Opening pandora's box: A sociological analysis of scientists' discourse.* Cambridge, England: Cambridge University Press.

Gillham, P. F., & Marx, G. T. (2000). Complexity and irony in policing and protesting: The World Trade Organization in Seattle. *Social Justice, 27*, 212–236.

Gray, V., & Lowrey, D. (1996). *The population ecology of interest representation: Lobbying communities in the American states.* Ann Arbor: University of Michigan Press.

Haines, H. H. (1988). *Black radicals and the civil rights mainstream, 1965–70.* Knoxville: University of Tennessee Press.

Hannan, M. T., & Freeman, J. (1977). The population ecology of organizations. *American Journal of Sociology, 82*, 929–964.

Hodgkinson, V., & Weitzman, M. S. (1996). *Nonprofit almanac, 1996–1997.* San Francisco: Jossey-Bass.

Imig, D. R. (1996). *Poverty and power: The political representation of poor Americans.* Lincoln: University of Nebraska Press.

Jasper, J. M. (1997). *The art of moral protest: Culture, biography and creativity in social movements.* Chicago: University of Chicago Press.

Jenkins, C. (1983). Resource mobilization theory and the study of social movements. *Annual Review of Sociology, 9*, 527–553.

Jenkins, J. C., & Eckert, C. M. (1986). Channeling black insurgency: Elite patronage and professional social movement organizations in the development of the black movement. *American Sociological Review, 51*, 812–829.

Jenkins, J. C., & Halci, A. (1999). Grassrooting the system? The development and impact of social movement philanthropy, 1953–1990. In *Philanthropic foundations: New scholarship, new possibilities* (pp. 229–256). Bloomington: Indiana University Press.

Jenkins, J. C., & Perrow, C. (1977). Insurgency of the powerless: Farm workers' movements (1946–1972). *American Sociological Review, 42*, 249–268.

Khawaja, M. (1994). Resource mobilization, hardship, and popular collective action in the West Bank. *Social Forces, 73*, 191–220.

Kitschelt, H. (1991). Resource mobilization theory: A critique. In *Research on Social Movements: The state of the art in Western Europe and the USA* (pp. 323–354). Frankfurt: Campus Verlag.

Klandermans, B. (1997). *The social psychology of protest.* Cambridge, MA: Blackwell.

Klandermans, B., & Oegema, D. (1987). Potentials, networks, motivations and barriers: Steps toward participation in social movements. *American Sociological Review, 52*, 519–531.

Knoke, D. (1989). Resource acquisition and allocation in U.S. national associations. *International Social Movements Research, 2*, 129–154.

Knoke, D. (1990). *Organizing for collective action: The political economies of associations.* New York: Aldine de Gruyter.

Koopmans, R. (1995). *Democracy from below: New social movements and the political system in West Germany.* Boulder, CO: Westview Press.

Kriesi, H. (1996). The organizational structure of new social movements in a political context. In D. McAdam, J. D. McCarthy, & M. N. Zald (Eds.), *Comparative perspectives on social movements: Political opportunities, mobilizing structures and cultural framings* (pp. 152–184). New York: Cambridge University Press.

Lahusen, C. (1996). *The rhetoric of moral protest: Public campaigns, celebrity endorsements and political mobilization.* Berlin: Walter de Gruyter.

Lofland, J. (1993). *Polite protesters: The American peace movement of the 1980s.* Syracuse, NY: Syracuse University Press.

Lofland, J. (1996). *Social movement organizations: Guide to research on insurgent realities.* New York: Aldine de Gruyter.

Lofland, J., & Jamison, M. (1985). Social movement locals: Modal membership structures. In J. Lofland, *Protest: Studies of collective behavior and social movements* (pp. 201–238). New Brunswick, NJ: Transaction Books.

March, J. G., & Simon, H. A. (1958). *Organizations.* New York: Wiley.

Martin, P. Y. (1990). Rethinking feminist organizations. *Gender and Society, 4*, 182–206.

Marullo, S., Pagnucco, R., & Smith, J. (1996). Frame changes and social movement contraction: US peace movement framing after the Cold War. *Sociological Inquiry, 66*, 1–28.

McAdam, D. (1982). *Political process and the development of black insurgency, 1930–1970.* Chicago: University of Chicago Press.

McAdam, D. (1988). *Freedom summer.* New York: Oxford University Press.

McAdam, D. (1996). Conceptual origins, current problems, future directions. In D. McAdam, J. D. McCarthy, & M. N. Zald (Eds.), *Comparative perspectives on social movements: Political opportunities, mobilizing structures, and cultural framings* (pp. 23–40). New York: Cambridge University Press.

McAdam, D., McCarthy, J. D., & Zald, M. N. (1988). Social movements. In N. Smelser (Ed.), *Handbook of sociology* (pp. 695–737). Beverly Hills, CA: Sage.

McAdam, D., McCarthy, J. D., & Zald, M. N. (Eds.). (1996). *Comparative perspectives on social movements: Political opportunities, mobilizing structures, and cultural framings.* New York: Cambridge University Press.

McCarthy, J. D. (1987). Pro-life and pro-choice mobilization: Infra-structure deficits and new technologies. In M. N. Zald & J. D. McCarthy (Eds.), *Social movements in an organizational society: Collected essays* (pp. 49–66). New Brunswick, NJ: Transaction Publishers.

McCarthy, J. D. (1997). The globalization of social movement theory. In J. Smith, C. Chatfield, & R. Pagnucco (Eds.),

Transnational social movements and global politics: Solidarity beyond the state (pp. 243–259). Syracuse, NY: Syracuse University Press.

McCarthy, J. D., & Castelli, J. (1994). *Working for justice: The campaign for human development and poor empowerment groups*. Washington, DC: Life Cycle Institute, The Catholic University of America.

McCarthy, J. D., & Castelli, J. (forthcoming). Studying non-profit advocacy organizations. In P. Flynn & V. Hodgkinson (Eds.), *Studying the impact of the nonprofit sector: An agenda for research*. San Francisco: Jossey-Bass.

McCarthy, J. D., & Harvey, D. (1989). Independent citizen advocacy: The past and the prospects. In *The Surgeon General's Workshop on Drunk Driving: Background Papers* (pp. 247–260). Office of the Surgeon General, U.S. Public Health Service. Washington, DC: Department of Health and Human Services.

McCarthy, J. D., & McPhail, C. (1998). The institutionalization of protest in the United States. In D. S. Meyer & S. Tarrow (Eds.), *The social movement society: Contentious politics for a new century* (pp. 83–110). Lanham, MD: Rowan and Littlefield.

McCarthy, J. D., & Wolfson, M. (1996). Resource mobilization by local social movement organizations: Agency, strategy and organization in the movement against drinking and driving. *American Sociological Review, 61,* 1070–1088.

McCarthy, J. D., & Zald, M. N. (1973). *The trend of social movements in America: Professionalization and resource mobilization*. Morristown, NJ: General Learning Press.

McCarthy, J. D., & Zald, M. N. (1977). Resource mobilization and social movements: A partial theory. *American Journal of Sociology, 82,* 1212–1241.

McCarthy, J. D., Wolfson, M., Baker, D. P., & Mosakowski, E. (1988). The founding of social movement organizations: Local citizens' groups opposing drunken driving. In *Ecological models of organizations* (pp. 71–84). Cambridge, MA: Ballinger.

McCarthy, J. D., Britt, D. W., & Wolfson, M. (1991). The institutional channeling of social movements by the state in the United States. *Research in Social Movements, Conflict and Change, 14,* 45–76.

Melucci, A. (1996). *Challenging codes: Collective action in the information age*. New York: Cambridge University Press.

Meyer, D. S., & Staggenborg, S. (1996). Movements, countermovements, and the structure of political opportunity. *American Journal of Sociology, 101,* 1628–1660.

Meyer, D. S., & Tarrow, S. (1998). A movement society: Contentious politics for a new century. In D. S. Meyer & S. Tarrow (Eds.), *The social movement society: Contentious politics for a new century* (pp. 1–28). Lanham, MD: Rowan and Littlefield.

Minkoff, D. (1995). *Organizing for equality: The evolution of women's and racial ethnic organizations in America, 1955–1985*. New Brunswick, NJ: Rutgers University Press.

Minkoff, D. (1997). The sequencing of social movements. *American Sociological Review, 62,* 779–799.

Minkoff, D. (1999). Bending in the wind: Strategic change and adaptation by women's and racial minority organizations. *American Journal of Sociology, 104,* 1666–1703.

Minkoff, D. (forthcoming). Macro-organizational analysis. In B. Klandermans & S. Staggenborg (Eds.), *Methods in social movements research*. Minneapolis: University of Minnesota Press.

Mitchell, R. C., Mertig, A. G., & Dunlap, R. E. (1992). Twenty years of environmental mobilization: Trends among national environmental organizations. In R. E. Dunlap & A. G. Mertig (Eds.), *American environmentalism: The U.S. environmental movement, 1970–1990* (pp. 11–26). Philadelphia: Taylor and Francis.

Morris, A. D. (1984). *The origins of the civil rights movement: Black communities organizing for change*. New York: Free Press.

Oberschall, A. (1973). *Social conflict and social movements*. Englewood Cliffs, NJ: Prentice-Hall.

Oliver, P. (1993). Formal models of collective action. *Annual Review of Sociology, 19,* 271–300.

Oliver, P., & Furman, M. (1989). Contradictions between national and local organization strength: The case of the John Birch Society. *International Social Movements Research, 2,* 155–177.

Oliver, P. E., & Marwell, G. (1992). Mobilizing technologies for collective action. In A. D. Morris & C. McClurg Mueller (Eds.), *Frontiers in social movement theory* (pp. 251–272). New Haven, CT: Yale University Press.

Ostrander, S. A. (1995). *Money for change: Social movement philanthropy at Haymarket People's Fund*. Philadelphia: Temple University Press.

Ostrander, S. A. (1999). When grantees becomes grantors: Accountability, democracy and social movement philanthropy. In *Philanthropic foundations: New scholarship, new possibilities* (pp. 257–270). Bloomington: Indiana University Press.

Perrow, C. (1979). The sixties observed. In *The dynamics of social movements* (pp. 192–211). Cambridge, MA: Winthrop Publishers.

Piven, F. F., & Cloward, R. (1977). *Poor people's movements*. New York: Pantheon.

Polletta, F. (1999). Snarls, quacks, and quarrels: Culture and structure in political process theory. *Sociological Forum*, *14*, 63–70.

Putnam, R. (2000). *Trends in civic engagement and social capital*. Cambridge, MA: Harvard University Press.

Rogers, M. B. (1990). *Cold anger: A story of faith and power politics*. Denton, TX: University of North Texas Press.

Ross, H. L. (1992). *Confronting drunk driving: Social policy for saving lives*. New Haven, CT: Yale University Press.

Rothschild-Whitt, J. (1979). The collectivist organization: An alternative to rational-bureaucratic models. *American Sociological Review*, *44*(August), 509–527.

Rucht, D. (1989). Environmental movement organizations in West Germany and France: Structure and interorganizational relations. *International Social Movements Research*, *2*, 61–94.

Rucht, D. (1996). The impact of national context on social movement structures: A cross-movement and cross-national comparison. In D. McAdam, J. D. McCarthy, & M. N. Zald (Eds.), *Comparative perspectives on social movements: Political opportunities, mobilizing structures, and cultural framings* (pp. 185–204). Cambridge, England: Cambridge University Press.

Rucht, D. (1999). Linking organization and mobilization: Michel's iron law of oligarchy reconsidered. *Mobilization: An International Journal*, *4*, 151–169.

Schneider, J. W. (1985). Social problems theory: The social constructionist view. *Annual Review of Sociology*, *11*, 209–229.

Scott, W. R. (1998). *Organizations: Rational, natural and open systems*, 4th ed. Englewood Cliffs, NJ: Prentice Hall.

Shanahan, S. E., & Brandon Tuma, N. (1994). The sociology of distribution and redistribution. In N. Smelser & R. Swedborg (Eds.), *The handbook of economic sociology* (pp. 733–765). Princeton, NJ: Princeton University Press.

Sherkat, D. E. (1998). What's in a frame: Towards an integrated social psychology of social movements. Unpublished paper, Department of Sociology, Vanderbilt University, Nashville, TN.

Sherkat, D. E., & Blocker, J. T. (1994). The political development of sixties' activists: Identifying the influence of class, gender, and socialization on protest participation. *Social Forces*, *76*, 1087–1115.

Simon, H. A. (1947). *Administrative behavior: A study of decision-making process in administrative organization*. New York: Macmillan.

Smith, D. H. (1997). The rest of the nonprofit sector: Grassroots associations as the dark matter ignored in prevailing "flat earth" maps of the sector. *Nonprofit and Voluntary Sector Quarterly*, *26*, 114–131.

Smith, J. (1997). Characteristics of the modern transnational social movement sector. In J. Smith, C. Chatfield, & R. Pagnucco (Eds.), *Transnational social movements and global politics: Solidarity beyond the state* (pp. 42–58). Syracuse, NY: Syracuse University Press.

Smith, J. (2001). Globalizing resistance: The battle of Seattle and the future of social movements. *Mobilization*, *6*, 1–19.

Smith, J., Pagnucco, R., & Romeril, W. (1994). Transnational social movement organizations in the global political area. *Voluntas*, *5*, 121–154.

Smith, J., Pagnucco, R., & Lopez, G. (1998). Globalizing human rights: Report on a survey of transnational human rights NGOs. *Human Rights Quarterly*, *20*, 379–412.

Snow, D. A., & Benford, R. D. (1988). Ideology, frame resonance, and participant mobilization. *International Social Movement Research*, *1*, 197–217.

Snow, D. A., & Benford, R. D. (1992). Master frames and cycles of protest. In A. D. Morris & C. M. Mueller (Eds.), *Frontiers in social movement theory* (pp. 133–155). New Haven, CT: Yale University Press.

Snow, D. A., Cress, D. M., Soule, S. A., & Baker, S. G. (2000). An event history analysis of homeless protest, 1980 to 1991: An assessment of strain, resource mobilization, political opportunity, and threshold theories. Unpublished paper. Tucson, AZ: Department of Sociology.

Snow, D. A., Rochford, E. B., Jr., Worden, S. K., & Benford, R. D. (1986). Frame alignment process, micromobilization, and movement participation. *American Sociological Review*, *51*, 464–481.

Snow, D. A., Zurcher, L. A., & Eckland-Olson, S. (1980). Social networks and social movements: A microstructural approach to differential recruitment. *American Sociological Review*, *45*, 787–801.

Staggenborg, S. (1988). The consequences of professionalization and formalization in the pro-choice movement. *American Sociological Review*, *53*, 585–606.

Staggenborg, S. (1991). *The pro-choice movement: Organization and activism in the abortion conflict*. New York: Oxford University Press.

Steinberg, M. W. (1999). The talk and back talk of collective action: A dialogic analysis of repertoires of discourse among nineteenth-century English cotton spinners. *American Journal of Sociology*, *105*, 736–780.

Stinchcombe, A. L. (1965). Social structure and organizations. In J. G. March (Ed.), *Handbook of organizations* (pp. 142–193). Chicago: Rand McNally.

Swanson, D. H. (1996). *An exploration of the causes and consequences of professionalization: Anti-drunken driving citizens' groups*. Washington, DC: Department of Sociology, Catholic University of America.

Tarrow, S. (1998). *Power in movement: Social movements and contentious politics*. New York: Cambridge University Press.

Tilly, C. (1978). *From mobilization to revolution*. New York: McGraw-Hill.

Tilly, C. (1979). Repertoires of contention in America and Britain, 1750–1830. In M. N. Zald & J. D. McCarthy (Eds.), *The dynamics of social movements: Resource mobilization, social control and tactics* (pp. 126–155). Cambridge, MA: Winthrop.

Tilly, C. (1998). *Durable inequality*. Berkeley: University of California Press.

Turner, R. H. (1981). Collective behavior and resource mobilization as approaches to social movements: Issues and continuities. *Research in Social Movements, Conflict and Change, 4*, 1–24.

Useem, B. (1998). Breakdown theories of collective action. *Annual Review of Sociology, 24*, 215–238.

Verba, S., Lehman Schlozman, K., & Brady, H. E. (1995). *Voice and equality: Civic voluntarism in American politics*. Cambridge, MA: Harvard University Press.

Walker, J. (1983). The origin and maintenance of interest groups in America. *American Political Science Review, 77*, 390–406.

Walker, J. L., Jr. (1991). *Mobilizing interest groups in America: Patrons, professions and social movements*. Ann Arbor: University of Michigan Press.

Warner, S. R. (1993). Work in progress toward a new paradigm for the sociological study of religion in the United States. *American Journal of Sociology, 98*, 1044–1093.

Weed, F. J. (1991). Organizational mortality in the anti-drunk-driving movement: Failure among local MADD chapters. *Social Forces, 69*, 851–868.

Weed, F. J. (1995). *Certainty of justice: Reform in the crime victim movement*. Hawthorne, NY: Aldine de Gruyter.

Wolfson, M. (2000). *The fight against big tobacco: The movement, the state, and the public's health*. New York: Aldine, de Gruyter.

Young, D. R. (1992). Organizing principles for international advocacy associations. *Voluntas, 3*, 1–28.

Young, D. R., Koenig, B. L., Najam, A., & Fisher, J. (1999). Strategy and structure in managing global associations. *Voluntas, 10*, 323–343.

Zald, M. N. (2000). Ideologically structured action: An enlarged agenda for social movement research. *Mobilization: The International Journal, 5*, 1–17.

Zald, M. N., & Ash, R. (1966). Social movement organizations: Growth, decay and change. *Social Forces, 40*, 327–340.

Zald, M. N., & McCarthy, J. D. (Eds.). (1979). *The dynamics of social movements: Resource mobilization, social control, and tactics*. Cambridge, MA: Winthrop.

Zald, M. N., & McCarthy, J. D. (1987). *Social movements in an organizational society*. New Brunswick, NJ: Transaction Books.

Zelizer, V. A. R. (1994). *The social meaning of money*. New York: Basic Books.

CHAPTER 26

Historical Analysis of Political Processes

CHARLES TILLY

Good sociology takes history seriously. Good political sociology, however, takes more than political history seriously. If political sociology is to escape from the cramped prison of the present, it must address directly the ways in which time and place affect the character of political processes. Reviewing visions of historical explanation before turning to specific political processes, this chapter urges a renewed search for robust causal mechanisms and processes in history.

Here is the plan. First, consider when explanation (as opposed to description, interpretation, and critique) should concern historical students of political processes. Second, review competing conceptions of explanation, arriving at reasons for concentrating on mechanism-based explanations. Third, inventory, compare, and refine strategies for historical analysis. Fourth, examine the practical explanatory program implied by historically grounded mechanism-based analysis. Finally, the bulk of the chapter illustrates that program by pursuing (1) robust mechanisms and processes, (2) explanation of puzzling features in historical episodes, (3) explanation of puzzling features in whole classes of historical episodes, and, very briefly, (4) detection of analogies among ostensibly dissimilar episodes. The enterprise centers on generation of visibly viable explanations for complex political processes.

Not all sociologists regard explanation as a feasible or laudable end for their inquiries. Sociology could, after all, probably survive as a valued discipline without offering powerful explanations of the phenomena its practitioners study. Sociologists can usefully describe current social conditions, unmask official claims, join moral and political debates, chart directions of change, document social differences, evaluate consequences of social interventions, or supply information to decision makers and social movement activists. All these useful sociological enterprises can proceed with no more than crude conceptions of cause–effect relations. In fact, most of what professional sociologists actually do these days belongs to one or more of these pursuits.

Historical analysis of political processes more often pursues cause–effect relations. Nevertheless, even it need not center on causes and effects. Consider the place of explanation

---

CHARLES TILLY • Department of Sociology, Columbia University, New York, New York 10027.

Handbook of Sociological Theory, edited by Jonathan H. Turner. Kluwer Academic / Plenum Publishers, New York, 2002.

in sociology's major contemporary forms of historical analysis: historical social criticism, pattern identification, scope extension, and process analysis.

Historical social criticism reconstructs the past on the way to informing human choices in the present and future. We do not need a compelling explanation of capitalism to reflect intelligently on its costs and benefits for human welfare. Historical pattern identification searches for recurrent structures and sequences across time and space: standard configurations and trajectories for industrialization, for revolution, for secularization, or perhaps for societal development as a whole. That venerable sociological enterprise usually makes some gestures toward explanation, but often settles practically for identifying parallels among cases. Historical scope extension applies techniques, models, or generalizations that sociologists have developed in studies of contemporary social life to historical situations. As in the case of pattern identification, the application of demographic or network models to past settings may involve explaining what happened in those settings, but it often ends with no more than identification of similarities and differences.

Finally, historical process analysis examines how social interactions impinge on each other in space and time. Instead of considering space and time as additional variables, it presumes that space–time connections define social processes and that social processes operate differently as a function of their placement in space and time. As in the previous modes of inquiry, process analysis may reasonably ask largely descriptive questions, for example, whether in a given period and region epidemics, fads, money, artifacts, and news, for whatever reasons, followed essentially the same communication lines. Process analysis lends itself to historical explanation more effectively than do historical social criticism, pattern identification, and scope extension because it explicitly draws attention to temporal and spatial interdependencies. But it is still possible to practice process analysis without much effort at explanation. None of sociology's standard modes of historical analysis, then, absolutely requires a focus on explanation.

Explanations begin to matter when sociologists become intellectually ambitious. Three circumstances make the character and quality of explanation crucial:

- Sociologists attempt to identify similarities and differences in the workings of ostensibly distinct social processes such as war, democratization, nationalism, ethnic conflict, and social movements.
- Sociologists seek to confront or integrate their accounts of social processes with those prevailing in adjacent disciplines such as anthropology, neuroscience, economics, evolutionary biology, linguistics, psychology, geography, history, or political science.
- Theorists in one or more of these adjacent disciplines propose to subsume sociological findings under their own explanatory schemes.

In all these circumstances, bad explanations cause serious trouble for sociologists. In the liveliest sectors of political sociology, as it happens, all three circumstances prevail.

That is notably true of historical analysis. There, sociologists face the challenge of explaining similarities and intersections of apparently disparate forms of politics, confront competing explanations in adjacent disciplines, and encounter many an economist, historian, political scientist, psychologist, or evolutionary biologist who claims to have identified the fundamental explanations of political processes. Sociologists who want to make advances in historical analyses of war, revolution, state formation, democratization, nationalism, social movements, and contentious politics at large have little choice but to take explanatory problems seriously. Both competing explanations and competing views of explanation confront each other in the historical analysis of political processes.

In the long run, a discipline's intellectual vivacity and viability depend on its capacity to generate superior explanations. This discussion therefore addresses students of sociological theory who actually want to recognize, fashion, or verify explanations of historically situated political processes. They have a choice of explanatory strategies. In sociology as a whole, four conceptions of explanation vie vigorously for attention:

1. *Covering law* accounts consider explanation to consist of subjecting robust empirical generalizations to higher and higher level generalizations, the most general of all standing as laws. In such accounts, models are invariant—they work the same in all conditions. Investigators search for necessary and sufficient conditions of stipulated outcomes, those outcomes often conceived of as "dependent variables." Studies of covariation among presumed causes and presumed effects therefore serve as validity tests for proposed explanations. Thus some students of democratization hope to state the general conditions under which any nondemocratic polity whatsoever becomes democratic.

2. *Propensity* accounts consider explanation to consist of reconstructing a given actor's state at the threshold of action, with that state variously stipulated as motivation, consciousness, need, organization, or momentum. Explanatory methods of choice then range from sympathetic interpretation to reductionism, psychological or otherwise. Thus some students of social movements compare the experiences of different social groupings with deindustrialization in an effort to explain why some groupings resist and others disintegrate.

3. Although authors of covering law and propensity accounts sometimes use the language of systems, *system* explanations strictly speaking consist of specifying the place of some event, structure, or process within a larger self-maintaining set of interdependent elements, showing how the event, structure, or process in question serves and/or results from interactions among the larger set of elements. Thus some students of peasant revolt explain its presence or absence by peasants' degree of integration into society as a whole

4. *Mechanism-based* accounts select salient features of episodes, or significant differences among episodes, and explain them by identifying robust mechanisms of relatively general scope within those episodes. As compared with covering law, propensity, and system approaches, mechanism-based explanations aim at modest ends: selective explanation of salient features by means of partial causal analogies. Thus some students of nationalism try to relate its intensity to the extent and character of competition among ethnic entrepreneurs. In such accounts, competition for political constituencies becomes a central (but not exclusive or sufficient) mechanism in the generation of nationalism.

System explanations have lost ground in sociology since the days of Pitirim Sorokin and Talcott Parsons, but they still figure prominently in some sorts of organizational analysis and demography. When today's sociologists fight about explanation, however, they generally pit covering law against propensity accounts, with the first often donning the costume of Science and the second the garb of Interpretation. Explanation by means of robust causal mechanisms has received much less self-conscious attention from sociological methodologists than have covering law, propensity, and system explanations. Nevertheless, a significant body of thought recommends the mechanistic approach (see e.g., Bunge 1997, 1998; Hedström & Swedberg, 1998; Elster, 1989; Little, 1991, 1998; Stinchcombe, 1991). This chapter accordingly pursues mechanisms and processes.

HISTORICAL ANALYSIS
OF POLITICAL PROCESSES?

Let us include as political all social processes in which governments figure significantly. (Governments are organizations controlling the principal concentrated means of coercion within substantial bounded territories and exercising priority in some regards over all other organizations operating within the same territories.) By such a criterion, war, revolution, and democratization clearly qualify as political processes, but communication, exploitation, and production only qualify as political processes when and if governments become parties to them. Of course, governments often do become parties to communication, exploitation, and production.

We can adopt either a weak or a strong definition of historical analysis. The weak version simply deals with events and processes that have taken place before the present. All study of the past, in the weak version, constitutes historical analysis. The strong version demands more. It identifies ways that (1) when and where an event or process occurs affect (2) how it occurs, (3) why it occurs, and (4) with what consequences it occurs. Strong-version historical studies of democratization, for example, examine how and why democratization takes various forms and has disparate impacts on the quality of life in different periods and regions. Although plenty of work in historical sociology—notably including much of scope extension—depends on the weak definition, here I stress the strong definition. Historical analysis of political processes, for present purposes, means systematic description and explanation of social processes involving governments, processes whose character varies significantly as a function of their location in space and time.

The strong definition excludes two extremes: random or unique events and processes that operate identically everywhere, every time they occur. But it excludes few if any significant political processes. All complex, major political processes operate differently in different times and places. That is so chiefly for three reasons: (1) all political processes incorporate institutions, understandings, and practices that have accumulated historically in their current sites; (2) prior iterations of a given process affect its subsequent iterations; and (3) processes that acquire the same names often result from different causes.

Why? Political processes such as social movements and civil wars incorporate institutions, understandings, and practices that have accumulated historically in their current sites; despite some family resemblances between 17th-century English civil wars and recent civil wars in the Congo/Zaïre, the two unfolded differently because of their historical settings. Prior iterations of a process, say, revolution or religious mobilization, affect subsequent iterations by providing models for participants, by altering possible participants' estimates of likely outcomes to various possible interactions, by transforming relations among possible participants and third parties. Finally, complex episodes that acquire the same names (e.g., genocide or nationalism) often result from different causes, as in the diverse sequences that produced political independence and international recognition for Algeria, Croatia, and Uzbekistan. Historical analysts therefore must examine how prior iterations of a process affect its subsequent iterations, how political processes incorporate locally accumulated institutions and practices, as well as how causally heterogeneous episodes acquire the same public names.

Interesting choices arise at precisely this point:

1. Since political processes incorporate institutions, understandings, and practices that accumulate historically in their current sites, analysts might plausibly follow the lead of historians, who remain skeptical about general analyses of those processes. Instead

of creating general schemata for all civil wars or all social movements, terre à terre historians prefer to integrate their civil wars and social movements into well-documented historical contexts.

2. Since prior iterations of a given process affect its subsequent iterations, however, analysts might plausibly follow the lead of historical sociologists by creating subfields to encompass distinct processes: a sociology of revolution, another sociology of democratization, a third sociology of war, and so on. This choice relies on the presumption that each of these forms has a distinctive, continuous organizational and causal structure, even if one iteration affects the next.

3. Since causally heterogeneous political processes often acquire the same names, finally, analysts might plausibly concentrate on a twofold strategy: get explanation right by regrouping processes into causally similar categories, but treat the application of a certain name (e.g., this is a revolution, that is genocide) to a political process as a phenomenon deserving explanation for its own sake.

My own preferred intellectual strategy combines 1 and 3, but subordinates 1 to 3. It searches for very general political mechanisms and processes—mechanisms and processes that transcend such categories as revolution, democratization, and war—but seeks to explain how they articulate with locally accumulated institutions, understandings, and practices. Strategy 2 then comes into play not as a form of explanation, but as a heuristic; it helps clarify what we must explain.

Notice the ambitious program of inquiry that follows. We must combine theoretical and empirical work as we identify significant mechanisms and processes that recur across a variety of times, places, and circumstances. We must specify interactions between those mechanisms and processes, on one side, and the contexts within which they operate: to what extent and how, for example, do outcomes of mobilization processes vary as a function of initial conditions? We must trace causal connections between one iteration of a mechanism or process and the next. We must finally examine how relatively general mechanisms and processes incorporate or respond to locally accumulated institutions, understandings, and practices. In short, we must undertake serious historical work without getting lost in historical particularism.

For the work at hand, let us adopt a simple conceptual apparatus: episodes (connected sets of events that include phenomena requiring explanation), causal mechanisms (events altering relations among some specified set of elements), processes (causal chains, sequences, and combinations), and explanation (identification of mechanisms and processes that produce crucial political phenomena). After explicating each of these concepts, we can turn to their use in accounting for concrete political events.

First we delineate one or more episodes: conveniently or conventionally bounded, connected sets of events that include phenomena requiring explanation. In some fields of political analysis, researchers already have developed standard ways of identifying comparable episodes: strikes, contentious gatherings, wars, events, revolutionary situations, and the like (Azar & Ben-Dak, 1973; Brockett, 1992; Cioffi-Revilla, 1990; Diani & Eyerman, 1992; Favre, Fillieule, & Mayer, 1997; Gurr & Harff, 1994; Shapiro & Markoff, 1998; Small & Singer, 1982; Sugimoto, 1981; Tilly & Rule, 1965; White, 1993). In these methods, researchers either accept conventional definitions of the events in question (e.g., official listings of strikes) or construct a priori definitions, applying them uniformly to the available evidence (as is common in the study of "protest events": Franzosi, 1998; Mueller, 1997; Oliver & Meyers, 1999; Olzak, 1989; Rucht & Koopmans, 1999; Rucht, Koopmans, & Neidhardt, 1998). In principle, it also should be possible to use criteria of internal connectedness to delineate comparable events (see, e.g., Bearman, Faris, & Moody, 1999). But that approach has not yet been much tried in historical studies of political processes.

After delineation of episodes, we proceed to locate causal mechanisms within the episodes. Mechanisms are events that alter relations among some specified set of elements, as, for example, a broker's creation of a connection between two previously unconnected groups alters the two groups' behavior. We can conveniently distinguish among cognitive, relational, and environmental mechanisms. Cognitive mechanisms operate through alterations of individual and collective perception; words like "recognize," "understand," "reinterpret," and "classify" characterize such mechanisms. Relational mechanisms alter connections among people, groups, and interpersonal networks; words like "ally," "attack," "subordinate," and "appease" convey a sense of relational mechanisms. Environmental mechanisms apply external influences on the conditions affecting political processes; words like "disappear," "enrich," "expand," and "disintegrate," applied not to actors but their settings, suggest the sorts of cause–effect connections in question. For explanatory purposes, then, we search especially for cognitive, relational, and environmental mechanisms that operate in similar fashion across a wide variety of settings.

Mechanisms concatenate into broader processes. Processes are causal chains, sequences, and combinations. They deserve recognition as robust when they occur in similar ways across a variety of settings and circumstances. Polarization provides an example of a fairly robust political process that recurs widely. Polarization combines mechanisms of category formation, coalition formation, opportunity/threat spirals, and brokerage: creation of a named boundary with organized relations across and on either side of the boundary; development of coordinated action among two or more actors on each side of the boundary; signaling–reaction sequences that increase distance between the two sides; establishment of interlocutors (brokers) representing each side.

Explanation, in this mechanism-based approach, follows two complementary paths. First, it pursues particular mechanisms and processes across different settings, investigating how they work. Thus a general interest in polarization processes leads to close investigation of category formation, coalition formation, opportunity/threat spirals, and brokerage in different conditions and locales. When do they arise, how do they operate, what produces their effects? Any such investigation is likely to establish that some of its premises erred: that category formation is not uniform across settings, that opportunity/threat spirals reduce to more elementary mechanisms, and so on.

Second, explanation entails identifying problematic features of episodes or classes of episodes, then discovering what mechanisms and processes produce those problematic features. The study of episodes is likely to involve close comparison, but not in the style of John Stuart Mill's classic methods of agreement, difference, residues, and concomitant variation. Instead, the most prized comparisons will show whether the mechanisms and processes in question do indeed qualify as robust, operating similarly in disparate conditions.

Put more schematically, the analytical program that follows has several different versions:

- Single out, describe, and explain a single robust mechanism or process, demonstrating its operation in a variety of episodes.
- Identify puzzling features of a given episode, then use systematic comparison with other episodes to locate robust mechanisms and processes producing those puzzling features.
- Do the same thing for a whole class of similar episodes.
- Identify partial causal analogies among ostensibly dissimilar episodes and classes of episodes by locating the same mechanisms and processes within them.

All four versions integrate theory with empirical investigation. None can begin without both some empirical sense of the phenomena under investigation and at least a crude theory of their operation. The remainder of this chapter illustrates those four procedures. It emphasizes relational (rather than cognitive or environmental) mechanisms on the ground that they have received insufficient attention from historical analysts of political processes. More narrowly, it concentrates on mechanisms and processes that create, transform, and activate political identities: public, collective answers to the questions "Who are we," "Who are you," and "Who are they." For the most part, analysts have treated political identities phenomenologically, considering them as aspects of individual or collective consciousness. A closer look, however, reveals the organizational bases of political identities.

ROBUST MECHANISMS AND PROCESSES

A number of identity processes depend on, among other things, the twinned mechanisms of certification and decertification: validation (or devalidation) of actors, their performances, and their claims by external authorities. It is the political version of a very general phenomenon. Pondering why weak, peripheral Sweden entered Europe's raging war in 1630, Erik Ringmar reflects on that general phenomenon:

> I will stress the social character of identities: people alone cannot decide who or what they are, but any such decision is always taken together with others. We need *recognition* for the persons we take ourselves to be, and only *as recognized* can we conclusively come to establish an identity. The quest for recognition will consequently come to occupy much of the time of people or groups who are uncertain regarding who they are. We all want to be taken seriously and be treated with respect; we all want to be recognized as the kinds of persons we claim to be. Yet recognition is rarely automatic and before we gain it we are often required to prove that our interpretations of ourselves indeed do fit us. In order to provide such proof we are often forced to *act*—we must *fight* in order to convince people regarding the applicability of our self-descriptions. (Ringmar, 1996, pp. 13–14)

Ringmar's language conveys the unfortunate implication that certification is chiefly a way of satisfying a psychological need. His analysis of Sweden's intervention in the Thirty Years War, however, amply demonstrates that much more than national self-satisfaction was at stake: international recognition of Sweden as a great power because of its war-making prowess altered its relations to all other European powers, gave its diplomacy credibility it previously lacked, and affected the policies of its European neighbors.

The treaties of Westphalia (1648) that ended the Thirty Years War, indeed, established a new set of powers, now identified as sovereign states, constituting both the certified major actors on the European scene and collectively the certifiers of arrivals and departures on the scene. At the same time, they decertified the Holy Roman Empire (which still nominally included a number of the newly sovereign states) as exclusive international interlocutor for its members. For two centuries thereafter, successors of the great powers continued the process of certification and eventually extended it to all the world's states.

Beginning with the French Revolution and Napoleon's conquests, the certification process took on a national twist. Increasingly, Europeans built national and international politics around the equation of nation with state. That equation appears in two competing versions: (1) we have a state and therefore have the right to create our own nation; and (2) we are a nation and therefore have the right to our own state. The first qualifies as state-led nationalism, the second as state-seeking nationalism. State-led nationalism encouraged rulers to impose national languages, official histories, ceremonies, legal systems, and sometimes other cultural forms, which meant subordinating or suppressing other languages, ceremonies, legal systems, and cultural forms. State-seeking nationalism encouraged aspiring leaders of autonomous political units to resist state-led nationalism in the name of distinctive languages, histories, cultural forms, and prior occupation of a territory. In both cases, external powers played pivotal parts: certifying current rulers as authentic rulers of their nations, certifying claimants to independence as valid representatives of authentic nations.

The certification/decertification process actually occurs in every polity, whether international, national, or local in scale. Every polity implicitly establishes a roster of those political actors that have rights to exist, to act, to make claims, and/or to draw routinely on government-controlled resources; it maps members and challengers. So doing, every polity also implicitly (and sometimes explicitly) broadcasts criteria for acceptable political organization, membership, identity, activity, and claim making. Some organizations specialize in surveillance and certification of acceptable or unacceptable versions of organization, membership, identity, activity, and claim making. To take an extreme but significant example, in 1945 the powers that settled World War II, redrawing the European map extensively as they did so, ceded their work of recognizing valid states to the United Nations. During the vast wave of decolonization that soon followed, United Nations officials spent much of their effort screening performances and claims in the form:

- We are a distinct nation and therefore we deserve a state of our own.
- We are an unjustly oppressed people and therefore we deserve a state of our own.
- We were once an independent state and deserve to be independent again.
- Our colonial masters are ready to concede independence to us.
- Our claims to lead a new state are more valid than our rivals'.

Each claim entailed performances by aspiring national leaders—performances displaying evidence of legal rights, leadership, administrative capacity, popular support, internal military control, economic viability, and backing from at least some great powers. Those performances had to be polyvalent, establishing credibility simultaneously with very different audiences, some of them at odds with each other. The minimum set included not only United Nations officials, but also leaders of former colonial powers, constituencies at home, rival claimants to represent the nation in question, and rulers of adjacent states, who were often making their own territorial claims at the same time. Coached by representatives of great powers, United Nations officials rejected far more claims in this vein than they accepted, but they still certified well over 100 new states, with their proposed rulers and forms of government, between 1945 and 1990.

In this extreme case, the world's great powers created an international bureaucracy that radically standardized claim making in its arena. But similar processes operate less bureaucratically and at a smaller scale throughout the world of contentious politics. Every regime sorts forms of organization, publicly asserted identities, and forms of collective interaction along the continuum from prescribed to tolerated to forbidden. Indeed, a good deal of political struggle concerns which forms of organization, which identities, and which forms of collective interaction the regime in power should prescribe, tolerate, or forbid.

Consider South Asia. What people loosely call Hindu nationalism in India centers on the demand for priority in these regards to Hinduism as defined by the Rashtriya Swayamsevak Sangh (RSS), a coordinating organization that originated in Nagpur in 1925. Since the RSS claims that Sikhs and Buddhists are actually Hindus, its program emphasizes state certification of the categorical pair Hindu/Muslim (Tambiah, 1996, pp. 244–245). It remains to be seen whether an RSS government in power would actually write its whole program into law. Meanwhile, in Pakistan, Bangladesh, and Sri Lanka representatives of other religious categories struggle for legal priority.

Regimes, including South Asian regimes, differ momentously in which kinds of organization, identity, and collective interaction they prescribe, tolerate, and forbid. But all of them create procedures for public screening of acceptability in these regards; those procedures crystallize as laws, registers, surveillance, police practice, subsidies, organizations of public space, and repressive policies. In South Asia and elsewhere, group certification as a valid interlocutor for a major religious category gives serious weight to an organization or a network of leaders.

Certification and decertification, then, appear to work in similar fashions over an enormous variety of situations. They qualify as robust mechanisms. In the company of other mechanisms such as brokerage, category formation, and object shift, furthermore, they concatenate into fairly robust, wide-ranging processes of identity formation and change. Theorists of nationalism, genocide, ethnic mobilization, state formation, social movements, revolution, coups d'état, and a variety of other historically grounded political processes have much to learn from close attention to certification and decertification.

PUZZLING FEATURES
OF PARTICULAR EPISODES

A second version of the mechanism-based analytical program identifies puzzling features of a given episode, then uses systematic comparison with other episodes to locate robust mechanisms and processes producing those puzzling features. Instead of resorting to historical particularism or searching for covering laws to subsume the entire episode, it focuses on causes of the puzzling features. The Soviet Union's disintegration poses just such puzzles:

1. How did a political economy that seemed so solid, centralized, authoritarian, and resourceful disintegrate visibly in 5 or 6 years?
2. Why did so much of the contentious claim making take the form of ethnic and national self-assertion?
3. How then did so many old regime power holders reappear in positions of power after the great transformation?

Partial answers lie in the intersection of four robust mechanisms: opportunity spirals, identity shift, competition, and brokerage. Opportunity spirals involve shifting and expanding likely consequences of available claim-making actions. Identity shift (often coupled with certification or decertification) realigns prevailing collective, public answers to the questions "Who are you," "Who are we," and "Who are they." Competition consists of striving among several actors within a reward-allocating arena. Brokerage finally consists of establishing, severing, or realigning connections among social sites. These familiar mechanisms intersected with weighty consequences in the Soviet Union and its successor states after the mid-1980s. My short sketch of Soviet history will concentrate on placing the four crucial mechanisms in historical context, without spelling out comparisons to other instances of imperial disintegration on which my analysis implicitly relies (Barkey & von Hagen, 1997). Furthermore, it will not make crucial regional distinctions, for example, the Baltics versus the Caucasus, that a more detailed analysis would require.

The Soviet Union formed in the ruins of war and revolution. Its imperial predecessor took heavy losses from its battering by Germany and Austria in World War I, losing control of

Russian Poland and the Baltic provinces in the process. Workers' strikes and soldiers' mutinies in 1917 coupled with resistance of the Duma (national assembly) in driving the tsar to abdicate and a conservative–liberal provisional government to take power. Soon insurrectionary countergovernments of workers and soldiers were forming at the local and regional level, as Bolshevik leaders such as Lenin and Trotsky returned from exile. Struggle swirled around multiple factions and issues, but by November 1917 the Bolsheviks had gained enough ground to seize power from the provisional government.

Between 1917 and 1921, the Bolsheviks had their hands full simply keeping together what remained of the Russian empire. Through civil war and peace settlements Russia lost Estonia, Lithuania, Latvia, Finland, and Poland. The new state only regained control of the Caucasus, Georgia, Azerbaijan, Armenia, Ukraine, and Moldavia through military conquest by a hastily assembled Red Army that enrolled 5 million men at its peak. With great effort Lenin, Trotsky, and their collaborators returned the country to civilian control by locating a tightly disciplined Communist party (itself recruited in part from former or present military men) within a large centralized bureaucracy. With Stalin's takeover (and expulsion of Trotsky) in 1927, the Soviet Union moved into a phase of forced-draft industrialization, agricultural collectivization, bureaucratic expansion, and increasingly authoritarian deployment of the Communist party as an instrument of central power.

Broadly speaking, Stalin's regime imposed direct centralized rule on Russia, but relied on a distinctive version of indirect rule elsewhere in the Union. In nominally autonomous political units of the Soviet Union outside of Russia, the Kremlin typically assigned one ethnic identity (e.g., Uzbek, Armenian) priority and appointed party bosses of those ethnicities who had proven their loyalty to the central party. Such regional leaders enjoyed great autonomy and priority within their regions so long as their constituencies delivered compliance, goods, and services to the center. In public life, the titular national language and culture enjoyed equal standing with Russian language and culture, at the expense of the many other cultural forms that ordinarily coexisted in any region.

The late 1930s and the 1940s brought momentous changes to the Soviet Union's national scope. Its leaders began one of history's most massive military mobilizations. Allied temporarily with Nazi Germany, the Soviets occupied half of Poland, reduced Finland to little more than a satellite state, and absorbed Latvia, Lithuania, and Estonia directly into the Union. As a devastating war ended, the peace settlement awarded a battered Soviet Union hegemony over former Axis allies Romania, Bulgaria, and Hungary, not to mention Axis conquests Czechoslovakia and Poland. Although Russian rule remained somewhat more indirect in its Central European satellites than within the Soviet Union's internationally recognized boundaries, the system of Communist party control, Russian presence, and heavy circulation between Moscow and peripheral capitals prevailed throughout what in 1955 became the Warsaw Pact.

Even more so than before World War II, the postwar Soviet economy and polity depended on the combination of three elements: (1) maintenance of formidable military might, (2) large-scale coordination and division of labor in the production and distribution of subsistence goods, and (3) close surveillance and control of all political expression. The three elements in their turn produced paradoxical results:

- Subordination of production for consumers to heavy industrial development.
- Movement of military and party authorities toward a modus vivendi after the chilly relations that had characterized them before the war.
- Enormous strength in the mathematics, physics, and engineering fields on which

military development in competition with the United States increasingly relied, a strength whose by-products were flows of mathematically trained intellectuals into adjacent fields and the creation of protected sites of quiet political dissent.

- Pockets of privilege for party officials, senior military officers, regional leaders, and key professionals, privilege all the more visible for its contrast with the physical hardships and incessant shortages of Soviet life experienced by most of the population.
- Immense underground networks of mutual assistance, information, evasion, and supply, almost all of them technically illegal, but most of them actually indispensable to the everyday survival of Soviet citizens and enterprises (see Feige, 1998; Ledeneva, 1998; Solnick, 1998).

All of these processes became more visible—and fateful—in the Soviet Union's disintegration.

How did it happen? At the time, Soviet assistance in Afghanistan's left-leaning military coup of 1979 seemed like just one more Cold War contretemps, but it proved crucial. As the United States poured in support for a variety of Afghan rebels, the Soviet military suffered a frustrating and humiliating stalemate. Before Mikhail Gorbachev cut Soviet losses by ratifying a precarious peace in 1988, the Soviet Union was maintaining between 100,000 and 120,000 of its own troops in Afghanistan as well as subsidizing unreliable Afghan forces without advancing against the enemies of its puppet regime.

Within the Soviet Union, the Afghan nightmare, a general economic slowdown, and rising international publicity for Soviet dissidents strengthened the case of would-be reformers in the party hierarchy. In 1985, liberalizer Gorbachev arrived at the party's head with a program of opening up public life: releasing political prisoners, accelerating exit visas for Jews, shrinking the military, reducing external military involvement, and ending violent repression of demands for political, ethnic, and religious autonomy. By 1987, he was promoting *perestroika*, a shift of the economy from military to civilian production, toward better and more abundant consumer goods, and in the direction of much higher productivity. In parallel, Gorbachev announced that the Soviet Union would no longer provide military support to Central European satellite regimes that came under attack from their own citizens.

Reduction of central controls over production and distribution promoted:

- Proliferation of small enterprises.
- Widespread attempts to set up joint ventures with foreign capitalists.
- More open operation of the black markets, gray markets, and mutual aid networks that had long linked individuals, households, and firms.
- Massive slowdowns of payments and goods deliveries to central organizations.
- Substitution of private media and systems of exchange for public means.
- Extensive diversion of government-owned stocks and facilities into profit-making or monopoly-maintaining private distribution networks to the benefit of existing managers, quick-thinking entrepreneurs, and members of organizations already enjoying preferential access to desirable goods, facilities, or foreign currencies.

All this happened as the government was attempting, on the contrary, to generalize and liberate national markets. As a consequence, the capacity of the central state to deliver rewards to its followers declined visibly from one month to the next. In response, officials and managers engaged in what Steven Solnick calls a run on the bank: wherever they could divert fungible assets to their own advantage, they increasingly did so. They set about "stealing the state" (Solnick, 1998).

On the political front, a parallel and interdependent collapse of central authority occurred.

As results of Gorbachev's economic program alienated not only producers who previously had benefited from emphasis on military enterprise, but also consumers who did not have ready access to one of the new distribution networks and officials whose previous powers were now under attack, his political program opened up space for critics and rivals such as Boris Yeltsin. From a Moscow base, Yeltsin rose to control the Russian federation. Gorbachev's own effort to check the threatened but still intact military and intelligence establishments through conciliation, caution, and equivocation encouraged defections of reformers without gaining him solid conservative support. Simultaneously, furthermore, he sought to acquire emergency powers that would free him to forward economic transformation. That brought him into conflict with rival reformers, political libertarians and defenders of the old regime alike. Although demands for guarantees of religious and political liberties arose almost immediately in 1986 and 1987, nevertheless, the rush of nationalities to assure their positions in relation to the emerging new political system destroyed the old regime.

Russia's Communists, after all, had dealt with non-Russian regions by co-opting regional leaders who were loyal to their cause, integrating them into the Communist party, recruiting their successors among the most promising members of designated nationalities but training them in Russia, dispatching many Russians to staff new industries, professions, and administrations, promoting Russian language and culture as media of administration and interregional communication, granting regional power holders substantial autonomy and military support within their own territories just so long as they assured supplies of state revenue, goods, and conscripts, striking immediately against any individual or group that called for liberties outside of this system. Such a system could operate effectively so long as regional leaders received powerful support from the center and their local rivals had no means or hope of appealing for popular backing.

The system's strength also proved to be its downfall. Gorbachev and collaborators simultaneously promoted opening of political discussion, reduced military involvement in political control, tolerated alternatives to the Communist connecting structure, made gestures toward truly contested elections, and acknowledged diminished capacity to reward faithful followers. As that happened, both regional power holders and their rivals suddenly acquired strong incentives to distance themselves from the center, to recruit popular support, to establish their credentials as authentic representatives of the local people, to urge priority of their own nationalities within territorial subdivisions of the USSR they happened to occupy, and to press for new forms of autonomy. In the Baltic republics and those along the USSR's western or southern tiers, furthermore, the possibility of special relations with kindred states and authorities outside the Soviet Union—Sweden, Finland, Turkey, Iran, the European Community, and NATO—offered political leverage and economic opportunity the Union itself was decreasingly capable of providing.

In political subdivisions containing more than one well-organized national population, threats mounted rapidly to those who lost the competition for certification as authentic regional citizens. Those who moved first could gain more. Escalation began, with each concession by the central government giving new incentives and precedents for further demands by other nationalities, increasingly threatening any connected population that shared a distinct identity but failed to mobilize effectively. As early as 1986, demands for autonomy and protection arose not only from Estonians, Latvians, Lithuanians, and Ukrainians, but also from Kazakhs, Crimean Tatars, Armenians, Moldavians, Uzbeks, and Russians themselves. Within such heterogeneous regions as Nagorno-Karabakh, a primarily Armenian enclave within Azerbaijan, militants of neighboring ethnicities battled for priority and did not scruple to kill. In addition to Azerbaijan, Moldavia, Georgia, and Tadjikistan grew mean with intergroup conflict. Between January 1988 and August 1989, ethnic clashes claimed 292 lives, leaving 5520 people injured and 360,000 homeless (Nahaylo & Swoboda, 1990, p. 336). The situation recalled the Empire's disaggregation in 1918.

Time horizons altered rapidly. On the large scale and the small, people could no longer count on payoffs from long-term investment in the existing system; they reoriented to short-term gains and exit strategies. Gorbachev's 1990 proposal of a new union treaty, with greater scope for the 15 republics but preservation of a federal government's military, diplomatic, and economic priority, simply accelerated the efforts of each potential national actor to assure its own position within (or, for that matter, just outside) the new system. When Gorbachev sought validation of his plans in a referendum of March 1991, leaders of six republics (Latvia, Lithuania, Estonia, Moldavia, Armenia, and Georgia, all of which had started the process of declaring themselves independent) boycotted the proceedings, as results for the rest confirmed the division between Russia and the non-Russian portions of the tottering federation. From outside, venture capitalists, development economists, world financial institutions, and great powers such as the United States, Turkey, Iran, and the European Union all strove for their pieces of the action and/or for containment of ugly spillover from Soviet turmoil.

In the face of ethnic disaggregation, economic collapse, and undermining of the old regime's powers, many observers and participants on the Soviet scene feared a bid of the military, intelligence, and Party establishment to reverse the flow of events. History realized their fears. The critical moment arrived in August 1991, when a junta backed by just those elements sequestered Gorbachev at his Crimean holiday retreat on the eve of his signing yet another union treaty for the nine republics that were still collaborating with the central state. Drawn especially from the military, intelligence, and police administrations, plotters declared the seizure of power by a shadowy emergency committee; its control of the state, such as it was, lasted only 3 days.

President Boris Yeltsin of the Russian federation had already been playing the nationalist card against central authority on behalf of Russia. During the abortive coup, Yeltsin braved the army's tanks and spoke to crowds in Moscow, calling for a general strike against the emergency committee. Several military units defected to Yeltsin's side, setting up a defensive line around the Russian republic's Moscow headquarters. The defection and defense shattered the junta's resolve. The attempted coup broke up without armed combat. Gorbachev's captors released him.

On his return, Gorbachev faced a wave of demands for accelerated reform, renewed efforts of organized nationalities to depart from the Union, intensified rivalries from Yeltsin and his counterparts in other republics, and utter collapse of the Kremlin's authority. Resigning as Party head, Gorbachev suspended Party activities throughout the USSR. Over the next 4 months Yeltsin sought to succeed Gorbachev, not as Party secretary but as chief of a confederation maintaining a measure of economic, military, and diplomatic authority. Even that effort ended with dissolution of the Soviet Union into an ill-defined and disputatious Commonwealth from which the Baltic states absented themselves entirely, while others began rushing toward exits.

Once the Soviet regime collapsed, Russian nationalists (including the opportunistic nationalist Yeltsin) faced a fierce dilemma: on the one hand, they claimed the right of Russians to rule the Russian federation, which actually included millions of people from non-Russian minorities. This claim supported the principle that titular nationalities should prevail. On the other hand, they vigorously criticized the treatment of Russians outside the Russian federation— for example, the large numbers of self-identified Russians in Estonia, Lithuania, Ukraine, and Kazakhstan—as second-class minorities facing a choice among assimilation to the titular nationality, lesser forms of citizenship, and emigration (Barrington, 1995). Unsurprisingly, newly independent neighbors often accused the Russian federation's authorities of imperialism.

Mark Beissinger's catalog of protest events from 1987 through 1992 throughout the Soviet Union's space identifies a crucial shift in popular participation. Protest demonstrations increased rapidly in numbers from 1987 to 1989, then reached their peak in 1990, only to swing wildly but in a generally downward direction thereafter. Mass violent events, in contrast, reached a minor peak in mid-1989, but began a powerful upward surge in 1991, remaining frequent through 1992; by 1992, the dominant issue of protest events had become the drawing of borders among republics (Beissinger, 1998, pp. 294–305). The shift corresponded to a switch from relatively peaceful, if massive, demands for reform and national representation to bitterly fought struggles over national rights. State-seeking nationalism (on the part of republics seeking exit from the Union) and state-led nationalism (on the part of republic leaders seeking to establish hegemony within their own territories) interacted powerfully.

As it happens, Beissinger explicitly interprets his events as a cycle of contention, with violence characteristically increasing in the cycle's later stages. Indeed, all four of our mechanisms—opportunity spirals, identity shift, competition, and brokerage—operated with a vengeance in Soviet disintegration. In the Soviet case, several spirals succeeded each other: first bids for external support of profit-making and rent-seeking enterprises under declining central controls, then outright assertions of rights to national autonomy on the parts of existing regional leaders and their local rivals, and finally seizure of fungible state resources by whomever could make off with them. Considering previous images of the Communist system as an unshakable block, identity shift occurred with startling rapidity, with longtime beneficiaries of Communist control backing off from identification with the party and its legacy in favor of a series of improvised alternatives among which ethnic labels (including Russian) assumed ever-increasing scope. Competition operated on two fronts: in attempts to gain external economic and political support; in related attempts to seize organizations and assets previously firmly under state control.

Brokerage may be less obvious, but it made a big difference in two regards. First, it helps account for the remarkable continuity of rulers through apparently revolutionary turmoil. Although gangsters and tycoons have appeared from the shadows of Soviet society, for the most part the people who run things in the former Soviet Union are the same sorts of people— and in many cases the very same people—who ran things during the 1980s. That is because as connectors in a vast centralized system they had privileged access to information, resources, and other centers of power; it was extremely difficult for anyone to match the advantages afforded them by their institutional positions. The second regard is the converse of the first: once regional leaders, entrepreneurs, work groups, and ordinary citizens started to resist yielding goods and services to central authorities, those authorities lost power as brokers; they could no longer redistribute resources to sustain their own positions, their allies, and the activities to which they were most committed. Thus opportunity spirals, identity shifts, competition, and brokerage interacted powerfully.

Notice the crucial importance of history in the actual operation of these mechanisms. Two examples only: First, given the USSR's vast, powerful military establishment, one might have expected the Soviet military to play a pivotal independent role in the transition from socialism. Despite the involvement of military, intelligence, and police officers in the 1991 coup, the military establishment figured only secondarily in the events we have reviewed. The historical creation of a massive governing party out of a fusion of revolutionary activism with military mobilization left the Soviet Union's military impressively subordinated to civilian power holders. (In fact, the military probably wield more autonomous political power in postsocialist

Russia and other fragments of the Union than they did during the 1980s.) Brokerage operated within limits set by previously established organizational relations.

Second, the Stalinist system of rule through titular nationalities had a double effect. In previously independent countries the USSR had incorporated wholesale—notably the Baltic states—even the massive diffusion of Russian-language communication and the substantial migration of ethnic Russian technicians and administrators did not destroy recognized non-Russian political identities. In multicultural, multilingual regions, the establishment of titular nationalities created recognized, dominant political identities where none had previously prevailed. As a consequence, political identities the regime had nurtured (rather than age-old solidarities and hatreds) became the bases of mobilization, opposition, and political reconstitution as the Soviet Union disintegrated. Opportunity spirals, identity shifts, and competition worked in the USSR as they do elsewhere, but as they incorporated and articulated with distinctive historical accumulations they led to rather different outcomes than, say, in the disbanding of the tsarist, Ottoman, or British empires. In this sense, time and place made a huge difference to the operation of very general political processes.

PUZZLING FEATURES
IN CLASSES OF EPISODES

Our third strategy is to identify puzzling features for a whole class of similar episodes, then use systematic comparison with other classes of episodes to locate robust mechanisms and processes producing those puzzling features. Social movements offer an excellent illustration. Whatever else happens in social movements, they center on projection of collective identities. For clarity and compactness, my discussion will concentrate on identity mechanisms and processes within social movements, neglecting their connections with social change, organizational bases, responses to threat and opportunity, forms of action, and strategic interactions (see Tarrow, 1998, for extensive discussions of these matters). It also will interweave comparisons with other classes of episodes instead of setting out those comparisons separately.

Although some analysts use the term "social movement" loosely for any sort of collective popular claim making, both the term and the phenomenon crystallized during the 19th century. The social movement consists of sustained interaction between power holders and activists who speak on behalf of a wronged population through collective public displays of determination and capacity coupled with explicit support for programs of action. At least as concretized in associations, public meetings, demonstrations, marches, petitions, slogans, writings, and statements to the media, no social movements occurred anywhere in the world before the late 18th century. Yet by 1850, social movement activity had become a well-established mode of political action in Western Europe and North America. By the end of the 20th century, the social movement had become a standard form of politics throughout the democratic world.

Oddly, no one has yet written a comprehensive history of this significant political innovation. From more fragmentary studies, nevertheless, some features of the social movement's history emerge: significant coincidence with the expansion of popular elections and parliamentary power; reliance on freedom of association and speech; early salience of labor and religious organizations, followed by proliferation of other special interests; overlap with the growth of interest group politics; displacement of relatively direct, and frequently violent, forms of claim making, by predominantly nonviolent shows of strength; interdependence with the formation of police forces specialized in control of public spaces; significant cross-national transfers of practices and personnel; and internal historical development in prevailing idioms, practices, and organizational structures. Like election campaigns and strikes, social movements have a well-defined political history.

They also present a puzzling feature that has generated plenty of debate but no resolution: Why do social movement participants spend so much of their shared time and organizing effort on public displays of solidarity when they could be engaging in interactions that in the short run are more likely to advance the programs they advocate? Opponents of particular social movements often have asked the question in a hostile mood, wondering out loud why young people waste their effort in disruptive marching and shouting when their elders are quietly doing their best to solve the problems about which the youngsters are complaining. Activists themselves often have split over the choice between concrete ameliorative efforts and contentious public displays of solidarity. Even generally enthusiastic participants ask themselves now and then whether meeting, demonstrating, and chanting slogans have any impact on the evils they seek to combat.

Many observers have thought that solidarity and shared identity bring intrinsic satisfaction, but that explanation ignores both (1) the many occasions on which identity displays offer little more than suffering to the participants, and (2) the effort that leaders invest in coordinating correct public performances in support of claimed identities. Some professional students of social movements have replied to the dilemma by rejecting instrumental accounts, at least for the new social movements of environmentalism, feminism, peace, and sexual preference. Social movements, they say, organize not around practical politics but around the production of new identities.

That critique almost gets things right. Yet it locates the identities in question wrongly. Political identities always erect boundaries between political actors, define relations across the boundaries, and organize relations on either side of the boundaries as well. The crucial mechanisms include those that Soviet experience has already brought to our attention: opportunity spirals, identity shift, competition, and brokerage. But they also include category formation and object shift.

Category formation creates identities. A social category consists of a set of sites that share a boundary distinguishing all of them from and relating all of them to at least one set of sites visibly excluded by the boundary. Category formation occurs by means of three different submechanisms, through invention, borrowing, and encounter. Invention involves authoritative drawing of a boundary and prescription of relations across that boundary, as when Bosnian Serb leaders decree who in Bosnia is a Serb and who not, then regulate how Serbs interact with non-Serbs. Borrowing involves importation of a boundary-cum-relations package already existing elsewhere and its installation in the local setting, as when rural French Revolutionaries divided along the lines patriot/aristocrat that had already split Paris and other major French cities.

Encounter involves initial contact between previously separate (but internally well-connected) networks in the course of which members of one network begin competing for resources with members of the other, interactively generating definitions of the boundary and relations across it. In social movements, invention, borrowing, and encounter all occur, but social movements specialize in combinations of invention and borrowing: creation of the Coalition of *X*s, United Citizens of *Y*, Front against *Z*, each of them paired with some set of authorities.

Object shift significantly affects contentious repertoires. Object shift means alteration in relations between claimants and objects of claims. Object shift often occurs in the short run during the strategic interaction of contention; battling gangs unite against the police, the intervention of an official in a market conflict diverts customers' attacks to him, a besieged tax clerk calls in the mayor. Of course, such shifts commonly alter the actors and the paired identities they deploy, but they likewise affect the forms of collective claim making that are available, appropriate, and likely to be effective. Object shift also occurs over the longer run and outside of contentious interaction. Social movements often involve object shift, as activists move among claims on local authorities, claims on national authorities, competition with rivals, and provision of services to their constituencies.

As we saw in the earlier discussion of certification and decertification, over a wide variety of polities recognition as a valid political actor provides collective benefits distinct from accomplishment of the particular programs around which people rally. Because certification matters, important elements of contentious politics that a strict means–end calculus renders mysterious actually make sense. To make a successful claim of collective worthiness, unity, numbers, and commitment brings recognition as a credible political player with the capacity to make a difference in the next political struggle.

To be sure, individual commitment and interpersonal bonds matter crucially to the collective life of any social movement. What is more, some people do experience intensive satisfaction and establish lifelong ties in social movement activism. Social movement involvement often alters people's own relations to others as well as their sense of who they are. But identity has a public, collective side that does not depend heavily on person-by-person transformation.

On the public side of social movement activity, what are the stakes? Recognition as a valid political actor makes those who represent the collective identity available as allies, carries the implicit threat of independent or disruptive action, and solidifies communication lines both within and across boundaries. In fact, those benefits are sufficiently substantial that, as Robert Michels noted long ago, leaders of recognized political actors often shift into advancing their own interests by means of the organizations and connections they control.

A social movement is a kind of campaign, parallel in many respects to an electoral campaign. This sort of campaign, however, demands righting of a wrong, most often a wrong suffered by a well-specified population. It constructs that population as a category, often as a categorical candidate for polity membership. The population in question can range from a single individual to all humans, or even all living creatures. Whereas an electoral campaign pays off chiefly in the votes that finally result from it, a social movement pays off in effective transmission of the message that its program's supporters are WUNC: (1) worthy, (2) unified, (3) numerous, and (4) committed. The four elements compensate one another to some degree, for example, with a high value on worthiness making up for small numbers. Yet a visibly low value on any one of them (a public demonstration of unworthiness, division, dwindling numbers, and/or outright defection) discredits the whole movement.

Social movement campaigning involves a familiar bundle of performances: creation of associations and coalitions, marches, demonstrations, petitions, public meetings, slogan-shouting, badge-wearing, pamphlet-writing, and more. Seen as means–end action, such a campaign has a peculiar diffuseness; as compared with striking, voting, smashing the loom of a nonstriking weaver, or running a miscreant out of town, its actions remain essentially symbolic, cumulative, and indirect, with almost no chance that any single event will achieve its stated objective of ending an injustice or persuading authorities to enact a needed law. Social movement mobilization gains its strength from an implicit threat to act in adjacent arenas: to withdraw support from public authorities, to provide sustenance to a regime's enemies, to ally with splinter parties, to move toward direct action or even rebellion. Skilled social movement organizers draw tacitly on such threats to bargain with the objects of their demands.

Social movements take place as conversations: not as solo performances but as inter-actions among parties. The most elementary set of parties consists of a claim-making actor, an object of the actor's claims, and an audience having a stake in the fate of at least one of them. Whatever else they do, movements dramatize categorical differences between claimants and objects of claims. But allies, competitors, enemies, authorities, and multiple audiences also frequently play parts in movement interactions. Therein lies the complexity of social move-ment organizing, not to mention of responses by authorities and objects of claims; third parties always complicate the interaction.

Examined from the viewpoint of challengers, social movement success depends in part on two varieties of mystification. First, as they increase, worthiness, unity, numbers, and commitment almost necessarily contradict each other; to gain numbers, for example, generally requires compromise on worthiness, unity, and/or commitment. The actual work of organizers consists recurrently of patching together provisional coalitions, suppressing risky tactics, negotiating which of the multiple agendas participants bring with them will find public voice in their collective action, and above all hiding backstage struggle from public view. They almost always exaggerate their coalition's worthiness, unity, numbers, and commitment.

Second, movement activists seek to present themselves and (if different) the objects of their solicitude as a solidary group, preferably as a group with a long history and with coherent existence outside the world of public claim making. In that regard, they resemble state-seeking nationalists with their constructions of long, coherent, distinctive cultural histories for their nations. Thus feminists identify themselves with women's age-old struggles for rights in the streets and in everyday existence, civil rights leaders minimize class and religious differences within their racial category, and environmentalists present most of humankind as their eternal community.

The two varieties of mystification address several different audiences. They encourage activists and supporters to make high estimates of the probability that fellow adherents will take risks and incur costs for the cause, hence that their own contributions will bear fruit. They warn authorities, objects of claims, opponents, rivals, and bystanders to take the movement seriously as a force that can affect their fates.

Movements differ significantly in the relative attention they give to these various audi-ences, from self-absorbed tests of daring organized by small clusters of terrorists to signature of petitions by transient participants who wish some authority to know their opinion. These orientations frequently vary in the course of a given social movement, for example, in transitions from (1) internal building to (2) ostentatious action to (3) fighting off competitors and enemies.

Mystification does not mean utter falsehood. Activists and constituents of social move-ments vary considerably in the extent to which they actually embody worthiness, unity, numbers, and commitment, in the degree to which they spring from a single solidary group with collective life outside the world of public politics. To the extent that the two varieties of mystification contain elements of truth, furthermore, social movements generally mobilize more effectively. A segregated ethnic community threatened by outside attack, on the average, mobilizes more readily than does the entire category consisting of all those who suffer from diverse attacks on civil liberties.

The process whereby social movement activists achieve recognition as valid interlocutors for unjustly deprived populations does not resemble the fact-finding inquiries of novelists, social scientists, or investigative reporters. It resembles a court proceeding, in which those who make such claims, however self-evident to them, must establish themselves in the eyes of others—authorities, competitors, enemies, and relevant audiences—as voices that require attention and must commonly establish themselves in the face of vigorous opposition. They must prove that they qualify. Almost all such proofs entail suppression of some evidence and exaggeration of other evidence concerning the claimants' worthiness, unity, numbers, commitment, and grounding in a durable, coherent, solidary, deprived population. Again, resemblances to state-seeking nationalism immediately strike the mind's eye.

Analysts of collective action, especially those who entertain sympathy for the actions they are studying, often insist on these mystified elements as intrinsic to social movements: the presence of solidarity, the construction of shared identities, the sense of grievance, the creation of sustaining organizations, and more; without such features, analysts say, we have nothing but ordinary politics. Sometimes the myths fulfill themselves, building up the lineaments of durable connection among core participants. But most social movements remain far more contingent and volatile than their mystifications allow; these other elements do not define the social movement as a distinctive political phenomenon.

What does? Social movements involve collective claims on authorities. A social movement consists of a sustained challenge to power holders in the name of a population living under the jurisdiction of those power holders by means of repeated public displays of that population's numbers, commitment, unity, and worthiness. We, the aggrieved, demand that you, perpetrators of evil or responsible authorities, act to alleviate a condition about which we are justly indignant. Although some of our actions may express support for proposals, programs, or persons that are already advancing our aims, most of our displays dramatize not only our own WUNC, but also the existence of conditions we oppose.

As they developed in Great Britain and other West European countries during the early 19th century, characteristic social movement displays included creation of special purpose associations, lobbying of officials, public meetings, demonstrations, marches, petitions, pamphlets, statements in mass media, posting or wearing of identifying signs, and deliberate adoption of distinctive slogans; while their relative weight varied considerably from movement to movement, these elements have coexisted since the early 19th century.

Note the importance of invention. For all its contentiousness, most of human history has proceeded without social movements, without sustained challenges to power holders in the names of populations living under the jurisdiction of those power holders by means of repeated public displays of those populations' numbers, commitment, unity, and worthiness. Rebellions, revolutions, avenging actions, rough justice, and many other forms of popular collective action have abounded, but not the associating, meeting, marching, petitioning, propagandizing, sloganeering, and brandishing of symbols that mark social movements.

With some 18th-century precedents, this complex of interactions emerge as a way of doing political business in Western Europe and North America during the 19th century; however we finally sort out the priorities, Britain shares credit for the invention. In Great Britain, the actual inventors were political entrepreneurs such as John Wilkes, Lord George Gordon, William Cobbett, and Francis Place. They, their collaborators, and their followers bargained out space for new forms of political action; bargained it out with local and national authorities, with rivals, with enemies, and with objects of their claims.

Social movements, then, center on construction of categorical identities. Identities in general are shared experiences of distinctive social relations and representations of those social relations. Workers become workers in relation to employers and other workers, women become women in relation to men and other women, Orthodox Jews become Orthodox Jews in relation to non-Jews, non-Orthodox Jews, and other Orthodox Jews.

Like social movements, nationalism and religious qualifications for citizenship involve the construction and enforcement of unequal paired categories. Clearly the study of identities in social movements leads directly to comparisons with identity mechanisms and processes in quite different classes of episodes.

ANALOGIES AMONG OSTENSIBLY
DISSIMILAR EPISODES

The fourth analytical strategy for historical treatment of political processes consists of identifying partial causal analogies among ostensibly dissimilar episodes and classes of episodes by locating the same mechanisms and processes within them. In fact, we have been pursuing that analytical strategy through the three previous examples. Consider the major causal mechanisms we have encountered along the way: certification, decertification, identity shift, object shift, opportunity spirals, competition, and brokerage. They constitute a small but widely applicable bundle of identity-shaping mechanisms. They certainly appear recurrently in episodes of nationalism, imperial disintegration, and social movements. They reappear, however, in unexpected places: in civil wars when each party claims to be the authentic embodiment of the rightful government, in revolutions when insurgents claim to speak for the oppressed, in state formation when one authority among many manages to eliminate or subordinate the rest, in democratization when previously excluded political actors acquire voice. Across a wide range of political processes, certification, decertification, identity shift, object shift, opportunity spirals, competition, and brokerage operate in similar fashions, with vastly dissimilar overall consequences.

Let me stress that conclusion. The mechanism-based program of inquiry into historical political processes does not return surreptitiously to the discovery of recurrent structures and processes on the large scale. It denies the possibility of general models and complete explanations for whole political episodes. It also negates the idea that war, revolution, social movements, nationalism, and democratization constitute phenomena *sui generis*, each springing in its own characteristic way from a distinctive set of causes. It concedes that as political constructions one war influences the next, one revolution influences the next, and so on. But that construction of politically meaningful forms and its consequences for political action become part of what historical analysts must explain.

Sociologists who take this program of inquiry seriously will have to abandon ingrained practices: creating *sui generis* models of major political processes, choosing among covering law, propensity, and system accounts of explanation; imagining history as a storage bin of raw materials for testing of contemporary political models; rejecting explanations because they neglect favorite variables; and supposing that exhaustion of variance is the criterion of solid explanation. Those who dare have a world to gain.

ACKNOWLEDGMENTS: I have adapted a few passages from the current draft of Doug McAdam, Sidney Tarrow, and Charles Tilly (2001), *Dynamics of Contention*, and more from material I originally prepared for that volume but later cut for lack of space. I also have adapted some passages from *Durable Inequality* (Tilly).

REFERENCES

Azar, E., & Ben-Dak, J. (Eds.). (1973). *Theory and practice of events research*. New York: Gordon & Breach.
Barkey, K., & von Hagen, M. (Eds.). (1997). *After empire. Multiethnic societies and nation-building*. Boulder, CO: Westview.
Barrington, L. (1995). The domestic and international consequences of citizenship in the Soviet successor states, *Europe-Asia Studies, 47*, 731–763.

Bearman, P., Faris, R., & Moody, J. (1999). Blocking the future: New solutions for old problems in historical social science. *Social Science History, 23*, 501–534.

Beissinger, M. (1998). Event analysis in transitional societies: Protest mobilization in the former soviet union. In D. Rucht, R. Koopmans, & F. Neidhardt (Eds.), *Acts of dissent. New developments in the study of protest* (pp. 284–316). Berlin: Sigma.

Brockett, C. D. (1992). Measuring political violence and land inequality in Central America. *American Political Science Review, 86*, 169–176.

Bunge, M. (1997). Mechanism and explanation. *Philosophy of the Social Sciences, 27*, 410–465.

Bunge, M. (1998). *Social science under debate: A philosophical perspective*. Toronto: University of Toronto Press.

Cioffi-Revilla, C. (1990). *The scientific measurement of international conflict. Handbook of datasets on crises and wars, 1495–1988 AD*. Boulder, CO: Lynne Rienner.

Diani, M., & Eyerman, R. (Eds.). (1992). *Studying collective action*. Newbury Park, CA: Sage.

Elster, J. (1989). *Nuts and bolts for the social sciences*. Cambridge: Cambridge University Press.

Favre, P., Fillieule, O, & Mayer, N. (1997). La fin d'une étrange lacune de la sociologie des mobilisations. L'étude par sondage des manifestants. Fondements théoriques et solutions techniques. *Revue Française de Science Politique, 47*, 3–28.

Feige, E. (1998). Underground activity and institutional change: Productive, protective, and predatory behavior in transition economies. In J. M. Nelson, C. Tilly, & L. Walker (Eds.), *Transforming Post-Communist Political Economies* (pp. 21–34). Washington, DC: National Academy Press.

Franzosi, R. (1998). Narrative as data: Linguistic and statistical tools for the quantitative study of historical events. *International Review of Social History, 43* (Suppl. 6), 81–104.

Gurr, T. R., & Harff, B. (1994). *Ethnic conflict in world politics*. Boulder, CO: Westview.

Hanagan, M. P., Moch, L. P., & te Brake, W. (Eds.). (1998). *Challenging authority. The historical study of contentious politics*. Minneapolis: University of Minnesota Press.

Hedström, P., & Swedberg, R. (Eds.). (1998). *Social mechanisms. An analytical approach to social theory*. Cambridge: Cambridge University Press.

Ledeneva, A. V. (1998). *Russia's economy of favours. Blat, networking and informal exchange*. Cambridge: Cambridge University Press.

Little, D. (1991). *Varieties of social explanation. An introduction to the philosophy of social science*. Boulder, CO: Westview.

Little, D. (1998). *On the philosophy of the social sciences. Microfoundations, method, and causation*. New Brunswick, NJ: Transaction.

McAdam, D., Tarrow, S., & Tilly, C. (2001). *Dynamics of contention*. Cambridge, UK: Cambridge University Press.

Mann, M. (1986, 1993). *The Sources of Social Power I. A History of Power from the Beginning to AD 1760*; II. *The Rise of Classes and Nation-States, 1760–1914*. Cambridge: Cambridge University Press.

Marx, A. W. (1998). *Making race and nation. A Comparison of the United States, South Africa, and Brazil*. Cambridge: Cambridge University Press.

Michels, R. (1949). *Political parties*. Glencoe, IL: Free Press. (Original publication 1915).

Mueller, C. (1997). International press coverage of East German protest events, 1989. *American Sociological Review, 62*, 820–832.

Nahaylo, B., & Swoboda, V. (1990). *Soviet disunion. A history of the nationalities problem in the USSR*. New York: Free Press

Oliver, P. E., & Myers, D. J. (1999). How events enter the public sphere: Conflict, location, and sponsorship in local newspaper coverage of public events. *American Journal of Sociology, 105*, 38–87.

Olzak, S. (1989). Analysis of events in the study of collective action. *Annual Review of Sociology, 15*, 119–141.

Ringmar, E. (1996). *Identity, interest and action. A cultural explanation of Sweden's intervention in the Thirty Years War*. Cambridge: Cambridge University Press.

Rucht, D., & Koopmans, R. (Eds.). (1999). Protest event analysis. *Mobilization, 4*(2), (entire issue).

Rucht, D., Koopmans, R., & Neidhardt, F. (Eds.). (1998). *Acts of dissent. New developments in the study of protest*. Berlin: Sigma Rainer Bohn Verlag.

Scott, J. C. (1998). *Seeing like a state. How certain schemes to improve the human condition have failed*. New Haven, CT: Yale University Press.

Shapiro, G., & Markoff, J. (1998). *Revolutionary demands. A content analysis of the Cahiers de Doléances of 1789*. Stanford, CA: Stanford University Press.

Sider, G., & Smith, G. (Eds.). (1997). *Between history and histories. The making of silences and commemorations*. Toronto: University of Toronto Press.

Skocpol, T. (Ed.). (1998) *Democracy, revolution, and history*. Ithaca, NY: Cornell University Press.

Small, M., & Singer, J. D. (1982). *Resort to arms. International and civil wars, 1816–1980*. Beverly Hills, CA: Sage.

Solnick, S. L. (1998). *Stealing the state: Control and collapse in Soviet institutions*. Cambridge, MA: Harvard University Press.

Stinchcombe, A. L. (1991). The conditions of fruitfulness of theorizing about mechanisms in social science. *Philosophy of the Social Sciences, 21*, 367–388.

Sugimoto, Y. (1981). *Popular disturbance in postwar Japan*. Hong Kong: Asian Research Service.

Tambiah, S. J. (1996). *Leveling crowds. Ethnonationalist conflicts and collective violence in South Asia*. Berkeley: University of California Press.

Tarrow, S. (1998). *Power in movement*. New York: Cambridge University Press.

Tilly, C. (1998). *Durable inequality*. Berkeley: University of California Press.

Tilly, C., & Rule, J. (1965). *Measuring political upheaval*. Princeton, NJ: Center of International Studies.

White, R. W. (1993). On measuring political violence: Northern Ireland, 1969 to 1980. *American Sociological Review, 58*, 575–585.

CHAPTER 27

World-Systems Theorizing

CHRISTOPHER CHASE-DUNN

The intellectual history of world-systems theorizing has roots in classical sociology, Marxian revolutionary theory, geopolitical strategizing, and theories of social evolution. But in explicit form the world-systems perspective emerged only in the 1970s when Samir Amin, Andre Gunder Frank, and Immanuel Wallerstein began to formulate the concepts and to narrate the analytic history of the modern world system. Especially for Wallerstein (1974), it was explicitly a perspective rather than a theory or a set of theories. A terminology was deployed to tell the story. The guiding ideas were explicitly *not* a set of precisely defined concepts being used to formulate theoretical explanations. Universalistic theoretical explanations were rejected and the historicity of all social science was embraced.[1] Indeed, Wallerstein radically collapsed the metatheoretical opposites of nomothetic ahistoricism/ideographic historicism into the contradictory unity of "historical systems." Efforts to formalize a theory or theories out of the resulting analytic narratives are only confounded if they assume that the changing meanings of "concepts" are unintentional.[2] Rather, there has been sensitivity to context and difference that has abjured specifying definitions and formalizing propositions.

Yet it has been possible to adopt a more nomothetic and systemic stance and then to proceed with world-systems theorizing with the understanding that this is a principled difference from more historicist world-systems scholars. Indeed, world-systems scholars, as with other macrosociologists, may be arrayed along a continuum from purely nomothetic ahistoricism to completely descriptive idiographic historicism. The possible metatheoretical stances are not two, but many, depending on the extent to which different institutional realms are thought to be lawlike or contingent and conjunctural. Fernand Braudel was more historicist than Wallerstein. Amin, an economist, is more nomothetic. Giovanni Arrighi's (1994) monumental work on 600 years of "systemic cycles of accumulation," sees qualitative differences in each hegemony, while Wallerstein, despite his aversion to explicating models, sees rather

---

[1]But see Hopkins and Wallerstein (1982).

[2]Thomas Richard Shannon's (1996) *Introduction to the World-Systems Perspective* remains the most valuable tool for introducing the main ideas to undergraduates. But Shannon displays a misplaced exasperation when he encounters apparently inconsistent terminological usages in Wallerstein's work. This is because Shannon's effort to explicate assumes a single and unvarying set of meanings, while Wallerstein allows his vocabulary to adapt to the historical context that it is being used to analyze.

CHRISTOPHER CHASE-DUNN • Department of Sociology, University of California, Riverside, California 92521.

Handbook of Sociological Theory, edited by Jonathan H. Turner. Kluwer Academic / Plenum Publishers, New York, 2002.

more continuity in the logic of the system, even extending to the most recent era of globalization. Gunder Frank (Frank & Gills, 1993) now claims that there was no transition to capitalism,
and that the logic of "capital imperialism" has not changed since the emergence of cities and
states in Mesopotamia 5000 years ago. Metatheory comes before theory. It focuses our theoretical spotlight on some questions while leaving others in the shadows. No overview of world-
systems theorizing can ignore the issue of metatheoretical stances on the problem of systemness.

In this chapter I will provide an intentionally inclusive characterization of the late 20th-
century cultural artifact that is designated by the words "world-systems/world system scholarship" (with and without the hyphen). Some reflections on the intellectual ancestors of this
artifact are included in the discussion below. An earlier overview of the several heritages that
provoked world-systems theorizing is to be found in Chase-Dunn (1998, Introduction). I also
will outline my own view as to where world-systems theorizing ought to be going. In his
instructions to the chapter authors of this *Handbook of Sociological Theory*, Jonathan Turner
(personal communication, January 8, 1999) said "... I am less interested in summaries of a
theoretical orientation per se than in what you are doing theoretically in this area." Thus the
theoretical research program I have been constructing with Tom Hall (Chase-Dunn & Hall,
1997) and my foray into praxis with Terry Boswell (Boswell & Chase-Dunn, 2000) will loom
large in what follows.

WHAT IT IS

The hyphen emphasizes the idea of the whole system, the point being that all the human
interaction networks small and large, from the household to global trade, constitute the world-
system. It is not just a matter of "international relations." This converts the internal–external
problem of the causes of social change into an empirical question. The world-systems
perspective emphatically does not deny the possibility of agency because everything is alleged
to be determined by the global system. What it does is to make it possible to understand where
agency is more likely to be successful and where not. This said, the hyphen also has come to
connote a degree of loyalty to Wallerstein's approach. Other versions often drop the hyphen.
Hyphen or not, the world(-)systems approach has long been far more internally differentiated
than most of its critics have understood.

The world-systems approach looks at human institutions over long periods of time and
employs the spatial scale that is necessary for comprehending whole interaction systems. It is
neither Eurocentric nor core-centric, at least in principle. The main idea is simple: Human
beings on Earth have been interacting with one another in important ways over broad expanses
of space since the emergence of ocean-going transportation in the 15th century. Before the
incorporation of the Americas into the Afroeurasian system there were many local and
regional world-systems (intersocietal networks). Most of these were inserted into the expanding European-centered system largely by force and their populations were mobilized to supply
labor for a colonial economy that was repeatedly reorganized according to the changing
geopolitical and economic forces emanating from the European and (later) North American
core societies.

This whole process can be understood structurally as a stratification system composed of
economically and politically dominant core societies (themselves in competition with one
another) and dependent peripheral and semiperipheral regions, some of which have been
successful in improving their positions in the larger core–periphery hierarchy, while most
have simply maintained their relative positions.

This structural perspective on world history allows us to analyze the cyclical features of social change and the long-term trends of development in historical and comparative perspective. We can see the development of the modern world-system as driven primarily by capitalist accumulation and geopolitics in which businesses and states compete with one another for power and wealth. Competition among states and capitals is conditioned by the dynamics of struggle among classes and by the resistance of peripheral and semiperipheral peoples to domination from the core. In the modern world-system the semiperiphery is composed of large and powerful countries in the Third World (e.g., Mexico, India, Brazil, China) as well as smaller countries that have intermediate levels of economic development (e.g., the East Asian newly industrialized countries). It is not possible to understand the history of social change in the system as a whole without taking into account both the strategies of the winners and the strategies and organizational actions of those who have resisted domination and exploitation.

It also is difficult to understand why and where innovative social change emerges without a conceptualization of the world-system as a whole. As with earlier regional intersocietal systems, new organizational forms that transform institutions and lead to upward mobility most often emerge from societies in semiperipheral locations. Thus all the countries that became hegemonic core states in the modern system formerly have been semiperipheral (the Dutch, the British, and the United States). This is a continuation of a long-term pattern of social evolution that Chase-Dunn and Hall (1997) call "semiperipheral development." Semiperipheral marcher states and semiperipheral capitalist city-states had acted as the main agents of empire formation and commercialization for millennia. This phenomenon arguably also includes the semiperipheral communist states as well as future organizational innovations in semiperipheral countries that will transform the now-global system.

This approach requires that we think structurally. We must be able to abstract from the particularities of the game of musical chairs that constitutes uneven development in the system to see the structural continuities. The core–periphery hierarchy remains, though some countries have moved up or down. The interstate system remains, though the internationalization of capital has further constrained the abilities of states to structure national economies. States have always been subjected to larger geopolitical and economic forces in the world-system, and as is still the case, some have been more successful at exploiting opportunities and protecting themselves from liabilities than others.

In this perspective many of the phenomena that have been called "globalization" correspond to recently expanded international trade, financial flows, and foreign investment by transnational corporations and banks. The globalization discourse generally assumes that until recently there were separate national societies and economies and that these have now been superseded by an expansion of international integration driven by information and transportation technologies. Rather than a wholly unique and new phenomenon, globalization is primarily international economic integration, and as such it is a feature of the world-system that has been oscillating as well as increasing for centuries. Chase-Dunn, Kawano, and Brewer (2000) have shown that trade globalization is both a cycle and a trend.

The Great Chartered Companies of the 17th century already were playing an important role in shaping the development of world regions. Certainly the transnational corporations of the present are much more important players, but the point is that "foreign investment" is not an institution that only became important since 1970 (nor since World War II). Giovanni Arrighi (1994) has shown that finance capital has been a central component of the commanding heights of the world-system since the 14th century. The current floods and ebbs of world money are typical of the late phase of very long "systemic cycles of accumulation."

An inclusive bounding of the circle of world(-)system scholarship should include all those who see the global system of the late 20th century as having important systemic continuities with the nearly global system of the 19th century. While this is a large and inter-disciplinary group, the temporal depth criterion excludes a large number of students of globalization who see such radical recent discontinuities that they need know nothing about what happened before 1960.

A second criterion that might be invoked to draw a boundary around world(-)systems scholarship is a concern for analyzing international stratification, what some world-systemists call the core–periphery hierarchy. Certainly this was a primary focus for Wallerstein, Amin, and the classical Gunder Frank. These progenitors themselves were influenced by the Latin American dependency school and by the Third Worldism of *Monthly Review* Marxism. Wallerstein was an Africanist when he discovered Fernand Braudel and Marion Malowist and the earlier dependent development of Eastern Europe. The epiphany that Latin America and Africa were like Eastern Europe—that they all had been peripheralized by core exploitation and domination over a period of centuries—mushroomed into the idea of the whole stratified system.

It is possible to have good temporal depth but still to ignore the periphery and the dynamics of global inequalities. The important theoretical and empirical work of political scientists George Modelski and William R. Thompson (1996) is an example. Modelski and Thompson theorize a "power cycle" in which "system leaders" rise and fall since the Portu-guese led European expansion in the 15th century. They also study the important phenomenon of "new lead industries" and the way in which the Kondratieff wave, a 40- to 60-year business cycle, is regularly related to the rise and decline of "system leaders." Modelski and Thompson largely ignore core–periphery relations to concentrate on the "great powers." But so does Giovanni Arrigui's (1994) masterful 600-year examination of "systemic cycles of accumula-tion."[3] Gunder Frank's (1998) latest reinvention, an examination of Chinese centrality in the Afroeurasian world system and the abrupt rise of European power around 1800, also largely ignores core–periphery dynamics.

So too does the "world polity school" led by sociologist John W. Meyer. This institu-tionalist approach adds a valuable sensitivity to the civilizational assumptions of Western Christendom and their diffusion from the core to the periphery. But rather than a dynamic struggle with authentic resistance from the periphery and the semiperiphery, the world polity school stresses how the discourses of resistance, national self-determination, and individual liberties are constructed out of the assumptions of the European Enlightenment.

I contend that leaving out the core–periphery dimension or treating the periphery as inert are grave mistakes, not only for reasons of completeness, but because the dynamics of all hierarchical world-systems involve a process of semiperipheral development in which a few societies "in the middle" innovate and implement new technologies of power that drive the processes of expansion and transformation. But I would not exclude scholars from the circle because of this mistake. Much is to be learned from those who focus primarily on the core.

It often is assumed that world-systems must necessarily be of large geographical scale. But systemness means that groups are tightly wound, so that an event in one place has important consequences for people in another place. By that criterion, intersocietal systems have only become global (Earth-wide) with the emergence of intercontinental seafaring. Earlier world-systems were smaller regional affairs. An important determinant of system size is the kind of transportation and communications technologies that are available. At the very

---

[3]The more recent work by Arrigui and Silver (1999) reintroduces the consideration of core–periphery and class struggle dynamics.

small extreme we have intergroup networks of sedentary foragers who primarily used "back-packing" to transport goods. This kind of hauling produces rather local networks. Such small systems still existed until the 19th century in some regions of North America and Australia (e.g., Chase-Dunn & Mann, 1998). But they were similar in many respects with small world-systems all over the Earth before the emergence of states. An important theoretical task is to specify how to bound the spatial scale of human interaction networks. Working this out makes it possible to compare small, medium-sized, and large world-systems and to use world-systems concepts to rethink theories of human social evolution on a millennial time scale.

Anthropologists and archaeologists have been doing just that. Kasja Ekholm and Jonathan Friedman (1982) have pioneered what they have called "global anthropology," by which they mean regional intersocietal systems that expanded to become the Earth-wide system of today. Archaeologists studying the US Southwest, provoked by the theorizing and excavations of Charles DiPeso, began using world-systems concepts to understand regional relations and interactions with Mesoamerica. It was archaeologist Phil Kohl (1987) who first applied and critiqued the idea of core–periphery relations in ancient Western Asia and Mesopotamia. Guillermo Algaze's (1993) *The Uruk World System* is a major contribution as is Gil Stein's (1999) careful examination of the relationship between his village on the upper Tigris and the powerful Uruk core state. Stein develops important new concepts for understanding core–periphery relations.[4] Research and theoretical debates among Mesoamericanists also have mushroomed. Peter Peregrine's (1992, 1995) innovative interpretation of the Mississippian world-system as a Friedmanesque prestige goods system has cajoled and provoked the defenders of local turf to reconsider the possibilities of larger-scale interaction networks in the territory that eventually became the United States of America (e.g., Neitzel, 1999).[5]

THE COMPARATIVE
WORLD-SYSTEMS PERSPECTIVE

Tom Hall and I have entered the fray by formulating a theoretical research program based on a reconceptualization of the world-systems perspective for the purposes of comparing the contemporary global system with earlier regional intersocietal systems (Chase-Dunn & Hall, 1997). We contend that world-systems, not single societies, always have been the relevant units in which processes of structural reproduction and transformation have occurred, and we have formulated a single model for explaining the changing scale and nature of world-systems over the past 12,000 years.[6]

---

[4]Stein's polemical use as a straw man of the alleged necessity of all world-systems to have very exploitative and spatially extensive core–periphery hierarchies is an unnecessary distraction from an otherwise intriguing analysis.
[5]This archaeological world-systems literature is reviewed in Hall and Chase-Dunn (1993).
[6]Though we are sociologists, we long have engaged in serious dialogue with social scientists from other disciplines, especially archaeologists, ethnographers, political scientists, historians and geographers. Our original intent may have been to raid these *auslanders* for their data, but in learning the required foreign languages we also have learned how the other tribes think, and our own thinking has been subsequently reconstituted. Our reconceptualization of world-systems concepts is obviously indebted to those who created the world-systems perspective: Fernand Braudel, Immanuel Wallerstein, Samir Amin, Andre Gunder Frank, and Giovanni Arrigui. We also draw heavily upon the evolutionary work of Marshall Sahlins, Morton Fried, Marvin Harris, Robert Carneiro, Robert Cohen, Patrick Kirch, and Stephen Sanderson. Our formulation was greatly influenced by world historians, especially William McNeill and Philip Curtin. The sociologists who have most influenced us have been Gerhard Lenski, Randall Collins, Janet Abu-Lughod, and Michael Mann. The geographers who inspired us were Owen Lattimore, David Harvey, and Peter

Institutional Materialism

Due in part to its multidisciplinary sources of inspiration, our formulation bridges many disciplinary chasms. The term we now use for our general approach is "institutional materialism." We see human social evolution as produced by an interaction among demographic, ecological, and economic forces and constraints that is expanded and modified by the institutional inventions that people devise to solve problems and to overcome constraints. Solving problems at one level usually leads to the emergence of new problems, and so the basic constraints are never really overcome, at least so far. This is what allows us to construct a single basic model that represents the major forces that have shaped social evolution over the last 12 millennia.

This perspective is obviously indebted to the "cultural materialism" of Marvin Harris and its elaboration by Robert Cohen, Robert Carneiro, and Stephen Sanderson. Our approach to conceptualizing and mapping world-systems is greatly indebted to David Wilkinson, though we have changed both his terminology and his meaning to some extent (see Chapters 1–3 in Chase-Dunn & Hall, 1997).

It is the whole package that is new, not its parts. We contend that world-systems have evolved because of the basic demographic, ecological, and economic forces emphasized by cultural materialism, but we do not thereby adopt the formalist and rational choice individual psychology that is bundled with the cultural materialism of Harris and Sanderson. Our approach is more institutional because we contend that there have been qualitatively different logics of accumulation (kin-based, tributary, and capitalist) and that these have transformed the nature of the social self and personality, as well as forms of calculation and rationality. We remain partisans of Polanyi's (1977) substantive approach to the embeddedness of economies in cultures. This does not mean that we subscribe to the idea that rationality was an invention of the modern world. We agree with Harris and Sanderson and many anthropologists that people in all societies are economic maximizers for themselves and their families, at least in a general sense. But it also is important to note the differences in the cultural constructions of personality, especially as between egalitarian and hierarchical societies. Here we follow the general line explicated by Jonathan Friedman (1994).

Semiperipheral Development

We also add the important hypothesis of semiperipheral development: that semiperipheral regions are fertile locations of the emergence of new innovations and transformational actors. This is the main basis of our claim that world-systems are the most important unit of analysis for explaining social evolution.

As we have said above, the units of analysis in which our model is alleged to operate are world-systems. These are defined as networks of interaction that have important, regularized consequences for reproducing and changing local social structures.[7] By this definition many small-scale regional world-systems have merged or been incorporated over the last 12,000 years into a single global system.

Taylor. From political science we have been most greatly influenced by George Modelski, William R. Thompson, and David Wilkinson. From archaeology Richard Blanton, Gary Feinman, Philip Kohl, Kristian Kristiansen, Robert Mc C. Adams, Joseph Tainter, and Peter Peregrine have inspired us. The ethnographers who have most influenced our theory are Jane Schneider, Kasja Ekholm, and Jonathan Friedman. Economist Ester Boserup also contributed greatly to our understanding of population pressure and evolution.

[7]Chase-Dunn and Hall (1997) proposed a set of nested networks for spatially bounding world-systems.

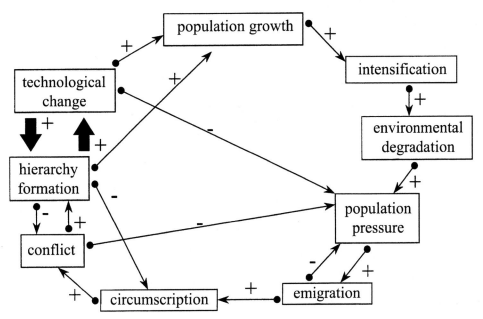

FIGURE 27.1. Basic iteration model.

The Iteration Model

Our basic explanatory model shows what we think are the main sources of causation in the development of more hierarchical and complex social structures, as well as technological changes in the processes of production. We call our schema an "iteration model" because the variables both cause and are caused by the main processes. It is a positive feedback model in which systemic expansion, hierarchy formation, and technological development are explained as consequences of population pressure, and in turn they cause population growth, and so the sequences of causes goes around again.[8] We use the term "iteration" because the positive feedback feature repeats the same process over and over on an expanding spatial scale. Figure 27.1 illustrates the variables and our hypotheses about the causal relations among them. Positive arrows signify that a variable increases another variable. Negative arrows indicate that a variable decreases another variable. Thicker arrows indicate stronger effects.

The model is not alleged to characterize what has happened in all world-systems. Many have gotten stuck at one level of hierarchy formation or technological development. Our model accounts for instances in which hierarchy formation and technological development occurred. There were many systems in which these outcomes did not occur. Our claim is not that every system evolved in the same way. Rather, we hold that those systems in which greater complexity and hierarchy and new technologies did emerge went through the processes described in our model.

At the top of Fig. 27.1 is *population growth*. We realize that procreation is socially regulated in all societies, but we contend, following Marvin Harris, that restricting population growth, especially by premodern methods, was always costly, and so the moral order tended to

[8]We have modified our specification of the iteration model slightly from what was presented in Chapter 6 of *Rise and Demise* (Chase-Dunn & Hall, 1997) in order to clarify the distinction between intensification and technological change.

let up when conditions temporarily improved. This led to a long-run tendency for population to grow. Population growth leads to *intensification*, defined by Marvin Harris (1977, p. 5) as "the investment of more soil, water, minerals, or energy per unit of time or area." Intensification of production leads to *environmental degradation* as the raw material inputs become scarcer and the unwanted byproducts of human activity modify the environment. Together intensification and environmental degradation lead to rising costs of producing the food and raw materials that people need, and this condition is called *population pressure*. In order to feed more people, hunters must travel farther because the game nearest to home becomes exhausted. Thus the cost in time and effort of bringing home a given amount of food increases. Some resources are less subject to depletion than others (e.g., fish compared to big game), but increased use usually causes eventual rising costs. Other types of environmental degradation are due to the side effects of production, such as the buildup of wastes and pollution of water sources. These also increase the costs of continued production or cause other problems.

As long as there were available lands to occupy, the consequences of population pressure led to *migration*. So humans populated the whole Earth. The costs of migration are a function of the availability of desirable alternative locations and the effective resistance to immigration that is mounted by those who already live in these locations.

Circumscription (Carneiro, 1970) occurs when the costs of leaving are higher than the costs of staying. This is a function of available lands, but lands are differentially desirable depending on the technologies that the migrants employ. Generally people have preferred to live in the way that they have lived in the past, but population pressure or other push factors can cause them to adopt new technologies in order to occupy new lands. The factor of resistance from extant occupants also is a complex matter of similarities and differences in technology, social organization, and military techniques between the occupants and the groups seeking to immigrate. When the incoming group knows a technique of production that can increase the productivity of the land (such as horticulture), they may be able to peacefully convince the existing occupants to coexist for a share of the expanded product (Renfrew, 1987).[9] Circumscription increases the likelihood of higher levels of conflict in a situation of population pressure because, though the costs of staying are great, the exit option is closed off. This can lead to several different kinds of warfare, but also to increasing intrasocietal struggles and conflicts (civil war, class antagonisms, clan war, etc.) A period of intense conflict tends to reduce population pressure if significant numbers of people are killed off. Some systems get stuck in a vicious cycle in which warfare and other forms of conflict operate as the demographic regulator, e.g., the Marquesas Islands (Kirch, 1991). This cycle corresponds to the path that goes from population pressure to migration to circumscription to conflict, and then a negative arrow back to population pressure. When population again builds up, the circle goes around again.

Under the right conditions a circumscribed situation in which the level of conflict has been high will be the locus of the emergence of more hierarchical institutions. Carneiro (1970) and Mann (1986) contend that people will tend to run away from hierarchy if they can in order to maintain autonomy and equality. But circumscription raises the costs of exit, and exhaustion from prolonged or extreme conflict may make a new level of hierarchy the least bad alternative. It often is better to accept a king than to continue fighting. So kings (and big men, chiefs, and emperors) emerged out of situations in which conflict has reduced the resistance to

---

[9]But there also are cases in which the technological differential and other differences are too great, and so the incoming group exterminates the locals instead of incorporating them. Such was the outcome in Northern California (Chase-Dunn & Mann, 1998) and in many other regions in North America.

centralized power. This is quite different from the usual portrayal of those who hold to the functional theory of stratification. The world-system insight here is that the newly emergent elites often come from regions that have been semiperipheral.

Semiperipheral actors are unusually able to put together effective campaigns for erecting new levels of hierarchy. This may involve both innovations in the "techniques of power" and innovations in productive technology (*technological change*). Newly emergent elites often implement new production technologies as well as new waves of intensification. This, along with the more peaceful regulation of access to resources organized by the new elites, creates the conditions for a new round of population growth, which brings us around to the top of Fig. 27.1 again.

Shortcutting: How Institutional Inventions Modified the Iteration Model

We also contend that the institutional inventions made and spread by semiperipheral actors qualitatively transform the logic of accumulation and alter the operation of the variables in the iteration model. But these qualitative changes are themselves the consequence of people trying to solve the basic problems produced by the forces and constraints contained in the model. The model displayed in Fig. 27.1 best explains the independent rise of complex chiefdoms, class distinctions, and states in at least four different regional world-systems. But these institutional adaptations modified to some extent the operation of the variables in the model. Likewise, the long rise of commercialization and capitalism again modified the operation of the processes and added new causal arrows to the basic model.

Figure 27.2 illustrates in a general way what we think happened with the emergence of new modes of accumulation, especially states and capitalism. The new modes allowed some

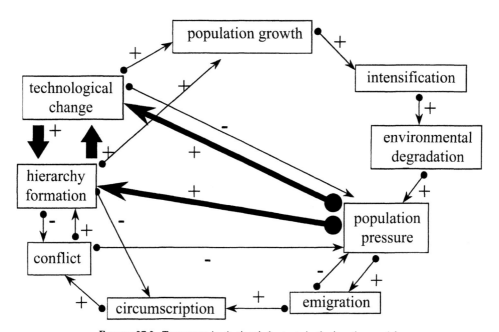

FIGURE 27.2. Temporary institutional shortcuts in the iteration model.

of the effects of population pressure to more directly cause changes in hierarchies and technologies of production, thus shortcutting the path that leads through migration, circumscription, and conflict. How can the emergence of states allow population pressure to more directly affect *hierarchy formation* and technological change? Once there are already states within a region, the phenomenon of secondary-state formation occurs. Population pressure in outlying semiperipheral areas combines with the threats and opportunities presented by interaction with the existing states to promote the formation of new states. This is the main way in which state formation short cuts the processes at the bottom of Fig. 27.2. We do not mean to say that conflict disappears, but rather that it does not need to reach the same levels of intensity in order to provoke the formation of new states once states are already present in a region.

State formation also articulates the rising costs due to intensification with changes in technology. The specialized organizations that states create (bureaucracies and armies) sometimes use their powers and organizational capabilities to invent new kinds of productive efficiency and to implement new kinds of production. Governing elites sometimes mobilize resources and labor for irrigation projects, clearing new land for agriculture, developing transportation facilities, and so forth. The portrayal of the early states and agrarian empires as technologically moribund is due mainly to comparing them with the much more powerful tendency of capitalist societies to revolutionize technology. But compared to earlier, less-hierarchical systems, the tributary empires increased the rate of technological innovations and implemented them across vast areas.

The emergence of market mechanisms and capitalism also articulated the forces produced by population pressure with new forms of hierarchy formation and technological change. Obviously markets provide incentives to economize and to develop cheaper substitutes for depleted resources that are becoming more expensive because of intensification. But markets and capitalism also alter the way in which hierarchy formation occurs. Once capitalist accumulation has become predominant in a system of regional core states, the sequence of the rise and fall of corewide empires is replaced by the rise and fall of hegemonic core powers in which hegemonic power is based as much on comparative advantage in the production of core commodities as on superior military capabilities. Capitalist hegemons more directly respond to the changing economic and political forces produced by ecological degradation and population pressure than tributary empires did. Again, conflict is not eliminated, but the intensity of conflict that is necessary to produce new levels of hierarchy formation is reduced. Competition comes to be based less on military factors and more on economic ones. Many now believe that this trend has gone so far that future hegemonic rivalry will not involve military conflict. Though we must all hope that this is true, there are good reasons to be somewhat skeptical (see Chase-Dunn & Podobnik, 1995). Another round of world war among core states might well prove to be fatal for the human species, but it also might lead to the formation of a global state that would outlaw warfare, as in the future scenario painted by Warren Wagar (1992). Our main point here is that capitalism transmits population pressure to the hierarchy formation process, creating incentives for the emergence of global governance.

The industrial capitalism of the late 19th and 20th centuries also has altered the operation of population pressure by producing the "demographic transition" in core countries. Harris (1977) contends that this has been the consequence of the concurrence and interaction of three forces: the fuel revolution, the job revolution, and the contraception revolution. The demographic transition means a decrease in mortality due to better public health measures and rising wages and then a decrease in fertility and family size. These changes lower population pressure in the core countries, and if they were replicable on a world scale, population pressure might cease to be such a driving force of social change. But Harris argues that the demographic transition in the core states since the latter quarter of the 19th century was due to conditions that will be difficult or impossible to replicate on a world scale.

Harris contends that average wages in the core did not rise above subsistence until the last quarter of the 19th century, but other studies of wages show that returns to labor rise and fall cyclically with long economic cycles such as the Kondratieff wave and the long cycles of price inflation–equilibrium studied by David Hackett Fischer (1996). Fischer (1996, p. 160) reports evidence of rising wages and returns to labor throughout the 19th century. The demographic transition was produced by a combination of rising wages with the invention of inexpensive and effective methods of birth control and the shift from coal to oil (which multiplied geometrically the amount of energy utilized in production).

Harris also emphasizes that these concurrent and interactive "revolutions" were probably a unique and time-bound phenomenon rather than the early stages of a global transcendence of population pressure. The nonrenewable character of oil-based energy, and the ecological impossibility of extending the contemporary American level of resource utilization to the vast populations of Asia, add up to what Peter Taylor (1996) has called "global impasse." The model of development to which the global majority has been encouraged to aspire is an ecological impossibility for all to attain. If the Chinese eat the same number of eggs and drive the same number of cars per capita as the United Statesians do, the biosphere will collapse. The best expert projection of proven oil reserves with current techniques and current consumption levels is around 50 years. That is not much time in the perspective of human social evolution.

All this is to say that the current system probably has not permanently transcended the nasty bottom part of the iteration model. As did states, capitalism has allowed the number of people on Earth to increase greatly. It also has produced the tantalizing possibility of a new system in which population pressure has been brought under control. But the failure to extend the demographic transition to the peripheral countries, or rather to reduce fertility after reducing mortality, has resulted in population pressure on a scale greater than ever before. Under such circumstances a return to some new version of the nasty route would seem to be likely.

Is our revised iteration model testable? In principle it is, but not with existing data sets. The Human Relations Area File might be a good place to start, but its unit of analysis is the society, not world-systems, and the characteristics of the societies are conceptualized as synchronic, whereas we would need to study processes of change over long periods of time. What is needed for formal comparative cross-world-systems research is a "representative sample" of each of the major types of world-systems.

In *Rise and Demise* (Chase-Dunn & Hall, 1997), we have begun to study bounded world-systems over long time periods, but the numbers of cases remain small. This problem can be overcome by doing time series analyses on individual world-systems, and this is the research design that holds the most immediate promise for being able to evaluate the causal propositions contained in our model. Time series analysis using structural equations models could disentangle the kind of reciprocal causation we hypothesize in our iteration models. It also would be desirable to study as many separate systems as possible in order to see if the causal structures hold across different systems.

MODELING THE MODERN SYSTEM

My *Global Formation* (Chase-Dunn, 1998) is an effort to make a single model of the constants, cycles, and trends of the modern world-system and to work out major conceptual issues and arguments regarding the "necessity of imperialism." This model of the structural constants, cycles, and secular trends specifies the basic and normal operations of the system. I argue that this basic scheme continues to accurately describe the system in the current period of global capitalism and the "information age" (Chase-Dunn, 1998).

Schema of World-System Constants, Cycles, and Trends

The structural constants are:

1. Capitalism: the accumulation of resources by means of the production and sale of commodities for profit.
2. The interstate system: a system of unequally powerful sovereign national states that compete for resources by supporting profitable commodity production and by engaging in geopolitical and military competition.
3. The core–periphery hierarchy: in which core regions have strong states and specialize in high-technology, high-wage production, while peripheral regions have weak states and specialize in labor-intensive and low-wage production.

These structural features of the modern world-system are continuous and reproduced. I argue that they are interlinked and interdependent with one another such that any real change in one would necessarily alter the others in fundamental ways (Chase-Dunn, 1998).

In addition to these structural constants, there are two other structural features that I see as continuities even though they involve patterned change. These are the systemic cycles and the systemic trends. The basic systemic cycles are:

1. The Kondratieff wave (K-wave): a worldwide economic cycle with a period of from forty to sixty years in which the relative rate of economic activity increases (during "A-phase" upswings) and then decreases (during "B-phase" periods of slower growth or stagnation).
2. The hegemonic sequence: the rise and fall of hegemonic core powers in which military power and economic comparative advantage are concentrated into a single hegemonic core state during some periods and these are followed by periods in which wealth and power are more evenly distributed among core states. Examples of hegemons are the Dutch in the 17th century, the British in the 19th century, and the United States in the 20th century.
3. The cycle of core war severity: the severity (battle deaths per year) of wars among core states (world wars) displays a cyclical pattern that has closely tracked the K-wave since the 16th century (Goldstein, 1988).
4. The oscillation between market trade versus more politically structured interaction between core states and peripheral areas. This is related to cycles of colonial expansion and decolonization and is manifesting itself in the current period in the form of emergent regional trading blocs that include both developed and less-developed countries.

The systemic trends that are normal operating procedure in the modern world-system are:

1. Expansion and deepening of commodity relations: land, labor, and wealth have been increasingly mediated by marketlike institutions in both the core and the periphery.
2. State-formation: the power of states over their populations has increased everywhere,

though this trend is sometimes slowed down by efforts to deregulate. State regulation has grown secularly, while political battles rage over the nature and objects of regulation.

3. Increased size of economic enterprises: while a large competitive sector of small firms is reproduced, the largest firms (those occupying what is called the monopoly sector) have continuously grown in size. This remains true even in the most recent period despite its characterization by some analysts as a new "accumulation regime" of "flexible specialization" in which small firms compete for shares of the global market.

4. International economic integration: the growth of trade interconnectedness and the transnationalization of capital. Capital has crossed state boundaries for millennia but the proportion of all production that is due to the operation of transnational firms has increased in every epoch. The contemporary focus on transnational sourcing and the single interdependent global economy is the heightened awareness produced by a trend long in operation.

5. Increasing capital intensity of production and mechanization (in several industrial revolutions since the 16th century) has increased the productivity of labor in agriculture, industry, and services.

6. Proletarianization: the world work force increasingly has depended on labor markets for meeting its basic needs. This long-term trend may be slowed temporarily or even reversed in some areas during periods of economic stagnation, but the secular shift away from subsistence production has a long history that continues in the most recent period. The expansion of the informal sector is part of this trend despite its functional similarities with earlier rural subsistence redoubts.

7. The growing gap: despite exceptional cases of successful upward mobility in the core–periphery hierarchy (e.g., the United States, Japan, Korea, Taiwan), the relative gap in incomes between core and peripheral regions has continued to increase, and this trend has existed since at least the end of the 19th century and probably before.

8. International political integration: the emergence of stronger international institutions for regulating economic and political interactions. This is a trend since the rise of the Concert of Europe after the defeat of Napoleon. The League of Nations, the United Nations, and such international financial institutions as the World Bank and the International Monetary Fund show an upward trend toward increasing global governance.

The comparative world-systems perspective developed by Chase-Dunn and Hall does not require the reformulation of this schema of structural constants, cycles, and trends. The very long-term perspective does reveal that many of the dynamic processes that operate in the modern world-system are analogous to patterns that can be seen in earlier systems. Kondratieff waves (40- to 60-year business cycles composed of A-phases of expansion and B-phases of stagnation) probably existed in 10th century China. The hegemonic sequence (rise and fall of hegemonic core powers) is the particular manifestation in the modern system of a general sequence of centralization and decentralization of power that is characteristic of all hierarchical world-systems. In all world-systems small and large, culturally different groups trade, fight, and make alliances with one another in ways that importantly condition processes of social change.

The cyclical trend of economic globalization (international economic integration) needs to be understood in the context of the other cycles and trends specified in the schema above.

The trends and cycles reveal important continuities and imply that future struggles for economic justice and democracy need to base themselves on an analysis of how earlier struggles changed the scale and nature of development in the world-system. This raises the question of the relevance of these theoretical approaches for possible human futures.

WHERE IS IT GOING?

The term "globalization" has been used to refer to "the globalization project": the abandoning of Keynesian models of national development and a new emphasis on deregulation and opening national commodity and financial markets to foreign trade and investment (McMichael, 1996). This is to point to the ideological aspects of the recent wave of international economic integration. The term I prefer for this turn in global discourse is "neoliberalism." The worldwide decline of the political left may have predated the revolutions of 1989 and the demise of the Soviet Union, but it certainly also was accelerated by these events. The structural basis of the rise of the globalization project is the new level of integration reached by the global capitalist class. The internationalization of capital has long been an important part of the trend toward economic globalization. There have been many claims to represent the general interests of business before. Indeed, every modern hegemon has made this claim. But the real integration of interests of the capitalists in each of the core states probably has reached a level greater than ever before.

This is the part of the model of a global stage of capitalism that must be taken most seriously, though it certainly can be overdone. The world-system has now reached a point at which both the old interstate system based on separate national capitalist classes and new institutions representing the global interests of capitalists exist and are powerful simultaneously. In this light, each country can be seen to have an important ruling class fraction that is allied with the transnational capitalist class.

Neoliberalism began as the Reagan–Thatcher attack on the welfare state and labor unions. It evolved into the structural adjustment policies of the International Monetary Fund and the triumphalism of the ideologues of corporate globalization after the demise of the Soviet Union. In United States foreign policy it has found expression in a new emphasis on "democracy promotion" in the periphery and semiperiphery. Rather than propping up military dictatorships in Latin America, the emphasis has shifted toward coordinated action between the Central Intelligence Agency (CIA) and the US National Endowment for Democracy to promote electoral institutions in Latin America and other semiperipheral and peripheral regions (Robinson, 1996). Robinson points out that the kind of "low intensity democracy" that is promoted is really best understood as "polyarchy," a regime form in which elites orchestrate a process of electoral competition and governance that legitimates state power and undercuts more radical political alternatives that might threaten the ability of national elites to maintain their wealth and power by exploiting workers and peasants. Robinson (1996) convincingly argues that polyarchy and democracy promotion are the political forms that are most congruent with a globalized and neoliberal world economy in which capital is given free reign to generate accumulation wherever profits are greatest.

The Spiral of Capitalism and Socialism

The interaction between expansive commodification and resistance movements can be denoted as "the spiral of capitalism and socialism." The world-systems perspective provides a view of the long-term interaction between the expansion and deepening of capitalism and the efforts of people to protect themselves from exploitation and domination. The historical development of the communist states is explained as part of a long-run spiraling interaction between expanding capitalism and socialist counterresponses. The Russian and Chinese revolutions were socialist movements in the semiperiphery that attempted to transform the basic logic of capitalism, but which ended up using socialist ideology to mobilize industrialization for the purpose of catching up with core capitalism.

The spiraling interaction between capitalist development and socialist movements is revealed in the history of labor movements, socialist parties, and communist states over the last 200 years. This long-run comparative perspective enables one to see recent events in China, Russia, and Eastern Europe in a framework that has implications for future efforts to institutionalize democratic socialism. The metaphor of the spiral means this: Both capitalism and socialism affect one another's growth and organizational forms. Capitalism spurs socialist responses by exploiting and dominating peoples, and socialism spurs capitalism to expand its scale of production and market integration and to revolutionize technology.

Defined broadly, socialist movements are those political and organizational means by which people try to protect themselves from market forces, exploitation, and domination and to build more cooperative institutions.[10] The several industrial revolutions, by which capitalism has restructured production and reorganized labor, have stimulated a series of political organizations and institutions created by workers and communities to protect their livelihoods and resources. This happened differently under different political and economic conditions in different parts of the world-system. Skilled workers created guilds and craft unions. Less skilled workers created industrial unions. Sometimes these coalesced into labor parties that played important roles in supporting the development of political democracies, mass education, and welfare states (Rueschemeyer, Stephens, and Stephens, 1992). In other regions workers and peasants were less politically successful, but managed at least to protect access to rural areas or subsistence plots for a fallback or hedge against the insecurities of employment in capitalist enterprises. To some extent the burgeoning contemporary "informal sector" in both core and peripheral societies provides such a fallback.

The mixed success of workers' organizations also had an impact on the further development of capitalism. In some areas workers and/or communities were successful at raising the wage bill or protecting the environment in ways that raised the costs of production for capital. When this happened capitalists either displaced workers by automating them out of jobs or capital migrated to where fewer constraints allowed cheaper production. The process of capital flight is not a new feature of the world-system. It has been an important force behind the uneven development of capitalism and the spreading scale of market integration for centuries. Labor unions and socialist parties were able to obtain some power in certain states, but capitalism became yet more international. Firm size increased. International markets became more and more important to successful capitalist competition. Fordism, the employment of large numbers of easily organizable workers in centralized production locations, has been partially supplanted by "flexible accumulation" (small firms producing small customized products) and global sourcing (the use of substitutable components from broadly dispersed competing producers). These new production strategies make traditional labor-organizing approaches much less viable.

Socialists were able to gain state power in certain semiperipheral states and to create

[10]The term "antisystemic movements" also has been used to designate this family of popular forms of resistance (Amin et al., 1982; Arrighi et al., 1989). The main movements I have in mind are anticolonial and anti-imperial national liberation movements, the global indigenous movement, labor movements, socialist parties, communist states, feminism, and environmentalism. The problem of counterhegemony is how to bring these interests together.

political mechanisms of protection against competition with core capital. This was not a wholly new phenomenon. As discussed below, capitalist semiperipheral states had done and were doing similar things. But the communist states claimed a fundamentally oppositional ideology in which socialism was allegedly a superior system that eventually would replace capitalism. Ideological opposition is a phenomenon that the capitalist world economy had seen before. The geopolitical and economic battles of the Thirty Years War were fought in the name of Protestantism against Catholicism. The content of the ideology may make some difference for the internal organization of states and parties, but every contender must be able to legitimate itself in the eyes and hearts of its cadre. The claim to represent a qualitatively different and superior socioeconomic system is not evidence that the communist states were ever able to become structurally autonomous from world capitalism.

The communist states severely restricted the access of core capitalist firms to their internal markets and raw materials, and this constraint on the mobility of capital was an important force behind the post-World War II upsurge in the spatial scale of market integration and a new revolution of technology. In certain areas capitalism was driven to further revolutionize technology or to improve living conditions for workers and peasants because of the demonstration effect of propinquity to a communist state. United States support for state-led industrialization in Japan and Korea (in contrast to US policy in Latin America) is only understandable as a geopolitical response to the Chinese revolution. The existence of "two superpowers"—one capitalist and one communist —in the period since World War II provided a fertile context for the success of international liberalism within the "capitalist" bloc. This was the political–military basis of the rapid growth of transnational corporations and the latest round of "time–space compression" made possible by radically lowered transportation and communications costs (Harvey, 1989). This technological revolution once again has restructured the international division of labor and created a new regime of labor regulation called "flexible accumulation." The process by which the communist states have become reintegrated into the capitalist world-system has been long, as described below. But the final phase of reintegration was provoked by the inability to be competitive with the new form of capitalist regulation. Thus, capitalism spurs socialism, which spurs capitalism, which spurs socialism again in a wheel that turns and turns, while getting larger.

The economic reincorporation of the communist states into the capitalist world-economy did not occur recently and suddenly. It began with the mobilization toward autarchic industrialization using socialist ideology, an effort that was quite successful in terms of standard measures of economic development. Most of the communist states were increasing their percentage of world product and energy consumption up until the 1980s (Boswell & Chase-Dunn, 2000).

The economic reincorporation of the communist states moved to a new stage of integration with the world market and foreign firms in the 1970s. Andre Gunder Frank (1980, Chapter 4) documented a trend toward reintegration in which the communist states increased their exports for sale on the world market, increased imports from the avowedly capitalist countries, and made deals with transnational firms for investments within their borders. The economic crisis in Eastern Europe and the Soviet Union was not much worse than the economic crisis in the rest of the world during the global economic downturn that began in the late 1960s (see Boswell & Peters, 1990, Table 1). Data presented by World Bank analysts indicates that gross domestic product (GDP) growth rates were positive in most of the "historically planned economies" in Europe until 1989 or 1990 (Marer et al., 1991, Table 7a).

Put simply, the big transformations that occurred in the Soviet Union and China after 1989 were part of a process that has been underway since the 1970s. The regime changes were a matter of the political superstructure catching up with the economic base. The democratization of these societies is, of course, a welcome trend, but democratic political forms do not automatically lead to a society without exploitation or domination. The outcomes of current political struggles are rather uncertain in most of the ex-communist countries. New types of authoritarian regimes seem at least as likely as real democratization.

As trends in the last two decades have shown, austerity regimes, deregulation, and marketization within nearly all the communist states occurred during the same period as similar phenomena in noncommunist states. The synchronicity and broad similarities between Reagan–Thatcher deregulation and attacks on the welfare state, austerity socialism in most of the rest of the world, and increasing pressures for marketization in the Soviet Union and China are all related to the B-phase downturn of the Kondratieff wave, as were the moves toward austerity and privatization in most semiperipheral and peripheral states. The trend toward privatization, deregulation, and market-based solutions among parties of the Left in almost every country is thoroughly documented by Lipset (1991). Nearly all socialists with access to political power have abandoned the idea of doing anything more than buffing off the rough edges of capitalism.

The way in which the pressures of a stagnating world economy impact on national policies certainly varies from country to country, but the ability of any single national society to construct collective rationality is limited by its interaction within the larger system. The most recent expansion of capitalist integration, termed "globalization of the economy," has made autarchic national economic planning seem anachronistic. Yet, political reactions against economic globalization are now under way in the form of revived ex-communist parties and economic nationalism in both the core and the periphery (e.g., Pat Buchanan, the Brazilian military, the Indonesian prime minister) and a growing coalition of popular forces who are critiquing the ideological hegemony of neoliberalism (e.g., Ralph Nader, environmentalists, and a resurgent labor movement that defeated the "Fast Track" legislation in the United States, etc.) (see Mander & Goldsmith, 1996). Antiglobalization demonstrations from Seattle to Prague have made the headlines and the glory days of neoliberal economics have passed even within the international financial institutions.

Political Implications of the World-Systems Perspective

The age of US hegemonic decline and the rise of postmodernist philosophy have cast the liberal ideology of the European Enlightenment (science, progress, rationality, liberty, democracy, and equality) into the dustbin of repressive totalizing universalisms. It is alleged that these values have been the basis of imperialism, domination, and exploitation, and thus they should be cast out in favor of each group asserting its own set of values. It is important to note that self-determination and a considerable dose of multiculturalism (especially regarding religion) were already central elements in Enlightenment liberalism.

A structuralist and historical materialist version of the world-systems approach poses this problem of values in a different way. The problem with the capitalist world-system has not been with its values. The philosophy of liberalism is fine. It quite often has been an embarrassment to the pragmatics of imperial power and frequently has provided justifications for resistance to domination and exploitation. The philosophy of the Enlightenment has never been, by itself, a major cause of exploitation and domination. Rather, it was the military and economic power generated by capitalism that made European hegemony possible. Power was legitimated in the eyes of the agents and some of the victims by recitation of the great liberal values, but it was not the values that mainly enabled conquest and exploitation, but rather the gunships and the cheap prices of commodities.

To humanize the world-system we may need to construct a new philosophy of democratic and egalitarian liberation. Of course, many of the principle ideals that have been the core of the Left's critique of capitalism are shared by non-European philosophies. Democracy, in the sense of popular control over collective decision making, was not invented in ancient Greece. It was a characteristic of all nonhierarchical human societies on every continent before the emergence of complex chiefdoms and states. My point is that a new egalitarian universalism can usefully incorporate quite a lot from the old universalisms. It is not liberal ideology that caused so much exploitation and domination. It was the failure of real capitalism to live up to its own ideals (liberty and equality) in most of the world.

A central question for any strategy of transformation is the question of agency. Who are the actors who will most vigorously and effectively resist capitalism and construct democratic socialism? Where is the most favorable terrain, the weak link, where concerted action could bear the most fruit? Samir Amin (1990, 1992) contends that the agents of socialism have been most heavily concentrated in the periphery. It is there that the capitalist world-system is most oppressive, and thus peripheral workers and peasants, the vast majority of the world proletariat, have the most to win and the least to lose.

On the other hand, Marx and many contemporary Marxists have argued that socialism will be most effectively built by the action of core proletarians. Since core areas already have attained a high level of technological development, the establishment of socialized production and distribution should be easiest in the core. Organized core workers have had the longest experience with industrial capitalism and the most opportunity to create socialist social relations.

I submit that both "workerist" and "Third-Worldist" positions have important elements of truth, but there is another alternative that is suggested by a structural and comparative theory of the world-system: the semiperiphery as the weak link. Core workers may have experience and opportunity, but a sizable segment of the core working classes lack motivation because they have benefited from a less confrontational relationship with core capital. The existence of a labor aristocracy has divided the working class in the core and, in combination with a large middle stratum, has undermined political challenges to capitalism. Also, the "long experience" in which business unionism and social democracy have been the outcome of a series of struggles between radical workers and the labor aristocracy has created a residue of trade union practices, party structures, legal and governmental institutions, and ideological heritages that act as barriers to new socialist challenges. These conditions have changed to some extent during the last two decades as hypermobile capital has attacked organized labor, dismantled welfare states, and downsized middle-class work forces. These developments have created new possibilities for popular movements within the core, and we can expect more confrontational stances to emerge as workers devise new forms of organization (or revitalize old forms). Economic globalization makes labor internationalism a necessity, and so we can expect to see the old idea take new forms and become more organizationally real. Even small victories in the core have important effects on peripheral and semiperipheral areas because of demonstration effects and the power of core states.

The main problem with "Third Worldism" is not motivation but opportunity. Powerful external forces that either overthrow them or force them to abandon most of their socialist program soon beset democratic socialist movements that take state power in the periphery. Liberation movements in the periphery most usually have been anti-imperialist class alliances that succeed in establishing at least the trappings of national sovereignty, but not socialism.

The low level of the development of the productive forces also makes it more difficult to establish socialist forms of accumulation, although this is not impossible in principle. It is simply harder to share power and wealth when there are very little of either. But, the emergence of democratic regimes in the periphery will facilitate new forms of mutual aid, cooperative development and popular movements to challenge the current ideological hegemony of neoliberalism.

Semiperipheral Democratic Socialism

In the semiperiphery both motivation and opportunity exist. Semiperipheral areas, especially those in which the territorial state is large, have sufficient resources to be able to stave off core attempts at overthrow and to provide some protection to socialist institutions if the political conditions for their emergence should arise. Tom Hall and I (Chase-Dunn & Hall, 1997, Chapter 5) found that semiperipheral societies have played transformational roles in many earlier world-systems, an observation that we dub "semiperipheral development." Some semiperipheral societies have continued to be both upwardly mobile and transformative of social relations in the modern world-system. All the hegemonic core powers (the Dutch, the British, and the United States) were former semiperipheral countries. John Markoff (1996) shows that innovations in democratic institutions tended to occur in semiperipheral countries in the 19th century. Semiperipheral regions (e.g., Russia and China) have experienced more militant class-based socialist revolutions because of their intermediate position in the core–periphery hierarchy. While core exploitation of the periphery creates and sustains alliances among classes in both the core and the periphery, in the semiperiphery an intermediate world-system position undermines class alliances and provides a fruitful terrain for strong challenges to capitalism. Semiperipheral revolutions and movements are not always socialist in character, as we have seen in Iran. But when socialist intentions are strong, there are greater possibilities for real transformation than in the core or the periphery. Thus, the semiperiphery is the weak link in the capitalist world-system. It is the terrain on which the strongest efforts to establish socialism have been made, and this is likely to be true of the future as well.

On the other hand, the results of the efforts so far, while they undoubtedly have been important experiments with the logic of socialism, have left much to be desired. The tendency for authoritarian regimes to emerge in the communist states betrayed Marx's idea of a freely constituted association of direct producers. The imperial control of Eastern Europe by the Russians was an insult to the idea of proletarian internationalism. Democracy within and between nations must be a constituent element of true socialism.

It does not follow that efforts to build socialism in the semiperiphery will always be so constrained and thwarted. The revolutions in the Soviet Union and the Peoples' Republic of China have increased our collective knowledge about how to build socialism despite their only partial successes and their obvious failures. It is important for all of us who want to build a more humane and peaceful world-system to understand the lessons of socialist movements in the semiperiphery, and the potential for future, more successful forms of socialism there.

Once again the core has developed new lead industries—computers and biotechnology —and much of large-scale heavy industry, the classic terrain of strong labor movements and socialist parties, has been moved to the semiperiphery (Silver, 1995). This means that new socialist bids for state power in the semiperiphery (e.g., South Africa, Brazil, Mexico, perhaps Korea) will be much more based on an urbanized and organized proletariat in large-scale industry than the earlier semiperipheral socialist revolutions were. This should have happy consequences for the nature of new socialist states in the semiperiphery because the relationship between the city and the countryside within these countries should be less antagonistic. Less internal conflict will make more democratic socialist regimes possible and will lessen the likelihood of core interference. The global expansion of communications has increased the salience of events in the semiperiphery for audiences in the core and this may serve to dampen core state intervention into the affairs of democratic socialist semiperipheral states.

Some critics of the world-systems perspective have argued that emphasis on the structural importance of global relations leads to political do-nothingism while we wait for socialism to emerge at the world level. The world-systems perspective does indeed encourage us to examine global constraints (and opportunities) and to allocate our political energies in ways that will be most productive when these structural constraints are taken into account. It does not follow that building socialism at the local or national level is futile, but we must expend resources on transorganizational, transnational, and international socialist relations. The environmental, feminist, and indigenous movements are now in the lead with regard to internationalism and labor needs to follow their example.

A simple domino theory of transformation to democratic socialism is misleading and inadequate. Suppose that all firms or all nation-states adopted socialist relations internally but continued to relate to one another through competitive commodity production and political–military conflict. Such a hypothetical world-system still would be dominated by the logic of capitalism, and that logic would be likely to repenetrate the "socialist" firms and states. This cautionary tale advises us to invest political resources in the construction of multilevel (transorganizational, transnational, and international) socialist relations lest we simply repeat the process of driving capitalism to once again perform an end run by operating on a yet larger scale.

A Market Socialist Global Democracy

These considerations lead us to a discussion of socialist relations at the level of the entire world-system. The emergence of democratic collective rationality (socialism) at the world-system level is likely to be a slow process. What might such a world-system look like and how might it emerge? It is obvious that such a system would require a democratically controlled world federation that can effectively adjudicate disputes among nation-states and eliminate warfare (Wagar, 1996). This is a bare minimum. There are many other problems that badly need to be coordinated at the global level: ecologically sustainable development, a more balanced and egalitarian approach to economic growth, and the lowering of population growth rates.

The idea of global democracy is important for this struggle. The movement needs to push toward a kind of popular democracy that goes beyond the election of representatives to include popular participation in decision making at every level. Global democracy can be real only if it is composed of civil societies and national states that are themselves truly democratic (Robinson, 1996). Global democracy is probably the best way to lower the probability of another war among core states. For that reason it is in everyone's interest.

How might such a global democracy come into existence? The process of the growth of international organizations, which has been going on for at least 200 years, will eventually result in a world state if we are not blown up first. Even international capitalists have some uses for global regulation, as attested to by the International Monetary Fund and the World Bank. Capitalists do not want the massive economic and political upheavals that would follow the collapse of the world monetary system, and so they support efforts to regulate "ruinous" competition and beggar-thy-neighborism. Some of these same capitalists also fear nuclear holocaust, and so they may support a strengthened global government that can effectively adjudicate conflicts among nation-states.

Of course, capitalists know as well as others that effective adjudication means the establishment of a global monopoly of legitimate violence. The process of state formation has a long history, and the king's army needs to be bigger than any combination of private armies that might be brought against him. While the idea of a world state may be a frightening specter to some, I am optimistic about it for several reasons. First, a world state is probably the most direct and stable way to prevent nuclear holocaust, a desideratum that must be at the top of everyone's list. Second, the creation of a global state that can peacefully adjudicate disputes among nations will transform the existing interstate system. The interstate system (multiple sovereignties in the core) is the political structure that stands behind the maneuverability of capital and its ability to escape organized workers and other social constraints on profitable accumulation (Chase-Dunn, 1998, Chapter 7). While a world state may at first be dominated by capitalists, the very existence of such a state will provide a single focus for struggles to socially regulate investment decisions and to create a more balanced, egalitarian, and ecologically sound form of production and distribution.

The progressive response to neoliberalism needs to be organized at national, international, and global levels if it is to succeed. Democratic socialists should be wary of strategies that focus only on economic nationalism and national autarchy as a response to economic globalization. Socialism in one country has never worked in the past and it certainly will not work in a world that is more interlinked than ever before. The old forms of progressive internationalism were somewhat premature, but internationalism finally has become not only desirable but necessary. This does not mean that local-, regional- and national-level struggles are irrelevant. They are just as relevant as they always have been. But, they also need to have a global strategy and global-level cooperation lest they be isolated and defeated. Communications technology certainly can be an important tool for the kinds of long-distance interactions that will be required for truly international cooperation and coordination among popular movements.

Boswell and Chase-Dunn (2000) imagine a feasible vision of a fairer and more sustainable world-system based on a modified version of the idea of market socialism proposed by John Roemer (1994). Roemer rethinks the institutional structure of socialism in the light of the problems of "soft budget constraints" produced by state ownership of the means of production. In Roemer's model all citizens at the age of majority would inherit 1000 shares of stock in large firms. These can be traded and so firms need to try to make profit in order to compete for additional capital. At the global level this model needs to be modified to take into account the inequalities of the core–periphery hierarchy. Boswell and Chase-Dunn (2000) introduce an element of worker control over large firms and socialist international financial institutions (a Peoples World Bank) that will help to reduce uneven development and degradation of the environment.

How could such a world come about? Wagar (1996) has proposed the formation of a "World Party" as an instrument of "mundialization": the creation of a global socialist commonwealth. His proposal has been critiqued from many angles: as a throwback to the Third International, and so forth.[11] Boswell and Chase-Dunn (2000) support a somewhat

[11]See the critiques of Wagar's proposals in the special issue on "Global Praxis" of the *Journal of World-Systems Research*, Volume 2, 1996 (http://csf.colorado.edu/wsystems/jwsr.html). The World Party web page is at http://csf.colorado.edu/wsystems/archive/praxis/wp/index.htm, and further discussion of the idea of a World Party during the months of October and November, 1999, is available at http://csf.colorado.edu./mail/wsn/.

modified version of Wagar's proposed World Party idea. Self-doubt and postmodern reticence, as well as the dominant rhetoric of neoliberalism, tar this approach as Napoleonic or worse (e.g., Stalinist, megalomaniac). It certainly is necessary to learn from past mistakes, but this should not prevent us from debating the pros and cons of concerted and organized action. There are many world parties already, but perhaps there needs to be one that understands the lessons of historical capitalist development and human social evolution. Members of such an organization would debate what we know from social science and what needs to be done to survive, prevail, and make good on Earth. They also might undertake special organizing projects in key areas that are being neglected by other progressives.

The international segment of the world capitalist class is moving haltingly toward global state formation. The Asian crisis has led to calls for institutions that can dampen or ameliorate the destabilizing effects of wild fluctuations in international capital flows from some capitalists who are in this very business, e.g., George Soros. The World Trade Organization, the World Bank, and the International Monetary Fund have come under increased attack from antiglobalizationists on the both the right and the left. Rather than simply oppose international political integration with a return to nationalism, progressives should make every effort to democratize the emerging global state. We need to prevent the normal operation of the interstate system and future hegemonic rivalry from causing another war among core powers (e.g., Wagar, 1992; see also Bornschier & Chase-Dunn, 1999). We need to shape the emerging world society into a global democratic commonwealth based on collective rationality, liberty, and equality. This possibility is present in existing and evolving structures. The agents are all those who are tired of wars and hatred and who desire a humane, sustainable, and fair world-system. This certainly is a majority of the people of the Earth.

REFERENCES

Abu-Lughod, J. (1989). *Before European hegemony*. New York: Oxford
Algaze, G. (1993). *The Uruk world system: The dynamics of expansion of early Mesopotamian civilization*. Chicago: University of Chicago Press.
Amin, S. (1980). *Class and nation, historically and in the current crisis*. New York: Monthly Review Press.
Amin, S., Arrighi, G., Gunder Frank, A., & Wallerstein, I. (1982). *Dynamics of global crisis*. New York: Monthly Review Press.
Amin, S. (1990). *Delinking: Towards a polycentric world*. London: Zed Press.
Amin, S. (1992). *Empire of chaos*. New York: Monthly Review Press.
Arrighi, G. (1994). *The long twentieth century*. London: Verso.
Arrighi, G. (1992). 1989, the continuation of 1968. *Review, 15*, 221–242.
Arrighi, G., & Silver, B. (1999). *Chaos and governance in the modern world-system: Comparing hegemonic transitions*. Minneapolis: University of Minnesota Press.
Arrighi, G., Hopkins, T. K., & Wallerstein, I. (1989a). *Antisystemic movements*. London and New York: Verso.
Arrighi, G., Hopkins, T. K., & Wallerstein, I. (1989b). 1968: The great rehearsal. In T. Boswell (Ed.), *Revolution in the world-system* (pp. 19–33). New York: Greenwood.
Bairoch, P. (1996). Globalization myths and realities: One century of external trade and foreign investment. In R. Boyer & D. Drache (Eds.), *States against markets: The limits of globalization* (pp. 173–192). London and New York: Routledge.
Bornschier, V., & Chase-Dunn, C. (Eds.). (1999). The Future of Global Conflict. London: Sage.
Boswell, T., & Chase-Dunn, C. (2000). *The spiral of capitalism and socialism: Toward global democracy*. Boulder, CO: Lynne Rienner.
Boswell, T., & Peters, R. (1990). State socialism and the industrial divide in the world-economy: A comparative essay on the rebellions in Poland and China. *Critical Sociology, 17*, 3–35.
Carneiro, R. L. (1970). A theory of the origin of the state. *Science, 169*, 733–738.
Chase-Dunn, C. (1998). *Global formation: Structures of the world-economy*, 2nd edition. Lanham, MD: Rowman and Littlefield.

Chase-Dunn, C., & Hall, T. D. (1997). *Rise and demise: Comparing world-systems.* Boulder, CO: Westview.

Chase-Dunn, C., & Mann, K. M. (1998). *The Wintu and their neighbors: A very small world-system in Northern California.* Tucson: University of Arizona Press.

Chase-Dunn, C., & Podobnik, B. (1995). The next world war: World-system cycles and trends. *Journal of World-Systems Research, 1,* 1–46.

Chase-Dunn, C., Kawano, Y., & Brewer, B. (2000). Trade globalization since 1795: Waves of integration in the world-system. *American Sociological Review,* 77–95.

Denemark, R., Friedman, J., Gills, B. K., & Modelski, G. (Eds.) (2000). *World system history: The social science of long-term change.* London: Routledge.

Ekholm, K., & Friedman, J. (1980). Toward a global anthropology. In L. Blusse, H. L. Wesseling, & G. D. Winius (Eds.). Leyden: Center for the History of European Expansion, Leyden University.

Ekholm, K., & Friedman, J. (1982). Capital imperialism and exploitation in the ancient world-systems. *Review, 6*(1), 87–110.

Fischer, D. H. (1996). *The great wave: Price revolutions and the rhythm of history.* New York: Oxford University Press.

Frank, A. G. (1980). *Crisis in the world economy.* New York: Holmes and Meier.

Frank, A. G. (1998). *Reorient: Global economy in the Asian age.* Berkeley: University of California Press.

Friedman, J. (1994). *Cultural identity and global process.* London: Sage.

Goldstein, J. S. (1988). *Long cycles: Prosperity and war in the modern age.* New Haven, CT: Yale University Press.

Hall, T. D. (Ed.). (2000) *A world-systems reader: New perspectives on gender, urbanism, cultures, indigenous peoples, and ecology.* Lanham, MD: Rowman and Littlefield.

Hall, T. D., & Chase-Dunn, C. (1993). The world-systems perspective and archaeology: Forward into the past. *Journal of Archaeological Research, 1*(2), 121–143.

Harris, M. (1977). *Cannibals and kings: The origins of culture.* New York: Random House.

Harvey, D. (1989). *The condition of postmodernity.* Cambridge, MA: Blackwell.

Hopkins, T. K., & Wallerstein, I. (1982). Cyclical rhythms and secular trends of the capitalist world-economy. In T. K. Hopkins & I. Wallerstein (Eds.), *World-systems analysis: Theory and methodology* (pp. 104–120). Beverly Hills, CA: Sage.

Kohl, P. L. (1987). The use and abuse of world systems theory: The case of the "pristine" West Asian state. In *Archeological advances in method and theory* (pp. 1–35). New York: Academic Press.

Lipset, S. M. (1991). No third way: A comparative perspective on the Left. In D. Chirot (Ed.), *The crisis of Leninism and the decline of the left: The revolutions of 1989* (pp. 183–232). Seattle: University of Washington Press.

Mander, J., & Goldsmith, E. (Eds.). (1996). *The case against the global economy and for a turn toward the local.* San Francisco: Sierra Club Books.

Mann, M. (1986). *Sources of social power.* Vol. 1. Cambridge: Cambridge University Press.

Marer, P., Arvay, J., O'Connor, J., & Swenson, D. (1991). Historically planned economies: A guide to the data. I.B.R.D. (World Bank), Socioeconomic Data Division and Socialist Economies Reform Unit.

Markoff, J. (1996). *Waves of democracy: Social movements and political change.* Thousand Oaks, CA: Pine Forge Press.

McMichael, P. (1996). *Development and social change: A global perspective.* Thousand Oaks, CA: Pine Forge.

Modelski, G., & Thompson, W. R. (1996). *Leading sectors and world powers: The coevolution of global economics and politics.* Columbia: University of South Carolina Press.

Murphy, C. (1994). *International organization and industrial change: Global governance since 1850.* New York: Oxford.

Neitzel, J. (Ed.). (1999). *Great towns and regional polities.* Albuquerque: University of New Mexico Press.

Peregrine, P. (1992). *Mississippian evolution: A world-system perspective.* Monographs in World Archaeology No. 9. Madison, WI: Prehistory Press.

Peregrine, P. (1995). Networks of power: The Mississippian world-system. In M. Nassaney & K. Sassaman (Eds.), *Native American interactions* (pp. 132–143). Knoxville: University of Tennessee Press.

Polanyi, K. (1977). *The livelihood of man,* ed. H. W. Pearson. New York: Academic Press.

Renfrew, C. R. (1987). *Archaelogy and language: The puzzle of Indo-European origins.* London: Jonathan Cape.

Robinson, W. I. (1996). *Promoting polyarchy: Globalization, U.S. intervention and hegemony.* Cambridge: Cambridge University Press.

Roemer, J. E. (1994). *A future for socialism.* Cambridge, MA: Harvard University Press. Albany: State University of New York Press.

Rueschemeyer, D., Stephens, E. H., & Stephens, J. D. (1992). *Capitalist development and democracy.* Chicago: University of Chicago Press.

Shannon, T. R. (1996). *An introduction to the world-system perspective.* Boulder, CO: Westview.

Silver, B. (1995). World-scale patterns of labor-capital conflict: Labor unrest, long waves and cycles of hegemony. *Review*, *18*, 53–92.

Soros, G. (1998). *The crisis of global capitalism*. New York: Pantheon.

Stein, G. J. (1999). *Rethinking world-systems: Diasporas, colonies and interaction in Uruk Mesopotamia*. Tucson: University of Arizona Press.

Taylor, P. J. (1996). *The way the modern world works: World hegemony to world impasse*. New York: Wiley.

Wagar, W. W. (1992). *A short history of the future*. Chicago: University of Chicago Press.

Wagar, W. W. (1996). Toward a praxis of world integration. *Journal of World-Systems Research*, *2*(1). http://csf.colorado.edu/wsystems/jwsr.html.

Wallerstein, I. (1974). *The modern world-system*, Volume 1. New York: Academic Press.

CHAPTER 28

Theoretical Understandings of Gender

A Third of a Century of Feminist Thought in Sociology

JANET SALTZMAN CHAFETZ

INTRODUCTION

Over the past 30 years, feminist sociologists, along with their counterparts in a variety of other disciplines, have produced a prodigious theoretical literature oriented to explaining gender differences and especially inequality. Within sociology, such theories reflect, revise, and extend almost every theoretical tradition extant in the field (see Chafetz, 1988, 1997, 1999a; England, 1993; Wallace, 1989, for reviews). In addition, some efforts have been made to integrate ideas from a number of very different theoretical traditions (e.g., Chafetz, 1990; Collins et al., 1993; Lorber, 1994; Connell 1987). Because gender permeates all levels of human existence, from the intrapsychic to the interactional, organizational, and societal, synthesizing efforts across micro–meso–macro levels of analysis and between varying theoretical orientations are virtually required in order to produce a meaningful understanding of the role of gender in social life. In this chapter, I focus on the myriad feminist sociological theories that attempt to explain gender differences and inequality, as they are manifest at all three levels of analysis.

Theorizing about gender does not require a feminist perspective. Indeed, most 19th and early 20th century founding fathers of sociology had something to say about gender (see Kandal, 1988), but much of it could scarcely be defined as feminist (Chafetz, 1999a). In order to be considered a *feminist* theory in addition to or instead of a focus on gender as difference, a theory must recognize gender as a system of inequality, assume that it is a mutable rather than constant or necessary feature of human societies, and normatively espouse a commitment to a gender equitable system. With only a few exceptions (e.g., much, but not all sociobiological

JANET SALTZMAN CHAFETZ • Department of Sociology, University of Houston, Houston, Texas 77204.

Handbook of Sociological Theory, edited by Jonathan H. Turner. Kluwer Academic / Plenum Publishers, New York, 2002.

theory), gender theories developed by sociologists since about 1970 have been feminist according to this definition (as were a number much earlier, written by the forgotten founding mothers of sociology and described in detail by Lengermann and Niebrugge-Brantley, 1998). Nonetheless, while normatively committed to social change, few feminist theories in our discipline attempt to systematically explain how it occurs, as distinct from what features of social life need to be changed. Moreover, many feminist theories that do suggest change mechanisms base their explanations on processes that logically presuppose that change has already occurred (Chafetz, 1999b).

This chapter is divided into two major sections, in addition to the introduction and conclusion. I will first address the major insights developed by feminist theorists, since about 1970, concerning how systems of gender difference and inequality maintain and reproduce themselves. I begin with a distillation of the important insights provided by macrolevel theories, subsequently exploring meso- and microlevel ideas. I then explore issues pertaining to gender system change. Logically, systems of gender inequality can change (and empirically have done so) to become more as well as less inequitable. However, I will discuss only what is today the dominant, long-term direction change in most contemporary, especially advanced industrial societies: that toward decreasing gender stratification (Jackson, 1998; for a theory that explicitly incorporates change toward increasing inequality, see Chafetz, 1990).

I begin at the macrolevel because, by definition, to assume gender inequality, as all feminists do, is to assume differences in the level of power and resources to which, on average, men and women have access, as well as in the amount and types of opportunities and constraints they typically confront. In turn, at least in contemporary societies, these are generated chiefly by major societal institutions, including the economy, polity, educational system, religious, and other cultural institutions, i.e., at the macrolevel. As will become apparent, most feminist theories suggest or imply that micro- and mesolevel processes are significantly shaped and constrained by macrolevel features and until a change process is underway serve primarily to reproduce the existing system.

Some General Issues

One major issue of general importance to a discussion of feminist theory concerns the concept "agency." In an effort to avoid depicting women as merely passive victims of male dominance, many feminist scholars use the term in discussing the myriad ways by which women have resisted their oppression and created freer social spaces for themselves. However, the term is typically undefined and used almost mystically. While it is undoubtedly the case that women have not simply lived as passive victims within male-dominated social contexts, theorists cannot logically argue that women are both oppressed within such systems and yet experience more than trivial amounts of "agency;" in fact, too often only choices between bad and worse options are available. By definition, dominance by any group implies that the dominated are highly constrained in the choices they are able to make without incurring serious social—even physical—penalty. When "deviant" acts (choices) result in heavy penalty, few will opt to imitate them; most will "choose" to remain largely conformist victims of the system, thereby reinforcing the very system that disadvantages them. I conceptualize agency as the opportunity to make choices among alternatives that are perceived as variably rewarding and that do not incur heavy penalties. Making the choice to relinquish one's purse rather than die does not demonstrate "agency" in a sociologically meaningful manner.

Further, I conceptualize the term as a *variable*, not as an assumed constant. In various times and places and among different subpopulations (e.g., gender, class, racial/ethnic) people enjoy varying amounts and types of choice opportunities, with those in socially dominant positions typically enjoying significantly more and better options than those in subordinate ones. Stated otherwise, the extent to which one can exercise agency is socially structured. Therefore, to the extent that "degree of agency" is the inverse of social ranking, e.g., that the more equal women are to men the more agency they experience, the result is virtually a tautological statement. On the other hand, when used—as many feminist (and other) theorists appear to— to mean that philosophically, one *can always* make choices and that to deny this constitutes "bad faith" all but ignores the issue of penalty, rendering the term sociologically vacuous (although morally necessary). Nonetheless, how women employ whatever level of agency they command and what kinds of choices they make when offered more and better alternatives are important questions to address, especially when trying to understand change in a gender system, as well as variation among women in how they respond to a given or changing opportunity structure (see Chafetz, 1999b, for a fuller discussion of this issue).

Another major issue for feminist theory pertains to the distinction between gender differences, on average, in the personalities, values, attitudes, aspirations, choices, behaviors, and/or other individual-level traits of women and men and disadvantages that women relative to men who are otherwise their social equals [e.g., in family socioeconomic status (SES), race/ ethnicity/religion] experience in their access to scarce and valued resources, including power, prestige, and property (i.e., the level of gender stratification). Inequality implies difference, or at least the widespread perception of it, although difference does not necessitate inequality. In the case of gender, both assumed differences and structured inequalities characterize virtually all contemporary societies, dating back at least to the inception of agriculture and the domestication of animals for food (Chafetz, 1984; Blumberg, 1978; Martin & Voorhies, 1975). Both the kinds of gender differences and the level of gender inequality vary among subpopulations within socially heterogeneous societies, especially between classes and racially/ ethnically/religiously defined subcultures. I concentrate solely on gender in this chapter, thereby ignoring intrasocietal variation in the level and nature of gender inequality, a topic explored extensively in the descriptive literature in recent years under the rubric of "the intersection of race, class, and gender," but as yet inadequately theorized (for a first attempt, see Hill Collins, 1990).

The extent to which gender differences are "real" versus perceived and the factors that produce whatever verifiable differences do exist are contested issues both among feminist theorists and between many feminists and those less sympathetic to their agenda (for an excellent discussion of the debate, see Epstein, 1988, 1999). On the one hand, "essentialists" assume that, whether biologically inherent or the result of early childhood experiences, men and women categorically differ in their preferences, values, personalities, behaviors, intellectual, and other individual-level qualities. On the other hand, "minimalists" argue that, regardless of widespread essentialist stereotypes, between-sex differences pale when contrasted to within-sex ones on virtually any individual-level trait. Moreover, those differences that do exist are not categorical but rather can best be described as highly overlapping normal curves of distribution. Finally, minimalists argue that these "real," albeit mostly minor between-sex differences can best be explained by features of social life that result on average in adult females and males performing different social roles, being involved in different types of networks, and confronting different opportunity and reward structures. Epstein (1988) (see also Kanter, 1977) makes an excellent case for the minimalist stance, one that I share.

MAINTAINING AND
REPRODUCING GENDER

Macrolevel Approaches

Men have long dominated—often monopolized—the central institutions of their societies, including the extended household in prestate times and places (Collins, 1975) and subsequently the polity, large-scale economic, and major culture-producing organizations (e.g., religious and educational, especially advanced-level, institutions, knowledge production, and the media of mass communication). Although only a small and privileged handful of their sex, elite men, who constitute the policy and decision makers of these institutions, represent what Connell (1987) calls "hegemonic masculinity." All forms of femininity are ranked below this and other forms of masculinity are generally ranked somewhere in between. Elsewhere, I (Chafetz, 1990) have argued that it does not require any conscious intent or deliberate effort on the part of elite men to denigrate or discriminate against women, although some may purposely do so, in order for them to maintain their privileges and more generally those of men categorically. Rather, because they are men and therefore define, perceive, and evaluate the world from the perspective of their (elite) male social position, the rules and standards of judgment they establish, the social, cultural, and organizational definitions they promulgate while performing their elite roles, will perforce be androcentric, thereby automatically advantaging members of their sex, especially those who share their elite status.

In a similar vein, Smith (1987, 1990) and Hill Collins (1990) emphasize the near male monopoly over that which is socially defined as legitimate knowledge production as the primary mechanism by which (white) males are able to maintain social hegemony in the modern world. Expanding on insights from Marx, Mannheim, Foucault, and others, these and other standpoint theorists (e.g., Cook & Fonow, 1986; Farganis, 1986; Haraway, 1988; Harding, 1986; Harstock, 1983) argue that all knowledge is partial in that it reflects the specific social position(s) of the knower, but only some knowledge is privileged by the broader society as "true," "real," or legitimate. Privileged knowledge has been produced overwhelmingly by males but broadly accepted as universally valid truth. In turn, such "truth" not only distorts the lived reality of women and other oppressed categories of people (e.g., racial minorities, nonheterosexuals, lower-class people), it serves to reproduce social definitions and expectations that contribute further to their oppression (see Sprague & Zimmerman, 1993; Sprague & Kobrynowicz, 1999, for reviews of feminist standpoint theory).

The macrolevel structure most frequently posited as central to the explanation of gender inequality (patriarchy) is the economy, although it is conceptualized in different ways by different theorists. Marxist-inspired socialist and world system feminist theories concentrate on how capitalism maintains and often, especially in peripheral third-world nations, exacerbates patriarchy. Most Socialist–feminist scholars (e.g., Hartmann, 1979, 1984; Sacks, 1974; Eisenstein, 1979; Vogel, 1983; Sokoloff, 1980) analytically distinguish between classes and gender-based structures of oppression, recognize that the latter both predated capitalism and has survived under socialism, but argue that within capitalist systems they are mutually interpenetrating and reinforcing. Classic Marxist theory is faulted for its failure to incorporate as a central theoretical construct the phenomenon of reproductive labor, which is performed overwhelmingly by women as unpaid work, alongside that of productive labor that directly produces surplus value. Every bit as necessary to capitalists as waged labor, reproductive labor (maintaining workers by fulfilling their daily needs and raising the next generation of workers) constitutes a fundamental service both to male workers and to capitalists. Nonetheless, because women are overwhelmingly responsible for its accomplishment, they are at best less able to compete in the waged labor force and therefore receive lower pay and at worst are excluded from the labor force, and thus from "social adulthood" (Sacks, 1974). Shelton and Agger (1993) define the contemporary situation in advanced industrial societies, in which women have added labor force work to reproductive labor, as one in which they create far more surplus value than men, and thus are doubly exploited by capitalism. The theoretical (and extensive empirical) literature on women and development (e.g., Ward, 1984, 1990, 1993; see Pyle, 1999, for a general review) uses a modified world systems approach to describe and explain the mostly negative impact of capitalist penetration on the status of women in peripheral nations.

While they do not define the primary issue as that of a specifically capitalist economy, other feminist structural theories (e.g., Blumberg, 1978, 1984, 1988; Collins et al., 1993; Chafetz, 1984, 1990; see Dunn et al., 1993, for a general review) focus on two issues central to Socialist feminist analyses: unpaid maintenance (domestic and child rearing) work and the gender division of labor within the economy (in contemporary societies, mostly the paid labor force). These, in fact, are interrelated aspects of the more general concept, gender division of labor. Two propositions summarize this perspective:

1. The greater the amount of domestic–reproductive labor for which women are responsible, the less access they have to and the lower the reward level they receive from economic roles (i.e., those that produce income or nondomestically exchangeable products/services), and vice versa.
2. The more women control exchangeable products–services or income derived from economic labor, the lower the level of gender inequality.

Several macrostructural approaches devote considerable attention to delineating the variables that explain the relative extent to which women enjoy economic opportunities and resources and to a lesser extent their level of domestic/reproductive labor. In my work (Chafetz, 1990), the gender division of labor—in the labor force and household—constitutes the single-most important construct for understanding how systems of gender stratification maintain and reproduce themselves. Blumberg (1984) suggests the women's ability to control economic resources (their economic power) is strongly affected by the strategic indispensibility of their work and constitutes the most important factor in predicting their level of autonomy and influence within the household. However, she notes that three other forms of power, coercive, political and ideological, although less important than economic, tend to flow from higher social levels (e.g., societal, community) downward to the lowest nested level: the household. These forms of power tend overwhelmingly to advantage men, thereby serving to "discount" the effects of women's economic power at the household level.

Virtually all macrolevel theories include cultural or ideological gender definitions as a crucial underpinning of systemic gender inequality. Neo-Marxist feminists argue that capitalists foster a patriarchal ideology that justifies women's nonwaged domestic labor with reference to biologically rooted reproductive differences between the sexes, and then justifies sex-based inequities in the labor market with reference to women's domestic obligations (e.g., Eisenstein, 1979). The advantages in the home and labor market that therefore accrue to working-class men are postulated as reducing their willingness to challenge the capitalist system (Sokoloff, 1980; Shelton & Agger, 1993). Chafetz (1984, 1990) argues that religious and secular ideologies, developed primarily by male elites, "explain," justify, and legitimate the gender division of labor, gender stereotypes, and gender norms, thus contributing to the maintenance of gender stratification. Likewise, one of Blumberg's (1984) four types of power that typically advantage males is ideology. Some anthropologists (e.g., Ortner, 1974; Rosaldo, 1974; Sanday, 1981) focus their explanations of gender stratification almost entirely on cultural belief systems, and standpoint theorists, as discussed earlier, focus on privilege knowledge production as the key to understanding contemporary systems of patriarchy.

Family structure variables comprise yet another focus of macrostructural feminist theories, especially those directed to a broader array of societal types than simply contemporary industrial/capitalistic ones. Blumberg (1978), Chafetz (1984), and Martin and Voorhies (1975) point to patrilineage and patrilocality as especially disadvantageous to women. Collins et al. (1993) include in their complex theory the construct "sexual alliance politics," which focuses on family systems that exchange women as wives, thereby cementing political alliances. In such cases, women's sexuality constitutes a form of property to be carefully protected by male family members, with the result that women are highly controlled.

Another group of variables considered by a number of these theories is demographic, including sex ratio (Guttentag & Secord, 1983; also Chafetz, 1984, 1990), population density (Harris, 1978; also Chafetz, 1984, 1990), and fertility rates (Huber, 1991, 1999). These variables affect one or both aspects of the gender division of labor. In general, women fare best where population density and fertility rates are low and where there is a shortage of men.

Using Lenski's (1966) typology, in which the dominant technology and resultant size of the economic surplus define societal types, several theorists (e.g., Blumberg, 1978; Chafetz, 1984; Huber, 1988, 1999) trace the effects of environment and technology on the variables described above, and hence on the level of gender stratification. In general, harsh physical environments (e.g., desert, tundra) and/or chronic warfare (i.e., a socially harsh environment) result in higher levels of gender inequality. Technological level is related in a curvilinear manner to the level of gender stratification: very low in most foraging (hunting–gathering) societies, rising in horticultural, peaking in agrarian, herding and early-stage industrial, and declining somewhat in later stage industrial societies.

Some of the most eclectic macrostructural feminist theories are highly complex in the number of constructs and nature of their linkages (e.g., Chafetz, 1984, 1990; Collins et al., 1993). All attempt to explain the structural features that produce systems of gender stratification and/or account for varying levels of gender inequality. Most therefore at least implicitly suggest how such systems change, a topic to which I will return later. While they vary somewhat in their emphases, most examples of this theory type focus strongly on the gender division of labor and especially on the relative control women exercise over economic surplus and/or income, using the other variables discussed in this section to explain the gender division of labor and/or to link it to the level of gender inequality. Although there has been some recognition of the independent importance of political structure or power for understanding the level of gender inequality (e.g., Collins, 1975; Collins et al., 1993; Blumberg, 1984), this variable, by and large, has been short shrifted by feminist theorists in our discipline (Dunn et al., 1993).

Mesolevel Theories

Mesolevel feminist approaches focus on how organizations and groups reproduce gender inequality. The earliest of these theories was Kanter's (1977) analysis of the impact of three structural variables on the work-related behaviors of women and men: opportunity structure, power, and relative numbers. She argues that the extent to which employees in a large corporate bureaucracy perceive promotion opportunities, enjoy adequate resources (power) to accomplish the tasks for which they are responsible and are numerically tokens/dominants in their ascribed (gender, racial) status within the work group, produce varying levels of job commitment, as well as differences in a variety of attitudes and behaviors on the job. Men and women respond the same way to these variables. However, given discriminatory hiring and promotion practices, the probabilities that women will be in positions where upward mobility is likely and their level of empowerment is high are much lower than those of men, while women are much more likely to find themselves tokens in the work setting. Thus, women's and men's work commitments, attitudes, and behaviors come to differ because the nature of their work and work setting differ (see also Miller et al., 1983). These differences, in turn, reinforce negative stereotypes about women's work performance, especially in higher-level, white-collar jobs, thereby justifying discriminatory practices.

Acker (1991, 1999) conceptualizes bureaucratic organizations as a set of fundamentally gendered processes. Gender inequality is continuously reproduced by the routine, mundane practices of organizations. The array of such practices include, among other things, screening tests for job applicants, evaluation criteria, job classification schemes, job design, "common-sense" conceptions of organizational features, and gender-specific definitions and expectations of employees. While organizations may appear to function in a gender-neutral fashion, in fact gender colors all aspects of their ongoing practices, largely because these practices have long been rooted in the assumption that workers are male. Finally, given the centrality of formal organizations to the economy and the centrality of the economy to all other aspects of contemporary life, these gendered practices, which mostly advantage men, have a profound impact on the broader gender system.

Task-oriented groups constitute the focus of status expectations theory, which explains the tendency for males to dominate mixed-sex groups (see Ridgeway, 1993; Ridgeway & Smith-Lovin, 1999, for reviews of this perspective). Given that males enter such groups with a higher socially ascribed status, group members of both sexes expect their performances to be more competent than those of women, unless the task is explicitly viewed as a traditionally feminine one. In turn, the expectation that males are more competent leads to a self-fulfilling prophecy that functions to reduce women's self-confidence, prestige, power, and influence in future, as well as present group interactions. Because gender-based expectations are defined by group members as legitimate, an individual woman's attempt to counteract them will be rejected by other group members as inappropriate. The result is that outcomes usually reflect the preferences of the group's male members. Moreover, the status and power of male group members are enhanced, which is often "the basis on which many of society's rewards of power, position and respect are distributed" (Ridgeway, 1993, p. 193).

Although network theory is typically unconcerned with the characteristics of actors, rather focusing on the linkages between them, nonetheless it recently has been applied to gender (Smith-Lovin & McPherson, 1993; see Ridgeway & Smith-Lovin, 1999, for a general review). The central argument is that "you are who you know," and that beginning in early childhood and cumulating over the life span most people are primarily embedded in gender-homophilous networks. In turn, because adult networks foster aspirations, behaviors, and opportunities, these come to differ by gender. Women typically have more network ties to kin and neighbors, and men to nonkin, especially co-workers and voluntary group members. Women are more densely interconnected, while men have more extensive but looser ties. Finally, occupational success and other benefits are associated with nonredundant ties, which are more characteristic of men's than women's networks (Ridgeway & Smith-Lovin, 1999, pp. 256–257).

In summary, formal organizations, long dominated and largely staffed by men, continue a set of mundane practices that are deeply and often subtly gendered, to the advantage of men. More overt discriminatory practices produce among women the very behaviors and attitudes that reinforce the negative stereotypes used to justify discrimination. Mixed-sex groups function to reproduce and strengthen the advantages with which men enter them. Finally, ubiquitous same-sex networks reproduce existing opportunity structures that advantage men, as well as shape aspirations and behaviors in a gender-traditional manner.

Microlevel Theories

A variety of theories concern the engenderment process by which children typically become traditionally and "appropriately" masculine or feminine and the ways in which dyadic interactions reproduce gender differences and inequities. Childhood engenderment theories reflect several psychological–psychoanalytical traditions (for a general review, see Stockard, 1999), including social learning, cognitive development, and object relations neo-Freudian theories. Among American sociologists, Chodorow's work (1978, 1989) has been the single-most influential neo-Freudian approach and has been widely used by feminist scholars as the major underpinning for essentialist arguments. This theory posits that because infant and toddler caretaking is overwhelmingly performed by women, youngsters of both sexes have a female as their primary love object. As a result, boys' and girls' Oedipal stage experiences are vastly different. Girls, who share their primary love object's sex, need not separate from her in order to attain a gendered identity. Because of this, girls grow into women whose primary concern is with connection to and nurturance of other people. In contrast, in order to develop a gendered identity, boys must separate from their female primary love object, a task that results in a lifelong emphasis on individuation, a denial of affect, misogyny, an orientation toward dominance, and striving for success outside the family. Based on Chodorow's theory, Gilligan (1982) argues that males and females engage in different types of moral reasoning: men employ abstract principles, while women focus on personal relationships and obligations when making moral decisions (see reviews of neo-Freudian feminist theory by Kurzweil, 1989; Williams, 1993).

Neo-Freudian explanations of gender differences focus on the unconscious processes that are said to create fundamentally different personalities, values, behaviors, and even cognitive styles in the two sexes. What I broadly label as socialization theory depicts many of the same outcomes as being produced by more deliberate processes and by a larger number of actors than just the primary caregiver. From this perspective, beginning at birth children receive a constant stream of information from significant others and later from peers, teachers, and the broader culture that informs them as to what their "proper" gender identity is and the "appropriate" behaviors based on that identity (e.g., Cahill, 1983; Lever, 1976; Constanti-nople, 1979; Coser, 1975, 1986; Sattel, 1976). Rewards, punishments, and modeling are postulated as major mechanisms that produce engenderment, which is said to become immut-able somewhere between the ages of three and six. Children actively participate in the process by categorizing their own sex as an "in-group" and the other as an "out-group" and on this basis seeking cues as to in-group "appropriate" toys, games, and behaviors, i.e., "gender schemas" (for a review, see Stockard, 1999).

Both the neo-Freudian and general socialization approaches assume that gender identity and a set of gendered behavioral orientations and values are firmly established during the preschool-aged years. These are said to continue throughout the life span to affect men's and women's choices and behaviors across virtually all types of situations. Many of these theories describe briefly the contributions of engenderment to the reproduction of gender inequality, primarily by discussing the relationship between presumably gendered personalities, values, and cognitive functioning, on the one hand, and the division of labor, on the other. Nonetheless, with a few exceptions, they focus more on difference than inequality.

This emphasis on difference also is manifested in feminist ethnomethodological theories. Kessler and McKenna (1978) argue that people are constantly engaged in creating a sense of gender difference and defining self and others through that lens. West and Zimmerman (1987) coined the term "doing gender" to refer to the work done during interactions in order to recreate each partner's sense of their own and the other's gender (see also West & Fenstermaker, 1993, 1995; Fenstermaker et al., 1991). Gender is "omnirelevant" in that any action can be interpreted as exemplifying it (West & Fenstermaker, 1993). Based on the taken-for-granted view that there are two (and only two) sexes to one (and only one) of which each person belongs, people automatically engage in gender attribution of self and other when they enter an interaction. On that basis, they interpret any and all kinds of behavior according to its normative gender "appropriateness," legitimating or discrediting it accordingly. This process is no less true for same-sex than cross-sex interactions (Gerson, 1985). The actual content of gender (i.e., that which is socially defined as masculinity and femininity) varies across time, space, and even situation, but for feminist ethnomethodologists, people's notion that males and females are fundamentally different does not. Indeed, the specific content associated with the two genders appears to be of little or no interest to these theorists, who are thus left with no basis on which to understand gender inequality (Hill Collins et al., 1995).

A variety of feminist theories are outgrowths of the symbolic interactionist tradition. More so than the ethnomethodological approaches, many of these focus on how interaction recreates gender inequality. Several feminist sociolinguists, social psychologists, and sociologists focus on how symbolic and nonverbal communication reinforce male privilege in interpersonal interactions (for a review, see Bonvillain, 1995, Chapter 9). Fishman (1982), Mayo and Henley (1981), and West and Zimmerman (1977), among others, argue that women work hard to sustain conversations, despite the fact that men dominate such interactions, and unlike men, women tend to use verbal and body language in a variety of ways that weaken their ability to assert themselves. Moreover, gender bias is built into most languages, including English. Fishman (1982, p. 178) concludes that, "the definition of what is appropriate conversation becomes men's choice. What part of the world [the interaction partners] ... maintain the reality of, is his choice" in short, men create the definition of the situation in their interactions with women.

Labeling theory is used by Schur (1984) to discuss how the stigmatized and devalued master status of femaleness results in the selective perception of women based on stereotypes and in their objectification as body parts and things rather than persons. Such objectification encourages the treatment of women in exploitative and degrading ways, which, in turn produce self-fulfilling prophecies by which women come to define themselves as inferior, suffer from low self-esteem and in-group hostility, and identify with their male oppressors.

Ferguson (1980) argues that men enter cross-sex interactions with superior power resources that allow them to define both specific situations and the generalized other. Women thus come to define themselves "by reference to standards that brand them as inferior" (p. 155), thereby assuming self-blame for their problems. In addition, women become highly skilled at taking the role of the male other, attempting to please and flatter him, anticipating his needs, and acquiescing to his demands in order to avoid punishment by their more powerful partners (Ferguson, 1980, pp. 161–162).

Scripting theory also is applied to gender reproduction because so many social roles are specifically associated with one sex. As people go about performing gender-specific roles, they automatically "do gender." For instance, the division of household labor, by which gendered scripts are provided for numerous tasks, makes this setting a veritable "gender factory" (Fenstermaker Berk, 1985). Many female roles, in the family and workforce, include scripts of "emotional labor" (Hochschild, 1983), which function to deny women an "integrated autonomous identity" (Kasper, 1986, p. 40).

Role theory was widely employed by feminist scholars in the 1970s, but it emanated primarily from the now discredited Parsonian conceptualization of generalized "sex or gender roles" that focused on highly scripted, trans-situational male and female roles. The most recent work to employ role theory springs instead from a symbolic interactionist perspective that conceptualizes social roles as negotiated performances (Lopata, 1994, 1999). Lopata focuses on the array of specific social roles contemporary women play (e.g., family, kinship, employment, student), comparing three ideal-typical kinds of women—modern, transitional, and traditional—but concentrating on the modern. Women perform the duties of their numerous roles within social circles composed of all those with whom they interact during the process of role enactment. Role salience changes over the life course, and therefore so do women's identifies, which are rooted in their roles. Unlike their more traditional sisters, modern role-players, who live in "modern" (i.e., advanced industrial) societies, deal with a more complex role set, a wider social circle, and therefore greater opportunities to negotiate role performances, although not all women in such societies are modern role-players. Lopata thereby relates role-playing to social change by linking the definitions, constraints, and opportunities generated at the macrostructural level with women's role negotiations, performances, and therefore identities. It is one of the few microlevel feminist theories to explicitly consider change, but the specific structural changes entailed by modernization and the actual processes that connect them with expanded role options for women are not well delineated.

Utilitarian theories of rational choice and social exchange also have been applied to the issue of the reproduction of gender inequality. Friedman and Diem (1993) demonstrate that many feminist empirical works concerning gender-related choices implicitly utilize such rational choice constructs as institutional constraints, opportunity costs, and preferences. Gender-related choices made by parents (e.g., regarding investments in sons' vs. daughter's education), employers (e.g., which sex to hire for which jobs), and individual women (e.g., whether to become a full-time homemaker), can be and often are analyzed from a rational choice theoretical perspective. My work with Hagan (Chafetz & Hagan, 1996) uses a modified rational choice perspective to explain a variety of family changes experienced in all advanced industrial nations (e.g., later average ages of first marriages and births; increasing divorce and cohabitation rates). We argue that these changes result from alterations in the rationally calculated choices large numbers of women make in such societies, in response to a new set of educational and occupational opportunities but a continuing set of traditional constraints in the family and workplace.

Social exchange theory has informed a considerable theoretical (and empirical) literature concerning spousal relationships and interactions (e.g., Bell & Newby, 1976; Chafetz, 1980, 1990; Curtis, 1986; Parker & Parker, 1979). The basic argument begins with the assertion that macrostructural arrangements traditionally have functioned to provide husbands with substantially more access than wives to the scarce and valued resources needed and desired by their families (especially income, but also prestige, knowledge, culturally legitimated authority, etc.). Men import this resource advantage into the family, where the spousal relationship is conceptualized as one of social exchange. In order for resource-poor wives to balance the exchange, they typically provide to their husbands compliance and deference, as well as domestic labor, thereby constantly recreating gender inequality within the family. In turn, depending on husbands' preferences, this can spill over into the economy by affecting whether wives are "permitted" to enter the labor force, and if so, the nature of jobs and number of hours they can accept (Chafetz, 1990).

At the microlevel, feminist theorists have focused on the reproduction of gender difference and inequality through childhood engenderment processes and the dynamics of interaction between men and women. Young children assume a gender identity and seek to express it behaviorally, presumably resulting in lifelong differences between the sexes in personality, cognitive style, values, and behaviors. As adults, men and women automatically attribute gender to interaction partners and by "doing gender" work to recreate situationally the shared sense of the reality of gender difference. Just as, at the mesolevel men bring greater status to mixed-sex groups then do women, at the microlevel men bring more resources than women to cross-sex dyadic interactions. This enables men to define situations, to extract compliance and deference, and therefore to recreate their superior position. Simultaneously, the same processes work to undermine women's self-identity and confidence, encouraging them to conspire in their own oppression.

UNDERSTANDING GENDER
SYSTEM CHANGE

Feminist scholars disagree about whether significant change has occurred in recent decades in the level of gender inequality, especially that characteristic of advanced industrial societies. Some, such as most socialist feminists, treat "patriarchy" as a virtual constant and seek to understand its various guises. From this kind of perspective, constant change in the manifestations of patriarchy mask an unchanging reality of inequality. In contrast, especially those theorists who take a broad historical and/or cross-cultural view, typically argue that the level, not simply manifestations, of gender stratification has decreased in wealthy nations during recent decades (e.g., Jackson, 1998; Chafetz, 1984, 1990; Huber, 1999). Because I agree with the second view, the question is: given that as recently as 150 years ago men monopolized control over the economy, polity, legal, and educational systems in virtually all nations, how did they come to relinquish at least some of it to women in many (Jackson, 1998)?

The Inadequacies of Micro- and Mesolevel Explanations

Childhood engenderment theories assume that the gendered personalities, cognitive styles, values, and behavioral orientations that accompany the development of a "proper" gender identity remain strong throughout life. In the neo-Freudian approach, caregiver sex (female) plays the crucial role in the reproduction of gender. In the general socialization approach, parents, significant others, and other actors recreate gendered selves in each new generation, thus reproducing systems of gender inequality. To create gender system change, logically one would have to alter the personalities, values, behaviors, and indeed self-concepts of a large proportion of an adult generation, but how could and why would this occur? Why, in the case of the neo-Freudians, would large numbers of "individuating," "misogynistic" men, who are oriented to denying affect and pursuing success, come to nurture infants and toddlers (and who would want them to do so)? Chodorow (1978) does recognize that different societal types (defined in terms of technology and political economy) vary in the extent to which men are involved in nurturing very young children, thereby implying that change can occur. However, this begs the question of *how* it occurs (although implying a macrolevel cause). Socialization theories imply or explicitly suggest that as significant others change their behaviors and as gendered cultural depictions change, the gendered content of the messages children learn will too, again begging the question of why these things would change. In fact, to the extent that childhood engenderment is said to produce strong, lifelong behavioral and other consequences, changes in adult attributes and behaviors are logically impossible to produce or explain on a large-scale basis.

When theories of cross-sex interaction are examined, it is clear that most imply that change is impossible, ignore the issue entirely, or locate its impetus outside of the interaction context. Feminist ethnomethodology conceptualizes the process of creating a sense of gender difference, by interaction partners continually "doing gender," as a constant. Scripting and sociolinguistic theories do not assert that the features they discuss are constants, but neither do they suggest any mechanism by which they might change. Many other theories inspired by symbolic interactionism, along with feminist versions of status attainment and social exchange theories, assume that men bring into dyadic relationships/interactions with women superior prestige, power, and/or resources generated in a usually untheorized "elsewhere." The implication of this kind of approach is that change in interaction patterns can occur, but only after changes in the surrounding environment had reduced men's or enhanced women's status, power, and/or resources.

Several meso- and microlevel theories do explicitly suggest how change can occur, but their suggestions presuppose an already-existing process of change in the gender system. Smith-Lovin and McPherson (1993), in their network analysis, assert that anything that alters women's networks could contribute to expanding their opportunities and raising their aspirations. As an example, they talk about public policy concerning equal employment opportunities, which begs the issue of what causes such favorable public policy changes. The same problem occurs with Ridgeway's (1993, pp. 187–188) analysis of change in task-oriented groups. She suggests three conditions that can reduce male dominance in this context, two of which reinforce traditional gender-based expectations of women: performance expectations will not favor men if the task is traditionally defined as feminine; and women can neutralize legitimacy effects by signaling that their motivations to contribute are cooperative rather than competitive with men. The third states that expectations can be modified if an outside authority imposes on the group a definition of the female as more competent than the male members in skills valued by the group. This, too, only leads to the question: Why would an outside authority be motivated to do so? Kanter (1977) offers numerous suggestions to organizations to reduce women's disadvantages (e.g., reorganizing work groups so women are not placed in token positions), but all presuppose a commitment on the part of (male) executives to gender equity. Why would they be so committed? Acker's (1999) suggestions for organizational change suffer from the same problem. In all these cases, the theorists are undoubtedly assuming that governmental pressure, based on antidiscrimination legislation, constitutes the major outside impetus. However, after centuries of publicly legitimated sex discrimination, how does one account for such legislation arising?

Given all these problems, I conclude that the basic impetus for gender system change must be located at the macrolevel. Once begun, change at this level has major ramifications for micro- and mesolevel processes, and as they begin to change, there are likely feedback mechanisms to the macrolevel. Nonetheless, one cannot understand how gender systems begin to change any place other than at the macro-level.

The Macrolevel Impetus

Not only must the impetus for gender system change be located at the macrostructural level, logically it cannot emphasize women's agency in producing it. To the extent that males control—in fact, often monopolize—power and resources in gender stratified systems, by definition women lack sufficient opportunities and resources (i.e., sufficient agency) to change the system to one less disadvantageous for their sex. Moreover, if one assumes (as I do) that no privileged category of people consciously and purposely relinquishes its privilege (except under duress), the source of gender system change must be located in the latent consequences of actions performed by (male) elites, as they go about the business of running major societal institutions and/or as the accidental outcome of processes under no direct human control.

Recently, Jackson (1998) subtitled his rational choice analysis of gender system change in wealthy nations (especially the United States), "The Inevitable Rise of Women's Status." He argues that in the rational pursuit of their institutions' interests, over the last 150 years politicians, business leaders, university, and other institutional administrators came to decouple organizational decision making from gender concerns. During the 19th century, families and households began a long-term decline as the basic units of society, as their functions were increasingly assumed by bureaucratic organizations. In turn, organizations' vested interests sometimes (often quite subtly) contradicted whatever interests their male leaders may have had in maintaining their gender's dominance. It was not that these men sought or even supported enhanced status and opportunities for women. Rather, they were often oblivious to the long-run ramifications of their decisions for women's status. In this way, women first gained a variety of legal and subsequently political rights, as well as access to higher education and labor force opportunities. The development of institutional and ideological emphases on individualism and meritocracy in the long run were antithetical to systemic gender inequality. The family, too, became more voluntaristic and contractual, hence individualistic, gradually losing its inherent interest in preserving gender inequality. While Jackson recognizes that women are still disadvantaged by their sex and refrains from predicting the end of gender inequality altogether, he nonetheless argues that major societal institutions have inadvertently lost their inherent interest in discriminating against women as an unanticipated consequence of their pursuit of rational self-interest.

Other theories of the initiation of gender system change emphasize conditions that inadvertently increase the demand for and/or the supply of women to the labor force. I (Chafetz, 1984, 1990; Oppenheimer, 1970) have theorized that in recent decades economic expansion and technological changes have led to enormous growth in the service sectors of all advanced industrial nations. This resulted in a significant increase in the demand for women's labor, beyond that which the traditional female labor pool (mostly young, single, and very poor married women) could provide. Married women with older children and subsequently those with preschool-aged children were induced to enter the workforce to meet labor demands that men could (or, less often would) not meet. Others (e.g., Huber, 1988, 1991, 1999) have examined the impact of enhanced educational opportunities for women and significantly reduced fertility rates, both of which are seen as latent effects of economic development, on women's willingness and ability to supply labor to the workforce. The combination of enhanced demand for and supply of women to the labor force provided increasing numbers of women with direct (as opposed to mediated via husbands and fathers) access to scarce and valued resources through an income of their own. However, all these factors were "accidental" outcomes of long-term alterations in the economies and other institutions of mature industrial nations. Although very low sex ratios in a community or nation (usually the result of war or male-specific out-migration) also can enhance women's opportunities, the effect is usually temporary (Chafetz, 1984, 1990).

Systemic Ramifications

Any type of structural change that has the latent consequence of increasing the direct access by a large proportion of women to scarce and valued societal resources can initiate a broader process of change in a system of gender inequality. The significant resource advantages men traditionally bring to mixed-sex groups and dyadic relationships then becomes mitigated, at least in part, and therefore group and interpersonal dynamics begin to change to less fully reproduce gender inequities. To the extent that the gender division of labor changes as women assume new, nontraditional roles, models for children become less traditional. Moreover, as Lopata (1994) theorizes, women come to enjoy greater opportunities to negotiate role performances according to their own preferences as their social circles widen in response to enhanced access to a variety of roles. The constraints and opportunities that shape rational choices also begin to alter, contributing to changes in what had been traditional, gender-based decisions, as does the nature of women's networks and therefore their aspirations and opportunities. In other words, many of the mechanisms that feminist theories identify to explain the micro- and mesolevel reproduction of gender differences and inequality are interrupted, at least in part. Stated differently, women come to enjoy enhanced agency that enables them to negotiate their interactions with men, thereby producing outcomes more favorable to themselves.

Perhaps more importantly, gender system change becomes a political goal for many women, and to the extent that they are successful, mesolevel as well as further macro- and microlevel change occurs. Chafetz and Dworkin (1986) (see also Jackson, 1998, Chapter 5) theorize that women's movements explicitly oriented to creating a system of gender equality arise and grow large only after women's resources and opportunities have begun to significantly expand. Once they grow beyond the small, "incipient" level, women's movements often impact public opinion and policy, thereby strengthening the impetus for gender system changes that are already underway (see also Chafetz, 1995). According to Chafetz and Dworkin (1986), as women's roles expand beyond those traditional to their sex, women begin to alter their comparative reference group from other women to male co-workers, fellow students, and so forth. They thereby "discover" their relatively disadvantaged position and develop an increasing sense of relative deprivation. They also tend to suffer "status/role conflicts" as they continue to be treated on the basis of traditional expectations associated with their gender rather than on the basis of their newly achieved statuses. Increasingly concentrated in schools and workplaces (rather than dispersed in private households), many women come to communicate these grievances with one another. In the process, some develop a "gender consciousness" that locates the source of their problems at the systemic level rather than in their individual shortcomings, and one or more ideologies countering the prevailing ones that justify and legitimate gender inequality. Armed with enhanced material and other resources (e.g., knowledge, public-speaking skills) that flow from their newly assumed roles, gender-conscious women create social movement organizations designed to bring about legal and other changes to fight gender inequality. Through overlapping membership networks, new movement organizations develop alliances with preexisting women's clubs and organizations, thereby expanding their support base. Women's movements are likely to be at least somewhat successful to the extent that the ongoing increase in their sex's opportunities creates a large pool of women who share a similar set of problems. With new laws and policies directed toward enhancing gender equality, organizations come to feel the kinds of pressures for change that several theories reviewed earlier appeared to have been taken for granted. However, the mechanisms that directly connect women's movement activism with legal and other policy changes are poorly theorized; the answer to the question, "How do women's movements actually produce change in a system of gender stratification" remains to be adequately developed.

In addition to their effects on law and organizational policies, women's movements affect large numbers of individuals by creating public awareness of gender inequality. As their "consciousness" is at least partially "raised," many people—especially women—attempt to alter their own lives, self-concepts, and aspirations, to raise children in less traditional ways, to change the manner in which they interact with members of the other sex, divide household labor, and so on, and they may try to change the professions and organizations in which they work and their children are educated (Chafetz, 1990). In short, once a woman's movement, with its new ideology concerning gender relations, begins to affect the broader public, it negatively affects many of the micro- and mesolevel processes that heretofore had reproduced gender difference and inequality.

Gender system changes that begin as unintended consequences of macrostructural change, by which women's access of opportunities and resources is enhanced, tend to directly spur both other changes in gender arrangements and the development of a women's movement. In turn, as such movements grow, they expedite and hasten changes at all levels—micro, meso, and macro—of the gender institution (as Lorber, 1994, calls it). To date, no one feminist theory adequately integrates all levels of analysis in a full explanation of gender system change, although there have been several attempts to do so (e.g., Chafetz, 1990; Collins et al., 1993; Connell, 1987; Lorber, 1994).

CONCLUSION

In this chapter I have devoted very little attention to the many versions of feminist epistemology that are collectively labeled "standpoint theory" and are in many instances treated as virtually synonymous with the term "feminist theory" in our discipline. Instead, I have attempted to demonstrate the wide array of contemporary feminists explanatory theories in sociology, theories that reflect, revise, and/or extend almost all of our discipline's fundamental perspectives. Collectively, these theories do an excellent job of explaining how systems of gender difference and inequality permeate all aspects and levels of social life and how they are continuously reproduced. In doing so, they provide a comprehensive list of the myriad things that require change in order to achieve a gender equitable society (see especially Lorber, 1994, Conclusion). Despite their authors' commitment to changing such systems, however, most feminist theories do a poor job of explaining how systems of gender inequality come to change, largely presupposing the existence of laws and policies mandating equal treatment and/or a gender-conscious segment of the population that actively works to produce change. As the last section of this chapter demonstrates, however, we now have most of the theoretical insights necessary to develop a comprehensive theory of gender system change by beginning with the latent consequences of macrostructural change and subsequently demonstrating how gender equitable laws, policies, and consciousness arise that spur further change at all levels of social life. This process does not go unchallenged and over time often takes two steps forward and one backward (Chafetz & Dworkin, 1989; also Chafetz, 1990; Rossi, 1982; Rupp & Taylor, 1987). It is, however, beyond the scope of this chapter to explore the theoretical reasons for this cyclical phenomenon.

Feminist theory has undergone substantial development during the last third of the 20th century and at century's end finally has begun to appear even in most contemporary theory textbooks in sociology, although substantial ghettoization remains. I hope soon to see the day that gender assumes its rightful position in sociological theory, alongside class/status, as equally important axes along which all surplus-producing societies to date have distributed scarce and valued resources and opportunities. When gender is fully integrated into "general" sociological theory, our discipline will achieve a much more robust understanding of social life.

REFERENCES

Acker, J. (1991). Hierarchies, jobs, bodies: A theory of gendered organizations. In J. Lorber & S. A. Farrell (Eds.), *The social construction of gender* (pp. 162–179). Newbury Park, CA: Sage.

Acker, J. (1999). Gender and organizations. In J. S. Chafetz (Ed.), *Handbook of the sociology of gender* (pp. 177–194). New York: Plenum Press.

Bell, C., & Newby, H. (1976). Husbands and wives: The dynamics of the deferential dialectic. In D. L. Baker & S. Allen (Eds.), *Dependence and exploitation in work and marriage* (pp. 152–168). London: Longman.

Blumberg, R. L. (1978). *Stratification: Socioeconomic and sexual inequality.* Dubuque, IA: Wm. C. Brown.

Blumberg, R. L. (1984). A general theory of gender stratification. In R. Collins (Ed.), *Sociological theory, 1984* (pp. 23–101). San Francisco: Jossey-Bass.

Blumberg, R. L. (1988). Income under female versus male control: Hypotheses from a theory of gender stratification and data from the third world. *Journal of Family Issues, 9,* 51–84.

Bonvillain, N. (1995). *Women and men: Cultural constructs of gender.* Englewood Cliffs, NJ: Prentice-Hall.

Cahill, S. (1983). Reexamining the acquisition of sex roles: A symbolic interactionist approach. *Sex Roles, 9,* 1–15.

Chafetz, J. S. (1980). Conflict resolution in marriage: Toward a theory of spousal strategies and marital dissolution rates. *Journal of Family Issues, 1,* 397–421.

Chafetz, J. S. (1984). *Sex and advantage: A comparative, macro-structural theory of sex stratification.* Totowa, NJ: Rowman and Allanheld.

Chafetz, J. S. (1988). *Feminist sociology: An overview of contemporary theories.* Itasca, IL: F. E. Peacock.

Chafetz, J. S. (1990). *Gender equity: A theory of stability and change.* Newbury Park, CA: Sage.

Chafetz, J. S. (1995). Chicken or egg? A theory of the relationship between feminist movements and family change in industrialized societies. In K. Oppenheimer Mason & A. Jensen (Eds.), *Gender and family change in industrialized societies* (pp. 63–81). Oxford: Clarendon Press.

Chafetz, J. S. (1997). Feminist theory and sociology. *Annual Review of Sociology, 23,* 97–120.

Chafetz, J. S. (1999a). The varieties of gender theory in sociology. In J. S. Chafetz (Ed.), *Handbook of the sociology of gender* (pp. 2–23). New York: Plenum Press.

Chafetz, J. S. (1999b). Structure, agency, consciousness and social change in feminist theories: A conundrum. *Current Perspectives in Social Theory, 19,* 145–164.

Chafetz, J. S., & Dworkin, A. G. (1986). *Female revolt: Women's movements in world and historical perspective.* Totowa, NJ: Rowman and Allanheld.

Chafetz, J. S., & Dworkin, A. G. (1989). Action and reaction: An integrated, comparative perspective on feminist and antifeminist movements. In M. Kohn (Ed.), *Cross-national research in sociology* (pp. 329–350). Beverly Hills, CA: Sage.

Chafetz, J. S., & Hagan, J. (1996). The gender division of labor and family change in industrial societies: A theoretical accounting. *Journal of Comparative Family Studies, 27,* 187–217.

Chodorow, N. (1978). *The reproduction of mothering: Psychoanalysis and the sociology of gender.* Berkeley: The University of California Press.

Chodorow, N. (1989). *Feminism and psychoanalytic theory.* New Haven: Yale University Press.

Collins, R. (1975). *Conflict sociology: Toward an explanatory science.* New York: Academic Press.

Collins, R., Chafetz, J. S., Blumberg, R. L., Coltrane, S., & Turner, J. (1993). Toward an integrated theory of gender stratification. *Sociological Perspectives, 36*, 185–216.

Connell, R. W. (1987). *Gender and power: Society, the person, and sexual politics*. Stanford, CA: Stanford University Press.

Constantinople, A. (1979). Sex-role acquisition: In search of the elephant. *Sex Roles, 5*, 121–133.

Cook, J. A., & Fonow, M. M. (1986). Knowledge and women's interests: Issues of epistemology and methodology in feminist sociological research. *Sociological Inquiry, 56*, 2–29.

Coser, R. L. (1975). Stay home, littler Sheba: On placement, displacement and social change. *Social Problems, 22*, 470–480.

Coser, R. L. (1986). Cognitive structure and the use of social space. *Sociological Forum, 1*, 1–26.

Curtis, R. (1986). Household and family in theory on inequality. *American Sociological Review, 51*, 168–183.

Dunn, D., Almquist, E., & Chafetz, J. S. (1993). Macrostructural perspectives on gender inequality. In P. England (Ed.), *Theory on gender/feminism on theory* (pp. 69–90). New York: Aldine de Gruyter.

Eisenstein, Z. (1979). Developing a theory of capitalist patriarchy and socialist feminism, and some notes on the relations of capitalist patriarchy. In Z. Eisenstein (Ed.), *Capitalist patriarchy and the case for socialist feminism* (pp. 5–55). New York: Monthly Review Press.

England, P. (1993). *Theory on gender/feminism on theory*. New York: Aldine De Gruyter.

Epstein, C. F. (1988). *Deceptive distinctions: Sex, gender, and the social order*. New Haven: Yale University Press.

Epstein, C. F. (1999). Similarity and difference: The sociology of gender distinction. In J. S. Chafetz (Ed.), *Handbook of the sociology of gender* (pp. 45–61). New York: Plenum Press.

Farganis, S. (1986). Social theory and feminist theory: The need for dialogue. *Sociological Inquiry, 56*, 50–68.

Fenstermaker Berk, S. (1985). *The gender factory*. New York: Plenum Press.

Fenstermaker, S., West, C., & Zimmerman, D. (1991). Gender inequality: New conceptual terrain. In R. Blumberg (Ed.), *Gender, family, and economy: The triple overlap* (pp. 289–307). Newbury Park, CA: Sage.

Ferguson, K. (1980). *Self, society, and womankind*. Westwood, CT: Greenwood Press.

Fishman, P. (1982). Interaction: The work women do. In R. Kahn-Hut, A. K. Daniels, & R. Colvard (Eds.), *Women and work: Problems and perspectives* (pp. 170–180). New York: Oxford University Press.

Friedman, D., & Diem, C. (1993). Feminism and the pro-(rational-) choice movement: rational-choice theory, feminist critiques, and gender inequality. In P. England (Ed.), *Theory on gender/feminism on theory* (pp. 91–114). New York: Aldine De Gruyter.

Gerson, J. M. (1985). Boundaries, negotiation, consciousness: Reconceptualizing gender relations. *Social Problems, 32*, 317–331.

Gilligan, C. (1982). *In a different voice*. Cambridge, MA: Harvard University Press.

Guttentag, M., & Secord, P. (1983). *Too many women? The sex ratio question*. Beverly Hills, CA: Sage.

Haraway, D. (1988). Situated knowledges: The science question in feminism and the privilege of partial perspective. *Feminist Studies, 14*, 575–599.

Harding, S. (1986). *The science question in feminism*. Ithaca, NY: Cornell University Press.

Harris, M. (1978). *Cannibals and kings: The origins of cultures*. London: Collins.

Harstock, N. C. M. (1983). The feminist standpoint: Developing the ground for a specifically feminist historical materialism. In S. Harding & M. B. Hintikka (Eds.), *Discovering reality: Feminist perspectives on epistemology, metaphysics, methodology and philosophy of science* (pp. 283–310). Boston: D. Reidel.

Hartmann, H. (1979). Capitalism, patriarchy, and job segregation by sex. In Z. Eisenstein (Ed.), *Capitalist patriarchy and the case for socialist feminism* (pp. 206–247). New York: Monthly Review Press.

Hartmann, H. (1984). The unhappy marriage of Marxism and feminism: Towards a more progressive union. In A. Jaggar & P. Rothenberg (Eds.), *Feminist frameworks: Alternative theorétical accounts of the relations between women and men* (pp. 172–189). New York: McGraw-Hill.

Hill Collins, P. (1990). *Black feminist thought: Knowledge, consciousness and the politics of empowerment*. Boston: Unwin Hyman.

Hill Collins, P., Maldonado, L., Takagi, D., Thorne, B., Weber, L., & Winant, H. (1995). Symposium on West and Fenstermaker's "Doing Difference." *Gender & Society, 9*, 491–513.

Hochschild, A. (1983). *The managed heart: Commercialization of human feeling*. Berkeley: University of California Press.

Huber, J. (1988). A theory of family, economy, and gender. *Journal of Family Issues, 9*, 9–26.

Huber, J. (1991). Macro–micro links in gender stratification. In J. Huber (Ed.), *Macro–micro linkages in sociology* (pp. 11–25). Newbury Park, CA: Sage.

Huber, J. (1999). Comparative gender stratification. In J. S. Chafetz (Ed.), *Handbook of the sociology of gender* (pp. 65–80). New York: Plenum Press.

Jackson, R. M. (1998). *Destined for equality: The inevitable rise of women's status*. Cambridge, MA: Harvard University Press.

Kandal, T. R. (1988). *The woman question in classical sociological theory*. Miami: Florida International University Press.

Kanter, R. M. (1977). *Men and women of the corporation*. New York: Basic Books.

Kasper, A. (1986). Consciousness re-evaluated: Interpretive theory and feminist scholarship. *Sociological Inquiry, 56,* 30–49.

Kessler, S., & McKenna, W. (1978). *Gender: An ethnomethodological approach*. New York: John Wiley and Sons.

Kurzweil, E. (1989). Psychoanalytic feminism: Implications for sociological theory. In R. Wallace (Ed.), *Feminism and sociological theory* (pp. 82–97). Newbury Park, CA: Sage.

Lengermann, P. M., & Niebrugge-Brantley, J. (1998). *The women founders: Sociology and social theory, 1830–1930*. Boston: McGraw-Hill.

Lenski, G. (1966). *Power and privilege: A theory of social stratification*. New York: McGraw-Hill.

Lever, J. (1976). Sex differences in the games children play. *Social Problems, 23–24,* 478–487.

Lopata, H. Z. (1994). *Circles and settings: Role changes of American women*. Albany: State University of New York Press.

Lopata, H. Z. (1999). Gender and social roles. In J. S. Chafetz (Ed.), *Handbook of the sociology of gender* (pp. 229–246). New York: Plenum Press.

Lorber, J. (1994). *Paradoxes of gender*. New Haven: Yale University Press.

Martin, M. K., & Voorhies, B. (1975). *Female of the species*. New York: Columbia University Press.

Mayo, C., & Henley, N. (1981). Nonverbal behavior: Barrier or agent for sex role change? In C. Mayo & N. Henley (Eds.), *Gender and nonverbal behavior* (pp. 3–13). New York: Springer-Verlag.

Miller. J., Schooler, C., Kohn, M., & Miller, K. (1983). Women and work: The psychological effects of occupational conditions. In M. Kohn & C. Schooler (Eds.), *Work and personality: An inquiry into the impact of social stratification*. Norwood, NJ: Ablex.

Oppenheimer, V. K. (1970). *The female labor force in the United States*. Berkeley: University of California Press.

Ortner, S. B. (1974) Is female to male as nature is to culture? In M. Z. Rosaldo & L. Lamphere (Eds.), *Woman, culture and society*. Stanford, CA: Stanford University Press.

Parker, S., & Parker, H. (1979). The myth of male superiority: Rise and demise. *American Anthropologist, 81,* 289–309.

Pyle, J. (1999). Third world women and global restructuring. In J. S. Chafetz (Ed.), *Handbook of the sociology of gender* (pp. 81–104). New York: Plenum Press.

Ridgeway, C. (1993). Gender, status, and the social psychology of expectations. In P. England (Ed.), *Theory on gender/feminism on theory* (pp. 175–197). New York: Aldine DeGruyter.

Ridgeway, C., & Smith-Lovin, L. (1999). Gender and interaction. In J. S. Chafetz (Ed.), *Handbook of the sociology of gender* (pp. 247–274). New York: Plenum Press.

Rosaldo, M. Z. (1974). Women, culture, and society: A theoretical overview. In M. Rosaldo & L. Lamphere (Eds.), *Women, culture and society*. Stanford, CA: Stanford University Press.

Rossi, A. (1982). *Feminists in politics*. New York: Academic Press.

Rupp, L. J., & Taylor, V. (1987). *Survival in the doldrums: The American women's rights movement, 1945 to the 1960s*. New York: Oxford University Press.

Sacks, K. (1974). Engels revisited: Women, the organization of production, and private property. In M. Z. Rosaldo & L. Lamphere (Eds.), *Women, culture and society* (pp. 207–222). Stanford: Stanford University Press.

Sanday, P. R. (1981). *Female power and male dominance: On the origins of sexual inequality*. Cambridge: Cambridge University Press.

Sattel, J. (1976) The inexpressive male: Tragedy or sexual politics? *Social Problems, 23–24,* 469–477.

Schur, E. (1984). *Labeling women deviant: Gender, stigma, and social control*. New York: Random House.

Shelton, B., & Agger, B. (1993). Shotgun wedding, unhappy marriage, no-fault divorce? Rethinking the feminism-Marxism relationship. In P. England (Ed.), *Theory on gender/feminism on theory* (pp. 25–41). New York: Aldine De Gruyter.

Smith, D. (1987). *The everyday world as problematic: A feminist sociology*. Boston: Northeastern University Press.

Smith, D. (1990). *The conceptual practices of power: A feminist sociology of knowledge*. Boston: Northeastern University Press.

Smith-Lovin, L., & McPherson, J. M. (1993). You are who you know: A network approach to gender. In P. England (Ed.), *Theory on gender/feminism on theory* (pp. 223–251). New York: Aldine De Gruyter.

Sokoloff, N. (1980). *Between money and love: The dialectics of women's home and market work*. New York: Praeger.

Sprague, J., & Kobrynowicz, D. (1999). A feminist epistemology. In J. S. Chafetz (Ed.), *Handbook of the sociology of gender* (pp. 25–43). New York: Plenum Press.

Sprague, J., & Zimmerman, M. K. (1993). Overcoming dualisms: A feminist agenda for sociological methodology. In P. England (Ed.), *Theory on gender/feminism on theory* (pp. 255–280). New York: Aldine De Gruyter.

Stockard, J. (1999). Gender socialization. In J. S. Chafetz (Ed.), *Handbook of the sociology of gender* (pp. 215–227). New York: Plenum Press.

Vogel, L. (1983). *Marxism and the oppression of women: Toward a unitary theory.* New Brunswick, NJ: Rutgers University Press.

Wallace, R. (1989). *Feminism and sociological theory.* Newbury Park, CA: Sage.

Ward, K. (1984). *Women in the world-system: Its impact on status and fertility.* New York: Praeger.

Ward, K. (1990). *Women workers and global restructuring.* Ithaca, NY: ILR Press.

Ward, K. (1993). Reconceptualizing world system theory to include women. In P. England (Ed.), *Theory on gender/feminism on theory* (pp. 43–68). New York: Aldine De Gruyter.

West, C., & Fenstermaker, S. (1993). Power, inequality and the accomplishment of gender: An ethnomethodological view. In P. England (Ed.), *Theory on gender/feminism on theory* (pp. 151–174). New York: Aldine De Gruyter.

West, C., & Fenstermaker, S. (1995). Doing difference. *Gender & Society, 9,* 8–37.

West, C., & Zimmerman, D. (1977). Women's place in everyday talk: Reflections on parent–child interaction. *Social Problems, 24,* 521–529.

West, C., & Zimmerman, D. (1987). Doing gender. *Gender & Society, 1,* 125–151.

Williams, C. L. (1993). Psychoanalytic theory and the sociology of gender. In P. England (Ed.), *Theory on gender/feminism on theory* (pp. 131–149). New York: Aldine De Gruyter.

PART VII

THEORIZING FROM ASSUMPTIONS OF RATIONALITY

CHAPTER 29

Social Rationality versus Rational Egoism

Siegwart Lindenberg

THE CONCEPTION OF RATIONALITY

Rationality means many different things to many different people. Some use the term to indicate individuals' ability to exercise reason. Others use it to indicate that something is the result of reasoning or even of conscious calculation. Some use the term to indicate that purposes are being served, so that "rational action" is the same as purposeful action. Still others already presuppose purposeful action and use the term in the much more restrictive sense that individuals "act rationally" by choosing the best means available for achieving a given end. Again, others see rationality as a form of consistency between what is wanted and what is chosen: individuals rank the options open to them according to their ordered preferences and choose according to this ranking. Each of these meanings of rationality has been criticized as being too vague (for example, "exercise reason") or too narrow (for example, "consistency") to cover the wider intuitive reach of the term. I believe that these criticisms have a point. The very wish to come up with a simple definition of rationality is to stress what one considers to be the most essential feature of rationality among a number of other features of rationality that are not stated. There is no need to begin with such a restrictive strategy because even in its restrictive form, a definition of rationality is not enough to be used as a theory of action. As a heuristic device, it would serve its function better if it included a greater number of important elements associated with an intuitive understanding of rationality. For this reason, I would like to take a different approach. I use the term "rationality" to indicate a particular heuristic device for asking questions and searching for and evaluating answers concerning human behavior. At a later stage, more specifications can be added to come to a theory of action. The heuristic device I would like to propose consists of six assumptions about human beings that jointly indicate the meaning of the phrase "human beings are endowed with rationality." For such a heuristic, the search is for elements which jointly cover most people's intuition of rationality as applied to humans. In fact, the list should be such that a human being who is lacking one or more of the elements would be considered pathological to various degrees by a

Siegwart Lindenberg • Department of Sociology/ICS, University of Groningen, Groningen, The Netherlands.

Handbook of Sociological Theory, edited by Jonathan H. Turner. Kluwer Academic / Plenum Publishers, New York, 2002.

broad consensus. Often, psychological "biases" (for example, the hindsight bias) are used to indicate deviations from rationality. In the concept I will develop in this paper, this goes much too far. Biases can be part and parcel of human rationality; they may even have an as yet undiscovered evolutionary advantage. Freedom from cognitive biases thus should not be an element of rationality. What, then, should go into such a list? Of course, it has to include the pursuit of goals in the face of restrictions, but it should also include the fact that human beings form expectations and quite generally attempt to make action situations meaningful. When we have a closer look at goals, we see that it is useful to distinguish three components. First, people evaluate events; second, they are motivated to realize conditions which they evaluate more highly than other events; and third, they are resourceful in doing so. Putting these components of goal pursuit next to restrictions, expectations and the pursuit of meaning, we get a set of six basic elements which have become increasingly consensual among scholars who deal with human rationality and can be expressed by the acronym RREEMM.[1] A human being, irrespective of time and place, is endowed with rationality, which means that he or she is:

- Resourceful: given human beings are motivated to pursue a goal, they will search for and often find possibilities to realize a state they evaluate more positively than the one they are in; they can be inventive.
- Restricted: human beings are confronted with scarcity and chooses (consciously or not) among exclusive options; choice implies costs in terms of forgone opportunities.
- Expecting: human beings form expectations about past, present, and future events; they can learn.
- Evaluating: human beings attach value to past, present, and future states of the world.
- Motivated: human beings are motivated to achieve a condition which they value more highly than the one they are in. This can be seen as an operational goal that expresses a general striving across different situational goals. It implies possible substitution of one option for another when restrictions, expectations and/or evaluations change.
- Meaning: human beings, when confronted with an unstructured situation, will try to improve the structure of this situation by making it meaningful in terms of the other elements of RREEM. For example, when they experience an unexpected event, they will try to fit the event into the knowledge that generates their expectations or else search for appropriate changes in the knowledge, i.e., they will search for reasons for the occurrence of the unexpected event.

These assumptions are by no means trivial. They stress important aspects that scholars of human behavior should take into account. They stress intelligent effort, initiative, and ability to learn; they stress limited resources and the need to choose; at the same time, they stress that this choice is guided by information (expectations) that is "updated" through search and learning; and that the choice is meaningful: to move toward what the individual finds good (or better) and away from what the individual finds bad (or worse), attempting to make the best of the fact that resources are scarce and that what is optimal now may not be optimal the next time (substitution). They also indicate that individuals actively interpret the world and structure their experience when it is ambiguous. The assumption of resourcefulness implies that the

---

[1]See Lindenberg (1990), where I follow and expand a suggestion by Meckling (1976). Here I introduce two changes. I substitute "motivated" for "maximizing" because the term "maximizing" is too much associated with its use in either neoclassical theory or the theory of rational egoists. I add "meaning" (the last M) to the set rather than to keep it a separate assumption. The reason for this is that I believe that between 1990 and now this assumption on meaning (the definition of the situation) has become widespread enough to include it in the consensual set, even though many rational choice scholars make no explicit use of it.

process of substitution is not restricted to readily available options but includes search and investment behavior. When trying to explain human behavior, we are driven to look for (or reconstruct) the restrictions, the expectations, the evaluations and their possible changes. We also are guided to consider the possibility that actions are directed at changing given restrictions and reducing uncertainty (i.e., increasing structure).

Even though these assumptions go a long way as a heuristic device, they are more like an interrelated list of essential features of human functioning than a theory of action. Deviating from any of the six can be considered a deviation from "normal" human functioning, and thus as pathological. For example, a person who has goals but is not motivated to pursue any of them would be seen as seriously impaired. Similarly, if the person does not search for ways to achieve his goals or does not learn, there is presumably something wrong with him. Also, if he does not generate expectations, he is severely cognitively impaired. Somebody also would be severely impaired if he believed he were not confronted with scarcity, could not evaluate any states of the world, or would not attempt to make sense of the situation he is in. In the past, attempts to formulate rational choice theories have specified the operational goal (the general motivation assumption) as "utility maximization" and given this assumption priority over the other elements of RREEMM. Due to the special history of rational choice theories, priority was given not just to the specification of maximization but also to the requirement that this specification should allow deductive tractability (formalization). Simplifications that have to be made in further specifications of the RREEMM assumptions had to answer first and foremost to the requirements of deductive tractability, to begin with the meaning of maximization. In this way, we get different version of rational choice theories, depending on how RREEMM is further specified and how the simplifications affect each element of RREEMM. The ultimate purpose of this chapter is to present a specification of RREEMM that is particularly suited for sociological analyses. Other specifications of RREEMM will be presented as contrast and I begin with these contrasting specifications.

RATIONAL CONSUMERS AND RATIONAL EGOISTS

There are a number of elaborations of RREEMM the most well-known of which is the microeconomic consumer theory and the most important of which in present-day rational choice analyses is the theory of rational egoists.[2] Standard neoclassical consumer theory fills in RREEMM roughly as follows. (1) Resourcefulness: there is no need to make any specific assumptions on resourcefulness because the consumer is assumed to be completely informed about alternatives and prices (see number 3). (2) Restrictions: own income (in terms of money) and scarcity of consumer goods (reflected in monetary prices) jointly form the only relevant restriction. (3) Expectations: they are trivial due to the assumption of complete information on alternatives and prices. (4) Evaluation: ordered preferences on (material) consumer goods, governed by subjective rates of substitution between goods (which, in turn, are governed by decreasing marginal value). The category of goods over which preferences are defined (i.e., material consumer goods) is not itself subject to theorizing and often presented as a pragmatic limitation of the subject matter of consumer economics.[3] The actual preference ordering is

---

[2]This division is akin to but not completely identical to what Green and Shapiro (1994, pp. 17ff.), following Ferejohn, call "thin-rational" (microeconomic theory) versus "thick-rational" (theory of rational egoists).
[3]Frank (190, p. 54) observed that economists are quick to defer to psychologists, sociologists, and philosophers when

exogenous to the theory and filled in through the assumption that these orderings are revealed through action. In principle, there are no a priori restrictions on what might be revealed.[4] (5) Motivated: the operational goal of the individuals is to maximize their utility and they do so by ranking the options open to them according to their ordered preferences and choose according to this ranking. Technically, this implies that individuals will, for any pair of goods, choose quantities such that the ratio of marginal utilities of these goods is equal to their relative prices (i.e., to the ratio of prices of these goods). (6) Meaning: trivial, because the consumer is assumed to be at all times confronted with well-structured situations.

It is clear that the major simplifications emanate from the requirement of giving a deductively tractable meaning to "maximization." The beauty of this way of specifying RREEMM is that it yields a very simple theory, one that allows a very transparent and tractable body or interlinked propositions on consumption. However, its usefulness is small for most sociological problems in which interaction and interdependencies play an important role. For sociological applications, other specifications of RREEMM have been made. The most prominent of these is best known under the label of "theory of rational egoists." Because it is this theory against which the theory of social rationality will be developed below, it is useful to have a closer look at it.

The Theory of Rational Egoists

The idea that individuals are often selfish is probably of all times. Individuals have passions, such as pride, envy, greed, avarice, cupidity, and ambition. As Hirschman (1977) observed, the idea of self-seeking governed by reason (i.e., rational pursuit of self-interest) is different from this general assumption of selfishness and relatively more recent. "La Rochefoucauld dissolved the passions *and* almost all virtues into self-interest, and in England Hobbes carried out a similar reductionist enterprise" (Hirschman, 1977, p. 42). Self-interest became mainly associated with economic interests (love of gain). The positive moral flavor these interests had acquired in the 18th-century defense of capitalism carried over into neoclassical economics. According to Stigler (1965, p. 256), the concept of perfect competition received its complete formulation in Frank Knight's (1921) *Risk, Uncertainty and Profit*. The market with perfect competition, however, is only made possible by the "proper" behavior of all participants. Knight makes is quite explicit that "we exclude all preying of individuals upon each other. There must be no way of acquiring goods except through production and free exchange in the open market" (Knight, 1921, p. 78). He adds that this excludes "fraud or deceit, theft or brigandage." Opportunities for this kind of opportunistic behavior, if they are present, by assumption do not influence behavior.

This "morally bounded" conception of self-interest only changed when economists, game theorists, and sociologists started to focus on nonmarket phenomena, especially on the explanation of norms and governance structures for human transactions. It became clear that the moral fiction built into neoclassical economics was in the way of explaining the "proper" behavior that had simply been assumed. For example, Williamson (1985) criticized neoclassical theory for assuming away the importance of economic organization:

---

asked what people really care abut: "As a practical matter, however, economists ... are content to assume the consumer's overriding objective is the consumption of goods, services, and leisure - in short, the pursuit of material self-interest."

[4]For example, Alchian and Allen (1974, pp. 24ff.) explicitly include the possibility of altruistic behavior in their definition of homo oeconomicus.

> Although neoclassical man confronts self-interested others across markets, this merely presumes that bargains are struck on terms that reflect original positions. But initial positions will be fully and candidly disclosed upon inquiry, state of the world declarations will be accurate, and execution is oath- or rule bound. (p. 49)

Instead, Williamson (1985) argues, what is needed is a more realistic view of human nature. This means self-interest seeking with guile, including the "calculated efforts to mislead, distort, disguise, obfuscate, or otherwise confuse" (p. 47). This explicit inclusion of strategically opportunistic behavior purposefully neglects attributes such as "kindness, sympathy, solidarity, and the like. Indeed to the extent that such factors are acknowledged, their costs, rather than their benefits, are emphasized" (Williamson, 1985, p. 391). Earlier on, Coleman (1964) had followed a similar track for the explanation of norms. He argued that sociologists usually take as their starting point social systems in which norms exists. In turn, these norms govern individual behavior. But that says nothing about why there are norms to begin with and how social order can emerge when there are no norms. For this reason, he argued for what he considered to be the opposite but possibly more fruitful error: to start with man wholly free, "unsocialized, entirely self-interested, not constrained by norms of a system, but only rationally calculating to further his own self interests" (Coleman 1964, p. 167). Coleman never abandoned this "fruitful error," also not in his magnum opus *Foundations of Social Theory* (1990). A similar stance had been taken by principal agent theory (Jensen & Meckling, 1976). Also, in the literature dealing with applications of "economic theory" to politics, "economic theory" is most often identified with the rational egoist version. The same can be said about game theory, especially when applied to the explanation of institutions (Raub & Weesie 2000).[5] Binmore (1994, p. 24) explicitly states that "greed and fear will suffice as motivations."

Not always, but quite generally, the theory of rational egoists also assumes "farsightedness." There is no exact (technical) meaning of this term, but it conveys the view that a theoretician does not have to worry about two interrelated adaptations of neoclassical theory: the explicit introduction of uncertainty and of time. First, when the highly simplifying assumption in neoclassical theory of complete information on prices and alternatives is withdrawn in favor of information as a scarce good or of the explicit possibility of uncertainty, then the assumption of farsightedness says "do not worry, nothing fundamentally damaging to the maximizing assumption is introduced by letting go the fiction of complete information." All that needs to be done is to factor peoples' ability to look ahead into the theory in a consistent way [say, by assuming a Bayesian notion of expected utility maximization, or as Binmore (1994, p. 25) puts it, by taking it for granted that the individual "has beliefs that accurately reflect the information available to him"]. Second, in the neoclassical consumer theory, time is not explicitly considered. In this theory, the meaning of "period" in "quantity per period" is conveniently left open, except for concrete empirical analyses. But when time is of the essence, as in contracting theory, in the theory of futures markets, in investment theory, or the economic theory of crime (with anticipated punishment), periods must be more explicitly introduced, at least ordinally. For example, contracting theories generally deal with at least two time periods (*ex ante* and *ex post*) and human capital theory assumes maximization over a lifetime (or work life cycle). Farsightedness means that the maximization assumption does not need to be seriously reconsidered when time is explicitly introduced. Individuals' ability to anticipate and evaluate future events is such that it does not interfere with the

---

[5]In evolutionary game theory, the assumption about self-interest mainly has been applied not to the individual but to the gene or its cultural equivalent, the *meme*. In the context of this chapter, there is no room to follow these developments in any detail.

extension of periods. Of course, individuals discount future events, but that is either rational (say, following the interest rate) or at least harmless for the predictions (as long as no reversal of choice is involved[6]). Williamson, who had explicitly introduced the possibility that *ex post* events often cannot be anticipated, still maintained that

> but for farsightedness, transaction cost economics would be denied access to one of the most important "tricks" in the economist's bag, namely the assumption that economic actors have the ability to look ahead, discern problems and prospects, and factor these back into the organizational/contractual design. (Williamson, 1993, p. 129)

In terms of RREEMM, the theory of rational egoists amounts to the following specifications: (1) Resourcefulness: individuals think of efficient solutions to their problems (this includes actively changing the given set of alternatives) and they learn efficiently from experience (see number 3). (2) Restrictions: a given set of alternatives with associated outcomes. (3) Expectations: many outcomes are uncertain but individuals estimate objective probabilities by and large correctly given the evidence available to them, at prices they are willing to pay for this evidence. Since individuals are farsighted, time has no influence on the way in which expectations are formed. (4) Evaluation: ordered preferences on goods that serve self-interest, governed by subjective rates of substitution between goods (which, in turn, are governed by value of a good diminishing with the quantity a person already has of that good). Farsightedness implies that time has no inherently distorting effects on evaluations (i.e., no effects that would lead to a preference reversal according to availability of goods over time). Evaluations are assumed not to be relative (with ordinal preferences) but absolute, so that expectations can influence evaluations in a systematic way (expected utility formed by weighting the utility of a good with the subjective probability of its occurrence). (5) Motivated: the operational goal of an individual is to maximize his or her expected utility across outcomes (which also presupposes ordered preferences and certain consistency requirements[7]). (6) Meaning: trivial, because the actor is at all times confronted with well-structured situations.

Notice that there are important differences between the *homo oeconomicus* of neoclassical economics and the theory of rational egoists regarding assumptions of preferences and regarding assumptions on uncertainty and time. Also, resourcefulness is a more important aspect in the theory of rational egoists than in the neoclassical consumer theory. Still, the two theories are often confused and confounded. Brennan (1990, p. 55) critically observes that economists (and, I might add, sociologists) often move unannounced back and forth between these two versions. When rational choice theory is attacked for assuming human beings to be much too egoistical, the answer often heard is that this theory does allow all sorts of preferences, including altruistic ones (as neoclassical theory in deed does). When rational choice theory is attacked for not coming up with any definite predictions because virtually all behavior can be "rationalized"[8] after the fact, the answer often is heard that the assumption of self-interest excludes assumptions on "soft" and "shifting" preferences (as is indeed the case in the theory of rational egoists) and that rational choice theory thus can come up in many

---

[6]See Parfit (1984).

[7]So-called Von Neuman-Morgenstern utility functions (see, for example, Harsanyi, 1977a).

[8]For example, in their critical review of rational choice theory in political science, Green and Shapiro (1994, p. 18) state against theories that allow all kinds of goals and preferences: "It will become clear, however, that what is gained by avoiding controversial assumptions about human nature can come at a considerable cost from the standpoint of measurement and empirical testing of rational choice theories." Later on in the book (p. 203), they find self-interest too restrictive "no doubt strategic calculation will be one [important variable, S.L.], but there will typically be many others, ranging from traditions of behavior, norms, and culture to differences among people's capacities and the contingencies of historical circumstances."

contexts with definite predictions. More recently, theories in which the egoism is shifted to another level, namely, to selfish genes, have gained in popularity. Selfish genes are compatible with some altruistic tendencies among their carriers. This has given legitimacy to the assumption that there are different types of individuals, some very selfish, some very cooperative, some in between. The theory of rational egoists has thus been pushed somewhat in the direction of *homo oeconomicus.*

Of course, the two versions of rational choice theory also have common elements. They are both specifications of RREEMM. More importantly, they share the view that maximization is the heart of rationality and should be kept as precise as possible in its operational meaning even if that necessitates highly unrealistic assumptions in the other elements of RREEMM. In other words, for both the neoclassical consumer theory and the theory of rational egoists, the maximization assumptions largely govern the way the other five assumptions are specified.

THE PRINCIPLE
OF SUFFICIENT COMPLEXITY

There has been much criticism of both versions of rational choice theory. Much of it is directed against the very unrealistic simplifications made by both of them. "We find ourselves sharing an increasingly widespread concern that the rationality attributed to homo economicus is too simplistic or else simply wrong when applied to actors in many political and social situations" (Levi et al., 1990, p. 2). Rather than repeat the literature on this criticism here, I will concentrate on what I consider to be the core element that causes the problem. It lies in the logic of simplification itself.

Why not simply make the model assumptions less simplistic? The answer to this question by model builders generally has been that complex assumptions often may be closer to reality but they also reduce the power of a theory. There is a trade-off that is not necessarily worth the bargain. With complex assumptions, it is more difficult (if at all possible) to deduce testable hypotheses and it is more difficult to use the theory as a unified heuristic device to guide analyses and generate relevant research questions. The maxim for making assumptions in good model building in the social sciences should be "as simple as possible and as complex as necessary." The problem with knowing when a model is as simple as possible and as complex as necessary has led to the method of decreasing abstraction (see Lindenberg, 1992b). It long has been widely used in applications of rational choice theory. You start with highly simplified assumptions and then make the assumptions successively more realistic (i.e., less abstracting from reality). For example, one may start with the assumption of complete information and then introduce some version of uncertainty at a later step in the model development. The advantage of doing it this way is that the tractability of the successive versions of the model remains high. Simplifications are made explicit and it generally is clear which assumptions need to be replaced by more realistic ones when the model turns out to be too simple. The theory of rational egoists has been hailed as a useful worst case scenario (Schüßler, 1988) and as a "fruitful error" (Coleman, 1964). When these simplifications seem too simplistic, one can, for example, withdraw the assumptions that all human beings are egoistical and instead assume that there are different types of individuals. In the literature, we find especially the following three types: "individualistic" (the goal is to maximize one's individual payoff); "competitive" (the goal is to maximize the positive difference between one's own and other's payoff); and "cooperative" (the goal is to maximize joint payoffs) (Liebrand et al., 1986).

The method of decreasing abstraction is vital for theory formation. However, there is a hitch. The method works well if, at least for some initial steps, the quality of the explanation increases with increasing complexity of an assumption. But where the method can go completely awry is when the simplifying assumption also assumes away what was to be explained. For example, if we want to explain institutions (all kinds of institutions) and we assume complete information, we cannot possibly explain institutions that deal with uncertainty. Our simplification has assumed away the phenomenon to be explained. For this very reason, the method of decreasing abstraction has to be accompanied by the principle of sufficient complexity. This principle states that the simplest model assumptions always should be realistic enough to allow a description of the phenomenon to be explained. Thus, if the explanandum contains uncertainty, the model may not exclude uncertainty by the simplifying assumption that individuals have complete information. This principle seems obvious enough, and yet it has considerable consequences. Basically it says that if human proclivities lead to interpersonal solutions for dealing with these proclivities, then these proclivities already must be represented in the simplest model assumptions. As we will see, the principle of sufficient complexity forces us to think differently about rationality as well, especially for sociological analyses, because these analyses very often directly confront a great variety of human proclivities and social attempts to deal with them.

THE THEORY OF SOCIAL RATIONALITY

To hold on to the idea that a deductively tractable concept of maximization is the heart of rationality might force us to make simplifications that violate the principle of sufficient complexity. At this point I reiterate the view that rationality should be seen as a collection of human characteristics, none of which is clearly more important than the other. When one takes this point of departure, assumptions concerning the operational goal will not dominate assumptions on, say, expectation, evaluation, and meaning. For example, there is no contrary-to-fact simplification that individuals are particularly farsighted, that they have well-ordered preferences, or that they are always confronted with well-structured situations simply for the sake of giving maximization a precise meaning.

A theory of social rationality would aim at the following: to elaborate RREEMM in such a way that we can see when, how, and to what extent the elements of RREEMM depend on the social context not just in the sense that other people constitute relevant restrictions and resources but also in the sense that social aspects may affect virtually all elements of RREEMM. In the remainder of the chapter, I will treat each element of RREEMM from this point of view. There is no normative definition of rational action (or choice) intended. Of course, there have been many contributions in the literature so far about deviations from (expected) utility maximization in the direction of "bounded rationality." Simon's "satisficing" may be the most famous of them. With regard to "expectations" and "meaning," Kahneman and Tversky's (1979) prospect theory in its various versions is widely known. There is no space to go into these contributions in this chapter. Instead, I will present the results of my own struggle with these and other contributions.

Resourcefulness

The role of resourcefulness is strongly influenced by the assumptions on other elements of RREEMM. As we have seen, in neoclassical consumer theory resourcefulness is made trivial by the assumption of complete information (which helps to give a precise meaning to maximization). Yet there are some versions of economics in which resourcefulness plays a role. For example, in the so-called Austrian economics (especially Von Mises) human beings are seen in a sense to be entrepreneurs who create alternatives. That takes resourcefulness. In Becker's (1996) conception of household production, human beings are seen as producers of their own well-being, and as such, resourcefulness becomes more important, even though Becker does not particularly stress this point. In the theory of rational egoists, uncertainty leads to a more pronounced but still relatively modest role of resourcefulness. As we will see, in the theory of social rationality, the operational goal of human being is seen to be "to improve one's condition." It is this goal that gives resourcefulness a central place in the conception of rationality, including learning in the sense of an active improvement of one's knowledge. However, the theory also points to limitations with regard to resourcefulness that stem from framing effects. In framing, attention focuses on some aspects and other aspects are pushed into the background. Resourcefulness is therefore topical, depending on the frame. Thus, the assumption on high resourcefulness with regard to some goals is perfectly compatible with low resourcefulness with regard to other goals (those that are often in the background). More importantly, resourcefulness is least when the goal to improve one's condition itself is pushed into the background, as it is in a "normative" frame in which the major objective is "to act appropriately." These points will come back in the discussion of the other elements of RREEMM.

Restrictions

Restrictions refer mainly to the scarcity of resources and to the need to allocate these resources to certain alternatives to the exclusion of other alternatives. Restrictions thus refer both to what is possible and what is not possible. The heuristic importance of restrictions is that (together with assumptions about other elements of RREEMM) they indicate what kinds of alternative we should pay particular attention to. In neoclassical theory, it is the feasible set of consumer goods. Given money prices, money income determines what can and cannot be bought. Less frequently, we find time and effort explicitly considered in a manner analogous to money income (with given or assumed shadow prices). In the theory of rational egoists, budgets are rarely made explicit. Budgets find their way into the analysis by the assumption the researcher makes on the set of feasible alternatives from which the individual chooses. There is thus no particular attention to budgets. Self-interest assumptions find their way into the analysis by the heuristic steering they offer for the selection of relevant alternatives and their ordering, often in terms of the neutral concept "payoff." In the theory of social rationality, restrictions take on a somewhat different meaning because of the strong emphasis on production and improvement of one's condition. As we will see below, goals are ordered hierarchically in terms of production functions (i.e., in terms of interrelated chains of means–end relationships) and the major operational goal is improvement of one's condition. Thus, rather than point to the feasible set of consumer goods or discrete alternatives, the theory of social rationality draws attention to production possibilities and associated possibilities (or impossibilities) of improvement. For example, if deviant behavior of youths would have to be explained, one would compare the youths' nondeviant and deviant possibilities to produce physical and social well-being (including their temperament and social skills) and one would search for possible path dependencies of declining possibilities for "nondeviant" improvement of the youths' condition. Availability of norms, social networks, and group memberships belong just as much to the scarce resources as do temperament and social skills and the quality of the production functions themselves (i.e., their efficiency, precariousness, compatibility, etc.). This may seem like a dazzling variety of sorts of resources. However, the theories on substantive and operational goals offer heuristic guidance on the search for the relevant menu of resources to be considered.[9]

Expectations: Social Sources and Content

Assumptions on expectations are trivial in the neoclassical theory due to the assumption of complete information. In the theory of rational egoists, there is uncertainty and expectations amount to various approximations to "objective" probabilities (depending on the information available to the individual). In most cases, the approximation is assumed to be sufficiently high in order not to worry about possible amounts, shapes, and sources of discrepancies between subjective and objective probabilities. In addition, farsightedness is strong enough to allow the introduction of long time periods without fundamental changes in the assumptions on the generation of expectations of preferences. An important question in the theory of rational egoists is how expectations relate to evaluations, namely, why would it be "rational" to consider probabilities at all and especially products of probabilities and utilities of outcomes. There is little concern with sources and content of expectations and thereby little concern for social influences on expectations.

In the theory of social rationality, the major point of attention is not the relation of expectations to evaluations but the generative processes of expectations.[10] Thus, sources and content (and their consequences) are most important because they show us the social influences at work. Five very different aspects are brought into play here. First, attentional processes called "framing" (i.e., goal-guided selective attention) make it likely that human beings are prone to give more attention to short-term outcomes than to long-term outcomes, especially when hedonic aspects are involved (see Loewenstein & Thaler, 1989; Loewenstein & Elster, 1992; Gattig, 2001). Thus, time cannot be introduced into the analysis without considering its effects on the selection of relevant aspects in decisions, and farsightedness can be severely restricted. If individuals can and do see far into the future, there thus is a strong presumption that one needs to look for (and will find) social arrangements that allow this farsightedness. For example, when a couple decides to have a child, it is impossible to consider all the ramifications into the distant future. However, due to standard trajectories of development, associated social arrangements of hospitals, child care, schooling, and so forth and due to social pressures to make corresponding private arrangements at standard junctions in time (such as applying for a kindergarten years ahead), people act seemingly with reasonable farsightedness. This is not a feat of their cognitive equipment but of their social environment.

Second, expectations are generated by experience, information, knowledge, theories, and ideologies. In daily life, interacting individuals are very much aware of the importance of situating the other so as to know something about his or her sources of expectations. For example, religious beliefs may lead to expectations about rewards or punishments in the hereafter for certain deeds. Contract partners may or may not be savvy with regard to what goes on in a particular industry. Managers may have read the newest hype in management technique and are now convinced that actions X will have consequences Y. People may have read about three cases of child molesters in one week in the newspapers and expect that their own child will be molested soon.

---

[9]For an example of this kind of analysis applied to revolutions see Lindendberg (1989b).

[10]The combination of expectations and evaluations is assumed to be as Kahneman and Tversky (1979) originally suggested: expectations are weights for evaluations. But there is no presumption that the weights fulfill all the axioms of probability theory.

Tacit knowledge and habits may be most difficult to trace in its impact on expectations (see Berry & Dienes, 1993; Reber, 1993). The heuristic guidance from neoclassical theory and the theory of rational egoists to pay attention to these sources of expectations are completely absent. In the theory of social rationality, there is no particularly sophisticated hypothesis about the sources of expectations, but it does push the commonsense idea that I need to find out about the relevant sources of expectations. In this spirit, Callon (1998) attempts to trace the influence of economics on the functioning of the market.

Third, the kind of information (including chunks of memory, knowledge, etc.) mobilized in any particular action situation depends not just on whether or not a person has that information but also on the frame that selects among the frame-relevant chunks of information. For example, when my goal right now is to feel better, I will mobilize mainly information about what actions are likely to improve my feeling. Information about the long-term effects of whatever I take to feel better will not be primed. For the same reason, the search for more information is likely to be highly selective according to the frame I am in. For this reason, it is fair to assume that expectations are generated in a frame-specific way (see also Kahneman & Tversky, 1979).

Fourth, in the theory of rational egoists, uncertainty is interpreted as a situation in which subjective probabilities must be assigned to outcomes. The possibility that the outcomes themselves are not known [what Knight (1921) called "fundamental uncertainty"] receives no serious consideration. From the point of view of formalization, this is understandable. However, the theory of social rationality does not have to give any priority to aspects of formalization and negate the relevance of fundamental uncertainty. For example, in complex contracting, many of the future contingencies cannot even be identified and therefore they cannot be factored into credible commitments *ex ante*. As Favereau (1997, p. 219) formulates poignantly: "the incompleteness of contracts is not the problem but (its acceptance is) the solution." The point is related to the principle of sufficient complexity discussed above. If there are important social situations in which people devise ways to deal with fundamental uncertainty, then the theory of action devised to explain these ways must allow fundamental uncertainty as well. Framing is likely to increase fundamental uncertainty in interactions in which the frames of interaction partners are not coordinated. For example, in organizations selective attention to aspects of joint problems may lead to an increase in actions that are unpredictable across subdivisions. Wittek (2000) even argues that periodic reorganization is necessary to decrease this kind of fundamental uncertainty in organizations.

Fifth, the generation of expectations often is socially orchestrated through joint categories and institutionalized rules (see Stinchcombe, 1986), creating "coorientation" (Scheff, 1967). This means that the expectations are locked in by the fact that they mesh. For example, the rule to drive on the right side of the road creates expectations about the other's behavior but also about the other's knowledge of the rule and about the other's expectations concerning me. Common categorizations create similar "cognitive interdependencies" (see Turner, 1991). In sum, the heuristics of a theory of social rationality should pay particular attention to sources of expectations and to framing and categorization effects, including fundamental uncertainty.

Evaluations: A Theory of Goals

In the neoclassical consumer theory, human goals are not theoretically specified and only pragmatically restricted to material consumer goods. In the theory of rational egoists, human goals are specified by the vague concept "self-interest," by many taken to mean "material gain."

As we will see, both solutions are wanting. If no goals are specified, explanations are open to all sorts of ad hoc assumptions about preferences (including the stability assumption that is necessary for revealed preferences). If goals are identified with self-interest, one has an indication of the ballpark but not much more. This is sufficient in contexts in which self-interest is relatively clearly defined by an institutionally supported maximand, as in "profit maximization" or by fiat (as in game theory). In Western economies, "profit" of a firm is defined by rules and the notion of "payoff" in game theory is often left unspecified or arbitrarily identified with money. But in most real-life contexts, it is not so evident what self-interest is, since the concept covers very heterogeneous goals. For example, when workers' hourly pay increases, they might work more to earn "more money" or work less to buy "more leisure." What, then, would be their self-interested choice? Things get even more complicated when one gets into relational goods. For example, social relationships may be taken to be valued goods. Are joint payoffs then part of self-interest? If attention to opportunity costs is the major theoretical vehicle by which individuals choose among goals,[11] there must be a menu of self-interest goals from which they can choose and there must be a way for the individual to assess the compatibility or incompatibility of goals. This implies that instrumental relationships between goals also must be known. It comes down to the requirement that the researcher must know the ordered preferences (or goals) that pertain to so-called self-interest in order to deal with choice among self-interest goals. What is this menu of ordered goals? The theory of rational egoists has no such auxiliary theory on goals. The other side of the coin is that the vague term self-interest necessarily creates an equally vague opposite of altruistic behavior. The vagueness of altruistic behavior is just as serious as the vagueness of self-interested behavior. Another problem is that the operational goal of maximization is not discussed as a goal and therefore not related to the substantive goals.

Clearly, in order to use REEMM in sociology, one needs a more refined theory of goals (evaluations) than that of the theory of rational egoists. There has been a considerable number of theories on human goals. However, for a social science using REEMM, the usefulness of this kind of work is limited. For such a social science (as opposed to a behavioral science) it is essential that the influence of the environmental restrictions (especially the social environment) on behavior can be traced. Theories of human goals rarely say anything about the role of restrictions on goal selection and goal achievement. For the same reason, these theories generally do not deal with the possibilities of substitution.

Development of a REEMM-compatible theory of human goals has greatly been aided by the work of Stigler and Becker (1977),[12] which introduces the important distinction between universal and instrumental goals. Universal goals are identical for all human beings and instrumental goals pertain to the means that lead to the ultimate goals. Instrumental goals are in fact constraints; they differ for different categories of people and they can change. Thus they

[11]Harsanyi is very explicit about this point. He maintains that the real progress in rational choice theory came from realizing that rational behavior could not be limited to choosing the most efficient means to a given end but that it had to include the choice of ends itself: "If I am choosing a given end ... then typically I have to give up many alternative ends. Giving up these alternative ends is the opportunity cost of pursuing this particular end. Thus, under this model, rational behavior consists in choosing one specific end, after careful consideration and in full awareness of the opportunity costs of this choice" (Harsanyi, 1977b, p. 319).

[12]More recently, Becker (1996) has put more emphasis on the influence of past consumption on today's preferences than on the hierarchy of goals. This new emphasis is quite compatible with a stronger emphasis on reference points and social comparisons which come in through the operational goal "to improve one's condition."

can be traced in an approach that emphasizes the impact of the action environment on the action (rather than the influence of preferences). Note that it is the combination of universal and instrumental goals that constitute the theoretical advantage. Technically speaking, there is only one utility function for all mankind but there are systematically different production functions for different kinds of people.[13] This conception also shifts the emphasis from consumption to production. Buying a particular good is now not an act of consumption but the purchase of a means of production, such as a CD for the production of music pleasure.

Stigler and Becker's (1977) approach may be called a "production function approach" and it leads to a hierarchy of goals. On top there is utility, below which are the universal goals, below which are means–end chains of instrumental goals. It also is clear that the hierarchy is not strict. Lower-order goals (such as money) may be instrumental for various higher-order goals.

As ingenious as Stigler and Becker's suggestion is, it has a serious drawback: the universal goals are not specified. This opens again the door to ad hoc theorizing. For example, goals can be arbitrarily assumed to be universal if one needs justification for particular instrumental goals or for particular substitutions. In the last 15 years, Becker's approach was further developed into what has been called the "theory of social production functions" (see Lindenberg, 1986; Lindenberg & Frey 1993; Ormel et al., 1999; Van Bruggen, 2001).

First, the top of the hierarchy—utility—has been replaced by "subjective well-being." The relevance of this move will become clearer shortly. Second, directly below the top, there are two general goals. The first major goal is physical well-being. It is this goal that drives the acquisition of many consumer goods, from buying bread to buying housing and medicine. By a silent assumption that effort brings about a reduction in physical well-being, economists at times introduce effort as cost, an important assumption, not just for labor market theory. There are, however, good reasons to assume that this identification of effort as cost is too restrictive. Human beings seem to prefer a certain level of activation above which effort is a cost and below which it is a benefit (see Hebb, 1958). Thus, physical well-being is not produced just by comfort but also by stimulation (see Scitovsky, 1976; Wippler, 1990). Even when stimulation is purely mental, it is here taken to be a means for physical well-being because of the importance of the level of activation. Comfort and stimulation can be seen as the major arguments in the production function of physical well-being. As goals, they are both instrumental (for physical well-being) and universal (i.e., the same for all mankind). Instrumental goals on a yet lower level (such as an armchair for comfort or a scary movie for stimulation) are more specific to a particular culture of group within a culture.

The other major goal has been stressed over and over again by sociologists as the most important universal goal: social well-being, produced by some form of social approval. It was already quite clear to Adam Smith (1976) that "nature, when she formed man for society, endowed him with an original desire to please, and an original aversion to offend his brethren. She taught him to feel pleasure in their favourable, and pain in their unfavourable regard" (p. 116). Marshall (1920, pp. 14–17) reiterated the importance of social approval, as did Parsons (1937, pp. 162ff.) and Parsons and Shils (1951, p. 69). "The struggle to preserve or enhance feelings of self-worth or prestige marks all men who live above a bare subsistence level," state Krech et al. (1962, p. 96), and William Goode (1978, p. vii) maintains that "all people share the universal need to gain the respect or esteem of others.... The foundations of social life rest in part on the universal need for respect, esteem, approval and honor." This is but a small selection of voices who all point in the same direction.

---

[13]For people with identical production functions relative prices may differ.

As in the case of physical well-being, the direct instruments for reaching social well-being are themselves universal goals. The direct instruments have a long pedigree within sociology and are also corroborated by evolutionary arguments: (1) *Status*, behavioral confirmation, and affection.[14] Status refers to a relative ranking (mainly based on control over scarce resources). (2) *Behavioral confirmation* is the feeling of doing or having done "the right thing" in the eyes of relevant others (including yourself). "Doing the right thing" is not restricted to overt action but also covers covert actions such as thinking certain thoughts, agreeing with certain maxims, and adopting certain attitudes. The term "behavioral" thus points to aspects the individual can be held responsible for in the eye of relevant others (including oneself). (3) *Affection* is the feeling of love and caring between people in a close relationship and the feeling of being accepted with regard to what one is (as opposed to what he or she has or does). All three universal instrumental goals are themselves emotional states or tied to emotional states, such as pride and dominance for status, guilt and shame for behavioral confirmation, and love and compassion for affection.[15]

Still, lower-level goals are entirely dependent on the opportunities and restrictions an individual faces. There are again instruments for reaching the higher-level instruments, and so forth. For example, for both comfort and stimulation, virtually every adult in our society needs money (in order to buy material goods, rest, amusement, etc.). In order to earn money, one may need a paying job, and for a particular job one may need a specific qualification. Goals thus are hierarchically structured, with the general human goals on top and with lower-level goals being tied to higher-level goals in production chains. Below the top (which is the same for everybody) there are many different sets of (nested) production functions each of which specifies the instrumental relationship between lower-order and higher-order goals for a particular category of people (see Fig. 29.1).

The sociologically important point is that the social production functions are affected by subjective judgments but they are not idiosyncratic. Rather they are social facts in Durkheim's (1950) sense of the word. For example, in our society, it was and partially still is true that by and large women can produce income either by working or by being tied to a male partner (for making a home), and women can produce social approval either by their own occupational status or by being tied to a male partner (they get behavioral confirmation for making a home and raising children and they participate in the occupational status of their partner). For men, the situation is different. They may get some behavioral confirmation from being tied to a female partner, but by and large they cannot produce income or status via their partner. When making a home and raising children yield less and less social well-being (especially behavioral confirmation), women will seek alternative means for the production of social well-being, for example by entering the labor market if they have not done so already for the sake of money (which may serve mainly physical well-being).[16]

The heuristics for identifying goals is thus driven by a guided search for systematic production possibilities for social well-being (in its three forms) and physical well-being (in its

[14]In the environment of evolutionary adaptation, inclusive fitness is likely to have been essentially served by (1) resource holding power (leading to status-striving), (2) reciprocal altruism (leading to a striving for behavior confirmation from relevant others), and (3) kin altruism (leading to a striving for affection from people to whom one is closely tied).

[15]Turner (2000) even argues that during evolutionary adaptation, rewiring of the hominid brain to gain control over emotions (especially anger and fear) and expanding the repertoire of emotions (to include complex emotions like guilt, shame, and pride) is likely to have had great advantages for inclusive fitness due to the effects of emotions on the ability to forge bonds of increased solidarity and thereby more stable local group structures.

[16]This analysis is worked out in more detail in Lindenberg (1991).

Top level Universal Goals	Subjective Well-being				
	Physical Well-being		Social Well-being		
Universal instrumental goals	Stimulation/ Activation (optimal level of arousal)	Comfort (absence of physiological needs and fears)	Status (control over scarce resources)	Behavioral Confirmation (approval for "doing the right things")	Affection (positive inputs from caring others)
Examples of activities and endowments (means of production for universal instrumental goals)	Physical and mental activities producing arousal; fantasy	Avoidance of fatigue; vitality	Excel in work or sports, life style, talent	Compliance with external and internal norms; conscience	Intimate ties, offering and receiving emotional support; empathy
Examples of resources + enhancing activities	physical and mental stamina; training	Food, health care eating	Education, unique skills schooling	Social kills, competence netwerking	Spouse, child listening

FIGURE 29.1. Top of the goal hierarchy with some examples of lower-order instrumental goals (activities, endowments, resources, and activities to get resources)

two forms). Substitutes and complements will show up as by-products of the construction of nested social production functions.

Motivation: Improving One's Condition

What about the operational goal (motivation)? Remember, for both the neoclassical theory and the theory of rational egoists, utility (or expected utility, respectively) maximization was the operational goal. The very concept of utility has a venerable tradition and great importance for dealing with both price and income effects and other important advantages (cf. Stigler, 1965). However, utility maximization as operational goal (i.e., as general motivator of action) can be separated from the concept of utility itself and the question here, then, is what is the assumed operational goal of the theory of social rationality? Do people maximize subjective well-being? Is subjective well-being just a stand-in for the concept of utility? Before answering this question, let us consider the special features of the top of the goal hierarchy. Physical and social well-being are not perfect substitutes and neither are they only universal instrumental goals for reaching the final goal of subjective well-being. Human beings must have both physical and social well-being, and within physical well-being they must have a certain amount of both comfort and stimulation. Within social well-being, human beings must have some level of status, behavioral confirmation, and affection. For these reasons, substitution is only possible beyond these minimum levels (whatever they are). This makes the top three layers of the hierarchy very special: On each level, the goals are being pursued for their own sake (they are intrinsic), and goals of the second and third layer also are pursued as instruments for the goal(s) above them. Thus, layers two and three of the hierarchy consist of goals that are both intrinsic and instrumental. Here is the catch. If formalization were our main objective, we could find a (mathematical) way to still work with a single maximand (utility or subjective well-being) even though goals in layers two and three are both intrinsic and instrumental. However, as stated above, formalization is not our main objective. To the contrary, we would like to see where we get if we do not allow the requirements for formalization to dictate our simplifying assumptions. From the point of view of the process by which individuals pursue goals, it is entirely possible that the assumption of utility (or subjective well-being) maximization as operational goal does not fit very well.

Consider that the pursuit of a goal is a complex process in which the goal itself exerts a considerable influence on what aspects of the situation are important, what aspects are attended to, what knowledge and memory chunks are being mobilized, and so on. Would it then make a difference whether the goal pursued was identical in all situations (as in the assumption of utility maximization) or whether it was, say, status achievement in one situation and the achievement of stimulation in another?[17] Surely, it would make a difference, and somehow we have to deal with this difference. In addition, we have to deal with the double nature of the high-level goals as both intrinsic and instrumental. That is, whatever the operational goal we assume, it would have to accommodate both aspects.

GOAL PURSUIT. It is by now commonplace in cognitive psychology that individuals cannot attend to everything at the same time. Simon (1997, pp. 368ff) stressed this point long ago but to little avail with regard to rational choice theory. Attention must be selective, and what is being attended to is particularly important for determining the kind of action that is taken (see also Fazio, 1990). Different bits of knowledge are mobilized and different categories activated, with the result that the individual is more sensitive to some kind of information than to another, relies more or less on stereotypes, places more value on certain outcomes, and so forth. For example, individuals' negotiating behavior is affected by instructions that tell them to be cooperative or competitive (see Carnevale & Lawler, 1986). Individuals can be primed, that is, certain stored knowledge, categories, or attitudes can selectively become more easily accessible thereby influencing a person's information processing (see Higgins & Brendl, 1995). At the same time, aspects not belonging to the selected construct are inhibited, thus creating a double selective effect (see Bodenhousen & Macrae, 1998; Houghton & Tipper, 1996). Note that although these effects steer attention, they need not be conscious or work via prior intention. For example, a person in a situation in which others speak highly of the value of achievement can get "primed" to focus on achievement without being aware of it (Bargh, 1997).

Most important for influencing a person's cognitive activity and thereby the action that is based on such activity are goals (see Gollwitzer & Moskowitz, 1996). One prominent researcher in this field claimed recently that most cognitive activity is goal dependent (Kruglanski, 1996). Goals can be influenced by the situation but they cannot be conjured up at will. At any given moment you have them or you do not. One might try to change one's goals

---

[17]Notice that this questions is not identical to the discussion of maximization of "present aims" versus self-interest (Partfit, 1984).

over time but that takes a great deal of effort, if it works at all. One also might try to avoid situations that mobilize goals one does not want to have mobilized (such as staying away from the sight of food if you want to lose weight). Thus goals are only accessible to rational choice in a very limited sense.

These insights from cognitive psychology make the assumption that utility maximization is the operational goal very problematic (even as an "as if" assumption). What we are looking for is an operational goal that can be situationally tied to the goal at hand, the goal that actually governs the cognitive processes at that moment. Utility maximization, by contrast, either refers to the choice of alternatives according to the ranking of options open to the individual according to his or her ordered preferences (in the neoclassical model) or it goes directly to the feature the present goal shares with all other goals, namely, context-free utility (in the theory of rational egoists), and there is no way one can relate it directly to the specific goal at hand with its specific features of selection of aspects, of specific knowledge chunks, and so forth.

A strong candidate for an operational goal that does allow situational specification is the general desire to improve one's condition. For example, somebody's status position at the moment is X (or feels low) and he would like to improve it (or feel better concerning his status). The operational goal in action thus is always tied to the specification of the status quo or some reference point of the present goal. Such a goal implies that if an individual chooses from a given set of alternatives, he or she will choose the subjectively most optimal one, as assumed in neoclassical theory. Settling for an alternative below the optimal one would still allow the individual improvement of his condition in that very decision situation. But an improvement-related operational goal also addresses nongiven alternatives. The individual will search for possibilities to improve his or her condition regarding a particular goal achievement (cf. Lindenberg & Frey, 1993). The operational goal thus is also connected to assumptions about resourcefulness in RREEMM ("a human being will search for and often find possibilities to realize a state he or she evaluates more positively than the one he or she is in; he or she can learn and be inventive").

Substantively, the operational goal implies that relative gain is more important than absolute gain, and therefore reference points and social comparisons are crucial for the utility an individual derives from goal achievement. Utility thus is not something that inheres in what is achieved but derives from the comparison of what is achieved to the status quo ante of the concrete goal that was pursued. Improvement thus also may be the prevention of deterioration of the present condition, or limiting the loss that would materialize if you did nothing.

The goal to improve one's condition has long been recognized as a major operational goal. Adam Smith (1976) already had drawn our attention to "that great purpose of human life which we call bettering our condition."[18] His suggestion, however, did not survive the marginal revolution in the 19th century. Sociologists and social psychologists also long have been arguing for the importance of social comparison processes (for example, Durkheim, 1951; Sherif, 1966; Merton, 1957; Festinger, 1954; Helson, 1964). Their discussions, however, were outside the context of goal achievement. Within the context of utility theory, more recent contributions have pushed in the same direction, arguing for relative rather than absolute conceptions of utility (for example, Scitovsky, 1976; Kahneman & Tversky, 1979; Frank, 1992).[19] Despite this long pedigree, the idea has not yet led to any serious change in the operational goal in rational choice theory. One reason for this may be the fact that the idea was never developed

---

[18]*Theory of Moral Sentiments* (I.iii.2.1). We find a similar notion in *The Wealth of Nations* as a desire that "comes with us from the womb, and never leaves us till we go into the grave" (II.iii.28).

[19]Observe that this discussion should not be identified with the question whether the Weber–Fechner law of the "just noticeable difference" (cf. Sigler, 1965, pp. 109ff) should be used in utility theory.

in the context of research on goals and goal hierarchies. It is through the more recent research on the impact of goals on cognitive processes and through the research on goal hierarchies that the context of the discussion of operational goals takes on a new significance. The increasing interest in merging theories of emotion with theories of goal-directed action (cf. Turner, 2000), and quite generally an evolutionary perspective, is likely to support a rethinking of operational goals. Emotions such as anger, disappointment, sadness, regret, which exist side-by-side with emotions such as happiness and satisfaction, would seem to fit well an operational goal of "improving one's condition" and the problems associated with failing to reach it. Such an operational goal contains a reference point against which achievement is assessed, whereas utility maximization contains no such reference point. The latter is always achieved and would make no evolutionary sense of the human emotions engendered by failure. Seen in this light, the operational goal of "improving one's condition" will enjoy increasing attention from scholars of various disciplines who are interested in social rationality.

Meaning: Structuring the Situation

Neither neoclassical consumer theory nor the theory of rational egoists deal with cognitive processes. However, if one does consider cognitive processes, a serious question arises with regard to the mechanism by which an overarching goal may work. As will be discussed at some more detail in a moment, the influence of goals on cognitive processing is such that there is only one overriding goal at a time (although routines that do not require attention can go on simultaneously with the pursuit of the "present" goal). This focus on one goal can be easily reconciled with having the goal "to improve one's condition" be operational at the same time as the "present goal" that is being pursued. The latter is the specification of a means for the former. For example, I improve my condition by earning more money. What about other goals that may be present in the action situation, for example, because they are affected by the present goal? It is well-known that, say, the goal to earn money through work is likely to be affected by "hedonic" aspects of the job in addition to money, such as the risk to be injured or to get dirty, the status of the work, and so on (see Rosen, 1974). The question is how it is possible to stick to the notion that, situationally, individuals focus attention only on one goal, whereas the operational goal should apply situationally to many other goals as well. The answer should be looked for in the same process that creates the limitation of attention in the first place: framing. Framing is a process of structuring the action situation and in that sense it governs "meaning."

FRAMING. The theory of framing (Lindenberg, 1989a, 1993) combines some elements of Kahneman and Tversky's prospect theory (1979) with a theory on how the definition of an action situation (a "frame") affects the selection of knowledge chunks, beliefs, attention to certain situational aspects, recall of situational aspects, as well as the choice of action. The basic idea is quite simple. There are two types of behavior: automatic and controlled (see, for example, Bargh, 1984; Fazio, 1990). For example, while driving a car, it is possible to register and judge the movement of traffic, shift gears, and give directional signals, while at the same time carrying on a conversation about, say, Mozart's Don Gionvanni. The controlled action requires a scarce resource: attention. Attention is selective. Automatic encoding processes focus our attention, and thus create in any action situation an attended foreground and an unattended background. The focus of attention is strongly influenced by goals. A goal is a desired state of affairs. In the foreground, there is a goal that "frames" or defines the action situation in the sense that it mobilizes certain knowledge chunks and beliefs, furnishes the criteria for the selection and ordering of alternatives, directs attention to certain attributes, and provides links to other action situations. Although the action situation is governed by a single goal, that does not mean that the "background" is unimportant. This background contains, among other things, goals that are potentially relevant in the situation, positively or negatively. For example, if one buys a new computer, the most salient goal might be to get the best computer below a certain price ceiling. But there also may be a goal concerning the pleasantness of design, another goal about having a computer better than one's colleague, and so forth. The crucial difference in the influence of goals on action thus is between direct and indirect. The background goals influence the frame indirectly in the sense that they increase or decrease the salience of the frame. Salience is a concept that acknowledges the possibility that other goals can distract from or intensify the pursuit of the major goals to varying degrees, depending on the direction and intensity of "externalities" of the goal pursued in the foreground on each of the background goals.

The salience of a frame strongly affects the distribution of choice probabilities over the alternative. For example, the nice design of a particular computer may decrease the likelihood that the "best" (but less attractive looking) computer will be bought. A very salient frame will lead to a very high probability that the "best" alternative for this frame is chosen because it increases the perceived difference between alternatives. Good reasons that might be embedded in chunks of memory and knowledge that are mobilized with the frame will, if present, increase the salience as well.[20] The lower the salience the more equal the choice probabilities over the various alternatives get (see Fig. 29.2). This indicates a "distraction" of the major goal by other goals in the background of the frame. For example, if you help a friend in need financially, then within the limits of your possibilities you may let yourself be guided mainly by what he needs. The opportunity costs for helping are not keenly perceived because they belong to goals in the background. As far as friendship norms are concerned, the high salience of "helping a friend in need" will lead to "optimal helping." However, if the friend keeps coming back for more, then the background goal of "improve your scarce resources" will become stronger and lower the salience of the frame "to help a friend in need" even if you are convinced that the friend's need is real. You may still help but you increasingly lower the amount (i.e., deviate more from the optimal amounts for friendship), and when you come into a situation where the salience of the frame approaches zero, i.e., when it gets close to a toss up whether you help or not, the frame is likely to switch to "improve your scarce resources." With the new frame, other alternatives come in with their own ordering, other knowledge chunks are being mobilized, and links to other kinds of situations come into view (see Fig. 29.3). You may regret not being able to see the friend as friend anymore when he turns up, but to see him only as a drain on your finances. But, like all constraints, the frame itself cannot be chosen at will, only influenced over time, for example, by trying to avoid situations that lower the salience of a particular frame.

The definition of a situation thus is governed by a situational goal that "frames" the situation. The frame also will heavily influence the kinds of beliefs that are being mobilized for the pursuit of the goal. For example, when my goal is "to help a friend in need," the beliefs that are mobilized along with this goal include beliefs about the general obligation to help a friend in need, about the legitimacy of asking a friend for help, and so on. If the frame is to "improve your scarce resources," then the beliefs that are mobilized include beliefs about the importance of guarding ones expenses, about the legitimacy of thinking of your own needs and financial worries, and so on. While all these beliefs are part of a person's repertoire of beliefs, the flashlight of framing shines only on some of them at any given point of time, which will

---

[20]A priori strength of the master frames, depicted in Fig. 29.2, will be explained later.

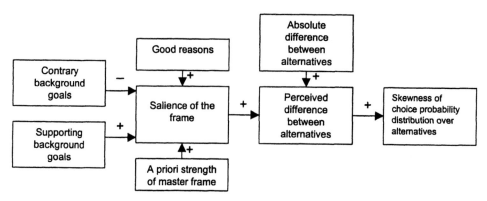

FIGURE 29.2 Simplified schema of framing effects on choice

create different weights for different beliefs at different times. This flashlight will not be equally selective for every goal. For example, Millar and Tesser (1989) found that in a context of instrumental action the focus on cognitive aspects of attitudes greatly increases the attitude–behavior correlation, whereas in a context of consummatory action (geared to feeling better) this correlation increases when the focus is on affective aspects of attitudes. The two contexts "pull out" different aspects of attitudes (see also Frisch, 1993).

In sum, the major direct influence on action comes from the frames, i.e., the selection of what is situationally relevant, of beliefs and attitudes and chunks of knowledge. This direct influence will be the stronger the more salient the frame. Other goals (i.e., those in the background) will play a role by influencing the salience of the frame. Their influence on action is indirect, and thus muted. When money plays a role only in the background, it will influence one's decisions much less than when it is part of frame itself. One can be penny-wise or pound-foolish, as the frame may be. In this way, the operational goal to improve one's condition cannot be linked just to the goal that is presently pursued (in the foreground) but at the same time also to many other goals (in the background). This point is very important because it describes the mechanism by which improvement with regard to the present goal is related to other higher-order goals. It is a "sluggish" relation in the sense that there is no direct way of thinking them through, no "calculation," only the indirect way via the influence on salience, and thus on choice probabilities. Still, the larger picture is not completely out of sight. Human beings thus are "sharp" in their goal pursuit only in a highly salient frame, less sharp in less salient frames, and quite fuzzy with regard to all the goals that happen not to be in the foreground. Depending on which one of these is chosen as an example of the way human beings pursue goals, one would come to very different conclusion about "rationality," not to speak about "maximizing."[21]

MASTER FRAMES

As described above, there is a goal hierarchy with subjective well-being at the top, physical and social well-being below the top, and so on. The operational goal for this hierarchy

---

[21]As argued earlier, this is one important reason why I reserve the term "rationality" for the set of human tendencies summarized in RREEMM rather than for the operational goal alone.

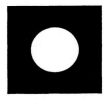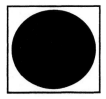

FIGURE 29.3 Schematic depiction of foreground (white) and background (black) goals in framing, with (from left to right) decreasing salience that leads to a frame switch.

of substantive goals (namely, to improve one's condition) can itself be seen as the top of a hierarchy, with chains of means for the achievement of the improvement below the top. This is useful because of framing effects. Let me briefly explain why.

There are many goals, big ones, small ones, abstract ones, concrete ones, and so forth. For example, one can have a goal of taking a walk, then there will be many smaller sub-goals such as putting on a coat, locking the door, lifting your feet from the ground step by step, and so on.[22] There is a confounding influence of automatic and controlled behavior with regard to goals. For example, if one's goal is to write a paper, then the frame will govern the activities (thinking, reading, writing, correcting); some of them will be automatic, others not. However, as one writes, automatic processes may increase the salience of a background goal (such as "getting something to eat") and lower the salience of the frame, leading to a frame switch. Thus, while some automatic processes are subject to the given goal, other automatic processes influence the goal selection itself.

I am most concerned here with high-level goals that are subject to automatic selection and that in turn govern the selection of lower-level goals. Such overarching goals may indirectly be influenced by willfully bringing oneself into a particular situation, just as sleep itself is not controlled by will but can be enticed by going to bed. High-level goals will influence the selective mobilization of beliefs and knowledge chunks for lower-level goals. One such higher-level goal (in the background) may affect the other (in the foreground) by increasing or decreasing its salience. We thus gain some ordering in overarching foreground and background goals. For this reason, it is useful to focus on higher-level frames that help us to manage the great variety of substantive goals people have with a small number of frames that count the most in terms of the meaning of the situation and behavioral and emotional consequences. What might the most important higher-level frames be?

The operational goal "to improve one's condition" is linked to classes of ways and means to actually improve one's condition, each with similar main features of selection in the framing process. We can divide the means roughly into two main classes. First, there are means to directly improve the state of goal achievement with regard to physical and social well-being. The general way to achieve this is to strive for an improvement in one's feeling (emotions). For example, if I feel hungry, I can improve my condition with regard to this feeling by eating. What all these means have in common in terms of framing is that they serve the high-level subgoal "to feel better." Second, there are means to improve one's condition with regard to the resources one has for reaching higher level goals. If I earn more money, I can use it to

---

[22]There are even considerations of optimality (i.e., good reasons) with regard to the level at which an action is identified. Vallacher and Wegner (1987) suggested an "action identification theory" in which there can be a mismatch between level of action identification and the difficulty of the task (difficult tasks should be identified on a low level, easy ones on a high, i.e., inclusive, level).

achieve more of the higher-level goals. This goal to improve one's resources will indirectly have consequences for the achievement of physical and social well-being but as a goal, it is very different from "feeling better." In a moment, both overarching goals will be dealt with in some more detail. Before I get to this, a third overarching goal has to be introduced that takes on a very special meaning: the goal to act appropriately. It is seemingly not directly linked to the operational goal to improve one's condition. As we will see, such a goal is the answer to a paradox: that improvement with regard to some goals (for example, behavioral confirmation and affection) can be achieved much better if it is the by-product of action rather than the intended result. The importance of this "twist" for the rule following and the role of morality can hardly be overestimated. Let me take up each of these overarching goals in turn.

Hedonic Frame

In a hedonic frame the goal is "to feel better." In other contexts such a frame has been called "consummatory." The goal "to feel better" may involve opposite tendencies: to increase/decrease arousal (i.e., seek stimulation, say, through engaging in a risky activity, or avoid a stimulation overdose) and increase pleasantness/decrease unpleasantness (i.e., seek improved feelings regarding comfort, status, behavioral confirmation, and affection). These two dimensions also have been identified as the main dimensions of affect and moods (see Russell, 1983; Watson & Tellegen, 1985). They may be involved in almost everything people do. For example, one may feel as unpleasant going against a norm by offending other people, or failing to gain resources. The crucial question is whether feelings play a role in the foreground or only in the background. In the background, the goal "to feels better" only influences the salience of the reigning frame. For example, if the frame is "to improve your resources," specified in terms of improving income in your present job, then the choice alternatives are likely to be ordered by the way the wage rate is specified, say, as hours of work per week. The effort you put into these hours is not directly considered. It comes in only indirectly via the background by reducing your feeling of comfort with increasing hours of work. This in turn will lower the salience (i.e., the strength) of the frame and thereby increase the likelihood that the second or third best alternative will be chosen. You might work fewer hours because of it. This looks like the same result one would get from putting "leisure" and "income" into the same utility function, but it is not. There are two important differences. First, the effect of "feeling better" (in terms of comfort) on the decision to work a certain number of hours is much reduced when it comes from the background. In such situations, people have been known to work themselves into illness. Second, there is a difference with regard to the alternatives that are being considered and therefore a difference in the aspect on which improvement focuses. Had "decrease your feeling of discomfort" been in the foreground rather than "increase your income," then the choice alternatives would in all likelihood have been ordered according aspects regarding comfort, that is, aspects having to do with effort. The person would search for effort-related aspects of the job (given the present number of hours he works per week), i.e., for possibilities to get by with putting less effort into it, and choose the one with the least effort.

Thus, only when feelings become the center of attention, i.e., when the situational goal is directly focused on arousal and/or pleasantness or unpleasantness, do they determine the aspects selected for attention, the chunks of knowledge that are activated, and the criteria for judging the success of one's plan of action. Then "hedonic" is an appropriate label. The time horizon of this frame is short because the goal is by definition linked to the here and now (see Loewenstein, 1996).

There is a particular kind of event that has a high likelihood of triggering a hedonic frame: loss. Loss is not the same as negative gain. The asymmetry between losses and gains in terms of utility (when both are subjectively medium or large) seems to be well established (see Kahneman et al., 1991). Losses weigh heavier than gains. But there seems to be another difference involved than just one of utility. Gains are by and large less disruptive than losses, and thus are less likely to be accompanied by a strong hedonic response (i.e., by being both aroused and feeling good/bad).[23] For this reason actual or expected losses are more likely to trigger a hedonic frame than actual or expected gains.[24]

Gain Frame

The goal to improve one's resources includes two subvariants. First, the goal is the increase of resources held, such as increasing the amount of money one has. The other is to improve the efficiency of one's production function, such as searching for a better paying job in order to increase the productivity of working time in terms of money. Although there are important differences between these aspects, they may be taken together in one master frame with the name of "gain frame." Such a frame is most typical of what people generally associate with self-interest. Gain as a goal is here defined in terms of increasing one's scarce resources for producing higher-level goals, such as money, disposable time, knowledge, skills, decision power, social influence, and so forth,[25] or of improving the productivity of the given production functions. Often, but by no means always, these two aspects of gain will go together.

Again, the kinds of knowledge chunks, beliefs, attention to situational aspects, and so on that are being mobilized in a situation where gain is the frame are specific to the task, the more so the more salient the frame. Above, we had discussed the example of going for income or leisure in a job. Another example is helping. If somebody is asked for help, then a person in a gain frame will not mobilize beliefs about the general obligation to help or about the legitimacy of asking for help, but rather, say, beliefs about the possibilities of making a profit and the legitimacy of making the best of the situation for yourself. How can you earn something by helping, or how can you increase your influence by doing so? Is this person able to harm you later on if you do not help now? Would not helping frustrate other plans to advance your condition? In a gain frame, the situational aspects that draw one's attention are in answer to such questions. Below, we will see that helping looks very different in a "normative" frame.

Normative Frame

There has been much discussion about the question whether there is a "moral dimension" in human action (for example, Etzioni, 1988; Elster, 1991). In rational choice theory, the

---

[23]Emotions have been linked to the interruption of goal chains (see Mandler, 1984). Medium and large losses are associated with negative interruptions of goal sequences, whereas medium and large gains are either the result of goal sequences or are likely to be interruptions that advance you closer to a goal.

[24]Of course, at times gain can be disruptive of the status quo (in a positive and negative way) and then also be linked to a hedonic frame rather than a gain frame. For example, getting a driver's license is often associated with a significant change in status quo and thus possibly linked to a hedonic frame.

[25]Status can be a valuable resource for achieving other instrumental goals (such as money, access, etc.), and thus status is both an aspect of social well-being and a resource, more so than behavioral confirmation and affection. For this reason, the marginal utility of status is likely to decrease less with increasing status than the marginal utility of the other respects of social welfare.

controversy does not seem to be anymore whether there is something like a sense of obligation but how it is compatible with the theory of rational egoists. In the theory of social rationality, it is not a question of compatibility with self-interest but with the operational goal "to improve one's condition."

Does following obligations belong to a separate master frame, not subsumable under a hedonic or a gain frame? If so, where is the connection to improving one's condition? The argument I would like to introduce here has been elaborated elsewhere (Lindenberg, 1983, 1992a). For the functioning of norms, it is essential that norm conformity does not rely exclusively on sanctions because the monitoring capacity of the group is never sufficient for that. Thus, it is important that people also keep to the norms when they are not observed. If it is obvious that a person only follows the norms in order to avoid negative and invite positive sanctions, he cannot be trusted to follow the norms when nobody watches. For this reason, wherever there are children, there is a regulatory interest by adults in them learning early on to consider doing what is "right" as a value of its own (even though that behavior is stabilized by social approval and disapproval and by common good type reasons).[26] In this way, trust and trustworthiness become attached to the ability to have no seemingly ulterior motives when behaving morally or following norms. A person who obviously conforms to norms in order to get social approval (behavioral confirmation and/or affection) or some other advantage is less likely to get it than is a person who seemingly is intrinsically motivated to act morally and follow the norms. He can expect much social approval and trust for the same reason that adults attempted to make children learn the "intrinsic" value of appropriate behavior in the first place. This lesson has been called the "by-product paradox of social goods" (Lindenberg, 1989a) and it is reinforced time and again during the life course: in the realm of morality and norms, it is genuine noninstrumental behavior that is rewarded. Whereas this is especially so for social approval and trust, it also holds for other advantages. In short, endowed with the ability to "internalize" social expectations and probably with the massive help of emotions like shame, guilt, and (fear of losing) love, children learn to develop a sense of obligation seemingly without any instrumental link to their other two master frames.

In terms of framing, we can say that individuals develop the ability to pursue the goal "to act appropriately" in such a way that other goals (especially the other two master frames) are pushed into the background and are thereby veiled (see Fig. 29.4). However, because of the simultaneous working of foreground and background goals, the social approval and other advantages achieved by norm conformity will have a positive effect on the salience of the normative frame. A friend asking for help is likely to trigger this overarching normative frame with the subgoal "to help a friend in need." Given the friendship norms, helping a friend in need is the appropriate thing to do and there is an appropriate range for the amount of help that the friend can legitimately ask. Within that range, the cost of helping is not sharply calculated because it belongs to a goal in the background (say, the goal "to improve one's scarce resources"). This veiled relation to any instrumental connection to the other master frames can explain why social scientists often have insisted that morality is nonutilitarian (value or

---

[26]Emotions such as guilt and shame probably play an important role in the ability to learn "to act appropriately" as a separate goal, strong enough to push many other goals into the background. But it is the central point of framing theory that the avoidance of the feelings of guilt and shame are not the driving motives in following norms and moral maxims. This may lead to an asymmetry in the role of shame before and after a deviant act. In a normative frame, shame is in the background and after a deviant act shame may be so strong that it creates a switch to a hedonic frame aimed at improving the depressed feeling and not at restoring what was normatively asked in the first lace. In his study of emotions, Elster (1999, pp. 153, 156) observed that "shame is weighted too little when anticipated and too much when experienced" and "in shame, the immediate impulse is to hide, to run away, to shrink—anything to avoid being seen."

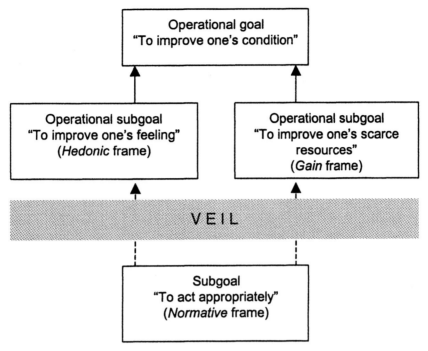

FIGURE 29.4. The three master frames in their relation to the main operational goal

axiologically rational, intrinsic, deontolocial), whereas even casual observation shows that conformity to norms is sensitive to rewards (especially social rewards).[27]

Ligthart (1995) could show this influence of norms on frames experimentally. In scenario experiments, he contrasted business transactions between, respectively, two friends, two acquaintances, and two strangers. The scenario is as follows. A customer comes into a second-hand bookshop and wants a book that is long out of print and not often seen in secondhand bookshops. He is willing to pay up to $65 for it. The owner of the shop does not have the book but promises to look for it. A week later he finds the book in a rummage sale for $35, a price the customer is, of course, not aware of. Question: what price will the bookseller ask of the customer? Notice that there is asymmetry of information and because of that the bookseller need not be concerned about the influence of the price he asks on future interactions as long as the price is seemingly still related to cost and not suspiciously close to the maximum offer. Standard rational choice theory would predict that he would ask the same price of a friend, an acquaintance and a stranger, namely, the highest possible price that is not outrightly suspicious, say between $60 and $65 dollars. Framing theory would predict that vis-à-vis "regular" customers (strangers and acquaintances), the bookseller is in a gain frame (i.e., he has to make a living off selling books). But when a close friend comes and asks for a favor, the bookseller would be in a normative frame and behave appropriately according to friendship norms (which generally exclude making a profit off a friend). The difference between acquaintance and stranger would show up in the strength of the salience of the gain frame: vis-

---

[27]Boudon (1996) is one prominent scholar who recently has reiterated a realm of noninstrumental rational action. However, he does not deal with the seeming paradox that this action is sensitive to rewards even through it is not oriented toward ulterior goals.

à-vis the acquaintance there are some relational concerns that lower the salience of the gain frame, while vis-à-vis the stranger, there are no such concerns (high salience). It is not appropriate to make profit off a friend; therefore the predicted price vis-à-vis the friend was cost price (thus $35). The predicted price vis-à-vis an acquaintance was a price that would split the difference (representing a compromise between profit making and relational concern). In the scenario, the customer was willing to pay $65 (which defines the upper limit for the price), the costs were $35 (which defines the lower limit of the price), the midpoint between these limits is $50, which then represents the "split-the-difference" price. Vis-à-vis the stranger, the bookseller is predicted to ask what the standard rational choice theory would predict for all three relations: the maximum nonsuspicious price, somewhere between $60 and $65. The results clearly rejected the predictions of the standard rational choice model for friend and acquaintance and favored the framing prediction: $40 was the average price asked of the friend, $52 of the acquaintance, and $57 of the stranger. These prices were statistically different from each other. A test of the appropriateness of prices vis-à-vis a friend and vis-à-vis an acquaintance corroborated the framing interpretation: cost price was considered the most appropriate price to ask of a friend and the split-the-difference price was considered the most appropriate price of an acquaintance (see Ligthart & Lindenberg, 1994).

There are aspects of instrumentality that can go along with following norms but they have nothing to do with the operational goal "to improve one's condition." For example, obligations may be embedded in public good arguments. Such "good reasons" may be mobilized with the frame along with other chunks of knowledge. They are likely to heighten the importance of conforming to the norm or moral maxim and thereby the salience of the normative frame. In this way, theories and ideologies can contribute to norm conformity and moral behavior. For example, the economist North (1981) argued that interconnected comprehensive views of the world (which he calls "ideologies") play an important role for human action, mainly through the link of ideology to legitimacy and fairness judgments and the role these two play in overcoming the free rider problem. For example, "if individuals believe in the value of political democracy they will vote as a matter of civic obligation" (North, 1981, p. 53), North, however, does not offer a mechanism how this acting out of obligation can exist side by side with self-interested behavior.

THE RELATIVE STRENGTH
MASTER FRAMES

When we consider the three master frames we must ask about their relative strength. Is there an a priori difference in their salience, and thus in their ability to displace each other? In the literature, this question has been discussed for a long time (see Hirschman, 1977) in terms of ordering passions, interests, and reason, three categories that come somewhat close in meaning to the three master frames because "reason" included morality. The most prominent view before the 18th century was that passions have the upper hand when compared to reason. Spinoza recounts this view:

> All men certainly seek their advantage, but seldom as sound reason dictates; in most cases appetite is their only guide, and in their desires and judgments of what is beneficial they are carried away by their passions, which take no account of the future or of anything else.[28]

[28]Tractatus theologicopoliticus, Chapter V. Quoted after Hirschman (1977, p. 44).

According to Hirschman, it was in the 18th century that the concept of "interest" was introduced in the sense of a nonvolatile passion: the love of material gain, which is ruled by reason. It is this combination of a soft passion with reason that is supposed to subdue all volatile passions and in addition is socially acceptable by the fact that it serves the ends of society at large (see Myers, 1983). Over the years, the love of gain has evolved into the main meaning of the term "self-interest." The discussion of passions had more or less vanished from the intellectual agenda of economics.

What should we make of the relative strength of the master frames? The a priori strength of a frame should be related mainly to two aspects. First, the role emotions play in its salience; second, the relation it has to the operational goal ("to improve one's condition"). Remember that the subgoals of physical well-being and of social well-being operate via emotions. Emotions can be tied directly to the frame (via the foreground) or only indirectly (via the background). A direct tie should have a strong positive impact on the salience of the frame. Emotions that only operate from the background have a reduced influence on the salience. The same is true with the operational goal "to improve one's condition" (see Table 29.1). In the hedonic frame the goal is "to feel better," and therefore it is directly tied both to feelings and to the operational goal. It should therefore be a priorily a very strong frame. In the gain frame the goal is "to improve one's resources." Resources are instruments for improving the condition with regard to the emotionally charged subgoals of physical and social well-being. However, gain does not itself improve the condition of hedonic goals; it only increases the potential for doing so. Its tie to emotions is thus indirect, whereas the tie to the operational goal is direct. On one count, it is thus weaker than a hedonic frame. For the normative frame, both ties are indirect because the instrumentality of following norms and moral codes for the improvement of one's condition (regarding hedonic goals and also regarding gain) is pushed into the background. Thus the a priori relative strength of the three frames should be in that order: hedonic, gain, normative.

The theory of rational egoists takes self-interest as the strongest motive. It could mean either a hedonic or a gain frame, but from the tradition of the concept it is clear that self-interest in rational choice theory is associated with gain rather than with the hedonic frame. In fact, the theory of rational egoists does not cover hedonic motives, and thus also offers no clue under what conditions a gain frame may be more salient than a hedonic frame. At times, a hedonic frame can be brushed aside as "irrational," but mostly it is simply ignored. The theory of rational egoists also has trouble dealing with normative frames. The existence of obligations is acknowledged but remains troublesome. Two ways of dealing with obligations have become popular in rational choice analyses. First, the attempt to concentrate on situations in which seemingly normative behavior can be shown to be motivated by self-interest after all. Consider, for example, a quote from Gary Becker (1996): "We have trouble understanding the people who take good care of elderly parents even when *not forced by social norms or altruism* ..." (p. 128, emphasis added). The context is that he wants to show that helping also can be

TABLE 29.1. Dimensions of Relative a Priori Strength of Master Frames

Master frame	Tie to emotions	Tie to operational goal	A priori frame strength
Hedonic	Direct	Direct	+++
Gain	Indirect	Direct	++
Normative	Indirect	Indirect	+

seen as utility-maximizing behavior. The expression "forced" is indeed curious but it shows the recent acceptance of obligations as something to be taken seriously without having to be dealt with. Second, there is the logical solution that normative frames become salient when the gain to be had in a situation is negligible. This view has become well-known under the name of "low-cost decisions" (see Kirchgässner, 1992). Morality can reign when gain is too weak to compete. This solution is quite acceptable in terms of the a priori ordering of master frames, but it says nothing about the cases in which the normative frame is surprisingly strong. Such cases are generally excluded from the analysis when the theory of rational egoists is applied. For example, Olson (1965) tells us that rational choice makes self-interested people free riders, but he immediately adds that "the theory is not at all sufficient where philanthropic lobbies ... or religious lobbies are concerned" (p. 160). Presumably, philanthropic and religious zealots are strongly motivated but in a way that does not lead to free riding out of rational self-interest.

The a priori strength of salience would indeed boil down to a hierarchy of motive strength were it not for the fact that the salience of frames also is affected by goals in the background. The a priori strength of a frame may be considerably altered by "good reasons" in the foreground and by goals in the background of a frame. For example, the salience of a normative frame may be significantly stabilized by the fear of disapproval from self and others (which is a hedonic factor), by the fear of being fined (which is a gain factor), and also by, say, a public good argument (see Varese & Yaish, 2000). *There is, in short, no fixed hierarchy of salience strength once we consider framing effects.* For this reason, the strategy of rational choice scholars to focus on self-interested action and leave the rest to people who deal with exceptions and fine-tuning only works reasonably well if we confine our analysis to situations of high-salience gain frames (such as spot markets and other situations of strong competition). One also can lump hedonic and gain frames together as "selfish motivation" when dealing with low-evidence situations, in which we have little information (at first) on possible hidden supports of a normative frame (see Lindenberg, 1996). In the latter case, selfishness as the guiding motive then can be interpreted as a heuristic device in the face of uncertainty on factors that change the a priori hierarchy of frame salience.

One could even argue that in any society considerable effort is made to create hidden supports for a priori weak but socially important frames. In addition to the sanctions (i.e., gain aspects) associated with rules of law, societies are eager to have these rules be legitimate (i.e., supported by fear of disapproval, normative obligation, and judgment). Weber's (1961) thesis on the impact of religion on the development of capitalism can be interpreted as a case in point. Hume had already observed that institutionalized standards and expectations can pull the gain frame above the hedonic frame: "It is an infallible consequence of all industrious professions, to ... make the love of gain prevail over the love of pleasure."[29] But for many occupations he does not go far enough because they also imply training in honor codes and other normative obligations for practitioners, greatly lowering the probability that the professional judgment is made in a gain frame.

In the literature, an important point had been made about the ability of "extrinsic" motivation (especially the pursuit of money) to displace "intrinsic" motivation (see Frey, 1997). With the help of framing, we can see that it is not really a matter of axiological motivation but a matter of veiled instrumental connections. If I pay my son for doing his duty in and around the house (say, paying $5 for mowing the lawn), I intrude into the normatively defined situation with a gain frame. The next time I ask my son to simply do his duty and mow the lawn for nothing, the prior payment is likely to lower the salience of the normative frame

---

[29]*Writings on Economics,* quoted after Hirschman (1977, p. 66).

and thereby draw attention to the opportunity costs of the time it takes my son to mow the lawn. In all likelihood, there will be a frame switch. In an environment in which there is strong consensus on norms and obligations, the frame switch is difficult to reverse because easily measurable opportunity costs (measured in terms of money) outweigh vague and fuzzy opportunity costs (measured in terms of what he forgoes by not doing his duty). Money takes on a special significance in such environments because it allows a much more precise measurement of costs than most other goods.

We may conclude that social scientists need to trace the social and institutional mechanisms that change the a priori ordering of master frames. Even a gain frame takes careful social and institutional support. Of course, there are many market situations in which one can safely take a gain frame as given and not bother about other frames. However, in any more detailed analysis of markets in a particular industry, the theory of rational egoists will simply miss a large part of the story. For example, for the functioning of modern markets with incomplete contracts, "balancing" of gain and normative frames may be the essence of complex transactions. Trust problems cannot be solved just by lowering strategic opportunism with credible commitments; it also takes strong normative frames (see Lindenberg, 2000). The two solutions are bound to each other. Unless strategic opportunism is lowered by credible commitments, we cannot expect a normative frame to be strong enough to hold its own against a gain frame. Research on the social and institutional conditions of the relative strength of master frames would have ramifications far beyond the study of markets.

SUMMARY AND CONCLUSION

There is growing consensus about the key elements of human behavior that jointly define what is meant by the phrase "human beings are endowed with rationality." These elements have been summarized by the acronym RREEMM: Human beings are Resourceful (search and learn); Restricted (confronted with scarcity and choose); Expecting (generate expectations), Evaluating (have goals which lead to preferences); Motivated (are motivated to achieve a condition which they value more highly than the one they are in); Meaning (try to make action situations meaningful in terms of other elements of RREEM).

Of course, these elements are interrelated. The specification of one limits the degrees of freedom for specifying the others. By specifying each key element in such an interrelated way, one turns RREEMM into a theory of action. The most well-known specifications are the neoclassical consumer theory and the theory of rational egoists. Both specify RREEMM in such a way that the exigencies of formalization and deductive tractability largely dictate the simplifying assumptions. In both, the specification of motivation is taken to be the most important element of RREEMM, and the requirements for a precise meaning of "maximization" strongly influence the specifications of the rest. It has been argued in this chapter that these requirements lead to theories that are less useful in many sociologically interesting contexts, and that for these contexts the specification of RREEMM should not be made according to the exigencies of formalization. Worries about deductive tractability should come only after the substantive specifications on RREEMM have been made. As an example of what such a substantive specification would look like the theory of social rationality was presented. What are the differences?

In *neoclassical consumer theory*, the assumption on perfect information on goods and prices renders the elements "resourceful," "expecting," and "meaning" trivial. Preferences are assumed to be ordered whatever they may be. There thus is only a pragmatic "selection" of goods (consumer goods) for study, without excluding any other goods over which preferences are defined. The assumption on restrictions also is pragmatic: it contains the relevant resources (budgets) available to acquire the priced goods over which preferences have been defined in any given study. With these specifications, "motivated" can be succinctly defined as maximization of utility by ranking the available options according to the ordered preferences and by choosing according to this ranking. This renders "rationality" mainly a matter of consistency.

In the *theory of rational egoists*, two key elements have been changed in comparison to the neoclassical consumer theory. First, the goods over which preferences are defined are narrowed down to goods that serve self-interest. Even though the meaning of self-interest is somewhat vague, it is still a considerable step away from the "open preference" assumption of neoclassical theory. The immediate consequence of this change is that restrictions are looked at in a different way. They are not seen as budgets to be optimally allocated over priced goods but as sets of discrete feasible alternatives with relevant outcomes. The researcher selects and orders the alternatives on the basis of assumptions made on self-interest (say, fear and greed in a prisoner's dilemma). Second, the assumption on perfect information is withdrawn and replaced by an assumption on uncertainty with regard to probabilities of occurrence. This change renders "resourcefulness" somewhat more important (because of search activity for uncertainty-reducing information) than in neoclassical theory and it changes the technical meaning of "maximization" to "maximizing expected utility."

Because these two theories seem so similar, they are often confused and confounded. Attacks against rational choice theory as assuming human beings to be much too egoistical are fought off by pointing to the open preference assumption. Conversely, attacks against the theory that it is so vague that it can only "predict" after the fact are countered with the definite predictions made on the basis of clear self-interest assumption.[30]

The *theory of social rationality* fills in RREEMM in quite a different way. The most critical key elements that are specified differently are the two elements on goals ("evaluating" and "motivated") and on "meaning." An explicit theory of substantive goals is introduced. It is based on the idea that human beings "produce" their own well-being and that the ultimate goals for which they strive are the same for mankind, whereas the means they use can be culture or subgroup specific. The means turn into "instrumental" goals if the individual does not have them but strives to acquire them. In this way, goals form a production hierarchy in which the most general goals (physical and social well-being) are on top and the more specific instrumental goals are below. Preferences for instrumental goals are not "tastes" but reflect social contexts, knowledge, and resources. They become the subject matter of genuine sociological analysis. In addition, processes of substitution can be traced, reflecting changes in relative production advantages (or costs).

The operational goal ("motivated") is assumed to be a general striving for the improvement of one's condition, not a general striving to choose the best given alternative. The difference is mainly twofold. First, the individual will search for possibilities to improve his or her condition regarding a particular goal achievement. This renders resourcefulness much more important than it is in either neoclassical theory or in the theory of rational egoists. Second, the operational goal implies that relative gain is more important than absolute gain, and therefore that reference points and social comparisons are crucial for the utility an individual derives from goal achievement, prominently the individual's own condition with regard to the foreground and background goals at the moment of choice.

---

[30]The possibility to shift selfishness up one level (to the genes) opens up possibilities for genuine cross-overs, in which the theory of rational egoists is applied to genes, whereas a menu of different kinds of preferences are assumed for human beings (including prosocial preferences).

Processes of selective attention lead to the structuring of situations in terms of goals. Thus, "meaning" in the sense of the definition of the situation is provided by the situationally strongest goal that "frames" the situation in terms of the relevant aspects and ordering of alternatives. However, the weaker but potentially relevant goals in the situation are still able to exert some influence from the background into which they have been pushed. They can increase or decrease the salience of the frame and thereby the degree to which the action is determined by the given ordering of alternatives. For example, the wish to improve one's resources may negatively affect the salience of the goal to help a friend without any direct weighing of costs against helping.

Because goals are so important for providing meaning to action situations, it is very important to know which major goals govern the definition (or structuring) of the situation. One can distinguish three master frames, one in which the major goal is "to improve one's feeling" (a hedonic frame), one in which the major goal is "to improve one's scarce resources" (a gain frame), and one in which the major goal is "to act appropriately" (a normative frame). Action emanating from a normative frame is what sociologists have usually called "acting out of a feeling of obligation." In such a frame (and only in this frame), the connection to "improving one's condition" is veiled. Therefore, actions are seemingly driven only by normative or moral concerns. The "gain frame" covers what is mostly assumed to be self-interest in the theory of rational egoists. The hedonic frame has been largely ignored by rational choice theorists. It is a different kind of "self-interest," tied to a short time horizon and feelings (i.e., emotions) as success criteria. Which frame wins out in any given action situation? One can argue that the hedonic frame is a priorily stronger than the gain frame, which in turn is a priorily stronger than the normative frame. The crucial question then is what social conditions are able to change this a priori ordering. In finding answers to these questions, one needs to consider social goals as well as social restrictions and social sources of expectations. It even takes favorable conditions to have a gain frame displace a hedonic frame. In general, then, the possibilities of producing physical and social well-being and the possibilities of improving this production belong to the most important bits of information for sociological analyses. The theory of social rationality thus leads to a very different heuristic guidance through the thicket of the social world, and that may make the (possibly temporary) reduction in deductive tractability worthwhile.

REFERENCES

Alchian, A. A., & Allen, W. R. (1974). *University economics*, 3rd edition. London: Prentice Hall.

Bargh, J. A. (1984). Automatic and conscious processing of social information. In R. S. Wyer, Jr. & T. K. Srull (Eds.), *Handbook of social cognition* (pp. 1–44). Hillsdale, NJ: Erlbaum.

Bargh, J. A. (1997). The automaticity of everyday life. In R. S. Wyer (Ed.), *The authomaticity of everyday life. Advances in social cognition* 10, (pp. 1–61). Mahwah, NJ: Erlbaum.

Becker, G. S. (1996). *Accounting for tastes*. Cambridge, MA: Harvard University Press.

Berry, D. C., & Dienes, Z. (1993). *Implicit learning*. Hove, England: Erlbaum.

Binmore, K. (1994). *Game theory and the social contract*. Volume I: *Playing Fair*. Cambridge, MA: MIT Press.

Bodenhousen, G. V., & Macrae, C. N. (1998). Stereotype activation and inhibition. In R. S. Wyer (Ed.). *Stereotype activation and inhibition. Advances in social cognition* 11 (pp. 1–52). Mahwah, NJ: Lawrence Erlbaum.

Boudon, R. (1996). The cognitivist model: A generalized rational-choice model. *Rationality and Society, 8*, 123–150.

Brennan, G. (1990). What might rationality fail to do? In K. S. Cook & M. Levy (Eds.). *The limits of rationality* (pp. 51–59). Chicago: The University of Chicago Press.

Callon, M. (1998). Introduction: The embeddedness of economic markets in economics. In M. Callon (Ed.). *The law of the markets* (pp. 1–57). Oxford: Blackwell Publishers.

Carnevale, P. J. D., & Lawler, E. J. (1986). Time pressure and the development of integrative agreements in bilateral negotiations. *Journal of Conflict Resolution, 30,* 636–659.

Coleman, J. S. (1986). Collective decisions. In *Individual interests and collective action* (pp. 15–32). Cambridge: Cambridge University Press.

Coleman, J. S. (1990). *Foundation of social theory.* Cambridge, MA: Harvard University Press.

Durkheim, E. (1950). *The rules of sociological method.* Glencoe, IL: Free Press.

Durkheim, E. (1951). *Suicide. A study in sociology.* Glencoe, IL: Free Press.

Elster, J. (1991). Rationality and social norms. *Europäisches Archief für Soziologie, 32,* 109–129.

Elster, J. (1999). *Alchemies of the mind. Rationality and the emotions.* Cambridge: Cambridge University Press.

Etzioni, A. (1988). *The moral dimension. Toward a new economics.* New York: Free Press.

Favereau, O. (1997). L'incomplètude n'est pas le problème, c'est la solution. In B. Reynaud (Ed.). *Les limites de la rationalité.* Tome 2, *Les Figures du collectief* (pp. 219–234). Colloque de Cerisy, Paris: La Decouverte.

Fazio, R. H. (1990). Multiple processes by which attitudes guide behavior: The mode model as an integrative framework. *Advances in Experimental Social Psychology, 23,* 75–109.

Festinger, L. (1954). A theory of social comparison processes. *Human Relations, 7,* 117–140.

Frank, R. (1990). Rethinking rational choice. In R. Friedland & A. F. Robertson (Eds.). *Beyond the marketplace* (pp. 53–87). New York: Aldine de Gruyter.

Frank, R. (1992). Frames of reference and the intertemporal wage profile. In G. Loewenstein & J. Elster (Eds.). *Choice over time* (pp. 371–382). New York: Russell Sage Foundation.

Frey, B. S. (1997). *Not just for the money. An economic theory of personal motivation.* Brookfield: Edward Elgar Publishing.

Frisch, D. (1993). Reasons for framing effects. *Organizational Behavior and Human Decision Processes, 54,* 399–429.

Gattig, A. (2001). *Intertemporal decision making.* Amsterdam: Thela Thesis.

Gollwitzer, P. M., & Moskowitz, G. B. (1996). Goal effects on action and cognition. In E. T. Higgins & A. W. Kruglanski (Eds.). *Social psychology. Handbook of basic principles* (pp. 361–399). London: Guilford Press.

Goode, W. (1978). *The celebration of heroes. Prestige as a control system.* Berkeley: University of California Press.

Green, D. P., & Shaprio, I. (1994). *Pathologies of rational choice theory. A critique of applications in political science.* New Haven, CT, and London: Yale University Press.

Harsanyi, J. C. (1977a). *Rational behavior and bargaining equilibrium in games and social situations.* Cambridge: Cambridge University Press.

Harsanyi, J. C. (1977b). Advances in understanding rational behavior. In R. E. Butts & J. Hintikka (Eds.). *Foundational problems in the special sciences* (pp. 315–343). Dordrecht: Reidel Publishing.

Hebb, D. O. (1958). *A textbook of psychology.* Philadelphia: W. B. Saunders.

Helson, H. (1964). *Adaptation level theory.* New York: Harper & Row.

Higgins, E. T., & Brendl, M. (1995). Accessibility and applicability: Some activation rules influencing judgment. *Journal of Experimental Social Psychology, 31,* 218–243.

Hirschman, A. O. (1977). *The passions and the interests: Political arguments for capitalism before its triumph.* Princeton, NJ: Princeton University Press.

Houghton, G., & Tipper, S. P. (1996). Inhibitory mechanisms of neural and cognitive control: applications to selective attention and sequential action. *Brain and Cognition, 30,* 20–43.

Jensen, M., & Meckling, W. (1976). Theory of the firm: Managerial behavior, agency costs and ownership structure, *Journal of Financial Economics, 3,* 305–360.

Kahneman, D., & Tversky, A. (1979). Prospect theory: an analysis of decision under risk. *Econometrica, 47,* 263–291.

Kahneman, D., Knetsch, J. L., & Thaler, R. H. (1991). Anomalies: the endowment effect, loss aversion, and status quo bias. *Journal of Economic Perspectives, 5,* 193–206.

Kirchgässner, G. (1992). Towards a theory of low-cost decisions. *European Journal of Political Economy, 8,* 305–320.

Knight, F. (1921). *Risk, uncertainty and profit.* Chicago: University of Chicago Press (reissue 1971).

Krech, D., Crutchfield, R. S., & Ballanchey, E. L. (1962). *Individual in society.* New York: McGraw-Hill.

Kruglanksi, A. W. (1996). Motivated social cognition: Principles of the interface. In E. T. Higgins & A. W. Kruglanski (Eds.). *Social psychology. Handbook of basic principles* (pp. 493–520). London: Guilford Press.

Levi, M., Cook, K. S., O'Brian, J. O., & Faye, H. (1990). Introduction: The limits of rationality. In K. S. Cook & M. Levi (Eds.). *The limits of rationality* (pp. 1–18). Chicago: The University of Chicago Press.

Liebrand, W. B. G., Jansen, R. W. T. L., Rijken, V. M., & Suhre, C. J. M. (1986). Might over morality: social values and the perception of other players in experimental games. *Journal of Experimental Social Psychology, 22,* 203–215.

Ligthart, P. A. M. (1995). *Solidarity in economic transactions: An experimental study of framing effects in bargaining and contracting.* Amsterdam: Thela Thesis.

Ligthart, P. A. M., & Lindenberg, S. (1994). Solidarity and gain maximization in economic transactions: Framing effects on selling prices. In A. Lewis & K. E. Wärneryd (Eds.). *Ethics and economic affairs* (pp. 215–230). London: Routledge.

Lindenberg, S. (1983). Utility and morality, *Kyklos, 36*(3), 450–468.

Lindenberg, S. (1986). The paradox of privatization in consumption. In Diekmann A. & Mitter P. (Eds.). *Paradoxical effects of social behavior. Essays in honor of Anatol Rapoport* (pp. 297–310). Heidelberg/Wien: Physica-Verlag.

Lindenberg, S. (1989a). Choice and culture: The behavioral basis of cultural impact on transactions. In H. Haferkamp (Ed.). *Social structure and culture* (pp. 175–200). Berlin: de Gruyter.

Lindenberg, S. (1989b). Social production functions, deficits, and social revolutions: pre-revolutionary France and Russia. *Rationality and Society, 1*(1), 51–77.

Lindenberg, S. (1990). Homo socio-oeconomicus: The emergence of a general model of man in the social sciences, *Journal of Institutional and Theoretical Economics, 146,* 727–748.

Lindenberg, S. (1991). Social approval, fertility and female labour market behaviour. In J. Siegers, J. de Jong-Gierveld, & E. van Imhoff (Eds.). *Female labour market behaviour and fertility: A rational choice approach* (pp. 32–58). Berlin/New York: Springer Verlag.

Lindenberg, S. (1992a). An extended theory of institutions and contractual discipline. *Journal of Institutional and Theoretical Economics, 148*(2), 125–154.

Lindenberg, S. (1992b). The method of decreasing abstraction. In J. S. Coleman & T. J. Fararo (Eds.). *Rational choice theory: Advocacy and critique* (pp. 3–20). Newbury Park, CA: Sage.

Lindenberg, S. (1993). Framing, empirical evidence, and applications. In: *Jahrbuch für Neue Politische Ökonomie* (pp. 11–38).Tübingen: Mohr (Siebeck).

Lindenberg, S. (1996). Low evidence situations in the social and historical sciences: Rational choice as a heuristic device. *The Netherlands' Journal of Social Sciences, 32*(1), 25–34.

Lindenberg, S. (2000). It takes both trust and lack of mistrust: The workings of solidarity and relational signaling in contractual relationships. *Journal of Management and Governance, 4,* 11–33.

Lindenberg, S., & Frey, B. (1993). Alternatives, frames, and relative prices: A broader view of rational choice. *Acta Sociologica, 36,* 191–205.

Loewenstein, G. F. (1996). Out of control: Visceral influences on behavior. *Organizational Behavior and Human Decision Processes, 65*(3), 272–292.

Loewenstein, G. F., & Elster, J. (Eds.) (1992). *Choice over time.* New York: Russell Sage Foundation.

Loewenstein G. F., & Thaler, R. (1989). Anomalies: Intertemporal choice. *Journal of Economic Perspectives, 3,* 181–193.

Mandler, G. (1984). *Mind and body: Psychology of emotions and stress.* New York: Norton.

Marshall, A. (1920). *Principles of economics,* 8th ed. London: Macmillan.

Meckling, W. (1976). Values and the choice of the model of the individual in the social sciences. *Schweizerische Zeitschrift für Volkswirtschaft und Statistik, 112,* 545–559.

Merton, R. (1957). *Social theory and social structure.* Glencoe, IL: Free Press.

Millar, M. G., & Tesser, A. (1989). The effects of affective-cognitive consistency and thought on the attitude-behavior relation. *Journal of Experimental Social Psychology, 25,* 189–202.

Myers, M. L. (1983). *The soul of modern economic man. Ideas of self-interest. Thomas Hobbes to Adam Smith.* Chicago: University of Chicago Press.

North, D. (1981). *Structure and change in economic history.* New York: Norton.

Olson, M. (1965). *The logic of collective action.* Cambridge, MA: Harvard University Press.

Ormel, J., Lindenberg, S., Steverink, N., & Verbrugge, L. M. (1999) Subjective well-being and social production functions. *Social Indicator Research, 46,* 61–90.

Parfit, D. (1984). *Reasons and persons.* Oxford: Clarendon Press.

Parsons, T. (1937). *The structure of social action.* Glencoe, IL: Free Press.

Parsons, T., & Shils, E. (1951) Values, motives and systems of action. In T. Parsons & E. Shils (Eds.), *Toward a general theory of action* (pp. 47–275. Cambridge, MA: Harvard University Press.

Raub W., & Weesie J. (2000). The management of matches: A research program on solidarity in durable relations. *Netherlands' Journal of Social Sciences, 36,* 71–88.

Reber, A. S. (1993). *Implicit learning and tacit knowledge.* Oxford: Oxford University Press.

Rosen, S. (1974). Hedonic prices and implicit markets. *Journal of Political Economy, 82,* 34–55.

Russell, J. A. (1983). Pancultural aspects of the human conceptual organization of emotions. *Journal of Personality and Social Psychology, 45,* 1281–1288.

Scheff, T. J. (1967). Towards a sociological model of consensus. *American Sociological Review, 32,* 32–46

Schüßler, R. (1988). Der Homo Oeconomicus als skeptische Fiktion. *Kölner Zeitschrift für Soziologie und Sozialpsychologie, 40,* 447–463.

Scitovsky, T. (1976). *The joyless economy*. Oxford: Oxford University Press.

Sherif, M. (1966). *In common predicament: Social psychology of intergroup conflict and cooperation*. Boston: Houghton-Mifflin.

Simon, H. (1997). Rationality in psychology and economics. In *Models of bounded rationality*. Vol. III: *Empirically grounded economic reason* (pp. 367–385). Cambridge, MA: MIT Press.

Smith, A. (1976). *The theory of moral sentiments*. Glasgow Edition, Vol. I. Oxford: Clarendon Press.

Stigler, G. (1965). *Essays in the history of economics*. Chicago: University of Chicago Press.

Stigler, G., & Becker, G. S. (1977). De gustibus non est disputandum. *The American Economic Review, 67*, 76–90.

Stinchcombe, A. (1986). Reason and rationality. *Sociological Theory, 4*(2), 151–166.

Turner, J. C. (1991). *Social influence*. Pacific Grove, CA: Brooks/Cole Publishing.

Turner J. H. (2000). *On the origins of human emotions. A sociological inquiry into the evolution of human affect*. Stanford, CA: Stanford University Press.

Vallacher, R. R., & Wegner, D. M. (1987). What do people think they are doing? Action identification and human behavior. *Psychological Review, 94*, 3–15.

Van Bruggen, A. (2001). *Individual production of social well-being*. Groningen; Dissertation.

Varese, F., & Yaish M. (2000). The importance of being asked: The rescue of Jews in Nazi Europe. *Rationality and Society, 12*, 307–334.

Watson, D., & Tellegen, A. (1985). Toward a consensual structure of mood. *Psychological Bulletin, 98*, 219–235.

Weber, M. (1961). *Genearl economic history*. New York: Collier.

Williamson, O. E. (1985). *The economic institutions of capitalism*. New York: Free Press.

Williamson, O. E. (1993). Calculativeness, trust, and economic organization. *Journal of Law and Economics, XXXVI*, 453–486.

Wippler, R. (1990). Cultural resources and participation in high culture. In M. Hechter, K.-D. Opp, & R. Wippler (Eds.). *Social institutions. Their emergence, maintenance, and effects* (pp. 187–204). New York: Aldine de Gruyter.

Wittek, R. (2000). Governance by reorganization. Research proposal, Groningen: ICS/University of Groningen.

Wright, R. (1994). *The moral animal. Why we are the way we are: The new science of evolutionary psychology*. New York: Vintage Books.

CHAPTER 30

Comparison Theory

Guillermina Jasso

INTRODUCTION

Comparison theory was born in 1988. It was born with the realization that the justice evaluation function, which in the previous decade had become a useful starting postulate for justice theory, is a special case of a substantially more general function—the comparison function—and therefore large portions of the justice theory apparatus can be put in the service of the larger set of comparison processes.

The basic idea underlying comparison theory—that humans compare themselves to others and/or to previous or envisioned selves, and thereby experience happiness, well-being, self-esteem, and the sense of justice—of course, is not new. This idea, which is at least as old as recorded history, has figured prominently in social thought, philosophy, and social science from *Genesis* to Benjamin Franklin, from classical Greek and Roman authors (especially Epictetus and the Spanish Romans, Marcus Aurelius and Seneca), to the pioneering 19th-century social scientists Marx (1849/1968), Baldwin (1899–1891), Durkheim (1893/1951, 1897/1964), and William James (1891/1952). For example, the first recorded social event in Judaeo-Christian literature (postcreation) involves a comparison ("if you eat this, you will be like gods, knowing good from evil"). After the fall, the next recorded social events are conjugal relations and a new comparison (Cain compares his reward to Abel's, and as a result kills him).

In the middle decades of the 20th century, comparison ideas spawned sparkling advances in social science, notably in the work of Stouffer et al. (1949), Merton and Rossi (1950), Festinger (1954), Thibaut and Kelley (1959), Merton (1957), Runciman (1961), Homans (1974), Wright (1963), Blau (1964), Hyman (1968), Lipset (1968), Sherif (1968), Zelditch (1968), and Berger, Zelditch, Anderson, and Cohen (1972). Across these decades, a shift began to occur, which was to prove enormously consequential. This was the shift from the formulation,

Humans compare themselves to others or to previous or envisioned selves,

to a revised formulation highlighting persons' *holdings of goods* rather than *persons themselves,*

Humans compare their holdings of goods to others' or their own previous or envisioned holdings of goods,

---

Guillermina Jasso • Department of Sociology, New York University, New York, New York 10003.

Handbook of Sociological Theory, edited by Jonathan H. Turner. Kluwer Academic / Plenum Publishers, New York, 2002.

669

and finally to a formulation that deletes persons altogether from the comparison holding,

> *Humans compare their actual levels of attributes and amounts of possessions to the levels/amounts expected or desired or thought just or appropriate.*

This shift would enable rigorous formalization of the basic comparison idea, and the new comparison function, embedded in the short postulate set inherited from justice theory, would in turn yield a wealth of implications. The implications would go far beyond the expected territory, to the larger world of phenomena and processes previously thought to reside, unconnected, in separate domains. Most would not even have the word "compare" in them. They would appear at every level of analysis, from individuals to dyads, small groups to large societies. They would include intuitive and counterintuitive implications, quantitative and qualitative implications. They would suggest the existence of fundamental constants. They would provide theoretical foundation for new measurement procedures. They would provide interpretations for rare events.

Today comparison theory is a robustly growing theory, with an abundance of implications making their way into the empirical trenches. It satisfies the theoretical criteria for a good theory: its few postulates yield a large and growing set of implications, including novel predictions. However, it is empirical test that will decide its validity, that will set limits to its applicability, suggest revisions, perhaps reject it. Comparison theory in the 21st century may grow more beautiful, its postulate set more spartan, and its prediction set more abundant; or it may disappear, giving way to more fundamental theories with greater explanatory power, leaving behind only the happy memory of a theoretical life well lived and substantial experience with the tools that will enable swift progress with the new theories.

This chapter provides an overview of comparison theory, describing its postulate set, summarizing the micromodel and macromodel methods for deriving predictions, and listing a few of the predictions derived to date. Though generating testable predictions is a theory's first purpose, comparison theory also does some of the other things that a good theory does— suggest the existence of fundamental constants, provide a foundation for measurement, provide interpretation for rare or nonrecurring events—and these are briefly discussed. The chapter concludes with a set of frequently asked questions (FAQs).

The order to be followed, however, departs from the logical order in one respect. The overview begins with a sampling of predictions, rather than proceeding systematically from the postulates to the derivation methods to the predictions. The reason is that a major purpose of this chapter is to invite the reader to work in comparison theory. The implications are sufficiently wide-ranging, and some of them novel, that they pique the reader's curiosity in a way that parallels the theorist's surprise: How could this sparse set of assumptions yield such predictions? Moreover, as spectacularly exciting as the comparison function may appear to someone already working with it, to a newcomer it may seem little more than the old idea it is underneath the formalization. What is new is that this old idea, which we knew from our own experience before we learned it in graduate school, can be made to surrender its secrets, to reveal how far its reach extends.

SOME PREDICTIONS
OF COMPARISON THEORY

Comparison theory yields predictions for virtually every area of the human experience. The predictions are testable, *ceteris paribus*, predictions. This section presents a sampling of the predictions of comparison theory, grouped by topical domain.

Note that many of the predictions derived from comparison theory pertain to two or more topical domains; for example, they may connect family behavior with health and with grief. In the listing that follows, to save space, we list each prediction in only one topical group (somewhat arbitrarily chosen) and we make no attempt to cross-reference them. If this were a comprehensive inventory of the theory's predictions, it would be important to cross-reference them completely. Here, however, our main purpose is to provide a flavor for the variety of topical areas touched by comparison processes.

Note also that although each prediction embodies a relationship that can be generated by many processes, the predictions share the feature that the comparison impulse plays a part in all of them.

Death

John Donne's (1923/1959) poem, "No Man Is an Island" (*Devotions XVII*), occupies a special place in English-language literature. The following lines are often quoted:

> Any man's death diminishes me,
> Because I am involved in mankind;
> And therefore never send to know for whom the bell tolls;
> It tolls for thee.

Thus, it was a surprise when, in the course of using micromodel procedures to derive implications from comparison theory for disaster phenomena, the following prediction popped up:

- *Prediction (Death and Grief)*: In a disaster, if there is no property loss but at least one death, then everyone experiences a loss in well-being.

Inheritance

In the novel *Don Quixote* (Cervantes, 1605, 1615/1968), as Don Quixote lies dying and all around are weeping uncontrollably, he summons the notary and, dictating his will, makes bequests to his niece, to the housekeeper, and to Sancho Panza (Part II, Chapter 74). Don Quixote lived for 3 more days and during this time,

> The house was all in confusion; but still the niece ate and the housekeeper drank and Sancho Panza enjoyed himself; for inheriting property wipes out or softens down in the heir the feeling of grief the dead man might be expected to leave behind him. (Cervantes, 1605, 1615/1952, p. 429)

Again, it was a surprise to notice, among the implications obtained in an application of comparison theory to gifts and bequests, the prediction:

- *Prediction (Inheritance and Grief)*: Inheritance tempers grief.

This implication in turn engenders a large set of special cases, including:

- *Prediction (Grief and Death of a Child)*: The death of an offspring is mourned more than the death of a parent.

- *Prediction (Grief and Death of a Parent)*: Under the condition that the parent who dies first leaves his estate to the surviving spouse, the parent who dies first is mourned more than the other parent. Thus, in historical epochs when wives predecease their husbands (as when death in childbirth is prevalent), mothers are mourned more than fathers, but when husbands predecease their wives (as when war is endemic), fathers are mourned more than mothers.

Gifts

There are two main occasions when parents give gifts to their children: at the children's birthdays and at some annual gift giving occasion, such as Christmas or Hanukkah or the Feast of the Three Kings. How do parents allocate their toy budget? More generally, how does gift giving operate? Comparison theory yields many implications about gift giving, including the following three (one of which echoes Virgil):

- *Prediction (Parental Giftgiving)*: Under the condition that parents love their children, parents of nontwin children will spend more of their toy budget at an annual gift giving occasion rather than at the children's birthdays.

- *Prediction (Rules against Gifts)*: Groups make rules restricting gifts from outsiders.

- *Prediction (Gifts and Greeks)*: Beware of Greeks bearing gifts.[1]

Theft

Theft appears to be a universal feature of human experience. It appears early in *Genesis*, for example, with Jacob's theft of Esau's birthright. Comparison theory yields a large set of theft predictions, including the following:

- *Prediction (Thief's Gain and Insider/Outsider Theft)*: A thief's gain from theft is greater when stealing from a fellow group member than when stealing from an outsider.

- *Prediction (Thief's Gain, Insider/Outsider Theft, and Group Wealth)*: A thief's extra gain when stealing from a fellow group member rather than from an outsider is larger in poor groups than in rich groups.

- *Prediction (Cross-Group Theft and Interpersonal Affinities)*: In cross-group theft, there are natural affinities (1) between thief and members of victim's group, and (2) between victim and members of thief's group.

- *Prediction (Theft and Society)*: Society loses when rich steal from poor.

Birth, Wealth, and Virtue

The decision whether to value birth, wealth, or virtue constitutes both a fundamental individual decision and a fundamental societal-organizing principle. Discussions abound in history, philosophy, social thought, literature, and the daily press. Don Quixote spends the better part of the novel lecturing Sancho Panza, who seeks wealth, on the superiority of virtue and heroic deeds. In contrast, an argument can be made, based on the reasonings of Veblen (1899/1953), Weber (1904–1905/1958), Rainwater (1974), and Rosenberg and Pearlin (1978), that cardinal goods are always the default valued goods because they are simpler to measure and the mind is drawn to simple mathematical solutions (Jasso 1983, 1987).[2]

Early in the development of justice theory, it became clear that it would be necessary to distinguish between cardinal goods, like wealth, and ordinal goods, like birth, beauty, athletic

---

[1]Or, as in the *Aeneid*, Book II, l. 49. *"Quidquid id est, timeo Danaos et dona ferentis."*

[2]Whether to value beauty, wealth, athletic skills, or virtue is a common topic in the daily press. Recent stories in *The New York Times*, for example, suggest that the valued good is wealth in Silicon Valley, beauty in Florida, and varies widely across schools.

skill, attractiveness, and so on. It also became clear that the characteristics we call virtues are ordinal goods, and therefore would not be distinguished in their operation from other nonvirtue ordinal goods. However, the distinction between cardinal and ordinal goods would be profound and would lead to important implications for the differential consequences of living in materialistic and nonmaterialistic societies. Some of these implications are:

- *Prediction (Overreward and Materialism)*: The most advantaged person in a materialistic society is happier than the most advantaged person in a nonmaterialistic society.

- *Prediction (Marital Happiness and Materialism)*: Marital happiness can achieve higher levels in materialistic societies than in nonmaterialistic societies.

- *Prediction (Happiness and Group Size in Nonmaterialistic Societies)*: In societies that value ordinal goods, the larger the group, the lower the average happiness.

- *Prediction (Conflict and Materialism)*: Given a conflict between the two subgroups of a two-subgroup society, in nonmaterialistic societies conflict severity decreases as the size of the lower subgroup increases, but in materialistic societies, the direction of the effect of subgroup size on conflict severity depends on the shape of the income distribution.

- *Prediction (Religious Institutions and Materialism)*: The salutary effect of religious institutions on the "world" differs systematically across materialistic and nonmaterialistic societies.

Marriage and Divorce

Most people marry and many people divorce. It thus is of interest whether comparison processes play a part in marital phenomena. It turns out that comparison theory yields many implications for marital phenomena, including the following:

- *Prediction (Employment and Marital Cohesiveness)*: The effects of employment, unemployment, and retirement depend on the spouses' earnings ratio.

- *Prediction (Opposite Effects on Individual Well-being and Marital Cohesiveness)*: Shifts that increase marital cohesiveness increase the well-being of one spouse but decrease the other's.

- *Prediction (Grief from Widowhood and Divorce)*: Losing a beloved spouse to death is less painful than losing a beloved spouse to divorce.

Health

Anecdotal accounts suggest the effects of comparison processes on physical and mental health. Comparison theory yields the following implications:

- *Prediction (Eating Disorders and Blindness)*: Blind persons are less vulnerable to eating disorders such as anorexia than are persons with sight.

- *Prediction (Disasters and Euphoria)*: In a disaster, if there is property loss but no deaths, nonvictims experience euphoria.

Conversation

Talk pervades the social life. Here, too, we see the hand of comparison processes, as in the following implications:

- *Prediction (Conversation Topics and Valued Goods)*: The topics raised in conversation signal the speaker's valued good(s). A prime example is that of a hereditary monarch discussing horse bloodlines.

- *Prediction (Interruptions and Valued Goods)*: The number of interruptions in a group depends on (1) the number of potential valued goods, (2) inequality in the distribution of cardinal goods, and (3) intercorrelations among the valued goods.

- *Prediction (Interruptions and Groups)*: Interruptions are group-specific; a given actor may interrupt repeatedly in one group, never in another.

- *Prediction (Courtesy in the City)*: Courtesy is lower in heterogeneous societies, and thus in urban settings.

Immigration

An interesting question in comparative social policy concerns the variability in immigration policies. Why do some societies welcome immigration and others not? Comparison theory yields a pertinent prediction:

- *Prediction (Immigration and Materialism)*: Societies that welcome immigration must be societies that value wealth.

Groups and the Changing Value of Things

All social scientists—but perhaps especially sociologists—assume that groups and group structure exert fundamental influence over individuals. The implications of comparison theory include the following:

- *Prediction (Groups and the Value of Things)*: A thing changes value as it, or its owner, moves from group to group.

- *Prediction (Gift's Value and Giver's Presence)*: A gift is more valuable to the receiver when the giver is present.

- *Prediction (Theft of a Gift)*: In an experiment, if a thing is given by the experimenter to a subject and subsequently stolen by a fellow participant, the loss from theft exceeds the gain from the gift.

International Relations

Some predictions apply to relations between countries. These include the following:

- *Prediction (Bilateral Migration Policy)*: In international migration, if origin and destination countries have equal wealth, they cannot both favor or both oppose migration; they can only both be indifferent to it.

- *Prediction (How to Punish a Foe)*: To punish a foe, kill its best people or send it your worst people.

- *Prediction (How to Incapacitate a Foe)*: To incapacitate a foe, kill its children.

War

The topic of international relations leads naturally to the topic of war. Some of the implications of comparison theory for war-related phenomena are:

- *Prediction (War and Games of Chance)*: In wartime, the favorite leisure-time activity of soldiers is playing games of chance.

- *Prediction (War and Gifts)*: Gift giving increases in wartime.

- *Prediction (War and Posttraumatic Stress)*: Posttraumatic stress is greater among veterans of wars fought away from home than among veterans of wars fought on home soil.

Inequality

Not surprisingly, given the strong links between comparison theory and justice theory, comparison theory yields implications about the social consequences of economic inequality. Some of these implications are:

- *Prediction (Conflict Severity and Economic Inequality)*: In materialistic societies, conflict severity is an increasing function of economic inequality.

- *Prediction (Emigration and Economic Inequality)*: In materialistic societies, the proportion of the population at risk of emigrating is an increasing function of economic inequality.

THE POSTULATES OF COMPARISON THEORY

The predictions reported in the previous section were deduced from the postulates of comparison theory. In this section we take a look at those postulates.

Individual-Level Postulates

COMPARISON FUNCTION. A theory begins with an assumption. Comparison theory begins with the assumption that humans compare the amounts or levels of their holdings of goods and bads to the amounts or levels they desire or expect or think appropriate (henceforth, simply "comparison holding"), thereby experiencing happiness, well-being, self-esteem, and the sense of justice. This assumption is represented by the comparison function, which specifies the comparison outcome (say, happiness or self-esteem), denoted Z, as the natural logarithm of the ratio of the actual holding, denoted A, to the comparison holding, denoted C.

- *Postulate 1 (Logarithmic Specification of Comparison Function)*: The comparison outcome varies with the logarithm of the ratio of the actual holding to the comparison holding,

$$Z = \theta \ln\left(\frac{A}{C}\right) \tag{1}$$

where θ is the signature constant, whose sign is positive for goods and negative for bads.[3]

---

[3]The absolute value of the signature constant measures the individual's expressiveness and is known as the expressiveness coefficient. Expressiveness plays an important part in empirical work. However, it has not played a part in the

TABLE 30.1. Mathematical Statement of Key Properties of the Comparison Function

1. *Additivity.* The function $Z = Z(A,C)$ is said to be additive if and only if the effect of A on Z is independent of C and the effect of C on Z is independent of A:

$$Z_{AC} = 0$$

2. *Scale Invariance.* The function $Z = Z(A,C)$ is said to be scale invariant if and only if it is homogeneous of degree zero:

$$AZ_A + CZ_C = 0$$

3. *Symmetry.* The function $Z = Z(A,C)$ is said to be symmetric if and only if it satisfies the condition:

$$Z(A,C) = -Z(A,C)$$

4. *Deficiency Is Felt More Keenly than Comparable Excess.* The function $Z = Z(A,C)$ is said to satisfy the property that deficiency is felt more keenly than comparable excess if and only if it satisfies the condition:

$$|Z_{(A=C_0-k)}| > Z_{(A=C_0+k)}$$

where C_0 is the comparison reward and k is a positive constant.

According to the comparison function, the Z outcomes assume values of zero when the actual holding equals the comparison holding, negative values when the actual holding is less than the comparison holding, and positive values when the actual holding exceeds the comparison holding. Thus, for example, the happiness dimension is represented by the full real-number line, with zero a neutral point, degrees of happiness represented by positive numbers, and degrees of unhappiness by negative numbers.

The logarithmic-ratio specification of the comparison function has several properties desirable in a comparison function; these are summarized in Table 30.1. For example, it quantifies the common human experience that deficiency is felt more keenly than comparable excess. Moreover, in the case of cardinal goods and bads, it is the only functional form that satisfies both scale-invariance and additivity.[4]

MEASUREMENT RULE FOR HOLDINGS. The logarithmic specification initially was proposed for cardinal things; it is easy to measure the actual and comparison holdings of, say, money or hectares of land. But the literature and everyday experience suggest that goods and bads not susceptible of cardinal measurement (beauty, intelligence, athletic skill, heroism) also play important parts in comparison processes. Therefore, the second postulate proposes a measurement rule (Jasso, 1980):

- *Postulate 2 (Measurement Rule):* Cardinal goods and bads are measured in their own units (the amount denoted by x), and ordinal goods and bads are measured by the individual's relative rank $[i/(N + 1)]$ within a specially selected comparison group, where i denotes the rank-order statistic in ascending order and N denotes the size of the group or population:

$$A,C \begin{cases} x, & \text{cardinal holding} \\ \dfrac{i}{N + 1}, & \text{ordinal holding} \end{cases} \qquad (2)$$

---

development of comparison theory to date. Accordingly, in this chapter, the signature constant is fixed at $+1$ for goods and -1 for bads.

[4] For fuller exposition of the comparison function and its roots in the justice evaluation function, see the original report of the justice evaluation function (Jasso, 1978) and the generalization to the comparison function (Jasso, 1990), as well as the further analysis in Jasso (1996b, 1999).

IDENTITY REPRESENTATION OF COMPARISON HOLDING. A substantial portion of theoretical derivation in comparison theory involves drawing out the implications of changes or differences in individuals' actual rewards and societal distributions of actual rewards. Such derivation was hampered by the absence of information about individuals' comparison holdings. The third postulate makes it possible to carry out theoretical derivation even without any knowledge about the comparison holdings and to do so without imposing any additional assumption about how individuals form their notions of the comparison holding (Jasso, 1986).

- *Postulate 3 (Identity Representation of Comparison Holding)*: The comparison holding C is identically equal to, and can be expressed as, the product of the arithmetic mean of the actual reward in the collectivity and an individual-specific constant, denoted Φ, which captures everything that is unknown about how the individual chooses his/her own comparison holding:

$$C = \phi E(A) \tag{3}$$

Because the arithmetic mean is itself equal to the total sum (S) of a thing divided by the population size (N), the comparison reward in the case of a cardinal reward can be written:

$$C = \phi E(A) = \phi S/N \tag{4}$$

Thus, the identity representation provides a way to incorporate into the basic comparison function two important factors: the group affluence S and the group size N.

The foregoing three individual-level postulates form the heart of the postulate set of comparison theory. For easy reference, they are summarized in panel A of Table 30.2.

BASIC COMPARISON FUNCTION FORMULAS. Combining the three postulates yields the basic comparison formulas, which express the comparison function for cardinal and ordinal holdings and which can be written in versions for small groups and large collectivities (the "small"-groups formulas include the population size N; the large-collectivities formulas are

TABLE 30.2. Fundamental Postulates of Comparison Theory

A. Individual-Level Postulates
   1. Postulate of Logarithmic Specification of the Comparison Function

$$Z = \theta \ln\left(\frac{A}{C}\right)$$

   2. Measurement Rule for Holdings

$$A, C \begin{cases} x, & \text{cardinal good/bad} \\ \dfrac{i}{N+1}, & \text{ordinal good/bad} \end{cases}$$

   3. Identity Representation of Comparison Holding

$$C = \phi E(A)$$

B. Social-Level Postulates
   4. Social Welfare

$$SW = E(Z)$$

   5. Social Cohesiveness

$$\text{Social Cohesiveness} = -GMD(Z)$$

NOTES: As described in the text, Z denotes the comparison outcome, A the actual reward, and C the just reward. The signature constant θ is positive for goods and negative for bads. For both actual and just rewards, x denotes the amount of a cardinal good or bad, i denotes the rank-order statistics arranged in ascending order, and N denotes the population size. ϕ denotes the individual-specific parameter, $E(\cdot)$ the expected value, and $GMD(\cdot)$ the Gini's mean difference.

TABLE 30.3. Fundamental Formulas of Comparison Theory

A. Comparison Function
    1. When the Comparison Reward Is Known

<table>
<tr><th>Small Groups</th><th>Large Groups</th></tr>
<tr>
<td>

$$Z = \begin{cases} \theta \ln \dfrac{x_A}{x_C}, & \text{cardinal holding} \\[2mm] \theta \ln \dfrac{i_A}{i_C}, & \text{ordinal holding} \end{cases}$$

</td>
<td>

$$Z = \begin{cases} \theta \ln \dfrac{x_A}{x_C}, & \text{cardinal holding} \\[2mm] \theta \ln \dfrac{\alpha_A}{\alpha_C}, & \text{ordinal holding} \end{cases}$$

</td>
</tr>
</table>

    2. When the Comparison Reward Is Unknown

<table>
<tr><th>Small Groups</th><th>Large Groups</th></tr>
<tr>
<td>

$$Z = \begin{cases} \theta \ln \dfrac{xN}{\phi S}, & \text{cardinal holding} \\[2mm] \theta \ln \dfrac{2i}{\phi(N+1)}, & \text{ordinal holding} \end{cases}$$

</td>
<td>

$$Z = \begin{cases} \theta \ln \dfrac{x}{\phi E(X)}, & \text{cardinal holding} \\[2mm] \theta \ln \dfrac{2\alpha}{\phi}, & \text{ordinal holding} \end{cases}$$

</td>
</tr>
</table>

B. Social Welfare Function
    1. When the Comparison Reward Is Known

<table>
<tr><th>Small Groups</th><th>Large Groups</th></tr>
<tr>
<td>

$$E(Z) = \begin{cases} \theta \ln \dfrac{G(X_A)}{G(X_C)}, & \text{cardinal holding} \\[2mm] \theta \ln \dfrac{G(i_A)}{G(i_C)}, & \text{ordinal holding} \end{cases}$$

</td>
<td>

$$E(Z) = \begin{cases} \theta \ln \dfrac{G(X_A)}{G(X_C)}, & \text{cardinal holding} \\[2mm] \theta \ln \dfrac{G(\alpha_A)}{G(\alpha_C)}, & \text{ordinal holding} \end{cases}$$

</td>
</tr>
</table>

    2. When the Comparison Reward Is Unknown

<table>
<tr><th>Small Groups</th><th>Large Groups</th></tr>
<tr>
<td>

$$E(Z) = \begin{cases} \theta \ln \dfrac{G(X_A)}{E(X_A)} - \theta \ln [G(\phi)], & \text{cardinal holding} \\[2mm] \theta \ln \dfrac{\sqrt[N]{N!}}{N+1} - \theta \ln [G(\phi)], & \text{ordinal holding} \end{cases}$$

</td>
<td>

$$E(Z) = \begin{cases} \theta \ln \dfrac{G(X_A)}{E(X_A)} - \theta \ln [G(\phi)], & \text{cardinal holding} \\[2mm] \theta \ln \dfrac{2}{e} - \theta \ln [G(\phi)], & \text{ordinal holding} \end{cases}$$

</td>
</tr>
</table>

NOTES: The relative rank is denoted α. The letter S denotes the total amount of the cardinal good(bad). $G(\cdot)$ denotes the geometric mean.

the limiting case as N goes to infinity). Formulas for the case in which the comparison reward is known (subpanel 1) are based on postulates 1 and 2; formulas for the case in which the comparison reward is unknown (subpanel 2) are based on postulates 1, 2, and 3. The formulas are presented in panel A of Table 30.3.

    To save space we do not discuss all the formulas, illustrating with only one: the formula for the comparison function for cardinal holdings in small groups when the comparison reward is unknown (Table 30.3, panel A.2, left column, top branch):

$$Z = \theta \ln \left(\frac{xN}{S\phi} \right) \tag{5}$$

Note that in this case the comparison outcome is expressed as a function of the individual's own holding x, the group size N, and the group's total amount S of the holding. Note, moreover, that the logarithmic form enables separating the effects of all factors, thus yielding predictions about the *ceteris paribus* effects of the individual's actual holding and the group size and group affluence, net of the individual's idiosyncrasy parameter ϕ. This particular formula is the starting point for one of the major techniques for deriving predictions, known as the *micro-*

model. The micromodel is used to investigate the effects of change in one or more of the three factors in the comparison function, thus enabling derivation of implications for a wide variety of situations involving change in own holding or group affluence or size (such as situations involving gifts, bequests, disasters, war, and so on).

Social-Level Postulates

An early insight in justice theory was that a society can be represented by the distribution of justice evaluations among its members and that parameters of this distribution may be importantly related to behavioral and social phenomena (Jasso, 1980). Comparison theory inherited this insight, and like justice theory highlights two parameters of the distribution of comparison outcomes—the expected value (or arithmetic mean) and the Gini's mean difference—forming two postulates around them. As will be seen below, a major technique for deriving implications, known as the *macromodel*, takes the comparison distribution for its starting point.

- *Postulate 4 (Social Welfare)*: The collectivity's social welfare SW varies with the expected value of the Z distribution:

$$SW = E(Z) \tag{6}$$

The social welfare postulate plays a part in some of the implications derived using macromodel procedures. Formulas for the social welfare function for both cardinal and ordinal holdings, in versions for small groups and large collectivities (where, as before, the "small"-groups formulas include the population size N, and the large-collectivities formulas are the limiting case as N goes to infinity), are reported in panel B of Table 30.3. As with the formulas for the comparison function, formulas for the case in which the comparison reward is known (subpanel 1) are based on postulates 1 and 2; formulas for the case in which the comparison reward is unknown (subpanel 2) are based on postulates 1, 2, and 3. Note that the social welfare is the same as the quantity that in justice analysis is known as the justice index (Jasso, 1999).

- *Postulate 5 (Social Cohesiveness)*: The collectivity's social cohesiveness SC varies with the Gini's mean difference of the Z distribution:

$$\text{Social Cohesiveness} = -GMD(Z) \tag{7}$$

TWO TECHNIQUES
FOR THEORETICAL DERIVATION

The second section presented a sampling of predictions of comparison theory and the third section presented the postulates of comparison theory. It is time now to discuss, albeit briefly, how to get from the postulates to the predictions.[5] We already have mentioned two main tools: the micromodel and the macromodel. The terms micromodel and macromodel are not exact, as both techniques use both micro and macro terms and both techniques yield predictions at both micro- and macrolevels. The terms are useful nonetheless, as the main task of derivation starts with an individual in the micromodel and with a population in the macromodel.

---

[5]Geoffrey Tootell has remarked in oral presentations that all the action lies between the postulates and the predictions.

Though there are other ways of deriving predictions, these two techniques have proved sufficiently useful in a variety of cases as to warrant brief summaries. But first, a few general remarks are in order.

Ceteris Paribus Predictions in a Multifactor World

All the predictions of comparison theory are *ceteris paribus* predictions. Without doubt, in most situations there are many factors at work. Comparison processes constitute only one of the possibly many influences shaping behavioral and social phenomena. The predictions of comparison theory represent only the operation of comparison processes.

The Role of Additional Assumptions

The implications presented above—with one exception, the prediction about parental gift giving, which as stated incorporates a condition and which is discussed below—are derived solely from one or more of the five postulates in the third section. Some of these implications describe events or actions that increase or decrease someone's well-being; such implications are of the form, "Such-and-such a behavior or event increases (or decreases) someone's well-being." These implications have the feature that they can be combined with an additional assumption in order to derive further implications that on occasion may prove more felicitous or more pertinent.

If the "someone" is the individual him or herself, then introducing two additional assumptions—(1) that individuals seek to increase their well-being, and (2) that individuals are aware of the behavioral relationship embodied in the implication—will produce a new implication that the individual will "prefer" the event, or will engage in the behavior, that increases (or decreases) his or her well-being.

Similarly, if the "someone" whose well-being is affected is someone else, then introducing two additional assumptions—about whether the first actor wishes to increase or decrease the other's well-being and about the first actor's knowledge of the behavioral relationship embodied in the implication—will produce a new prediction.

Let us illustrate. Application of micromodel procedures to theft yields the prediction that a thief's gain from theft is greater when stealing from a fellow group member than when stealing from an outsider. Incorporating the additional assumptions that individuals seek to increase their well-being and that prospective thieves are aware (however vaguely) of the link between the gain in well-being and the victim's group leads to a new prediction, "A thief will prefer to steal from a fellow group member rather than from an outsider." Obviously, if the thief seeks to decrease his gain from theft, he or she will prefer the opposite. Moreover, the new prediction may be more applicable to experienced thieves, who may have noticed the link between the gain in well-being and the victim's group, or to thieves in a thief culture that may impart to apprentice thieves the knowledge gained by their predecessors.

Similarly, application of micromodel procedures to gifts yields the prediction that if a child in a sibship of young children receives a gift from outside the sibship, then the other children will experience a loss in well-being. Incorporating the additional assumptions that parents seek to prevent a loss in well-being among their children and that they are aware of the link between gifts and well-being leads to the prediction that they will give more gifts at an annual gift giving occasion than at the children's birthdays. This is a case in which parents quickly learn about the implied link, though many also benefit from the cultural transmission of parenting lore.

Of course, many of the predictions of comparison theory end, so to speak, within the confines of comparison theory; they are not amenable to the type of manipulation to which the implications about individual well-being are susceptible. For example, the prediction that blind persons are less susceptible to eating disorders cannot readily be used to generate additional predictions.

Micromodel Procedures

The micromodel approach begins with investigation of the effects of an event on an individual, where the event may be a human action (such as giving a gift or stealing a radio), or the outcome of a human action (such as receiving a gift or having a radio stolen), or an event not traceable to human agency (such as a natural disaster). The objective is to assess the effects of the event on a comparison outcome. The micromodel thus makes it possible to ascertain change in well-being, or in self-esteem, or in the sense of being justly or unjustly rewarded, establishing, for example, who becomes better-off and who becomes worse-off, and by how much. The basic equation in the micromodel approach is an equation that compares the individual at two points in time:

$$CZ = Z_2 - Z_1 \tag{8}$$

where, as before, Z denotes the comparison outcome (e.g., well-being) and CZ denotes change in Z. Thus, the micromodel investigates the change in Z between time 1 and time 2. If CZ is zero, then whatever transpired between the two time periods has had no effect on the individual; if, however, CZ is negative, then the individual has become worse-off, and, if positive, better-off.[6]

The micromodel can be used for both cardinal and ordinal goods, for both small groups and large groups, and for both the case in which the comparison reward is known and the case in which the comparison reward is unknown; that is, the micromodel can be formulated with any of the basic individual-level formulas as its starting-point (panel A, Table 30.3). To date, however, most derivations using the micromodel have been based on the formula for the comparison function for cardinal holdings in small groups when the comparison reward is unknown [Table 30.3, panel A.2., left column, top branch, and also shown in Eq. (5)]. Thus, in this brief summary, Eq. (5) is the basic formula that will be incorporated into the change equation in Eq. (8). The events and actions whose effects on the individual's well-being can be investigated via the micromodel approach are not limited to events or actions that alter the individual's actual reward, but encompass as well events and actions that affect the population size and the population's total amount of the reward, for example, the population's total wealth or total gross domestic product (GDP).

Because there are many events and actions that affect the constituent factors of Z (that affect, for example, in the case of a cardinal good or bad, own wealth, population wealth, and population size), the micromodel procedure can be used for a wide variety of cases. To illustrate, theft affects own wealth x and may affect group wealth S (depending on whether the thief and victim are from the same group); murder affects population size N, may affect x and

---

[6]Note that the change equation refers exclusively to one individual at two points in time. The individual may become better-off or worse-off relative to his or her own situation at time 1.

S (depending on bequests and relationship to the victim), and may affect the individual's rank i in an ordinal good (bad) regime. Similarly, giving and receiving a gift affect x and may affect S, depending on whether giver and receiver are together or apart; and when a fellow group member gives or receives a gift, S is altered. Note that when S or N is altered, *all* group members experience a change in Z, not merely the protagonists in the situation (such as thief and victim in the theft case or giver and receiver in the gift case).

Plugging Eq. (5) into Eq. (8) yields the basic equation for the change in well-being, in this case of a cardinal good in a small group with the comparison reward unknown:

$$CZ = \ln\left(\frac{x_2 N_2 S_1 \phi_1}{x_1 N_1 S_2 \phi_2}\right) \tag{9}$$

Table 30.4 outlines the protocol for the micromodel strategy, applied to a cardinal-good regime. As shown, the micromodel approach begins with the formulas for Z (step 1, Table 30.4) and for CZ (step 2, Table 30.4). The goal is to systematically draw out the implications of basic comparison processes for a wide range of disparate domains. Accordingly, at the next step the theorist chooses a field of application (step 3, Table 30.4). In general, any domain involving alterations in own wealth, population wealth, or population size is a candidate. Once the theorist has selected the particular domain, the theorist identifies the kinds of actors involved and the kinds of situations and provides the pertinent special notation. The ensuing setup and analysis is referred to as a model of _____ phenomena based on comparison theory, often abbreviated to _____ model. Examples include the comparison-based theft model, the comparison-based gift model, and the comparison-based disaster model.

TABLE 30.4. **The Micromodel Strategy for Generating Predictions in Comparison Theory: Studying the Effects of an Event or Action in a Cardinal-Good Regime**

---

1. Write basic comparison-function formula, cardinal-good case.

$$Z = \ln\frac{xN}{S\phi}$$

where Z denotes the comparison-based response (say, happiness or well-being), x denotes the individual's own amount of the cardinal good (say, wealth), S denotes the total amount of the cardinal good in the collectivity, N denotes the population size, and ϕ denotes the individual-specific parameter capturing idiosyncratic elements in the comparison standard used by the individual for him- or herself.

2. Express change in Z from time 1 to time 2.

$$CZ = Z_2 - Z_1$$

$$CZ = \ln\frac{x_2 N_2}{S_2 \phi_2} - \ln\frac{x_1 N_1}{S_1 \phi_1}$$

$$CZ = \ln\frac{x_2 N_2 S_1 \phi_1}{x_1 N_1 S_2 \phi_2}$$

3. Analyze the particular event or action.
4. Write the formulas for CZ for each kind of person in each situation or special case.
5. Is CZ positive or negative? (This requires an assumption about phi; for example, assume $\phi_1 = \phi_2$.)
6. In which situation does each kind of actor have the higher CZ? (For each actor, evaluate the inequalities across all situations.)
7. Within situation, which actor has the higher CZ and absolute value of CZ?
8. Obtain first and second partial derivatives of CZ with respect to each factor in the CZ formulas.
9. The results obtained in 5–8 comprise the predictions.

Space constraints do not permit comprehensive exposition of the micromodel. However, detailed exposition is found in Jasso (2000). Micromodel procedures have been used to derive implications for theft (Jasso, 1988b, 2000), gifts (Jasso, 1993c), disasters (Jasso, 1993b), and migration (Jasso, 1996a).

Macromodel Procedures

The macromodel method begins with the *distribution* of a comparison outcome—as before, let us call it Z—together with the parameters, subdistribution structure, and other features of that distribution. For example, the macromodel may begin with the distribution of justice evaluations in a society or with the happiness distribution in a group. In general, the macromodel is used whenever a problem is posed that focuses on aspects of the distribution as a whole or on connections between aspects of the subdistribution structure.[7] Four examples will provide concreteness.

First, in justice theory an appealing idea is that a society can be usefully represented and characterized by the distribution of justice evaluations among its member. Interest thus centers on the Z distribution. Because Z is a function of the actual and comparison holdings—A and C—characterizing the Z distribution requires information about the A and C distributions and their intercorrelations. A theoretical problem for which macromodel procedures are well suited is the problem of establishing a priori what happens to the Z distribution in the following cases: (1) if A and C refer to cardinal versus ordinal goods, (2) if A and C have positive or negative or zero correlation, (3) in the cardinal-good case, if inequality in A and C varies, or (4) in the cardinal-good case, if A and C have particular distributional shapes.

Second, one approach to the study of conflict posits a society with two subgroups in which the two subgroups are nonoverlapping in the distribution of a valued good. For example, the physicians and nurses on staff at a hospital may value earnings, and the earnings of the highest-paid nurse may be less than the earnings of the lowest-paid physician. This approach suggests that the severity of the conflict between the physicians and the nurses will vary with the difference between the mean Z for the advantaged group (the physicians) and the mean Z for the disadvantaged group (the nurses). To investigate conflict severity, we study the censored subdistribution structure, in which the distribution yields two censored subdistributions, with the censoring point set at the proportion in the disadvantaged group (e.g., the proportion nurses among the staff). We obtain expressions for the expected value of the right-censored subdistribution (the nurses) and the expected value of the left-censored subdistribution (the physicians) and we address a priori questions about how the difference between the two expected values may vary with the subgroup split (the proportion who are nurses and the proportion who are physicians) and with the earnings inequality.

Third, in theoretical justice analysis it often is of interest to investigate the proportions who are underrewarded and overrewarded and the expected values of each subset. In this case, the relevant subdistribution structure is a truncated subdistribution structure, with the truncation point fixed at zero, the point of perfect justice, which divides the underrewarded from the overrewarded. As in the previous problem, attention centers on analyzing how the proportions

---

[7]The macromodel makes use of censored and truncated subdistributions. There is some confusion about terminology in the literature, and we follow the usage in Moses (1966) and in Johnson and Kotz (1969, p. 27). Truncation refers to selection of the units by values of the variate. Censoring refers to selection of the units by their ranks or percentage (or probability) points. For example, the group with incomes less than $20,000 forms a truncated subdistribution; the top 5% of the population forms a censored subdistribution.

underrewarded and overrewarded and their means differ across societies with cardinal versus ordinal valued goods and in the cardinal case vary with inequality in the valued good.

Fourth, an appealing idea is that there may be a "mainstream" in the Z distribution, and that this mainstream consists of individuals with Z scores between -1 and $+1$. The question arises how the proportions in the mainstream and in the "underclass" and the "overclass" differ across types of valued-good regimes. As in the third example, this question is addressed via the truncated subdistribution structure, which in this case yields three subdistributions, with truncation points at -1 and $+1$.

There are two main goals in the macromodel approach. The first is to obtain distribution-independent results; the second is to obtain results for a wide variety of distributional forms that can be regarded as approximations to real-world distributions of valued goods at different times and places. It has been shown that for ordinal holdings, the correct modeling distribution is the rectangular (Jasso, 1980). As for cardinal goods and bads, a useful selection of modeling distributions would consist of continuous nonnegative distributions that exemplify combinations of features considered important a priori. Two such features are whether the variate approaches zero from the right and whether the variate tends to positive infinity: in ordinary (and imprecise) language, whether or not the society has a minimum income and whether or not it has a maximum income. Treating each dimension as a dichotomy, this approach leads to four combinations. Distributions that exemplify these combinations—the exponential, lognormal, Pareto, power-function, and quadratic variates—have been used for several years in comparison theory research. Ongoing work is extending the set of modeling distributions to include other distributional families. Candidates for modeling distributions are found in the standard sources (Johnson & Kotz, 1970a,b; Hastings & Peacock, 1974; Evans, Hastings, & Peacock, 1993; Stuart & Ord, 1987; articles in the *Encyclopedia of Statistical Sciences*, e.g., Kotz, Johnson, & Read, 1985; etc.).[8]

As in the micromodel, the starting point for theoretical derivation may be a formula for Z when the comparison reward is explicitly included or, alternatively, a formula for Z when the comparison reward is unknown (see Table 30.3, panel A). It is considerably easier, both mechanically and in terms of substantive modeling, to base application of macromodel procedures on the formula when the comparison reward is unknown or is fixed at a common quantity for everyone and early applications did that. When the comparison reward is treated as unknown, the results are interpreted as the predictions net of the operation of the idiosyncrasy parameter φ. Examples include Jasso (1991, 1993a–c, 1996a). More recent theoretical derivation using macromodel procedures has been based on the formula for Z that explicitly includes the comparison reward (Jasso, 1997a, 1999).

Whatever the substantive question that will be addressed via macromodel procedures, some basic information about the Z distribution is required. Table 30.5 reports the results of investigating the shape of the Z distribution when the formula for Z includes both the actual and the comparison rewards. As shown, two important features are (1) whether A and C are identical or different, and (2) the relation between A and C, in particular whether A and C are independent, perfectly positively associated, or perfectly negatively associated, producing six special cases. Panel A reports distribution-independent results. For example, if A and C are identically and independently distributed, the Z distribution will be symmetric about zero (equal proportions underrewarded and overrewarded). Panel B reports the results for four cases in which A and C belong to the same variate family, the variates investigated being the rectangular (which models ordinal holdings), the Pareto, the power-function, and the lognor-

---

[8]Comprehensive exposition of the macromodel approach is provided in Jasso (1997b).

TABLE 30.5. Distribution of $Z = \ln\left(\dfrac{A}{C}\right)$

A,C Variate	Relation between A and C		
	A & C Independent	rho(A,C) = +1	rho(A,C) = −1
A. Distribution-Independent Results			
Identical	Z symmetric about zero	Z degenerate at zero	Z symmetric about zero
Different	Z asymmetric/symmetric about any number	Z asymmetric/symmetric about any number	Z asymmetric/symmetric about any number
B. A and C from Same Variate Family			
Rectangular			
Identical	Laplace	Equal	Logistic
Different	—	—	—
Pareto			
Identical	Laplace	Equal	Logistic
Different	Asymmetrical Laplace	Positive/negative exponential	Quasi-logistic
Power-function			
Identical	Laplace	Equal	Logistic
Different	Asymmetrical Laplace	Postive/negative exponential	Quasi-logistic
Lognormal			
Identical	Normal	Equal	Normal
Different	Normal	Normal	Normal

mal. Table 30.5 shows the distribution of Z for each of these special cases. The special macromodel application can then proceed to establish the subdistribution structure, the subdistribution means, and so on.

BESIDES PREDICTIONS: OTHER HIGHLIGHTS OF COMPARISON THEORY

A theory's first purpose is to provide testable predictions. A good theory, however, goes beyond providing predictions. A good theory provides a foundation for measurement, and a good theory provides interpretation of rare or nonrecurring events. Comparison theory does both. It also suggests the existence of fundamental constants.

Foundation for Measurement

Comparison theory provides a foundation for measurement of a number of quantities. Here we provide three examples.

MEASURING THE JUST REWARD.   It long has been thought that asking respondents to provide their idea of the just reward—say, the just earnings for self or other—may invite biased measurement, as response mechanisms, together with rhetorical and socialization elements, may interfere. Comparison theory, via the justice evaluation function, makes it possible to measure the just reward in an indirect way that appears to be relatively more protected against bias. This indirect way builds on Jasso and Rossi's (1977) empirical justice design, and instead of asking respondents to provide their idea of the just reward asks respondents to judge the fairness or unfairness of reward amounts randomly associated with target recipients. Algebraic procedures utilizing the justice evaluation function can then estimate the "true" just reward.

MEASURING FRAMING.   Individuals may frame rewards differently. While most persons may frame earnings as a good, some may frame it as a bad; and while most individuals may frame time in prison as a bad, some may frame it as a good. Until recently, respondents were not allowed the freedom to frame rewards as goods or as bads; the investigator, via the analysis procedures, imposed a single view on all respondents. Comparison theory, via the comparison function, makes it possible to estimate for each respondent a *framing coefficient*; the framing coefficient can assume values of -1, which indicates that the respondent frames the reward as a bad, and $+1$, which indicates that the respondent frames the reward as a good.

JUSTICE INDEXES AND INJUSTICE DECOMPOSITIONS.   Comparison theory, in the justice version, makes it possible to measure the total amount of injustice experienced in a society, via two justice indexes recently proposed (Jasso, 1999). Additionally, one of the two justice indexes yields two distinct decompositions. The first decomposition enables measurement of the amount of injustice due to poverty and the amount of injustice due to inequality. The second decomposition enables measurement of the amount of injustice due to reality and the amount of injustice due to ideology.

Interpretation of Rare Events

Comparison theory, along with its predictions, provides a framework for interpreting rare or nonrecurring events. We provide three examples.

MENDICANT INSTITUTIONS.   Comparison theory suggests that the invention, in the late 12th century, of mendicant institutions (Franciscans, Dominicans) was a response to the switch from valuing birth and nobility to valuing wealth. This interpretation arises from an application of comparison theory in which the public benefit of religious institutions varies with the difference between the mean well-being of a society before and after a subset become cloistered and renounce the valued good. When the valued good is birth or nobility, the archetypal monastic institutions (Benedictine, with individual poverty but not corporate poverty) provide a public benefit, but when the valued good is wealth, the monasteries, some of which can be quite wealthy, fail to provide a public benefit. It was the genius of Francis of Assisi and Dominic to invent an institution in which the house itself and not merely the monks embraced total poverty. Valued goods rise and ebb, and the history of total poverty in religious institutions (e.g., the great debates among the Franciscans, in which William of Ockham made an inspired defense of total poverty,[9] and the great Teresian reforms of the Carmelites[10]) may be interpreted as a response to the valued-good regime around them.

DETECTIVE FICTION.   Comparison theory suggests that when cardinal goods are valued, murder needs a motive. Thus, it is no accident that the search for a motive in the murderer-

---

[9]It is not without interest that the great champion of parsimony in intellectual structures was also the great champion of total poverty in religious institutions.

[10]See St. Teresa's *Camino de Perfección* and the *Constituciones* (Teresa de Ávila, 1546–1582/1982).

detection enterprise and the associated literary genre seem to have arisen in 19th century England.

MARIEL EMIGRATION. Comparison theory suggests that there are two ways to punish a foe, by reducing its good and by increasing its bad. Suppose that from the perspective of nation-states, some members of the population constitute a good (e.g., able-bodied, upright, skilled soldiers) and others constitute a bad (e.g., felons and social or political undesirables). Then an aggressor nation has two possible instruments: (1) going to war and killing some of the target nation's soldiers (or scientists), thus reducing its good, and (2) sending social undesirables to the target nation, thus increasing its bad. According to comparison theory, then, in the Mariel emigration of 1980, Castro used a "punish-via-bad" strategy against the United States, sending "social misfits" among the Mariel emigrants. As a White House aide put it, "Castro in a way, is using people like bullets aimed at this country" (Rivera, 1991, p. 7).

Fundamental Constants

Comparison theory suggests the existence of two sets of fundamental constants.

CRITICAL INEQUALITY LEVEL. Comparison theory suggests the existence of a critical inequality level, occurring when Atkinson's inequality equals $1 - (2/e)$, or approximately .264.[11] This critical inequality level is thought to govern the switch between valuing cardinal goods and valuing ordinal goods, for example, the switch between valuing birth and valuing wealth. In a society that values a cardinal good, when inequality in that cardinal good approaches the critical level, a switch is triggered from valuing that cardinal good to valuing another good. Conversely, in a society that values an ordinal good, when economic inequality declines comfortably below .264, a switch is triggered from valuing any ordinal good to valuing wealth. In the exponential, lognormal, and Pareto distributions, the critical inequality level occurs when the Gini coefficient is approximately .42; in the power-function variate, the critical inequality level occurs when the Gini coefficient is approximately .33.

SOCIETAL MAINSTREAM. Comparison theory suggests that the societal mainstream lies between Z values of -1 and $+1$. In the special case in which the comparison reward is the mean reward (i.e., equality), the critical Z values occur at relative ranks or ratios of $1/e$, or approximately .368, and e, or approximately 2.72. In this case, ordinal-good societies have no "overclass"; cardinal-good societies may have no "underclass," or no "overclass," or neither.

Ongoing Extensions

Current work, besides continuing to derive new predictions, is extending comparison theory in two new directions. The first involves analyzing the policy implications of comparison theory. It turns out that some of the predictions are amenable to interventions (and others not). For example, the prediction that conflict severity increases with the gap in mean Z

---

[11]Atkinson's (1970, 1975) inequality refers to the measure of inequality defined as one minus the ratio of the geometric mean to the arithmetic mean. See also Jasso (1982, 1999) for exposition and elaboration.

between nonoverlapping subgroups is amenable to design of an intervention. To illustrate, in the case of physicians and nurses discussed above, one possible intervention strategy is to destroy the nonoverlappingness; this can be accomplished by one or both of two tactics: create new nursing positions that are highly paid (paid more than some physician positions) and create new physician positions that are poorly paid (paid less than some nursing positions).

A second new direction involves scrutinizing the predictions to see what light they may shed on the emergence of social norms. This activity, whose initial report appears in Jasso (2000), yields a set of new predictions, including the prediction that the rule, "Thou shalt not steal," is not likely to arise unless it is imposed by Guardians.

FREQUENTLY ASKED QUESTIONS

FAQ 1. What Is the Exact Relation between Justice Theory and Comparison Theory?

To answer this question precisely, we first identify three elements—justice theory, comparison theory, and the justice version of comparison theory—noting that the first two are families of theories while the third is a single theory. To visualize their relations, Fig. 30.1 provides a Venn diagram.

As depicted in Fig. 30.1, justice theory consists of many theories, of which the justice version of comparison theory is only one (see Chapter 3). Meanwhile, the justice version of comparison theory also is a member of the comparison theory family, differing from it in that the larger comparison theory, of which this chapter provides an overview, encompasses not only justice but also all other comparison outcomes, such as happiness, well-being, and self-esteem.

Another way to describe the exact relations between comparison theory, justice theory, and the justice version of comparison theory is by examining their postulates. The first postulate of the larger comparison theory is the comparison function and the first postulate of the justice version of comparison theory is the justice evaluation function, which is a special

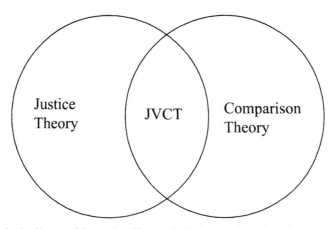

FIGURE 30.1. The Justice Version of Comparison Theory (JVCT) is a member of both the Justice-Theory family and the Comparison-Theory family.

case of the comparison function. Note, however, that both the comparison function and the justice evaluation function used in the justice version of comparison theory are *reflexive* functions, in which the observer reflects about his or her own situation. A larger version—the original justice evaluation function that applies to justice evaluations about both self and other—appears as the first postulate of other members of the justice theory family (see Chapter 3). Thus, the comparison function is both broader and narrower than the justice evaluation function. It is broader in that it applies to a larger set of outcomes, not only the justice evaluation but also happiness, self-esteem, and so on. But it is narrower in that it applies only to reflexive assessments, while the justice evaluation function applies to both reflexive and nonreflexive assessments.[12]

FAQ 2. How Can Comparison Theory Make Predictions about So Many Things Like Gifts and Theft and Religious Institutions When It Cannot Predict the Underlying Happiness or Justice Evaluation?

Comparison theory cannot predict an individual's happiness or justice evaluation without information about the actual holding and the comparison holding. Happiness, the justice evaluation, and other outcomes are predicted to vary with the actual reward and the comparison reward, as in the basic comparison function,

$$Z = \theta \ln \left(\frac{A}{C} \right) \tag{10}$$

but while the actual reward may be known, the comparison reward often is not known and cannot be predicted (there is not yet a theory that predicts what a person will think is just or appropriate for him- or herself).

However, due to the separability of terms inherent in the logarithmic specification of the comparison function, we can predict the effect of a change in the actual reward on the Z outcome. Moreover, when we incorporate the identity representation of the comparison holding, as in the basic comparison function formula for the cardinal-good case,

$$Z = \theta \ln \left(\frac{xN}{S\phi} \right) \tag{11}$$

we also can predict the effect of a change in the population size and wealth. Further, when we embed this formula in the micromodel and macromodel sets of procedures, we can derive large sets of additional predictions, concerning, for example, whether a person's gain (or loss) in well-being is greater in one or another group or situation and which actors gain (or lose) more in each group or situation (see the micromodel protocol in Table 30.4). To illustrate, comparison theory cannot predict a thief's gain from theft, but it can predict that the gain from theft will be greater when stealing from a fellow group member than when stealing from an outsider. Similarly, comparison theory cannot predict a gift-receiver's gain from the gift, but it can predict that the gain will be greater when the giver is present.

It seems remarkable that even though we are unable to predict the basic quantity Z or the change CZ, it nevertheless is straightforward to derive so many other predictions. Moreover,

[12]This leads to a related point. While in comparison theory there are two main methods for deriving predictions—the micromodel and macromodel—which both begin with reflexive comparison outcomes, in justice theory there is a third method—the matrixmodel—which begins with the full matrix of justice evaluations about both self and others.

the predictions that can be derived are for phenomena that may be even more interesting (to a sociologist, at least) than the ones that cannot be derived; that is, predictions about parental gift giving, bereavement across historical eras, posttraumatic stress among combat veterans, and theft victims may be more pertinent to sociology than predictions about the magnitude of an individual's happiness. To illustrate, the prediction that a thief's gain from theft is greater when stealing from a fellow group member than when stealing from an outsider may be more pertinent to sociology than a prediction about the thief's exact gain from theft. Similarly, the prediction that a gift-receiver's gain from the gift is greater when the giver is present than when the giver is absent may be more pertinent to sociology than a prediction about the gift-receiver's exact gain from the gift.

Technically, looking at the comparison function formula in Eq. (11), the reason that we cannot predict Z or CZ is that we do not know ϕ, and the reason that we can predict so many other things is that the logarithmic specification makes it possible to separate the effects of ϕ from the other effects. Moreover, in many derivations, notably those involving a comparison of two CZs, ϕ vanishes outright.

FAQ 3. Isn't It Unrealistic to Assume That People Are Always Comparing Themselves to Others?

Yes, and comparison theory does not make such an assumption. As noted in the first section, the starting idea for comparison theory is indeed the idea that humans compare themselves to others and/or to previous or envisioned selves and thereby experience a variety of judgments and sentiments, including happiness, well-being, self-esteem, and the sense of justice. Note that even in that unformalized expression, the starting idea covered individuals who never compare themselves to others, only to themselves at some past or future time.

But comparison theory takes an additional and important step. It shifts the comparison from a comparison of self to other or self to previous/envisioned self to a comparison of the actual levels of attributes and amounts of possessions to the levels/amounts expected or desired or thought just or appropriate. This shift both makes possible the mathematical formalization and also has profound implications for the substantive coverage of comparison theory and correct interpretation of its assumptions and predictions. This shift implies, among other things, that individuals who never compare themselves to others are fully within the theoretical umbrella, as are individuals devoid of any concern for relative rank, provided they compare what they have to some standard or referent, whatever its source.

FAQ 4. How Can We Interpret the Predictions of Comparison Theory Given That So Many Important Factors Are Omitted?

The predictions of comparison theory are *ceteris paribus* predictions. They inform us about the part played by comparison processes in the social life. Our basic premise is that, following the view advanced by Newton for understanding physical nature, observed behavioral and social phenomena may be regarded as the product of the joint operation of several basic forces. Put differently, we believe that the world we seek to understand is a multifactor world, a view widely accepted in modern social science.[13]

This multifactor view of the world poses two main scientific challenges: one theoretical, the other empirical. The theoretical challenge is to identify the basic forces governing human

---

[13]For example, see Parsons (1968) on Durkheim as a multifactor theorist.

behavior, to describe their operation, and to derive their implications. The empirical challenge is to test the derived implications. The theoretical and empirical work jointly lead to the accumulation of reliable knowledge about human behavioral and social phenomena.

Comparison processes are not at the level of fundamental forces; thus, comparison theory lies in the Mertonian middle range (Merton, 1949/1968). The basic research challenge is to discover how fundamental forces generate the comparison impulse.

Empirically, the multifactor view poses special challenges, for the operation of two factors may lead to opposite effects. It may at first appear that one prediction is rejected, but in fact it may be that one of the two effects is stronger than the other. For example, suppose that comparison theory predicts that Y is an increasing function of X and a theory about another mechanism B predicts that Y is a decreasing function of X. The empirical finding that Y is an increasing function of X does not constitute, in a multifactor world, evidence that mechanism B is not operating, but rather is consistent with the operation of both mechanisms such that the effect of the comparison mechanism is stronger, or "dominates" mechanism B. And conversely.[14]

The multifactor view of the world leads to a deeper understanding about the importance of theoretical development on many fronts. Put starkly, we cannot know the precise operation and effects of comparison processes without empirically pitting the predictions of comparison theory against the predictions of other theories about other processes. Probably, one mechanism will dominate in some contexts, a second in other contexts, a third in still others, and so on. But it will not be possible to isolate and measure the exact effects of comparison processes unless the predictions of other theories are simultaneously tested. For example, in any of the topical domains for which comparison theory yields implications—family, gifts, crime, religious institutions—there are likely to be other basic processes at work. Correct understanding of the part played by comparison processes requires simultaneous test of the operation of those other processes.

Thus, there is a jointness about theoretical work. Progress in comparison theory depends on progress in other theories. As John Donne would have understood, the fate of comparison theory is inextricably bound with the fate of other theories.

FAQ 5. How Do We Know Which Is the Group to Which a Prediction Applies?

Many of the predictions of comparison theory refer to a group or groups. In some cases, the group is made explicit (for example, predictions about families, parents, and children make explicit the group to which they refer), but in others, not. Consider, for example, the prediction about a thief's gain from theft being greater when stealing from a fellow group member. What is meant by "group?"

All predictions that leave the group unspecified are predicted to hold for whatever group or groups is salient to the particular actor. Suppose the prospective thief is a college student living on the west wing of the third floor of a dormitory; the prospective thief is also female and of Etruscan ethnicity.[15] What does "group" refer to? Our protagonist could think of herself as belonging to any of the following groups: all college students; college students at

---

[14]This is one of the reasons why it is easier to test a theory the more fruitful it is. As Danto (1967, pp. 299–300), observes, "Indeed, it is by and large the ability of a theory to permit derivations far afield from its original domain which serves as a criterion for accepting a theory, for in addition to the obvious fruitfulness such a criterion emphasizes, such derivations permit an increasingly broad and diversified basis for testing the theory."

[15]The reader will forgive the time travel. It is best not to ascribe thieving designs to contemporary ethnicities.

this college; all residents of her dormitory; all residents of the third floor of her dormitory; all residents of the west wing of the third floor of her dormitory; all women; all female college students; all Etruscans; all female Etruscans; all female Etruscan college students; and so on.

The prediction holds for whichever groups are salient to her. Following the classic W. I. Thomas idea of "definition of the situation," the prediction applies to whatever groups she defines herself as belonging to.[16] Now, it may happen that three of the possible groups are salient to her, and thus the prediction applies to those three—say, dorm co-residents, college students, and female Etruscans. However, it also may be the case that these three are differentially salient; college students is the salient group 30% of the time, dorm coresidents 35% of the time, and female Etruscans 35% of the time. Then, according to comparison theory, she would prefer to steal from a college student rather than from a noncollege student, from a dorm coresident rather than from anyone else, and from a female Etruscan rather than from males and non-Etruscans. Moreover, the preference would be stronger for the latter two, which are more salient to her (35% of the time for each vs. 30% of the time for the college student group).

The empirical challenges are evident. Because each thief or prospective thief in a population would have a different configuration of group definitions, the research design must be especially clever—the hallmark of theory-driven research is cleverness—in order to discern operation of the comparison effect and measure it.

That is not all. Meanwhile, other factors in this multifactor world are at work. Some of these will militate against stealing from a fellow group member in some groups. For example, there may be a strong Etruscan ethic against stealing from a fellow Etruscan. Accurate measurement of the comparison theory effects in each group requires inclusion in the empirical work of the predicted effects of other factors, as discussed in FAQ 4 above.

It is easy to see that if our prospective thief thinks of herself as an Etruscan all of the time and concomitantly there is a strong Etruscan ethic against insider theft, then it will not be possible to measure the comparison theory effect unless one also measures the Etruscan-ethic effect, conducting the research in a way that permits identification of the two opposite effects.

FAQ 6. Is Comparison Theory Limited to Things That Can Be Summed?

No. However, it is easy to get this impression from work that uses the micromodel set of procedures for deriving predictions, because even though the micromodel applies also to ordinal goods and bads, most derivations to date that have used the micromodel have applied it to situations involving cardinal holdings (in fact, cardinal goods). Moreover, even though these applications are usually labeled (saying, for example, "cardinal-good regime" or "quantity-good" or some synonym), the existence of the counterpart ordinal-holding procedures may be overlooked.

The macromodel, however, has had a different application history. Here, a central feature of the theoretical derivation has been to establish systematic differences between groups that value cardinal things (like wealth) and groups that value ordinal things (like beauty, health, virtue, intelligence). Predictions have included the prediction that the most advantaged person in an ordinal world feels less overrewarded than the most advantaged person in a cardinal world (for example, the most beautiful person feels less advantaged than the richest person);

[16]This idea, called the Thomas Theorem by Robert K. Merton (1942/1973, 1995), states, "If men define situations as real, they are real in their consequences." The Thomas Theorem, owed to W. I. Thomas, first appeared in Thomas and Thomas (1928); Merton (1995) provides the history of the theorem and its ascription.

the prediction that, given a conflict between the two subgroups of a two-subgroup society, in nonmaterialistic societies conflict severity decreases as the size of the lower subgroup increases, but in materialistic societies, the direction of the effect of subgroup size on conflict severity depends on the shape of the income distribution.

Thus, the question in this frequently asked question typically is asked by readers of micromodel-based derivations, but never by readers of macromodel-based derivations.

FAQ 7. How Do We Test Comparison Theory?

Accumulation of reliable knowledge about human behavioral and social phenomena requires empirical work. However coherent or elegant a theoretical structure, ultimately it stands or falls on its fidelity to empirical reality.

In general, two kinds of issues arise in testing a scientific theory: philosophical and practical. The philosophical ground has been cogently and carefully covered in the 20th century; social science is particularly indebted to Karl R. Popper (1959, 1963), Thomas S. Kuhn (1970), and Imre Lakatos (1970).[17] If one considers the empirical assessment of a single theory in isolation, then the questions that arise are: (1) how many tests? (2) of how many predictions? (3) with what combination of results? There is widespread agreement that rejecting a prediction is not a sufficient condition for rejecting a theory. Moreover, rejecting a prediction is not a necessary condition for rejecting a theory; even if all of a theory's predictions survive test unrejected, one may still reject the theory, in favor of a better theory, one with "excess corroborated content" (Lakatos, 1970). Indeed, the view known as "sophisticated falsificationism" holds that it is not possible to judge the empirical merits of a theory in isolation; falsification requires comparison of the relative merits of two theories (Lakatos, 1970, p. 116).

Consider now the special problem faced by all theories of a single process or a single force: it can be difficult to discern whether discrepancies between the theory's predictions and empirical data are due to a defective theory or instead to the operation of another basic process. Of course, design of empirical work usually takes into account the possibility that many other factors may be at work; courses in the empirical methods of the social sciences routinely teach procedures for guarding against omitted-variables bias. For example, design of the test of the comparison theory prediction that a married couple's earnings ratio affects marital cohesiveness, as manifested in the couple's sexual activity, explicitly incorporated the operation of a wide range of other factors possibly implicated in sexual activity, including the unobserved sexual drive and the presence of young children (Jasso, 1988a). Nonetheless, interpreting tests of the predictions of a theory of a single process, given the near certainty that we live in a multifactor world, requires judiciousness and circumspection.

Practical issues that arise in testing scientific theories include (1) selection of predictions to test and the order in which they will be tested; (2) for each prediction to be tested, choosing between two strategies (designing new explicit tests versus conducting meta-analyses of extant studies); and (3) for each prediction to be tested, deciding whether the test is best conducted by the theorist (who may be a general theorist with no special knowledge of the subject matter of the prediction) or by empirical scientists who specialize in the topic of the prediction. Ironically, when the theory is fruitful and yields many implications for many disparate phenomena, the practical problems are compounded. For example, rigorous test of

---

[17]For brief discussions of the philosophical issues that arise in testing, see Reynolds (1971) and Jasso (1988b, pp. 3–5, 1989, pp. 139–141).

even a few predictions across several topical domains almost certainly will require leadership from empirical experts in those topical domains.[18]

FAQ 8. What Is the Current Evidentiary Status of Comparison Theory?

First, a few predictions have received rigorous, explicit test. One is the prediction that, *ceteris paribus*, marital cohesiveness declines, the greater the disparity between husband and wife in their holdings of valued goods (deduced in Jasso, 1983, tested in Jasso, 1988a). Another is the prediction that each individual has a unique signature constant in the comparison function (proposed in Jasso, 1980, tested in Jasso, 1990). In both cases, the empirical results were consistent with the predictions.

Second, several predictions are consistent with the results of rigorous empirical work that was not designed to test them. These include the prediction that the response to gains is concave and the response to losses is convex, as documented by Tversky and Kahneman (Kahneman & Tversky, 1979; Tversky & Kahneman, 1986) in extensive experimental work; and the prediction that the rate of vocations to the religious life is higher in societies with poverty and gross economic inequality than in societies with less inequality and a "safety net," a prediction consistent with Ebaugh's (1993) findings concerning the dearth of religious vocations in the United States and the abundance in Third World countries.

Third, several predictions are consistent with known facts. These include the prediction that parents of two or more children (who do not all have the same birthday) will spend more of their toy budget at a single annual gift giving occasion (such as Christmas) than at the children's birthdays, a prediction borne out by published toy sales figures (Jasso, 1993c).

Fourth, several predictions are consistent with notions that although not rigorously documented appear to be widely believed. These include the prediction that the incidence of gift giving is greater during courtship than after marriage and greater in wartime than in peacetime.

Finally, some predictions are novel and there seems to be no hint of them in any literature, technical or lay. These include the prediction that posttraumatic stress syndrome is less severe among veterans of wars fought on home soil than among veterans of wars fought away from home. Interestingly, a distinguished journalist, chronicling a recent trip to Vietnam, observes that Vietnamese veterans of the Vietnam War appear to be better adjusted than American veterans of the Vietnam War (Sheehan, 1991), but does not make the connection to the battle site. Another novel prediction is the prediction that blind persons are less susceptible to eating disorders than are the nonblind. Still another novel prediction is the prediction that games of chance are salutary, contrary to the view that gambling is a vice.

Of the foregoing five sets of predictions, only the first two have a rigorous evidentiary status. The rest require rigorous, explicit test. Note that the predictions are amenable to testing via many empirical strategies. Some are amenable to testing via traditional survey research, others via classical experiments, still others via comparative historical work. For example, predictions about gifts and theft would appear suitable for survey research, predictions about how things change value would seem ideally suited to experiments, and predictions about differential mourning for mothers and fathers across historical periods would seem to require comparative historical research.

Creative, clever empirical research will illuminate the part played by comparison pro-

---

[18]For a brief discussion of these and other practical problems that arise in testing, see Jasso (1993b, pp. 258–263).

cesses in the behavioral and social life and at the same time advance understanding of the confluence of several basic processes in shaping observed phenomena.

FAQ 9. How Do I Get Started Doing Comparison Theory?

You may be interested in studying comparison processes in general, that is, in doing comparison analysis, in which case you may be interested both in doing theoretical work (theoretical comparison analysis) and in doing empirical work (empirical comparison analysis). As this chapter is in a handbook on theory, however, we will have no more to say about empirical analysis (beyond the general comments in FAQs 7 and 8).

You want to do theoretical work on comparison processes. The best training and not coincidentally often the most important contribution involves undertaking a new derivation. The temptation to contribute a new assumption is always strong among young theorists, yet it should be resisted, in part because it provides no training in the activity that occupies 99% of a theorist's time—derivation—in part because it runs counter to parsimony, and in part because it is often derivation that triggers formulation of useful new assumptions. (For example, it was theoretical derivation that led to both the second and third postulates of comparison theory, as derivation quickly ran into obstacles that these postulates later resolved.)

So you will undertake derivation. Again, the best training is to use a tried-and-true method, such as the micromodel or the macromodel. Later you may well devise a new method for deriving predictions. (Again, these methods were developed to overcome deficiencies in other methods.) For now, however, choose either the micromodel or the macromodel.

Which method you choose depends on personal taste. If you love to work with probability distributions, if there is magic in "Gamma" or excitement in "Logistic," or if your idea of the perfect weekend is to outwit an integral, then the macromodel is for you. On the other hand, if your tessitura is in the land of partial derivatives, or if you like to imagine small groups and how the well-being of their members changes with actions or events that alter individuals' wealth and total wealth and group size, then the micromodel will be greatly satisfying. To be sure, sooner or later you will work with both micromodel and macromodel, as well as with other techniques, and may invent your own. For now, however, choose either the micromodel or the macromodel.

Here is a three-step plan to help you get started doing comparison theory. The micromodel plan and the macromodel plan are the same except for the first and third steps.

- *Micromodel Step One*: Work carefully through the protocol and the application reported in Jasso (2000). The application is a rigorous restatement and elaboration of the theft application. Derive every expression and every effect. Restate every single expression and effect in words (to save space, Jasso, 2000, only describes a fraction of the results). Become fluent with words like "intensifies" and "attenuates" and so on.
- *Macromodel Step One*: Work carefully through the protocol in Jasso (1997b) and the application reported in Jasso (1993a). The application is to conflict phenomena. Derive every expression and every effect. Restate every single expression and effect in words. Become fluent with phrases like "censored subdistribution" and "upper mean" and so on.
- *Between Step One and Step Two*: When you have finished step one, put all thought of comparison theory aside. Catch up on your coursework (as student or teacher). Go to the movies. Read novels. Watch TV. Do empirical work. Run a few regressions.

- *Step Two*: Read the abstracts of every article in *American Sociological Review* and *American Journal of Sociology* for the last full calendar year.[19] If any article piques your interest, read it. If the topic intrigues you, think about it.
- *Between Step Two and Step Three*: When you have finished step two, put all thought of the *American Sociological Review* or *American Journal of Sociology* articles aside. Catch up on your coursework (as student or teacher). Go to the movies. Read novels. Watch TV. Do empirical work. Run a few regressions.
- *Step Three*: If you do nothing at all—merely enjoy the movies, novels, and TV, and master some new empirical technique—chances are very good that you will wake up one day with lots of ideas for a new micromodel or macromodel analysis (or the ideas may greet you when you return from class). You will be excited and anxious, you will feel strange things in your chest and stomach. Write down everything that comes to mind—everything. Do not stop to correct errors or typos or to rephrase things. Mull over these thoughts, but not too long.

The time has come to undertake a systematic analysis. Follow the protocol exactly. For example, if you are working in the micromodel, define each situation and each actor precisely. Take some care in choosing notation. Of course, everything can be revised later, but the experience gained from hard thinking at every step will later prove invaluable.

Doing theory is like writing a poem. Great emotion precedes it and great emotion follows it. In between there is "emotion recollected in tranquillity," as Wordsworth put it, and the discipline imposed by the rules of deduction or of the rhyming form. What begins as vague unspecified tension is transformed into precise predictions that promise new insights and new perspectives.

Then you send them out to be tested.

ACKNOWLEDGMENTS: This chapter was written in part while the author was a Fellow at the Center for Advanced Study in the Behavioral Sciences, Stanford, California. I gratefully acknowledge the Center's support.

REFERENCES

Atkinson, A. B. (1970). On the measurement of inequality. *Journal of Economic Theory, 2*, 244–263.
Atkinson, A. B. (1975). *The economics of inequality*. London: Oxford.
Baldwin, J. M. (1889–1891). *Handbook of psychology* (2 volumes). New York: Holt.
Berger, J., Zelditch, M., Jr., Anderson, B., & Cohen, B. P. (1972). Structural aspects of distributive justice: A status-value formulation. In J. Berger, M. Zelditch, & B. Anderson (Eds.), *Sociological theories in progress*, Volume 2 (pp. 119–246). Boston: Houghton Mifflin.
Blau, P. M. (1964). *Exchange and power in social life*. New York: Wiley.
Cervantes de Saavedra, M. (1968). *Don Quijote de la Mancha*, annot. Martin de Riquer. Barcelona: Juventud.
Cervantes, M. de. (1605, 1615/1952). *The history of Don Quixote de la Mancha*, John Ormsby (Trans.). Chicago: Britannica.
Danto, A. C. (1967). Philosophy of science, problems of. In Paul Edwards (Ed.), *Encyclopedia of philosophy, Volume 6* (pp. 296–300). New York: Macmillan.

[19]From a theoretical point of view, it does not matter if you read all of 2000 or instead the April 2000 to February 2001 issues. But calendars were invented for a purpose, and you will feel good about yourself if you can tell your fellow graduate students or assistant professors that you surveyed all of 2000 without burdening your sentence with the names of months.

Donne, J. (1623/1959). *Devotions upon emergent occasions.* Ann Arbor, MI: University of Michigan Press.

Durkheim, É. (1893/1964). *The division of labor in society.* George Simpson (Trans.). New York: Free Press.

Durkheim, É. (1897/1951). *Suicide: A study in sociology.* J. A. Spaulding & G, Simpson (Trans.). G. Simpson (Ed.). New York: Free Press.

Ebaugh, H. R. (1993). The growth and decline of catholic religious orders of women worldwide: The impact of women's opportunity structures." *Journal for the Scientific Study of Religion, 32,* 68–75.

Evans, M., Hastings, N., & Peacock, B. (1993). *Statistical distributions,* 2nd edition. New York: Wiley & Sons.

Festinger, L. (1954). A theory of social comparison processes. *Human Relations, 7,* 117–140.

Hastings, N. A. J., & Peacock, J. B. (1974). *Statistical distributions: A handbook for students and practitioners.* London: Butterworth.

Homans, G. C. (1974). *Social behavior: Its elementary forms,* revised edition. New York: Harcourt, Brace, Jovanovich.

Hyman, H. H. (1968). Reference groups. In David L. Sills (Ed.), *International encyclopedia of the social sciences,* Volume 13 (pp. 353–361). New York: Macmillan.

James, W. (1891/1952). *The principles of psychology.* Chicago: Britannica.

Jasso, G. (1978). On the justice of earnings: A new specification of the justice evaluation function. *American Journal of Sociology, 83,* 1398–1419.

Jasso, G. (1980). A new theory of distributive justice. *American Sociological Review, 45,* 3–32.

Jasso, G. (1982). Measuring inequality by the ratio of the geometric mean to the arithmetic mean. *Sociological Methods and Research, 10,* 303–326.

Jasso, G. (1983). Social consequences of the sense of distributive justice: Small-group applications. In D. M. Messick & K. S. Cook (Eds.), *Theories of equity: psychological and sociological perspectives* (pp. 243–294). New York: Praeger.

Jasso, G. (1986). A new representation of the just term in distributive-justice theory: Its properties and operation in theoretical derivation and empirical estimation. *Journal of Mathematical Sociology, 12,* 251–274.

Jasso, G. (1987). Choosing a good: Models based on the theory of the distributive-justice force. Advances in group processes: *Theory and Research, 4,* 67–108.

Jasso, G. (1988a). Distributive-justice effects of employment and earnings on marital cohesiveness: An empirical test of theoretical predictions. In M. Webster & M. Foschi (Eds.), *Status generalization: New theory and research* (pp. 123–162). Palo Alto, CA: Stanford University Press.

Jasso, G. (1988b). Principles of theoretical analysis. *Sociological Theory, 6,* 1–20.

Jasso, G. (1989). Notes on the advancement of theoretical sociology (reply to Turner). *Sociological Theory, 7,* 135–144.

Jasso, G. (1990). Methods for the theoretical and empirical analysis of comparison processes, *Sociological Methodology, 20,* 369–419.

Jasso, G. (1991). Cloister and society: Analyzing the public benefit of monastic and mendicant institutions. *Journal of Mathematical Sociology, 16,* 109–136.

Jasso, G. (1993a). Analyzing conflict severity: Predictions of distributive-justice theory for the two-subgroup case. *Social Justice Research, 6,* 357–382.

Jasso, G. (1993b). Building the theory of comparison processes: Construction of postulates and derivation of predictions. In J. Berger & M. Zelditch, Jr. (Eds.), *Theoretical research programs: Studies in the growth of theory* (pp. 474–478). Stanford, CA: Stanford University Press.

Jasso, G. (1993c). Choice and emotion in comparison theory. *Rationality and Society, 5,* 231–274.

Jasso, G. (1996a). Deriving implications of comparison theory for demographic phenomena: A first step in the analysis of migration. *The Sociological Quarterly, 37,* 19–57.

Jasso, G. (1996b). Exploring the reciprocal relations between theoretical and empirical work (paper in honor of Robert K. Merton). *Sociological Methods and Research, 24,* 253–303.

Jasso, G. (1997a). The common mathematical structure of disparate sociological questions. *Sociological Forum, 12,* 37–51.

Jasso, G. (1997b). Derivation of predictions in comparison theory: Foundations of the macromodel approach. In J. Szmatka, J. Skvoretz, & J. Berger (Eds.). *Status, network, and structure: Theory development in group processes* (pp. 241–270). Stanford, CA: Stanford University Press.

Jasso, G. (1999). How much injustice is there in the world? Two new justice indexes. *American Sociological Review, 64,* 133–168.

Jasso, G. (2000). Rule-finding about rule-making: Comparison processes and the making of norms. In K.-D. Opp & M. Hechter (Eds.), *Emergence of norms* (pp. 348–393). New York: Russell Sage Foundation.

Jasso, G., & Rossi, P. H. (1977). Distributive justice and earned income. *American Sociological Review, 42,* 639–651.

Johnson, N. L., & Kotz, S. (1969). *Distributions in statistics: Discrete distributions.* New York: Houghton Mifflin.

Johnson, N. L. (1970a). *Distributions in statistics: Continuous univariate distributions—1.* New York: Wiley & Sons.

Johnson, N. L. (1970b). *Distributions in statistics: Continuous univariate distributions—2.* New York: Wiley & Sons.

Kahneman, D., & Tversky, A. (1979). Prospect theory: An analysis of decision under risk. *Econometrica, 47,* 263–291.

Kotz, S., Johnson, N. L., & Read, C. B. (1985). Log-laplace distribution. In S. Kotz, N. L. Johnson, & C. B. Read (Eds.). *Encyclopedia of statistical sciences,* Vol. 5 (pp. 133–134). New York: Wiley & Sons.

Kuhn, T. S. (1970). *The structure of scientific revolutions,* 2nd edition, enlarged. Chicago: University of Chicago Press.

Lakatos, I. (1970). Falsification and the methodology of scientific research programmes. In I. Lakatos & A. Musgrave (Eds.), *Criticism and the growth of knowledge* (pp. 91–195). Cambridge: Cambridge University Press.

Lipset, S. M. (1968). Stratification, social: Social class. In D. L. Sills (Ed.), *International encyclopedia of the social sciences,* Vol. 15 (pp. 296–316). New York: Macmillan.

Marx, K. (1849/1968). Wage labour and capital. In *Karl Marx and Frederick Engels: Selected works* (pp. 74–97). New York: International Publishers.

Merton, R. K. (1949/1968). *Social theory and social structure.* New York: Free Press.

Merton, R. K. (1957). Continuities in the theory of reference groups and social structure. In R. K. Merton (Ed.), *Social theory and social structure,* 2nd edition, revised and enlarged (pp. 281–386). New York: Free Press.

Merton, R. K. (1942/1973, 1995). The normative structure of science. In R. K. Merton, *The sociology of science* (pp. 267–278). Chicago: University of Chicago Press.

Merton, R. K. (1995). The Thomas theorem and the Matthew effect. *Social Forces, 74,* 379–422.

Merton, R. K., & Rossi, A. S. (1950). Contributions to the theory of reference group behavior. In R. K. Merton & P. Lazarsfeld (Eds.), *Continuities in social research: Studies in the scope and method of "the American soldier"* (pp. 40–105). New York: Free Press. [Reprinted in R. K. Merton, *Social Theory and Social Structure,* 2nd edition, revised and enlarged (pp. 225–280). New York: Free Press.

Moses, L. E. (1966). Statistical analysis: Truncation and censorship. In D. L. Sills (Ed.), *International encyclopedia of the social sciences,* Vol. 15 (pp. 169–201). New York: Macmillan.

Parsons, T. (1968). Émile Durkheim. In D. L. Sills (Ed.), *International encyclopedia of the social sciences,* Vol. 4 (pp. 311–320). New York: Macmillan.

Popper, K. R. (1959). *The logic of scientific discovery.* New York: Basic Books.

Popper, K. R. (1963). *Conjectures and refutations: The growth of scientific knowledge.* New York: Basic Books.

Rainwater, L. (1974). *What money buys: Inequality and the social meanings of income.* New York: Basic Books.

Reynolds, P. D. (1971). *A primer in theory construction.* New York: Macmillan.

Rivera, M. A. (1991). *Decision and structure: U.S. refugee policy in the Mariel crisis.* Lanham, MD: University Press of America.

Rosenberg, M., & Pearlin, L. I. (1978). Social class and self-esteem among children and adults. *American Journal of Sociology, 84,* 53–77.

Runciman, W. G. (1961). Problems of research on relative deprivation. *Archives Européennes de Sociologie, 2,* 315–323.

Sheehan, N. (1991). *After the war was over: Hanoi and Saigon.* New York: Random House.

Sherif, M. (1968). Self concept. In D. L. Sills (Ed.), *International encyclopedia of the social sciences,* Vol. 14 (pp. 150–159). New York: Macmillan.

Stouffer, S. A. (1949). *The American soldier,* 2 volumes. *Studies in Social Psychology in World War II.* Princeton, NJ: Princeton University Press.

Stuart, A., & Ord, J. K. (1987). *Kendall's advanced theory of statistics,* Vol. 1, *Distribution Theory,* 5th ed. New York: Oxford University Press.

Teresa de Ávila, S. (1546–1582/1982). *Obras completas.* The Quatercentenary Edition. Madrid: Aguilar.

Thibaut, J. W., & Kelley, H. H. (1959). *The social psychology of groups.* New York: Wiley.

Thomas, W. I., & Thomas, D. S. (1928). *The child in America: Behavior problems and programs.* New York: Knopf.

Tversky, A., & Kahneman, D. (1986). Rational choice and the framing of decisions. In R. M. Hogarth & M. W. Reder (Eds.), *Rational choice: The contrast between economics and psychology* (pp. 67–94). Chicago: University of Chicago Press.

Veblen, T. (1899/1953). *The theory of the leisure class: An economic study of institutions.* New York: New American Library.

Virgil. (c. 30–19 BC/1916). *The Aeneid.* Two vol., H. Rushton Fairclough (Trans.). Cambridge, MA: Loeb Classical Library.

Weber, M. (1904–1905/1958). *The Protestant ethic and the spirit of capitalism.* T. Parsons (Trans.). New York: Scribner's.

von Wright, G. H. (1963). *The varieties of goodness.* London: Routledge and Kegan Paul.

Zelditch, M., Jr. (1968). Status, social. In D. L. Sills (Ed.), *International encyclopedia of the social sciences,* Vol. 15 (pp. 250–257). New York: Macmillan.

CHAPTER 31

Exchange and Power

Issues of Structure and Agency

Karen S. Cook and Eric R. W. Rice

INTRODUCTION

Social exchange theory has a long and venerable history in sociology dating back to the 1950s when various theorists in the social sciences came up with the idea of focusing on the world of interpersonal relations from a "scientific" perspective. For Homans this meant taking the small group as the laboratory in which social processes such as power and the exercise of influence, the emergence of stratified rights and privileges, cooperation and competition, social disruption, and anger and feelings of fairness could be examined under the microscope to provide insights into these same processes as they were played out in larger social contexts. Blau took a similar tack, more aggressively trying to formulate the principles operating at the microlevel that informed social processes at more macrolevels of social organization. Others joined the enterprise in sociology, most notably, Emerson, and in the 1970s and 1980s, Cook, Molm, Yamagishi, Willer, Markovsky, Skvoretz, Stolte, Bonacich, Bienenstock, Friedkin, and their collaborators. In this chapter we examine briefly the roots of exchange theory in related disciplines as well as in sociology and then comment more fully on topics of central concern to exchange theorists today. We reserve a major part of the text for a discussion of the most recent work covering topics only briefly researched up until now and we link this work to developments in related subfields in sociology, most prominently, what is now called economic sociology.

THE ROOTS OF
THE EXCHANGE TRADITION

Social exchange theory derives from several lines of work in the social sciences, including utilitarianism, functionalism, and social behaviorism (Turner, 1986). George C. Homans (1974), Peter M. Blau (1964, 1986), and Richard M. Emerson (1962, 1972) generally are

Karen S. Cook and Eric R. W. Rice • Department of Sociology, Stanford University, Stanford, California 94305.

Handbook of Sociological Theory, edited by Jonathan H. Turner. Kluwer Academic / Plenum Publishers, New York, 2002.

thought of as the major developers of the exchange perspective within sociology. But psychology, anthropology, and economics also made significant contributions. Thibaut and Kelley (1959) and Kelley and Thibaut (1978) in psychology, for example, developed a theoretical framework that emphasized the interdependence of actors and the social implications of different forms of interdependence. Though focused primarily on dyadic interaction, this framework had much in common with subsequent developments in social exchange theory.

The anthropologists, Malinowski (1922), Mauss (1925), Schneider (1974), and Levi-Strauss (1969), have contributed to the emergence of this theoretical perspective (see Ekeh, 1974) in the social sciences though the anthropological work focused on a broader range of systems of exchange, such as kinship systems, gift exchange, and systems of generalized exchange. As Heath (1976) argues, the basic foundation of microeconomics has much in common with some variants of social exchange theory. This affinity is clearest in Blau's (1964) book, *Exchange and Power in Social Life*, though it also is reflected in some of the more recent work in sociology (e.g., Cook & Emerson, 1978; Coleman, 1990, Yamaguchi, 1996). A more thorough treatment of the contributions of Homans, Blau, and Emerson will set the stage for a discussion of the current research in this field.

HOMANS: ELEMENTARY
FORMS OF BEHAVIOR

Homans introduced a new theoretical orientation into mainstream sociology with the publication of his classic, "Social Behavior as Exchange," in 1958. This perspective was elaborated further in the subsequent volume *Social Behavior: Its Elementary Forms* (1974, originally published 1961). The use of operant psychology as the behavioral basis of the theory created much of the early controversy surrounding the utility of this work for sociologists. Homans' bold claim that the laws of social behavior could be "reduced to" the basic underlying principles of psychological behaviorism generated intense debate (e.g., Deutsch, 1964). Even though Homans took a reductionistic approach, he explicitly defined his major theoretical task as the explanation of social phenomena, not individual behavior. The emphasis on social behavior and the social structures generated and altered by human social interaction has been the main focus of exchange theory in sociology despite Homans' efforts to ground the theory in a psychology of operant behavior.

Homans' (1974) theoretical formulation portrayed human behavior as a function of its payoffs, the consequent rewards and punishments. The first proposition, the "success proposition" states that behavior that generates positive consequences is likely to be repeated. The "stimulus proposition" states that behavior that has been rewarded on such occasions in the past will be performed in similar situations. The "value proposition" specifies that the more valuable the result of an action is to the actor, the more likely that action is to be performed. The "deprivation–satiation" proposition, which follows, qualifies the stimulus proposition introducing the general ideal of diminishing marginal utility: the more often a person has recently received a particular reward for an action, the less valuable is an additional unit of that reward. Thus some rewards become less effective over time in eliciting specific actions. The fifth theoretical proposition in Homans' (1974, p. 37) basic framework specifies when individuals will react emotionally to different reward situations. People will become angry and aggressive when they do not receive what they anticipate (see the frustration–aggression hypothesis in Miller and Dollard, 1941). Those who receive more than they expect or do not receive anticipated punishments will be happy and will behave approvingly. These propositions represent the core of Homan's version of social exchange theory and they provide one microlevel theoretical foundation for predictions concerning exchange processes.

Using this set of theoretical ideas, Homans (1974) developed explanations for a wide range of phenomena including cooperation, conformity, and competition, structures of sentiment and interaction, status and influence, satisfaction and productivity, leadership, the exercise of power and authority, distributive justice, and the emergence of stratification. He focused on the nature of the interpersonal relations involved, emphasizing "elementary" forms of behavior. By studying such forms of behavior he hoped to illuminate the informal "subinstitutional" bases of more complex social behavior, typically more formal and often institutionalized. A major goal of Homans' work was to explicate the microfoundations of social structures and social change. Other theorists have attempted to offer coherent views of microlevel interaction that form the basis of macrosocial processes and structures. A notable effort quite different from the work of Homans, was Collins' (1981) attempt to treat interaction ritual chains as the primary basis for macrosocial processes. Blau's work on exchange and power provided a more comprehensive framework.

BLAU: EMERGENT PROCESSES
AND A NON-REDUCTIONISTIC VIEW
OF SOCIAL EXCHANGE

Whereas Homans focused on elementary forms of behavior and the subinstitutional level of analysis, Blau (1964, 1986) moved beyond the microlevel to the institutional level, dealing with authority and power, conflict, and change in the context of institutionalized systems of exchange. Reacting against Homans' reductionistic strategy, Blau (1986, p. ix) claimed that his own "theory is rooted in the peculiarly social nature of exchange, which implies that it cannot be reduced to or derived from psychological principles that govern the motives of individuals, as Homans aims to do." Rejecting reductionism, Blau asserted that social structures had "emergent" properties that could not be explained by characteristics or processes involving only the subunits.

Blau's work can be distinguished from Homans' in two major ways. First, his framework was not based on principles of behavioral psychology; instead, he introduced some microeconomic reasoning into the analysis of distinctly social exchange. Second, he explicitly introduced the notion of emergent processes into his theoretical treatise, not only rejecting reductionism, but also expanding the theory to extend far beyond what Homans referred to as its subinstitutional base. We discuss both of these key features of Blau's perspective before moving to more recent theoretical contributions.

Blau's analysis relied on the assumption of rational actors who act to maximize their utility in exchanges with others, unlike Homans, who based his theory of exchange explicitly on principles of operant psychology. This early rational choice approach, derived from microeconomics, focused on exchange rates and the quantities exchanged when two actors who are in possession of unique socially desirable resources engage in trade. But Blau was aware that all dyadic exchanges are embedded in a set of alternative opportunities. Because certain social resources are more scarcely distributed in a population than others (i.e., valuable advice), exchange for these goods often comes at the price of subordination on the part of those in need of a good to those in possession of the good:

> Exchange processes proliferate from bilateral monopolies into wider circles not only as a result of the search for more profitable opportunities but also because of limitations of resources. A person can obtain a service in return for either another service or compliance, that is, subordination. (Blau, 1986, p. 177).

Blau thus offers a rudimentary explanation for the emergence of inequality in social relations.

Blau carefully distinguished between what he considered to be the properties of social exchanges and those of economic exchange. Social exchange, he claimed, involves unspecified obligations and the reciprocal return of favors, unlike economic exchanges, which depend on specific negotiations over the terms of trade: "Social exchange, in contrast [to economic exchange] involved the principle that one person does another a favor, and while there is a general expectation of some future return, its exact nature is definitely not stipulated in advance" (Blau, 1986, p. 93). Since there is no way to ensure that others "discharge" their obligations and return favors, trusting relationships may emerge from ongoing relations of social exchange, something not characteristic of economic exchanges according to Blau. Moreover, the benefits people acquire in social exchange are not subject to quantification in terms of a price because there is no easy equivalent to money as a medium of exchange in social relations. Finally, economic relations generate value that can and often is extrinsic to the specific relation in which a good is acquired. Social exchange relations, however, often generate intrinsic value insofar as social exchange becomes a part of the process of sociability not simply the acquisition of resources. In this sense the resources become nonfungible.

For Blau, many aspects of social relations are emergent properties of interactions. Actors become involved in social exchange with others because each possesses social resources that the other cannot acquire alone (e.g., advice and deference). For example, people exchange these resources in the form of favors. The successful "discharging" of obligations created by the giving and receiving of such favors creates the reciprocal relations that characterize ongoing relations of social exchange. While some generalized expectations for reciprocity may exist in societies, reciprocity as action is an emergent phenomenon. Inequalities can result from exchange because some actors possess more socially valuable resources than others do. As a result they may incur social debts that can be most effectively discharged through the subordination of these others. It is the emergence of such relations of subordination and domination and their self-perpetuating character that Blau believed was the basis for power inequality "more evident in the class structure of entire societies than in the differentiation of status in small groups (Blau, 1986, p. 197).

Macrostructures and Microprocesses

Blau (1964) developed a general framework for analyzing macrostructures and processes based on an extension of his microlevel theory of social exchange. Developing a coherent framework that linked levels of analysis was one of Blau's primary goals. Drawing on Simmel's understanding of social life he explained the general structure of social associations rooted in psychological processes like attraction, approval, reciprocation, and rational conduct. Group formation, cohesion, and social integration as well as processes of opposition, conflict, and dissolution were all explained in terms of social exchange. The forms of social association generated by exchange processes over time come to constitute very complex social structures (and substructures). Blau examined these more complex social structures as they are created and changed by power processes and the dynamics of legitimization and political opposition. Common values mediate and make possible indirect exchanges, and thus the coordination of action in large collectivities. They also "legitimate the social order." Blau compares social exchange processes in simple structures with those in more complex social structures and institutions.

At the end of *Exchange and Power in Social Life*, Blau provides a provocative sketch of a more complete theory for linking micro- and macrostructures through processes of social exchange. Blau argued that societies are composed of substructures that contain individuals or groups that together combine to form the macrostructure of a society. Moreover, there are universalistic values that are shared by all members of a society that act to differentiate and stratify actors within substructures, while particularistic values unite actors within substructures and stratify across substructures within a society. The mobility of individuals between positions in these structures helps to shape the macrostructural level, while the tension between particularistic and individualistic values helps to promote and/or constrain this mobility. In his discussion, Blau became particularly concerned with how these values constitute constraints as well as opportunities for change and how the movement of people between substructures could affect the macrostructures present in society. These ideas have yet to be fully explored.

The strategy of building a theory of macrostructure and processes on an explicitly microlevel theory was a distinguishing feature of Blau's (1964) original work that also became the focus of a major stream of theoretical work in sociology on the "micro–macro link" in the 1980s and 1990s. Ironically, Blau (1986) himself challenged the utility of his approach in his subsequent writings (see also Blau, 1987) fueling the debate. In his introduction to the second printing of his book on exchange and power, he argued that microsociological and macrosociological theories "require different approaches and conceptual schemes though their distinct perspectives enrich each other" (1986, p. xv). This theoretical debate continues as scholars work out the ways in which theories at distinct levels of analysis inform one another.

Blau (1964), and subsequently Emerson (1962, 1972), made power the central focus of analysis as have most of the current exchange theorists. Power, authority, opposition and legitimization were all viewed as major topics in Blau's (1964) discussion of microprocesses, macrostructures, and the dynamics of structural change. Emerson's approach to power also was developed primarily to explain structural change.

EMERSON: HOMANS' ACTOR, BLAU'S EMPHASIS

Emerson's (1962) theory of power-dependence relations was partially incorporated into Blau's (1964) treatment of power imbalance and the strategies for maintaining social independence. For Emerson (1962) these strategies were power-balancing mechanisms. The central proposition in Emerson's (1962) citation classic was that power, defined in relational terms, was a function of the dependence of one actor on another. In a two-party exchange relation, the power of one party (A) over another party (B) is a function of the dependence of B on A. Dependence is a function of the value one actor places on the resources (or valued behavior) mediated by the other and the availability of those resources from alternate sources: the greater the availability of these resources from other actors (i.e., or alternative sources), the lower one actor's dependence on another. Two features of this approach to power are important: (1) it treats power as relational, a feature of a social relation and not simply a property of an actor, and (2) it treats power as potential power; that is, it may or may not be exercised. This relational conception of power became the basis for most of the subsequent work on exchange and power. It is even the basis for much of the more recent structural work on power since network approaches are inherently relational.

Emerson (1972) expanded his treatment of power and dependence to form a more extensive exchange theory of social relations. In many ways his work was a composite of the approaches of Homans (1974) and Blau (1964). In the original formulation Emerson (1972) adopted the language and principles of behavioral psychology to form a theory of social relations. However, he moved quickly beyond behavioral principles to the formation of more complex propositions regarding the emergence of various kinds of social structures. Here the theory adopts the Simmelian focus of Blau's work as well as the concern with emergent properties and complex social structures. Emerson (1972), like Blau (1964, 1986), viewed the major task of exchange theory as the creation of a framework in which the primary dependent variable was social structure and structural change. This major task was eminently sociological, not psychological.

Early debates about the value of exchange theory in the social sciences focused on the role of rationality, tautology, and reductionism (see Emerson, 1976). These debates gave way during the last two decades to more sophisticated arguments in the field concerning theoretical strategy and the best ways to develop microlevel models of exchange that inform macrolevel processes. More complex theoretical formulations emerged during the 1980s and 1990s based on the results of careful empirical work, much of it experimental, testing the fundamental propositions derived from exchange theory. Emerson's formulation provided the impetus for much of this empirical work primarily because he formalized the theory to make it more precise and therefore testable. Subsequent formulations adopted a similar theoretical strategy, though there is variation in the underlying conceptions of the process of exchange and its structural determinants as well as in the specific ways in which the theory has been formalized (e.g., Markovsky, Willer & Patton, 1988; Bonacich, 1998; Bienenstock & Bonacich, 1992; Friedkin, 1992; Skvoretz & Willer, 1993; Yamaguchi, 1996).

EXCHANGE RELATIONS AND
THE NETWORKS THEY FORM

Exchange theory, though originally dyadic in focus, has been extended over the past three decades to apply to the analysis of exchange networks The definition of exchange relations as "connected" in various ways to form network structures was a key development in the theory. Emerson defined two major types of connections between exchange relations: negative and positive connections. (Subsequent theorists included "null" connection as a third category referring to the lack of a connection between exchange relations.) Two relations are negatively connected if the amount or frequency of exchange in one is negatively correlated with the magnitude or frequency of exchange in the other relation. In essence the two relations are strictly alternatives. If a buyer gets parts in an exchange with one vendor, then she or he does not need the same parts from another supplier. Negatively connected relations thus are competitive in nature. Two suppliers in such a case compete for access to the same buyer or market. In contrast, when two relations are positively connected, exchange in one relation enhances exchange in the other. For example, the resources one party gets in exchange with one supplier can be used to obtain needed goods from another supplier. In this case a positive connection exists and the two exchange relations are positively correlated. Such exchange relations are more cooperative in nature than competitive and they form the basis for some types of division of labor and specialization within exchange networks. Subsequent theorists (e.g., Willer, Markovsky, Bonacich, & Yamaguchi) have developed other ways of classifying types of exchange connections. Willer, for example, speaks of inclusive and exclusive exchange relations, while Yamaguchi refers to complementary and substitutable sources in exchange networks (see the discussion below on related formulations). These formulations are quite similar to Emerson's formulation.

INEQUALITY IN EXCHANGE AND POWER

A key concept in Emerson's exchange theory of power is the idea that exchange relations can be balanced or imbalanced. A power inequality results from an imbalance in power relations between two or more actors. An exchange relation is balanced if both parties are equally dependent on each other for exchange (or resources of value). If they are equally dependent, they have equal power. The central idea that power is based on dependence allows for the specification of ways in which dependencies can be altered to affect the balance of power in the exchange relation and in the network of connected exchange relations.

Structurally induced power inequalities and the behavioral consequences of such inequalities have been the most enduring theme in power-dependence research (e.g., Cook & Emerson, 1978; Cook, Emerson, Gillmore, & Yamagishi, 1983; Yamagishi, Gillmore, & Cook, 1988; Bienenstock & Bonacich, 1992). This focus began with Emerson's (1972) introduction of social network concepts explicitly into the framework of social exchange. The move from theorizing about dyadic relations to more complex networks of interdependent actors shifted the focus of power-dependence theory from a theory concerned with power balance to a theory primarily interested in explaining the creation and maintenance of imbalanced power structures, that is, structures of inequality.

Dyadic exchange relationships, Emerson (1972, 1981) argued, have a tendency to move toward a balance of power. Reciprocity is inherent in any enduring dyadic relation, since without it exchange is not likely to continue. "Reciprocity as such is not a variable attribute of exchange relations, and, once recognized, it is of little theoretical interest" (Emerson 1972, p. 62). But once exchange relations become embedded in more complex network structures, despite the existence of reciprocity, power imbalance can occur for a number of reasons. Emerson argued these imbalanced relations have a tendency to move toward a state of power balance (but see Molm, 1997a). "The use of a power advantage reduces the power advantage across time. In short, exchange relations tend to change toward balance" (Emerson 1972, p. 66). Power imbalance when it does exist, he argued, must be explained by forces exogenous to the particular imbalanced relation and is an anomaly which theory must explain. To quote Emerson again, "imbalance stems from events outside the relation, and its 'survival' is a problem to be explained when it occurs" (Emerson 1972, p. 67). Subsequent research clearly demonstrates that in network structures imbalance often persists. Thus more recent work clarifies the nature of the embeddedness of dyadic relations and the concomitant constraints on power-balancing processes within dyads.

Emerson proposed four alternative balancing operations that can reduce power imbalance in dyads and networks of exchange relations. If the dependence of actor A on actor B for some good y is greater than the dependence of B on A for another good x ($D_{AB} > D_{BA}$), the four following operations are possible. First, there can be a decrease in the value of good y for A, which he calls "withdrawal." Second, there can be an increase in the value of x for B, called "status-giving." These two processes can occur in dyadic or network relations. Third, there can be an increase in the number of alternatives open to A that can provide good y, which he referred to as "network extension." Finally, a reduction in alternatives open to B can occur, called "coalition formation" by A (presumably with another structurally similar actor). Notice that the first two mechanisms stress change in the values actors attach to social goods (hence, they can operate in dyads), while the second two mechanisms stress a change in the structure of the social network to balance power (hence, they can only occur in networks of exchange opportunities). But what happens if such changes are not possible?

When the value of goods exchanged is stable over time and the network of alternative exchange partners is static, power imbalance can be an enduring feature of social exchange relations (Cook & Emerson, 1978; Cook et al., 1983; Yamagishi et al., 1988). When Cook and Emerson moved the study of exchange into the experimental laboratory, the focus of exchange theory shifted from Emerson's earlier discussions of the dynamic properties of imbalanced exchange relations to explanations of the emergence of power imbalance within networks of exchange opportunities. Several findings characterize this early empirical work. The use of power by actors can be structurally induced (Cook & Emerson, 1978; Cook et al., 1983; Yamagishi et al., 1988). The power of a particular position depends on its location in the network of alternative exchange partners. Thus power imbalance is a function of differential opportunities for exchange across a social network (Cook & Emerson, 1978; Cook et al., 1983). The location of powerful positions in a social network is contingent on the kind of connections (negative or positive) that characterize the exchanges (Yamagishi et al., 1988) and power is a function of one's position in the network of exchanges (Cook et al., 1983). Powerful positions cannot simply be reduced to the points of highest network centrality (or some other purely graph theoretic principle), but depend on an actor's own alternatives, as well as the alternatives available to the alternatives (Cook et al., 1983).

Comparatively little research has been conducted on how power imbalances in social networks may cause changes to those structures and no research has been conducted on the effects of changes in values (but see Emerson, 1987). The important exception to this trend was the work done by Cook and Gillmore (1984) on the process of coalition formation. They found that power imbalance does indeed promote coalition formation. Coalitions that incorporate all weak actors in a social network against a strong actor balance power in a network. Those coalitions that do not include all of the power-disadvantaged actors in a coalition do not create balanced structures. Coalitions that produce balanced power structures tend to be the most stable over time, while those that do not create balance tend to decline in frequency over time. Moreover, as relations become increasingly competitive, the formation of coalitions becomes increasingly difficult as actors have a harder time aligning their interests to achieve the common goal of coalition formation and maintenance (see also Simpson & Macy, 2001, for a new treatment of coalitions in exchange networks).

Other mechanisms besides coalition formation among actors can alter the fundamental power distribution in the network of exchange relations. Division of labor, or specialization within the network, may operate as a power-balancing mechanism, since it can result in changes in the distribution of power in a network through modifications in the distribution of resources and the structure of the alternative exchange opportunities. For example, two suppliers of the same resource who had been competitors may decide to specialize and offer different services in a way that makes them no longer competitive with each other in a particular network. Network extension also can alter the balance of power in a network, as new exchange partners become available. In addition, when other strategies are not available actors can devalue what it is they obtain from a more powerful actor as a way of reducing their dependence on the relation. This strategy may be a precursor to exit from the relation in many instances. Various theorists have continued this line of work, specifying the principles that predict the distribution of power in different exchange structures and processes that modify it (e.g., Cook et al., 1983; Cook, Gillmore, & Yamagishi, 1986; Bonacich, 1998; Yamaguchi, 1996).

EXCHANGE NETWORKS:
RELATED FORMULATIONS

Theorists have offered related and sometimes conflicting accounts of the determinants of power in networks of exchange. The works of Homans, Blau, and Emerson explicitly influenced some; others attempted to derive new theoretical formulations drawing in distinct ways from varied sources of the core ideas in exchange theory. Most notable among these efforts was the work of Willer and Anderson in the early 1980s, which was subsequently developed more fully by Willer and his colleagues over the years, including Markovsky, Skvoretz, Patton, and Lovaglia, among others.

Elementary Theory

Willer and Anderson (1981), for example, proposed the "elementary theory" as an explicit alternative to power-dependence theory. Their intent was to create a general theory of the relationship between social structure and actor behavior that would be broader in its scope than exchange theory. Exchange phenomena were thus a subset of behaviors that could be explained by their theory.[1] Like Blau, they rejected operant psychology as a reasonable basis for a theory of exchange, arguing instead that elementary theory had the capacity to explain exchange from a purely structural basis. Values, they argued, were epiphenomenal and unnecessary for the development of a rigorous theory of exchange relations. Here they also parted company with Emerson's work. Instead, they viewed actors as having "interests" in achieving their first-ranked "system state," a set of ideas conceptually similar to the rank-ordering of preferences and utility maximization common in microeconomic theory. Like microeconomists, they tended to view the transaction as the primary unit of analysis rather than the exchange relation, the central focus of Emerson's theoretical endeavors. Until the early 1990s, this distinction clearly differentiated the work of Willer and his collaborators from the theoretical and empirical work of those who based their research on Emerson's theory of exchange.

The exchange theory derived from the "elementary theory," developed by Willer and Anderson, was premised first on the idea that social structures are a concrete aspect of social phenomena. The actors who occupy positions in social structures transmit and receive positive and/or negative sanctions from other actors in different positions in the social structure.[2] Exchange, they argue, can be "defined as a network in which only positive sanctions are potential" (Willer & Anderson, 1981, p. 26). This focus on social structure as the primary determinant of exchange behavior complemented nicely the developments of power-dependence

---

[1] From its inception, the elementary theory was highly formal and mathematical, taking advantage of the mechanics of graph theory in particular.

[2] The explicit use of coercion, in the form of negative sanctions, set elementary theory apart from many other early exchange theories that were concerned exclusively (or at least primarily) with social exchange processes as the distribution of rewards. Subsequently, Molm (e.g., 1987, 1989, 1997a,b) has written extensively about coercion and the use of punishment power in social exchange relations.

theory by Cook and Emerson (1978) who also had moved to an increasingly structural explanation for exchange behaviors with their focus on relative positions in networks as determinants of the distribution of power in social structures. Despite the explicit differences delineated by Willer and Anderson (1981), in practice, elementary theory manifested many parallels to developments in power-dependence theory.

Friedkin (1992, 1995) and Bienenstock and Bonacich (1992, 1993, 1997) have developed other alternative formulations in the intervening years. Friedkin developed a more general formal theory of social influence in networks that he applied in various ways to the analysis of exchange and power in network structures. Bonacich and Bienenstock produced a game theoretic analysis of the distribution of power in different types of network structures. In addition, they provide an interesting formal analysis of coalitions in exchange networks from a game theoretic point of view. Further development of game theoretic analyses of the outcomes of exchange processes in various networks will be a very useful addition to the empirical work on exchange and may help bridge the gap between the different theoretical formulations.

Extensions of Power-Dependence Exchange Network Formulations

Subsequent extensions of the exchange theory originally developed by Emerson (1972, 1976) have focused on the links between structure and process and on other bases of power. In a major research program extending over a 10-year period, for example, Molm (1997a) investigated the role of coercive power in social exchange. Emerson's work and that of most of the exchange theorists focused almost exclusively on reward power or the control over positively valued goods and services. Coercive power is the ability to control negative events (e.g., to withhold rewards) or to inflict punishment on another in an exchange relation. Unlike reward power, coercive power is used less often in exchange relations especially by those in power-advantaged positions, who seem to understand that it may be viewed as unjustified in many circumstances. The fear of retaliation also is a deterrent to the use of coercive reward power. The use of coercive power is more costly, since it imposes losses on the exchange partner in addition to the opportunity costs involved. Molm's major accomplishment was to expand the treatment of power in the classic power-dependence formulation to include forms of coercion. Since exchange relations often involve control over things we value and as well as things we wish to avoid this is a significant extension of the theory.

Strategy and Structure: The Dynamics of Power Use

Developments in the theory of exchange during the last decade include the formulation of explicit propositions concerning the use of power in different types of exchange network structures and specification of some of the determinants of power use. These factors include concern over the fairness of the distribution of outcomes, uncertainty, and the commitments that emerge between actors (e.g., Yamagishi, Cook, & Watabe, 1998; Lawler & Yoon, 1996), the formation of coalitions, particular strategies of action, and whether or not the power is reward power or punishment power, as noted above. Developments over the past decade also focus attention on methods for specifying more precisely the distribution of power in complex network structures (e.g., Lovaglia, Skvoretz, Willer, & Markovsky, 1995; Markovsky, 1987, 1995; Markovsky, Skvoretz, Willer, Lovaglia, & Erger, 1993; Markovsky et al., 1988; Skvoretz & Lovaglia, 1995; Willer, 1987, 1992). Interest in this topic, in part, is driven by the potential for synthesizing exchange theoretic conceptions of power with network models of social structure (see Cook, 1987; Cook & Whitmeyer, 1992; Whitmeyer 1994, 1999), and more recently game theoretic formalizations (e.g., Bienenstock & Bonacich, 1993).

A topic of continued interest is the specification of dynamic models of power use and structural change that include more sophisticated models of the actors involved and the strategies they adopt in their attempts to obtain resources and services of value (e.g., Molm, 1997b; Whitmeyer, 1994). A major effort is now underway to study the cognitive and affective components of exchange such as emotion, cohesion, risk, uncertainty, and trust, factors that received less attention while theorists were concentrating on the structural determinants of exchange processes and outcomes.

EMOTION, AFFECT, AND RELATIONAL COHESION IN EXCHANGE RELATIONS

In recent work, Lawler and Yoon (1993, 1996, 1998) have developed a theory of how affect oriented toward specific exchange relations is a proximal mechanism, intervening between structural factors and the outcomes of exchange. Relational cohesion theory, as they refer to it, specifies the effects of a set of endogenous affective mechanisms on exchange processes. Structural power affects exchange frequency, which in turn positively affects the creation of positive, everyday emotions, which then positively affect relational cohesion, and cohesion positively affects commitment behaviors (Lawler & Yoon, 1996, 1998). Explicit in this theory is the argument that each of these effects is dependent on the previous effects. The variables in this causal chain affect commitment behaviors through relational cohesion, the only variable that is expected to manifest direct effects on commitment (but see Lawler, Thye, & Yoon, 2000).

Lawler and Yoon have found substantial empirical support for the basic premise that affect mediates the effects of structural power on commitment to particular exchange relations. That relational cohesion, in particular, is a proximal mechanism in the manner described by the theory has received empirical support. But two caveats need to be added. First, their 1996 study found that perceptions of uncertainty and frequency of exchange still manifested independent effects on relational cohesion and commitment, despite the claims of the theory. While they found support for their contention that relational cohesion is a proximal mechanism, they could not rule out the existence of uncertainty reduction as an alternative.

Second, with the expansion of their experimental design to include network structures, reported in Lawler and Yoon (1998), the effect of relational cohesion becomes more complicated than they originally anticipated. In egalitarian relationships relational cohesion did affect commitment behaviors as they theorize. Exploitative relations, however, are not as cohesive. The relational cohesion expressed by exploiting actors had a positive effect on their commitment behaviors, whereas the relational cohesion expressed by exploited actors had a negative effect, a result that violates the relation-specific nature of the theory. This finding is consistent with some earlier research that suggests that power-advantaged actors view their exchange relations differently than do power-disadvantaged actors (see Cook, Hegtvedt, & Yamagishi, 1988; Stolte 1993) in terms of fairness and legitimacy of the inequality.

This line of research presents an important development in exchange theory, just as much for its novelty as for its connection to classical themes in exchange theory. The work of Lawler and Yoon reminds modern exchange theorists that even within the context of negotiated exchanges, exchange relations have emergent properties. The focus on affect, in particular, as such an emergent property mirrors Blau's concern with explaining how exchange relations are closely related to the process of sociability and over time develop an intrinsic value to the participants. People often come to care about the relationship for its own sake not just for the extrinsic benefits they can obtain through their exchanges. Emerson (1972, 1981) also argued for similar emergent phenomena. Trust, liking, and commitment could all potentially emerge out of ongoing exchange relationships. Through the development of relational cohesion theory, Lawler and Yoon have returned to these older themes in exchange theory and have given them new life, adding theoretical and empirical rigor.

The research on affect, cohesion, and commitment offers an explicit step beyond the power and position theories that were popular in the late 1980s and early 1990s. Lawler and Yoon, along with a handful of other researchers (Molm, 1997a; Molm, Peterson, & Takahashi, 1999; Molm, Takahashi, & Peterson, 2000; Kollock, 1994; Yamagishi et al., 1998) have moved beyond theorizing only about the distribution of power and rewards in social exchange networks toward theorizing about other important exchange outcomes, namely, commitment behavior. An explicit return to the relation as the focus of analysis has facilitated the delineation of what they believe to be important proximal causes for exchange outcomes. They have made explicit how aspects of the exchange process endogenous to the actors in a relation can affect outcomes, not just exogenous structural forces. This move presents the potential to make more explicit the mechanisms by which microlevel interactions can affect macrolevel structures.

Structural power is generated by the contingencies of alternative exchange relations within an opportunity structure of potential relations. Such structural aspects of exchange relations are typically thought to lie outside the control of actors within particular opportunity structures. This structurally generated power, however, affects the ways actors orient themselves toward particular relations, inducing positive affect and relational cohesion in recurring, successful exchange partnerships. This relational cohesion in turn affects commitment behaviors. If commitment behaviors are strongly affected, potential exchange relations within the opportunity structure of relations may fall away as actors increasingly favor those exchange relations toward which they have developed feelings of relational cohesion. As certain relations within the opportunity structure atrophy, the patterns of exchange relations and the connections among them may be altered, perhaps radically. In this way, the theory proposed by Lawler and Yoon (1993, 1996, 1998) may provide a powerful lens through which we can begin to view structural changes and the impact that processes endogenous to relations may have on these structural outcomes.

EMOTION AS AN OUTCOME OF EXCHANGE: AN ALTERNATIVE APPROACH

Molm et al. (2000) are also interested in delineating the connections between exchange behaviors and emotion. Their conceptual model, however, is quite different from the one proposed by Lawler and Yoon (1993, 1996, 1998). Whereas Lawler and Yoon's (1993, 1996, 1998) relational cohesion theory posits emotion directed toward exchange relations, as a proximal mechanism intervening between factors that influence structural cohesion and commitment behaviors, Molm and colleagues (2000) argue that affect is an outcome in its own right, one affected by commitment behaviors. Molm et al. (2000) argue that structural arrangements, not emotional responses, are largely responsible for differences in commitment behaviors that can be observed across different social structures. They argue that affect toward one's exchange partners is driven simultaneously by the form of exchange (i.e., negotiated or reciprocal) and the level of behavioral commitment induced by the structure of available alternatives in the network of exchange relations.

Molm and collaborators stress the existence of two distinct aspects to commitment. First, there is a purely behavioral outcome, which they define as "patterns of exchange in which pairs of actors choose to exchange repeatedly with one another rather than with alternative partners" (Molm et al., 2000, p. 1405). Second, there is an affective component to commitment, which they define as "bonds that develop from repeated experiences with successful exchanges between the same partners" (Molm et al., 2000, p. 1405). They are careful to point out that their conception of the affective component of commitment differs from that of Lawler and Yoon's (1993, 1996, 1998) in so far as they orient their discussion of affect as directed toward a particular partner, not the relation as a whole, as in relational cohesion theory. The relationship between these two alternative conceptions needs exploration. Both may be significantly involved in the emergence of commitment. That is, affect may be endogenously involved as well as an important outcome of exchange processes. Furthermore, in the end it may be difficult for people to clearly differentiate their emotions toward their partners from their emotional orientations to their relationships with these partners.

Each of these two aspects of commitment is argued to be affected by different social psychological mechanisms. Behavioral commitment, as we have already mentioned, is largely determined by the structure of the exchange relations. In networks where there is a large power imbalance, commitments tend to be lower, relative to those networks in which the power imbalance between positions is lower. These lowered levels of commitment are the result of the greater availability of alternative partners to power-advantaged positions in networks in which the power imbalance is greater, as compared to networks with a greater balance of power, in which alternative partners tend to be less available to those in power-advantaged positions.

Affective commitment, however, is the joint function of two simultaneous influences, the form of the exchange and the level of behavioral commitment. Molm and her collaborators argue that the form of exchange, whether the relationship can be characterized as negotiated or reciprocal exchange, affects actors' feelings of trust and their positive evaluations of their partners. Because rewards from exchange are not guaranteed in reciprocal exchanges, this form of exchange allows actors to establish their trustworthiness in their continued reciprocation of valued resources. Relative to negotiated exchange environments, in which rewards are more often assured due to the binding nature of such agreements, positive evaluations of one's exchange partners are higher in reciprocated exchange. Moreover, they argue that as the level of behavioral commitment goes up in exchange relations, actor's positive evaluations of their partners will likewise increase. Frequent exchanges enhance positive feelings (as Lawler and Yoon also argue) and affective commitment increases.

The work of Molm and colleagues (2000) calls into question the specific connection between commitment behaviors and affect proposed by Lawler and Yoon (1993, 1996, 1998). These differences appear to be due, at least partly, to Molm and collaborators' conviction that commitment can be broken into two component parts: an affective and a behavioral dimension. But this difference seems to reflect a deeper division over the extent to which structural factors are the dominating force determining the level of behavioral commitments. For Molm et al. (2000), affect comes last in the causal chain that links structure, behavior, and emotion. The removal of affect as an endogenous process and proximal mechanism in the formation of commitments limits the extent to which their theoretical work can generate the sort of connections between microlevel interactions and macrolevel structural changes that Lawler and Yoon's (1993, 1996, 1998) research suggests.

Yamagishi et al. (1998) provide experimental evidence that one of the key factors driving commitment behaviors is the degree of uncertainty in the exchange setting. The uncertainty they study is uncertainty over the possible exploitative behavior of an exchange partner rather than uncertainty over the quality of the goods to be traded, the primary form of uncertainty in the Kollock (1994) study. Uncertainty, however, of both types appears to foster the formation of committed relations as a mechanism for reducing uncertainty. This factor, as suggested above, remains significant as a determinant of commitment formation even when other factors are taken into account (e.g., the emergence of positive affect between successful exchange partners). We return to this finding in our discussion of the integration of exchange theory and recent work in economic sociology in which uncertainty and risk play a role in fostering the embeddedness of transactions and in the emergence of various forms of social structure that facilitate exchange in uncharted territories. Risk and uncertainty also are at the center of some of the recent discussions of trust (e.g., Heimer, 2001), a topic of interest to both exchange theorists and economic sociologists. Before examining this literature we comment briefly on other applications of exchange theory to related subfields in sociology.

APPLICATIONS OF EXCHANGE THEORY: BEYOND THE LABORATORY

The application of exchange theory to a variety of social phenomena "outside the laboratory" has increased over the past three decades as exchange concepts and propositions have been used in various subfields in sociology including organizational behavior, life course analysis, aging, family, medical sociology, international relations, and economic sociology. For example, early work in social psychology focused on the explanation of the initiation and termination of personal relations such as romantic involvements and social relations in the workplace. Topics of interest to researchers included conceptions of fairness in social exchange relations and its link to satisfaction and relationship dissolution (e.g., Sprecher, 1988). Power also was an important topic as investigators attempted to apply the work on power-dependence relations and the structural determinants of power in exchange networks to an understanding of power processes in family and work settings. Studying the abuse of power, particularly in relations of extreme dependence, and examining the use of control over both rewards and costs (or the withdrawal or withholding of rewards) in exchange relations expanded as investigators found the exchange approach to provide useful insights into both the processes involved and the outcomes in various settings. In particular, Molm's work on the use of coercive power in exchange relations has made new applications in this arena possible. Extreme dependence often invites the abuse of power in social relations, since the power disadvantaged view themselves as having few alternatives.

Beyond the application to family and work settings, the theory also has been applied in many different contexts to the study of organizations and interorganizational relations. Similar applications exist at the level of international relations as well. Since organizations typically require resources from other entities much of their time is devoted to the strategic management of these dependencies. The resource-dependence perspective (Pfeffer & Salancik, 1978) in the field of organizations is a straightforward application of exchange reasoning to the strategic actions of organizations and their subunits (e.g., at the divisional level). The developing field of economic sociology also is now drawing to some extent on ideas derived from exchange theory to explain the emergence of network forms of organization and the nature of the power processes that emerge in such networks. Network effects on labor practices, informal influence among organizations, the organization of business groups, and the formation of international linkages that cross traditional national boundaries of economic and productive activity are central topics of inquiry in economic sociology. Some of these efforts involve understanding the effects of network location on outcomes and the various strategies actors use to enhance bargaining power and influence. These efforts derive, in part, from power-dependence reasoning first introduced by Emerson and Blau into exchange theorizing. We comment in more detail on the close linkages between exchange theory and some of the current developments in economic sociology below.

Other applications of exchange theory in fields like medical sociology include broad efforts to investigate the balance of power in the health care industry, the strategic role of insurance companies in the era of managed care, and the response of physicians to the loss of power and autonomy. In addition, several researchers have attempted to analyze the nature of physician referrals in network exchange terms and to characterize the nature of the physician–patient interaction as an exchange relation in which power is asymmetric (or imbalanced) and in which trust plays a key role in "balancing" this power differential. The patient must place her fate in the hands of a more competent, more informed actor and trust that the physician will "do no harm." The research on these topics is expanding as the health care system undergoes severe economic pressures and new legal challenges. Applications of the exchange model of interaction and of network exchange in other domains in the future will help to clarify and extend the underlying theoretical framework. In the concluding section of our chapter we comment in greater detail on the developing links between exchange theory and several important subfields of sociology including economic sociology and the emerging work on the sociology of Internet exchanges.

EXCHANGE THEORY AND ECONOMIC SOCIOLOGY

Exchange theory and economic sociology (e.g., Granovetter, 1985; Uzzi, 1996; White, 1981; Burt, 1992; Fligstein, 1996) share more in common substantively and theoretically than either subfield recognizes. With rare exceptions (e.g., Kollock, 1994; Lawler & Yoon, 1996) these two streams of work have developed in relative isolation despite the centrality of social networks and transactions to theory and methods in each tradition. Similarities between the two bodies of work, however, extend far deeper to the core of each group's theoretical concerns and explanatory accounts. Swedberg and Granovetter (1992) explicitly lay out what they believe to be the three central propositions of economic sociology: (1) economic action is a form of social action; (2) economic action is socially situated; and (3) economic institutions are social constructions. The first two propositions share a great deal of intellectual, common ground with modern versions of exchange theory.

In explaining the first proposition, Swedberg and Granovetter stress that while economic action is not devoid of instrumental behavior and market dynamics (i.e., the pull of supply and demand on price), a sociological analysis of economic action must concern itself with structural and social issues: "From a sociological perspective, it is clear that economic action cannot, in principle, be separated from the quest for approval, status, sociability, and power" (Swedberg & Granovetter, 1992, p. 7). Exchange theory, likewise, not only maintains the integrity of the instrumental aspects of transactions, but also attempts to explain how transactions are tied to other noninstrumental, social processes (e.g., trust in exchange). How the relations between transacting partners produce power and how differences in power affect exchange behaviors and the distribution of rewards have long been a concern of exchange theory. Moreover, the recent work on affect in exchange (Lawler & Yoon, 1996, 1998; Molm et al., 2000), described briefly above, provides insights into how outcomes from transactions influence sociability and affect in exchange relations.

Issues of power and dependence have taken on an increasingly central role in economic sociology over the past decade. Baker (1990), for example, argues that corporate actors engage in tactics to increase interorganizational power, not merely profit maximization. In his study of corporate dealings with investment banks he makes this argument quite explicit: "The central problem for corporations is how to manage their relations with investment banks to reduce their dependence *and* exploit power advantages. The observed configuration of market ties is the revealed result of efforts to do so [italics in original]" (Baker, 1990, p. 592). This stream of research within economic sociology shares an obvious concern for power and dependence with classical and experimental research on exchange theory. Economic sociologists, in particular Baker (1990), Burt (1992), and Leiffer (1991), argue that economic actors strategically manipulate power within the context of network structures, altering these structures along the way. Although exchange theorists often stress the stability of structure and its effects on the distribution of power among actors, as we have already discussed, Emerson's (1962, 1972) early theoretical work emphasizes the ways in which relations and structures can be modified to alter the nature of the power differences among the actors. In addition, more recent experimental research in the exchange tradition has begun to examine more fully the role of actor strategy in altering the structure of the exchange relations in a network, and thus the nature of the distribution of power.

Swedberg and Granovetter (1992) claim that reference to individual motives alone (or the mere aggregation of individually motivated acts) cannot explain economic action, according to economic sociology. Economic action is situated in social networks of ongoing personal relations. This last point is perhaps the primary insight and the main area of theoretical development within economic sociology. This issue is the central focus of Granovetter's (1985) "embeddedness" argument. It is here that the similarity to exchange theory is most easily conveyed. One of the core methodological as well as theoretical agendas of each field is to explain how concrete social structures, in the form of social networks, affect the instrumental behaviors pursued by social actors in transactions with one another. Both reject the primacy of individualist motivations favored by economics and focus instead on how social relations and social networks mediate and shape the outcomes of exchanges.

The research conducted under the umbrella of "embeddedness" shares an enormous intellectual common ground with recent developments in exchange theory. Uzzi (1996) argues that "embeddedness" has profound behavioral consequences, affecting the shape of economic relations and the success of firms, which rely on ongoing exchange relations across a relatively stable set of alternative partners. As Uzzi states: "A key behavioral consequence of embeddedness is that it becomes separate from the narrow economic goals that originally constituted the exchange and generates outcomes that are independent of the narrow economic interests of the relationship" (Uzzi, 1996, p. 681). The recent research conducted by Lawler and Yoon (1996, 1998) on emotions and relational cohesion in exchange networks reflects a similar theoretical orientation. They argue that actors who develop feelings of relational cohesion directed toward ongoing exchange relationships are more likely to engage in a host of behaviors not easily explained in strictly economic terms, such as gift giving, forming new joint ventures across old ties, and staying in relations despite the presence of new, potentially more profitable partners (see the previous discussion on relational cohesion for more detail on this and related research in exchange theory).

That these two subfields have developed in relative isolation from one another is likely the result of several key factors. First, the old notion that exchange theory is concerned only with the explanation of the dynamics of social and not economic exchanges still lingers in the discipline. When one considers the convergence of theoretical concerns just discussed, the usefulness of this distinction becomes suspect.[3] Second, and more important, the two subfields tend to adopt quite distinct styles of research and theorizing. Exchange theory often has been associated with rational choice theory (e.g., Blau, 1964; Coleman, 1972; Marsden, 1983) and economic sociology often uses rational choice theory as a theoretical foil. Moreover, even when exchange theory does not rely on rational choice assumptions, opting for operant mechanisms instead, these theories are still focused primarily on predicting behaviors from relations. Economic sociologists, on the other hand, tend to prefer *ex post* explanations of empirically observed phenomenon. Moreover, exchange theorists frequently have collected data primarily in the laboratory on constructed exchange systems, while economic sociologists have tended to be resolute about the collection of data from naturally occurring economic phenomena.

These theoretical and methodological divergences, however, are what make a marriage of exchange theory and economic sociology so promising. Each has tools and insights from which the other can benefit. Primarily, economic sociology can benefit from the predictive nature of exchange theory and the explicit mechanisms proposed by exchange theory for explaining transaction behaviors and the structures in which they are embedded. Moreover, exchange theory has delineated a set of interesting dependent variables, such as the distribution of power and the cohesiveness of relations that economic sociology at times ignores in favor of explaining how economic action deviates from "maximizing" behaviors. Exchange theory gains from this marriage the richness and complexity inherent in the analysis of more macrolevel phenomenon outside the laboratory. Exchange theorists in mid-century, particularly Homans (1958, 1974) and Blau (1964) were not as divorced from such an endeavor as are modern practitioners. An engagement with "real-world" economic phenomena presents the possibility of new venues in which to test the predictions of exchange theory as well as the impetus to explore new problems and mechanisms that such an endeavor would necessarily encourage. In conclusion we discuss briefly one example of such an endeavor.

EXCHANGE RELATIONS AND ONLINE MARKETS: THE STUDY OF EMERGENT PHENOMENA

Online markets and auction houses (e.g., eBay) present such a context for new sociological research in which the marriage of economic sociology and exchange theory may be particularly fruitful. Although some initial work (e.g., Kollock, 1999) has begun to tackle the complicated sociological issues to be found in these emerging markets, there certainly is ample

---

[3]It must be acknowledged that not all exchange theorists are so catholic in their visions of economic and social transactions. Molm and colleagues (1999, 2000) have reaffirmed the importance of such an analytic division between economic and social exchange. They make a clear distinction between reciprocal (i.e., nonnegotiated) exchanges and negotiated exchanges, viewing the former as a more accurate representation of social exchange and the latter as more reflective of strictly economic exchange.

room for more theory and research. Economic sociology has a long-standing interest in the social construction of markets (e.g., White, 1981; Granovetter, 1985; Fligstein, 1996). The focus of much of this theorizing has been on how the formation of market structures represents social "solutions" to complex social problems surrounding the distribution and control of resources. As Fligstein (1996) puts it, "The creation of markets implies societal solutions to the problems of property rights, governance structures, conceptions of control and rules of exchange" (p. 670). Such insights are taken quite seriously, although only implicitly, by Kollock (1999) in his recent work on the emergence of trust in online markets. He points to the emergence of reputation systems as a solution to the problem of trust in this new economic arena. Online environments, according to Kollock, represent particularly risky environments for exchange. Enforcement by third parties (i.e., the government) is difficult, firsthand knowledge of one's trading partners is rare, and the field of potential exchange relations often literally spans the globe.

Online market participants have created a host of endogenous solutions to these uncertainties in their exchanges. The most prominent and effective solution appears to be the creation of reputation systems, in which market participants create public biographies, focused on their history of exchanges as an attempt to establish themselves as trustworthy exchange partners. Actors involved in these exchanges have various mechanisms for contributing to the information base on which reputations are formed. Kollock suggests that such reputation systems not only help transactions proceed smoothly with a minimum of opportunism, but the development of a strong reputation may enhance the value of one's goods placed on the market (see Kollock, 1999, for more discussion on these points).

Both economic sociologists and exchange theorists have abundant reason to begin researching this new phenomenon. First, both groups of researchers have a long-standing interest in the formation and outcomes of exchange relations. Online markets certainly provide a wealth of potential exchanges to study. Second, both groups theorize about the formation or emergence of social structures, such as markets and exchange networks. The relative infancy of online markets presents an opportunity for both sets of researchers to study the formation of such structures in an extremely public domain. Finally, online markets present special problems for economic sociologists as well as exchange theorists, because this "real world" of exchange partners tends to exist outside the bounds of traditional conceptions of social networks.

Both sets of theorists have devoted an enormous amount of time and energy to theorizing about the effects that concrete social structures have on the outcomes of economic and social exchange. In the world of online markets, transactions take place not in an anonymous world, but in a world that exists without network ties in the traditional sense. It is a social world in which identity is part of the constitution of the market itself and reputations are built up and torn down through the exchanges they are intended to facilitate. As difficult as theorizing about this arena may appear on first examination, the work of economic sociology on the social construction of markets (e.g., White, 1981; Granovetter, 1985; Fligstein, 1996) and the recent work in exchange theory on solutions to uncertainty in social exchange settings (Kollock, 1994, 1999; Molm et al., 2000; Yamagishi et al., 1998) present promising starting points for the creation of a rigorous sociological theory of online transactions and the new forms of social structure they create, even if some would view them as "virtual social structures."

At the more microlevel, reputation systems serve to foster trust in both the specific social relations in which the transactions actually occur and in the institutions that are emerging to maintain and monitor the store of knowledge on which the reputations are based. The latter focuses attention more on matters of credibility and legitimacy both of which are critical in any emergent social system. In fact, to the extent that the transactions are embedded in networks that are monitored and where defection or cheating is sanctioned through reputational mechanisms, the need for "pure" trust based interactions is reduced. The initial offerings, however, in many circumstances require some form of risk taking or trust, often viewed as more of a "leap of faith" in one's fellow human being (see Yamagishi & Yamagishi, 1994). Beyond trust and reputational mechanisms, future research also may draw on the developing work on the role of affect in exchange systems. Does it emerge in online systems of exchange as anecdotal evidence implies or do online relations serve the role of an alternative to affective attachments in the real world of social encounters? Many interesting questions remain unanswered at the microlevel as well as at more macrolevels regarding the development of new systems of exchange anchored as much in cyberspace as in the traditional realms of economic and social exchange. In fact, the distinction between economic and social exchange may become blurred over time in such a context. Both exchange theory and economic sociology are likely to contribute a great deal in the future to our understanding of these newest forms of exchange and the structures that emerge to facilitate them.

REFERENCES

Bienenstock, E. J., & Bonacich, P. (1992). The core as a solution to exclusionary networks. *Social Networks, 14,* 231–243.

Bienenstock, E., & Bonacich, P. (1993). Game-theory models for exchange networks: Experimental results. *Sociological Perspectives, 36,* 117–135.

Bienenstock, E., & Bonacich, P. (1997). Network exchange as a cooperative game. *Rationality and Society, 9,* 937–965.

Baker, W. (1990). Market networks and corporate behavior. *American Journal of Sociology, 96,* 589–625.

Blau, P. M. (1964). *Exchange and power in social life.* New York: Wiley.

Blau, P. M. (1986). *Exchange and power in social life,* 2nd printing. New Brunswick, NJ: Transaction Books.

Blau, P. M. (1987). Microprocess and macrostructure. In K. S. Cook, (Ed.), *Social exchange theory* (pp. 83–100). Newbury Park, CA: Sage.

Blau, P. M. (1998). Behavioral foundation for a structural theory of power in exchange networks. *Social Psychology Quarterly, 61,* 185–198.

Burt, R. (1992). *Structural holes: The social structure of competition.* Cambridge, MA: Harvard University Press.

Coleman, J. S. (1990). *Foundations of social theory.* Cambridge, MA: Harvard University Press.

Coleman, J. S. (1972). Systems of social exchange. *Journal of Mathematical Sociology, 2,* 145–163.

Collins, R. (1981). On the microfoundations of microsociology. *American Journal of Sociology, 86,* 984–1014.

Cook, K. S. (Ed.) (1987). *Social exchange theory.* Newbury Park, CA: Sage.

Cook, K. S., & Emerson, R. M. (1978). Power, equity and commitment in exchange networks. *American Sociological Review, 43,* 712–39.

Cook, K. S., & Gillmore, M. (1984). Power, dependence, and coalitions. In E. J. Lawler (Ed.), *Advances in group processes,* Vol. 1 (pp. 27–58). Greenwich, CT: JAI Press.

Cook, K. S., & Whitmeyer, J. M. (1992). Two approaches to social structure: Exchange theory and network analysis. *Annual Review of Sociology, 18,* 109–127.

Cook, K. S., Emerson, R. M., Gillmore, M. R., & Yamagishi, T. (1983). The distribution of power in exchange networks: Theory and experimental results. *American Journal of Sociology, 89,* 275–305.

Cook, K. S., Gillmore, M. R., & Yamagishi, T. (1986). Point and line vulnerability as bases for predicting the distribution of power in exchange networks: Reply to Willer. *American Journal of Sociology, 92,* 445–448.

Cook, K., Hegtvedt, K. A., & Yamagishi, T. (1988). Structural inequality, legitimation, and reactions to inequities in exchange networks. In M. Webster & M. Foschi (Eds.), *Status generalization: New theory and reason* (pp. 291–308). Stanford, CA: Stanford University Press.

Deutsch, M. (1964). Homans in the skinner box. *Sociological Inquiry, 34,* 156–165.

Ekeh, P. P. (1974). *Social exchange theory: The two traditions.* Cambridge, MA: Harvard University Press.

Emerson, R. M. (1962). Power-dependence relations. *American Sociological Review, 27,* 31–41.

Emergson, R. M. (1972). Exchange theory, part I and II. In J. Berger, M. Zelditch Jr., & B. Anderson (Eds.), *Sociological theories in progress*, Vol. 2 (pp. 38–87). Boston: Houghton Mifflin.

Emerson, R. M. (1987). Toward a theory of value in social exchange. In K. S. Cook (Eds.), *Social exchange theory* (pp. 11–46). Newbury Park, CA: Sage.

Emerson, R. M. (1976). Social exchange theory. *Annual Review of Sociology, 2*, 335–362.

Emerson, R. M. (1981). Social exchange theory. In M. Rosenberg & R. Turner (Eds.), *Social psychology: Sociological perspectives* (pp. 30–65). New York: Basic Books.

Fligstein, N. (1996). Market politics: A political-cultural approach to market institutions. *American Sociological Review, 61*, 656–673.

Friedkin, N. E. (1992). An expected value model of social power: Predictions for selected exchange networks. *Social Networks, 14*, 213–229.

Friedkin, N. E. (1995). The incidence of exchange networks. *Social Psychology Quarterly, 58*, 213–222.

Granovetter, M. (1985). Economic action and social structure: The problem of embeddedness. *American Journal of Sociology, 91*, 481–510.

Heimer, C. (2001). Solving the problem of trust. In K. S. Cook (Ed.), *Trust in society* (pp. 40–48). New York: Russell Sage Foundation.

Homans, G. C. (1958). Social behavior as exchange. *American Journal of Sociology, 62*, 597–606.

Homans, G. C. (1974). *Social behavior: Its elementary forms*, 2nd ed. New York: Harcourt, Brace & World. (Original publication 1961)

Kelley, H. H., & Thibaut, J. (1978). *Interpersonal relations: A theory of interdependence*. New York: John Wiley.

Kollock, P. (1994). The emergence of exchange structures: An experimental study of uncertainty, commitment and trust. *American Journal of Sociology, 100*, 313–345.

Kollock, P. (1999). The production of trust in online markets. In E. J. Lawler et al. (Eds.), *Advances in group process* (pp. 99–123). Greenwich, CT: JAI Press.

Lawler, E. J., & Yoon, J. (1993). Power and the emergence of commitment Behavior in negotiated exchange. *American Sociological Review, 58*, 465–481.

Lawler, E. J., & Yoon, J. (1996). Commitment in exchange relations: A test of a theory of relational cohesion. *American Sociological Review, 61*, 89–108.

Lawler, E. J., & Yoon, J. (1998). Network structure and emotion in exchange relations. *American Sociological Review, 63*, 871–894.

Lawler, E. J., Thye, S. R., & Yoon, J. (2000). Emotion and group cohesion in productive exchange. *American Journal of Sociology, 106*(3), 616–657.

Leiffer, E. M. (1991). *Actors as observers: A theory of skill in social relationships*. New York and London: Garland.

Lovaglia, M. J., Skvoretz, J., Willer, D., & Markovsky, B. (1995). Negotiated exchanges in social networks. *Social Forces, 74*, 123–155.

Malinowski, B. (1922). *Argonauts of the Western Pacific*. New York: E. P. Dutton.

Markovsky, B. (1987). Toward multilevel sociological theories: Simulations of actor and network effects. *Sociological Theory, 5*, 101–117.

Markovsky, B. (1995). Developing an exchange network simulator. *Sociological Perspectives, 38*, 519–545.

Markovsky, B, Willer, D., & Patton, T. (1988). Power relations in exchange networks. *American Sociological Review, 53*, 220–236.

Markovsky, B., Skvoretz, J., Willer, D., Lovaglia, M. J., & Erger, J. (1993). The seeds of weak power: Extending network exchange theory. *American Sociological Review, 1993*, 197–209.

Marsden, P. V. (1983). Restricted access in networks and models of power. *American Journal of Sociology, 88*, 686–717.

Mauss, M. (1925). *Essai sur le Don en Sociologie et Anthropologie*. Paris: Presses Universitaires de France.

Miller, N. E., & Dollard, J. (1941). *Social learning and imitation*. New Haven, CT: Yale University Press.

Molm, L. D. (1989). Punishment power: A balancing process in power-dependence relations. *American Journal of Sociology, 94*(6), 1392–1418.

Molm, L. D. (1987). Power-dependence theory: Power processes and negative outcomes. In E. J. Lawler & B. Markovsky (Eds.), *Advances in group processes*, Vol. 4 (pp. 171–198). Greenwich, CT: JAI Press.

Molm, L. D. (1991). Affect and social exchange: Satisfaction in power-dependence relations. *American Sociological Review, 56*, 475–493.

Molm, L. D. (1997a). *Coercive power in social exchange*. Cambridge, England: Cambridge University Press.

Molm, L. D. (1997b). Risk and power use: Constraints on the use of coercion in exchange. *American Sociological Review, 62*, 113–133.

Molm, L. D., Peterson, G., & Takahashi, N. (1999). Power in negotiated and reciprocal exchange. *American Sociological Review, 64*, 876–890.

Molm, L. D., Takashi, N., & Peterson, G. (2000). Risk and trust in social exchange: An experimental test of a classical proposition. *American Journal of Sociology, 105*, 1396–1427.

Pfeffer, J., & Salancik, G. R. (1978). *The external control of organizations: A resource dependence perspective.* New York: Harper & Row.

Schneider, H. K. (1974). *Economic man: The anthropology of economics.* New York: Free Press.

Simpson, B., & Macy, M. (2000). Collective action and power inequality coalition in exchange networks. *Social Psychology Quarterly, 64*, 88–100.

Skvoretz, J., & Lovaglia, M. J. (1995). Who exchanges with whom: Structural determinants of exchange frequency in negotiated exchange networks. *Social Psychology Quarterly, 58*, 163–177.

Skvoretz, J., & Willer, D. (1993). Exclusion and power: A test of four theories of power in exchange networks. *American Sociological Review, 58*, 801–818.

Stolte, J. (1983). The legitimation of structural inequality: Reformulation and test of the self-evaluation argument. *American Sociological Review, 48*, 331–342.

Sprecher, S. (1988). Investment model, equity, and social support determinants of relationship commitments. *Social Psychology Quarterly, 51*, 318–328.

Swedberg, R., & Granovetter, M. (1992). Introduction. In M. Granovetter & R. Swedberg (Eds.), *The sociology of economic life* (pp. 1–26). Boulder, CO, San Francisco, Oxford: Westview Press.

Thibaut, J. W., & Kelley, H. H. (1959). *The social psychology of groups.* New York: Wiley.

Turner, J. (1986). *The structure of sociological theory,* 4th ed. Homewood, IL: Dorsey.

Uzzi, B. (1996). The sources and consequences of embeddedness for the economic performance of organizations: The network effect. *American Sociological Review, 61*, 674–698.

White, H. C. (1981). Where do markets come from? *American Journal of Sociology, 87*, 517–547.

Whitmeyer, J. M. (1994). Social structure and the actor: The case of power in exchange networks. *Social Psychology Quarterly, 57*, 177–189.

Whitmeyer, J. M. (1999). Interest-network structures in exchange networks. *Sociological Perspectives, 42*, 23–47.

Willer, D. (1987). The location of power in exchange networks. *Social Networks, 14*, 187–341

Willer, D. (1992). Predicting power in exchange networks: A brief history and introduction to the issues. *Social Networks, 14*, 187–211.

Willer, D., & Anderson, B. (1981). *Networks, exchange and coercion: The elementary theory and its applications.* New York: Elsevier.

Yamagishi, T., Cook, K. S., & Watabi, M. (1998). Uncertainty, trust and commitment formation in the United States and Japan. *American Journal of Sociology, 104*, 165–194.

Yamagishi, T., & Yamagishi, M. (1994). Trust and commitment in the United States and Japan. *Motivation and Emotion, 18*, 129–166.

Yamagishi, T., Gillmore, M. R., & Cook, K. S. (1988). Network connections and the distribution of power in exchange networks. *American Journal of Sociology, 93*, 833–851.

Yamaguchi, K. (1996). Power in networks of substitutable and complementary exchange relations: A rational-choice model and an analysis of power centralization. *American Sociological Review, 61*, 308–332.

Index